FREE Online Courses —

Available in BlackBoard, WebCT, & CourseCompass!

Are you teaching an online course now? Or would you like to teach a Web-enhanced course? Here's how Prentice Hall can help you to optimize your class!

- **Online Quizzes** that automatically feed results into the Gradebook
- **Bulletin Boards** that let you and your students post critical messages
- **An Online Syllabus** that keeps students aware of deadlines and updates
- **Discussion Groups** that enable instructors to hold synchronous or asynchronous meetings with classes, speakers, or groups of students
- **Links** that connect your students (via the syllabus) to key Internet sites

Most important, you can include any of your own materials—create and post your own lectures, assignment options, and class projects!

Premium CourseCompass with eBook

Now you get even more when you team up with CourseCompass to teach your accounting courses! You'll have all the quality course content and easy-to-use management tools of CourseCompass—plus a searchable, Web-based e-book:

- **Easy-to-use, anytime, anywhere.** Students can access their textbook from any computer 24 hours a day, 7 days a week.
- **One integrated study experience for students.** With one click, students have access to complete course materials (text, quizzes, research links), all in one place.
- **Affordable, searchable e-textbook.** Prentice Hall and MetaText have partnered to provide a unique Web-based study experience that, when combined with the online study guide and tools of CourseCompass, provides a value for students.

Cost Accounting

A Managerial Emphasis

Charles T. Horngren Series in Accounting

Charles T. Horngren, *Consulting Editor*

Auditing and Assurance Services: An Integrated Approach, 8th ed. ▲ Arens/Elder/Beasley

Advanced Accounting, 8th ed. ▲ Beams/Anthony/Clement/Lowensohn

Financial Statement Analysis, 2nd ed. ▲ Foster

Governmental and Nonprofit Accounting: Theory and Practice, 7th ed. ▲ Freeman/Shoulders

Financial Accounting, 4th ed. ▲ Harrison/Horngren

Cases in Financial Reporting, 3rd ed. ▲ Hirst/McAnally

Cost Accounting: A Managerial Emphasis, 11th ed. ▲ Horngren/Datar/Foster

Accounting, 5th ed. ▲ Horngren/Harrison/Bamber

Introduction to Financial Accounting, 8th ed. ▲ Horngren/Sundem/Elliott

Introduction to Management Accounting, 12th ed. ▲ Horngren/Sundem/Stratton

EDITION 11

Cost Accounting

A Managerial Emphasis

Charles T. Horngren
Stanford University

Srikant M. Datar
Harvard University

George Foster
Stanford University

PRENTICE HALL
Upper Saddle River, NJ 07458

Library of Congress Cataloging-in-Publication Data

Horngren, Charles T., 1926-
Cost accounting: a managerial emphasis / Charles T. Horngren, Srikant M. Datar, George Foster; with annotations by Robert Caperttini—11th ed.
p. cm.
"Annotated instructor's edition."
Includes index.
ISBN 0-13-064815-9
1. Cost accounting. I. Datar, Srikant M. II. Foster, George,. III. Title.

HF5686.C8H59 2002
658.15'11—dc21 2001056577

Acquisitions Editor: Thomas Sigel
Editor-in-Chief: P. J. Boardman
Editorial and Supplements Assistance: Fran Toepfer and Linda Albelli
Senior Development Editor: Mike Elia
Director of Development Steve Deitmer
Senior Media Project Manager: Nancy Welcher
Executive Marketing Manager: Beth Toland
Managing Editor (Production): Cindy Regan
Senior Production Editor: Anne Graydon
Production Assistant: Dianne Falcone
Permissions Coordinator: Suzanne Grappi
Associate Director, Manufacturing: Vincent Scelta
Production Manager: Arnold Vila
Design Manager: Pat Smythe
Interior Design: Amanda Kavanagh
Cover Design: John Romer
Cover Photo: Bob Thomason/Getty Images Stone
Illustrator (Interior): Progressive Information Technologies
Manager, Multimedia Production: Christy Mahon
Senior Formatter: Ashley Scattergood
Photo Researcher: Teri Stratford
Photo Permissions Coordinator: Reynold Rieger
Composition: Progressive Information Technologies
Full-Service Project Management: Progressive Publishing Alternatives
Printer/Binder: R. R. Donnelley, Willard

Credits and acknowledgments borrowed from other sources and reproduced, with permission:
The cover image is a photo of Denver, Colorado. **page 1** Regal Marine Industries, Inc. **page 14** Toshiyuki Aizawa/Reuters NewMedia/CORBIS **page 29** Three Dog Bakery **page 35** AP/Wide World Photos **page 61** The Store24 Companies Inc. **page 73** Toru Yamanaka/AFP Photo/CORBIS **page 95** Courtesy Gigabyte Technology **page 104** Colorscope **page 135** Ed Kashi/CORBIS **page 154** AP/Wide World Photos **page 175** Farrell Grehan/CORBIS **page 188** FRx Software Corporation **page 215** ©Teri Stratford. All rights reserved. **page 226** Charles O'Rear/CORBIS **page 251** Teva-Deckers Outdoor Corporation **page 261** Henry Horenstein/Stock Boston **page 285** Collins Industries, Inc. **page 297** Michael Rosenfeld/Getty Images Inc. **page 323** AP/Wide World Photos **page 338** Bill Varie/CORBIS **page 369** The Store24 Companies Inc. **page 378** Ricardo Azoury/Corbis/SABA Press Photos, Inc. **page 409** Lynn Eodice/Index Stock Imagery, Inc. **page 430** Index Stock Imagery, Inc. **page 445** Frank Siteman/PhotoEdit **page 461** AP/Wide World Photos **page 481** Nantucket Nectars/Allserve, Inc. **page 493** AP/Wide World Photos **page 521** Loren Santow/Getty Images Inc. **page 536** Steven Starr/Stock Boston **page 555** Micron Technology, Inc. **page 570** AP/Wide World Photos **page 585** Nantucket Nectars/Allserve, Inc. **page 608** Jim Leynse/Corbis/SABA Press Photos, Inc. **page 625** Used with permission of Pilkington 2001. **page 640** DuPont **page 653** Nik Wheeler/CORBIS **page 662** Stock Illustration Source, Inc. **page 685** Regal Marine Industries, Inc. **page 698** AP/Wide World Photos **page 717** Karl Weatherly/CORBIS **page 735** AP/Wide World Photos **page 753** SuperStock, Inc. **page 771** Alan Oddie/PhotoEdit **page 785** AP/Wide World Photos **page 802** Christina Lantry/Getty Images Inc.

Pearson Education LTD
Pearson Education Australia PTY, Limited
Pearson Education Singapore, Pte. Ltd
Pearson Education North Asia Ltd
Pearson Education, Canada, Ltd
Pearson Educación de Mexico, S. A. de C. V.
Pearson Education – Japan
Pearson Education Malaysia, Pte. Ltd

10 9 8 7 6 5 4 3 2 1
ISBN 0-13-064815-9

TO OUR FAMILIES

Joan, Scott, Mary, Susie, Cathy (CH)
Swati, Radhika, Gayatri, Sidharth (SD)
The Foster Family (GF)

BRIEF CONTENTS

PART ONE Cost Accounting Fundamentals

1 The Accountant's Role in the Organization 1
2 An Introduction to Cost Terms and Purposes 29
3 Cost-Volume-Profit Analysis 61
4 Job Costing 95
5 Activity-Based Costing and Activity-Based Management 135

PART TWO Tools for Planning and Control

6 Master Budget and Responsibility Accounting 175
7 Flexible Budgets, Variances, and Management Control: I 215
8 Flexible Budgets, Variances, and Management Control: II 251
9 Inventory Costing and Capacity Analysis 285

PART THREE Cost Information for Decisions

10 Determining How Costs Behave 323
11 Decision Making and Relevant Information 369
12 Pricing Decisions and Cost Management 409

PART FOUR Cost Allocation and Revenues

13 Strategy, Balanced Scorecard, and Strategic Profitability Analysis 445
14 Cost Allocation, Customer-Profitability Analysis, and Sales-Variance Analysis 481
15 Allocation of Support Department Costs, Common Costs, and Revenues 521
16 Cost Allocation: Joint Products and Byproducts 555
17 Process Costing 585

PART FIVE Quality and JIT

18 Spoilage, Rework, and Scrap 625
19 Quality, Time, and the Theory of Constraints 653
20 Inventory Management, Just-in-Time, and Backflush Costing 685

PART SIX Investment Decisions and Management Control Systems

21 Capital Budgeting and Cost Analysis 717
22 Management Control Systems, Transfer Pricing, and Multinational Considerations 753
23 Performance Measurement, Compensation, and Multinational Considerations 785

PREFACE xvii

PART ONE
Cost Accounting Fundamentals

1 The Accountant's Role in the Organization 1

Management Accounting, Financial Accounting, and Cost Accounting 2
Cost Management and Accounting Systems 3
Strategic Decisions and the Management Accountant 3
Developing a Strategy 4
Building Resources and Capabilities 4
The Management Accountant's Role in Implementing Strategy 6
Feedback: Linking Planning and Control 6
An Example: Planning and Control and the Management Accountant 6
Problem-Solving, Scorekeeping, and Attention-Directing Roles 8
Enhancing the Value of Management Accounting Systems 9
▲ ***Surveys of Company Practice: "A Day in the Life" of a Management Accountant 11***
Key Management Accounting Guidelines 13
Cost-Benefit Approach 13
Behavioral and Technical Considerations 13
Different Costs for Different Purposes 13
▲ ***Concepts in Action: E-Business Strategies and the Management Accountant 14***
Organization Structure and the Management Accountant 15
Line and Staff Relationships 15
The Chief Financial Officer and the Controller 15
Professional Ethics 16
Ethical Guidelines 17
Typical Ethical Challenges 17
Problem for Self-Study 19 • Summary 20 • Terms to Learn 20 • Assignment Material 21 • Video Case: Regal Marine 26

2 An Introduction to Cost Terms and Purposes 29

Costs and Cost Terminology 30
Direct Costs and Indirect Costs 31
Cost Tracing and Cost Allocation 31
Factors Affecting Direct/Indirect Cost Classifications 32
Cost-Behavior Patterns: Variable Costs and Fixed Costs 32
▲ ***Surveys of Company Practice: Purposes for Companies Distinguishing Between Variable Costs and Fixed Costs 34***
Cost Drivers 34
▲ ***Concepts in Action: How Application Service Providers (ASPs) Influence Cost Structures 35***
Relevant Range 35
Relationships of Types of Costs 36
Total Costs and Unit Costs 36
Unit Costs and Average Costs 36
Use Unit Costs Cautiously 37
Manufacturing-, Merchandising-, and Service-Sector Companies 38
Financial Statements, Inventoriable Costs, and Period Costs 38
Types of Inventory 38
Commonly Used Classifications of Manufacturing Costs 39
Inventoriable Costs 39
Period Costs 39
Illustrating the Flow of Inventoriable Costs and Period Costs 40
Manufacturing-Sector Example 40
Recap of Inventoriable Costs and Period Costs 42
Prime Costs and Conversion Costs 43

Measuring Costs Requires Judgment 43
Measuring Labor Costs 43
Overtime Premium 44
Benefits of Defining Accounting Terms 45
The Many Meanings of Product Costs 45
A Framework for Cost Management 46
Problem for Self-Study 48 • Summary 50 • Terms to Learn 51 • Assignment Material 51 • Video Case: Three Dog Bakery 60

3 Cost-Volume-Profit Analysis 61

Cost-Volume-Profit Assumptions and Terminology 62
Essentials of CVP Analysis 63
The Breakeven Point 64
Equation Method 65
Contribution Margin Method 65
Graph Method 66
Target Operating Income 67
Target Net Income and Income Taxes 67
Using CVP Analysis for Decision Making 69
Decision to Advertise 69
Decision to Reduce Selling Price 69
Sensitivity Analysis and Uncertainty 70
Cost Planning and CVP 71
Alternative Fixed-Cost/Variable-Cost Structures 71
▲ ***Concepts In Action: Influencing Cost Structures to Manage the Risk-Return Trade-off at Amazon.com 73***
Effect of Time Horizon 73
Effects of Sales Mix on Income 74
CVP Analysis in Service and Nonprofit Organizations 75
Multiple Cost Drivers 76
Contribution Margin Versus Gross Margin 77
Merchandising Sector 77
Manufacturing Sector 77
Problem for Self-Study 78 • Summary 79
APPENDIX: Decision Models and Uncertainty 80
Coping with Uncertainty 80
Terms to Learn 83 • Assignment Material 83 • Video Case: Store 24 93

4 Job Costing 95

Building-Block Concepts of Costing Systems 96
Two Major Cost Objects: Products and Departments 97
Job-Costing and Process-Costing Systems 98
Job Costing in Manufacturing 99
General Approach to Job Costing 99
▲ ***Surveys of Company Practice: Cost-Allocation Bases Used for Manufacturing Overhead 100***
Source Documents 101
The Role of Technology 103
▲ ***Concepts in Action: Pricing and Efficiency Gains from Job Costing at Colorscope 104***
Time Period Used to Compute Indirect-Cost Rates 105
Normal Costing 106
A Normal Job-Costing System in Manufacturing 107
General Ledger and Subsidiary Ledgers 107
Explanations of Transactions 107
Nonmanufacturing Costs and Job Costing 114
Budgeted Indirect Costs and End-of-Period Adjustments 114
Adjusted Allocation-Rate Approach 115
Proration Approach 116
Write-Off to Cost of Goods Sold Approach 117
Choice Among Approaches 117
Multiple Overhead Cost Pools 118
Variations from Normal Costing: A Service-Sector Example 118
Problem for Self-Study 119 • Summary 121 • Terms to Learn 122 • Assignment Material 122 • Video Case: Dell Computer 133

5 Activity-Based Costing and Activity-Based Management 135

Broad Averaging via Peanut-Butter Costing Approaches 136
Undercosting and Overcosting 136
Product-Cost Cross-Subsidization 136
Costing System at Plastim Corporation 137
Design, Production, and Distribution Processes 137
Existing Single Indirect-Cost Pool System 138
Refining a Costing System 140
Activity-Based Costing Systems 141
Cost Hierarchies 143
Implementing Activity-Based Costing at Plastim 144
Comparing Alternative Costing Systems 148
Using ABC Systems for Improving Cost Management and Profitability 148
Activity-Based Costing and Department-Costing Systems 151

Implementing ABC Systems 151
ABC in Service and Merchandising Companies 152
▲ ***Surveys of Company Practice: Growing Interest in Activity-Based Costing 153***
▲ ***Concepts in Action: Measuring and Managing E-Retailing with Activity-Based Costing 154***
Problem for Self-Study 155 • Summary 157 • Terms to Learn 158 • Assignment Material 158 • Video Case: Dell Computer 173

PART TWO
Tools for Planning and Control

6 Master Budget and Responsibility Accounting 175

Budgets and the Budgeting Cycle 176
Advantages of Budgets 177
  Strategic Planning and Implementation of Plans 177
  Framework for Judging Performance 178
  Motivating Managers and Employees 178
  Coordination and Communication 178
  Administration of Budgets 179
▲ ***Surveys of Company Practice: Budget Practices Around the Globe 179***
Time Coverage of Budgets 180
Steps in Developing an Operating Budget 180
  Stylistic Furniture 181
Computer-Based Financial Planning Models 187
▲ ***Concepts in Action: Putting Budgeting on the Fast Track with Web Technology 188***
Kaizen Budgeting 189
Activity-Based Budgeting 189
Budgeting and Responsibility Accounting 191
  Organization Structure and Responsibility 191
  Feedback 192
Responsibility and Controllability 192
  Definition of Controllability 192
  Emphasis on Information and Behavior 193
Human Aspects of Budgeting 193
Problem for Self-Study 194 • Summary 195
APPENDIX: The Cash Budget 195
  Preparation of Budgets 197
  Sensitivity Analysis and Cash Flows 200
Terms to Learn 200 • Assignment Material 200 • Video Case: Ritz-Carlton Hotel Company 214

7 Flexible Budgets, Variances, and Management Control: I 215

The Use of Variances 216
Static Budgets and Flexible Budgets 216
  Accounting System at Webb 217
Static-Budget Variances 217
Steps in Developing a Flexible Budget 218
Flexible-Budget Variances and Sales-Volume Variances 219
  Sales-Volume Variances 220
  Flexible-Budget Variances 221
Price Variances and Efficiency Variances for Direct-Cost Inputs 221
  Obtaining Budgeted Input Prices and Budgeted Input Quantities 222
▲ ***Surveys of Company Practice: The Widespread Use of Standard Costs 223***
  Data for Calculating Webb's Price Variances and Efficiency Variances 223
  Price Variances 224
  Efficiency Variance 225
▲ ***Concepts in Action: Comparing Efficiency Variances and Yield Improvements at Analog Devices 226***
  Summary of Variances 226
  Impact of Inventories 227
Management Uses of Variances 228
  Performance Measurement Using Variances 228
  Multiple Causes of Variances and Organization Learning 228
  When to Investigate Variances 229
  Continuous Improvement 230
  Financial and Nonfinancial Performance Measures 230
Journal Entries Using Standard Costs 230
  Standard Costing and Information Technology 232
  Wide Applicability of Standard Costing Systems 232
Flexible Budgeting and Activity-Based Costing 232
  Relating Batch Costs to Product Output 232
  Price and Efficiency Variances 233
  Focus on Hierarchy 234
Benchmarking and Variance Analysis 234
Problem for Self-Study 235 • Summary 237 • Terms to Learn 237 • Assignment Material 238 • Video Case: McDonald's Corporation 248

8 Flexible Budgets, Variances, and Management Control: II 251

Planning of Variable and Fixed Overhead Costs 252

Planning Variable Overhead Costs 252

Planning Fixed Overhead Costs 252

Standard Costing at Webb Company 253

Developing Budgeted Variable Overhead Cost-Allocation Rates 253

Variable Overhead Cost Variances 254

Flexible-Budget Analysis 254

Variable Overhead Efficiency Variance 255

Variable Overhead Spending Variance 255

Developing Budgeted Fixed Overhead Cost-Allocation Rates 257

Fixed Overhead Cost Variances 258

Production-Volume Variance 258

Computation of Production-Volume Variance 258

Interpreting the Production-Volume Variance 259

Integrated Analysis of Overhead Cost Variances 260

▲ ***Concepts in Action: Standard Costing and Variance Analysis at Polysar 261***

4-, 3-, 2-, and 1-Variance Analysis 262

Different Purposes of Manufacturing Overhead Cost Analysis 263

Variable Manufacturing Overhead Costs 263

Fixed Manufacturing Overhead Costs 264

Journal Entries for Overhead Costs and Variances 264

Recording Overhead Costs 264

▲ ***Surveys of Company Practice: Variance Analysis and Control Decisions 265***

Financial and Nonfinancial Performance 267

Overhead Cost Variances in Nonmanufacturing and Service Settings 267

Activity-Based Costing and Variance Analysis 268

Flexible Budget and Variance Analysis for Variable Setup Overhead Costs 268

Flexible Budget and Variance Analysis for Fixed Setup Overhead Costs 270

Problem for Self-Study 271 • Summary 273 • Terms to Learn 274 • Assignment Material 274 • Video Case: Teva Sport Sandals 283

9 Inventory Costing and Capacity Analysis 285

PART ONE: Inventory Costing for Manufacturing Companies 286

Variable Costing and Absorption Costing 286

Data for One-Year Example 286

Comparing Income Statements 288

Explaining Differences in Operating Income 289

Data for Three-Year Example 289

Comparing Income Statements 290

Effect of Sales and Production on Operating Income 292

Performance Measures and Absorption Costing 293

Undesirable Buildup of Inventories 293

Proposals for Revising Performance Evaluation 295

Throughput Costing 295

Capsule Comparison of Inventory-Costing Methods 296

▲ ***Concepts in Action: Yield Improvements and the Production-Volume Variance at Analog Devices 297***

▲ ***Surveys of Company Practice: Usage of Variable Costing by Companies 298***

Problem for Self-Study 299

PART TWO: Denominator-Level Capacity Concepts and Fixed-Cost Capacity Analysis 300

Alternative Denominator-Level Capacity Concepts for Absorption Costing 300

Theoretical Capacity and Practical Capacity 300

Normal Capacity Utilization and Master-Budget Capacity Utilization 300

Effect on Budgeted Fixed Manufacturing Overhead Cost Rate 301

Choosing a Capacity Level 301

Effect on Product Costing and Capacity Management 302

Pricing Decisions and the Downward Demand Spiral 303

Effect on Performance Evaluation 303

Effect on Financial Statements 304

Regulatory Requirements 306

Difficulties in Forecasting Chosen Denominator-Level Concept 306

Capacity Costs and Denominator-Level Issues 306

Problem for Self-Study 307 • Summary 308

APPENDIX: Breakeven Points in Variable Costing and Absorption Costing 309

Terms to Learn 311 • Assignment Material 311 • Video Case: Wheeled Coach 320

PART THREE
Cost Information for Decisions

10 Determining How Costs Behave 323

General Issues in Estimating Cost Functions 324
- Basic Assumptions and Examples of Cost Functions 324
- Brief Review of Cost Classification 326
- Cost Estimation 326

The Cause-and-Effect Criterion in Choosing Cost Drivers 327

▲ ***Surveys of Company Practice: International Comparison of Cost Classification by Companies 328***

Cost Estimation Methods 328
- Industrial Engineering Method 329
- Conference Method 329
- Account Analysis Method 329
- Quantitative Analysis Methods 330

Steps in Estimating a Cost Function Using Quantitative Analysis 330
- High-Low Method 332
- Regression Analysis Method 333

Evaluating Cost Drivers of the Estimated Cost Function 335

Cost Drivers and Activity-Based Costing 337

Nonlinearity and Cost Functions 337

▲ ***Concepts in Action: Activity-Based Costing, Cost Drivers, and Revenue Drivers 338***

Learning Curves and Nonlinear Cost Functions 339
- Cumulative Average-Time Learning Model 340
- Incremental Unit-Time Learning Model 340
- Setting Prices, Budgets, and Standards 342

Data Collection and Adjustment Issues 343

Problem for Self-Study 345 • Summary 346

APPENDIX: Regression Analysis 347
- Estimating the Regression Line 347
- Goodness of Fit 347
- Significance of Independent Variables 348
- Specification Analysis of Estimation Assumptions 349
- Using Regression Output to Choose Cost Drivers of Cost Functions 351
- Multiple Regression and Cost Hierarchies 351
- Multicollinearity 353

Terms to Learn 354 • Assignment Material 354 • Case: U.S. Brewing Industry 367

11 Decision Making and Relevant Information 369

Information and The Decision Process 370

The Concept of Relevance 370
- Relevant Costs and Relevant Revenues 370
- Qualitative and Quantitative Relevant Information 372

An Illustration of Relevance: Choosing Output Levels 372
- One-Time-Only Special Orders 373
- Potential Problems in Relevant-Cost Analysis 374

Insourcing-Versus-Outsourcing and Make-Versus Buy Decisions 375
- Outsourcing and Idle Facilities 375
- Strategic and Qualitative Factors 377

Opportunity Costs, Outsourcing, and Capacity Constraints 377

▲ ***Concepts in Action: VW Takes Outsourcing to the Limit 378***
- Carrying Costs of Inventory 380

▲ ***Concepts in Action: American Airlines, the Internet, and Opportunity Costs 381***

Product-Mix Decisions Under Capacity Constraints 382

Customer Profitability, Activity-Based Costing, and Relevant Costs 383
- Relevant-Revenue and Relevant-Cost Analysis of Discontinuing a Customer 384
- Relevant-Revenue and Relevant-Cost Analysis of Adding a Customer 385
- Relevant-Revenue and Relevant-Cost Analysis of Discontinuing or Adding Branches or Segments 386

Irrelevance of Past Costs and Equipment-Replacement Decisions 386

Decisions and Performance Evaluation 388

Problem for Self-Study 389 • Summary 391

APPENDIX: Linear Programming 391
- Steps in Solving an LP Problem 392
- Sensitivity Analysis 394

Terms to Learn 395 • Assignment Material 395 • Video Case: Store 24 407

12 Pricing Decisions and Cost Management 409

Major Influences on Pricing Decisions 410
- Customers, Competitors, and Costs 410
- Time Horizon of Pricing Decisions 411

Cost and Pricing for The Short Run 411
Relevant Costs for Pricing a Special Order 411
Strategic and Other Factors in Pricing a Special Order 412
Costing and Pricing for The Long Run 413
Calculating Product Costs 413
Alternative Long-Run Pricing Approaches 414
Target Costing for Target Pricing 415
Implementing Target Pricing and Target Costing 416
Value Engineering, Cost Incurrence, and Locked-In Costs 417
Achieving the Target Cost Per Unit for Provalue 419
Cost-Plus Pricing 421
Cost-Plus Target Rate of Return on Investment 421
Alternative Cost-Plus Methods 422
Cost-Plus Pricing and Target Pricing 423
▲ ***Surveys of Company Practice: Differences in Pricing Practices and Cost Management Methods in Various Countries 424***
Life-Cycle Product Budgeting and Costing 425
Life-Cycle Budgeting and Pricing Decisions 425
Uses of Life-Cycle Budgeting and Costing 426
Considerations Other Than Costs in Pricing Decisions 427
Effects of Antitrust Laws on Pricing 428
▲ ***Concepts in Action: Pricing and the Internet 430***
Problem for Self-Study 430 • Summary 431 • Terms to Learn 432 • Assignment Material 432 • Video Case: Grand Canyon Railway 443

PART FOUR
Cost Allocation and Revenues

13 Strategy, Balanced Scorecard, and Strategic Profitability Analysis 445

What Is Strategy? 446
Implementation of Strategy and the Balanced Scorecard 447
The Balanced Scorecard 447
Quality Improvement and Reengineering at Chipset 448
The Four Perspectives of the Balanced Scorecard 449
Aligning the Balanced Scorecard to Strategy 451
Implementing a Balanced Scorecard 451
Features of a Good Balanced Scorecard 452
Pitfalls in Implementing a Balanced Scorecard 453
Evaluating the Success of a Strategy 453
▲ ***Surveys of Company Practice: Widening the Performance Measurement Lens Using the Balanced Scorecard 454***
Strategic Analysis of Operating Income 454
Growth Component 456
Price-Recovery Component 457
Productivity Component 458
Further Analysis of Growth, Price-Recovery, and Productivity Components 459
Downsizing and The Management of Capacity 460
▲ ***Concepts in Action: Growth Versus Profitability Choices of Dot-com Companies 461***
Relationships Between Inputs and Outputs 462
Identifying Unused Capacity for Engineered and Discretionary Overhead Costs 463
Managing Unused Capacity 464
Problem for Self-Study 464 • Summary 467
APPENDIX: Productivity Measurement 468
Partial Productivity Measures 468
Evaluating Changes in Partial Productivities 469
Total Factor Productivity 470
Calculating and Comparing Total Factor Productivity 470
Using Partial and Total Factor Productivity Measures 471
Terms to Learn 471 • Assignment Material 471 • Video Case: McDonald's Corporation 479

14 Cost Allocation, Customer-Profitability Analysis, and Sales-Variance Analysis 481

Purposes of Cost Allocation 482
Criteria to Guide Cost-Allocation Decisions 484
Role of Dominant Criteria 484
Cost-Benefit Approach 485
Cost Allocation and Costing Systems 485
Allocating Corporate Costs to Divisions and Products 486
▲ ***Surveys of Company Practice: Why Allocate Corporate and Other Support Costs to Divisions and Departments 488***
Implementing Corporate Cost Allocations 489
Customer Revenues and Customer Costs 490
Customer Revenue Analysis 491
Customer Cost Analysis 491
Customer-Level Costs 492
▲ ***Concepts in Action: Customer Profitability at PHH and Federal Express 493***

Customer-Profitability Profiles 494
Assessing Customer Value 495
Sales Variances 496
Static-Budget Variance 497
Flexible-Budget Variance and Sales-Volume Variance 497
Sales-Mix and Sales-Quantity Variances 498
Sales-Mix Variance 498
Sales-Quantity Variance 499
Market-Share and Market-Size Variances 500
Market-Share Variance 500
Market-Size Variance 501
Problem for Self-Study 502 • Summary 504
APPENDIX: Mix and Yield Variances for Substitutable Inputs 504
Direct Materials Price and Efficiency Variances 505
Direct Materials Mix and Materials Yield Variances 505
Terms to Learn 507 • Assignment Material 508 • Video Case: Nantucket Nectars 519

15 Allocation of Support Department Costs, Common Costs, and Revenues 521

Allocating Costs of a Support Department to Operating Divisions 522
Single-Rate and Dual-Rate Methods 522
Budgeted Versus Actual Rates 524
Budgeted Usage, Actual Usage, and Capacity-Level Allocation Bases 525
Allocating Costs of Multiple Support Departments 526
Operating and Support Departments 526
Direct Allocation Method 527
Step-Down Allocation Method 528
Reciprocal Allocation Method 529
Overview of Methods 532
▲ ***Surveys of Company Practice: Allocation of Support Department Costs 533***
Allocating Common Costs 533
Stand-Alone Cost-Allocation Method 533
Incremental Cost-Allocation Method 534
Cost Allocations and Contracts 535
Contracting with the U.S. Government 535
Fairness of Pricing 535
▲ ***Concepts in Action: Contract Disputes over Reimbursable Costs for U.S. Government Agencies 536***
Revenue Allocation and Bundled Products 537
Revenue-Allocation Methods 537
Stand-Alone Revenue-Allocation Method 538
Incremental Revenue-Allocation Method 539
Other Revenue-Allocation Methods 540
Problem for Self-Study 540 • Summary 542 • Terms to Learn 543 • Assignment Material 543 • Case: Stanford University 553

16 Cost Allocation: Joint Products and Byproducts 555

Joint-Cost Basics 556
Why Allocate Joint Costs? 558
Approaches to Allocating Joint Costs 558
Sales Value at Splitoff Method 560
Physical-Measure Method 560
Net Realizable Value (NRV) Method 561
Constant Gross-Margin Percentage NRV Method 563
Choosing a Method 564
Not Allocating Joint Costs 565
▲ ***Surveys of Company Practice: Joint-Cost Allocation in the Oil Patch 566***
Irrelevance of Joint Costs for Decision Making 566
Sell or Process Further 567
Joint-Cost Allocation and Performance Evaluation 567
Accounting for Byproducts 568
Method A: Byproducts Recognized at Time Production Is Completed 569
▲ ***Concepts in Action: Chicken Processing: Costing of Joint Products and Byproducts 570***
Method B: Byproducts Recognized at Time of Sale 570
Problem for Self-Study 571 • Summary 573 • Terms to Learn 573 • Assignment Material 573 • Case: Memory Manufacturing Company 584

17 Process Costing 585

Illustrating Process Costing 586
▲ ***Surveys of Company Practice: Process Costing in Different Industries 587***
Case 1: Process Costing with Zero Beginning and Zero Ending Work-in-Process Inventory 588
Case 2: Process Costing with Zero Beginning but Some Ending Work-in-Process Inventory 588
Physical Units and Equivalent Units (Steps 1 and 2) 589

Calculation of Product Costs (Steps 3, 4, and 5) 590
Journal Entries 591
Case 3: Process Costing with Some Beginning and Some Ending Work-in-Process Inventory 592
Weighted-Average Method 593
First-in, First-Out Method 596
Comparison of Weighted-Average and FIFO Methods 599
Standard-Costing Method of Process Costing 600
Computations under Standard Costing 600
Accounting for Variances 601
Transferred-in Costs in Process Costing 603
Transferred-In Costs and the Weighted-Average Method 604
Transferred-In Costs and the FIFO Method 606
Points to Remember about Transferred-In Costs 607
▲ ***Concepts in Action: Hybrid Costing for Customized Products at Levi Strauss 608***
Hybrid-Costing Systems 608
Problem for Self-Study 609 • Summary 611
APPENDIX: Operation Costing 612
Overview of Operation-Costing Systems 612
Illustration of an Operation-Costing System 612
Journal Entries 613
Terms to Learn 614 • Assignment Material 614 • Video Case: Nantucket Nectars 623

PART FIVE
Quality and JIT

18 Spoilage, Rework, and Scrap 625

Terminology 626
Different Types of Spoilage 626
▲ ***Surveys of Company Practice: Rejection in the Electronics Industry 627***
Normal Spoilage 628
Abnormal Spoilage 628
Process Costing and Spoilage 628
Count All Spoilage 629
The Five-Step Procedure for Process Costing with Spoilage 630
Weighted-Average Method and Spoilage 631
FIFO Method and Spoilage 631
Standard-Costing Method and Spoilage 631
Journal Entries 634
Inspection Points and Allocating Costs of Normal Spoilage 634
Job Costing and Spoilage 636
Rework 637
Accounting for Scrap 638
Recognizing Scrap at the Time of Its Sale 638
Recognizing Scrap at the Time of Its Production 639
▲ ***Concepts in Action: Managing Waste and Environmental Costs at the DuPont Corporation 640***
Problem for Self-Study 641 • Summary 641
APPENDIX: Inspection and Spoilage at Intermediate Stages of Completion in Process Costing 642
Terms to Learn 644 • Assignment Material 644 • Case: The United Libbey-Nippon Plant 651

19 Quality, Time, and the Theory of Constraints 653

Quality as a Competitive Tool 654
Costs of Quality 655
Techniques Used to Analyze Quality Problems 657
Control Charts 657
Pareto Diagrams 658
Cause-and-Effect Diagrams 659
Relevant Costs and Benefits of Quality Improvement 659
Costs of Design Quality 661
Nonfinancial Measures of Quality and Customer Satisfaction 661
Nonfinancial Measures of Customer Satisfaction 661
Nonfinancial Measures of Internal Performance 662
▲ ***Concepts in Action: Dell Computer's QUEST 662***
Evaluating Quality Performance 663
Advantages of COQ Measures 663
Advantages of Nonfinancial Measures of Quality 663
Time as a Competitive Tool 663
Customer-Response Time 664
On-Time Performance 664
Time Drivers and Costs of Time 664
Uncertainty and Bottlenecks as Drivers of Time 665
▲ ***Concepts in Action: Overcoming Bottlenecks on the Internet 665***
Relevant Revenues and Costs of Time 667

Theory of Constraints and Throughput Contribution Analysis 668

Problem for Self-Study 671 • Summary 672 • Terms to Learn 673 • Assignment Material 673 • Video Case: Ritz-Carlton Hotel Company 683

20 Inventory Management, Just-in-Time, and Backflush Costing 685

Inventory Management in Retail Organizations 686
- Costs Associated with Goods for Sale 686

Economic-Order-Quantity Decision Model 687
- When to Order, Assuming Certainty 688
- Safety Stock 689

Estimating Inventory-Related Costs and Their Effects 691
- Considerations in Obtaining Estimates of Relevant Costs 691
- Cost of a Prediction Error 691
- Evaluating Managers and Goal-Congruence Issues 692

Just-in-Time Purchasing 692
- JIT Purchasing and EOQ Model Parameters 692
- Relevant Benefits and Relevant Costs of JIT Purchasing 693
- Supplier Evaluation and Relevant Costs of Quality and Timely Deliveries 693

Inventory Management and Supply-Chain Analysis 695

▲ ***Surveys of Company Practice: Challenges in Obtaining the Benefits from a Supply-Chain Analysis 696***

Inventory Management and MRP 696

Inventory Management and JIT Production 697

▲ ***Concepts in Action: Writing a Book Is as Easy as Making a Cup of Latté 698***
- Enterprise Resource Planning (ERP) Systems 698
- Financial Benefits of JIT and Relevant Costs 699
- Performance Measures and Control in JIT Production 699
- JIT's Effect on Costing Systems 700

Backflush Costing 700
- Simplified Normal or Standard Job Costing 700
- Accounting for Variances 703
- Special Consideration in Backflush Costing 706

Problems for Self-Study 707 • Summary 708 • Terms to Learn 709 • Assignment Material 709 • Video Case: Regal Marine 716

PART SIX
Investment Decisions and Management Control Systems

21 Capital Budgeting and Cost Analysis 717

Two Dimensions of Cost Analysis 718

Stages of Capital Budgeting 719

Discounted Cash Flow 720
- Net Present Value Method 720
- Internal Rate-of-Return Method 722
- Comparison of Net Present Value and Internal Rate-of-Return Methods 723

Sensitivity Analysis 724

Payback Method 724
- Uniform Cash Flows 724
- Nonuniform Cash Flows 725

Accrual Accounting Rate-of-Return Method 726

▲ ***Surveys of Company Practice: International Comparison of Capital Budgeting Methods 727***

Evaluating Managers and Goal-Congruence Issues 727

Relevant Cash Flows in Discounted Cash Flow Analysis 728
- Relevant After-Tax Flows 729

Managing the Project 733
- Management Control of Investment Activity 733
- Management Control of the Project—Postinvestment Audit 733

Strategic Considerations in Capital Budgeting 734
- Intangible Assets and Capital Budgeting 734

▲ ***Concepts in Action: Capital Budgeting for Pollution Prevention 735***

Problem for Self-Study 736 • Summary 738

APPENDIX: Capital Budgeting and Inflation 739
- Net Present Value Method and Inflation 739

Terms to Learn 741 • Assignment Material 741 • Video Case: Deer Valley Resort 751

22 Management Control Systems, Transfer Pricing, and Multinational Considerations 753

Management Control Systems 754

Evaluating Management Control Systems 755

Organization Structure and Decentralization 755
- Benefits of Decentralization 756

Costs of Decentralization 756
Comparison of Benefits and Costs 757
Decentralization in Multinational Companies 757
Choices About Responsibility Centers 758
Transfer Pricing 758
Transfer-Pricing Methods 759
An Illustration of Transfer Pricing 759
Market-Based Transfer Prices 762
Perfectly Competitive Market Case 762
Distress Prices 762
Cost-Based Transfer Prices 763
Full-Cost Bases 763
Variable Cost Bases 765
Prorating the Difference Between Maximum and Minimum Transfer Prices 765
Dual Pricing 765
Negotiated Transfer Prices 766
▲ ***Surveys of Company Practice: Domestic and Multinational Transfer-Pricing Practices 767***
A General Guideline for Transfer-Pricing Situations 768
Multinational Transfer Pricing and Tax Considerations 769
▲ ***Concepts in Action: U.S. Internal Revenue Service, Japanese National Tax Agency, and Transfer-Pricing Games 771***
Problem for Self-Study 772 • Summary 773 • Terms to Learn 774 • Assignment Material 774 • Case: Information Systems Corporation 783

23 Performance Measurement, Compensation, and Multinational Considerations 785

Financial and Nonfinancial Performance Measures 786
Choosing Among Different Performance Measures: Step 1 787
Return on Investment 788
Residual Income 789
Economic Value Added 790
Return on Sales 791
Comparing Performance Measures 792
▲ ***Surveys of Company Practice: Examples of Key Financial Performance Measures in Different Companies Around the Globe 792***
Choosing the Time Horizon of the Performance Measures: Step 2 793
Choosing Alternative Definitions for Performance Measures: Step 3 794
Choosing Measurement Alternatives for Performance Measures: Step 4 794
Current Cost 794
Long-Term Assets: Gross or Net Book Value? 795
Choosing Target Levels of Performance: Step 5 797
Choosing the Timing of Feedback: Step 6 797
Performance Measurement in Multinational Companies 797
Calculating the Foreign Division's ROI in the Foreign Currency 798
Calculating the Foreign Division's ROI in U.S. Dollars 798
Distinction Between Managers and Organization Units 799
The Basic Trade-Off: Creating Incentives Versus Imposing Risk 800
Intensity of Incentives and Financial and Nonfinancial Measurements 800
Benchmarks and Relative Performance Evaluation 801
▲ ***Concepts in Action: Should Companies Force Rank Employees? 802***
Performance Measures at the Individual Activity Level 802
Performing Multiple Tasks 803
Team-Based Compensation Arrangements 803
Executive Performance Measures and Compensation 803
Intrinsic Motivation and Organization Culture 805
Environmental and Ethical Responsibilities 805
Problem for Self-Study 806 • Summary 807 • Terms to Learn 808 • Assignment Material 808

Appendix A: Surveys of Company Practice 819
Appendix B: Recommended Readings 822
Appendix C: Notes on Compound Interest and Interest Tables 825
Appendix D: Cost Accounting in Professional Examinations 832
Glossary 835
Author Index 846
Company Index 847
Subject Index 849

PREFACE

Studying cost accounting is one of the best business investments a student can make. Why? Because success in any organization — from the smallest corner store to the largest multinational corporation — requires the use of cost accounting concepts and practices. Cost accounting provides key data to managers for planning and controlling, as well as costing products, services, and customers. Topics covered in this book also are of great value in personal financial management. For example, gaining an understanding of budgeting yields lifelong returns.

The central focus of this book is how cost accounting helps managers make better decisions. Cost accountants are increasingly becoming integral members of decision-making teams instead of just data providers. To link to this decision-making emphasis, the "different costs for different purposes" theme is used throughout this book. By focusing on basic concepts, analyses, uses, and procedures instead of procedures alone, we recognize cost accounting as a managerial tool for business strategy and implementation. We also prepare students for the rewards and challenges facing them in the professional cost accounting world both today and tomorrow.

STRENGTHS OF THE TENTH EDITION RETAINED AND ENHANCED

Reviewers of the tenth edition praised the following features, which have been retained and strengthened in the eleventh edition:

- Exceptionally strong emphasis on managerial uses of cost information
- Clarity and understandability of the text
- Excellent balance in integrating modern topics with existing content
- Emphasis on human behavior aspects
- Extensive use of real-world examples
- Ability to teach chapters in difference sequences
- Excellent quantity, quality and range of assignment material

The first thirteen chapters provide the essence of a one-term (quarter or semester) course. There is ample text and assignment material in the book's twenty-three chapters for a two-term course. This book can be used immediately after the student has had an introductory course in financial accounting. Alternatively, this book can build on an introductory course in managerial accounting.

Deciding on the sequence of chapters in a textbook is a challenge. Every instructor has a favorite way of organizing his or her course. Hence, we present a modular, flexible organization that permits a course to be custom-tailored. *This organization facilitates diverse approaches to teaching and learning.*

As an example of the book's flexibility, consider our treatment of process costing. Process costing is described in Chapters 17 and 18. Instructors interested in filling out a student's perspective of costing systems can move directly from job-order costing described in Chapter 4 to Chapter 17 without interruption in the flow of material. Other instructors may want their students to delve into activity-based costing and budgeting and more decision-oriented topics early in the course. These instructors may prefer to postpone discussion of process costing.

CHANGES IN CONTENT AND PEDAGOGY OF THE ELEVENTH EDITION

The pace of change in organizations continues to be rapid. The eleventh edition of *Cost Accounting* reflects changes occurring in the role of cost accounting in organizations and in research on cost accounting. Examples of key additions and changes in the topic areas of the eleventh edition are:

1. *Increased coverage of strategy and strategic uses of cost information.* Chapter 13, entitled "Strategy, Balanced Scorecard, and Strategic Profitability Analysis," has been revised and simplified. In addition, Chapter 1 describes strategy and strategy implementation; Chapter 3 presents the application of cost-volume-profit analysis to strategic decisions such as in pricing, product promotion, and choosing cost structures; Chapters 6, 7, and 8 discuss how budgets and variances provide managers with feedback about the validity of their strategies; Chapter 9 describes how managers make strategic decisions regarding capacity; Chapters 11 and 12 show the application of relevant costs and relevant revenues to strategic decisions such as opening and closing divisions and pricing of products; Chapters 19 and 20 address the strategic benefits of quality and just-in-time inventory systems. Chapter 21 shows how capital budgeting techniques help in strategic decisions such as long-term customer relationships.

2. *A framework for cost accounting and cost management introduced in Chapter 2* provides a bridge between the concepts introduced in Chapters 1 and 2 and the topics presented in Chapters 3 through 12. The framework emphasizes three key ideas for the study of cost accounting and cost management: (1) calculating the cost of products, services, and other cost objects, (2) obtaining information for planning and control and performance evaluation, and (3) identifying relevant information for decision making. The framework provides a structure for discussing topics in later chapters such as strategy evaluation, quality, and just-in-time that invariably have product costing, planning and control, and decision-making perspectives.

3. *Activity-based costing (ABC) presented in a single chapter (Chapter 5)* with links to simpler job-costing systems (presented in Chapter 4). New ABC-related material has been added on budgeting (Chapter 6), capacity choices for calculating activity rates (Chapter 9), cost estimation (Chapter 10), and customer profitability analysis (Chapter 14). Activity-based costing and activity-based management material is also included in Chapters 7 and 8 on variance analysis; Chapter 11 on outsourcing and adding or dropping business segments; Chapter 12 on design decisions; Chapter 13 on reengineering and downsizing; Chapter 19 on quality costs and quality improvements; and Chapter 20 on supplier analysis.

4. *Increased discussion of decision uses of cost accounting information.* This increase occurs in many topic areas, such as activity-based costing (Chapter 5), variance analysis (Chapters 7 and 8), capacity analysis (Chapter 9), cost estimation (Chapter 10), relevant costs and prices (Chapters 11 and 12), joint cost allocations (Chapter 16), process costing (Chapter 17), quality management (Chapter 19), and transfer pricing (Chapter 22).

5. *Systematic incorporation of new and evolving management thinking* including capacity decisions (Chapter 9), supply chain analysis, vendor managed inventory, and enterprise resource planning systems (Chapter 20), and long-term customer relationships (Chapter 21).

6. *Incorporating advances in technology* into coverage of topics. Many of the Concepts in Action boxes focus on technology, information systems, and the Internet—for example e-business strategies and the management accountant (Chapter 1); how application service providers (ASPs) influence cost structures (Chapter 2); cost structures and the risk-return trade-off at Amazon.com (Chapter 3); using activity-based costing to measure and manage e-retailing (Chapter 5); budgeting using web-based technology (Chapter 6); pricing on the Internet (Chapter 12); growth versus profitability choices of dot.com companies (Chapter 13); making custom-fit jeans at Levi Strauss (Chapter 17); overcoming bottlenecks on the Internet (Chapter 19); printing books on demand (Chapter 20).

7. *Increased attention to behavioral issues* such as reducing budgetary slack, motivating managers and employees, and building a culture for learning and support (Chapter 6), trade-offs between setting attainable versus ideal standards (Chapter 7), effect of joint-cost allocations on performance measurement and managerial behavior (Chapter 16), effect of management control and transfer pricing on managers' behavior (Chapter 22), and the role of organization culture, values, and intrinsic motivation in motivating managers (Chapter 23).

Major Changes in Content and Sequence

Special attention has been given to streamlining presentations in every chapter of the book as well as providing better and clearer explanations. Each chapter was scrutinized by knowledgeable critics before a final draft was completed. The result is a shorter and more student-friendly book. Specific major changes in content and in the sequence of individual chapters are:

1. Chapter 2 presents a framework for studying and understanding cost accounting and cost management.
2. Chapters 6 and 7 have more coverage on the behavioral effects of budgeting including how budgets motivate managers and employees, how managers can reduce budgetary slack, and the trade-offs between attainable versus ideal standards.
3. Chapter 7 shows how variances can be used to reconcile static-budget operating income and actual operating income.
4. Chapter 8 shows how the production-volume variance is related to the sales-volume variance and what each variance seeks to explain.
5. Part 2 in Chapter 9 on denominator-level choices has been significantly reorganized and new material on the effect of denominator-level choices for product costing, capacity management, and pricing has been added.
6. The Chapter 13 example that runs throughout the chapter has been simplified by reducing the number of cost categories.
7. Chapters 14 and 16 of the tenth edition have been restructured and appear as Chapters 14 and 15 in the eleventh edition. Chapter 15 in the tenth edition was on joint costs, and is now Chapter 16 in the eleventh edition. Chapter 14 focuses on macro issues in cost and revenue analysis. It includes material on allocating corporate costs to divisions (from Chapter 14 in the tenth edition) and customer profitability analysis and sales revenue analysis (from

Chapter 16 in the tenth edition). Chapter 15 focuses on micro issues in cost and revenue allocations, such as allocating support department costs to operating departments and common cost and common revenue allocations. Chapters 14 and 15 retain the modular structure of the rest of the book. Instructors who want to focus on cost and revenue allocations can move directly from the first part of Chapter 14 to Chapter 15 without interruption in the flow of material. Chapter 15 also contains new material on using practical capacity to compute cost-allocation rates, a second approach to doing reciprocal allocations, and the Shapley value for common cost allocations.

8. Chapter 21 on capital budgeting has been restructured. The presentation of relevant cash flow analysis in capital budgeting has been consolidated in one section that includes a discussion of income tax effects. This section follows the presentation of all four capital budgeting methods, net present value, internal rate of return, payback, and accrual accounting rate of return.
9. Numerical company examples in key chapters have been updated or revised to streamline the exposition and provide better explanations.

The Solutions Manual for instructors includes a chapter-by-chapter listing of the major changes in the text of the eleventh edition.

Assignment Material

The eleventh edition continues the widely applauded close connection between text and assignment material formed in previous editions. We have also significantly expanded the assignment material, provided more structure, and added greater variety.

End-of-chapter assignment material is divided into six groups: Questions, Exercises, Problems, a Collaborative Learning Problem, Internet Exercises, and a Video Case. Additional assignment material will be posted on the Web site www.prenhall.com/horngren. Questions require students to understand basic concepts and the meaning of key terms. Exercises are short, structured assignments that test basic issues presented in the chapter. Problems are longer and more difficult assignments. Each chapter has an ethics-related problem. Each chapter also has an exercise or problem linked to an Excel application. The Excel application gives students step-by-step directions to creating an Excel spreadsheet to work the exercise or problem. The Collaborative Learning Problem is the last assignment in each chapter and requires students to think critically about a particular problem or specific business situation. The Internet Exercise leads students to a Web site related to the material presented in the chapter. Students use information available at the Web site to answer questions that are also available on the Web. The Video Case is an in-depth description of a particular company, in most chapters, accompanied by a video on the company. Instructors may choose to use the case without requiring students to view the video or have students view the video tape that accompanies the text. The case questions challenge students to apply the concepts learned in the chapter to a specific business situation.

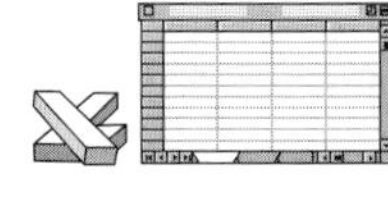

Other Pedagogical Changes

1. *Margin notes that appear throughout the book* provide students with helpful hints and clarifications for understanding the material and give additional examples of key concepts.
2. *Learning objectives that appear in the text's margins now contain* brief descriptions of the key concepts and ideas that relate to a learning objective.
3. A new feature, *Decision Points, uses a question-and-answer format to summarize* the chapter's learning objectives. The question is related to a learning objective and is framed in the form of a decision. The answer to the question is framed as guidelines for the decision.
4. Each *chapter opens with a vignette* describing a specific situation or problem faced by managers at a company. For most chapters, a video clip related to the vignette can be accessed at www.prenhall.com/horngren. The goal is to interest and motivate students to learn the chapter material. The *case at the end of the chapter* assignment material is on the same company described in the vignette and develops issues raised in the vignette. Students can answer the case questions based on the concepts presented in the chapter.

ILLUSTRATIONS OF ACTUAL BUSINESSES

Students become highly motivated to learn cost accounting if they can relate the subject matter to the real world. We have spent considerable time interacting with the business community, investigating new uses of cost accounting information, and gaining insight into how changes in technology are affecting the roles of cost accounting information. Real-world illustrations are found in many parts of the text.

Concepts in Action Boxes. Found in every chapter, these boxes discuss how cost accounting concepts are applied by individual companies. Examples are drawn from many different countries, including the *United States* (Amazon.com on p. 73, Colorscope on p. 104, Analog Devices on p. 297, American Airlines on p. 381, and Federal Express on p. 493), *Brazil* (Volkswagen on p. 378), *Canada* (Polysar on p. 281), *Japan* (Nissan Motor Company on p. 771), *Switzerland* (Novartis on p. 338), and the *United Kingdom* (Cooperative Bank on p. 338).

New boxes covering the use by managers of the Internet have been added in several chapters.

These Concepts in Action boxes cover a diverse set of industries including airline transportation, automobiles, banking, chemicals, computers, electronics, e-retailing, Internet equipment, manufacturing, publishing, and textiles.

Surveys of Company Practice Boxes. Results from surveys in more than 15 countries are cited in the many Surveys of Company Practice boxes found throughout the book. Examples include:

- Management purposes for classifying costs (p. 34)—cites evidence from Australia, Japan, and the United Kingdom.
- Activity-based cost information (p. 153)—cites evidence from United States, Canada, Holland, Ireland, New Zealand, and the United Kingdom.
- Standard costs (p. 223)—cites evidence from United States, Canada, Ireland, Japan, Sweden, and the United Kingdom.
- Variable costing (p. 298)—cites evidence from the United States, Canada, Australia, Japan, Sweden, and the United Kingdom.
- Balanced scorecard (p. 454)—cites evidence from the United States, Canada, Finland, Portugal, and Scandinavia.
- Purposes of cost allocation (p. 488)—cites evidence from the United States, Australia, Canada, and the United Kingdom.
- Capital budgeting practices (p. 727)—cites evidence from the United States, Australia, Canada, Ireland, Japan, Scotland, South Korea, and the United Kingdom.
- Transfer pricing practices (p. 767)—cites evidence from the United States, Australia, Canada, India, Japan, New Zealand, and the United Kingdom.
- Performance measures (p. 792)—cites evidence from the United States, Canada, Australia, Germany, Italy, Japan, Sweden, and the United Kingdom.

This extensive survey evidence enables students to see that many of the concepts they are learning are widely used around the globe.

Photos from Actual Companies. Each chapter opens with a photograph that illustrates an important concept discussed in that chapter. These photos feature many different companies including Regal Marine (p. 1), Store 24 (p. 61), Dell Computer (p. 136), Ritz Carlton (p. 175), McDonalds (p. 215), Nantucket Nectars (p. 481), Deer Valley Resort (p. 717).

Each Concepts in Action box also has an accompanying photo.

SUPPLEMENTS TO THE ELEVENTH EDITION

A complete package of supplements is available to assist students and instructors in using this book.

Student Resources

- **Student Guide and Review Manual** by John K. Harris helps reinforce key concepts.
- **Student Solutions Manual** by Charles T. Horngren, Srikant M. Datar, George Foster, and M. Zafar Iqbal assists with select end-of-chapter problems.
- **ABC CD-ROM** EasyABC Quick™ helps you create a model of a business and identify and analyze the real costs associated with activities, processes, and products. EasyABC Quick includes extensive online help and is an important tool to help accelerate learning about and the understanding of activity-based costing.
- **Prentice Hall Companion Web Site** offers access to online quizzes, tutorial assistance, current events, links to key accounting sites, writing resources, research center, study tips, downloads, and much more! To visit the site go to www.prenhall.com/horngren.
- **Spreadsheet Templates** by Albert Fisher of Community College of Southern Nevada are available on the Web site.
- *NEW* **Streaming Videos** (from www.prenhall.com/horngren) are linked with the **Chapter-Opening Vignettes.** Students can see how real companies are wrestling with cost accounting issues; these On-Location clips and the chapter-opening vignettes set the stage for the chapter content that follows.
- *NEW* **Student CD-ROM** contains a rich assortment of tools (PowerPoints, spreadsheets, and videos) to aid students in learning cost accounting topics!

Instructor Resources

- **Instructor's Manual and Media Guide** by Jean L. Hawkins of William Jewell College offers helpful classroom suggestions and teaching tips.

- **Test Item File** by Karen Schoenebeck of Southwestern College offers an array of questions ranging from easy to difficult. An electronic version of these questions is also available.
- **Solutions Manual** by Charles T. Horngren, Srikant M. Datar, George Foster, and M. Zafar Iqbal provides instructors with answers to all end-of-chapter material.
- **Solutions Transparencies** are also available to instructors.
- **Solutions to Spreadsheet Templates** provide instructors with answers to problems.
- **On-Location Videos** produced by Beverly Amer of Northern Arizona University and Aspenleaf Productions provide real-company scenarios. A full set of videos is available, and instructors and students can also access brief digitized clips of these videos at www.prenhall.com/horngren.
- **PowerPoint Presentation** created by Olga Quintana of University of Miami, provides you with a slide show ready for classroom use! Use the slides as they are, or edit them to meet your classroom needs.
- *NEW* **Excel for Management & Cost Accounting** provides a rich assortment of tools to master Excel.
- **Prentice Hall Companion Web Site** offers access to online quizzes, tutorial assistance, current events, links to key accounting sites, writing resources, research center, study tips, downloads, and much more! To visit the site go to www.prenhall.com/horngren. To obtain a password, contact your Prentice Hall book representative.
- *NEW* **Instructor Course Organizer CD-ROM** contains every print and technology ancillary. This makes it extremely easy for faculty to (1) customize any supplement, (2) access any supplement while using a computer, and (3) transport "the entire package" from home, to class, to office. **Free upon adoption.**
- *NEW* **eBook with CourseCompass** provides you and your students with 24/7 access to their text from any computer. In addition, the ***NEW* Online Course in BlackBoard or CourseCompass** enables you to use the text in an online (or Web-enhanced course). For more information, contact your Prentice Hall book representative.

ACKNOWLEDGMENTS

We are indebted to many for their ideas and assistance. Our primary thanks go to the many academics and practitioners who have advanced our knowledge of cost accounting.

The package of teaching materials we present is the work of many skillful and valued team members. John K. Harris aided us immensely at all stages in the development and production of this book. He critiqued the tenth edition and gave a detailed review of the manuscript for the eleventh edition. M. Zafar Iqbal reviewed the manuscript and gave suggestions for improvement in addition to developing some excellent end-of-chapter assignment material. Sheryl Powers gave much valued input on both the text and solutions manual. Beverly Amer proved to be an invaluable resource in researching and writing the video cases. Eric Blazer creatively developed the Internet exercises and Dennis Campbell methodically crafted the Excel applications. Jeremy Cott and Edie Prescott provided outstanding research assistance on technical issues and current developments. The book is much better because of the efforts of these colleagues.

Professors providing detailed written reviews of the previous edition or comments on our drafts of this edition include:

Robyn Alcock
Central Queensland University

David S. Baglia
Grove City College

Charles Bailey
University of Central Florida

Dennis Caplan
Columbia University

Donald W. Gribbin
Southern Illinois University

Rosalie Hallbauer
Florida International University

Jean Hawkins
William Jewell College

Jiunn C. Huang
San Francisco State University

Larry N. Killough
Virginia Polytechnic Inst. & State Univ.

Sandra Lazzarini
University of Queensland

Gary J. Mann
University of Texas at El Paso

Ronald Marshall
Michigan State University

Marjorie Platt
Northeastern University

Gim S. Seow
University of Connecticut

Rebekah A. Sheely
Northeastern University

Robert J. Shepherd
University of California, Santa Cruz

Vic Stanton
California State Univ.–Hayward

Carolyn Streuly
Marquette University

Peter D. Woodlock
Youngstown State University

James Williamson
San Diego State University

Sung-Soo Yoon
UCLA at Los Angeles

The faculty participating in the many focus groups on the tenth edition provided highly valued feedback. Many students provided input on this and the previous edition including Sudhakar Balachandran, Laura Donahue, Susan Kulp, Elizabeth Demers, Philip Joos, Patricia Joseph, Kazbi Kothaval, Mee Sook Lee, Erik Steiner, and Kenton Yee. The assistance of Dennis Campbell in checking the Solutions Manual was much appreciated. In addition we have received helpful suggestions from many users, unfortunately too numerous to be mentioned here. The eleventh edition is much improved by the feedback and interest of all these people. We are very appreciative of this support.

Our association with CAM-I has been a source of much stimulation as well as enjoyment. CAM-I has played a pivotal role in extending the frontiers of knowledge on cost management. We appreciate our extended and continued interaction with Jim Brimson, Callie Berliner, Charles Marx, R. Steven Player, Tom Pryor, Mike Roberts, and Pete Zampino.

We thank the people at Prentice Hall for their hard work and dedication, including Thomas Sigel, Mike Elia, Anne Graydon, Beth Toland, Arnold Vila, Linda Albelli, Fran Toepfer, and Pat Smythe. We would also like to thank Cindy Regan, Vincent Scelta, Steve Deitmer, P. J. Boardman, Michael Weinstein, and Annie Todd for their support and encouragement throughout the process, and Donna King at Progressive Publishing Alternatives.

Aza Gevorkian, Ariel Shoresh, and Jiranee Tongudai managed the production aspects of all the manuscript preparation with superb skill and much grace. We are deeply appreciative of their good spirits, loyalty, and ability to stay calm in the most hectic of times. The constant support of Bianca Baggio, Niesha Bryant, Katie Haskin, Chris Lion, Luz Velasquez, Carla West, and Debbie Wheeler is greatly appreciated.

Appreciation also goes to the American Institute of Certified Public Accountants, the Institute of Management Accountants, the Society of Management Accountants of Canada, the Certified General Accountants Association of Canada, the Financial Executive Institute of America, and many other publishers and companies for their generous permission to quote from their publications. Problems from the Uniform CPA examinations are designated (CPA); problems from the Certified Management Accountant examination are designated (CMA); problems from the Canadian examinations administered by the Society of Management Accountants are designated (SMA); problems from the Certified General Accountants Association are designated (CGA). Many of these problems are adapted to highlight particular points.

We are grateful to the professors who contributed assignment material for this edition. Their names are indicated in parentheses at the start of their specific problems.

Comments from users are welcome.

Charles T. Horngren
Srikant M. Datar
George Foster

Charles T. Horngren is the Edmund W. Littlefield Professor of Accounting, Emeritus, at Stanford University. A Graduate of Marquette University, he received his MBA from Harvard University and his Ph.D. from the University of Chicago. He is also the recipient of honorary doctorates from Marquette University and DePaul University.

A Certified Public Accountant, Horngren served on the Accounting Principles Board for six years, the Financial Accounting Standards Board Advisory Council for five years, and the Council of the American Institute of Certified Public Accountants for three years. For six years, he served as a trustee of the Financial Accounting Foundation, which oversees the Financial Accounting Standards Board and the Government Accounting Standards Board.

Horngren is a member of the Accounting Hall of Fame.

A member of the American Accounting Association, he has been its President and its Director of Research. He received its first annual Outstanding Accounting Educator Award.

The California Certified Public Accountants Foundation gave Horngren its Faculty Excellence Award and its Distinguished Professor Award. He is the first person to have received both awards.

The American Institute of Certified Public Accountants presented its first Outstanding Educator Award to Horngren.

Horngren was named Accountant of the Year, Education, by the national professional accounting fraternity, Beta Alpha Psi.

Professor Horngren is also a member of the Institute of Management Accountants, from whom he received its Distinguished Service Award. He was also a member of the Institutes' Board of Regents, which administers the Certified Management Accountant examinations.

Horngren is the author of other accounting books published by Prentice Hall: *Introduction to Management Accounting,* 12th ed. (with Sundem and Stratton); *Introduction to Financial Accounting,* 8th ed. (with Sundem and Elliott); *Accounting,* 5th ed. (with Harrison and Bamber); and *Financial Accounting,* 4th ed. (with Harrison).

Horngren is the Consulting Editor for the Charles T. Horngren Series in Accounting.

Srikant M. Datar is the Arthur Lowes Dickinson Professor of Business Administration at Harvard University. A graduate with distinction from the University of Bombay, he received gold medals upon graduation from the Indian Institute of Management, Ahmedabad, and the Institute of Cost and Works Accountants of India. A Chartered Accountant, he holds two masters degrees and a Ph.D. from Stanford University.

Cited by his students as a dedicated and innovative teacher, Datar received the George Leland Bach Award for Excellence in the Classroom at Carnegie Mellon University and the Distinguished Teaching Award at Stanford University.

Datar has published his research in various journals, including *The Accounting Review, Contemporary Accounting Research, Journal of Accounting, Auditing and Finance, Journal of Accounting and Economics, Journal of Accounting Research,* and *Management Science.* He has also served on the editorial board of several journals and presented his research to corporate executives and academic audiences in North America, South America, Asia, and Europe.

Datar has worked with many organizations, including Apple Computer, AT&T, Boeing, British Columbia Telecommunications, The Cooperative Bank, Du Pont, Ford, General Motors, Hewlett-Packard, Kodak, Mellon Bank, Novartis, Solectron, Store 24, TRW, Visa, and the World Bank. He is a member of the American Accounting Association and the Institute of Management Accountants.

George Foster is the Paul L. and Phyllis Wattis Professor of Management at Stanford University. He graduated with a university medal from the University of Sydney and has a Ph.D. from Stanford University. He has been awarded honorary doctorates from the University of Ghent, Belgium, and from the University of Vaasa, Finland. He has received the Outstanding Educator Award from the American Accounting Association.

Foster has received the Distinguished Teaching Award at Stanford University and the Faculty Excellence Award from the California Society of Certified Public Accountants. He has been a Visiting Professor to Mexico for the American Accounting Association.

Research awards Foster has received include the Competitive Manuscript Competition Award of the American Accounting Association, the Notable Contribution to Accounting Literature Award of the American Institute of Certified Public Accountants, and the Citation for Meritorious Contribution to Accounting Literature Award of the Australian Society of Accountants.

He is the author of *Financial Statement Analysis,* published by Prentice Hall. He is co-author of *Activity-Based Management Consortium Study (APQC and CAM-I)* and *Marketing, Cost Management and Management Accounting (CAM-I)*. He is also co-author of two monographs published by the American Accounting Association-*Security Analyst Multi-Year Earnings Forecasts and The Capital Market and Market Microstructure and Capital Market Information Content Research*. Journals publishing his articles include *Abacus, The Accounting Review, Harvard Business Review, Journal of Accounting and Economics, Journal of Accounting Research, Journal of Cost Management, Journal of Management Accounting Research, Management Accounting,* and *Review of Accounting Studies.*

Foster works actively with many companies, including Apple Computer, ARCO, BHP, Digital Equipment Corp., Exxon, Frito-Lay Corp., Hewlett-Packard, McDonalds Corp., Octel Communications, PepsiCo, Santa Fe Corp., and Wells Fargo. He also has worked closely with Computer Aided Manufacturing-International (CAM-I) in the development of a framework for modern cost management practices. Foster has presented seminars on new developments in cost accounting in North and South America, Asia, Australia, and Europe.

CHAPTER 1

The Accountant's Role in the Organization

LEARNING OBJECTIVES

1. Describe how cost accounting supports management accounting and financial accounting
2. Understand how management accountants affect strategic decisions
3. Distinguish between the planning and control decisions of managers
4. Distinguish among the problem-solving, scorekeeping, and attention-directing roles of management accountants
5. Identify four themes managers need to consider for attaining success
6. Describe the set of business functions in the value chain
7. Describe three ways management accountants support managers
8. Understand how management accounting fits into an organization's structure
9. Understand what professional ethics mean to management accountants

www.prenhall.com/horngren

If you think of accounting as lists of numbers to be totaled, sorted, and tracked, you're in for a surprise. Modern cost accounting is more than numbers, much more. It's a major player in management decision making. From providing information for planning new products to evaluating the success of the latest marketing campaign, cost accounting plays a major role.

Regal Marine uses cost accounting information in all parts of its Florida-based boat-manufacturing operation. The research and development team needs to examine the costs of alternative boat designs. The production department must control its materials and labor costs to stay on budget. The marketing group wants to evaluate different advertising media to make the best choice, and distribution needs to manage the costs of delivering finished watercraft to customers. Managers in each of these areas within Regal Marine rely on cost accounting information to make decisions to keep the company afloat.

Modern cost accounting provides information managers need when making decisions. The study of modern cost accounting yields insights into what managers and accountants do in an organization. Many large companies—such as Fidelity Investments, GTE Corporation, Loral Aerospace, and Nike—have senior executives who have accounting backgrounds.

The purpose of these "margin notes," which run parallel to the text, is to facilitate your understanding of cost accounting. The notes include: points to emphasize, examples, focus questions with answers, and study tips.

This book focuses on management decision making. Managers use management accounting information to choose strategy, to communicate it, and to determine how best to implement it. They use management accounting information to coordinate their decisions about designing, producing, and marketing a product or service. This chapter describes the challenges managers face and how management accounting can provide the financial and nonfinancial information that helps managers decide how to best deal with those challenges.

MANAGEMENT ACCOUNTING, FINANCIAL ACCOUNTING, AND COST ACCOUNTING

Accounting systems take economic events and transactions that have occurred and process the data in those transactions into information that is helpful to managers and other users, such as sales representatives and production supervisors. Processing any economic transaction entails collecting, categorizing, summarizing, and analyzing. For example, costs are collected by cost categories (materials, labor, and shipping); summarized to determine total costs by month, quarter, or year; and analyzed to evaluate how costs have changed relative to revenues, say, from one period to the next. Accounting systems provide information such as financial statements (the income statement, balance sheet, and statement of cash flows) and performance reports (such as the cost of operating a plant or providing a service). Managers use accounting information (a) to administer each of the activity or functional areas for which they are responsible and (b) to coordinate those activities or functions within the framework of the organization as a whole. This book focuses on how accounting assists managers in these tasks.

Unlike the remainder of this book, Chapter 1 has no "number crunching." Its purpose is to emphasize the accountant's role in providing information for managers.

Individual managers often require the information in an accounting system to be presented or reported differently. Consider, for example, sales order information. A sales manager may be interested in the total dollar amount of sales to determine the commissions to be paid. A distribution manager may be interested in the sales order quantities by geographic region and customer-requested delivery dates to ensure timely deliveries. A manufacturing manager may be interested in the quantities of various products and their desired delivery dates to schedule production. An ideal database—sometimes called a data warehouse or infobarn—consists of small, detailed bits of information that can be used for multiple purposes. For example, the sales order database will contain detailed information about product, quantity ordered, selling price, and delivery details (place and date) for each sales order. The data warehouse stores information in a way that allows managers to access the information that each needs.

Management accounting and financial accounting have different goals. **Management accounting** measures and reports financial and nonfinancial information that helps managers make decisions to fulfill the goals of an organization. Managers use management accounting information to choose, communicate, and implement strategy. They also use management accounting information to coordinate product design, production, and marketing decisions. Management accounting focuses on internal reporting.

1 Describe how cost accounting supports management accounting and financial accounting

...measures costs of acquiring or utilizing resources

Financial accounting focuses on reporting to external parties. It measures and records business transactions and provides financial statements that are based on generally accepted accounting principles (GAAP). Managers are responsible for the financial statements issued to investors, government regulators, and other parties outside the organization. Executive compensation is often directly affected by the numbers in these financial statements. It is not difficult to see that managers are interested in both management accounting and financial accounting.

Cost accounting provides information for management accounting and financial accounting. Cost accounting measures and reports financial and nonfinancial information relating to the cost of acquiring or utilizing resources in an organization. Cost accounting includes those parts of both *management accounting* and *financial accounting* in which cost information is collected or analyzed.

In financial accounting courses, the product costs used to calculate cost of goods sold are given. In this book you will learn how these product costs are calculated.

The internal reporting–external reporting distinction just mentioned is only one of several significant differences between management accounting and financial accounting. Other distinctions include management accounting's emphasis on the future—that's budgeting—and management accounting's emphasis on influencing the behavior of managers and employees. Another distinction is that management accounting is not nearly as restricted by GAAP as is financial accounting. For example, managers may charge interest on owners' capital to help judge a division's performance, even though such a charge is not allowable under GAAP.

Reports such as balance sheets, income statements, and statements of cash flow are common to both management accounting and financial accounting. Most companies adhere to, or only mildly depart from, GAAP for their basic internal financial statements. Why? Because accrual accounting provides a uniform way to measure an organization's financial performance for internal and external purposes. However, management accounting is more wide-ranging than financial accounting's emphasis on financial statements. Management accounting embraces more extensively such topics as the development and implementation of strategies and policies, budgeting, special studies and forecasts, influence on employee behavior, and nonfinancial as well as financial information.

Cost Management and Accounting Systems

The term *cost management* is widely used in businesses today. Unfortunately, there is no uniform definition. We use **cost management** to describe the approaches and activities of managers in short-run and long-run planning and control decisions that increase value for customers and lower costs of products and services. For example, managers make decisions regarding the amount and kind of material being used, changes of plant processes, and changes in product designs. Information from accounting systems helps managers make such decisions, but the information and the accounting systems themselves are not cost management.

Cost management refers to using information (for example, product costs and number and type of customer complaints) for management decisions.

Cost management has a broad focus. For example, it includes—but is not confined to—the continuous reduction of costs. The planning and control of costs is usually inextricably linked with revenue and profit planning. For instance, to enhance revenues and profits, managers often deliberately incur additional costs for advertising and product modifications.

Cost management is not practiced in isolation. It's an integral part of general management strategies and their implementation. Examples include programs that enhance customer satisfaction and quality, as well as programs that promote "blockbuster" new-product development.

STRATEGIC DECISIONS AND THE MANAGEMENT ACCOUNTANT

A company earns profit by attracting customers willing to pay for the goods and services it offers. Customers compare the goods and services offered by a company to the same goods and services offered by other companies. The key to a company's success is creating

2 Understand how management accountants affect strategic decisions

...provide information about competitive advantages and resources

value for customers while differentiating itself from its competitors. Identifying how a company will do this is what strategy is all about. However, a chosen strategy is only as good as how effectively it is implemented. The management accountant provides input that aids in developing strategy, building resources and capabilities, and implementing strategy. To understand the management accountant's role, we must first understand the manager's tasks in more detail.

Developing a Strategy

"The 1999 Practice Analysis of Management Accounting," a survey of management accountants in the United States, cites strategic planning as the most critical work activity for success as a management accountant.

Strategy specifies how an organization matches its own capabilities with the opportunities in the marketplace to accomplish its objectives. In other words, strategy describes how a company will compete and the opportunities its employees should seek and pursue. Companies follow one of two broad strategies. Some companies, such as Southwest Airlines and Vanguard Investments, compete on the basis of providing a quality product or service at low prices. Other companies such as EMC Corporation, the manufacturer of data-storage equipment, and Pfizer, the pharmaceutical giant, compete on their ability to offer unique products or services that are often priced higher than the products or services of competitors.

Deciding between these strategies is a big part of what managers do. Management accountants work closely with managers in formulating strategy by providing information about the sources of competitive advantage—for example, the cost, productivity, or efficiency advantage of their company relative to competitors or the premium prices a company can charge relative to the costs of adding features that make its products or services distinctive. The management accountant also helps formulate a strategy by answering questions such as:

- Who are our most important customers?
- How sensitive are their purchases to price, quality, and service?
- Who are our most important suppliers?
- What substitute products exist in the marketplace, and how do they differ from our product in terms of price and quality?
- Is the industry demand growing or shrinking?
- Is there overcapacity?

Strategic cost management is often used to describe cost management that specifically focuses on strategic issues such as these.

Building Resources and Capabilities

Managers must match their knowledge of the opportunities and threats that exist in the marketplace with the resources and capabilities of their company. Such an analysis usually begins on the asset side of the balance sheet, where the management accountant finds the information to help managers recognize both the company's strengths and weaknesses and the opportunities to build new capabilities.

Current Assets Current assets are cash or assets that usually will be turned into cash in less than one year. Current assets include cash, accounts receivable, and inventory. Cash is needed to pay suppliers and employees and to repay lenders. Any strategy must be tested against the cash needed to implement it. For example, will adequate cash be available to fund the strategy or will additional funds need to be raised?

Reducing inventories also helps a company build capability. Many companies, such as Dell Computer, General Electric, and Toyota, have implemented *just-in-time (JIT) production and purchasing* techniques. JIT production is a manufacturing system in which each component in a production line is produced as soon as, and only when, needed by the next step in the production line. A customer order triggers each step of the production process, from purchase of materials to the finished product. The absence of inventories means that if any step in the production process fails, the entire production line grinds to a halt. Companies that implement JIT work hard to improve their manufacturing processes and product quality, thereby strengthening their ability to compete in the marketplace.

Long-Term Productive Assets These are assets held longer than one year and used to produce goods and services for customers. Productive assets include buildings, manufacturing equipment, computers, and information and technology infrastructures, such as the hardware and software used to automate production and enable salespersons to access a company's database while visiting customers.

In computer-integrated manufacturing (CIM) plants, computers give instructions that automatically set up and run equipment. The role of manufacturing labor in CIM plants is largely computer programming, engineering support, and maintenance of robotic machinery. CIM technology makes the manufacturing system flexible. For example, a CIM plant can make major design modifications, such as switching from manufacturing a two-door car to a four-door car, quickly. The ability to produce a variety of products using the same equipment results in greater flexibility and faster response to changes in customer preferences.

Computers in CIM plants monitor a product as it progresses through manufacturing, and they directly control the manufacturing process to achieve high-quality output. The continuous monitoring and control of the manufacturing processes allow computers to report real-time information regarding process parameters (such as temperature and pressure), units produced, defects, and product costs. Any time a defect occurs, managers use process information to identify reasons for the defect and change the process so that the defects do not recur. Similarly, information technology enables managers to have access to timely and accurate information about costs, product development, manufacturing, marketing, and distribution. Management accountants use this information to analyze trends and measure efficiencies.

The Internet and the World Wide Web make it possible for a company to facilitate contact with its customers and its suppliers. Many companies have begun to use the Internet's advantages of distribution, its enormous reach, and its ease of access to become more productive, to cut costs, to innovate, and to globalize. Companies such as Amazon.com, Barnes and Noble, and Toys Я Us sell books and toys directly to customers who order online. Customers can also follow online the status of their orders, such as when products are expected to ship. Other companies such as Wal-Mart and Sears are using the Internet to coordinate their relationships with suppliers, such as Procter & Gamble, for jointly managing their inventory levels. Developing a network of relationships with customers and suppliers is a valuable source of competitive advantage for a company.

Making the right investments in productive assets is among the most important strategic decisions that managers make. How much should the company invest in advanced manufacturing technologies? In information technology? In Internet applications? The management accountant aids the manager in these decisions by identifying the financial and nonfinancial costs and benefits associated with the alternative choices.

Intangible Assets These are assets such as patents and trademarks. Often a company has other intangible resources that are not recorded as assets because their future value cannot be easily measured. Examples of such intangible resources include the capabilities to perform research (for example, Merck & Company, the pharmaceutical giant), to create a brand (Nike and McDonald's Corporation), to build distribution networks (Kraft Foods), and to develop information systems (American Airlines' customer-reservation system).

In designing its strategy, a company must match the opportunities and threats it sees in the marketplace with its resources and capabilities. Sometimes a company may see opportunities and threats that require it to build capabilities. For example, after Amazon.com's success in selling books online, Barnes and Noble also developed capabilities to sell online. At other times, companies use their existing capabilities to create new opportunities. For example, Kellogg Company uses the reputation of its brand to introduce new types of cereals. However, the best-designed strategies and the best-developed capabilities are useless unless they are effectively executed.

3 **Distinguish between the planning decisions**

...how to attain goals

and the control decisions of managers

...implementing decisions and using feedback

THE MANAGEMENT ACCOUNTANT'S ROLE IN IMPLEMENTING STRATEGY

Managers implement strategy by translating it into actions. Managers do this using planning systems and control systems designed to help the collective decisions throughout the organization.

Planning comprises (a) selecting organization goals, predicting results under various alternative ways of achieving those goals, deciding how to attain the desired goals and (b) communicating the goals and how to attain them to the entire organization.

One common planning tool is a *budget*. A **budget** is the quantitative expression of a proposed plan of action by management and is an aid to coordinating what needs to be done to implement that plan. The information used to project budgeted amounts includes past financial and nonfinancial information routinely recorded in accounting systems. The budget expresses the strategy by describing the sales plans, the costs and investments that would be needed to achieve sales goals, the anticipated cash flows, and the potential financing needs. The process of preparing a budget forces coordination and communication across the business functions of a company, as well as with the company's suppliers and customers.

Control comprises (a) taking actions that implement the planning decisions and (b) deciding how to evaluate performance and what feedback to provide that will help future decision making.

Planning and control are distinct activities, but they go hand in hand. To maximize the benefit from planning (for example, a cost budget), the manager should use that plan for control. It is difficult to control a cost without a plan.

Individuals pay attention to how they are measured. They tend to favor those measures that make their performance look best. Performance measures tell managers how well they and the subunits they are managing are doing. Linking rewards to performance helps to motivate managers. These rewards are both intrinsic (self-satisfaction for a job well done) and extrinsic (salary, bonuses, and promotions linked to performance). A budget serves as much as a control tool as a planning tool. Why? Because a budget is a benchmark against which actual performance can be compared.

Feedback: Linking Planning and Control

Planning and control are linked by feedback: **Feedback** involves managers examining past performance (the control function) and systematically exploring alternative ways to make better-informed decisions and plans in the future. Feedback can lead to changes in goals, changes in the ways decision alternatives are identified, and changes in the range of information collected when making predictions. Management accountants play an active role in linking control to future planning.

An Example: Planning and Control and the Management Accountant

A daily newspaper, the *Daily News* has a strategy to differentiate itself from its competitors by focusing on in-depth analyses of news by its highly rated journalists, using color to enhance attractiveness to readers and advertisers, and developing its Web site to deliver up-to-the-minute news, interviews, and analyses. It has substantial capabilities to deliver on this strategy. It owns an automated, computer-integrated, state-of-the-art printing facility and has developed a Web-based information technology infrastructure. Its distribution network is one of the best in the business. For its strategy to be successful, the *Daily News* must be able to increase its revenues.

Let's see how the *Daily News* will implement its strategy. The left side of Exhibit 1-1 provides an overview of the *planning* and *control* decisions at the *Daily News*. The right side of Exhibit 1-1 highlights how the management accounting system facilitates decisions.

Consider first the planning decisions. To increase operating income and be consistent with its strategy, two main alternatives were evaluated:

1. Increase the selling price per newspaper
2. Increase the rate per page charged to advertisers

The *Daily News*'s manager, Naomi Crawford, decided to increase advertising rates by 4% to \$5,200 per page for March 2004. She budgeted advertising revenues to be \$4,160,000 (\$5,200 per page × 800 pages predicted to be sold in March 2004).

Now consider the *Daily News*'s control decisions. One control decision is communicating the new advertising rate schedule to its sales representatives and advertisers.

EXHIBIT 1-1

How Accounting Facilitates Planning and Control at the *Daily News*

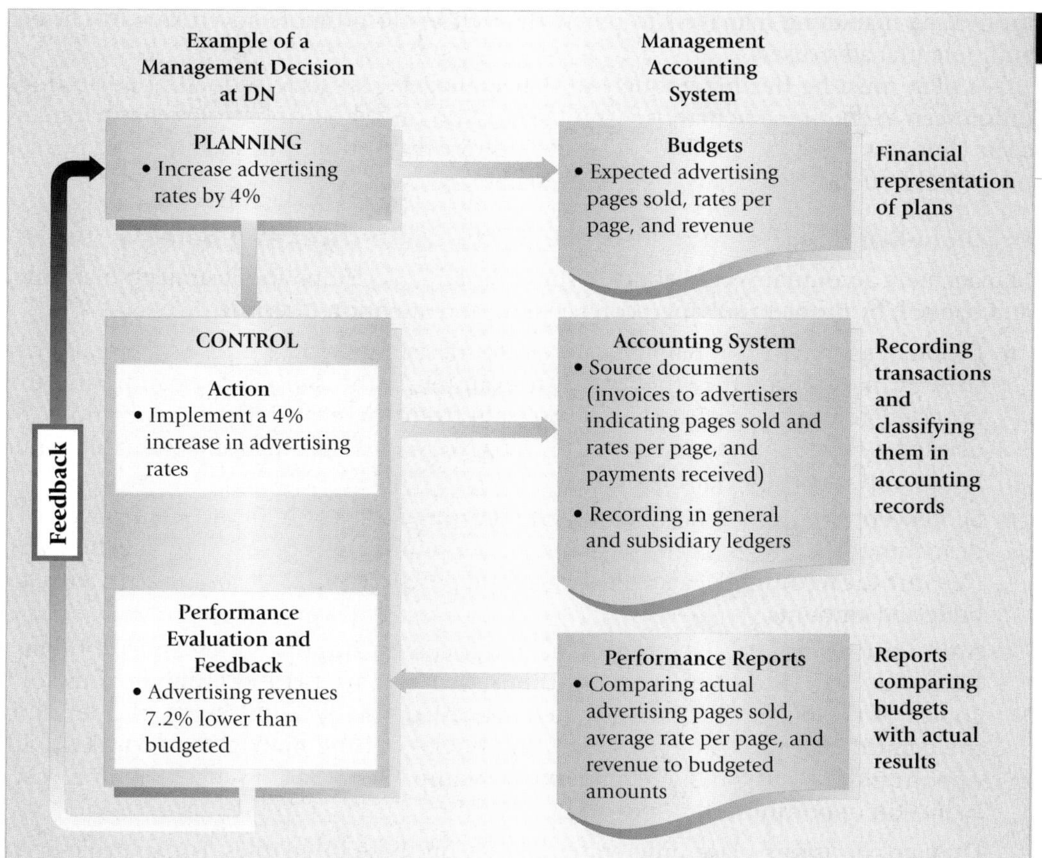

Another control decision is performance evaluation, such as a monthly "attainment of manager objectives" review, in which actual results for a period are compared with amounts budgeted for that period. During March 2004, the newspaper sold advertising, issued invoices, and received payments. These invoices and receipts were recorded in the accounting system. Advertising revenues for March are the aggregate of the advertising done that month for each individual account. Exhibit 1-2 shows the *Daily News*'s performance report of advertising revenues for March 2004. This report indicates that 760 pages of advertising (40 pages less than the budgeted 800 pages) were sold. The average rate per page was $5,080, compared with the budgeted $5,200 rate, yielding actual advertising revenues of $3,860,800. The actual advertising revenues are $299,200 less than the budgeted $4,160,000.

The performance report in Exhibit 1-2 spurs investigation and more decisions. For example, did the marketing department make sufficient efforts to convince advertisers that, even with the new higher rate of $5,200 per page, advertising in the *Daily News* was a good buy? Why was the actual average rate per page $5,080 instead of the budgeted rate of $5,200? Did some sales representatives offer discounted rates? Did economic conditions cause the decline in advertising revenues? Answers to these questions could prompt the newspaper's publisher to take subsequent actions, including, for example,

EXHIBIT 1-2 **Performance Report of Advertising Revenues at the *Daily News* for March 2004**

	Actual Result (1)	Budgeted Amount (2)	Difference: (Actual Result − Budgeted Amount) (3) = (1) − (2)	Difference as a Percentage of Budgeted Amount (4) = (3) ÷ (2)
Advertising pages sold	760 pages	800 pages	40 pages Unfavorable	5.0% Unfavorable
Average rate per page	$5,080	$5,200	$120 Unfavorable	2.3% Unfavorable
Advertising revenues	$3,860,800	$4,160,000	$299,200 Unfavorable	7.2% Unfavorable

motivating marketing managers to renew their efforts to promote advertising by current and potential advertisers.

A plan must be flexible enough so that managers can seize sudden opportunities unforeseen at the time the plan is formulated. In no case should control mean that managers cling to a plan when unfolding events indicate that actions not encompassed by that plan would offer better results for the company.

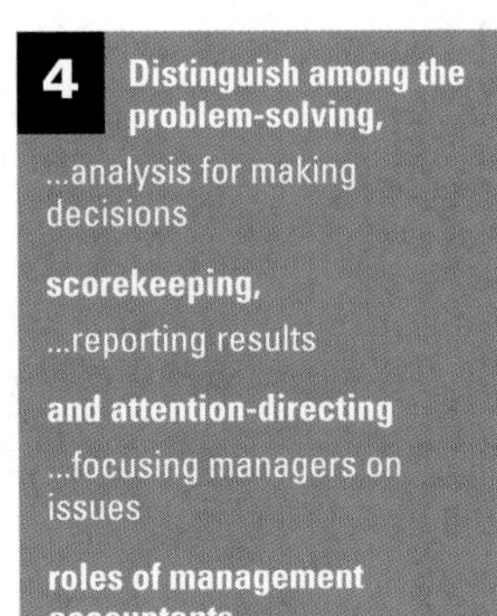

Problem-Solving, Scorekeeping, and Attention-Directing Roles

Management accountants contribute to the company's decisions about strategy, planning, and control, by problem solving, scorekeeping, and attention directing.

- **Problem solving**—Comparative analysis for decision making: Of the several alternatives available, which is the best? An example is the *Daily News* comparing the expected revenues and costs of proposals from three different organizations to develop a new Internet version of the *Daily News*. This information is valuable input for an important strategic decision.
- **Scorekeeping**—Accumulating data and reporting results to all levels of management describing how the organization is doing. Examples of scorekeeping at the *Daily News* are the recording of actual revenues and purchases of newsprint paper relative to budgeted amounts.
- **Attention directing**—Helping managers focus on opportunities and problems. Examples of attention directing at the *Daily News* are (a) the number of unsold copies of the paper returned per day and (b) the daily utility costs of operating the printing presses. Attention directing means getting managers to focus on all opportunities that would add value to the company and not to focus only on cost-reduction opportunities.

Different decisions place different emphases on these three roles. For strategic decisions and planning decisions, the problem-solving role is most prominent. Consider the *Daily News*'s strategic decision to increase operating income by increasing advertising rates per page (Exhibit 1-1). The newspaper's management accountant serves as a problem-solver to help make this strategic decision by providing information about past increases or decreases in advertising rates and the subsequent changes in advertising revenues, as well as by collecting and analyzing information on advertising rates charged by competing media outlets (including other newspapers). The goal is to assist the manager in making a better decision about whether to increase the advertising rate per page, and, if so, the magnitude of the increase.

For control decisions at the *Daily News* (which include both actions to implement planning decisions and decisions about performance evaluation), the scorekeeping and attention-directing roles are most prominent because they provide feedback to managers. An example of scorekeeping at the *Daily News* is recording in the accounting system the details of advertising revenues and reporting a summary in the monthly income statement. An example of the attention-directing role is a report highlighting the reduced March 2004 advertising revenues, with details of the specific advertisers that cut back or stopped advertising after the rate-increase went into effect. This feedback helps managers decide which advertisers to target for intensive follow-up by sales representatives.

Feedback from scorekeeping and attention directing often leads managers to revise planning decisions and sometimes make new strategic decisions. Information that prompts a planning decision is frequently reanalyzed and supplemented by the management accountant in the problem-solving role. The ongoing interaction among strategic decisions, planning decisions, and control decisions means that management accountants often are simultaneously doing problem-solving, scorekeeping, and attention-directing activities.

Management accounting information must be relevant and timely to be useful to managers. For example, a management accounting group at Johnson & Johnson (manufacturer of many consumer products, such as Band-Aids) has as its explicit goals: "delight our customers" and "be the best." Management accounting is successful when it provides information to managers that improves their strategic, planning, and control decisions. Nortel Networks, the global telecommunications company, has its managers evaluate the management accounting group when major changes in the management accounting systems are made. The relationship between managers and management accounting goes both ways. Managers who support their management accountants allocate the resources (such as for computer software) they need to do their jobs. With these resources, management accountants are able to better provide the support managers need to make their decisions. The Surveys of Company Practice (p. 12) indicates the increasingly important role management accountants are playing in helping managers develop and implement strategy. It also describes the abilities and skills needed to be a successful management accountant in the future.

ENHANCING THE VALUE OF MANAGEMENT ACCOUNTING SYSTEMS

The design of a management accounting system should be guided by the challenges facing managers. Exhibit 1-3 presents four themes common to many companies. The customer-focus theme is particularly critical. The other three themes—value-chain and supply-chain analysis, key success factors, and continuous improvement and benchmarking—are geared to improving customer focus and customer satisfaction. Management accounting helps managers focus on these four themes.

5 Identify four themes managers need to consider for attaining success

...examples are customer focus and quality improvement

1. Customer focus. The number of organizations aiming to be "customer-driven" is large and increasing. For example, Asea Brown Boveri (ABB)—a global manufacturer of industrial products—gives high priority to customer focus:

> *Customer Focus is a guiding principle to the way we do business. It is an attitude about everything we do that prompts us to constantly ask ourselves: "How can I add value for the customer?" Our commitment to Customer Focus has been reinforced by the measurable impacts it has had on employee morale and the bottom line.*

The challenge facing managers is to continue investing sufficient resources in customer satisfaction such that customers who provide a company the most profits are attracted and retained. It is for this reason that airline companies pay special attention to their most frequent travelers. The management accounting system must also track whether the internal business functions are adding value to customers.

Customer focus aims to achieve customer satisfaction. Without customer satisfaction guiding the way companies do business, they will go out of business.

2. Value-chain and supply-chain analysis. Value chain refers to the sequence of business functions in which usefulness is added to the products or services of a company. The term value refers to the increase in the usefulness of the product or service and, as a result, its value to the *customer.* Exhibit 1-4 shows six business functions—research and development (R&D), design, production, marketing, distribution, and customer service. Management accountants provide information managers need to make decisions in each of these six business functions. We illustrate these business functions using the example of SONY Corporation's television division.

6 Describe the set of business functions in the value chain

...examples are R&¡D, manufacturing, and marketing

- **Research and development**—Generating and experimenting with ideas related to new products, services, or processes. At SONY, this function includes research on alternative ways of television signal transmission (analog, digital, high definition) and on the clarity of different shapes of television screens.

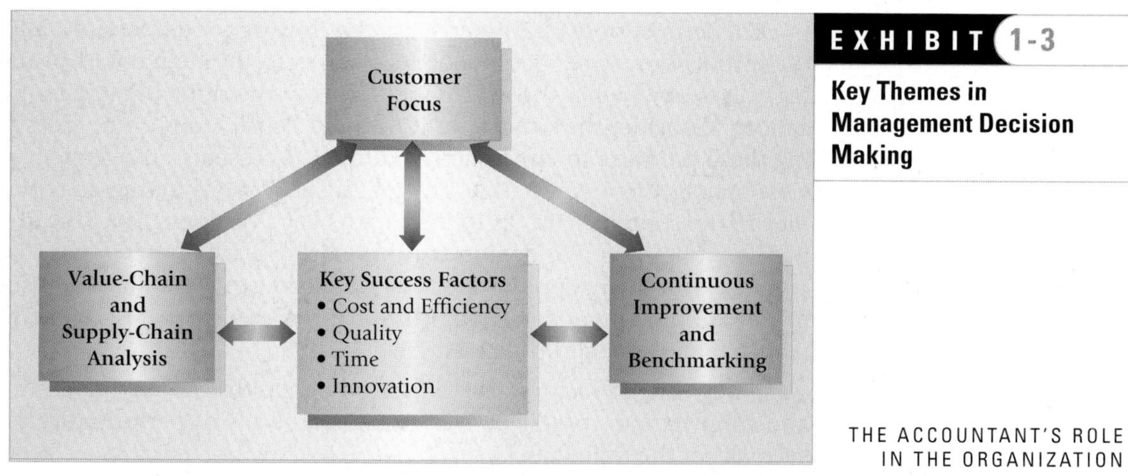

EXHIBIT 1-3

Key Themes in Management Decision Making

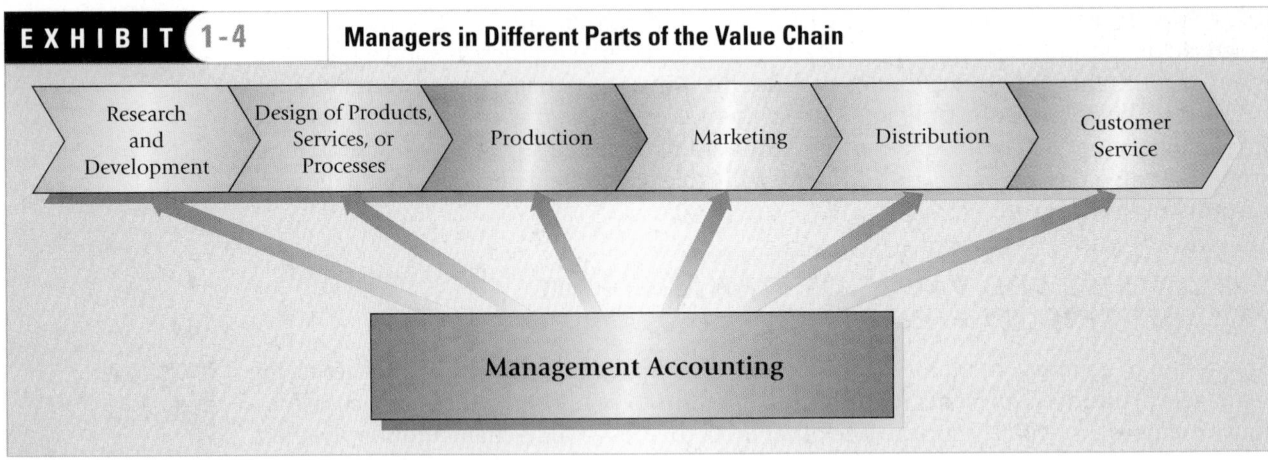

Understand the distinctions between research and development (R&D) and design. R&D is basic research and idea generation. Design turns those ideas into reality. It encompasses development of prototype products and the manufacturing process by which the products are produced.

The value chain in Exhibit 1-4 could be expanded to separately highlight costs implicitly included in one or more of the individual business functions. Examples include administrative costs and future cash outlays associated with actions of the current period (such as environmental-cleanup costs).

Some companies subcontract some of the six business functions. Nike subcontracts its production (manufacturing) function. Even with subcontracting, the challenge of coordinating all of the business functions remains.

Accounting helps managers coordinate across business functions of the value chain, for example, by analyzing whether more money spent on R&D and design will reduce subsequent production and customer-service costs.

Toyota often loans its engineers to suppliers to help suppliers streamline their production processes. In return, Toyota expects to receive a share of the suppliers' cost savings in the form of reduced prices.

- **Design of products, services, or processes**—Detailed planning and engineering of products, services, or processes. Design at Sony includes determining the number of component parts in a television set and the effect of alternative product designs on manufacturing costs.
- **Production**—Acquiring, coordinating, and assembling resources to produce a product or deliver a service. Production of a SONY television set includes the acquisition and assembly of the electronic parts, the cabinet, and the packaging used for shipping.
- **Marketing**—Promoting and selling products or services to customers or prospective customers. SONY markets its televisions through trade shows, advertisements in newspapers and magazines, and on the Internet.
- **Distribution**—Delivering products or services to customers. Distribution for SONY includes shipping to retail outlets, catalog vendors, direct sales via the Internet, and other channels through which customers purchase televisions.
- **Customer service**—Providing after-sale support to customers. SONY provides customer service on its televisions in the form of customer-help telephone lines, support on the Internet, and warranty repair work.

Each function is essential to SONY satisfying its customers and keeping them satisfied (and even delighted) over time. Exhibit 1-4 depicts the usual order in which different business-function activities physically occur. Do not, however, interpret Exhibit 1-4 as implying that managers should proceed sequentially through the value chain when planning and managing their activities. Companies gain (in terms of cost, quality, and the speed with which new products are developed) if two or more of the individual business functions of the value chain work concurrently as a team. For example, inputs into design decisions by managers in production, marketing, distribution, and customer service often lead to design choices that reduce costs in all value-chain functions.

The term **supply chain** describes the flow of goods, services, and information from the initial sources of materials and services to the delivery of products to consumers, regardless of whether those activities occur in the same organization or in other organizations. Consider the soft drinks, Coke and Pepsi. Many companies play a role in bringing these products to consumers. Exhibit 1-5 presents an overview of the supply chain. Cost management emphasizes integrating and coordinating activities across all companies in the supply chain, as well as across each business function in an individual company's *value chain*. For example, both Coca-Cola Company and Pepsi Bottling Group contract with their suppliers (such as glass and can companies and sugar manufacturers) to frequently deliver small quantities of materials directly to the production floor to reduce materials-handling costs.

3. Key success factors. Customers are demanding that companies use the value chain and supply chain to deliver ever-improving levels of performance regarding several (or even all) of the following:

EXHIBIT 1-5 **Supply Chain for a Cola Bottling Company**

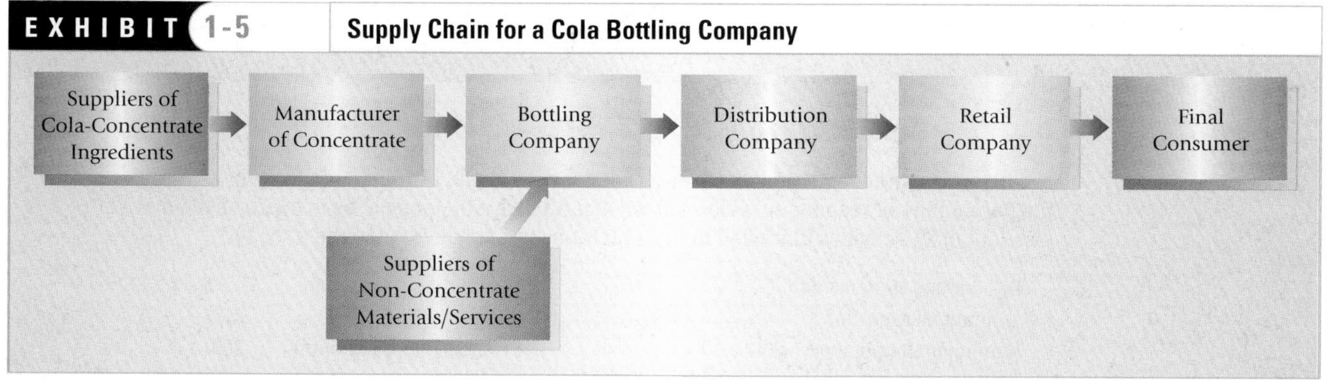

- **Cost and efficiency**—Companies face continuous pressure to reduce the cost of the products or services they sell. Understanding the tasks or activities (such as setting up machines or distributing products) that cause costs to arise is useful for calculating and managing the cost of products. To set cost-reduction targets, managers start by scanning the market to determine prices that customers are willing to pay for products or services. From this "target price," managers subtract the operating income they want to earn to arrive at the target cost. Managers strive to achieve the target cost by eliminating some activities (such as rework) and by reducing the costs of performing activities. They do so across all value-chain functions and over the entire life cycle of the product—from its initial R&D to when customer service and support for the product are no longer offered.
- **Quality**—Customers expect high levels of quality. Total quality management (TQM) is a philosophy in which management improves operations throughout the value chain to deliver products and services that exceed customer expectations. TQM encompasses designing the product or service to meet the needs and wants of customers, as well as making products with zero (or minimal) defects and waste. Management accountants evaluate the costs and revenue benefits of TQM initiatives.
- **Time**—Time has many components. *New-product development time* is the time to develop and bring new products to market. The increasing pace of technological innovation has led to shorter product life cycles and the need for companies to bring new products to market more rapidly.

  Customer-response time describes the speed at which an organization responds to customer requests. To increase customer satisfaction, organizations must complete activities faster and meet promised delivery dates reliably. Delays or bottlenecks occur when the work to be performed exceeds the available capacity. To increase output, managers need to increase the capacity of the bottleneck operation. The management accountant's role is to quantify the cost and benefits of relieving the bottleneck constraints.
- **Innovation**—A constant flow of innovative products or services is the basis for ongoing company success. The management accountant helps managers evaluate alternative investment decisions and R&D decisions.

  Management accountants help managers track performance on the chosen key success factors vis-à-vis the performance of competitors on the same factors. Tracking what is happening in other companies alerts managers to changes in what their own customers are observing and evaluating.

4. Continuous improvement and benchmarking. Continuous improvement by competitors creates a never-ending search for higher levels of performance to satisfy customers. Some phrases that typify this theme are "We are running harder just to stand still" and "If you're not going forward, you're going backward."

To compete, many companies are concentrating on improving different aspects of their own operations. Keep in mind, though, that different industries will focus on improving different operating factors. Airline companies, such as Southwest Airlines, seek to improve the percentage of their flights that arrive on time. Internet companies, such as eBay, seek to improve the percentage of each 24-hour period that customers can access

SURVEYS OF COMPANY PRACTICE

"A Day in the Life" of a Management Accountant

What do management accountants do? The following table, based on a survey of CMAs,[a] shows the percentage of respondents who named a particular work activity as in the top five work activities (out of 29 activities identified to them) in terms of time devoted to the activity.

Activity	%	Activity	%
Accounting systems and financial reporting	62%	Computer systems and operations	21%
Managing the accounting/ finance function	42%	Process improvement	20%
Internal consulting	42%	Performance evaluation	17%
Short-term budgeting	37%	Tax compliance	14%
Long-term strategic planning	25%	Accounting policy	13%
Financial and economic analysis	24%	Project accounting	11%
		Consolidations	11%

In terms of importance, management accountants ranked the abilities and skills needed to succeed as follows:

- Communication (oral, written, and presentation) skills
- Ability to work on a team
- Analytical/problem-solving skills
- Solid understanding of accounting
- Understanding of how a business functions
- Computer skills

What changes in work activities are projected in the future for management accountants? Projected to become more important are

- Internal consulting
- Long-term strategic planning
- Computer systems and operations
- Process improvement
- Performing financial and economic analysis

Projected to become less important are

- Accounting systems and financial reporting
- Consolidations
- Managing the accounting/finance function
- Accounting policy
- Short-term budgeting
- Project accounting

The increasing use of information technology in the future was seen from the survey as helping management accountants spend a lower percentage of their time on data collection and financial statement preparation and a higher percentage on financial analysis.

The survey indicates a clear shift away from activities we traditionally think of as the core of the controller's responsibilities—managing the function, ensuring business controls, and planning and reporting—toward activities we think of as business partnering—strategic planning, business leadership, analyzing and interpreting information, decision making, process improvements, and performance evaluation.

The controller of USWest supported this finding, "We're becoming more business people and less just accountants". The controller of Caterpillar described the job as a "business advisor to...help the team develop strategy and focus the team all the way through recommendations and implementation."

[a] G. Siegel and J. Sorensen, "The 1999 Practice Analysis of Management Accounting." Full citations are in Appendix A at the end of the book.

their online systems without delay. Sumitomo Electric Industries, the Japanese manufacturer of electric wire and cable, has daily meetings so that all employees maintain a continuous focus on cost reduction.

The continuous improvement targets often are set by benchmarking, or measuring the quality of the products, services, and activities of the company against the best levels of performance found in competing companies. For example, Continental Airlines sets its target for on-time arrival percentage based on the airline that has the best percentage in the industry.

At times, a company may have to make more-fundamental changes in its operations and restructure—also referred to as reengineer—its processes to achieve improvements in cost, quality, timeliness, or service. Management accountants provide the financial and nonfinancial information that helps managers make decisions about reengineering and continuous improvement.

Think of these four themes as overlapping and interacting with one another. For example, customer focus (theme 1) is a key ingredient in new-product development (theme 2) at all companies. Product designers are encouraged to search for cost-reduction opportunities at all stages in the value chain and the supply chain (themes 3 and 4). The Concepts in Action (p. 14) describes how companies choose their e-business strategies to integrate the four themes.

KEY MANAGEMENT ACCOUNTING GUIDELINES

Three important guidelines help management accountants provide the most value when problem solving, scorekeeping, and attention directing: employ a cost-benefit approach, give full recognition to behavioral considerations as well as technical considerations, and use different costs for different purposes.

7 Describe three ways management accountants support managers

...for example, by calculating different costs for different purposes

Cost-Benefit Approach

Management accountants continually face resource-allocation decisions, such as whether to purchase a new software package or hire a new employee. The **cost-benefit approach** should be used in making these decisions: Resources should be spent if they are expected to better attain company goals in relation to the expected costs of those resources. The expected benefits from spending should exceed the expected costs. The expected benefits and costs may not be easy to quantify. Nevertheless, the cost-benefit approach is useful for making resource-allocation decisions.

Consider the installation of a company's first budgeting system. Previously, the company used historical recordkeeping and little formal planning. A major benefit of installing a budgeting system is that it compels managers to plan more formally. This may lead to different decisions that create more profits than the decisions that would have been made using the historical system. The expected benefits exceed the expected costs of the new budgeting system. These costs include investments in physical assets, in training people, and in ongoing operating costs.

Although it is difficult to quantify the costs and benefits of a budgeting system, the question is, Will costs and benefits be considered implicitly (as part of a "gut feeling")? or explicitly, in which effects of different estimates can be examined? It is better to be as explicit as feasible, but with some gut feeling.

Behavioral and Technical Considerations

The cost-benefit approach is the criterion that assists managers in deciding whether, say, to install a proposed budgeting system instead of continuing to use an existing historical system. Consider the human (the behavioral) side of why budgeting is used. Budgets induce a different set of collective decisions because of compelled planning. A management accounting system should have two simultaneous missions for providing information: (a) to help managers make wise economic decisions and (b) to motivate managers and other employees to aim and strive for goals of the organization (when managers emphasize a particular measure or goal, employees pay more attention to it).

Do not underestimate the role of individuals and groups in management planning and control systems. Both accountants and managers should always remember that management systems are not confined exclusively to technical matters, such as the type of computer software systems used and the frequency with which reports are prepared. Management is primarily a human activity that should focus on how to help individuals do their jobs better, for example, by helping them to understand the activities that add value (product design, say) and those that do not (defects and rework). Similarly, it is often better for managers to personally discuss how to improve performance with underperforming workers instead of sending those workers a report highlighting their underperformance.

Different Costs for Different Purposes

This book examines alternative ways to compute costs, which is why we are concerned with different costs for different purposes. This theme is the management accountant's

CONCEPTS IN ACTION

E-Business Strategies and the Management Accountant

How should a company choose its e-business strategy? Should it focus on initiatives that reduce costs, make the company more responsive to customers, or integrate the value chain and the supply chain? The opportunities of e-business touch all four themes—customer focus; value-chain and supply-chain analysis; continuous improvement; and key success factors—cost and efficiency, quality, time, and innovation—that are important to managers attaining success in their planning and control decisions.

One way to think about strategic choices is the E-Business Value Matrix, which is organized into four quadrants along the dimensions of business criticality and practice innovation.

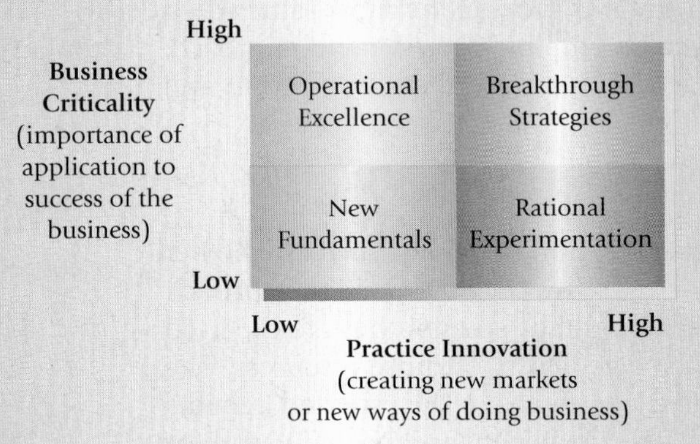

New Fundamentals include such e-business applications as creating an employee directory or putting information about employee benefits on a company's internal Web site so that employees can access information easily. These applications are not critical to the success of the business nor do they create new markets. But they will probably reduce costs and require only a small investment.

Rational Experimentation refers to strategies such as those pursued by pharmaceutical companies, including Merck, Novartis, and Pfizer, to provide information and literature about their products to doctors and insurers. Such practices are innovative but not critical to business success because the companies' sales representatives can also provide the doctors with this information. Such initiatives can be justified on the basis of their revenue potential and lower costs.

Breakthrough Strategies are strategies like those pursued by Amazon.com, which sells books and toys over the Internet, or Yahoo, which organizes and aggregates information about content on the Internet. These strategies are innovative, critical, and risky and are motivated by opportunities for rapid revenue growth.

Operational Excellence includes strategies pursued by companies such as Dell Computer. Dell uses the Internet to sell computers directly to customers and to efficiently acquire material and components from suppliers. Managing customer relationships and the supply chain are critical to Dell's business, but its use of the Internet is now standard practice at Dell. Dell's operational excellence leads to lower costs and, consequently, more sales, and it is central to sustaining competitive advantage.

Most successful companies have tried to populate all four quadrants with their e-business initiatives. Management accountants have helped identify the costs and benefits of these alternative investment strategies. As a broad generalization, the benefits of e-business initiatives on the left side of the matrix have emphasized cost reductions; the benefits on the right side have emphasized revenue growth from distinctive product offerings.

Source: A. Hartman, J. Sifonis, and J. Kador, *Net Ready* (McGraw Hill, New York, 2000). Used by permission.

version of the "one size does not fit all" notion. A cost concept used for the external-reporting purpose of accounting may not be an appropriate concept for internal, routine reporting to managers.

Consider the advertising costs associated with launching a major new Microsoft Corporation product. The product is expected to have a useful life of two years or more. For external reporting to shareholders, television advertising costs are fully expensed in the income statement in the year they are incurred. This immediate expensing is a requirement of GAAP governing U.S. external reporting. In contrast, for internal purposes of evaluating management performance, the television advertising costs could be capitalized and then amortized, or written off as expenses over several years. Microsoft could capitalize these advertising costs if it believes doing so better represents the performance of the managers launching the new product.

There are multiple external parties and multiple internal parties for whom financial reports are prepared. Any specific accounting method (such as immediate expensing of television advertising costs) is unlikely to be the preferred method for all external and internal parties. Even an individual manager may prefer accounting method A for one decision and accounting method B for another decision.

We now discuss how organization structure affects the reporting responsibilities of the management accountant.

ORGANIZATION STRUCTURE AND THE MANAGEMENT ACCOUNTANT

Line and Staff Relationships

8 **Understand how management accounting fits into an organization's structure**

...for example, the responsibilities of the controller

Most organizations distinguish between line management and staff management. **Line management,** such as manufacturing, marketing, and distribution management, is directly responsible for attaining the goals of the organization. For example, managers of manufacturing divisions may target particular levels of budgeted operating income, certain levels of product quality and safety, and compliance with environmental laws. **Staff management,** such as management accountants and information technology and human-resources management, exists to provide advice and assistance to line management. A plant manager (a line function) may be responsible for investing in new equipment. A management accountant (a staff function) assists the plant manager by preparing detailed operating-cost comparisons of alternative pieces of equipment.

Increasingly, organizations are using teams to achieve their objectives. These teams can include both line and staff management, with the result that the traditional distinctions between line and staff are less clear-cut than they were a decade ago.

The Chief Financial Officer and the Controller

The **chief financial officer (CFO)**—also called the **finance director** in many countries—is the executive responsible for overseeing the financial operations of an organization. The responsibilities of the CFO vary among organizations, but they usually include the following areas:

- *Controllership*—includes providing financial information for reports to managers and reports to shareholders and overseeing the overall operations of the accounting system.
- *Treasury*—includes banking and short- and long-term financing, investments, and management of cash.
- *Risk management*—includes managing the financial risk of interest-rate and exchange-rate changes and derivatives management.
- *Taxation*—includes income taxes, sales taxes, and international tax planning.
- *Internal audit*—includes reviewing and analyzing financial and other records to attest to the integrity of the organization's financial reports and to adherence to its policies and procedures.

In some organizations, the CFO is also responsible for information systems. In other organizations, an officer of equivalent rank to the CFO—called the chief information officer—is responsible for information systems.

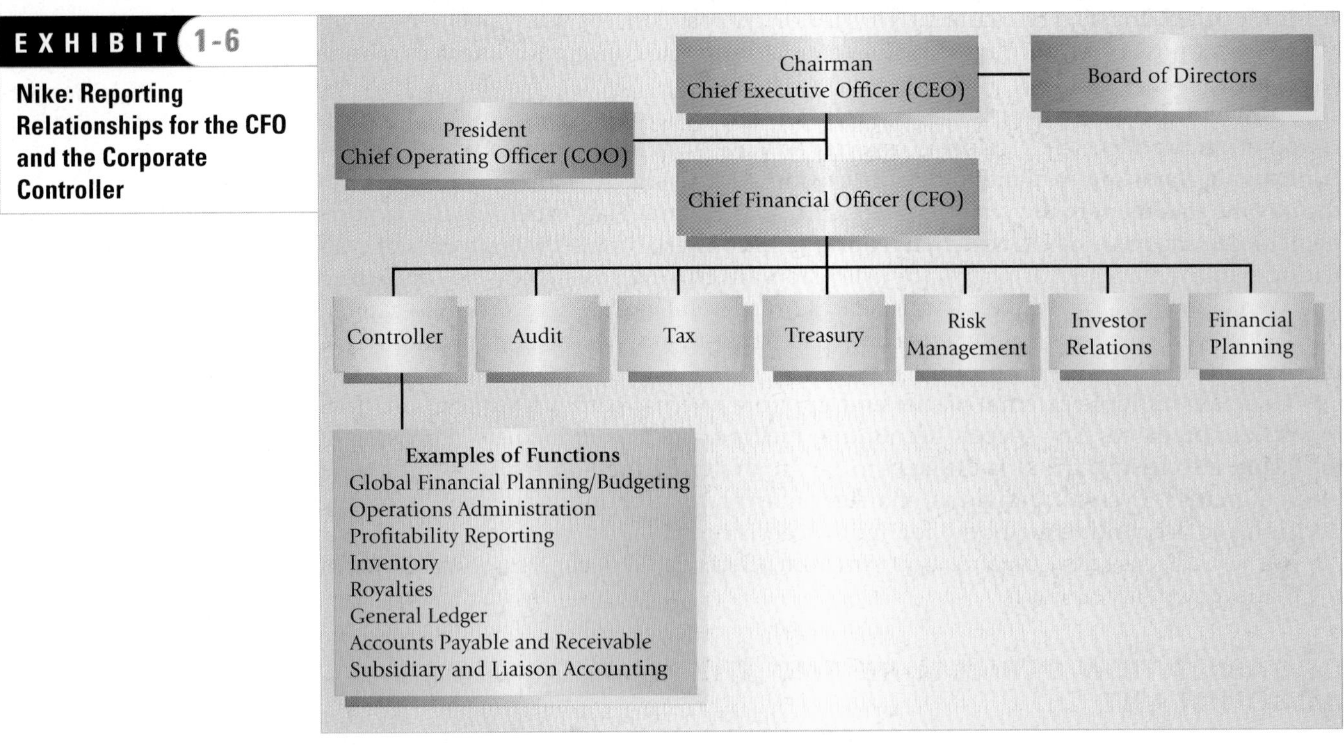

EXHIBIT 1-6

Nike: Reporting Relationships for the CFO and the Corporate Controller

The **controller** (also called the *chief accounting officer*) is the financial executive primarily responsible for management accounting and financial accounting. This book focuses on the controller as the chief management accounting executive. Modern controllers do not do any controlling in terms of line authority except over their own departments. Yet, the modern concept of controllership maintains that the controller does control in a special sense. That is, by reporting and interpreting relevant data (problem-solving and attention-directing roles), the controller exerts a force or influence that impels management toward making better-informed decisions.

You may not be aware of the variety of jobs available to accountants. Exhibit 1-6 illustrates the diverse areas that report to the CFO. An understanding of accounting is essential in many of these areas.

Exhibit 1-6 is an organization chart of the CFO and the corporate controller at Nike, the leading footwear and apparel company. The CFO is a staff management function that reports to the Chief Operating Officer (COO), who reports to the Chief Executive Officer (CEO). As in most organizations, the corporate controller at Nike reports to the CFO. Organization charts such as the one in Exhibit 1-6 show formal reporting relationships. In most organizations, there are also informal relationships that must be understood when managers attempt to implement their decisions. Examples of informal relationships are friendships among managers (friendships of a professional or personal kind) and the personal preferences of top management about the type of managers they choose to rely on in decision making.

The CFO at Nike is one of the corporate officers. These include the CEO, the COO, the CFO; the heads of geographic regions in the United States, Asia Pacific, the Americas, and Europe; the heads of its apparel and footwear products; and sports marketing management; and a chief legal counsel. Exhibit 1-6 provides examples of the functions undertaken in the controller's group. Each of Nike's major geographic groups (United States, Asia Pacific, the Americas, and Europe) has its own regional controller. Many individual countries within each geographic group also have a country controller.

All members in a company, whether in line management or staff management, are responsible to ensure compliance with the organization's ethical standards.

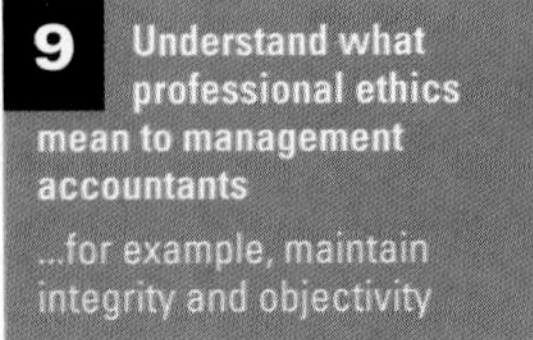

PROFESSIONAL ETHICS

Accountants have special responsibilities regarding ethics, given their responsibility for the integrity of financial information provided to internal and external parties. Accountants consistently rank high in public opinion surveys on the ethics exhibited by members of different professions.

Ethical Guidelines

Professional accounting organizations promote high ethical standards. Professional accounting organizations representing management accountants exist in many countries. Appendix D discusses professional organizations in the United States, Canada, Australia, Japan, and the United Kingdom. Each of these organizations provides certification programs. For example, the **Institute of Management Accountants (IMA)**—the largest association of management accountants in the United States—provides programs leading to the **Certified Management Accountant (CMA)** certificate and the **Certified in Financial Management (CFM)** certificate. These certificates indicate that the holder has demonstrated the competency of technical knowledge required by the IMA in management accounting and financial management, respectively.

The IMA has issued a *Standards of Ethical Conduct for Management Accountants.* Exhibit 1-7 on the next page presents the IMA's guidance on issues relating to competence, confidentiality, integrity, and objectivity. The IMA provides its members with an ethics hotline service. Members can call professional counselors at the IMA's Ethics Counseling Service to discuss their ethical dilemmas. The counselors help identify the key ethical issues and possible alternative ways of resolving them, and confidentiality is guaranteed.

Details of the IMA's guidance on ethical issues, including its ethics hotline service, are on its Web site (www.imanet.org).

Typical Ethical Challenges

Ethical issues can confront management accountants in many ways. Here are two examples:

- **Case A:** A management accountant, knowing that reporting a loss for a software division will result in yet another "rightsizing initiative" (a gentler term than "layoffs"), has concerns about the commercial potential of software for which R&D costs are currently being capitalized as an asset rather than being shown as an expense for internal reporting purposes. The division manager argues that the new product will be a "winner" but presents little evidence to support her argument. The last two products from this division have been unsuccessful. The management accountant has many friends in the division and wants to avoid a personal confrontation with the division manager.
- **Case B:** A packaging supplier, bidding for a new contract, offers the management accountant of the purchasing company an all-expenses-paid weekend to the Super Bowl. The supplier does not mention the new contract when giving the invitation. The accountant is not a personal friend of the supplier. He knows cost issues are critical in approving the new contract and is concerned that the supplier will ask for details about bids by competing packaging companies.

In each case the management accountant is faced with an ethical dilemma. Case A involves competence, objectivity, and integrity. The management accountant should request that the division manager provide credible evidence that the new product is commercially viable. If the manager does not provide such evidence, expensing R&D costs in the current period is appropriate. Case B involves confidentiality and integrity. Ethical issues are not always clear-cut. The supplier in Case B may have no intention of raising issues associated with the bid. However, the appearance of a conflict of interest in Case B is sufficient for many companies to prohibit employees from accepting "favors" from suppliers. Exhibit 1-8 on page 19 presents the IMA's guidance on "Resolution of Ethical Conflict." The accountant in Case B should discuss the invitation with his immediate supervisor. If the visit is approved, the supplier should be informed that the invitation has been officially approved subject to his following corporate policy (which includes the confidentiality of information).

Most professional accounting organizations around the globe issue statements about professional ethics. These statements include many of the same issues discussed by the IMA in Exhibits 1-7 and 1-8. For example, the Chartered Institute of Management Accountants (CIMA) in the United Kingdom identifies the same four fundamental principles as in Exhibit 1-7—competency, confidentiality, integrity, and objectivity.

EXHIBIT 1-7 Standards of Ethical Conduct for Management Accountants

Practitioners of management accounting and financial management have an obligation to the public, their profession, the organization they serve, and themselves to maintain the highest standards of ethical conduct. In recognition of this obligation, the Institute of Management Accountants has promulgated the following standards of ethical conduct for practitioners of management accounting and financial management. Adherence to these standards, both domestically and internationally, is integral to achieving the Objectives of Management Accounting. Practitioners of management accounting and financial management shall not commit acts contrary to these standards, nor shall they condone the commission of such acts by others within their organizations.

Competence

Practitioners of management accounting and financial management have a responsibility to:

- Maintain an appropriate level of professional competence by ongoing development of their knowledge and skills.
- Perform their professional duties in accordance with relevant laws, regulations, and technical standards.
- Prepare complete and clear reports and recommendations after appropriate analysis of relevant and reliable information.

Confidentiality

Practitioners of management accounting and financial management have a responsibility to:

- Refrain from disclosing confidential information acquired in the course of their work except when authorized, unless legally obligated to do so.
- Inform subordinates as appropriate regarding the confidentiality of information acquired in the course of their work and monitor their activities to assure the maintenance of that confidentiality.
- Refrain from using or appearing to use confidential information acquired in the course of their work for unethical or illegal advantage either personally or through third parties.

Integrity

Practitioners of management accounting and financial management have a responsibility to:

- Avoid actual or apparent conflicts of interest and advise all appropriate parties of any potential conflict.
- Refrain from engaging in any activity that would prejudice their ability to carry out their duties ethically.
- Refuse any gift, favor, or hospitality that would influence or would appear to influence their actions.
- Refrain from either actively or passively subverting the attainment of the organization's legitimate and ethical objectives.
- Recognize and communicate professional limitations or other constraints that would preclude responsible judgment or successful performance of an activity.
- Communicate unfavorable as well as favorable information and professional judgments or opinions.
- Refrain from engaging in or supporting any activity that would discredit the profession.

Objectivity

Practitioners of management accounting and financial management have a responsibility to:

- Communicate information fairly and objectively.
- Disclose fully all relevant information that could reasonably be expected to influence an intended user's understanding of the reports, comments, and recommendations presented.

Source: Institute of Management Accountants, "Standards of Ethical Conduct for Practitioners of Management Accounting and Financial Management," *Management Accounting,* Vol. LXXIX, No. 1.

EXHIBIT 1-8 Resolution of Ethical Conflict

In applying the standards of ethical conduct, practitioners of management accounting and financial management may encounter problems in identifying unethical behavior or in resolving an ethical conflict. When faced with significant ethical issues, practitioners of management accounting and financial management should follow the established policies of the organization bearing on the resolution of such conflict. If these policies do not resolve the ethical conflict, such practitioners should consider the following courses of action:

- Discuss such problems with the immediate superior except when it appears that the superior is involved, in which case the problem should be presented initially to the next higher managerial level. If satisfactory resolution cannot be achieved when the problem is initially presented, submit the issues to the next higher managerial level.
  If the immediate superior is the chief executive officer, or equivalent, the acceptable reviewing authority may be a group such as the audit committee, executive committee, board of directors, board of trustees, or owners. Contact with levels above the immediate superior should be initiated only with the superior's knowledge, assuming the superior is not involved. Except where legally prescribed, communication of such problems to authorities or individuals not employed or engaged by the organization is not considered appropriate.
- Clarify relevant ethical issues by confidential discussion with an objective advisor (e.g., IMA Ethics Counseling Service) to obtain a better understanding of possible courses of action.
- Consult your own attorney as to legal obligations and rights concerning the ethical conflict.
- If the ethical conflict still exists after exhausting all levels of internal review, there may be no other recourse on significant matters than to resign from the organization and to submit an informative memorandum to an appropriate representative of the organization. After resignation, depending on the nature of the ethical conflict, it may also be appropriate to notify other parties.

Source: Institute of Management Accountants, "Standards of Ethical Conduct for Practitioners of Management Accounting and Financial Management," *Management Accounting,* Vol. LXXIX, No. 1.

PROBLEM FOR SELF-STUDY

Campbell Soup Company incurs the following costs:

a. Purchase of tomatoes by a canning plant for Campbell's tomato-soup products
b. Materials purchased for redesigning Pepperidge Farm biscuit containers to make biscuits stay fresh longer
c. Payment to Backer, Spielvogel, Bates, the advertising agency, for advertising work on Healthy Request line of soup products
d. Salaries of food technologists researching feasibility of a Prego pizza sauce that has minimal calories
e. Payment to Safeway for obtaining shelf space to display Campbell's food products
f. Cost of a toll-free telephone line used for customer inquiries about possible product defects in Campbell's soups
g. Cost of gloves used by line operators on the Swanson Fiesta breakfast-food production line
h. Cost of hand-held computers used by Pepperidge Farm delivery staff serving major supermarket accounts

Required

Classify each cost item (**a–h**) as one of the business functions in the value chain shown in Exhibit 1-4 (p. 10).

SOLUTION

a. Production
b. Design of products, services, or processes
c. Marketing
d. Research and development
e. Marketing
f. Customer service
g. Production
h. Distribution

DECISION POINTS — SUMMARY

The following question-and-answer format summarizes the chapter's learning objectives. Each decision presents a key question related to a learning objective. The guidelines are the answer to that question.

Decision	Guidelines
1. What information does cost accounting provide?	Cost accounting measures and reports financial information and other information related to the acquisition or consumption of an organization's resources. Cost accounting provides information to both management accounting and financial accounting.
2. How do management accountants support strategic decisions?	Management accountants contribute to strategic decisions by providing information about the sources of competitive advantage and by helping managers identify and build a company's resources and capabilities.
3. How do managers implement strategy?	Managers make planning decisions and control decisions. Planning decisions include deciding on organization goals, predicting results under various alternative ways of achieving those goals, and then deciding how to attain the desired goals. Control decisions include taking actions to implement the planning decisions and deciding on performance evaluation and feedback that will help future decision making.
4. What roles do management accountants perform?	In most organizations, management accountants perform multiple roles: problem solving (comparative analyses for decision making), scorekeeping (accumulating data and reporting reliable results), and attention directing (helping managers properly focus their attention).
5. What should managers do to compete effectively?	Four themes for managers to attain success are customer focus, value-chain and supply-chain analysis, key success factors, and continuous improvement and benchmarking.
6. How do companies add value?	Companies add value through R&D; design of products, services, or processes; production; marketing; distribution; and customer service. Managers in all business functions of the value chain are customers of management accounting information.
7. What guidelines do management accountants use?	Three guidelines that help management accountants increase their value to managers are (a) employ a cost-benefit approach, (b) recognize behavioral as well as technical considerations, and (c) identify different costs for different purposes.
8. Where does the management accounting function fit into an organization's structure?	Management accounting is an integral part of the controller's function in an organization. In most organizations, the controller reports to the chief financial officer, who is a key member of the top management team.
9. What are the ethical responsibilities of management accountants?	Management accountants have ethical responsibilities that are related to competence, confidentiality, integrity, and objectivity.

TERMS TO LEARN

Each chapter will include this section. Like all technical terms, accounting terms have precise meanings. Learn the definitions of new terms when you initially encounter them. The meaning of each of the following terms is given in this chapter and in the Glossary at the end of this book.

attention directing (8)
budget (6)
Certified in Financial Management (CFM) (17)
Certified Management Accountant (CMA) (17)
chief financial officer (CFO) (15)
control (6)
controller (16)
cost accounting (3)
cost-benefit approach (13)
cost management (3)
customer service (10)
design of products, services, or processes (10)
distribution (10)
feedback (6)
finance director (15)
financial accounting (3)
Institute of Management Accountants (IMA) (17)
line management (15)
management accounting (2)
marketing (10)
planning (6)
problem solving (8)
production (10)
research and development (9)
scorekeeping (8)
staff management (15)
strategic cost management (4)
strategy (4)
supply chain (10)
value chain (9)

Questions

1-1 How can a management accountant help in formulating a stategy?

1-2 How does management accounting differ from financial accounting?

1-3 Distinguish planning decisions from control decisions.

1-4 What are three roles that management accountants perform?

1-5 "Management accounting should not fit the straitjacket of financial accounting." Explain and give an example.

1-6 Describe the business functions in the value chain.

1-7 A leading management observer stated that the most successful companies are those that have an obsession for their customers. Is this statement pertinent to management accountants? Explain.

1-8 Describe four themes that are important to managers attaining success and in which management accounting can play a significant role in decision support.

1-9 Explain the term supply chain and its importance to cost management.

1-10 What three guidelines help management accountants provide the most value to managers?

1-11 "Knowledge of technical issues such as computer technology is a necessary but not sufficient condition to becoming a successful management accountant." Do you agree? Why?

1-12 As a new controller, reply to this comment by a plant manager: "As I see it, our accountants may be needed to keep records for shareholders and Uncle Sam, but I don't want them sticking their noses in my day-to-day operations. I do the best I know how. No bean-counter knows enough about my responsibilities to be of any use to me."

1-13 As used in accounting, what do IMA and CMA stand for?

1-14 Name the four areas in which standards of ethical conduct exist for management accountants in the United States. What organization sets forth these standards?

1-15 What steps should a management accountant take if established written policies provide insufficient guidance on how to handle an ethical conflict?

Exercises

1-16 **Planning and control decisions.** Barnes & Noble is a book retailing company. Most of its sales are made at its own stores, located in shopping malls or in central business districts. A small but increasing percentage of sales is made via BarnesandNoble.com, in which its major competitor is Amazon.com.

The following five reports were recently prepared by the management accounting group at Barnes & Noble:

1. Annual financial statements
2. Weekly report to vice president of operations for each Barnes & Noble's store—includes revenues, gross margin, and operating costs
3. Study for vice president of new business development of the expected revenues and costs of BarnesandNoble.com, selling music products (CDs, cassettes, etc.) as well as books
4. Weekly report to book publishers and trade magazines on the sales of the top 10 selling fiction and nonfiction books at both its own stores and BarnesandNoble.com.
5. Report to insurance company on losses Barnes & Noble suffered at its three San Francisco stores due to an earthquake

Required

For each report, identify both a planning-decision and a control-decision use by a Barnes & Noble manager.

1-17 **Problem solving, scorekeeping, and attention directing.** For each of the following activities, identify the main role the accountant is performing—problem solving, scorekeeping, or attention directing.

1. Preparing a monthly statement of Australian sales for the IBM marketing vice president
2. Interpreting differences between actual results and budgeted amounts on a performance report for the Customer Warranty Department of General Electric
3. Preparing a schedule of depreciation for forklift trucks in the Receiving Department of a Hewlett-Packard Company plant in Scotland

4. Analyzing, for a Mitsubishi international-manufacturing manager, the desirability of having some auto parts made in Korea
5. Interpreting why a Birmingham distribution center exceeded its delivery-costs budget
6. Explaining a Xerox Corporation Shipping Department's performance report
7. Preparing, for the manager of production control of a U.S. steel plant, a cost comparison of two computerized-manufacturing control systems
8. Preparing a scrap report for the Finishing Department of a Toyota parts plant
9. Preparing the budget for the Maintenance Department of Mount Sinai Hospital
10. Analyzing for a General Motors product designer the impact on product costs of a new headlight

1-18 **Problem solving, scorekeeping, and attention directing.** For each of the following activities, identify the main role the accountant is performing—problem solving, scorekeeping, or attention directing.

1. Interpreting differences between actual results and budgeted amounts on a shipping manager's performance report at a Daewoo distribution center
2. Preparing a report showing the benefits from leasing motor vehicles rather than owning them
3. Preparing journal entries for depreciation on the personnel manager's office equipment at Citibank
4. Preparing a customer's monthly statement for a Sears store
5. Processing the weekly payroll for the Harvard University Maintenance Department
6. Explaining the product-design manager's performance report at a Chrysler division
7. Analyzing the costs of different ways to blend materials in the foundry of a General Electric plant
8. Tallying sales, by branches, for the sales vice president of Unilever
9. Analyzing, for the president of Microsoft, the impact of a contemplated new product on net income
10. Interpreting why an IBM sales district did not meet its sales quota

1-19 **Value chain and classification of costs, computer company.** Compaq Computer incurs the following costs:

a. Electricity costs for the plant assembling the Presario computer line of products
b. Transportation costs for shipping the Presario line of products to a retail chain
c. Payment to David Kelley Designs for design of the Armada Notebook
d. Salary of computer scientist working on the next generation of minicomputers
e. Cost of Compaq employees' visit to a major customer to demonstrate Compaq's ability to interconnect with other computers
f. Purchase of products of competitors for testing against potential Compaq products
g. Payment to television network for running Compaq advertisements
h. Cost of cables purchased from outside supplier to be used with the Compaq printer

Required Classify each of the cost items (**a–h**) into one of the business functions of the value chain shown in Exhibit 1-4 (p. 10).

1-20 **Value chain and classification of costs, pharmaceutical company.** Merck, a pharmaceutical company, incurs the following costs:

a. Cost of redesigning blister packs to make drug containers more tamper-proof
b. Cost of videos sent to doctors to promote sales of a new drug
c. Cost of a toll-free telephone line used for customer inquiries about usage, side effects of drugs, and so on
d. Equipment purchased to conduct experiments on drugs yet to be approved by the government
e. Payment to actors on an infomercial to be shown on television promoting a new hair-growing product for balding men
f. Labor costs of workers in the packaging area of a production facility
g. Bonus paid to a salesperson for exceeding monthly sales quota
h. Cost of Federal Express courier service to deliver drugs to hospitals

Required Classify each of the cost items (**a–h**) as one of the business functions of the value chain shown in Exhibit 1-4 (p. 10).

1-21 **Management accounting system and customer focus.** A recent annual report of Ford Motor Company included the following comments:

- Delivering great value to our customers. That's our passion.
- Throughout Ford Motor Company, we're focused on improving the quality and value of our products and speeding delivery to market.
- All our efforts are aimed at exceeding customer expectations. That's the best way to attract and keep customers.

1. Who are the customers of management accounting functions?

2. How may the value of management accounting systems to its customers be enhanced?

Required

1-22 Management themes and changes in management accounting. A survey on ways organizations are changing their management accounting systems reported the following:

a. Company A now prepares a value-chain income statement for each brand it sells.

b. Company B now presents in a single report all costs related to achieving high quality levels of its products.

c. Company C now presents in its performance reports estimates of the manufacturing costs of its two most important competitors, in addition to its own manufacturing costs.

d. Company D reduces by 1% each month the budgeted labor-assembly cost of a product when evaluating the performance of a plant manager.

e. Company E now reports profitability and satisfaction measures (as assessed by a third party) on a customer-by-customer basis.

Link each of these changes to one of the key themes that are important to managers attaining success (see Exhibit 1-3, p. 9).

Required

1-23 Professional ethics and reporting divisional performance. Marcia Miller is division controller and Tom Maloney is division manager of the Ramses Shoe Company. Miller has line responsibility to Maloney, but she also has staff responsibility to the company controller.

Maloney is under severe pressure to achieve the budgeted division income for the year. He has asked Miller to book $200,000 of revenues on December 31. The customers' orders are firm, but the shoes are still in the production process. They will be shipped on or about January 4. Maloney says to Miller, "The key event is getting the sales order, not shipping of the shoes. You should support me, not obstruct my reaching division goals."

1. Describe Miller's ethical responsibilities.

2. What should Miller do if Maloney gives her a direct order to book the sales?

Required

Problems

1-24 Management accounting guidelines. For each of the following items, identify which of the management guidelines applies—cost-benefit approach, behavioral and technical considerations, or different costs for different purposes.

1. Analyzing whether to keep the billing function within the organization or outsourcing it
2. Deciding to give bonuses for superior performance to the employees in a Japanese subsidiary and extra vacation time to the employees in a Swedish subsidiary
3. Including costs of all the value-chain functions before deciding to launch a new product but including only its manufacturing costs in determining its inventory valuation
4. Considering the desirability of hiring one more salesperson
5. Giving each salesperson the compensation option of choosing either from a low salary and a high-percentage sales commission or a high salary and a low-percentage sales commission
6. Selecting the costlier computer system after considering two systems
7. Installing a participatory budgeting system in which managers set their own performance targets, instead of top management imposing performance targets on them
8. Recording research costs as an expense for financial reporting purpose (as required by U.S. GAAP) but capitalizing and expensing them over a longer period for management performance-evaluation purposes
9. Introducing a profit-sharing plan for employees

1-25 Planning and control decisions, Internet company. WebNews.com is an Internet company. It offers subscribers multiple online services ranging from an annotated TV guide to local-area information on restaurants and movie theaters. It has two main revenue sources:

- Monthly fees from subscribers. Recent data are:

Month/Year	Actual Number of Subscribers	Actual Monthly Fee per Subscriber
June 2001	28,642	$14.95
December 2001	54,813	$19.95
June 2002	58,178	$19.95
December 2002	86,437	$19.95
June 2003	146,581	$19.95

- Banner advertising fees from companies advertising on WebNews.com page sites. Recent data are:

Month/Year	Advertising Revenues
June 2001	$ 400,988
December 2001	833,158
June 2002	861,034
December 2002	1,478,072
June 2003	2,916,962

The following decisions were made from June to October 2003:

a. June. Decision to raise the monthly subscription fee from $19.95 per month to $24.95 per month in July. The $19.95 fee began in December 2001.

b. June. Decision to inform existing subscribers that the July subscription fee would be $24.95.

c. July. Decision to upgrade the content of its online services and to offer better Internet mail services.

d. October. Demotion of vice president of marketing after significant slowing of subscriber growth in accounts and revenues. Results include:

Month/Year	Actual Number of Subscribers	Actual Monthly Fee per Subscriber
July 2003	128,933	$24.95
August 2003	139,419	$24.95
September 2003	143,131	$24.95

Budgeted amounts (set in June 2003) for the number of subscribers were 140,000 for July 2003, 150,000 for August 2003, and 160,000 for September 2003.

e. October 2003. Decision to reduce the monthly subscription fee from $24.95 per month in September 2003 to $21.95 in October 2003.

Required

1. Distinguish between planning decisions and control decisions at WebNews.com.
2. Classify each of the (**a**) to (**e**) decisions as a planning or a control decision.

1-26 Problem solving, scorekeeping, attention directing, and feedback, Internet company (continuation of 1-25). Management accountants at WebNews.com can play three roles in each of the five decisions described in Problem 1-25: problem solving, scorekeeping, and attention directing.

Required

1. Distinguish between the problem-solving, scorekeeping, and attention-directing roles of a management accountant at WebNews.com.
2. For each of the five decisions outlined in 1-25, describe a problem-solving, scorekeeping, or attention-directing role. When possible, provide your own example of an information item that a management accountant could provide for each decision.
3. What was the role of feedback in the decisions made in the period?
4. What further action might WebNews.com take based on feedback from the July to September subscription information?

1-27 The chief financial officer and the controller. Juan Rodriguez used to be the controller of Allied Electronics and has just been promoted to the position of Chief Financial Officer (CFO) of the company.

Required

1. Describe Rodriguez's major responsibilities in his former position as a controller.
2. As CFO, what is the scope of Rodriguez's new responsibilities?

1-28 Software-procurement decision, ethics. Jorge Michaels is the Chicago-based controller of Fiesta Foods, a rapidly growing manufacturer and marketer of Mexican food products. Michaels is currently considering the purchase of a new cost-management package for use by each of the company's six manufacturing plants and its many marketing personnel. Four major, competing products are being considered by Michaels.

Horizon 1-2-3 is an aggressive software developer. It views Fiesta as a target of opportunity. Every six months, Horizon has a three-day users' conference in a Caribbean location. Each conference has substantial time allowed for "rest and recreation." Horizon offers Michaels an all-expenses-paid visit to the upcoming conference in Cancun, Mexico. Michaels accepts the offer believing it will be very useful to talk to other users of Horizon software. He is especially looking forward to the visit because he has close relatives in the Cancun area.

Prior to leaving, Michaels receives a visit from the president of Fiesta. She shows him an anonymous letter sent to her. It argues that Horizon is receiving unfair favorable treatment in Fiesta's software decision-making process. The letter specifically mentions Michaels' upcoming "all-expenses-paid package to Cancun during Chicago's cold winter." Michaels is deeply offended. He says he has made no decision and believes he is very capable of making a software choice on the merits of each product. Fiesta currently does not have a formal, written code of ethics.

1. Do you think Michaels faces an ethical problem in regard to his forthcoming visit to the Horizon user's group meeting? Refer to Exhibit 1-7 (p. 18). Explain.
2. Should Fiesta allow executives to attend user meetings while negotiating with other vendors about a purchase decision? Explain. If yes, what conditions on attending should apply?
3. Would you recommend that Fiesta develop its own code of ethics to handle situations such as this? What are the pros and cons of having such a written code?

Required

1-29 Professional ethics and end-of-year games. Janet Taylor is the new division controller of the snack-foods division of Gourmet Foods. Gourmet Foods has reported a minimum 15% growth in annual earnings for each of the past five years. The snack-foods division has reported annual earnings growth of more than 20% each year in this same period. During the current year, the economy went into a recession. The corporate controller estimates a 10% annual earnings growth rate for Gourmet Foods this year. One month before the December 31 fiscal year-end of the current year, Taylor estimates the snack-foods division will report an annual earnings growth of only 8%. Warren Ryan, the snack-foods division president, is less than happy, but he says with a wry smile, "Let the end-of-year games begin."

Taylor makes some inquiries and is able to compile the following list of end-of-year games that were more or less accepted by the previous division controller:

a. Deferring December's routine monthly maintenance on packaging equipment by an independent contractor until January of next year
b. Extending the close of the current fiscal year beyond December 31 so that some sales of next year are included in the current year
c. Altering dates of shipping documents of next January's sales to record them as sales in December of the current year
d. Giving salespeople a double bonus to exceed December sales targets
e. Deferring the current period's advertising by reducing the number of television spots run in December and running more than planned in January of next year
f. Deferring the current period's reported advertising costs by having Gourmet Foods' outside advertising agency delay billing December advertisements until January of next year or having the agency alter invoices to conceal the December date
g. Persuading carriers to accept merchandise for shipment in December of the current year although they normally would not have done so

Required

1. Why might the snack-foods division president want to play the end-of-year games?
2. The division controller is deeply troubled and reads the "Standards of Ethical Conduct for Management Accountants" in Exhibit 1-7 (p. 18). Classify each of the end-of-year games (**a–g**) as (i) acceptable or (ii) unacceptable according to that document.
3. What should Taylor do if Ryan suggests that end-of-year games are played in every division of Gourmet Foods and that she would greatly harm the snack-foods division if she does not play along and paint the rosiest picture possible of the division's results?

Collaborative Learning Problem

1-30 Global company, ethical challenges with bribery. In June 2003, the government of Safistan invited bids for construction of two hydroelectric plants. Norris Energy Company obtained the necessary information and specifications. Because Norris was eager to enter the market in the region where Safistan is located, the company's bid was prepared very carefully with an expected profit margin only one-half of the normal profit on similar projects. The bid was submitted before the deadline. After two weeks, Norris received an acknowledgment from the Safistan's Ministry of Water and Electricity that its bid had been received. Several weeks went by without any further communication. After waiting what Norris thought was a reasonable period, Stan Cheng, vice president of global operations, wrote letters to the appropriate government officials of Safistan but received no response. He talked by telephone to several officials at the ministry but they were not helpful. Finally, Cheng sought assistance from the U.S. commercial attaché in Safistan. The commercial attaché advised Cheng to visit Safistan because: "In this culture they only deal with business people they know personally." Cheng immediately left for Safistan. The U.S. commercial attaché was able to arrange a meeting for Cheng with the deputy minister of water and electricity. Cheng made himself thoroughly familiar with the project specifications and the bid in preparation for the meeting with the deputy minister. He was anxious for the meeting to go well because it was a multimillion-dollar project.

Cheng went to the deputy minister's office and from there was escorted to the meeting room. Soon the deputy minister arrived with his second-in-command, Sufi Gharib. After introductions and exchanging pleasantries, the deputy minister asked Cheng a few questions about Norris Energy's bid. After listening to Cheng's responses, the deputy minister said, "I am favorably inclined toward your bid, but a few details need to be worked out. I have to go to another meeting, but Mr. Gharib is authorized to negotiate with you."

After the departure of the deputy minister, Gharib said to Cheng, "I can guarantee that your bid will be accepted if you pay a $1 million commission." It was clear to Cheng that "commission" was nothing else than a bribe. He told Gharib that it would be impossible for his company to make such a payment due to U.S. laws and corporate policy. Gharib stood up, shook Cheng's hand, and wished him a pleasant trip home.

Required

1. As a shareholder of the company, would you prefer that Norris Energy make the payment?
2. Cheng shared his experience in Safistan with Charlie Short, who is manager of global operations in another company. Charlie told him that his "personal philosophy" is to make such payments if such a practice is part of the local culture. Do you think that Charlie's comment has some merit?
3. Why would Norris Energy have a corporate policy against such payments?

CHAPTER 1 INTERNET EXERCISE

Accountants consistently rank high in public opinion surveys on the ethics exhibited by members of different professions. Professional accounting organizations play an important role in promoting high ethical standards. To learn more about the Institute of Management Accountants, go to www.prenhall.com/horngren, click on *Cost Accounting,* 11th ed., and access the Internet exercise for Chapter 1.

CHAPTER 1 VIDEO CASE

REGAL MARINE: The Accountant's Role

Regal Marine is one of the United States' leading luxury performance-boat manufacturers. Sales of all models in a recent year topped $100 million, with their biggest customer, Boat Tree, buying close to 90% of all boats produced by Regal Marine. Headquartered in Orlando, Florida, Regal Marine currently makes 22 different models, ranging from a 14-foot runabout sport boat to the 40-foot Commodore yacht. The product life cycle for each of Regal Marine's boats is three to five years, depending on the size of the boat, with smaller boats having shorter life cycles. This variation in life cycle results in a continuing stream of new products that work their way through the company's value chain.

Cross-functional design teams with representatives from R&D, production, purchasing, design, accounting, marketing, customer service, upholstery, and cabinetry work together to fine-tune prototype designs. Customer feedback is gathered at boat shows, and suppliers regularly present their new product innovations to the company for potential use in future boat models. The team also tries to make sure manufacturing requirements are met by using existing components and production processes, when feasible, to streamline manufacturing. Computer-aided design (CAD) systems are used for all designs. When the design of a new model is finished, Regal Marine makes a prototype of it before producing the new models.

To make a new boat model, a foam-based carving called a *plug* is created. CAD system specifications are used to drive the automated carving of plugs. The plug becomes the basis for making the molds for fiberglass hulls and decks. The finished molds are then used to make thousands of fiberglass hulls and decks. Regal Marine has

QUESTIONS

1. For each of the following activities, identify the main role the accountant is performing—problem solving (P), scorekeeping (S), or attention directing (A).
   a. Preparing a schedule of depreciation for boat hull and deck molds
   b. Analyzing the desirability of using standard Volvo-Penta boat engines in a new boat model
   c. Preparing the daily report of the number of hull defects found during the quality check on the Sport Boat assembly line
   d. Explaining the Commodore Yacht Division's monthly performance report
   e. Interpreting differences between actual results and budgeted amounts on the Prototyping Department's monthly performance report.
   f. Preparing a monthly statement of boat sales, by model and customer, for the company's vice president of sales
   g. Analyzing for the Design Team the impact on product costs for a new dashboard-odometer display
   h. Preparing a cost comparison of two plywood manufacturers for use by the purchasing manager
2. Classify each of the cost items (**a–h**) into one of the business functions of the value chain.

several hundred molds, representing their largest capital investment. Molds are kept even after production of outdated models is stopped.

At the Orlando factory, production begins by coating the molds with gelcoat and then spraying the dried gelcoat with chopped fiberglass and resin. Then the fiberglass hulls and decks are popped off the molds and wheeled into assembly stations that move in synch each day. While hulls and decks are being crested, other manufacturing departments—such as upholstery, cabinetry, electrical, and small part fabrication—prepare the components that will be installed in each boat during assembly. Trained workers install required components—fasteners, electrical, upholstered seats, and cabinets, for example—according to a strict schedule that assures each assembly station's work is done each day so the lines keep moving. It takes anywhere from 2 to 20 days to complete production, depending on boat size. In the smaller sport-boat category, for example, 10 boats a day roll off the assembly line. As soon as boats are quality-checked and approved for delivery, they are loaded onto trucks for delivery to customers such as Boat Tree. No boats are kept in finished-goods inventory.

a. Cost of a toll-free telephone line used for customer inquiries about product specifications, performance, and warranty coverage
b. Cost of sales and promotional materials for use at boat shows
c. Labor costs of workers in the Cabinetry Department of the production facility
d. Cost of an industry research report on boat industry trends
e. Equipment and trucks purchased for transporting finished boats to retail outlets such as the Boat Tree
f. Boat hull and deck mold-fabrication costs
g. Cost of a new CAD design station used by the Design Department
h. Costs of upholstered seats for Commodore yachts

CHAPTER 2

An Introduction to Cost Terms and Purposes

LEARNING OBJECTIVES

1. Define and illustrate a cost object
2. Distinguish between direct costs and indirect costs
3. Explain variable costs and fixed costs
4. Interpret unit costs cautiously
5. Distinguish among manufacturing companies, merchandising companies, and service-sector companies
6. Describe the three categories of inventories commonly found in manufacturing companies
7. Differentiate between inventoriable costs and period costs
8. Explain why product costs are computed in different ways for different purposes
9. Present key features of cost accounting and cost management

www.prenhall.com/horngren

What do dogs and dollars have in common? At Three Dog Bakery, they combine to form one of the most unique business concepts around. The bakery specializes in making gourmet baked treats—for dogs. When founders Dan Dye and Mark Beckloff started the company, cost accounting was not part of their business recipe. But today, company managers understand cost objects, direct costs and indirect costs, fixed costs and variable costs, and more. Their costs are now accumulated, analyzed, and reported on a regular basis. The reports are used by production managers to understand and control product manufacturing costs. Externally, bankers and shareholders use the reports to evaluate company performance. There is not a decision made today that isn't somehow influenced by the accounting information associated with their tasty treats—tasty for canine consumers.

An understanding of this chapter's cost terms and concepts provides the foundation for this course.

Accounting reports contain a variety of cost concepts and terms representing a lot of information. Managers who understand these concepts and terms are able to best use the information provided, as well as to avoid misuse of that information. A common understanding on the meaning of cost concepts and terms facilitates communication among managers and management accountants. This chapter discusses cost concepts and terms expressed in accounting information used for internal and external reporting.

COSTS AND COST TERMINOLOGY

In the definition of *cost,* "sacrificed" refers to a resource that is consumed—say $3,000 to lease a warehouse. "Forgone" refers to giving up an opportunity for using a resource. For example, the $3,000 spent on the warehouse lease cannot be used for another purpose.

Accountants define **cost** as a resource sacrificed or forgone to achieve a specific objective. A cost (such as direct materials or advertising) is usually measured as the monetary amount that must be paid to acquire goods or services. An **actual cost** is the cost incurred (a historical cost), as distinguished from a budgeted (or forecasted) cost.

To guide their decisions, managers want to know how much a particular thing (such as a product, machine, service, or process) costs. We call this "thing" a **cost object,** which is anything for which a measurement of costs is desired. Exhibit 2-1 lists examples of seven different types of cost objects for which Procter & Gamble, the consumer-products company, wants to know the costs.

1 Define and illustrate a cost object
... examples are products, services, activities, processes, parts of the organization, and customers

A costing system typically accounts for costs in two basic stages: accumulation followed by assignment. **Cost accumulation** is the collection of cost data in some organized way by means of an accounting system. For example, a publisher that purchases paper rolls for printing magazines collects (accumulates) the costs of individual rolls bought in any one month to obtain the total monthly cost of paper. Beyond accumulating costs, managers assign costs to designated cost objects (such as the different magazines the publisher publishes) to help decision making (such as the pricing of different magazines). Managers assign costs to cost objects for many purposes. Costs assigned to a department facilitate decisions about department efficiency. Costs assigned to products help in pricing decisions and in analyzing how profitable different products are. Costs assigned to customers help managers to understand the profit earned from different customers and to make decisions about how to allocate resources to support different customers. **Cost assignment** is a general term that encompasses both (1) tracing accumulated costs that have a direct relationship to a cost object and (2) allocating accumulated costs that have an indirect relationship to a cost object.

In the following questions, the cost objects are in italics: What selling price should be charged for a *product*? Which *machine* is the least expensive to operate?

EXHIBIT 2-1 Examples of Cost Objects at Procter & Gamble

Cost Object	Illustration
Product	*Crest Tartar Control*: Original Flavor toothpaste product
Service	Telephone hotline providing information and assistance to users of *Pampers Diapers* products
Project	R&D project on alternative scent-free formulations of *Tide* detergent products
Customer	Safeway, the retailer, which purchases a broad range of Procter & Gamble products
Brand category	*Vidal Sassoon* range of hairstyle products
Activity	Development and updating Web site on the Internet or setting up machines for production
Department	Environmental, Health, and Safety Department

DIRECT COSTS AND INDIRECT COSTS

Cost Tracing and Cost Allocation

- **Direct costs of a cost object** are related to the particular cost object and can be traced to that cost object in an economically feasible (cost-effective) way. For example, the cost of the cans or bottles is a direct cost of Pepsi-Colas. The cost of the cans or bottles can be easily traced to or identified with the drink. The term **cost tracing** is used to describe the assignment of direct costs to the particular cost object.
- **Indirect costs of a cost object** are related to the particular cost object but cannot be traced to that cost object in an economically feasible (cost-effective) way. For example, the salaries of supervisors who oversee production of the many different soft drink products bottled at a Pepsi plant is an indirect cost of Pepsi-Colas. Supervision costs are related to the cost object (Pepsi-Colas) because supervision is necessary for managing the production and sale of Pepsi-Colas. Supervision costs are indirect costs because supervisors also oversee the production of other products, such as 7-Up. Unlike the cost of cans or bottles, it is difficult to trace supervision costs to the Pepsi-Cola line. The term **cost allocation** is used to describe the assignment of indirect costs to a particular cost object.

2 **Distinguish between direct costs**
... that are traced to the cost object
and indirect costs
... that are allocated to the cost object

Consider the audits performed by a public accounting firm. The firm traces direct professional labor costs to each audit by means of time records. In contrast, rent on the firm's office space and depreciation on its computers cannot be traced to individual audits. These are indirect costs that must be allocated to the audits.

Exhibit 2-2 depicts direct costs and indirect costs and both forms of cost assignment—cost tracing and cost allocation—using the example of *Sports Illustrated* magazine, which is published by AOL Time Warner. The cost object is the *Sports Illustrated* magazine. The paper on which the magazine is printed is a direct cost. This paper can be traced in a cost-effective way to *Sports Illustrated* magazine. Consider the cost of leasing the building that houses the senior editorial staff of such magazines as *Time, People,* and *Sports Illustrated.* This leasing cost is an indirect cost of *Sports Illustrated.* Time Warner can *trace* the lease amount paid for the entire building, but there is no separate lease agreement for the space used by the editorial staff of *Sports Illustrated.* Therefore, Time Warner cannot trace the lease cost for *Sports Illustrated.* Time Warner can, however, *allocate* to *Sports Illustrated* a part of the lease cost of the entire building, for example, on the basis of an estimate of the relative percentage of the building's total floor space occupied by the editorial staff of *Sports Illustrated.*

Managers want to accurately assign costs to cost objects. Inaccurate product costs will mislead managers about the profitability of different products; as a result, managers might promote products that are not profitable while deemphasizing products that are profitable. Generally, managers are more confident about the accuracy of direct costs of cost objects, such as the paper cost of the *Sports Illustrated* magazine. Indirect costs pose more problems. For some indirect costs such as lease cost, allocating costs on the basis of the total floor space occupied by the editorial staff of each magazine measures the building resources demanded by each magazine reasonably accurately. This allocation assumes that the quality of the space (such as views from window(s), upkeep, etc.) used by the different magazines is fairly similar. Accurately allocating other overhead costs, such as the costs of AOL Time Warner's top management, to the *Sports Illustrated* magazine is more difficult. Should these costs be allocated on the basis of the size of the editorial staff? The

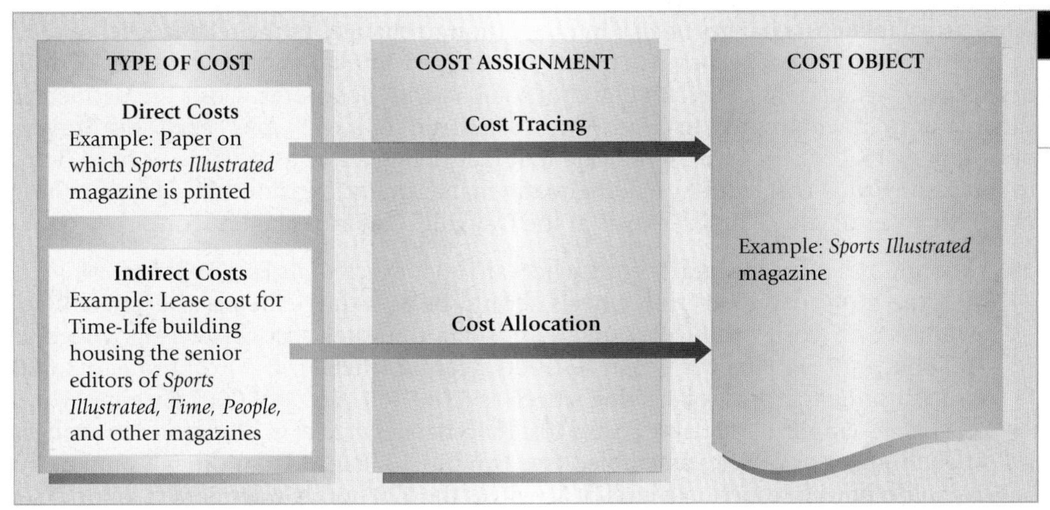

EXHIBIT 2-2
Cost Assignment to a Cost Object

number of magazines sold? Some other measure? It is not so clear how to measure the share of top management's time demanded by each magazine.

Factors Affecting Direct/Indirect Cost Classifications

Several factors affect the classification of a cost as direct or indirect:

1. *The materiality of the cost in question.* The larger the amount of a cost, the more likely that it is economically feasible to trace that cost to a particular cost object. Consider a mail-order catalog company. It would probably be economically feasible to trace the courier charges for delivering each package directly to the individual customer. In contrast, the cost of invoice paper included in the package sent to the customer is likely to be classified as an indirect cost. Why? Because although the cost of the paper can be traced to each customer, it is not cost-effective to trace the cost of this small quantity of paper to each customer. The benefits of knowing the exact number of, say, 0.5 cents worth of paper included in each package do not exceed the costs of money and time in tracing the cost to each package.

2. *Available information-gathering technology.* Improvements in information-gathering technology are making it possible to consider more and more costs as direct costs. Bar codes, for example, allow many manufacturing plants to treat certain materials, previously classified as indirect costs, as direct costs of products. Many component parts display a bar code that can be scanned at every point in the production process. Bar codes can be read into a manufacturing cost file by waving a "wand" in the same quick and efficient way supermarket checkout clerks enter the cost of each item purchased by a customer.

3. *Design of operations.* Classifying a cost as direct is easier if a company's facility (or some part of it) is used exclusively for a specific cost object, such as a specific product or a particular customer.

This book examines different ways to assign costs to cost objects. For now, be aware that a specific cost may be both a direct cost of one cost object and an indirect cost of another cost object. *That is, the direct/indirect classification depends on the choice of the cost object.* For example, the salary of an Assembly Department supervisor at Ford is a direct cost if the cost object is the Assembly Department, but it is an indirect cost if the cost object is a product such as the Ford Windstar because the Assembly Department assembles many different models. A useful rule of thumb is that the broader the definition of the cost object—the Assembly Department rather than the Windstar—the higher the proportion of total costs that are direct costs and the more confidence management has in the accuracy of the resulting cost amounts. We now discuss costs and their behavior.

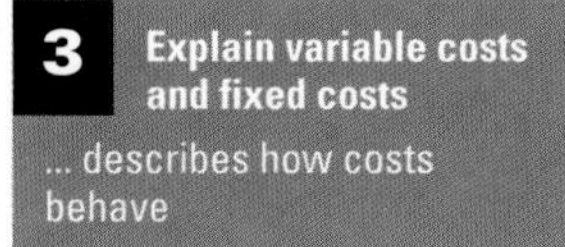

The distinction between variable costs and fixed costs is necessary to address basic questions, such as how much would manufacturing costs change if the output level increases by 5%.

COST-BEHAVIOR PATTERNS: VARIABLE COSTS AND FIXED COSTS

Costing systems record the costs of resources acquired and track how they are then used. Recording the costs of resources acquired and used allows managers to see how costs behave. Consider two basic types of cost-behavior patterns found in many accounting systems. A **variable cost** changes *in total* in proportion to changes in the related level of total activity or volume. A **fixed cost** remains unchanged *in total* for a given time period, despite wide changes in the related level of total activity or volume. Costs are defined as variable or fixed with respect to *a specific cost object* and for *a given time period*. The Surveys of Company Practice on page 34 indicate that identifying a cost as variable or fixed helps in forecasting total costs and in making many management decisions. To illustrate these two basic types of costs, consider costs at the Oakville, Ontario, plant of Ford.

- *Variable Costs*: If Ford buys a steering wheel at $60 for each of its Ford Windstar vehicles, then the total cost of steering wheels should be $60 times the number of vehicles assembled. If Ford produces 1,000 Windstars, the total cost of steering wheels is $60,000 ($60 per steering wheel × 1,000 steering wheels). If Ford produces 3,000 Windstars, the total cost of steering wheels is $180,000 ($60 × 3,000). Steering wheel cost is an example of a variable cost, a cost that changes *in total* in proportion to changes in the number of vehicles assembled (see Exhibit 2-3, Panel A). Another example of a variable cost with respect to a level of activity is the $20 hourly wage paid to labor to set

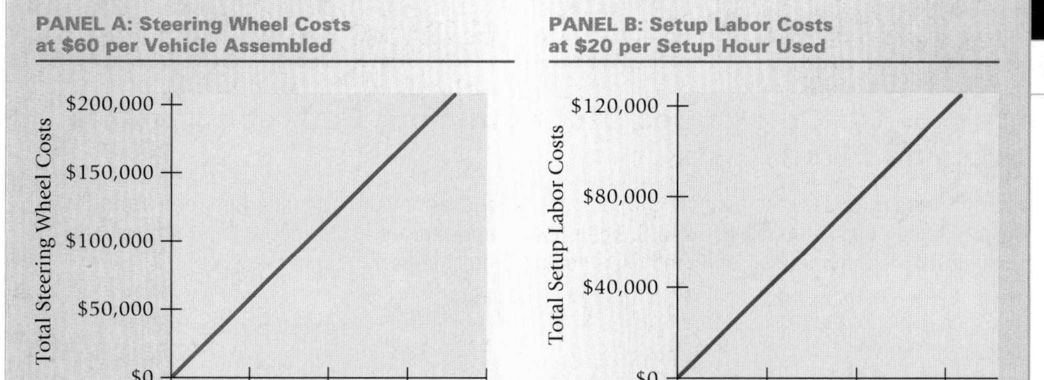

EXHIBIT 2-3

Examples of Variable Costs

up machines at the Oakville plant. Setup labor cost is a variable cost, a cost that changes *in total* in proportion to the number of setup hours used (see Exhibit 2-3, Panel B). In Panels A and B, the costs are represented by a straight line. The phrases "strictly variable" or "proportionately variable" are sometimes used to describe the variable costs represented in Exhibit 2-3. Note that in both Panels A and B, the cost per unit of a variable cost is the same: $60 for each vehicle assembled in Panel A and $20 per setup hour in Panel B. However, total costs change with the level of activity or volume.

- *Fixed Costs*: Ford may incur in a given year a total of $100 million in leasing cost for its Oakville plant. This cost is unchanged *in total* over a designated range of the number of vehicles assembled during a given time span. Fixed costs become smaller and smaller on a *per unit basis* as the number of vehicles assembled increases. For example, if Ford assembles 10,000 vehicles at this plant in a year, the fixed cost for leasing per vehicle would be $10,000 ($100,000,000 ÷ 10,000 vehicles). If 50,000 vehicles are assembled, the fixed cost per vehicle would be $2,000 ($100,000,000 ÷ 50,000). Do not be misled by the change in fixed cost per unit. *When considering fixed costs, always focus on total costs.* Costs are fixed when total costs remain unchanged despite changes in the level of total activity or volume.

Why are some costs variable and other costs fixed? Recall, a cost is usually measured as the amount of money that must be paid to acquire goods and services. Total steering wheel costs are variable costs because Ford buys the steering wheels only when they are needed. As more Windstars are produced, proportionately more steering wheels are acquired and proportionately more costs are incurred.

Contrast the description of variable costs with the $100 million of fixed costs incurred by Ford to lease its Oakville plant for a year. This plant capacity is acquired well before Ford uses the capacity to produce Windstars and before Ford even knows how much of the capacity it will use. Let us say the plant has the capacity to turn out 50,000 Windstars each year. If the demand is for only 45,000 Windstars, not all of the capacity will be needed or used. However, Ford must pay for the capacity it is not using. If demand is even lower, say only 40,000 Windstars, plant leasing costs will not change; they will continue to be $100 million. However, now even less of the capacity will be used. Unlike variable costs, fixed costs pay for resources, such as for plant capacity, that cannot be quickly and easily changed to match the resources needed or used. Over time, of course, managers can take actions to reduce fixed costs. For example, Ford may choose to lease only part of the plant or to sublease part of the plant to other companies.

Do not assume that individual cost items are inherently variable or fixed. Consider labor costs. Labor costs can be purely variable with respect to units produced when workers are paid on a piece-unit (piece-rate) basis. Some garment workers are paid on a per-shirt-sewed basis. In contrast, labor costs at a plant in the coming year are appropriately classified as fixed when a labor union agreement or an implicit contract with employees has set annual salaries and conditions, contains a no-layoff clause, and severely restricts a company's flexibility to assign workers to any other plant that has demand for labor. Japanese companies, for example, for a long time have had a policy of lifetime

Suppose you make belts using leather that costs $5/belt (a variable cost) in a workshop with $450/month rent (a fixed cost). Calculate total and per unit costs for

	1 Belt		10 Belts	
	Total	Per Unit	Total	Per Unit
Leather	$ 5	$ 5	$ 50	$ 5
Rent	450	450	450	45
Total	$455	$455	$500	$50

Total VC vary with the number of belts produced (from $5 to $50 as volume increases from 1 to 10 belts), but *per unit VC are constant* at $5/belt (for both 1 and 10 belts). *Total FC are constant* at $450 (for both 1 and 10 belts), but *per unit FC vary* with the number of belts produced (from $450 to $45 as volume increases from 1 to 10 belts). Thus, total cost per belt depends on the number of belts produced.

SURVEYS OF COMPANY PRACTICE

Purposes for Companies Distinguishing Between Variable Costs and Fixed Costs

Many chapters in this book illustrate the insights gained from distinguishing between variable costs and fixed costs. One survey of U.S. companies reported the following ranking of purposes for distinguishing between variable and fixed costs (15 most important purposes).[a]

Rank	Purpose	Chapter(s) in This Book Discussing the Purpose in Detail
1 (equal)	Pricing	4, 5, 11, 12, and 13
1 (equal)	Budgeting	6
3	Profitability analysis—existing products	4, 5, 11, 12, and 13
4	Profitability analysis—new products	11, 12, and 13
5	Cost-volume-profit (CVP) analysis	3
6	Variance analysis	7, 8, and 14

Surveys of Australian, Japanese, and United Kingdom companies provide additional evidence on the ranking by managers of the many purposes for distinguishing between variable costs and fixed costs (1 = most important purpose):[b]

Purpose	Australian Companies	Ranking by Japanese Companies	United Kingdom Companies
Pricing decisions	1	5	1
Budgeting	2	2	3
Making profit plans	3	1	2
Cost reduction	6	3	5 (equal)
CVP analysis	4 (equal)	4	4
Cost-benefit analysis	4 (equal)	6	5 (equal)

These surveys highlight the wide range of decisions for which managers feel an understanding of cost behavior is important.

[a]Adapted from Mowen, *Accounting for Costs as Fixed and Variable*.

[b]Blayney and Yokoyama, "Comparative Analysis of Japanese and Australian Cost Accounting and Management Practices." Full citations are in Appendix A at the end of the book.

employment for their workers. Although such a policy entails higher labor costs, particularly in economic downturns, the benefits are increased loyalty and dedication to the company and higher productivity. The Concepts in Action feature on page 35 describes how the Internet offers companies the opportunity to convert fixed costs of application software into variable costs by renting software applications on an as-needed basis.

A particular cost item could be a variable cost with respect to one level of activity and fixed with respect to another. Consider annual registration and license costs for a fleet of planes owned by an airline company. Registration and license costs would be a variable cost with respect to the number of planes owned. But registration and license costs for a particular plane are fixed with respect to the miles flown by that plane during a year.

Cost Drivers

A **cost driver** is a variable, such as the level of activity or volume, that causally affects costs over a given time span. That is, there is a cause-and-effect relationship between a change in the level of activity or volume and a change in the level of total costs. For example, if product-design costs change with the number of parts in a product, the number of parts is a cost driver of product-design costs. Similarly, miles driven is often a cost driver of distribution costs.

CONCEPTS IN ACTION

How Application Service Providers (ASPs) Influence Cost Structures[a]

Do you foresee a day when companies will not be buying computers or software, instead renting the software they need from a service provider? If so, you are looking ahead to the world of Application Service Providers (ASPs).[b] ASPs allow companies to access application software from a remote server via the Internet. According to *ASP News.com*, an online newsletter, "Within a few years, users will not want to install applications locally. Instead, they will access the applications they need, on demand, from on-line providers who will charge them by the second for the precise value of the specific features and resources they choose to use."

Let's think about what this development means. Consider application software, such as e-mail and messaging, supply chain and procurement planning, human resource management, customer-relationship management, or budgeting, required by a small to medium-sized company of 250 employees. What options does the company have? It could (1) choose to build its own proprietary systems at a very high cost, or (2) purchase a packaged software, recruit and retain in-house information technology (IT) resources to install and maintain the software, and build and maintain the IT infrastructure necessary to support the application. Both solutions entail high fixed costs, leading many small businesses to not automate basic processes such as financial reporting and human resources.

ASPs such as Corio, Jamcracker, Microsoft, and Sprint design, develop, maintain, and upgrade application packages and then charge companies a price for using the package. From the perspective of their customers, ASPs convert fixed costs of software applications to variable costs. If business declines, ASP customers are not saddled with the fixed costs of the applications software. Of course, if customers use more of the software applications, they wind up paying more overall than they would have paid if they had developed the applications themselves.

Three nonfinancial reasons why companies may not use ASPs are (1) concerns about security of data sent over the Internet, (2) losing control over important applications, and (3) lack of reliability of the network (this is why ASPs offer service agreements that guarantee 99.9% uptime).

[a]T. Eisenmann and S. Pothen, *Application Service Providers,* Harvard Business School Note, 2001.

[b]R. Lavery, "The ABCs of ASPs," *Strategic Finance,* May 2001.

The cost driver of a variable cost is the level of activity or volume whose change causes proportionate changes in (variable) costs. For example, the number of vehicles assembled is the cost driver of the cost of steering wheels. If setup workers are paid an hourly wage, the number of setup hours is the cost driver of (variable) setup costs.

Costs that are fixed in the short run have no cost driver in the short run but may have a cost driver in the long run. Consider the costs of testing personal computers at Dell. These costs consist of Testing Department equipment and staff costs that are difficult to change and, hence, fixed in the short run with respect to changes in the volume of production. In this case, volume of production is not a cost driver of testing costs in the short run. But in the long run, Dell will increase or decrease the Testing Department's equipment and staff to the levels needed to support future production volumes. In the long run, volume of production is a cost driver of testing costs.

Relevant Range

Relevant range is the band of normal activity level or volume in which there is a specific relationship between the level of activity or volume and the cost in question. For example, a fixed cost is fixed only in relation to a given range (usually wide) of the total activity or volume (at which the company is expected to operate) and for a given time span (usually a particular budget period). Consider Thomas Transport Company (TTC), which rents

EXHIBIT 2-4

Fixed Cost Behavior at Thomas Transport Company

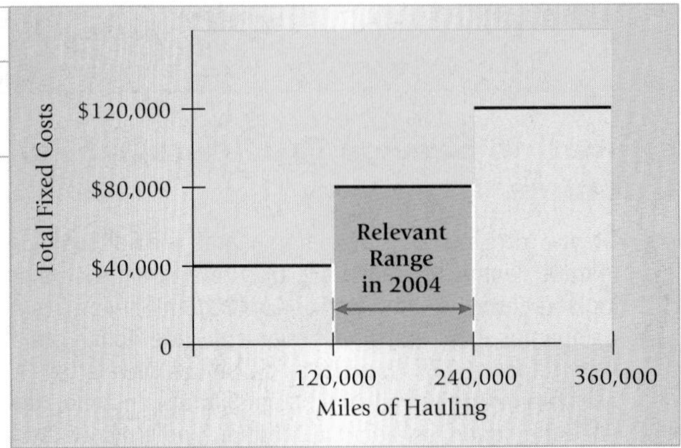

two refrigerated trucks that carry agricultural produce to market. Each truck has annual fixed rental costs of $40,000. The maximum annual usage of each truck is 120,000 miles. In the current year (2004), the predicted combined total hauling of the two trucks is 170,000 miles.

Exhibit 2-4 shows how annual fixed costs behave at different levels of miles of hauling. Up to 120,000 miles, TTC can operate with one truck; from 120,001 to 240,000 miles, it operates with two trucks; from 240,001 to 360,000 miles, it operates with three trucks. This pattern would continue as TTC adds trucks to its fleet to provide more miles of hauling. Given the predicted 170,000-mile usage for 2004, the range from 120,001 to 240,000 miles hauled is the range in which TTC expects to operate, resulting in fixed truck costs of $80,000. Within this relevant range, changes in miles hauled will not affect the annual fixed costs.

Fixed costs may change from one year to the next. For example, if the total rental fees for the two refrigerated trucks is increased by $2,000 in 2005, the total level of fixed costs will increase to $82,000 (all else remaining the same). However, if that increase were to occur, total truck costs would be fixed at this new level of $82,000 in 2005 for miles hauled in the 120,001–240,000 range.

The basic assumption of the relevant range also applies to variable costs. That is, outside the relevant range, variable costs, such as direct materials, may not change proportionately with changes in production volume. For example, above a certain volume, direct material costs may increase at a lower rate because of price discounts on direct-materials purchases greater than a certain quantity.

Relationships of Types of Costs

We have introduced two major classifications of costs: direct/indirect and variable/fixed. Costs may simultaneously be

- Direct and variable
- Direct and fixed
- Indirect and variable
- Indirect and fixed

Exhibit 2-5 shows examples of costs in each of these four cost classifications for the Ford Windstar.

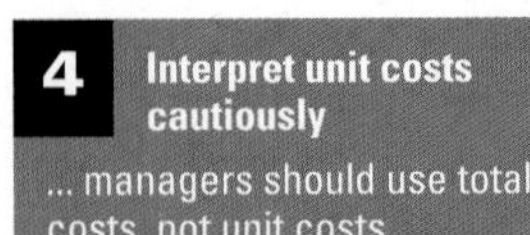
4 Interpret unit costs cautiously

... managers should use total costs, not unit costs

TOTAL COSTS AND UNIT COSTS

Unit Costs and Average Costs

The preceding section concentrated on the behavior patterns of total costs in relation to activity or volume levels. Generally, the decision maker should think in terms of total costs rather than unit costs. In many decision contexts, however, calculating a unit cost is essential. Consider the chairman of the social committee of a fraternity trying to decide whether to hire a musical group for an upcoming party. The total fee may be

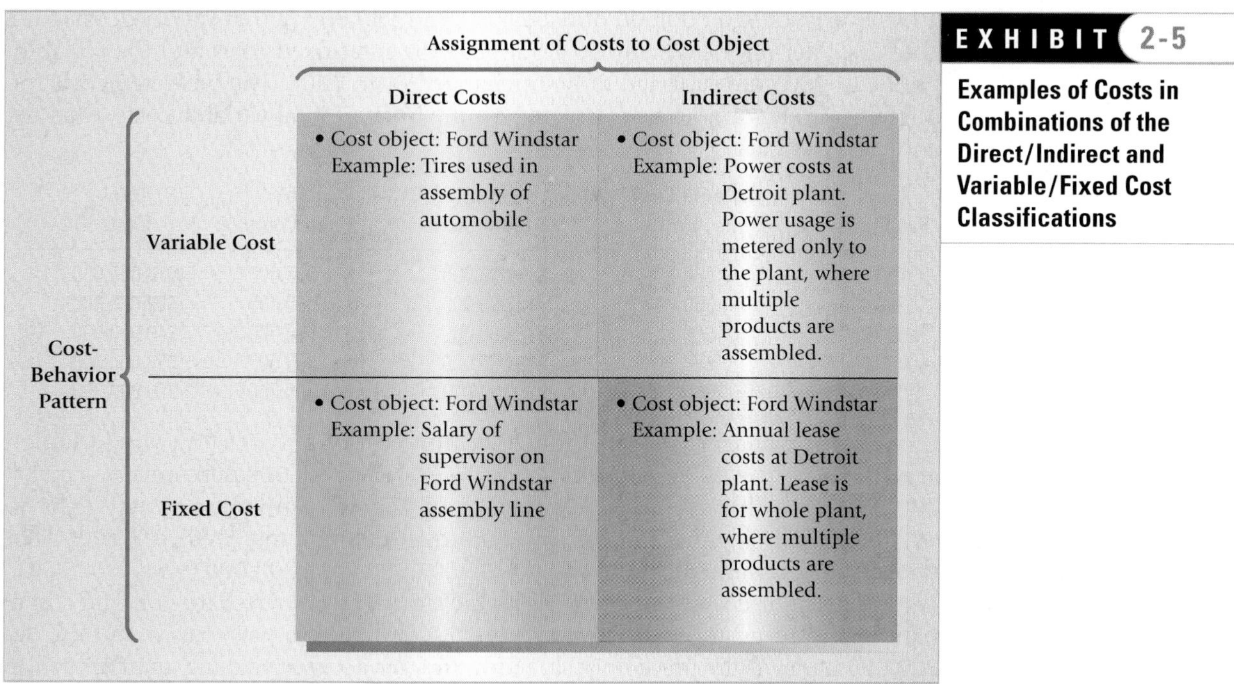

EXHIBIT 2-5

Examples of Costs in Combinations of the Direct/Indirect and Variable/Fixed Cost Classifications

predicted with certainty to be $1,000. This knowledge is helpful for the decision, but it may not be enough.

Before a decision can be reached, the chairman must predict both the total cost and the probable number of people who will attend. Without knowledge of both, he cannot decide intelligently on a possible admission price or even on whether to have a party at all. So he computes the unit cost by dividing the total cost by the expected number of people who will attend. If 1,000 people attend, the unit cost is $1 per person; if 100 attend, the unit cost soars to $10.

Unless the total cost is "unitized" (that is, averaged with respect to the cost object), the $1,000 cost is difficult to interpret. The unit cost combines the total cost and the number of people in a handy, communicative way.

Accounting systems typically report both total-cost amounts and average cost-per-unit amounts. A **unit cost**, also called an **average cost**, is computed by dividing some amount of total costs by the related number of units. The units might be expressed in various ways. Examples are automobiles assembled, packages delivered, or hours worked. Suppose $40,000,000 of manufacturing costs are incurred in 2004 to produce 500,000 cellular phones at the Memphis plant of Tennessee Products. Then the unit cost is $80:

You will discover that it is necessary to *understand* the material in this course rather than *memorize* it. It's a good idea to consider using the *Student Guide* (*SG*) that accompanies this book. The *SG* (ISBN 013-064928-7) is a self-study aid that helps (1) reinforce and clarify your understanding of the text material, (2) develop your analytical thinking skills, and (3) prepare you for exams. So you can evaluate the *SG*, see the first three chapters that are available free at Prentice Hall's Web site (www.prenhall.com/harris).

$$\frac{\text{Total manufacturing costs}}{\text{Number of units manufactured}} = \frac{\$40{,}000{,}000}{500{,}000 \text{ units}} = \$80 \text{ per unit}$$

If 480,000 units are sold and 20,000 units remain in ending inventory, the unit-cost concept helps in determining total costs in the income statement and balance sheet:

Cost of goods sold in the income statement, 480,000 units × $80 per unit	$38,400,000
Ending inventory on the balance sheet, 20,000 units × $80 per unit	1,600,000
Total manufacturing costs of 500,000 units	$40,000,000

Unit costs are found in all areas of the value chain—for example, unit cost of product design, of sales visits, and of customer-service calls.

Use Unit Costs Cautiously

Unit costs are regularly used in financial reports. *However, for many decisions, managers should think in terms of total costs rather than unit costs.* Consider the manager of the Memphis manufacturing plant of Tennessee Products. Assume the $40,000,000 costs in

2004 consist of $10,000,000 of fixed costs and $30,000,000 of variable costs (at $60 variable costs per phone assembled). Suppose the total fixed costs and the variable cost per phone in 2005 are expected to be unchanged from 2004. The budgeted costs for 2005 at different production levels calculated on the basis of total variable costs, total fixed costs, and total costs are:

Units Produced	Variable Cost Per Unit	Total Variable Costs	Total Fixed Costs	Total Costs	Unit Cost
100,000	$60	$ 6,000,000	$10,000,000	$16,000,000	$160.00
200,000	$60	$12,000,000	$10,000,000	$22,000,000	$110.00
500,000	$60	$30,000,000	$10,000,000	$40,000,000	$ 80.00
800,000	$60	$48,000,000	$10,000,000	$58,000,000	$ 72.50
1,000,000	$60	$60,000,000	$10,000,000	$70,000,000	$ 70.00

For many decisions, managers should think in terms of total costs rather than unit costs because fixed cost per unit change when the related level of total volume changes. Consequently, unit costs should be interpreted with caution when they include a fixed-cost component.

A plant manager who uses the 2004 unit cost of $80 per unit would underestimate actual total costs if 2005 output is below the 2004 level of 500,000 units. If actual volume is 200,000 units due to, say, the presence of a new competitor, actual costs would be $22,000,000. Using the unit cost of $80 times 200,000 units predicts $16,000,000, which underestimates the actual total costs by $6,000,000 ($22,000,000 − $16,000,000). *The unit cost of $80 only applies when 500,000 units are produced.* An overreliance on unit cost in this situation could lead to insufficient cash being available to pay costs if volume declines to 200,000 units. As the preceding table indicates, for decision making, managers should think in terms of total variable costs, total fixed costs, and total costs rather than unit cost.

We now discuss cost concepts used in different sectors of the economy.

MANUFACTURING-, MERCHANDISING-, AND SERVICE-SECTOR COMPANIES

5 Distinguish among manufacturing companies, merchandising companies, and service-sector companies

... different types of companies give rise to different accounting issues

We first define three different sectors and provide examples of companies in each sector.

- **Manufacturing-sector companies** purchase materials and components and convert them into various finished goods. Examples are automotive companies, food-processing companies, and textile companies.
- **Merchandising-sector companies** purchase and then sell tangible products without changing their basic form. This sector includes companies engaged in retailing (such as bookstores or department stores), distribution, or wholesaling.
- **Service-sector companies** provide services or intangible products—for example, legal advice or audits—to their customers. Examples are law firms, accounting firms, banks, insurance companies, transportation companies, advertising agencies, radio and television stations, and Internet-based companies.

FINANCIAL STATEMENTS, INVENTORIABLE COSTS, AND PERIOD COSTS

The distinction between *inventoriable costs* and *period costs* is necessary for financial reporting in both the manufacturing and merchandising sectors of the economy. As background, we will first look at the different types of inventory that companies hold and some commonly used classifications of manufacturing costs.

Types of Inventory

6 Describe the three categories of inventories commonly found in manufacturing companies

... direct materials, work-in-process, finished goods

Manufacturing-sector companies purchase materials and components and convert them into various finished goods. These companies typically have one or more of the following three types of inventory:

1. **Direct materials inventory.** Direct materials in stock and awaiting use in the manufacturing process (for example, the computer chips and components needed to manufacture cellular phones).
2. **Work-in-process inventory.** Goods partially worked on but not yet fully completed (for example, cellular phones at various stages of completion in the manufacturing process). Also called **work in progress.**

3. **Finished-goods inventory**. Goods (for example, cellular phones) fully completed but not yet sold.

Merchandising-sector companies purchase tangible products and then sell them without changing their basic form. They hold only one type of inventory, which are products in their original purchased form called *merchandising inventory*. Service-sector companies provide only services or intangible products; they do not hold inventories of tangible products for sale.

Commonly Used Classifications of Manufacturing Costs

Three terms commonly used when describing manufacturing costs are direct material costs, direct manufacturing labor costs, and indirect manufacturing costs.

1. **Direct material costs** are the acquisition costs of all materials that eventually become part of the cost object (work in process and then finished goods) and that can be traced to the cost object in an economically feasible way. Acquisition costs of direct materials include freight-in (inward delivery) charges, sales taxes, and custom duties. Examples of direct material costs are the aluminum used to make Pepsi cans and the paper used to print *Sports Illustrated*.

2. **Direct manufacturing labor costs** include the compensation of all manufacturing labor that can be traced to the cost object (work in process and then finished goods) in an economically feasible way. Examples include wages and fringe benefits paid to machine operators and assembly-line workers who convert direct materials purchased to finished goods.

3. **Indirect manufacturing costs** are all manufacturing costs that are related to the cost object (work in process and then finished goods) but that cannot be traced to that cost object in an economically feasible way. Examples include electric power, supplies, indirect materials such as lubricants, indirect manufacturing labor such as plant maintenance and cleaning labor, plant rent, plant insurance, property taxes on plants, plant depreciation, and the compensation of plant managers. This cost category is also referred to as **manufacturing overhead costs** and **factory overhead costs**. We use *indirect manufacturing costs* and *manufacturing overhead costs* interchangeably in this book.

This book uses the term *direct manufacturing labor* because labor used in other business functions of the value chain can also be traced directly to cost objects. For example, in some cases salespersons' salaries can be traced directly to specific customers.

We next describe the important distinction between inventoriable and period costs.

Inventoriable Costs

7 **Differentiate between inventoriable costs**
... assets when incurred, then cost of goods sold
and period costs
... expenses of the period when incurred

Inventoriable costs are all costs of a product that are regarded as assets when they are incurred and then become cost of goods sold when the product is sold. For manufacturing-sector companies, all manufacturing costs are inventoriable costs. Costs of direct materials issued to production from direct materials inventory, direct manufacturing labor costs, and indirect manufacturing costs create new assets, beginning as work in process and becoming finished goods. Hence manufacturing costs are included in work-in-process inventory and in finished-goods inventory (they are "inventoried") to accumulate the costs of creating these assets. When finished goods are sold, the cost of manufacturing the goods sold is matched against the revenues from the sale. The cost of goods sold includes all manufacturing costs (direct materials, direct manufacturing labor, and indirect manufacturing costs) incurred to produce the goods sold. Finished goods may be sold during a different accounting period than the period in which the goods were manufactured. Thus, inventorying manufacturing costs during the period when they were manufactured and expensing the manufacturing costs of goods sold later when revenues are recognized achieves matching of revenues and expenses.

For merchandising-sector companies, inventoriable costs are the costs of purchasing the goods that are resold in their same form. These costs are the costs of the goods themselves and any incoming freight, insurance, and handling costs for those goods. For service-sector companies, the absence of inventories means there are no inventoriable costs.

Inventoriable costs are assets. They have value as long as the company owns them. When the inventory (finished goods) is sold, its cost is transferred from the balance sheet to the income statement as cost of goods sold.

Period Costs

Period costs are all costs in the income statement other than cost of goods sold. Period costs are treated as expenses of the period in which they are incurred because they are expected to benefit revenues in the current period and are not expected to benefit revenues in future periods (perhaps because there is not sufficient evidence to conclude that such benefit exists). Expensing these costs in the current period matches expenses to revenues.

For manufacturing-sector companies, period costs in the income statement are all nonmanufacturing costs (for example, design costs and distribution costs). For merchandising-sector companies, period costs in the income statement are all costs not related to the cost of goods purchased for resale. Examples of period costs are labor costs of sales floor personnel and marketing costs. Because there are no inventoriable costs for service-sector companies, all their costs in the income statement are period costs.

ILLUSTRATING THE FLOW OF INVENTORIABLE COSTS AND PERIOD COSTS

Manufacturing-Sector Example

The income statement of a manufacturer, Cellular Products, is shown in Exhibit 2-6. Revenues of Cellular are (in thousands) $210,000. **Revenues** are inflows of assets (usually cash or accounts receivable) received for products or services provided to customers. Cost of goods sold in a manufacturing company is usually computed as:

Beginning finished goods inventory	+	Cost of goods manufactured	−	Ending finished goods inventory	=	Cost of goods sold

For Cellular Products in 2004, the corresponding amounts (in thousands) in Exhibit 2-6 Panel A are:

$$\$22,000 + \$104,000 - \$18,000 = \$108,000$$

Cost of goods manufactured refers to the cost of goods brought to completion, whether they were started before or during the current accounting period. In 2004, these costs amount to $104,000 for Cellular Products (see the Schedule of Cost of Goods Manufactured in Exhibit 2-6 Panel B). A line item in Panel B is "Manufacturing costs incurred during the period" of $105,000. This item refers to the sum of the direct manufacturing costs and the indirect manufacturing costs that were incurred during 2004 for all goods worked on during that year, regardless of whether all those goods were fully completed during 2004.

Cellular Products classifies its manufacturing costs into the three categories described earlier:

1. *Direct material costs.* The cost of direct materials used is computed in Exhibit 2-6 Panel B as:

Beginning direct materials inventory	+	Purchase of direct materials	−	Ending direct materials inventory	=	Direct materials used
$11,000	+	$73,000	−	$8,000	=	$76,000

2. *Direct manufacturing labor costs.* Exhibit 2-6 Panel B reports these costs as $9,000.
3. *Indirect manufacturing costs.* Exhibit 2-6 Panel B reports these costs as $20,000.

Exhibit 2-7 shows related general-ledger T-accounts for Cellular Products' manufacturing cost flow. Note how the cost of goods manufactured of $104,000 is the cost of all goods completed during the accounting period. These costs are all inventoriable costs. Goods completed during the period are transferred to finished goods inventory. These costs become cost of goods sold when the goods are sold.

The $70,000 comprising marketing costs, distribution costs, and customer-service costs are the period costs of Cellular Products. These period costs include, for example, salaries of salespersons, depreciation on computers and other equipment used in marketing, and the cost of leasing warehouse space for distribution. Operating income of Cellular Products is $32,000. **Operating income** is total revenues from operations minus cost of goods sold and operating costs (excluding interest expense and income taxes).

EXHIBIT 2-6 Income Statement and Schedule of Cost of Goods Manufactured of a Manufacturing-Sector Company, Cellular Products

PANEL A: INCOME STATEMENT

Cellular Products
Income Statement
For the Year Ended December 31, 2004 (in thousands)

Revenues		$210,000
Cost of goods sold:		
Beginning finished goods, January 1, 2004	$ 22,000	
Cost of goods manufactured (see Panel B)	104,000	
Cost of goods available for sale	126,000	
Ending finished goods, December 31, 2004	18,000	
Cost of goods sold		108,000
Gross margin (or gross profit)		102,000
Operating costs:		
Marketing, distribution, and customer-service costs	70,000	
Total operating costs		70,000
Operating income		$ 32,000

PANEL B: COST OF GOODS MANUFACTURED

Cellular Products
Schedule of Cost of Goods Manufactured[a]
For the Year Ended December 31, 2004 (in thousands)

Direct materials:		
Beginning inventory, January 1, 2004	$ 11,000	
Purchases of direct materials	73,000	
Cost of direct materials available for use	84,000	
Ending inventory, December 31, 2004	8,000	
Direct materials used		$ 76,000
Direct manufacturing labor		9,000
Indirect manufacturing costs:		
Indirect manufacturing labor	7,000	
Supplies	2,000	
Heat, light, and power	5,000	
Depreciation—plant building	2,000	
Depreciation—plant equipment	3,000	
Miscellaneous	1,000	
Total indirect manufacturing costs		20,000
Manufacturing costs incurred during 2004		105,000
Add beginning work-in-process inventory, January 1, 2004		6,000
Total manufacturing costs to account for		111,000
Deduct ending work-in-process inventory, December 31, 2004		7,000
Cost of goods manufactured (to Income Statement)		$104,000

[a]Note that the term *cost of goods manufactured* refers to the cost of goods brought to completion (finished) during the year, whether they were started before or during the current year. Some of the manufacturing costs incurred during the year are held back as costs of the ending work-in-process inventory; similarly, the costs of the beginning work-in-process inventory become part of the cost of goods manufactured for the year. Note, too, that this schedule can become a Schedule of Cost of Goods Manufactured and Sold simply by including the beginning and ending finished goods inventory figures in the supporting schedule rather than in the body of the income statement.

EXHIBIT 2-7 General-Ledger T-Accounts for Cellular Products' Manufacturing Cost Flow

Work-in-Process Inventory

Debit		Credit	
Bal. Jan. 1, 2004	6,000	Cost of goods manufactured	104,000
Direct materials used	76,000		
Direct manuf. labor	9,000		
Indirect manuf. costs	20,000		
Bal. Dec. 31, 2004	7,000		

Finished Goods Inventory

Debit		Credit	
Bal. Jan. 1, 2004	22,000	Cost of goods sold	108,000
	104,000		
Bal. Dec. 31, 2004	18,000		

Cost of Goods Sold

Debit	Credit
108,000	

Newcomers to cost accounting frequently assume that indirect costs such as rent, telephone, and depreciation are always costs of the period in which they are incurred and are not associated with inventories. When these costs are incurred in marketing or in corporate headquarters, they are period costs. However, when these costs are related to manufacturing, they are indirect manufacturing costs and are inventoriable.

Recap of Inventoriable Costs and Period Costs

Exhibit 2-8 highlights the differences between inventoriable costs and period costs.

EXHIBIT 2-8 Relationships of Inventoriable Costs and Period Costs

PANEL A: MANUFACTURING COMPANY

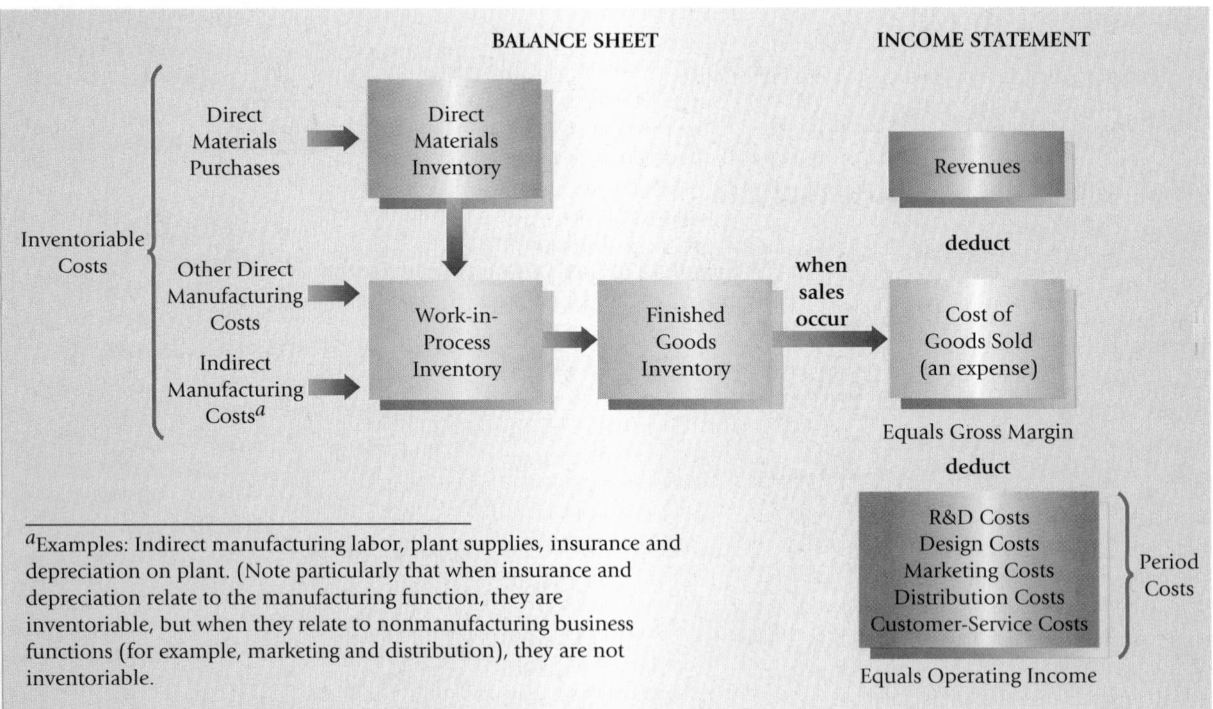

[a]Examples: Indirect manufacturing labor, plant supplies, insurance and depreciation on plant. (Note particularly that when insurance and depreciation relate to the manufacturing function, they are inventoriable, but when they relate to nonmanufacturing business functions (for example, marketing and distribution), they are not inventoriable.

PANEL B: MERCHANDISING COMPANY (RETAILER OR WHOLESALER)

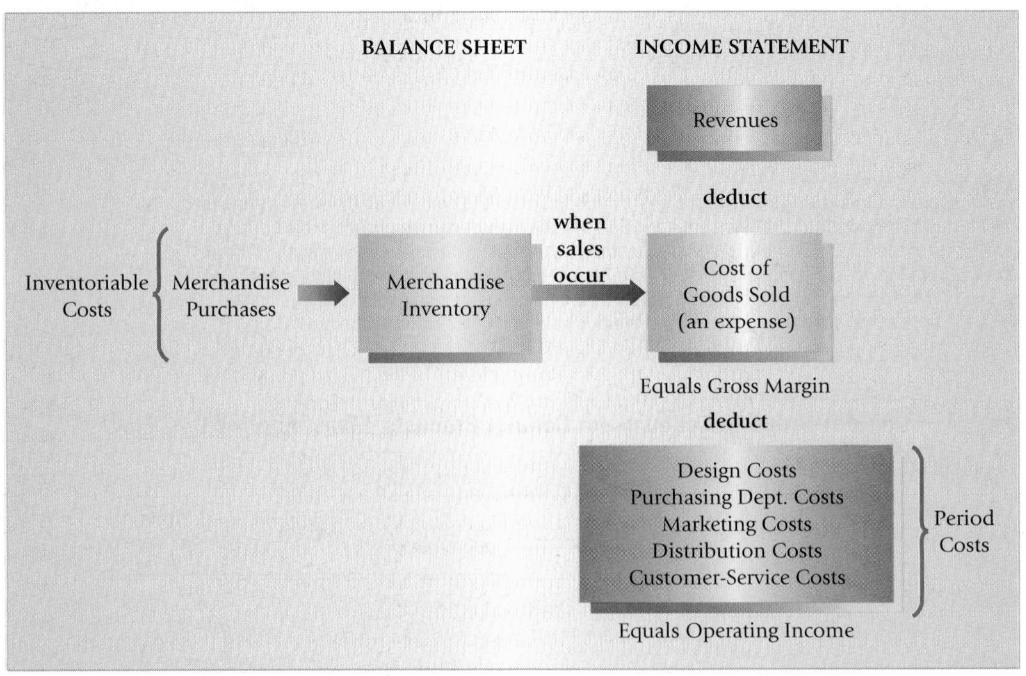

Panel A uses the manufacturing sector to illustrate these differences. The merchandising sector is shown in Panel B. First study Panel A. The manufacturing costs of the finished goods include direct materials, other direct manufacturing costs such as direct manufacturing labor, and indirect manufacturing costs. All these costs are inventoriable: They are assigned to work-in-process inventory or finished goods inventory until the goods are sold.

Consider now Panel B. A retailer or wholesaler buys goods for resale. The *only* inventoriable cost is the cost of merchandise. Unsold goods are held as merchandise inventory whose cost is shown as an asset in the balance sheet. As the goods are sold, their costs are shown in the income statement as cost of goods sold. A retailer or wholesaler also has a variety of marketing, distribution, and customer-service costs, which are period costs. In the income statement, period costs are deducted from revenues without ever having been included as part of inventory.

Prime Costs and Conversion Costs

Two terms used to describe costs classifications in manufacturing costing systems are prime costs and conversion costs. **Prime costs** are all direct manufacturing costs. For Cellular Products, prime costs are $85,000 ($76,000 direct material costs + $9,000 direct manufacturing labor costs). As we have already discussed, the greater the proportion of prime costs in a company's cost structure, the more confident managers can be about the accuracy of the costs of various cost objects such as products. As information-gathering technology improves, companies can add more and more direct-cost categories. For example, power costs might be metered in specific areas of a plant that are dedicated totally to the manufacture of separate products. In this case, prime costs would include direct materials, direct manufacturing labor, and direct metered power (assuming there are already direct materials and direct manufacturing labor categories). Computer software companies often have a "purchased technology" direct manufacturing cost item. This item, which represents payments to suppliers who develop software algorithms for a product, is also included in prime costs. **Conversion costs** are all manufacturing costs other than direct material costs. These costs represent all manufacturing costs incurred to convert direct materials into finished goods. For Cellular Products, conversion costs are $29,000 ($9,000 direct manufacturing labor costs + $20,000 of indirect manufacturing costs).

Some manufacturing companies use conversion costs to simplify their accounting. They have only two classifications of costs: direct material costs and conversion costs. For these companies, all conversion costs are indirect manufacturing costs. An example is costing systems in computer-integrated manufacturing (CIM) plants. CIM plants have very few workers. The workers' role is to monitor the manufacturing process and maintain the equipment that produces multiple products. Costing systems in CIM plants do *not* have a direct manufacturing labor cost category because direct manufacturing labor costs are small and because it is difficult to trace these costs to products.

Question: Do prime costs + conversion costs = total manufacturing costs?
Answer: Only under the two-part classification: prime costs = direct material costs, and conversion costs = indirect manufacturing costs (which include direct manufacturing labor). Under the three-part classification, direct manufacturing labor is both a prime cost and a conversion cost.

MEASURING COSTS REQUIRES JUDGMENT

Measuring costs requires judgment. That's because there are alternative ways in which costs can be defined and classified. Different companies or sometimes even different subunits within the same company may define and classify costs differently. Be careful to define and understand the way costs are measured in a company or situation. We first illustrate this point with respect to labor cost measurement.

Measuring Labor Costs

Although manufacturing labor cost classifications vary among companies, most companies have the following categories:

- Direct manufacturing labor (labor that can be traced to individual products)
- Manufacturing overhead (examples of prominent labor components of this manufacturing overhead follow):
  - Indirect labor (compensation)
    Forklift truck operators (internal handling of materials)
    Plant janitors

Plant guards
Rework labor (time spent by direct laborers redoing defective work)
Overtime premium paid to plant workers (explained below)
Idle time (explained below)

- Managers', department heads', and supervisors' salaries
- Payroll fringe costs (for example, health care premiums, pension costs)

All manufacturing labor compensation other than for direct labor, managers' salaries, department heads' salaries, and supervisors' salaries is usually classified as *indirect labor costs,* a major component of manufacturing overhead. The indirect labor costs are commonly divided into many subclassifications to retain information on different categories of indirect labor. For example, the wages of forklift truck operators generally are not commingled with janitors' wages, although both are regarded as indirect labor costs.

Managers' salaries usually are not classified as indirect labor costs. Instead, the compensation of supervisors, department heads, and all others who are regarded as manufacturing management is placed in a separate classification of manufacturing overhead.

Overtime Premium

The purpose of classifying costs in detail is to associate an individual cost with a specific cause or reason for why it was incurred. Two classes of indirect labor—overtime premium and idle time—need special mention. **Overtime premium** is the wage rate paid to workers (for both direct labor and indirect labor) in *excess* of their straight-time wage rates. All overtime premium is usually considered a part of indirect costs or overhead. Consider an example from the service sector. George Flexner does home repairs for Sears Appliance Services. He is paid $20 per hour for straight-time and $30 per hour (time and a half) for overtime. His premium is $10 per overtime hour. If he works 44 hours, including 4 overtime hours, in one week, his gross compensation would be classified as follows:

Direct service labor: 44 hours × $20 per hour	$880
Overtime premium: 4 hours × $10 per hour	40
Total compensation for 44 hours	$920

Why is the overtime premium of direct labor usually considered an indirect rather than a direct cost? After all, it can be traced to specific batches of work. Overtime premium is generally not considered a direct charge because the scheduling of repair jobs is generally either random or in accordance with minimizing overall travel time. For example, assume that jobs 1–5 are scheduled to be completed on a specific workday of 10 hours, including 2 overtime hours. Each job (service call) requires 2 hours. Should the job scheduled during hours 9 and 10 be assigned the overtime premium? Or should the premium be prorated over all five jobs? Prorating the overtime premium does not "penalize"—add to the cost of—a particular batch of work solely because it happened to be worked on during the overtime hours. *Instead, the overtime premium is considered to be attributable to the heavy overall volume of work. Its cost is regarded as part of service overhead, which is borne by all repair jobs.*

Sometimes overtime is not random. For example, a customer demanding a "rush job" may clearly be the sole source of the overtime. In such instances, the overtime premium is regarded as a direct cost of that job.

Another subclassification of indirect labor is the *idle time* of both direct and indirect manufacturing or service labor. **Idle time** is wages paid for unproductive time caused by lack of orders, machine breakdowns, material shortages, poor scheduling, and the like. For example, if the Sears repair truck broke down for 3 hours, Flexner's earnings would be classified as follows:

Direct service labor: 41 hours × $20/hour	$820
Idle time (service overhead): 3 hours × $20/hour	60
Overtime premium (service overhead): 4 hours × $10/hour	40
Total earnings for 44 hours	$920

Clearly, the idle time is not related to a particular job, nor as we have already discussed, is the overtime premium. Both overtime premium and idle time are considered indirect costs.

Benefits of Defining Accounting Terms

Managers, accountants, suppliers, and others will avoid many problems if they thoroughly understand and agree on the classifications and the meanings of the cost terms introduced in this chapter and later in this book.

Consider the classification of manufacturing labor *payroll fringe costs* (for example, employer payments for employee benefits such as Social Security, life insurance, health insurance, and pensions). Some companies classify these costs as manufacturing overhead costs. In other companies, the fringe benefits related to direct manufacturing labor are treated as an additional direct manufacturing labor cost. Consider, for example, a direct laborer, such as a lathe operator whose gross wages are computed on the basis of a stated wage rate of $20 an hour and fringe benefits totaling, say, $5 per hour. Some companies classify the $20 as direct manufacturing labor cost and the $5 as manufacturing overhead cost. Other companies classify the entire $25 as direct manufacturing labor cost. The latter approach is preferable because the stated wage and the fringe costs together are a fundamental part of acquiring direct manufacturing labor services.

Caution: In every situation, pinpoint clearly and exactly what direct manufacturing labor includes and what direct manufacturing labor excludes. Achieving clarity may prevent disputes regarding cost-reimbursement contracts, income tax payments, and labor union matters. Consider that some countries offer substantial income tax savings to companies such as Intel that locate plants within their borders. To qualify, the direct manufacturing labor costs of these companies in that country must equal at least a specified percentage of the total manufacturing costs of their products. Disputes have arisen regarding how to calculate the direct manufacturing labor percentage for qualifying for such tax benefits. For instance, are payroll fringe benefits on direct manufacturing labor part of direct manufacturing labor costs, or are they part of manufacturing overhead? Depending on how companies classify costs, you can see how they may show direct manufacturing labor as different percentages of total manufacturing costs. Consider a company with $5 million of payroll fringe costs (figures are assumed, in millions):

CLASSIFICATION A			CLASSIFICATION B		
	Costs	Percentage		Costs	Percentage
Direct materials	$ 40	40%	Direct materials	$ 40	40%
Direct manufacturing labor	20	20	Direct manufacturing labor	25	25
Manufacturing overhead	40	40	Manufacturing overhead	35	35
Total manufacturing costs	$100	100%	Total manufacturing costs	$100	100%

Classification A assumes that payroll fringe costs are part of manufacturing overhead costs. In contrast, classification B assumes that payroll fringe costs are part of direct manufacturing labor costs. If a country sets the minimum percentage of direct labor costs at 25%, the company would receive a tax break using classification B, but no tax break using classification A. In addition to fringe benefits, other debated items are compensation for training time, idle time, vacations, sick leave, and overtime premium. To prevent disputes, contracts and laws should be as specific as feasible regarding definitions and measurements.

The Many Meanings of Product Costs

Many cost terms found in practice have ambiguous meanings. Consider the term *product cost*. A **product cost** is the sum of costs assigned to a product for a specific purpose. Different purposes can result in different measures of product cost, as the brackets on the value chain in Exhibit 2-9 illustrate:

8 **Explain why product costs are computed in different ways for different purposes**

... pricing and product-mix decisions, government contracts, and financial statements

1. *Pricing and product-mix decisions.* For the purposes of making decisions about pricing and which products yield the most profits, the manager is interested in the overall (total) profitability of different products and, consequently, assigns costs incurred in all business functions of the value chain to the different products.
2. *Contracting with government agencies.* Government contracts often reimburse contractors on the basis of the "costs of a product" plus a prespecified margin of profit. Because of the cost-plus nature of the contract, government agencies provide detailed guidelines on the items of cost they will allow and those they will disallow when calculating the cost of a product. For example, some government agencies explicitly exclude marketing costs

EXHIBIT 2-9

Different Product Costs for Different Purposes

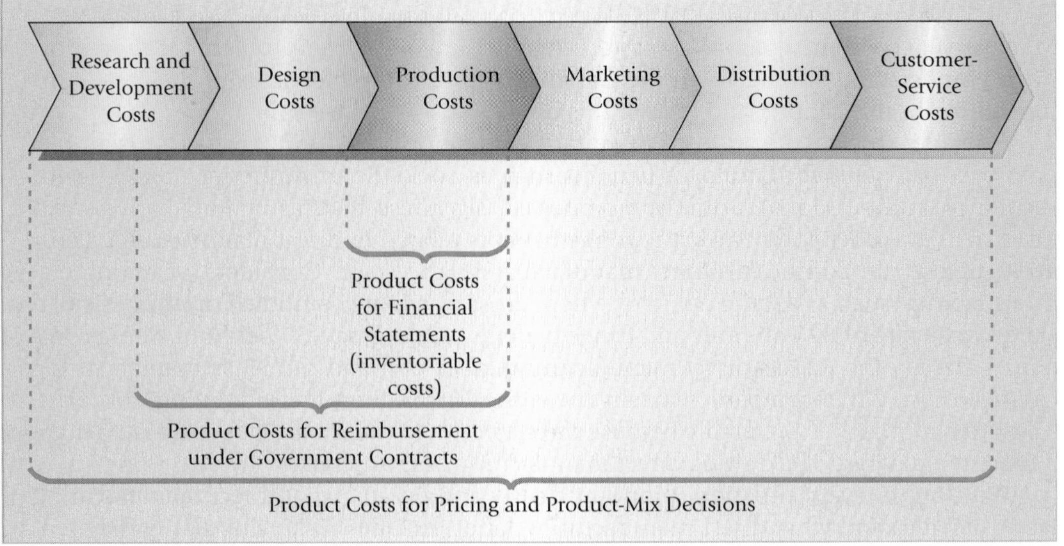

from the product costs that qualify for reimbursement and may reimburse only a part of R&D costs. These agencies want to reimburse contractors for only those costs most closely related to delivering products under the contract. The second bracket in Exhibit 2-9 shows how the product-cost calculations for a specific contract may allow for all design and production costs and only a part of R&D costs.

Inventoriable costs are called *product costs* in financial accounting courses.

3. *Preparing financial statements for external reporting under GAAP.* Under GAAP, only manufacturing costs can be assigned to inventories in the financial statements. For the purposes of calculating inventory costs, product costs include only inventoriable (manufacturing) costs.

Here is a numerical example to illustrate the concepts in Exhibit 2-9. The inventoriable cost of a product is $100 per unit, the product's cost for reimbursement under a government contract is $180, and the product's cost from throughout the value chain for a pricing decision is $300 per unit.

Exhibit 2-9 illustrates how product-cost measures range from a narrow set of costs for financial reporting that includes only inventoriable costs to a broader set of costs for reimbursement under a government contract to a still broader set of costs for pricing and product-mix decisions.

This section has focused on how different purposes can result in the inclusion of different items of the value chain of business functions when calculating product costs. The same caution about the need to be clear and precise about cost concepts and their measurement applies to each cost classification introduced in this chapter. Exhibit 2-10 summarizes the key cost classifications. The next section describes how the basic concepts introduced in this chapter lead to a framework for understanding cost accounting and cost management that can then be applied to the study of many topics, such as strategy evaluation, quality, and investment decisions.

A FRAMEWORK FOR COST MANAGEMENT

Three features of cost accounting and cost management across a wide range of applications are:

1. Calculating the cost of products, services, and other cost objects
2. Obtaining information for planning and control and performance evaluation
3. Analyzing the relevant information for making decisions

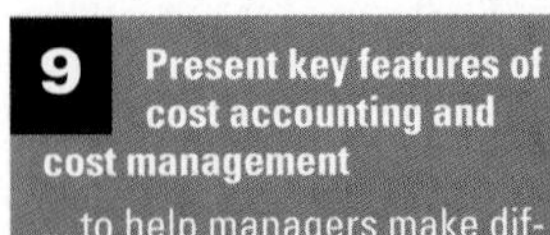
9 Present key features of cost accounting and cost management

... to help managers make different decisions

We develop these ideas in Chapters 3 through 12. These ideas also form the foundation for the study of various topics later in the book.

Calculating the cost of products, services, and other cost objects We have already seen the different purposes and measures of product costs. Whatever the purpose, the costing system traces direct costs and allocates indirect costs to products. Chapters 4 and 5 describe basic systems used to calculate total and unit costs of products and services and how managers use this information for pricing, product mix, and cost management decisions.

EXHIBIT 2-10 Alternative Classifications of Costs

1. Business function
   a. Research and development
   b. Design of products, services, or processes
   c. Production
   d. Marketing
   e. Distribution
   f. Customer service
2. Assignment to a cost object
   a. Direct costs
   b. Indirect costs
3. Behavior pattern in relation to changes in the level of activity or volume
   a. Variable costs
   b. Fixed costs
4. Aggregate or average
   a. Total costs
   b. Unit costs
5. Assets or expenses
   a. Inventoriable costs
   b. Period costs

Obtaining information for planning and control and performance evaluation Budgeting is the most commonly used tool for planning and control. A budget forces managers to look ahead, to translate strategy into plans, to coordinate and communicate within the organization, and to provide a benchmark for evaluating performance. Chapter 6 describes budgeting systems.

At the end of a reporting period, managers compare actual results to planned performance. The manager's task is to understand why differences between actual and planned performance (called variances) arise and to use the information provided by these variances as feedback to promote learning and future improvement. Managers also use variances as well as nonfinancial measures, such as defect rates and customer satisfaction ratings, to control and evaluate the performance of various departments, divisions, and managers. Chapters 7 and 8 discuss variance analysis. Chapter 9 describes the planning and control and inventory costing issues relating to capacity.

Analyzing the relevant information for making decisions When making decisions, managers must understand which revenues and costs to consider and which ones to ignore. Management accountants help managers identify what information is relevant and what information is irrelevant. Consider a decision about whether to buy a product from an outside vendor or to make it in-house. The costing system indicates that it costs $25 per unit to make the product in-house. A vendor offers the product for $22 per unit. At first glance, it seems it will cost less for the company to buy the product than to make it. However, suppose that, of the $25 to make it in-house, $5 consists of plant lease payments that the company will have to make whether the product is made or is bought. Under this condition, it will cost less to make the product than to buy it. Why? Because making the product only costs an additional $20 per unit ($25 − $5), compared with an additional $22 per unit if it is bought. The $5 per unit of lease payments is irrelevant to the decision because it will be incurred whether the product is made or bought. Analyzing relevant information is a key aspect of making decisions.

When making decisions about what products to produce, managers need to know how revenues and costs vary with changes in output levels. For this purpose, managers need to distinguish between which costs are fixed and which costs are variable. Chapter 3 analyzes how operating income changes with changes in output levels and how managers use this information to make decisions such as how much to advertise. Chapter 10 describes methods to estimate fixed and variable components of costs. Chapter 11 applies the concept of relevance to making decisions in many different situations. Chapter 12 describes how management accountants help managers determine prices and manage costs across the value chain and over a product's life.

Later chapters in the book discuss topics such as strategy evaluation, customer profitability, quality, JIT systems, investment decisions, transfer pricing, and performance evaluation. Each of these topics invariably has product costing, planning and control, and decision-making perspectives. A command of the first 12 chapters is helpful to master these topics. For example, Chapter 13 on strategy describes a balanced set of financial and nonfinancial measures used to implement strategy that builds on the planning and control functions. The section on strategic analysis of operating income builds on ideas of product costing and variance analysis. The section on downsizing and managing capacity builds on ideas of relevant revenues and relevant costs.

PROBLEM FOR SELF-STUDY

Campbell Company is a metal and wood cutting manufacturer, selling products to the home construction market. Consider the following data for the year 2004:

Sandpaper	$ 2,000
Materials-handling costs	70,000
Lubricants and coolants	5,000
Miscellaneous indirect manufacturing labor	40,000
Direct manufacturing labor	300,000
Direct materials, Jan. 1, 2004	40,000
Direct materials, Dec. 31, 2004	50,000
Finished goods, Jan. 1, 2004	100,000
Finished goods, Dec. 31, 2004	150,000
Work in process, Jan. 1, 2004	10,000
Work in process, Dec. 31, 2004	14,000
Plant-leasing costs	54,000
Depreciation—plant equipment	36,000
Property taxes on plant equipment	4,000
Fire insurance on plant equipment	3,000
Direct materials purchased	460,000
Revenues	1,360,000
Marketing promotions	60,000
Marketing salaries	100,000
Distribution costs	70,000
Customer-service costs	100,000

Required

1. Prepare an income statement with a separate supporting schedule of cost of goods manufactured. For all manufacturing items, indicate by V or F whether each is basically a variable cost or a fixed cost (when the cost object is a product unit). If in doubt, decide on the basis of whether the total cost will change substantially over a wide range of units produced.
2. Suppose that both the direct material costs and the plant-leasing costs are for the production of 900,000 units. What is the direct material cost of each unit produced? What is the plant-leasing cost per unit? Assume the plant-leasing cost is a fixed cost.
3. Suppose Campbell Company manufactures 1,000,000 units next year. Repeat the computation in requirement 2 for direct materials and plant-leasing costs. Assume the implied cost-behavior patterns persist.
4. As a management consultant, explain concisely to the company president why the unit cost for direct materials did not change in requirements 2 and 3 but the unit cost for plant-leasing costs did change.

SOLUTION

1.

Campbell Company
Income Statement
For the Year Ended December 31, 2004

Revenues		$1,360,000
Cost of goods sold:		
Beginning finished goods, January 1, 2004	$ 100,000	
Cost of goods manufactured (see schedule below)	960,000	
Cost of goods available for sale	1,060,000	
Ending finished goods, December 31, 2004	150,000	910,000
Gross margin (or gross profit)		450,000
Marketing, distribution, and customer-service costs		
Marketing promotions	60,000	
Marketing salaries	100,000	
Distribution costs	70,000	
Customer-service costs	100,000	330,000
Operating income		$ 120,000

Campbell Company
Schedule of Cost of Goods Manufactured
For the Year Ended December 31, 2004

Direct materials:		
Beginning inventory, January 1, 2004		$ 40,000
Purchases of direct materials		460,000
Cost of direct materials available for use		500,000
Ending inventory, December 31, 2004		50,000
Direct materials used		450,000 (V)
Direct manufacturing labor		300,000 (V)
Indirect manufacturing costs:		
Sandpaper	$ 2,000 (V)	
Materials-handling costs	70,000 (V)	
Lubricants and coolants	5,000 (V)	
Miscellaneous indirect manufacturing labor	40,000 (V)	
Plant-leasing costs	54,000 (F)	
Depreciation—plant equipment	36,000 (F)	
Property taxes on plant equipment	4,000 (F)	
Fire insurance on plant equipment	3,000 (F)	214,000
Manufacturing costs incurred during 2004		964,000
Add beginning work in process, January 1, 2004		10,000
Total manufacturing costs to account for		974,000
Deduct ending work in process, December 31, 2004		14,000
Cost of goods manufactured (to Income Statement)		$960,000

2.
$$\begin{aligned}\text{Direct material unit cost} &= \text{Direct materials used} \div \text{Units produced}\\ &= \$450{,}000 \div 900{,}000 \text{ units} = \$0.50 \text{ per unit}\\ \text{Plant-leasing unit cost} &= \text{Plant-leasing cost} \div \text{Units produced}\\ &= \$54{,}000 \div 900{,}000 \text{ units} = \$0.06 \text{ per unit}\end{aligned}$$

3. The direct material costs are variable, so they would increase in total from \$450,000 to \$500,000 (1,000,000 units × \$0.50 per unit). However, their unit cost would be unaffected: \$500,000 ÷ 1,000,000 units = \$0.50 per unit.

In contrast, the plant-leasing cost of \$54,000 are fixed, so they would not increase in total. However, the plant-leasing cost per unit would decline from \$0.060 to \$0.054: \$54,000 ÷ 1,000,000 = \$0.054.

4. The explanation would begin with the answer to requirement 3. As a consultant, you should stress that the unitizing (averaging) of costs that have different behavior patterns can be misleading. A common error is to assume that a total unit cost, which is often a sum of variable unit cost and fixed unit cost, is an indicator that total costs change in proportion to changes in production levels. The next chapter demonstrates the necessity for distinguishing between cost-behavior patterns. You must be wary, especially about average fixed cost per unit. Too often, unit fixed cost is erroneously regarded as being indistinguishable from unit variable cost.

DECISION POINTS

SUMMARY

The following question-and-answer format summarizes the chapter's learning objectives. Each decision presents a key question related to a learning objective. The guidelines are the answer to that question.

Decision	Guidelines
1. How do managers decide on a cost object?	A cost object is anything for which a separate measurement of costs is needed. Examples include product, service, project, customer, brand category, activity, and department.
2. How do managers decide whether a cost is a direct or an indirect cost?	A direct cost is any cost that is related to a particular cost object and can be traced to that cost object in an economically feasible way. Indirect costs are related to the particular cost object but cannot be traced to it in an economically feasible way. The same cost can be direct for one cost object and indirect for other cost objects. This book uses *cost tracing* to describe the assignment of direct costs to a cost object and *cost allocation* to describe the assignment of indirect costs to a cost object.
3. How do managers decide whether a cost is a variable or a fixed cost?	A variable cost changes in total in proportion to changes in the related level of total activity or volume. A fixed cost remains unchanged in total for a given time period despite wide changes in the related level of total activity or volume.
4. How should costs be estimated?	In general, focus on total costs, not unit costs. When making total cost estimates, think of variable costs as an amount per unit and fixed costs as a total amount. The unit cost of a cost object should be interpreted cautiously when it includes a fixed-cost component.
5. How do you distinguish among manufacturing, merchandising, and service companies?	Manufacturing-sector companies purchase materials and components and convert them into finished goods. Merchandising-sector companies purchase and then sell tangible products without changing their basic form. Service-sector companies provide services or intangible products to their customers.
6. How do manufacturing companies categorize inventories?	The three categories of inventories found in many manufacturing companies depict stages in the conversion process—direct materials, work in process, and finished goods.
7. Which costs are initially treated as assets for external reporting, and which costs are expensed as they are incurred?	Inventoriable costs are all costs of a product that are regarded as an asset when they are incurred and then become cost of goods sold when the product is sold. Period costs are expensed in the period in which they are incurred and are all costs in an income statement other than cost of goods sold.
8. How do managers assign costs to cost objects?	Managers can assign different costs to the same cost object depending on the purpose. For example, for the external reporting purpose in a manufacturing company, the inventoriable cost of a product includes only manufacturing costs. In contrast, costs from all business functions of the value chain are assigned to a product for pricing and product-mix decisions.
9. What are the features of cost accounting and cost management systems?	Three features of cost accounting and cost management are (1) calculating the cost of products, services, and other cost objects, (2) obtaining information for planning and control and performance evaluation, and (3) analyzing the relevant information for making decisions.

TERMS TO LEARN

This chapter contains more basic terms than any other in this book. Do not proceed before you check your understanding of the following terms. Both the chapter and the Glossary at the end of the book contain definitions.

actual cost (p. 30)
average cost (37)
conversion costs (43)
cost (30)
cost accumulation (30)
cost allocation (31)
cost assignment (30)
cost driver (34)
cost object (30)
cost of goods manufactured (40)
cost tracing (31)
direct costs of a cost object (31)
direct manufacturing labor costs (39)
direct material costs (39)
direct materials inventory (38)
factory overhead costs (39)
finished-goods inventory (39)
fixed cost (32)
idle time (44)
indirect costs of a cost object (31)
indirect manufacturing costs (39)
inventoriable costs (39)
manufacturing overhead costs (39)
manufacturing-sector companies (38)
merchandising-sector companies (38)
operating income (40)
overtime premium (44)
period costs (39)
product cost (45)
prime costs (43)
relevant range (35)
revenues (40)
service-sector companies (38)
unit cost (37)
variable cost (32)
work-in-process inventory (38)
work in progress (38)

ASSIGNMENT MATERIAL

Questions

2-1 Define *cost object* and give three examples.

2-2 Define *direct costs* and *indirect costs.*

2-3 Why do managers consider direct costs to be more accurate than indirect costs?

2-4 Name three factors that will affect the classification of a cost as direct or indirect.

2-5 Describe how manufacturing-, merchandising-, and service-sector companies differ from each other.

2-6 What is a *cost driver*? Give one example.

2-7 Define *variable cost* and *fixed cost.* Give an example of each.

2-8 What is the *relevant range*? What role does the relevant-range concept play in explaining how costs behave?

2-9 Explain why *unit costs* must often be interpreted with caution.

2-10 What are three different types of inventory that manufacturing companies hold?

2-11 Distinguish between *inventoriable costs* and *period costs.*

2-12 Do service-sector companies have inventoriable costs? Explain.

2-13 Define the following: *direct materials costs, direct manufacturing-labor costs, indirect manufacturing costs, prime costs,* and *conversion costs.*

2-14 Describe the overtime-premium and idle-time categories of indirect labor.

2-15 Define *product cost.* Describe three different purposes for computing product costs.

Exercises

2-16 **Computing and interpreting manufacturing unit costs.** Minnesota Forest Products (MFP) produces three different paper products at its Vaasa lumber plant—Supreme, Deluxe, and Regular. Each product has its own dedicated production line at the plant. It currently uses the following three-part classification for its manufacturing costs: direct materials, direct manufacturing labor, and indirect manufacturing costs. Total indirect manufacturing costs of the plant in July 2004 are $150 million ($20 million of which is fixed). This total amount is allocated to each product line on the basis of direct manufacturing labor costs of each line. Summary data (in millions) for July 2004 are as follows:

	Supreme	Deluxe	Regular
Direct material costs	$84.0	$54.0	$62.0
Direct manufacturing labor costs	$14.0	$28.0	$ 8.0
Indirect manufacturing costs	$42.0	$84.0	$24.0
Units produced	80	120	100

Required

1. Compute the manufacturing cost per unit for each product produced in July 2004.
2. Suppose that in August 2004, production was 120 million units of Supreme, 160 million units of Deluxe, and 180 million units of Regular. Why might the July 2004 manufacturing unit cost information be misleading when predicting total manufacturing costs in August 2004?

2-17 Direct and indirect costs, effect of changing the classification of a cost item. Minnesota Forest Products (MFP) employs a consultant to help reduce energy costs at its St. Cloud plant. Currently, MFP does not trace energy costs to each of its three different paper products—Supreme, Deluxe, and Regular. The energy consultant notes that each production line at the St. Cloud plant has multiple energy meters and that tracing of energy costs to each line is possible. Of the $150 million of indirect manufacturing costs in July 2004, $90 million is for energy costs traceable to individual production lines. The remaining $60 million of indirect manufacturing costs of the plant (including the $20 million fixed costs) is allocated to each product line on the basis of direct manufacturing-labor costs at each line. Using this information, MFP's cost analyst reports the following numbers (in millions) for July 2004.

	Supreme	Deluxe	Regular
Direct materials	$84.0	$54.0	$62.0
Direct manufacturing labor	$14.0	$28.0	$ 8.0
Direct energy costs	$39.8	$40.7	$ 9.5
Indirect manufacturing costs	$16.8	$33.6	$ 9.6
Units produced	80	120	100

Required

1. Distinguish a direct cost from an indirect cost?
2. Why might MFP's managers prefer energy costs to be a direct cost rather than an indirect manufacturing cost?
3. Compute the manufacturing cost per unit for each of the product lines.

2-18 Classification of costs, service sector. Consumer Focus is a marketing research firm that organizes focus groups for consumer-product companies. Each focus group has eight individuals who are paid $50 per session to provide comments on new products. These focus groups meet in hotels and are led by a trained, independent, marketing specialist hired by Consumer Focus. Each specialist is paid a fixed retainer to conduct a minimum number of sessions and a per session fee of $2,000. A Consumer Focus staff member attends each session to ensure that all the logistical aspects run smoothly.

Required Classify each of the following cost items as:

a. Direct or indirect (D or I) costs with respect to each individual focus group.
b. Variable or fixed (V or F) costs with respect to how the total costs of Consumer Focus change as the number of focus groups conducted changes. (If in doubt, select on the basis of whether the total costs will change substantially if there is a large change in the number of groups conducted.)

You will have two answers (D or I; V or F) for each of the following items:

Cost Item	D or I	V or F
A. Payment to individuals in each focus group to provide comments on new products		
B. Annual subscription of Consumer Focus to *Consumer Reports* magazine		
C. Phone calls made by Consumer Focus staff member to confirm individuals will attend a focus group session (Records of individual calls are not kept.)		
D. Retainer paid to focus group leader to conduct 20 focus groups per year on new medical products		
E. Meals provided to participants in each focus group		
F. Lease payment by Consumer Focus for corporate office		
G. Cost of tapes used to record comments made by individuals in a focus group session (These tapes are sent to the company whose products are being tested.)		
H. Gasoline costs of Consumer Focus staff for company-owned vehicles (staff members submit monthly bills with no mileage breakdowns.)		

2-19 Classification of costs, merchandising sector. Home Entertainment Center (HEC) operates a large store in San Francisco. The store has both a video section and a musical (compact disks, and tapes) section. HEC reports revenues for the video section separately from the musical section.

Required Classify each of the following cost items as:

a. Direct or indirect (D or I) costs with respect to the video section.
b. Variable or fixed (V or F) costs with respect to how the total costs of the video section change as the number of videos sold changes. (If in doubt, select on the basis of whether the total costs will change substantially if there is a large change in the number of videos sold.)

You will have two answers (D or I; V or F) for each of the following items:

Cost Item	D or I	V or F
A. Annual retainer paid to a video distributor		
B. Electricity costs of HEC store (single bill covers entire store)		
C. Costs of videos purchased for sale to customers		
D. Subscription to *Video Trends* magazine		
E. Leasing of computer software used for financial budgeting at HEC store		
F. Cost of popcorn provided free to all customers of HEC		
G. Earthquake insurance policy for HEC store		
H. Freight-in costs of videos purchased by HEC		

2-20 Classification of costs, manufacturing sector. The Fremont, California, plant of New United Motor Manufacturing, Inc. (NUMMI), a joint venture of General Motors and Toyota, assembles two types of cars (Corollas and Geo Prisms). Separate assembly lines are used for each type of car.

Classify each of the following cost items as: **Required**

a. Direct or indirect (D or I) costs with respect to the type of car assembled (Corolla or Geo Prism).

b. Variable or fixed (V or F) costs with respect to how the total costs of the plant change as the number of cars assembled changes. (If in doubt, select on the basis of whether the total costs will change substantially if there is a large change in the number of cars assembled.)

You will have two answers (D or I; V or F) for each of the following items:

Cost Item	D or I	V or F
A. Cost of tires used on Geo Prisms		
B. Salary of public relations manager for NUMMI plant		
C. Annual awards dinner for Corolla suppliers		
D. Salary of engineer who monitors design changes on Geo Prism		
E. Freight costs of Corolla engines shipped from Toyota City, Japan, to Fremont, California		
F. Electricity costs for NUMMI plant (single bill covers entire plant)		
G. Wages paid to temporary assembly-line workers hired in periods of high production (paid on hourly basis)		
H. Annual fire-insurance policy cost for NUMMI plant		

2-21 Variable costs and fixed costs. Consolidated Minerals (CM) owns the rights to extract minerals from beach sands on Fraser Island. CM has costs in three areas:

a. Payment to a mining subcontractor who charges $80 per ton of beach sand mined and returned to the beach (after being processed on the mainland to extract three minerals—ilmenite, rutile, and zircon).

b. Payment of a government mining and environmental tax of $50 per ton of beach sand mined.

c. Payment to a barge operator. This operator charges $150,000 per month to transport each batch of beach sand—up to 100 tons per batch per day—to the mainland and then return to Fraser Island. (That is, 0–100 tons per day = $150,000 per month; 101–200 tons per day = $300,000 per month, and so on.) Each barge operates 25 days per month. The $150,000 monthly charge must be paid even if fewer than 100 tons are transported on any day and even if Consolidated Minerals requires fewer than 25 days of barge transportation in that month.

CM is currently mining 180 tons of beach minerals per day for 25 days per month.

Required

1. What is the variable cost per ton of beach sand mined? What is the fixed cost to CM per month?
2. Plot a graph of the variable costs and another graph of the fixed costs of Consolidated Minerals. Your graphs should be similar to Exhibits 2-3 (p. 33) and 2-4 (p. 34). Is the concept of relevant range applicable to your graphs? Explain.
3. What is the unit cost per ton of beach sand mined (a) if 180 tons are mined each day, or (b) if 220 tons are mined each day? Explain the difference in the unit-cost figures.

2-22 Cost drivers and the value chain. A Johnson & Johnson analyst is preparing a presentation on cost drivers at its pharmaceutical drug subsidiary. Unfortunately, both the list of its business functions and the accompanying list of representative cost drivers are accidentally randomized. The two lists now on the computer screen are

Business Function	Representative Cost Driver
A. Production	**1.** Minutes of T.V. advertising time on "*60 Minutes*"
B. Research and development	**2.** Number of calls to toll-free customer phone line
C. Marketing	**3.** Hours the Tylenol packaging line is in operation
D. Distribution	**4.** Number of packages shipped
E. Design of products/processes	**5.** Hours spent designing tamper-proof bottles
F. Customer service	**6.** Number of patents filed with U.S. Patent Office

Required

1. Match each business function with its representative cost driver.
2. Give a second example of a cost driver for each business function of Johnson & Johnson's pharmaceutical drug subsidiary.

2-23 Cost drivers and functions. The list of representative cost drivers in the right column below are randomized with respect to the list of functions in the left column. That is, they do not match.

Function	Representative Cost Driver
1. Accounting	A. Number of invoices sent
2. Personnel	B. Number of purchase orders
3. Data processing	C. Number of research scientists
4. Research and development	D. Hours of computer processing unit (CPU)
5. Purchasing	E. Number of new hires
6. Billing	F. Number of transactions processed

Required

1. Match each function with its representative cost driver.
2. Give a second example of a cost driver for each function.

2-24 Total costs and unit costs. A student association has hired a musical group for a graduation party. The cost will be a fixed amount of $4,000.

Required

1. Suppose 500 people attend the party. What will be the total cost of the musical group? The unit cost per person?
2. Suppose 2,000 people attend. What will be the total cost of the musical group? The unit cost per person?
3. For prediction of total costs, should the manager of the party use the unit cost in requirement 1? The unit cost in requirement 2? What is the major lesson of this exercise?

2-25 Total costs and unit costs. Susan Wang is a well-known software engineer. Her specialty is writing software code used in maintaining the security of credit-card information. Wang is approached by the Electronic Commerce Group (ECG). They offer to pay her $100,000 for the right to use her code under license in their *e.procurement* software package. Wang rejects this offer because it provides her with no upside if the *e.procurement* package is a runaway success. Both parties eventually agree to a contract in which ECG pays Wang a flat fee of $100,000 for the right to use her code in up to 10,000 packages. If *e.procurement* sells more than 10,000 packages, Wang receives an additional $8 for each package sold beyond the 10,000 level.

Required

1. What is the unit cost to ECG of Wang's software code included in its *e.procurement* package if it sells (a) 2,000 packages, (b) 6,000 packages, (c) 10,000 packages, and (d) 20,000 packages? Comment on the results.
2. To predict ECG's total cost of using Wang's software code in *e.procurement*, which unit cost (if any) of (a) to (d) in requirement 1 would you recommend ECG use? Explain.

2-26 Inventoriable costs versus period costs. Each of the following cost items pertains to one of these companies: General Electric (a manufacturing-sector company), Safeway (a merchandising-sector company), and AOL (a service-sector company):

a. Perrier mineral water purchased by Safeway for sale to its customers
b. Electricity used to provide lighting for assembly-line workers at a General Electric refrigerator-assembly plant
c. Depreciation on AOL's computer equipment used to update directories of Web sites
d. Electricity used to provide lighting for Safeway's store aisles
e. Depreciation on General Electric's computer equipment used for quality testing of refrigerator components during the assembly process
f. Salaries of Safeway's marketing personnel planning local-newspaper advertising campaigns
g. Perrier mineral water purchased by AOL for consumption by its software engineers
h. Salaries of AOL's marketing personnel selling banner advertising

Required

1. Distinguish between manufacturing-sector, merchandising-sector, and service-sector companies.
2. Distinguish between inventoriable costs and period costs.
3. Classify each of the cost items (**a–h**) as an inventoriable cost or a period cost. Explain your answers.

2-27 Computing cost of goods purchased and cost of goods sold. The data below are for Marvin Department Store. The account balances (in thousands) are for 2004.

Marketing, distribution, and customer-service costs	$ 37,000
Merchandise inventory, January 1, 2004	27,000
Utilities	17,000
General and administrative costs	43,000
Merchandise inventory, December 31, 2004	34,000
Purchases	155,000
Miscellaneous costs	4,000
Transportation-in	7,000
Purchase returns and allowances	4,000
Purchase discounts	6,000

Compute (a) cost of goods purchased and (b) cost of goods sold. Required

2-28 Cost of goods manufactured. Consider the following account balances (in thousands) for the Canseco Company:

	Beginning of 2004	End of 2004
Direct materials inventory	$22,000	$26,000
Work-in-process inventory	21,000	20,000
Finished goods inventory	18,000	23,000
Purchases of direct materials		75,000
Direct manufacturing labor		25,000
Indirect manufacturing labor		15,000
Plant insurance		9,000
Depreciation—plant building and equipment		11,000
Repairs and maintenance—plant		4,000
Marketing, distribution, and customer-service costs		93,000
General and administrative costs		29,000

Required

1. Prepare a schedule of cost of goods manufactured for 2004.
2. Revenues in 2004 were $300 million. Prepare the income statement for 2004.

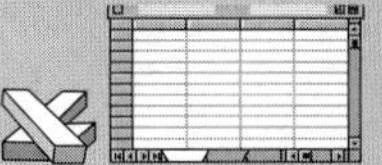

Excel Application For students who wish to practice their spreadsheet skills, the following is a step-by-step approach to creating an Excel spreadsheet to work this problem.

Step-by-Step

1. In a new spreadsheet, create an income statement and a schedule of cost of goods manufactured in the same format as Exhibit 2-6 on page 41. Your categories of indirect manufacturing costs will differ from those in Exhibit 2-6 and should be the following: indirect manufacturing labor, plant insurance, depreciation, and repairs and maintenance.
2. In your schedule of cost of goods manufactured, enter the amounts for beginning direct materials inventory, purchases of direct materials, ending direct materials inventory, direct manufacturing labor, indirect manufacturing labor, plant insurance, depreciation, repairs and maintenance, beginning work-in-process inventory, and ending work-in-process inventory. Follow the format in Panel B of Exhibit 2-6.

(Program your spreadsheet to perform all necessary calculations. Do not "hard-code" any amounts, such as gross margin or operating income, requiring addition or subtraction operations.)

3. In your schedule of cost of goods manufactured, enter calculations for (a) cost of direct materials available for use and (b) direct materials used.
4. In your schedule of cost of goods manufactured, enter calculations for (a) total indirect manufacturing costs, (b) manufacturing costs incurred during the period, (c) total manufacturing costs to account for, and (d) cost of goods manufactured.
5. In your income statement, enter the calculation that sets the amount of cost of goods manufactured equal to the amount in the cell where you calculated cost of goods manufactured in step 4.
6. To complete the income statement: enter revenues, and enter the amounts for marketing, distribution, and customer-service costs, general and administrative costs, beginning finished goods inventory, and ending finished goods inventory. Enter a calculation for cost of goods available for sale. Finally, enter calculations for gross margin, operating costs, and operating income.
7. *Verify the accuracy of your spreadsheet.* Go to your schedule of cost of goods manufactured and change direct manufacturing labor from $25,000 to $35,000. If your spreadsheet is programmed correctly, cost of goods manufactured should change to $146,000, and operating income should change to $37,000.

2-29 Income statement and schedule of cost of goods manufactured. The Howell Corporation has the following account balances (in millions):

For Specific Date		For Year 2004	
Direct materials, Jan. 1, 2004	$15	Purchases of direct materials	$325
Work in process, Jan. 1, 2004	10	Direct manufacturing labor	100
Finished goods, Jan. 1, 2004	70	Depreciation—plant building and equipment	80
Direct materials, Dec. 31, 2004	20	Plant supervisory salaries	5
Work in process, Dec. 31, 2004	5	Miscellaneous plant overhead	35
Finished goods, Dec. 31, 2004	55	Revenues	950
		Marketing, distribution, and customer-service costs	240
		Plant supplies used	10
		Plant utilities	30
		Indirect manufacturing labor	60

Required Prepare an income statement and a supporting schedule of cost of goods manufactured for the year ended December 31, 2004. (For additional questions regarding these facts, see the next problem.)

2-30 Interpretation of statements (continuation of 2-29).

Required

1. How would the answer to Problem 2-29 be modified if you were asked for a schedule of cost of goods manufactured and sold instead of a schedule of cost of goods manufactured? Be specific.
2. Would the sales manager's salary (included in marketing, distribution, and customer-service costs) be accounted for any differently if the Howell Corporation were a merchandising-sector company instead of a manufacturing-sector company? Using the flow of manufacturing costs outlined in Exhibit 2-7 (p. 41), describe how the wages of an assembler in the plant would be accounted for in this manufacturing company.
3. Plant supervisory salaries are usually regarded as indirect manufacturing costs. When might some of these costs be regarded as direct manufacturing costs? Give an example.
4. Suppose that both the direct materials used and the plant depreciation are related to the manufacture of 1 million units of product. What is the unit cost for the direct materials assigned to those units? What is the unit cost for plant building and equipment depreciation? Assume that yearly plant depreciation is computed on a straight-line basis.
5. Assume that the implied cost-behavior patterns in requirement 4 persist. That is, direct material costs behave as a variable cost, and depreciation behaves as a fixed cost. Repeat the computations in requirement 4, assuming that the costs are being predicted for the manufacture of 1.2 million units of product. How would the total costs be affected?
6. As a management accountant, explain concisely to the president why the unit costs differed in requirements 4 and 5.

2-31 Income statement and schedule of cost of goods manufactured. The following items (in millions) pertain to Chan Corporation:

For Specific Date		For Year 2004	
Work in process, Jan. 1, 2004	$10	Plant utilities	$ 5
Direct materials, Dec. 31, 2004	5	Indirect manufacturing labor	20
Finished goods, Dec. 31, 2004	12	Depreciation—plant, building, and equipment	9
Accounts payable, Dec. 31, 2004	20	Revenues	350
Accounts receivable, Jan. 1, 2004	50	Miscellaneous manufacturing overhead	10
Work in process, Dec. 31, 2004	2	Marketing, distribution, and customer-service costs	90
Finished goods, Jan. 1, 2004	40	Direct materials purchased	80
Accounts receivable, Dec. 31, 2004	30	Direct manufacturing labor	40
Accounts payable, Jan. 1, 2004	40	Plant supplies used	6
Direct materials, Jan. 1, 2004	30	Property taxes on plant	1

Chan's manufacturing costing system uses a three-part classification of direct materials, direct manufacturing labor, and indirect manufacturing costs.

Required Prepare an income statement and a supporting schedule of cost of goods manufactured. (For additional questions regarding these facts, see the next problem.)

2-32 Terminology, interpretation of statements (continuation of 2-31).

Required

1. Calculate total prime costs and total conversion costs.
2. Compute total inventoriable costs and period costs.
3. Design costs and R&D costs are not considered product costs for financial reporting purposes. When might some of these costs be regarded as product costs? Give an example.
4. Suppose that both the direct materials used and the plant depreciation are related to the manufacture of 1 million units of product. Determine the unit cost for the direct materials assigned to those units and the unit cost for plant, building, and equipment depreciation. Assume that yearly depreciation is computed on a straight-line basis.
5. Assume that the implied cost-behavior patterns in requirement 4 persist. That is, direct materials costs behave as a variable cost and plant depreciation behaves as a fixed cost. Repeat the computations in requirement 4, assuming that the costs are being predicted for the manufacture of 1.5 million units of product. Determine the effect on total costs.
6. Assume depreciation on the equipment (but not the plant and building) is computed based on number of units produced because the equipment deteriorates with units produced. The depreciation rate is $4 per unit. Calculate the equipment depreciation assuming (a) 1 million units of product are produced and (b) 1.5 million units of product are produced.

2-33 Overtime premium. Gwen Benson and Ian Blacklaw are sales representatives for Electronic Manufacturing, Inc. (EMI). Each sales representative receives a base salary plus a bonus based on 20% of the actual gross margin of each order they sell. Indirect manufacturing costs excluding overtime premium are determined as 200% of direct manufacturing labor cost.

Summary data for two recent orders are as follows:

Customer	Westec	BBC
Sales Representative	**Blacklaw**	**Benson**
Revenues	$420	$480
Direct materials	$250	$270
Direct manufacturing labor	$ 40	$ 40
Indirect manufacturing	$ 80	$ 80
Direct labor-hours	2 hours	2 hours

EMI charges an overtime premium to the rush orders that cause work to be done overtime. In cases when overtime is caused by overall heavy production volume, and not due to any rush orders, the overhead premium is allocated to all orders. The direct manufacturing labor straight-time rate is $20 per hour, and the overtime rate is 50% higher.

Required

1. Calculate the gross margin EMI would report on each of the two orders if only BBC was a rush order that caused overtime.
2. Assume that only Westec was a rush order that caused overtime. Compute the revised gross margin EMI would report on each of the two orders.
3. Assume that neither Westec nor BBC was a rush order. Calculate the revised gross margin EMI would report on each of the two orders. There were no other orders. There was a total of two overtime hours.

2-34 Finding unknown amounts. An auditor for the Internal Revenue Service is trying to reconstruct some partially destroyed records of two taxpayers. For each of the cases in the accompanying list, find the unknowns designated by the letters A through D.

	Case 1 (in thousands)	Case 2
Accounts receivable, 12/31	$ 6,000	$ 2,100
Cost of goods sold	A	20,000
Accounts payable, 1/1	3,000	1,700
Accounts payable, 12/31	1,800	1,500
Finished goods inventory, 12/31	B	5,300
Gross margin	11,300	C
Work in process, 1/1	0	800
Work in process, 12/31	0	3,000
Finished goods inventory, 1/1	4,000	4,000
Direct material used	8,000	12,000
Direct manufacturing labor	3,000	5,000
Indirect manufacturing costs	7,000	D
Purchases of direct material	9,000	7,000
Revenues	32,000	31,800
Accounts receivable, 1/1	2,000	1,400

2-35 Fire loss, computing inventory costs. A distraught employee, Fang W. Arson, put a torch to a manufacturing plant on a blustery February 26. The resulting blaze destroyed the plant and its contents. Fortunately, certain accounting records were kept in another building. They reveal the following for the period from January 1, 2004, to February 26, 2004:

Direct materials purchased	$160,000
Work in process, 1/1/2004	$34,000
Direct materials, 1/1/2004	$16,000
Finished goods, 1/1/2004	$30,000
Indirect manufacturing costs	40% of conversion costs
Revenues	$500,000
Direct manufacturing labor	$180,000
Prime costs	$294,000
Gross margin percentage based on revenues	20%
Cost of goods available for sale	$450,000

The loss is fully covered by insurance. The insurance company wants to know the historical cost of the inventories as a basis for negotiating a settlement, although the settlement is actually to be based on replacement cost, not historical cost.

Required Calculate the cost of:

1. Finished goods inventory, 2/26/2004
2. Work-in-process inventory, 2/26/2004
3. Direct materials inventory, 2/26/2004

2-36 Comprehensive problem on unit costs, product costs. Tampa Office Equipment manufactures and sells metal shelving. It began operations on January 1, 2004. Costs incurred for 2004 are as follows (V stands for variable; F stands for fixed):

Direct material costs	$140,000 V
Direct manufacturing-labor costs	30,000 V
Plant energy costs	5,000 V
Indirect manufacturing-labor costs	10,000 V
Indirect manufacturing-labor costs	16,000 F
Other indirect manufacturing costs	8,000 V
Other indirect manufacturing costs	24,000 F
Marketing, distribution, and customer-service costs	122,850 V
Marketing, distribution, and customer-service costs	40,000 F
Administrative costs	50,000 F

Variable manufacturing costs are variable with respect to units produced. Variable marketing, distribution, and customer-service costs are variable with respect to units sold.

Inventory data are

	Beginning, January 1, 2004	Ending, December 31, 2004
Direct materials	0 lb.	2,000 lbs.
Work in process	0 units	0 units
Finished goods	0 units	? units

Production in 2004 was 100,000 units. Two pounds of direct materials are used to make one unit of finished product.

Revenues in 2004 were $436,800. The selling price per unit and the purchase price per pound of direct materials were stable throughout the year. The company's ending inventory of finished goods is carried at the average unit manufacturing costs for 2004. Finished-goods inventory at December 31, 2004, was $20,970.

Required

1. Calculate direct materials inventory, total cost, December 31, 2004.
2. Calculate finished-goods inventory, total units, December 31, 2004.
3. Calculate selling price per unit, 2004.
4. Calculate operating income, 2004.

2-37 Product costs, effect of changing the cost classification (continuation of problem 2-36). Assume the same facts as in 2-36, except that fixed indirect manufacturing costs are not considered inventoriable costs. There are 9,000 units of finished goods inventory on December 31, 2004.

Required

1. Calculate finished goods inventory, total costs, December 31, 2004.
2. Calculate operating income, 2004.

Problems

2-38 Cost analysis, litigation risk, ethics. Sam Nash is the manager of new product development of Forever Young (FY). Nash is currently considering Enhance, which would be FY's next major product. All FY's current products are cosmetics applied to the skin by the consumer. In contrast, Enhance is inserted via a needle into the skin by a doctor. Each treatment is planned to cost patients $300 and will last three months. Enhance fills out the skin so that fewer wrinkles are observable.

FY plans to sell Enhance to doctors for $120 a treatment, providing the doctor with a large incentive to promote the product. Nash, however, questions the economics of this product. At present, all the costs recognized, including manufacturing by a third party, are $100 per treatment. Nash's main concern is that the current costing proposal excludes potential litigation costs in defending lawsuits related to Enhance. Elisabeth Savage, the CEO of the company, totally disagrees with Nash. She maintains she has total confidence in her medical research team and directs Nash not to include any amount from his potential litigation cost of $110 per treatment in his upcoming presentation to the board of directors on the economics and pricing of the Enhance product. Nash was previously controller of FY.

Required

1. What reasons might Savage have for not wanting Nash to include potential litigation costs on the product in a presentation on Enhance's economics and pricing?
2. FY sets prices by adding 20% to total costs. What would be the selling price per unit if Nash's proposal for including potential litigation costs are also included? How might this price affect promotion of Enhance?

3. Savage directs Nash to drop any further discussion of the litigation issue. Nash is to focus on making Enhance the blockbuster product that field research has suggested it will be. Nash is uneasy with this directive. He tells Savage it is an "ostrich approach" (head-in-the-sand) to a real problem that could potentially bankrupt the company. Savage tells Nash to go and think about her directive. What should Nash do next?

Collaborative Learning Problem

2-39 Missing data. Shaheen Plastics, Inc.'s selected data for the month of August 2004 are presented below (in millions):

Work-in-process inventory 8/1/2004	$ 200
Direct materials inventory 8/1/2004	90
Direct materials purchased	360
Direct materials used	375
Variable manufacturing overhead	250
Total manufacturing overhead	480
Total manufacturing costs	1,600
Cost of goods manufactured	1,650
Cost of goods sold	1,700
Finished goods inventory 8/1/2004	125

Required

Calculate the following costs:

1. Direct materials inventory 8/31/2004
2. Fixed manufacturing overhead costs for August
3. Direct manufacturing labor costs for August
4. Work-in-process inventory 8/31/2004
5. Goods available for sale in August
6. Finished-goods inventory 8/31/2004

CHAPTER 2 INTERNET EXERCISE

A great way to understand the concepts of fixed and variable costs is to tour a manufacturing plant. To tour Gibson Guitars' manufacturing production line, go to www.prenhall.com/horngren, click on *Cost Accounting,* 11th ed., and access the Internet exercise for Chapter 2.

CHAPTER 2 VIDEO CASE

THREE DOG BAKERY: Understanding Cost Terms

For Three Dog Bakery, "going to the dogs" has been a good thing! Founded by Dan Dye and Mark Beckloff in 1989 with little more than the desire to satisfy the finicky palate of their beloved 114-pound, deaf Great Dane, Gracie, the company has grown from a single store in downtown Kansas City, Missouri, to more than 30 worldwide locations. Their dog treats are made from wholesome ingredients such as flour, eggs, carrots, spinach, peanut butter, and carob, and they have clever names such as Snickerpoodles, Scottie Biscottis, Rollovers, Pup Tarts, and Great Danish. Some of the treats are frosted with honey-yogurt icings and decorated with colorful, edible flourishes. Special-occasion cakes, such as carrot cake or carob chip, can be personalized by an in-store pastry chef. More than a few customers have entered the bakery stores to buy snacks before realizing the treats were for dogs, not people. In all, the company makes more than 125 different low-fat treats. Selling prices range from a few cents for a small dog biscuit to more than $20 for a special-order cake.

Three Dog Bakery has a 40,000-square-foot centralized baking commissary in downtown Kansas City that prepares 70% of the goodies sold. Except for slower summer months, the commissary runs 24 hours a day, seven days a week. Items consist of baked biscuits and carob-dipped goodies that can pack and ship well. The commissary has one main assembly line with stations for mixing ingredients, mechanized cutting of shapes, extruding doughnut-shaped biscuits, manual placement of cut or extruded biscuits on baking sheets, baking ovens, cooling, manual carob dipping (for selected items), hand-packing into trays or containers, shrink-wrapping, and boxing. Most trays hold 12 specialty biscuits each and are packed by hand. There is also a conveyer belt for the automated packing of small biscuits into 7-ounce tubs. Employees are cross-trained to perform multiple assembly-line functions and can work on every type of biscuit the plant produces.

For the remaining 30% of finished goods, each store has a specially outfitted kitchen that prepares cakes, brownies, tarts, and other delicate or frosted items. Prepackaged mixes, created at the commissary, are used to assure consistent quality from store to store. Retail bakeries also sell nonedible pet items, such as collars, leashes, shampoo, logo t-shirts, hats, and coffee mugs. Some of the stores host birthday parties and "yappy hours" for in-store dog socialization. Customers do not have to come to a Three Dog Bakery retail store to buy merchandise, however. The company has a whimsical Web site (www.threedog.com) and a healthy mail-order business through its cat—oops!—*Dogalog.* PetsMart stores in the United States stock Three Dog Bakery treats, too. Sales are split evenly between the three sales channels: retail, direct-to-consumer, and wholesale.

Annual revenues exceed $20 million for this privately held company. As for the pet market itself, there are more than 60 million pet dogs in the United States, with nearly every owner buying anywhere from one to five packages of treats per month. Two-thirds of pet owners give their pets gifts, more than half give Christmas presents, and 25% give birthday gifts. Pet owners spend in excess of $20 billion annually industrywide on animal products, food, and services. Owners who spend more than $300 per year on their dogs tend to be younger, earn higher incomes, be married, and have no children.

QUESTIONS

1. To what cost objects could Three Dog Bakery trace its costs?
2. Classify the following cost items as direct (D) or indirect (I), and fixed (F) or variable (V) with respect to the production department (you'll have two answers for each item (D or I; F or V):

	Cost Item	D or I	F or V
a.	Salary of the production-department manager who oversees manufacturing		
b.	Salaries of founders Dan Dye and Mark Beckloff		
c.	Cardboard trays used to package sets of 12 specialty biscuits		
d.	Salary of the graphic designer who prepares the Dogalog illustrations and layout		
e.	Annual maintenance service agreement for the shrink-wrap machine		
f.	Wages paid to assembly line workers who mix Snickerpoodle ingredients in batches		
g.	Air conditioning costs for the entire baking commissary		
h.	Cost of flour, eggs, and carob icing for Rollover biscuits		

3. The company produces its *Dogalog* on a quarterly basis and mails copies to customers on the company's mailing list. Is the cost of producing and mailing the *Dogalog* considered an inventoriable cost or a period cost? Why?
4. What sectors—manufacturing, merchandising, or service—does Three Dog Bakery operate in? Why are they classified this way?

CHAPTER 3

Cost-Volume-Profit Analysis

LEARNING OBJECTIVES

1. Understand the assumptions of cost-volume-profit (CVP) analysis
2. Explain the features of CVP analysis
3. Determine the breakeven point and output level needed to achieve a target operating income
4. Understand how income taxes affect CVP analysis
5. Explain CVP analysis in decision making and how sensitivity analysis helps managers cope with uncertainty
6. Use CVP analysis to plan variable and fixed costs
7. Apply CVP analysis to a company producing different products
8. Adapt CVP analysis to situations in which a product has more than one cost driver
9. Distinguish contribution margin from gross margin

www.prenhall.com/horngren

How can managers of the Store 24 convenience store chain see the effects of selling a new flavor of coffee during the morning rush hour, increasing milk prices, or opening stores in a new neighborhood? Sound a bit like peering into a crystal ball? But there's no magic to gaining this knowledge, and the cost is nothing more than a bit of time. The knowledge comes from a technique called* cost-volume-profit (CVP) analysis*, and you can learn how to use it in the time it takes to read this chapter. CVP analysis helps managers plan by evaluating various alternatives. No crystal ball needed!

Surveys show more than 50% of responding companies use some form of CVP analysis.

Cost-volume-profit (CVP) analysis examines the behavior of total revenues, total costs, and operating income as changes occur in the output level, the selling price, the variable cost per unit, and/or the fixed costs of a product. Managers use CVP analysis to help answer questions such as: How will total revenues and total costs be affected if the output level (the *volume* in CVP analysis) changes—for example, if we sell 1,000 more units? If we raise or lower our selling price, how will that affect the output level? If we expand our business into foreign markets, how will that affect costs, selling price, and output level? These questions have a common "what-if" theme. By examining the results of these what-if possibilities and alternatives, CVP analysis illustrates the profits from those possibilities and alternatives. In this way, CVP analysis guides managers' planning.

COST-VOLUME-PROFIT ASSUMPTIONS AND TERMINOLOGY

1 Understand assumptions of cost-volume-profit (CVP) analysis

...for example, all costs are either variable or fixed with respect to output units

CVP analysis is based on several assumptions.

1. Changes in the levels of revenues and costs arise only because of changes in the number of product (or service) units produced and sold—for example, the number of television sets produced and sold by Sony Corporation. The number of output units is the only *revenue driver* and the only *cost driver.* Just as a cost driver is any factor that affects costs, a **revenue driver** is a variable, such as volume, that causally affects revenues.
2. Total costs can be separated into a fixed component that does not vary with the output level and a component that is variable with respect to the output level. Furthermore, you know from Chapter 2 (Exhibit 2-5, p. 37) that variable costs include both direct variable costs and indirect variable costs of a product. Similarly, fixed costs include both direct fixed costs and indirect fixed costs of a product. (We discuss details of determining fixed and variable components of costs in Chapter 10.)
3. When represented graphically, the behaviors of total revenues and total costs are linear (meaning they can be represented as a straight line) in relation to output level within a relevant range (and time period).
4. Selling price, variable cost per unit, and fixed costs (within a relevant range and period) are known and constant. (This assumption is discussed later in the chapter and in the appendix to this chapter.)
5. The analysis either covers a single product or assumes that the proportion of different products when multiple products are sold will remain constant as the level of total units sold changes. (This assumption is discussed later in the chapter.)
6. All revenues and costs can be added and compared without taking into account the time value of money. (Chapter 21 considers time value of money.)

Assumption 3 holds if selling price and costs of production inputs are constant within the relevant range. Assumption 3 does not hold if reductions in selling price are necessary to spur sales at higher output levels or if variable cost per unit declines when output increases as employees learn to work more efficiently.

Many companies (and divisions and plants of companies) in industries such as airlines, automobiles, chemicals, plastics, and semiconductors have found that even the simplest possible CVP analysis can be helpful in making decisions about strategic and long-range planning, as well as decisions about product features and pricing. In some real-world settings, the six assumptions just described may not hold. For example, predicting total revenues and total costs may require multiple drivers of revenues and costs (such as number of output units, number of sales visits made to customers, and number of advertisements placed). CVP analysis still may be useful in these situations, but the analysis becomes more complex. Always assess whether a simplified CVP analysis generates sufficiently accurate predictions of how total revenues and total costs behave. Use a more complex approach with multiple revenue drivers, multiple cost drivers, and cost functions that are not linear only if doing so will significantly improve decisions.

Before explaining the basics of CVP analysis, we first clarify some terms. As described in Chapter 2,

$$\text{Operating income} = \text{Total revenues from operations} - \text{Cost of goods sold and operating costs (excluding income taxes)}$$

Net income is operating income plus nonoperating revenues (such as interest revenue) minus nonoperating costs (such as interest cost) minus income taxes. For simplicity, throughout this chapter we assume nonoperating revenues and nonoperating costs are zero. Thus, net income is computed as:

$$\text{Net income} = \text{Operating income} - \text{Income taxes}$$

ESSENTIALS OF CVP ANALYSIS

2 Explain the features of CVP analysis

...how operating income changes with changes in output level, selling price, variable costs, or fixed costs

To start, we use an example to show how CVP analysis works.

> ***Example:*** *Mary Frost plans to sell Do-All Software, a home-office software package, at a two-day computer convention in Chicago. Mary can purchase this software from a computer software wholesaler at \$120 per package, with the privilege of returning all unsold packages and receiving a full \$120 refund per package. The packages will be sold for \$200 each. She has already paid \$2,000 to Computer Conventions, Inc., for the booth rental for the two-day convention. Assume there are no other costs. What profits will Mary make for different quantities of packages sold?*

In the Do-All Software example, the privilege of returning unsold packages means that cost of goods sold is variable with respect to the number of units sold.

The booth-rental cost of \$2,000 is a fixed cost because it will not change no matter how many packages Mary sells. The cost of the package itself is a variable cost because it increases in proportion to the number of packages sold. For each package that Mary sells, she incurs a cost of \$120 to purchase it. If Mary sells 5 packages, the variable purchase costs are \$600 (\$120 × 5).

Mary can use CVP analysis to examine changes in operating income as a result of selling different quantities of packages. If Mary sells 5 packages, she will receive revenues of \$1,000 (\$200 per package × 5 packages), incur variable costs of \$600 (\$120 per package × 5 packages), incur fixed costs of \$2,000, and report an operating loss of \$1,600 (\$1,000 − \$600 − \$2,000). If Mary sells 40 packages, she will receive revenues of \$8,000 (\$200 per package × 40 packages), incur variable costs of \$4,800 (\$120 per package × 40 packages), incur the same fixed costs of \$2,000, and report an operating income of \$1,200 (\$8,000 − \$4,800 − \$2,000).

The only numbers that change from selling different quantities of packages are *total revenues* and *total variable costs*. The difference between total revenues and total variable costs is called **contribution margin.** Contribution margin indicates why operating income changes as the number of units sold changes. The contribution margin when Mary sells 5 packages is \$400 (\$1,000 in total revenues minus \$600 in total variable costs); the contribution margin when Mary sells 40 packages is \$3,200 (\$8,000 in total revenues minus \$4,800 in total variable costs). Be sure to subtract all variable costs when calculating the contribution margin. For example, if Mary had variable selling costs because she paid salespersons a commission on each package they sold at the convention, variable costs would include the cost of the package plus the sales commission.

Contribution margin per unit is a useful tool for calculating contribution margin. The **contribution margin per unit** is the difference between the selling price and the variable cost per unit. In the Do-All Software example, the contribution margin per package, or per unit, is \$200 − \$120 = \$80. Contribution margin can be calculated as:

$$\text{Contribution margin} = \text{Contribution margin per unit} \times \text{Number of units sold}$$

For example, when 40 packages are sold, contribution margin = \$80 per unit × 40 units = \$3,200.

Contribution margin represents the amount of revenues minus variable costs that *contributes* to recovering fixed costs. Once fixed costs are fully recovered, the remaining

EXHIBIT 3-1 **Contribution Income Statement for Different Quantities of Do-All Software Packages Sold**

	Number of Packages Sold				
	0	1	5	25	40
Revenues at $200 per package	$ 0	$ 200	$ 1,000	$5,000	$8,000
Variable costs at $120 per package	0	120	600	3,000	4,800
Contribution margin at $80 per package	0	80	400	2,000	3,200
Fixed costs	2,000	2,000	2,000	2,000	2,000
Operating income	$(2,000)	$(1,920)	$(1,600)	$ 0	$1,200

Question: What is the basic difference between the income statement prepared under generally accepted accounting principles (IS/GAAP) and the contribution income statement (CIS)? *Answer:* In the IS/GAAP, costs are separated into inventoriable costs and period costs. In the CIS, costs are separated according to how they behave (variable or fixed).

contribution margin increases operating income. Exhibit 3-1 tabulates contribution margins for different quantities of packages sold and shows how contribution margin recovers fixed costs and generates operating income with increasing numbers of packages sold. The income statement in Exhibit 3-1 is called a **contribution income statement** because it groups costs into variable costs and fixed costs to highlight the contribution margin. See how each additional package sold from 0 to 1 to 5 increases contribution margin by $80 per package, recovering more of the fixed costs and reducing the operating loss. If Mary sells 25 packages, the contribution margin equals $2,000 ($80 per package × 25 packages), exactly recovering the fixed costs and resulting in $0 operating income. If Mary sells 40 packages, the contribution margin increases by another $1,200 ($3,200 − $2,000), all of which becomes operating income. As you look across Exhibit 3-1 from left to right, you see that the increase in contribution margin exactly equals the increase in operating income (or the decrease in operating loss).

Note from Exhibit 3-1 that contribution margin percentage (CM%) can also be calculated as contribution margin divided by total revenues. If 40 packages are sold, CM% = $3,200 ÷ $8,000 = 40%.

Instead of expressing contribution margin as a dollar amount per unit, we can express it as a percentage. **Contribution margin percentage** (also called **contribution margin ratio**) is contribution margin per unit divided by selling price.

In our example,

$$\text{Contribution margin percentage} = \frac{\$80}{\$200} = 0.40, \text{ or } 40\%$$

The complement of the contribution margin percentage (CM%) is the variable cost percentage (VC%). That is, CM% + VC% = 1. In the Do-All Software example, CM% = 40%, so VC% = 60%. Given a variable cost of $120 per unit and a VC% of 60%, the selling price is $200 ($120 ÷ 0.60).

Contribution margin percentage is contribution margin per dollar of revenues. In this example, it indicates that 40% of each dollar of revenues (equal to 40 cents) is contribution margin.

Mary can calculate the total contribution margin for different output levels by multiplying the contribution margin percentage by the total revenues shown in Exhibit 3-1. For example, if Mary sells 25 packages, revenues would be $5,000 and contribution margin would equal 40% of $5,000, or 0.40 × $5,000 = $2,000, exactly offsetting fixed costs. Mary breaks even by selling 25 packages for a total of $5,000.

3 **Determine the breakeven point and output level needed to achieve a target operating income**

...by comparing contribution margin and fixed costs

THE BREAKEVEN POINT

The **breakeven point (BEP)** is that quantity of output sold at which total revenues equal total costs—that is, the quantity of output sold at which the operating income is $0. Managers are interested in the breakeven point because they want to avoid operating losses. The breakeven point tells them how much output they must sell to avoid a loss. We will continue to use the preceding data for Do-All Software to examine three methods for determining the breakeven point: the equation method, the contribution margin method, and the graph method. However, we will use the more general term "quantity of output *units* sold," rather than quantity of *packages* sold.

Get familiar with these abbreviations. You will find them helpful as we present CVP analysis.

SP = Selling price
VCU = Variable cost per unit
CMU = Contribution margin per unit (SP − VCU)

$CM\%$ = Contribution margin percentage ($CMU \div SP$)
FC = Fixed costs
Q = Quantity of output units sold (and manufactured)
OI = Operating income
TOI = Target operating income
TNI = Target net income

Equation Method

To use the equation method to determine breakeven, the income statement is expressed as the following equation:

$$\text{Revenues} - \text{Variable cost} - \text{Fixed costs} = \text{Operating income}$$

$$\left(\begin{matrix}\text{Selling}\\\text{price}\end{matrix} \times \begin{matrix}\text{Quantity of output}\\\text{units sold}\end{matrix}\right) - \left(\begin{matrix}\text{Variable cost}\\\text{per unit}\end{matrix} \times \begin{matrix}\text{Quantity of output}\\\text{units sold}\end{matrix}\right) - \text{Fixed costs} = \text{Operating income}$$

$$(SP \times Q) - (VCU \times Q) - FC = OI \qquad (1)$$

Just remember the format of the contribution income statement and you can reconstruct this equation.

This equation provides the most general—and easiest to remember—approach to any CVP situation. Using Do-All Software data and setting operating income equal to $0, we obtain:

$$\$200Q - \$120Q - \$2{,}000 = \$0$$
$$\$80Q = \$2{,}000$$
$$Q = \$2{,}000 \div \$80 \text{ per unit} = 25 \text{ units}$$

If Mary sells fewer than 25 units, she will have a loss; if she sells 25 units, she will break even; and if she sells more than 25 units, she will make a profit. This breakeven point is expressed in units. It can also be expressed in terms of revenues: 25 units × $200 selling price = $5,000.

Contribution Margin Method

The contribution margin method simply rearranges the terms in equation 1, which is

$$(SP \times Q) - (VCU \times Q) - FC = OI$$

Rewriting equation 1:

$$(SP - VCU) \times Q = FC + OI$$

That is,

$$CMU \times Q = FC + OI$$
$$Q = \frac{FC + OI}{CMU} \qquad (2)$$

At the breakeven point, operating income is, by definition, $0. Setting $OI = 0$, we obtain:

$$Q = \frac{FC}{CMU} \qquad (3)$$

$$\begin{matrix}\text{Breakeven}\\\text{number of units}\end{matrix} = \frac{\text{Fixed costs}}{\text{Contribution margin per unit}}$$

The calculation in the equation method and the calculation in the contribution margin method appear similar because one equation is merely a restatement of the other. In our example, fixed costs are $2,000, and the contribution margin per unit is $80 ($200 − $120). Therefore,

$$\begin{matrix}\text{Breakeven}\\\text{number of units}\end{matrix} = \frac{\$2{,}000}{\$80 \text{ per unit}} = 25 \text{ units}$$

Although the text and common usage refer to three methods for CVP analysis, think of the methods not as distinct approaches but rather as different forms of exposition and different variations of the equation for the contribution-income statement.

To calculate the breakeven in terms of revenues, recall that in the Do-All Software example, $CM\% = \frac{CMU}{SP} = \frac{\$80}{\$200} = 0.40$, or 40%; that is, 40% of each dollar of revenues, or 40 cents, is contribution margin. To break even, contribution margin must equal fixed costs of \$2,000. To earn \$2,000 of contribution margin, revenues must equal \$2,000 ÷ 0.40 = \$5,000.

$$\text{Breakeven revenues} = \frac{FC}{CM\%} = \frac{\$2,000}{0.40} = \$5,000$$

Graph Method

In the graph method, we represent total costs and total revenues graphically. Each is shown as a line on a graph. The point where they intersect is the breakeven point. Exhibit 3-2 illustrates the graph method for Do-All Software. Because we have assumed that total costs and total revenues behave in a linear fashion, we need only two points to plot the line representing each.

1. **Total costs line.** The total costs line is the sum of the fixed costs and the variable costs. Fixed costs are \$2,000 at all output levels within the relevant range. To plot fixed costs, measure \$2,000 on the vertical axis (point *A*) and extend a line horizontally to the right from \$2,000 on the vertical axis. Variable costs are \$120 per unit. To plot the total costs line, use as one point the \$2,000 fixed costs at zero units sold (point *A*), because variable costs are \$0 when no units are sold. Select a second point by choosing any other convenient output level (say, 40 units sold) and determining the corresponding total costs. The total variable costs at this output level are \$4,800 (40 units × \$120 per unit). Because fixed costs are \$2,000 at all output levels within the relevant range, total costs at 40 units sold are \$6,800 (\$2,000 + \$4,800), which is point *B* in Exhibit 3-2. The total costs line is the straight line from point A through point B.
2. **Total revenues line.** One convenient starting point is \$0 revenues at 0 units sold, which is point *C* in Exhibit 3-2. Select a second point by choosing any other convenient output level and determining the corresponding total revenues. At 40 units sold, total revenues are \$8,000 (\$200 per unit × 40 units), which is point *D* in Exhibit 3-2. The total revenues line is the straight line from point *C* through point *D*.

The breakeven point is the quantity of units sold at which the total revenues line and the total costs line intersect. At this point (25 units sold in Exhibit 3-2), total revenues equal total costs. Exhibit 3-2, however, shows the profit or loss outlooks for a wide range of quantities of units sold besides the breakeven point. The profits or losses at sales levels

EXHIBIT 3-2

Cost-Volume-Profit Graph for Do-All Software

Even if total revenues and total costs are not linear throughout the range of 0 to 50 units as in Exhibit 3-2, a linear approximation may be acceptable within a relevant range, say, 15 to 40 units. If so, an alternative presentation is as follows:

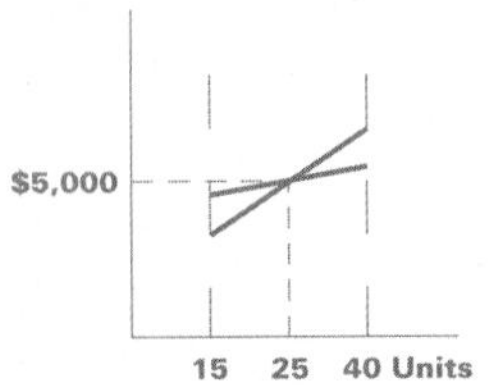

This format shows that making inferences outside the range of 15 to 40 units is dangerous.

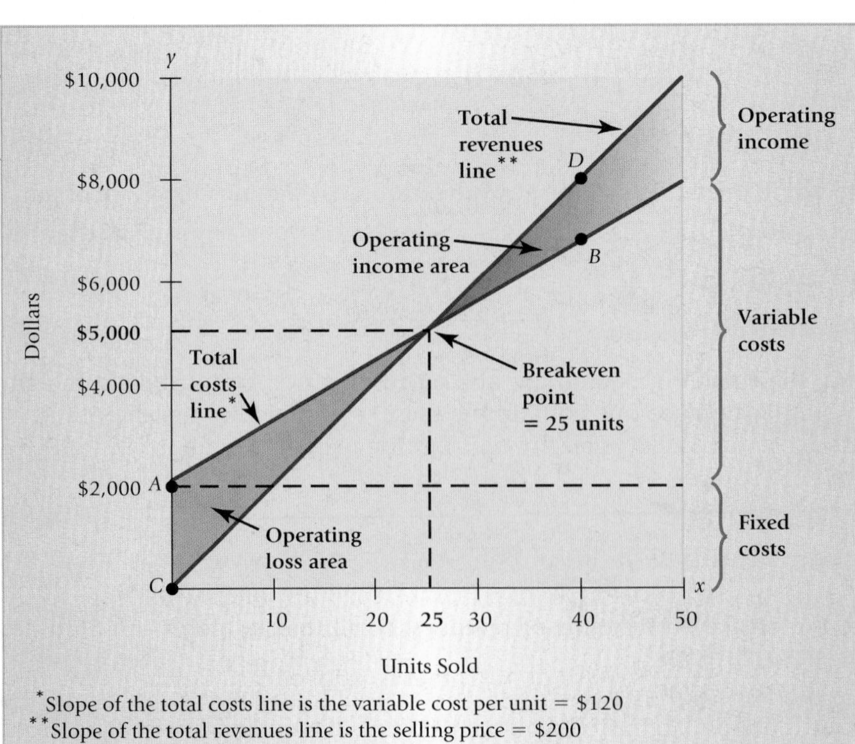

*Slope of the total costs line is the variable cost per unit = \$120
**Slope of the total revenues line is the selling price = \$200

other than 25 units can be determined by the vertical distances between the two lines at those levels. For quantities fewer than 25 units sold, total costs exceed total revenues, and the mauve area indicates operating losses. For quantities greater than 25 units sold, total revenues exceed total costs, and the blue-green area indicates operating incomes.

Target Operating Income

We introduce a profit element into our CVP analysis for Do-All Software by asking, How many units must be sold to earn an operating income of $1,200? Using equation 1, we need to find Q where:

$$\$200Q - \$120Q - \$2{,}000 = \$1{,}200$$
$$\$80Q = \$2{,}000 + \$1{,}200 = \$3{,}200$$
$$Q = \$3{,}200 \div \$80 \text{ per unit} = 40 \text{ units}$$

Alternatively, we could use the contribution margin method and equation 2, in which the numerator consists of fixed costs plus target operating income:

$$Q = \frac{\text{Fixed costs} + \text{Target operating income}}{\text{Contribution margin per unit}} = \frac{FC + TOI}{CMU}$$

$$Q = \frac{\$2{,}000 + \$1{,}200}{\$80 \text{ per unit}} = \frac{\$3{,}200}{\$80 \text{ per unit}} = 40 \text{ units}$$

The intuition for the formula is, "How many units must be sold to generate enough contribution margin to cover fixed costs and target operating income?"

Proof:	
Revenues, $200 per unit × 40 units	$8,000
Variable costs, $120 per unit × 40 units	4,800
Contribution margin, $80 per unit × 40 units	3,200
Fixed costs	2,000
Operating income	$1,200

The revenues needed to earn an operating income of $1,200 can also be calculated directly by recognizing (1) that $3,200 of contribution margin must be earned (given fixed costs of $2,000) and (2) that each dollar of revenue earns 40 cents of contribution margin. To earn $3,200 of contribution margin, revenues must equal $3,200 ÷ 0.40 = $8,000.

$$\text{Revenues needed to earn } \$1{,}200 = \frac{FC + TOI}{CM\%} = \frac{\$2{,}000 + \$1{,}200}{0.40} = \frac{\$3{,}200}{0.40} = \$8{,}000$$

The graph in Exhibit 3-2 is not helpful in answering the question of how many units Mary must sell to earn an operating income of $1,200. Why isn't it helpful? Because it is not easy to determine in the graph the point at which the difference between the total revenues line and the total costs line is $1,200. However, recasting Exhibit 3-2 in the form of a profit-volume (PV) graph makes it possible to answer this question.

A **PV graph** shows how changes in the quantity of units sold affects operating income. Exhibit 3-3 is the PV graph for Do-All Software (fixed costs, $2,000; selling price, $200; and variable cost per unit, $120). The PV line can be drawn using two points. One convenient point (*X*) is the operating loss at 0 units sold, which is equal to the fixed costs of $2,000, shown at −$2,000 on the vertical axis. A second convenient point (*Y*) is the breakeven point, which is 25 units in our example (see p. 68). The PV line is the straight line from point *X* through point *Y*. To find the number of units Mary must sell to earn an operating income of $1,200, draw a horizontal line corresponding to $1,200 on the vertical axis (that's the *y*-axis). At the point where this line intersects the PV line, draw a vertical line to the horizontal axis (that's the *x*-axis). The vertical line intersects the horizontal axis at 40 units, indicating that by selling 40 units Mary will earn an operating income of $1,200.

Target Net Income and Income Taxes

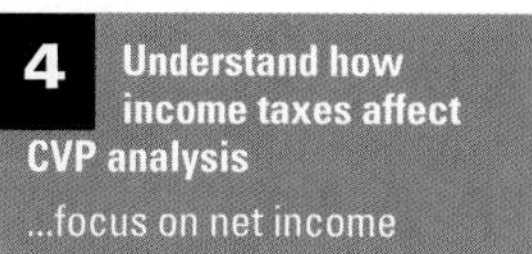

Thus far, we have ignored the effect of income taxes in our CVP analysis. At times, managers want to know the effect of their decisions on operating income after income taxes are paid. Net income is operating income minus income taxes. To make these evaluations, CVP calculations for target income must be stated in terms of target net income instead of target operating income. For example, Mary may be interested in knowing the quantity of units she must sell to earn a net income of $960, assuming an income tax rate of 40%. We

EXHIBIT 3-3

Profit-Volume Graph for Do-All Software

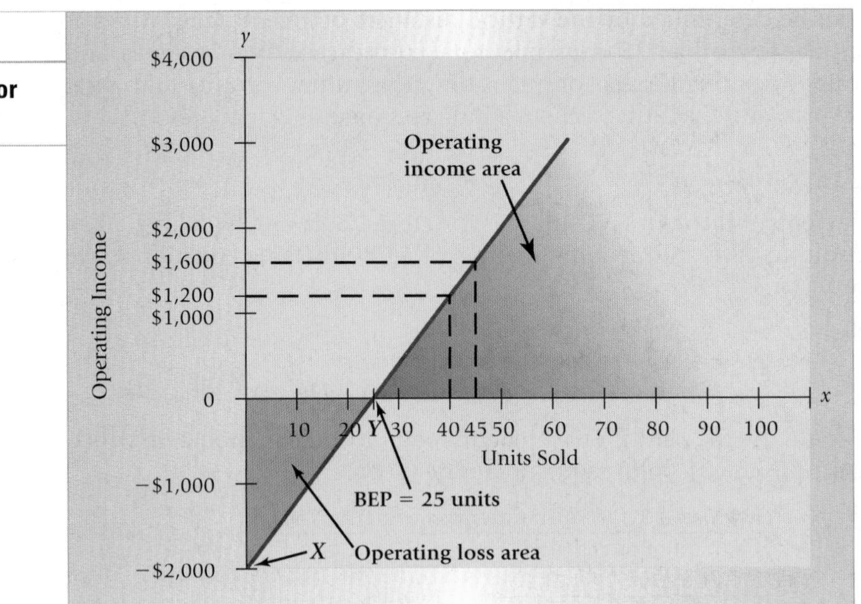

modify the target operating income calculations of the previous section so we can consider the effect of income taxes. Using the equation method,

$$\text{Revenues} - \text{Variable costs} - \text{Fixed costs} = \text{Target operating income}$$

Because no income taxes are paid at the breakeven point (BEP), income taxes do not affect the BEP. However, an increase in income tax rates increases the number of units that must be sold to generate a given net income (NI). In the Do-All Software example, when income tax is 40%, sales of 45 units generate $960 NI. If the income tax rate were 50%, an extra 4 units (49 − 45) must be sold to generate $960 NI:
TOI = $960 / (1 − 0.50) = $1,920
Q = ($2,000 + $1,920) / $80/unit = 49 units

Furthermore,

$$\text{Target net income} = (\text{Target operating income}) - (\text{Target operating income} \times \text{Tax rate})$$
$$\text{Target net income} = (\text{Target operating income})\,(1 - \text{Tax rate})$$
$$\text{Target operating income} = \frac{\text{Target net income}}{1 - \text{Tax rate}}$$

Substituting for target operating income:

$$\text{Revenues} - \text{Variable costs} - \text{Fixed costs} = \frac{\text{Target net income}}{1 - \text{Tax rate}}$$

Substituting numbers from our Do-All Software example:

$$\$200Q - \$120Q - \$2{,}000 = \frac{\$960}{1 - 0.40}$$
$$\$200Q - \$120Q - \$2{,}000 = \$1{,}600$$
$$\$80Q = \$3{,}600$$
$$Q = \$3{,}600 \div \$80 \text{ per unit} = 45 \text{ units}$$

Alternatively, we can use the contribution margin method of equation 2 and substitute:

$$\text{Target operating income} = \frac{\text{Target net income}}{1 - \text{Tax rate}}$$

$$\text{That is, } Q = \frac{\text{Fixed costs} + \dfrac{\text{Target net income}}{1 - \text{Tax rate}}}{\text{Contribution margin per unit}} = \frac{FC + \dfrac{TNI}{1 - \text{Tax rate}}}{CMU}$$

$$Q = \frac{\$2{,}000 + \dfrac{\$960}{1 - 0.40}}{\$80} = \frac{\$2{,}000 + \$1{,}600}{\$80 \text{ per unit}} = 45 \text{ units}$$

Proof:	
Revenues, $200 per unit × 45 units	$9,000
Variable costs, $120 per unit × 45 units	5,400
Contribution margin	3,600
Fixed costs	2,000
Operating income	1,600
Income taxes, $1,600 × 0.40	640
Net income	$ 960

Focusing the analysis on target net income instead of target operating income will not change the breakeven point. It doesn't because, by definition, operating income at the breakeven point is $0, and no income taxes are paid when there is no operating income.

Mary can also use the PV graph in Exhibit 3-3. For a target net income of $960,

$$\text{Target operating income} = \frac{\text{Target net income}}{1 - \text{Tax rate}} = \frac{\$960}{1 - 0.40} = \$1,600$$

From Exhibit 3-3, to earn target operating income of $1,600, Mary needs to sell 45 units.

USING CVP ANALYSIS FOR DECISION MAKING

5 Explain CVP analysis in decision making and how sensitivity analysis helps managers cope with uncertainty

...effect on operating income of different assumptions

We have shown how CVP analysis is useful to determine breakeven quantities and to determine the quantities for achieving target operating income and target net income. Managers also use CVP analysis to guide other decisions, many of them strategic decisions. Consider a decision about which features to add to an existing product. Different choices can affect selling prices, variable cost per unit, fixed costs, units sold, and operating income. CVP analysis helps managers make this decision by estimating the expected long-term profitability of the choices. CVP analysis also helps managers decide how much to advertise, whether to expand into new markets, and how to price the product.

Strategic decisions invariably entail risk. CVP analysis evaluates how operating income will be affected if the original predicted data are not achieved—say, if sales are 10% lower than estimated. Evaluating this risk affects other strategic decisions a company might make. For example, if the probability of a decline in sales seems high, a manager may take actions to shift the cost structure to have more variable costs and fewer fixed costs.

Decision to Advertise

Consider Do-All Software. Suppose Mary anticipates selling 40 units. Exhibit 3-3 indicates that Mary's operating income would be $1,200. Mary is considering placing an advertisement describing the product and its features in the convention brochure. The advertisement will cost $500. This cost will be fixed because it must be paid and will not change regardless of the number of units Mary sells. She anticipates that advertising will increase sales by 10% to 44 packages. Should Mary advertise? The following table presents the CVP analysis.

	40 Packages Sold with No Advertising (1)	44 Packages Sold with Advertising (2)	Difference (3) = (2) − (1)
Contribution margin ($80 × 40; $80 × 44)	$3,200	$3,520	$ 320
Fixed costs	2,000	2,500	500
Operating income	$1,200	$1,020	$(180)

Operating income decreases by $180, so Mary should not advertise. Note that Mary could focus only on the difference column (3) and come to the same conclusion: If Mary advertises, contribution margin will increase by $320 ($80 per unit × 4 additional units), and fixed costs will increase by $500, resulting in a $180 decrease in operating income.

Decision to Reduce Selling Price

Having decided not to advertise, Mary is contemplating whether to reduce the selling price to $175. At this price, she thinks she will sell 50 units. At this quantity, the software wholesaler who supplies Do-All Software will sell the packages to Mary for $115 per unit instead of $120. Should Mary reduce the selling price? No, as the following CVP analysis shows.

Contribution margin from lowering price to $175: ($175 − $115) per unit × 50 units	$3,000
Contribution margin from maintaining price at $200: ($200 − $120) per unit × 40 units	3,200
Change in contribution margin from lowering price	$ (200)

Decreasing the price will reduce contribution margin by $200 and, because the fixed costs of $2,000 do not change, it will also reduce operating income by $200.

Mary can examine other alternatives to increase operating income, such as simultaneously increasing advertising costs and lowering prices. In each case, Mary will compare the changes in contribution margin (through the effects on selling prices, variable costs, and quantities of units sold) to the changes in fixed costs, and she will choose the alternative that gives the highest operating income.

SENSITIVITY ANALYSIS AND UNCERTAINTY

When values of the CVP model's components are not known with certainty, they will need to be estimated. These estimates require judgment, and reasonable managers might disagree on their estimates of, say, variable cost per unit (VCU). Accountants perform sensitivity analysis to find out whether these different estimates of VCU significantly affect the results of CVP analysis.

An electronic spreadsheet application such as Excel greatly facilitates sensitivity analysis.

Before choosing among alternatives, managers frequently analyze the sensitivity of their decisions to changes in underlying assumptions. **Sensitivity analysis** is a "what-if" technique that managers use to examine how a result will change if the original predicted data are not achieved or if an underlying assumption changes. In the context of CVP analysis, sensitivity analysis answers such questions as, What will operating income be if the quantity of units sold decreases by 5% from the original prediction? and, What will operating income be if variable cost per unit increases by 10%? The sensitivity of operating income to various possible outcomes broadens managers' perspectives about what might actually occur *before* they commit costs.

Electronic spreadsheets enable managers to conduct CVP-based sensitivity analyses in a systematic and efficient way. Using spreadsheets, managers can conduct sensitivity analysis to examine the effect and interaction of changes in selling price, variable cost per unit, fixed costs, and target operating income. Exhibit 3-4 displays a spreadsheet for the Do-All Software example. Mary can immediately see the revenues that need to be generated to reach particular operating-income levels, given alternative levels of fixed costs and variable cost per unit. For example, revenues of $6,400 ($200 per unit × 32 units) are required to earn an operating income of $1,200 if fixed costs are $2,000 and variable cost per unit is $100. Mary can also use Exhibit 3-4 to assess what revenues she needs to break even (earn operating income of $0) if, for example, the booth rental at the Chicago convention is raised to $2,800 (increasing fixed costs to $2,800) or if the software supplier raises its price to $150 (increasing variable cost to $150 per unit).

An aspect of sensitivity analysis is **margin of safety,** the amount of budgeted revenues over and above breakeven revenues. Expressed in units, margin of safety is the sales quantity minus the breakeven quantity. The margin of safety answers the "what-if" question: If budgeted revenues are above breakeven and drop, how far can they fall below budget before the breakeven point is reached? Such a fall could be due to a competitor

EXHIBIT 3-4

Spreadsheet Analysis of CVP Relationships for Do-All Software

Fixed Costs	Variable Cost per Unit	Revenues Required at $200 Selling Price to Earn Operating Income of 0	$1,200	$1,600	$2,000
$2,000	$100	$ 4,000	$ 6,400[a]	$ 7,200	$ 8,000
	120	5,000	8,000	9,000	10,000
	150	8,000	12,800	14,400	16,000
2,400	100	4,800	7,200	8,000	8,800
	120	6,000	9,000	10,000	11,000
	150	9,600	14,400	16,000	17,600
2,800	100	5,600	8,000	8,800	9,600
	120	7,000	10,000	11,000	12,000
	150	11,200	16,000	17,600	19,200

[a] $$\text{Number of units required to be sold} = \frac{\text{Fixed costs} + \text{Target operating income}}{\text{Contribution margin per unit}} = \frac{\$2,000 + \$1,200}{\$200 - \$100} = 32\text{ units}$$

$$\text{Revenues required} = \text{Number of units required to be sold} \times \text{Selling price} = 32\text{units} \times \$200 = \$6,400$$

introducing a better product, or to poorly executed marketing programs, and so on. Assume that Mary has fixed costs of $2,000, a selling price of $200, and variable cost per unit of $120. For 40 units sold, the budgeted revenues are $8,000 and the budgeted operating income is $1,200. The breakeven point for this set of assumptions is 25 units ($2,000 ÷ $80 per unit), or $5,000 ($200 per unit × 25 units). The margin of safety is 15 (40 − 25) units or $3,000 ($8,000 − $5,000).

Sensitivity analysis is one approach to recognizing **uncertainty,** which is the possibility that an actual amount will deviate from an expected amount. Another approach to recognizing uncertainty is to compute expected values using probability distributions. This is illustrated in the appendix to this chapter.

COST PLANNING AND CVP

Alternative Fixed-Cost/Variable-Cost Structures

6 **Use CVP analysis to plan variable and fixed costs**

...compare risk of losses versus higher returns

CVP-based sensitivity analysis highlights the risks and returns as fixed costs are substituted for variable costs in a company's cost structure. In Exhibit 3-4, Compare line 2 (fixed costs, $2,000; variable cost per unit, $120) and line 7 (fixed costs, $2,800; variable cost per unit, $100) See how the revenues required to break even are *higher* for line 7 ($5,600 versus $5,000 in line 2) whereas the revenues required to earn $2,000 of operating income are *lower* in line 7 ($9,600 versus $10,000 in line 2). Line 7, with higher fixed costs, has more risk of loss (has a higher breakeven point) but offers a greater return (more profits) as revenues increase. CVP analysis can help managers evaluate various fixed-cost/variable-cost structures. To consider these choices in more detail, let's return to Do-All Software. Mary is paying a $2,000 booth-rental fee. Suppose Computer Conventions offers Mary three rental alternatives:

- *Option 1:* $2,000 fixed fee
- *Option 2:* $800 fixed fee plus 15% of convention revenues
- *Option 3:* 25% of convention revenues with no fixed fee

Mary anticipates selling 40 units (packages). She is interested in how her choice of a rental agreement will affect the income she earns and the risks she faces. Exhibit 3-5 graphically depicts the profit-volume relationship for each option. The line representing the relationship between units sold and operating income for option 1 is the same as the line in the PV graph shown in Exhibit 3-3 (fixed costs of $2,000 and contribution margin

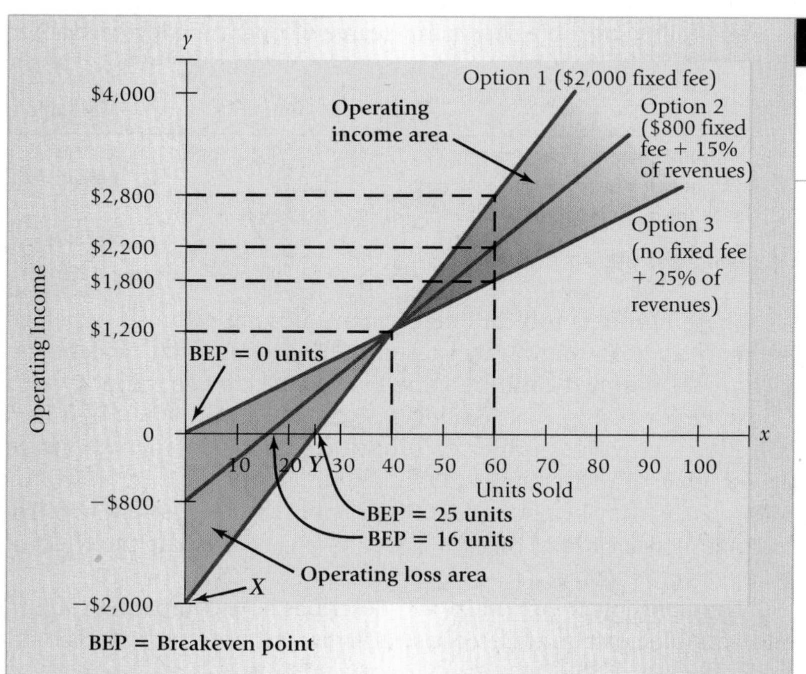

EXHIBIT 3-5

Profit-Volume Graph for Alternative Rental Options for Do-All Software

per unit of $80). The line representing option 2 shows fixed costs of $800 and a contribution margin per unit of $50 [selling price, $200, minus variable cost per unit, $120, minus variable rental fees per unit, $30, (0.15 × $200)]. The line representing option 3 has fixed costs of $0 and a contribution margin per unit of $30 [$200 − $120 − $50 (0.25 × $200)].

If Mary sells 40 units, she should be indifferent across the various options. Each option results in operating income of $1,200. The CVP analysis, however, highlights the different risks of loss and different returns associated with each option if sales differ from 40 units. The higher risk of a loss in option 1 is because of its higher fixed costs ($2,000), which result in a higher breakeven point (25 units) and a lower margin of safety (40 − 25 = 15 units) relative to the other options. The line representing option 1 intersects the horizontal axis farther to the right than the lines representing options 2 and 3.

Consider operating income under each option if the number of units sold drops to 20. Exhibit 3-5 shows that option 1 leads to an operating loss, whereas options 2 and 3 continue to generate operating incomes. (A vertical line from $X = 20$ units sold cuts the option 1 line below the horizontal axis in the mauve area and cuts the options 2 and 3 lines above the horizontal axis in the blue-green area.) The higher risk of loss in option 1, however, must be evaluated against its potential benefits. Option 1 has the highest contribution margin per unit because of its low variable costs. Once fixed costs are recovered at sales of 25 units, each additional unit sold adds $80 of contribution margin and, therefore, $80 of operating income per unit. For example, at sales of 60 units, option 1 shows an operating income of $2,800, greater than the operating incomes for sales of 60 units under options 2 and 3. By moving from option 1 toward option 3, Mary faces less risk of loss when demand is low, both because of lower fixed costs and because she loses less contribution margin per unit. She must, however, accept less operating income when demand is high because of the higher variable costs of option 3 compared with options 1 and 2. The choice among options 1, 2, and 3 will be influenced by her confidence in the level of demand for the software package and her willingness to risk losses if demand is low.

Degree of operating leverage (DOL) is specific to a given level of sales as a starting point. If the starting point changes, the DOL changes. For example, if the starting point was sales of 50 units, the DOL for option 1 would be:

$$\frac{CM}{CM - FC} = \frac{\$80 \times 50}{(\$80 \times 50) - \$2{,}000} = 2.00$$

The risk-return tradeoff across alternative cost structures can be measured as *operating leverage*. **Operating leverage** describes the effects that fixed costs have on changes in operating income as changes occur in units sold and, hence, in contribution margin. Organizations with a high proportion of fixed costs in their cost structures, as is the case under option 1, have high operating leverage. The line representing option 1 in Exhibit 3-5 is the steepest of the three lines. Small increases in sales lead to large increases in operating incomes. Small decreases in sales result in relatively large decreases in operating incomes, leading to a greater risk of operating losses. *At any given level of sales,* the **degree of operating leverage** equals contribution margin divided by operating income.

The following table shows the degree of operating leverage at sales of 40 units for the three rental options.

	Option 1	Option 2	Option 3
1. Contribution margin per unit (pp. 71–72)	$ 80	$ 50	$ 30
2. Contribution margin (Row 1 × 40 units)	$3,200	$2,000	$1,200
3. Operating income (from Exhibit 3-5)	$1,200	$1,200	$1,200
4. Degree of operating leverage	$\frac{\$3{,}200}{\$1{,}200} = 2.67$	$\frac{\$2{,}000}{\$1{,}200} = 1.67$	$\frac{\$1{,}200}{\$1{,}200} = 1.00$

These numbers indicate that, when sales are 40 units, a percentage change in sales and contribution margin will result in 2.67 times that percentage change in operating income for option 1, but the same percentage change in operating income for option 3. Consider, for example, a sales increase of 50% from 40 to 60 units. Contribution margin will increase by 50% under each option. Operating income, however, will increase by 2.67 × 50% = 133% from $1,200 to $2,800 in option 1, but it will increase only by 1.00 × 50% = 50% from $1,200 to $1,800 in option 3 (see Exhibit 3-5). The degree of operating leverage at a given level of sales helps managers calculate the effect of fluctuations in sales on operating incomes.

The Concepts in Action (p. 73) describes how companies can influence the fixed costs and variable costs in their cost structures and how such decisions affect the risk-return tradeoff.

CONCEPTS IN ACTION

Influencing Cost Structures to Manage the Risk-Return Trade-off at Amazon.com

Building up too many fixed costs can be hazardous to a company's health. Because fixed costs, unlike variable costs, do not automatically decrease as volume declines, companies with too many fixed costs can lose a considerable amount of money during lean times. Amazon.com, the Internet retailer, understood this concept well. Amazon began business using a "virtual" business model. When Amazon received a customer order for a book on its Web site, it immediately turned around and placed an order with a book wholesaler, which shipped the book directly to the customer. The "virtual" in Amazon's business model referred to the fact that Amazon was able to sell books from its Web site without having to invest in warehouses or inventory. Amazon only incurred the cost of acquiring books on an as-needed basis after it had received a confirmed order from a customer. Amazon essentially had a variable-cost structure—costs were high when sales were strong, and costs were low when sales were weak. Without warehousing and inventory costs, Amazon avoided being stuck with costs if business was slow. But this low-risk strategy came at a price—purchasing books from wholesalers cost significantly more than purchasing books directly from publishers.

The competitive disadvantage from the higher cost of books became apparent in 1997, when Barnes & Noble, the largest "bricks and mortar" based book retailer, opened an online store. Barnes & Noble already had a large distribution center to supply books to its "bricks and mortar" stores. It planned to use the same warehouse facility to fill the orders it received from online customers. Moreover, Barnes & Noble paid less for its books than Amazon because its distribution-center capacity enabled it to order books in the minimum-order quantities required by publishers. When it opened its online store, Barnes & Noble claimed it would offer "the lowest everyday prices of any online bookseller," as well as better service because it controlled the product itself, rather than having to rely on a wholesaler to supply it. Barnes & Noble had higher fixed costs but lower variable costs than Amazon. At high volume levels, Barnes & Noble's costs would be less than Amazon's costs.

In response to Barnes & Noble's threat, Amazon decided to build and acquire distribution centers of its own. Doing so increased Amazon's fixed costs, operating leverage, and risk but decreased its variable costs. Amazon was counting on a rapid and dramatic expansion in sales. How rapid? At the beginning of 2000, stock analysts estimated that Amazon's warehouse capacity was three to five times more than it then needed. In early 2001, Amazon acknowledged that 2000 sales had fallen short of expectations, projected even lower sales growth in 2001, and announced the closing of two of its distribution facilities. As sales decreased, Amazon had to cut its fixed costs to increase its chances to break even.

Source: Amazon.com financial statements, stock-analyst reports, and conversations with company management.

Effect of Time Horizon

In CVP analysis, we assume that costs are either variable or fixed. But whether a cost is variable or fixed depends on the time period for a decision. The shorter the time horizon, the higher the percentage of total costs considered as fixed. Suppose an American Airlines plane will depart from its gate in the next 60 minutes and currently has 20 seats unsold. A potential passenger arrives with a transferable ticket from a competing airline. What are the variable costs to American of placing one more passenger in an otherwise empty seat? Variable costs (such as one more meal) would be negligible. Virtually all the costs in this decision situation (such as crew costs and baggage-handling costs) are fixed. Alternatively, suppose American must decide whether to include another city in its routes. This decision may have a one-year planning horizon. Many more costs, including crew costs, baggage-handling costs, and airport fees, would be regarded as variable; and fewer costs (for example, corporate-office costs) would be regarded as fixed in this

In the American example, note that a seemingly short-run decision can have long-run consequences. If American accepts last-minute passengers at reduced fares (because the contribution margin from these passengers is positive), this decision could have long-run consequences if future passengers expect reduced fares at the last minute.

decision. This example should make clear that whether a cost is fixed depends heavily on the relevant range, the length of time horizon being considered, and the specific decision situation.

7 Apply CVP analysis to a company producing many different products

...assume sales mix of products remains constant as total units sold changes

EFFECTS OF SALES MIX ON INCOME

Sales mix is the quantities of various products (or services) that constitute total unit sales of a company. Suppose Mary is now budgeting for the next convention. She plans to sell two different software products—Do-All and Superword—and budgets the following:

	Do-All	Superword	Total
Units sold	60	40	100
Revenues, $200 and $100 per unit	$12,000	$4,000	$16,000
Variable costs, $120 and $70 per unit	7,200	2,800	10,000
Contribution margin, $80 and $30 per unit	$ 4,800	$1,200	6,000
Fixed costs			4,500
Operating income			$ 1,500

What is the breakeven point? Unlike in the single product (or service) situation, there is no unique breakeven number of total units for a company selling multiple products. The number of total units that must be sold to break even depends on the sales mix—the number of units of Do-All sold compared with the number of units of Superword sold. One possible assumption is that the budgeted sales mix (3 units of Do-All sold for every 2 units of Superword sold) will not change at different levels of total unit sales. That is, if 5 total units are sold, 3 units will be Do-All and 2 units will be Superword. If 10 times as many total units are sold ($5 \times 10 = 50$ units), $3 \times 10 = 30$ units will be Do-All and $2 \times 10 = 20$ units will be Superword. In general, if $5 \times S$ (written as $5S$) total units are sold, $3 \times S$ ($3S$) units will be Do-All and $2 \times S$ ($2S$) units will be Superword. To calculate the breakeven point:

$$\text{Revenues} - \text{Variable costs} - \text{Fixed costs} = \text{Operating income} = 0$$

Where,

$$\begin{aligned}
\text{Revenues} &= \left(\begin{matrix}\text{Selling price}\\ \text{of Do-All}\end{matrix} \times \begin{matrix}\text{Number of units}\\ \text{of Do-All sold}\end{matrix}\right) + \left(\begin{matrix}\text{Selling price}\\ \text{of Superword}\end{matrix} \times \begin{matrix}\text{Number of units}\\ \text{of Superword sold}\end{matrix}\right)\\
&= \$200 \text{ per unit} \times 3S \text{ units} + \$100 \text{ per unit} \times 2S \text{ units}\\
&= \$600S + \$200S\\
&= \$800S
\end{aligned}$$

To help understand the product-mix concept, imagine the software being sold only in bundles of five units: 3 Do-Alls and 2 Superwords. Such "bundling" is a good way to think of the product-mix concept, even though the bundling need not be literally true.

$$\begin{aligned}
\text{Variable costs} &= \left(\begin{matrix}\text{Variable cost}\\ \text{per unit of}\\ \text{Do-All}\end{matrix} \times \begin{matrix}\text{Number of units}\\ \text{of Do-All sold}\end{matrix}\right) + \left(\begin{matrix}\text{Variable cost}\\ \text{per unit of}\\ \text{Superword}\end{matrix} \times \begin{matrix}\text{Number of units}\\ \text{of Superword sold}\end{matrix}\right)\\
&= \$120 \text{ per unit} \times 3S \text{ units} + \$70 \text{ per unit} \times 2S \text{ units}\\
&= \$360S + \$140S\\
&= \$500S
\end{aligned}$$

To calculate the breakeven point,

$$\begin{aligned}
\text{Revenues} - \text{Variable costs} - \text{Fixed costs} &= 0\\
\$800S - 500S - \$4,500 &= 0\\
\$800S - \$500S &= \$4,500\\
\$300S &= \$4,500\\
S &= 15 \text{ units}
\end{aligned}$$

$$\text{Number of units of Do-All to break even} = 3S = 3 \times 15 = 45 \text{ units}$$
$$\text{Number of units of Superword to break even} = 2S = 2 \times 15 = 30 \text{ units}$$

The breakeven point is 75 total units when the sales mix is 45 units of Do-All and 30 units of Superword. That's the sales mix that maintains the ratio of 3 units of Do-All to 2 units of Superword. At this mix, the contribution margin of $4,500 (Do-All $80 per unit × 45 units = $3,600 + Superword $30 per unit × 30 units = $900) equals the fixed costs of $4,500.

Another way to compute the breakeven point is to calculate the *weighted-average contribution margin per unit* for the two products together.

$$\text{Weighted-average contribution margin per unit} = \frac{\left(\text{Do-All's CMU} \times \begin{array}{c}\text{Number of units}\\ \text{of Do-All}\\ \text{sold}\end{array}\right) + \left(\text{Superword's CMU} \times \begin{array}{c}\text{Number of units}\\ \text{of Superword}\\ \text{sold}\end{array}\right)}{\text{Number of units of Do-All sold} + \text{Number of units of Superword sold}}$$

$$= \frac{(\$80 \times 60) + (\$30 \times 40)}{60 + 40} = \frac{\$6,000}{100} = \$60$$

We then have

$$\text{Breakeven point} = \frac{\text{Fixed costs}}{\text{Weighted-average contribution margin per unit}} = \frac{\$4,500}{\$60} = 75 \text{ units}$$

Because the ratio of Do-All sales to Superword sales is 60:40, or 3:2, the breakeven point is 45 (0.60 × 75) units of Do-All and 30 (0.40 × 75) units of Superword.

We can also calculate the breakeven point in revenues for the multiple-product situation using the weighted-average contribution margin percentage.

$$\text{Weighted-average contribution margin percentage} = \frac{\text{Total contribution margin}}{\text{Total revenues}} = \frac{\$6,000}{\$16,000} = 0.375, \text{ or } 37.5\%$$

$$\text{Total revenues required to break even} = \frac{\text{Fixed costs}}{\text{Weighted-average contribution margin percentage}} = \frac{\$4,500}{0.375} = \$12,000$$

The $16,000 of total revenues are in the ratio of 3:1 ($12,000:$4,000), or 75%:25% (p. 74). Hence the breakeven revenues of $12,000 should be split in the same ratio, 75%:25%. This amounts to breakeven revenues of $9,000 (75% × $12,000) of Do-All and $3,000 (25% × $12,000) of Superword. At a selling price of $200 for Do-All and $100 for Superword, breakeven equals 45 units ($9,000 ÷ $200) of Do-All and 30 units ($3,000 ÷ $100) of Superword.

Alternative sales mixes (in units) that have a contribution margin of $4,500 and cause Mary to break even include:

Companies that sell multiple products adjust their mix to respond to demand changes. For example, as gas prices increase and customers want smaller cars, auto companies shift their production mix to produce additional smaller cars.

	Units									
Do-All	54	48	42	36	30	24	18	12	6	0
Superword	6	22	38	54	70	86	102	118	134	150
Total	60	70	80	90	100	110	120	130	140	150

None of these sales mixes, however, describes the breakeven point in our example. Why? Because they do not match the budgeted sales mix of 3 units of Do-All for every 2 units of Superword. If the sales mix changes to 3 units of Do-All for every 7 units of Superword, you can see in the preceding table that the breakeven point increases from 75 units to 100 units, comprising 30 units of Do-All and 70 units of Superword. The breakeven quantity increases because the sales mix has shifted toward the lower contribution-margin product, Superword, decreasing the weighted-average contribution margin per unit.

In general, other things being equal, for any given total quantity of units sold, as the sales mix shifts toward units with higher contribution margins, operating income will be higher. If the mix shifts toward Do-All (say to 70% Do-All from 60% Do-All), which has a contribution margin of more than twice that of Superword, Mary's operating income will increase.

CVP ANALYSIS IN SERVICE AND NONPROFIT ORGANIZATIONS

Thus far, our CVP analysis has focused on a merchandising company. CVP can also be applied to decisions by manufacturing, service, and nonprofit organizations. To apply CVP analysis in service and nonprofit organizations, we need to focus on measuring their output, which is different from the tangible units sold in a merchandising company. Examples of output measures in various service and nonprofit industries are

Industry	Measure of Output
Airlines	Passenger miles
Hotels/motels	Room-nights occupied
Hospitals	Patient days
Universities	Student credit-hours

Consider a social welfare agency of the government with a $900,000 budget appropriation (its revenues) for 2003. This nonprofit agency's purpose is to assist handicapped people seeking employment. On average, the agency supplements each person's income by $5,000 annually. The agency's fixed costs are $270,000. It has no other costs. The agency manager wants to know how many people could be assisted in 2003. We can use CVP analysis here by setting operating income to $0. Let *Q* be the number of handicapped people to be assisted:

$$\begin{aligned} \text{Revenues} - \text{Variable costs} - \text{Fixed costs} &= 0 \\ \$900{,}000 - \$5{,}000Q - \$270{,}000 &= 0 \\ \$5{,}000Q &= \$900{,}000 - \$270{,}000 = \$630{,}000 \\ Q &= \$630{,}000 \div \$5{,}000 \text{ per person} = 126 \text{ people} \end{aligned}$$

Suppose the manager is concerned that the total budget appropriation for 2004 will be reduced by 15% to $900,000 × (1 − 0.15) = $765,000. The manager wants to know how many handicapped people could be assisted with this reduced budget. Assume the same amount of monetary assistance per person:

$$\begin{aligned} \$765{,}000 - \$5{,}000Q - \$270{,}000 &= \$0 \\ \$5{,}000Q &= \$765{,}000 - \$270{,}000 = \$495{,}000 \\ Q &= \$495{,}000 \div \$5{,}000 \text{ per person} = 99 \text{ people} \end{aligned}$$

Note the following two characteristics of the CVP relationships in this nonprofit situation:

1. The percentage drop in the number of people aided, (126 − 99) ÷ 126, or 21.4%, is more than the 15% reduction in the budget appropriation. Why? Because the $270,000 in fixed costs still must be paid, leaving a proportionately lower budget to aid people. The percentage drop in service exceeds the percentage drop in budget appropriation.
2. Given the reduced budget appropriation (revenues) of $765,000, the manager can adjust operations to stay within this appropriation in one or more of three basic ways: (a) reduce the number of people assisted from the current 126, (b) reduce the variable cost (the extent of assistance per person) from the current $5,000 per person, or (c) reduce the total fixed costs from the current $270,000.

MULTIPLE COST DRIVERS

8 **Adapt CVP analysis to situations in which a product has more than one cost driver**

...basic concepts apply but not the simple formulas

Throughout the chapter we have assumed that the number of output units is the only revenue driver and the only cost driver. Now we describe how some aspects of CVP analysis can be adapted to the general case of multiple cost drivers.

Consider again the single-product Do-All Software example. Suppose Mary will incur a variable cost of $10 for preparing documents (including an invoice) for each customer who buys Do-All Software. That is, the cost driver of document-preparation costs is the number of customers who buy Do-All Software. Mary's operating income can then be expressed in terms of revenues and these costs:

$$\text{Operating income} = \text{Revenues} - \left(\begin{array}{c}\text{Cost of each}\\ \text{Do-All software}\\ \text{package}\end{array} \times \begin{array}{c}\text{Number of}\\ \text{packages}\end{array}\right) - \left(\begin{array}{c}\text{Cost of preparing}\\ \text{documents}\\ \text{for each customer}\end{array} \times \begin{array}{c}\text{Number of}\\ \text{customers}\end{array}\right) - \begin{array}{c}\text{Fixed}\\ \text{costs}\end{array}$$

If Mary sells 40 packages to 15 customers, then

$$\begin{aligned} \text{Operating income} &= (\$200 \text{ per package} \times 40 \text{ packages}) - (\$120 \text{ per package} \times 40 \text{ packages}) \\ &\quad - (\$10 \text{ per customer} \times 15 \text{ customers}) - \$2{,}000 \\ &= \$8{,}000 - \$4{,}800 - \$150 - \$2{,}000 = \$1{,}050 \end{aligned}$$

If instead Mary sells 40 packages to 40 customers, then

$$\begin{aligned}\text{Operating income} &= (\$200 \times 40) - (\$120 \times 40) - (\$10 \times 40) - \$2{,}000 \\ &= \$8{,}000 - \$4{,}800 - \$400 - \$2{,}000 = \$800\end{aligned}$$

The number of packages sold is not the only determinant of Mary's operating income. For a given number of packages sold, Mary's operating income will be lower if she sells Do-All Software to more customers. Mary's costs depend on two cost drivers—the number of packages sold and the number of customers.

Just as in the case of multiple products, there is no unique breakeven point when there are multiple cost drivers. For example, Mary will break even if she sells 26 packages to 8 customers or 27 packages to 16 customers:

$$(\$200 \times 26) - (\$120 \times 26) - (\$10 \times 8) - \$2{,}000 = \$5{,}200 - \$3{,}120 - \$80 - \$2{,}000 = \$0$$
$$(\$200 \times 27) - (\$120 \times 27) - (\$10 \times 16) - \$2{,}000 = \$5{,}400 - \$3{,}240 - \$160 - \$2{,}000 = \$0$$

This example illustrates that CVP analysis can be adapted to multiple cost-driver situations. However, in cases involving multiple cost drivers, the simple formulas described earlier in the chapter, for example, to calculate the breakeven point, cannot be used.

CONTRIBUTION MARGIN VERSUS GROSS MARGIN

This section describes the distinction between contribution margin and gross margin in manufacturing and merchandising companies. This distinction does not apply to service companies because they have no cost of goods sold and hence no gross margin.

Let's contrast contribution margin, which provides information for CVP analysis, with gross margin discussed in Chapter 2.

$$\text{Gross margin} = \text{Revenues} - \text{Cost of goods sold}$$
$$\text{Contribution margin} = \text{Revenues} - \text{All variable costs}$$

Cost of goods sold in the merchandising sector is made up of goods purchased and then sold. Cost of goods sold in the manufacturing sector consists entirely of manufacturing costs (including fixed manufacturing costs). The phrase "all variable costs" refers to variable costs in each of the business functions of the value chain.

Service-sector companies can compute a contribution margin but not a gross margin. That's because service-sector companies do not have a cost of goods sold line item in their income statement.

Merchandising Sector

The most common difference between contribution margin and gross margin for companies in the merchandising sector is variable cost items that are not included in cost of goods sold. An example of such a variable cost item is commissions paid to salespersons as a percentage of revenues. Contribution margin is computed by deducting all variable costs from revenues, whereas gross margin is computed by deducting only cost of goods sold from revenues. The following example (figures assumed and in thousands) illustrates this difference:

Contribution Income Statement Emphasizing Contribution Margin			**Financial Accounting Income Statement Emphasizing Gross Margin**	
Revenues		$200	Revenues	$200
Variable cost of goods sold	$120		Cost of goods sold	120
Variable operating costs	43	163		
Contribution margin		37	Gross margin	80
Fixed operating costs		19	Operating costs ($43 + $19)	62
Operating income		$ 18	Operating income	$ 18

Variable operating costs of $43,000 are deducted from revenues when calculating contribution margin but are not deducted when calculating gross margin.

Manufacturing Sector

For companies in the manufacturing sector, contribution margin and gross margin differ in two respects: fixed manufacturing costs and variable nonmanufacturing costs. The following example (figures assumed and in thousands) illustrates this difference:

Income Statement Emphasizing Contribution Margin			Income Statement Emphasizing Gross Margin	
Revenues		$1,000	Revenues	$1,000
Variable manufacturing costs	$250		Cost of goods sold ($250 + $160)	410
Variable nonmanufacturing costs	270	520		
Contribution margin		480	Gross margin	590
Fixed manufacturing costs	160		Nonmanufacturing costs	
Fixed nonmanufacturing costs	138	298	($270 + $138)	408
Operating income		$ 182	Operating income	$ 182

Fixed manufacturing costs of $160,000 are not deducted from revenues when computing contribution margin but are deducted when computing gross margin. Cost of goods sold in a manufacturing company includes all variable manufacturing costs and all fixed manufacturing costs ($250,000 + $160,000). Variable nonmanufacturing costs of $270,000 are deducted from revenues when computing contribution margin but are not deducted when computing gross margin.

Like contribution margin, *gross margin* can be expressed as a total, as an amount per unit, or as a percentage. For example, the **gross margin percentage** is the gross margin divided by revenues—59% ($590 ÷ $1,000) in our manufacturing-sector example.

PROBLEM FOR SELF-STUDY

Wembley Travel Agency specializes in flights between Los Angeles and London. It books passengers on United Airlines at $900 per round-trip ticket. Until last month, United paid Wembley a commission of 10% of the ticket price paid by each passenger. This commission was Wembley's only source of revenues. Wembley's fixed costs are $14,000 per month (for salaries, rent, and such), and its variable costs are $20 per ticket purchased for a passenger. This $20 includes a $15 per ticket delivery fee paid to Federal Express. (To keep the analysis simple, we assume each round-trip ticket purchased is delivered in a separate package. Thus, the $15 delivery fee applies to each ticket.)

United Airlines has just announced a revised payment schedule for travel agents. It will now pay travel agents a 10% commission per ticket up to a maximum of $50. Any ticket costing more than $500 generates only a $50 commission, regardless of the ticket price.

Required

1. Under the old 10% commission structure, how many round-trip tickets must Wembley sell each month (a) to break even and (b) to earn an operating income of $7,000?
2. How does United's revised payment schedule affect your answers to (a) and (b) in requirement 1?

SOLUTION

1. Wembley receives a 10% commission on each ticket: 10% × $900 = $90. Thus,

$$\begin{aligned} SP &= \$90 \text{ per ticket} \\ VCU &= \$20 \text{ per ticket} \\ CMU &= \$90 - \$20 = \$70 \text{ per ticket} \\ FC &= \$14{,}000 \text{ per month} \end{aligned}$$

a. $$Q = \frac{FC}{CMU} = \frac{\$14{,}000}{\$70 \text{ per ticket}} = 200 \text{ tickets per month}$$

b. When target operating income (TOI) = $7,000 per month:

$$\begin{aligned} Q &= \frac{FC + TOI}{CMU} \\ &= \frac{\$14{,}000 + \$7{,}000}{\$70 \text{ per ticket}} = \frac{\$21{,}000}{\$70 \text{ per ticket}} \\ &= 300 \text{ tickets per month} \end{aligned}$$

2. Under the new system, Wembley would receive only $50 on the $900 ticket. Thus,

$$SP = \$50 \text{ per ticket}$$
$$VCU = \$20 \text{ per ticket}$$
$$CMU = \$50 - \$20 = \$30 \text{ per ticket}$$
$$FC = \$14{,}000 \text{ per month}$$

a. $$Q = \frac{\$14{,}000}{\$30 \text{ per ticket}} = 467 \text{ tickets (rounded up)}$$

b. $$Q = \frac{\$21{,}000}{\$30 \text{ per ticket}} = 700 \text{ tickets}$$

The $50 cap on the commission paid per ticket causes the breakeven point to more than double (from 200 to 467 tickets) and the tickets sold to earn $7,000 per month to also more than double (from 300 to 700 tickets). Travel agents reacted very negatively to the United Airlines announcement to change commission payments.

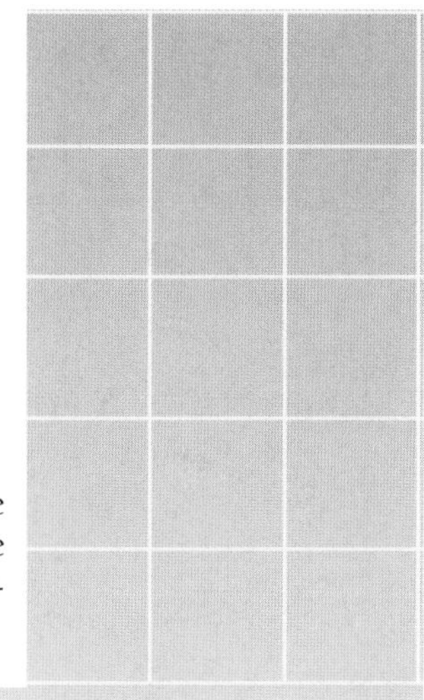

DECISION POINTS — SUMMARY

The following question-and-answer format summarizes the chapter's learning objectives. Each decision presents a key question related to a learning objective. The guidelines are the answer to that question.

Decision	Guidelines
1. What assumptions must hold for applying CVP analysis?	CVP analysis requires simplifying assumptions, such as costs are either fixed or variable with respect to the number of output units (units produced and sold) and the relationship between total revenues and total costs is linear.
2. How can CVP analysis assist managers?	CVP analysis assists managers in understanding the behavior of a product's total costs, total revenues, and operating income as changes occur in that product's output level, selling price, variable costs, or fixed costs.
3. How do companies determine the breakeven point or the output needed to achieve a target operating income?	The breakeven point is the quantity of output at which total revenues equal total costs. The three methods for computing the breakeven point and the quantity of output to achieve target operating income are the equation method, the contribution margin method, and the graph method. Each method is merely a restatement of the others. Managers often select the method they find easiest to use in their specific situation.
4. How should companies incorporate income taxes into CVP analysis?	Income taxes can be incorporated into CVP analysis by using target net income rather than target operating income. The breakeven point is unaffected by the presence of income taxes because no income taxes are paid if there is no operating income.
5. How should companies cope with uncertainty or changes in underlying assumptions?	Sensitivity analysis, a "what-if" technique, examines how a result will change if the original predicted data are not achieved or if an underlying assumption changes. When making decisions, managers use CVP analysis to compare contribution margins and fixed costs under different assumptions.
6. How should companies choose between different variable-cost/fixed-cost structures?	CVP analysis highlights the risk of losses when revenues are low and the upside return when revenues are high of different proportions of variable and fixed costs in a company's cost structure.
7. Can CVP analysis be applied to a company producing multiple products?	CVP analysis can be applied to a company producing multiple products by assuming the sales mix of products sold remains constant as the total quantity of units sold changes. There is no unique breakeven number of units for a company producing multiple products.
8. Can CVP analysis be applied to a product that has multiple cost drivers?	The basic concepts of CVP analysis can be applied to multiple cost-driver situations, but the simple formulas of the single cost-driver case, for example, to calculate the breakeven point, cannot be used.
9. Can contribution margin and gross margin be used interchangeably?	No. Contribution margin is revenues minus all variable costs (throughout the value chain); gross margin is revenues minus cost of goods sold.

APPENDIX: DECISION MODELS AND UNCERTAINTY

This appendix explores the characteristics of uncertainty and describes an approach managers can use to make decisions in a world of uncertainty. We'll also illustrate the insights gained when uncertainty is recognized in CVP analysis.

Coping with Uncertainty[1]

Role of a decision model *Uncertainty* is the possibility that an actual amount will deviate from an expected amount. In the Do-All example, Mary might forecast sales at 40 units, but actual sales may turn out to be 30 units or 60 units. A *decision model* helps managers deal with such uncertainty. It is a formal method for making a choice, commonly involving both quantitative and qualitative analyses. The quantitative analysis usually includes the following steps:

Question: What is the difference between *events* and *actions?* *Answer:* Events are possible relevant occurrences; they are uncontrollable states of nature. Managers assess the probabilities of various events occurring. Actions are choices made by managers. For a given decision, one action is selected and the other action(s) is not selected.

Step 1: **Identify a choice criterion.** A **choice criterion** is an objective that can be quantified. This objective can take many forms. Most often the choice criterion is to maximize income or to minimize costs. The choice criterion provides a basis for choosing the best alternative action. Mary's choice criterion is to maximize expected operating income at the computer convention.

Step 2: **Identify the set of alternative actions to be considered.** We use the letter a with subscripts $_1$, $_2$, and $_3$ to distinguish each of Mary's three possible actions:

a_1 = Pay \$2,000 fixed fee
a_2 = Pay \$800 fixed fee plus 15% of convention revenues
a_3 = Pay 25% of convention revenues with no fixed fee

Step 3: **Identify the set of events that can occur.** An **event** is a possible relevant occurrence, such as the actual number of packages Mary may sell at the convention. The set of events should be mutually exclusive and collectively exhaustive. Events are mutually exclusive if they cannot occur at the same time. Events are collectively exhaustive if, taken together, they make up the entire set of possible relevant occurrences (no other event can occur). Examples of mutually exclusive and collectively exhaustive events are growth, decline, or no change in industry demand, and increase, decrease, or no change in interest rates. Only one event out of the entire set of mutually exclusive and collectively exhaustive events will actually occur. Suppose Mary's only uncertainty is the number of units of Do-All Software that she can sell. For simplicity, suppose Mary estimates that sales will be either 30 or 60 units. We use the letter x with subscripts $_1$ and $_2$ to distinguish the set of mutually exclusive and collectively exhaustive events:

x_1 = 30 units
x_2 = 60 units

Step 4: **Assign a probability to each event that can occur.** A **probability** is the likelihood or chance that an event will occur. The decision model approach to coping with uncertainty assigns probabilities to events. A **probability distribution** describes the likelihood, or the probability that each of the mutually exclusive and collectively exhaustive set of events will occur. In some cases, there will be much evidence to guide the assignment of probabilities. For example, the probability of obtaining a heads in the toss of a coin is $\frac{1}{2}$ and that of drawing a particular playing card from a standard, well-shuffled deck is $\frac{1}{52}$. In business, the probability of having a specified percentage of defective units may be assigned with great confidence on the basis of production experience with thousands of units. In other cases, there will be little evidence supporting estimated probabilities—for example, expected sales of a new pharmaceutical product next year. Suppose that Mary, on the basis of past experience, assesses a 60% chance, or a $\frac{6}{10}$ probability, that she will sell 30 units and a 40% chance, or a $\frac{4}{10}$ probability, that

[1]The presentation here draws (in part) from teaching notes prepared by R. Williamson.

she will sell 60 units. Using $P(x)$ as the notation for the probability of an event, the probabilities are

$$P(x_1) = \frac{6}{10} = 0.60$$
$$P(x_2) = \frac{4}{10} = 0.40$$

The probabilities of these events add to 1.00 because they are mutually exclusive and collectively exhaustive.

Step 5: **Identify the set of possible outcomes.** **Outcomes** measure, in terms of the choice criterion, the predicted economic results of the various possible combinations of actions and events. The outcomes in the Do-All Software example take the form of six possible operating incomes that are displayed in a *decision table* in Exhibit 3-6. A **decision table** is a summary of the alternative actions, events, outcomes, and probabilities of events.

Distinguish actions from events. Actions are choices available to managers—for example, the particular rental alternatives that Mary can choose. Events are the set of all relevant occurrences that can happen—for example, the different quantities of software packages that may be sold at the convention. The outcome is the operating income the company makes, which depends both on the action the manager selects (rental alternative chosen) and the event that occurs (the quantity of packages sold).

Exhibit 3-7 presents an overview of relationships among a decision model, the implementation of a chosen action, its outcome, and subsequent performance evaluation.

Expected value An **expected value** is the weighted average of the outcomes, with the probability of each outcome serving as the weight. When the outcomes are measured in monetary terms, *expected value* is often called **expected monetary value**. Using information in Exhibit 3-6, the expected monetary value of each booth-rental alternative denoted by $E(a_1)$, $E(a_2)$, and $E(a_3)$ is

Pay \$2,000 fixed fee:	$E(a_1) = 0.60\ (\$400) + 0.40\ (\$2{,}800) = \$1{,}360$
Pay \$800 fixed fee plus 15% of revenues:	$E(a_2) = 0.60\ (\$700) + 0.40\ (\$2{,}200) = \$1{,}300$
Pay 25% of revenues with no fixed fee:	$E(a_3) = 0.60\ (\$900) + 0.40\ (\$1{,}800) = \$1{,}260$

To maximize expected operating income, Mary should select action a_1—pay Computer Conventions a \$2,000 fixed fee.

To interpret the expected value of selecting action a_1, imagine that Mary attends many conventions, each with the probability distribution of operating incomes given in Exhibit 3-6. For a specific convention, Mary will earn operating income of either \$400, if she sells 30 units, or \$2,800, if she sells 60 units. But if Mary attends 100 conventions, she will expect to earn \$400 operating income 60% of the time (at 60 conventions), and \$2,800

EXHIBIT 3-6

Decision Table for Do-All Software

	Probability of Events	
Actions	x_1 = 30 units sold $P(x_1) = .60$	x_2 = 60 units sold $P(x_2) = .40$
a_1: Pay \$2,000 fixed fee	\$400[l]	\$2,800[m]
a_2: Pay \$800 fixed fee plus 15% of convention revenues	\$700[n]	\$2,200[p]
a_3: Pay 25% of convention revenues with no fixed fee	\$900[q]	\$1,800[r]

[l] Operating income = (\$200 − \$120)(30) − \$2,000 = \$400
[m] Operating income = (\$200 − \$120)(60) − \$2,000 = \$2,800
[n] Operating income = (\$200 − \$120 − \$30*)(30) − \$800 = \$700
[p] Operating income = (\$200 − \$120 − \$30*)(60) − \$800 = \$2,200
[q] Operating income = (\$200 − \$120 − \$50**)(30) = \$900
[r] Operating income = (\$200 − \$120 − \$50**)(60) = \$1,800
*\$30 = 15% of selling price of \$200
**\$50 = 25% of selling price of \$200

EXHIBIT 3-7 A Decision Model and Its Link to Performance Evaluation

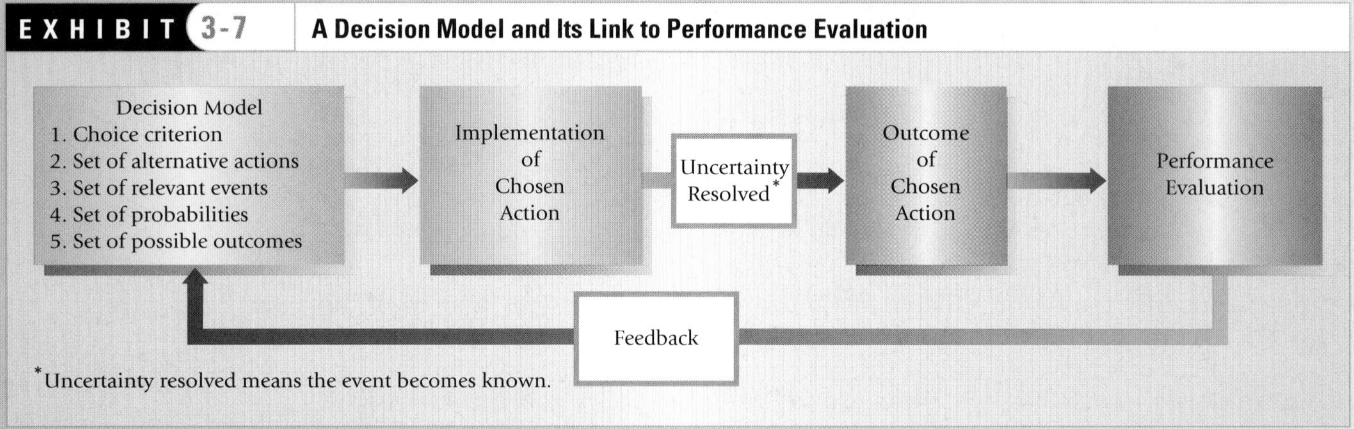

*Uncertainty resolved means the event becomes known.

operating income 40% of the time (at 40 conventions), for a total operating income of \$136,000 (\$400 × 60 + \$2,800 × 40). The expected value of \$1,360 is the operating income per convention that Mary will earn when averaged across all conventions (\$136,000 ÷ 100).

Consider the effect of uncertainty on the preferred action choice. If Mary were certain she would sell only 30 units (that is, $P(x_1)= 1$), she would prefer alternative a_3—pay 25% of convention revenues with no fixed fee. To follow this reasoning, examine Exhibit 3-6. When 30 units are sold, alternative a_3 yields the maximum operating income of \$900. Because fixed costs are \$0, booth-rental costs are lower, equal to \$1,500 (25% of revenues = 0.25 × \$200 per unit × 30 units) when sales are low.

However, if Mary were certain she would sell 60 software packages (that is, $P(x_2) = 1$), she would prefer alternative a_1—pay a \$2,000 fixed fee. Exhibit 3-6 indicates that when 60 units are sold, alternative a_1 yields the maximum operating income of \$2,800. Rental payments under a_2 and a_3 increase with units sold but are fixed under a_1.

Despite the high probability of selling only 30 units, Mary still prefers to take action a_1, that is, pay a fixed fee of \$2,000. That's because the high risk of low operating income (the 60% probability of selling only 30 units) is more than offset by the high return from selling 60 units, which occurs with 40% probability. If Mary were more averse to risk (measured in our example by the difference between operating incomes when 30 versus 60 units are sold), she might have preferred action a_2 or a_3. For example, action a_2 ensures an operating income of at least \$700, greater than the operating income of \$400 that she would earn under action a_1 if only 30 units are sold. Of course, choosing a_2 limits the upside potential to \$2,200 relative to \$2,800 under a_1, if 60 units are sold. If Mary is very concerned about downside risk, however, she may be willing to forgo some upside benefits to protect against a \$400 outcome by choosing a_2.[2]

Good decisions and good outcomes Always distinguish between a good decision and a good outcome. One can exist without the other. Suppose you are offered a one-time-only gamble tossing a coin. You will win \$20 if the event is heads, but you will lose \$1 if the event is tails. As a decision maker, you proceed through the logical phases: gathering information, assessing outcomes, and making a choice. You accept the bet. Why? Because the expected value is \$9.50 [0.5(\$20) + 0.5(−\$1)]. The coin is tossed and the event is tails. You lose. From your viewpoint, this was a good decision but a bad outcome.

A decision can be made only on the basis of information available at the time of evaluating and making the decision. By definition, uncertainty rules out guaranteeing, after the fact, that the best outcome will always be obtained. As in our example, it is possible that bad luck will produce bad outcomes even when good decisions have been made. A bad outcome does not mean a bad decision was made. The best protection against a bad outcome is a good decision.

[2] For more formal approaches, refer to G. Eppen, F. Gould, C. Schmidt, J. Moore, and L. Weatherford, *Introductory Management Science: Decision Modeling with Spreadsheets*, 4th ed. (Upper Saddle River, NJ: Prentice Hall, 1998).

TERMS TO LEARN

This chapter and the Glossary at the end of the book contain definitions of the following important terms:

breakeven point (BEP) (64)
choice criterion (80)
contribution income statement (64)
contribution margin (63)
contribution margin per unit (63)
contribution margin percentage (64)
contribution margin ratio (64)
cost-volume-profit (CVP) analysis (62)
decision table (81)
degree of operating leverage (72)
event (80)
expected monetary value (81)
expected value (81)
gross margin percentage (78)
margin of safety (70)
net income (63)
operating leverage (72)
outcomes (81)
probability (80)
probability distribution (80)
PV graph (67)
revenue driver (62)
sales mix (74)
sensitivity analysis (70)
uncertainty (71)

ASSIGNMENT MATERIAL

Note: To underscore the basic CVP relationships, the assignment material ignores income taxes unless stated otherwise.

Questions

3-1 Define cost-volume-profit analysis.

3-2 Describe the assumptions underlying CVP analysis.

3-3 Distinguish between operating income and net income.

3-4 Define contribution margin, contribution margin per unit, and contribution margin percentage.

3-5 Describe three methods that can be used to calculate the breakeven point.

3-6 Why is it more accurate to describe the subject matter of this chapter as CVP analysis rather than as breakeven analysis?

3-7 "CVP analysis is both simple and simplistic. If you want realistic analysis to underpin your decisions, look beyond CVP analysis." Do you agree? Explain.

3-8 How does an increase in the income tax rate affect the breakeven point?

3-9 Describe sensitivity analysis. How has the advent of the electronic spreadsheet affected its use?

3-10 Give an example of how a manager can decrease variable costs while increasing fixed costs.

3-11 Give an example of how a manager can increase variable costs while decreasing fixed costs.

3-12 What is operating leverage? How is knowing the degree of operating leverage helpful to managers?

3-13 "There is no such thing as a fixed cost. All costs can be 'unfixed' given sufficient time." Do you agree? What is the implication of your answer for CVP analysis?

3-14 How can a company with multiple products compute its breakeven point?

3-15 "In CVP analysis, gross margin is a less useful concept than contribution margin." Do you agree? Explain briefly.

Exercises

3-16 **CVP computations.** Fill in the blanks for each of the following independent cases.

Case	Revenues	Variable Costs	Fixed Costs	Total Costs	Operating Income	Contribution Margin Percentage
a.	$ —	$ 500	$ —	$ 800	$1,200	—
b.	2,000	—	300	—	200	—
c.	1,000	700	—	1,000	—	—
d.	1,500	—	300	—	—	40%

3-17 **CVP computations.** Patel Manufacturing sold 180,000 units of its product for $25 per unit in 2003. Variable cost per unit is $20 and total fixed costs are $800,000.

Required

1. Calculate (a) contribution margin and (b) operating income.
2. Patel's current manufacturing process is labor intensive. Kate Schoenen, Patel's production manager, has proposed investing in state-of-the-art manufacturing equipment, which will increase the annual fixed costs to $2,500,000. The variable costs are expected to decrease to $10 per unit. Patel expects to maintain the same sales volume and selling price next year. How would acceptance of Ms. Schoenen's proposal affect your answers to (a) and (b) in requirement 1?
3. Should Patel accept Schoenen's proposal? Explain.

3-18 CVP analysis, changing revenues and costs. Sunshine Travel Agency specializes in flights between Toronto and Jamaica. It books passengers on Canadian Air. Sunshine's fixed costs are $22,000 per month. Canadian Air charges passengers $1,000 per round-trip ticket.

Required

Calculate the number of tickets Sunshine must sell each month to (a) break even and (b) make a target operating income of $10,000 per month in each of the following independent cases.

1. Sunshine's variable costs are $35 per ticket. Canadian Air pays Sunshine 8% commission on ticket price.
2. Sunshine's variable costs are $29 per ticket. Canadian Air pays Sunshine 8% commission on ticket price.
3. Sunshine's variable costs are $29 per ticket. Canadian Air pays $48 fixed commission per ticket to Sunshine. Comment on the results.
4. Sunshine's variable costs are $29 per ticket. It receives $48 commission per ticket from Canadian Air. It charges its customers a delivery fee of $5 per ticket. Comment on the results.

3-19 Gross margin and contribution margin, making decisions. Schmidt Men's Clothing's revenues and cost data for 2004 appear below.

Revenues		$ 500,000
Cost of goods sold (40% of sales)		200,000
Gross margin		300,000
Operating costs:		
Salaries and wages	$150,000	
Sales commissions (10% of sales)	50,000	
Depreciation of equipment and fixtures	12,000	
Store rent ($4,000 per month)	48,000	
Other operating costs	50,000	310,000
Operating income (loss)		$ (10,000)

Mr. Schmidt, the owner of the store, is unhappy with the operating results. An analysis of other operating costs reveals that it includes $40,000 variable costs, which vary with sales volume, and $10,000 fixed costs.

Required

1. Compute the contribution margin of Schmidt Men's Clothing.
2. Compute the contribution margin percentage.
3. Mr. Schmidt estimates he can increase revenues by 20% by incurring additional advertising costs of $10,000. Calculate the impact on operating income of this action.

3-20 CVP exercises. The Super Donut owns and operates six doughnut outlets in and around Kansas City. You are given the following corporate budget data for next year:

Revenues	$10,000,000
Fixed costs	1,700,000
Variable costs	8,200,000

Variable costs change with respect to the number of doughnuts sold.

Required

Compute the budgeted operating income for each of the following deviations from the original budget data. (Consider each case independently.)

1. A 10% increase in contribution margin, holding revenues constant
2. A 10% decrease in contribution margin, holding revenues constant
3. A 5% increase in fixed costs
4. A 5% decrease in fixed costs
5. An 8% increase in units sold
6. An 8% decrease in units sold
7. A 10% increase in fixed costs and a 10% increase in units sold
8. A 5% increase in fixed costs and a 5% decrease in variable costs

3-21 CVP exercises. The Doral Company manufactures and sells pens. Currently, 5,000,000 units are sold per year at $0.50 per unit. Fixed costs are $900,000 per year. Variable costs are $0.30 per unit.

Required

Consider each case separately:

1. **a.** What is the present operating income for a year?

b. What is the present breakeven point in revenues?

Compute the new operating income for each of the following changes:

2. A $0.04 per unit increase in variable costs
3. A 10% increase in fixed costs and a 10% increase in units sold
4. A 20% decrease in fixed costs, a 20% decrease in selling price, a 10% decrease in variable cost per unit, and a 40% increase in units sold

Compute the new breakeven point in units for each of the following changes:

5. A 10% increase in fixed costs
6. A 10% increase in selling price and a $20,000 increase in fixed costs

3-22 CVP analysis, income taxes. The Bratz Company has fixed costs of $300,000 and a variable-cost percentage of 80%. The company earns net income of $84,000 in 2002. The income tax rate is 40%.

Compute (1) operating income, (2) contribution margin, (3) total revenues, and (4) breakeven revenues. **Required**

3-23 CVP analysis, income taxes. The Rapid Meal has two restaurants that are open 24 hours a day. Fixed costs for the two restaurants together total $450,000 per year. Service varies from a cup of coffee to full meals. The average sales check per customer is $8.00. The average cost of food and other variable costs for each customer is $3.20. The income tax rate is 30 percent. Target net income is $105,000.

Required

1. Compute the revenues needed to obtain the target net income.
2. How many customers are needed to break even? To earn net income of $105,000?
3. Compute net income if the number of customers is 150,000.

3-24 CVP analysis, sensitivity analysis. Hoot Washington is the newly elected leader of the Republican Party. He is the darling of the right-wing media. His attitude has left many an opponent on talk shows feeling run over by a Mack truck.

Media Publishers is negotiating to publish *Hoot's Manifesto*, a new book that promises to be an instant best-seller. The fixed costs of producing and marketing the book will be $500,000. The variable costs of producing and marketing will be $4.00 per copy sold. These costs are before any payments to Hoot. Hoot negotiates an up-front payment of $3 million, plus a 15% royalty rate on the net sales price of each book. The net sales price is the listed bookstore price of $30, minus the margin paid to the bookstore to sell the book. The normal bookstore margin of 30% of the listed bookstore price is expected to apply.

Required

1. Prepare a PV graph for Media Publishers.
2. How many copies must Media Publishers sell to (a) break even and (b) earn a target operating income of $2 million?
3. Examine the sensitivity of the breakeven point to the following changes:
   a. Decreasing the normal bookstore margin to 20% of the listed bookstore price of $30.
   b. Increasing the listed bookstore price to $40 while keeping the bookstore margin at 30 percent.
   c. Comment on the results.

3-25 CVP analysis, margin of safety. Suppose Lattin Corp.'s breakeven point is revenues of $1,000,000. Fixed costs are $400,000.

Required

1. Compute the contribution margin percentage.
2. Compute the selling price if variable costs are $12 per unit.
3. Suppose 80,000 units are sold. Compute the margin of safety.

3-26 Operating leverage. Color Rugs is holding a two-week carpet sale at Jerry's Club, a local warehouse store. Color Rugs plans to sell carpets for $500 each. The company will purchase the carpets from a local distributor for $350 each, with the privilege of returning any unsold units for a full refund. Jerry's Club has offered Color Rugs two payment alternatives for the use of space.

Option 1: A fixed payment of $5,000 for the sale period.
Option 2: 10% of total revenues earned during the sale period.

Assume Color Rugs will incur no other costs.

Required

1. Calculate the breakeven point in units for (a) option 1 and (b) option 2.
2. At what level of revenues will Color Rugs earn the same operating income under either option?
3. a. For what range of unit sales will Color Rugs prefer option 1?
   b. For what range of unit sales will Color Rugs prefer option 2?
4. Calculate the degree of operating leverage at sales of 100 units for the two rental options.
5. Briefly explain and interpret your answer to requirement 4.

3-27 CVP analysis, international cost structure differences. Knitwear, Inc., is considering three countries for the sole manufacturing site of its new sweater: Singapore, Thailand, and the United States. All sweaters are to be sold to retail outlets in the United States at $32 per unit. These retail outlets add their own markup when selling to final customers. The three countries differ in their fixed cost and their variable cost per sweater.

Country	Annual Fixed Costs	Variable Manufacturing Cost per Sweater	Variable Marketing & Distribution Cost per Sweater
Singapore	$ 6.5 million	$ 8.00	$11.00
Thailand	4.5 million	5.50	11.50
United States	12.0 million	13.00	9.00

Required

1. Compute the breakeven point of Knitwear, Inc., in (a) units sold for each country and (b) revenues for each country.
2. If Knitwear, Inc., sells 800,000 sweaters in 2002, what is the budgeted operating income for each countrry? Comment on the results.

3-28 Sales mix, new and upgrade customers. Zapo 1-2-3 is a top-selling electronic spreadsheet product. Zapo is about to release version 5.0. It divides its customers into two groups: new customers and upgrade customers (those who previously purchased Zapo 1-2-3, 4.0 or earlier versions). Although the same physical product is provided to each customer group, sizable differences exist in selling prices and variable marketing costs:

	New Customers		Upgrade Customers	
Selling price		$210		$120
Variable costs				
Manufacturing	$25		$25	
Marketing	65	90	15	40
Contribution margin		$120		$ 80

The fixed costs of Zapo 5.0 are $14,000,000. The planned sales mix in units is 60% new customers and 40% upgrade customers.

Required

1. What is the Zapo 1-2-3 5.0 breakeven point in units, assuming that the planned 60%/40% sales mix is attained?
2. If the sales mix is attained, what is the operating income when 200,000 units are sold?
3. Show how the breakeven point in units changes with the following customer mixes:
   a. New 50%/Upgrade 50% **b.** New 90%/Upgrade 10% **c.** Comment on the results.

3-29 Athletic scholarships, CVP analysis. Midwest University has an annual budget of $5,000,000 for athletic scholarships. Each athletic scholarship is for $20,000 per year. Fixed operating costs of the athletic scholarship program are $600,000, and variable operating costs are $2,000 per scholarship offered.

Required

1. Determine the number of athletic scholarships Midwest University can offer each year.
2. Suppose the total budget for next year is reduced by 22%. Fixed costs are to remain the same. Calculate the number of athletic scholarships that Midwest can offer next year.
3. As in requirement 2, assume a budget reduction of 22% and the same fixed costs. If Midwest wanted to offer the same number of athletic scholarships as it did in requirement 1, calculate the amount that will be paid to each student who receives a scholarship.

3-30 CVP analysis, multiple cost drivers. Susan Wong is a distributor of brass picture frames. For 2002, she plans to purchase frames for $30 each and sell them for $45 each. Susan's fixed costs for 2002 are expected to be $240,000. Susan's only other costs will be variable costs of $60 per shipment for preparing the invoice and delivery documents, organizing the delivery, and following up for collecting accounts receivable. The $60 cost will be incurred each time Susan ships an order of picture frames, regardless of the number of frames in the order.

Required

1. **a.** Suppose Susan sells 40,000 picture frames in 1,000 shipments in 2002. Calculate Susan's 2002 operating income.
   b. Suppose Susan sells 40,000 picture frames in 800 shipments in 2002. Calculate Susan's 2002 operating income.
2. Suppose Susan anticipates making 500 shipments in 2002. How many picture frames must Susan sell to break even in 2002?
3. Calculate another breakeven point for 2002, different from the one described in requirement 2. Explain briefly why Susan has multiple breakeven points.

3-31 Gross margin and contribution margin. (R. Lambert, adapted) Foreman Fork, Inc.'s income statement for 2003 on production and sales of 200,000 units is as follows:

Revenues	$2,600,000
Cost of goods sold	1,600,000
Gross margin	1,000,000
Marketing and distribution costs	1,150,000
Operating income (loss)	$ (150,000)

Foreman's fixed manufacturing costs are $500,000, and variable marketing and distribution costs are $4 per unit.

Required

1. a. Calculate Foreman's variable manufacturing cost per unit in 2003.
   b. Calculate Foreman's fixed marketing and distribution costs in 2003.
2. Foreman's gross margin per unit is $5 ($1,000,000 ÷ 200,000 units). Sam Hogan, Foreman's president, believes that if production and sales had been 230,000 units, it would have covered the $1,150,000 of marketing and distribution costs ($1,150,000 ÷ 5 = 230,000) and enabled Foreman to break even for the year. Calculate Foreman's operating income if production and sales equal 230,000 units. Explain briefly why Sam Hogan is wrong.
3. Calculate the breakeven point for 2003 in units and in revenues.

3-32 **Uncertainty, CVP analysis.** (Chapter Appendix) Angela King is the Las Vegas promoter for boxer Mike Foreman. King is promoting a new world championship fight for Foreman. The key area of uncertainty is the size of the cable pay-per-view TV market. King will pay Foreman a fixed fee of $2 million and 25% of net cable pay-per-view revenues. Every cable TV home receiving the event pays $29.95, of which King receives $16. King pays Foreman 25% of the $16.

King estimates the following probability distribution for homes purchasing the pay-per-view event:

Demand	Probability
100,000	0.05
200,000	0.10
300,000	0.30
400,000	0.35
500,000	0.15
1,000,000	0.05

Required

1. What is the expected value of the payment King will make to Foreman?
2. Assume the only uncertainty is about cable TV demand for the fight. King wants to know the breakeven point, given her own fixed costs of $1 million and her own variable costs of $2 per home. (Also include King's payments to Foreman in calculating your answer.)

Problems

3-33 **CVP analysis, service firm.** Wildlife Escapes generates average revenue of $4,000 per person on its five-day package tours to wildlife parks in Kenya. The variable costs per person are

Airfare	$1,500
Hotel accommodations	1,000
Meals	300
Ground transportation	600
Park tickets and other costs	200
Total	$3,600

Annual fixed costs total $480,000.

Required

1. Calculate the number of package tours that must be sold to break even.
2. Calculate the revenue needed to earn a target operating income of $100,000.
3. If fixed costs increase by $24,000, what decrease in variable costs must be achieved to maintain the breakeven point calculated in requirement **1**?

3-34 **CVP, target income, service firm.** Teddy Bear Daycare provides daycare for children Mondays through Fridays. Its monthly variable costs per child are

Lunch and snacks	$ 100
Educational supplies	75
Other supplies (paper products, toiletries, etc.)	25
Total	$ 200

Monthly fixed costs consist of

Rent	$2,000
Utilities	300
Insurance	300
Salaries	2,500
Miscellaneous	500
	$5,600

Teddy Bear charges each parent $600 per child

Required

1. Calculate the breakeven point.
2. Teddy Bear's target operating income is $10,400 per month. Compute the number of children that must be enrolled to achieve the target operating income.

3. Teddy Bear lost its lease and had to move to another building. Monthly rent for the new building is $3,000. At the suggestion of parents, Teddy Bear plans to take children on field trips. Monthly costs of the field trips are $1,000. By how much should Teddy Bear increase fees per child to meet the target operating income of $10,400 per month, assuming the same number of children as in requirement 2?

3-35 CVP analysis. (CMA, adapted) Galaxy Disk's projected operating income for 2003 is $200,000, based on a sales volume of 200,000 units. Galaxy sells disks for $16 each. Variable costs consist of the $10 purchase price and a $2 shipping and handling cost. Galaxy's annual fixed costs are $600,000.

Required

1. Calculate Galaxy's breakeven point in units.
2. Calculate the company's operating income in 2003 if there is a 10% increase in projected unit sales.
3. For 2004, management expects that the unit purchase price of the disks will increase by 30%. Calculate the sales revenue Galaxy must generate in 2004 to maintain the current year's operating income if the selling price remains unchanged.

3-36 CVP analysis, income taxes. (CMA, adapted) R. A. Ro and Company, a manufacturer of quality handmade walnut bowls, has had a steady growth in sales for the past five years. However, increased competition has led Mr. Ro, the president, to believe that an aggressive marketing campaign will be necessary next year to maintain the company's present growth. To prepare for next year's marketing campaign, the company's controller has prepared and presented Mr. Ro with the following data for the current year, 2003:

Variable costs (per bowl)	
Direct materials	$ 3.25
Direct manufacturing labor	8.00
Variable overhead (Manufacturing, marketing, distribution, and customer service)	2.50
Total variable costs	$ 13.75
Fixed costs	
Manufacturing	$ 25,000
Marketing, distribution, and customer service	110,000
Total fixed costs	$135,000
Selling price	$25.00
Expected sales, 20,000 units	$500,000
Income tax rate	40%

Required

1. What is the projected net income for 2003?
2. What is the breakeven point in units for 2003?
3. Mr. Ro has set the revenue target for 2004 at a level of $550,000 (or 22,000 bowls). He believes an additional marketing cost of $11,250 for advertising in 2004, with all other costs remaining constant, will be necessary to attain the revenue target. What is the net income for 2004 if the additional $11,250 is spent and the revenue target is met?
4. What is the breakeven point in revenues for 2004 if the additional $11,250 is spent for advertising?
5. If the additional $11,250 is spent, what are the required 2004 revenues for 2004's net income to equal 2003's net income?
6. At a sales level of 22,000 units, what maximum amount can be spent on advertising if a 2004 net income of $60,000 is desired?

3-37 CVP analysis, decision making. (M. Rajan, adapted) Tocchet Company manufactures CB1, a citizens band radio. The company's plant has an annual capacity of 50,000 units. Tocchet currently sells 40,000 units at a price of $105. It has the following cost structure:

Variable manufacturing cost per unit	$45
Fixed manufacturing costs	$800,000
Variable marketing and distribution cost per unit	$10
Fixed marketing and distribution costs	$600,000

Required Consider each requirement independently.

1. The Marketing Department indicates that decreasing the selling price to $99 would increase sales to 50,000 units. This strategy will require Tocchet to increase its fixed marketing and distribution costs. Calculate the *maximum* increase in fixed marketing and distribution costs that will allow Tocchet to reduce the selling price to $99 and maintain its operating income.
2. The Manufacturing Department proposes changes in the manufacturing process to add new features to the CB1 product. These changes will increase fixed manufacturing costs by $100,000 and variable manufacturing cost per unit by $2. At its current sales quantity of 40,000 units, compute the *minimum* selling price that will allow Tocchet to add these new features and maintain its operating income.

3-38 Margin of safety. Cooper Company manufactures footballs. Its budget data for a popular brand "Cornhusker" for the next year are

Sales (10,000 units)	$1,000,000
Variable costs	600,000
Contribution margin	400,000
Fixed costs	250,000
Operating income	$ 150,000

Required

1. Calculate breakeven point in units and dollars.
2. Calculate margin of safety in units and dollars.
3. Calculate Cooper's contribution margin ratio. If actual sales are $200,000 above the budgeted amount, use the contribution margin ratio to calculate the incremental operating income.

3-39 CVP analysis, shoe stores. The Walk Rite Shoe Company operates a chain of shoe stores. The stores sell 10 different styles of inexpensive men's shoes with identical unit costs and selling prices. A unit is defined as a pair of shoes. Each store has a store manager who is paid a fixed salary. Individual salespeople receive a fixed salary and a sales commission. Walk Rite is trying to determine whether to open another store, which is expected to have the following revenue and cost relationships:

Unit variable data (per pair of shoes)	
Selling price	$ 30.00
Cost of shoes	$ 19.50
Sales commissions	1.50
Variable costs per unit	$ 21.00
Annual fixed costs	
Rent	$ 60,000
Salaries	200,000
Advertising	80,000
Other fixed costs	20,000
Total fixed costs	$360,000

Consider each question independently.

Required

1. What is the annual breakeven point in (a) units sold and (b) revenues?
2. If 35,000 units are sold, what will be the store's operating income (loss)?
3. If sales commissions were discontinued for individual salespeople in favor of an $81,000 increase in fixed salaries, what would be the annual breakeven point in (a) units sold and (b) revenues?
4. Refer to the original data. If the store manager were paid $0.30 per unit sold in addition to his current fixed salary, what would be the annual breakeven point in (a) units sold and (b) revenues?
5. Refer to the original data. If the store manager were paid $0.30 per unit commission on each unit sold in excess of the breakeven point, what would be the store's operating income if 50,000 units were sold? (This $0.30 is in addition to both the commission paid to the sales staff and the store manager's fixed salary.)

Excel Application For students who wish to practice their spreadsheet skills, the following is a step-by-step approach to creating an Excel spreadsheet to work this problem.

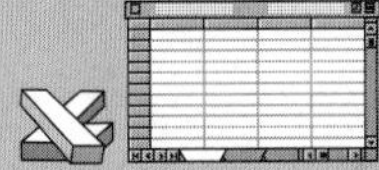

Step-by-Step

1. At the top of a new spreadsheet, create an "Original Data" section for the data provided by Walk Rite. Create rows for the unit variable data and annual fixed cost data in the same format as shown for Walk Rite above.
   (Program your spreadsheet to perform all necessary calculations. Do not "hard-code" any amounts, such as breakeven quantities or revenues, requiring addition, subtraction, multiplication, or division operations.)
2. Skip down rows. Create a new section labeled "Problem 1." Create rows for "Contribution margin per unit," "a. Breakeven units," and "b. Breakeven revenues." Use the data in the "Original Data" section and enter calculations for contribution margin, breakeven units, and breakeven revenues in rows a and b.
3. Skip two rows and create a new section labeled "Problem 2." Create rows for revenues, cost of shoes, sales commissions, total variable costs , contribution margin, total fixed costs, and operating income. The format should be similar to the contribution income statement in the "Merchandising Sector" section on page 77. Enter calculations for cost of shoes and sales commissions, total revenues, total variable costs, contribution margin, total fixed costs, and operating income.
4. Skip two rows. Create a new section labeled "Problem 3" using the same format created for "Problem 1." Enter calculations for contribution margin, breakeven units, and breakeven revenues that reflect the discontinuance of sales commissions and increase in fixed salaries.
5. Skip two rows. Create a new section labeled "Problem 4" using the same format as steps 2 and 4. Enter calculations for contribution margin, breakeven units, and breakeven revenues that reflect the new fixed-salary plus commission structure.
6. Skip two rows. Create a new section labeled "Problem 5." Create a contribution income statement using the same format as created for "Problem 2." Enter the same calculations as in step 3, reflecting the new salary plus commission structure and the 50,000 units sold.

7. *Verify the accuracy of your spreadsheet.* Go to your "Original Data" section and change the cost of shoes from $19.50 to $20.00. If your spreadsheet is programmed correctly, breakeven revenues in Problem 1 should change to $1,270,588 and operating income in Problem 5 should change to $62,706.

3-40 CVP analysis, shoe stores (continuation of 3-39). Refer to requirement 3 of 3-39.

Required

1. Calculate the number of units sold at which the operating income under the fixed-salary plan and the lower fixed-salary-and-commission plan (for salespeople only) would be equal. Above that number of units sold, one plan would be more profitable than the other; below that number of units sold, the reverse would occur.
2. Compute the operating income or loss under each plan in requirement 1 at sales levels of (a) 50,000 units and (b) 60,000 units.
3. Suppose the target operating income is $168,000. How many units must be sold to reach the target under (a) the fixed-salary plan and (b) the lower fixed-salary-and-commission plan?

3-41 Sensitivity and inflation (continuation of 3-40). As president of Walk Rite, you are concerned that inflation may squeeze your profitability. Specifically, you feel committed to the $30 selling price and fear that decreasing the quality of the shoes in the face of rising costs would be an unwise move. You expect the cost of shoes to rise by 10% during the coming year. You are tempted to avoid the cost increase by placing a noncancelable order with a large supplier that would provide 50,000 units of the specified quality for each store at $19.50 per unit. (To simplify this analysis, assume that all stores will face identical demands.) These shoes could be acquired and paid for as delivered throughout the year. However, all shoes must be delivered to the stores by the end of the year.

As a shrewd merchandiser, you foresee some risks. If sales were less than 50,000 units, you feel that markdowns of the unsold merchandise would be necessary to sell the goods. You predict that the average selling price of the leftover units would be $18.00. The regular commission of 5% of revenues would be paid to salespeople.

Required

1. Suppose that actual sales for the year are 48,000 units at $30 per unit and that you contracted for 50,000 units. What is the operating income for the store?
2. If you had perfect forecasting ability, you would have contracted for 48,000 units rather than 50,000 units. What would the operating income have been if you had ordered 48,000 units?
3. Given actual sales of 48,000 units, by how much would the average cost per unit have had to rise before you would have been indifferent to having the contract for 50,000 units or not having the contract?

3-42 CVP analysis, income taxes, sensitivity. (CMA, adapted) Almo Company manufactures and sells adjustable canopies that attach to motor homes and trailers. For its 2004 budget, Almo estimated the following:

Selling price	$400
Variable cost per canopy	$200
Annual fixed costs	$100,000
Net income	$240,000
Income tax rate	40%

The May financial statements reported that sales were not meeting expectations. For the first five months of the year, only 350 units had been sold at the established price, with variable costs as planned, and it was clear that the net income projection for 2004 would not be reached unless some actions were taken. A management committee presented the following mutually exclusive alternatives to the president.

a. Reduce the selling price by $40. The sales organization forecasts that at this significantly reduced price, 2,700 units can be sold during the remainder of the year. Total fixed costs and variable cost per unit will stay as budgeted.

b. Lower variable cost per unit by $10 through the use of less expensive direct materials and slightly modified manufacturing techniques. The selling price will also be reduced by $30, and sales of 2,200 units are expected for the remainder of the year.

c. Reduce fixed costs by $10,000 and lower the selling price by 5%. Variable cost per unit will be unchanged. Sales of 2,000 units are expected for the remainder of the year.

Required

1. If no changes are made to the selling price or cost structure, determine the number of units that Almo Company must sell (a) to break even and (b) to achieve its net income objective.
2. Determine which alternative Almo should select to achieve its net income objective. Show your calculations.

3-43 Choosing between compensation plans, operating leverage. (CMA, adapted) Marston Corporation manufactures pharmaceutical products that are sold through a network of sales agents. The agents are paid a commission of 18% of revenues. The income statement for the year ending December 31, 2002, is as follows:

Marston Corporation
Income Statement
For the Year Ended December 31, 2002

Revenues		$26,000,000
Cost of goods sold		
Variable	$11,700,000	
Fixed	2,870,000	14,570,000
Gross margin		11,430,000
Marketing costs		
Commissions	4,680,000	
Fixed costs	3,420,000	8,100,000
Operating income		$ 3,330,000

Marston is considering hiring its own sales staff to replace the network of sales agents. Marston would pay its salespeople a commission of 10% of revenues and incur additional fixed costs of $2,080,000.

Required

1. Calculate Marston Corporation's breakeven point in revenues for 2002.
2. Calculate Marston Corporation's breakeven point in revenues for 2002 if the company had hired its own sales force in 2002 to replace the network of sales agents.
3. Calculate the degree of operating leverage at revenues of $26,000,000 if (a) Marston uses sales agents and (b) Marston employs its own sales staff. Describe the advantages and disadvantages of each alternative.
4. If Marston had hired its own sales staff and increased the commission paid to them to 15%, keeping all other cost behavior patterns the same, how much revenue would Marston have to generate to earn the same operating income as in 2002?

3-44 Sales mix, three products. The Ronowski Company has three product lines of belts: A, B, and C, with contribution margins of $3, $2, and $1, respectively. The president foresees sales of 200,000 units in the coming period, consisting of 20,000 units of A, 100,000 units of B, and 80,000 units of C. The company's fixed costs for the period are $255,000.

Required

1. What is the company's breakeven point in units, assuming that the given sales mix is maintained?
2. If the sales mix is maintained, what is the total contribution margin when 200,000 units are sold? What is the operating income?
3. What would operating income be if 20,000 units of A, 80,000 units of B, and 100,000 units of C were sold? What is the new breakeven point in units if these relationships persist in the next period?

3-45 Multiproduct breakeven, decision making. Evenkeel Corporation manufactures and sells one product—an infant car seat called Plumar—at a price of $50. Variable costs equal $20 per car seat. Fixed costs are $495,000. Evenkeel manufactures Plumar upon the receipt of orders from its customers. In 2003, it sold 30,000 units of Plumar. One of Evenkeel's customers, Glaston Corporation, has asked if in 2004 Evenkeel will manufacture a different style of car seat called Ridex. Glaston will pay $25 for each unit of Ridex. The variable costs for Ridex are estimated to be $15 per seat. Evenkeel has enough capacity to manufacture all the units of Plumar it can sell as well as the units of Ridex that Glaston wants and will thus incur no additional fixed costs. Evenkeel estimates that in 2004 it will sell 30,000 units of Plumar (assuming the same price and variable costs in 2003) and 20,000 units of Ridex.

Andy Minton, the president of Evenkeel, checked the effect of accepting Glaston's offer on the breakeven revenues for 2004. Using the planned sales mix for 2004, he was surprised to find that the revenues required to break even appeared to increase. He was not sure that his numbers were correct, but if they were, Andy felt inclined to reject Glaston's offer. He asks for your advice.

Required

1. Calculate the breakeven point in units and in revenues for 2003.
2. Calculate the breakeven point in units and in revenues for 2004 at the planned sales mix.
3. Explain why the breakeven point in revenues calculated in requirements 1 and 2 are different.
4. Should Andy accept Glaston's offer? Provide supporting computations.

3-46 Sales mix, two products. The Goldman Company retails two products, a standard and a deluxe version of a luggage carrier. The budgeted income statement for next period is as follows:

	Standard Carrier	Deluxe Carrier	Total
Units sold	150,000	50,000	200,000
Revenues at $20 and $30 per unit	$3,000,000	$1,500,000	$4,500,000
Variable costs at $14 and $18 per unit	2,100,000	900,000	3,000,000
Contribution margins at $6 and $12 per unit	$ 900,000	$ 600,000	1,500,000
Fixed costs			1,200,000
Operating income			$ 300,000

Required

1. Compute the breakeven point in units, assuming that the planned sales mix is attained.
2. Compute the breakeven point in units (a) if only standard carriers are sold and (b) if only deluxe carriers are sold.
3. Suppose 200,000 units are sold, but only 20,000 of them are deluxe. Compute the operating income. Compute the breakeven point in units. Compare your answer with the answer to requirement 1. What is the major lesson of this problem?

3-47 CVP analysis under uncertainty. (Chapter Appendix, R. Jaedicke and A. Robichek, adapted) The Jaro Company is considering two new colors for their umbrella products: emerald green and shocking pink. Either can be produced using present facilities. Each product requires an increase in annual fixed costs of $400,000. The products have the same $10 selling price and the same $8 variable cost per unit.

Management, after studying past experience with similar products, has prepared the following probability distribution:

	Probability for	
Event (Units Demanded)	**Emerald Green Umbrella**	**Shocking Pink Umbrella**
50,000	0.0	0.1
100,000	0.1	0.1
200,000	0.2	0.1
300,000	0.4	0.2
400,000	0.2	0.4
500,000	0.1	0.1
	1.0	1.0

Required

1. What is the breakeven point in units for each product?
2. Which product should be chosen, assuming the objective is to maximize expected operating income? Why? Show your computations.
3. Suppose management is absolutely certain that 300,000 units of shocking pink will be sold, but it still faces the same uncertainty about the demand for emerald green as outlined in the problem. Which product should be chosen? Why? What benefits are available to management from having the complete probability distribution instead of just an expected value?

3-48 Ethics, CVP analysis. Allen Corporation produces a molded plastic casing, LX201, for desktop computers. Summary data from its 2003 income statement are as follows:

Revenues	$5,000,000
Variable costs	3,000,000
Fixed costs	2,160,000
Operating income	$ (160,000)

Jane Woodall, Allen's president, is very concerned about Allen's poor profitability. She asks Max Lemond, production manager, and Lester Bush, controller, to see if there are ways to reduce costs.

After two weeks, Max returns with a proposal to reduce variable costs to 52% of revenues by reducing the costs Allen currently incurs for safe disposal of wasted plastic. Lester is concerned that this would expose the company to potential environmental liabilities. He tells Max, "We would need to estimate some of these potential environmental costs and include them in our analysis." "You can't do that," Max replies. "We are not violating any laws. There is some possibility that we may have to incur environmental costs in the future, but if we bring it up now, this proposal will not go through because our senior management always assumes these costs to be larger than they turn out to be. The market is very tough, and we are in danger of shutting down the company. We don't want all our colleagues to lose their jobs. The only reason our competitors are making money is because they are doing exactly what I am proposing."

Required

1. Calculate Allen's breakeven revenues for 2003.
2. Calculate Allen's breakeven revenues if variable costs are 52% of revenues.
3. Calculate Allen's operating income in 2003 if variable costs had been 52% of revenues.
4. Given Max Lemond's comments, what should Lester Bush do?

Collaborative Learning Problem

3-49 Deciding where to produce. (CMA, adapted) The PTO Division produces the same power takeoff units in two plants, a new plant in Peoria, and an older plant in Moline. The PTO Division expected to produce and sell 192,000 power takeoff units during the coming year. The following data are available for the two plants.

	Peoria		Moline	
Selling price		$150.00		$150.00
Variable manufacturing cost per unit	$72.00		$88.00	
Fixed manufacturing cost per unit	30.00		15.00	
Variable marketing and distribution cost per unit	14.00		14.00	
Fixed marketing and distribution cost per unit	19.00		14.50	
Total cost per unit		135.00		131.50
Operating income per unit		$ 15.00		$ 18.50
Production rate per day	400 units		320 units	

All fixed costs per unit are calculated based on a normal year consists of 240 working days. When the number of working days exceeds 240, variable manufacturing costs increase by $3.00 per unit in Peoria and $8.00 per unit in Moline. Capacity for each plant is 300 working days per year.

Wishing to take advantage of the higher operating income per unit at Moline, PTO's production manager has decided to manufacture 96,000 units at each plant. This production plan results in Moline operating at capacity (320 units per day x 300 days) and Peoria operating at its normal volume (400 units per day × 240 days).

Required

1. Calculate the breakeven point in units for the Peoria and Moline plants.
2. Calculate the operating income that would result from the production manager's plan to produce 96,000 units at each plant.
3. Determine how the production of the 192,000 units should be allocated between the Peoria and Moline plants to maximize operating income for the PTO Division. Show your calculations.

CHAPTER 3 INTERNET EXERCISE

Southwest Airlines enjoys the distinction of having the lowest operating cost structure in the domestic airline industry. Its costs structure influences its overall profitability, and has important strategic implications. To better understand these concepts, go to www.prenhall.com/horngren, click on *Cost Accounting,* 11th ed., and access the Internet exercise for Chapter 3.

CHAPTER 3 VIDEO CASE

STORE 24: Cost-Volume-Profit Analysis

Modern convenience stores realize they have to offer more than late-night hours and diverse product assortment; they have to change with the times or face extinction. Over the years, they have added new products and services, such as motor fuel, lottery tickets, and even Internet shopping and delivery services. A walk through any convenience store is likely to reveal in excess of 3,000 different products and services, available, in many cases, 24 hours a day, seven days a week. There are over 24,000 convenience stores scattered across the United States. The convenience store industry generated $269.4 billion in sales in 2000.

Store 24, headquartered in Waltham, Massachusetts, operates 82 stores in its chain of convenience stores. Locations are primarily in the Northeastern United States, where there are about 2,200 convenience stores—approximately 9% of the country's total. The average sale is $3.00, with a gross margin of 30%. As part of an accounting class assignment, Maria Lopez made a visit to the Store 24 headquarters to learn more about the company. The class instructor directed the students to find a local business that uses cost-volume-profit (CVP) analysis for decision-making, and identify a scenario where CVP analysis was used. Since Maria worked part-time at the Store 24 in her neighborhood after school, she wanted to use her employer for the assignment.

Paul Doucette, Store 24's chief financial officer, agreed to meet Maria and help with her assignment. Paul assembled a set of reports and information Maria might find useful for the assignment. Paul told Maria that Store 24 uses CVP analysis in many situations. For example, company managers recently evaluated preparing in-store deli sandwiches for lunchtime customers versus pre-packaged deli sandwiches provided by an outside supplier. The effect on income of the store's sales mix also had been reviewed, and sensitivity analysis had been performed to see the effect of changing the selling price of milk.

One recent use of CVP analysis that Paul thought would make a good illustration for Maria was its decision surrounding the sale of money orders at its stores. Paul explained this was a new product area for the company—a "financial service," much like what a bank would offer. By offering this new service, Store 24 hoped to boost its customer count. Previous studies had shown that

Continued

customers were likely to buy more than just the items they originally intended to purchase. Store 24 wanted to boost sales revenue by giving customers another reason to come into the store—and buy more than intended.

Paul outlined for Maria the following information related to the analysis. The price of renting the machine used in each store to prepare money orders is $25 per month. For each money order processed, Store 24 paid a processing fee of five cents. After conducting an informal survey of banks and other local businesses that offered money order services, Store 24 found most charging 99 cents for each money order transaction. Store 24 decided to price its money order fee at 69 cents to undercut the local competition. Paul estimated that a money order transaction would take one counter clerk 90 seconds to complete, versus only 30 seconds for ringing up a product sale. The average hourly wage rate for a store clerk is $9.00 per hour.

QUESTIONS

1. What kinds of customers might be attracted to the money order service? Would you expect these customers to be typical of a convenience store such as Store 24?
2. What is the contribution margin per unit (money order)?
3. Using both the equation method and contribution margin method, how many money orders would each Store 24 location have to sell each month in order to break even on the service?
4. How many money orders would each Store 24 location need to sell to earn an operating income of $100 per month?
5. Studies have found that convenience store customers don't like to wait in line for service. What effect might the offering of money orders have if there's only one clerk staffed at the cash register each shift?

CHAPTER

4

Job Costing

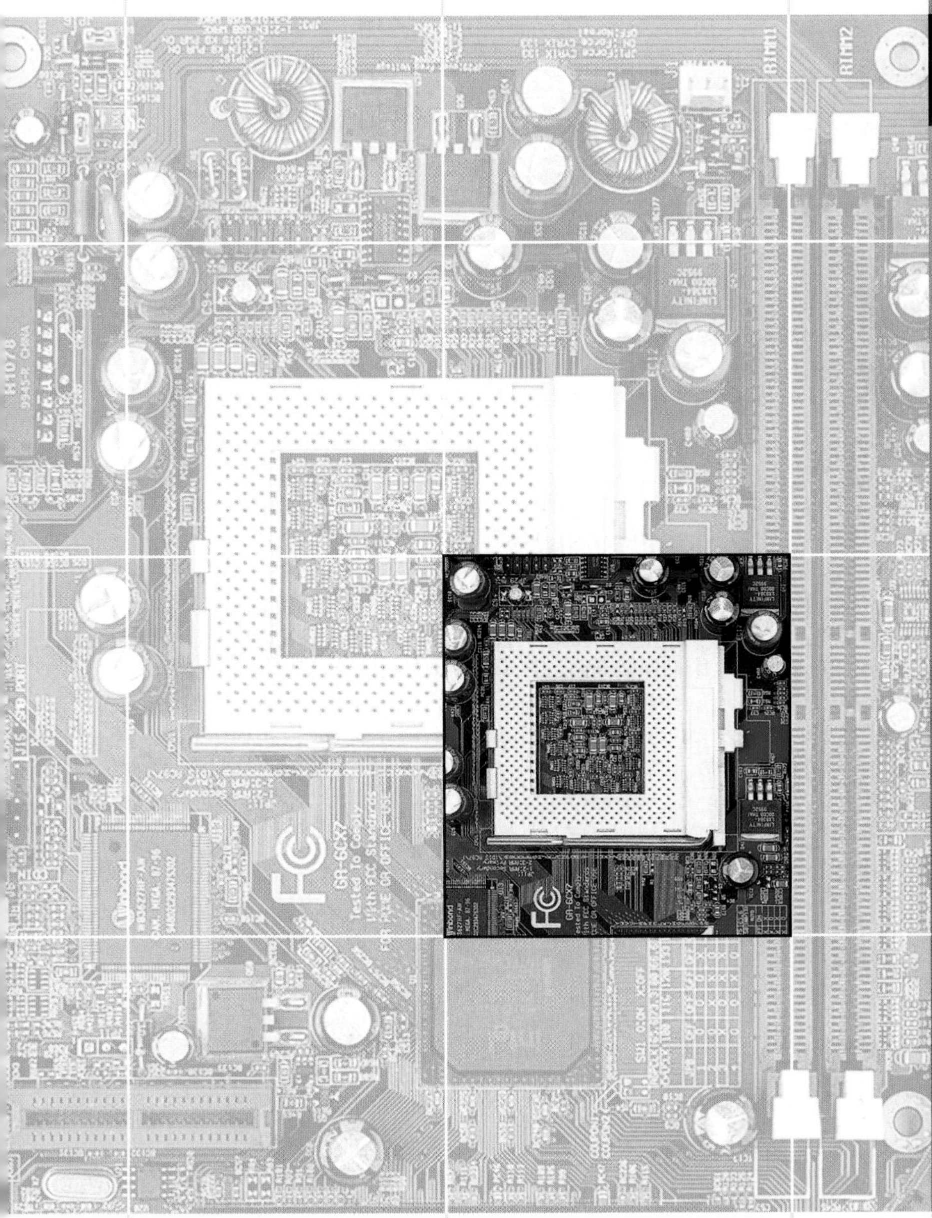

LEARNING OBJECTIVES

1. Describe the building-block concepts of costing systems
2. Distinguish job costing from process costing
3. Outline the seven-step approach to job costing
4. Distinguish actual costing from normal costing
5. Track the flow of costs in a job-costing system
6. Account for end-of-period underallocated or overallocated indirect costs using alternative methods
7. Apply variations from normal costing

www.prenhall.com/horngren

How much does it cost DaimlerChrysler to manufacture a PT Cruiser? How much does it cost PriceWaterhouseCoopers to tabulate the results of Academy Award voting? How much does it cost Wal-Mart to sell different products from its Web site? How much does it cost Dell Computer to assemble and sell its newest laptop computer model? Managers ask such questions for many purposes, including developing strategies, making pricing and cost-management decisions, and meeting external-reporting requirements. Each of these questions relate to a "job," with specific costs associated with completing the work to do that specific job.

Dell produces many models and types of computers, ranging from the least expensive of the Inspiron laptop line to the most expensive of the Dimension desktop series; but not without first receiving customer orders specifying the features each customer wants. Each computer consists of specified hardware components, such as circuit boards, processing and memory chips, and secondary storage devices, that will fulfill a customer's specified features. Each hardware item has a cost attached to it. There are also wages paid to the workers who assemble each computer. These hardware and labor costs are considered direct costs related to the job of assembling a specific computer to meet a customer's order. There are also indirect costs, such as heat and lighting costs of the manufacturing facility. Dell considers each computer order as a separate job, and tracks the costs of each order. This accounting helps Dell managers answer questions related to current-period profitability, as well as to devise future strategic directions.

To begin to explore the details of costing systems, you will find it helpful to keep these four points in mind.

1. *The cost-benefit approach we discussed in Chapter 1 (p. 13) is essential in designing and choosing costing systems.* The costs of a complex costing system, including the costs of educating managers and other personnel to use it, can be high. Managers should install a more complex system only if they believe that its additional benefits—such as making better informed decisions—will outweigh the additional costs.

Each company's costing system needs to be designed to supply managers with information for running the business. The company's strategy and processes guide accountants in designing the costing system. The costing system should *never* dictate the choice of strategy or processes.

2. *Costing systems should be tailored to the underlying operations; the operations should not be tailored to fit the costing systems.* Any significant change in operations is likely to justify a corresponding change in the costing system. Designing the best system begins with a study of how operations are conducted and then determining from that study what information to gather and report.

3. *Costing systems accumulate costs to facilitate decisions.* Because it's not always possible to foresee specific decisions that might be necessary, costing systems are designed to fulfill several general needs of managers. In this chapter, we will focus on decisions regarding product costing. Therefore, we pay most attention to the part of the costing system that aims to report cost numbers that indicate the manner in which particular cost objects—such as products or services—use the resources of an organization. Managers use product-costing information to make decisions and strategy, and for planning and control, cost management, and inventory valuation.

4. *Costing systems are only one source of information for managers.* When making decisions, managers combine information on costs with other noncost information, such as personal observation of operations, and nonfinancial performance measures, such as setup times, absentee rates, and number of customer complaints.

1 Describe the building-block concepts of costing systems

...cost object, direct costs, indirect costs, cost pools, and cost-allocation bases

BUILDING-BLOCK CONCEPTS OF COSTING SYSTEMS

Let's review some terms discussed in Chapter 2 that we'll now use to introduce costing systems:

- *Cost object*—anything for which a measurement of costs is desired; an example is a product, such as an iMac computer, or a service, such as the cost of repairing an iMac computer.

- *Direct costs of a cost object*—costs related to a particular cost object that can be traced to that cost object in an economically feasible (cost-effective) way.
- *Indirect costs of a cost object*—costs related to a particular cost object that cannot be traced to that cost object in an economically feasible (cost-effective) way. Indirect costs are allocated to the cost object using a cost-allocation method.

Cost assignment is a general term for assigning costs, whether direct or indirect, to a cost object. Cost tracing is a specific term for assigning direct costs; cost allocation specifically refers to assigning indirect costs. The relationship among these three concepts can be graphically represented as

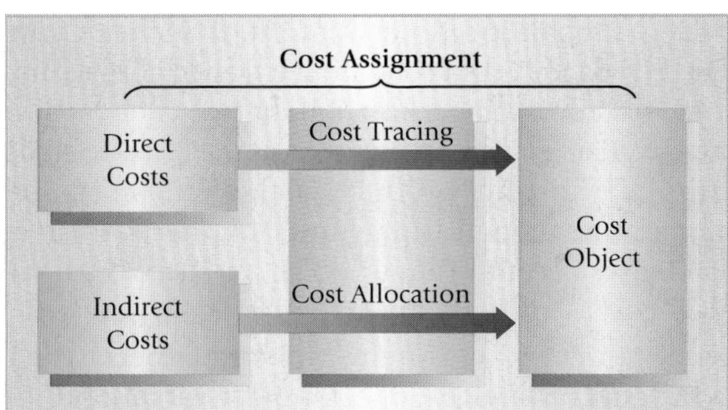

We need to introduce and explain two more terms to discuss costing systems:

- *Cost pool.* A **cost pool** is a grouping of individual cost items. Cost pools can range from broad, such as all costs of the manufacturing plant, to narrow, such as the costs of operating metal-cutting machines.
- *Cost-allocation base.* How should a company allocate costs to operate metal-cutting machines collected in a single cost pool among different products? One way would be to allocate the costs on the basis of the number of machine-hours used to produce the different products. The **cost-allocation base** (in our example, the number of machine-hours) is a factor that links in a systematic way an indirect cost or group of indirect costs (in our example, operating costs of all metal-cutting machines) to a cost object (in our example, different products). Companies often use the cost driver of indirect costs (number of machine-hours) as the cost-allocation base because of the cause-and-effect link between changes in the level of the cost driver and changes in indirect costs. A cost-allocation base can be either financial (such as direct labor costs) or nonfinancial (such as the number of machine-hours). When the cost object is a job, product, or customer, the cost-allocation base is also called a **cost-application base.**

The concepts represented by these five terms constitute the building blocks that we will use to design the costing systems described in this chapter.

Two Major Cost Objects: Products and Departments

Costs are recorded in an accounting system to help managers make decisions. Cost objects are chosen to help make those decisions. One major cost object of an accounting system is *products*. Another major cost object is *responsibility centers*, which are parts, segments, or subunits of an organization whose managers are accountable for specified activities. Examples of responsibility centers are departments, groups of departments, divisions, or geographic territories.

The most common responsibility center is a department. Identifying department costs helps managers control the costs for which they are responsible. It also enables senior managers to evaluate the performance of their subordinates and the performance of subunits as economic investments. In manufacturing companies, the costs of the Manufacturing Department include all costs of materials, manufacturing labor, supervision, engineering, production, and quality control.

You should be aware that supervision, engineering, and quality control costs, considered indirect or overhead costs when costing individual jobs, are considered direct costs of

These two cost objects (departments and products) illustrate two purposes of management accounting: providing information for (1) planning and control and (2) determining the cost of products. To illustrate, when manufacturing custom furniture, the cost of lumber and workers' wages are assigned to (1) the Production Department for control and performance evaluation (for example, did workers cut lumber and assemble furniture efficiently?) and (2) the finished pieces of furniture for inventory valuation. Estimating the cost of a piece of furniture *before* manufacturing occurs often is the basis of the pricing decision.

the Manufacturing Department. The reason is these costs are difficult to trace in an economically feasible way to individual jobs within the Manufacturing Department, but they are easily identified with and traced to the department itself.

2 Distinguish job costing ...to cost a distinct product **from process costing** ...to cost masses of identical or similar units

JOB-COSTING AND PROCESS-COSTING SYSTEMS

Two basic types of costing systems are used to assign costs to products or services:

- **Job-costing system.** In this system, the cost object is a unit or multiple units of a *distinct* product or service called a **job.** The product or service is often a single unit, such as a specialized machine made at Hitachi, a construction project managed by Bechtel Corporation, a repair job done at an Audi Service Center, or an advertising campaign produced by Saatchi and Saatchi. Each special machine made by Hitachi is unique and distinct. An advertising campaign for one client at Saatchi and Saatchi differs greatly from advertising campaigns for other clients. Job costing is also used to cost multiple units of a distinct product, such as the costs incurred by Raytheon Corporation to manufacture multiple units of the Patriot missile for the U.S. Department of Defense. Because the products and services are distinct, job-costing systems accumulate costs separately for each product or service.
- **Process-costing system.** In this system, the cost object is masses of *identical* or *similar* units of a product or service. For example, Citibank provides the same service to all its customers when processing customer deposits. Intel provides the same product (say, a Pentium 4 chip) to each of its customers. Customers of General Chemicals all receive the same product (say, soda ash). In each period, process-costing systems divide the total costs of producing an identical or similar product or service by the total number of units produced to obtain a per-unit cost. This per-unit cost is the average unit cost that applies to each of the identical or similar units produced.

Exhibit 4-1 presents examples of job costing and process costing in the service, merchandising, and manufacturing sectors.

These two types of costing systems are best considered as opposite ends of a continuum; in between, one type of system can blur into the other to some degree.

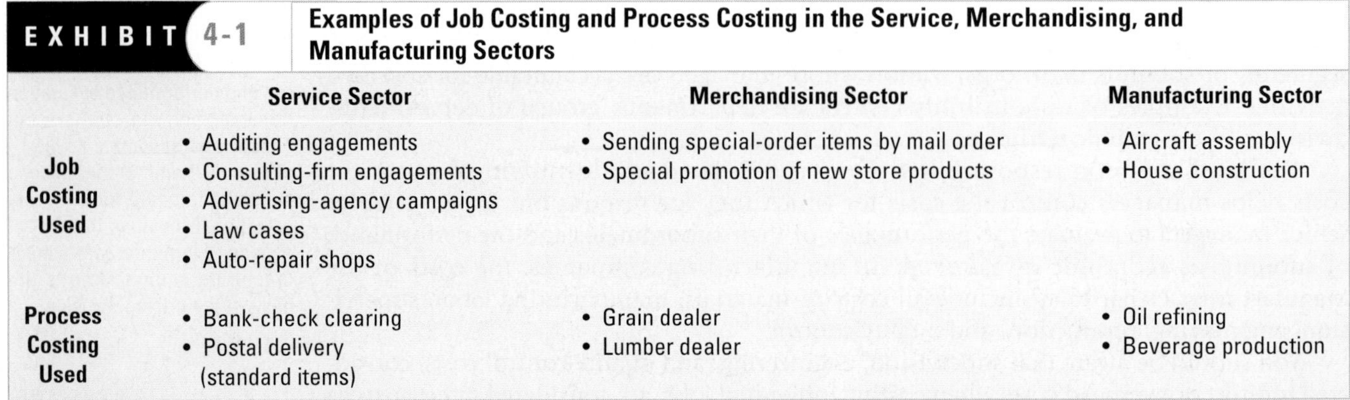

EXHIBIT 4-1 Examples of Job Costing and Process Costing in the Service, Merchandising, and Manufacturing Sectors

	Service Sector	Merchandising Sector	Manufacturing Sector
Job Costing Used	• Auditing engagements • Consulting-firm engagements • Advertising-agency campaigns • Law cases • Auto-repair shops	• Sending special-order items by mail order • Special promotion of new store products	• Aircraft assembly • House construction
Process Costing Used	• Bank-check clearing • Postal delivery (standard items)	• Grain dealer • Lumber dealer	• Oil refining • Beverage production

Many companies have costing systems that are neither pure job costing nor pure process costing but have elements of both. For example, Kellogg Corporation uses job costing to calculate the total cost to manufacture each of its different and distinct types of products—such as Cornflakes, Crispix, and Froot Loops—but process costing to calculate the per-unit cost of each box of Cornflakes, say. In this chapter, we focus on job-costing systems. Chapters 17 and 18 discuss process-costing systems.

JOB COSTING IN MANUFACTURING

We illustrate job costing using the Robinson Company, which operates at capacity to manufacture and install specialized machinery for the paper-making industry at its Green Bay, Wisconsin, plant. In its job-costing system, Robinson accumulates costs incurred on a job (the manufacture and installation of each machine) in different parts of the value chain—for example, manufacturing, marketing, and customer service. To start, we focus on Robinson's manufacturing and installation functions. To make a machine, Robinson purchases some of the components from outside suppliers and makes others itself. Each of Robinson's jobs has a service element: installing a machine at a customer's site, integrating it with the customer's other machines and processes, and ensuring it works as the customer expects. Our example spans both manufacturing operations and service operations.

The specific job we will focus on is the manufacture and installation of a small pulp machine, which converts wood to pulp, for Western Pulp and Paper Company in 2003. Based on a cost estimate, Robinson prices the job at $15,000. Knowledge about its own costs helps Robinson select a price that will make a profit, as well as make informed estimates of the costs of future jobs.

Consider Robinson's *actual costing* system, a job-costing system that uses *actual costs* to determine the cost of individual jobs. **Actual costing** is a costing method that traces direct costs to a cost object by using the actual direct-cost rates times the actual quantity of the direct-cost inputs. It allocates indirect costs based on the actual indirect-cost rates times the actual quantity of the cost-allocation bases. The next section describes the calculation of direct- and indirect-cost rates and actual costs.

General Approach to Job Costing

3 Outline the seven-step approach to job costing
...to compute direct and indirect costs of a job

There are seven steps to assigning costs to an individual job. This seven-step procedure applies equally to assigning costs to a job in the manufacturing, merchandising, and service sectors.

Step 1: **Identify the Job That Is the Chosen Cost Object.** The cost object in the Robinson Company example is Job Number WPP 298, manufacturing a pulp machine for the Western Pulp and Paper Company in 2003.

Step 2: **Identify the Direct Costs of the Job.** Robinson identifies two direct-manufacturing cost categories: direct materials and direct manufacturing labor. Direct materials costs for the WPP 298 job are $4,606; direct manufacturing labor costs are $1,579. Direct materials costs are calculated by multiplying the quantity of each material used for the WPP 298 job by its unit cost (the direct-cost rate) and adding together the costs of all the materials. Similarly, direct manufacturing labor costs are calculated by multiplying the hours worked by each employee on the WPP 298 job by his or her wage rate and adding these costs together.

Step 3: **Select the Cost-Allocation Bases to Use for Allocating Indirect Costs to the Job.** Indirect manufacturing costs are necessary costs to do a job that cannot be traced to a specific job. It would be impossible to complete a job without incurring indirect costs such as supervision, manufacturing engineering, utilities, and repairs. Because these costs cannot be traced to a specific job, they must be allocated to all jobs but not in a blanket way. Different jobs require different quantities of indirect resources. The objective is to allocate the costs of indirect resources in a systematic way to their related jobs.

SURVEYS OF COMPANY PRACTICE

Cost-Allocation Bases Used for Manufacturing Overhead

How do companies around the world allocate manufacturing overhead costs to products? The percentages in the following table indicate how frequently particular cost-allocation bases are used in costing systems in five countries. The reported percentages for each country exceed 100% because many companies surveyed use more than one cost-allocation base.

	United States[a]	Australia[b]	Ireland[c,d]	Japan[b]	United Kingdom[b]
Direct labor-hours	31%	36%	38%	50%	31%
Direct labor dollars	31	21	13	7	29
Machine-hours	12	19	22	12	27
Direct materials dollars	4	12	7	11	17
Units of production	5	20	28	16	22
Prime costs (%)	—	1	—	21	10
Other	17	—	21	—	—

Surveys[e] indicate that as companies begin to identify activity drivers of manufacturing overhead costs, such as setup hours and inspection hours, more of the manufacturing overhead costs are allocated to products using measures other than direct labor-hours and machine-hours.

[a]Adapted from Cohen and Paquette, "Management Accounting."
[b]Blayney and Yokoyama, "Comparative Analysis."
[c]Clarke, "A Survey of."
[d]Clarke and Brislane, "An Investigation into."
[e]T. Groot, "Activity-Based Costing."
Full citations are given in Appendix A at the end of the book.

Companies often use multiple cost-allocation bases to allocate indirect costs (see Surveys of Company Practice above). Robinson, however, chooses direct manufacturing labor-hours as the sole allocation base for linking all indirect manufacturing costs to jobs. Why? Because Robinson believes that the number of direct manufacturing labor-hours is a measure of how individual jobs use all the manufacturing overhead resources, such as salaries paid to supervisors, engineers, production support staff, and quality management staff. There is a strong cause-and-effect relationship between the direct manufacturing labor-hours required by an individual job—that's the cause—and the indirect manufacturing resources demanded by that job—that's the effect. In 2003, Robinson records 27,000 actual direct manufacturing labor-hours.

Step 4: **Identify the Indirect Costs Associated with Each Cost-Allocation Base.** Because Robinson believes that a single cost-allocation base—direct manufacturing labor-hours—can be used to allocate indirect manufacturing costs to products, it creates a single cost pool called *manufacturing overhead costs*. This pool represents the indirect costs of the Green Bay Manufacturing Department that are difficult to trace directly to individual jobs. In 2003, actual indirect manufacturing costs total $1,215,000.

Step 5: **Compute the Rate per Unit of Each Cost-Allocation Base Used to Allocate Indirect Costs to the Job.** For each cost pool, the **indirect-cost rate** is calculated by dividing total overhead costs in the pool (determined in step 4) by the total quantity of the cost-allocation base (determined in step 3). Robinson calculates the allocation rate for its single manufacturing overhead cost pool as follows:

$$\text{Actual indirect-cost rate} = \frac{\text{Actual total costs in indirect-cost pool}}{\text{Actual total quantity of cost-allocation base}}$$

$$= \frac{\$1,215,000}{27,000 \text{ direct manufacturing labor-hours}}$$

$$= \$45 \text{ per direct manufacturing labor-hour}$$

Step 6: Compute the Indirect Costs Allocated to the Job. The indirect costs of a job are computed by multiplying the actual quantity of each different allocation base (one allocation base for each cost pool) associated with the job by the indirect-cost rate of each allocation base (computed in step 5). To make the pulp machine, Robinson uses 88 direct manufacturing labor-hours, the cost-allocation base for its only indirect-cost pool (out of the 27,000 total direct manufacturing labor-hours for 2003). Indirect costs allocated to the pulp machine job equal \$3,960 (\$45 per direct manufacturing labor-hour × 88 hours).

Step 7: Compute the Total Cost of the Job by Adding All Direct and Indirect Costs Assigned to the Job. The cost of the Western Pulp job is \$10,145.

Direct manufacturing costs		
Direct materials	\$4,606	
Direct manufacturing labor	1,579	\$ 6,185
Indirect manufacturing costs		
(\$45 per direct manuf. labor-hour × 88 hours)		3,960
Total manufacturing costs of job		\$10,145

Recall, Robinson was paid \$15,000 for the job. With that revenue, the actual costing system shows a gross margin of \$4,855 (\$15,000 − \$10,145) and a gross margin percentage of 32.4% (\$4,855 ÷ \$15,000 = 0.324).

Robinson can use the gross margin and gross margin percentage calculations to compare profitability of jobs and the reasons why some jobs show low profitability: Have direct materials been wasted? Is direct manufacturing labor too high? Are there ways to improve the efficiency of these jobs? Or were these jobs simply underpriced? Job-cost analysis provides the information needed for judging performance and making future improvements. (The Concepts in Action, p. 104, describes pricing and efficiency gains from job costing at Colorscope, a special effects photography laboratory.)

Exhibit 4-2 is an overview of Robinson Company's job-costing system. This exhibit represents the concepts comprising the five building blocks—*cost object, direct costs of a cost object, indirect costs of a cost object, indirect-cost pool, and cost-allocation base*—of job-costing systems. Costing-system overviews such as Exhibit 4-2 are important learning tools. We urge you to sketch one when you need to understand a costing system in manufacturing, merchandising, or service companies. (The symbols in Exhibit 4-2 are used consistently in the costing-system overviews presented in this book. For example, a triangle always identifies a direct cost; a rectangle, the indirect-cost pool; and an octagon, the cost-allocation base.) Note the parallel between the exhibit diagram and the cost of the pulp machine job described in step 7. Exhibit 4-2 shows two direct-cost categories (direct materials and direct manufacturing labor) and one indirect-cost category (manufacturing overhead) used to allocate indirect costs. The costs in step 7 also have three dollar amounts, each corresponding respectively to the two direct-cost and one indirect-cost categories.

Source Documents

Robinson's managers and accountants gather information that goes into their costing systems through *source documents.* A **source document** is an original record (such as a labor time card on which an employee's work hours are recorded) that supports journal entries in an accounting system. The main source document in a job-costing system is a *job-cost record.* A **job-cost record,** also called a **job-cost sheet,** records and accumulates all the costs assigned to a specific job, starting when work begins. Exhibit 4-3, Panel A, shows the job-cost record for the pulp machine ordered by Western Pulp and Paper Company.

Various individual items in a job-cost record also have source documents. Consider direct materials. On the basis of the engineering specifications and drawings provided by Western Pulp, a manufacturing engineer orders materials from the storeroom. This is done using a basic source document called a **materials-requisition record,** which contains information about the cost of direct materials used on a specific job and in a specific department. Exhibit 4-3, Panel B, shows a materials-requisition record for the Robinson Company. See how the record specifies the job for which the material is

EXHIBIT 4-2

Job-Costing Overview for Determining Manufacturing Costs of Jobs at Robinson Company

Exhibit 4-2 presents concepts that appear throughout this book in a similar format. In this example, the cost object (a pulp machine for Western Pulp and Paper Company) has two direct costs (direct materials and direct manufacturing labor) and one indirect cost (manufacturing overhead) allocated on the basis of direct manufacturing labor-hours.

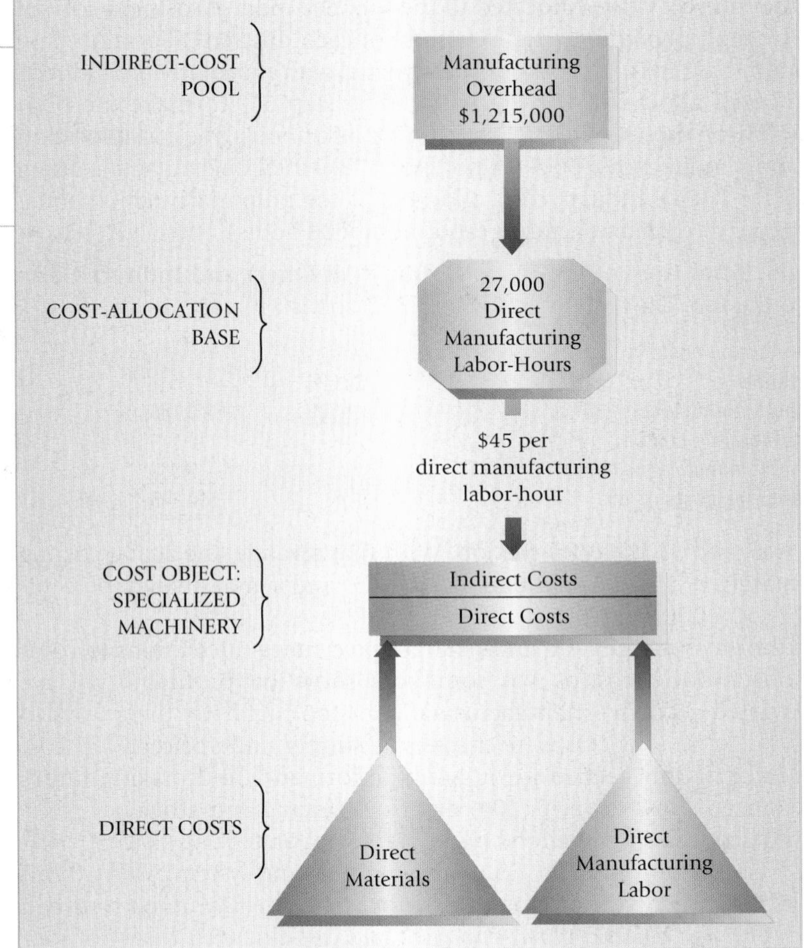

requested (WPP 298), the description of the material (Part Number MB 468-A, Metal brackets), the actual quantity (8), the actual unit cost ($14), and the actual total cost ($112). The $112 actual total cost also appears on the job-cost record. Adding the cost of all the material requisitions gives the actual direct materials costs of $4,606 shown on the job-cost record.

The accounting for direct manufacturing labor is similar to the accounting described for direct materials. The basic source document for direct manufacturing labor is a **labor-time record,** which contains information about the labor time used on a specific job and in a specific department. Exhibit 4-3, Panel C, shows a typical weekly labor-time record for a particular employee (G. L. Cook). Each day Cook records the time spent on individual jobs (in this case WPP 298 and JL 256), as well as the time spent on other tasks, such as maintenance of machines or cleaning, that are not related to a specific job.

The 25 hours that Cook spends on Job WPP 298 appear on the job-cost record in Panel A at a cost of $450 (25 hours × $18 per hour). Similarly, the job-cost record for Job JL256 will carry a cost of $216 (12 hours × $18 per hour). The three hours of time spent on maintenance and cleaning at $18 per hour equal $54; this cost is part of indirect manufacturing costs because it is not traceable to any particular job. This indirect cost is included as part of the manufacturing-overhead cost pool allocated to jobs using direct manufacturing labor-hours. The total direct manufacturing labor costs of $1,579 for the pulp machine that appears on the job-cost record in Panel A is the sum of all the direct manufacturing labor costs charged to this job by different employees.

Companies pay special attention to the accuracy of source documents because the reliability of job-cost records depends on the reliability of the inputs. Problems occur with respect to the accuracy of information in source documents, such as incorrect job numbers assigned to materials or labor inputs.

In many costing systems, the source documents exist only in the form of computer records. Bar coding and other forms of online information recording reduce human

EXHIBIT 4-3 **Source Documents at Robinson Company: Job-Cost Record, Materials-Requisition Record, and Labor-Time Record**

PANEL A:

JOB- COST RECORD

JOB NO: WPP 298 CUSTOMER: Western Pulp and Paper

Date Started: Feb. 3, 2003 Date Completed: Feb. 28, 2003

DIRECT MATERIALS

Date Received	Materials Requisition No.	Part No.	Quantity Used	Unit Cost	Total Costs
Feb. 3, 2003	2003: 198	MB 468-A	8	$14	$ 112
Feb. 3, 2003	2003: 199	TB 267-F	12	63	756
					•
					•
Total					$ 4,606

DIRECT MANUFACTURING LABOR

Period Covered	Labor Time Record No.	Employee No.	Hours Used	Hourly Rate	Total Costs
Feb. 3–9, 2003	LT 232	551-87-3076	25	$18	$ 450
Feb. 3–9, 2003	LT 247	287-31-4671	5	19	95
					•
					•
Total					$ 1,579

MANUFACTURING OVERHEAD*

Date	Cost Pool Category	Allocation Base	Allocation-Base Units Used	Allocation-Base Rate	Total Costs
Dec. 31, 2003	Manufacturing	Direct Manufacturing Labor-Hours	88 hours	$45	$ 3,960
Total					$ 3,960
TOTAL JOB COST					$10,145

PANEL B:

MATERIALS-REQUISITION RECORD

Materials-Requistion Record No. 2003: 198

Job No.: WPP 298 Date: Feb. 3, 2003

Part No.	Part Description	Quantity	Unit Cost	Total Cost
MB 468-A	Metal Brackets	8	$14	$112

Issued By: B. Clyde Date: Feb. 3, 2003

Received By: L. Daley Date: Feb. 3, 2003

PANEL C:

LABOR-TIME RECORD

Labor-Time Record No.: LT 232

Employee Name: G. L. Cook Employee No.: 551-87-3076

Employee Classification Code: Grade 3 Machinist

Hourly Rate: $18

Week Start: Feb. 3, 2003 Week End: Feb. 9, 2003

Job. No.	M	T	W	Th	F	S	Su	Total
WPP 298	4	8	3	6	4	0	0	25
JL 256	3	0	4	2	3	0	0	12
Maintenance	1	0	1	0	1	0	0	3
Total	8	8	8	8	8	0	0	40

Supervisor: R. Stuart Date: Feb. 10, 2003

*The Robinson Company uses a single manufacturing-overhead cost pool. The use of multiple overhead cost pools would mean multiple entries in the "Manufacturing Overhead" section of the job-cost record.

intervention and facilitate greater accuracy in the records of materials and labor time used on jobs.

Exhibit 4-3 shows how Robinson's job-cost record uses information from materials requisitions and labor time records.

The Role of Technology

To improve the efficiency of their operations, managers use product-costing information to control materials, labor, and overhead costs. Modern information technology provides managers with quick and accurate product-cost information that makes it easier to manage and control jobs.

Consider, for example, direct materials charged to jobs for product-costing purposes. Managers control these costs well before the materials are used. Through technologies such as Electronic Data Interchange (EDI), companies like Robinson can order materials

CONCEPTS IN ACTION

Pricing and Efficiency Gains from Job Costing at Colorscope

Colorscope, Inc., is a special-effects photography laboratory that designs printed advertisements for companies such as Saatchi & Saatchi, J. Walter Thompson, Walt Disney, and R. H. Macy. Competitive pressures and thin profit margins make understanding costs critical in pricing decisions. Each job must be estimated individually because the unique end products demand different amounts of Colorscope's resources.

Previously, Colorscope charged the same price for all its jobs. That's because, regardless of the end result, every customer job goes through five stages—job preparation, scanning, assembly, film developing, and quality control. In the *job preparation* stage, the template of the job is created by physically cutting and pasting text, graphics, and photographs and by specifying the layout, font, color, and shading. The job template is then *scanned* into a computer, where the job is *assembled* using archives of scanned images adjusted for color and shades. The assembled job is then transferred and *developed* on a large sheet of four-color film. *Quality control* ensures that the job fully satisfies the customer's specifications. If not, or if the customer's requirements have changed, quality control initiates rework.

Andrew Cha, Colorscope's founder and chief executive, observed large differences in the amount of image-scanning and processing activity required by different jobs, as well as varying amounts of rework across jobs. Although the jobs used different amounts of resources, the same price (roughly) was charged for all jobs—so Colorscope lost money on certain jobs. Cha concluded that a job-costing system measuring costs based on the labor-hours spent at each operation would give him better information about costs incurred on various jobs. Colorscope's job-costing system now traces direct materials to jobs and allocates all other costs (wages, rent, depreciation, and so on) to jobs using an overhead rate per labor-hour for each operation.

Besides better tracing of costs to specific jobs, Colorscope's new job-costing system has provided the additional benefit of improving efficiency through process changes. For example, the job-costing system highlighted the significant resources Colorscope had been spending on rework. Colorscope's management discovered that most rework was caused by faulty scanning. These defects were not detected until the job was completed, by which time significant additional resources had also been incurred on the job. Colorscope implemented process changes to reduce faulty scanning and to test for quality immediately after the scanning stage. Thus, Colorscope's job-costing system improves its profitability by pricing jobs better and by increasing efficiency and quality.

Source: Colorscope, Inc., Harvard Business School Case Number 9-197-040.

from their suppliers by clicking a few keys on a computer keyboard. EDI, an electronic computer link between a company and its suppliers, ensures that the order is transmitted quickly and accurately with minimum paper work and costs. A bar code scanner records the receipt of incoming materials. The computer matches the receipt with the order, prints out a check to the supplier, and records the material received. When an operator on the production floor transmits a request for materials via a computer terminal, the computer prepares a materials-requisition record, instantly recording the issue of materials in the materials and job-cost records. Each day, the computer sums the materials-requisition records charged to a particular job or manufacturing department. A performance report is then prepared comparing budgeted costs versus actual costs of direct materials. Direct materials usage might be reported hourly—if there is an economic payoff for such frequent reporting.

Similarly, information about manufacturing labor is obtained as employees log into computer terminals and punch in the job numbers, their employee numbers, and start and end times of their work on different jobs. The computer automatically prints the labor-time record and, using hourly rates stored for each employee, calculates the labor costs of individual jobs. Information technology also provides managers with instantaneous feedback to control manufacturing overhead, jobs in process, jobs completed, and jobs shipped and installed at customer sites.

TIME PERIOD USED TO COMPUTE INDIRECT-COST RATES

Robinson Company computes indirect-cost rates in step 5 (p. 100) on an annual basis. Why does Robinson wait until the end of the year to calculate indirect-cost rates? Why can't Robinson calculate indirect-cost rates each week? or each month? Using weekly rates or monthly rates, Robinson would be able to calculate actual costs of jobs much earlier and not have to wait until the end of the year. There are two reasons for using longer periods to calculate indirect-cost rates, one related to the dollar amount in the numerator and one related to the quantity in the denominator of the calculation.

1. *The numerator reason* (indirect-cost pool). The shorter the period, the greater the influence of seasonal patterns on the amount of costs. For example, if indirect-cost rates were calculated each month, costs of heating (included in the numerator) would be charged only to production during the winter months. But an annual period incorporates the effect of all four seasons into a single, annual indirect-cost rate.

   Levels of total indirect costs are also affected by nonseasonal erratic costs. Examples of nonseasonal erratic costs include costs incurred in a particular month that benefit operations during future months, costs of repairs and maintenance of equipment, and costs of vacation and holiday pay. If monthly indirect-cost rates were calculated, jobs done in a month with high, nonseasonal, erratic costs would be loaded with these costs. Pooling all indirect costs together over the course of a full year and calculating a single annual indirect-cost rate helps to smooth some of the erratic bumps in costs associated with specific periods.

2. *The denominator reason* (quantity of the allocation base). Another reason for longer periods is the need to spread monthly fixed indirect costs over fluctuating levels of monthly output. Some indirect costs may be variable each month with respect to the cost-allocation base (for example, supplies), whereas other indirect costs are fixed each month (for example, property, taxes, and rent).

Question: Should a product's cost depend on when production takes place during the year? *Answer:* Probably not, unless economic factors cause the cost to fluctuate during the year. For example, no obvious economic reason exists why the cost of a personal computer should depend on the month it is produced.

Suppose a company deliberately schedules its production to correspond with a highly seasonal sales pattern. Assume the following mix of variable indirect costs (such as supplies, repairs, and indirect manufacturing labor) and fixed indirect costs (plant depreciation and engineering support):

	Indirect Costs			Direct Manufacturing Labor-Hours	Allocation Rate per Direct Manufacturing Labor-Hour
	Variable (1)	Fixed (2)	Total (3)	(4)	(5) = (3) ÷ (4)
High-output month	$40,000	$60,000	$100,000	3,200	$31.25
Low-output month	10,000	60,000	70,000	800	87.50

You can see that variable indirect costs change in proportion to changes in direct manufacturing labor-hours. Therefore, the variable indirect-cost rate is the same in both the high-output months and the low-output months ($40,000 ÷ 3,200 labor-hours = $12.50 per labor-hour; $10,000 ÷ 800 labor-hours = $12.50 per labor-hour). Because of the fixed costs of $60,000, monthly total indirect-cost rates vary considerably—from $31.25 per hour to $87.50 per hour. Few managers believe that identical jobs done in different months should be allocated indirect-cost charges per hour that differ so significantly ($87.50 ÷ $31.25 = 2.80, or 280%). In our example, management chooses a specific level of capacity based on a time horizon far beyond a mere month. An average, annualized rate based on the relationship of total annual indirect costs to the total annual level of output will smooth the effect of monthly variations in output levels.

In this example, the change in the indirect cost-allocation rate arises solely because of fixed costs. Variable cost per unit = $12.50 at both 3,200 and 800 hours. However, fixed cost per unit = $18.75 at 3,200 hours and = $75.00 at 800 hours. Fluctuations in the denominator affect only the fixed cost portion of the cost rate.

The calculation of monthly indirect-cost rates is affected by the number of Monday-to-Friday workdays in a month. The number of workdays per month varies from 20 to 23 during a year. If separate rates are computed each month, jobs in February, having the fewest workdays in a month, would bear a greater share of indirect costs (such as depreciation and property taxes) than jobs in other months. Many managers believe such results to be an unrepresentative and unreasonable way to assign indirect costs to jobs. An annual period reduces the effect that the number of working days per month has on unit costs.

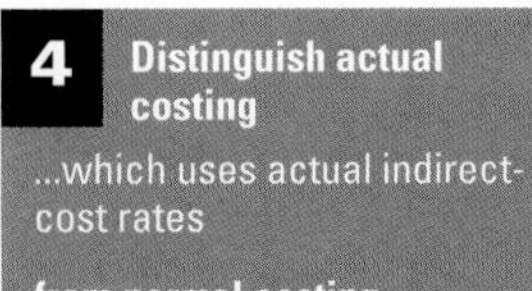

NORMAL COSTING

The difficulty of calculating actual indirect-cost rates on a weekly or monthly basis means managers cannot calculate the actual costs of jobs as they are completed. However, managers want a close approximation of the manufacturing costs of various jobs regularly during the year, not just at the end of the year. Managers want manufacturing costs (and other costs, such as marketing costs) for ongoing uses, including pricing jobs, managing costs, and preparing interim financial statements. Because of these benefits of immediate access to job costs, few companies wait until the *actual* manufacturing overhead is finally known (at year-end) before allocating overhead costs to compute job costs. Instead, a *predetermined* or *budgeted* indirect-cost rate is calculated for each cost pool at the beginning of a fiscal year, and overhead costs are allocated to jobs as work progresses. For the numerator and denominator reasons already described, the **budgeted indirect-cost rate** is computed for each cost pool by dividing the budgeted *annual* indirect cost by the budgeted *annual* quantity of the cost-allocation base. Using budgeted indirect-cost rates gives rise to *normal costing*.

Normal costing is a costing method that traces direct costs to a cost object by using the actual direct-cost rates times the actual quantity of the direct-cost inputs, and allocates indirect costs based on the budgeted indirect-cost rates times the actual quantity of the cost-allocation bases. Both actual costing and normal costing trace direct costs to jobs in the same way. The actual quantities and actual rates of direct materials and direct manufacturing labor used on a job are known from the source documents as the work is done. The only difference between actual costing and normal costing is that actual costing uses *actual* indirect-cost rates, whereas normal costing uses *budgeted* indirect-cost rates to cost jobs. Exhibit 4-4 distinguishes between actual costing and normal costing.

We illustrate normal costing for the Robinson Company example using the seven-step procedure. The following budgeted data for 2003 are for the manufacturing operations of Robinson Company:

	Budget
Total manufacturing overhead costs	$1,120,000
Total direct manufacturing labor-hours	28,000

Steps 1 and 2 are exactly as before: Step 1 identifies WPP 298 as the cost object; Step 2 calculates actual direct material costs of $4,606, and actual direct manufacturing labor costs of $1,579. Recall from Step 3 that Robinson uses a single cost-allocation base, direct manufacturing labor-hours, to allocate all manufacturing overhead costs to jobs. The budgeted quantity of direct manufacturing labor-hours for 2003 is 28,000 hours. In Step 4, Robinson groups all the indirect manufacturing costs into a single manufacturing overhead cost pool. In Step 5, the budgeted indirect-cost rate for 2003 is calculated as:

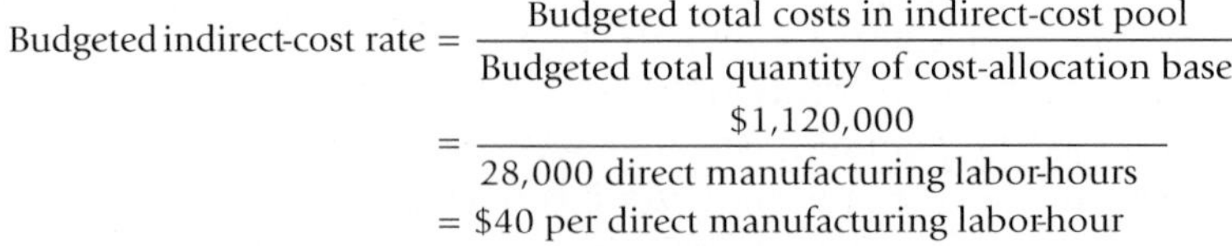

$$\begin{aligned}\text{Budgeted indirect-cost rate} &= \frac{\text{Budgeted total costs in indirect-cost pool}}{\text{Budgeted total quantity of cost-allocation base}}\\ &= \frac{\$1{,}120{,}000}{28{,}000 \text{ direct manufacturing labor-hours}}\\ &= \$40 \text{ per direct manufacturing labor-hour}\end{aligned}$$

In Step 6, under a normal-costing system, indirect costs allocated to the WPP 298 job are calculated as the *actual* quantity of direct manufacturing labor-hours used on the job times the budgeted indirect-cost rate, $40 per direct manufacturing labor-hour × 88 direct manufacturing labor-hours = $3,520. In Step 7, the cost of the job under normal-costing is $9,705, calculated as

EXHIBIT 4-4 **Actual-Costing and Normal Costing Methods**

	Actual Costing	Normal Costing
Direct Costs	Actual direct-cost rates × actual quantity of direct-cost inputs	Actual direct-cost rates × actual quantity of direct-cost inputs
Indirect Costs	Actual indirect-cost rates × actual quantity of cost-allocation bases	Budgeted indirect-cost rates × actual quantity of cost-allocation bases

Direct manufacturing costs		
Direct materials	$4,606	
Direct manufacturing labor	1,579	$6,185
Indirect manufacturing costs ($40 × 88 actual direct manufacturing labor-hours)		3,520
Total manufacturing costs of job		$9,705

The manufacturing cost of the WPP 298 job is lower by $440 under normal costing ($9,705) than it is under actual costing ($10,145) because the budgeted indirect-cost rate is $40 per hour, whereas the actual indirect-cost rate is $45 per hour.

A NORMAL JOB-COSTING SYSTEM IN MANUFACTURING

5 **Track the flow of costs in a job-costing system** ...from purchase of materials to sale of finished goods

We now explain how a normal job-costing system operates in manufacturing. Continuing with the Robinson Company example, the following illustration considers events that occurred in February 2003.

General Ledger and Subsidiary Ledgers

You know by this point that a job-costing system has a separate job-cost record for each job. A summary of the job-cost record is typically found in a subsidiary ledger. The general ledger account, Work-in-Process Control, presents the totals of these separate job-cost records pertaining to all unfinished jobs. The job-cost records and Work-in-Process Control account track job costs from the time jobs are started until they are completed.

Exhibit 4-5 shows T-account relationships for Robinson Company's general ledger and examples of how the records appear in the subsidiary ledgers. Panel A shows the general ledger section that gives a "bird's-eye view" of the costing system; the amounts shown here are based on the illustration that follows. Panel B shows the subsidiary ledgers and the basic source documents that contain the underlying details—the "worm's-eye view." General ledger accounts with *"Control"* in the titles (such as Materials Control and Accounts Payable Control) have underlying subsidiary ledgers that contain additional details, such as each type of material in inventory and individual suppliers that Robinson must pay. The total of all entries in underlying subsidiary ledgers equals the amounts in the corresponding general ledger control account.

Think of subsidiary ledger accounts as little T-accounts that support the general ledger control T-account; for example, individual job-cost records are the support for Work-in-Process Control.

Software programs drive how transactions are processed in most accounting systems. Some programs make general ledger entries simultaneously with entries in the subsidiary ledger accounts. Other software programs make general ledger entries at, say, weekly or monthly intervals, with entries made in the subsidiary ledger accounts more frequently. The Robinson Company makes entries in its subsidiary ledger when transactions occur and then makes entries in its general ledger on a monthly basis.

A general ledger should be viewed as only one of many tools that assist management in planning and control. To control operations, managers use not only the source documents used to record amounts in the subsidiary ledgers, but also nonfinancial variables such as the percentage of jobs requiring rework.

Explanations of Transactions

The following transaction-by-transaction analysis explains how a job-costing system serves the twin goals of (1) product costing and (2) department responsibility and control. These transactions track stages (a) through (d) from the purchase of materials and other manufacturing inputs, to conversion to work-in-process and finished goods, to the eventual sale of finished goods:

This graphic, which shows the *physical flow* of product through a manufacturing process, clarifies the economic transactions occurring. To more easily understand the first eight journal entries that follow, link the discussion of each entry to the graphic.

(a)
Purchases of Materials and Other Manufacturing Inputs
(b)
Conversion into Work-in-Process Inventory
(c)
Conversion into Finished Goods Inventory
(d)
Sale of Finished Goods

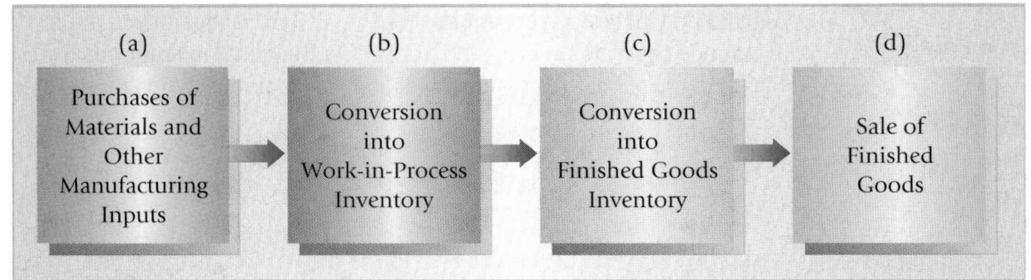

1. *Transaction:* Purchases of materials (direct and indirect) on credit, $89,000.

   Analysis: The asset Materials Control is increased (debited) by $89,000, and the liability Accounts Payable Control is increased (credited) by $89,000. Both accounts have the word *Control* in their title in the general ledger because they have detailed records in the subsidiary ledger. The subsidiary records for materials at Robinson Company—called *Materials Records*—maintain a continuous record of additions to, and deductions from, inventory. At a minimum, these records would contain information about quantity received, quantity issued to jobs, and balance (see Panel B of Exhibit 4-5). There is a

EXHIBIT 4-5 **Manufacturing Job-Costing System Using Normal Costing: Diagram of Ledger Relationships for February 2003**

PANEL A: GENERAL LEDGER

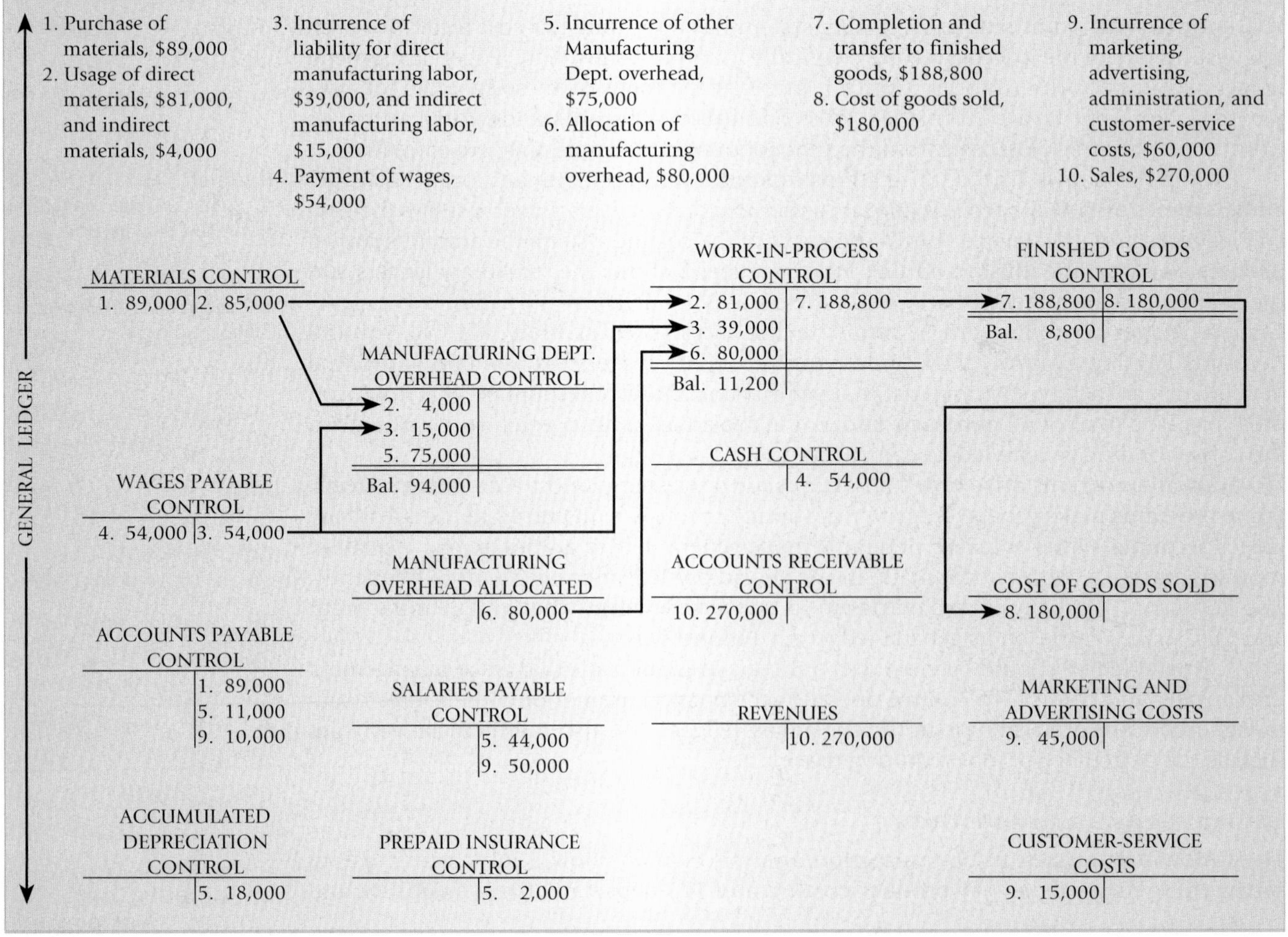

1. Purchase of materials, $89,000
2. Usage of direct materials, $81,000, and indirect materials, $4,000
3. Incurrence of liability for direct manufacturing labor, $39,000, and indirect manufacturing labor, $15,000
4. Payment of wages, $54,000
5. Incurrence of other Manufacturing Dept. overhead, $75,000
6. Allocation of manufacturing overhead, $80,000
7. Completion and transfer to finished goods, $188,800
8. Cost of goods sold, $180,000
9. Incurrence of marketing, advertising, administration, and customer-service costs, $60,000
10. Sales, $270,000
GENERAL LEDGER
MATERIALS CONTROL
1. 89,000 | 2. 85,000
WORK-IN-PROCESS CONTROL
2. 81,000 | 7. 188,800
3. 39,000
6. 80,000
Bal. 11,200
FINISHED GOODS CONTROL
7. 188,800 | 8. 180,000
Bal. 8,800
MANUFACTURING DEPT. OVERHEAD CONTROL
2. 4,000
3. 15,000
5. 75,000
Bal. 94,000
CASH CONTROL
| 4. 54,000
WAGES PAYABLE CONTROL
4. 54,000 | 3. 54,000
MANUFACTURING OVERHEAD ALLOCATED
| 6. 80,000
ACCOUNTS RECEIVABLE CONTROL
10. 270,000 |
COST OF GOODS SOLD
8. 180,000 |
ACCOUNTS PAYABLE CONTROL
| 1. 89,000
| 5. 11,000
| 9. 10,000
SALARIES PAYABLE CONTROL
| 5. 44,000
| 9. 50,000
REVENUES
| 10. 270,000
MARKETING AND ADVERTISING COSTS
9. 45,000 |
ACCUMULATED DEPRECIATION CONTROL
| 5. 18,000
PREPAID INSURANCE CONTROL
| 5. 2,000
CUSTOMER-SERVICE COSTS
9. 15,000 |

EXHIBIT 4-5 (continued)

PANEL B: SUBSIDIARY LEDGERS

MATERIALS RECORDS BY TYPE OF MATERIALS

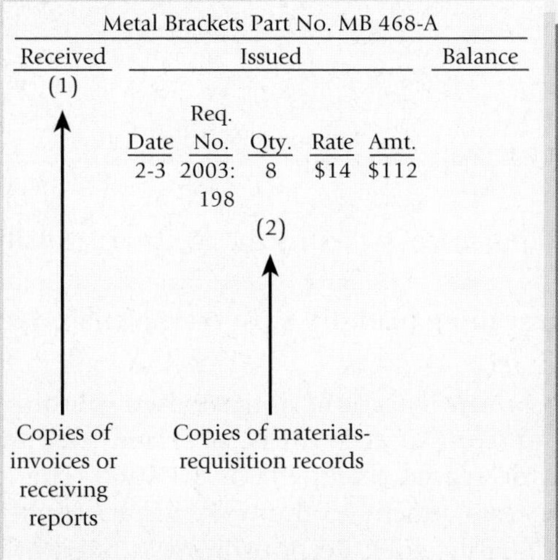
Metal Brackets Part No. MB 468-A

Received	Issued					Balance
	Date	Req. No.	Qty.	Rate	Amt.	
(1)	2-3	2003: 198	8	$14	$112	
		(2)				

Total cost of all types of materials received in February, $89,000

Total cost of all types of materials issued in February, $85,000

WORK-IN-PROCESS RECORDS BY JOBS

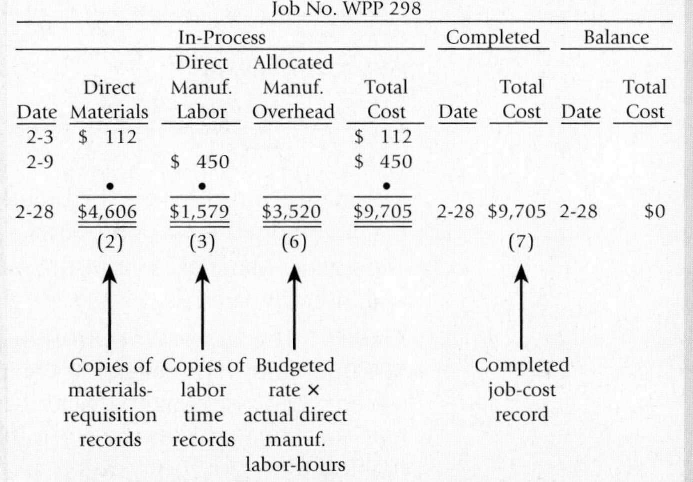
Job No. WPP 298

In-Process					Completed		Balance	
Date	Direct Materials	Direct Manuf. Labor	Allocated Manuf. Overhead	Total Cost	Date	Total Cost	Date	Total Cost
2-3	$ 112			$ 112				
2-9		$ 450		$ 450				
	•	•		•				
2-28	$4,606	$1,579	$3,520	$9,705	2-28	$9,705	2-28	$0
	(2)	(3)	(6)			(7)		

Total cost of direct materials issued to all jobs in Feb., $81,000

Total cost of direct manuf. labor used on all jobs in Feb., $39,000

Total manuf. overhead allocated to all jobs in Feb., $80,000

Total cost of all jobs completed and transferred to finished goods in Feb., $188,800

Finished Goods Records by Job

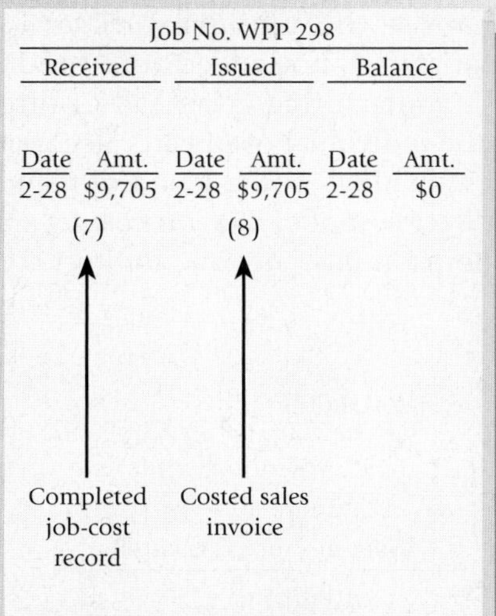
Job No. WPP 298

Received		Issued		Balance	
Date	Amt.	Date	Amt.	Date	Amt.
2-28	$9,705	2-28	$9,705	2-28	$0
	(7)		(8)		

Total cost of all jobs transferred to finished goods in Feb., $188,800

Total cost of all jobs sold and invoiced in Feb., $180,000

Labor Records by Employee

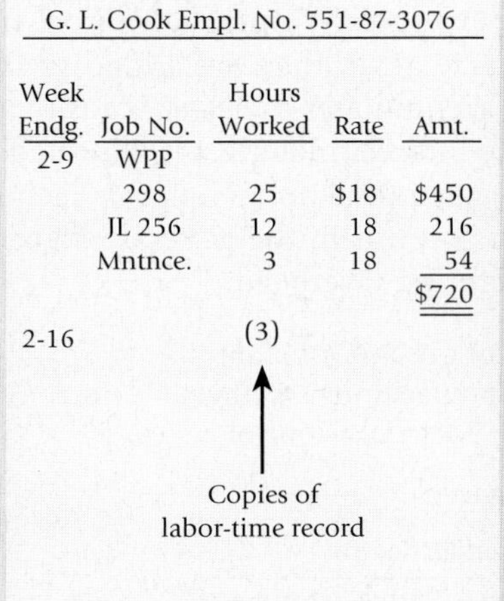
G. L. Cook Empl. No. 551-87-3076

Week Endg.	Job No.	Hours Worked	Rate	Amt.
2-9	WPP 298	25	$18	$450
	JL 256	12	18	216
	Mntnce.	3	18	54
				$720
2-16		(3)		

Total cost of all direct and indirect manufacturing labor incurred in February, $54,000 ($39,000 + $15,000)

Manufacturing Dept. Overhead Records by Month

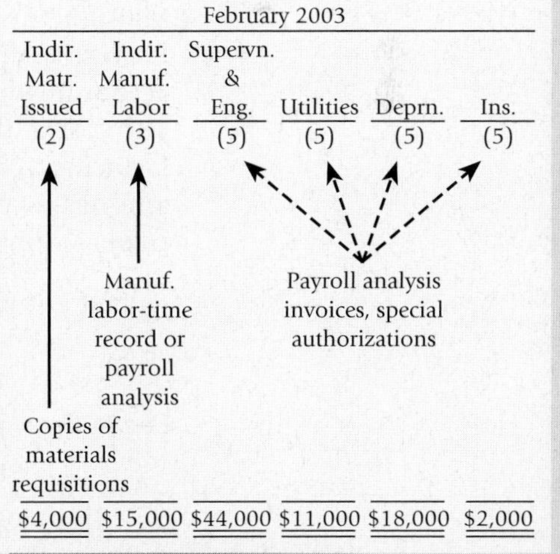
February 2003

Indir. Matr. Issued	Indir. Manuf. Labor	Supervn. & Eng.	Utilities	Deprn.	Ins.
(2)	(3)	(5)	(5)	(5)	(5)
$4,000	$15,000	$44,000	$11,000	$18,000	$2,000

Other manufacturing overhead costs incurred in February, $75,000

separate materials record for each type of material in the subsidiary ledger. For example, the subsidiary records contain details of the Metal Brackets (Part No. MB 468-A) issued for the Western Pulp machine job. The following journal entry aggregates all the February 2003 entries made for purchases in the materials subsidiary ledger:

Journal Entry:		
Materials Control	89,000	
Accounts Payable Control		89,000

Post to General Ledger:

Materials Control			
①	89,000		

Accounts Payable Control			
		①	89,000

Materials Control includes all material purchases, whether the items are classified as direct or indirect costs of products.

2. *Transaction:* Materials sent to the manufacturing plant floor: direct materials, $81,000, and indirect materials, $4,000.

Analysis: The asset Work-in-Process Control account is increased (debited) by $81,000, and Manufacturing Overhead Control account is increased (debited) by $4,000. The asset Materials Control is decreased (credited) by $85,000. The idea is that costs incurred on the work in process "attach" to the work in process, thereby making the work in process a more valuable asset. Responsibility is fixed by using *materials-requisition records* as a basis for charging departments for the materials issued to them. Requisitions posted in the Materials Records of the subsidiary ledger are accumulated and posted monthly to the general ledger.

As direct materials are used, they are charged to individual job records, which are the subsidiary ledger accounts for the Work-in-Process Control account in the general ledger account. For example, the metal brackets used in the Western Pulp machine job appear as direct materials costs of $112 in the subsidiary ledger under the job-cost record for WPP 298. The cost of direct materials used across all job-cost records for February 2003 is $81,000.

Indirect materials (for example, lubricants) are charged to the Manufacturing Department's overhead-cost records, which comprise the subsidiary ledger for Manufacturing Overhead Control. Indirect materials are not added to Work-in-Process Control. Instead, they are added to the Manufacturing Overhead Control account, which accumulates the *actual costs* in all the individual overhead categories. The cost of these indirect materials is allocated to individual jobs as a part of manufacturing overhead (transaction 6 below). Each indirect-cost pool in a job-costing system has its own account in the general ledger. Robinson has only one indirect-cost pool—Manufacturing Overhead.

Journal Entry:		
Work-in-Process Control	81,000	
Manufacturing Overhead Control	4,000	
Materials Control		85,000

Post to General Ledger:

Materials Control			
①	89,000	②	85,000

Work-in-Process Control			
②	81,000		

Manufacturing Overhead Control			
②	4,000		

3. *Transaction:* Total manufacturing payroll for February: direct, $39,000; indirect, $15,000.

Analysis: The asset Work-in-Process Control is increased (debited) by the direct manufacturing labor amount of $39,000, and Manufacturing Overhead Control is increased (debited) by the $15,000 of indirect manufacturing labor. The liability Wages Payable Control is increased (credited) by $54,000. Direct manufacturing labor costs increase Work-in-Process Control because these costs increase the cost of the work-in-process asset. Direct manufacturing labor helps to transform one asset—direct materials—into another asset—work in process—and eventually into finished goods. Labor-time records are used to trace direct manufacturing labor to Work-in-Process Control (see

Panel B of Exhibit 4-5) and to accumulate the indirect manufacturing labor in Manufacturing Overhead Control. The subsidiary ledger for employee labor records shows the $750 of wages owed to G. L. Cook, Employee No. 551-87-3076, for the week ending February 9. The sum of total wages owed to all employees for February 2003 is $54,000. The job-cost record for WPP 298 shows direct manufacturing labor costs of $450 for the time Cook spent on the Western Pulp machine job. Total direct manufacturing labor costs recorded on all job-cost records (the subsidiary ledger for Work-in-Process Control) for February 2003 is $39,000. The total indirect manufacturing labor costs of $15,000 for February 2003 is, by definition, not traced to an individual job. It is instead allocated to individual jobs as a part of manufacturing overhead (transaction 6 below).

Journal Entry:		Debit	Credit
	Work-in-Process Control	39,000	
	Manufacturing Overhead Control	15,000	
	Wages Payable Control		54,000

Post to General Ledger:

Wages Payable Control

		③	54,000

Work-in-Process Control

②	81,000		
③	39,000		

Manufacturing Overhead Control

②	4,000		
③	15,000		

4. *Transaction:* Payment of total manufacturing payroll for February, $54,000. (For simplicity, payroll withholdings from employees are ignored in this example.)

Analysis: The liability Wages Payable Control is decreased (debited) by $54,000, and the asset Cash Control is decreased (credited) by $54,000.

Journal Entry:		Debit	Credit
	Wages Payable Control	54,000	
	Cash Control		54,000

Post to General Ledger:

Wages Payable Control

④	54,000	③	54,000

Cash Control

		④	54,000

For convenience here, wages payable for the month is assumed to be completely paid at month's end.

5. *Transaction:* Additional manufacturing overhead costs incurred during February, $75,000. These costs consist of engineering and supervisory salaries, $44,000; plant utilities and repairs, $11,000; plant depreciation, $18,000; and plant insurance, $2,000.

Analysis: The indirect-cost account, Manufacturing Overhead Control, is increased (debited) by $75,000. The liability, Salaries Payable Control, is increased (credited) by $44,000; the liability, Accounts Payable Control, is increased (credited) by $11,000; the asset Equipment Control is decreased (credited) by means of a related contra asset account Accumulated Depreciation Control by $18,000; and the asset Prepaid Insurance Control is decreased (credited) by $2,000. The detail of each of these costs is entered in the appropriate columns of the individual manufacturing overhead cost records that make up the subsidiary ledger for Manufacturing Overhead Control (see Exhibit 4-5, Panel B). The source documents for these distributions include invoices (for example, a utility bill) and special schedules (for example, a depreciation schedule) from the responsible accounting officer.

Items such as utilities, depreciation, and insurance are debited to Manufacturing Overhead Control only if they are related to *producing the products;* these costs are inventoriable costs (assets) until the products are sold. In contrast, utilities for a sales office or depreciation on executives' automobiles are not part of manufacturing overhead; these costs are period costs.

Journal Entry:		Debit	Credit
	Manufacturing Overhead Control	75,000	
	Salaries Payable Control		44,000
	Accounts Payable Control		11,000
	Accumulated Depreciation Control		18,000
	Prepaid Insurance Control		2,000

Post to General Ledger:

Accounts Payable Control

	①	89,000
	⑤	11,000

Manufacturing Overhead Control

②	4,000	
③	15,000	
⑤	75,000	

Accumulated Depreciation Control

	⑤	18,000

Prepaid Insurance Control

	⑤	2,000

Salaries Payable Control

	⑤	44,000

6. *Transaction:* Allocation of manufacturing overhead to jobs, $80,000.

   Analysis: The asset Work-in-Process Control is increased (debited) by $80,000. Manufacturing Overhead Control is, in effect, decreased (credited) by $80,000 via its contra account, Manufacturing Overhead Allocated. **Manufacturing overhead allocated** (also called **manufacturing overhead applied**) is the amount of indirect manufacturing costs allocated to individual jobs based on the budgeted rate multiplied by actual quantity used of the allocation base. Manufacturing overhead allocated comprises all manufacturing costs that are assigned to a product (or service) using a cost-allocation base, because these costs cannot be traced specifically to it in an economically feasible way. Under Robinson's normal-costing system, the budgeted manufacturing overhead rate for 2003 is $40 per direct manufacturing labor-hour. The job-cost record for each individual job in the subsidiary ledger will include a debit item for manufacturing overhead allocated for the actual direct manufacturing labor-hours used on that job. For example, the job-cost record for Job WPP 298 shows Manufacturing Overhead Allocated of $3,520 (budgeted rate of $40 per labor-hour × 88 actual direct manufacturing labor-hours used). We assume 2,000 actual direct manufacturing labor-hours were used for all jobs in February 2003, resulting in a total manufacturing overhead allocation of $40 per labor-hour × 2,000 direct manufacturing labor-hours = $80,000.

Journal Entry:			
	Work-in-Process Control	80,000	
	Manufacturing Overhead Allocated		80,000

Post to General Ledger:

Manufacturing Overhead Allocated

	⑥	80,000

Work-in-Process Control

②	81,000	
③	39,000	
⑥	80,000	

Actual manufacturing overhead (MOH) is debited to MOH Control as incurred; the total actual MOH is not known until the *end* of the period. Allocated MOH is the budgeted MOH rate (known at the *beginning* of the period) times the actual quantity of the MOH allocation base recorded upon *completion* of jobs (or the *end* of the period)—when usage of the allocation base is known.

Keep in mind the distinct difference between transactions 5 and 6. In transaction 5, actual overhead costs incurred throughout the month are added (debited) to the Manufacturing Overhead Control account and the subsidiary manufacturing overhead records. These costs are not debited to Work-in-Process Control or the individual job-cost records. Manufacturing overhead costs are added (debited) to Work-in-Process Control and individual job-cost records *only when* manufacturing overhead costs are allocated in transaction 6. At the time those costs are allocated, Manufacturing Overhead Control is, *in effect*, decreased (credited). Under the normal-costing system described in our illustration, the budgeted indirect-cost rate of $40 per direct manufacturing labor-hour is calculated at the beginning of the year on the basis of predictions of annual manufacturing overhead costs and predictions of the annual quantity of the cost-allocation base. Almost certainly, the actual amounts allocated will differ from the predictions.

7. *Transaction:* Completion and transfer to finished goods of 12 individual jobs, $188,800.

   Analysis: The asset Finished Goods Control is increased (debited) by $188,800, and the asset Work-in-Process Control is decreased (credited) by $188,800 to recognize the completion of jobs. The Work-in-Process records in the subsidiary ledger indicate that the costs of the 12 individual jobs completed in February 2003 equal $188,800. Exhibit 4-5, Panel B, shows that Job WPP 298 was one of the jobs completed at a cost of $9,705. Given Robinson's use of normal costing, cost of goods completed consists of *actual* direct materials, *actual* direct manufacturing labor, and the manufacturing overhead allocated to each job based on the *budgeted* manufacturing overhead rate times the *actual* direct manufacturing labor hours. Job WPP 298 also simultaneously appears as one of the 12 jobs in the finished goods records of the subsidiary ledger.

Journal Entry:	Finished Goods Control	188,800	
	Work-in-Process Control		188,800

In transaction 7, the completed goods are moved *out of* the manufacturing area and *into* the finished goods area. The $188,800 cost of completed goods is the "cost of goods manufactured." A *schedule* of cost of goods manufactured (for a different company) is presented in Exhibit 2-6, p. 41.

Post to General Ledger:

Work-in-Process Control			
②	81,000	⑦ 188,800	
③	39,000		
⑥	80,000		
Bal.	11,200		

Finished Goods Control		
⑦	188,800	

The debit balance of $11,200 in the Work-in-Process Control account represents the total costs of all jobs (per the job-cost records in the subsidiary ledger) that have not been completed as of the end of February 2003.

8. *Transaction:* Cost of Goods Sold, $180,000.

Analysis: The account Cost of Goods Sold is increased (debited) by $180,000. The asset Finished Goods Control is decreased (credited) by $180,000. The $180,000 amount represents the total cost of all goods sold during February 2003. Exhibit 4-5, Panel B, indicates that Job WPP 298 was one of the jobs sold and delivered to the customer in February 2003.

Journal Entry:	Cost of Goods Sold	180,000	
	Finished Goods Control		180,000

Post to General Ledger:

Finished Goods Control			
⑦	188,800	⑧ 180,000	
Bal.	8,800		

Cost of Goods Sold		
⑧	180,000	

The debit balance of $8,800 in the Finished Goods Control account represents the costs of all jobs that have been completed but not sold as of the end of February 2003.

9. *Transaction:* Marketing and customer-service payroll and advertising costs accrued for February:

Marketing Department salaries	$35,000
Advertising costs	10,000
Customer-Service Department salaries	15,000

Analysis: As described in Chapter 2, for financial accounting purposes, marketing and advertising costs of $45,000 ($35,000 + $10,000) and customer-service costs of $15,000 are *period costs* for February 2003 to be matched against February 2003's revenues. Unlike manufacturing costs, these costs are not added to Work-in-Process Control because these costs are not incurred to transform materials into a finished product. Robinson records the following entries.

Journal Entries:	Marketing and Advertising Costs	45,000	
	Customer-Service Costs	15,000	
	Salaries Payable Control		50,000
	Accounts Payable Control		10,000

Post to General Ledger:

Marketing and Advertising Costs	
⑨ 45,000	

Salaries Payable Control	
	⑨ 50,000

Customer-Service Costs	
⑨ 15,000	

Accounts Payable Control	
	⑨ 10,000

10. *Transaction:* Sales revenues, all on credit, \$270,000.

Analysis: The \$270,000 represents total amounts due from customers for sales made in February 2003, including \$15,000 due from the sale of WPP 298.

Journal Entry:	Accounts Receivable Control	270,000	
	Revenues		270,000

Post to General Ledger:

Accounts Receivable Control	
⑩ 270,000	

Revenues	
	⑩ 270,000

At this point, you should review all 10 entries in this illustration. Be sure to trace each journal entry, step by step, to accounts in the general ledger section in Panel A of Exhibit 4-5 (p. 108).

Nonmanufacturing Costs and Job Costing

Chapter 2 (pp. 45 – 46) pointed out that companies use product costs for different purposes. The product costs reported as inventoriable costs to shareholders may differ from product costs reported to tax authorities and may also differ from product costs reported to managers for guiding pricing and product-mix decisions. We emphasize that, even though as described previously, marketing and customer-service costs are expensed when incurred for financial accounting purposes, companies often trace or allocate these costs to individual jobs for pricing, product-mix, and cost-management decisions.

To identify marketing and customer-service costs of individual jobs, Robinson can use the same approach to job costing described earlier in this chapter in the context of manufacturing. Robinson can trace the direct-marketing and customer-service costs to jobs. Robinson can then calculate a budgeted indirect-cost rate by dividing budgeted indirect-marketing cost plus customer-service costs by the budgeted quantity of the cost-allocation base, say, revenues. Robinson can use this rate to allocate these indirect costs to jobs. For example, if this rate were 15% of revenues, Robinson would allocate \$2,250 to Job WPP 298 (0.15 × \$15,000, the revenue from the job). By assigning both manufacturing costs and nonmanufacturing costs to jobs, Robinson can compare all costs of the different jobs against the revenues they generate.

6 Account for end-of-period underallocated or overallocated indirect costs using alternative methods

...to make indirect costs allocated based on budgeted rates equal to actual indirect costs incurred

BUDGETED INDIRECT COSTS AND END-OF-PERIOD ADJUSTMENTS

Using budgeted indirect-cost rates and normal costing instead of actual costing has the advantage that indirect costs can be assigned to individual jobs on an ongoing and timely basis, rather than only at the end of the accounting period when actual costs are known. However, budgeted rates are likely to be inaccurate because they are based on estimates made up to 12 months before actual costs are incurred. We now consider adjustments that need to be made when, at year-end, indirect costs allocated differ from actual indirect costs incurred. Recall that for the numerator and denominator reasons discussed earlier (pp. 105 – 106), we do *not* expect actual overhead costs incurred each month to equal overhead costs allocated each month.

Underallocated indirect costs occur when the allocated amount of indirect costs in an accounting period is less than the actual (incurred) amount. **Overallocated indirect costs** occur when the allocated amount of indirect costs in an accounting period is greater than the actual (incurred) amount.

Underallocated (overallocated) indirect costs = Indirect costs incurred − Indirect costs allocated

Underallocated (overallocated) indirect costs are also called **underapplied (overapplied) indirect costs** and **underabsorbed (overabsorbed) indirect costs.**

Consider the manufacturing overhead indirect-cost pool at Robinson Company. There are two indirect-cost accounts in the general ledger that have to do with manufacturing overhead:

- Manufacturing Overhead Control, the record of the actual costs in all the individual overhead categories (such as indirect materials, indirect manufacturing labor, supervision, engineering, power, and rent)
- Manufacturing Overhead Allocated, the record of the manufacturing overhead allocated to individual jobs on the basis of the budgeted rate multiplied by actual direct manufacturing labor-hours

Assume the following annual data for the Robinson Company:

Manufacturing Overhead Control		Manufacturing Overhead Allocated	
Bal. Dec. 31, 2003 1,215,000			Bal. Dec. 31, 2003 1,080,000

The $1,080,000 credit balance in Manufacturing Overhead Allocated results from multiplying the 27,000 actual direct manufacturing labor-hours worked on all the jobs in 2003 by the budgeted rate of $40 per direct manufacturing labor-hour.

The $135,000 difference (a net debit) is an underallocated amount because actual manufacturing overhead costs are greater than the allocated amount. This difference arises from two reasons related to the computation of the $40 budgeted hourly rate:

1. *Numerator reason (indirect-cost pool).* Actual manufacturing-overhead costs of $1,215,000 are greater than the budgeted amount of $1,120,000.
2. *Denominator reason (quantity of allocation base).* Actual direct manufacturing labor-hours of 27,000 are fewer than the budgeted 28,000 hours.

There are three main approaches to accounting for the $135,000 underallocated manufacturing overhead caused by Robinson underestimating indirect costs and overestimating the quantity of the cost-allocation base: (1) the adjusted allocation-rate approach, (2) the proration approach, and (3) the write-off to cost of goods sold approach.

Adjusted Allocation-Rate Approach

The **adjusted allocation-rate approach** restates all overhead entries in the general ledger and subsidiary ledgers using actual cost rates rather than budgeted cost rates. First, the actual indirect-cost rate is computed at the end of the year. Then, the indirect costs allocated to every job during the year are recomputed using the actual indirect-cost rate (rather than the budgeted indirect-cost rate). Finally, end-of-year closing entries are made. The result is that at year-end, every job-cost record and finished goods record—as well as the ending Work-in-Process Control, Finished Goods Control, and Cost of Goods Sold accounts—accurately represents actual indirect costs incurred.

The widespread adoption of computerized accounting systems has greatly reduced the cost of using the adjusted allocation-rate approach. Consider the Robinson example. The actual manufacturing overhead ($1,215,000) exceeds the manufacturing overhead allocated ($1,080,000) by 12.5% [($1,215,000 − $1,080,000) ÷ $1,080,000]. The actual 2003 manufacturing overhead rate is $45 per direct manufacturing labor-hour ($1,215,000 ÷ 27,000 hours) rather than the budgeted $40 per direct manufacturing labor-hour. At year-end, Robinson could increase the manufacturing overhead allocated to each job in 2003 by 12.5% using a single software directive. The directive would affect both the subsidiary ledgers and the general ledger.

The adjusted allocation-rate approach "corrects" all MOH entries in the general and subsidiary ledgers to what they would have been if accountants had had a crystal ball and perfectly forecasted actual MOH costs and the actual quantity of the allocation base used. The feasibility of implementing the adjusted allocation-rate approach increases as technology decreases information processing costs.

Consider the Western Pulp Machine Job WPP 298. Under normal costing, the manufacturing overhead allocated to the job is $3,520 (the budgeted rate of $40 per direct manufacturing labor-hour × 88 hours). Increasing the manufacturing overhead allocated by 12.5%, or $440 ($3,520 × 0.125), means the adjusted amount of manufacturing overhead allocated to Job WPP 298 equals $3,960 ($3,520 + $440). Note from p. 101 that under actual costing, manufacturing overhead allocated on this job is also $3,960 (the actual rate of $45 per direct manufacturing labor-hour × 88 hours). Making this adjustment under normal costing for each job in the subsidiary ledgers ensures that all $1,215,000 of manufacturing overhead is allocated to jobs.

The adjusted allocation-rate approach yields the benefits of both *the timeliness and convenience of normal costing during the year and the accuracy of actual costing at the end of the year.* Each individual job-cost record and the end-of-year account balances for inventories and cost of goods sold are adjusted to actual costs. After-the-fact analysis of actual profitability of individual jobs provides managers with accurate and useful insights for future decisions about job pricing, which jobs to emphasize, and ways to manage costs.

Proration Approach

MOH Allocated is $135,000 less than MOH Control. That is, MOH Allocated is *underallocated*—its balance is smaller than the balance of MOH Control. This understated MOH Allocated flowed into Work-in-Process Control, which in turn flowed into Finished Goods Control and Cost of Goods Sold. Because all three of these accounts are understated, they would be increased under the proration approach.

Proration spreads underallocated overhead or overallocated overhead among ending work in process, finished goods and cost of goods sold. Materials inventories are not allocated manufacturing overhead costs, so they are not included in this proration. In our Robinson example, end-of-period proration is made to the ending balances in Work-in-Process Control, Finished Goods Control, and Cost of Goods Sold. Assume the following actual results for Robinson Company in 2003:

	Account Balance (Before Proration)	Manufacturing Overhead Allocated Included in the Account Balance (Before Proration)
Work in process	$ 50,000	$ 16,200
Finished goods	75,000	31,320
Cost of goods sold	2,375,000	1,032,480
	$2,500,000	$1,080,000

How should Robinson prorate the underallocated $135,000 of manufacturing overhead at the end of 2003?

Robinson should prorate underallocated or overallocated amounts on the basis of the total amount of manufacturing overhead allocated (before proration) in the ending balances of Work-in-Process Control, Finished Goods Control, and Cost of Goods Sold. The $135,000 underallocated overhead is prorated over the three affected accounts in proportion to their total amount of manufacturing overhead allocated (before proration) in column 2 of the following table, resulting in the ending balances (after proration) in column 4 at actual costs.

Account	Account Balance (Before Proration) (1)	Manufacturing Overhead Included in the Account Balance in Column (1) (2)		Proration of $135,000 Underallocated Manufacturing Overhead (3)	Account Balance (After Proration) (4) = (1) + (3)
Work in process	$ 50,000	$ 16,200	(1.5%)	0.015 × $135,000 = $ 2,025	$ 52,025
Finished goods	75,000	31,320	(2.9%)	0.029 × 135,000 = 3,915	78,915
Cost of goods sold	2,375,000	1,032,480	(95.6%)	0.956 × 135,000 = 129,060	2,504,060
	$2,500,000	$1,080,000	100.0%	$135,000	$2,635,000

Recall that the actual manufacturing overhead ($1,215,000) exceeds the manufacturing overhead allocated ($1,080,000) by 12.5%. The proration amounts in column 3 can also be derived by multiplying the balances in column 2 by 0.125. For example, the $3,915 proration to Finished Goods is 0.125 × $31,320. The journal entry to record this proration is

Work-in-Process Control	2,025	
Finished Goods Control	3,915	
Cost of Goods Sold	129,060	
Manufacturing Overhead Allocated	1,080,000	
Manufacturing Overhead Control		1,215,000

If manufacturing overhead had been overallocated, the Work-in-Process, Finished Goods, and Cost of Goods Sold accounts would be decreased (credited) instead of increased (debited).

This journal entry restates the 2003 ending balances for Work in Process, Finished Goods, and Cost of Goods Sold to what they would have been, if actual indirect-cost rates had been used rather than budgeted indirect-cost rates. This method reports the same 2003 ending balances in the general ledger as the adjusted allocation-rate approach.

Some companies use the proration approach but base it on the column 1 amounts of the preceding table—that is, the ending balances of Work in Process, Finished Goods, and Cost of Goods Sold before proration. It gives the same results as the previous proration *only if* the proportions of manufacturing overhead costs to total costs, and therefore direct costs, are the same in the Work-in-Process, Finished Goods, and Cost of Goods Sold accounts. In general, the proportion of direct costs to manufacturing overhead costs in the various accounts are not constant. For example, direct materials in the Work in Process ending balance may be a higher proportion than the direct materials in the Cost of Goods Sold ending balance, while manufacturing overhead is allocated using a cost-allocation base other than direct materials, say direct manufacturing labor. The following table shows that prorations based on ending account balances will not be the same as the more accurate prorations calculated earlier based on manufacturing overhead.

Account	Account Balance (Before Proration) (1)	Proration of $135,000 Underallocated Manufacturing Overhead (2)	Account Balance (After Proration) (3) = (1) + (2)
Work in process	$ 50,000 (2%)	0.02 × $135,000 = $ 2,700	$ 52,700
Finished goods	75,000 (3%)	0.03 × 135,000 = 4,050	79,050
Cost of goods sold	2,375,000 (95%)	0.95 × 135,000 = 128,250	2,503,250
	$2,500,000 100%	$135,000	$2,635,000

However, proration based on ending balances is frequently justified as being a less-complex way of approximating the more accurate results from using indirect costs allocated.

Write-Off to Cost of Goods Sold Approach

In this case, the total underallocated overhead or overallocated overhead is included in this year's Cost of Goods Sold. For Robinson, the journal entry would be:

Cost of Goods Sold	135,000	
Manufacturing Overhead Allocated	1,080,000	
Manufacturing Overhead Control		1,215,000

Robinson's two Manufacturing Overhead accounts are closed with the difference between them included in cost of goods sold. The Cost of Goods Sold account after the write-off equals $2,510,000, the balance before the write-off of $2,375,000 *plus* the *underallocated* overhead amount of $135,000.

No matter which approach is used, the underallocated overhead is not carried in the overhead accounts beyond the end of the year because the ending balances in Manufacturing Overhead Control and Manufacturing Overhead Allocated are closed to Work-in-Process Control, Finished Goods Control, and Cost of Goods Sold, and consequently become zero at the end of each year.

Choice Among Approaches

Which of these three approaches is the best one to use? In making this decision, managers should be guided by how the resulting information will be used. If managers intend to develop the most accurate record of individual job costs for profitability analysis purposes, the adjusted allocation-rate approach is preferred. If the purpose is confined to reporting the most accurate inventory and cost of goods sold figures in the financial statements, proration based on the manufacturing overhead-allocated component in the ending balances should be used because it adjusts the balances to what they would have been under actual costing. Note that the proration approach does not adjust individual job-cost records.

Proration based on the total amount of MOH Allocated in the ending balances of Work-in-Process Control, Finished Goods Control, and Cost of Goods Sold corrects these accounts to what they would have been under actual costing, which are the same ending balances as under the adjusted allocation-rate approach.

The write-off to Cost of Goods Sold is the simplest approach for dealing with underallocated or overallocated overhead. If the amount of underallocated or overallocated overhead is small — in comparison to total operating income or some other measure of materiality — the write-off to Cost of Goods Sold approach yields a good approximation to more accurate, but more complex, approaches. Modern companies are also becoming increasingly conscious of inventory control. Thus, quantities of inventories are lower than they were in earlier years, and Cost of Goods Sold tends to be higher in relation to the dollar amount of work-in-process and finished goods inventories. Also, the inventory balances of job-costing companies are usually small because goods are often made in response to customer orders. Consequently, as is true in our Robinson example, writing off underallocated or overallocated overhead instead of prorating it is unlikely to cause significant distortions in financial statements. For all these reasons, the cost-benefit test would favor the simplest approach — write-off to Cost of Goods Sold — because the more complex attempts at accuracy represented by the other two approaches do not appear to provide sufficient additional useful information.

MULTIPLE OVERHEAD COST POOLS

The Robinson Company illustration assumed that a single manufacturing overhead cost pool with direct manufacturing labor-hours as the cost-allocation base was appropriate for allocating indirect manufacturing costs to jobs. Robinson could have used multiple cost-allocation bases, say, direct manufacturing labor-hours *and* machine-hours, to allocate indirect costs to jobs. But Robinson would do something like that only if its managers believed that the benefits of the information generated by adding one or more pools (more accurate costing and pricing of jobs and better ability to manage costs) exceeded the costs of a costing system with two or more cost pools. (We discuss these issues in Chapter 5.)

To implement a normal-costing system with two overhead cost pools, Robinson would determine, say, the budgeted total direct manufacturing labor-hours and the budgeted total machine-hours for 2003, and identify the associated budgeted indirect total costs for each cost pool. It would then calculate two budgeted indirect-cost rates, one based on direct manufacturing labor-hours and the other on machine-hours. Indirect costs would be allocated to jobs using these budgeted indirect-cost rates and the actual direct manufacturing labor-hours and actual machine-hours used by various jobs. The general ledger would contain Manufacturing Overhead Control and Manufacturing Overhead Allocated amounts for each cost pool. End-of-period adjustments for underallocated or overallocated indirect costs would then be made separately for each cost pool.

7 Apply variations from normal costing

...costing systems that use budgeted direct-cost rates

VARIATIONS FROM NORMAL COSTING: A SERVICE-SECTOR EXAMPLE

Job-costing is very useful in service industries such as accounting and consulting firms, advertising agencies, auto repair shops, and hospitals. In an accounting firm, each audit is a job. The costs of each audit are accumulated on a job-cost record, much like the document used by Robinson Company, following the seven-step approach described earlier. On the basis of labor-time records, direct labor costs of the professional staff — audit partners, audit managers, and audit staff — are traced to individual jobs. Other direct costs such as travel, out-of-town meals and lodging, phone, fax, and copying are also traced to jobs. The costs of secretarial support, office staff, rent, and depreciation of furniture and equipment are indirect costs because these costs cannot be traced to jobs in an economically feasible way. Indirect costs are allocated to jobs, for example, using a cost-allocation base such as professional labor-hours.

In some service, merchandising, and manufacturing organizations, a variation from normal costing is helpful because actual direct-labor costs — the largest component of total costs — are difficult to trace to jobs as they are completed. For example, in our audit illustration, the actual direct-labor costs may include bonuses that become known only at the end of the year (a numerator reason). Also, the hours worked each period might vary significantly depending on the number of working days each month and the demand from clients (a denominator reason). Because of situations like these, a company needing timely information during the progress of an audit (and not wanting to wait until the end of the year) will use budgeted rates for some direct costs and budgeted rates for indirect costs. All budgeted rates are calculated at the start of the budget year. In contrast, normal costing uses actual cost rates for all direct costs and budgeted cost rates only for indirect costs.

The mechanics of using budgeted rates for direct costs are similar to the methods employed when using budgeted rates for indirect costs in normal costing. We illustrate this for Lindsay and Associates, a public accounting firm. At the start of 2003, Lindsay budgets total direct-labor costs of $14,400,000, total indirect costs of $12,960,000, and total direct (professional) labor-hours of 288,000 for the year. In this case,

$$\text{Budgeted direct-labor cost rate} = \frac{\text{Budgeted total direct-labor costs}}{\text{Budgeted total direct labor-hours}}$$

$$= \frac{\$14{,}400{,}000}{288{,}000 \text{ direct labor-hours}} = \$50 \text{ per direct labor-hour}$$

Assuming only one indirect-cost pool and total direct-labor costs as the cost-allocation base,

$$\text{Budgeted indirect-cost rate} = \frac{\text{Budgeted total costs in indirect-cost pool}}{\text{Budgeted total quantity of cost-allocation base (direct-labor costs)}}$$

$$= \frac{\$12{,}960{,}000}{\$14{,}400{,}000} = 0.90, \text{ or } 90\% \text{ of direct-labor costs}$$

Suppose an audit of Tracy Transport, a client of Lindsay, completed in March 2003, uses 800 direct labor-hours. Lindsay calculates the direct-labor costs of the Tracy Transport audit by multiplying the budgeted direct-labor cost rate, $50 per direct labor-hour by 800, the actual quantity of direct labor-hours. It allocates indirect costs to the Tracy Transport audit by multiplying the budgeted indirect-cost rate (90%) by the direct-labor costs of the Tracy Transport job ($40,000). Assuming no other direct costs for travel and the like, the cost of the Tracy Transport audit is:

Direct-labor costs, $50 × 800	$40,000
Indirect costs allocated, 90% × $40,000	36,000
Total	$76,000

At the end of the year, the direct costs traced to jobs using budgeted rates will generally not equal the actual direct costs because the actual rate and the budgeted rate are developed at different times using different information. End-of-period adjustments for underallocated or overallocated direct costs would need to be made in the same way that adjustments are made for underallocated or overallocated indirect costs.

The Lindsay and Associates example illustrates that all costing systems do not exactly match either the actual-costing system or the normal-costing system described earlier in the chapter. As another example, engineering consulting firms often have some actual direct costs (cost of making blueprints or fees paid to outside experts), other direct costs traced to jobs using a budgeted rate (professional labor costs), and indirect costs allocated to jobs using a budgeted rate (engineering and office-support costs).

PROBLEM FOR SELF-STUDY

You are asked to bring the following incomplete accounts of Endeavor Printing, Inc., up to date through January 31, 2004. Consider the data that appear in the T-accounts as well as the following information in items (a) through (i).

Endeavor's normal-costing system has two direct-cost categories (direct material costs and direct manufacturing labor costs) and one indirect-cost pool (manufacturing overhead costs, which are allocated using direct manufacturing labor costs).

Continued

Materials Control	
12-31-2003 Bal. 15,000	

Wages Payable Control	
	1-31-2004 Bal. 3,000

Work-in-Process Control	

Manufacturing Overhead Control	
1-31-2004 Bal. 57,000	

Manufacturing Overhead Allocated	

Finished Goods Control	
12-31-2003 Bal. 20,000	

Costs of Goods Sold	

Additional Information

a. Manufacturing overhead is allocated using a budgeted rate that is set every December. Management forecasts next year's manufacturing overhead costs and next year's direct manufacturing labor costs. The budget for 2004 is $600,000 for manufacturing overhead costs and $400,000 for direct manufacturing labor costs.

b. The only job unfinished on January 31, 2004, is No. 419, on which direct manufacturing labor costs are $2,000 (125 direct manufacturing labor-hours) and direct material costs are $8,000.

c. Total direct material costs placed into production during January are $90,000.

d. Cost of goods completed during January is $180,000.

e. Materials inventory as of January 31, 2004, is $20,000.

f. Finished goods inventory as of January 31, 2004, is $15,000.

g. All plant workers earn the same wage rate. Direct manufacturing labor-hours used for January total 2,500 hours. Other labor costs and supervision costs total $10,000.

h. The gross plant payroll paid in January equals $52,000. Ignore withholdings.

i. All "actual" manufacturing overhead incurred during January has already been posted.

Required

Calculate:

1. Materials purchased during January
2. Cost of Goods Sold during January
3. Direct manufacturing labor costs incurred during January
4. Manufacturing Overhead Allocated during January
5. Balance, Wages Payable Control, December 31, 2003
6. Balance, Work-in-Process Control, January 31, 2004
7. Balance, Work-in-Process Control, December 31, 2003
8. Manufacturing Overhead Underallocated or Overallocated for January 2004

SOLUTION

Amounts from the T-accounts are labeled "(T)."

1. From Materials Control T-account, Materials purchased: $90,000 (c) + $20,000 (e) − $15,000 (T) = $95,000
2. From Finished Goods Control T-account, Cost of Goods Sold: $20,000 (T) + $180,000 (d) − $15,000 (f) = $185,000
3. Direct manufacturing wage rate: $2,000 (b) ÷ 125 direct manufacturing labor-hours (b) = $16 per direct manufacturing labor-hour

   Direct manufacturing labor costs: 2,500 direct manufacturing labor-hours (g) × $16 per hour = $40,000
4. Manufacturing overhead rate: $600,000 (a) ÷ $400,000 (a) = 150%

   Manufacturing Overhead Allocated: 150% of $40,000 = 1.50 × $40,000 (see 3) = $60,000
5. From Wages Payable Control T-account, Wages Payable Control, December 31, 2003: $52,000 (h) + $3,000 (T) − $40,000 (see 3) − $10,000 (g) = $5,000
6. Work-in-Process Control, January 31, 2004: $8,000 (b) + $2,000 (b) + 150% of $2,000 (b) = $13,000 (This answer is used in item 7.)

7. From Work-in-Process Control T-account, Work-in-Process Control, December 31, 2003: \$180,000 (d) + \$13,000 (see 6) − \$90,000 (c) − \$40,000 (see 3) − \$60,000 (see 4) = \$3,000
8. Manufacturing overhead overallocated: \$60,000 (see 4) − \$57,000 (T) = \$3,000

Entries in T-accounts are lettered in accordance with the preceding additional information and are numbered in accordance with the requirements above.

Materials Control

December 31, 2003 Bal. (given)		15,000		
	(1)	95,000*	(c)	90,000
January 31, 2004 Bal.	(e)	20,000		

Work-in-Process Control

December 31, 2003 Bal.	(7)	3,000	(d)	180,000
Direct materials	(c)	90,000		
Direct manufacturing labor	(b) (g) (3)	40,000		
Manufacturing overhead allocated	(g) (a) (4)	60,000		
January 31, 2004 Bal.	(b) (6)	13,000		

Finished Goods Control

December 31, 2003 Bal.	(given)	20,000		
	(d)	180,000	(2)	185,000
January 31, 2004 Bal	(f)	15,000		

Wages Payable Control

	(h)	52,000	December 31, 2003 (5)	5,000
			(g), (3)	40,000
			(g)	10,000
			January 31, 2004 (given)	3,000

Manufacturing Overhead Control

Total January charges	(given)	57,000		

Manufacturing Overhead Allocated

			(g) (a) (4)	60,000

Cost of Goods Sold

	(f) (2)	185,000		

*Can be computed only after all other postings in the account have been found.

DECISION POINTS SUMMARY

The following question-and-answer format summarizes the chapter's learning objectives. Each decision presents a key question related to a learning objective. The guidelines are the answer to that question.

Decision	Guidelines
1. What are the building-block concepts of costing systems?	The building-block concepts of a costing system are cost object, direct costs of a cost object, indirect costs of a cost object, cost pool, and cost-allocation base. Costing-system overview diagrams represent these concepts in a systematic way. Costing systems aim to report cost numbers that reflect the way chosen cost objects (such as products or services) use the resources of an organization.

Continued

2. How do you distinguish job-costing from process costing?	Job-costing systems assign costs to distinct units of a product or service. Process-costing systems assign costs to masses of identical or similar units and compute unit costs on an average basis. These two costing systems represent opposite ends of a continuum. The costing systems of many companies combine some elements of both job costing and process costing.
3. How do you implement a job-costing system?	A general approach to job-costing requires identifying (a) the job, (b) the direct-cost categories, (c) the cost-allocation bases, (d) the indirect-cost categories, (e) the cost-allocation rates, (f) the allocated indirect costs of a job, and (g) the total direct and indirect costs of a job.
4. How do you distinguish actual costing from normal costing?	Actual costing and normal costing differ in the way each uses actual or budgeted indirect-cost rates:

	Actual Costing	Normal Costing
Direct-cost rates	Actual rates	Actual rates
Indirect-cost rates	Actual rates	Budgeted rates

Both methods use actual quantities of inputs for tracing direct costs and actual quantities of the allocation bases for allocating indirect costs.

5. What are the stages for recording transactions in a job-costing system?	The transactions in a job-costing system in manufacturing track: (a) the acquisition of materials and other manufacturing inputs; (b) their conversion into work in process; (c) their eventual conversion into finished goods; and (d) the sale of finished goods. Each of the (a) to (d) stages in the manufacture/sale cycle are represented by journal entries in the costing system.
6. How should you account for underallocated or overallocated manufacturing overhead costs?	The two theoretically correct approaches to disposing of underallocated or overallocated manufacturing overhead costs are to adjust the allocation rate and to prorate on the basis of the total amount of the allocated manufacturing overhead cost in the ending balances of Work-in-Process Control, Finished Goods Control, and Cost of Goods Sold. Many companies simply write off amounts of underallocated or overallocated manufacturing overhead to Cost of Goods Sold on the basis of practicality.
7. What variations from normal costing can be used?	In some variations from normal-costing, organizations use budgeted rates to assign direct costs, as well as indirect costs, to jobs.

TERMS TO LEARN

This chapter and the Glossary at the end of this book contain definitions of:

actual costing (p. 99)
adjusted allocation-rate approach (115)
budgeted indirect-cost rate (106)
cost-allocation base (97)
cost-application base (97)
cost pool (97)
indirect-cost rate (100)
job (98)
job-cost record (101)
job-cost sheet (101)
job-costing system (98)
labor-time record (102)
manufacturing overhead allocated (112)
manufacturing overhead applied (112)
materials-requisition record (101)
normal costing (106)
overabsorbed indirect costs (115)
overallocated indirect costs (114)
overapplied indirect costs (115)
process-costing system (98)
proration (116)
source document (101)
underabsorbed indirect costs (115)
underallocated indirect costs (114)
underapplied indirect costs (115)

ASSIGNMENT MATERIAL

Questions

4-1 Define cost pool, cost tracing, cost allocation, and cost-allocation base.

4-2 How does a job-costing system differ from a process-costing system?

4-3 Why might an advertising agency use job costing for an advertising campaign by Pepsi, whereas a bank uses process costing to determine the cost of checking account withdrawals?

4-4 Describe the seven steps in job costing.

4-5 What are the two major cost objects that managers focus on in companies using job-costing?

4-6 Describe three major source documents used in job-costing systems.

4-7 What is the main concern about source documents used to prepare job-cost records?

4-8 Give two reasons why most organizations use an annual period rather than a weekly or monthly period to compute budgeted indirect-cost rates.

4-9 Distinguish between actual costing and normal costing.

4-10 Describe two ways in which a house construction company may use job-cost information.

4-11 Comment on the following statement: "In a normal costing system, the amounts in the Manufacturing Overhead Control account will always equal the amounts in the Manufacturing Overhead Allocated account."

4-12 Describe three different debit entries to the Work-in-Process Control general ledger T-account under normal costing.

4-13 Describe three alternative ways to dispose of under- or overallocated indirect costs.

4-14 When might a company use budgeted costs rather than actual costs to compute direct labor rates?

4-15 Describe briefly why modern technology such as Electronic Data Interchange (EDI) is helpful to managers.

Exercises

4-16 **Job order costing, process costing.** In each of the following situations, determine whether job-costing or process costing would be more appropriate.

a. A CPA firm
b. An oil refinery
c. A custom furniture manufacturer
d. A tire manufacturer
e. A textbook publisher
f. A pharmaceutical company
g. An advertising agency
h. An apparel manufacturing plant
i. A flour mill
j. A paint manufacturer
k. A medical care facility
l. A landscaping company
m. A cola-drink-concentrate producer
n. A movie studio
o. A law firm
p. A commercial aircraft manufacturer
q. A management consulting firm
r. A breakfast-cereal company
s. A catering service
t. A paper mill
u. An auto repair garage

4-17 **Actual costing, normal costing, accounting for manufacturing overhead.** Destin Products uses a job-costing system with two direct-cost categories (direct materials and direct manufacturing labor) and one manufacturing overhead cost pool. Destin allocates manufacturing overhead costs using direct manufacturing labor costs. Destin provides the following information:

	Budget for 2004	Actual Results for 2004
Direct materials costs	$1,500,000	$1,450,000
Direct manufacturing labor costs	1,000,000	980,000
Direct manufacturing overhead costs	1,750,000	1,862,000

Required

1. Compute the actual and budgeted manufacturing overhead rates for 2004.
2. During March, the job-cost record for Job 626 contained the following information:

Direct materials used	$40,000
Direct manufacturing labor costs	$30,000

Compute the cost of Job 626 using (a) actual costing and (b) normal-costing.

3. At the end of 2004, compute the under- or overallocated manufacturing overhead under normal costing. Why is there no under- or overallocated overhead under actual costing?

4-18 **Job-costing, normal and actual costing.** Anderson Construction assembles residential houses. It uses a job-costing system with two direct-cost categories (direct materials and direct labor) and one indirect-cost pool (assembly support). Direct labor-hours is the allocation base for assembly support costs. In December 2003, Anderson budgets 2004 assembly-support costs to be $8,000,000 and 2004 direct labor-hours to be 160,000.

At the end of 2004, Anderson is comparing the costs of several jobs that were started and completed in 2004.

	Laguna Model	Mission Model
Construction period	Feb–June 2004	May–Oct 2004
Direct materials	$106,450	$127,604
Direct labor	$36,276	$41,410
Direct labor-hours	900	1,010

Direct materials and direct labor are paid for on a contract basis. The costs of each are known when direct materials are used or direct labor-hours are worked. The 2004 actual assembly-support costs were $6,888,000, and the actual direct labor-hours were 164,000.

Required

1. Compute the (a) budgeted and (b) actual indirect-cost rates. Why do they differ?
2. What is the job cost of the Laguna Model and the Mission Model using (a) normal costing and (b) actual costing?
3. Why might Anderson Construction prefer normal costing over actual costing?

4-19 Budgeted manufacturing overhead rate, allocated manufacturing overhead. Waheed Company uses normal costing. It allocates manufacturing overhead costs using a budgeted rate per machine-hour. The following data are available for 2003:

Budgeted manufacturing overhead costs	$2,850,000
Budgeted machine-hours	190,000
Actual manufacturing overhead costs	2,910,000
Actual machine-hours	195,000

Required

1. Calculate the budgeted manufacturing overhead rate.
2. Compute the manufacturing overhead allocated during 2003.
3. Calculate the amount of underallocated or overallocated manufacturing overhead.

4-20 Job-costing, accounting for manufacturing overhead, budgeted rates. The Lynn Company uses a job-costing system at its Minneapolis plant. The plant has a Machining Department and an Assembly Department. Its job-costing system has two direct-cost categories (direct materials and direct manufacturing labor) and two manufacturing overhead cost pools (the Machining Department overhead, allocated to jobs based on actual machine-hours, and the Assembly Department overhead, allocated to jobs based on actual direct manufacturing labor cost). The 2004 budget for the plant is:

	Machining Department	Assembly Department
Manufacturing overhead	$1,800,000	$3,600,000
Direct manufacturing labor cost	$1,400,000	$2,000,000
Direct manufacturing labor-hours	100,000	200,000
Machine-hours	50,000	200,000

Required

1. Present an overview diagram of Lynn's job-costing system. Compute the budgeted manufacturing overhead rate for each department.
2. During February, the job-cost record for Job 494 contained the following:

	Machining Department	Assembly Department
Direct materials used	$45,000	$70,000
Direct manufacturing labor costs	$14,000	$15,000
Direct manufacturing labor-hours	1,000	1,500
Machine-hours	2,000	1,000

   Compute the total manufacturing overhead costs allocated to Job 494.
3. At the end of 2004, the actual manufacturing overhead costs were $2,100,000 in Machining and $3,700,000 in Assembly. Assume that 55,000 actual machine-hours were used in Machining and that actual direct manufacturing labor costs in Assembly were $2,200,000. Compute the over- or underallocated manufacturing overhead for each department.

4-21 Job-costing, consulting firm. Taylor & Associates, a consulting firm, has the following condensed budget for 2004:

Revenues		$20,000,000
Total costs:		
Direct costs		
Professional labor	$ 5,000,000	
Indirect costs		
Consulting support	13,000,000	18,000,000
Operating income		$ 2,000,000

Taylor has a single direct-cost category (professional labor) and a single indirect-cost pool (client support). Indirect costs are allocated to jobs on the basis of professional labor costs.

1. Present an overview diagram of the job-costing system. Compute the 2004 budgeted indirect-cost rate for Taylor & Associates. **Required**
2. The markup rate for pricing jobs is intended to produce operating income equal to 10% of revenues. Compute the markup rate as a percentage of professional labor costs.
3. Taylor is bidding on a consulting job for Red Rooster, a fast-food chain specializing in poultry meats. The budgeted breakdown of professional labor on the job is as follows:

Professional Labor Category	Budgeted Rate per Hour	Budgeted Hours
Director	$200	3
Partner	100	16
Associate	50	40
Assistant	30	160

Compute the budgeted cost of the Red Rooster job. How much will Taylor bid for the job if it is to earn its target operating income of 10% of revenues?

4-22 Computing indirect-cost rates, job-costing. Mike Rotundo, the president of Tax Assist, is examining alternative ways to compute indirect-cost rates. He collects the following information from the budget for 2003:

- Budgeted variable indirect costs: $10 per hour of professional labor time
- Budgeted fixed indirect costs: $50,000 per quarter

The budgeted billable professional labor-hours per quarter are

January–March	20,000 hours
April–June	10,000 hours
July–September	4,000 hours
October–December	6,000 hours

Rotundo pays all tax professionals employed by Tax Assist on an hourly basis ($30 per hour, including all fringe benefits).

Tax Assist's job-costing system has a single direct-cost category (professional labor at $30 per hour) and a single indirect-cost pool (office support that is allocated using professional labor-hours).

Tax Assist charges clients $65 per professional labor-hour.

1. Compute the budgeted indirect-cost rate per professional labor-hour using **Required**
   a. Quarterly budgeted billable hours as the denominator
   b. Annual budgeted billable hours as the denominator
2. Compute the operating income for the following four customers using
   a. Quarterly indirect-cost rates
   b. An annual indirect-cost rate
      - Stan Hansen: 10 hours in February
      - Lelani Kai: 6 hours in March and 4 hours in April
      - Ken Patera: 4 hours in June and 6 hours in August
      - Evelyn Stevens: 5 hours in January, 2 hours in September, and 3 hours in November
3. Comment on your results in requirement 2.

4-23 Accounting for manufacturing overhead. Consider the following selected cost data for the Pittsburgh Forging Company for 2003.

Budgeted manufacturing overhead	$7,000,000
Budgeted machine-hours	200,000
Actual manufacturing overhead	$6,800,000
Actual machine-hours	195,000

The company uses normal costing. Its job-costing system has a single manufacturing overhead cost pool. Costs are allocated to jobs using a budgeted machine-hour rate. Any amount of under- or overallocation is written off to cost of goods sold.

1. Compute the budgeted manufacturing overhead rate. **Required**
2. Prepare the journal entries to record the allocation of manufacturing overhead.
3. Compute the amount of under- or overallocation of manufacturing overhead. Is the amount significant? Prepare a journal entry to dispose of this amount.

4-24 Job costing, journal entries. The University of Chicago Press is wholly owned by the university. It performs the bulk of its work for other university departments, which pay as though the press were an outside business enterprise. The press also publishes and maintains a stock of books for general sale. A job-costing system is used to cost each job. There are two direct-cost categories (direct materials and direct manufacturing labor) and one indirect-cost pool (manufacturing overhead, allocated on the basis of direct manufacturing labor costs).

The following data (in thousands) pertain to 2004:

Direct materials and supplies purchased on account	$800
Direct materials used	710
Indirect materials issued to various production departments	100
Direct manufacturing labor	1,300
Indirect manufacturing labor incurred by various departments	900
Depreciation on building and manufacturing equipment	400
Miscellaneous manufacturing overhead* incurred by various departments (ordinarily would be detailed as repairs, photocopying, utilities, etc.)	550
Manufacturing overhead allocated at 160% of direct manufacturing labor costs	?
Cost of goods manufactured	4,120
Revenues	8,000
Cost of goods sold	4,020
Inventories, December 31, 2003 (not 2004):	
Materials control	100
Work-in-process control	60
Finished goods control	500

* The term *manufacturing overhead* is not used uniformly. Other terms that are often encountered in printing companies include job overhead and shop overhead.

Required

1. Present an overview diagram of the job-costing system at the University of Chicago Press.
2. Prepare journal entries to summarize 2004 transactions. As your final entry, dispose of the year-end under- or overallocated manufacturing overhead as a write-off to Cost of Goods Sold. Number your entries. Explanations for each entry may be omitted.
3. Show posted T-accounts for all inventories, Cost of Goods Sold, Manufacturing Overhead Control, and Manufacturing Overhead Allocated.

4-25 **Job costing, journal entries, and source documents (continuation of 4-24).** For each journal entry in your answer to Exercise 4-24, (a) indicate the source document that would most likely authorize the entry, and (b) give a description of the entry in the subsidiary ledgers, if any entry needs to be made there.

4-26 **Job costing, journal entries.** Donnell Transport assembles prestige manufactured homes. Its job-costing system has two direct-cost categories (direct materials and direct manufacturing labor) and one indirect-cost pool (manufacturing overhead allocated at a budgeted $30 per machine-hour in 2004). The following data (in millions) pertain to operations for 2004:

Materials Control, December 31, 2003	$ 12
Work-in-Process Control, December 31, 2003	2
Finished Goods Control, December 31, 2003	6
Materials and supplies purchased on account	150
Direct materials used	145
Indirect materials (supplies) issued to various production departments	10
Direct manufacturing labor	90
Indirect manufacturing labor incurred by various production departments	30
Depreciation on plant and manufacturing equipment	19
Miscellaneous manufacturing overhead incurred (ordinarily would be detailed as repairs, utilities, etc., with a corresponding credit to various liability accounts)	9
Manufacturing overhead allocated, 2,100,000 actual machine-hours	?
Cost of goods manufactured	294
Revenues	400
Cost of goods sold	292

Required

1. Present an overview diagram of Donnell Transport's job-costing system.
2. Prepare journal entries. Number your entries. Post to T-accounts. What is the ending balance of Work-in-Process Control?
3. Show the journal entry for disposing of under- or overallocated manufacturing overhead directly as a year-end write-off to Cost of Goods Sold. Post the entry to T-accounts.

4-27 **Job costing, unit cost, ending work in process.** Raymond Company worked on only two jobs during May. Information on the jobs is given below:

	Job M1	Job M2
Direct materials	$ 75,000	$ 50,000
Direct manufacturing labor	$270,000	$210,000
Direct manufacturing labor-hours	6,000	5,000

Manufacturing overhead costs are allocated at the budgeted rate of $30 per direct manufacturing labor-hour. Job M1 was completed in May.

Required

1. Compute the total cost of Job M1.
2. Calculate per unit cost for Job M1 assuming it has 15,000 units.
3. Prepare the journal entry transferring Job M1 to Finished Goods.
4. Determine the ending balance in the Work-in-Process account.

4-28 **Job costing; actual, normal, and variation from normal costing.** Chirac & Partners is a Quebec-based public accounting partnership specializing in audit services. Its job-costing system has a single direct-cost category (professional labor) and a single indirect-cost pool (audit support, which contains all the costs in the Audit Support Department). Audit support costs are allocated to individual jobs using actual professional-labor hours. Chirac & Partners employs 10 professionals who perform their auditing services.

Budgeted and actual amounts for 2004 are as follows:

Budget for 2004

Professional labor compensation	$960,000
Audit support department costs	$720,000
Professional labor-hours billed to clients	16,000 hours

Actual results for 2004

Audit support department costs	$744,000
Professional labor-hours billed to clients	15,500 hours
Actual professional labor cost rate	$58 per hour

Required

1. Compute the direct-cost rate per professional labor-hour and the indirect-cost rate per professional labor-hour for 2004 under (a) actual costing, (b) normal costing, and (c) the variation from normal costing that uses budgeted rates for direct costs.
2. The audit of Pierre Enterprises done in 2004 was budgeted to take 110 hours of professional labor time. The actual professional labor time on the audit was 120 hours. Compute the 2004 job cost using (a) actual costing, (b) normal costing, and (c) the variation from normal costing that uses budgeted rates for direct costs. Explain any differences in the job cost.

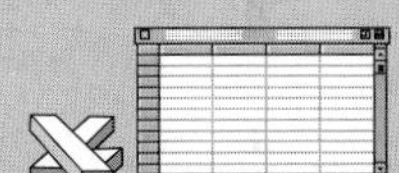

Excel Application For students who wish to practice their spreadsheet skills, the following is a step-by-step approach to creating an Excel spreadsheet to work this problem.

Step-by-Step

1. At the top of a new spreadsheet, create an "Original Data" section for the data provided by Chirac & Partners. Create rows for the budgeted and actual amounts for the period in exactly the same format as shown for Chirac & Partners above.

(Program your spreadsheet to perform all necessary calculations. Do not "hard-code" any amounts, such as direct and indirect cost rates, requiring addition, subtraction, multiplication, or division operations.)

2. Skip two rows. Create a new section labeled "Problem 1". Set up rows for direct-cost rate and indirect-cost rate. Set up columns "Actual costing," "Normal costing," and "Variation from normal costing." Use data in the "Original Data" section to compute the direct and indirect cost rates under actual costing, normal costing, and variation from normal costing that uses budgeted rates for direct costs.
3. Skip two rows and create a new section labeled "Problem 2", with rows for professional labor costs, audit support costs, and total job costs, and columns for "Actual Costing," "Normal Costing," and "Variation from Normal Costing." Use the direct and indirect cost rates in your "Problem 1" section to calculate professional labor costs, audit support costs, and total job cost for the Pierre Enterprises audit under actual costing, normal costing, and variation from normal costing that uses budgeted rates for direct costs.
4. *Verify the accuracy of your spreadsheet.* Go to your "Original Data" section and change the budgeted professional labor-hours billed from 16,000 to 17,000. If your spreadsheet is programmed correctly, the indirect cost rate under normal costing should change to $42, and total job cost for the Pierre Enterprises audit under the variation from normal costing should change to $11,859.

4-29 **Job costing, service industry, actual, normal, variation from normal costing.** Web Creations, a Web-site design and maintenance company, uses job-costing. Its job-costing system has a single direct-cost category (professional services) and a single indirect-cost pool (client support). Client support costs are allocated to individual jobs using actual professional service-hours. Budgeted and actual amounts for 2004 are as follows:

Budget for 2004

Professional services staff compensation	$10,000,000
Client support costs	$6,500,000
Professional service-hours billed to clients	50,000 hours

Actual results for 2004

Client support costs	$6,220,000
Professional service-hours billed to clients	55,000 hours
Actual professional services staff rate	$225 per hour

Required

1. Compute the direct-cost rate per professional service-hour and the indirect-cost rate per professional service-hour for 2004 under (a) actual costing, (b) normal costing, and (c) the variation from normal costing that uses budgeted rates for direct costs.
2. In 2004, Web Creations provided services to Amazing.com. Web Creations budgeted to spend 500 professional service-hours. Actual professional service-hours were 575. Compute the job cost of Amazing.com project using (a) actual costing, (b) normal costing, and (c) the variation from normal costing that uses budgeted rates for direct costs. Explain any differences in the job cost.

Problems

4-30 **Job costing, accounting for manufacturing overhead, budgeted rates.** The Solomon Company uses a job-costing system at its Dover, Delaware, plant. The plant has a Machining Department and a Finishing Department. Solomon uses normal-costing with two direct-cost categories (direct materials and direct manufacturing labor) and two manufacturing overhead cost pools (the Machining Department, with machine-hours as the allocation base, and the Finishing Department, with direct manufacturing labor costs as the allocation base). The 2003 budget for the plant is as follows:

	Machining Department	Finishing Department
Manufacturing overhead	$10,000,000	$8,000,000
Direct manufacturing labor costs	$900,000	$4,000,000
Direct manufacturing labor-hours	30,000	160,000
Machine-hours	200,000	33,000

Required

1. Present an overview diagram of Solomon's job-costing system.
2. What is the budgeted overhead rate that should be used in the Machining Department? In the Finishing Department?
3. During the month of January, the job-cost record for Job 431 shows the following:

	Machining Department	Finishing Department
Direct materials used	$14,000	$3,000
Direct manufacturing labor costs	$600	$1,250
Direct manufacturing labor-hours	30	50
Machine-hours	130	10

   Compute the total manufacturing overhead allocated to Job 431.
4. Assuming that Job 431 consisted of 200 units of product, what is the unit product cost of Job 431?
5. Amounts at the end of 2003 are as follows:

	Machining Department	Finishing Department
Manufacturing overhead incurred	$11,200,000	$7,900,000
Direct manufacturing labor costs	$950,000	$4,100,000
Machine-hours	220,000	32,000

   Compute the under- or overallocated manufacturing overhead for each department and for the Dover plant as a whole.
6. Why might Solomon use two different manufacturing overhead cost pools in its job-costing system?

4-31 **Service industry, job costing, law firm.** Keating & Associates is a law firm specializing in labor relations and employee-related work. It employs 25 professionals (5 partners and 20 associates) who work directly with its clients. The average budgeted total compensation per professional for 2002 is $104,000. Each professional is budgeted to have 1,600 billable hours to clients in 2002. Keating is a highly respected firm, and all professionals work for clients to their maximum 1,600 billable hours available. All professional labor costs are included in a single direct-cost category and are traced to jobs on a per-hour basis.

All costs of Keating & Associates other than professional labor costs are included in a single indirect-cost pool (legal support) and are allocated to jobs using professional labor-hours as the allocation base. The budgeted level of indirect costs in 2002 is $2,200,000.

Required

1. Present an overview diagram of Keating's job-costing system.
2. Compute the 2002 budgeted direct-cost rate per hour of professional labor.
3. Compute the 2002 budgeted indirect-cost rate per hour of professional labor.
4. Keating & Associates is considering bidding on two jobs:
   a. Litigation work for Richardson, Inc., which requires 100 budgeted hours of professional labor
   b. Labor contract work for Punch, Inc., which requires 150 budgeted hours of professional labor

   Prepare a cost estimate for each job.

4-32 Service industry, job costing two direct- and two indirect-cost categories, law firm (continuation of 4-31). Keating has just completed a review of its job-costing system. This review included a detailed analysis of how past jobs used the firm's resources and interviews with personnel about what factors drive the level of indirect costs. Management concluded that a system with two direct-cost categories (professional partner labor and professional associate labor) and two indirect-cost categories (general support and secretarial support) would yield more accurate job costs. Budgeted information for 2002 related to the two direct-cost categories is as follows:

	Professional Partner Labor	Professional Associate Labor
Number of professionals	5	20
Hours of billable time per professional	1,600 per year	1,600 per year
Total compensation (average per professional)	$200,000	$80,000

Budgeted information for 2002 relating to the two indirect-cost categories is

	General Support	Secretarial Support
Total costs	$1,800,000	$400,000
Cost-allocation base	Professional labor-hours	Partner labor-hours

Required

1. Compute the 2002 budgeted direct-cost rates for (a) professional partners and (b) professional associates.
2. Compute the 2002 budgeted indirect-cost rates for (a) general support and (b) secretarial support.
3. Compute the budgeted costs for the Richardson and Punch jobs, given the following information:

	Richardson, Inc.	Punch, Inc.
Professional partners	60 hours	30 hours
Professional associates	40 hours	120 hours

4. Comment on the results in requirement 3. Why are the job costs different from those computed in Problem 4-31?

4-33 Proration of overhead. (Z. Iqbal, adapted) The Zaf Radiator Company uses a normal-costing with a single manufacturing overhead cost pool and machine-hours as the cost-allocation base. The following data are for 2004:

Budgeted manufacturing overhead	$4,800,000
Overhead allocation base	Machine-hours
Budgeted machine-hours	80,000
Manufacturing overhead incurred	$4,900,000
Actual machine-hours	75,000

Machine-hours data and the ending balances (before proration of under- or overallocated overhead) are as follows:

	Actual Machine-Hours	2004 End of Year Balance
Cost of Goods Sold	60,000	$8,000,000
Finished Goods	11,000	1,250,000
Work in Process	4,000	750,000

Required

1. Compute the budgeted manufacturing overhead rate for 2004.

2. Compute the under- or overallocated manufacturing overhead of Zaf Radiator in 2004. Dispose of this amount using
   a. Write-off to Cost of Goods Sold
   b. Proration based on ending balances (before proration) in Work in Process, Finished Goods, and Cost of Goods Sold
   c. Proration based on the allocated overhead amount (before proration) in the ending balances of Work in Process, Finished Goods, and Cost of Goods Sold
3. Which method do you prefer in requirement 2? Explain.

4-34 Normal costing, overhead allocation, working backwards. (M. Rajan, adapted) Gibson Company uses normal costing. Its job-costing system has two direct-cost categories (direct materials and direct manufacturing labor) and one indirect-cost category (manufacturing overhead). The following information is obtained from the company's records for 2004:

- Total manufacturing costs, $8,000,000
- Cost of finished goods manufactured, $7,920,000
- Manufacturing overhead allocated, $3,600,000
- Manufacturing overhead was allocated to production at a rate of 200% of direct manufacturing labor costs
- The dollar amount of work-in-process inventory on January 1, 2004, was $320,000.

Required

1. Compute the total direct manufacturing labor costs in 2004.
2. Calculate the total cost of direct materials used in 2004.
3. Determine the dollar amount of work-in-process inventory on December 31, 2004.

4-35 Proration of overhead, two indirect-cost pools. Glavine Corporation uses two manufacturing overhead cost pools—one for the overhead costs incurred in the Machining Department and another for overhead costs incurred in the Assembly Department. Glavine uses normal costing. It allocates overhead costs to jobs from the Machining Department using a budgeted machine-hour (MH) overhead rate, and from the Assembly Department using a budgeted direct manufacturing labor-hour (DLH) rate.

The following data are for 2003:

	Machining Department	Assembly Department
Budgeted manufacturing overhead rate	$60 per machine-hour	$40 per direct manuf. labor-hour
Actual manufacturing overhead costs	$6,200,000	$4,700,000

Machine-hours and direct manufacturing labor-hours data and ending balances are as follows:

	Actual Machine-Hours	Actual Direct Manufacturing Labor-Hours	Balance Before Proration, December 31, 2003
Cost of Goods Sold	67,500	90,000	$16,000,000
Finished Goods Control	4,500	4,800	750,000
Work-in-Process Control	18,000	25,200	3,250,000

Required

1. Compute the underallocated or overallocated overhead in *each* department in 2003. Dispose of the underallocated or overallocated amount in *each* department using:
   a. Write-off to Cost of Goods Sold.
   b. Proration based on ending balances (before proration) in Cost of Goods Sold, Finished Goods Control, and Work-in-Process Control.
   c. Proration based on the allocated overhead amount (before proration) in the ending balances of Cost of Goods Sold, Finished Goods Control, and Work-in-Process Control.
2. Explain which proration method you prefer in requirement 1.

4-36 General ledger relationships, under- and overallocation. (S. Sridhar, adapted) Needham Company uses normal costing in its job-costing system. Partially completed T-accounts and additional information for Needham for 2003 are as follows:

Materials Control (Dr.)	Materials Control (Cr.)	Work-in-Process Control (Dr.)	Work-in-Process Control (Cr.)	Finished Goods Control (Dr.)	Finished Goods Control (Cr.)
1-1-2003 30,000	380,000	1-1-2003 20,000		1-1-2003 10,000	900,000
400,000		Dir. manuf. labor 360,000		940,000	

Manufacturing Overhead Control (Dr.)	Manufacturing Overhead Control (Cr.)	Manufacturing Overhead Allocated (Dr.)	Manufacturing Overhead Allocated (Cr.)	Cost of Goods Sold (Dr.)	Cost of Goods Sold (Cr.)
540,000					

Additional Information:

a. Direct manufacturing labor wage rate was $15 per hour.
b. Manufacturing overhead was allocated at $20 per direct manufacturing-labor hour.
c. During the year, sales revenues were $1,090,000, and marketing and distribution costs were $140,000.

Required

1. What was the amount of direct materials issued to production during 2003?
2. What was the amount of manufacturing overhead allocated to jobs during 2003?
3. What was the cost of jobs completed during 2003?
4. What was the balance of work-in-process inventory on December 31, 2003?
5. What was the cost of goods sold before proration of under- or overallocated overhead?
6. What was the under- or overallocated manufacturing overhead in 2003?
7. Dispose of the under- or overallocated manufacturing overhead using
   a. Write-off to Cost of Goods Sold
   b. Proration based on ending balances (before proration) in Work in Process, Finished Goods, and Cost of Goods Sold
8. Using each of the approaches in requirement 7, calculate Needham's operating income for 2003.
9. Which approach in requirement 7 do you recommend Needham use? Explain your answer briefly.

4-37 Overview of general ledger relationships. The Blakely Company is a small machine shop that uses normal costing in its job-costing system. The total debits and credits in certain accounts *one day before year-end* are as follows:

	December 30, 2002	
	Total Debits	**Total Credits**
Materials Control	$100,000	$ 70,000
Work-in-Process Control	320,000	305,000
Manufacturing Department Overhead Control	85,000	—
Finished Goods Control	325,000	300,000
Cost of Goods Sold	300,000	—
Manufacturing Overhead Allocated	—	90,000

All materials purchased are direct materials. Note that "total debits" in the inventory accounts would include beginning inventory balances, if any.

The total debits and total credits above *do not* include the following:

a. The manufacturing labor costs for the December 31 working day: direct manufacturing labor, $5,000, and indirect manufacturing labor, $1,000.
b. Miscellaneous manufacturing overhead incurred on December 31: $1,000.

Additional Information:

a. Manufacturing overhead has been allocated as a percentage of direct manufacturing labor costs through December 30.
b. Direct materials purchased during 2002 were $85,000.
c. No direct materials were returned to suppliers.
d. Direct manufacturing labor costs during 2002 totaled $150,000, not including the December 31 working day described previously.

Required

1. Compute the inventories (December 31, 2001) of Materials Control, Work-in-Process Control, and Finished Goods Control. Show T-accounts.
2. Prepare all adjusting and closing journal entries for the preceding accounts. Assume that all under- or overallocated manufacturing overhead is closed directly to Cost of Goods Sold.
3. Compute the ending inventories (December 31, 2002), after adjustments and closing, of Materials Control, Work-in-Process Control, and Finished Goods Control.

4-38 General ledger relationships, under- and overallocation, service industry. Brody and Co., an engineering consulting firm, uses a variation from normal costing in its job-costing system. It charges jobs for fees paid to outside experts at actual costs, professional direct-labor costs at a budgeted direct-labor rate, and engineering support overhead costs at a budgeted indirect-cost rate.

Brody maintains a "Jobs-in-Process Control" account in its general ledger that accumulates all costs of jobs. As a job is completed, Brody immediately bills the client and transfers the costs of the completed job to a "Cost of Jobs Billed" account.

The following data pertain to 2004:

1. Direct costs of fees (all cash)	$150,000
2. Actual direct professional labor costs (all cash)	$1,500,000
3. Direct professional labor allocated at $50 per actual direct professional labor-hour	$1,450,000
4. Actual engineering support overhead costs (all cash)	$1,180,000

Continued

5. Engineering support overhead allocated at 80% of actual direct professional labor costs — $1,200,000
6. Cost of jobs billed — $2,500,000

Required

1. Prepare summary journal entries for the above transactions using these accounts:

   Jobs-in-Process Control, Cost of Jobs Billed, Direct Professional Labor Control, Direct Professional Labor Allocated, Engineering Support Overhead Control, Engineering Support Overhead Allocated, and Cash Control.

2. As your final entry, dispose of the year-end under- or overallocated account balances as direct write-offs to Cost of Jobs Billed.

4-39 Allocation and proration of manufacturing overhead. (SMA, heavily adapted) Nicole Limited is a company that produces machinery to customer order. Its job-costing system (using normal costing) has two direct-cost categories (direct materials and direct manufacturing labor) and one indirect-cost pool (manufacturing overhead, allocated using a budgeted rate based on direct manufacturing labor costs). The budget for 2004 was:

Direct manufacturing labor	$420,000
Manufacturing overhead	$252,000

At the end of 2004, two jobs were incomplete: No. 1768B (total direct manufacturing labor costs were $11,000) and No. 1819C (total direct manufacturing labor costs were $39,000). Machine time totaled 287 hours for No. 1768B and 647 hours for No. 1819C. Direct materials issued to No. 1768B amounted to $22,000. Direct materials for No. 1819C were $42,000.

Total charges to the Manufacturing Overhead Control account for the year were $186,840. Direct manufacturing labor costs of all jobs were $400,000, representing 20,000 direct manufacturing labor-hours.

There were no beginning inventories. In addition to the ending work in process, the ending finished goods showed a balance of $156,000 (including direct manufacturing labor costs of $40,000). Revenues for 2004 totaled $2,700,680, cost of goods sold was $1,600,000, and marketing costs were $857,870. Nicole prices on a cost-plus basis. It currently uses a guideline of cost plus 40% of cost.

Required

1. Prepare a detailed schedule showing the ending balances in the inventories and Cost of Goods Sold (before considering any under- or overallocated manufacturing overhead). Show also the manufacturing overhead allocated in these ending balances.
2. Compute the under- or overallocated manufacturing overhead for 2004.
3. Prorate the amount computed in requirement 2 on the basis of
   a. The ending balances (before proration) of Work-in-Process Control, Finished Goods Control, and Cost of Goods Sold.
   b. The allocated overhead amount (before proration) in the ending balances of Work-in-Process Control, Finished Goods Control, and Cost of Goods Sold.
4. Assume that Nicole decides to write off to Cost of Goods Sold any under- or overallocated manufacturing overhead. Will operating income be higher or lower than the operating income that would have resulted from the proration in requirements 3a and 3b?
5. Calculate the cost of job No. 1819C if Nicole Limited had used the adjusted allocation-rate approach to dispose of under- or overallocated manufacturing overhead in 2004.

4-40 Job costing, contracting, ethics. Jack Halpern is the owner and CEO of Aerospace Comfort, a firm specializing in the manufacture of seats for air transport. He has just received a copy of a letter written to the General Audit Section of the U.S. Navy. He believes it is from an ex-employee of Aerospace.

Dear Sir,

Aerospace Comfort manufactured 100 X7 seats for the Navy in 2004. You may be interested to know the following:

1. *Direct materials costs billed for the 100 X7 seats were $25,000.*
2. *Direct manufacturing labor costs billed for 100 X7 seats were $6,000. These costs include 16 hours of setup labor at $25 per hour, an amount included in the manufacturing overhead cost pool as well. The $6,000 also includes 12 hours of design time at $50 an hour. Design time was explicitly identified as a cost the Navy would not reimburse.*
3. *Manufacturing overhead costs billed for 100 X7 seats were $9,000 (150% of direct manufacturing labor costs). This amount includes the 16 hours of setup labor at $25 per hour that is incorrectly included as part of direct manufacturing labor costs.*

You may also want to know that over 40% of the direct materials is purchased from Frontier Technology, a company that is 51% owned by Jack Halpern's brother. For obvious reasons, this letter will not be signed.

cc: The Wall Street Journal
Jack Halpern, CEO of Aerospace Comfort

Aerospace Comfort's contract states that the Navy reimburses Aerospace at 130% of total manufacturing costs. Assume that the facts in the letter are correct as you answer the following questions.

Required

1. What is the cost amount per X7 seat that Aerospace Comfort billed the Navy? Assume that the actual direct material costs were $25,000.
2. What is the amount per X7 seat that Aerospace Comfort should have billed the Navy? Assume that the actual direct material costs were $25,000.
3. What should the Navy do to tighten its procurement procedures to reduce the likelihood of such situations recurring in the future?

Collaborative Learning Problem

4-41 **Service industry, job costing, accounting for overhead costs, budgeted rates.** Jefferson Company, a painting contractor, uses normal costing to cost each job. Jefferson's job-costing system has two direct-cost categories (direct materials and direct labor) and one indirect-cost pool called overhead costs. Jefferson's budgeted overhead rate for allocating overhead costs to jobs is 80% of direct labor costs.

Jefferson provides the following additional information:

1. As of January 31, 2004, Job A21 was the only job in process, with direct materials costs of $30,000 and direct labor costs of $50,000.
2. Jobs A22, A23, and A24 were started during February.
3. Direct materials used during February were $150,000.
4. Direct-labor costs for February were $120,000.
5. Actual overhead costs for February were $102,000.
6. The only job still in process February 29, 2004, was job A24, with direct materials costs of $20,000 and direct labor costs of $40,000.

Jefferson maintains a "Jobs-in-Process Control" account in its general ledger. When a job is completed, Jefferson transfers the cost of the completed job to "Cost of Jobs Billed" account. Each month, Jefferson closes any underallocated or overallocated overhead to "Cost of Jobs Billed."

Required

1. Calculate the overhead allocated to Job A21 as of January 31, 2004, and the overhead allocated to Job A24 as of February 29, 2004.
2. Calculate the underallocated or overallocated overhead for February 2004.
3. Calculate the Cost of Jobs Billed for February 2004.

CHAPTER 4 INTERNET EXERCISE

The basis for allocating overhead in a job-costing system depends on a company's manufacturing process. To better understand factors that influence the choice of cost-allocation bases, go to www.prenhall.com/horngren, click on *Cost Accounting*, 11th ed., and access the Internet exercise for Chapter 4.

CHAPTER 4 VIDEO CASE

DELL COMPUTER: Cost Accounting Fundamentals and Job Costing

What does it cost to produce a computer for a customer? What are the costs of manufacturing, and how are they being managed? How can corporate performance be improved? These are a few of the questions managers at Dell Computer are called upon to answer. In most cases, the source of their replies can be traced back to the company's management accounting systems, which collect data on the many aspects of Dell's operations and provide information that managers use to answer questions and make decisions.

Dell Computer, headquartered in Austin, Texas, is a global manufacturing company. Dell does not make computer components, such as processor chips or disk drives. Instead, Dell focuses on the assembly of the components into computers that are distributed and sold worldwide. Dell produces four categories of personal computers: (1) the Optiplex line of high-end desktop computers, (2) the Dimension line of value-priced computers, (3) notebook computers such as the Inspiron series, and (4) network servers. The company's manufacturing facilities (located in Austin, Ireland, and Malaysia) serve customers around the globe from these locations. Each computer is built to a customer's order, so no finished goods inventory exists at Dell. Direct materials inventory is turned over every 30 days.

Dell's goal is to fill each customer's order in an average of five to six days. Each computer in an order is considered a separate job because the total cost of the components that make up each unit will vary, based on the customer's specifications. For example, costs are tracked to the computer unit level and include direct materials,

Continued

direct manufacturing labor, and a standard manufacturing overhead rate. The manufacturing overhead rate is developed in conjunction with Dell's Engineering Group, based on cost levels in its product manufacturing work cells or "mods." The overhead rates are revised every quarter. Product assembly mods are responsible for computer unit assembly, including putting together individual-unit direct materials and testing the components in each computer. Fully assembled and tested units pass out of each assembly mod to the shipping mod, where they are packed and prepared for shipment to the customer.

To be competitive, Dell maintains a Product Group, responsible for R&D of new product ideas. This group works in conjunction with its strategic partners, such as Intel Corporation, a major microprocessor chip manufacturer, to create products that can continue to meet the demands of the marketplace for more processing power and speed. New products that have the latest technology command higher margins, so Dell works hard to minimize the time it takes to develop and produce them. Often, new products are announced the same day component manufacturers unveil their new technological advances.

QUESTIONS

1. Using the seven-step approach to job costing, give an overview of manufacturing costs for Dell Computer.
2. What journal entries would you expect Dell to make in its job-costing system?
3. In which business functions of its value chain would you expect Dell to add the most value? Why?
4. Give examples of Dell's costs that would be considered (1) inventoriable costs and (2) period costs.

CHAPTER

5

Activity-Based Costing and Activity-Based Management

LEARNING OBJECTIVES

1. Explain undercosting and over-costing of products or services
2. Present three guidelines for refining a costing system
3. Distinguish between the traditional and the activity-based costing approaches to designing a costing system
4. Describe a four-part cost hierarchy
5. Cost products or services using activity-based costing
6. Use activity-based costing systems for activity-based management
7. Compare activity-based costing systems and department-costing systems
8. Evaluate the costs and benefits of implementing activity-based costing systems

www.prenhall.com/horngren

Dell Computer's personal computers are categorized into different lines, such as desktops, laptops, and servers. The three basic activities for manufacturing personal computers are (a) designing computers, (b) ordering component parts, and (c) configuring the assembly line so the manufacturing process is as efficient as possible. Finished machines are packed and shipped to buyers. That sounds simple. And it is. But not simple enough so managers can assume that the costs to manufacture all computers are the same. If they assumed that, they'd be making product decisions with flawed information. That's because different activities are needed to produce different computers in the different product lines.

Chapter 4 described a job-costing system that uses a single cost pool and a single indirect-cost rate to allocate indirect costs to jobs. That's an introduction to a basic job-costing system, but it raises the question, Does a single indirect-cost rate provide misleading job cost numbers? If the jobs, products, or services are alike in the way they consume indirect costs of a company, then a simple costing system, as in Chapter 4, will suffice for job-costing purposes. If they are not alike, then a simple costing system will yield inaccurate cost numbers for different jobs, products, or services being costed.

It's easy to determine "accurate" costs of products (or services) when a company has only a few products. When companies expand their product offerings and these products use different amounts of resources (such as supervision and quality control), it is more difficult to determine accurate costs of products. This situation is a main reason why companies use activity-based costing.

As global competition intensifies, companies are producing an increasing variety of products and services. They are finding that producing different products and services places varying demands on their resources. The need to measure more accurately how different products and services use resources has led companies such as American Express, Boeing, General Motors, and Exxon Mobil to refine their costing systems. One of the main ways companies around the globe have refined their costing systems is through activity-based costing (ABC). We describe how ABC systems help companies make better decisions about pricing and product mix. And we also show how ABC systems assist in cost management decisions by improving product designs and efficiency.

1 Explain undercosting and overcosting of products or services

...arise when reported costs of products do not equal their actual costs

BROAD AVERAGING VIA PEANUT-BUTTER COSTING APPROACHES

Companies that use a broad average—for example, a single indirect-cost rate—to allocate costs to products often do not produce reliable cost data. The term **cost smoothing,** or **peanut-butter costing** (yes, that's what it's called), describes a particular costing approach that uses broad averages for assigning (or spreading, as in spreading peanut butter) the cost of resources uniformly to cost objects (such as products or services) when the individual products or services, in fact, use those resources in a nonuniform way.

Undercosting and Overcosting

Cost smoothing can lead to undercosting or overcosting of products or services:

- **Product undercosting**—a product consumes a high level of resources but is reported to have a low cost per unit.
- **Product overcosting**—a product consumes a low level of resources but is reported to have a high cost per unit.

Companies that undercost products may make sales that actually result in losses, although they may have the impression—an incorrect impression—that these sales are profitable. These sales bring in fewer revenues than the cost of the resources they use. Companies that overcost products may overprice their products, losing market share to competitors producing similar products.

Product-Cost Cross-Subsidization

Product-cost cross-subsidization means that if a company undercosts one of its products, then it will overcost at least one of its other products. Similarly, if a company overcosts one of its products, it will undercost at least one of its other products. Product-cost cross-subsidization occurs when a cost is uniformly spread—meaning it is broadly averaged—across multiple products without recognizing which products require what resources in what amounts. Consider the costing of a restaurant bill for four colleagues who meet once a month to discuss business developments. Each diner orders separate entrees, desserts, and drinks. The restaurant bill for the most recent meeting is

	Entree	Dessert	Drinks	Total
Emma	$11	$ 0	$ 4	$ 15
James	20	8	14	42
Jessica	15	4	8	27
Matthew	14	4	6	24
Total	$60	$16	$32	$108
Average	$15	$ 4	$ 8	$ 27

If the $108 total restaurant bill is divided evenly, $27 is the average cost per dinner. This crude cost-smoothing approach treats each diner the same. Emma would probably object to paying $27 because her actual cost is only $15; she ordered the lowest-cost entree, had no dessert, and had the lowest-cost drinks. When costs are averaged across all four diners, both Emma and Matthew are overcosted, James is undercosted, and Jessica is (by coincidence) accurately costed.

In this example, the amount of cost cross-subsidization of each diner can be readily computed given that all cost items can be *traced* as direct costs to each diner. Calculating the account of cost cross-subsidization is not as simple when there are indirect costs to be considered that make the costing more complex. Why? Because the resources represented by the indirect costs are used by two or more individual diners, and the amounts to be allocated to each diner are not so clear-cut—for example, the cost of a bottle of wine shared by two or more diners.

To see the effects of cost smoothing on direct and indirect costs, we consider Plastim Corporation's costing system.

COSTING SYSTEM AT PLASTIM CORPORATION

Plastim Corporation manufactures lenses for the rear lamps (taillights) of automobiles. The lens, made from black, red, orange, or white plastic, is the part of the lamp visible on the automobile's exterior. Lenses are made by injecting molten plastic into a mold to give the lamp its desired shape. The mold is cooled to allow the molten plastic to solidify, and the lens is removed.

Under its contract with Giovanni Motors, a major automobile manufacturer, Plastim makes two types of lenses: a complex lens, CL5, and a simple lens, S3. The complex lens is a large lens with special features, such as multicolor molding (when more than one color is injected into the mold) and complex shapes that wrap around the corner of the car. Manufacturing CL5 lenses is more complex because various parts in the mold must align and fit precisely. The S3 lens is simpler to make because it is a single color and has few special features.

Design, Production, and Distribution Processes

The sequence of steps to design, produce, and distribute lenses, whether simple or complex, is

1. *Design products and processes.* Each year Giovanni Motors specifies some modifications to the simple and complex lenses. Plastim's Design Department designs the molds from which the lenses will be made and specifies the processes needed (details of the manufacturing operations).
2. *Manufacturing operations.* The lenses are molded, finished, cleaned, and inspected.
3. *Shipping and distribution.* Finished lenses are packed and sent to Giovanni Motors.

Plastim is operating at capacity and incurs very low marketing costs. Because of its high-quality products, Plastim has minimal customer-service costs. Plastim's business environment is very competitive with respect to simple lenses. At a recent meeting,

Giovanni's purchasing manager indicated that a new competitor, who makes only simple lenses, was offering to supply the S3 lens to Giovanni at a price of $53, well below Plastim's $63. Unless Plastim lowers its selling price, it will probably lose the Giovanni business for the simple lens for the upcoming model year. Plastim's management is very concerned. Fortunately, the same competitive pressures do not exist for the complex lens, which Plastim currently sells to Giovanni at $137 per lens.

Plastim's management has various options available. For example, Plastim can give up the Giovanni business in simple lenses if it is unprofitable. Or, Plastim can reduce the price of the simple lens and either accept a lower margin or aggressively seek to reduce costs. But to make these decisions management needs to first understand the costs to make and sell the S3 and CL5 lenses. To guide their pricing and cost management decisions, Plastim's managers assign all costs, both manufacturing and nonmanufacturing, to the S3 and CL5 lenses. Had the purpose been inventory costing, they would have assigned only manufacturing costs to the lenses.

Existing Single Indirect-Cost Pool System

Plastim currently uses a costing system with a single indirect-cost rate, the same as the system described in Chapter 4. The steps are

Step 1: Identify the Products That Are the Chosen Cost Objects. The cost objects are the 60,000 simple S3 lenses and the 15,000 complex CL5 lenses. Plastim's goal is to calculate the *total* costs of manufacturing and distributing these lenses. Plastim determines the unit cost of each lens by dividing total costs of each lens by 60,000 units for S3 lenses and 15,000 units for CL5 lenses.

Step 2: Identify the Direct Costs of the Products. Plastim identifies the direct costs—direct materials and direct manufacturing labor—of the lenses as follows:

	60,000 Simple Lenses (S3)		15,000 Complex Lenses (CL5)		
	Total (1)	per Unit (2) = (1) ÷ 60,000	Total (3)	per Unit (4) = (3) ÷ 15,000	Total (5) = (1) + (3)
Direct materials	$1,125,000	$18.75	$675,000	$45.00	$1,800,000
Direct manufacturing labor	600,000	10.00	195,000	13.00	795,000
Total direct costs	$1,725,000	$28.75	$870,000	$58.00	$2,595,000

Step 3: Select the Cost-Allocation Bases to Use for Allocating Indirect Costs to the Products. Most of the indirect costs consist of salaries paid to supervisors, engineers, manufacturing support, and maintenance staff, all supporting direct manufacturing labor. Plastim decides to use direct manufacturing labor-hours as the only allocation base to allocate all indirect costs to S3 and CL5. In the current year 2003, Plastim used 39,750 actual direct manufacturing labor-hours.

Step 4: Identify the Indirect Costs Associated with Each Cost-Allocation Base. Because Plastim uses only a single cost-allocation base, Plastim groups all indirect costs, totaling $2,385,000, into a single overhead cost pool.

Step 5: Compute the Rate per Unit of Each Cost-Allocation Base Used to Allocate Indirect Costs to the Products.

$$\text{Actual indirect-cost rate} = \frac{\text{Actual total costs in indirect-cost pool}}{\text{Actual total quantity of cost-allocation base}}$$

$$= \frac{\$2,385,000}{39,750 \text{ dir. manuf. labor-hours}} = \$60 \text{ per direct manufacturing labor-hour}$$

Exhibit 5-1, Panel A, shows an overview of Plastim's costing system.

Allocating indirect costs to both products at the $60 rate per direct manufacturing labor-hour used is the peanut-butter costing approach.

Step 6: Compute the Indirect Costs Allocated to the Products. Plastim uses 30,000 total direct manufacturing labor-hours to make the S3 lenses and 9,750 direct manufacturing labor-hours to make the CL5 lenses. Exhibit 5-1, Panel B, shows indirect costs of $1,800,000 ($60 per direct manufacturing labor-hour × 30,000 direct manufacturing labor-hours) allocated to the simple lens and $585,000

($60 per direct manufacturing labor-hour × 9,750 direct manufacturing labor-hours) allocated to the complex lens.

Step 7: Compute the Total Cost of the Products by Adding All Direct and Indirect Costs Assigned to the Products. Exhibit 5-1, Panel B, presents the product costs for the simple and complex lenses. The direct costs are calculated in step 2 and the indirect costs in step 6. Be sure you see the parallel between the costing system overview diagram (Exhibit 5-1, Panel A) and the costs calculated in step 7. Panel A shows two direct-cost categories and one indirect-cost category. Hence, the cost of each type of lens in step 7 (Panel B) has three line items: two for direct costs and one for allocated indirect costs.

EXHIBIT 5-1 **Product Costs at Plastim, Inc., Using Existing Single Overhead Cost Pool**

PANEL A: OVERVIEW OF PLASTIM'S EXISTING COSTING SYSTEM

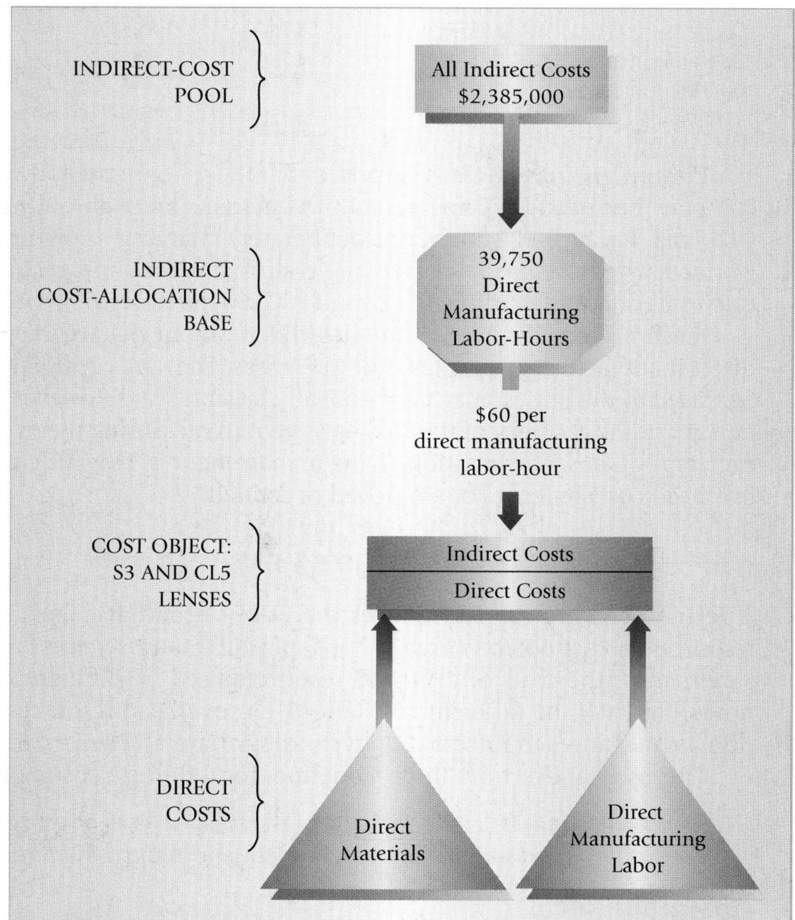

PANEL B: PRODUCT COSTS USING THE EXISTING COSTING SYSTEM

	60,000 Simple Lenses (S3)		15,000 Complex Lenses (CL5)		
	Total (1)	per Unit (2) = (1) ÷ 60,000	Total (3)	per Unit (4) = (3) ÷ 15,000	Total (5) = (1) + (3)
Direct materials	$1,125,000	$18.75	$ 675,000	$45.00	$1,800,000
Direct manufacturing labor	600,000	10.00	195,000	13.00	795,000
Total direct costs	1,725,000	28.75	870,000	58.00	2,595,000
Indirect costs allocated	1,800,000	30.00	585,000	39.00	2,385,000
Total costs	$3,525,000	$58.75	$1,455,000	$97.00	$4,980,000

Plastim's management begins investigating why the unit cost of the S3 lens is $58.75, well above the $53 selling price quoted by Plastim's competitor. A possible explanation is that Plastim's technology and processes are inefficient in manufacturing and distributing the S3 lens. Further analysis indicates that such inefficiency is not the reason. Plastim has years of experience in manufacturing and distributing lenses such as S3. Because Plastim often makes process improvements, management is confident that their simple-lens technology and processes are not inferior to those of their competitors. However, management is less certain about Plastim's capabilities in manufacturing and distributing complex lenses. Plastim has only recently started making this type of lens. Management is pleasantly surprised to learn that Giovanni Motors considers the price of the CL5 lens to be very competitive. Although puzzling, even at these prices, Plastim earns a very large profit margin percentage (operating income ÷ revenues) on the CL5 lenses:

	60,000 Simple Lenses (S3)		15,000 Complex Lenses (CL5)		
	Total (1)	per Unit (2) = (1) ÷ 60,000	Total (3)	per Unit (4) = (3) ÷ 15,000	Total (5) = (1) + (3)
Revenues	$ 3,780,000	$63.00	$2,055,000	$137.00	$5,835,000
Costs	3,525,000	58.75	1,455,000	97.00	4,980,000
Operating income	$ 255,000	$ 4.25	$ 600,000	$ 40.00	$ 855,000
Operating income ÷ Revenues		6.75%		29.20%	

Accountants need to reevaluate the costing system if it yields numbers that don't agree with what operating and marketing managers intuitively expect or if costs/prices appear to be out of line with competitors' costs/prices.

Plastim's management is surprised that the margins are low for the S3 lens, where the company has strong capabilities, but the margins are high on the newer, less-established CL5 lens. Because Plastim is not deliberately charging a low price for S3, management wonders whether the costing system is overcosting the simple S3 lens (assigning too much cost to it) and undercosting the complex CL5 lens (assigning too little cost to it).

Plastim's management is quite confident about the accuracy of direct materials and direct manufacturing labor costs of the lenses. They are confident because these costs can be traced to the lenses in an economically feasible way. However, management is less certain about the accuracy of the costing system in measuring the overhead resources used by each type of lens. The question facing management is, How might the system of allocating overhead costs to lenses be improved or refined?

2 **Present three guidelines for refining a costing system**

...classify more costs as direct costs, expand the number of indirect-cost pools, and identify cost drivers

REFINING A COSTING SYSTEM

A **refined costing system** reduces the use of broad averages for assigning the cost of resources to cost objects (such as jobs, products, and services) and provides better measurement of the costs of overhead resources used by different cost objects—no matter how differently the different cost objects use overhead resources. More intense competition and advances in information technology have accelerated these refinements.

This chapter describes three guidelines for refining a costing system:

1. *Direct-cost tracing.* Classify as many of the total costs as direct costs of the cost object as is economically feasible. This guideline aims to reduce the amount of costs classified as indirect.
2. *Indirect-cost pools.* Expand the number of indirect-cost pools until each of these pools is more homogeneous. In a *homogeneous cost pool,* all of the costs have the same or a similar cause-and-effect (or benefits-received) relationship with the cost-allocation base. Thus, a single cost pool containing both indirect machining costs and distribution costs that are allocated to products using machine hours is not homogeneous because machining costs and distribution costs do not have the same cause-and-effect relationship with machine hours. Increases in machine hours—the cause—have the effect of increasing machining costs but not distribution costs. Now suppose machining costs and distribution costs are separated into two cost pools with machine-hours as the cost-allocation base for the machining cost pool and the number of shipments as the cost-allocation base for the distribution cost pool. Each cost pool would now be homogeneous—within each cost pool, all costs have the same cause-and-effect relationship with their respective cost-allocation bases.

3. *Cost-allocation bases.* Use the cause-and-effect criterion, when possible, to identify the cost-allocation base for each indirect-cost pool.

ACTIVITY-BASED COSTING SYSTEMS

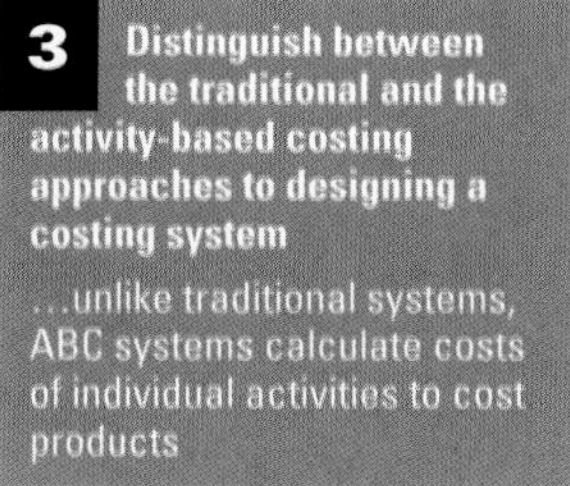

One of the best tools for refining a costing system is *activity-based costing.* **Activity-based costing (ABC)** refines a costing system by focusing on individual activities as the fundamental cost objects. An **activity** is an event, task, or unit of work with a specified purpose; for example, designing products, setting up machines, operating machines, and distributing products. ABC systems calculate the costs of individual activities and assign costs to cost objects such as products and services on the basis of the activities needed to produce each product or service:[1]

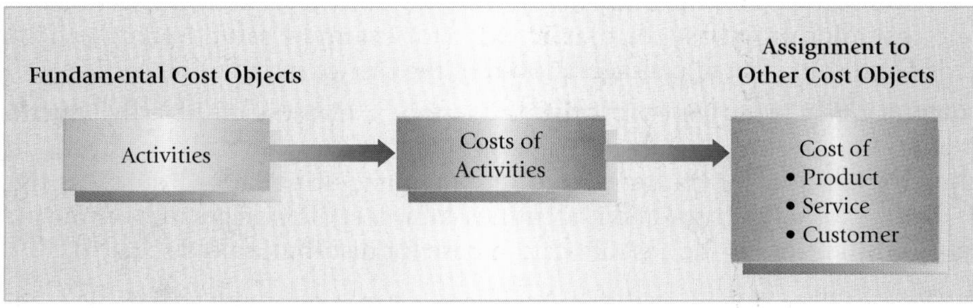

Activities consume resources (for example, workers are paid to pack and ship finished goods to customers). Then, products that consume the activities (packing and shipping) are allocated the costs of those activities.

Direct costs can be traced to products and jobs easily, so ABC systems focus on indirect costs, refining the assignment of indirect costs to departments, processes, products, and other cost objects. Plastim's ABC system identifies various activities that help explain why Plastim incurs the costs it currently classifies as indirect. To identify these activities, Plastim organizes a team from design, manufacturing, distribution, accounting, and administration. The team identifies the following seven activities by developing a flowchart of all the steps and processes needed to design, manufacture, and distribute lenses.

a. Design products and processes
b. Set up molding machines to ensure the molds are properly held in place and parts are properly aligned before manufacturing starts
c. Operate machines to manufacture lenses
d. Clean and maintain the molds after lenses are manufactured
e. Set up batches of finished lenses for shipment
f. Distribute lenses to customers
g. Administer and manage all processes at Plastim

By identifying activities and the costs of performing each activity, ABC systems seek a greater level of detail to understand how an organization uses its resources. As we describe ABC systems, keep in mind the three guidelines for refining a costing system described on pages 140 – 141.

1. *Direct-cost tracing.* A feature of ABC systems is aiming to identify some costs or cost pools that can be reclassified as direct costs instead of indirect costs. ABC systems do this by subdividing existing cost pools. Costs in some new pools may qualify as direct costs. In the Plastim example, the cleaning and maintenance activity consists of salaries and wages paid to workers responsible for cleaning the mold. These costs can be traced directly to the specific mold used to produce the lens. Direct tracing of costs improves cost accuracy and is simpler because, unlike indirect costs, cost pools and cost-allocation bases do not have to be identified.

[1]For more details on ABC systems, see R. Cooper and R. S. Kaplan, *The Design of Cost Management Systems,* (Upper Saddle River, NJ: Prentice Hall, 1999).

2. *Indirect-cost pools.* ABC systems create smaller cost pools linked to the different activities. Plastim subdivides its original single overhead cost pool into one direct activity-cost pool and six indirect activity-related cost pools, each one pool corresponding to one of the seven activities described earlier.

The single overhead cost pool is *not* homogeneous. It's not homogeneous because the costs of some of the activities (for example, designing products and processes, setting up machines, and distributing lenses) that are lumped into the single cost pool have a weak cause-and-effect relationship with direct manufacturing labor-hours—for example, changes in direct manufacturing labor-hours have no effect on the costs of designing products and processes. Consequently, measuring the direct manufacturing labor-hours used by the S3 and CL5 lenses does not represent the costs of the overhead resources required by these two different lenses.

Each of the activity-related cost pools are homogeneous. Why? Because each activity cost pool includes only a narrow and focused set of costs (for example, setup or distribution). Over time, the costs in each activity-cost pool have a cause-and-effect relationship with the cost-allocation base for that activity (for example, setup-hours in the case of setup costs and cubic feet of packages moved in the case of distribution costs).

3. *Cost-allocation bases.* For each activity-cost pool, a measure of the activity performed serves as the cost-allocation base. For example, Plastim identifies setup-hours, the measure of setup activity (rather than direct manufacturing labor-hours), as the cost-allocation base for setup costs; and it identifies cubic feet of packages moved, the measure of distribution activity, as the cost-allocation base for distribution costs.

The logic of ABC systems is that more finely structured activity-cost pools with activity-specific cost-allocation bases, which are cost drivers for the cost pool, lead to more accurate costing of activities. Allocating costs to products by measuring the cost-allocation bases of different activities used by different products leads to more accurate product costs. We illustrate this logic by focusing on the setup activity.

Setting up molding machines frequently entails trial runs, fine-tuning, and adjustments. Improper setups cause quality problems such as scratches on the surface of the lens. The resources needed for each setup depend on the complexity of the manufacturing operation. Complex lenses require more setup resources per setup than simple lenses. Furthermore, complex lenses can be produced only in small batches because the molds for complex lenses need to be cleaned more often than molds for simple lenses. Relative to simple lenses, complex lenses not only use more resources per setup, they also need more frequent setups.

Setup data for the simple S3 lens and the complex CL5 lens are

		Simple S3 Lens	Complex CL5 Lens	Total
1	Quantity of lenses produced	60,000	15,000	
2	Number of lenses produced per batch	240	50	
3 = (1) ÷ (2)	Number of batches	250	300	
4	Setup time per batch	2 hours	5 hours	
5 = (3) × (4)	Total setup-hours	500 hours	1,500 hours	2,000 hours

Plastim identifies the total costs of setups (consisting mainly of allocated costs of process engineers, quality engineers, supervisors, and setup equipment) of $300,000. The following table illustrates the effect of using direct manufacturing labor-hours—the cost-allocation base for all overhead costs in Plastim's pre-ABC costing system—versus setup-hours—the cost-allocation base for setup costs in the ABC system—to allocate setup costs to the simple and complex lenses. The setup cost per direct manufacturing labor-hour equals $7.54717 ($300,000 ÷ 39,750 direct manufacturing labor-hours). The setup cost per setup-hour equals $150 ($300,000 ÷ 2,000 setup-hours).

	Simple S3 Lens	Complex CL5 Lens	Total
Cost allocated using direct manufacturing labor-hours: $7.54717 × 30,000; $7.54717 × 9,750	$226,415	$ 73,585	$300,000
Cost allocated using setup-hours: $150 × 500; $150 × 1,500	$ 75,000	$225,000	$300,000

Which allocation base should Plastim use? Answer: Setup-hours because, following guidelines 2 and 3, there is a strong cause-and-effect relationship between setup-hours and setup-related overhead costs, but there is almost no relationship between direct manufacturing labor-hours and setup-related overhead costs. Setup costs depend on the number of batches and the complexity of the setups, so that's why setup-hours drive setup costs. The simple S3 lens is allocated more of the setup costs when costs are allocated on the basis of direct manufacturing labor-hours. The reason? Because more direct manufacturing labor-hours are needed to produce S3 lenses. However, direct manufacturing labor-hours required by the S3 and CL5 lenses bear no relationship to the setup-hours (and setup costs) demanded by the S3 and CL5 lenses.

Note that setup-hours are related to batches (or groups) of lenses made, not individual lenses. Activity-based costing highlights the different levels of activities—for example, individual units of output versus batches of output—when identifying cause-and-effect relationships. As our discussion of setups illustrates, limiting the drivers of costs to only units of output, or cost-allocation bases related to units of output (such as direct manufacturing labor-hours), frequently will weaken the cause-and-effect relationship between the cost-allocation base and the costs in a cost pool. When the cost in a cost pool relates to batches of output (such as setup costs), the cost-allocation base must also relate to batches of output (for example, setup-hours). The *cost hierarchy* distinguishes costs by whether the cost driver is a unit of output (or variables such as machine-hours or direct manufacturing labor-hours that are a function of units of output); or a *group* of units of a product, such as a batch in the case of setup costs; or the *product itself*, such as the complexity of the mold in the case of design costs.

Cost Hierarchies

4 Describe a four-part cost hierarchy

...used to categorize costs based on different types of cost drivers—for example, costs that vary with each unit of a product versus costs that vary with each batch of products

A **cost hierarchy** categorizes costs into different cost pools on the basis of the different types of cost drivers, or cost-allocation bases, or different degrees of difficulty in determining cause-and-effect (or benefits-received) relationships. ABC systems commonly use a cost hierarchy having four levels—output unit-level costs, batch-level costs, product-sustaining costs, and facility-sustaining costs—to identify cost-allocation bases that are, whenever possible, cost drivers of costs in activity cost pools.

Output unit-level costs are the cost of activities performed on each individual unit of a product or service. Manufacturing operations costs (such as the costs of energy, machine depreciation, and repair) related to the activity of running the automated molding machines are output unit-level costs. They are output unit-level costs because, over time, the cost of this activity increases with additional units of output produced (or machine-hours used).

Suppose that in our Plastim example, each S3 lens requires 0.15 molding machine-hours. Then S3 lenses require a total of 9,000 molding machine-hours (0.15 molding machine-hours per lens × 60,000 lenses). Similarly, suppose each CL5 lens requires 0.25 molding machine-hours. Then the CL5 lenses require 3,750 molding machine-hours (0.25 molding machine-hours per lens × 15,000 lenses). The *total* manufacturing operations costs allocated to S3 and CL5 depend on the quantity of each type of lens produced, regardless of the number of batches in which the lenses are made. Plastim's ABC system uses machine-hours—an output unit-level cost-allocation base—to allocate manufacturing operation costs to products.

Batch-level costs are the costs of activities related to a group of units of products or services rather than to each individual unit of product or service. In the Plastim example, setup costs are batch-level costs. They are batch-level costs because, over time, the cost of this setup activity increases with setup-hours needed to produce batches of lenses. The S3 lens requires 500 setup-hours (2 setup-hours per batch × 250 batches). The CL5 lens requires 1,500 setup-hours (5 setup-hours per batch × 300 batches). The total setup costs allocated to S3 and CL5 depend on the total setup-hours required by each type of lens, not on the number of units of S3 and CL5 produced. Plastim's ABC system uses setup-hours—a batch-level cost-allocation base—to allocate setup costs to products.

In companies that purchase many different types of direct materials (Plastim purchases mainly plastic pellets), procurement costs can be significant. Procurement costs include the costs of placing purchase orders, receiving materials, and paying suppliers. These costs are batch-level costs because they are related to the number of purchase orders placed rather than to the quantity or value of materials purchased.

Product-sustaining costs (or **service-sustaining costs**) are the costs of activities undertaken to support individual products or services regardless of the number of units or batches in which the units are produced. In the Plastim example, design costs are product-sustaining costs. Over time, design costs depend largely on the time spent by designers on designing and modifying the product, the mold, and the process. These design costs are a function of the complexity of the mold, measured by the number of parts in the mold multiplied by the area (in square feet) over which the molten plastic must flow (12 parts × 2.5 square feet, or 30 parts-square feet for the S3 lens, and 14 parts × 5 square feet, or 70 parts-square feet for the CL5 lens). In 2003, the *total* design costs allocated to S3 and CL5 depend on the complexity of the mold, regardless of the number of units or batches of production. Design costs cannot be linked in any cause-and-effect way to individual units of products or to individual batches of products. Plastim's ABC system uses parts-square feet—a product-sustaining cost-allocation base—to allocate design costs to products. Another example of product-sustaining costs is engineering costs incurred to change product designs, although such changes are infrequent at Plastim.

A major reason low-volume products are often undercosted is that low-volume products' *batch-level costs and product-sustaining costs* should be spread over the relatively few units of low-volume products rather than spread like peanut butter over all products using *output unit-level cost-allocation bases.*

Facility-sustaining costs are the cost of activities that cannot be traced to individual products or services but support the organization as a whole. In the Plastim example, the general administration costs (including rent and building security) are facility-sustaining costs. It is usually difficult to find good cause-and-effect relationships between these costs and a cost-allocation base. This lack of a cause-and-effect relationship causes some companies not to allocate these costs to products and instead to deduct them from operating income. Other companies, such as Plastim, allocate facility-sustaining costs to products on some basis—for example, direct manufacturing labor-hours—because management believes all costs should be allocated to products. Allocating all costs to products or services becomes important when management wants to set selling prices on the basis of an amount of cost that includes all costs.

5 Cost products or services using activity-based costing

...use cost rates for different activities to compute indirect costs of a product

IMPLEMENTING ACTIVITY-BASED COSTING AT PLASTIM

Now that you understand the basic concepts of ABC, let's use them to refine the costing system Plastim has been using. We again follow the seven-step approach to costing and the three guidelines for refining costing systems (the guidelines are increasing direct-cost tracing, creating homogeneous indirect-cost pools, and identifying cost-allocation bases that have cause-and-effect relationships with costs in the cost pool).

Step 1: Identify the Products That Are the Chosen Cost Objects. The cost objects are the S3 and CL5 lenses. Plastim's goal is to calculate, first, the total costs, and second, the per-unit costs of manufacturing and distributing these lenses.

Step 2: Identify the Direct Costs of the Products. Plastim identifies as direct costs of the lenses: direct materials costs, direct manufacturing labor costs, and mold cleaning and maintenance costs. In the costing system it has been using, Plastim classified mold cleaning and maintenance costs as indirect costs and allocated them to products using direct manufacturing labor-hours. However, these costs can be traced directly to a lens because each type of lens can only be produced from a specific mold. You should see that because mold cleaning and maintenance costs consist of workers' wages for cleaning molds after each batch of lenses is produced, the costs for cleaning and maintenance are direct batch-level costs. Complex lenses incur more cleaning and maintenance costs than simple lenses because Plastim produces more batches of complex lenses than simple lenses and because the molds of complex lenses are more difficult to clean. Direct manufacturing labor-hours is not a good cost driver of the demand that simple and complex lenses place on mold cleaning and maintenance resources.

Plastim's direct costs are

Description	Cost Hierarchy Category	60,000 Simple Lenses (S3) Total (1)	per Unit (2) = (1) ÷ 60,000	15,000 Complex Lenses (CL5) Total (3)	per Unit (4) = (3) ÷ 15,000	Total (5) = (1) + (3)
Direct materials	Output unit-level	$1,125,000	$18.75	$ 675,000	$45.00	$1,800,000
Direct manuf. labor	Output unit-level	600,000	10.00	195,000	13.00	795,000
Cleaning & maintenance	Batch-level	120,000	2.00	150,000	10.00	270,000
Total direct costs		$1,845,000	$30.75	$1,020,000	$68.00	$2,865,000

Step 3: Select the Cost-Allocation Bases to Use for Allocating Indirect Costs to the Products. Plastim identifies six activities—design, molding machine setups, manufacturing operations, shipment setup, distribution, and administration—for allocating indirect costs to products. Exhibit 5-2, column 4, shows the cost-allocation base and the quantity of the cost-allocation base for each activity described in column 1.

Identifying the cost-allocation bases defines the number of activity pools into which costs must be grouped in an ABC system. For example, rather than define the design activities of product design, process design, and prototyping as separate activities, Plastim defines these three activities together as a combined design activity. Why? Because the complexity of the mold is an appropriate cost driver for costs incurred in each of the three separate design activities.

Identifying activities and cost drivers is not easy but necessary. Operating personnel have the best understanding of the company's production processes. In ABC, accountants often interview operating personnel to help identify activities and the related cost-allocation bases.

EXHIBIT 5-2 Activity-Cost Rates for Indirect-Cost Pools

Activity (1)	Cost Hierarchy Category (2)	(Step 4) Total Costs (3)	(Step 3) Quantity of Cost-Allocation Base (4)	(Step 5) Overhead Allocation Rate (5) = (3) ÷ (4)	Brief Explanation of the Cause-and-Effect Relationship That Motivates the Choice of the Allocation Base (6)
Design	Product-sustaining	$450,000	100 parts-square feet	$4,500 per part-square foot	Complex molds (more parts and larger surface area) require greater Design Department resources
Setups of molding machines	Batch-level	$300,000	2,000 setup-hours	$150 per setup-hour	Overhead costs of the setup activity increase as setup-hours increase
Manufacturing operations	Output unit-level	$637,500	12,750 molding machine-hours	$50 per molding machine-hour	Plastim has mostly automated molding machines. Manufacturing overhead costs support automated molding machines and, hence, increase with molding machine usage
Shipment setup	Batch-level	$ 81,000	200 shipments	$405 per shipment	Costs incurred to prepare batches for shipment increase with the number of shipments
Distribution	Output unit-level	$391,500	67,500 cubic feet	$5.80 per cubic foot shipped	Overhead costs of the distribution activity increase with cubic feet of packages shipped
Administration	Facility-sustaining	$255,000	39,750 direct manuf. labor-hours	$6.4151 per direct manuf. labor-hour	Administration Department resources support direct manufacturing labor-hours because the demand for these resources increases with direct manufacturing labor-hours

A second consideration in choosing a cost-allocation base is the availability of reliable data and measures. Consider the problem of determining a cost-allocation base for the design activity. The driver of design cost, which is a product-sustaining cost, is the complexity of the mold; more complex molds take more time to design. In its ABC system, Plastim measures complexity in terms of the number of parts in the mold and the surface area of the mold. If these data are difficult to obtain or measure, Plastim may be forced to use some other measure of complexity, such as the amount of material flowing through the mold. A potential problem with this measure of complexity is that the quantity of material flow may not adequately represent the complexity of the design activity.

Companies that have successfully implemented ABC usually limit the number of activities to 5 to 10 per department, at least in the initial implementation. More activities can be added later if additional complexity is warranted. Identifying too many activities initially may bog the company down in too much detail, which might cause the ABC implementation to fail.

Step 4: Identify the Indirect Costs Associated with Each Cost-Allocation Base. In this step, overhead costs incurred by Plastim are assigned to activities (see Exhibit 5-2, column 3), to the extent possible, on the basis of a cause-and-effect relationship between the cost-allocation base for an activity and the costs of the activity. For example, costs are assigned to the distribution-cost pool on the basis of a cause-and-effect relationship to cubic feet of packages moved. Of course, the strength of the cause-and-effect relationship between the cost-allocation base and the respective costs of the activity varies across cost pools. For example, the cause-and-effect relationship between direct manufacturing labor-hours and administration activity costs is not as strong as the relationship between setup-hours and setup activity costs.

Some costs can be directly identified with a particular activity. For example, salaries paid to design engineers are directly identified with the design activity.

EXHIBIT 5-3 Product Costs at Plastim, Inc., Using Activity-Based Costing

PANEL A: OVERVIEW OF PLASTIM'S ACTIVITY-BASED COSTING SYSTEM

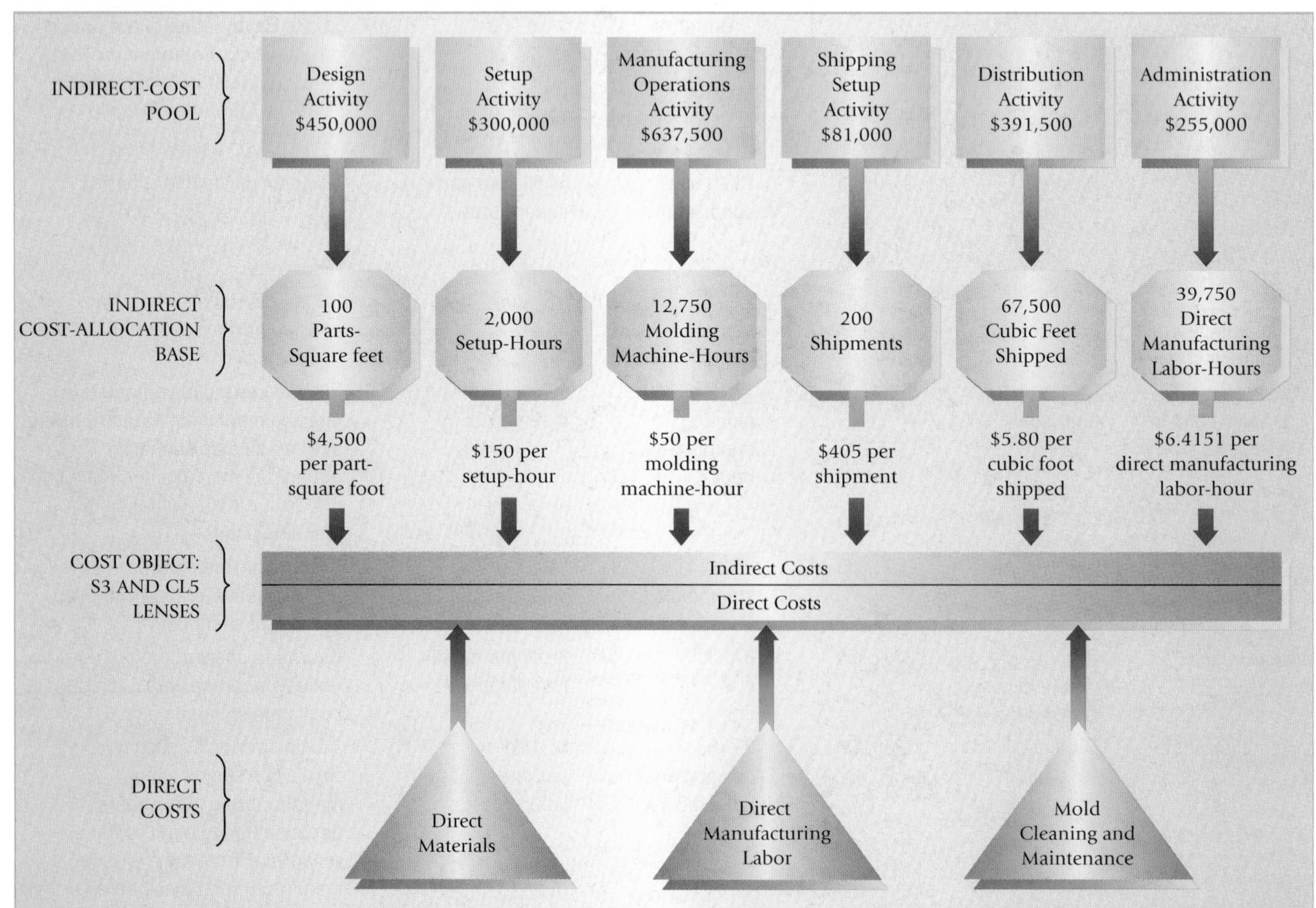

Continued

Other costs need to be allocated across activities. For example, on the basis of interviews or time records, manufacturing engineers and supervisors identify the time spent on design activities, molding machine setup activity, and manufacturing operations. The time spent on these activities serves as a basis for allocating manufacturing engineers' and supervisors' salary costs to various activities. Similarly, other costs are allocated to activity-cost pools using allocation bases that best describe the costs incurred to support the different activities. For example, rent cost is allocated on the basis of square-feet area used for different activities.

The point here is that all costs do not fit neatly into activity categories. Often, costs may first need to be allocated to activities before the costs of the activities can be allocated to products.

Step 5: Compute the Rate per Unit of Each Cost-Allocation Base Used to Allocate Indirect Costs to the Products. Exhibit 5-2, column 5, summarizes the calculation of the activity-cost rates using the cost-allocation bases selected in step 3 and the indirect costs of each activity calculated in step 4. Exhibit 5-3, Panel A, presents an overview of Plastim's ABC system.

Step 6: Compute the Indirect Costs Allocated to the Products. Exhibit 5-3, Panel B, shows total indirect costs of $1,153,953 allocated to the simple lens and $961,047 allocated to the complex lens. To calculate total indirect costs of each lens, the total quantity of the cost-allocation base used for each activity by each type of lens (using data provided by Plastim's operations personnel) is multiplied

EXHIBIT 5-3 (continued)

PANEL B: PRODUCT COSTS USING THE ACTIVITY-BASED COST SYSTEM

	60,000 Simple Lenses (S3)		15,000 Complex Lenses (CL5)		
Description of Cost and the Quantity of Activity Used by Each Type of Lens	**Total (1)**	**per Unit (2) = (1) ÷ 60,000**	**Total (3)**	**per Unit (4) = (3) ÷ 15,000**	**Total (5) = (1) + (3)**
Direct costs					
Direct materials	$1,125,000	$18.75	$ 675,000	$ 45.00	$1,800,000
Direct manufacturing labor	600,000	10.00	195,000	13.00	795,000
Direct mold cleaning and maintenance costs	120,000	2.00	150,000	10.00	270,000
Total direct costs	1,845,000	30.75	1,020,000	68.00	2,865,000
Indirect costs					
Design activity costs					
S3, 30 parts-sq.ft. × $4,500	135,000	2.25			450,000
CL5, 70 parts-sq.ft. × $4,500			315,000	21.00	
Setup activity costs					
S3, 500 setup-hours × $150	75,000	1.25			300,000
CL5, 1,500 setup-hours × $150			225,000	15.00	
Manufacturing operations activity costs					
S3, 9,000 molding machine-hours × $50	450,000	7.50			637,500
CL5, 3,750 molding machine-hours × $50			187,500	12.50	
Shipping setup activity					
S3, 100 shipments × $405	40,500	0.67			81,000
CL5, 100 shipments × $405			40,500	2.70	
Distribution activity					
S3, 45,000 cubic feet shipped × $5.80	261,000	4.35			391,500
CL5, 22,500 cubic feet shipped × $5.80			130,500	8.70	
Administration activity					
S3, 30,000 dir. manuf. labor-hours × $6.4151	192,453	3.21			255,000
CL5, 9,750 dir. manuf. labor-hours × $6.4151			62,547	4.17	
Total indirect costs	1,153,953	19.23	961,047	64.07	2,115,000
Total costs	$2,998,953	$49.98	$1,981,047	$132.07	$4,980,000

by the cost-allocation rate calculated in step 5 (see Exhibit 5-2, column 5). For example, of the 2,000 hours of the setup activity (Exhibit 5-2, column 4), the S3 lens uses 500 setup-hours and the CL5 lens uses 1,500 setup-hours. Therefore, the total costs of the setup activity allocated to the S3 lens are $75,000 (500 setup-hours × $150 per setup-hour) and to the CL5 lens are $225,000 (1,500 setup-hours × $150 per setup-hour). The setup cost per unit can then be calculated as $1.25 ($75,000 ÷ 60,000 units) for the S3 lens and $15 ($225,000 ÷ 15,000 units) for the CL5 lens.

Step 7: Compute the Total Costs of the Products by Adding All Direct and Indirect Costs Assigned to the Products. Exhibit 5-3, Panel B, presents the product costs for the simple and complex lenses. The direct costs are calculated in step 2, and the indirect costs are calculated in step 6. The ABC system overview in Exhibit 5-3, Panel A, shows three direct-cost categories and six indirect-cost categories. The cost of each lens type in Exhibit 5-3, Panel B, has nine line items, three for direct costs and six for indirect costs. The differences between the ABC product costs of S3 and CL5 calculated in Exhibit 5-3, Panel B, highlight how each of these products uses different amounts of direct costs and indirect costs in each activity area.

We emphasize two key features of ABC systems. First, these systems identify all costs used by products, whether the costs are variable or fixed in the short run. That's because the focus of ABC systems is on long-run decisions when more of the costs can be managed and fewer costs are regarded as fixed. Hence, ABC systems identify all resources used by products, regardless of how individual costs behave in the short run. Second, recognizing the hierarchy of costs is critical when allocating costs to products. It is easiest to use the cost hierarchy to calculate total costs. For this reason, we recommend calculating total costs first. The per-unit costs can then be easily calculated by dividing total costs by the number of units produced.

COMPARING ALTERNATIVE COSTING SYSTEMS

Exhibit 5-4 compares the single indirect-cost pool system (Exhibit 5-1) Plastim had been using and the ABC system (Exhibit 5-3) that replaced it. We emphasize three points in Exhibit 5-4, consistent with the guidelines for refining a costing system: (1) ABC systems trace more costs as direct costs; (2) ABC systems create homogeneous cost pools linked to different activities; and (3) for each activity-cost pool, ABC systems seek a cost-allocation base that has a cause-and-effect relationship with costs in the cost pool.

The homogeneous cost pools and the choice of cost-allocation bases, tied to the cost hierarchy, give Plastim's managers greater confidence in the activity and product cost numbers from the ABC system. Exhibit 5-4 shows that allocating costs to lenses using only an output unit-level allocation base—direct manufacturing labor-hours, as in the single indirect-cost pool system used prior to ABC—overcosts the simple S3 lens by $8.77 per unit and undercosts the complex CL5 lens by $35.07 per unit. The CL5 lens uses a disproportionately larger amount of output-unit-level, batch-level, and product-sustaining costs than is represented by the direct manufacturing labor-hour cost-allocation base. The S3 lens uses a disproportionately smaller amount of these three costs.

The benefit of an ABC system is that it provides information to make better decisions. But this benefit must be weighed against the measurement costs and implementation costs of an ABC system.

6 Use activity-based costing systems for activity-based management

...such as pricing decisions, product-mix decisions, and cost reduction

USING ABC SYSTEMS FOR IMPROVING COST MANAGEMENT AND PROFITABILITY

The emphasis of this chapter so far has been on the role of ABC systems in obtaining better product costs. **Activity-based management (ABM)** describes management decisions that use activity-based costing information to satisfy customers and improve profitability. We define ABM broadly to include decisions about pricing and product mix, decisions about how to reduce costs, decisions about how to improve processes, and decisions relating to product design.

EXHIBIT 5-4 Comparing Alternative Costing Systems

	Existing Single Indirect-Cost Pool System (1)	ABC System (2)	Difference (3) = (2) − (1)
Direct-cost categories	2	3	+1
	Direct materials Direct manufacturing labor	Direct materials Direct manufacturing labor Direct cleaning and maintenance labor	
Total direct costs	$2,595,000	$2,865,000	$270,000
Indirect-cost pools	1	6	5
	Single indirect-cost pool allocated using direct manufacturing labor-hours	Design cost pool allocated using parts-square feet Molding machine setup cost pool allocated using setup-hours Manufacturing operations cost pool allocated using machine-hours Shipment setup cost pool allocated using number of shipments Distribution cost pool allocated using cubic feet of packages shipped Administration cost pool allocated using direct manufacturing labor-hours.	
Total indirect costs	$2,385,000	$2,115,000	($270,000)
Total costs assigned to simple (S3) lens	$3,525,000	$2,998,953	($526,047)
Cost per unit of simple (S3) lens	$58.75	$49.98	($8.77)
Total costs assigned to complex (CL5) lens	$1,455,000	$1,981,047	$526,047
Cost per unit of complex (CL5) lens	$97.00	$132.07	$35.07

Pricing and Product-Mix Decisions An ABC system gives managers cost information that is helpful for making and selling diverse products. With this information, managers can make pricing and product-mix decisions. For example, the ABC system indicates that Plastim can reduce the price of S3 to the $53 range and still make a profit, because the ABC cost of S3 is $49.98. Without this information from the ABC system, Plastim managers might conclude erroneously that they would incur an operating loss on the S3 lens at $53. This incorrect conclusion might cause Plastim to reduce its business in simple lenses and focus instead on complex lenses, where its existing single indirect-cost pool system indicates it is very profitable.

Focusing on complex lenses would be a mistake. The ABC system indicates that the cost of making the complex lens is much higher—$132.07 versus $97 under the direct manufacturing labor-hour-based costing system Plastim had been using. As Plastim's operations staff had thought all along, Plastim has no competitive advantage in making CL5 lenses. At a price of $137 per lens for CL5, the profit margin is very small ($137.00 − $132.07 = $4.93). As Plastim reduces prices on simple lenses, it will probably have to negotiate a higher price for the complex lenses.

The core of the ABC approach is the analysis of activities. When Plastim analyzes its activity—setups of molding machines—the company may find ways to reduce setup time (the cost-management benefit of ABC) and better estimate setup cost per unit of product (the product-costing benefit of ABC). Remember, activities consume resources, and products consume activities.

Cost Reduction and Process Improvement Decisions Manufacturing and distribution personnel use ABC systems to focus on how and where to reduce costs. Managers set cost reduction targets in terms of reducing the cost per unit of the cost-allocation base in different activity areas. For example, the supervisor of the distribution activity area at Plastim could have a performance target of decreasing the distribution cost per cubic foot of products shipped from $5.80 to $5.40 by reducing distribution labor and warehouse rental costs.

Doing an analysis of the factors that cause costs to be incurred (cost drivers and cost-allocation bases) reveals many opportunities for improving the way work is done. Management can evaluate whether particular activities can be reduced or eliminated. Each of the indirect cost-allocation bases in the ABC system is a nonfinancial variable (number of setup-hours, cubic feet shipped, and so on). Controlling physical items such as setup-hours or cubic feet shipped is often the most fundamental way that operating personnel manage costs. For example, Plastim can decrease distribution costs by packing the lenses in a way that reduces the bulkiness of the shipment.

The following table shows the reduction in distribution costs of the S3 and CL5 lenses as a result of actions that lower the cost per cubic foot shipped (from $5.80 to $5.40) and the total cubic feet of shipments (from 45,000 to 40,000 for S3 and 22,500 to 20,000 for CL5).

	60,000 S3 lenses		15,000 CL5 lenses	
	Total (1)	per Unit (2) = (1) ÷ 60,000	Total (3)	per Unit (4) = (3) ÷ 15,000
Distribution costs (from Exh. 5-3, Panel B)	$261,000	$4.35	$130,500	$8.70
Distribution costs as a result of process improvements				
S3, 40,000 cubic feet × $5.40	216,000	3.60		
CL5, 20,000 cubic feet × $5.40			108,000	7.20
Savings in distribution costs from process improvements	$ 45,000	$0.75	$ 22,500	$1.50

Design Decisions Management can evaluate how its current product and process designs affect activities and costs as a way of identifying new designs to reduce costs. For example, design decisions that decrease the complexity of the mold reduce the costs of design, materials, labor, setups, molding machine operations, and mold cleaning and maintenance. Plastim's customers may be willing to give up some features of the lens in exchange for a lower price.

There are often more opportunities for cost reduction in the design stage before final design decisions are made than in production.

Had Plastim continued to use its direct manufacturing labor-hour-based system to choose among alternative designs, which design choices would Plastim favor? Answer: Those designs that reduce direct manufacturing labor-hours the most. That's because the costing system would signal that reducing direct manufacturing labor-hours reduces overhead costs. However, this is a false signal. As our discussion of Plastim's ABC system reveals, the cause-and-effect relationship between direct manufacturing labor-hours and Plastim's overhead costs is weak.

Planning and Managing Activities As was the case with Plastim, most companies implementing ABC systems for the first time analyze actual costs to identify activity-cost pools and activity-cost rates. Many companies then use ABC systems for planning and managing activities. These companies specify budgeted costs for activities and use budgeted cost rates to cost products using normal costing. At year-end, budgeted costs and actual costs are compared to provide feedback on how well activities were managed. As activities and processes are changed, new activity-cost rates may need to be calculated. At the end of the year, adjustments will also need to be made for underallocated or overallocated indirect costs for each activity area using either the adjusted allocation-rate approach, proration, or write-off to cost of goods sold—approaches described in Chapter 4.

We will return to activity-based management in later chapters. Management decisions that use activity-based costing information are described in Chapter 11, where we discuss outsourcing and adding or dropping business segments; in Chapter 12, where we evaluate alternative design choices to improve efficiency and reduce nonvalue-added costs; in Chapter 13, where we cover reengineering and downsizing; in Chapter 14, where we explore managing customer profitability; in Chapter 19, where we explain quality improvements; and in Chapter 20, where we describe how to evaluate suppliers.

ACTIVITY-BASED COSTING AND DEPARTMENT-COSTING SYSTEMS

7 Compare activity-based costing systems and department-costing systems

...these systems provide similar costs when products use different activities within a department in a similar way

Companies often use costing systems that have features of ABC systems—such as multiple cost pools and multiple cost-allocation bases—but do not emphasize individual activities. Many companies have evolved their costing systems from using a single indirect-cost rate system to using separate indirect-cost rates for each department (for example, design, manufacturing, distribution, and so on) or each subdepartment (for example, machining and assembly departments within manufacturing). Why do companies use department cost rates? They do so because the cost drivers of resources in each department or subdepartment differ from the single, companywide, cost-allocation base. ABC systems are a further refinement of department-costing systems. In this section, we compare ABC systems and department-costing systems.

Plastim uses the Design Department indirect-cost rate to cost its design activity. Plastim calculates the design activity rate by dividing total Design Department costs by total parts-square feet, a measure of the complexity of the mold and the driver of Design Department costs. Plastim does not find it worthwhile to calculate separate activity rates within the Design Department for the different design activities, such as designing products, making a temporary mold, and designing processes. Why not? Because the complexity of the mold is an appropriate cost-allocation base for costs incurred for all those design activities. The Design Department costs are homogeneous with respect to this cost-allocation base.

In contrast, using ABC, Plastim identifies in the Manufacturing Department, two activity-cost pools—a setup-cost pool and a manufacturing operations-cost pool—instead of using a single Manufacturing Department indirect-cost pool. It identifies these activity-cost pools for two reasons. First, each of these activities within manufacturing incurs significant costs and has a different cost driver. Second, the S3 and CL5 lenses do not use resources from these two activity areas in the same proportion. For example, CL5 uses 75% (1,500 ÷ 2,000) of the setup-hours but only 29.4% (3,750 ÷ 12,750) of the machine-hours. Using only machine-hours, say, to allocate all Manufacturing Department costs at Plastim would result in CL5 being undercosted because it would not be charged for the significant setup resources it actually uses.

Based on what we just explained, consider the following: Using department indirect-cost rates to allocate costs to products results in the same product costs as activity-cost rates if: (1) a single activity accounts for a sizable fraction of the department's costs; or (2) significant costs are incurred on different activities within a department but each activity has the same cost-allocation base (as was the case in Plastim's Design Department); or (3) significant costs are incurred on different activities with different cost-allocation bases within a department but different products use resources from the different activity areas in the same proportions (for example, if CL5 had used 65% (say) of the setup-hours and 65% of the machine-hours).

When any one of these three conditions holds, department indirect-cost rates and activity-cost rates will give the same or similar cost information. In companies where none of these conditions hold, department-costing systems can be refined using ABC. Emphasizing activities leads to more focused and homogeneous cost pools and aids in identifying cost-allocation bases for activities that have a better cause-and-effect relationship with the costs in activity-cost pools. But the benefits of an ABC system must be balanced against its costs and limitations.

IMPLEMENTING ABC SYSTEMS

8 Evaluate the costs and benefits of implementing activity-based costing systems

...measurement difficulties versus more accurate costs that aid in decision making

Managers choose the level of detail to use in a costing system by evaluating the expected costs of the costing system against the expected benefits that will accrue from using it to make better decisions. There are telltale signs that indicate when an ABC system is likely to provide the most benefits. Here are some of these signs:

1. Significant amounts of indirect costs are allocated using only one or two cost pools.
2. All or most indirect costs are identified as output unit-level costs (i.e., few indirect costs are described as batch-level costs, product-sustaining costs, or facility-sustaining costs).
3. Products make diverse demands on resources because of differences in volume, process steps, batch size, or complexity.
4. Products that a company is well suited to make and sell, show small profits; whereas products that a company is less suited to produce and sell show large profits.
5. Operations staff have significant disagreements with the accounting staff about the costs of manufacturing and marketing products and services.

Even when a company decides to implement ABC, it must make important choices about the level of detail to use. Should it choose many finely specified activities, cost drivers, and cost pools, or would a few suffice? For example, Plastim could identify a different molding machine-hour rate for each different type of molding machine. In making such choices, managers consider the costs and limitations of refining costing systems.

The main costs and limitations of an ABC system are the measurements necessary to implement it. ABC systems require management to estimate costs of activity pools and to identify and measure cost drivers for these pools to serve as cost-allocation bases. Even basic ABC systems require many calculations to determine costs of products and services. These measurements are costly. Activity-cost rates also need to be updated regularly.

As ABC systems get very detailed and more cost pools are created, more allocations are necessary to calculate activity costs for each cost pool. This increases the chances of misidentifying the costs of different activity-cost pools. For example, supervisors are more prone to incorrectly identify the time they spent on different activities if they have to allocate their time over five activities rather than only two activities.

At times, companies are also forced to use allocation bases for which data are readily available rather than the allocation bases they would have liked to use. For example, a company might be forced to use the number of loads moved, instead of the complexity and distance of different loads moved, as the allocation base for material-handling costs because the number of loads moved is easier to measure. When measurement errors are large, activity-cost information can be misleading. For example, if the cost per load moved decreases, a company may conclude that it has become more efficient in its materials-handling operations. In fact, the lower cost per load moved may have resulted solely from moving many lighter loads over shorter distances.

Refined costing systems are cost-effective when (1) different cost objects (products, services, customers, etc.) consume resources differently, (2) competition in the output marketplace is keen (for example, accurate cost information helps managers decide how to price products), and (3) information processing costs are low.

Many companies find the benefits of a less detailed ABC system to be good enough to not warrant incurring the costs and complexities of a more detailed system. However, as improvements in information technology and accompanying declines in measurement costs continue, more detailed ABC systems have become a practical alternative in many companies. (See Surveys of Company Practice, p. 153.) As such trends continue, more detailed ABC systems should be better able to pass the cost-benefit test.

ABC IN SERVICE AND MERCHANDISING COMPANIES

ABC was originally developed in the manufacturing sector, but it is now also applied to all business functions in the value chain.

Although many of the early examples of ABC originated in manufacturing, ABC has many applications in service and merchandising companies. In addition to manufacturing activities, the Plastim example includes the application of ABC to a service activity—design—and to a merchandising activity—distribution. Companies such as the Cooperative Bank, Braintree Hospital, BCTel in the telecommunications industry, and Union Pacific in the railroad industry have implemented some form of ABC system to identify profitable product mixes, improve efficiency, and satisfy customers. Similarly, many retail and wholesale companies—for example, Fleming, a wholesaler of grocery store products—have used ABC systems.

SURVEYS OF COMPANY PRACTICE

Growing Interest in Activity-Based Costing

Activity-based costing is being implemented by a growing number of companies around the globe. Specific ABC applications vary from organization to organization. A few organizations use ABC as their basic, ongoing cost accounting system. But many ABC applications are selective—special studies within subparts of the organization, such as business divisions or particular functions.

One study[a] of 162 U.S.-based companies (including 29 service-sector implementations) reported the following ranking of the primary applications: (1) product/service costing, (2) cost reduction, and (3) process improvement. Areas in which ABC-based information produced "significant" or "very significant" changes in decisions ranked as follows: (1) pricing strategy, (2) processes, and (3) product mix. A survey[b] of U.S. companies in the food and beverage industry found 18% of the respondents implementing ABC and 58% considering it. A survey of Dutch companies in the food and beverage industry found 12% currently using ABC and 25% considering it. Managers at the Dutch companies indicated that information similar to that developed by ABC systems already existed in Dutch companies. Dutch companies that implemented ABC did so mainly for (1) process improvement, (2) cost reduction, and (3) product costing.

Among Canadian companies, one survey[c] indicates that 14% of the interviewed businesses have implemented ABC and another 15% are considering using it. What attracts Canadian firms to ABC?

More accurate cost information for product pricing	61%
More accurate profit analysis	61
By product	22
By customer	20
By process	24
By department	43
Improved performance measures	43
Improved insight into cost causation	37

The ABC system has replaced existing systems for 24% of the Canadian respondents, and it is a supplementary (off-line) system for 76%.

A United Kingdom survey[d] found that "just under 20% of 251 respondents had used ABC." The ranking of the application areas was (1) cost management, (2) performance measurement, (3) product/service pricing, and (4) cost modeling. A New Zealand survey[e] ranked the benefits of ABC as (1) cost management, (2) product/service pricing, and (3) inventory valuation.

A survey[f] of Irish manufacturing companies that have implemented ABC reported the following percentages for the actual benefits experienced: (1) more accurate cost information for product costing and pricing (71%), (2) improved cost control and management (66%), (3) improved insight into cost drivers (58%), (4) better performance measures (46%), and (5) more accurate customer profitability analysis (25%). A survey[g] of Irish service-sector companies reports similar percentages for the benefits experienced. An Australian survey[h] found that 43% of the respondents were either using ABC or implementing it.

The Canadian survey reported the two most common implementation problems were difficulties in defining activities and difficulties in selecting cost drivers. Implementation problems in the Irish survey included difficulties in identifying activities and assigning costs to those pools, difficulties in identifying and selecting cost drivers, inadequate computer software, and lack of adequate resources. The two top-ranked problems in the New Zealand survey were difficulties in obtaining reliable data and lack of middle management acceptance. The Dutch survey cited problems of other priorities and lack of time, as well as the difficulty and cost of collecting data.

[a]Adapted from APQC/CAM-I, "Activity-Based Management"

[b]Adapted from T. Groot, "Activity-Based Costing"

[c]Adapted from Armitage, H., and R. Nicholson, "Activity-Based Costing"

[d]Adapted from Innes, J., and F. Mitchell, "A Survey of Activity-Based Costing"

eAdapted from Cotton, W., "Activity-Based Costing"

[f]Adapted from Clarke, P., "A Survey of."

[g]Adapted from Clarke, P., and T. Mullins, "Activity-based costing."

[h]Adapted from Clarke, B., and M. Lokman, "Activity-Based Costing"

Full citations are in Appendix A at the end of the book.

CONCEPTS IN ACTION

Measuring and Managing E-Retailing with Activity-Based Costing

Activity-based costing (ABC) can help Internet retailers, such as Amazon.com, Toys 'Я' Us.com, and Walmart.com, in strategic analysis, execution, and implementation. ABC can help answer questions such as, What profits are earned by selling standardized products versus unique products? Which type of advertising is most cost effective for a service or product? How much does it cost to get a new Internet customer? How much does it cost to build a relationship with a customer and to get repeat business? To answer these questions, ABC systems identify and measure the costs of activities aimed at serving the customer.

Some of the activities and the cost drivers of activities at online stores are similar to bricks and mortar stores. Examples are

Activity	Cost Driver
1. Servicing routine customers—helping a customer select a product; answering questions about the product via telephone or e-mail; placing an order	Number of orders processed
2. Merchandise inventory selection and management—selecting inventory items; negotiating contracts with suppliers; creating and developing new products	Number of new products
3. Purchasing and receiving—placing orders with suppliers; receiving and documenting received goods; working with suppliers regarding damaged goods	Number of orders
4. Customer acquisition and retention—acquiring customers and putting together deals to gain customers	Number of targeted customers
5. Sustaining business—for example, managing operations, employees, information systems, and inventory	Number of products

Other activities are special and unique to online stores. Examples are

Activity	Cost Driver
1. Electronic customer-order processing—maintaining hardware, software, and telephone systems necessary for a customer to place an order online; maintaining the Web site	Number of orders placed online
2. Imaging and annotation—putting selected merchandise on the Web site by scanning and marking inventory images; removing images from the site	Number of changes to inventory database
3. Virtual storefront optimization—continuously improving the design and setup of the Web site to keep it fresh	Hours of Web page development
4. Affiliate marketing for customer acquisition and retention—establishing links to the online store from other Web sites; negotiating affiliate marketing arrangements	Number of affiliate links

The activity costs are used to identify costs of different products and product groupings on the basis of the activities needed to support different products. (Cost of capacity that has been created but is not currently needed to support various products is not allocated to products.) For example, Amazon.com could use ABC information to evaluate (1) its profitability from selling books versus toys versus CDs; (2) the profits earned on different types of books (nonfiction versus mystery versus children's); or (3) the effectiveness of television advertising versus affiliate marketing in obtaining new customers. Amazon could also use ABC information to reduce the cost of different activities (for example, imaging and annotation), or to evaluate whether it should reduce some activities (for example, storefront optimization).

Source: T. L. Zeller, "Measuring and Managing E-Retailing with Activity-Based Costing," *Journal of Cost Management,* January/February 2000. Used by permission.

The general approach to ABC in service and merchandising companies is similar to the ABC approach in manufacturing. Costs are divided into homogeneous cost pools and classified as output unit-level costs, batch-level costs, product-sustaining costs, service-sustaining costs, or facility-sustaining costs. The cost pools correspond to activities. Costs are allocated to products or customers using cost drivers or cost-allocation bases that have a cause-and-effect relationship with the costs in the cost pool. Service and merchandising companies also must confront the problems of measuring activity-cost pools and identifying and measuring allocation bases.

The Cooperative Bank in the United Kingdom followed this approach when it implemented ABC in its retail bank. It calculated the costs of various activities, such as performing ATM transactions, opening and closing accounts, administering mortgages, and processing Visa transactions. It then used the activity-cost rates to calculate costs of various products, such as checking accounts, mortgages, and Visa cards. ABC information helped Cooperative Bank to improve its processes and to identify profitable products and customer segments. The Problem for Self-Study describes an application of ABC in the merchandising sector. The Concepts in Action (p. 154) describes ABC analysis in e-retailing.

PROBLEM FOR SELF-STUDY

Family Supermarkets (FS) has decided to increase the size of its Memphis store. It wants information about the profitability of individual product lines: soft drinks, fresh produce, and packaged food.

FS provides the following data for 2003 for each product line:

	Soft Drinks	Fresh Produce	Packaged Food
Revenues	$317,400	$840,240	$483,960
Cost of goods sold	240,000	600,000	360,000
Cost of bottles returned	4,800	0	0
Number of purchase orders placed	144	336	144
Number of deliveries received	120	876	264
Hours of shelf-stocking time	216	2,160	1,080
Items sold	50,400	441,600	122,400

FS also provides the following information for 2003:

Activity (1)	Description of Activity (2)	Total Costs (3)	Cost-Allocation Base (4)
1. Bottle returns	Returning of empty bottles to store	$ 4,800	Direct tracing to soft-drink line
2. Ordering	Placing of orders for purchases	$ 62,400	624 purchase orders
3. Delivery	Physical delivery and receipt of merchandise	$100,800	1,260 deliveries
4. Shelf-stocking	Stocking of merchandise on store shelves and ongoing restocking	$ 69,120	3,456 hours of shelf-stocking time
5. Customer support	Assistance provided to customers, including checkout and bagging	$122,880	614,400 items sold
Total		$360,000	

Required

1. Family Supermarkets currently allocates store support costs (all costs other than cost of goods sold) to product lines on the basis of cost of goods sold of each product line. Calculate the operating income and operating income as a percentage of revenues for each product line.
2. If Family Supermarkets allocates store support costs (all costs other than cost of goods sold) to product lines using an ABC system, calculate the operating income and operating income as a percentage of revenues for each product line.
3. Comment on your answers in requirements 1 and 2.

Continued

SOLUTION

1. The following table shows the operating income and operating income as a percentage of revenues for each product line. All store support costs (all costs other than cost of goods sold) are allocated to product lines using cost of goods sold of each product line as the cost-allocation base. Total store support costs equal \$360,000 (cost of bottles returned, \$4,800 + cost of purchase orders, \$62,400 + cost of deliveries, \$100,800 + cost of shelf-stocking, \$69,120 + cost of customer support, \$122,880). The allocation rate for store support costs = \$360,000 ÷ \$1,200,000 = 30% of cost of goods sold. To allocate support costs to each product line, FS multiplies the cost of goods sold of each product line by 0.30.

	Soft Drinks	Fresh Produce	Packaged Food	Total
Revenues	\$317,400	\$840,240	\$483,960	\$1,641,600
Cost of goods sold	240,000	600,000	360,000	1,200,000
Store support cost				
(\$240,000; \$600,000; \$360,000) × 0.30	72,000	180,000	108,000	360,000
Total costs	312,000	780,000	468,000	1,560,000
Operating income	\$ 5,400	\$ 60,240	\$ 15,960	\$ 81,600
Operating income ÷ Revenues	1.70%	7.17%	3.30%	4.97%

2. Under an ABC system, FS identifies bottle-return costs as a direct cost because these costs can be traced to the soft drink product line. FS then calculates cost-allocation rates for each activity area (as in step 5 described in the chapter, p. 147). The activity rates are as follows:

Activity (1)	Cost Hierarchy (2)	Total Costs (3)	Quantity of Cost-Allocation Base (4)	Overhead Allocation Rate (5) = (3) ÷ (4)
Ordering	Batch-level	\$ 62,400	624 purchase orders	\$100 per purchase order
Delivery	Batch-level	\$100,800	1,260 deliveries	\$80 per delivery
Shelf-stocking	Output unit-level	\$ 69,120	3,456 shelf-stocking-hours	\$20 per stocking-hour
Customer support	Output unit-level	\$122,880	614,400 items sold	\$0.20 per item sold

Store support costs for each product line by activity are obtained by multiplying the total quantity of the cost-allocation base for each product line by the activity-cost rate. Operating income and operating income as a percentage of revenues for each product line are as follows:

	Soft Drinks	Fresh Produce	Packaged Food	Total
Revenues	\$317,400	\$840,240	\$483,960	\$1,641,600
Cost of goods sold	240,000	600,000	360,000	1,200,000
Bottle-return costs	4,800	0	0	4,800
Ordering costs				
(144; 336; 144) purchase orders × \$100	14,400	33,600	14,400	62,400
Delivery costs				
(120; 876; 264) deliveries × \$80	9,600	70,080	21,120	100,800
Shelf-stocking costs				
(216; 2,160; 1,080) stocking-hours × \$20	4,320	43,200	21,600	69,120
Customer support costs				
(50,400; 441,600; 122,400) items sold × \$0.20	10,080	88,320	24,480	122,880
Total costs	283,200	835,200	441,600	1,560,000
Operating income	\$ 34,200	\$ 5,040	\$ 42,360	\$ 81,600
Operating income ÷ Revenues	10.78%	0.60%	8.75%	4.97%

3. Managers believe the ABC system is more credible than its previous costing system. The ABC system distinguishes the different types of activities at FS more precisely. It also tracks more accurately how individual product lines use resources. Rankings of relative profitability—that's the percentage of operating income to revenues—of the three product lines under the previous costing system and under the ABC system are

Previous Costing System		ABC System	
1. Fresh produce	7.17%	1. Soft drinks	10.78%
2. Packaged food	3.30%	2. Packaged food	8.75%
3. Soft drinks	1.70%	3. Fresh produce	0.60%

The percentage of revenues, cost of goods sold, and activity costs for each product line are as follows:

	Soft Drinks	Fresh Produce	Packaged Food
Revenues	19.34%	51.18%	29.48%
Cost of goods sold	20.00	50.00	30.00
Bottle returns	100.00	0	0
Activity areas:			
Ordering	23.08	53.84	23.08
Delivery	9.53	69.52	20.95
Shelf-stocking	6.25	62.50	31.25
Customer support	8.20	71.88	19.92

Soft drinks consume less resources than either fresh produce or packaged food. Soft drinks have fewer deliveries and require less shelf-stocking time than required for either fresh produce or packaged food. Most major soft-drink suppliers deliver merchandise to the store shelves and stock the shelves themselves. In contrast, the fresh produce area has the most deliveries and consumes a large percentage of shelf-stocking time. It also has the highest number of individual sales items. The previous costing system assumed that each product line used the resources in each activity area in the same ratio as their respective individual cost of goods sold to total cost of goods sold. Clearly, this assumption is incorrect. The previous costing system is an example of broad averaging via cost smoothing.

FS managers can use the ABC information to guide their decisions, such as how to allocate a planned increase in floor space. An increase in the percentage of space allocated to soft drinks is warranted. Note, however, that ABC information should be but one input into decisions about shelf-space allocation. FS may have minimum limits on the shelf space allocated to fresh produce because of shoppers' expectations that supermarkets will carry products from this product line. In many situations, companies cannot make product decisions in isolation but must consider the effect that dropping a product might have on customer demand for other products.

Pricing decisions can also be made in a more informed way with ABC information. For example, suppose a competitor announces a 5% reduction in soft-drink prices. Given the 10.77% margin FS currently earns on its soft-drink product line, it has flexibility to reduce prices and still make a profit on this product line. In contrast, the previous costing system erroneously implied that soft drinks only had a 1.70% margin, leaving little room to counter a competitor's pricing initiatives.

DECISION POINTS — SUMMARY

The following question-and-answer format summarizes the chapter's learning objectives. Each decision presents a key question related to a learning objective. The guidelines are the answer to that question.

Decision	Guidelines
1. When does product undercosting or product overcosting occur?	Product undercosting (overcosting) occurs when a product or service consumes a high (low) level of resource but is reported to have a low (high) cost. Cost smoothing, or peanut-butter costing, a common cause of undercosting or overcosting, is the result of using broad averages that uniformly assign, or spread, the cost of resources to products when the individual products use those resources in a nonuniform way. Product-cost cross-subsidization exists when one undercosted (overcosted) product results in at least one other product being overcosted (undercosted).
2. How do you refine a costing system?	Refining a costing system means making changes that result in cost numbers that better measure the way different cost objects, such as products, use different amounts of resources of the company. These changes can require additional direct-cost tracing, the choice of more homogeneous indirect-cost pools, or the use of different cost-allocation bases.

Continued

3. What is the difference between the traditional approach and the activity-based costing (ABC) approach to designing costing systems?	The ABC approach differs from the traditional approach by its fundamental focus on activities. The ABC approach typically results in more homogeneous indirect-cost pools than the traditional approach and more cost drivers used as cost-allocation bases.
4. What is a cost hierarchy?	A cost hierarchy categorizes costs into different cost pools on the basis of the different types of cost-allocation bases or different degrees of difficulty in determining cause-and-effect (or benefits-received) relationships. A four-part cost hierarchy consists of output unit-level costs, batch-level costs, product-sustaining or service-sustaining costs, and facility-sustaining costs.
5. How do you cost products or services using ABC systems?	In ABC, costs of activities are used to assign costs to other cost objects such as products or services based on the activities the products or services consume.
6. How do you use ABC systems to manage better?	Activity-based management (ABM) describes management decisions that use ABC information to satisfy customers and improve profits. ABC systems are used for such management decisions as pricing, product-mix, cost reduction, process improvement, product and process redesign, and planning and managing activities.
7. When can you use department-costing systems instead of ABC systems?	Cost information in department-costing systems approximates cost information in ABC systems only when each department has a single activity, or a single cost-allocation base for different activities, or when different products use the different activities of the department in the same proportions.
8. When should you use ABC systems?	ABC systems are likely to yield the most benefits when indirect costs are a high percentage of total costs or products and services make diverse demands on indirect resources. The main costs of ABC systems are the measurements necessary to implement and update the systems.

TERMS TO LEARN

This chapter and the Glossary at the end of this book contain definitions of:

activity (p. 141)
activity-based costing (ABC) (141)
activity-based management (ABM) (148)
batch-level costs (143)
cost hierarchy (143)
cost smoothing (136)
facility-sustaining costs (144)
output unit-level costs (143)
peanut-butter costing (136)
product-cost cross-subsidization (136)
product overcosting (136)
product-sustaining costs (144)
product undercosting (136)
refined costing system (140)
service-sustaining costs (144)

ASSIGNMENT MATERIAL

Questions

5-1 Define cost smoothing, and explain how managers can determine whether it occurs with their costing system.

5-2 Why should managers worry about product over- or undercosting?

5-3 What is costing system refinement? Describe three guidelines for refinement.

5-4 What is an activity-based approach to designing a costing system?

5-5 Describe four levels of a cost hierarchy.

5-6 "The existence of costs other than output unit-level costs means that managers should not compute unit product costs based on total manufacturing costs in all levels of the cost hierarchy." Do you agree? Explain.

5-7 What are the key reasons for product cost differences between traditional costing systems and ABC systems?

5-8 Describe four decisions for which ABC information is useful.

5-9 "Department indirect-cost rates are never activity-cost rates." Do you agree? Explain.

5-10 Describe four signs that help indicate when ABC systems are likely to provide the most benefits.

5-11 What are the main costs and limitations of implementing ABC systems?

5-12 "ABC systems only apply to manufacturing companies." Do you agree? Explain.

5-13 "Activity-based costing is the wave of the present and the future. All companies should adopt it." Do you agree? Explain.

5-14 "Increasing the number of indirect-cost pools is guaranteed to sizably increase the accuracy of product or service costs." Do you agree? Why?

5-15 The controller of a retail company has just had a $50,000 request to implement an ABC system quickly turned down. A senior vice president, in rejecting the request, noted, "Given a choice, I will always prefer a $50,000 investment in improving things a customer sees or experiences, such as our shelves or our store layout. How does a customer benefit by our spending $50,000 on a supposedly better accounting system?" How should the controller respond?

Exercises

5-16 Cost smoothing or peanut-butter costing, cross-subsidization. For many years, five former classmates—Steve Armstrong, Lola Gonzales, Rex King, Elizabeth Poffo, and Gary Young—have had a reunion dinner at the annual meeting of the American Accounting Association. The details of the bill for the most recent dinner at the Seattle Space Needle Restaurant break down as follows:

Diner	Entree	Dessert	Drinks	Total
Armstrong	$27	$8	$24	$59
Gonzales	24	3	0	27
King	21	6	13	40
Poffo	31	6	12	49
Young	15	4	6	25

For at least the last 10 dinners, King has put the total restaurant bill on his American Express card. He then mails the other four a bill for the average cost. They have shared the gratuity at the restaurant by paying cash. King continued this practice for the Seattle dinner. However, just before he sent the bill to the other diners, Young phoned him to complain. He was livid at Poffo for ordering the steak and lobster entree ("She always does that!") and at Armstrong for having three glasses of imported champagne ("What's wrong with domestic beer?").

Required

1. Why is the average-cost approach in the context of the reunion dinner an example of cost smoothing or peanut-butter costing?
2. Compute the average cost to each of the five diners. Who is undercharged and who is overcharged under the average-cost approach? Is Young's complaint justified?
3. Give an example of a dining situation in which King would find it more difficult to compute the amount of under- or overcosting. How might the behavior of the diners be affected if each person paid his or her own bill instead of continuing with the average-cost approach?

5-17 Cost hierarchy. Telecom, Inc., manufactures boom boxes (music systems with radio, cassette, and compact disc players) for several well-known companies. The boom boxes differ significantly in their complexity and their manufacturing batch sizes. The following costs were incurred in 2003.

a. Designing processes, drawing process charts, making engineering process changes for products, $800,000
b. Procurement costs of placing purchase orders, receiving materials, and paying suppliers related to the number of purchase orders placed, $500,000
c. Direct materials costs, $6,000,000
d. Costs incurred to set up machines each time a different product needs to be manufactured, $600,000
e. Direct manufacturing labor costs, $1,000,000
f. Machine-related overhead costs such as depreciation, maintenance, production engineering, $1,100,000 (These resources relate to the activity of running the machines.)
g. Plant management, plant rent, and plant insurance, $900,000

Required

1. Classify each of the preceding costs as output unit-level, batch-level, product-sustaining, or facility-sustaining. Explain each answer.
2. Consider two types of boom boxes made by Telecom, Inc. One boom box is complex to make and is produced in many batches. The other boom box is simple to make and is produced in few batches. Suppose that Telecom needs the same number of machine-hours to make each type of boom box and that Telecom allocates all overhead costs using machine-hours as the only allocation base. How, if at all, would the boom boxes be miscosted? Briefly explain why.
3. How is the cost hierarchy helpful to Telecom in managing its business?

5-18 ABC, distribution. (W. Bruns, adapted) Sonoma Winery makes two wines: a regular wine and a premium wine. Sonoma distributes the regular wine and the premium wine through different distribution channels. It distributes 120,000 cases of regular wine through 10 general distributors and 80,000 cases of the premium wine through 30 specialty distributors. Sonoma incurs $2,130,000 in distribution costs. Under its existing costing system, Sonoma allocates distribution costs to products on the basis of cases shipped.

To understand better the demands on its resources in the distribution area, Sonoma identifies three activities and related activity costs:

a. Promotional costs—Somoma estimates it incurs $8,000 per distributor.
b. Order handling costs—Somoma estimates costs of $300 pertaining to each order. Sonoma's records show that distributors of regular wine place an average of 10 orders per year, whereas distributors of premium wine place an average of 20 orders per year.
c. Delivery costs—$8 per case.

Required

1. Using Sonoma's existing costing system, calculate the total distribution costs and distribution cost per case for the regular wine and the premium wine.
2. Using Sonoma's activity-based costing system, calculate the total distribution costs and distribution cost per case for the regular wine and the premium wine.
3. Explain the cost differences and the accuracy of the product costs calculated using the existing costing system and the ABC system. How might Sonoma's management use the information from the ABC system to manage its business better?

5-19 **ABC, cost hierarchy, service.** (CMA, adapted) Plymouth Test Laboratories does heat testing (HT) and stress testing (ST) on materials. Under its current costing system, Plymouth aggregates all operating costs of $1,200,000 into a single overhead cost pool. Plymouth calculates a rate per test-hour of $15 ($1,200,000 ÷ 80,000 total test-hours). HT uses 50,000 test-hours, and ST uses 30,000 test-hours. Gary Celeste, Plymouth's controller, believes that there is enough variation in test procedures and cost structures to establish separate costing and billing rates for HT and ST. The market for test services is becoming competitive. Without this information, any miscosting and mispricing of its services could cause Plymouth to lose business. Celeste divides Plymouth's costs into four activity-cost categories.

a. Direct-labor costs, $240,000. These costs can be directly traced to HT, $180,000, and ST, $60,000.
b. Equipment-related costs (rent, maintenance, energy, and so on), $400,000. These costs are allocated to HT and ST on the basis of test-hours.
c. Setup costs, $350,000. These costs are allocated to HT and ST on the basis of the number of setup-hours required. HT requires 13,500 setup-hours, and ST requires 4,000 setup-hours.
d. Costs of designing tests, $210,000. These costs are allocated to HT and ST on the basis of the time required to design the tests. HT requires 2,800 hours, and ST requires 1,400 hours.

Required

1. Classify each activity cost as output unit-level, batch-level, product- or service-sustaining, or facility-sustaining. Explain each answer.
2. Calculate the cost per test-hour for HT and ST. Explain briefly the reasons why these numbers differ from the $15 per test-hour that Plymouth calculated using its existing costing system.
3. Explain the accuracy of the product costs calculated using the existing costing system and the ABC system. How might Plymouth's management use the cost hierarchy and ABC information to manage its business better?

5-20 **Alternative allocation bases for a professional services firm.** The Wolfson Group (WG) provides tax advice to multinational firms. WG charges clients for (a) direct professional time (at an hourly rate) and (b) support services (at 30% of the direct professional costs billed). The three professionals in WG and their rates per professional hour are

Professional	Billing Rate per Hour
Myron Wolfson	$500
Ann Brown	120
John Anderson	80

WG has just prepared the May 2002 bills for two clients. The hours of professional time spent on each client are as follows:

	Hours per Client	
Professional	Seattle Dominion	Tokyo Enterprises
Wolfson	15	2
Brown	3	8
Anderson	22	30
Total	40	40

Required

1. What amounts did WG bill to Seattle Dominion and Tokyo Enterprises for May 2002?
2. Suppose support services were billed at $50 per professional labor-hour (instead of 30% of professional labor costs). How would this change affect the amounts WG billed to the two clients for May 2002? Comment on the differences between the amounts billed in requirements 1 and 2.

3. How would you determine whether professional labor costs or professional labor-hours is the more appropriate allocation base for WG's support services?

5-21 Plantwide indirect-cost rates. Automotive Products (AP) designs, manufactures, and sells automotive parts. It has three main operating departments: design, engineering, and production.

- *Design*—the design of parts, using state of the art, computer-aided design (CAD) equipment
- *Engineering*—the prototyping of parts and testing of their specifications
- *Production*—the manufacture of parts

For many years, AP had long-term contracts with major automobile assembly companies. These contracts had large production runs. AP's costing system allocates variable manufacturing overhead on the basis of machine-hours. Actual variable manufacturing overhead costs for 2004 were $308,600. AP had three contracts in 2004, and its machine-hours used in 2004 were assigned as follows:

United Motors	120
Holden Motors	2,800
Leland Vehicle	1,080
Total	4,000

Required

1. Compute the plantwide variable manufacturing overhead rate for 2004.
2. Compute the variable manufacturing overhead allocated to each contract in 2004.
3. What conditions must hold for machine-hours to provide an accurate estimate of the variable manufacturing overhead incurred on each individual contract at AP in 2004?

5-22 Department indirect-cost rates as activity rates (continuation of 5-21). The controller of Automotive Parts (AP) decides to interview key managers of the Design, Engineering, and Production departments. Each manager is to indicate the consensus choice among department personnel of the cost driver of variable manufacturing overhead costs for his or her department. Summary data are

Department	Variable Manufacturing Overhead in 2004	Cost Driver
Design	$ 39,000	CAD design-hours
Engineering	29,600	Engineering-hours
Production	240,000	Machine-hours
	$308,600	

Details pertaining to usage of these cost drivers for each of the three 2004 contracts are:

Department	Cost Driver	United Motors	Holden Motors	Leland Vehicle
Design	CAD design-hours	110	200	80
Engineering	Engineering-hours	70	60	240
Production	Machine-hours	120	2,800	1,080

Required

1. What is the variable manufacturing overhead rate for each department in 2004?
2. What is the variable manufacturing overhead allocated to each contract in 2004 using department variable manufacturing overhead rates?
3. Compare your answer in requirement 2 to that in requirement 2 of Exercise 5-21. Comment on the results.

5-23 ABC, process costing. Parker Company produces mathematical and financial calculators. Data related to the two products is presented below.

	Mathematical	Financial
Annual production in units	50,000	100,000
Direct materials costs	$150,000	$300,000
Direct manufacturing labor costs	$50,000	$100,000
Direct manufacturing labor-hours	2,500	5,000
Machine-hours	25,000	50,000
Number of production runs	50	50
Inspection hours	1,000	500

Both products pass through Department 1 and Department 2. The departments' combined manufacturing overhead costs are

	Total
Machining costs	$375,000
Setup costs	120,000
Inspection costs	105,000

Required

1. Compute the manufacturing overhead cost per unit for each product.
2. Compute the manufacturing cost per unit for each product.

5-24 ABC, retail product-line profitability. Family Supermarkets (FS) decides to apply ABC analysis to three product lines: baked goods, milk and fruit juice, and frozen foods. It identifies four activities and activity-cost rates for each activity as:

Ordering	$100 per purchase order
Delivery and receipt of merchandise	$80 per delivery
Shelf-stocking	$20 per hour
Customer support and assistance	$0.20 per item sold

The revenues, cost of goods sold, store support costs, and activity-area usage of the three product lines are

	Baked Goods	Milk and Fruit Juice	Frozen Products
Financial data			
Revenues	$57,000	$63,000	$52,000
Cost of goods sold	38,000	47,000	35,000
Store support	11,400	14,100	10,500
Activity-area usage (cost-allocation base)			
Ordering (purchase orders)	30	25	13
Delivery (deliveries)	98	36	28
Shelf-stocking (hours)	183	166	24
Customer support (items sold)	15,500	20,500	7,900

Under its previous costing system, FS allocated support costs to products at the rate of 30% of cost of goods sold.

Required

1. Use the previous costing system to prepare a product-line profitability report for FS.
2. Use the ABC system to prepare a product-line profitability report for FS.
3. What new insights does the ABC system in requirement 2 provide to FS managers?

5-25 ABC, wholesale, customer profitability. Villeagas Wholesalers sells furniture items to four department-store chains. Mr. Villeagas commented, "We apply ABC to determine product-line profitability. The same ideas apply to customer profitability, and we should find out our customer profitability as well." Villeagas Wholesalers sends catalogs to the corporate purchasing departments on a monthly basis. The customers are entitled to return unsold merchandise within a six-month period from the purchase date and receive a full purchase price refund. The following data were collected from last year's operations:

	Chain			
	1	2	3	4
Gross sales	$50,000	$30,000	$100,000	$70,000
Sales returns:				
Number of items	100	26	60	40
Amount	$10,000	$ 5,000	$ 7,000	$ 6,000
Number of orders:				
Regular	40	150	50	70
Rush	10	50	10	30

Villeagas has calculated the following activity rates.

Activity	Cost Driver Rate
Regular order processing	$20 per regular order
Rush order processing	$100 per rush order
Returned items processing	$10 per item
Catalogs and customer support	$1,000 per customer

Customers pay the transportation costs. The cost of goods sold averages 80% of sales.

Required Determine the contribution to profit from each chain last year. Comment on your solution.

5-26 ABC, activity area cost-driver rates, product cross-subsidization. Idaho Potatoes (IP) processes potatoes into potato cuts at its highly automated Pocatello plant. It sells potatoes to the retail consumer market and to the institutional market, which includes hospitals, cafeterias, and university dormitories.

IP's existing costing system has a single direct-cost category (direct materials, which are the raw potatoes) and a single indirect-cost pool (production support). Support costs are allocated on the basis of pounds of potato cuts processed. Support costs include packaging materials. The 2003 total actual costs for producing 1,000,000 pounds of potato cuts (900,000 for the retail market and 100,000 for the institutional market) are

Direct materials used	$150,000
Production support	$983,000

The existing costing system does not distinguish between potato cuts produced for the retail and the institutional markets.

At the end of 2003, IP unsuccessfully bid for a large institutional contract. Its bid was reported to be 30% above the winning bid. This feedback came as a shock because IP included only a minimum profit margin on its bid. Moreover, the Pocatello plant was acknowledged as the most efficient in the industry.

As a result of its review process of the lost contract bid, IP decided to explore ways to refine its costing system. First, it identified that $188,000 of the $983,000 pertaining to packaging materials could be traced to individual jobs ($180,000 for retail and $8,000 for institutional). These costs will now be classified as direct material. The $150,000 of direct materials used were classified as $135,000 for retail and $15,000 for institutional. Second, it used ABC to examine how the two products (retail potato cuts and institutional potato cuts) used indirect support resources. The finding was that three activity areas could be distinguished.

- *Cleaning Activity Area*—IP uses 1,200,000 pounds of raw potatoes to yield 1,000,000 pounds of potato cuts. The cost-allocation base is pounds of raw potatoes cleaned. Costs in the cleaning activity area are $120,000.
- *Cutting Activity Area*—IP processes raw potatoes for the retail market independently of those processed for the institutional market. The production line produces (a) 250 pounds of retail potato cuts per cutting-hour and (b) 400 pounds of institutional potato cuts per cutting-hour. The cost-allocation base is cutting-hours on the production line. Costs in the cutting activity area are $231,000.
- *Packaging Activity Area*—IP packages potato cuts for the retail market independently of those packaged for the institutional market. The packaging line packages (a) 25 pounds of retail potato cuts per packaging-hour and (b) 100 pounds of institutional potato cuts per packaging-hour. The cost-allocation base is packaging-hours on the production line. Costs in the packaging activity area are $444,000.

Required

1. Using the existing costing system, what is the cost per pound of potato cuts produced by IP?
2. Calculate the cost rate per unit of the cost driver in the (a) cleaning, (b) cutting, and (c) packaging activity areas.
3. Suppose IP uses information from its activity-cost rates to calculate costs incurred on retail potato cuts and institutional potato cuts. Using the ABC system, what is the cost per pound of (a) retail potato cuts and (b) institutional potato cuts?
4. Comment on the cost differences between the two costing systems in 1 and 3. How might IP use the information in 3 to make better decisions?

5-27 Activity-based costing, job-costing system. The Hewlett-Packard (HP) plant in Roseville, California, assembles and tests printed-circuit (PC) boards. The job-costing system at this plant has two direct-cost categories (direct materials and direct manufacturing labor) and seven indirect-cost pools. These indirect-cost pools represent the seven activity areas that operating personnel at the plant determined are sufficiently different (in terms of cost-behavior patterns or individual products being assembled) to warrant separate cost pools. The cost-allocation base chosen for each activity area is the cost driver at that activity area.

Debbie Berlant, a newly appointed marketing manager at HP, is attending a training session that describes how an activity-based costing approach was used to design the Roseville plant's job-costing system. Berlant is provided with the following incomplete information for a specific job (an order for a single PC board, No. A82):

Direct materials	$75.00	
Direct manufacturing labor	15.00	$90.00
Manufacturing overhead (see below)		?
Total manufacturing cost		$?

Manufacturing Overhead Cost Pool	Cost-Allocation Base	Cost-Allocation Rate	Units of Cost-Allocation Base Used on Job No. A82	Manufacturing Overhead Allocated to Job
1. Axial insertion	Axial insertions	0.08	45	?
2. Dip insertion	Dip insertions	0.25	?	6.00
3. Manual insertion	Manual insertions	?	11	5.50
4. Wave solder	Boards soldered	3.50	?	3.50
5. Backload	Backload insertions	?	6	4.20
6. Test	Budgeted time board is in test activity	90.00	0.25	?
7. Defect analysis	Budgeted time for defect analysis and repair	?	0.10	8.00

Required

1. Present an overview diagram of the activity-based job-costing system at the Roseville plant.
2. Fill in the blanks (noted by question marks) in the cost information provided to Berlant for Job No. A82.
3. Why might manufacturing managers and marketing managers favor this ABC job-costing system over the previous costing system, which had the same two direct-cost categories but only a single indirect-cost pool (manufacturing overhead allocated using direct manufacturing labor costs)?

5-28 ABC, product-costing at banks, cross-subsidization. First International Bank (FIB) is examining the profitability of its Premier Account, a combined savings and checking account. Depositors receive a 7% annual interest rate on their average deposit. FIB earns an interest rate spread of 3% (the difference between the rate at which it lends money and the rate it pays depositors) by lending money for home loan purposes at 10%. Thus, FIB would gain \$60 on the interest spread if a depositor has an average Premier Account balance of \$2,000 in 2002 (\$2,000 × 3% = \$60).

The Premier Account allows depositors unlimited use of services such as deposits, withdrawals, checking accounts, and foreign currency drafts. Depositors with Premier Account balances of \$1,000 or more receive unlimited free use of services. Depositors with minimum balances of less than \$1,000 pay a \$20-a-month service fee for their Premier Account.

FIB recently conducted an activity-based costing study of its services. It assessed the following costs for six individual services. The use of these services in 2002 by three customers is as follows:

	Activity-Based Cost per "Transaction"	Account Usage		
		Robinson	Skerrett	Farrel
Deposit/withdrawal with teller	\$2.50	40	50	5
Deposit/withdrawal with automatic teller machine (ATM)	0.80	10	20	16
Deposit/withdrawal on prearranged monthly basis	0.50	0	12	60
Bank checks written	8.00	9	3	2
Foreign currency drafts	12.00	4	1	6
Inquiries about account balance	1.50	10	18	9
Average Premier Account balance for 2002		\$1,100	\$800	\$25,000

Assume Robinson and Farrel always maintain a balance above \$1,000, whereas Skerrett always has a balance below \$1,000.

Required

1. Compute the 2002 profitability of the Robinson, Skerrett, and Farrel Premier Accounts at FIB.
2. What evidence is there of cross-subsidization among the three Premier Accounts? Why might FIB worry about this cross-subsidization if the Premier Account product offering is profitable as a whole?
3. What changes would you recommend for FIB's Premier Account?

Problems

5-29 Job costing with single direct-cost category, single indirect-cost pool, law firm. Wigan Associates is a recently formed law partnership. Ellery Hanley, the managing partner of Wigan Associates, has just finished a tense phone call with Martin Offiah, president of Widnes Coal. Offiah strongly complained about the price Wigan charged for some legal work done for Widnes Coal.

Hanley also received a phone call from its only other client (St. Helen's Glass), which was very pleased with both the quality of the work and the price charged on its most recent job.

Wigan Associates uses a cost-based approach to pricing (billing) each job. Currently it uses a single direct-cost category (professional labor-hours) and a single indirect-cost pool (general support). Indirect costs are allocated to cases on the basis of professional labor-hours per case. The job files show the following:

	Widnes Coal	St. Helen's Glass
Professional labor	104 hours	96 hours

Professional labor costs at Wigan Associates are \$70 an hour. Indirect costs are allocated to cases at \$105 an hour. Total indirect costs in the most recent period were \$21,000.

Required

1. Why is it important for Wigan Associates to understand the costs associated with individual jobs?
2. Compute the costs of the Widnes Coal and St. Helen's Glass jobs using Wigan's existing job-costing system.

5-30 Job costing with multiple direct-cost categories, single indirect-cost pool, law firm (continuation of 5-29). Hanley asks his assistant to collect details on those costs included in the \$21,000 indirect-cost pool that can be traced to each individual job. After analysis, Wigan is able to reclassify \$14,000 of the \$21,000 as direct costs:

Other Direct Costs	Widnes Coal	St. Helen's Glass
Research support labor	$1,600	$ 3,400
Computer time	500	1,300
Travel and allowances	600	4,400
Telephones/faxes	200	1,000
Photocopying	250	750
Total	$3,150	$10,850

Hanley decides to calculate the costs of each job had Wigan used six direct-cost pools and a single indirect-cost pool. The single indirect-cost pool would have $7,000 of costs and would be allocated to each case using the professional labor-hours base.

Required

1. What is the revised indirect-cost allocation rate per professional labor-hour for Wigan Associates when total indirect costs are $7,000?
2. Compute the costs of the Widnes and St. Helen's jobs if Wigan Associates had used its refined costing system with multiple direct-cost categories and one indirect-cost pool.
3. Compare the costs of Widnes and St. Helen's jobs in 2 above with those in requirement 2 of Problem 5-29. Comment on the results.

5-31 Job costing with multiple direct-cost categories, multiple indirect-cost pools, law firm (continuation of 5-29 and 5-30). Wigan has two classifications of professional staff: partners and associates. Hanley asks his assistant to examine the relative use of partners and associates on the recent Widnes Coal and St. Helen's jobs. The Widnes job used 24 partner-hours and 80 associate-hours. The St. Helen's job used 56 partner-hours and 40 associate-hours. Therefore, totals of the two jobs together were 80 partner-hours and 120 associate-hours. Hanley decides to examine how using separate direct-cost rates for partners and associates and using separate indirect-cost pools for partners and associates would have affected the costs of the Widnes and St. Helen's jobs. Indirect costs in each indirect-cost pool would be allocated on the basis of total hours of that category of professional labor. From the total indirect-cost pool of $7,000, $4,600 is attributable to the activities of partners, and $2,400 is attributable to the activities of associates.

The rates per category of professional labor are as follows:

Category of Professional Labor	Direct Cost per Hour	Indirect Cost per Hour
Partner	$100.00	$4,600 ÷ 80 hours = $57.50
Associate	50.00	$2,400 ÷ 120 hours = $20.00

Required

1. Compute the costs of the Widnes and St. Helen's cases using Wigan's further refined system, with multiple direct-cost categories and multiple indirect-cost pools.
2. For what decisions might Wigan Associates find it more useful to use this job-costing approach rather than the approaches in Problems 5-29 or 5-30?

5-32 Plantwide, department, and activity-cost rates. (CGA, adapted) The Sayther Company manufactures and sells two products, A and B. The manufacturing activity is organized in two departments. Manufacturing overhead costs at its Portland plant are allocated to each product using a plantwide rate of $17 per direct manufacturing labor-hour. This rate is based on budgeted manufacturing overhead of $340,000 and 20,000 budgeted direct manufacturing labor-hours:

Manufacturing Department	Budgeted Manufacturing Overhead	Budgeted Direct Manufacturing Labor-Hours
1	$240,000	10,000
2	100,000	10,000
Total	$340,000	20,000

The number of direct manufacturing labor-hours required to manufacture each product is

Manufacturing Department	Product A	Product B
1	4	1
2	1	4
Total	5	5

Per-unit costs for the two categories of direct manufacturing costs are

Direct Manufacturing Costs	Product A	Product B
Direct materials costs	$120	$150
Direct manufacturing labor costs	80	80

At the end of the year, there was no work in process. There were 200 finished units of product A and 600 finished units of product B on hand. Assume that the budgeted production level of the Portland plant was exactly attained.

Sayther sets the selling price of each product by adding 120% to its unit manufacturing costs; that is, if the unit manufacturing costs are $100, the selling price is $220 ($100 + $120). This 120% markup is designed to cover costs upstream to manufacturing (R&D and design) and costs downstream from manufacturing (marketing, distribution, and customer service), as well as to provide a profit.

Required

1. How much manufacturing overhead cost would be included in the inventory of products A and B if Sayther used (a) a plantwide overhead rate and (b) department overhead rates?
2. By how much would the selling prices of product A and product B differ if Sayther used a plantwide overhead rate instead of department overhead rates?
3. Should Sayther Company prefer plantwide or department overhead rates?
4. Under what conditions should Sayther Company further subdivide the department cost pools into activity-cost pools?

5-33 Plantwide versus department overhead cost rates. (CMA, adapted) The MumsDay Corporation manufactures a complete line of fiberglass suitcases. MumsDay has three manufacturing departments (molding, component, and assembly) and two support departments (maintenance and power).

The sides of the cases are manufactured in the Molding Department. The frames, hinges, locks, and so forth are manufactured in the Component Department. The cases are completed in the Assembly Department. Varying amounts of materials, time, and effort are required for each of the various cases. The Maintenance Department and Power Department provide services to the three manufacturing departments.

MumsDay has always used a plantwide manufacturing overhead rate. Direct manufacturing labor-hours are used to allocate the overhead to each product. The budgeted rate is calculated by dividing the company's total budgeted manufacturing overhead cost by the total budgeted direct manufacturing labor-hours to be worked in the three manufacturing departments.

Whit Portlock, manager of Cost Accounting, has recommended that MumsDay use department overhead rates. Portlock has projected operating costs and production levels for the coming year. They are presented (in thousands) by department in the following table:

	Manufacturing Department		
	Molding	**Component**	**Assembly**
Department Operating Data			
Direct manufacturing labor-hours	500	2,000	1,500
Machine-hours	875	125	–
Department Costs			
Direct manufacturing materials	$12,400	$30,000	$ 1,250
Direct manufacturing labor	3,500	20,000	12,000
Manufacturing overhead	21,000	16,200	22,600
Total departmental costs	$36,900	$66,200	$35,850
Use of Support Departments			
Estimated usage of maintenance resources in labor-hours for coming year	90	25	10
Estimated usage of power (in kilowatt-hours) for coming year	360	320	120

Estimated costs are $4,000 for the Maintenance Department and $18,400 for the Power Department.

Required

1. Calculate the plantwide overhead rate for MumsDay Corporation for the coming year using the same method as used in the past.
2. Whit Portlock has been asked to develop department overhead rates for comparison with the plantwide rate. Follow these steps in developing the department rates:
   a. Allocate the Maintenance Department and Power Department costs to the three manufacturing departments.
   b. Calculate department overhead rates for the three manufacturing departments using a machine-hour allocation base for the Molding Department and a direct manufacturing labor-hour allocation base for the Component Department and Assembly Department.
3. Should the MumsDay Corporation use a plantwide rate or department rates to allocate overhead cost to its products? Explain your answer.
4. Under what conditions should MumsDay Corporation further subdivide the department cost pools into activity-cost pools?

5-34 Activity-based costing, merchandising. Figure Four, Inc., specializes in the distribution of pharmaceutical products. Figure Four buys from pharmaceutical companies and resells to each of three different markets:

a. General supermarket chains
b. Drugstore chains
c. Ma and Pa single-store pharmacies

Rick Flair, the new controller of Figure Four, reported the following data for August 2002:

	General Supermarket Chains	Drugstore Chains	Ma and Pa Single Stores
Average revenue per delivery	$30,900	$10,500	$1,980
Average cost of goods sold per delivery	$30,000	$10,000	$1,800
Number of deliveries	120	300	1,000

For many years, Figure Four has used gross margin percentage [(Revenue − Cost of goods sold) ÷ Revenue] to evaluate the relative profitability of its customer groups (distribution outlets).

Flair recently attended a seminar on activity-based costing and decides to consider using it at Figure Four. Flair meets with all the key managers and many staff members. Generally, these individuals agree that there are five key activity areas at Figure Four:

Activity Area	Cost Driver
1. Customer purchase order processing	Purchase orders by customers
2. Line-item ordering	Line items per purchase order
3. Store delivery	Store deliveries
4. Cartons shipped to stores	Cartons shipped to a store per delivery
5. Shelf-stocking at customer store	Hours of shelf-stocking

Each customer purchase order consists of one or more line items. A line item represents a single product (such as Extra-Strength Tylenol Tablets). Each store delivery entails the delivery of one or more cartons of products to a customer. Each product is delivered in one or more separate cartons. Figure Four staff stack cartons directly onto display shelves in a store. Currently, there is no charge for this service, and not all customers use Figure Four for this activity.

The August 2002 operating costs (other than cost of goods sold) of Figure Four are $301,080. These operating costs are assigned to the five activity areas. The costs in each area and the quantity of the cost-allocation base used in that area for August 2002 are as follows:

Activity Area	Total Costs in August 2002	Total Units of Cost-Allocation Base Used in August 2002
1. Customer purchase order processing	$ 80,000	2,000 orders
2. Line-item ordering	63,840	21,280 line items
3. Store deliveries	71,000	1,420 store deliveries
4. Cartons shipped to stores	76,000	76,000 cartons
5. Shelf-stocking at customer stores	10,240	640 hours
	$301,080	

Other data for August 2002 include the following:

	General Supermarket Chains	Drugstore Chains	Ma and Pa Single Stores
Total number of orders	140	360	1,500
Average number of line items per order	14	12	10
Total number of store deliveries	120	300	1,000
Average number of cartons shipped per store delivery	300	80	16
Average number of hours of shelf-stocking per store delivery	3	0.6	0.1

Required

1. Compute the August 2002 gross-margin percentage for each of its three distribution markets and compute Figure Four's operating income.
2. Compute the August 2002 rate per unit of the cost-allocation base for each of the five activity areas.
3. Compute the operating income of each distribution market in August 2002 using the activity-based costing information. Comment on the results. What new insights are available with the activity-based information?

4. Describe four challenges Flair would face in assigning the total August 2002 operating costs of $301,080 to the five activity areas.

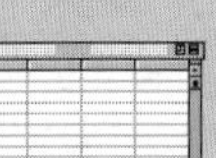

Excel Application For students who wish to practice their spreadsheet skills, the following is a step-by-step approach to creating an Excel spreadsheet to work this problem.

Step-by-Step

1. In a new spreadsheet, create a "Financial Data" section for the financial data provided by Rick Flair, with rows for average revenue per delivery, average cost of goods sold per delivery, and number of deliveries, and columns for "General Supermarket Chains," "Drugstore Chains," and "Ma and Pa Single Stores." When you are finished, this section should look just like the table provided by Rick Flair on page 167.
2. Skip two rows. Create a "Cost-Allocation Data" section with columns labeled "Activity Area," "Total Cost in August 2002," and "Total Units of Cost-Allocation Base Used in August 2002." Set up rows for each activity area in the same format as in the middle of page 167. Next, set up a column beside the "Total Units of Cost-Allocation Base Used in August 2002" column and call the new column "Rate per Unit of Cost-Allocation Base."
3. Skip down two rows and create an "Activity Data" section in the same format as presented by Rick Flair at the bottom of page 167. Set up columns for "General Supermarket Chains," "Drugstore Chains," and "Ma and Pa Single Stores." Set up separate rows for each activity area. Enter the quantity of each activity used by each market during the period.
4. Skip two rows. Create a "Profitability Analysis" section; columns for "General Supermarket Chains," "Drugstore Chains," "Ma and Pa Single Stores," and "Figure Four, Inc."; rows for revenues, cost of goods sold, gross margin, gross margin percentage, each of the five activity areas, operating costs, operating income, and operating margin percentage.
5. For Problem 1, go to the "Profitability Analysis" section, enter calculations for revenues, cost of goods sold, and gross margin percentage for each market. Next calculate operating income for Figure Four, Inc., as a whole and enter this number in the operating income row of the "Figure Four, Inc." column.
6. For Problem 2, go to the "Cost-Allocation Data" section, enter calculations for the rate per unit of the cost-allocation base for each of the five activity areas in the "Rate per Unit of Cost-Allocation Base" column.
7. Enter calculations for the total cost of each activity in each of the different markets in your "Profitability Analysis" section.
8. For Problem 3, compute operating income for each market by entering the appropriate calculation in the operating income row of the "Profitability Analysis" section.
9. *Verify the accuracy of your spreadsheet:* Go to your "Cost-Allocation Data" section and change total order processing costs from $80,000 to $100,000. If you programmed your spreadsheet correctly, operating income for Figure Four, Inc., should change to $116,920.

5-35 **Activity-based costing, product-cost cross-subsidization.** Baker's Delight (BD) has been in the food-processing business three years. For its first two years (2002 and 2003), its sole product was raisin cake. All cakes were manufactured and packaged in one-pound units. BD used a normal costing system. The two direct-cost categories were direct materials and direct manufacturing labor. The sole indirect manufacturing cost category—manufacturing overhead—was allocated to products using units of production as the allocation base.

In its third year (2004), BD added a second product—layered carrot cake—which was packaged in one-pound units. This product differs from raisin cake in several ways:

- More expensive ingredients are used.
- More direct manufacturing labor time is required.
- More-complex manufacturing processing is required.

In 2004, BD continued to use its existing costing system, in which it allocated manufacturing overhead using total units produced of raisin and layered carrot cakes.

Direct materials costs in 2004 were $0.60 per pound of raisin cake and $0.90 per pound of layered carrot cake. Direct manufacturing labor cost in 2004 was $0.14 per pound of raisin cake and $0.20 per pound of layered carrot cake.

During 2004, BD sales staff reported greater-than-expected sales of layered carrot cake and less-than-expected sales of raisin cake. The budgeted and actual sales volume for 2004 is as follows:

	Budgeted	**Actual**
Raisin cake	160,000 pounds	120,000 pounds
Layered carrot cake	40,000 pounds	80,000 pounds

The budgeted manufacturing overhead for 2004 is $210,800.

At the end of 2004, Jonathan Davis, the controller of BD, decided to investigate how an activity-based costing system would affect the product-cost numbers. After consultation with operating personnel, the single manufacturing overhead cost pool was subdivided into five activity areas. These activity areas, the cost-allocation base, the budgeted 2004 cost-allocation rate, and the quantity of the cost-allocation base used by the raisin and layered carrot cakes are as follows:

Activity	Cost-Allocation Base	Budgeted 2004 Cost per Unit of Cost-Allocation Base	Quantity of Cost-Allocation Base: Raisin Cake	Quantity of Cost-Allocation Base: Layered Carrot Cake
Mixing	Labor-hours	$0.04	600,000	640,000
Cooking	Oven-hours	$0.14	240,000	240,000
Cooling	Cool room-hours	$0.02	360,000	400,000
Creaming/Icing	Machine-hours	$0.25	0	240,000
Packaging	Machine-hours	$0.08	360,000	560,000

Required

1. Compute the 2004 unit-product cost of raisin cake and layered carrot cake using the existing costing system used in the 2002 to 2004 period.
2. Compute the 2004 unit-product cost of raisin cake and layered carrot cake using the activity-based costing system.
3. Explain the differences in unit-product costs computed in requirements 1 and 2.
4. Describe three uses Baker's Delight might make of the activity-based cost numbers.

5-36 **ABC, health care.** Uppervale Health Center runs three programs: (1) alcoholic rehabilitation, (2) drug-addict rehabilitation, and (3) aftercare (counseling and support of patients after release from a mental hospital).

The center's budget for 2003 follows:

Professional salaries:		
4 physicians × $150,000	$ 600,000	
18 psychologists × $75,000	1,350,000	
20 nurses × $30,000	600,000	$2,550,000
Medical supplies		300,000
General overhead (administrative salaries, rent, utilities, etc.)		880,000
		$3,730,000

Muriel Clayton, the director of the center, is keen on determining the cost of each program. Clayton compiled the following data describing employee allocations to individual programs:

	Alcohol	Drug	Aftercare	Total Employees
Physicians		4		4
Psychologists	6	4	8	18
Nurses	4	6	10	20

Eighty patients are in residence in the alcohol program, each staying about six months. Thus, the clinic provides 40 patient-years of service in the alcohol program. Similarly, 100 patients are involved in the drug program for about six months each. Thus, the clinic provides 50 patient-years of service in the drug program.

Clayton has recently become aware of activity-based costing as a method to refine costing systems. She asks her accountant, Huey Deluth, how she should apply this new technique. Deluth obtains the following information:

1. Consumption of medical supplies depends on the number of patient-years.
2. General overhead costs consists of

Rent and clinic maintenance	$ 180,000
Administrative costs to manage patient charts, food, laundry	600,000
Laboratory services	100,000
Total	$ 880,000

3. Other information about individual departments:

	Alcohol	Drug	Aftercare	Total
Square feet of space occupied by each program	9,000	9,000	12,000	30,000
Patient-years of service	40	50	60	150
Number of laboratory tests	400	1,400	700	2,500

Required

1. **a.** Selecting cost-allocation bases that you believe are the most appropriate for allocating indirect costs to programs, calculate the indirect-cost rates for medical supplies, rent, and clinic maintenance; administrative costs for patient charts, food, and laundry; and laboratory services.
   b. Using an activity-based costing approach to cost analysis, calculate the cost of each program and the cost per patient-year of the alcohol and drug programs.
   c. What benefits can Uppervale Health Center obtain by implementing the ABC system?
2. What factors, other than cost, do you think Uppervale Health Center should consider in allocating resources to its programs?

5-37 Activity-based job costing. Schramka Company manufactures a variety of prestige boardroom chairs. Its job-costing system uses an activity-based approach. There are two direct-cost categories (direct materials and direct manufacturing labor) and three indirect-cost pools. The cost pools represent three activity areas at the plant.

Manufacturing Activity Area	Budgeted Costs for 2004	Cost Driver Used as Allocation Base	Cost-Allocation Rate
Materials handling	$ 200,000	Parts	$ 0.25
Cutting	2,000,000	Parts	2.50
Assembly	2,000,000	Direct manufacturing labor-hours	25.00

Two styles of chairs were produced in March: the executive chair and the chairman chair. Their quantities, direct material costs, and other data for March 2004 are as follows:

	Units Produced	Direct Material Costs	Number of Parts	Direct Manufacturing Labor-Hours
Executive chair	5,000	$600,000	100,000	7,500
Chairman chair	100	25,000	3,500	500

The direct manufacturing labor rate is $20 per hour. Assume no beginning or ending inventory.

Required

1. Compute the March 2004 total manufacturing costs and unit costs of the executive chair and the chairman chair.
2. The upstream activities to manufacturing (R&D and design) and the downstream activities (marketing, distribution, and customer service) are analyzed, and the unit costs in 2004 are budgeted to be

	Upstream Activities	Downstream Activities
Executive chair	$ 60	$110
Chairman chair	146	236

   Compute the full costs per unit of each chair. (Full costs of each chair are the sum of the costs of all business functions.)
3. Compare the per unit cost figures for the executive chair and the chairman chair computed in requirements 1 and 2. Why do the costs differ for each chair? Why might these differences be important to Schramka Company?

5-38 Activity-based job costing, unit-cost comparisons. The Tracy Corporation has a machining facility specializing in jobs for the aircraft-components market. The previous job-costing system had two direct-cost categories (direct materials and direct manufacturing labor) and a single indirect-cost pool (manufacturing overhead, allocated using direct manufacturing labor-hours). The indirect cost-allocation rate of the previous system for 2004 would have been $115 per direct manufacturing labor-hour.

Recently a team with members from product design, manufacturing, and accounting used an ABC approach to refine its job-costing system. The two direct-cost categories were retained. The team decided to replace the single indirect-cost pool with five indirect-cost pools. The cost pools represent five activity areas at the facility, each with its own supervisor and budget responsibility. Pertinent data are as follows:

Activity Area	Cost-Allocation Base	Cost-Allocation Rate
Material handling	Parts	$ 0.40
Lathe work	Lathe turns	0.20
Milling	Machine-hours	20.00
Grinding	Parts	0.80
Testing	Units tested	15.00

Information-gathering technology has advanced to the point at which the data necessary for budgeting in these five activity areas are collected automatically.

Two representative jobs processed under the ABC system at the facility in the most recent period had the following characteristics:

	Job 410	Job 411
Direct materials cost per job	$ 9,700	$59,900
Direct manufacturing labor cost per job	$750	$11,250
Number of direct manufacturing labor-hours per job	25	375
Parts per job	500	2,000
Lathe turns per job	20,000	60,000
Machine-hours per job	150	1,050
Units per job (all units are tested)	10	200

Required

1. Compute the manufacturing costs per unit for each job under the previous job-costing system.
2. Compute the manufacturing costs per unit for each job under the activity-based costing system.
3. Compare the per unit cost figures for Jobs 410 and 411 computed in requirements 1 and 2. Why do the previous and the activity-based costing systems differ in the manufacturing costs per unit for each job? Why might these differences be important to Tracy Corporation?
4. How might Tracy Corporation use information from its ABC system to manage its business better?

5-39 ABC, implementation, ethics. (CMA, adapted) Applewood Electronics, a division of Elgin Corporation, manufactures two large-screen television models, the Monarch, which has been produced since 1998 and sells for $900, and the Regal, a newer model introduced in early 2001 that sells for $1,140. Based on the following income statement for the year ended November 30, 2002, senior management at Elgin have decided to concentrate Applewood's marketing resources on the Regal model and to begin to phase out the Monarch model.

Applewood Electronics
Income Statement
For the Fiscal Year Ended November 30, 2002

	Monarch	Regal	Total
Revenues	$19,800,000	$4,560,000	$24,360,000
Cost of goods sold	12,540,000	3,192,000	15,732,000
Gross margin	7,260,000	1,368,000	8,628,000
Selling and administrative expense	5,830,000	978,000	6,808,000
Operating income	$ 1,430,000	$ 390,000	$ 1,820,000
Units produced and sold	22,000	4,000	
Net income per unit sold	$65.00	$97.50	

Unit costs for Monarch and Regal are as follows:

	Monarch	Regal
Direct materials	$208	$584
Direct manufacturing labor		
Monarch (1.5 hours × $12)	18	
Regal (3.5 hours × $12)		42
Machine costs[a]		
Monarch (8 hours × $18)	144	
Regal (4 hours × $18)		72
Manufacturing overhead other than machine costs[b]	200	100
Total cost	$570	$798

[a]Machine costs include lease costs of the machine, repairs, and maintenance.
[b]Manufacturing overhead was allocated to products based on machine-hours at the rate of $25 per hour.

Applewood's controller, Susan Benzo, is advocating the use of activity-based costing and activity-based management and has gathered the following information about the company's manufacturing overhead costs for the year ended November 30, 2002.

Activity Center (Cost-Allocation Base)	Total Activity Costs	Units of the Cost-Allocation Base: Monarch	Regal	Total
Soldering (number of solder points)	$ 942,000	1,185,000	385,000	1,570,000
Shipments (number of shipments)	860,000	16,200	3,800	20,000
Quality control (number of inspections)	1,240,000	56,200	21,300	77,500
Purchase orders (number of orders)	950,400	80,100	109,980	190,080
Machine power (machine-hours)	57,600	176,000	16,000	192,000
Machine setups (number of setups)	750,000	16,000	14,000	30,000
Total manufacturing overhead	$4,800,000			

After completing her analysis, Benzo shows the results to Fred Duval, the Applewood division president. Duval does not like what he sees. "If you show headquarters this analysis, they are going to ask us to phase out the Regal line, which we have just introduced. This whole costing stuff has been a major problem for us. First Monarch was not profitable and now Regal."

"Looking at the ABC analysis, I see two problems. First, we do many more activities than the ones you have listed. If you had included all activities, maybe your conclusions would be different. Second, you used number of setups and number of inspections as allocation bases. The numbers would be different had you used setup-hours and inspection-hours instead. I know that measurement problems precluded you from using these other cost-allocation bases, but I believe you ought to make some adjustments to our current numbers to compensate for these issues. I know you can do better. We can't afford to phase out either product."

Benzo knows her numbers are fairly accurate. On a limited sample, she calculated the profitability of Regal and Monarch using more and different allocation bases. The set of activities and activity rates she had used resulted in numbers that closely approximate those based on more detailed analyses. She is confident that headquarters, knowing that Regal was introduced only recently, will not ask Applewood to phase it out. She is also aware that a sizable portion of Duval's bonus is based on division revenues. Phasing out either product would adversely affect his bonus. Still, she feels some pressure from Duval to do something.

Required

1. Using activity-based costing, calculate the profitability of the Regal and Monarch models.
2. Explain briefly why these numbers differ from the profitability of the Regal and Monarch models calculated using Applewood's existing costing system.
3. Comment on Duval's concerns about the accuracy and limitations of ABC.
4. How might Applewood find the ABC information helpful in managing its business?
5. What should Susan Benzo do?

Collaborative Learning Problem

5-40 **Activity-based costing, cost hierarchy.** (CMA, adapted) Coffee Bean, Inc., (CBI) buys coffee beans from around the world and roasts, blends, and packages them for resale. The major cost is direct materials; however, there is substantial manufacturing overhead in the predominantly automated roasting and packing process. The company uses relatively little direct labor.

Some of the coffees are very popular and sell in large volumes, whereas a few of the newer blends sell in very low volumes. CBI prices its coffee at budgeted cost, including allocated overhead, plus a markup on cost of 30%.

Data for the 2003 budget include manufacturing overhead of $3,000,000, which has been allocated on the basis of each product's budgeted direct-labor cost. The budgeted direct-labor cost for 2003 totals $600,000. Purchases and use of materials (mostly coffee beans) are budgeted to total $6,000,000.

The budgeted direct costs for one-pound bags of two of the company's products are

	Mauna Loa	Malaysian
Direct materials	$4.20	$3.20
Direct labor	0.30	0.30

CBI's controller believes the existing costing system may be providing misleading cost information. She has developed an activity-based analysis of the 2003 budgeted manufacturing overhead costs shown in the following table:

Activity	Cost Driver	Cost Driver Rate
Purchasing	Purchase orders	$500
Materials handling	Setups	400
Quality control	Batches	240
Roasting	Roasting-hours	10
Blending	Blending-hours	10
Packaging	Packaging-hours	10

Data regarding the 2003 production of the Mauna Loa and Malaysian coffee follow. There will be no beginning or ending materials inventory for either of these coffees.

	Mauna Loa	Malaysian
Expected sales	100,000 pounds	2,000 pounds
Purchase orders	4	4
Batches	10	4
Setups	30	12
Roasting-hours	1,000	20
Blending-hours	500	10
Packaging-hours	100	2

Required

1. Using CBI's existing costing system:
   a. Determine the company's 2003 budgeted manufacturing overhead rate using direct-labor cost as the single allocation base.
   b. Determine the 2003 budgeted costs and selling prices of 1 pound of Mauna Loa coffee and 1 pound of Malaysian coffee.
2. Use the controller's activity-based approach to estimate the 2003 budgeted cost for 1 pound of
   a. Mauna Loa coffee
   b. Malaysian coffee

   Allocate all costs to the 100,000 pounds of Mauna Loa and the 2,000 pounds of Malaysian. Compare the results with those in requirement 1.
3. Examine the implications of your answers to requirement 2 for CBI's pricing and product-mix strategy.

CHAPTER 5 INTERNET EXERCISE

Activity-Based Costing. Southwest Airlines provides an excellent example of the important role that activity-based costing (ABC) can play in strategic planning and pricing decisions. To better understand these concepts, go to www.prenhall.com/horngren, click on *Cost Accounting*, 11th ed., and access the Internet exercise for Chapter 5.

CHAPTER 5 VIDEO CASE

DELL COMPUTER: Implementing Activity–Based Costing

When Dell embarked on its ABC change initiative in 1994, few managers knew what to expect. The Austin, Texas-based maker of made-to-order personal computers had "hit a wall," according to Ken Hashman, director of service logistics. Net revenues for 1994 were $2.9 billion, but the year ended with a $36 million loss. The company was poised for tremendous growth, yet managers weren't sure which products and markets were going to produce the greatest profitability. Managers needed to know which product lines were driving profits and which were not.

So, when management chose to implement an ABC system, few people resisted. Dell managers recognized the value of better product-cost information and wanted to work out the details of implementing ABC in dozens of areas. In reflecting on this enthusiasm, Ken Hashman noted that the company actually had to pull back at first to get managers to focus on "the critical few" areas that held the greatest promise for big gains.

To begin the ABC process, cross-functional employee teams identified about 10 key activities. The activities comprised the logical flow of production, starting with inbound freight and duty, receiving, parts issuance, assembly, shipping, outbound distribution, and warranty. The assembly activity was further broken down for different product lines.

When it came time to estimate total indirect costs of the activities, the Dell teams went to work gathering data. Cost driver identification followed indirect-cost estimation. Some of the cost drivers required rethinking by managers. For example, the purchasing function supports all product lines and acquires hundreds of parts for the computer assembly process. The cost of acquiring a part, whether the part costs $1 or $100, is pretty much the same. So, the number of *part numbers* for each line of business became relevant. Before ABC, the cost of the purchasing function was simply part of overhead and was not identified with individual product lines.

Total cost-driver quantities were collected through Dell's internal computer information system. Initially, spreadsheets were used to create the ABC models and to analyze the data collected about the cost drivers. The spreadsheets made it easy to create the formulas to calculate the estimated indirect costs for each activity. The spreadsheets were also used to allocate the cost of activities to cost objects, such as different computer lines, based on the actual quantities used.

Five years later, the effort paid off big time! Net revenues for fiscal year 1998 were $12.3 billion, an increase of 329% from 1994. Net income for 1998 topped $944 million. Even more significant, managers now say they have a much better understanding of where the company makes money and where it doesn't. John Jones, vice president and controller of Dell Americas Operations, says it best. "Activity-based costing has really allowed Dell to go to the next level of understanding the profitability of each product it sells." Through the efforts of Dell's teams, managers can use the resulting ABC information to perform activity-based management to truly affect profitability and decision making.

QUESTIONS

1. Why did Dell use cross-functional employee teams to identify company activities?
2. Prior to implementing activity-based costing and activity-based management, Dell used a simple job-costing system. How does job costing differ from activity-based costing, and why was it important for Dell to make this change? What would Dell have risked by not making the change?
3. Dell focused its initial ABC efforts on about 10 key activities. Was this a good decision? Why or why not?

CHAPTER 6

Master Budget and Responsibility Accounting

LEARNING OBJECTIVES

1. Understand what a master budget is and explain its benefits
2. Describe the advantages of budgets
3. Prepare the operating budget and its supporting schedules
4. Use computer-based financial planning models in sensitivity analysis
5. Explain kaizen budgeting and how it is used for cost management
6. Prepare an activity-based budget
7. Describe responsibility centers and responsibility accounting
8. Explain how controllability relates to responsibility accounting

www.prenhall.com/horngren

The revenues budget for each hotel in the Ritz-Carlton Hotel chain drives decision making for all other budgets. Managers in every department, from housekeeping to the administrative office, use their hotel's revenues budget to prepare their own department budgets. Each department budget supports the anticipated occupancy, banquets, and restaurant activity described in the revenues budget.

The general manager and controller of each hotel have ultimate responsibility for assuring that all the department plans accurately reflect the coming year's expected—planned—business activities. The general manager challenges department managers to defend their budgets. Only when the general manager becomes convinced the budgets are accurate and sound will the overall plan be approved.

Budgeting is the common accounting tool companies use for planning and controlling what they must do to satisfy their customers and succeed in the marketplace. Budgets provide a measure of the financial results a company expects from its planned activities. By planning for the future, managers learn to anticipate potential problems and how to avoid them. Instead of subsequently facing problems, managers can focus their energies on exploiting opportunities. Remember that, "Few businesses plan to fail, but many of those that flop, failed to plan."

BUDGETS AND THE BUDGETING CYCLE

A *budget* is (a) the quantitative expression of a proposed plan of action by management for a specified period and (b) an aid to coordinating what needs to be done to implement that plan. A budget can cover both financial and nonfinancial aspects of the plan and serves as a blueprint for the company to follow in an upcoming period. A budget that covers financial aspects quantifies management's expectations regarding income, cash flows, and financial position. Just as financial statements are prepared for past periods, so can financial statements be prepared for future periods—for example, a budgeted income statement, a budgeted statement of cash flows, and a budgeted balance sheet. Underlying these financial budgets can be nonfinancial budgets for, say, units manufactured or sold, number of employees, and number of new products being introduced to the marketplace.

Well-managed companies usually cycle through the following budgeting steps:

1. Planning the performance of the company as a whole, as well as planning the performance of its subunits (such as departments or divisions). Management at all levels agrees on what is expected.
2. Providing a frame of reference, a set of specific expectations against which actual results can be compared.
3. Investigating variations from plans. If necessary, corrective action follows investigation.
4. Planning again, in light of feedback and changed conditions.

1 Understand what a master budget is
...initial budget prepared before the start of a period
and explain its benefits
...for example, planning, coordination, and control

The **master budget** expresses management's operating and financial plans for a specified period (usually a year) and comprises a set of budgeted financial statements. The master budget gets its name because it is the initial plan of what the company intends to accomplish in the period. The master budget reflects the impact of both operating and financing decisions.

- Operating decisions deal with the use of scarce resources.
- Financing decisions deal with how to obtain the funds to acquire those resources.

The focus of this book is on how accounting helps managers make operating decisions. That's why this chapter emphasizes operating budgets. Managers spend a big part of their time in preparing budgets and analyzing budgets. The many advantages of budgeting make this a wise investment of their energy.

Terminology used to describe budgets varies among companies. For example, budgeted financial statements are sometimes called **pro forma statements.** Some companies, such as Hewlett-Packard, refer to budgeting as *targeting*. And many companies, such as Nissan Motor and Owens Corning, give a positive thrust to budgeting by referring to a budget as a *profit plan*.

ADVANTAGES OF BUDGETS

Budgets are a big part of most management control systems. When administered wisely, a budget

a. compels strategic planning and implementation of plans
b. provides a framework for judging performance
c. motivates managers and employees
d. promotes coordination and communication among subunits within the company

2 Describe the advantages of budgets

...for example, helping to develop and implement strategic plans and motivate employees

Strategic Planning and Implementation of Plans

Budgeting is most useful when it is an integral part of a company's strategy analysis. *Strategy* specifies how an organization matches its own capabilities with the opportunities in the marketplace to accomplish its objectives. It includes consideration of such questions as:

1. What are the objectives of the company?
2. Are the markets for a company's products local, regional, national, or global? What trends affect its markets? How is the company affected by the economy, its industry, and its competitors?
3. What form of organization and financial structure serves the company best?
4. What are the risks of alternative strategies, and what are the company's contingency plans if its preferred plan fails?

As shown in Exhibit 6-1, a company's strategy affects both its long-run and short-run planning. And the company's planning is expressed through its long-run and short-run budgets. But there is more to the story! See in the exhibit those arrowheads pointing backward as well as forward? The backward arrows are a way of graphically indicating that budgets can lead to changes in plans and strategies. Budgets provide managers with feedback about the likely effects of their strategies and plans. And sometimes the feedback signals to managers that they need to revise their plans and possibly their strategies. DaimlerChrysler's decision relating to the pricing of its Dodge Durango illustrates the relationship between strategy, plans, and budgets. The Durango competes in the sport-utility vehicle (SUV) market with the lower-priced Subaru Forrester and Isuzu Rodeo, as well as the comparably priced Chevrolet Blazer. By reducing the Durango's price, DaimlerChrysler expected to increase the demand for the Durango. The budget, however, indicated that, even at the forecast higher sales quantities, DaimlerChrysler would be unable to meet its financial targets for the Durango. For its strategy of reducing price to succeed, DaimlerChrysler also would need to reduce its manufacturing and marketing

Planning is setting goals and developing strategies to achieve those goals. *Budgets* show how resources will be deployed to implement strategy. The master budget is not in itself a strategic plan, rather, it helps managers *implement* their strategic plans.

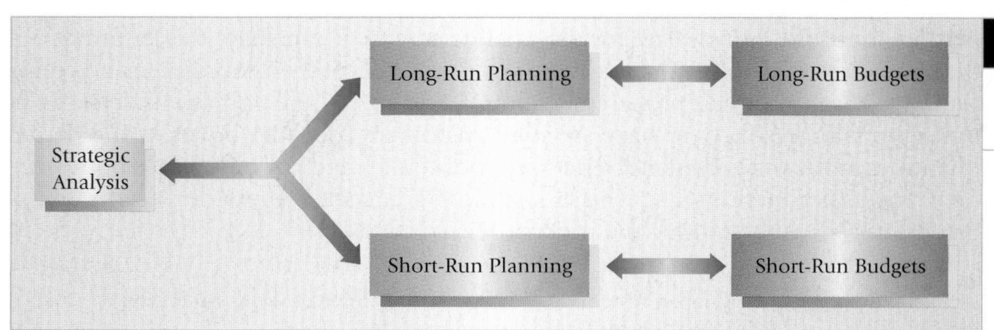

EXHIBIT 6-1
Strategy, Planning, and Budgets

costs. This feedback led the Durango team to develop plans to use materials and labor more efficiently.

Framework for Judging Performance

Once plans are in place, a company's performance can be measured against the budgets established for those plans. Budgets can overcome two limitations of using past performance as a basis for judging actual results. One limitation is that past results incorporate past miscues and substandard performance. Consider a cellular telephone company (Mobile Communications) examining the current year 2004 performance of its sales force. Suppose the past performance in 2003 incorporates the efforts of many salespeople who left Mobile because they did not have a good understanding of the marketplace. (The president of Mobile said, "They could not sell ice cream in a heat wave.") Using the sales record of those departed employees would set the performance bar for 2004 much too low.

The other limitation of using past performance is that future conditions may be expected to differ from the past. Consider again Mobile Communications. Suppose, in 2004, Mobile had a 20% revenue increase, compared with a 10% revenue increase in 2003. Does this increase indicate outstanding sales performance? Before you say yes, consider the following facts. In November 2003, an industry trade association forecast that the 2004 growth rate in industry revenues would be 40%, which also turned out to be the actual growth rate. Mobile's 20% actual revenue gain in 2004 takes on a negative connotation, even though it exceeded the 2003 actual growth rate of 10%. Using the 40% budgeted sales growth rate provides a better measure of the 2004 sales performance than using the 2003 actual growth rate of 10%.

Motivating Managers and Employees[1]

Research shows that budgets that are challenging improve performance. An inability to achieve budgeted numbers is viewed as a failure. Most individuals are motivated to work more intensely to avoid failure than to achieve success. As individuals get closer to a goal, they work harder to achieve it. For these reasons, many executives like to set challenging but achievable goals for their subordinates. Creating a little anxiety improves performance. But overly ambitious and unachievable budgets increase anxiety without motivation—that's because individuals see little chance of avoiding failure. General Electric's former CEO, Jack Welch, describes setting challenging budgets as energizing, motivating, and satisfying for managers and employees while unleashing out-of-the-box and creative thinking.

Coordination and Communication

Coordination is meshing and balancing all factors of production or service and all departments and business functions in the best way for the company to meet its goals. *Communication* is getting those goals to be understood and accepted by all the employees.

The master budget helps coordinate the various business functions, such as production and marketing. Management accountants usually coordinate the complex budgeting process.

Coordination forces executives to think of relationships among individual operations, departments, the company as a whole, and across companies. Consider budgeting at Pace, a United Kingdom-based manufacturer of electronic products. A key product is their decoder boxes for cable television. The production manager can achieve more timely production by coordinating and communicating with the company's marketing personnel to understand when decoder boxes will be needed. In turn, the marketing personnel can make better predictions of future demand for decoder boxes by coordinating and communicating with Pace's customers.

Suppose BSKYB, one of Pace's largest customers, is planning to launch a new digital satellite service nine months from now. If Pace's marketing group is able to obtain information about the launch date for the satellite service, it can share this information with the manufacturing group. The manufacturing group must then coordinate and communicate with Pace's materials procurement group, and so on. The point to understand here is that Pace is more likely to have satisfied customers (decoder boxes in the demanded quantities at the times demanded) if Pace coordinates and communicates both within its own business functions and with its suppliers and customers during the budgeting process as well as the production process.

[1] For a more detailed discussion, see R. Larnick, G. Wu, and C. Heath. "Raising the Bar on Goals," Graduate School of Business Publication, University of Chicago, Spring 1999.

Administration of Budgets

Budgeting takes up a lot of management time. Top managers want lower-level managers to participate in the budget process because lower-level managers have valuable knowledge about the day-to-day aspects of running the business. Participation also creates greater commitment and responsibility toward the budget among lower-level managers.

There are costs (as well as benefits) of budgeting. For example, managers often spend much time working on budgets. Studies of large companies report about 5% of staff positions are devoted to budgeting.

The widespread prevalence of budgets indicates that the advantages of budgeting systems outweigh their costs. (See Surveys of Company Practice, below.) *To gain the benefits of*

SURVEYS OF COMPANY PRACTICE

Budget Practices Around the Globe[a]

Surveys of financial officers of the largest industrial companies in the United States, Australia, Holland, Japan, and the United Kingdom indicate some interesting similarities and differences in budgeting practices across countries. The use of master budgets is widespread in all countries. Differences arise with respect to other dimensions of budgeting. U.S. controllers and managers prefer more participation and regard return on investment as the most important budget goal. In contrast, Japanese controllers and managers prefer less participation and regard sales revenues as the most important budget goal. Surveys of Australian[b] and Japanese[c] managers report that budgeting is the management accounting practice that has the highest benefit to them.

	United States	Japan	Australia	United Kingdom	Holland
1. Percentage of companies that prepare a complete master budget	91%	93%	100%	100%	100%

	United States	Japan	Holland
2. Percentage of companies reporting division manager participation in budget committee discussions	78%	67%	82%

	United States	Japan
3. Ranking of the most important budget goals for division managers (1 is most important)		
Return on investment	1	4
Operating income	2	2
Sales revenues	3	1
Production costs	4	3

What reduces the effectiveness of the planning and budgeting processes of companies? A survey of chief financial officers (CFOs) in the United States reported the following four factors in order of importance:[d]

1. Lack of a well-defined strategy
2. Lack of a clear linkage of strategy to operational plans
3. Lack of individual accountability for results
4. Lack of meaningful performance measures

Two planning methodologies viewed as "significant to extremely valuable" by more than 60% of CFO's surveyed were "activity-based budgeting" and "rolling budget forecasts."

[a]Adapted from (1) Asada, Bailes, and Amano, "An Empirical Study"; Blayney and Yokoyama, "Comparative Analysis"; and de With and Ijskes "Current Budgeting."

[b]Chenhal and Langfield-Smith, "Adoption and Benefits of Management Accounting Practices."

[c]Inoue, "A Comparative Study of Recent Development of Cost Management Problems in U.S.A., U.K., Canada, and Japan."

[d]Lazere, "All Together Now."

Full citations are in Appendix A at the end of the book.

budgeting, management at all levels of the company should understand and support the budget and all aspects of the management control system. Top management support is critical for obtaining active line-management participation in the formulation of budgets and for successful administration of the budget. Line managers who feel that top management does not "believe" in the budget are unlikely to be active participants in the budget process.

Line management, such as manufacturing and marketing management, is directly responsible for attaining the goals of the organization.

Budgets should not be administered rigidly. Changing conditions usually call for changes in plans. A manager may commit to the budget, but a situation might develop in which some unplanned repairs or an unplanned advertising program would better serve the interests of the company. The manager should not defer the repairs or the advertising as a way of meeting the budget — not if doing so will hurt the company in the long run. Attaining the budget should not be an end in itself.

TIME COVERAGE OF BUDGETS

Budgets typically have a set period, such as a month, quarter, year, and so on. The set period can itself be broken into subperiods. For example, a 12-month cash budget may be broken into 12 monthly periods so that cash inflows and cash outflows can be coordinated more regularly.

The purposes of budgeting should guide the period chosen for the budget. Consider budgeting for a new Harley-Davidson 500-cc motorcycle. If the purpose is to budget for the total profitability of this new model, a five-year period (or more) may be appropriate and long enough to cover the product from design through to manufacture, sales, and after-sales support. In contrast, consider budgeting for producing a school play. If the purpose is to estimate all cash outlays, a six-month period from planning to stage the play to opening curtain may be adequate.

The most frequently used budget period is one year. The annual budget is often subdivided by months for the first quarter and by quarters for the remainder of the year. The budgeted data for a year are frequently revised as the year goes on. For example, at the end of the first quarter, the budget for the next three quarters is changed in light of new information obtained during the first quarter.

Businesses are increasingly using *rolling budgets*. A **rolling budget,** also called a **continuous budget,** is a budget or plan that is always available for a specified future period, by adding a period (month, quarter, or year) in the future as the period just ended is dropped. Consider Electrolux, the global appliance company, which has a three- to five-year strategic plan and a four-quarter rolling budget. A four-quarter rolling budget for the April 2004 to March 2005 period is superceded by a four-quarter rolling budget for July 2004 to June 2005 the next quarter, and so on. There is always a 12-month budget (for the next year) in place. Rolling budgets constantly force Electrolux's management to think about the forthcoming 12 months, regardless of the quarter at hand.

STEPS IN DEVELOPING AN OPERATING BUDGET

3 Prepare the operating budget
...the budgeted income statement
and its supporting schedules
...such as cost of goods sold and marketing costs

The best way to explain how to prepare budgets is with an example. Stylistic Furniture is a manufacturer of prestige coffee tables. Its job-costing system for manufacturing costs has two direct-cost categories — direct materials and direct manufacturing labor — and one indirect-cost category — manufacturing overhead. Manufacturing overhead, both variable and fixed, is allocated to each coffee table using direct manufacturing labor-hours as the allocation base.

Exhibit 6-2 shows a diagram of the various parts of the master budget for Stylistic Furniture. The master budget comprises the financial projections of all the individual budgets for a company. The result is a set of related financial statements for a specified period, usually a year. Most of what you see in Exhibit 6-2 comprises a set of budgets — the budgeted income statement and its supporting budget schedules — together called the **operating budget.** These schedules are budgets for various business functions of the value chain, from research and development to customer service. The **financial budget** is that part of the master budget made up of the capital expenditures budget, the cash budget, the budgeted balance sheet, and the budgeted statement of cash flows. A financial budget

EXHIBIT 6-2 **Overview of the Master Budget for Stylistic Furniture**

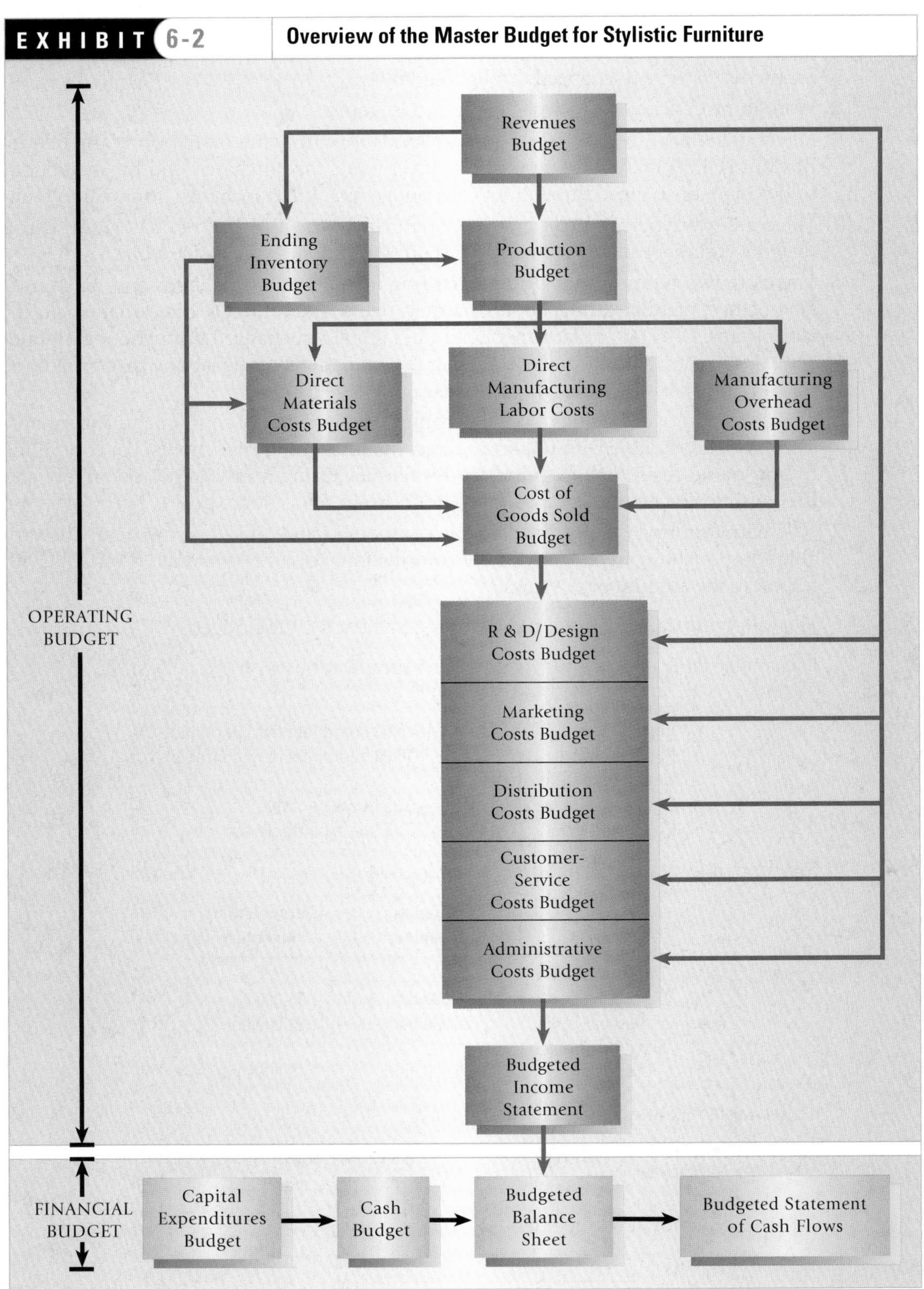

focuses on how operations and planned capital outlays affect cash. The master budget is finalized only after several rounds of discussions between top management and managers responsible for various business functions of the value chain.

Stylistic Furniture

We now present the steps in preparing an operating budget for Stylistic Furniture for 2004. The appendix to this chapter presents Stylistic's cash budget, which is another key component of the master budget. We assume the following:

1. The only source of revenues is sales of coffee tables. Nonsales-related revenues, such as interest income, is assumed to be zero. Units sold is the driver of revenues because prices are predicted to be unchanged throughout 2004.
2. Work-in-process inventory is negligible and is ignored.
3. Direct materials inventory and finished goods inventory are costed using the first-in, first-out (FIFO) method. Unit costs of direct materials purchased and finished goods sold remain unchanged throughout each budget year but can change from year to year.
4. There are two types of direct materials: particle board (PB) and red oak (RO). Direct material costs are variable with respect to units of output—the coffee tables.
5. There are two types of direct manufacturing labor: laminating labor and machining labor. Direct manufacturing labor costs are variable with respect to direct manufacturing labor-hours. Direct manufacturing labor rates remain unchanged throughout each budget year but can change from year to year. Direct manufacturing labor workers are hired on an hourly basis; no overtime is worked.
6. Manufacturing overhead has a variable component and a fixed component. The variable component is variable with respect to direct manufacturing labor-hours. For computing inventoriable costs, Stylistic allocates all manufacturing overhead costs, variable and fixed, using direct manufacturing labor-hours as the allocation base.
7. Nonmanufacturing costs have a variable component and a fixed component. The variable component, consisting mostly of commissions to sales personnel, is variable with respect to the amount of revenues.[2]

The following data are used in developing Stylistic's 2004 budget:

a. Each coffee table has the following product specifications:

Direct Materials	
Particle board (PB)	9.00 board feet (b.f.) per table
Red oak (RO)	10.00 board feet (b.f.) per table
Direct manufacturing labor	
Laminating labor	0.25 hours per table
Machining labor	3.75 hours per table

Ending inventory is not just a "leftover"; it is a budgeted amount.

b. Inventory information in physical units for 2004 is

	Beginning Inventory	Target Ending Inventory
Direct materials		
Particle board	20,000 b.f	18,000 b.f
Red oak	25,000 b.f.	22,000 b.f.
Finished goods		
Coffee tables	5,000 units	3,000 units

c. Coffee table revenues expected for 2004 are

Selling price	$392 per table
Units sold	52,000 coffee tables

d. Costs expected for 2004 include:

	2003	2004
Particle board (per b.f.)	$ 3.90	$ 4.00
Red oak (per b.f.)	$ 5.80	$ 6.00
Laminating labor (per hour)	$24.00	$25.00
Machining labor (per hour)	$29.00	$30.00

e. Other budgeted cost rates and amounts for 2004 are

[2] To keep the Stylistic budget example straightforward, we assume all nonmanufacturing costs are variable with respect to amount of revenues. In practice, some of these costs may be variable with respect to nonrevenue-based factors. For example, some distribution costs may be variable with respect to the weight of the item distributed or the distance to be moved to distribute the product. For case studies, see S. Player and D. Keys (ed.), *Activity-Based Management* (New York: MasterMedia, 1995).

- Variable manufacturing overhead costs — $9.50 per direct manufacturing labor-hour
- Variable nonmanufacturing costs — 13.5% of revenues
- Fixed manufacturing overhead costs — $1,600,000
- Fixed nonmanufacturing costs — $1,400,000

f. The inventoriable (manufacturing) cost is $275 per coffee table in 2003.

The budgeted cost per coffee table of $275 is based on the cost Stylistic expects to incur on its new production line. Stylistic could have set the budgeted cost based on the cost per coffee table at the most efficient plant owned by Stylistic or the cost per coffee table at the most efficient plant owned by any company in the industry. Companies differ in how they compute their budgeted amounts. Some companies rely heavily on past results when developing budgeted amounts; others rely on detailed engineering studies.

Most companies have a budget manual; it contains a company's particular instructions and relevant information for preparing its budgets. Although the details differ among companies, the following basic steps are common for developing the operating budget for a manufacturing company. Beginning with the revenues budget, each of the other budgets follows step by step in logical fashion.

Step 1: Prepare the Revenues Budget. A revenues budget, calculated in Schedule 1, is the usual starting point for budgeting. That's because the production level and the inventory level — and hence manufacturing costs — as well as nonmanufacturing costs, generally depend on the forecasted level of unit sales or revenues. Many factors influence the sales forecast, including the sales volume in recent periods, general economic and industry conditions, market research studies, pricing policies, advertising and sales promotions, competition, and regulatory policies.

Because all budgets in Exhibit 6-2 flow from the revenues budget, accurate sales forecasts are needed. However, factors outside the company's control (such as competition and economic conditions) make it difficult to accurately forecast sales.

Schedule 1: Revenues Budget
For the Year Ended December 31, 2002

	Selling Price	Units Sold	Total Revenues
Coffee tables	$392	52,000	$20,384,000

The $20,384,000 is the amount of revenues in the budgeted income statement. The revenues budget is often the outcome of elaborate information gathering and discussions among sales managers and sales representatives who have a detailed understanding of customer needs, market potential, and competitors' products. Statistical approaches such as regression and trend analysis can also help in sales forecasting. These techniques use indicators of economic activity and past sales data to forecast future sales. Managers should use statistical analysis only as one input to forecast sales. In the final analysis, the sales forecast should represent the collective experience and judgement of managers.

Regression and trend analysis are techniques that use sales data from recent periods to fit a line that best represents how sales have changed over those periods. Extending this line into the future helps in predicting future sales.

The usual starting point for step 1 is to base revenues on expected demand. Occasionally, a factor other than demand limits budgeted revenues. For example, when demand is greater than available production capacity or a resource factor is in short supply, the revenues budget would be based on the maximum units that could be produced. Why? Because sales would be limited by the amount produced.

Step 2: Prepare the Production Budget (in Units). After revenues are budgeted, the production budget, calculated in Schedule 2, can be prepared. The total finished goods units to be produced depends on budgeted sales and expected changes in inventory levels:

$$\text{Budgeted production (units)} = \text{Budgeted sales (units)} + \text{Target ending finished goods inventory (units)} - \text{Beginning finished goods inventory (units)}$$

The nature of the product makes it difficult for some companies to synchronize production levels with expected sales. When inputs are available only seasonally, production occurs "in season." For example, a manufacturer of jellies makes the year's supply of strawberry jelly during strawberry harvest season.

There is no need to memorize this schedule if you understand that the number of units to be produced is equal to the number of units needed (budgeted sales + ending FG inventory) minus the units already on hand (beginning FG inventory). The same idea applies to the purchases of each type of direct material. Keep all these computations in units and then multiply by the cost per unit at the end.

Schedule 2: Production Budget (in Units)
For the Year Ended December 31, 2004

	Coffee Tables
Budgeted unit sales (Schedule 1)	52,000
Add target ending finished goods inventory	3,000
Total requirements	55,000
Deduct beginning finished goods inventory	5,000
Units to be produced	50,000

Step 3: Prepare the Direct Materials Usage Budget and Direct Materials Purchases Budget. The number of units to be produced, calculated in Schedule 2, is the key to computing the usage of direct materials in quantities and in dollars.

Schedule 3A: Direct Materials Usage Budget
For the Year Ended December 31, 2004

	Particle Board (PB)	Red Oak (RO)	Total
Physical Units Budget			
PB: 50,000 units × 9.00 b.f. per unit	450,000		
RO: 50,000 units × 10.00 b.f. per unit		500,000	
To be used in production, b.f.	450,000	500,000	
Cost Budget			
(Available from beginning inventory)			
PB: \$3.90 per b.f. × 20,000 b.f.	\$ 78,000		
RO: \$5.80 per b.f. × 25,000 b.f.		\$ 145,000	
To be obtained from purchases of this period:			
PB: \$4.00 per b.f. × (450,000 b.f. − 20,000 b.f.)	1,720,000		
RO: \$6.00 per b.f. × (500,000 b.f. − 25,000 b.f.)		2,850,000	
Direct materials to be used	\$1,798,000	\$2,995,000	\$4,793,000

Schedule 3B computes the budget for direct materials purchases, which depends on the budgeted direct materials to be used, the beginning inventory of direct materials, and the target ending inventory of direct materials:

$$\text{Purchases of direct materials} = \text{Direct materials used in production} + \text{Target ending inventory of direct materials} - \text{Beginning inventory of direct materials}$$

Once we determine the number of units to be produced from the production budget (Schedule 2), we can budget manufacturing inputs—direct materials, direct labor, and overhead.

Schedule 3B: Direct Materials Purchases Budget
For the Year Ended December 31, 2004

	Particle Board (PB)	Red Oak (RO)	Total
Physical Units Budget			
Production usage (from Schedule 3A)	450,000 b.f.	500,000 b.f.	
Add target ending inventory	18,000 b.f.	22,000 b.f.	
Total requirements	468,000 b.f.	522,000 b.f.	
Deduct beginning inventory	20,000 b.f.	25,000 b.f.	
Purchases	448,000 b.f.	497,000 b.f.	
Cost Budget			
PB: 448,000 b.f. × \$4.00 per b.f.	\$1,792,000		
RO: 497,000 b.f. × \$6.00 per b.f.		\$2,982,000	
Purchases	\$1,792,000	\$2,982,000	\$4,774,000

Step 4: Prepare the Direct Manufacturing Labor Budget. These costs depend on wage rates, production methods, and hiring plans. The computations of budgeted direct manufacturing labor costs appear in Schedule 4:

Schedule 4: Direct Manufacturing Labor Budget
For the Year Ended December 31, 2004

	Laminating Labor (LL)	Machining Labor (ML)	Total
Labor-Hours Budget			
LL: 50,000 units × 0.25 hours/unit	12,500 hours		
ML: 50,000 units × 3.75 hours/unit		187,500 hours	
	12,500 hours	187,500 hours	200,000 hours
Cost Budget			
LL: $25.00 per hour × 12,500 hours	$312,500		
ML: $30.00 per hour × 187,500 hours		$5,625,000	
	$312,500	$5,625,000	$5,937,500

Step 5: Prepare the Manufacturing Overhead Budget. The total of these costs depends on how individual overhead costs vary with respect to the cost driver—direct manufacturing labor-hours, in this example. The calculations of budgeted manufacturing overhead costs appear in Schedule 5. The individual amounts for variable manufacturing overhead costs and fixed manufacturing overhead costs are based on input from Stylistic's operating personnel. The starting point for these amounts is Stylistic's costs in the current and prior years. Management makes adjustments for cost changes expected in the future.

Stylistic treats both variable manufacturing overhead and fixed manufacturing overhead as inventoriable costs. It inventories manufacturing overhead at the budgeted rate of $17.50 per direct manufacturing labor-hour (total budgeted manufacturing overhead, $3,500,000 ÷ 200,000 budgeted direct manufacturing labor-hours). Stylistic does not use a separate variable manufacturing overhead rate and a separate fixed manufacturing overhead rate. The budgeted manufacturing overhead cost per coffee table is $70 ($3,500,000 ÷ 50,000 coffee tables budgeted to be produced in 2004). The $70 budgeted manufacturing overhead cost per coffee table can also be calculated as $17.50 budgeted cost per direct manufacturing labor-hour × 4 budgeted direct manufacturing labor-hours per coffee table = $70.

Total variable overhead costs fluctuate in proportion to the quantity of the cost-allocation base (direct manufacturing labor-hours in the Stylistic example), whereas total fixed overhead costs remains constant over a relevant range of output.

Schedule 5: Direct Manufacturing Overhead Budget
For the Year Ended December 31, 2004

	At Budgeted Level of 200,000 Direct Manufacturing Labor-Hours	
Variable manufacturing overhead costs		
Supplies	$240,000	
Indirect manufacturing labor	620,000	
Power and energy	460,000	
Maintenance	300,000	
Miscellaneous	280,000	$1,900,000
Fixed manufacturing overhead costs		
Depreciation	$500,000	
Property taxes	350,000	
Property insurance	260,000	
Plant supervision	210,000	
Miscellaneous	280,000	1,600,000
Total manufacturing overhead costs		$3,500,000

Step 6: Prepare the Ending Inventories Budget. Schedule 6A shows the computation of the unit cost of coffee tables started and completed in 2004. Under the first-in,

first-out method (FIFO), this unit cost is used to calculate the cost of target ending inventories of finished goods in Schedule 6B.

Schedule 6A: Computation of Unit Costs of Ending Inventory of Finished Goods
December 31, 2004

	Cost per Unit of Input	Input		Total
Direct materials				
Particle board	$4.00 per b.f.	9.00 b.f.	$36.00	
Red oak	6.00 per b.f.	10.00 b.f.	60.00	$ 96.00
Direct manufacturing labor				
Laminating labor	$25.00 per hour	0.25 hours	$ 6.25	
Machining labor	30.00 per hour	3.75 hours	112.50	118.75
Manufacturing overhead	17.50 per hour	4.00 hours		70.00
Total				$284.75

This $284.75 unit cost for 2004 compares to $275.00 unit cost for 2003.

Schedule 6B: Ending Inventories Budget
December 31, 2004

	Cost per Unit	Units		Total
Direct materials				
Particle board	$4.00 per b.f.	18,000 b.f.	$ 72,000	
Red oak	6.00 per b.f.	22,000 b.f.	132,000	$ 204,000
Finished goods				
Coffee tables	$284.75 per unit	3,000 units	$854,250	854,250
Total ending inventory				$1,058,250

Step 7: Prepare the Cost of Goods Sold Budget. The information from Schedules 3 through 6 is used in Schedule 7.

The cost of goods manufactured portion of the cost of goods sold budget in Schedule 7 is a summarized form of the cost of goods manufactured schedule (for a different company) in Exhibit 2-6, Panel B, p. 41. (Note, the Stylistic example assumes there is no beginning or ending work-in-process inventory.)

Schedule 7: Cost of Goods Sold Budget
For the Year Ended December 31, 2004

Beginning finished goods inventory, January 1, 2004, $275 × 5,000	Given		$ 1,375,000
Direct materials used	Schedule 3A	$4,793,000	
Direct manufacturing labor	Schedule 4	5,937,500	
Manufacturing overhead	Schedule 5	3,500,000	
Cost of goods manufactured			14,230,500
Cost of goods available for sale			15,605,500
Deduct ending finished goods inventory, December 31, 2004	Schedule 6B		854,250
Cost of goods sold			$14,751,250

Step 8: Prepare the Nonmanufacturing Costs Budget. Schedules 2 through 7 cover budgeting for Stylistic's production function part of the value chain. For brevity, other parts of the value chain are combined into a single schedule. Variable nonmanufacturing costs are variable with respect to the amount of revenues at the rate of 13.5% of revenues: $20,384,000 from Schedule 1 × 0.135 = $2,751,840. For example, variable product design costs represent royalty payments of 1.5% of revenues paid to the company that designed the table; variable marketing costs are 8% sales commission on revenues paid to salespersons; variable distribution costs are 2.5% of revenues for insurance and freight; and variable customer service costs equal 1.3% of revenues paid to an outside party to service all warranty claims. The individual fixed cost amounts are based on input from Stylistic's business function managers in different parts of its value chain.

EXHIBIT 6-3

Budgeted Income Statement for Stylistic Furniture for the Year Ended December 31, 2004

Revenues	Schedule 1		$20,384,000
Cost of goods sold	Schedule 7		14,751,250
Gross margin			5,632,750
Operating costs			
R & D/Product design	Schedule 8	$ 555,760	
Marketing costs	Schedule 8	1,920,720	
Distribution costs	Schedule 8	729,600	
Customer-service costs	Schedule 8	504,992	
Administrative costs	Schedule 8	440,768	4,151,840
Operating income			$ 1,480,910

Schedule 8: Nonmanufacturing Costs Budget
For the Year Ended December 31, 2004

Value-Chain Function	Variable Costs	Fixed Costs	Total Costs
R & D/Product design	$ 305,760	$ 250,000	$ 555,760
Marketing	1,630,720	290,000	1,920,720
Distribution	509,600	220,000	729,600
Customer service	264,992	240,000	504,992
Administrative	40,768	400,000	440,768
	$2,751,840	$1,400,000	$4,151,840

Step 9: Prepare the Budgeted Income Statement. Schedules 1, 7, and 8 provide the information needed to complete the budgeted income statement, shown in Exhibit 6-3. More details could be included in the income statement: The more details put in the income statement, the fewer supporting schedules needed for the income statement.

Top management's strategies for achieving revenue and operating income goals influence the costs planned for the different business functions of the value chain. As strategies change, the budgeted costs for different elements of the value chain will also change. For example, a shift in strategy toward emphasizing product development and customer service will result in increased costs in these parts of the operating budget.

COMPUTER-BASED FINANCIAL PLANNING MODELS

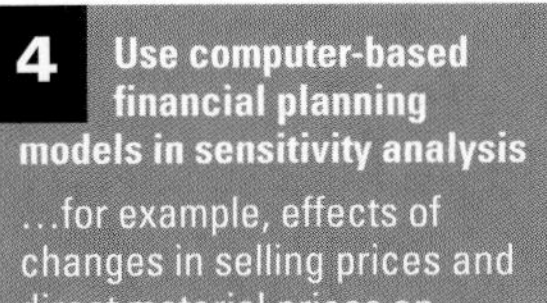

Web-based budgeting tools (see Concepts in Action, p. 188) and software packages are available to reduce the computational burden and time required to prepare budgets. The software packages perform calculations for **financial planning models,** which are mathematical representations of the relationships among operating activities, financing activities, and other factors that affect the master budget. Software packages assist managers with sensitivity analyses in their planning and budgeting activities. *Sensitivity analysis* is a "what-if" technique that examines how a result will change if the original predicted data are not achieved or if an underlying assumption changes.

Accounting Software Comparison provides comparisons of numerous vendors' accounting software packages, many of which include budgeting modules. If interested, see their Web site (www.excelco.com).

To see how sensitivity analysis works, let's consider two parameters in Stylistic Furniture's budget model for 2004:

1. Selling price per table of $392.
2. Direct material prices of $4 per b.f. for particle board and $6 per b.f. for red oak.

What if either or both of these parameters were to change? Exhibit 6-4 presents the budgeted operating income for nine combinations of different inputs for parameters 1 and 2:

a. Selling prices per table of (i) $431.20 (10% increase), (ii) $392.00 (original budgeted price), and (iii) $352.80 (10% decrease).
b. Direct material purchase prices (i) decreasing by 5% to $3.80 per b.f. for particle board and $5.70 per b.f. for red oak, (ii) remaining at the original budgeted price of $4.00 per

CONCEPTS IN ACTION

Putting Budgeting on the Fast Track with Web Technology

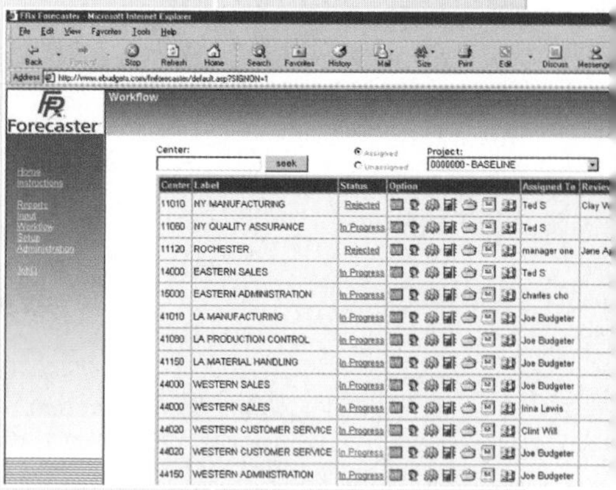

Tired of the time it takes to get the mechanics of budgeting straight? Frustrated by noncompatible software packages used by different parts of a company that significantly slow down budgeting? FRx® Forecaster, an online Web-enabled budgeting tool from FRx Software Corp. could relieve some of these problems.

With FRx Forecaster, a line manager signs on to the application from his or her office through the corporate intranet. Security is tight—access is limited to only the accounts that a manager is authorized to budget. The most recent "actuals" are available on the screen. Links are provided to other data the manager needs to know. For example, the manufacturing manager will have access to budgeted sales and human resources data. Managers enter their budget data and can use the software to perform what-if and sensitivity analyses. When managers submit budget information, all the data are stored on the Web server at headquarters. There is no need to communicate across multiple software packages.

During the year, FRx Forecaster interacts with FRx® Financial Reporting, accesses financial results from the general ledger, automatically transfers data to the budgeting application, and reports actual results versus budgeted amounts. FRx® Forecaster monitors budgets and actuals. For example, if a manager's purchase request exceeds the budgeted limit, the software alerts the manager to this situation.

How costly is the FRx Forecaster to implement? FRx Software Corp. makes FRx Forecaster available from an application service provider (described in the Concepts in Action on p. 35). With this setup, a company can rent the application over the Internet rather than buy it, at a cost of 10% of the investment needed for a typical budgeting system. Moreover, the company does not have to maintain or upgrade the system and software. All maintenance is done by the application service provider that provides the software.

FRx Software Corp. reports that its Web-based budgeting approach frees the finance department to focus on strategy, analysis, and decision making (rather than on spreadsheets). FRx Software Corp. claims that FRx Forecaster increases service levels to employees, reduces costs, accelerates the budget cycle, and improves the value from budgeting.

Source: T. Powell, "Software Trends," *Journal of Cost Management* (January/February, 1999) pp. 36–37; http://www.prnewswire.com, March 16, 2001, and May 29, 2001.

b.f. for particle board and $6.00 per b.f. for red oak, and (iii) increasing by 5% to $4.20 per b.f. for particle board and $6.30 per b.f. for red oak.

The nine combinations in Exhibit 6-4 show how budgeted operating income will change considerably with changes in selling prices and direct material costs.

EXHIBIT 6-4

Effect of Changes in Budget Assumptions on Budgeted Operating Income for Stylistic Furniture

		Direct Material Purchase Costs		Budgeted Operating Income	
Scenario	Selling Price	Particle Board	Red Oak	Amount	Change from Master Budget
1	$431.20	$3.80	$5.70	$3,458,226	134% Increase
2	431.20	4.00	6.00	3,244,126	119% Increase
3	431.20	4.20	6.30	3,030,026	105% Increase
4	392.00	3.80	5.70	1,695,010	14% Increase
5[a]	392.00	4.00	6.00	1,480,910	—
6	392.00	4.20	6.30	1,266,810	14% Decrease
7	352.80	3.80	5.70	(68,206)	105% Decrease
8	352.80	4.00	6.00	(282,306)	119% Decrease
9	352.80	4.20	6.30	(496,406)	134% Decrease

[a]Base case from Exhibit 6-3.

- Scenario 5 is the base case from Exhibit 6-3.
- Scenarios 2 and 8 illustrate the effect of changes in only the selling price.
- Scenarios 4 and 6 examine the effect of changes in only the direct material costs.
- Scenarios 1, 3, 7, and 9 pertain to simultaneous changes in both parameters.

Note that a change in Stylistic's selling price per table affects the variable nonmanufacturing costs, such as sales commissions, as well as revenues. Sensitivity analysis is especially useful in incorporating such interrelationships into budgeting decisions by managers. When the success or viability of a venture is highly dependent on attaining one or more targets, managers should frequently update their budgets as uncertainty is resolved. These updated budgets can assist managers to adjust expenditure levels, change marketing strategies, and so on as circumstances change.

Sensitivity analysis is also used in cash budgeting, which is discussed in the appendix to this chapter.

One of the first PC spreadsheets was developed by graduate students who wanted to perform sensitivity analysis on a master budget case assignment. They decided there had to be a better way than recomputing all the numbers by hand!

KAIZEN BUDGETING

5 Explain kaizen budgeting
...budgeting for continuous improvement in labor-hours per unit

and how it is used for cost management
...to reduce costs

Chapter 1 noted how continuous improvement is one of the key themes managers face (p. 12). The Japanese use *kaizen* to mean continuous improvement. **Kaizen budgeting** explicitly incorporates continuous improvement during the budget period into the budget numbers.

Throughout our nine budgeting steps for Stylistic Furniture, we assumed 3.75 hours of machining labor time to manufacture each table. A kaizen budgeting approach would incorporate continuous improvement, that is, reduction, in these manufacturing labor-hour requirements during 2004. For example:

	Budgeted Machining Labor-Hours per Table
January–March 2004	3.75
April–June 2004	3.70
July–September 2004	3.65
October–December 2004	3.60

Unless Stylistic meets these continuous improvement goals, actual hours used will exceed budgeted hours in the latter quarters of the year. Note, in Stylistic's budget, the implications of these direct labor-hour reductions would extend to reductions in variable manufacturing overhead costs, because direct manufacturing labor-hours is the driver of these costs.

Much of the cost reduction associated with kaizen budgeting arises from many small improvements rather than "quantum leaps." A significant aspect of kaizen budgeting is the quantity and quality of employees' suggestions.

Kaizen at Citizen Watch

Citizen Watch is the world's largest manufacturer of watches. The assembly areas at its plants are highly automated. Component part costs are 50% to 60% of the unit cost of each watch. A central part of Citizen's cost management system is kaizen budgeting. All parts of its entire supply chain, including component suppliers, are required to continually seek cost-reduction opportunities. For example, at its Tokyo plant, Citizen budgets steady cost reductions of 3% per year for purchased materials. Citizen's engineers work with suppliers to help the suppliers reduce their own costs by 3%.[3] Suppliers who achieve costs reductions greater than 3% earn more profits.

ACTIVITY-BASED BUDGETING

6 Prepare an activity-based budget
...by budgeting the cost of activities needed to produce a product

Most budgeting models to date have used a small number of cost drivers that are predominantly output-based (units produced, units sold, or revenues). Due, in part, to the growing use of activity-based costing (ABC), companies are incorporating activity-based cost drivers into budgets. ABC focuses on the reporting and analysis of past and current costs. A natural extension of activity-based costing is to use an activity-based approach to

[3]See R. Cooper, "Citizen Watch Company, Ltd.: Cost Reduction for Mature Products" (Harvard Business School case, 9-194-033).

budgeting future costs. **Activity-based budgeting (ABB)** focuses on the budgeted cost of activities necessary to produce and sell products and services. Adopting an ABB approach to developing Stylistic's operating budget entails formulating budgets for each activity in its activity management system. To illustrate ABB, we consider the setup activity of Stylistic. In Stylistic's operating budget outlined in steps 1 through 9 (pp. 183–187), the costs of the setup activity are included in step 5 (the Manufacturing Overhead Budget). In ABB, the costs of this setup activity (as well as the costs of each of the other activities) would be separately estimated. The following information assists in estimating the budgeted costs in this setup activity for 2004:

a. The plant operates two shifts per day for 250 working days a year. There are 4 workers in laminating activities per shift and 50 workers in machining activities per shift.

b. Setup worker time in both laminating and machining activities requires 0.5 hours when a new batch of tables is manufactured. In the laminating area, 25 tables per worker are started and completed per batch. Work on two tables per worker is started and completed in the machining area per batch.

c. The same hourly rates are paid to workers for setup time as for time spent on laminating or machining—that is, $25 per hour for laminating labor and $30 per hour for machining labor.

d. Supervisory labor, an indirect cost for the activity, is paid $60 per hour. Stylistic believes there is a cause-and-effect relationship such that 10 hours of worker labor-hours in setup require 1 hour of supervisory labor time.

This information enables Stylistic to prepare an activity-based budget for the setup activity in its manufacturing plant.

Given that Stylistic budgets to produce 50,000 tables in 2004, the information in **a** and **b** enables the total budgeted setup-hours for 2004 to be determined:

	Laminating Setup	Machining Setup
1. Quantity of tables to be produced	50,000 tables	50,000 tables
2. Number of tables to be produced per batch	25 tables/batch	2 tables/batch
3. Number of batches (1) ÷ (2)	2,000 batches	25,000 batches
4. Setup time per batch	0.5 hour/batch	0.5 hour/batch
5. Total setup-hours (3) × (4)	1,000 hours	12,500 hours

Combining this information with the hourly rates paid per worker from **c** yields the budgeted costs for setup worker time for 2004:

Laminating setup labor costs	
$25 per hour × 1,000 hours	$ 25,000
Machining setup labor costs	
$30 per hour × 12,500 hours	375,000
Total	$400,000

This $400,000 amount is currently included in the indirect manufacturing labor category of the variable manufacturing overhead costs of Stylistic's existing budget (see step 5, p. 185).

The total costs of the setup activity for Stylistic also include the costs of supervisory time. For 2004, Stylistic budgets 13,500 hours of setup time (1,000 hours for laminating + 12,500 hours for machining) for production of 50,000 tables. Supervision time in the setup activity is budgeted to be 1,350 hours (13,500 hours × 0.10) because it takes 1 hour of supervision for every 10 hours of setup labor. At a cost of $60 per hour, the budgeted cost for supervision in the setup activity for 2004 is

$$1,350 \text{ supervisory hours} \times \$60 \text{ per hour} = \$81,000$$

This $81,000 amount is currently included in the plant supervision category of fixed manufacturing overhead costs of Stylistic's budget (see step 5, p. 185).

Total budgeted cost in Stylistic's setup activity is $481,000, consisting of $400,000 for setup labor-hours and $81,000 for supervision. As we discussed in Chapter 5, ABC analysis makes no distinction between short-run variable costs and short-run fixed costs. ABC analysis takes a long-run perspective in which all costs of an activity are treated as variable costs of that activity. The activity-cost buildup makes it easier for Stylistic to see how to reduce its budgeted setup costs for 2004. Ways to reduce budgeted costs include:

1. Increase the length of the production run per batch so that fewer batches and fewer setups are needed for the budgeted production of 50,000 tables.
2. Decrease the setup time per batch. Shorter setup times mean lower total setup-hours for the budgeted production of 50,000 tables.
3. Reduce the supervisory time needed per worker setup-hour. Investments to increase the skill base of laminating or machining workers can result in less supervisory time required per worker-hour.
4. Reduce the hourly labor rates paid to workers and the salaries paid to supervisors.

This illustration shows how ABB can provide more detailed information that can improve decision making compared with budgeting based solely on output-based cost drivers. Should companies adopt ABC and ABB? As always, the answer for a specific company depends on a management evaluation of whether the expected benefits—for every department affected by the change—exceed the expected costs of installing and operating such systems.[4]

BUDGETING AND RESPONSIBILITY ACCOUNTING

7 Describe responsibility centers

...a part of an organization that a manager is accountable for

and responsibility accounting

...measurement of plans and actual results that a manager is accountable for

Organization Structure and Responsibility

To attain the goals described in the master budget, a company must coordinate the efforts of all its employees—from the top executive through all levels of management to every supervised worker. Coordinating the company's efforts means assigning responsibility to managers who are accountable for their actions in planning and controlling human and physical resources. How each company structures its own organization significantly shapes how the company's efforts will be coordinated.

Organization structure is an arrangement of lines of responsibility within the organization. A company such as British Petroleum may be organized primarily by business function: exploration, refining, and marketing. Another company, such as Procter & Gamble, the household-products giant, may be organized by product line or brand. The managers of the individual divisions (toothpaste, soap, and so on) would each have decision-making authority concerning all the business functions (manufacturing, marketing, and so on) within that division.

Each manager, regardless of level, is in charge of a *responsibility center*. A **responsibility center** is a part, segment, or subunit of an organization whose manager is accountable for a specified set of activities. The higher the manager's level, the broader the responsibility center and, generally, the larger the number of his or her subordinates. **Responsibility accounting** is a system that measures the plans—by budgets—and actions—by actual results—of each responsibility center. Four types of responsibility centers are

Surveys have shown that 95% of companies with definite budget goals establish budgetary reporting by responsibility center.

1. **Cost center**—the manager is accountable for costs only.
2. **Revenue center**—the manager is accountable for revenues only.
3. **Profit center**—the manager is accountable for revenues and costs.
4. **Investment center**—the manager is accountable for investments, revenues, and costs.

The Maintenance Department of a Marriott hotel is a cost center because the maintenance manager is responsible only for costs, so this budget emphasizes costs. The Sales Department is a revenue center because the sales manager is responsible primarily for revenues, so this budget emphasizes revenues. The hotel manager is in charge of a profit center because the manager is accountable for both revenues and costs, so this budget

[4]For illustrative purposes, the ABB example uses the setup costs included in Stylistic's variable manufacturing overhead costs budget and fixed manufacturing overhead costs budget. ABB implementations in practice may incorporate costs across many parts of the value chain. For an example, see S. Borjesson, "A Case Study on Activity-Based Budgeting," *Journal of Cost Management*, Vol. 10, No. 4, pp. 7–18.

emphasizes revenues and costs. The regional manager responsible for investments in new hotel projects and for revenues and costs is in charge of an investment center, so this budget emphasizes revenues, costs, and the investment base.

A responsibility center can be structured to promote better alignment of individual and company goals. Until recently, OPD, an office products distributor, operated its Sales Department as a revenue center. Each salesperson received an incentive of 3% of the revenues per order, regardless of its size, the cost of processing it, or the cost of delivering the office products. An analysis of customer profitability at OPD found many customers were unprofitable. The reason was the high ordering and delivery costs of small orders. OPD decided to make the Sales Department a profit center, changing the incentive system for salespeople to 15% of the monthly profitability per customer. The costs charged to each customer included the ordering and delivery costs. The effect of this change was immediate. Salespeople at OPD actively encouraged customers to make fewer orders, with each order producing larger revenues. Customer profitability increased because of a 40% reduction in ordering and delivery costs in one year.

Feedback

Budgets coupled with responsibility accounting provide feedback to top management about the performance relative to the budget of different responsibility center managers.

Differences between actual results and budgeted amounts—also called *variances*—if properly used, can be helpful in three ways:

1. *Early warning.* Variances alert managers early to events not easily nor immediately evident. Managers can then take corrective actions or exploit the available opportunities. For example, is a small decline in sales this period an indication of an even steeper decline to follow later in the year?
2. *Performance evaluation.* Variances inform managers about how well the company has performed in implementing its strategies. Were materials and labor used efficiently? Was R&D spending increased as planned? Did product warranty costs decrease as planned?
3. *Evaluating strategy.* Variances sometimes signal to managers that their strategies are ineffective. For example, a company seeking to compete by reducing cost and improving quality may find that it is achieving these goals but having little effect on sales and profits. Top management may then want to reevaluate the strategy.

8 Explain how controllability relates to responsibility accounting

...managers cannot control all costs they are accountable for; responsibility accounting focuses on obtaining information, not fixing blame

RESPONSIBILITY AND CONTROLLABILITY

Definition of Controllability

Controllability is the degree of influence that a specific manager has over costs, revenues, and related items for which he or she is responsible. A **controllable cost** is any cost that is primarily subject to the influence of a given *responsibility center manager* for a given *period*. A responsibility accounting system could either exclude all uncontrollable costs from a manager's performance report or segregate such costs from the controllable costs. For example, a machining supervisor's performance report might be confined to quantities—not costs—of direct materials, direct manufacturing labor, power, and supplies.

If the purchasing manager forgets to order a direct material item and must then place a rush order, the cost of the rush order is *controllable* by the purchasing manager. On the other hand, if suppliers increase their prices, that's something the purchasing manager cannot control. However, the manager is still *responsible* in the sense that he is in the best position to explain the price increases, and he can influence prices and quality by bargaining and maintaining good supplier relations.

In practice, controllability is difficult to pinpoint for at least two reasons:

1. Few costs are clearly under the sole influence of one manager. For example, *prices* of direct materials may be influenced by a purchasing manager, but these prices also depend on market conditions beyond the manager's control. *Quantities* used may be influenced by a production manager, but quantities used also depend on the quality of materials purchased. Moreover, managers often work in teams. How can individual responsibility be evaluated in a team situation?

2. With a long enough time span, all costs will come under somebody's control. However, most performance reports focus on periods of a year or less. A current manager may have inherited a predecessor's problems and inefficiencies. For example, present managers may have to work under undesirable contracts with suppliers or labor unions that were negotiated by their predecessors. How can we separate what the current manager actually controls from the results of decisions made by others? Exactly what is the current manager accountable for? Answers may not be clear-cut.

Executives differ in how they embrace the controllability notion when evaluating those reporting to them. Some company presidents regard the budget as a firm commitment that must be met. Failure to meet the budget is viewed unfavorably. Other presidents believe a more risk-sharing approach with managers is preferable, in which noncontrollable factors and performance relative to competitors are taken into account when judging the performance of managers who fail to meet their budgets.

Emphasis on Information and Behavior

Managers should avoid overemphasizing controllability. Responsibility accounting is more far-reaching. It focuses on *information and knowledge*, not on control. *Responsibility accounting helps managers to first focus on whom they should ask to obtain information and not on whom they should blame.* For example, if actual revenues at a Marriott hotel are less than budgeted revenues, the managers of the hotel may be tempted to blame the sales manager for the poor performance. The fundamental purpose of responsibility accounting, however, is not to fix blame but to gather information.

The question is, Who can tell us the most about the specific item in question, regardless of that person's ability to exert personal control over that item? For instance, purchasing managers may be held accountable for total purchase costs, not because of their ability to control market prices, but because of their ability to predict uncontrollable prices and explain uncontrollable price changes. Similarly, managers at a Pizza Hut unit may be held responsible for operating income of their units, even though they (a) do not fully control selling prices nor the costs of many food items and (b) have minimal flexibility about what items to sell or the ingredients in what they sell. That's because unit managers are in the best position to explain differences between their actual operating incomes and their budgeted operating incomes.

Performance reports for responsibility centers also may include uncontrollable items because this approach could change managers' behavior in the direction top management desires. For example, some companies have changed the accountability of a cost center to a profit center. That's because the manager will probably behave differently. A cost-center manager may emphasize production efficiency and deemphasize the pleas of sales personnel for faster service and rush orders. In a profit center, the manager is responsible for costs and revenues, so, even though the manager still has no control over sales personnel, the manager will now more likely weigh the impact of decisions on costs and revenues, rather than solely on costs.

HUMAN ASPECTS OF BUDGETING

Why did we discuss the two major topics, master budgets and responsibility accounting, in the same chapter? Primarily to emphasize that human factors are crucial parts of budgeting. Too often, students study budgeting as though it were a mechanical tool.

The budgeting techniques themselves are free of emotion. However, the administration of budgeting requires education, persuasion, and intelligent interpretation.

To be effective, budgeting requires "honest" communication about the business from subordinates and lower-level managers to their bosses. But subordinates may try to build in *budgetary slack*. **Budgetary slack** describes the practice of underestimating budgeted revenues, or overestimating budgeted costs, to make budgeted targets more easily achievable. It frequently occurs when budget variances (the differences between actual results and budgeted amounts) are used to evaluate performance. Line managers are also unlikely to be "fully honest" in their budget communications if top management mechanically institutes across-the-board cost reductions (say, a 10% reduction in all areas) in the face of projected revenue reductions. Budgetary slack provides managers with a hedge against unexpected adverse circumstances. But budgetary slack also misleads top management about the true profit potential of the company.

What can top management do to obtain accurate budget forecasts from lower-level managers? There are several options.

To explain one approach, let's consider the plant manager of a beverage bottler who is suspected by top management of understating the productivity potential of the bottling lines in his forecasts for the coming year. His presumed motivation is to increase the likelihood of meeting next year's production bonus targets. Suppose top management could purchase a consulting firm's study that reports productivity levels—such as the number of bottles filled per hour—at a number of comparable plants owned by other bottling companies. This report shows that their own plant manager's productivity forecasts are well below actual productivity levels being achieved at other comparable plants.

Top management could share this independent information source with their plant manager and ask him to explain why his productivity differs from that at other comparable plants. They could also base part of the plant manager's compensation on his plant's productivity vis-a-vis other "benchmark" plants rather than on the forecasts he provided. Using external benchmark performance measures reduces a manager's ability to set budget levels that are easy to achieve.[5]

Another approach to reducing budgetary slack is for managers to involve themselves regularly in understanding what their subordinates are doing. Such involvement should not result in managers dictating the decisions and actions of subordinates. Rather, a manager's involvement should take the form of providing support, challenging in a motivational way the assumptions subordinates make, and enhancing mutual learning about the operations. Regular interaction with subordinates allows managers to become knowledgeable about the operations and diminishes the ability of subordinates to create slack in their budgets.

Part of top management's responsibility is to promote organization commitment to a set of core values and norms. The values and norms describe what constitutes acceptable and unacceptable behavior. Companies such as General Electric and Johnson & Johnson have developed values and a culture that discourages budgetary slack.

Some companies, such as IBM and Kodak, have designed innovative performance evaluation measures that reward managers based on the subsequent accuracy of the forecasts used in preparing budgets. For example, the *higher and more accurate* the budgeted profit forecasts of division managers, the higher their incentive bonuses.

Many of the best performing companies set "stretch" or "challenge" targets. Stretch targets are actually overestimates of expected performance, intended to motivate employees to exert extra effort and attain better performance.

Many managers regard budgets negatively. To them, the word *budget* is about as popular as, say, *downsizing, layoff,* or *strike*. Top managers must convince their subordinates that the budget is a tool designed to help them set and reach goals. But budgets are not remedies for weak management talent, faulty organization, or a poor accounting system.

The management style of executives is a factor in how budgets are perceived in companies. Some CEOs argue that "numbers always tell the story." An executive once noted that "you can miss your plan once, but you wouldn't want to miss it twice." Other CEOs believe "too much focus on making the numbers in a budget" can lead to poor decision making.

[5]For an excellent discussion of these issues, see Chapter 14 ("Formal Models in Budgeting and Incentive Contracts") of R. S. Kaplan and A. A. Atkinson, *Advanced Management Accounting*, 3rd ed. (Upper Saddle River, NJ: Prentice Hall, 1998).

PROBLEM FOR SELF-STUDY

Prepare a budgeted income statement, including all necessary detailed supporting budget schedules. Use the data given in the chapter illustration of an operating budget to prepare the budget schedules. (See pp. 180–187.)

DECISION POINTS — SUMMARY

The following question-and-answer format summarizes the chapter's learning objectives. Each decision presents a key question related to a learning objective. The guidelines are the answer to that question.

Decision	Guidelines
1. What is a master budget and why is it useful?	The master budget summarizes the financial projections of all the company's budgets and plans. It expresses management's operating and financing plans—the formalized outline of the company's financial objectives and how they will be attained. Budgets are tools that, by themselves, are neither good nor bad. Budgets are useful when administered skillfully.
2. When should a company prepare budgets? What are the advantages?	Budgets should be prepared when their expected benefits exceed their expected costs. The advantages of budgets include: (a) they compel strategy analysis and planning, (b) they provide a framework for judging performance, (c) they motivate managers and employees, and (d) they promote coordination and communication among subunits of the company.
3. What is an operating budget and why is it useful?	The starting point for the operating budget is generally the revenues budget. The following supporting schedules are derived from the revenues budget: production budget, direct materials usage budget, direct materials purchases budget, direct manufacturing labor budget, manufacturing overhead costs budget, ending inventory budget, cost of goods sold budget, R&D/design budget, marketing budget, distribution budget, and customer-service budget. The operating budget results in the budgeted income statement that measures the profits a company expects to make.
4. How should managers consider what might happen if the assumptions underlying the budget change?	Managers should use computer-based financial planning models—mathematical statements of the relationships among operating activities, financing activities, and other factors that affect the budget. These models make it possible for management to conduct what-if (sensitivity) analysis of the effects on the master budget of changes in the original predicted data or changes in underlying assumptions and to develop plans to respond to changed conditions.
5. How can budgets include the effects of future improvements?	Kaizen budgeting is based on the idea that it is possible to continuously reduce costs over time. Costs in kaizen budgeting are based on improvements that are yet to be implemented rather than on current practices or methods.
6. How can a company prepare a budget based on costs of different activities?	Activity-based budgeting focuses on the budgeted costs of activities needed to produce and sell products and services. It is linked to activity-based costing but differs in its emphasis on future costs and future use of activity areas.
7. How do companies use responsibility centers and responsibility accounting?	A responsibility center is a part, segment, or subunit of an organization, whose manager is accountable for a specified set of activities. Four types of responsibility centers are cost centers, revenue centers, profit centers, and investment centers. Responsibility accounting systems are useful because they measure the plans—by budgets—and actions—by actual results—of each responsibility center.
8. Should performance reports of responsibility-center managers only include costs the manager can control?	Controllable costs are costs primarily subject to the influence of a given manager of a given responsibility center for a given time span. Performance reports of responsibility-center managers often include costs, revenues, and investments that the managers cannot control. Responsibility accounting associates financial items with managers on the basis of which manager has the most knowledge and information about the specific items, regardless of the manager's ability to exercise full control.

APPENDIX: THE CASH BUDGET

The chapter covered the operating budget, one part of the master budget. The other part is the financial budget, which includes the capital expenditures budget, the cash budget, the budgeted balance sheet, and the budgeted statement of cash flows. This appendix focuses on the cash budget and the budgeted balance sheet. Capital budgeting is discussed in Chapter 21. We don't cover the budgeted statement of cash flows because it is beyond the scope of this book. But we will cover the cash budget, which contains most of the items normally included in the statement of cash flows using the direct method.

Suppose Stylistic Furniture had the balance sheet for the year ended December 31, 2003, shown in Exhibit 6-5. The budgeted cash flows for 2004 are

	Quarters			
	1	2	3	4
Collections from Customers	$5,331,200	$4,704,000	$4,704,000	$6,272,000
Disbursements				
Direct materials	960,000	1,152,000	1,152,000	1,536,000
Payroll	1,626,300	1,626,300	1,888,600	1,626,300
Other costs	1,580,460	1,580,460	1,580,460	1,580,460
Machinery purchase	0	0	1,800,000	0
Interest expense on long-term debt	60,000	60,000	60,000	60,000
Income taxes	100,000	120,460	100,000	100,000

The quarterly data are based on the budgeted cash effects of the operations formulated in Schedules 1 through 8 in the chapter, but the details of that formulation are not shown here to keep this illustration as brief and as focused as possible.

Long-term debt is $2.4 million at an annual interest rate of 10%, with $60,000 interest payable every quarter. The company wants to maintain a $100,000 minimum cash balance at the end of each quarter. The company can borrow or repay money at an interest rate of 12% per year. Management does not want to borrow any more short-term cash than is necessary. By special arrangement, interest is computed and paid when the principal is repaid. Assume that borrowing takes place (in multiples of $1,000) at the beginning and repayment at the end of the quarter we are considering. Interest is computed to the nearest dollar.

Suppose an accountant at Stylistic is given the preceding data and the other data contained in the budgets in the chapter (pp. 180–187). She is instructed as follows:

1. Prepare a cash budget for 2004 by quarter. That is, prepare a statement of cash receipts and disbursements by quarter, including details of borrowing, repayment, and interest.

EXHIBIT 6-5

Balance Sheet for Stylistic Furniture, December 31, 2003

Assets			
Current assets			
Cash		$ 500,000	
Accounts receivable		1,881,600	
Direct materials		223,000	
Finished goods		1,375,000	$3,979,600
Property, plant, and equipment			
Land		1,200,000	
Building and equipment	$2,300,000		
Accumulated depreciation	(800,000)	1,500,000	2,700,000
Total			$6,679,600
Liabilities and Stockholders' Equity			
Current liabilities			
Accounts payable		$ 384,000	
Income taxes payable		20,460	
Total current liabilities		404,460	
Long-term debt (interest at 10% per year)		2,400,000	
Total current and long-term liabilities			$2,804,460
Stockholders' equity			
Common stock, $0.01 par value, 300,000 shares outstanding		3,000	
Retained earnings		3,872,140	3,875,140
Total			$6,679,600

2. Prepare a budgeted balance sheet on December 31, 2004.
3. Prepare a budgeted income statement for the year ended December 31, 2004. This statement should include interest expense and income taxes (at a rate of 36% of operating income). In April 2004, Stylistic will pay $120,640 of income taxes. This amount is the remaining payment due for the 2003 income tax year. Stylistic pays $100,000 each quarter of 2004 toward its 2004 income tax bill. Any remaining amount due is paid in April 2005.

PREPARATION OF BUDGETS

1. The **cash budget** (Exhibit 6-6) is a schedule of expected cash receipts and disbursements. It predicts the effects on the cash position at the given level of operations. Exhibit 6-6 presents the cash budget by quarters to show the impact of cash flow timing on bank loans and their repayment. In practice, monthly—and sometimes weekly or even daily—cash budgets are very helpful for cash planning and control. Cash budgets help avoid unnecessary idle cash and unexpected cash deficiencies. They thus keep cash balances in line with needs. Ordinarily, the cash budget has these main sections:

a. The beginning cash balance plus cash receipts equals the total cash available before financing. Cash receipts depend on collections of accounts receivable, cash sales, and miscellaneous recurring sources, such as rental or royalty receipts. Information on the expected collectibility of accounts receivable is needed for accurate predictions. Key factors include bad-debt (uncollectible accounts) experience and average time lag between sales and collections.

b. Cash disbursements include:

i. *Direct material purchases.* Suppliers are paid in full three weeks after the goods are delivered.

Keep in mind three points about cash budgets: (1) The ending balance (EB) of cash in one quarter is the beginning balance (BB) of cash the next quarter. (2) In the "Year as a whole" column, receipts and disbursements are totaled for the four quarters. However, the BB in that column is the BB for quarter 1, and the EB is the EB for quarter 4. (3) Depreciation is *not* a cash disbursement.

EXHIBIT 6-6 Cash Budget for Stylistic Furniture for the Year Ended December 31, 2004

	Quarters				Year as a Whole
	I	II	III	IV	
Cash balance, beginning	$ 500,000	$1,504,440	$1,669,220	$ 100,160	$ 500,000
Add receipts					
Collections from customers	5,331,200	4,704,000	4,704,000	6,272,000	21,011,200
Total cash available for needs (x)	5,831,200	6,208,440	6,373,220	6,372,160	21,511,200
Deduct disbursements					
Direct materials	960,000	1,152,000	1,152,000	1,536,000	4,800,000
Payroll	1,626,300	1,626,300	1,888,600	1,626,300	6,767,500
Other costs	1,580,460	1,580,460	1,580,460	1,580,460	6,321,840
Interest costs (long-term debt)	60,000	60,000	60,000	60,000	240,000
Machinery purchase	0	0	1,800,000	0	1,800,000
Income taxes	100,000	120,460	100,000	100,000	420,460
Total disbursements (y)	4,326,760	4,539,220	6,581,060	4,902,760	20,349,800
Minimum cash balance desired	100,000	100,000	100,000	100,000	100,000
Total cash needed	4,426,760	4,639,220	6,681,060	5,002,760	20,449,800
Cash excess (deficiency)[a]	$1,404,440	$1,569,220	$ (307,840)	$1,369,400	$ 1,061,400
Financing					
Borrowing (at beginning)	$ 0	$ 0	$ 308,000	$ 0	$ 308,000
Repayment (at end)	0	0	0	(308,000)	(308,000)
Interest (at 12% per annum)[b]	0	0	0	(18,480)	(18,480)
Total effects of financing	$ 0	$ 0	$ 308,000	$ (326,480)	$ (18,480)
Cash balance, ending[c]	$1,504,440	$1,669,220	$ 100,160	$1,142,920	$ 1,142,920

[a]Excess of total cash available over total cash needed before current financing.

[b]Note that the short-term interest payments pertain only to the amount of principal being repaid at the end of a quarter: $\$308{,}000 \times 0.12 \times \frac{1}{2} = \$18{,}480$.

[c]Ending cash balance = Total cash available for needs (x) − Total disbursements (y) + Total effects of financing.

There's no need to memorize the format of the cash budget if you remember that it's similar to the way your bank statement works: beginning balance + deposits (receipts) − disbursements = ending balance (before financing). This ending balance reveals how much must be borrowed or can be repaid/invested.

ii. *Direct labor and other wage and salary outlays.* All payroll-related costs are made in two equal cash installments—on the fifth and on the last day of the same month in which the labor effort occurs.

iii. *Other costs.* These depend on timing and credit terms. *Note, depreciation does not require a cash outlay.*

iv. *Other disbursements.* These include outlays for property, plant, equipment, and other long-term investments.

v. *Interest on long-term borrowing.*

vi. *Income tax payments.*

c. Short-term financing requirements depend on how the total cash available for needs (keyed as (x) in Exhibit 6-6) compares with the total cash disbursements (keyed as (y)), plus the minimum ending cash balance desired. The financing plans will depend on the relationship between total cash available for needs and total cash needed. If there is a deficiency of cash, loans will be taken. If there is excess cash, any outstanding loans will be repaid.

d. The ending cash balance.

The cash budget in Exhibit 6-6 shows the pattern of short-term "self-liquidating" cash loans. In quarter III, Stylistic budgets a $307,840 cash deficiency. Hence, it undertakes short-term borrowing of $308,000 for six months. Seasonal peaks of production or sales often result in heavy cash disbursements for purchases, payroll, and other operating outlays as the products are produced and sold. Cash receipts from customers typically lag behind sales. The loan is *self-liquidating* in the sense that the borrowed money is used to acquire resources that are used to produce and sell finished goods, and the proceeds from sales are used to repay the loan. This **self-liquidating cycle** is the movement from cash to inventories to receivables and back to cash.

2. The budgeted income statement is presented in Exhibit 6-7. It is merely the budgeted operating income statement in Exhibit 6-3 (p. 187) expanded to include interest expense and income taxes.

3. The budgeted balance sheet is presented in Exhibit 6-8. Each item is projected in light of the details of the business plan as expressed in all the previous budget schedules. For example, the ending balance of accounts receivable of $1,254,400 is computed by adding the budgeted revenues of $20,384,000 (from Schedule 1) to the beginning balance of $1,881,600 (given) and subtracting cash receipts of $21,011,200 (from Exhibit 6-6).

For simplicity, the cash receipts and disbursements were given explicitly in this illustration. Usually, the receipts and disbursements are calculated based on the lags between the items reported on the accrual basis of accounting in an income statement and balance sheet and their related cash receipts and disbursements. In the Stylistic

EXHIBIT 6-7

Budgeted Income Statement for Stylistic Furniture for Year Ending December 31, 2004

Revenues	Schedule 1		$20,384,000
Cost of goods sold	Schedule 7		14,751,250
Gross margin			5,632,750
Operating costs			
R & D/Product design costs	Schedule 8	555,760	
Marketing costs	Schedule 8	1,920,720	
Distribution costs	Schedule 8	729,600	
Customer-service costs	Schedule 8	504,992	
Administrative costs	Schedule 8	440,768	4,151,840
Operating income			1,480,910
Interest expense			258,480
Income before income taxes			1,222,430
Income taxes			440,075
Net income			$ 782,355

EXHIBIT 6-8

Budgeted Balance Sheet for Stylistic Furniture, December 31, 2004

Assets			
Current assets			
Cash		$1,142,920	
Accounts receivable		1,254,400	
Direct materials		204,000	
Finished goods		854,250	$3,455,570
Property, plant, and equipment			
Land		1,200,000	
Building and equipment	$4,100,000		
Accumulated depreciation	(1,300,000)	2,800,000	4,000,000
Total			$7,455,570
Liabilities and Stockholders' Equity			
Current liabilities			
Accounts payable		$ 358,000	
Income taxes payable		40,075	$ 398,075
Long-term debt (interest at 10% per year)			2,400,000
Stockholders' equity			
Common stock, $0.01 par value, 300,000 shares outstanding		$ 3,000	
Retained earnings		4,654,495	4,657,495
Total			$7,455,570

example, collections from customers are derived under two assumptions: (1) In any month, 20% of sales are cash and 80% of sales are on credit, and (2) the total credit sales are collected in the month after sale. For example, the cash collections in the third quarter (July – September) are

- July: the 80% of June's sales that were credit sales plus the 20% of July's sales that were cash sales
- August: the 80% of July's sales that were credit sales plus the 20% of August's sales that were cash sales
- September: the 80% of August's sales that were credit sales plus the 20% of September's sales that were cash sales

Note that the 80% of September's sales that were credit sales are not part of third-quarter cash collections because this cash will only be collected in October (the fourth quarter).

EXHIBIT 6-9

Sensitivity Analysis: Effects of Key Budget Assumptions in Exhibit 6-4 on Short-Term Borrowing for Stylistic Furniture

		Direct Materials Purchase Cost			Short-Term Borrowing by Quarter			
Scenario	Selling Price	Particle Board	Red Oak	Budgeted Operating Income	Quarter I	Quarter II	Quarter III	Quarter IV
1	$431.20	$3.80	$5.70	$3,458,226	$0	$0	$ 0	$ 0
2	431.20	4.00	6.00	3,244,126	0	0	0	0
3	431.20	4.20	6.30	3,030,026	0	0	0	0
4	392.00	3.80	5.70	1,695,010	0	0	145,000	0
5	392.00	4.00	6.00	1,480,910	0	0	308,000	0
6	392.00	4.20	6.30	1,266,810	0	0	472,000	0
7	352.80	3.80	5.70	(68,206)	0	0	1,413,000	717,000
8	352.80	4.00	6.00	(282,306)	0	0	1,576,000	997,000
9	352.80	4.20	6.30	(496,406)	0	0	1,739,000	1,276,000

SENSITIVITY ANALYSIS AND CASH FLOWS

Exhibit 6-4 (p. 188) shows how differing assumptions about selling prices and direct material costs for Stylistic Furniture led to differing amounts for budgeted operating income. A key use of sensitivity analysis is in cash-flow budgeting. Exhibit 6-9 outlines the short-term borrowing implications of the nine combinations examined in Exhibit 6-4. Scenarios 7 to 9, with the lower selling price per table ($352.80), require large amounts of short-term borrowing in quarters III and IV. Scenario 9, with the combination of a 10% lower selling price and 5% higher direct material costs, requires the largest amount of borrowing by Stylistic Furniture. Sensitivity analysis helps managers anticipate such outcomes and take steps to minimize the effects of expected reductions in cash flows from operations.

TERMS TO LEARN

The chapter and the Glossary at the end of the book contain definitions of:

activity-based budgeting (ABB) (p. 190)
budgetary slack (193)
cash budget (197)
continuous budget (180)
controllability (192)
controllable cost (192)
cost center (191)
financial budget (180)
financial planning models (187)
investment center (191)
kaizen budgeting (189)
master budget (176)
operating budget (180)
organization structure (191)
pro forma statements (177)
profit center (191)
responsibility accounting (191)
responsibility center (191)
revenue center (191)
rolling budget (180)
self-liquidating cycle (198)

ASSIGNMENT MATERIAL

Questions

6-1 What are the four elements of the budgeting cycle?

6-2 Define master budget.

6-3 "Strategy, plans, and budgets are unrelated to one another." Do you agree? Explain.

6-4 "Budgeted performance is a better criterion than past performance for judging managers." Do you agree? Explain.

6-5 "Production managers and marketing managers are like oil and water. They just don't mix." How can a budget assist in reducing battles between these two areas?

6-6 How might a company benefit by sharing its own internal budget information with other companies?

6-7 "Budgets meet the cost-benefit test. They force managers to act differently." Do you agree? Explain.

6-8 Define rolling budget. Give an example.

6-9 Outline the steps in preparing an operating budget.

6-10 "The sales forecast is the cornerstone for budgeting." Why?

6-11 How can sensitivity analysis be used to increase the benefits of budgeting?

6-12 What factors reduce the effectiveness of companies' budgeting?

6-13 Define kaizen budgeting.

6-14 Describe how nonoutput-based cost drivers can be incorporated into budgeting.

6-15 Explain how the choice of the type of responsibility center (cost, revenue, profit, or investment) affects behavior.

Exercises

6-16 **Advantages of budgeting.** (CMA, adapted) A major objective of budgeting is to substitute deliberate, well-conceived business judgment for accidental success or failure in managing an organization. Implicit in this objective is the confidence that a competent management team can plan for, manage, and control in large measure the relevant variables that dominate the life of a business. Managers must grapple with uncertainties, whether or not they have a budget.

Describe at least three benefits, other than improved cost control, that an organization can expect to realize from implementing a budget. **Required**

6-17 Sales and production budget. The Mendez Company expects sales in 2005 of 100,000 units of serving trays. Mendez's beginning inventory for 2005 is 7,000 trays; target ending inventory, 11,000 trays. Compute the number of trays budgeted for production in 2005.

6-18 Direct materials budget. Inglenook Co. produces wine. The company expects to produce 1,500,000 two-liter bottles of Chablis in 2005. Inglenook purchases empty glass bottles from an outside vendor. Its target ending inventory of such bottles is 50,000; its beginning inventory is 20,000. For simplicity, ignore breakage. Compute the number of bottles to be purchased in 2005.

6-19 Budgeting material purchases. The Mahoney Company has prepared a sales budget of 42,000 finished units for a three-month period. The company has an inventory of 22,000 units of finished goods on hand at December 31 and has a target finished goods inventory of 24,000 units at the end of the succeeding quarter.

It takes 3 gallons of direct materials to make one unit of finished product. The company has an inventory of 90,000 gallons of direct materials at December 31 and has a target ending inventory of 110,000 gallons at the end of the succeeding quarter. How many gallons of direct materials should be purchased during the three months ending March 31?

6-20 Revenues and production budget. Purity, Inc., bottles and distributes mineral water from the company's natural springs in northern Oregon. Purity markets two products: 12-ounce disposable plastic bottles and 4-gallon reusable plastic containers.

Required

1. For 2004, Purity marketing managers project monthly sales of 400,000 twelve-ounce units and 100,000 four-gallon units. Average selling prices are estimated at $0.25 per twelve-ounce unit and $1.50 per four-gallon unit. Prepare a revenues budget for Purity, Inc., for the year ending December 31, 2004.
2. Purity begins 2004 with 900,000 twelve-ounce units in inventory. The vice president of operations requests that twelve-ounce ending inventory on December 31, 2004, be no less than 600,000 units. Based on sales projections as budgeted above, what is the minimum number of twelve-ounce units Purity must produce during 2004?
3. The VP of Operations requests that ending inventory of four-gallon units on December 31, 2004, be 200,000 units. If the production budget calls for Purity to produce 1,300,000 four-gallon units during 2004, what is the beginning inventory of four-gallon units on January 1, 2004?

6-21 Direct materials usage, unit costs, and gross margins (continuation of 6-20). Purity, Inc., bottles and distributes mineral water from the company's natural springs in northern Oregon. Purity markets two products: 12-ounce disposable plastic bottles and 4-gallon reusable plastic containers. The 12-ounce bottles are purchased from Plastico, a plastics manufacturer, at a cost of 6 cents per unit. The 4-gallon containers are sterilized and put back into service at a cost of 30 cents per container. Spring water is extracted at a direct labor cost of 1 cent per 8 ounces (there are 128 ounces in a gallon). Manufacturing overhead is allocated at the rate of 15 cents per unit. (Note: A unit can be a 12-ounce bottle *or* a 4-gallon container). In 2004, the production budget calls for the production of 4,500,000 twelve-ounce units and 1,300,000 four-gallon units.

Required

1. Assume four-gallon containers are fully depreciated, so that the only cost incurred is that of sterilization. Beginning and ending inventories for four-gallon containers are zero. There are 500,000 empty twelve-ounce bottles in beginning inventory on January 1, 2004. The vice president of operations would like to end 2004 with 300,000 empty twelve-ounce bottles in inventory. Accounting for sterilization as the only cost of the four-gallon containers, prepare a direct materials usage budget (relating to both bottles and containers) in both units and dollars.
2. The cost of direct manufacturing labor is captured through the extraction cost as detailed above. Based on the data given, prepare a direct manufacturing labor budget for 2004.
3. Calculate the manufacturing cost per unit for each product.
4. Assuming average selling prices as in Exercise 6-20, what is the expected average gross margin per unit for each product?
5. Consider Purity's choice of a cost allocation base for manufacturing overhead. Can you suggest alternative cost allocation bases?

6-22 Revenues, production, and purchases budgets. The Suzuki Co. in Japan has a division that manufactures two-wheel motorcycles. Its budgeted sales for Model G in 2005 are 800,000 units. Suzuki's target ending inventory is 100,000 units, and its beginning inventory is 120,000 units. The company's budgeted selling price to its distributors and dealers is 400,000 yen (¥) per motorcycle.

Suzuki buys all its wheels from an outside supplier. No defective wheels are accepted. (Suzuki's needs for extra wheels for replacement parts are ordered by a separate division of the company.) The company's target ending inventory is 30,000 wheels, and its beginning inventory is 20,000 wheels. The budgeted purchase price is 16,000 yen(¥) per wheel.

Required

1. Compute the budgeted revenues in yen.

2. Compute the number of motorcycles to be produced.
3. Compute the budgeted purchases of wheels in units and in yen.

6-23 **Budgets for production and direct manufacturing labor.** (CMA, adapted) Roletter Company makes and sells artistic frames for pictures of weddings, graduations, and other special events. Bob Anderson, the controller, is responsible for preparing Roletter's master budget and has accumulated the following information for 2005:

	2005				
	January	**February**	**March**	**April**	**May**
Estimated sales in units	10,000	12,000	8,000	9,000	9,000
Selling price	$54.00	$51.50	$51.50	$51.50	$51.50
Direct manufacturing labor-hours per unit	2.0	2.0	1.5	1.5	1.5
Wage per direct manufacturing labor-hour	$10.00	$10.00	$10.00	$11.00	$11.00

Besides wages, direct manufacturing labor-related costs include pension contributions of $0.50 per hour, worker's compensation insurance of $0.15 per hour, employee medical insurance of $0.40 per hour, and social security taxes. Assume that as of January 1, 2005, the social security tax rates are 7.5% for employers and 7.5% for employees. The cost of employee benefits paid by Roletter on its employees is treated as a direct manufacturing labor cost.

Roletter has a labor contract that calls for a wage increase to $11 per hour on April 1, 2005. New labor-saving machinery has been installed and will be fully operational by March 1, 2005. Roletter expects to have 16,000 frames on hand at December 31, 2004, and it has a policy of carrying an end-of-month inventory of 100% of the following month's sales plus 50% of the second following month's sales.

Required Prepare a production budget and a direct manufacturing labor budget for Roletter Company by month and for the first quarter of 2005. Both budgets may be combined in one schedule. The direct manufacturing labor budget should include labor-hours and show the details for each labor cost category.

6-24 **Activity-based budgeting.** Family Supermarkets (FS) is preparing its activity-based budget for January 2005. Its current concern is with its four activities (which are also indirect-cost categories in its product profitability reporting system):

1. Ordering—covers purchasing activities. The cost driver is number of purchase orders.
2. Delivery—covers the physical delivery and receipt of merchandise. The cost driver is number of deliveries.
3. Shelf-stocking—covers the stocking of merchandise on store shelves and the ongoing restocking before sale. The cost driver is hours of stocking time.
4. Customer support—covers assistance provided to customers, including checkout and bagging. The cost driver is number of items sold.

Assume FS has only three product types: soft drinks, fresh produce, and packaged food. The budgeted usage of each cost driver in these three product types and the January 2005 budgeted cost-driver rates are

	Cost-Driver Rates		Jan. 2005 Budgeted Amount of Driver Used		
Activity and Driver	**2004 Actual Rate**	**Jan. 2005 Budgeted Rate**	**Soft Drinks**	**Fresh Produce**	**Packaged Food**
Ordering (per purchase order)	$100	$90	14	24	14
Delivery (per delivery)	$80	$82	12	62	19
Shelf-stocking (per hour)	$20	$21	16	172	94
Customer support (per item sold)	$0.20	$0.18	4,600	34,200	10,750

Required

1. What is the total budgeted cost for each activity in January 2005?
2. What advantages might FS gain by using an activity-based budgeting approach over, say, an approach that allocates the cost of these activities to products as a percentage of the cost of goods sold?

6-25 **Kaizen approach to activity-based budgeting (continuation of 6-24).** Family Supermarkets (FS) has a kaizen (continuous improvement) approach to budgeting monthly activity costs for each month of 2005. February's budgeted cost-driver rate is 0.998 times the budgeted January 2005 rate. March's budgeted cost-driver rate is 0.998 times the budgeted February 2005 rate, and so on. Assume that March 2005 has the same budgeted amount of cost-driver usage as January 2005.

Required

1. What is the total budgeted cost for each activity in March 2005?
2. What are the benefits of FS adopting a kaizen budgeting approach? What are the limitations?

6-26 **Responsibility and controllability.** Consider each of the following independent situations:

1. A purchasing agent forgot to order a part. A rush order had to be placed for the part, resulting in extra costs.
2. A supplier has increased prices of the materials ordered by a purchasing agent, resulting in higher costs of the materials purchased.
3. A higher-than-budgeted quantity of direct materials was used for the output. The supervisor of the production department correctly pointed out that it was due to the substandard quality of materials purchased by the purchasing department.
4. A higher-than-budgeted quantity of direct materials was used for the output. The cause was traced to abnormal spoilage resulting from a faulty machine setting by the machine operator.
5. A higher-than-budgeted quantity of direct materials was used for the output. This happened because of the spoilage occurring from the machine breakdown. The machine was to undergo regular maintenance last month. However, maintenance was not performed because the maintenance department is behind schedule due to heavy labor turnover.
6. A newly appointed division manager has high labor costs as a result of the unfavorable terms of a labor contract negotiated by her predecessor. Her predecessor, who was retiring, according to one observer, "gave the store away during labor contract negotiations."
7. A production department operated only at 80% of its capacity during a month. This was done at the instructions of the plant superintendent, who commented that increasing the department output will only build up inventory in the next production department, which is a bottleneck department.

Determine for each situation where (a) responsibility and (b) controllability lie. **Required**

6-27 Cash flow analysis, chapter appendix. (CMA, adapted) TabComp, Inc., is a retail distributor for MZB-33 computer hardware and related software and support services. TabComp prepares annual sales forecasts of which the first six months for 2005 are presented below.

Cash sales account for 25% of TabComp's total sales, 30% of the total sales are paid by bank credit card, and the remaining 45% are on open account (TabComp's own charge accounts). The cash sales and cash from bank credit-card sales are received in the month of the sale. Bank credit-card sales are subject to a 4% discount deducted at the time of the daily deposit. The cash receipts for sales on open account are 70% in the month following the sale and 28% in the second month following the sale. The remaining accounts receivable are estimated to be uncollectible.

TabComp's month-end inventory requirements for computer hardware units are 30% of the next month's sales. A one-month lead time is required for delivery from the manufacturer. Thus, orders for computer hardware units are placed on the 25th of each month to assure that they will be in the store by the first day of the month needed. The computer hardware units are purchased under terms of n/45 (payment in full within 45 days of invoice), measured from the time the units are delivered to TabComp. TabComp's purchase price for the computer units is 60% of the selling price.

TabComp Inc.—Sales Forecast First Six Months of 2005

	Hardware Sales		Software	Total
	Units	Dollars	Sales and Support	Revenues
January	130	$ 390,000	$160,000	$ 550,000
February	120	360,000	140,000	500,000
March	110	330,000	150,000	480,000
April	90	270,000	130,000	400,000
May	100	300,000	125,000	425,000
June	125	375,000	225,000	600,000
Total	675	$2,025,000	$930,000	$2,955,000

1. Calculate the cash that TabComp, Inc., can expect to collect during April 2005. Be sure to show all of your calculations. **Required**
2. TabComp, Inc., is determining how many MZB-33 computer hardware units to order on January 25, 2005.
   a. Determine the projected number of computer hardware units that will be ordered.
   b. Calculate the dollar amount of the order that TabComp will place for these computer hardware units.
3. As part of the annual budget process, TabComp prepares a cash budget by month for the entire year. Explain why a company such as TabComp prepares a cash budget by month for the entire year.

Problems

6-28 Budget schedules for a manufacturer. Sierra Furniture is an elite desk manufacturer. It makes two products:

- Executive desks—3′ × 5′ oak desks
- Chairman desks—6′ × 4′ red oak desks

The budgeted direct-cost inputs for each product in 2005 are

	Executive Line	Chairman Line
Oak top	16 square feet	0
Red oak top	0	25 square feet
Oak legs	4	0
Red oak legs	0	4
Direct manufacturing labor	3 hours	5 hours

Unit data pertaining to the direct materials for March 2005 are

Actual Beginning Direct Materials Inventory (3/1/2005)

	Executive Line	Chairman Line
Oak top (square feet)	320	0
Red oak top (square feet)	0	150
Oak legs	100	0
Red oak legs	0	40

Target Ending Direct Materials Inventory (3/31/2005)

	Executive Line	Chairman Line
Oak top (square feet)	192	0
Red oak top (square feet)	0	200
Oak legs	80	0
Red oak legs	0	44

Unit cost data for direct-cost inputs pertaining to February 2005 and March 2005 are

	February 2005 (actual)	March 2005 (budgeted)
Oak top (per square feet)	$18	$20
Red oak top (per square feet)	23	25
Oak legs (per leg)	11	12
Red oak legs (per leg)	17	18
Manufacturing labor cost per hour	30	30

Manufacturing overhead (both variable and fixed) is allocated to each desk on the basis of budgeted direct manufacturing labor-hours per desk. The budgeted variable manufacturing overhead rate for March 2005 is $35 per direct manufacturing labor-hour. The budgeted fixed manufacturing overhead for March 2005 is $42,500. Both variable and fixed manufacturing overhead cost are allocated to each unit of finished goods.

Data relating to finished goods inventory for March 2005 are

	Executive	Chairman Line
Beginning inventory in units	20	5
Beginning inventory in dollars (cost)	$10,480	$4,850
Target ending inventory in units	30	15

Budgeted sales for March 2005 are 740 units of the executive line and 390 units of the chairman line. The budgeted selling prices per unit in March 2005 are $1,020 for the executive line desk and $1,600 for the chairman line desk. Assume the following in your answer:

- Work-in-process inventories are negligible and ignored.
- Direct materials inventory and finished goods inventory are costed using the first-in first-out (FIFO) method.
- Unit costs of direct materials purchased and finished goods are constant in March 2005.

Required

1. Prepare the following budgets for March 2005:

a. Revenues budget
b. Production budget in units
c. Direct materials usage budget and direct materials purchases budget
d. Direct manufacturing labor budget
e. Manufacturing overhead budget
f. Ending inventory budget
g. Cost of goods sold budget

2. Suppose Sierra Furniture decides to incorporate continuous improvement into its budgeting process. Describe two areas where Sierra could incorporate continuous improvement into the budget schedules in requirement 1.

6-29 Sensitivity analysis, changing budget assumptions, and kaizen approach. Choco Chips produces two brands of chocolate chip cookies: Chippo and Choco. Choco Chips's cookies are produced from two ingredients: chocolate chips and cookie dough. Chippo is 50% chips and 50% dough, whereas Choco is 25% chips and 75% dough.

Packages of either brand weigh 1 pound. Choco Chips's master budget projects sales of 500,000 packages of each product in 2004. According to the master budget, estimated selling prices are $3 per package for each product. Forecasted 2004 ingredients' costs are as follows: 1 pound of chocolate will cost $2, and 1 pound of cookie dough will cost $1. A total of 5,000 direct manufacturing labor-hours—2,000 hours for Chippo and 3,000 hours for Choco—are budgeted at the hourly rate of $20 per hour. Indirect manufacturing costs are expected to be $160,000. The indirect manufacturing costs are allocated equally between Chippo and Choco on the basis of packages produced in 2004.

Required

1. Use the preceding information to calculate Choco Chips's budgeted gross margins for 2004.
2. By working with suppliers, Choco Chip was able to reduce the purchase cost of ingredients by 3%. Calculate Choco Chips's revised gross margin for 2004.
3. Assume that in addition to the 3% reduction in the purchase cost of ingredients mentioned in requirement 2, Choco Chips plans a 1% cost reduction in direct manufacturing labor-hours and a 2% cost reduction in the indirect manufacturing costs from the original data. These revisions to the original budget resulted from an analysis of all activities by a cross-functional team as a part of Choco Chips's efforts toward continuous improvement. Compute Choco Chips's revised gross margin for 2004 under these assumptions.

Excel Application For students who wish to practice their spreadsheet skills, the following is a step-by-step approach to creating an Excel spreadsheet to work this problem.

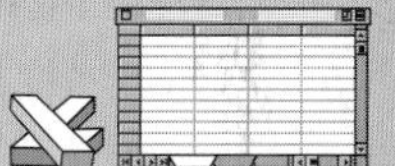

Step-by-Step

1. At the top of a new spreadsheet, create an "Original Data" section with columns for "Chippo" and "Choco" and rows for "% chips," "% dough," "Projected sales," "Estimated selling price per package," "Cost of chocolate ($/lb)," "Cost of cookie dough ($/lb)," "Budgeted direct manuf. labor hours," "Direct manuf. labor rate ($/hr)," and "Indirect manufacturing costs." Enter the data provided for Problem 6-29 in this section.

(Program your spreadsheet to perform all necessary calculations. Do not "hard-code" any amounts, such as total revenue or gross margin, requiring addition or subtraction operations.)

2. Skip two rows, create a section "Problem 1." Create rows for revenues and each of the categories of cost of goods sold, including chocolate chips, cookie dough, direct manuf. labor, and indirect manufacturing costs. Next, create rows for total cost of goods sold and gross margin. Create columns labeled "Chippo," "Choco," and "Total." Format as necessary.
3. Use the data from the original data section to calculate budgeted revenues for the Chippo product line, the Choco product line, and total revenues from both product lines.
4. Use the data from the original data section to calculate the cost of chocolate chips, cost of cookie dough, direct manuf. labor cost, and indirect manufacturing costs for each of the Chippo and Choco product lines, and total costs for each of these categories respectively. Use this data to calculate cost of goods sold for each product line and total cost of goods sold. Finally, calculate gross margins for each product line and total gross margins.
5. Skip two rows, create a section "Problem 2." Follow steps 2 through 4, but make the appropriate adjustments to the cost of chocolate chips and cookie dough.
6. Skip down two rows, create a section "Problem 3." Again, follow steps 2 through 4, but make the appropriate adjustments to direct manuf. labor and indirect manufacturing costs.
7. *Verify the accuracy of your spreadsheet:* Go to your original data section and change the cost of cookie dough from $1.00/lb to $1.25/lb. If you programmed your spreadsheet correctly, gross margin for the Chippo product line, Choco product line, and total gross margins should change to $567,500, $641,250, and $1,208,750 respectively.

6-30 Revenue and production budgets. (CPA, adapted) The Scarborough Corporation manufactures and sells two products, Thingone and Thingtwo. In July 2005, Scarborough's Budget Department gathered the following data to prepare budgets for 2006:

2006 Projected Sales

Product	Units	Price
Thingone	60,000	$165
Thingtwo	40,000	$250

2006 Inventories in Units

Product	Expected Target January 1, 2006	December 31, 2006
Thingone	20,000	25,000
Thingtwo	8,000	9,000

The following direct materials are used in the two products:

Direct Material	Unit	Amount Used per Unit Thingone	Thingtwo
A	pound	4	5
B	pound	2	3
C	each	0	1

Projected data for 2006 with respect to direct materials are as follows:

Direct Material	Anticipated Purchase Price	Expected Inventories January 1, 2006	Target Inventories December 31, 2006
A	$12	32,000 lb.	36,000 lb.
B	$ 5	29,000 lb.	32,000 lb.
C	$ 3	6,000 units	7,000 units

Projected direct manufacturing labor requirements and rates for 2006 are as follows:

Product	Hours Per Unit	Rate Per Hour
Thingone	2	$12
Thingtwo	3	16

Manufacturing overhead is allocated at the rate of $20 per direct manufacturing labor-hour.

Required Based on the preceding projections and budget requirements for Thingone and Thingtwo, prepare the following budgets for 2006:

1. Revenues budget (in dollars)
2. Production budget (in units)
3. Direct materials purchases budget (in quantities)
4. Direct materials purchases budget (in dollars)
5. Direct manufacturing labor budget (in dollars)
6. Budgeted finished goods inventory at December 31, 2006 (in dollars)

6-31 Budgeted income statement. (CMA, adapted) Easecom Company is a manufacturer of video-conferencing products. Regular units are manufactured to meet marketing projections, and specialized units are made after an order is received. Maintaining the video-conferencing equipment is an important area of customer satisfaction. With the recent downturn in the computer industry, the video-conferencing equipment segment has suffered, leading to a decline in Easecom's financial performance. The following income statement shows results for 2004.

Easecom Company
Income Statement
For the Year Ended December 31, 2004 (in thousands)

Revenues:		
Equipment	$6,000	
Maintenance contracts	1,800	
Total revenues		$7,800
Cost of goods sold		4,600
Gross margin		3,200
Operating costs		
Marketing	600	
Distribution	150	
Customer maintenance	1,000	
Administration	900	
Total operating costs		2,650
Operating income		$ 550

Easecom's management team is in the process of preparing the 2005 budget and is studying the following information:

1. Selling prices of equipment are expected to increase by 10% as the economic recovery begins. The selling price of each maintenance contract is unchanged from 2004.
2. Equipment sales in units are expected to increase by 6%, with a corresponding 6% growth in units of maintenance contracts.
3. Cost of each unit sold is expected to increase by 3% to pay for the necessary technology and quality improvements.
4. Marketing costs are expected to increase by $250,000, but administration costs are expected to remain at 2004 levels.
5. Distribution costs vary in proportion to the number of units of equipment sold.
6. Two maintenance technicians are to be added at a total cost of $130,000, which covers wages and related travel costs. The objective is to improve customer service and shorten response time.
7. There is no beginning or ending inventory of equipment.

Required

Prepare a budgeted income statement for 2005.

6-32 Responsibility of purchasing agent. (Adapted from a description by R. Villers) Mark Richards is the purchasing agent for the Hart Manufacturing Company. Kent Sampson is head of the Production Planning and Control Department. Every six months, Sampson gives Richards a general purchasing program. Richards gets specifications from the Engineering Department. He then selects suppliers and negotiates prices. When he took this job, Richards was informed very clearly that he bore responsibility for meeting the general purchasing program once he accepted it from Sampson.

During week 24, Richards is advised that Part No. 1234—a critical part—would be needed for assembly on Tuesday morning of week 32. He found that the regular supplier could not deliver. He called everywhere and finally found a supplier in the Midwest who accepted the commitment.

He followed up by e-mail. Yes, the supplier assured him, the part would be ready. The matter was so important that on Thursday of week 31, Richards checked by phone. Yes, the shipment had left in time. Richards was reassured and did not check further. But on Tuesday of week 32, the part had not arrived. Inquiry revealed that the shipment had been misdirected by the railroad and was still in Chicago.

Required

What department should bear the costs of time lost in the plant due to the delayed shipment? Why? As purchasing agent, do you think it fair that such costs be charged to your department?

6-33 Activity-based budgeting. Anderson Manufacturing, Inc, uses activity-based costing and activity-based budgeting. Budgetary information for selected activities for 2004 is provided below.

Activity	Cost Driver	Items in Cost Pool (fixed cost + cost per unit of cost driver)
Machining	Machine hours	Indirect materials $0 + $10 per hour
		Indirect labor $20,000 + $15 per hour
		Utilities $0 + $5 per hour
Setups and quality assurance	Production runs	Indirect materials $0 + $1,000 per run
		Indirect labor $0 + $1,200 per run
		Inspection $80,000 + $2,000 per run
Procurement	Purchase orders	Indirect materials $0 + $4 per order
		Indirect labor $45,000 + $0 per order
Design	Design hours	Engineering $75,000 + $50 per hour
Material handling	Square feet of materials handled	Indirect materials $0 + $2 per sq ft
		Indirect labor $30,000 + $0 per sq ft

Additional budget data for 2004:

Activity	Cost driver budgeted volume
a. Machining	10,000 machine hours
b. Setups and quality assurance	40 production runs
c. Procurement	15,000 purchase orders
d. Design	100 engineering hours
e. Material handling	100,000 square feet

Required

Calculate the budgeted amount for each activity in 2004.

6-34 Comprehensive operating budget, budgeted balance sheet. Slopes, Inc., manufactures and sells snowboards. Slopes manufactures a single model, the Pipex. In the summer of 2003, Slopes's accountant gathered the following data to prepare budgets for 2004:

Materials and labor requirements	
Direct materials	
Wood	5 board feet per snowboard

Continued

Fiberglass	6 yards per snowboard
Direct manufacturing labor	5 hours per snowboard

Slopes's CEO expects to sell 1,000 snowboards during 2004 at an estimated retail price of $450 per board. Further, he expects 2004 beginning inventory of 100 boards and would like to end 2004 with 200 snowboards in stock.

Direct materials inventories

	Beginning Inventory 1/1/2004	Ending Inventory 12/31/2004
Wood	2,000	1,500
Fiberglass	1,000	2,000

Variable manufacturing overhead is allocated at the rate of $7 per direct manufacturing labor-hour. There are also $66,000 in fixed manufacturing overhead costs budgeted for 2004. Slopes combines both variable and fixed manufacturing overhead into a single rate based on direct manufacturing labor-hours. Variable marketing costs are allocated at the rate of $250 per sales visit. The marketing plan calls for 30 sales visits during 2004. Finally, there are $30,000 in fixed nonmanufacturing costs budgeted for 2004.

Other data includes:

	2003 Unit Price	2004 Unit Price
Wood	$28.00 per b.f.	$30.00 per b.f.
Fiberglass	$4.80 per yard	$5.00 per yard
Direct manufacturing labor	$24.00 per hour	$25.00 per hour

The inventoriable unit cost for ending finished goods inventory on December 31, 2003, is $374.80. Assume Slopes uses a FIFO inventory method for both direct materials and finished goods. Ignore work in process in your calculations.

Budgeted balances at December 31, 2004, in the selected accounts are

Cash	$ 10,000
Property, plant, and equipment (net)	850,000
Current liabilities	17,000
Long-term liabilities	178,000
Stockholders' equity	800,000

Required

1. Prepare the 2004 revenues budget (in dollars).
2. Prepare the 2004 production budget (in units).
3. Prepare the direct materials usage and purchases budgets.
4. Prepare a direct manufacturing labor budget.
5. Prepare a manufacturing overhead budget.
6. What is the budgeted manufacturing overhead rate?
7. What is the budgeted manufacturing overhead cost per output unit?
8. Calculate the cost of a snowboard manufactured in 2004.
9. Prepare an ending inventory budget for both direct materials and finished goods.
10. Prepare a cost of goods sold budget.
11. Prepare the budgeted income statement for Slopes, Inc., for 2004.
12. Prepare the budgeted balance sheet for Slopes, Inc., for the year-end 2004.

6-35 Cash budgeting, chapter appendix. Retail outlets purchase snowboards from Slopes, Inc., throughout the year. However, in anticipation of late summer and early fall purchases, outlets ramp up inventories from May through August. Outlets are billed when boards are ordered. Invoices are payable within 60 days. From past experience, Slopes's accountant projects 20% of invoices are paid in the month invoiced, 50% are paid in the following month, and 30% of invoices are paid two months after the month of invoice. The average selling price per snowboard is $450.

To meet demand, Slopes increases production from April through July, because the snowboards are produced a month prior to their projected sale. Direct materials are purchased in the month of production and paid for during the following month (terms are payment in full within 30 days of the invoice date). During this period there is no production for inventory, and no materials are purchased for inventory.

Direct manufacturing labor and manufacturing overhead are paid monthly. Variable manufacturing overhead is incurred at the rate of $7 per direct manufacturing labor-hour. Variable marketing costs are driven by the number of sales visits. However, there are no sales visits during the months studied. Slopes, Inc., also incurs fixed manufacturing overhead costs of $5,500 per month and fixed nonmanufacturing overhead costs of $2,500 per month.

Projected Sales

May	80 units	August	100 units
June	120 units	September	60 units
July	200 units	October	40 units

Direct Materials and Direct Manufacturing Labor Utilization and Cost

	Units per Board	Price per Unit	Unit
Wood	5	$30	Board feet
Fiberglass	6	5	Yard
Direct manufacturing labor	5	25	Hour

The beginning cash balance for July 1, 2003, is $10,000. On September 1, 2003, Slopes had a cash crunch and borrowed $30,000 on a 6% one-year note with interest payable monthly. The note is due October 1, 2004. Using the information provided above, you must determine whether Slopes will be in a position to pay off this short-term debt on October 1, 2004.

Required

1. Prepare a cash budget for the months of July through September, 2004. Show supporting schedules for the calculation of receivables and payables.
2. Will Slopes be in a position to pay off the $30,000 one-year note on October 1, 2004? If not, what actions would you recommend to Slopes's management?
3. Suppose Slopes is interested in maintaining a minimum cash balance of $10,000. Will the company be able to maintain such a balance during all three months analyzed? If not, suggest a suitable cash management strategy.

6-36 Cash budget, fill in the blanks, chapter appendix. Starport manufactures and launches space stations. Use the following information to complete Starport's cash budget in Problem Exhibit 6-36 for the year ending December 31, 2004.

- Starport's CEO insists that Starport maintain a minimum monthly cash balance of $15 million.
- In the event of a cash deficiency, you are instructed to borrow exactly as much as is needed to return Starport to the minimum cash balance required. Short-term loans carry an interest rate of 12% per year, calculated from the beginning of the quarter in which the loan is initiated and through the end of the quarter in which the loan is repaid.

PROBLEM EXHIBIT 6-36 Cash Budget for Starport (in thousands)

For the Year Ended December 31, 2004

	Quarters				Year as a Whole
	I	II	III	IV	
Cash balance, beginning	$ 15,000	?	?	?	?
Add receipts					
Collections from customers	385,000	?	?	$365,000	$1,360,000
Total cash available for needs	?	$347,000	$310,000	?	?
Deduct disbursements					
Direct materials	175,000	125,000	?	155,000	?
Payroll	?	110,000	95,000	118,000	448,000
Other costs	50,000	45,000	40,000	49,000	?
Interest costs (bond)	?	?	?	?	?
Machinery purchase	0	?	0	0	85,000
Income taxes	15,000	14,000	12,000	?	61,000
Total disbursements	368,000	?	260,000	345,000	?
Minimum cash balance desired	?	?	?	?	15,000
Total cash needed	?	?	?	?	1,370,000
Cash excess (deficiency)	?	$(50,000)	?	?	$ 5,000
Financing					
Borrowing (at beginning)	$ 0	?	$ 0	0	?
Repayment (at end)	0	$ 0	0	$(50,000)	$ (50,000)
Interest (at 12% per annum)	0	0	0	(4,500)	(4,500)
Total effects of financing	$ 0	?	$ 0	$(54,500)	$ (4,500)
Cash balance, ending	$ 32,000	?	?	$ 15,500	?

- In the second quarter Starport makes a major investment in machinery amounting to $85 million.
- On January 1, 2002, Starport raised $100 million through the issue of a five-year 12% bond. Interest on this long-term debt is payable quarterly.

Required There is enough information available for you to complete Starport's cash budget. If you are unable to calculate any of the missing numbers, make an assumption and continue.

6-37 Cash budgeting, chapter appendix. On December 1, 2004, the Itami Wholesale Co. is attempting to project cash receipts and disbursements through January 31, 2005. On this latter date, a note will be payable in the amount of $100,000. This amount was borrowed in September to carry the company through the seasonal peak in November and December.

Selected general ledger balances on December 1 are

Cash	$ 10,000	
Accounts receivable	280,000	
Allowance for bad debts		$15,800
Inventory	87,500	
Accounts payable		92,000

Sales terms call for a 2% discount if payment is made within the first 10 days of the month after purchase, with the balance due by the end of the month after purchase. Experience has shown that 70% of the billings will be collected within the discount period, 20% by the end of the month after purchase, and 8% in the following month. The remaining 2% will be uncollectable. There are no cash sales.

The average selling price of the company's products is $100 per unit. Actual and projected sales are

October actual	$ 180,000
November actual	250,000
December estimated	300,000
January estimated	150,000
February estimated	120,000
Total estimated for year ended June 30, 2005	1,500,000

All purchases are payable within 15 days. Thus, approximately 50% of the purchases in a month are due and payable in the next month. The average unit purchase cost is $70. Target ending inventories are 500 units plus 25% of the next month's unit sales.

Total budgeted marketing, distribution, and customer-service costs for the year are $400,000. Of this amount, $150,000 are considered fixed (and includes depreciation of $30,000). The remainder vary with sales. Both fixed and variable marketing, distribution, and customer-service costs are paid as incurred.

Required Prepare a cash budget for December and January. Supply supporting schedules for collections of receivables; payments for merchandise; and marketing, distribution, and customer-service costs.

6-38 Comprehensive budget; fill in schedules. The following information is for Newport Stationery Store:

1. Balance sheet information as of September 30, 2004:

Current assets	
Cash	$ 12,000
Accounts receivable	10,000
Inventory	63,600
Equipment—net	100,000
Liabilities as of September 30	None

2. Recent and anticipated sales:

September	$40,000
October	48,000
November	60,000
December	80,000
January	36,000

3. Credit sales: Sales are 75% cash and 25% on credit. Assume that credit accounts are all collected within 30 days from sale. The accounts receivable on September 30 are the result of the credit sales for September (25% of $40,000).
4. Gross margin averages 30% of revenues. Newport treats cash discounts on purchases in the income statement as "other income."
5. Operating costs: Salaries and wages average 15% of monthly revenues; rent, 5%; other operating costs, excluding depreciation, 4 percent. Assume that these costs are disbursed each month. Depreciation is $1,000 per month.
6. Purchases: Newport keeps a minimum inventory of $30,000. The policy is to purchase each month additional inventory in the amount necessary to provide for the following month's sales. Terms on

purchases are 2/10, n/30. (Payments on purchases are to be made in 30 days; a 2% discount is available if the payment is made within 10 days after purchase.) Assume that payments are made in the month of purchase and that all discounts are taken.

7. Light fixtures: In October, $600 is spent for light fixtures, and in November, $400 is to be expended for this purpose. These amounts are to be capitalized.

Assume that a minimum cash balance of $8,000 must be maintained. Assume also that all borrowing is effective at the beginning of the month and all repayments are made at the end of the month of repayment. Loans are repaid when sufficient cash is available. Interest is paid only at the time of repaying principal. The interest rate is 18% per year. Management does not want to borrow any more cash than is necessary and wants to repay as soon as cash is available.

Required

On the basis of the preceding facts:

1. Complete Schedule A.

Schedule A
Budgeted Monthly Cash Receipts

Item	September	October	November	December
Total sales	$40,000	$48,000	$60,000	$80,000
Credit sales	10,000	12,000		
Cash sales				
Receipts:				
Cash sales		$36,000		
Collections on accounts receivable		10,000		
Total		$46,000		

2. Complete Schedule B. Note that purchases are 70% of next month's sales.

Schedule B
Budgeted Monthly Cash Disbursements for Purchases

Item	October	November	December	4th Quarter
Purchases	$42,000			
Deduct 2% cash discount	840			
Disbursements	$41,160			

3. Complete Schedule C.

Schedule C
Budgeted Monthly Cash Disbursements for Operating Costs

Item	October	November	December	4th Quarter
Salaries and wages	$ 7,200			
Rent	2,400			
Other cash operating costs	1,920			
Total	$11,520			

4. Complete Schedule D.

Schedule D
Budgeted Total Monthly Cash Disbursements

Item	October	November	December	4th Quarter
Purchases	$41,160			
Cash operating costs	11,520			
Light fixtures	600			
Total	$53,280			

5. Complete Schedule E.

Schedule E
Budgeted Cash Receipts and Disbursements

Item	October	November	December	4th Quarter
Receipts	$46,000			
Disbursement	53,280			
Net cash increase				
Net cash decrease	$7,280			

6. Complete Schedule F (assume that borrowings must be made in multiples of $1,000).

Schedule F
Financing Required

Item	October	November	December	Total
Beginning cash balance	$12,000			
Net cash increase				
Net cash decrease	7,280			
Cash position before borrowing	4,720			
Minimum cash balance required	8,000			
Excess/Deficiency	(3,280)			
Borrowing required	4,000			
Interest payments				
Borrowing repaid				
Ending cash balance	$ 8,720			

7. What do you think is the most logical type of loan needed by Newport? Explain your reasoning.
8. Prepare a budgeted income statement for the fourth quarter and a budgeted balance sheet as of December 31. Ignore income taxes.
9. Some simplifications have been included in this problem. What complicating factors might arise in a typical business situation?

6-39 Budgetary slack and ethics. (CMA) Marge Atkins, the budget manager at Norton Company, a manufacturer of infant furniture and carriages, is working on the budget for 2004. In discussions with Scott Ford, the sales manager, Atkins discovers that Ford's sales projections are lower than what Ford actually believes are achievable. When Atkins asks Ford about this, Ford says: "Well, we don't want to fall short of the sales projections, so we generally give ourselves a little breathing room by lowering the sales projections anywhere from 5 to 10 percent." Atkins also finds that Pete Granger, the production manager, makes similar adjustments. He pads budgeted costs, adding 10% to estimated costs.

Required As a management accountant, should Marge Atkins take the position that the behavior described by Scott Ford and Pete Granger is unethical? Refer to the Standards of Ethical Conduct for Management Accountants described in Chapter 1 (p. 18).

Collaborative Learning Problem

6-40 Comprehensive review of budgeting, cash budgeting, chapter appendix. Wilson Beverages bottles two soft drinks under license to Cadbury Schweppes at its Manchester plant. All inventory is in direct materials and finished goods at the end of each working day. There is no work-in-process inventory.

The two soft drinks bottled by Wilson Beverages are lemonade and diet lemonade. The syrup for both soft drinks is purchased from Cadbury Schweppes.

Wilson Beverages uses a lot size of 1,000 cases as the unit of analysis in its budgeting. (Each case contains 24 bottles.) Direct materials are expressed in terms of lots, in which one lot of direct materials is the input necessary to yield one lot (1,000 cases) of beverage. The following purchase prices are forecast for direct materials in 2005:

	Lemonade	Diet Lemonade
Syrup	$1,200 per lot	$1,100 per lot
Containers (bottles, caps, etc.)	$1,000 per lot	$1,000 per lot
Packaging	$ 800 per lot	$ 800 per lot

All direct material purchases are on account.

The two soft drinks are bottled using the same equipment. The only difference in the bottling process for the two soft drinks is the syrup.

Summary data used in developing budgets for 2005 are

1. Sales
- Lemonade, 1,080 lots at $9,000 selling price per lot
- Diet lemonade, 540 lots at $8,500 selling price per lot

All sales are on account.

2. Beginning (January 1, 2005) inventory of direct materials
- Syrup for lemonade, 80 lots at $1,100 purchase price per lot
- Syrup for diet lemonade, 70 lots at $1,000 purchase price per lot
- Containers, 200 lots at $950 purchase price per lot
- Packaging, 400 lots at $900 purchase price per lot

3. Beginning (January 1, 2005) inventory of finished goods
- Lemonade, 100 lots at $5,300 per lot
- Diet lemonade, 50 lots at $5,200 per lot

4. Target ending (December 31, 2005) inventory of direct materials
- Syrup for lemonade, 30 lots
- Syrup for diet lemonade, 20 lots
- Containers, 100 lots
- Packaging, 200 lots

5. Target ending (December 31, 2005) inventory of finished goods
- Lemonade, 20 lots
- Diet lemonade, 10 lots

6. Each lot requires 20 direct manufacturing labor-hours at the 2005 budgeted rate of $25 per hour. Direct manufacturning labor costs are paid at the end of each month.

7. Variable manufacturing overhead is forecast to be $600 per hour of bottling time; bottling time is the time the filling equipment is in operation. It takes two hours to bottle one lot of lemonade and two hours to bottle one lot of diet lemonade. Assume all variable manufacturing overhead costs are paid during the same month when incurred.

Fixed manufacturing overhead is forecast to be $1,200,000 for 2005. Included in the fixed manufacturing overhead forecast is $400,000 for depreciation. All manufacturing overhead costs are paid as incurred.

8. Hours of budgeted bottling time is the sole cost-allocation base for all fixed manufacturing overhead.

9. Administration costs are forecast to be 10% of the cost of goods manufactured for 2005. Marketing costs are forecast to be 12% of revenues for 2005. Distribution costs are forecast to be 8% of revenues for 2005. All these costs are paid during the month when incurred. Assume there are no depreciation or amortization expenses.

10. Budgeted beginning balances on January 1, 2005:

Accounts receivable (from sales)	$550,000
Accounts payable (for direct materials)	300,000
Cash	100,000

11. Budgeted ending balances on December 31, 2005:

Accounts receivable (from sales)	$600,000
Accounts payable (for direct materials)	400,000

12. Budgeted equipment purchase in May $1,350,000

13. Estimated income tax expense for 2005 $ 625,000

Required

Assume Wilson Beverages uses the first-in, first-out method for costing all inventories. On the basis of the preceding data, prepare the following budgets for 2005:

a. Revenues budget (in dollars)
b. Production budget (in units)
c. Direct materials usage budget (in units and dollars)
d. Direct materials purchases budget (in units and dollars)
e. Direct manufacturing labor budge
f. Manufacturing overhead costs budget
g. Ending finished goods inventory budget
h. Cost of goods sold budget
i. Marketing costs budget
j. Distribution costs budget
k. Administration costs budget
l. Budgeted income statement
m. Cash budget

CHAPTER 6 INTERNET EXERCISE

Budgeting is the most widely used accounting tool for planning and control organizations. Mark's Work Warehouse Ltd. provides a rare glimpse of budgeting and responsibility accounting in action. To take a look, go to www.prenhall.com/horngren, click on *Cost Accounting*, 11th ed., and access the Internet Exercise for Chapter 6.

CHAPTER 6 VIDEO CASE

RITZ-CARLTON HOTEL COMPANY: Budgets and Responsibility Accounting

"Ladies and gentlemen serving ladies and gentlemen." That's the motto of the Ritz-Carlton, based in Atlanta, Georgia, a region known for Southern hospitality and old-world elegance. It may seem a bit inelegant to talk about costs and budgets when referring to the activities of this hotel. Yet it is the attention given to these inelegant items that helps make it possible for the Ritz-Carlton to provides its elegance so successfully.

Each hotel's performance is the responsibility of the general manager and controller at each of 31 worldwide locations. Local forecasts and budgets are prepared annually and are the basis of subsequent performance evaluation. Preparation of the annual budget begins with the sales budgets, prepared by the hotel's sales director. Budgeted sources of revenue include hotel rooms; convention, wedding, and meeting facilities; merchandise; and food and beverage. The controller then seeks input from all employees, from maintenance staff to kitchen workers, about anticipated payroll changes, operating expenses, and planned events or promotions that might affect costs. Standard costs, based on cost per occupied room, are used to build the budget for guest room stays. Other standards are used for meeting rooms and food and beverage. After employee input is provided, the completed sales budget and annual operating budget are sent to corporate headquarters. From there, actual monthly performance against plan is monitored. Each Ritz-Carlton hotel is allowed a 5% variance in profitability goals each month and must provide explanations when targets are not met.

On the twenty-fifth of each month, budgets for the next three months are reviewed to be sure goals are still accurate. Accuracy can be critical for a business whose occupancy can fluctuate significantly from day to day, depending on group or company bookings, special events, or changes in local competition. The changes are communicated to corporate headquarters, with explanations of revisions provided as needed. Local hotel managers also meet daily to review performance to date, and they have the ability to adjust prices in the reservation system at any time to make sure profitability targets are met. Adjusting prices can be particularly important if a large group cancels at the last minute or if other unforeseen events cause occupancy to drop suddenly.

Meeting the monthly budgeted goals is primarily the responsibility of each hotel's controller. The controller at each location receives a monthly report from corporate headquarters that shows how all 31 hotels performed against their goals. Controllers compare their performance against their own budgets, as well as actual performance against the other Ritz-Carlton hotels. Ideas for boosting revenue and reducing costs are regularly shared among the company's controllers, who recognize the value of contributing to the entire organization's success, not just the success of their own hotels.

QUESTIONS

1. How would you expect the Ritz-Carlton Company to develop its standard costs per occupied room? How would these standards differ among locations?
2. The Ritz-Carlton recently started giving all employees at each of its hotels the chance to meet with their hotel's controller to review budgets and reports on actual performance, as a form of participatory budgeting. What advantages or disadvantages do you see with this approach?
3. How might the Ritz-Carlton use benchmarking within its own chain to improve efficiency?
4. What factors might affect the Ritz-Carlton's annual sales forecast for room occupancy, restaurants, and use of meeting rooms and conference facilities?
5. How is uncertainty handled in the budget process?
6. The Ritz-Carlton uses responsibility accounting for its worldwide hotel and resort operations. What levels of responsibility reports would you expect to see throughout the company?

CHAPTER 7

Flexible Budgets, Variances, and Management Control: I

LEARNING OBJECTIVES

1. Distinguish a static budget from a flexible budget
2. Develop flexible budgets and compute flexible-budget variances and sales-volume variances
3. Explain why standard costs are often used in variance analysis
4. Compute price variances and efficiency variances for direct-cost categories
5. Explain why purchasing performance measures should focus on more factors than just price variances
6. Integrate continuous improvement into variance analysis
7. Perform variance analysis in activity-based costing systems
8. Describe benchmarking and how it is used in cost management

www.prenhall.com/horngren

"Would you like fries with that?" is more than an inquiry about your food preferences. At McDonald's, it's part of a technique called "upselling," encouraging buyers to add items to their purchase, thereby generating more revenues for the company. More often than not, diners respond "yes," making more contributions to the restaurant's budgeted sales targets and profitability.

Behind the scenes, managers track these sales, as well as the costs associated with them. Standard food costs and labor costs are budgeted, and actual restaurant performance is compared against planned performance based on those budgeted costs. Any significant variances from the budget must be explained and addressed. If the actual sales volume of french fries differs from budgeted sales volume, the budgeted volume is adjusted to actual sales volume before examining costs. In this way, the budget is flexible, and managers can't simply use high sales volume to explain away high food costs or labor cost problems.

No cooking the books here!

Master the material in this chapter before moving on to the next chapter. Chapter 8 builds on concepts introduced here.

In Chapter 6, you saw how budgets assist managers in their function as planners. We now turn to how budgets—specifically flexible budgets—are used to evaluate feedback on variances, aiding managers in their control function. Feedback enables managers to compare actual results—that is, what is happening—with planned performance—what should have been happening according to plans. Flexible budgets and variances help managers gain insights into *why* the actual results differ from the planned performance. That "why" is what this chapter and the next are about.

THE USE OF VARIANCES

Each **variance** we compute is the difference between an amount based on an actual result and the corresponding budgeted amount—that is, the actual amount of something and the amount it was supposed to be according to the budget. The budgeted amount is a point of reference from which comparisons may be made.

Variances assist managers in their planning and control decisions. **Management by exception** is the practice of concentrating on areas not operating as expected (such as a shortfall in sales of a product) and giving less attention to areas operating as expected. Managers use information provided by variances to allocate their energies: They regularly pay more attention to areas with large variances. For example, assume the actual costs associated with scrap and rework at a Maytag appliances plant are well above the budgeted costs for scrap and rework. These variances will guide managers to seek explanations and to take early corrective action, ensuring that future operations result in less scrap and rework.

Variances are also used in performance evaluation. Production-line managers at Maytag may have quarterly efficiency incentives linked to achieving a budgeted amount of operating costs.

Sometimes variances suggest a change in strategy. Excessive defect rates for a new product may suggest a flawed product design. Executives may then want to reevaluate their product strategies.

STATIC BUDGETS AND FLEXIBLE BUDGETS

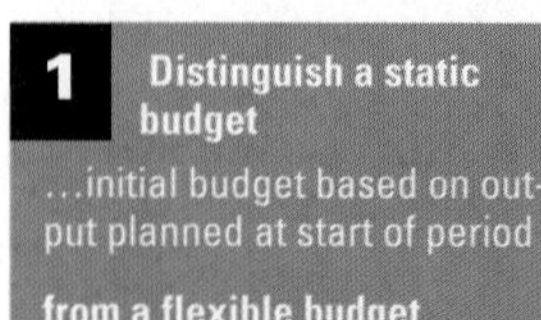

The *master budget,* or **static budget,** discussed in Chapter 6, is based on *the level of output planned at the start of the budget period.* The master budget for Stylistic Furniture is a static budget (pp. 180–187). It's static in the sense that the budget is developed for a single planned output level. When variances are computed from a static budget at the end of the period, adjustments are not made to the budgeted amounts for the actual output level in the budget period. In this chapter we emphasize flexible budgets.

A **flexible budget** calculates budgeted revenues and budgeted costs based on *the actual output level in the budget period.* A *flexible budget* is calculated at the end of the period when the actual output is known; a *static budget is developed at the start of the budget period based on the planned output level* for the period. As we show, a flexible budget enables managers to compute variances that provide more information than the information from variances in a static budget.

Budgets, both static and flexible, can differ in the level of detail they report. Companies present budgets with broad summary figures that can then be broken down into progressively more detailed figures via computer software programs. The level of detail increases in the number of line items examined in the income statement and the number of variances computed.

In this book, "level" followed by a number denotes the amount of detail shown by a variance analysis. Level 0 reports the least detail, Level 1 offers more information, and so on. We will use the example of Webb Company to illustrate static budgets and flexible budgets and their related variances.

Accounting System at Webb

Webb manufactures and sells a designer jacket that requires tailoring and many hand operations. Sales are made to distributors who sell to independent clothing stores and retail chains. Webb's only costs are manufacturing costs; it incurs no costs in other value chain functions such as marketing and distribution. We assume that all units manufactured in April 2003 are sold in April 2003. There are no beginning inventories or ending inventories. Webb has three variable-cost categories. The budgeted variable cost per jacket for each category is

Cost Category	Variable Cost per Jacket
Direct materials costs	$60
Direct manufacturing labor costs	16
Variable manufacturing overhead costs	12
Total variable costs	$88

The *number of units manufactured* is the cost driver for direct materials, direct manufacturing labor, and variable manufacturing overhead. The relevant range for the cost driver is from 0 to 12,000 jackets. The budgeted fixed manufacturing costs are $276,000 for production between 0 and 12,000 jackets. The budgeted selling price is $120 per jacket. This selling price is the same for all distributors. The static budget for April 2003 is based on selling 12,000 jackets. Actual sales for April 2003 were 10,000 jackets. Exhibit 7-1, column 3, presents the static budget for Webb Company for April 2003.

STATIC-BUDGET VARIANCES

A **static-budget variance** is the difference between an actual result and the corresponding budgeted amount in the static budget. Exhibit 7-1 shows the Level 0 and Level 1 variance analyses for April 2003. Level 0 gives the least detailed comparison of the actual and budgeted operating income.

A **favorable variance**—denoted F in this book—has the effect of increasing operating income relative to the budgeted amount. For revenue items, F means actual revenues exceed budgeted revenues. For cost items, F means actual costs are less than budgeted costs. An **unfavorable variance**—denoted U in this book—has the effect of decreasing operating income relative to the budgeted amount. Unfavorable variances are also called *adverse variances* in some countries, for example, the United Kingdom.

The unfavorable variance of $93,100 in Exhibit 7-1 for Level 0 is simply the result of subtracting the static-budget operating income ofh $108,000 from the actual operating income of $14,900:

$$\begin{aligned}\text{Static-budget variance for operating income} &= \text{Actual result} - \text{Static-budget amount}\\ &= \$14{,}900 - \$108{,}000\\ &= -\$93{,}100\text{, or }\$93{,}100\text{ U}\end{aligned}$$

Level 1 analysis in Exhibit 7-1 provides managers with more detailed information on the static-budget variance for operating income of $93,100 U. The additional information

EXHIBIT 7-1

Static-Budget-Based Variance Analysis for Webb Company for April 2003[a]

LEVEL 0 ANALYSIS

Actual operating income	$ 14,900
Budgeted operating income	108,000
Static-budget variance for operating income	$ 93,100 U

LEVEL 1 ANALYSIS

	Actual Results (1)	Static-Budget Variances (2) = (1) − (3)	Static Budget (3)
Units sold	10,000	2,000 U	12,000
Revenues	$1,250,000	$190,000 U	$1,440,000
Variable costs			
Direct materials	621,600	98,400 F	720,000
Direct manufacturing labor	198,000	6,000 U	192,000
Variable manufacturing overhead	130,500	13,500 F	144,000
Total variable costs	950,100	105,900 F	1,056,000
Contribution margin	299,900[b]	84,100 U	384,000[c]
Fixed costs	285,000	9,000 U	276,000
Operating income	$ 14,900	$ 93,100 U	$ 108,000

$93,100 U
Static-budget variance

[a]F = favorable effect on operating income; U = unfavorable effect on operating income.
[b]Contribution margin percentage = $299,900 ÷ $1,250,000 = 24.0%
[c]Contribution margin percentage = $384,000 ÷ $1,440,000 = 26.7%

added in Level 1 indicates how each of the line items of operating income—revenues, individual variable costs, and fixed costs—add up to the static-budget variance of $93,100. The budgeted contribution margin percentage of 26.7% decreases to 24.0% for the actual results.

Although Level 1 analysis provides more information than Level 0 analysis, managers often desire still more detail about the causes of variances. That's when a flexible budget helps.

2 Develop flexible budgets
...proportionately increase variable costs; keep fixed costs the same

and compute flexible-budget variances
...difference between actual result and flexible budget amount

and sales-volume variances
...difference between flexible-budget amount and static-budget amount

STEPS IN DEVELOPING A FLEXIBLE BUDGET

The flexible budget is prepared at the end of the period (April 2003) after the actual output level of 10,000 jackets is known. The flexible budget is the budget that Webb would have prepared at the start of the budget period had it correctly forecast the actual output level of 10,000 jackets. In preparing the flexible budget:

1. The budgeted selling price is the same $120 per jacket used in preparing the static budget.
2. The budgeted variable costs are the same $88 per jacket used in the static budget.
3. The budgeted fixed costs are the same static budget amount of $276,000 (because the 10,000 jackets produced falls within the relevant range of 0 to 12,000 jackets for which fixed costs are $276,000).

The *only* difference between the static budget and the flexible budget is that the static budget is prepared for the planned output of 12,000 jackets, whereas the flexible budget is based on the actual output of 10,000 jackets: The static budget is being "flexed" or adapted from 12,000 jackets to 10,000 jackets. In preparing the flexible budget for 10,000 jackets, all costs are assumed to be either variable or fixed with respect to the number of jackets produced.

Webb develops its flexible budget in three steps.

Step 1: **Identify the Actual Quantity of Output.** In April 2003, Webb produced and sold 10,000 jackets.

Step 2: Calculate the Flexible Budget for Revenues Based on Budgeted Selling Price and Actual Quantity of Output.

$$\text{Flexible-budget revenues} = \$120 \text{ per jacket} \times 10{,}000 \text{ jackets} = \$1{,}200{,}000$$

Step 3: Calculate the Flexible Budget for Costs Based on Budgeted Variable Cost per Output Unit, Actual Quantity of Output, and Budgeted Fixed Costs.

Flexible-budget variable costs	
Direct materials, \$60 per jacket × 10,000 jackets	\$ 600,000
Direct manufacturing labor, \$16 per jacket × 10,000 jackets	160,000
Variable manufacturing overhead, \$12 per jacket × 10,000 jackets	120,000
Total flexible-budget variable costs	880,000
Flexible-budget fixed costs	276,000
Flexible-budget total costs	\$1,156,000

Question: If the flexible budget (FB) is based on *actual output,* which isn't known until the end of the period, how can it be a *budget*?
Answer: The FB shows the costs that should have been incurred (the budgeted costs) to achieve the actual output level. The FB is the budget we would have made at the beginning of the period if we had perfectly predicted the actual output level.

These three steps enable Webb to prepare a flexible budget as shown in Exhibit 7-2, column 3. Webb uses the flexible budget to move to a Level 2 variance analysis that further subdivides the \$93,100 unfavorable static-budget variance for operating income.

FLEXIBLE-BUDGET VARIANCES AND SALES-VOLUME VARIANCES

Exhibit 7-2 shows the Level 2 flexible-budget-based variance analysis for Webb. The Level 2 variances subdivide the Level 1 \$93,100 unfavorable static-budget variance for operating income into two parts: a flexible-budget variance of \$29,100 U and a sales-volume variance of \$64,000 U.

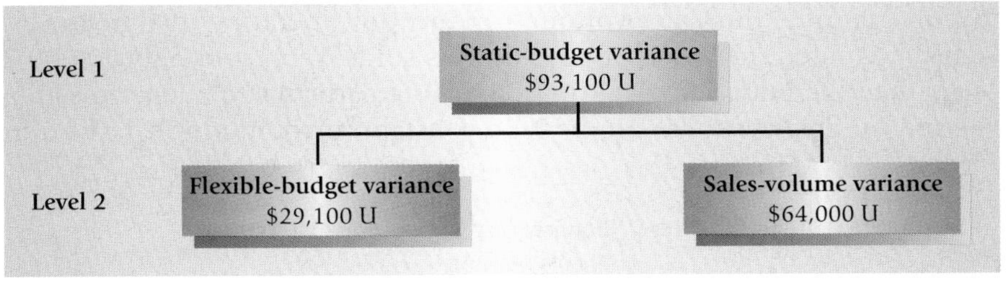

The levels of variance analysis can be likened to peeling an onion. With each deeper level of analysis, the manager peels away another layer, gaining further insight.

EXHIBIT 7-2 Level 2 Flexible-Budget-Based Variance Analysis for Webb Company for April 2003[a]

LEVEL 2 ANALYSIS

	Actual Results (1)	Flexible-Budget Variances (2) = (1) − (3)	Flexible Budget (3)	Sales-Volume Variances (4) = (3) − (5)	Static Budget (5)
Units sold	10,000	0	10,000	2,000 U	12,000
Revenues	\$1,250,000	\$50,000 F	\$1,200,000	\$240,000 U	\$1,440,000
Variable costs					
Direct materials	621,600	21,600 U	600,000	120,000 F	720,000
Direct manufacturing labor	198,000	38,000 U	160,000	32,000 F	192,000
Variable manufacturing overhead	130,500	10,500 U	120,000	24,000 F	144,000
Total variable costs	950,100	70,100 U	880,000	176,000 F	1,056,000
Contribution margin	299,900	20,100 U	320,000	64,000 U	384,000
Fixed costs	285,000	9,000 U	276,000	0	276,000
Operating income	\$ 14,900	\$29,100 U	\$ 44,000	\$ 64,000 U	\$ 108,000

\$29,100 U — Flexible-budget variance; \$ 64,000 U — Sales-volume variance

\$ 93,100 U — Static-budget variance

[a]F = favorable effect on operating income; U = unfavorable effect on operating income.

The **sales-volume variance** is the difference between a flexible-budget amount and the corresponding static-budget amount. The **flexible-budget variance** is the difference between an actual result and the corresponding flexible-budget amount based on the actual output level in the budget period.

What useful information comes from subdividing the static-budget variance into its two components? Remember, Webb actually produced and sold 10,000 jackets, although the static budget had anticipated an output of 12,000 jackets. *Managers would like to know how much of the static-budget variance is due to inaccurate forecasting of output units sold and how much of the static-budget variance is due to Webb's performance for 2003*. Creating a flexible budget makes it possible for managers to learn these two amounts.

Sales-Volume Variances

Keep in mind the flexible-budget amounts in column 3 of Exhibit 7-2 and the static-budget amounts in column 5 are both computed using budgeted selling prices, budgeted variable cost per jacket, and budgeted fixed costs. The only distinction is that the flexible-budget amount is calculated using the actual output level, whereas the static-budget amount is calculated using the budgeted output level. The difference between these two amounts is called the sales-volume variance because it represents the difference caused solely by the difference in the 10,000 actual quantity (or volume) of jackets sold and the 12,000 quantity of jackets expected to be sold in the static budget.

$$\begin{aligned}\text{Sales-volume variance for operating income} &= \text{Flexible-budget amount} - \text{Static-budget amount}\\ &= \$44{,}000 - \$108{,}000\\ &= -\$64{,}000, \text{ or } \$64{,}000\text{ U}\end{aligned}$$

In our Webb example, this sales-volume variance for operating income arises solely because of inaccurate forecasting of output units sold: Webb sold only 10,000 jackets, 2,000 fewer than the budgeted 12,000 jackets. Note particularly, budgeted selling price and budgeted variable cost per unit are held constant in computing sales-volume variances. Hence:

Sales-volume variances arise solely from the differences between the budgeted output level used to develop the static budget and the actual output level used to develop the flexible budget.

$$\begin{aligned}\text{Sales-volume variance for operating income} &= \left(\text{Budgeted selling price} - \text{Budgeted variable cost per unit}\right) \times \left(\text{Actual units sold} - \text{Static-budget units sold}\right)\\ &= (\$120\text{ per jacket} - \$88\text{ per jacket}) \times (10{,}000\text{ jackets} - 12{,}000\text{ jackets})\\ &= \$32\text{ per jacket} \times (-2{,}000\text{ jackets})\\ &= -\$64{,}000, \text{ or } \$64{,}000\text{ U}\end{aligned}$$

Webb's unfavorable sales-volume variance could be due to one or more of the following:

1. The overall demand for jackets is not growing at the rates that were anticipated.
2. Competitors are taking away market share from Webb.
3. Webb did not adapt quickly to changes in customer preferences and tastes.
4. Quality problems developed that led to customer dissatisfaction with Webb's jackets.
5. Budgeted sales targets were set without careful analysis of market conditions.

How Webb responds to the unfavorable sales-volume variance will be influenced by what is presumed to be the cause of the variance. For example, if Webb believes the variance was caused by market-related reasons (reasons 1 or 2), the sales manager would be in the best position to explain what happened and to suggest corrective actions, such as sales promotions, that may be needed. If however, the unfavorable variance was caused by quality problems, the manufacturing manager would be in the best position to analyze the causes and to suggest strategies for improvement, such as changes in the manufacturing process or investments in new machines.

Exhibit 7-2, column 4, shows a sales-volume variance for each of the line items in the income statement. Taking out the effects of inaccurate forecasting of output units sold—the sales-volume variance—from the static-budget variance enables managers to compare actual revenues and costs incurred for April 2003 against revenues and costs Webb would have budgeted for the 10,000 jackets actually produced and sold—the flexible budget. *These flexible-budget variances are a better measure of operating performance because they compare actual revenues to budgeted revenues and actual costs to budgeted costs for the same 10,000 jackets of output*. In contrast, the static-budget variance compares actual revenues and costs for 10,000 jackets against budgeted revenues and costs for 12,000 jackets.

Flexible-Budget Variances

The first three columns of Exhibit 7-2 compare actual results with flexible-budget amounts. Flexible-budget variances are in column 2 for each line item in the income statement:

$$\text{Flexible-budget variance} = \text{Actual results} - \text{Flexible-budget amount}$$

The operating income line in Exhibit 7-2 shows the flexible-budget variance is \$29,100 U (\$14,900 − \$44,000). The \$29,100 U arises because actual selling price, variable cost per unit, and fixed costs differ from their budgeted amounts. The actual and budgeted amounts for the selling price and variable cost per unit are

	Actual Amount	Budgeted Amount
Selling price	\$125.00 (\$1,250,000 ÷ 10,000 jackets)	\$120.00 (\$1,200,000 ÷ 10,000 jackets)
Variable cost per jacket	\$ 95.01 (\$ 950,100 ÷ 10,000 jackets)	\$ 88.00 (\$ 880,000 ÷ 10,000 jackets)

The flexible-budget variance for revenues is called the **selling-price variance** because it arises solely from differences between the actual selling price and the budgeted selling price:

$$\begin{aligned}\text{Selling-price variance} &= \left(\text{Actual selling price} - \text{Budgeted selling price}\right) \times \text{Actual units sold}\\ &= (\$125 \text{ per jacket} - \$120 \text{ per jacket}) \times 10,000 \text{ jackets}\\ &= \$50,000, \text{ or } \$50,000 \text{ F}\end{aligned}$$

Webb has a favorable selling-price variance because the \$125 actual selling price exceeds the \$120 budgeted amount, which increases operating income. Marketing managers are generally in the best position to understand and explain the reason for this selling price difference, for example, due to better workmanship or because of an overall increase in market prices.

The flexible-budget variance for variable costs is unfavorable for the actual output of 10,000 jackets. It's unfavorable because either (a) Webb used more quantities of inputs (such as direct manufacturing labor-hours) relative to the budgeted quantities of inputs, or (b) Webb incurred higher prices per unit for the inputs (such as the wage rate per direct manufacturing labor-hour) relative to the budgeted prices per unit for the inputs, or (c) both (a) and (b). Higher input quantities relative to the budget and/or higher input prices relative to the budget could be the result of Webb deciding to produce a superior product to what was planned in the budget, or the result of inefficiencies in Webb's manufacturing and purchasing, or both. *You should always think of variance analysis as providing suggestions for further investigation rather than as establishing conclusive evidence of good or bad performance*.

The actual fixed costs of \$285,000 are \$9,000 more than the budgeted amount of \$276,000. This higher fixed cost decreases operating income, making this flexible-budget variance unfavorable.

PRICE VARIANCES AND EFFICIENCY VARIANCES FOR DIRECT-COST INPUTS

We now illustrate how the Level 2 flexible-budget variance for direct-cost inputs can be further subdivided into two more detailed variances, which are Level 3 variances:

1. A price variance that reflects the difference between an actual input price and a budgeted input price

Managers generally have more control over efficiency variances than price variances. That's because the quantity of inputs used is primarily affected by factors *inside* the company, whereas price changes are primarily due to market forces *outside* the company.

2. An efficiency variance that reflects the difference between an actual input quantity and a budgeted input quantity

The information available from these Level 3 variances helps managers better understand past performance and better plan for future performance.

Obtaining Budgeted Input Prices and Budgeted Input Quantities

To calculate price and efficiency variances, Webb needs to obtain budgeted input prices and budgeted input quantities. Webb's three main sources of information are

1. Actual input data from past periods. Most companies have past data on actual input prices and actual input quantities. These past prices and quantities could be used as the budgeted prices and quantities in a flexible budget. Past data are typically available at low cost. Nevertheless, there are limitations to using this source of data: (i) past data can include inefficiencies, and (ii) past data do not incorporate any expected changes for the budget period.

2. Data from other companies that have similar processes. The main limitation of using this source is that input price and input quantity data from other companies may not be available.

3 **Explain why standard costs are often used in variance analysis**

...standard costs exclude past inefficiencies and take into account future changes

3. Standards developed by Webb. A **standard** is a carefully determined price, cost, or quantity. A standard is usually expressed on a per unit basis. Consider how Webb determines its standards. Using engineering studies, Webb conducts a detailed breakdown of the steps required to make a jacket. Each step is assigned a *standard* time based on work performed by a skilled operator using equipment operating in an efficient manner. There are two advantages of using standard times: (i) they aim to exclude past inefficiencies, and (ii) they aim to take into account changes expected to occur in the budget period. An example of (ii) is the leasing of new sewing machines that operate at a faster speed and enable output to be produced with lower defect rates. The standard manufacturing labor cost for each jacket is computed by multiplying the standard time allowed to produce a jacket by the standard wage rate that Webb expects to pay its operators. Similarly, Webb determines the standard quantity of square yards of cloth required by a skilled operator to make each jacket, the standard price per square yard of cloth, and (by multiplying them together) the standard direct material cost of a jacket.

Surveys show that more than 85% of responding U.S. companies use standard costs.

The term "standard" refers to many different things. Always clarify its meaning and how it is being used. A **standard input** is a carefully determined quantity of input—such as square yards of cloth or direct manufacturing labor-hours—required for one unit of output, such as a jacket. A **standard price** is a carefully determined price that a company expects to pay for a unit of input. In the Webb example, the standard wage rate is an example of a standard price of a direct manufacturing labor-hour. A **standard cost** is a carefully determined cost of a unit of output—for example the standard direct manufacturing labor cost of a jacket at Webb.

$$\text{Standard cost per jacket for each variable direct-cost input} = \text{Standard input allowed for one output unit} \times \text{Standard price per input unit}$$

Standard direct material cost per jacket: 2 square yards of cloth input allowed per output unit (jacket) manufactured, at $30 standard price per square yard

$$\text{Standard direct material cost per jacket} = 2 \text{ square yards} \times \$30 \text{ per square yard} = \$60$$

Standard direct manufacturing labor cost per jacket: 0.8 manufacturing labor-hour of input allowed per output unit manufactured, at $20 standard price per hour.

$$\text{Standard direct manufacturing labor cost per jacket} = 0.8 \text{ hour} \times \$20 \text{ per hour} = \$16$$

How are the words "budget" and "standard" related? Budget is the broader term. As the description above indicates, budgeted input prices, budgeted input quantities, and budgeted costs need not be based on standards. However, when standards are used to obtain budgeted input quantities and budgeted input prices, the terms "standard" and "budget" mean the same thing and are used interchangeably. The standard quantity of each input per unit of output and the standard price of each input determine the standard, or budgeted, cost of each input per unit of output. See how the standard cost computations for direct materials and direct manufacturing labor equal the budgeted direct

SURVEYS OF COMPANY PRACTICE

The Widespread Use of Standard Costs

Surveys of company practice across the globe report widespread use of standard costs by manufacturers. The following data are representative of surveys conducted in five countries:

	Percentage of Respondents Using Standard Costs in Their Accounting System
United States[a]	86
Ireland[b]	85
United Kingdom[c]	76
Sweden[d]	73
Japan[e]	65

What explains the popularity of standard costs? Companies based in four countries report the following reasons for using standard costs (1, most important; 4, least important):[f]

	United States	Canada	Japan	United Kingdom
Cost management	1	1	1	2
Pricing decisions	2	3	2	1
Budgetary planning and control	3	2	3	3
Financial statement preparation	4	4	4	4

The materials price and efficiency variances discussed in this chapter illustrate the use of standard costs in promoting cost management.

[a]Cornick, Cooper, and Wilson, "How Do Companies."
[b]Clarke and Brisbane, "An Investigation into."
[c]Drury, Braund, Osborne, and Tayles, "A Survey."
[d]Ask and Ax, "A Survey of."
[e]Scarbrough, Nanni, and Sakurai, "Japanese Management."
[f]Inoue, "A Comparative Study." [g]Gosselin, "Performance Measurement."
Full citations are in Appendix A at the end of the book.

material cost per jacket of $60 and the budgeted direct manufacturing labor cost of $16 referred to earlier in this chapter (p. 217).

In its standard costing system, Webb uses standards that are attainable through efficient operations but allow for normal disruptions. Some companies use ideal standards or theoretical standards that assume peak operating conditions with no machine breakdowns and no defective production. Obviously, these kinds of standards are difficult to achieve. As we discussed in Chapter 6, setting difficult standards increases worker frustration and hurts motivation and performance. The Surveys of Company Practice above describes the widespread use of standard costs.

4 Compute price variances ...difference between actual input price and budgeted input price **and efficiency variances** ...difference between actual input quantity and budgeted input quantity for actual output **for direct-cost categories**

Data for Calculating Webb's Price Variances and Efficiency Variances

Consider Webb's two direct-cost categories. The actual cost for each of these categories for the 10,000 jackets manufactured and sold in April 2003 is

Direct material purchased and used

1. Square yards of cloth input purchased and used	22,200
2. Actual price incurred per square yard	$28
3. Direct material costs (1 × 2) [Exhibit 7-2, column 1]	$ 621,600

Direct manufacturing labor

1. Direct manufacturing labor-hours	9,000
2. Actual price incurred per direct manufacturing labor-hour	$22
3. Direct manufacturing labor costs (1 × 2) [Exhibit 7-2, column 1]	$198,000

For simplicity, we assume the quantity of direct material used equals the quantity of direct material purchased. Let's use this Webb Company data to illustrate the price variance and the efficiency variance.

A **price variance** is the difference between the actual price and the budgeted price multiplied by the actual quantity of input, such as direct material purchased or used. A price variances is sometimes called an **input-price variance** or **rate variance,** especially when referring to a price variance for direct labor. An **efficiency variance** is the difference between the actual quantity of input used—such as square yards of cloth of direct materials—and the budgeted quantity of input that should have been used to produce the actual output, multiplied by the budgeted price. An efficiency variance is sometimes called a **usage variance.**

We use a columnar solution format as a helpful and intuitive approach to compute variances. Examples: Exhibits 7-3 and 7-6.

Exhibit 7-3 shows how the price variance and the efficiency variance subdivide the flexible-budget variance. Consider the panel for direct materials. The direct material flexible-budget variance of $21,600 U is the difference between the actual costs incurred (actual input quantity × actual price) shown in column 1 and the flexible budget (budgeted input quantity allowed for actual output × budgeted price) shown in column 3. Column 2 (actual input quantity × budgeted price) is inserted between column 1 and column 3. The difference between columns 1 and 2 is the price variance of $44,400 F because the same actual input quantity is multiplied by the *actual price* in column 1 and the *budgeted price* in column 2. The difference between columns 2 and 3 is the efficiency variance of $66,000 U because the same budgeted price is multiplied by the *actual input quantity* in column 2 and the *budgeted input quantity allowed for actual output* in column 3. See how the direct material price variance, $44,400 F, plus the direct material efficiency variance, $66,000 U, equals the direct material flexible-budget variance, $21,600 U. We next discuss the price variances and the efficiency variances in greater detail.

Price Variances

The formula for computing the price variance is

$$\text{Price variance} = \left(\text{Actual price of input} - \text{Budgeted price of input}\right) \times \text{Actual quantity of input}$$

EXHIBIT 7-3 **Columnar Presentation of Variance Analysis: Direct Costs for Webb Company for April 2003**[a]

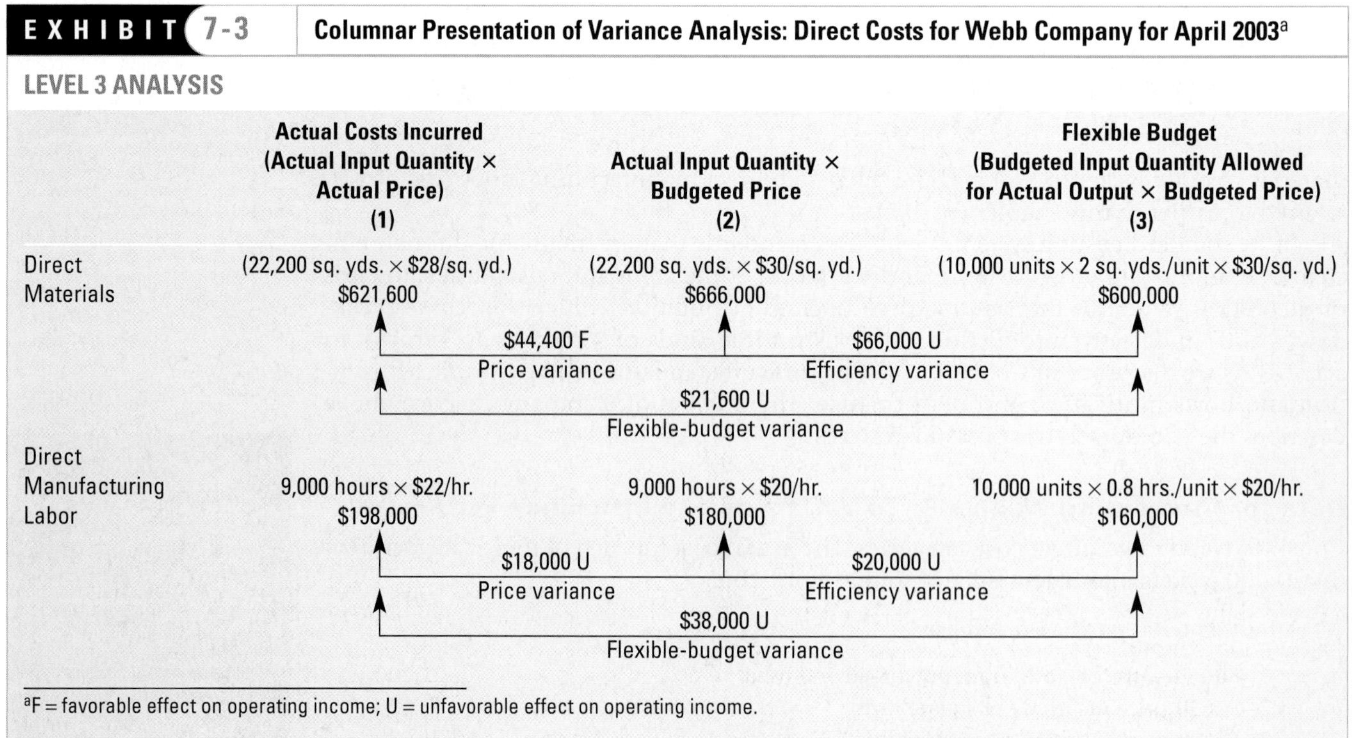

[a]F = favorable effect on operating income; U = unfavorable effect on operating income.

Price variances for Webb's two direct-cost categories are

Direct-Cost Category	(Actual price of input − Budgeted price of input)	×	Actual quantity of input	=	Price Variance
Direct material	($28 per sq. yard − $30 per sq. yard)	×	22,200 square yards	=	$44,400 F
Direct manufacturing labor	($22 per hour − $20 per hour)	×	9,000 hours	=	18,000 U
					$26,400 F

Always consider a broad range of possible causes for a price variance. For example, Webb's favorable direct material price variance could be due to one or more of the following:

- Webb's purchasing manager negotiated the direct material price more skillfully than was planned for in the budget.
- The purchasing manager changed to a lower-price supplier.
- Webb's purchasing manager bought in larger quantities than the quantities budgeted, thereby obtaining quantity discounts.
- Direct material prices decreased unexpectedly due to, say, industry oversupply.
- Budgeted purchase prices for direct material were set without careful analysis of market conditions.
- The purchasing manager received unfavorable terms on factors other than price (such as lower quality material).

How Webb responds to a material price variance will be vitally affected by what is presumed to be the cause of the variance. Assume Webb's managers attribute the favorable variance to the purchasing manager ordering in larger quantities than budgeted, thereby receiving quantity discounts. Webb could examine if purchasing in these larger quantities resulted in higher storage costs. If the increase in storage and inventory holding costs exceeds the quantity discounts, purchasing in larger quantities is not beneficial. For this reason, some companies have reduced their materials storage to prevent their purchasing managers from ordering in larger quantities.

Efficiency Variance

For any actual level of output, the *efficiency variance* is the difference between the input that was actually used and the input that should have been used to produce the actual output, holding input price constant at the budgeted price:

$$\text{Efficiency variance} = \left(\begin{array}{c}\text{Actual}\\ \text{quantity of}\\ \text{input}\end{array} - \begin{array}{c}\text{Budgeted quantity}\\ \text{of input allowed}\\ \text{for actual output}\end{array}\right) \times \begin{array}{c}\text{Budgeted price}\\ \text{of input}\end{array}$$

The idea here is that a company is inefficient if it uses a larger quantity of input than the budgeted quantity for the actual output units produced; the company is efficient if it uses fewer inputs than budgeted for the actual output units produced.

The efficiency variances for each of Webb's direct-cost categories are

Direct-Cost Category	(Actual quantity of input − Budgeted quantity of input allowed for actual output)	× Budgeted price of input	= Efficiency Variance
Direct material	[22,200 sq. yds. − (10,000 units × 2 sq. yds. unit)]	× $30 per sq. yard	
	= (22,200 sq. yds. − 20,000 sq. yds.)	× $30 per sq. yard	= $66,000 U
Direct manuf. labor	[9,000 hours − (10,000 units × 0.8 hour/unit)]	× $20 per hour	
	= (9,000 hours − 8,000 hours)	× $20 per hour	= 20,000 U
			$86,000 U

The flexible budget for inputs is based on the *budgeted quantity of inputs allowed for actual output level (BQIA)*. To understand BQIA in the Webb example, distinguish *inputs* (square yards of cloth, direct manufacturing labor-hours) from *output* (jackets). BQIA is computed by multiplying the actual quantity of output produced times how much of each input should have been used per output unit.

The two manufacturing efficiency variances—direct material efficiency variance and direct manufacturing labor efficiency variance—are unfavorable because more input was used than was budgeted, resulting in a decrease in operating income.

As with price variances, there is a broad range of possible causes for these efficiency variances (see also Concepts in Action, p. 226). For example, Webb's unfavorable efficiency variance for direct manufacturing labor could be due to one or more of the following:

CONCEPTS IN ACTION

Comparing Efficiency Variances and Yield Improvements at Analog Devices

Analog Devices, Inc., (ADI) produces integrated circuits and systems used in computer disc drives, medical instruments, and consumer electronics. To be successful, ADI must deliver high-quality products to its customers on time and at low cost. To control cost, ADI must improve yield—the quantity of good die produced on a silicon wafer divided by the total number of die that could be printed and produced on the wafer.

ADI's cost system tracks costs by major production cost centers. Each production cost center classifies costs into direct materials, direct labor, and fixed indirect costs. ADI uses a standard-costing system and has standard costs for each of the products it produces. Each month, ADI calculates price and efficiency variances for materials, and efficiency and rate variances for labor. Preparing a flexible budget is key to isolating these variances.

Most operating managers at ADI pay more attention to physical yields than the direct materials efficiency variance computations. They believe that a higher yield is a more direct measure of their performance and that if they improve yield, efficiency gains will follow. Indeed, in most periods, higher yields are associated with favorable direct materials efficiency variances.

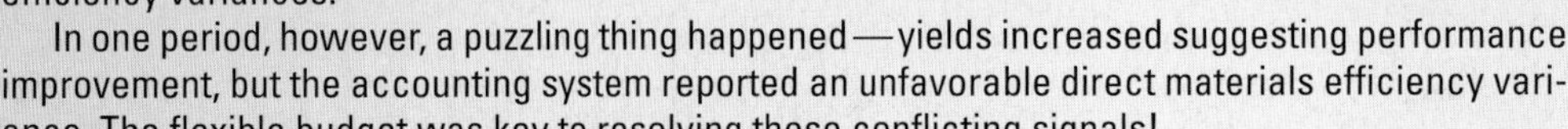

In one period, however, a puzzling thing happened—yields increased suggesting performance improvement, but the accounting system reported an unfavorable direct materials efficiency variance. The flexible budget was key to resolving these conflicting signals!

In the period in question, ADI had begun producing high-volume standardized products in place of the low-volume, nonstandardized products it previously produced. Standardized products are easier to manufacture and have higher yields than nonstandardized products, so it's not surprising that yields improved, but did performance improve? To find out, ADI looked at the actual quantity of wafers started and compared it to the flexible budget—the budgeted quantity of wafers allowed for the actual quantity of standardized product produced. ADI discovered that it actually started more wafers than the flexible-budget amount, resulting in the unfavorable direct materials efficiency variance. Performance was weak because, although yield increased, it did not increase as much as it should have for the actual quantity and type of output produced.

Source: Analog Devices: The Half-Life System, Harvard Business School case number 9-190-061 and discussions with company management.

- Webb's personnel manager hired underskilled workers.
- Webb's production scheduler inefficiently scheduled work, resulting in more manufacturing labor time than budgeted being used per jacket.
- Webb's Maintenance Department did not properly maintain machines, resulting in more manufacturing labor time than budgeted being used per jacket.
- Budgeted time standards were set too tight without careful analysis of the operating conditions and the employees' skills.

Suppose Webb's managers determine that the unfavorable variance is due to poor machine maintenance. Webb may then have a team consisting of plant engineers and machine operators develop a future maintenance schedule so that there will be fewer breakdowns adversely affecting labor time and product quality.

Summary of Variances

Exhibit 7-4 is a summary of the Level 1, 2, and 3 variances. Note how the variances in Level 3 aggregate to the variances in Level 2 and how the variances in Level 2 aggregate to the variances in Level 1.

The variances show why actual operating income is $14,900 when the static budget operating income is $108,000. Recall, a favorable variance has the effect of increasing

We will continue with the data in the Webb Company illustration with one change: During April 2003, Webb purchases 25,000 square yards of cloth. Recall, the actual quantity used is 22,200 square yards, and the standard quantity allowed for the 10,000 jackets of actual output manufactured at 2 square yards per jacket is 20,000 square yards. The actual purchase price is $28 per square yard, and the standard price is $30.

Note, in each of the following entries, unfavorable variances are always debits (they decrease operating income), and favorable variances are always credits (they increase operating income).

Journal Entry 1a: Isolate the direct materials price variance at the time of purchase by debiting Materials Control at standard prices. This is the earliest time possible to isolate this variance.

1a. Materials Control		
(25,000 square yards × $30 per square yard)	750,000	
Direct Materials Price Variance		
(25,000 square yards × $2 per square yard)		50,000
Accounts Payable Control		
(25,000 square yards × $28 per square yard)		700,000
To record direct materials purchased.		

Unfavorable variances reduce operating income, so they're debits, like expenses. Favorable variances increase operating income, so they're credits, like revenues (or contra-expenses).

Journal Entry 1b: Isolate the direct materials efficiency variance at the time the direct materials are used by debiting Work-in-Process Control at standard quantities allowed for actual output units manufactured times standard prices.

1b. Work-in-Process Control		
(10,000 jackets × 2 yards per jacket × $30 per square yard)	600,000	
Direct Materials Efficiency Variance		
(2,200 square yards × $30 per square yard)	66,000	
Materials Control		
(22,200 square yards × $30 per square yard)		666,000
To record direct materials used.		

Journal Entry 2: Isolate the direct manufacturing labor price and efficiency variances at the time this labor is used by debiting Work-in-Process Control at standard quantities allowed for actual output units manufactured at standard prices. Note, Wages Payable Control measures the payroll liability and, hence, is always at actual wage rates.

2. Work-in-Process Control		
(10,000 jackets × 0.80 hour per jacket × $20 per hour)	160,000	
Direct Manufacturing Labor Price Variance		
(9,000 hours × $2 per hour)	18,000	
Direct Manufacturing Labor Efficiency Variance		
(1,000 hours × $20 per hour)	20,000	
Wages Payable Control		
(9,000 hours × $22 per hour)		198,000
To record liability for direct manufacturing labor costs.		

Unlike materials, labor cannot be stored for future use, so there is only one entry for both the purchase and use of direct manufacturing labor.

From the preceding section, you know about the performance evaluation, learning, and continuous improvement advantages of standard costing systems. The journal entries here point to another advantage of standard costing systems—standard costs simplify product costing. As each unit is manufactured, costs are assigned to it using the standard cost of direct materials, the standard cost of direct manufacturing labor and, as you will see in Chapter 8, standard overhead cost. Actual costs do not have to be tracked for product costing purposes.

Recall from Chapter 4 that under both actual costing and normal costing, direct materials and direct manufacturing labor are calculated at actual costs.

From the perspective of control, all variances are isolated at the earliest possible time. For example, by isolating the direct materials price variance at the time of purchase, corrective actions—such as seeking cost reductions from the current supplier or obtaining price quotes from other potential suppliers—can be taken immediately when a large unfavorable variance is first known rather than waiting until after the materials are used in production.

At the end of each year, the variance accounts are either written off to cost of goods sold if immaterial in amount or prorated between cost of goods sold and various inventory accounts using the methods described in Chapter 4 (pp. 114 – 118). For example, the Direct Materials Price Variance is prorated between Materials Control, Work-in-Process Control, Finished Goods Control and Cost of Goods Sold on the basis of the standard costs of direct materials in each account's ending balance. The Direct Materials Efficiency Variance is prorated among Work-in-Process Control, Finished Goods Control and Cost of Goods Sold on the basis of the direct material costs in each account's ending balance (after proration of the direct materials price variance).

Standard Costing and Information Technology

Modern information technology greatly facilitates the use of standard costing systems for product costing and control. A company's standard prices and standard quantities are stored in its computer systems. A bar code scanner records the receipt of materials, immediately costing each material using its stored standard price. The receipt of materials is matched with the purchase order to record Accounts Payable and to isolate the direct materials price variance.

As output is completed, the standard quantity of direct materials that should have been used is computed and compared with the computerized request for direct materials submitted by an operator on the production floor. This difference multiplied by the standard direct material price is the direct materials efficiency variance. Labor variances are calculated as employees log into production floor terminals and punch in their employee numbers, start and end times, and the quantity of product they helped produce. Managers use this instantaneous feedback on variances to initiate immediate corrective action, as needed.

Wide Applicability of Standard Costing Systems

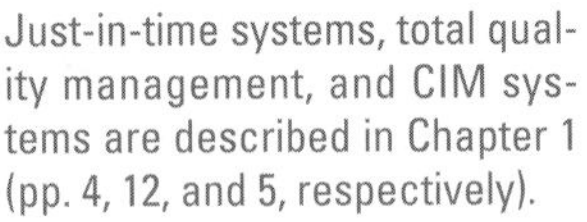
Just-in-time systems, total quality management, and CIM systems are described in Chapter 1 (pp. 4, 12, and 5, respectively).

Companies that have implemented just-in-time systems, total quality management, and computer-integrated manufacture (CIM) systems, as well as companies in the service sector, find standard costing to be a useful tool. It provides valuable information for the management and control of materials, labor, and other activities related to production. Companies implementing total quality management programs use standard costing to control materials costs. Service-sector companies are labor intensive and use standard costs to control labor costs. Companies implementing CIM use flexible budgeting and standard costing to manage activities such as materials handling and setups.

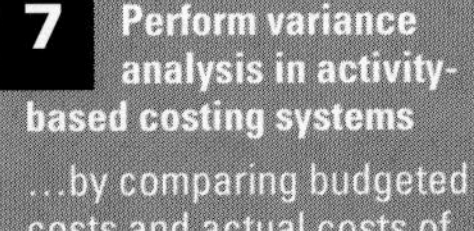
7 Perform variance analysis in activity-based costing systems

...by comparing budgeted costs and actual costs of activities

Because many companies use ABC, knowing how to compute variances arising in those systems is important.

FLEXIBLE BUDGETING AND ACTIVITY-BASED COSTING

Activity-based costing (ABC) systems focus on individual activities as the fundamental cost objects. ABC systems classify the costs of various activities into a cost hierarchy — output unit-level costs, batch-level costs, product-sustaining costs, and facility-sustaining costs (see pp. 143 – 144). Webb's two direct-cost categories — direct material costs and direct manufacturing labor costs — are examples of output unit-level costs. In this section, we show how the basic principles and concepts of flexible budgets and variance analysis can be applied to other levels of the cost hierarchy. We focus on batch-level costs. Batch-level costs are the costs of activities related to a group of units of products or services rather than to each individual unit of product or service.

Relating Batch Costs to Product Output

Consider Lyco Brass Works, which manufactures Jacutaps, a line of decorative brass faucets for home spas. Lyco produces Jacutaps in batches. For each product line, Lyco dedicates material-handling labor to bring materials to the manufacturing area, transport work in process from one work center to the next, and take the finished product to the shipping area. Hence, material-handling labor costs for Jacutaps are direct costs of Jacutaps. Because the materials for a batch are moved together, material-handling labor costs vary with the number of batches rather than with the number of units in a batch. Material-handling labor costs are variable direct batch-level costs.

Information regarding Jacutaps for 2004 follows:

	Static-Budget Amounts	Actual Amounts
1. Units of Jacutaps produced and sold	180,000	151,200
2. Batch size (units per batch)	150	140
3. Number of batches (Line 1 ÷ Line 2)	1,200	1,080
4. Material-handling labor-hours per batch	5	5.25
5. Total material-handling labor-hours (Line 3 × Line 4)	6,000	5,670
6. Cost per material-handling labor-hour	$14	$14.50
7. Total material-handling labor costs (Line 5 × Line 6)	$84,000	$82,215

To prepare the flexible budget for material-handling labor costs, Lyco starts with the actual units of output produced, 151,200 units, and proceeds in the following steps.

Step 1: Using Budgeted Batch Size, Calculate the Number of Batches That Should Have Been Used to Produce the Actual Output. At the budgeted batch size of 150 units per batch, Lyco should have produced the 151,200 units of output in 1,008 batches (151,200 units ÷ 150 units per batch).

Step 2: Using Budgeted Material-Handling Labor-Hours per Batch, Calculate the Number of Material-Handling Labor-Hours That Should Have Been Used. At the budgeted quantity of 5 hours per batch, 1,008 batches should have required 5,040 material-handling labor-hours (1,008 batches × 5 hours per batch).

Step 3: Using Budgeted Cost per Material-Handling Labor-Hour, Calculate the Flexible-Budget Amount for Material-Handling Labor-Hours. The flexible-budget amount is 5,040 material-handling labor-hours × $14 budgeted cost per material-handling labor-hour = $70,560.

Note how the flexible-budget calculations for material-handling costs focus on batch-level quantities (material-handling labor-hours) rather than on output unit-level amounts (such as material-handling labor-hours per unit of output). The flexible-budget variance for material-handling costs can then be calculated as:

$$\begin{aligned}\text{Flexible-budget variance} &= \text{Actual costs} - \text{Flexible-budget costs}\\ &= (5{,}670 \text{ hours} \times \$14.50 \text{ per hour}) - (5{,}040 \text{ hours} \times \$14 \text{ per hour})\\ &= \$82{,}215 - \$70{,}560\\ &= \$11{,}655, \text{ or } 11{,}655 \text{ U}\end{aligned}$$

The unfavorable variance indicates that material-handling labor costs were $11,655 higher than the flexible-budget target.

Price and Efficiency Variances

We can get some insight into the possible reasons for this $11,655 unfavorable variance by examining the price and efficiency components of the flexible-budget variance.

$$\begin{aligned}\text{Price variance} &= \left(\text{Actual price of input} - \text{Budgeted price of input}\right) \times \text{Actual quantity of input}\\ &= (\$14.50 \text{ per hour} - \$14 \text{ per hour}) \times 5{,}670 \text{ hours}\\ &= \$0.50 \text{ per hour} \times 5{,}670 \text{ hours}\\ &= \$2{,}835, \text{ or } \$2{,}835 \text{ U}\end{aligned}$$

The unfavorable price variance for material-handling labor indicates that the $14.50 actual cost per material-handling labor-hour exceeds the $14.00 budgeted cost per material-handling labor-hour. This variance could be due, for example, to (1) Lyco's human resources manager negotiating less skillfully than was planned in the budget and (2) wage rates increasing unexpectedly due to scarcity of labor.

$$\begin{aligned}\text{Efficiency variance} &= \left(\text{Actual quantity of input used} - \text{Budgeted quantity of input allowed for actual output}\right) \times \text{Budgeted price of input}\\ &= (5{,}670 \text{ hours} - 5{,}040 \text{ hours}) \times \$14 \text{ per hour}\\ &= 630 \text{ hours} \times \$14 \text{ per hour}\\ &= \$8{,}820, \text{ or } \$8{,}820 \text{ U}\end{aligned}$$

The unfavorable efficiency variance indicates that the 5,670 actual material-handling labor-hours exceeded the 5,040 material-handling labor-hours that Lyco should have used for the number of units it produced. Two reasons for the unfavorable efficiency variance are (1) smaller actual batch sizes of 140 units, instead of the budgeted batch sizes of 150 units, resulting in Lyco producing the 151,200 units in 1,080 batches instead of 1,008 (151,200 ÷ 150) batches; and (2) higher actual material-handling labor-hours per batch of 5.25 hours instead of budgeted material-handling labor-hours of 5 hours.

Reasons for smaller than budgeted batch sizes could include (1) quality problems, if batch sizes exceed 140 faucets, and (2) high costs of carrying inventory.

Reasons for larger actual material-handling labor-hours per batch could include (1) inefficient layout of the Jacutap production line relative to the layout proposed in the budget; (2) material-handling labor having to wait at work centers before picking up or delivering materials; (3) unmotivated, inexperienced, and underskilled employees; and (4) too tight standards for material-handling time.

Identifying the reasons for the efficiency variance helps Lyco's managers develop a plan for improving material-handling labor efficiency.

Focus on Hierarchy

The idea is to focus the flexible-budget quantity computations at the appropriate level of the cost hierarchy. For example, because material handling is a batch-level cost, the flexible-budget quantity calculations are made at the batch level—the quantity of material-handling labor-hours that Lyco should have used based on the number of batches it should have taken to produce the actual quantity of 151,200 units. If a cost had been a product-sustaining cost—such as product design cost—the flexible-budget quantity computations would focus at the product-sustaining level, for example, by evaluating the actual complexity of product design relative to the budget.

BENCHMARKING AND VARIANCE ANALYSIS

8 Describe benchmarking and how it is used in cost management

...compares actual performance against the best levels of performance

The budgeted amounts in the Webb Company and Lyco Brass Works illustrations are based on analysis of operations within their own respective companies. We now turn to the situation in which the budgeted amounts are based on an analysis of operations at other companies. **Benchmarking** is the continuous process of comparing the levels of performance in producing products and services and executing activities against the best levels of performance. The best levels of performance are commonly found in competing companies or in companies having similar processes.

Companies develop benchmarks and calculate variances on items that are the most important to their businesses. For example, McDonald's calculates average waiting-to-order time, order-delivery time, and window time for their drive-through lines.

We will examine United Airlines and eight other U.S. airlines to illustrate the use of benchmarks based on other companies. Knowledge of cost differences across airlines and of changes over time in these differences is important to planning and control decisions at United. Consider the unit cost per available seat mile (ASM) for United Airlines. Assume United uses data from each of eight competing airlines in its benchmark cost comparisons. Summary data are in Exhibit 7-5. The benchmark companies are ranked from lowest unit cost to highest unit cost per ASM in column 1. Also reported in Exhibit 7-5 are revenue per ASM, gross margin per ASM, labor cost per ASM, fuel cost per ASM, and total available seat miles (a measure of airline size).

Inferences about United's cost management are highly dependent on which specific benchmark is being used for comparison. United's actual cost of $0.1066 per ASM is $0.0004 higher than the average cost of $0.1062 per ASM of the eight other airlines. The magnitude of this difference is less than 0.5% of the average cost per ASM of the other airlines. This small difference implies United is similar, in cost competitiveness, to the average of these eight airlines. A very different, and less favorable, picture emerges if United compares itself solely to Southwest Airlines, the lowest-cost airline at $0.0772 per ASM. United's cost per ASM is $0.0294 higher ($0.1066 − $0.0772). This difference is 38% of Southwest's cost per ASM. Using this benchmark, United appears to have a much higher cost structure than the lowest-cost competitor.

Finding appropriate benchmarks is a major issue in implementing benchmarking. Many companies purchase benchmark data from consulting firms.

Using benchmarks such as those in Exhibit 7-5 is not without problems. For example, one problem is ensuring the benchmark numbers are comparable. That is, they need to be "apples to apples" comparisons. Differences can exist across companies in their strategies, inventory costing methods, depreciation methods, and so on. In our United example,

EXHIBIT 7-5 Available Seat Mile (ASM) Benchmark Comparison of United Airlines with Eight Other Airlines

Airline	Unit Cost per ASM (1)	Revenue per ASM (2)	Gross Margin per ASM (3) = (2) − (1)	Labor Cost per ASM (4)	Fuel Cost per ASM (5)	Total ASM (Millions) (6)
United Airlines	$0.1066	$0.1103	$0.0037	$0.0392	$0.0143	175,485
Airlines Used as Benchmarks:						
Southwest Airlines	$0.0772	$0.0943	$0.0171	$0.0281	$0.0134	59,910
America West Airlines	0.0862	0.0865	0.0003	0.0205	0.0138	27,112
Delta Airlines	0.0975	0.1080	0.0105	0.0385	0.0127	154,974
Northwest Airlines	0.1049	0.1104	0.0055	0.0349	0.0181	103,356
Continental Airlines	0.1070	0.1150	0.0080	0.0330	0.0167	86,100
American Airlines	0.1095	0.1178	0.0083	0.0405	0.0149	167,286
Alaska Airlines	0.1269	0.1257	(0.0012)	0.0413	0.0221	17,315
U.S. Airways	0.1400	0.1392	(0.0008)	0.0546	0.0193	66,574
Average of airlines used as benchmarks	$0.1062	$0.1121	$0.0060	$0.0364	$0.0164	85,328

Source: Individual companies' 10-K reports. All data are for the year ending December 31, 2000.

columns 4 and 5 report data for two of the costs included in the unit-cost comparisons: labor cost and fuel cost. On both these cost components, United has a higher cost than Southwest Airlines. For example, United's labor cost per ASM is 39.5% above Southwest's labor cost per ASM ($0.0392 compared with $0.0281). These benchmarking data highlight United's need for savings in labor costs as a big step in becoming more cost competitive with its lower-cost competitors.

The effect on costs of plane size and type, duration of flights, and so on, could also be considered. An analyst could also examine whether revenue differences per ASM across airlines are due to, say, differences in perceived quality of service or due to differences in monopoly power at specific airports. The analyst could further analyze the data to consider ways to improve performance via process changes. For example, the analyst could evaluate if performance could be improved by rerouting flights, using different types of aircraft on different routes, changing the composition of the flight crews, or changing the frequency or timing of specific flights.

Benchmark-type comparisons make clear that the management accountant must be able to direct attention to understanding "why" observed cost or revenue differences exist across companies. An analyst could examine whether airlines differ in their fixed costs and variable costs. Similarly, an analyst could determine whether airlines with higher cost per ASM are also able to generate higher revenue per ASM. Management accountants are more valuable to managers when they provide insight into *why* costs or revenues differ across companies, or within plants of the same company, as distinguished from simply reporting the magnitude of such differences.

PROBLEM FOR SELF-STUDY

O'Shea Company manufactures ceramic vases. It uses its standard costing system when developing its flexible-budget amounts. In April 2004, 2,000 finished units were produced. The following information is related to its two direct manufacturing cost categories: direct materials and direct manufacturing labor.

Direct materials used were 4,400 kilograms (kg). The standard direct materials input allowed for one output unit is 2 kg at $15 per kg. 5,000 kg of materials were purchased at $16.50 per kg, a total of $82,500.

Actual direct manufacturing labor-hours were 3,250 at a total cost of $66,300. Standard manufacturing labor time allowed is 1.5 hours per output unit, and the standard direct manufacturing labor cost is $20 per hour.

Continued

Required

1. Calculate the direct materials price variance and efficiency variance, and the direct manufacturing labor price variance and efficiency variance. The direct materials price variance will be based on a flexible budget for the actual quantity purchased, but the direct materials efficiency variance will be based on a flexible budget for the actual quantity used.
2. Prepare journal entries for a standard-costing system that isolates variances at the earliest possible time.

SOLUTION

1. Exhibit 7-6 shows how the columnar presentation of variances introduced in Exhibit 7-3 can be adjusted for the difference in timing between the purchase and use of materials. Note, in particular, the two sets of computations in column 2 for direct materials—the $90,000 for the direct materials purchased and the $66,000 for the direct materials used.
2. Materials Control

Materials Control (5,000 kg × $15 per kg)	75,000	
Direct Materials Price Variance (5,000 kg × $1.50 per kg)	7,500	
Accounts Payable Control (5,000 kg × $16.50 per kg)		82,500
Work in Process Control (2,000 units × 2 kg per unit × $15 per kg)	60,000	
Direct Materials Efficiency Variance (400 kg × $15 per kg)	6,000	
Materials Control (4,400 kg × $15 per kg)		66,000
Work in Process Control (2,000 units × 1.5 hours per unit × $20 per hour)	60,000	
Direct Manufacturing Labor Price Variance (3,250 hours × $0.40 per hour)	1,300	
Direct Manufacturing Labor Efficiency Variance (250 hours × $20 per hour)	5,000	
Wages Payable Control (3,250 hours × $20.40 per hour)		66,300

EXHIBIT 7-6 **Columnar Presentation of Variance Analysis for O'Shea Company: Direct Materials and Direct Manufacturing Labor for April 2004[a]**

LEVEL 3 ANALYSIS

	Actual Costs Incurred (Actual Input × Actual price) (1)	Actual Input × Budgeted Price (2)		Flexible Budget (Budgeted Input Allowed for Actual Output × Budgeted Price) (3)
Direct Materials	(6,000 kg × $16.50/kg) $99,000	(6,000 kg × $15.00/kg) $90,000	(4,400 kg × $15.00/kg) $66,000	(2,000 units × 2 kg/unit × $15.00) $60,000
	$9,000 U Price variance (1)–(2)		$6,000 U Efficiency variance (2)–(3)	
Direct Manufacturing Labor	(3,250 hrs. × $20.40/hr.) $66,300	(3,250 hrs. × $20.00/hr.) $65,000		(2,000 unit × 1.50 hrs./unit × $20.00/hr.) $60,000
	$1,300 U Price variance (1)–(2)		$5,000 U Efficiency variance (2)–(3)	

[a]F = favorable effect on operating income; U = unfavorable effect on operating income.

DECISION POINTS — SUMMARY

The following question-and-answer format summarizes the chapter's learning objectives. Each decision presents a key question related to a learning objective. The guidelines are the answer to that question.

Decision	Guidelines
1. How do flexible budgets differ from static budgets, and why should companies use flexible budgets?	A static budget is based on the level of output planned at the start of the budget period. A flexible budget is adjusted (flexed) to recognize the actual output level of the budget period. Flexible budgets help managers gain more insight into the causes of variances than is available from static budgets.
2. How can you develop a flexible budget and compute the flexible-budget variance and the sales-volume variance?	Use a three-step procedure to develop a flexible budget. When all costs are either variable with respect to output units or fixed, these three steps require only information about budgeted selling price, budgeted variable cost per output unit, budgeted fixed costs, and the actual quantity of output units. The static-budget variance can be subdivided into a flexible-budget variance (the difference between an actual result and the corresponding flexible-budget amount) and a sales-volume variance (the difference between the flexible-budget amount and the corresponding static-budget amount).
3. What is a standard cost, and why should a company use standard costs?	A standard cost is a carefully determined cost based on efficient operations. Standard costs aim to exclude past inefficiencies and aim to take into account changes expected to occur in the budget period.
4. Why should a company calculate price variances and efficiency variances?	The computation of price variances and efficiency variances helps managers gain insight into two different—but not independent—aspects of performance. The price variance focuses on the difference between the actual input price and the budgeted input price. The efficiency variance focuses on the difference between the actual quantity of input and the budgeted quantity of input allowed for the actual output.
5. Should a purchasing manager's performance be evaluated only on the basis of the price variance?	The price variance captures only one aspect of a purchasing manager's performance. Other aspects include the quality of the inputs the manager purchases and his or her ability to get suppliers to deliver on time.
6. Can managers integrate continuous improvement budgets into variance analysis?	Managers can use continuous improvement budgeted costs in their accounting system to signal to all employees that they are constantly seeking ways to reduce total costs.
7. Can variance analysis be used with an activity-based costing system?	Variance analysis can be applied to activity costs (such as setup costs) to gain insight into why actual activity costs differ from activity costs in the static budget or in the flexible budget. Interpreting cost variances for different activities requires understanding whether the costs are output unit-level, batch-level, product-sustaining, or facility-sustaining costs.
8. What is benchmarking and why is it useful?	Benchmarking is the continuous process of comparing the level of performance in producing products and services and executing activities against the best levels of performance. Benchmarking measures how well a company and its managers are doing.

TERMS TO LEARN

This chapter and the Glossary at the end of the book contain definitions of:

benchmarking (p. 234)
continuous improvement budgeted cost (230)
effectiveness (228)
efficiency (228)
efficiency variance (224)
favorable variance (217)
flexible budget (216)
flexible-budget variance (220)
input-price variance (224)
management by exception (216)
price variance (224)
rate variance (224)
sales-volume variance (220)
selling-price variance (221)
standard (222)
standard cost (222)
standard input (222)
standard price (222)
static budget (216)
static-budget variance (217)
unfavorable variance (217)
usage variance (224)
variance (216)

Questions

7-1 What is the relationship between *management by exception* and *variance analysis*?

7-2 What are two possible sources of information a company might use to compute the *budgeted amount* in variance analysis?

7-3 Distinguish between a *favorable variance* and an *unfavorable variance*.

7-4 What is the key difference between a *static budget* and a *flexible budget*?

7-5 Why might managers find a Level 2 flexible-budget analysis more informative than a Level 1 static-budget analysis?

7-6 Describe the steps in developing a flexible budget.

7-7 List four reasons for using standard costs.

7-8 How might a manager gain insight into the causes of a flexible-budget variance for direct materials?

7-9 List three causes of a favorable materials price variance.

7-10 Describe why materials price and materials efficiency variances may be computed with reference to different points in time.

7-11 How might the continuous improvement theme be incorporated into the process of setting budgeted costs?

7-12 Why might an analyst examining variances in the production area look beyond that business function for explanations of those variances?

7-13 Comment on the following statement made by a plant supervisor: "Meetings with my plant accountant are frustrating. All he wants to do is pin the blame on someone for the many variances he reports."

7-14 How can variances be used to analyze costs in individual activity areas?

7-15 "Benchmarking against other companies enables a company to identify the lowest-cost producer. This amount should become the performance measure for next year." Do you agree?

Exercises

7-16 **Flexible budget.** Brabham Enterprises manufactures tires for the Formula I motor racing circuit. For August 2003, it budgeted to manufacture and sell 3,000 tires at a variable cost of $74 per tire and total fixed costs of $54,000. The budgeted selling price was $110 per tire. Actual results in August 2003 were 2,800 tires manufactured and sold at a selling price of $112 per tire. The actual total variable costs were $229,600, and the actual total fixed costs were $50,000.

Required

1. Prepare a performance report (akin to Exhibit 7-2, p. 219) that uses a flexible budget and a static budget.
2. Comment on the results in requirement 1.

7-17 **Flexible budget.** Connor Company's budgeted prices for direct materials, direct manufacturing labor, and direct marketing (distribution) labor per attaché case are $40, $8, and $12, respectively. The president is pleased with the following performance report:

	Actual Costs	Static Budget	Variance
Direct materials	$364,000	$400,000	$36,000 F
Direct manufacturing labor	78,000	80,000	2,000 F
Direct marketing (distribution) labor	110,000	120,000	10,000 F

Required Actual output was 8,800 attaché cases. Is the president's pleasure justified? Prepare a revised performance report that uses a flexible budget and a static budget. Assume all three direct-cost items above are variable costs.

7-18 **Flexible budget.** The Virtual Candy Company sells sweets in bulk over the Web. Virtual Candy's budgeted operating income for the year ended December 31, 2004, was $3,150,000. As a result of continued explosive growth on the Web, actual operating income totaled $6,556,000.

Required

1. Calculate the total static-budget variances.
2. Flexible-budget operating income was $6,930,000. Calculate the total flexible-budget and total sales-volume variances.

3. Comment on the total flexible-budget variance in the light of the Web's explosive growth.

7-19 Price and efficiency variances. Peterson Foods manufactures pumpkin scones. For January 2004, it budgeted to purchase and use 15,000 pounds of pumpkin at $0.89 a pound. Actual purchase and usage for January 2004 was 16,000 pounds at $0.82 a pound. It budgets for 60,000 pumpkin scones. Actual output was 60,800 pumpkin scones.

Required

1. Compute the flexible-budget variance.
2. Compute the price and efficiency variances.
3. Comment on the results in requirements 1 and 2.

7-20 Materials and manufacturing labor variances. Consider the following data collected for Great Homes, Inc.:

	Direct Materials	Direct Manufacturing Labor
Cost incurred: actual inputs × actual prices	$200,000	$90,000
Actual inputs × standard prices	214,000	86,000
Standard inputs allowed for actual outputs × standard prices	225,000	80,000

Required

Compute the price, efficiency, and flexible-budget variances for direct materials and direct manufacturing labor.

Excel Application For students who wish to practice their spreadsheet skills, the following is a step-by-step approach to creating an Excel spreadsheet to work this problem.

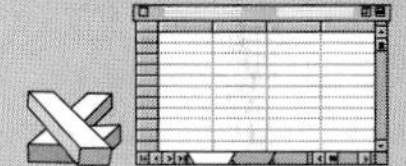

Step-by-Step

1. At the top of a new spreadsheet, create an "Original Data" section for the data provided by Great Homes, Inc., in exactly the same format as shown above, with rows labeled "Cost Incurred: Actual Inputs × Actual Prices," "Actual Inputs × Standard Prices," and "Standard Inputs Allowed for Actual Outputs × Standard Prices," and columns labeled "Direct Materials" and "Direct Manufacturing Labor."
2. Skip two rows, create a section, "Variance Calculations." Create rows for "Price Variance," "Efficiency Variance," and "Flexible-Budget Variance." Create columns for "Direct Materials" and "Direct Manufacturing Labor."

(Program your spreadsheet to perform all necessary calculations. Do not "hard-code" any of your variance calculations.)

3. Use the data in the Original Data section to calculate price variance, efficiency variance, and flexible-budget variance for direct materials and direct manufacturing labor. For example, to calculate direct materials price variance, in the cell corresponding to the "Price Variance" row and the "Direct Materials" column, enter a formula to subtract cost incurred from actual inputs times standard prices.
4. Unfavorable variances will show up as negative numbers. If you want to remain consistent with the format for calculating variances presented throughout this chapter, when calculating variances, take the absolute value of any differences you calculate in step 3 and label favorable variances with an "F" and unfavorable variances with a "U."
5. *Verify the accuracy of your spreadsheet.* Go to your Original Data section and change costs incurred for direct manufacturing labor from $90,000 to $100,000. If you programmed your spreadsheet correctly, the flexible-budget variance for direct manufacturing labor should change to $20,000 (unfavorable).

7-21 Price and efficiency variances. CellOne is a cellular phone service reseller. CellOne contracts with major cellular operators for airtime in bulk and then resells service to retail customers. CellOne budgeted to sell 7,800,000 minutes in the month ended March 31, 2004. Actual minutes sold totaled only 7,500,000. Due to fluctuations in hourly usage, CellOne "overbuys" airtime from cellular operators. CellOne plans to buy 10% more airtime than it plans to sell. For example, CellOne's budgets called for the purchase of 8,580,000 minutes, based on the plan to sell 7,800,000 minutes. In what follows, think of purchased airtime as direct materials.

CellOne budgets purchased airtime to cost 4.5 cents per minute. Actual purchased airtime in 2004 averaged 5.0 cents per minute. CellOne incurs direct labor costs due to the employment of technicians. One hour of technical support is required for every 5,000 minutes of airtime sold. In practice, only 1,600 hours of technical support were used. Technical support was planned at $60 per hour. Actual technical support costs averaged $62 per hour.

Required

1. Calculate the flexible-budget variance for direct materials and direct labor costs. (Use the 8,250,000 (7,500,000 × 1.10) minutes in the flexible budget.)
2. Calculate the price and efficiency variances for direct materials and labor costs.

7-22 Flexible budgets, variance analysis. You have been hired as a consultant by Mary Flanagan, the president of a small manufacturing company that makes automobile parts. Flanagan is an excellent engineer, but she has been frustrated by working with inadequate cost data.

You helped install flexible budgeting and standard costs. Flanagan has asked you to consider the following May data and recommend how variances might be computed and presented in performance reports:

Static budget in output units	20,000
Actual output units produced and sold	23,000
Budgeted selling price per output unit	\$40
Budgeted variable costs per output unit	\$25
Budgeted total fixed costs per month	\$200,000
Actual revenue	\$874,000
Actual variable costs	\$630,000
Favorable variance in fixed costs	\$5,000

Flanagan was disappointed. Although output units sold exceeded expectations, operating income did not. Assume that there was no beginning or ending inventory.

Required

1. You decide to present Flanagan with alternative ways to analyze variances so that she can decide what level of detail she prefers. The reporting system can then be designed accordingly. Prepare an analysis similar to Levels 0, 1, and 2 in Exhibit 7-1 and Exhibit 7-2.
2. What are some likely causes for the variances you report in requirement 1?

7-23 Flexible-budget preparation and analysis. Bank Management Printers, Inc., produces luxury checkbooks with three checks and stubs per page. Each checkbook is designed for an individual customer and is ordered through the customer's bank. The company's operating budget for September 2004 included these data:

Number of checkbooks	15,000
Selling price per book	\$20
Variable cost per book	\$8
Fixed costs for the month	\$145,000

The actual results for September 2004 were

Number of checkbooks produced and sold	12,000
Average selling price per book	\$21
Variable cost per book	\$7
Fixed costs for the month	\$150,000

The executive vice president of the company observed that the operating income for September was much less than anticipated, despite a higher-than-budgeted selling price and a lower-than-budgeted variable cost per unit. You have been asked to provide explanations for the disappointing September results.

Bank Management develops its flexible budget on the basis of budgeted per-output-unit revenue and per-output-unit variable costs without detailed analysis of budgeted inputs.

Required

1. Prepare a Level 1 analysis of the September performance.
2. Prepare a Level 2 analysis of the September performance.
3. Why might Bank Management find the Level 2 analysis more informative than the Level 1 analysis? Explain your answer.

7-24 Flexible budget, working backward. The Specialty Balls Company designs and manufactures ball bearings for extreme performance machinery. Exercise Exhibit 7-24 is a partially complete Level 2 variance analysis of Specialty Balls budgeted and actual results from sales of platinum ball bearings for the year ended December 31, 2004.

Required

1. Complete the analysis in Exercise Exhibit 7-24. Calculate all the required variances. If your work is accurate, you will find that the total static-budget variance is \$0.
2. What are the actual and budgeted selling prices? What are the actual and budgeted variable costs per unit?
3. Specialty Balls CEO was delighted with the lack of a static-budget variance. Is his reaction appropriate? Review the variances you have calculated and discuss possible causes and potential problems.
4. What is the most important lesson one can learn from performing this exercise?

	Actual Results (1)	Flexible-Budget Variances (2) = (1) − (3)	Flexible Budget (3)	Sales-Volume Variances (4) = (3) − (5)	Static Budget (5)
Units sold	650,000				600,000
Revenues (sales)	$3,575,000				$2,100,000
Variable costs	2,575,000				1,200,000
Contribution margin	1,000,000				900,000
Fixed Costs	700,000				600,000
Operating income	$ 300,000				$ 300,000

Total flexible-budget variance

Total sales-volume variance

Total static-budget variance

EXERCISE EXHIBIT 7-24

Schedule 1: Level 2 Variance Analysis for Specialty Balls for 2004 (Incomplete)

7-25 Price and efficiency variances, journal entries. Chemical, Inc., has set up the following standards per finished unit for direct materials and direct manufacturing labor:

Direct materials: 10 lbs. at $3 per lb.	$30.00
Direct manufacturing labor: 0.5 hours at $20 per hour	10.00

The number of finished units budgeted for March 2004 was 10,000; 9,810 units were actually produced.

Actual results in March 2004 were

Direct materials: 98,073 lbs. used	
Direct manufacturing labor: 4,900 hours	$102,900

Assume that there was no beginning inventory of either direct materials or finished units.

During the month, materials purchases amounted to 100,000 lbs., at a total cost of $310,000. Input-price variances are isolated upon purchase. Input-efficiency variances are isolated at the time of usage.

Required

1. Compute the March 2004 price and efficiency variances of direct materials and direct manufacturing labor.
2. Prepare journal entries to record the variances in requirement 1.
3. Comment on the March 2004 price and efficiency variances of Chemical, Inc.
4. Why might Chemical, Inc., calculate materials price variances and materials efficiency variances with reference to different points in time?

7-26 Continuous improvement (Continuation of 7-25). Chemical, Inc., adopts a continuous improvement approach to setting monthly standards costs. Assume the direct materials standard costs of $30 per unit and the direct manufacturing labor cost of $10 per unit pertain to January 2004. The standard amounts for February 2004 are 0.997 of the January standard amount. The standard amounts for March 2004 are 0.997 of the February standard amount. Assume the same information for March 2004 as in Exercise 7-25, except for these revised standard amounts.

Required

1. Compute the March 2004 standard amounts for direct materials and direct manufacturing labor.
2. Compute the March 2004 price and efficiency variances for direct materials and direct manufacturing labor.

7-27 Materials and manufacturing labor variances, standard costs. Consider the following selected data regarding the manufacture of a line of upholstered chairs:

	Standards per Chair
Direct materials	2 square yards of input at $10 per square yard
Direct manufacturing labor	0.5 hour of input at $20 per hour

The following data were compiled regarding actual performance: actual output units (chairs) produced, 20,000; square yards of input purchased and used, 37,000; price per square yard, $10.20; direct manufacturing labor costs, $176,400; actual hours of input, 9,000; labor price per hour, $19.60.

Required

1. Show computations of price and efficiency variances for direct materials and direct manufacturing labor. Give a plausible explanation of why the variances occurred.
2. Suppose 60,000 square yards of materials were purchased (at $10.20 per square yard), even though only 37,000 square yards were used. Suppose further that variances are identified at their most likely control point; accordingly, direct materials price variances are isolated and traced to the Purchasing Department rather than to the Production Department. Compute the price and efficiency variances under this approach.

7-28 Journal entries and T-accounts. (Continuation of 7-27). Prepare journal entries and post them to T-accounts for all transactions in Exercise 7-27, including requirement 2. Summarize in three sentences how these journal entries differ from the normal costing entries described in Chapter 4, pages 107–118.

7-29 Flexible budget. (Refer to Exercise 7-27.) Suppose the static budget was for 24,000 units of output. The general manager is thrilled about the following report:

	Actual Results	Static Budget	Variance
Direct materials	$377,400	$480,000	$102,600 F
Direct manufacturing labor	$176,400	$240,000	$63,600 F

Required Is the manager's glee warranted? Prepare a report that provides a more detailed explanation of why the static budget was not achieved. Actual output was 20,000 units.

7-30 Activity-based costing, flexible-budget variances for finance function activities. Josh Sanchez is the chief financial officer of Bouquets.com, an Internet company that enables customers to order deliveries of flowers by accessing its Web site. Sanchez is concerned with the efficiency and effectiveness of the finance function. He collects the following information for three finance activities in 2004:

Activity	Activity Level	Cost Driver	Rate per unit of Cost Driver: Static Budget	Rate per unit of Cost Driver: Actual
Receivables	Output unit	Remittances	$0.639	$0.75
Payables	Batch	Invoices	2.900	2.80
Travel expenses	Batch	Travel claims	7.600	7.40

The output measure is the number of deliveries, which is the same as the number of remittances. The following is additional information.

	Static-Budget Amounts	Actual Amounts
Number of deliveries	1,000,000	948,000
Batch size in terms of deliveries:		
Payables	5	4.468
Travel expenses	500	501.587

Required

1. Calculate the flexible-budget variance for each activity in 2004.
2. Calculate the price and efficiency variances for each activity in 2004.

7-31 Finance function activities, benchmarking (continuation of 7-30). Josh Sanchez, CFO of Bouquets.com, engages The Hackett Group, a consulting firm specializing in benchmarking. He asks Hackett to provide benchmark data of the finance function at "world-class" retail companies (both traditional retail and Internet-based retail). Hackett's cost benchmarks for Bouquet.com's three finance activities are

Finance Activity	"World-Class" Cost Performance
Payables	$0.71 per invoice
Receivables	$0.10 per remittance
Travel expenses	$1.58 per travel claim

Required

1. What new insights might arise with the Hackett benchmark data using the amounts in Exercise 7-30?
2. Assume you are in charge of travel-claim processing. What concerns might you have with Sanchez using the Hackett benchmark of $1.58 per travel claim as the key to evaluate your performance next period?

Problems

7-32 Flexible budget, direct materials and direct manufacturing labor variances. Tuscany Statuary manufactures bust statues of famous historical figures. All statues are the same size. Each unit requires the same amount of resources. The following information is from the static budget for 2004:

Expected production and sales	5,000 units
Direct materials	50,000 pounds
Direct manufacturing labor	20,000 hours
Total fixed costs	$1,000,000

Standard quantities, standard prices, and standard unit costs follow for direct materials and direct manufacturing labor.

	Standard Quantity	Standard Price	Standard Unit Cost
Direct materials	10 pounds	$10 per pound	$100
Direct manufacturing labor	4 hours	$40 per hour	$160

During 2004, actual number of units produced and sold was 6,000. Actual cost of direct materials used was $594,000, based on 54,000 pounds purchased at $11 per pound. Direct manufacturing labor-hours actually used were 25,000, at the rate of $38 per hour. This resulted in actual direct manufacturing labor cost of $950,000. Actual fixed costs were $1,005,000. There were no beginning or ending inventories.

Required

1. Calculate sales volume variance and flexible-budget variance.
2. Compute price and efficiency variances for direct materials and direct manufacturing labor.

7-33 **Static budget, flexible budget, service sector, professional labor efficiency and effectiveness.** Meridian Finance helps prospective homeowners find low-cost financing and assists existing homeowners in refinancing their current loans at lower interest rates.

Meridian charges clients 0.5% of the loan amount it arranges. In its 2004 static budget, Meridian assumes the average loan amount will be $200,000. Budgeted cost data per loan application for 2004 are

- Professional labor: 6 hours at a rate of $40 per hour
- Loan filing fees: $100
- Credit-worthiness checks: $120
- Courier mailings: $50

Office support is budgeted to be $31,000 per month. Meridian Finance views this amount as a fixed cost.

Required

1. Prepare a static budget for November 2004 assuming 90 loan applications.
2. Prepare a Level 2 variance analysis identifying sales-volume and flexible-budget variances for Meridian Finance for November 2004. Actual loan applications in November 2004 were 120, and the average loan amount was $224,000. Other actual data for November 2004 were
   - Revenue: $134,400
   - Professional labor: 7.2 hours per loan application at $42 per hour; total cost $36,288
   - Loan filing fees: $100 per loan application; total cost $12,000
   - Credit-worthiness checks: $125 per loan application; total cost $15,000
   - Courier mailings: $54 per loan application; total cost $6,480
   - Office support costs: $33,500
3. Compute professional labor price and efficiency variances for November 2004. (Compute labor price on a per-hour basis.)
4. What factors would you consider in evaluating the effectiveness of professional labor in November 2004?

7-34 **Comprehensive variance analysis responsibility issues** (CMA, adapted). Horizons Unlimited manufactures a full line of well-known sunglasses frames and lenses. Horizons uses a standard-costing system to set attainable standards for direct materials, labor, and overhead costs. Standards have been reviewed and revised annually, as necessary. Departmental managers, whose evaluations and bonuses are affected by their department's performance, have been held responsible to explain variances in their department performance reports.

Recently, the manufacturing variances in the Visionaire prestige line of sunglasses have caused some concern. For no apparent reason, unfavorable material and labor variances have occurred. At the monthly staff meeting, Jim Denton, manager of the Visionaire line, will be expected to explain his variances and suggest ways of improving performance. Denton will be asked to explain the following performance report for 2004:

	Actual Results	Static-Budget Amounts
Units sold	4,850	5,000
Revenues	$397,700	$400,000
Variable manufacturing costs	234,643	216,000
Fixed manufacturing costs	72,265	75,000
Gross margin	90,792	109,000

Denton collected the following information:

a. The standard variable manufacturing costs in 2004 comprised three items:
   - Direct materials: Frames. Static budget cost of $33,000. The standard input for 2004 is 3.00 ounces per unit.
   - Direct materials: Lenses. Static budget costs of $93,000. The standard input for 2004 is 6.00 ounces per unit.

- Direct manufacturing labor. Static budget costs of $90,000. The standard input for 2004 is 1.20 hours per unit.

Assume there are no indirect variable manufacturing costs.

b. The actual variable manufacturing costs in 2004 were
- Direct materials: Frames. Actual costs of $37,248. Actual ounces used per frame were 3.20 ounces per unit.
- Direct materials: Lenses. Actual costs of $100,492. Actual ounces used per frame were 7.00 ounces per unit.
- Direct manufacturing labor. Actual costs of $96,903. The actual labor rate was $14.80 per hour.

Required

1. Prepare a report that includes:
   a. Selling-price variance
   b. Sales-volume variance and flexible-budget variance in the format of the Level 2 analysis in Exhibit 7-2.
   c. Price and efficiency variances for
   - direct materials: frames
   - direct materials: lenses
   - direct manufacturing labor
2. Give three possible explanations for each of the three price and efficiency variances at Horizons in requirement 1c.

7-35 Continuous improvement (continuation of 7-34). Horizon receives a suggestion that continuous improvement standard costs be used that are updated monthly. Consider monthly revisions in 2005 for the three variable manufacturing cost items.

Required

1. The January 2005 standard input usage is 0.995 times the December 2004 standard. The February 2005 standard input usage is 0.995 times the January 2005 standard. Using the data from Problem 7-34, what is the standard for the direct materials usage for each variable cost item in January and February 2005?
2. What are the pros and cons of using the approach in requirement 1 as the primary approach to drive the cost competitiveness of Horizon?

7-36 Level 2 variance analysis, solve for unknowns. Homerun Headgear manufactures and distributes baseball caps to ballparks and other sports venues. Homerun's plan for 2005 forecast sales of 600,000 caps. However, only 500,000 caps were sold. Based on the data provided in Problem Exhibit 7-36, calculate the missing numbers and complete the analysis.

Required

1. Calculate the budgeted and actual selling prices.
2. Assuming that the driver for variable costs is units sold, what are the budgeted and actual variable costs per unit?
3. Calculate the flexible-budget operating income
4. Calculate the total flexible-budget variance
5. Calculate the total sales-volume variance
6. Calculate the total static-budget variance

7-37 Direct labor and direct materials variances, missing data. (CMA, heavily adapted).

Morro Bay Surfboards manufactures fiberglass surfboards. The standard cost of direct materials and direct manufacturing labor is $100 per board. This includes 20 pounds of direct materials, at the budgeted price of

PROBLEM EXHIBIT 7-36

Schedule 1: Level 2 Variance Analysis for Homerun Headgear for 2005, Incomplete

	Actual Results (1)	Flexible-Budget Variances (2) = (1) − (3)	Flexible Budget (3)	Sales-Volume Variances (4) = (3) − (5)	Static Budget (5)
Units sold	500,000				600,000
Revenues (sales)	$5,000,000				$4,800,000
Variable costs	1,400,000				1,800,000
Contribution margin		1,100,000 F		500,000 U	
Fixed Costs	1,150,000		1,000,000		1,000,000
Operating income					

Total flexible-budget variance (between columns 1 and 3); Total sales-volume variance (between columns 3 and 5); Total static-budget variance (between columns 1 and 5)

$2 per pound, and five hours of direct manufacturing labor, at the budgeted rate of $12 per hour. Following are the data for the month of July:

Units completed	6,000 units
Direct material purchases	150,000 pounds
Cost of direct material purchases	$292,500
Actual direct manufacturing labor-hours	32,000 hours
Actual direct-labor cost	$368,000
Direct materials efficiency variance	$ 12,500 U

There were no beginning inventories.

Required

1. Compute direct manufacturing labor variances for July.
2. Compute the actual pounds of direct materials used in production in July.
3. Calculate the actual price per pound of direct materials purchased.
4. Calculate direct materials price variance.

7-38 Comprehensive variance analysis review. FlexMem, Inc., manufactures diskettes. The CFO has provided you with the following budgeted standards for the month of February 2004:

Average selling price per diskette	$4.00
Total direct material cost per diskette	$0.85
Direct manufacturing labor	
Direct manufacturing labor cost per hour	$15.00
Average labor productivity rate (diskettes per hour)	300
Direct marketing cost per unit	$0.30
Fixed overhead	$900,000

Sales of 1,500,000 units are budgeted for February. Actual February results are as follows:

- Unit sales totaled 80% of plan.
- Actual average selling price declined to $3.70.
- Productivity dropped to 250 diskettes per hour.
- Actual direct manufacturing labor cost is $15 per hour.
- Actual total direct material cost per unit dropped to $0.80.
- Actual direct marketing costs were $0.30 per unit.
- Fixed costs were $30,000 below plan.

Calculate the following:

Required

1. Static-budget and actual operating income
2. Total static-budget variance
3. Flexible-budget operating income
4. Total flexible-budget variance
5. Total sales-volume variance
6. Total static-budget variance
7. Price and efficiency variances for direct manufacturing labor
8. Flexible-budget variance for direct manufacturing labor.

7-39 Direct materials and manufacturing labor variances, solving unknowns. (CPA, adapted) On May 1, 2004, Bovar Company began the manufacture of a new paging machine known as Dandy. The company installed a standard-costing system to account for manufacturing costs. The standard costs for a unit of Dandy follow:

Direct materials (3 lbs. at $5 per lb.)	$15.00
Direct manufacturing labor ($\frac{1}{2}$ hour at $20 per hour)	10.00
Manufacturing overhead (75% of direct manufacturing labor costs)	7.50
	$32.50

The following data were obtained from Bovar's records for the month of May:

	Debit	Credit
Revenues		$125,000
Accounts payable control (for May's purchases of direct materials)		68,250
Direct materials price variance	$3,250	
Direct materials efficiency variance	2,500	
Direct manufacturing labor price variance	1,900	
Direct manufacturing labor efficiency variance		2,000

Actual production in May was 4,000 units of Dandy, and actual sales in May were 2,500 units.

The amount shown earlier for direct materials price variance applies to materials purchased during May. There was no beginning inventory of materials on May 1, 2004.

Required Compute each of the following items for Bovar for the month of May. Show your computations.

1. Standard direct manufacturing labor-hours allowed for actual output produced
2. Actual direct manufacturing labor-hours worked
3. Actual direct manufacturing labor wage rate
4. Standard quantity of direct materials allowed (in pounds)
5. Actual quantity of direct materials used (in pounds)
6. Actual quantity of direct materials purchased (in pounds)
7. Actual direct materials price per pound

7-40 Comprehensive variance analysis. (CMA) Aunt Molly's Old Fashioned Cookies bakes cookies for retail stores. The company's best-selling cookie is Chocolate Nut Supreme, which is marketed as a gourmet cookie and regularly sells for $8 per pound. The standard cost per pound of Chocolate Nut Supreme, based on Aunt Molly's normal monthly production of 400,000 pounds, follows:

Cost Item	Quantity	Standard Unit Costs	Total Standard Cost
Direct materials			
Cookie mix	10 oz.	$0.02/oz.	$0.20
Milk chocolate	5 oz.	0.15/oz.	0.75
Almonds	1 oz.	0.50/oz.	0.50
			1.45
Direct manufacturing labor[a]			
Mixing	1 min.	14.40/hr.	0.24
Baking	2 min.	18.00/hr.	0.60
			0.84
Variable			
Overhead[b]	3 min.	32.40 hr.	1.62
Total standard cost per pound			$3.91

[a]Direct manufacturing labor rates include employee benefits.
[b]Allocated on the basis of direct labor-hours.

Aunt Molly's management accountant, Karen Blair, prepares monthly budget reports based on these standard costs. Presented below is April's report.

Performance Report, April 2004

	Actual	Budget	Variance
Units (in pounds)	450,000	400,000	50,000 F
Revenues	$3,555,000	$3,200,000	$355,000 F
Direct materials	865,000	580,000	285,000 U
Direct manufacturing labor	348,000	336,000	12,000 U

Justine Molly, president of the company, is disappointed with the results. Despite a sizable increase in the number of cookies sold, the product's expected contribution to the overall profitability of the company decreased. Molly has asked Blair to identify the reasons why the contribution margin decreased. Blair has gathered the following information to help in her analysis of the decrease.

Usage Report, April 2004

Cost Item	Quantity	Actual Cost
Direct materials		
Cookie mix	4,650,000 oz.	$ 93,000
Milk chocolate	2,660,000 oz.	532,000
Almonds	480,000 oz.	240,000
Direct manufacturing labor		
Mixing	450,000 min.	108,000
Baking	800,000 min.	240,000

Compute and comment on the following variances: **Required**

1. Selling-price variance
2. Direct material price variance
3. Direct material efficiency variance
4. Direct manufacturing labor efficiency variance

7-41 Flexible budgeting, activity-based costing, variance analysis. Toymaster, Inc., produces a toy car, TGC, in batches. After each batch of TGC is run, the molds are cleaned. The labor costs of cleaning the molds can be traced to TGC because TGC can only be produced from a specific mold. The following information pertains to June 2004:

	Static-Budget Amounts	Actual Amounts
Units of TGC produced and sold	30,000	22,500
Batch size (units per batch)	250	225
Cleaning labor-hours per batch	3	3.5
Cleaning labor cost per hour	$14	$12.50

Required

1. Calculate the flexible-budget variance for total cleaning labor costs in June 2004.
2. Calculate the price and efficiency variances for total cleaning labor costs in June 2004. Comment on the results.

7-42 Flexible budgeting, activity-based costing, variance analysis. King Taste is a manufacturer of fruitcakes. One of its plants produces five different cake products. Each cake product differs in terms of material inputs. They are identical in terms of the cooking and changeover processes.

The changeover process entails switching the production line from the manufacture of one product to another product. The costs of a changeover are a batch cost. They comprise the labor cost of the workers who clean the equipment so that the contents of each different product are not mixed together. The following information pertains to March 2003:

	Static-Budget Amounts	Actual Amounts
Units of cakes produced and sold	240,000	330,000
Average batch size (cakes per batch)	6,000	10,000
Changeover labor-hours per batch	20	24
Changeover labor cost per hour	$20	$21

Required

1. Compute the flexible-budget variance for total changeover labor costs in March 2003. Comment on the results.
2. Compute the price and efficiency variances for total changeover labor costs in March 2003. Comment on the results.
3. Provide two explanations for each of the price and efficiency variances in requirement 2.

7-43 Procurement costs, variance analysis, ethics. Rick Daley is the manager of the athletic shoe division of Raider Products. Raider is a U.S.-based company that has just purchased Fastfoot, a leading European shoe company. Fastfoot has long-term production contracts with suppliers in two Eastern Europe countries—Hergovia and Tanistan. Daley receives a request from Kevin Neal, president of Raider Products. Daley and his controller, Brooke Mullins, are to make a presentation to the next Board of Directors meeting on the cost competitiveness of the Fastfoot subsidiary. This report should include budgeted and actual procurement costs for 2004 at its Hergovia and Tanistan supply sources.

Mullins decides to visit the two supply operations. The budgeted average procurement cost for 2004 was $12 per pair of shoes. This cost includes payments to the shoe manufacturer and all other payments to conduct business in each country. Mullins reports the following to Daley:

- *Hergovia.* Total 2004 procurement costs for 250,000 pairs of shoes were $3,325,000. Payment to the shoe manufacturer was $2,650,000. Very few receipts existed for the remaining $675,000. Kickback payments are viewed as common in Hergovia.
- *Tanistan.* Total 2004 procurement costs for 900,000 pairs of shoes were $10,485,000. Payment to the shoe manufacturer was $8,640,000. Receipts existed for $705,000 of the other costs, but Mullins said he is skeptical of their validity. Kickback payments are a "way of business" at Tanistan.

At both the Hergovia and Tanistan plants, Mullins was disturbed by the employment of young children (many of them younger than 15 years). He was told that all major shoe-producing companies had similar low-cost employment practices in both countries.

Daley is uncomfortable about the upcoming presentation to the board. He was a leading advocate of the acquisition. A recent business magazine reported that the Fastfoot acquisition would make Raider Products the global low-cost producer in its market lines. The stock price of Raider Products jumped 21% the day the Fastfoot acquisition was announced. Mullins likewise is widely identified as a proponent of the acquisition. He is seen as a "rising star" due for a promotion to a division manager in the near future.

Required

1. What summary procurement cost variances could be reported to the Board of Directors of Raider Shoes?
2. What ethical issues do (a) Daley and (b) Mullins face when preparing and making a report to the Board of Directors?
3. How should Mullins address the issues you identify in requirement 2?

Collaborative Learning Exercise

7-44 Price and efficiency variances, problems in standard setting, benchmarking. Savannah Fashions manufactures shirts for retail chains. Jorge Andersen, the controller, is becoming increasingly disenchanted with Savannah's standard-costing system. The budgeted and actual amounts for direct materials and direct manufacturing labor for July 2004 were

	Budgeted Amounts	Actual Amounts
Shirts manufactured	4,000	4,488
Direct materials cost	\$20,000	\$20,196
Direct materials units (rolls of cloth)	400	408
Direct manufacturing labor costs	\$18,000	\$18,462
Direct manufacturing labor-hours	1,000	1,020

There were no beginning or ending inventories of materials.

The standard-costing system is based on a study of the operations conducted by an independent consultant six months earlier. Andersen observes that since then he has rarely seen an unfavorable variance of any magnitude. He notes that even at their current output levels, the workers seem to have a lot of time for sitting around and gossiping.

At a recent industry conference, a consultant for the Benchmarking Clearing House showed Andersen how she could develop six-month benchmark reports on the estimated costs of Savannah's major competitors. This information would be available by subscribing to the Benchmarking Clearing House monthly service.

Required

1. Compute the price and efficiency variances of Savannah Fashions for direct materials and direct manufacturing labor in July 2004.
2. Describe the types of actions the employees at Savannah Fashions may have taken to reduce the accuracy of the standards set by the independent consultant. Why would employees take those actions? Is this behavior ethical?
3. Describe how Savannah might use information from the Benchmarking Clearing House when computing the variances in requirement 1.
4. Discuss the pros and cons of Savannah using the Benchmarking Clearing House information to help increase its cost competitiveness.

CHAPTER 7 INTERNET EXERCISE

Flexible-budgeting variances help managers gain insights into why actual results differ from planned performance. To better understand these concepts, go to www.prenhall.com/horngren, click on *Cost Accounting*, 11th ed., and access the Internet exercise for Chapter 7.

CHAPTER 7 VIDEO CASE

McDONALD'S CORPORATION: Flexible Budgets, Standards, and Variances

The store manager at the new McDonald's restaurant in north Phoenix, Arizona, doesn't spend much time thinking about cost accounting. But that doesn't mean she's not familiar with the concepts. Instead, she's busy living them, every minute of the workday, at her busy store.

At the core of every McDonald's store manager's training is an in-depth education in store operations that has cost accounting fundamentals at the center. Surprised? Think about it. Why do you suppose a Big Mac is the same every time it's served, whether it's purchased in Detroit, Dallas, or Denver? The simple answer is "standards."

Customers have come to expect a certain level of quality (Q), service (S), cleanliness (C), and value (V) in every restaurant, every time they visit. McDonald's simply calls it "QSCV." Those expectations can be traced back to the high standards the company sets for stores, which link back to cost accounting.

Jerry Calabrese, vice president of accounting for McDonald's, says that the company has to differentiate itself in the fast-food market through "great execution." To do this, licensees and store managers in each of the company's 28,000-plus stores compare their actual performance in QSCV against standards and budgeted levels of performance. Any difference between actual and expected levels is a variance. And variances have everything to do with cost accounting.

Let's look at two examples. Materials and labor comprise the two largest costs for McDonald's. Budgets, standards, and variances are used to control both of them at the store level. There are standard costs and quantities for every ingredient used for menu items. The costs and quantities of condiments, french fries, hamburger patties, and buns are monitored. Each store manager receives a report called the "Quality Cost Report" that contains actual food costs versus budgeted food cost standards. Of course, managers don't use the report to figure out why pickle costs are 50 cents too high at the end of the day, although they could. Instead, the Quality Cost Report focuses attention on the bigger areas of opportunity, where there are larger dollar amounts, by comparing the costs of the items sold to the costs of items used. One example of its use might be to highlight higher hamburger patty costs. If the higher cost is way out of line, the store manager might investigate to see if cases of hamburgers are "walking out the back door" instead of being sold through the counter at the front.

Labor levels are carefully monitored also. For each level of expected sales, the store manager budgets a corresponding level of standard labor-hours spread across the different operational areas of the restaurant. Variances can occur here, too, when there is a difference between the standard hourly wage multiplied by the difference in actual quantity used and the budgeted quantity for the actual sales levels. So, if sales are significantly different from expected levels, either up or down, adjustments must be made to minimize the effect on both the customer and the store's profitability.

Nonfinancial measures are also monitored by store managers. One of the most challenging measures concerns cleanliness. How often is "often enough" for keeping public areas clean? According to Mr. Calabrese, if a restaurant isn't clean when the next customers come in, their perception of that restaurant and their dining experience will be marred. Store managers get feedback from customer surveys taken by "mystery shoppers," who drop into stores without notice and rate their entire dining experience, including cleanliness.

Strict adherence to standards, along with consistent monitoring, is critical to the success of McDonald's. Although they may not call it "cost accounting" in their restaurants, their daily pursuit of QSCV has its roots in the time-honored and proven techniques used by organizations of all sizes and types the world over.

QUESTIONS

1. The Quality Cost Report used by store managers to monitor food costs contains the basic elements of a particular type of cost accounting report. Which report does it resemble?
2. Labor costs are carefully monitored by every McDonald's store manager. Which type of cost accounting report was described in the case? What decision might a store manager use it to make?
3. Nonfinancial measures are important to the operations of each McDonald's store. Cleanliness of public areas is one such measure. What other nonfinancial measures do you think the company has? Why do nonfinancial measures matter in cost accounting?

CHAPTER 8

Flexible Budgets, Variances, and Management Control: II

LEARNING OBJECTIVES

1. Explain in what ways the planning of variable overhead costs and fixed overhead costs are similar and in what ways they differ
2. Identify the features of a standard-costing system
3. Compute the variable overhead efficiency variance and the variable overhead spending variance
4. Explain how the efficiency variance for a variable indirect-cost item differs from the efficiency variance for a direct-cost item
5. Compute a budgeted fixed overhead cost rate
6. Explain two concerns when interpreting the production-volume variance as a measure of the economic cost of unused capacity
7. Show how the 4-variance analysis approach reconciles the actual overhead incurred with the overhead amounts allocated during the period
8. Illustrate how the flexible-budget variance approach can be used in activity-based costing

www.prenhall.com/horngren

Teva Sport Sandals creates its new shoe designs from the ground up, literally—well, nearly literally. Each sandal starts with a footbed base, to which straps and hooks are added. Sandals range from rugged outdoor adventure styles to refined casual wear for men, women, and children. From prototype designs, managers at Teva negotiate the final cost of each component with its production facility in China. These costs are part of the company's standard-costing system, which traces direct costs to each type of sandal manufactured at the plant. As negotiations take place, plant managers also determine the planned variable overhead costs and fixed overhead costs so they'll know what their standard costs will be before a single sandal walks off the production line—not literally.

It is not unusual for more than 50% of a company's total product costs throughout the value chain to be classified as indirect. Increased automation, more complexity of production and distribution processes, and product proliferation usually increase the proportion of total product costs that are indirect. However, the lower cost of information processing works against this trend by facilitating more direct-cost tracing.

Overhead costs are a big part of the costs of many companies. Chemical, paper, and steel companies incur large costs to construct and maintain their physical plant and equipment: These costs are part of their overhead costs. Companies like Amazon.com and Yahoo! invest large amounts in software that enables them to provide a broad range of services to their customers in a timely and reliable way. These costs are part of their overhead costs.

This chapter shows how flexible budgets and variance analysis can help managers plan and control the overhead costs of their companies. Chapter 7 emphasized the direct-cost categories of direct materials and direct manufacturing labor. In this chapter, we focus on the indirect-cost categories of variable manufacturing overhead and fixed manufacturing overhead. And we explain why managers should be careful when interpreting variances based on overhead cost concepts developed primarily for financial reporting purposes.

1 Explain in what ways the planning of variable overhead costs and fixed overhead costs are similar and in what ways they differ

...for both, plan only essential activities and be efficient; fixed overhead costs are usually determined well before the budget period begins

PLANNING OF VARIABLE AND FIXED OVERHEAD COSTS

We'll continue to use the Webb Company to illustrate how concepts are analyzed and applied. Webb manufactures a designer jacket that is sold to distributors. Recall, Webb's only costs are manufacturing costs. Variable manufacturing overhead costs for Webb include energy, machine maintenance, engineering support, indirect materials, and indirect manufacturing labor. Fixed manufacturing overhead costs include plant-leasing costs, some administrative costs (such as the plant manager's salary), and depreciation on plant equipment.

Planning Variable Overhead Costs

The two ways of managing variable overhead costs are (1) eliminate nonvalue-added costs (for example, consume less electricity by using more energy-efficient equipment) and (2) reduce consumption of the cost-allocation bases (for example, redesign products to require fewer machine-hours of processing time).

Effective planning of variable overhead costs for a product or service means that a company only does those variable overhead activities that add value for customers using that product or service. Clorox (the bleach-manufacturing company) reported the following in its annual report: "Our work simplification initiative is pretty direct—it's about getting the gunk out of our internal systems by eliminating nonvalue-added work so that all of us at Clorox can spend our energy on value-adding activities that will move the business ahead."

In our example, Webb Company should examine how each of the activities in its variable overhead cost pools is related to delivering a product or service to customers. For example, customers know sewing to be an essential activity at Webb. Hence, maintenance activities for sewing machines—included in Webb's variable overhead costs—are also essential activities. Such maintenance should be done in a cost-effective way. This means, for example, scheduling equipment maintenance in a systematic way rather than waiting for sewing machines to break down.

Planning Fixed Overhead Costs

Effective planning of fixed overhead costs is much the same as effective planning for variable overhead costs—planning to undertake only essential activities and then planning to be efficient in that undertaking. But with planning fixed overhead costs, there is one more consideration: choosing the appropriate level of capacity or investment that will benefit the company over a long time. This third item is a key strategic decision. Consider Webb's leasing of sewing machines, each having a fixed cost per year. Leasing insufficient machine capacity—say, because Webb underestimates demand—will result in an inability to meet demand and lost sales of jackets. Leasing more machines than necessary—if Webb overestimates demand—will result in additional fixed leasing costs on machines not fully utilized during the year.

At the start of a budget period, management will have made most of the decisions that determine the level of fixed overhead costs to be incurred. But, it's the day-to-day, ongoing operating decisions that mainly determine the level of variable overhead costs incurred in that period.

The two ways of managing fixed overhead costs are (1) eliminate nonvalue-added costs (for example, arrange to have vendors deliver direct materials to the production floor just when needed, which enables a warehouse lease to be terminated) and (2) plan for appropriate capacity levels.

STANDARD COSTING AT WEBB COMPANY

2 Identify the features of a standard-costing system

...use standard prices and standard quantities of inputs to cost products

Webb uses standard costing. The development of standards for Webb's direct-cost categories was described in Chapter 7. This chapter discusses Webb's indirect-cost categories. **Standard costing** is a costing method that (a) traces direct costs to output produced by multiplying the standard prices or rates by the standard quantities of inputs allowed for actual outputs produced and (b) allocates indirect costs on the basis of the standard indirect rates times the standard quantities of the allocation bases allowed for the actual outputs produced.

With a standard-costing system, the standard costs of every product or service planned to be worked on during the period can be computed at the start of that period. This feature of standard costing makes it possible to use a simple recording system. For calculating the cost of products or services, no record need be kept of the actual costs of items used or of the actual quantities of the cost-allocation bases used on individual products or services worked on during the period. Once standards have been set, the costs of operating a standard-costing system can be low relative to the costs of operating an actual or a normal-costing system.

DEVELOPING BUDGETED VARIABLE OVERHEAD COST-ALLOCATION RATES

Variable overhead cost-allocation rates can be developed in four steps.

Step 1: Choose the Period to Be Used for the Budget. Webb uses a 12-month budget period that includes a full calendar-year cycle that includes different seasons.

Step 2: Select the Cost-Allocation Bases to Use in Allocating Variable Overhead Costs to Output Produced. Webb's operating managers believe that machine-hours is the cost driver of variable manufacturing overhead. Using the cause-and-effect criterion, Webb selects standard machine-hours as the cost-allocation base. Webb budgets 57,600 machine-hours for a budgeted output of 144,000 jackets in 2003.

Step 3: Identify the Variable Overhead Costs Associated with Each Cost-Allocation Base. Webb groups in a single pool all its variable manufacturing overhead costs, including costs of energy, machine maintenance, engineering support, indirect materials, and indirect manufacturing labor. Webb's budgeted variable manufacturing costs for 2003 are $1,728,000.

Step 4: Compute the Rate per Unit of Each Cost-Allocation Base Used to Allocate Variable Overhead Costs to Output Produced. Dividing the amount in step 3 ($1,728,000) by the amount in step 2 (57,600 machine-hours), Webb estimates a rate of $30 per standard machine-hour for its variable manufacturing overhead costs.

The budgeted variable manufacturing overhead (BVMOH) cost rate differs from the budgeted price of direct materials (DM) or direct manufacturing labor (DML). The BVMOH cost rate encompasses costs of *many diverse VMOH items per unit of the cost-allocation base.* In the Webb example, the BVMOH cost rate is $30 per machine-hour: That is, Webb expects to spend about $30 on a "market basket" of VMOH items. The market basket aspect of the BVMOH cost rate makes VMOH variances more difficult to interpret than DM and DML variances.

In standard costing, the variable overhead rate per unit of the cost-allocation base (machine-hours for Webb) is generally expressed as a standard rate per output unit. This standard rate depends on the number of units of the cost-allocation base (that's the input units) allowed per output unit. On the basis of an engineering study, Webb estimates it will take 0.40 machine-hours per actual output unit.

$$\begin{aligned}\text{Budgeted variable overhead cost rate per output unit} &= \text{Budgeted inputs allowed per output unit} \times \text{Budgeted variable Overhead cost rate per input unit}\\ &= 0.40 \text{ hours per jacket} \times \$30 \text{ per hour}\\ &= \$12 \text{ per jacket (output unit)}\end{aligned}$$

Webb uses $12 per jacket in both its static budget for 2003 and in the monthly performance reports it prepares during 2003.

VARIABLE OVERHEAD COST VARIANCES

The MOH variances in this chapter subdivide the underallocated/overallocated MOH in Chapter 4.

Be sure to distinguish budgeted VMOH cost per unit of output ($12 per jacket) from budgeted VMOH cost per unit of the input cost-allocation base ($30 per machine-hour). Either cost rate can be used to compute VMOH allocated: 10,000 × (0.40 × $30) = $120,000, or 10,000 × $12 = $120,000.

We now illustrate how the budgeted variable manufacturing overhead rate is used in computing Webb's variable manufacturing overhead cost variances. The following data are for April 2003, when Webb produced and sold 10,000 jackets:

Cost Item/Allocation Base	Actual Result	Flexible-Budget Amount
1. Output units (jackets)	10,000	10,000
2. Machine-hours	4,500	4,000
3. Machine-hours per output unit (2 ÷ 1)	0.45	0.40
4. Variable manufacturing overhead costs	$130,500	$120,000
5. Variable manufacturing overhead costs per machine-hour (4 ÷ 2)	$29.00	$30.00
6. Variable manufacturing overhead costs per output unit (4 ÷ 1)	$13.05	$12.00

The flexible-budget enables Webb to highlight the effect of differences between actual costs and actual quantities versus budgeted costs and budgeted quantities for the actual output level of 10,000 jackets.

Flexible-Budget Analysis

In this chapter, we again use a columnar solution format as a helpful and intuitive approach to compute variances. Examples include Exhibits 8-1, 8-2, 8-3.

As you saw in Chapter 7, the **variable overhead flexible-budget variance** measures the difference between actual variable overhead costs and flexible-budget variable overhead costs. As Exhibit 8-1 shows:

$$\begin{aligned}\text{Variable overhead flexible-budget variance} &= \text{Actual costs incurred} - \text{Flexible-budget amount}\\ &= \$130{,}500 - \$120{,}000\\ &= \$10{,}500, \text{ or } \$10{,}500\text{ U}\end{aligned}$$

EXHIBIT 8-1

Columnar Presentation of Variable Manufacturing Overhead Variance Analysis: Webb Company for April 2003[a]

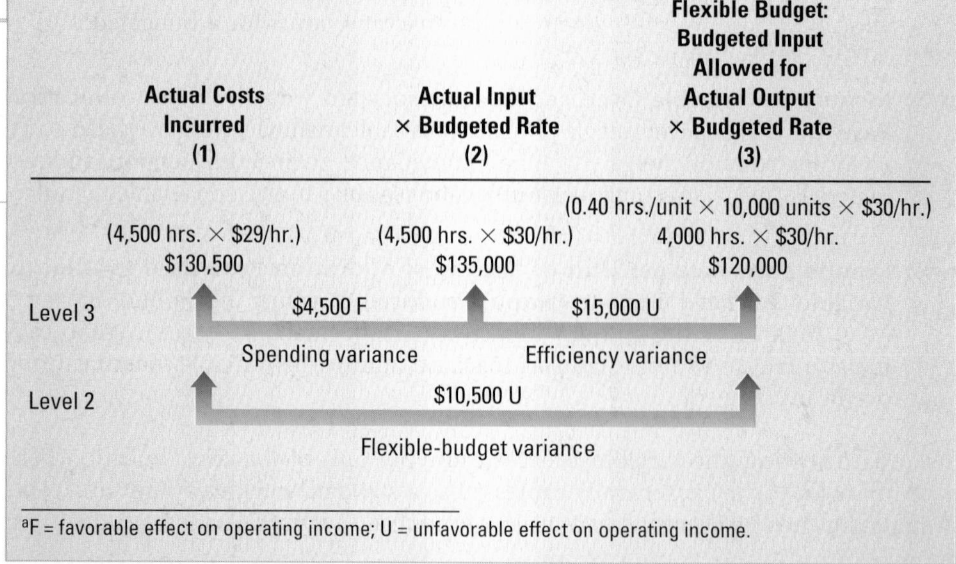

[a]F = favorable effect on operating income; U = unfavorable effect on operating income.

This $10,500 unfavorable flexible-budget variance means Webb's actual variable manufacturing overhead exceeded its flexible-budget amount by $10,500 for the 10,000 jackets actually produced and sold.

Just as we did in Chapter 7 with the flexible-budget variance for direct-cost items, we will now obtain additional information by subdividing the Level 2 variable manufacturing overhead flexible-budget variance into its Level 3 efficiency variance and spending variance.

Variable Overhead Efficiency Variance

The **variable overhead efficiency variance** is the difference between the actual quantity of the cost-allocation base used and the budgeted quantity of the cost-allocation base that should have been used to produce the actual output, multiplied by budgeted variable overhead cost per unit of cost-allocation base.

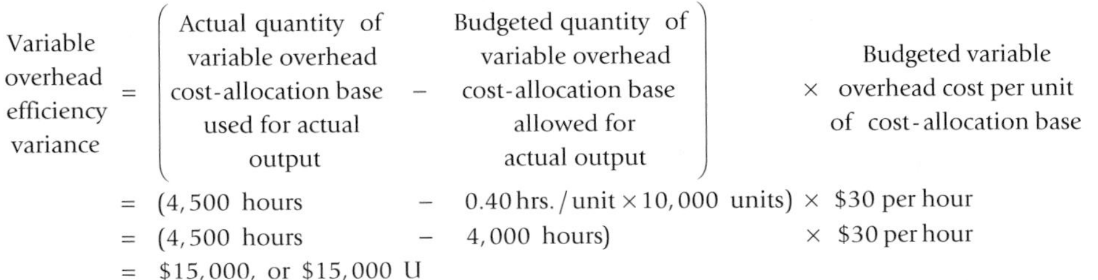

$$\text{Variable overhead efficiency variance} = \left(\begin{array}{c}\text{Actual quantity of}\\ \text{variable overhead}\\ \text{cost-allocation base}\\ \text{used for actual}\\ \text{output}\end{array} - \begin{array}{c}\text{Budgeted quantity of}\\ \text{variable overhead}\\ \text{cost-allocation base}\\ \text{allowed for}\\ \text{actual output}\end{array}\right) \times \begin{array}{c}\text{Budgeted variable}\\ \text{overhead cost per unit}\\ \text{of cost-allocation base}\end{array}$$

$$= (4,500 \text{ hours} - 0.40 \text{ hrs./unit} \times 10,000 \text{ units}) \times \$30 \text{ per hour}$$

$$= (4,500 \text{ hours} - 4,000 \text{ hours}) \times \$30 \text{ per hour}$$

$$= \$15,000, \text{ or } \$15,000 \text{ U}$$

Columns 2 and 3 of Exhibit 8-1 show the variable overhead efficiency variance. The variable overhead efficiency variance is computed in the same way as the efficiency variance for direct-cost items (Chapter 7, pp. 225–226). But the interpretation of the direct-cost efficiency variances differs from the interpretation of the variable overhead efficiency variance. In Chapter 7, efficiency variances for direct-cost items are based on differences between actual inputs used and the budgeted inputs allowed for actual output produced. For example, an efficiency variance for direct manufacturing labor for Webb will indicate whether more or less direct manufacturing labor is used per jacket than was budgeted for the actual output produced. In contrast, here in Chapter 8 the efficiency variance for variable overhead cost is based on *the efficiency with which the cost-allocation base is used*. Webb's unfavorable variable overhead efficiency variance of $15,000 means that actual machine-hours (the cost-allocation base) turned out to be higher than the budgeted machine-hours allowed to manufacture 10,000 jackets. Possible causes for Webb's actual machine-hours used exceeding budgeted machine-hours include:

(i) Workers were less skillful than expected in using the machines.
(ii) The production scheduler inefficiently scheduled jobs, resulting in more machine-hours used than budgeted.
(iii) Machines were not maintained in good operating condition.
(iv) Webb promised a distributor a rush delivery, which resulted in more machine-hours used than budgeted.
(v) Budgeted machine time standards were set too tight.

Management's response to this $15,000 U variance would be guided by which causes best describe the April 2003 results.

- Cause (i) has implications for employee-hiring practices and training procedures.
- Causes (ii) and (iii) relate to plant operations and include the possible use of software packages for production scheduling and plant maintenance.
- Cause (iv) has implications for coordinating production schedules with distributors and sharing information with them.
- Cause (v) requires managers to commit more resources to developing reliable standards.

3 Compute the variable overhead efficiency variance

...difference between actual quantity of cost-allocation base and budgeted quantity of cost-allocation base

and the variable overhead spending variance

...difference between actual variable overhead cost rate and budgeted variable overhead cost rate

In this chapter, we use the general term cost-allocation base, instead of cost driver. A cost-allocation base is a cost driver only if the relationship between the cost-allocation base and the cost pool is strong. In the case of overhead costs, the cause-and-effect relationship between the cost-allocation base (such as machine-hours) and some overhead costs (such as plant rent, engineering support, and production scheduling) may not be strong.

4 Explain how the efficiency variance for a variable indirect-cost item

...focuses on quantity of cost-allocation base used

differs from the efficiency variance for a direct-cost item

...focuses on quantity of materials and labor-hours used

The unfavorable VMOH efficiency variance doesn't mean workers wasted VMOH items and used more VMOH per machine-hour. This variance arose because Webb used too much of the cost-allocation base, machine-hours. Because the machines ran an extra 500 hours, they used extra VMOH items, such as electricity, maintenance, and supplies.

Variable Overhead Spending Variance

The **variable overhead spending variance** is the difference between the actual variable overhead cost per unit of the cost-allocation base and the budgeted variable overhead cost per unit of the cost-allocation base, multiplied by the actual quantity of variable overhead cost-allocation base used for actual output.

$$\begin{aligned}\text{Variable overhead spending variance} &= \left(\begin{array}{c}\text{Actual variable}\\ \text{overhead cost per}\\ \text{unit of cost-allocation base}\end{array} - \begin{array}{c}\text{Budgeted variable}\\ \text{overhead cost per}\\ \text{unit of cost-allocation base}\end{array}\right) \times \begin{array}{c}\text{Actual quantity of}\\ \text{variable overhead}\\ \text{cost-allocation base}\\ \text{used for actual output}\end{array}\\ &= (\$29 \text{ per machine-hour} - \$30 \text{ per machine-hour}) \times 4{,}500 \text{ machine-hours}\\ &= (-\$1 \text{ per machine-hour}) \times 4{,}500 \text{ machine-hours}\\ &= -\$4{,}500, \text{ or } \$4{,}500\text{F}\end{aligned}$$

Webb operated in April 2003 with a lower-than-budgeted variable overhead cost per machine-hour. Hence, there is a favorable variable overhead spending variance. Columns 1 and 2 in Exhibit 8-1 depict this variance.

To understand the variable overhead spending variance, you need to recognize why the *actual* variable overhead cost per unit of the cost-allocation base is *lower* than the *budgeted* variable overhead cost per unit of the cost-allocation base. Here's why: Relative to the flexible budget, the percentage increase in the actual quantity of the cost-allocation base is *more* than the percentage increase in actual total costs of individual items in the indirect-cost pool. In the Webb example, the 4,500 actual machine-hours are 12.5% greater than the flexible-budget amount of 4,000 machine hours [(4,500 – 4,000) ÷ 4,000 = 0.125, or 12.5%]. Actual variable overhead costs of $130,500 are only 8.75% greater than the flexible-budget amount of $120,000 [($130,500 – $120,000) ÷ $120,000 = 0.0875. or 8.75%]. Because the percentage increase in actual variable overhead costs is less than the percentage increase in machine-hours, the actual variable overhead cost per machine-hour is lower than the budgeted amount.

Variable manufacturing overhead costs include costs of energy, machine maintenance, indirect materials, and indirect manufacturing labor. Two reasons why the percentage increase in actual variable manufacturing overhead costs is less than the percentage increase in machine-hours in the Webb example are

1. The actual prices of individual inputs included in variable overhead, such as the price of energy, indirect materials, or indirect manufacturing labor, are lower than the budgeted prices of these inputs. For example, the actual price of electricity may only be $0.09 per kilowatt-hour, compared with a price of $0.10 per kilowatt-hour in the flexible budget.
2. Relative to the flexible budget, the percentage increase in the actual quantity usage of individual items in the variable overhead-cost pool is less than the percentage increase in machine-hours. Suppose actual energy used is 32,400 kilowatt-hours compared with the flexible-budget amount of 30,000 kilowatt-hours. The 8% [(32,400 – 30,000) ÷ 30,000] increase in energy usage compared with the 12.5% [(4,500 – 4,000) ÷ 4,000] increase in machine-hours will lead to a favorable variable overhead spending variance. The spending variance can be partially or completely traced to the efficient use of energy and other variable overhead items.

Price effects have implications for Webb's purchasing decisions. Quantity effects have implications for Webb's production decisions. Distinguishing these two effects for a variable overhead spending variance requires detailed information about the budgeted prices and budgeted quantities of the individual items in the variable overhead cost pool.

To clarify the concepts of variable overhead efficiency variance and variable overhead spending variance, consider the following example, assuming that (a) energy is the only item of variable overhead and machine-hours is the cost-allocation base, (b) the actual machine-hours used to produce the actual output equals the budgeted machine-hours, and (c) the actual price of energy equals the budgeted price. Under those assumptions, there would be no efficiency variance, but there could be a spending variance. The company has been efficient with respect to the number of machine-hours used to produce the actual output. But it could be using too much energy—not because of excessive machine-hours but because of wastage (more energy per machine-hour). The cost of this higher energy usage would be measured by the spending variance.

The variable manufacturing overhead variances computed in this section can be summarized as follows:

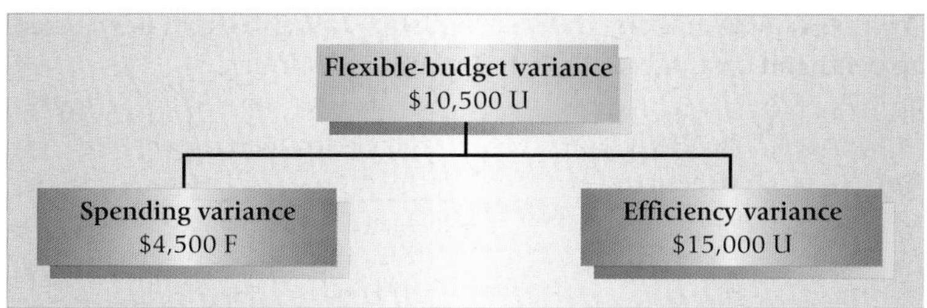

The cause for Webb's unfavorable flexible-budget variance was using a higher-than-budgeted number of machine-hours. Webb found out later that the machines in April 2003 operated below budgeted efficiency levels due to insufficient maintenance performed in February and March. A former plant manager delayed maintenance in a presumed attempt to meet monthly budget cost targets. Webb has since strengthened its internal maintenance procedures so that failure to do monthly maintenance as completely as needed raises a "red flag" that must be immediately explained to top management.

From variable overhead costs we now turn our attention to fixed overhead costs.

DEVELOPING BUDGETED FIXED OVERHEAD COST-ALLOCATION RATES

5 **Compute a budgeted fixed overhead cost rate**
...budgeted fixed costs divided by level of cost-allocation base

Fixed overhead costs are, by definition, a lump sum of costs that remains unchanged in total for a given period despite wide changes in the level of total activity or volume related to those overhead costs. Total fixed costs are usually included in flexible budgets, but they remain the same total amount within the relevant range of activity regardless of the output level chosen to "flex" the variable costs and revenues. The steps in developing the budgeted fixed overhead rate are

Step 1: **Choose the Period to Use for the Budget.** As with variable overhead costs, the budget period for fixed costs is typically 12 months. Chapter 4 (pp. 105–106) provides several reasons for using annual overhead rates rather than, say, monthly rates: numerator reasons—such as reducing the influence of seasonality—and denominator reasons—such as reducing the effect of varying output and number of days in a month. In addition, setting annual overhead rates once a year saves management time from being tied up 12 times during the year if budget rates had to be set monthly.

Step 2: **Select the Cost-Allocation Base to Use in Allocating Fixed Overhead Costs to Output Produced.** Webb uses standard machine-hours as the cost-allocation base for fixed manufacturing overhead costs. This is the denominator of the budgeted fixed overhead rate computation and is called the **denominator level**. In manufacturing settings, the denominator level is called more specifically, the **production-denominator level**. Standard machine-hours is also the allocation base Webb uses for its variable manufacturing overhead costs. For simplicity, we assume Webb expects to operate at capacity in 2003—budgeted machine-hours of 57,600 hours for a budgeted output of 144,000 jackets.[1]

Step 3: **Identify the Fixed Overhead Costs Associated with Each Cost-Allocation Base.** Webb groups all its fixed manufacturing overhead costs in a single cost pool. Costs in this pool include depreciation on plant and equipment, plant and equipment leasing costs, the plant manager's salary, and some administrative costs. Webb's fixed manufacturing budget for 2003 is $3,312,000.

Step 4: **Compute the Rate per Unit of Each Cost-Allocation Base Used to Allocate Fixed Overhead Costs to Output Produced.** Dividing the $3,312,000 from step

[1]Because Webb plans its capacity over multiple periods, anticipated demand in 2003 could be such that budgeted output for 2003 is less than capacity. The analysis presented in this chapter is unchanged if the master budget level is used as the denominator level. If capacity is used as the denominator level, some additional issues arise that are beyond the scope of this chapter. Chapter 9 discusses choice of a denominator level in more detail.

3 by the 57,600 machine-hours from step 2, Webb estimates a fixed manufacturing overhead cost rate of $57.50 per machine-hour:

$$\begin{aligned}\text{Budgeted fixed overhead cost per unit of cost-allocation base} &= \frac{\text{Budgeted total costs in fixed overhead cost pool}}{\text{Budgeted total quantity of cost-allocation base}} \\ &= \frac{\$3{,}312{,}000}{57{,}600} \\ &= \$57.50 \text{ per machine-hour}\end{aligned}$$

In standard costing, the $57.50 fixed overhead cost per machine-hour is usually expressed as a standard cost per output unit:

$$\begin{aligned}\text{Budgeted fixed overhead cost per output unit} &= \text{Budgeted quantity of cost-allocation base allowed per output unit} \times \text{Budgeted fixed overhead cost per unit of cost-allocation base} \\ &= 0.40 \text{ machine-hours per jacket} \times \$57.50 \text{ per machine-hour} \\ &= \$23.00 \text{ per jacket}\end{aligned}$$

When preparing monthly budgets for 2003, Webb divides the $3,312,000 annual total fixed costs into 12 equal monthly amounts of $276,000.

FIXED OVERHEAD COST VARIANCES

The flexible-budget amount for a fixed-cost item is also the amount included in the static budget prepared at the start of the period. No adjustment is required for differences between the actual output and the budgeted output for fixed costs. By definition, fixed costs are unaffected by changes in the output level within the relevant range. At the start of 2003, Webb budgeted fixed manufacturing overhead costs to be $276,000 per month. The actual amount for April 2003 turns out to be $285,000. As we saw in Chapter 7, the **fixed overhead flexible-budget variance** is the difference between actual fixed overhead costs and the fixed overhead costs in the flexible budget:

$$\begin{aligned}\text{Fixed overhead flexible-budget variance} &= \text{Actual costs incurred} - \text{Flexible-budget amount} \\ &= \$285{,}000 - \$276{,}000 \\ &= \$9{,}000, \text{ or } \$9{,}000 \text{ U}\end{aligned}$$

As Exhibit 8-2 shows, the variance is unfavorable because $285,000 actual fixed manufacturing overhead costs exceed the $276,000 budgeted for April 2003, which decreases that month's operating income compared to the budget by $9,000.

The flexible-budget variance for fixed manufacturing overhead (FMOH) is not subdivided into separate price and efficiency variances. The $9,000 unfavorable flexible-budget variance for FMOH arose because Webb incurred more FMOH costs than the lump-sum amount budgeted. That's why it's called a spending variance.

The variable overhead flexible-budget variance described earlier in this chapter was subdivided into a spending variance and an efficiency variance. There is not an efficiency variance for fixed costs. That's because a given lump sum of fixed costs will be unaffected by how efficiently machine-hours are used to produce output in a given budget period. As Exhibit 8-2 shows, the **fixed overhead spending variance,** a Level 3 variance, is the same amount as the Level 2 fixed overhead flexible-budget variance:

$$\begin{aligned}\text{Fixed overhead spending variance} &= \text{Actual costs incurred} - \text{Flexible-budget amount} \\ &= \$285{,}000 - \$276{,}000 \\ &= \$9{,}000, \text{ or } \$9{,}000 \text{ U}\end{aligned}$$

6 Explain two concerns when interpreting the production-volume variance as a measure of the economic cost of unused capacity

...extra capacity may be needed to satisfy uncertain demand surges; does not take into account the effect of price decreases that may be needed to fill capacity

Webb investigated this variance and found that there was a $9,000 per month unexpected increase in its equipment leasing costs. However, management concluded that the new lease rates were competitive with lease rates available elsewhere.

PRODUCTION-VOLUME VARIANCE

Computation of Production-Volume Variance

Webb's budgeted fixed manufacturing overhead costs are allocated to actual output produced during the period at the budgeted rate of $57.50 per standard machine-hour. We

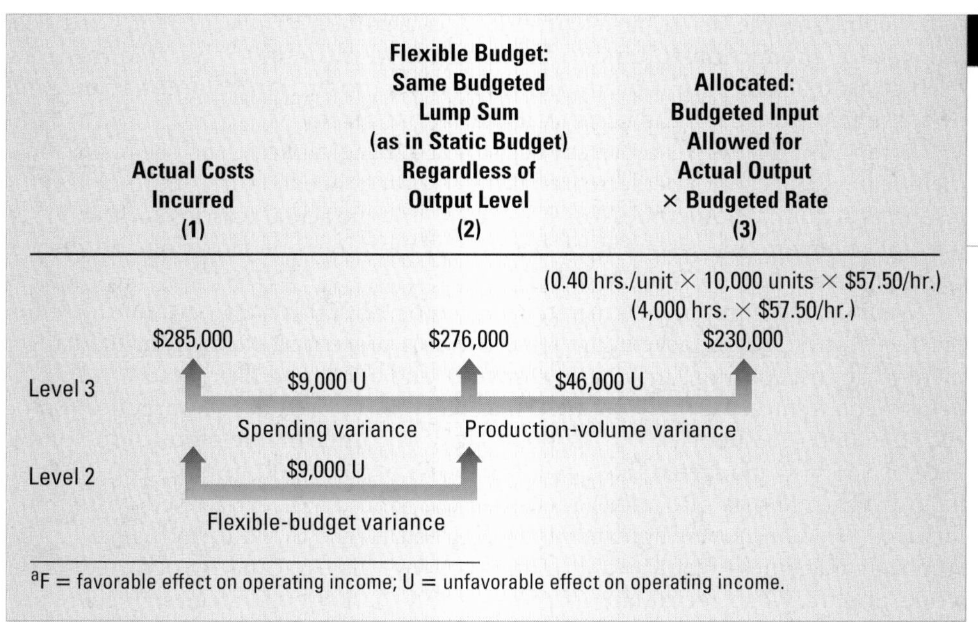

EXHIBIT 8-2

Columnar Presentation of Fixed Manufacturing Overhead Variance Analysis: Webb Company for April 2003[a]

now consider a variance that arises when the actual level of the cost-allocation base for allocating fixed overhead costs differs from the budgeted level of the cost-allocation base chosen at the start of the period. This budgeted level for Webb in April 2003 was 4,800 hours (0.40 machine-hours per output unit × 12,000 budgeted output units).

The **production-volume variance** is the difference between budgeted fixed overhead and fixed overhead allocated on the basis of actual output produced. The production-volume variance is also referred to as **denominator-level variance,** as well as **output-level overhead variance.**

The formula for calculating the production-volume variance, expressed in terms of allocation base units (machine-hours for Webb), is

$$\begin{aligned}\text{Production-volume variance} &= \text{Budgeted fixed overhead} - \text{Fixed overhead allocated using budgeted input allowed for actual output units produced}\\ &= \$276{,}000 - (0.40 \text{ hours per unit} \times 10{,}000 \times \$57.50 \text{ per hour})\\ &= \$276{,}000 - \$230{,}000\\ &= \$46{,}000, \text{ or } \$46{,}000\text{ U}\end{aligned}$$

The formula can also be expressed in terms of the budgeted fixed cost *per output unit:*

$$\begin{aligned}\text{Production-volume variance} &= \text{Budgeted fixed overhead} - \text{Fixed overhead allocated using budgeted cost per output unit allowed for actual output produced}\\ &= \$276{,}000 - (\$23 \text{ per jacket} \times 10{,}000 \text{ jackets})\\ &= \$276{,}000 - \$230{,}000\\ &= \$46{,}000, \text{ or } \$46{,}000\text{ U}\end{aligned}$$

As shown in Exhibit 8-2, the amount used for budgeted fixed overhead will be the same lump sum shown in the static budget and also in any flexible budget within the relevant range. Fixed overhead allocated is the amount of the fixed overhead costs allocated to each unit of output multiplied by the number of output units produced during the budget period.

Interpreting the Production-Volume Variance

The production-volume variance arises whenever the actual level of the denominator used for allocating fixed overhead costs differs from the level used to calculate the budgeted fixed overhead cost rate. We compute this budgeted fixed overhead rate because inventory costing and some types of contracts require fixed overhead costs to be expressed on a unit-of-output basis. The production-volume variance results from "unitizing" fixed costs. In

Question: When the production-volume variance is unfavorable, what is the realation between FMOH allocated and budgeted FMOH?
Answer: FMOH allocated is *less than* budgeted FMOH, as in the Webb example.

our Webb example, each jacket produced is assumed to use $23 of fixed costs. An unfavorable production-volume variance means we have underallocated the fixed overhead costs to actual output produced. A favorable production-volume variance indicates overallocated fixed overhead costs to actual output produced.

Lump-sum fixed costs represent costs of acquiring capacity, such as plant and equipment leases, that cannot be decreased if the resources needed turn out to be less than the resources acquired. Sometimes, costs are fixed for contractual reasons such as a lease contract; at other times, costs are fixed because of lumpiness in acquiring and disposing of capacity (as we discussed in Chapter 2).

Webb leased equipment capacity to produce 12,000 jackets per month. Although it produced only 10,000 jackets, the lease contract prevented Webb from reducing equipment lease costs during April 2003. Unitizing and allocating fixed costs at $23 per jacket helps Webb to measure the amount of fixed-cost resources it used to produce 10,000 jackets, $230,000 ($23 per jacket × 10,000 jackets). The unfavorable production-volume variance of $46,000 (budgeted fixed overhead costs of $276,000 minus $230,000 budgeted fixed overhead costs allocated) measures the amount of extra fixed costs that Webb incurred for manufacturing capacity it planned to use but did not use in April 2003. Webb's management would want to analyze why this overcapacity occurred. Is demand weak? Should Webb reevaluate its product and marketing strategies? Is there a quality problem? Or did Webb make a strategic mistake and acquire too much capacity?

Be careful, when making inferences about a company's decisions about capacity planning and how that capacity was used from the sign (that is, favorable, F, or unfavorable, U) or the magnitude associated with a production-volume variance. To interpret the $46,000 unfavorable variance, Webb should consider why it only sold 10,000 jackets in April. Suppose a new competitor had gained market share by pricing below Webb's selling price. To sell the budgeted 12,000 jackets, Webb may have had to reduce its own selling price on all 12,000 jackets. Suppose it decided that selling 10,000 jackets at a higher price yielded higher operating income than selling 12,000 jackets at a lower price. The production-volume variance does not take into account such information. That's why Webb should not interpret the $46,000 U amount as the *total economic cost* of selling 2,000 jackets less than the 12,000-jacket denominator level.

Companies plan their plant capacity strategically on the basis of expectations of how much capacity will be needed over some future time horizon. For 2003, Webb's budgeted quantity of output is equal to the maximum capacity of the plant for that budget period. Actual demand (and quantity produced) turned out to be below the budgeted quantity of output. Webb reports an unfavorable production-volume variance for April 2003. However, it would be incorrect to infer this means that Webb's management made a bad planning decision regarding the plant capacity. Demand for Webb's jackets might be highly uncertain. Given this uncertainty and the cost of not having sufficient capacity to meet sudden demand surges (for example, lost contribution margins and reduced follow-on business), Webb's management may have made a wise choice in planning 2003 plant capacity.

Always explore the *why* of a variance before concluding that the label unfavorable or favorable necessarily indicates, respectively, poor or good management performance. Understanding the reasons for a variance also helps managers decide on future courses of action (see Concepts in Action, p. 261). Should they try to reduce capacity, increase sales, or do nothing? Chapter 9 and Chapter 13 examine these issues in more detail.

7 Show how the 4- variance analysis approach reconciles the actual overhead incurred with the overhead amounts allocated during the period

...identify spending and efficiency variances for variable overhead costs and spending and production-volume variances for fixed overhead costs

INTEGRATED ANALYSIS OF OVERHEAD COST VARIANCES

As our discussion indicates, the variance calculations for variable manufacturing overhead and fixed manufacturing overhead differ.

- Variable manufacturing overhead has no production-volume variance.
- Fixed manufacturing overhead has no efficiency variance.

Exhibit 8-3 presents an integrated summary of the variable overhead variances and the fixed overhead variances computed using standard costs at the end of April 2003.

CONCEPTS IN ACTION

Standard Costing and Variance Analysis at Polysar

Chemical companies regularly use standard costing. That's because they often produce standardized products using standardized processes. The inputs needed to produce a unit of output are well known. Variances help isolate performances that are better and worse than expected. But there are a few choices that need to be made. For example, how often should standards be set? And who should be responsible for the production-volume variance?

Polysar, based in Ontario, Canada, is one of the world's largest producers of synthetic rubber and latex. Rubber products such as butyl and halobutyl are sold primarily to manufacturers of tires, belting, hoses, and footwear.

Butyl rubbers are costed using standard costing for both variable and fixed costs. Variable costs are feedstocks, chemicals, and energy. For each input, the standard variable cost per ton of butyl is calculated by multiplying the standard input per ton of butyl by the standard price of the input. Standard prices for chemical and energy are set annually, but standard prices for feedstock are a different story. Feedstock represents the largest component of cost, but feedstock prices vary significantly based on worldwide demand and supply. It is impossible for Polysar to set a standard price annually that will be valid for the whole year. Instead, Polysar resets the standard price of feedstock each month to parallel the market price.

Polysar allocates fixed costs, including depreciation, engineering, and planning, to production using a standard fixed cost per ton, and it calculates a production-volume variance equal to the difference between budgeted fixed costs and fixed overhead allocated to production.

Which manager should be responsible for an unfavorable production-volume variance: the sales manager for not booking enough orders to fill up the plant? Or, the production manager for not reducing excess capacity?

Polysar's plant is computerized and efficient, but it needs to employ the same number of persons and incur the same amount of fixed overhead costs whether or not it is operating at capacity. The production manager can do very little about the production-volume variance. The sales manager can probably provide some insight into the reasons for the budget shortfall. But, in effect, the production-volume variance is the result of a long-term strategic decision made by top management about the capacity needed to meet the demand for butyl over multiple periods.

Source: Polysar Limited, Harvard Business School case number 9-188-098 and discussions with company management.

Exhibit 8-3 indicates the columns for which no variances are calculated. Panel A shows the variances for variable manufacturing overhead; Panel B shows the variances for fixed manufacturing overhead. As you study Exhibit 8-3, note how the columns in Panels A and B are aligned to measure the different variances. In both Panels A and B,

1. The difference between columns 1 and 2 measures the spending variance.
2. The difference between columns 2 and 3 measures the efficiency variance (when applicable).
3. The difference between columns 3 and 4 measures the production-volume variance (when applicable).

Panel A has an efficiency variance; Panel B has no efficiency variance. A lump-sum amount of fixed costs will be unaffected by the degree of operating efficiency in a given budget period.

Panel A does not have a production-volume variance. That's because the amount of variable overhead allocated is always the same as the flexible-budget amount. Variable costs never have any unused capacity. When production and sales of jackets decline from 12,000 jackets to 10,000 jackets, budgeted variable overhead costs proportionately decline. Fixed costs are different. Panel B has a production-volume variance because Webb

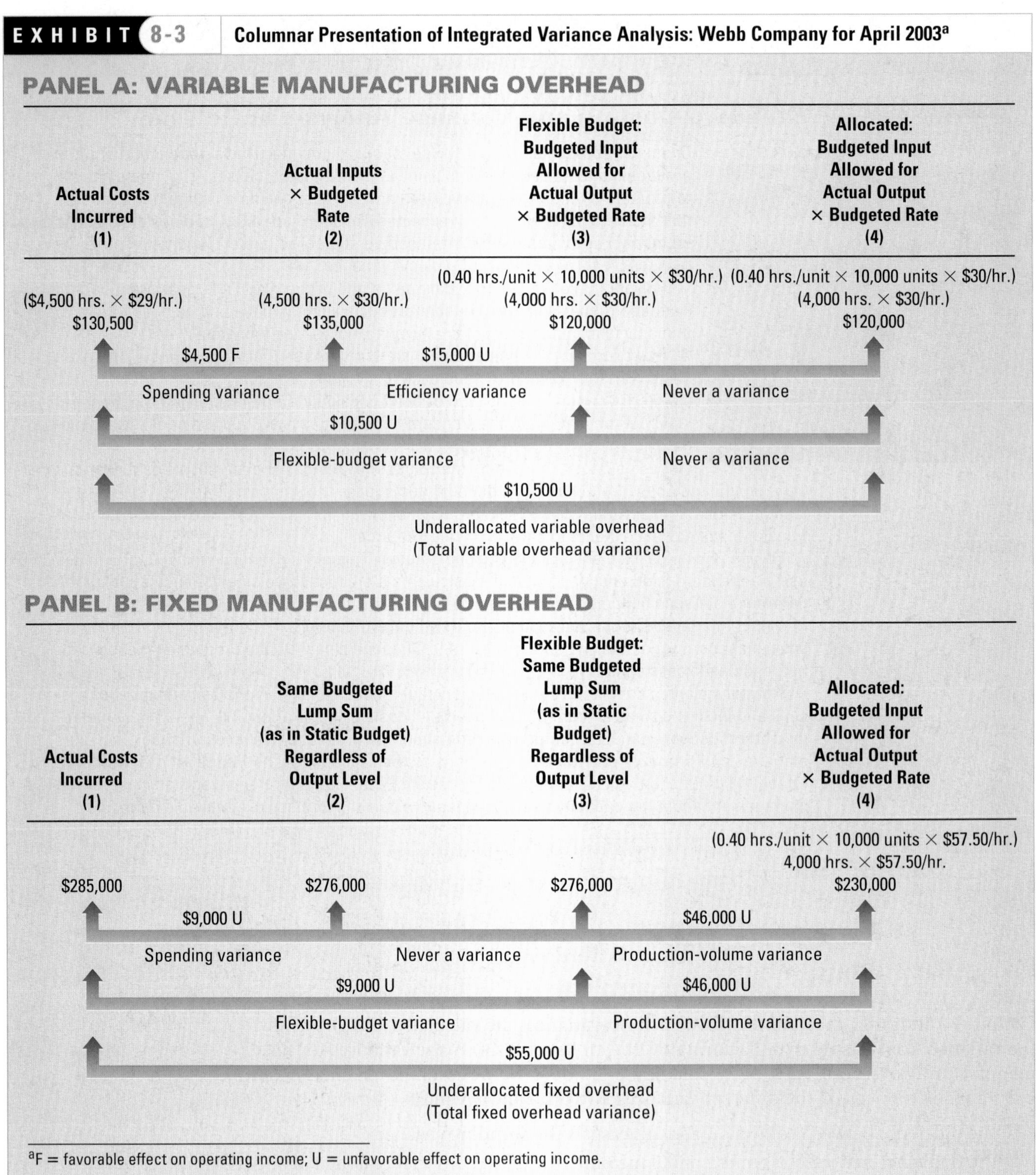

had to pay for the fixed manufacturing overhead resources it had committed to when it planned production of 12,000 jackets, even though it produced only 10,000 jackets and did not need nor use some of its capacity.

4-, 3-, 2-, and 1-Variance Analysis

When all four overhead variances in Exhibit 8-3 are presented together, it is called a 4-variance analysis:

4-Variance Analysis

	Spending Variance	Efficiency Variance	Production-Volume Variance
Variable Manufacturing Overhead	$4,500 F	$15,000 U	Never a variance
Fixed Manufacturing Overhead	$9,000 U	Never a variance	$46,000 U

Note "Never a variance," for production-volume variance in the case of variable manufacturing overhead, and "Never a variance," for efficiency variance for fixed manufacturing overhead.

We can modify this 4-variance analysis by combining the two spending variances. A 3-variance analysis is

3-Variance Analysis

	Spending Variance	Efficiency Variance	Production-Volume Variance
Total Manufacturing Overhead	$4,500 U	$15,000 U	$46,000 U

The 3-variance analysis simplifies the accounting for variances relative to 4-variance analysis, but some information is lost. Because 3-variance analysis combines variable and fixed overhead spending variances when reporting overhead cost variances, it is sometimes called *combined variance analysis*. A 2-variance analysis combines the spending and efficiency variances from the 3-variance analysis:

2-Variance Analysis

	Flexible-Budget Variance	Production-Volume Variance
Total Manufacturing Overhead	$19,500 U	$46,000 U

A 1-variance analysis combines the flexible-budget variance and the production-volume variance from 2-variance analysis:

1-Variance Analysis

	Total Overhead Variance
Total Manufacturing Overhead	$65,500 U

The single variance of $65,500 U in the 1-variance analysis is called **total-overhead variance.** Using figures from Exhibit 8-3, the $65,500 U total-overhead variance is the difference between (a) the total actual manufacturing overhead incurred ($130,500 + $285,000 = $415,500) and (b) the manufacturing overhead allocated ($120,000 + $230,000 = $350,000) to the actual output produced.

As you have seen in the case of other variances, the variances in Webb's 4-variance analysis are not necessarily independent of each other. For example, Webb may purchase lower-quality machine fluids (leading to a favorable variable overhead spending variance), which results in the machines taking longer to operate than budgeted (causing an unfavorable variable overhead efficiency variance).

DIFFERENT PURPOSES OF MANUFACTURING OVERHEAD COST ANALYSIS

Different types of cost analysis are used for different purposes (see Surveys of Company Practice, p. 265). We consider two purposes for variable manufacturing overhead and fixed manufacturing overhead: (1) planning and control and (2) inventory costing for financial reporting.

Variable Manufacturing Overhead Costs

In Exhibit 8-4, Panel A, Webb's variable manufacturing overhead is shown as variable with respect to output units (jackets) for the planning and control purpose and also for

EXHIBIT 8-4

Behavior of Variable and Fixed Manufacturing Overhead Costs for Planning and Control and for Inventory Costing for Webb Company for April 2003

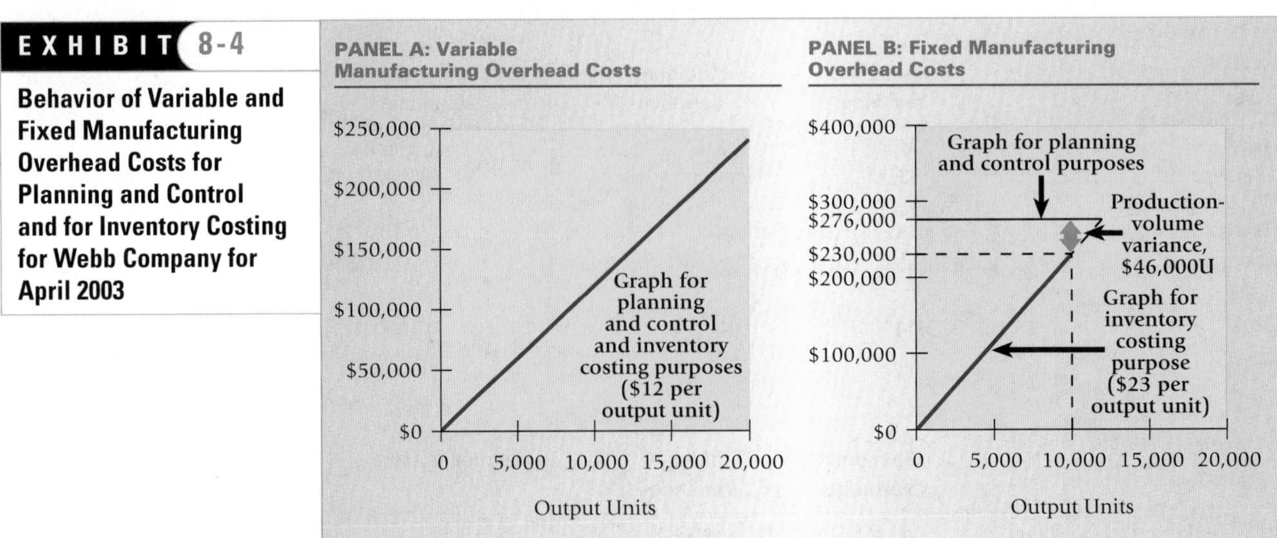

the inventory costing purpose. The greater the number of output units manufactured, the higher the budgeted variable manufacturing overhead costs and the higher the variable manufacturing overhead costs allocated to output units.

Panel A presents an overall picture of how *total* variable overhead might behave. Of course, variable overhead consists of many items, including energy costs, repairs, indirect labor, and so on. Managers help control variable overhead costs by budgeting each line item and then investigating possible causes for any significant variances.

Fixed Manufacturing Overhead Costs

When allocating FMOH for the inventory costing purpose, we "unitize" FMOH (we treat it *as if* it were a variable cost). In contrast, budgeted FMOH is fixed over a wide range of output levels. The production-volume variance is zero only if FMOH allocated *equals* budgeted FMOH. If so, the actual output level (expressed in terms of the FMOH cost-allocation base) is equal to the denominator level used to compute the budgeted FMOH cost rate.

Exhibit 8-4, Panel B, shows that for the planning and control purpose, fixed overhead costs do not change in the 0- to 12,000-unit relevant range. Consider the monthly leasing costs for building and equipment included in Webb's budgeted fixed manufacturing overhead costs of $276,000. Managers control this fixed leasing cost at the time the lease is signed. For any month during the leasing period, management can do little—most likely can do nothing—to change the lease payment. Contrast this description of fixed overhead with how these costs are depicted for the inventory costing purpose in Panel B. Under generally accepted accounting principles, fixed manufacturing costs are allocated as an inventoriable cost based on the level of output units produced. Every output unit that Webb manufactures will increase the fixed overhead allocated to products by $23. Because Webb produces 10,000 jackets, only $230,000 ($23 per jacket × 10,000 jackets) will be allocated to products. As the graph in Panel B shows, the difference between the fixed manufacturing overhead costs budgeted of $276,000 and the $230,000 of costs allocated is the $46,000 U production-volume variance, which will be written off to the Cost of Goods Sold account or prorated among Work in Process, Finished Goods and Cost of Goods Sold accounts.

Inventoriable costs are all costs of a product that are regarded as assets and expensed as cost of goods sold when the product is sold.

Managers should not use the unitization of fixed manufacturing overhead costs for planning and control. However, computing the fixed manufacturing overhead costs allocated of $230,000 allows managers to identify the production-volume variance of $46,000 U, representing unused fixed manufacturing overhead capacity.

JOURNAL ENTRIES FOR OVERHEAD COSTS AND VARIANCES

Recording Overhead Costs

The example for job costing (Robinson Company pp. 99–118) in Chapter 4 used a single Manufacturing Overhead Control account. Here, we illustrate separate accounts for Variable Manufacturing Overhead Control and Fixed Manufacturing Overhead Control. Each overhead control account requires its own overhead allocated account.

SURVEYS OF COMPANY PRACTICE

Variance Analysis and Control Decisions

There is widespread usage of the variances discussed in Chapters 7 and 8. A survey of United Kingdom companies reported the following percentages:

Variance	Percentage of Companies Computing Variance	Percentage of Companies Viewing the Variance as "Above Average Importance" or "Vitally Important" in Control Decisions
Sales volume	77%	70%
Selling price	75	69
Materials price	94	69
Materials efficiency	80	66
Labor price	63	36
Labor efficiency	73	65
Overhead spending	89	69
Production volume	41	28

The overhead spending variance reported is from a 3-variance analysis in which no distinction is made between variable and fixed costs. The survey did not report details on variable or fixed overhead spending variances. The low percentage use for control decisions of the production-volume variance is consistent with its purpose being predominantly financial reporting.

Source: Drury et. al., "A Survey of Management Accounting Practices in UK Manufacturing Companies." Full citation is in Appendix A at the end of the book.

Consider the journal entries for Webb Company. Recall that for April 2003,

	Actual Costs Incurred	Flexible Budget (10,000 units)	Allocated Amount
Variable manufacturing overhead	$130,500	$120,000[a]	$120,000
Fixed manufacturing overhead	285,000	276,000[b]	230,000[c]

[a] 0.40 machine-hour per unit × 10,000 units × $30 per machine-hour = $120,000

[b] $276,000 is the budgeted fixed manufacturing overhead

[c] 0.40 machine-hour per unit × 10,000 units × $57.50 per machine-hour = $230,000

As you have seen (p. 253–254), the budgeted variable overhead cost is $30 per machine-hour (or $12 per jacket). The denominator level for fixed manufacturing overhead is 57,600 machine-hours, with a budgeted cost of $57.50 per machine-hour (or $23 per jacket). Webb uses 4-variance analysis.

During the accounting period, actual variable overhead costs and actual fixed overhead costs are accumulated in the two separate control accounts. As each unit is manufactured, the variable overhead budgeted cost rate and the fixed overhead budgeted cost rate are used to record the amounts in the respective overhead allocated accounts. Webb isolates variances in its accounts on a monthly basis to provide timely feedback to managers.

Entries for variable manufacturing overhead for April 2003 are

1. Variable Manufacturing Overhead Control	130,500	
Accounts Payable Control and various other accounts		130,500
To record actual variable manufacturing overhead costs incurred.		
2. Work-in-Process Control	120,000	
Variable Manufacturing Overhead Allocated		120,000
To record variable manufacturing overhead cost allocated, (0.40 machine-hour/unit × 10,000 units × $30/machine-hour).		

3. Variable Manufacturing Overhead Allocated	120,000	
Variable Manufacturing Overhead Efficiency Variance	15,000	
Variable Manufacturing Overhead Control		130,500
Variable Manufacturing Overhead Spending Variance		4,500
To isolate variances for the accounting period. Calculation of these variances is in Exhibit 8-1.		

Entries for fixed manufacturing overhead for April 2003 are

4. Fixed Manufacturing Overhead Control	285,000	
Salaries Payable, Accumulated Depreciation, and various other accounts		285,000
To record actual fixed overhead costs incurred.		
5. Work-in-Process Control	230,000	
Fixed Manufacturing Overhead Allocated		230,000
To record fixed manufacturing overhead costs allocated, (0.40 machine-hour/unit × 10,000 units × $57.50/machine-hour).		
6. Fixed Manufacturing Overhead Allocated	230,000	
Fixed Manufacturing Overhead Spending Variance	9,000	
Fixed Manufacturing Overhead Production-Volume Variance	46,000	
Fixed Manufacturing Overhead Control		285,000
To isolate variances for the accounting period. Calculation of these variances is in Exhibit 8-2.		

To see how the production-volume variance fits into Webb's financial accounting system, consider the following basic budget data from pp. 217–218.

Budgeted selling price		$120
Standard direct material cost per jacket	$60	
Standard direct manufacturing labor cost per jacket	16	
Standard variable manufacturing overhead cost per jacket	12	
Standard fixed manufacturing overhead cost per jacket ($276,000 ÷ 12,000)	23	
Standard cost per jacket		111
Budgeted profit per jacket		$ 9*

*Note that the static-budget operating income is $9 per jacket × 12,000 jackets = $108,000.

Each jacket that Webb sells results in a budgeted profit of $9 per jacket, based on the budgeted selling price of $120 and the standard cost of $111 assigned to each jacket. For the 10,000 jackets that Webb sells, the operating income based on budgeted profit per jacket is $90,000 ($9 per jacket × 10,000 jackets). To see this differently, note that the debits to Work-in-Process Control for the 10,000 jackets produced, which are then transferred to Finished Goods and finally to Cost of Goods Sold are $1,110,000:

Direct materials (Chapter 7, p. 231, Entry 1b)	$ 600,000
Direct manufacturing labor (Chapter 7, p. 231, Entry 2)	160,000
Variable manufacturing overhead (Chapter 8, p. 265, Entry 2)	120,000
Fixed manufacturing overhead (Chapter 8, Entry 5 above)	230,000
Cost of goods sold at standard cost	$1,110,000

Operating income based on budgeted selling price and standard cost per jacket is

Revenues at budgeted selling price ($120 per jacket × 10,000 jackets)	$1,200,000
Cost of goods sold at standard cost	1,110,000
Operating income based on budgeted profit per jacket	$ 90,000

Of course, in calculating the budgeted operating income of $90,000, fixed manufacturing overhead allocated is only $230,000 ($23 per jacket × 10,000 jackets), whereas the budgeted fixed manufacturing overhead costs are $276,000. The $46,000 production-volume variance (the difference between budgeted fixed manufacturing overhead costs, $276,000, and allocated fixed manufacturing overhead costs, $230,000) helps explain why actual operating income is only $14,900 (p. 218) when the budgeted operating income is $90,000. The complete reconciliation is

Operating income based on budgeted profit per jacket ($9 per jacket × 10,000 jackets)	$90,000
Unfavorable production-volume variance	(46,000)
Flexible-budget operating income	44,000
Unfavorable flexible-budget variance for operating income (p. 219)	(29,100)
Actual operating income	$14,900

Compare the sales-volume variance and the production-volume variance. The $64,000 U sales-volume variance explains the difference between the static-budget operating income and the flexible-budget operating income (see, pp. 219–220). The $46,000 U production-volume variance explains the difference between the operating income based on the budgeted profit per jacket and the flexible-budget operating income.

Although Webb isolates variances in its accounts on a monthly basis, it waits until the end of each year to make adjustments so that variance accounts end up with zero balances. Chapter 4 (pp. 114 – 118) explains alternative approaches to making these adjustments.

FINANCIAL AND NONFINANCIAL PERFORMANCE

The overhead variances discussed in this chapter are examples of financial performance measures. Managers also find that nonfinancial measures provide useful information. Nonfinancial measures that Webb likely would find useful in planning and controlling its overhead costs are

(i) actual indirect materials used per machine-hour, relative to budgeted indirect materials used per machine-hour;

(ii) actual energy used per machine-hour, relative to budgeted energy used per machine-hour; and

(iii) actual machine time per jacket, relative to budgeted machine time per jacket.

MOH cost items can be controlled on the production floor through personal observation and timely nonfinancial measures of individual items (for example, overtime authorization, idle time, defect rates). The accounting system transforms these nonfinancial measures into financial measures that inform managers of the materiality (significance) of the variances.

These performance measures, like the financial variances discussed in this chapter and Chapter 7, are best considered as signals to direct managers' attention to problems. These nonfinancial performance measures probably would be reported on the production floor on a daily or hourly basis. The manufacturing overhead variances we discussed in this chapter capture the financial effects of items such as (i), (ii), and (iii), which in many cases first appear as nonfinancial performance measures.

Both financial and nonfinancial performance measures are used to evaluate the performance of managers. Exclusive reliance on either is always too simplistic.

There is debate over the relative weights to be given to financial and nonfinancial measures. For example, some experts maintain that nonfinancial measures, such as product quality and customer satisfaction, should be given more emphasis than financial measures. Chapter 13 considers this issue in detail.

OVERHEAD COST VARIANCES IN NONMANUFACTURING AND SERVICE SETTINGS

Our Webb Company example examines variable manufacturing overhead costs and fixed manufacturing overhead costs. Should the overhead costs of the nonmanufacturing areas of the company be examined using the variance analysis framework discussed in this chapter? Variable-cost information pertaining to nonmanufacturing as well as manufacturing costs is often used in pricing decisions and decisions about which products to push or deemphasize. Variance analysis of all variable overhead costs is a main consideration when making such decisions. For example, managers in industries in which distribution costs are high may invest in standard-costing systems that give reliable and timely information on variable distribution overhead spending variances and efficiency variances.

Variance analysis of fixed nonmanufacturing overhead costs, such as design costs, is helpful when a company does contract work that is reimbursed on the basis of full actual costs plus a percentage of those costs. Information on variances enables more accurate estimates of future costs. Variance analysis of fixed nonmanufacturing costs, such as distribution costs, is also useful in capacity planning and utilization decisions, as well as for managing these costs.

Consider service-sector companies such as airlines, hospitals, and railroads. The measures of output commonly used in these companies are passenger-miles flown, patient-days provided, and ton-miles of freight hauled, respectively. Very few costs can be traced to these outputs in a cost-effective way. The majority of costs are fixed overhead costs (for example, costs of equipment, buildings, and staff). Utilizing capacity effectively is the key to profitability.

In other service-sector companies such as banking, measures of output are more difficult to identify. Banks provide a variety of different products to their customers—checking accounts, savings accounts, mortgages, loans, and credit cards. Cost analysis focuses on the different activities and transactions of the bank, such as opening accounts, maintaining accounts, granting loans, and issuing credit cards. Most of the costs of these activities and transactions are overhead costs. Information technology has made it much easier to track and identify overhead costs to activities. Consider the assignment of staff costs to activities. Employees record in an activity database the time they spend on different activities. By accessing the salary database, the computer generates the total staff cost of each activity. As we discuss in the next section, managers can then use standard-costing techniques to manage the overhead costs of these activities.

8 **Illustrate how the flexible-budget variance approach can be used in activity-based costing**

...compare budgeted and actual overhead costs of activities

ACTIVITY-BASED COSTING AND VARIANCE ANALYSIS

ABC systems classify costs of various activities into a cost hierarchy: output-unit level, batch level, product sustaining, and facility sustaining (see pp. 143–144). The basic principles and concepts for variable manufacturing overhead costs and fixed manufacturing overhead costs presented earlier in the chapter can be applied to ABC systems. In this section, we illustrate variance analysis for variable batch-level setup overhead costs and fixed batch-level setup overhead costs. Batch-level costs are costs of activities that are related to a group of units of products or services rather than to each individual unit.

We continue the Chapter 7 example of Lyco Brass Works, which manufactures Jacutaps, a line of decorative brass faucets for home spas. Lyco produces Jacutaps in batches. To manufacture a batch of Jacutaps, Lyco must set up the machines and molds. Setups are a skilled activity. Hence, a separate Setup Department is responsible for setting up machines and molds for different types of Jacutaps. Lyco regards setup costs as overhead costs of products.

Setup costs consist of some costs that are variable and some that are fixed with respect to the number of setup-hours. Variable setup costs consist of wages paid to direct setup labor and indirect support labor, costs of maintenance of setup equipment, and costs of indirect materials and energy used during setups. Fixed setup costs consist of salaries paid to engineers and supervisors and costs of leasing setup equipment.

Information regarding Jacutaps for 2004 follows:

	Static-Budget Amount	Actual Amount
1. Units of Jacutaps produced and sold	180,000	151,200
2. Batch size (units per batch)	150	140
3. Number of batches (Line 1 ÷ Line 2)	1,200	1,080
4. Setup-hours per batch	6	6.25
5. Total setup-hours (Line 3 × Line 4)	7,200	6,750
6. Variable overhead cost per setup-hour	$20	$21
7. Variable setup overhead costs (Line 5 × Line 6)	$144,000	$141,750
8. Total fixed setup overhead costs	$216,000	$220,000

Flexible Budget and Variance Analysis for Variable Setup Overhead Costs

To prepare the flexible budget for variable setup overhead costs, Lyco starts with the actual units of output produced, 151,200 units, and proceeds in the following steps.

Step 1: Using Budgeted Batch Size, Calculate the Number of Batches That Should Have Been Used to Produce the Actual Output. Lyco should have manufactured the 151,200 units of output in 1,008 batches (151,200 units ÷ 150 units per batch).

Step 2: Using Budgeted Setup-Hours per Batch, Calculate the Number of Setup-Hours That Should Have Been Used. At the budgeted quantity of 6 setup-hours per batch, 1,008 batches should have required 6,048 setup-hours (1,008 batches × 6 setup-hours per batch).

Step 3: Using Budgeted Variable Cost per Setup-Hour, Calculate the Flexible Budget for Variable Setup Overhead Costs. The flexible-budget amount is 6,048 setup-hours × $20 per setup-hour = $120,960.

$$\begin{aligned}\text{Flexible-budget variance for variable setup overhead costs} &= \text{Actual costs incurred} - \text{Flexible-budget costs}\\ &= (6{,}750 \text{ hours} \times \$21 \text{ per hour}) - (6{,}048 \text{ hours} \times \$20 \text{ per hour})\\ &= \$141{,}750 - \$120{,}960\\ &= \$20{,}790, \text{ or } \$20{,}790 \text{ U}\end{aligned}$$

Exhibit 8-5 presents the variances for variable setup overhead costs in columnar form.

The flexible-budget variance for variable setup overhead costs can be subdivided into efficiency and spending variances.

$$\begin{aligned}\text{Variable setup overhead efficiency variance} &= \left(\begin{array}{c}\text{Actual quantity of variable overhead}\\ \text{cost-allocation base used for actual output}\end{array} - \begin{array}{c}\text{Budgeted quantity of variable overhead}\\ \text{cost-allocation base allowed for actual output}\end{array}\right) \times \begin{array}{c}\text{Budgeted variable overhead cost per}\\ \text{unit of cost-allocation base}\end{array}\\ &= (6{,}750 \text{ hours} - 6{,}048 \text{ hours}) \times \$20 \text{ per hour}\\ &= 702 \text{ hours} \times \$20 \text{ per hour}\\ &= \$14{,}040, \text{ or } \$14{,}040 \text{ U}\end{aligned}$$

The unfavorable variable setup overhead efficiency variance of $14,040 arises because the 6,750 actual setup-hours exceed the 6,048 setup-hours Lyco should have used for the number of units it produced. Two reasons for the unfavorable efficiency variance are (1) smaller actual batch sizes of 140 units per batch, instead of budgeted batch sizes of 150 units, which results in Lyco producing the 151,200 units in 1,080 batches instead of 1,008 batches; and (2) higher actual setup-hours per batch of 6.25 hours instead of the budgeted 6 hours.

Explanations for smaller-than-budgeted batch sizes include (1) quality problems if batch sizes exceed 140 units (faucets) and (2) high costs of carrying inventory. Explanations for higher actual setup-hours per batch include (1) problems with equipment; (2) undermotivated, inexperienced, or underskilled employees; and (3) inappropriate setup-time standards.

Because setup costs are at the batch level, the budgeted quantity of input allowed for actual output is calculated at the batch level. The quantity of setup-hours allowed is based on the number of batches it should have taken to produce the actual quantity of output. Although both ABC systems and traditional costing systems allocate MOH costs to output units produced, ABC has the advantage that there are better cause-and-effect relationships between the cost-allocation bases chosen and the related cost pools.

EXHIBIT 8-5

Columnar Presentation of Variable Setup Overhead Variance Analysis for Lyco Brass Works for 2004[a]

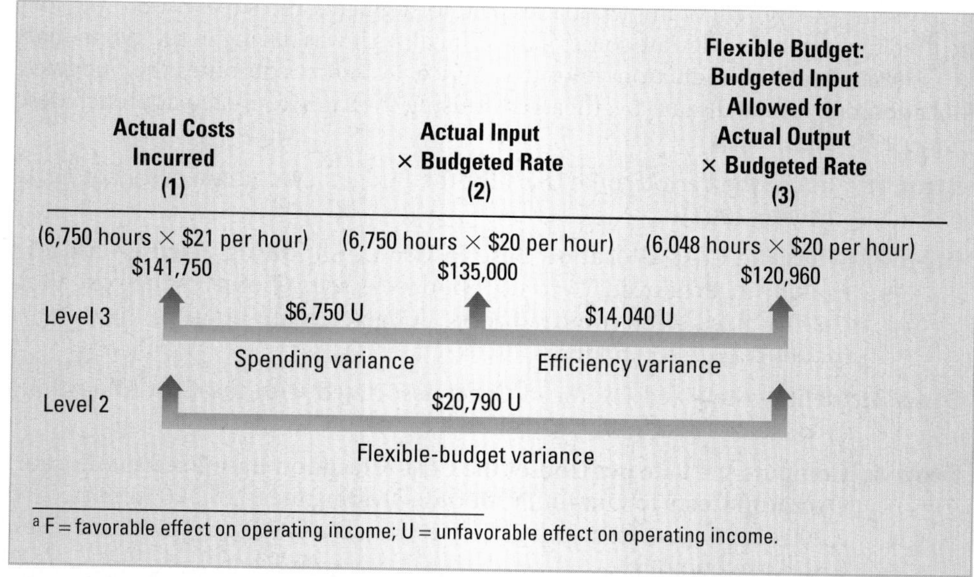

[a] F = favorable effect on operating income; U = unfavorable effect on operating income.

$$\begin{aligned}\text{Variable setup overhead spending variance} &= \left(\begin{array}{c}\text{Actual variable}\\ \text{overhead cost per}\\ \text{unit of cost-allocation}\\ \text{base}\end{array} - \begin{array}{c}\text{Budgeted variable}\\ \text{overhead cost per}\\ \text{unit of cost-allocation}\\ \text{base}\end{array}\right) \times \begin{array}{c}\text{Actual quantity of}\\ \text{variable overhead}\\ \text{cost-allocation base}\\ \text{used for actual output}\end{array}\\ &= (\$21 \text{ per hour} - \$20 \text{ per hour}) \times 6{,}750 \text{ hours}\\ &= \$1 \text{ per hour} \times 6{,}750 \text{ hours}\\ &= \$6{,}750, \text{ or } \$6{,}750 \text{ U}\end{aligned}$$

The unfavorable spending variance indicates that Lyco operated in 2004 with a higher-than-budgeted variable overhead cost per setup-hour. Two main reasons that could account for the unfavorable spending variance are (1) the actual prices of individual items included in variable overhead, such as setup labor, indirect support labor, or energy, are higher than the budgeted prices; and (2) the actual quantity usage of individual items, such as indirect support labor and energy, increased more than the increase in setup-hours, due perhaps to setups becoming more complex because of equipment problems. Thus, equipment problems could lead to an unfavorable efficiency variance because setup-hours increase, but they could also lead to an unfavorable spending variance, because each setup-hour requires more resources from the setup cost pool than the budgeted amounts.

Identifying the reasons for the variances is important because it helps managers take corrective action that will be incorporated in future budgets. We now consider fixed setup overhead costs.

Flexible Budget and Variance Analysis for Fixed Setup Overhead Costs

For fixed setup overhead costs, the flexible-budget amount equals the static-budget amount of $216,000. Why? Because there is no "flexing" of fixed costs.

$$\begin{aligned}\text{Fixed-setup overhead flexible-budget variance} &= \begin{array}{c}\text{Actual costs}\\ \text{incurred}\end{array} - \begin{array}{c}\text{Flexible-budget}\\ \text{costs}\end{array}\\ &= \$220{,}000 - \$216{,}000\\ &= \$4{,}000, \text{ or } \$4{,}000 \text{ U}\end{aligned}$$

The fixed setup overhead spending variance is the same amount as the fixed overhead flexible-budget variance (because fixed overhead costs have no efficiency variance).

$$\begin{aligned}\text{Fixed setup overhead spending variance} &= \begin{array}{c}\text{Actual costs}\\ \text{incurred}\end{array} - \begin{array}{c}\text{Flexible-budget}\\ \text{costs}\end{array}\\ &= \$220{,}000 - \$216{,}000\\ &= \$4{,}000, \text{ or } \$4{,}000 \text{ U}\end{aligned}$$

The unfavorable fixed setup overhead spending variance could be due to higher lease costs of new setup equipment or higher salaries paid to engineers and supervisors. Lyco may have incurred these costs to alleviate some of the difficulties it was having in setting up machines.

To calculate the production-volume variance, Lyco first computes the budgeted cost-allocation rate for fixed setup overhead costs using the same four-step approach described on pp. 257–258.

Step 1: Choose the Period to Be Used for the Budget. Lyco uses a period of 12 months (the year 2004).

Step 2: Select the Cost-Allocation Base to Use in Allocating Fixed Overhead Costs to Output Produced. Lyco uses budgeted setup-hours as the cost-allocation base for fixed setup overhead costs. Budgeted setup-hours in the static budget for 2004 are 7,200 hours.

Step 3: Identify the Fixed Overhead Costs Associated with the Cost-Allocation Base. Lyco's fixed setup overhead cost budget for 2004 is $216,000.

Step 4: Compute the Rate per Unit of the Cost-Allocation Base Used to Allocate Fixed Overhead Costs to Output Produced. Dividing the $216,000 from step 3 by the 7,200 setup-hours from step 2, Lyco estimates a fixed setup overhead cost rate of $30 per setup-hour:

EXHIBIT 8-6

Columnar Presentation of Fixed Setup Overhead Variance Analysis: Lyco Brass Works for 2004[a]

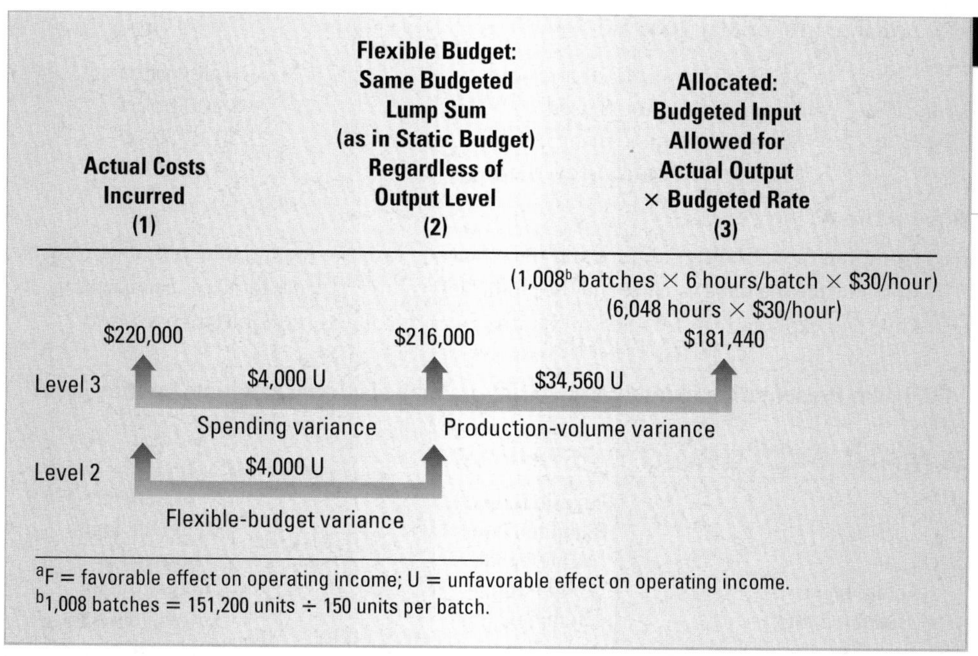

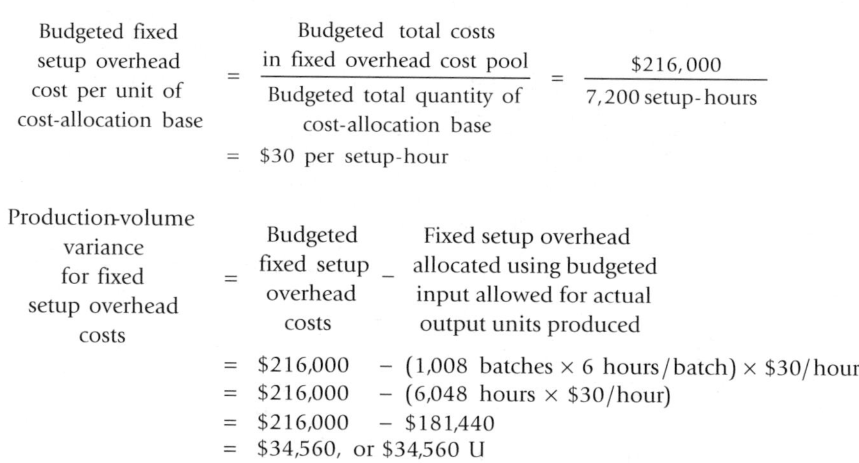

$$\begin{aligned}\text{Budgeted fixed setup overhead cost per unit of cost-allocation base} &= \frac{\text{Budgeted total costs in fixed overhead cost pool}}{\text{Budgeted total quantity of cost-allocation base}} = \frac{\$216{,}000}{7{,}200 \text{ setup-hours}} \\ &= \$30 \text{ per setup-hour}\end{aligned}$$

$$\begin{aligned}\text{Production-volume variance for fixed setup overhead costs} &= \text{Budgeted fixed setup overhead costs} - \text{Fixed setup overhead allocated using budgeted input allowed for actual output units produced} \\ &= \$216{,}000 - (1{,}008 \text{ batches} \times 6 \text{ hours/batch}) \times \$30/\text{hour} \\ &= \$216{,}000 - (6{,}048 \text{ hours} \times \$30/\text{hour}) \\ &= \$216{,}000 - \$181{,}440 \\ &= \$34{,}560, \text{ or } \$34{,}560 \text{ U}\end{aligned}$$

Exhibit 8-6 presents the variances for fixed setup overhead costs in columnar form.

During 2004, Lyco planned to produce 180,000 units of Jacutaps but actually produced only 151,200 units. The unfavorable production-volume variance measures the amount of extra fixed setup costs that Lyco incurred for setup capacity it had but did not use. One interpretation is that the unfavorable $34,560 production-volume variance represents inefficient use of setup capacity. However, Lyco may have earned higher operating income by selling 151,200 units at a higher price than 180,000 units at a lower price. The production-volume variance should be interpreted cautiously because it does not consider such information.

PROBLEM FOR SELF-STUDY

Maria Lopez is the newly appointed president of Laser Products. She is examining the May 2004 results for the Aerospace Products Division. This division manufactures wing parts for satellites. Lopez's current concern is with manufacturing overhead costs at the Aerospace Products Division. Both variable manufacturing overhead costs and fixed manufacturing overhead costs are allocated to the wing parts on the basis of laser-cutting-hours. The budgeted cost rates are variable manufacturing overhead of $200 per hour and fixed manufacturing overhead of $240 per hour. The budgeted laser-cutting time per wing part is 1.5 hours. Budgeted production and sales for May 2004 is 5,000 wing parts. Budgeted fixed manufacturing overhead costs for May 2004 is $1,800,000.

Continued

Actual results for May 2004 are

Wing parts produced and sold	4,800 units
Laser-cutting-hours used	8,400 hours
Variable manufacturing overhead costs	$1,478,400
Fixed manufacturing overhead costs	$1,832,200

Required

1. Compute the spending variance and the efficiency variance for variable manufacturing overhead.
2. Compute the spending variance and the production-volume variance for fixed manufacturing overhead.
3. Give two explanations for each of the variances calculated in requirements 1 and 2.

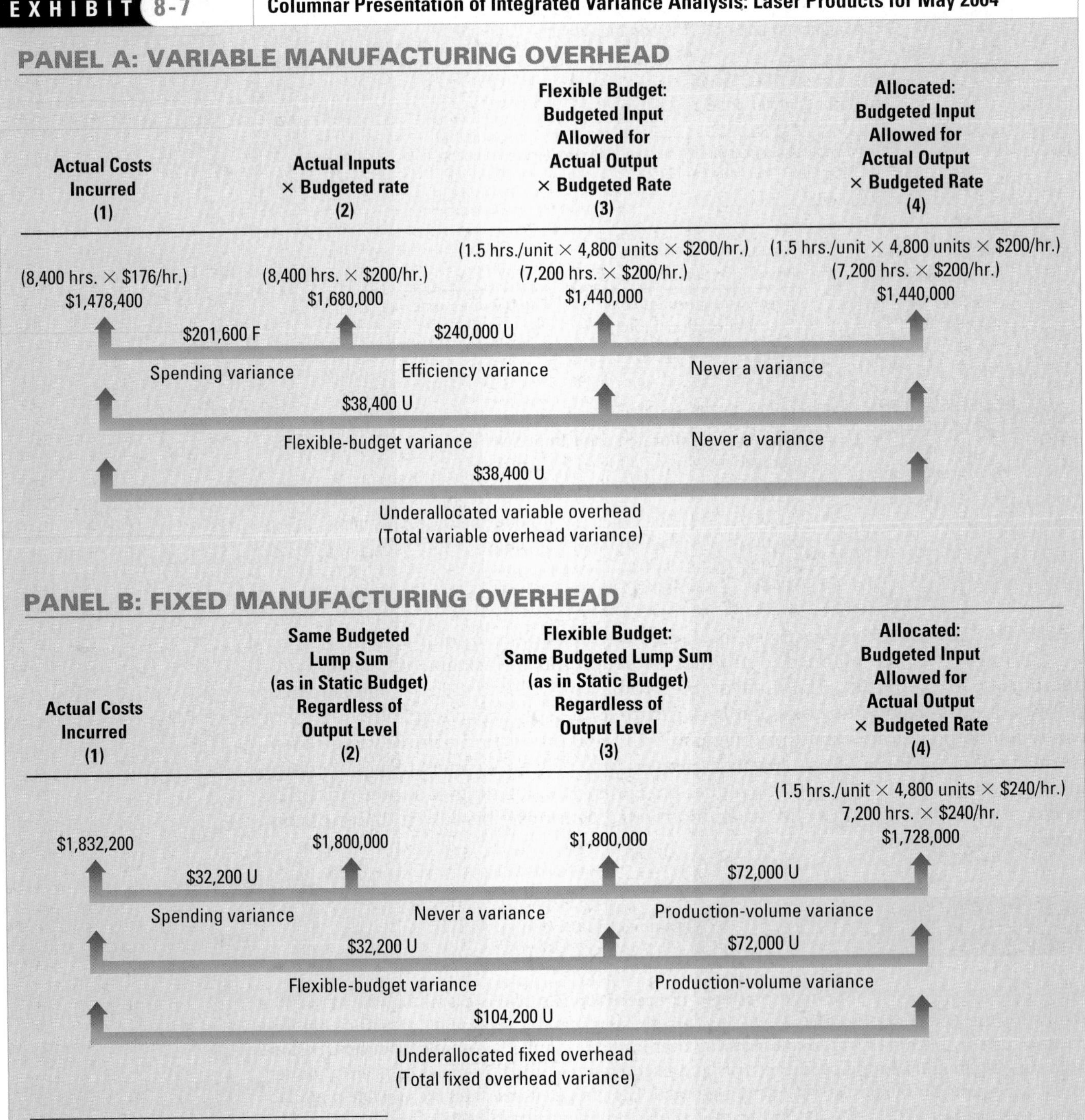

SOLUTION

1. and **2.** See Exhibit 8-7.

3. a. Variable manufacturing overhead spending variance, $201,600 F. One possible reason for this variance is that actual prices of individual items included in variable overhead (such as cutting fluids) are lower than budgeted prices. A second possible reason is that the percentage increase in the actual quantity usage of individual items in the variable overhead cost pool is less than the percentage increase in machine-hours compared to the flexible budget.

b. Variable manufacturing overhead efficiency variance, $240,000 U. One possible reason for this variance is inadequate maintenance of laser machines, causing them to take more laser time per wing part. A second possible reason is use of undermotivated, inexperienced, or underskilled workers with the laser-cutting machines, resulting in more laser-time per wing part.

c. Fixed manufacturing overhead spending variance, $32,200 U. One possible reason for this variance is that the actual prices of individual items in the fixed-cost pool unexpectedly increased from the prices budgeted (such as an unexpected increase in machine leasing costs). A second possible reason is misclassification of items as fixed that are in fact variable.

d. Production-volume variance, $72,000 U. Actual production of wing parts is 4,800 units, compared with the 5,000 units budgeted. One possible reason for this variance is demand factors, such as a decline in an aerospace program that led to a decline in the demand for aircraft parts. A second possible reason is supply factors, such as a production stoppage due to labor problems or machine breakdowns.

DECISION POINTS SUMMARY

The following question-and-answer format summarizes the chapter's learning objectives. Each decision presents a key question related to a learning objective. The guidelines are the answer to that question.

Decision	Guidelines
1. How do managers plan variable overhead costs and fixed overhead costs?	Planning of both variable overhead costs and fixed overhead costs involves undertaking only activities that add value and then being efficient in that undertaking. The key difference is that for variable-cost planning, ongoing decisions during the budget period play a larger role; whereas for fixed-cost planning, most key decisions must be made before the start of the period.
2. Why do companies use standard costing?	A standard-costing system traces direct costs to a cost object by multiplying the standard prices or rates times the standard inputs allowed for actual output produced and allocates indirect costs on the basis of the standard indirect rates times the standard quantities of the allocation bases allowed for the actual output produced. The standard costs of products are known at the start of the period. To manage costs, managers compare actual costs to standard costs.
3. What variances can be calculated for variable overhead?	When the flexible budget for variable overhead is developed, an overhead efficiency variance and an overhead spending variance can be computed. The variable overhead efficiency variance evaluates the actual quantity of the cost-allocation base used relative to the budgeted quantity of the cost-allocation base. The variable overhead spending variance evaluates the actual cost per unit of the cost-allocation base relative to the budgeted cost per unit of the cost-allocation base.
4. Is the efficiency variance for indirect-cost items similar to the efficiency variance for direct-cost items?	These two efficiency variances are not similar. The efficiency variance for a variable indirect-cost item indicates whether more or less of the cost-allocation base per output unit was used than was included in the flexible budget. The efficiency variance for a direct-cost item indicates whether more or less of the input per unit of output of that direct-cost item was used than was included in the flexible budget.

Continued

5. How is a budgeted fixed overhead cost rate calculated?	The budgeted fixed overhead cost rate is calculated by dividing the budgeted fixed overhead costs by the denominator level of the cost-allocation base.
6. How should you interpret the production-volume variance?	Interpret cautiously the production-volume variance as a measure of the economic cost of unused capacity. One caution: management may have maintained some extra capacity to meet uncertain demand surges that are important to satisfy. Another caution: the production-volume variance focuses only on fixed overhead costs. The production-volume variance does not take into account any decreases in the selling price of output necessary to spur extra demand that would, in turn, make use of any idle capacity.
7. What is the most detailed way for a company to reconcile actual overhead incurred with the amount allocated during a period?	A 4-variance analysis presents spending and efficiency variances for variable overhead costs and spending and production-volume variances for fixed overhead costs. By analyzing these four variances together, managers can reconcile the actual overhead costs with the amount of overhead allocated to output produced during a period.
8. Can the flexible-budget variance approach for analyzing overhead costs be used in activity-based costing?	Flexible budgeting in ABC systems gives insight into why actual overhead activity costs differ from budgeted overhead activity costs. Using output and input measures for an activity, a 4-variance analysis can be conducted.

TERMS TO LEARN

The chapter and the Glossary at the end of the book contain definitions of:

denominator level (p. 257)
denominator-level variance (259)
fixed overhead flexible-budget variance (258)
fixed overhead spending variance (258)
output-level overhead variance (259)
production-denominator level (257)
production-volume variance (259)
standard costing (253)
total-overhead variance (263)
variable overhead efficiency variance (255)
variable overhead flexible-budget variance (254)
variable overhead spending variance (255)

ASSIGNMENT MATERIAL

Questions

8-1 What are the steps in planning variable overhead costs?

8-2 How does the planning of fixed overhead costs differ from the planning of variable overhead costs?

8-3 How does a standard-costing system differ from an actual-costing system?

8-4 What are the steps in developing a budgeted variable overhead cost-allocation rate?

8-5 The spending variance for variable manufacturing overhead is affected by several factors. Explain.

8-6 Assume variable manufacturing overhead is allocated using machine-hours. Give three possible reasons for a $25,000 favorable variable overhead efficiency variance.

8-7 Describe the difference between a direct materials efficiency variance and a variable manufacturing overhead efficiency variance.

8-8 What are the steps in developing a budgeted fixed overhead rate?

8-9 Why is the flexible-budget variance the same amount as the spending variance for fixed manufacturing overhead?

8-10 Describe one caveat that will affect whether a production-volume variance is a good measure of the economic cost of unused capacity.

8-11 What are the variances in a 4-variance analysis?

8-12 Why is there no efficiency variance for fixed manufacturing overhead costs?

8-13 "Overhead variances should be viewed as interdependent rather than independent." Give an example.

8-14 Explain how the analysis of fixed overhead costs differs for (a) planning and control on the one hand and (b) inventory costing for financial reporting on the other hand.

8-15 Describe how flexible-budget variance analysis can be used in the control of costs in the activity areas.

Exercises

8-16 **Variable manufacturing overhead, variance analysis.** Esquire Clothing is a manufacturer of designer suits. The cost of each suit is the sum of three variable costs (direct materials costs, direct manufacturing labor costs and manufacturing overhead costs) and one fixed-cost category (manufacturing overhead costs). Variable manufacturing overhead cost is allocated to each suit on the basis of budgeted direct manufacturing labor-hours per suit. For June 2004, each suit is budgeted to take four labor-hours. Budgeted variable manufacturing overhead cost per labor-hour is $12. The budgeted number of suits to be manufactured in June 2004 is 1,040.

Actual variable manufacturing costs in June 2004 were $52,164 for 1,080 suits started and completed. There were no beginning or ending inventories of suits. Actual direct manufacturing labor-hours for June were 4,536.

Required

1. Compute the flexible-budget variance, the spending variance, and the efficiency variance for variable manufacturing overhead.
2. Comment on the results.

8-17 **Fixed manufacturing overhead, variance analysis (continuation of 8-16).** Esquire Clothing allocates fixed manufacturing overhead to each suit using budgeted direct manufacturing labor-hours per suit. Data pertaining to fixed manufacturing overhead costs for June 2004 are budgeted, $62,400, and actual, $63,916.

Required

1. Compute the spending variance for fixed manufacturing overhead. Comment on the results.
2. Compute the production-volume variance for June 2004. What inferences can Esquire Clothing draw from this variance?

8-18 **Variable manufacturing overhead variance analysis.** The French Bread Company bakes baguettes for distribution to upscale grocery stores. The company has two direct-cost categories, direct materials and direct manufacturing labor. Variable manufacturing overhead is allocated to products on the basis of standard direct manufacturing labor-hours. Following is some pertinent data for the French Bread Company:

Direct manufacturing labor use	0.02 hours per baguette
Variable manufacturing overhead	$10.00 per direct manufacturing labor-hour

The French Bread Company recorded the following additional data for the year ended December 31, 2004:

Planned (budgeted) output	3,200,000 baguettes
Actual production	2,800,000 baguettes
Direct manufacturing labor	50,400 hours
Actual variable manufacturing overhead	$680,400

Required

1. What is the denominator used for allocating variable manufacturing overhead? (That is, for how many direct manufacturing labor-hours is French Bread budgeting?)
2. Prepare a variance analysis of variable manufacturing overhead. Use Exhibit 8-3 (p. 262) for reference.
3. Discuss the variances you have calculated and give possible explanations for them.

8-19 **Fixed manufacturing overhead variance analysis.** The French Bread Company bakes baguettes for distribution to upscale grocery stores. The company has two direct-cost categories, direct materials and direct manufacturing labor. Fixed manufacturing overhead is allocated to products on the basis of standard direct manufacturing labor-hours. Following is some pertinent budgeted data for the French Bread Company:

Direct manufacturing labor use	0.02 hours per baguette
Fixed manufacturing overhead	$4.00 per direct labor-hour

The French Bread Company recorded the following additional data for the year ended December 31, 2004:

Planned (budgeted) output	3,200,000 baguettes
Actual production	2,800,000 baguettes
Direct manufacturing labor	50,400 hours
Actual fixed manufacturing overhead	$272,000

Required

1. Prepare a variance analysis of fixed manufacturing overhead cost. Use Exhibit 8-3 (p. 262) as a guide.
2. Is fixed overhead underallocated or overallocated? By what amount?
3. Comment on your results. Discuss the variances and explain what may be driving them.

8-20 **Manufacturing overhead, variance analysis.** Zyton assembles its CardioX product at its Scottsdale plant. Manufacturing overhead (both variable and fixed) is allocated to each CardioX unit using budgeted assembly-hours. Budgeted assembly time per CardioX product is two hours. The budgeted variable manufacturing overhead cost per assembly-hour is $40. The budgeted number of CardioX units to be assembled in March 2004 is 8,000. Budgeted fixed manufacturing overhead costs are $480,000.

Actual variable manufacturing overhead costs for March 2004 were $610,500 for 7,400 units actually assembled. Actual assembly-hours were 16,280. Actual fixed manufacturing overhead costs were $503,420.

Required

1. Prepare a 4-variance analysis for Zyton's Scottsdale plant.
2. Comment on the results in requirement 1.
3. How does the planning and control of variable manufacturing overhead costs differ from that of fixed manufacturing overhead costs?

8-21 4-variance analysis, fill in the blanks. Use the following manufacturing overhead data to fill in the following blanks:

	Variable	Fixed
Actual costs incurred	$11,900	$6,000
Costs allocated to products	9,000	4,500
Flexible budget: Budgeted input allowed for actual output produced × budgeted rate	9,000	5,000
Actual input × budgeted rate	10,000	5,000

Use F for favorable and U for unfavorable:

	Variable	Fixed
(1) Spending variance	$____	$____
(2) Efficiency variance	____	____
(3) Production-volume variance	____	____
(4) Flexible-budget variance	____	____
(5) Underallocated (overallocated) manufacturing overhead	____	____

8-22 Straightforward 4-variance overhead analysis. The Lopez Company uses a standard-costing system in its manufacturing plant for auto parts. Its standard cost of an auto part, based on a denominator level of 4,000 output units per year, included 6 machine-hours of variable manufacturing overhead at $8 per hour and 6 machine-hours of fixed manufacturing overhead at $15 per hour. Actual output produced was 4,400 units. Variable manufacturing overhead incurred was $245,000. Fixed manufacturing overhead incurred was $373,000. Actual machine-hours were 28,400.

Required

1. Prepare an analysis of all variable manufacturing overhead and fixed manufacturing overhead variances, using the 4-variance analysis in Exhibit 8-3 (p. 262).
2. Prepare journal entries using the 4-variance analysis.
3. Describe how individual variable manufacturing overhead items are controlled from day to day. Also, describe how individual fixed manufacturing overhead items are controlled.

8-23 Straightforward coverage of manufacturing overhead, standard-costing system. The Singapore division of a Canadian telecommunications company uses a standard-costing system for its machine-paced production of telephone equipment. Data regarding production during June are as follows:

Variable manufacturing overhead costs incurred	$155,100
Variable manufacturing overhead cost rate	$12 per standard machine-hour
Fixed manufacturing overhead costs incurred	$401,000
Fixed manufacturing overhead budgeted	$390,000
Denominator level in machine-hours	13,000
Standard machine-hour allowed per unit of output	0.30
Units of output	41,000
Actual machine-hours used	13,300
Ending work-in-process inventory	0

Required

1. Prepare an analysis of all manufacturing overhead variances. Use the 4-variance analysis framework illustrated in Exhibit 8-3 (p. 262)
2. Prepare journal entries for manufacturing overhead.
3. Describe how individual variable manufacturing overhead items are controlled from day to day. Also, describe how individual fixed manufacturing overhead items are controlled.

8-24 Spending and efficiency overhead variances, service sector. Meals on Wheels (MOW) operates a home meal delivery service. It has agreements with 20 restaurants to pick up and deliver meals to customers who phone or fax orders to MOW. MOW is currently examining its overhead costs for May 2004.

Variable overhead costs for May 2004 were budgeted at $2 per hour of home delivery time. Fixed overhead costs were budgeted at $24,000. The budgeted number of home deliveries (MOW's output measure) was 8,000. Delivery time, the allocation base for variable and fixed overhead costs, is budgeted to be 0.80 hour per delivery.

Actual results for May 2004 were

Variable overhead	$14,174
Fixed overhead	$27,600
Number of home deliveries	7,460
Hours of delivery time	5,595

Customers are charged $12 per delivery. The delivery driver is paid $7 per delivery.

MOW receives a 10% commission on the meal costs that the restaurants charge the customers who use MOW.

Required

1. Compute spending and efficiency variances for MOW's variable overhead in May 2004. Comment on the results.
2. Compute the spending variance for MOW's fixed overhead in May 2004. Comment on the results.
3. How might MOW manage its variable overhead costs differently from its fixed overhead costs?

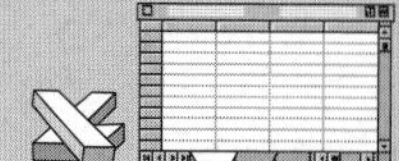

Excel Application For students who wish to practice their spreadsheet skills, the following is a step-by-step approach to creating an Excel spreadsheet to work this problem.

Step-By-Step

(Program your spreadsheet to perform all necessary calculations. Do not "hard-code" any of your variance calculations.)

1. At top of new spreadsheet, create an "Original Data" section for the data provided for Meals On Wheels, with rows labeled "Output Units (number of deliveries)," "Hours of Delivery Time," "Hours per Delivery," "Variable Overhead Costs," "Variable Overhead Costs per Hour of Delivery Time," and "Fixed Overhead Costs." Create columns for "Actual Results" and "Flexible Budget Amounts." Enter the data provided for MOW in this section. You will have to enter calculations for actual hours per delivery, budgeted hours of delivery time, budgeted variable overhead costs per hour of delivery time, and actual variable overhead cost per hour of delivery time.
2. Skip two rows, create a section, "Variance Calculations," with rows for "Actual Costs Incurred," "Actual Input × Budgeted Rate," "Budgeted Input Allowed for Actual Output × Budgeted Rate," "Spending Variance," "Efficiency Variance," and "Fixed Overhead Spending Variance." Use the data from the Original Data section to calculate actual costs incurred, actual input times budgeted rate, and budgeted input allowed for actual output times budgeted rate.
3. For Problem 1, use the data you created in step 2 to calculate spending and efficiency variances for Meals on Wheels variable overhead in May 2004. For Problem 2, use the actual and budgeted fixed overhead costs in the Original Data section to calculate the spending variance for Meals on Wheels fixed overhead in May 2004.
4. *Verify the accuracy of your spreadsheet.* Go to your Original Data section and change the actual number of deliveries from 7,460 to 7,600. If you programmed your spreadsheet correctly, then efficiency variance for MOW should change to $970 (favorable).

8-25 Total overhead, 3-variance analysis. Wright-Patterson Air Force Base has an extensive repair facility for jet engines. It developed standard costing and flexible budgets to account for this activity. Budgeted variable overhead at a level of 8,000 standard monthly direct labor-hours was $64,000; budgeted total overhead at 10,000 standard direct labor-hours was $197,600. The standard cost allocated to repair output included a total overhead rate of 120% of standard direct labor costs. Total overhead incurred for October was $249,000. Direct labor costs incurred were $202,440. The direct labor price variance was $9,640 unfavorable. The direct labor flexible-budget variance was $14,440 unfavorable. The standard labor price was $16 per hour. The production-volume variance was $14,000, favorable.

Required

1. Compute the direct labor efficiency variance and the spending, efficiency, and production-volume variances for overhead. Also, compute the denominator level.
2. Describe how individual variable manufacturing overhead items are controlled from day to day. Also, describe how individual fixed manufacturing overhead items are controlled.

8-26 Overhead variances, missing information. Blakely Printing prepared its budget at 10,000 machine hours. Blakely reported a $750 unfavorable spending variance for fixed overhead and a $250 unfavorable spending variance for variable overhead. The budgeted variable overhead rate is $5 per machine hour. The input allowed for actual output was 9,900 machine hours. Actual machine hours were 9,800, and actual total overhead costs were $80,000.

Required

1. Compute variable overhead efficiency variance, flexible-budget variance, and the amount underallocated or overallocated.
2. Calculate fixed overhead production-volume variance, flexible-budget variance, and the amount underallocated or overallocated.

8-27 4-variance analysis, working backwards. Lookmeup.com is striving to become a Web portal. The site allows surfers to find anything they wish to look up—be it a person, a site, a company, or a news article—through one interactive and easy-to-use interface. Most of Lookmeup.com's operating overhead is due to Internet connection costs. Lookmeup.com faces fixed as well as variable Internet connection charges. Following is the 4-variance analysis of Lookmeup.com's operating overhead:

	Spending Variance	Efficiency Variance	Production-Volume Variance
Variable Operating Overhead	$37,000 F	$24,000 F	Never a variance
Fixed Operating Overhead	$14,000 U	Never a variance	$17,000 U

Required

1. For total operating overhead, compute the following:
   a. Spending variance
   b. Efficiency variance
   c. Production-volume variance
   d. Flexible-budget variance
   e. Total-overhead variance

   Arrange your results in a suitable format for presenting 3-variance, 2-variance, and 1-variance analyses.
2. If Lookmeup.com's total actual operating overhead were $420,000, what was the operating overhead allocated to actual output units provided?
3. Can you say whether fixed operating overhead was underallocated or overallocated? If so, by what amount?
4. Are Lookmeup.com's different variances in the 4-variance analysis given necessarily independent? Explain and provide an example.

8-28 **Flexible-budget variances, review of Chapters 7 and 8.** *The Monthly Herald* budgets to produce 300,000 copies of its monthly newspaper (the output unit) for August 2004. It is budgeted to have 50 print pages per newspaper. Actual production was 320,000 copies, with 17,280,000 print pages run. Each paper was only 50 print pages, but quality problems with paper led to many pages being unusable.

Variable costs are direct materials, direct labor, and variable indirect costs. Variable and fixed indirect costs are allocated to each copy on the basis of good print pages. The driver for all variable costs is the number of print pages.

Data pertaining to August 2004 are

	Budgeted	Actual
Direct materials	$180,000	$224,640
Direct labor costs	45,000	50,112
Variable indirect costs	60,000	63,936
Fixed indirect costs	90,00	97,000

The actual direct labor rate was $29 per hour. Actual and budgeted pages produced per direct labor-hour were 10,000 print pages. Data pertaining to revenues for *The Monthly Herald* in August 2004 are

	Budgeted	Actual
Circulation revenue	$140,000	$154,000
Advertising revenue	360,000	394,600

The Monthly Herald sells for $0.50 per copy. Copies produced but not sold have no value. Advertising revenues covers receipts from all advertising sources.

Required

1. Prepare a comprehensive set of flexible-budget variances for the two direct-cost items (using Exhibit 7-3, p. 224) and the two indirect-cost items (using Exhibit 8-3, p. 262) for *The Monthly Herald*.
2. Comment on the results in requirement 1.

Problems

8-29 **Comprehensive variance analysis.** FlatScreen manufactures flat-panel LCD displays. The displays are sold to major PC manufacturers. Following is some manufacturing overhead data for FlatScreen for the year ended December 31, 2003:

Manufacturing Overhead	Actual	Flexible Budget	Allocated Amount
Variable	$1,532,160	$1,536,000	$1,536,000
Fixed	7,004,160	6,961,920	7,526,400

FlatScreen's budget was based on the assumption that 17,760 units (panels) will be manufactured during 2003. The planned allocation rate was 2 machine-hours per unit. Actual number of machine-hours used during 2003 was 36,480. The static-budget variable manufacturing overhead costs equal $1,420,800.

Compute the following quantities (you should be able to do so in the prescribed order):

Required

a. Budgeted number of machine-hours planned
b. Budgeted fixed manufacturing overhead costs per machine-hour
c. Budgeted variable manufacturing overhead costs per machine-hour
d. Budgeted number of machine-hours allowed for actual output produced
e. Actual number of output units
f. Actual number of machine-hours used per panel

8-30 Journal entries (continuation of 8-29).

Required

1. Prepare journal entries for variable and fixed manufacturing overhead (you will need to calculate the various variances to accomplish this).
2. Overhead variances are written off to Cost of Goods Sold (COGS) account at the end of the fiscal year. COGS is then entered in the income statement. Show how COGS is adjusted through journal entries.

8-31 Graphs and overhead variances. The Carvelli Company is a manufacturer of housewares. In its job-costing system, manufacturing overhead (both variable and fixed) is allocated to products on the basis of budgeted machine-hours. The budgeted amounts are taken from Carvelli's standard-costing system. The budget for 2004 included:

Variable manufacturing overhead	$9 per machine-hour
Fixed manufacturing overhead	$72,000,000
Denominator level	4,000,000 machine-hours

Required

1. Prepare two graphs, one for variable manufacturing overhead and one for fixed manufacturing overhead. Each graph should display how Carvelli's total manufacturing overhead costs will be depicted for the purposes of (a) planning and control and (b) inventory costing.
2. Suppose that 3,500,000 machine-hours were allowed for actual output produced in 2004, but 3,800,000 actual machine-hours were used. Actual manufacturing overhead was $36,100,000, variable, and $72,200,000, fixed. Compute (a) variable manufacturing overhead spending and efficiency variances and (b) the fixed manufacturing overhead spending and production-volume variances. Use the columnar presentation illustrated in Exhibit 8-3 (p. 262).
3. What is the amount of the underallocated or overallocated variable manufacturing overhead? Of the underallocated or overallocated fixed manufacturing overhead? Why are the flexible-budget variance and the underallocated or overallocated overhead amount always the same for variable manufacturing overhead but rarely the same for fixed manufacturing overhead?
4. Suppose the denominator level was 3,000,000 rather than 4,000,000 machine-hours. What variances in requirement 2 would be affected? Recompute them.

8-32 Variance analysis, graphs. Homer Metal Stamping budgets and allocates overhead costs using machine-hours. Homer's budget for 2003 was 10,000 machine-hours. Following is additional information relating to overhead for 2003:

Budgeted fixed overhead	$600,000
Actual fixed overhead	$590,000
Budgeted variable overhead	$1,000,000
Actual variable overhead	$1,100,000
Budgeted machine-hours allowed for actual output	9,800
Actual machine-hours used	9,500

Required

1. Compute the variable overhead spending variance and efficiency variance.
2. Compute the fixed overhead spending variance and production-volume variance.
3. Draw graphs similar to those in Exhibit 8-4, Panel A (variable overhead) and Panel B (fixed overhead).

8-33 4-variance analysis, find the unknowns. Consider each of the following situations—cases A, B, and C—independently. Data refer to operations for April 2004. For each situation, assume a standard-costing system. Also assume the use of a flexible budget for control of variable and fixed manufacturing overhead based on machine-hours.

	Cases		
	A	B	C
(1) Fixed manufacturing overhead incurred	$10,600	—	$12,000
(2) Variable manufacturing overhead incurred	$ 7,000	—	—
(3) Denominator level in machine-hours	500	—	1,100
(4) Standard machine-hours allowed for actual output achieved	—	650	—
Flexible-budget data:			
(5) Fixed manufacturing overhead	—	—	—
(6) Variable manufacturing overhead (per standard machine-hour)	—	$8.50	$5.00
(7) Budgeted fixed manufacturing overhead	$10,000	—	$11,000
(8) Budgeted variable manufacturing overhead[a]	—	—	—
(9) Total budgeted manufacturing overhead[a]	—	$12,525	—
Additional data:			
(10) Standard variable manufacturing overhead allocated	$7,500	—	—
(11) Standard fixed manufacturing overhead allocated	$10,000	—	—
(12) Production-volume variance	—	$500 U	$500 F
(13) Variable manufacturing overhead spending variance	$950 F	$0	$350 U
(14) Variable manufacturing overhead efficiency variance	—	$0	$100 U
(15) Fixed manufacturing overhead spending variance	—	$300 F	—
(16) Actual machine-hours used	—	—	—

[a] For standard machine-hours allowed for actual output produced.

Required Fill in the blanks under each case. (Hint: Prepare a worksheet similar to that in Exhibit 8-3 (p. 262). Fill in the knowns and then solve for the unknowns.)

8-34 Flexible budgets, 4-variance analysis. (CMA, adapted) Nolton Products uses a standard-costing system. It allocates manufacturing overhead (both variable and fixed) to products on the basis of standard direct manufacturing labor-hours (DLH). Nolton develops its manufacturing overhead rate from the current annual budget. The manufacturing overhead budget for 2004 is based on budgeted output of 720,000 units, requiring 3,600,000 DLH. The company is able to schedule production uniformly throughout the year.

A total of 66,000 output units requiring 315,000 DLH was produced during May 2004. Manufacturing overhead (MOH) costs incurred for May amounted to $375,000. The actual costs, compared with the annual budget and $^1/_{12}$ of the annual budget, are as follows:

Annual Manufacturing Overhead Budget 2004

	Total Amount	Per Output Unit	Per DLH Input Unit	Monthly MOH Budget May 2004	Actual MOH Costs for May 2004
Variable MOH					
Indirect manufacturing labor	$ 900,000	$1.25	$0.25	$ 75,000	$ 75,000
Supplies	1,224,000	1.70	0.34	102,000	111,000
Fixed MOH					
Supervision	648,000	0.90	0.18	54,000	51,000
Utilities	540,000	0.75	0.15	45,000	54,000
Depreciation	1,008,000	1.40	0.28	84,000	84,000
Total	$4,320,000	$6.00	$1.20	$360,000	$375,000

Required Calculate the following amounts for Nolton Products for May 2004:

1. Total manufacturing overhead costs allocated
2. Variable manufacturing overhead spending variance
3. Fixed manufacturing overhead spending variance
4. Variable manufacturing overhead efficiency variance
5. Production-volume variance

Be sure to identify each variance as favorable (F) or unfavorable (U).

8-35 Overhead analysis. Armstrong Corporation uses standard costing. The following information is for 2004:

Static-budget machine-hours	33,000
Fixed overhead budget costs	$4,950,000
Fixed overhead actual costs	$4,500,000
Variable overhead actual costs	$9,600,000
Variable overhead rate per machine-hour	$300
Actual machine-hours used	30,000
Budgeted machine-hours allowed for actual output	35,000

Required

1. Calculate variable overhead spending variance and efficiency variance.
2. Compute fixed overhead spending variance and production-volume variance.

8-36 Sales-volume variance, production-volume variance. Morano Company prepared its budgeted output and sales at its maximum capacity of 20,000 units for 2003. However, due to efficiency improvements, Morano was able to sell 22,000 units for the year. Other data for 2003 follow:

Budgeted fixed overhead costs	$500,000
Budgeted selling price	$100
Budgeted variable cost per unit	$40

Required

1. Calculate the budgeted profit per unit, the operating income based on the budgeted profit per unit, and the flexible-budget operating income.
2. Compute sales-volume variance and production-volume variance. What do each of these variance measure?

8-37 Activity-based costing, variance analysis. Toymaster, Inc., produces a plastic toy car, TGC, in batches. To manufacture a batch of TGCs, Toymaster must set up the machines. Setup costs are batch-level costs. A separate Setup Department is responsible for setting up machines for TGC.

Setup overhead costs consist of some costs that are variable and some that are fixed with respect to the number of setup-hours. The following information pertains to 2004.

	Static-Budget Amounts	Actual Amounts
Units of TGC produced and sold	30,000	22,500
Batch size (number of units per batch)	250	225
Setup-hours per batch	5	5.25
Variable overhead cost per setup-hour	$25	$24
Total fixed setup overhead costs	$18,000	$17,535

Required

1. For variable setup overhead costs, compute the efficiency and spending variances. Comment on the results.
2. For fixed setup overhead costs, compute the spending and the production-volume variances. Comment on the results.

8-38 Activity-based costing, variance analysis. Asma Surgical Instruments, Inc., makes a special line of forceps, SFA, in batches. Asma randomly selects forceps from each SFA batch for quality-testing purposes. Quality testing costs are batch-level costs. A separate quality-testing section is responsible for SFA quality testing.

Quality-testing costs consist of some variable and some fixed costs in relation to the quality-testing hours. The following information is for 2004:

	Static-Budget Amounts	Actual Amounts
Units of SFA produced and sold	21,000	22,000
Batch Size (number of units per batch)	500	550
Testing-hours per batch	5.5	5.4
Variable overhead cost per testing-hour	$40	$42
Total fixed testing overhead costs	$28,875	$27,216

Required

1. For variable testing overhead costs, compute the efficiency and spending variances. Comment on the results.
2. For fixed testing overhead costs, compute the spending and the production-volume variances. Comment on the results.

8-39 Comprehensive review of Chapters 7 and 8, working backward from given variances. The Mancusco Company uses a flexible budget and standard costs to aid planning and control of its machining manufacturing operations. Its normal-costing system for manufacturing has two direct-cost categories (direct materials and direct manufacturing labor—both variable) and two indirect-cost categories (variable manufacturing overhead and fixed manufacturing overhead, both allocated using direct manufacturing labor-hours).

At the 40,000 budgeted direct manufacturing labor-hour level for August, budgeted direct manufacturing labor is $800,000, budgeted variable manufacturing overhead is $480,000, and budgeted fixed manufacturing overhead is $640,000.

The following actual results are for August:

Direct materials price variance (based on purchases)	$176,000 F
Direct materials efficiency variance	69,000 U
Direct manufacturing labor costs incurred	522,750
Variable manufacturing overhead flexible-budget variance	10,350 U
Variable manufacturing overhead efficiency variance	18,000 U
Fixed manufacturing overhead incurred	597,460
Fixed manufacturing overhead spending variance	42,540 F

The standard cost per pound of direct materials is $11.50. The standard allowance is three pounds of direct materials for each unit of product. During August 30,000 units of product were produced. There was no beginning inventory of direct materials. There was no beginning or ending work in process. In August, the direct materials price variance was $1.10 per pound.

In July, labor unrest caused a major slowdown in the pace of production, resulting in an unfavorable direct manufacturing labor efficiency variance of $45,000. There was no direct manufacturing labor price variance. Labor unrest persisted into August. Some workers quit. Their replacements had to be hired at higher rates, which had to be extended to all workers. The actual average wage rate in August exceeded the standard average wage rate by $0.50 per hour.

Required

1. Compute the following for August:
   a. Total pounds of direct materials purchased
   b. Total number of pounds of excess direct materials used
   c. Variable manufacturing overhead spending variance
   d. Total number of actual direct manufacturing labor-hours used
   e. Total number of standard direct manufacturing labor-hours allowed for the units produced
   f. Production-volume variance
2. Describe how Mancusco's control of variable manufacturing overhead items differs from its control of fixed manufacturing overhead items.

8-40 Review of Chapters 7 and 8, 3-variance analysis. (CPA, adapted) The Beal Manufacturing Company's job-costing system has two direct-cost categories: direct materials and direct manufacturing labor. Manufacturing overhead (both variable and fixed) is allocated to products on the basis of standard direct manufacturing labor-hours (DLH). At the beginning of 2004, Beal adopted the following standards for its manufacturing costs:

	Input	Cost per Output Unit
Direct materials	3 lbs. at $5 per lb.	$ 15.00
Direct manufacturing labor	5 hrs. at $15 per hr.	75.00
Manufacturing overhead:		
Variable	$6 per DLH	30.00
Fixed	$8 per DLH	40.00
Standard manufacturing cost per output unit		$160.00

The denominator level for total manufacturing overhead per month in 2004 is 40,000 direct manufacturing labor-hours. Beal's flexible budget for January 2004 was based on this denominator level. The records for January indicated the following:

Direct materials purchased	25,000 lbs. at $5.20 per lb.
Direct materials used	23,100 lbs.
Direct manufacturing labor	40,100 hrs. at $14.60 per hr.
Total actual manufacturing overhead (variable and fixed)	$600,000
Actual production	7,800 output units

1. Prepare a schedule of total standard manufacturing costs for the 7,800 output units in January 2004.

Required

2. For the month of January 2004, compute the following variances, indicating whether each is favorable (F) or unfavorable (U):
   a. Direct materials price variance, based on purchases
   b. Direct materials efficiency variance
   c. Direct manufacturing labor price variance
   d. Direct manufacturing labor efficiency variance
   e. Total manufacturing overhead spending variance
   f. Variable manufacturing overhead efficiency variance
   g. Production-volume variance

Collaborative Learning Problem

8-41 **Overhead variances, ethics.** New Mexico Company uses a standard-costing system. The company prepared its static budget for 2004 at 1,000,000 machine-hours for the year. Total budgeted overhead cost is $12,500,000. The variable overhead rate is $10 per machine-hour ($20 per unit). Actual results for 2004 follow:

Machine-hours	960,000 hours
Output	498,000 units
Variable overhead	$10,080,000
Fixed overhead spending variance	$600,000 U

Required

1. Compute for the fixed overhead
   a. Budgeted amount
   b. Budgeted cost per machine-hour
   c. Actual cost
   d. Production-volume variance
2. Compute variable overhead spending variance and variable overhead efficiency variance.
3. Jerry Remich, the controller, prepares the variance analysis. It is common knowledge in the company that he and Ron Monroe, the production manager, are not on the best of terms. In a recent executive committee meeting, Monroe had complained about the lack of usefulness of the accounting reports he receives. To get back at him, Remich manipulated the actual fixed overhead amount by assigning a greater-than-normal share of allocated costs to the production area. And, he decided to depreciate all of the newly acquired production equipment using the double-declining balance method rather than the straight-line method, contrary to the company practice. As a result, there was a sizable unfavorable fixed overhead spending variance. He boasted to one of his confidants, "I am just returning the favor." Discuss Remich's actions and their ramifications.

CHAPTER 8 INTERNET EXERCISE

Managers use flexible budgets to evaluate and control costs at varying levels of production. Gain some hands-on experience calculating flexible-budget variances using FedEx Corporation's 1999 financial statements: go to www.prenhall.com/horngren, click on *Cost Accounting*, 11th ed., and access the Internet exercise for Chapter 8.

CHAPTER 8 VIDEO CASE

TEVA SPORT SANDALS: Variable Overhead Variances

Teva Sport Sandals was founded in the 1980s by a seasoned river guide, Mark Thatcher, who was tired of losing his flip-flop sandals every time he took a raft ride down the Colorado River. Thatcher knew first-hand how thong-style rubber sandals abandoned his feet when slogging through mud and water. He figured a thong-style sandal with a heel strap on the back would be the answer to keeping sandals on. His new sandal creation was called the "Teva" (which means "nature" in Hebrew), and it was an immediate hit with water sports enthusiasts on the river and with others nowhere near a river.

Today Teva sandals are manufactured under license by Deckers Outdoor Corporation of Goleta, California. More than 60 styles for men, women, and children are available through retail sports stores, catalogs, and department stores around the world. The entire line of sandals also is sold direct to consumers through Teva's Web site at www.teva.com. Sandal styles are updated by designers at Deckers annually for each new selling season. Those new sandal specifications are converted into sandal prototypes by the in-house fabrication department.

Continued

Upon approval of the prototype designs, detailed sandal specifications are given to Pat Devaney, Deckers' vice president of production, development, and sourcing. Pat has responsibility for negotiating the best possible prices for finished sandals with the factories in China that manufacture the sandals. The specifications are critical to the negotiations! Some of the raw materials are sourced within China to help reduce the prices of finished goods. Other raw materials must be imported. Either way, Deckers and the manufacturing facility in China work with each other to arrive at the best price. Once the specification and price negotiations are finished, the factory begins production according to the schedule set during negotiations.

The managers at the manufacturing facility in China have responsibility for controlling production costs. For illustration purposes, let's assume the following data apply to a recent month of sandal manufacturing for the factory (all amounts in U.S. dollars). Overhead is allocated based on machine-hours.

Cost Item/ Allocation Base	Actual Results	Flexible-Budget Amount
Output units (pairs of sandals)	150,000	150,000
Machine-hours	67,500	60,000
Machine-hours per output unit	0.45	0.40
Variable manufacturing overhead costs	$1,950,000	$1,800,000
Variable manufacturing overhead costs per machine-hour	$28.89	$30.00
Variable manufacturing overhead costs per output unit	$13.00	$12.00

The plant manager's performance bonus is tied, in part, to his or her control of manufacturing overhead costs. There is an unfavorable variable overhead flexible-budget variance of $150,075 for this month's production of 150,000 pairs of sandals. The manager is interested in finding out what happened and why.

QUESTIONS

1. Compute the spending variance and the efficiency variance for variable manufacturing overhead.
2. What do the spending and efficiency variances mean? What are possible causes?
3. What explanation(s) should the plant manager give for the unfavorable variable overhead flexible-budget variance this month?

CHAPTER 9

Inventory Costing and Capacity Analysis

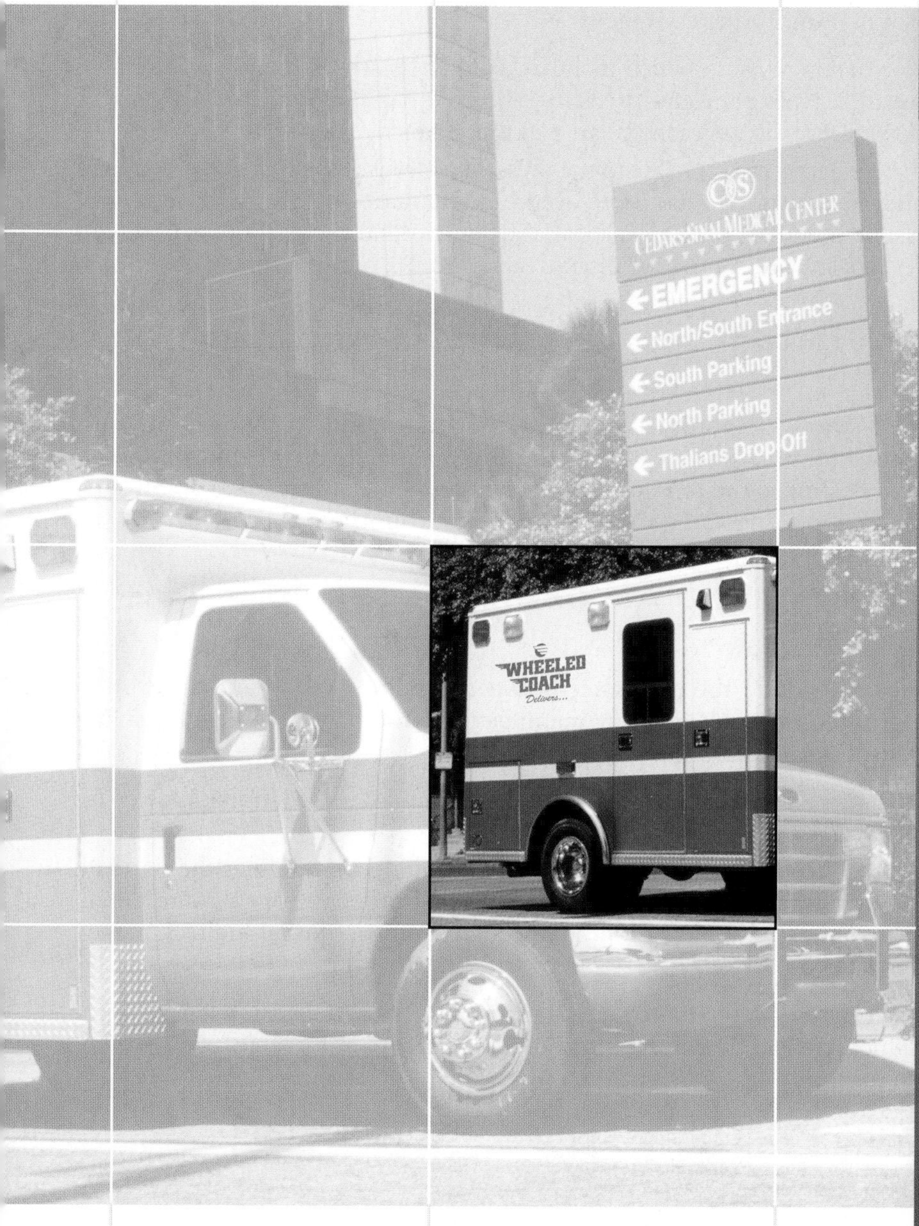

LEARNING OBJECTIVES

1. Identify what distinguishes variable costing from absorption costing
2. Prepare income statements under absorption costing and variable costing
3. Explain differences in operating income under absorption costing and variable costing
4. Understand how absorption costing can provide undesirable incentives for managers to build up finished goods inventory
5. Differentiate throughput costing from variable costing and from absorption costing
6. Describe the various capacity concepts that can be used in absorption costing
7. Understand the major factors management considers in choosing a capacity level to compute the budgeted fixed overhead cost rate
8. Describe how attempts to recover fixed costs of capacity may lead to price increases and lower demand
9. Explain how the capacity level chosen to calculate the budgeted fixed overhead cost rate affects the production-volume variance

www.prenhall.com/horngren

As the world's largest manufacturer of made-to-order ambulances, Wheeled Coach Industries of Winter Park, Florida, configures every ambulance to meet the exacting specifications of its buyers. Thousands of parts can be combined into a finished ambulance—from electrical wiring and siren systems to custom cabinets and medical equipment. The costs of those components, along with variable manufacturing costs, are useful in determining the company's contribution margin under variable costing. If gross margin is desired, absorption costing accumulates variable and fixed manufacturing costs and deducts them from revenues. Managers keep a close eye on finished goods inventory because they know the effect it can have on the health of the bottom line.

The reported income number captures the attention of managers in a way few other numbers do. Consider these examples:

- Planning decisions typically include analysis of how the alternatives under consideration would affect future reported income.
- Reported income is often used to evaluate the performance of managers.

This chapter examines two types of cost accounting choices for inventories that affect the reported income of manufacturing companies:

Choosing between absorption costing (AC) and variable costing (VC) is only one of several issues pertaining to inventory costing in manufacturing companies. For example, it is necessary to choose a cost flow assumption such as FIFO, LIFO, or weighted average. (The abbreviations AC and VC are used throughout the margin notes in this chapter.)

1. *Inventory-costing choices* relate to which manufacturing costs are treated as inventoriable costs. There are three types of inventory costing: absorption costing, variable costing, and throughput costing. We discuss each in Part 1 of this chapter.
2. *Denominator-level capacity choices* relate to the preselected level of the cost-allocation base used to set budgeted fixed manufacturing overhead cost rates. There are four choices of capacity levels: theoretical capacity, practical capacity, normal capacity utilization, and master-budget capacity utilization. We discuss each in Part 2 of this chapter.

PART ONE: INVENTORY COSTING FOR MANUFACTURING COMPANIES

The two common methods of costing inventories in manufacturing companies are variable costing and absorption costing. We discuss them first and then explain throughput costing. Absorption costing is the required method under generally accepted accounting principles for external reporting and tax reporting in most countries.

VARIABLE COSTING AND ABSORPTION COSTING

Data for One-Year Example

The easiest way to understand the difference between variable costing and absorption costing is via an example. Stassen Company manufactures and markets optical consumer products. Stassen uses a standard costing system in which:

a. Direct costs are traced to products using standard prices and standard inputs allowed for actual outputs produced.
b. Indirect (overhead) costs are allocated using standard indirect rates times the standard inputs allowed for the actual outputs produced. The allocation base for all indirect manufacturing costs is budgeted units produced; the allocation base for all indirect marketing costs is budgeted units sold.

Stassen wants you to prepare an income statement for 2003 (the year just ended) for the telescope product line. The operating information for the year is

	Units
Beginning inventory	0
Production	800
Sales	600
Ending inventory	200

Actual price and cost data for 2003 are

Selling price	$ 100
Variable manufacturing cost per unit produced	
Direct material cost	$ 11
Direct manufacturing labor cost	4
Indirect manufacturing cost	5
Total variable manufacturing cost per unit produced	$ 20
Variable marketing cost per unit sold (all indirect)	$ 19
Fixed manufacturing costs (all indirect)	$12,000
Fixed marketing costs (all indirect)	$10,800

We assume the following at Stassen:

1. The cost driver for all variable manufacturing costs is units produced; the cost driver for variable marketing costs is units sold. There are no batch-level costs and no product-sustaining costs.
2. Work in process is zero.
3. The budgeted level of production for 2003 is 800 units, which is used to calculate the budgeted fixed-manufacturing cost per unit. The actual production for 2003 is 800 units.
4. Stassen budgeted sales of 600 units for 2003, which is the same as the actual sales for 2003.
5. There are no price variances, no efficiency variances, no spending variances. Hence, the budgeted (standard) price and cost data for 2003 are the same as the actual price and cost data as given. Our first example (2003) has no production-volume variance for manufacturing costs. Later examples (for 2004 and 2005) have production-volume variances.
6. All variances are written off to cost of goods sold in the period (year) in which they occur.

Be aware that variable manufacturing costs often vary with the output level produced, whereas variable nonmanufacturing costs (for example, sales commissions) often vary with the amount of revenues.

Variable costing is a method of inventory costing in which all variable manufacturing costs are included as inventoriable costs. All fixed manufacturing costs are excluded from inventoriable costs; fixed manufacturing costs are instead treated as costs of the period in which they are incurred. As explained in Chapter 2 (p. 39), *inventoriable costs* are all costs of a product that are regarded as assets when they are incurred and expensed as cost of goods sold when the product is sold.

Absorption costing is a method of inventory costing in which all variable manufacturing costs and all fixed manufacturing costs are included as inventoriable costs. That is, inventory "absorbs" all manufacturing costs.

Under both variable costing and absorption costing, all variable manufacturing costs are inventoriable costs and all nonmanufacturing costs in the value chain (such as research and development and marketing), whether variable or fixed, are costs of the period and recorded as expenses when incurred.

The accounting for fixed manufacturing costs is the main difference between variable costing and absorption costing.

1 Identify what distinguishes variable costing

...fixed manufacturing costs excluded from inventoriable costs

from absorption costing

...fixed manufacturing costs included in inventoriable costs

Question: Under VC, are variable nonmanufacturing costs inventoriable?
Answer: No, only *variable manufacturing costs* are inventoriable under VC.

- Under variable costing, fixed manufacturing costs are treated as an expense of the period.
- Under absorption costing, fixed manufacturing costs are inventoriable costs. In our example, the standard fixed manufacturing overhead cost is $15 per unit ($12,000 ÷ 800 units) produced.

Inventoriable costs per unit produced in 2003 under the two methods for Stassen are

	Variable Costing		Absorption Costing	
Variable manufacturing cost per unit produced				
Direct material	$11.00		$11.00	
Direct manufacturing labor	4.00		4.00	
Indirect manufacturing cost	5.00	$20.00	5.00	$20.00
Fixed indirect manufacturing cost per unit produced		—		15.00
Total inventoriable cost per unit produced		$20.00		$35.00

2 **Prepare income statements under absorption costing**

...using the gross-margin format

and variable costing

... using the contribution-margin format

Comparing Income Statements

Exhibit 9-1 shows the variable-costing income statement, Panel A, and the absorption-costing income statement, Panel B, for the telescope product of Stassen Company for 2003. The variable-costing income statement uses the contribution-margin format introduced in Chapter 3. The absorption-costing income statement uses the gross-margin format introduced in Chapter 2. Why these differences in format? The distinction between variable costs and fixed costs is central to variable costing, and is highlighted by the contribution-margin format. Similarly, the distinction between manufacturing and nonmanufacturing costs is central to absorption costing, and is highlighted by the gross-margin format.

Absorption-costing income statements need not differentiate between variable and fixed costs. However, the Stassen Company exhibits in this chapter make the distinction between variable and fixed costs to highlight how individual line items are classified differently under variable costing and absorption costing. See in Exhibit 9-1, Panel B, that under absorption costing, inventoriable cost is \$35 per unit because fixed manufacturing cost, \$15 per unit, as well as variable manufacturing cost, \$20 per unit, are assigned to each unit of product.

See how the fixed manufacturing costs of \$12,000 are accounted for under variable costing and absorption costing in Exhibit 9-1. The income statement under variable costing deducts the \$12,000 lump sum as an expense for 2003. In contrast, the income statement

EXHIBIT 9-1

Comparison of Variable Costing and Absorption Costing for Stassen Company: Telescope Product-Line Income Statements for 2003

PANEL A: VARIABLE COSTING

Revenues: \$100 × 600 units		\$60,000
Variable costs		
Beginning inventory	\$ 0	
Variable manufacturing costs: \$20 × 800 units	16,000	
Cost of goods available for sale	16,000	
Deduct ending inventory: \$20 × 200 units	(4,000)	
Variable cost of goods sold	12,000	
Variable marketing costs: \$19 × 600 units	11,400	
Adjustment for variable-cost variances	0	
Total variable costs		23,400
Contribution margin		36,600
Fixed costs		
Fixed manufacturing costs	12,000	
Fixed marketing costs	10,800	
Adjustment for fixed-cost variances	0	
Total fixed costs		22,800
Operating income		\$13,800

PANEL B: ABSORPTION COSTING

Revenues: \$100 × 600 units		\$60,000
Cost of goods sold		
Beginning inventory	\$ 0	
Variable manufacturing costs: \$20 × 800 units	16,000	
Fixed manufacturing costs: \$15 × 800 units	12,000	
Cost of goods available for sale	28,000	
Deduct ending inventory: (\$20 + \$15) × 200 units	(7,000)	
Adjustment for manufacturing variances	0	
Cost of goods sold		21,000
Gross margin		39,000
Operating costs		
Variable marketing costs: \$19 × 600 units	11,400	
Fixed marketing costs	10,800	
Adjustment for operating cost variances	0	
Total operating costs		22,200
Operating income		\$16,800

The VC income statement uses the contribution-margin format that distinguishes variable costs from fixed costs. This format highlights the lump-sum fixed manufacturing overhead (FMOH) costs that are expensed in the period incurred. The AC income statement uses the gross-margin format that distinguishes manufacturing costs from nonmanufacturing costs.

Two items distinguish gross margin (GM) from contribution (CM): (1) FMOH costs and (2) variable nonmanufacturing (VNM) costs. AC expenses FMOH costs related to units sold (as part of cost of goods sold) in calculating GM. In contrast, VC expenses total FMOH costs after calculating CM. Also, in AC, all nonmanufacturing costs are subtracted from GM; but in VC, VNM costs are subtracted in calculating CM.

under absorption costing regards each finished unit as absorbing $15 of fixed manufacturing cost. Under absorption costing, the $12,000 ($15 per unit × 800 units) is initially treated as an inventoriable cost in 2003. Given the preceding data for Stassen, $9,000 ($15 per unit × 600 units) subsequently becomes a part of cost of goods sold in 2003, and $3,000 ($15 per unit × 200 units) remains an asset—part of ending finished goods inventory on December 31, 2003. Operating income is $3,000 higher under absorption costing compared with variable costing, because only $9,000 of fixed manufacturing costs are expensed under absorption costing, whereas all $12,000 of fixed manufacturing costs are expensed under variable costing.

The variable manufacturing cost of $20 per unit is accounted for the same way in both income statements in Exhibit 9-1.

These points can be summarized as follows:

	Variable Costing	**Absorption Costing**
Variable manufacturing costs: $20 per telescope produced	Inventoriable	Inventoriable
Fixed manufacturing costs: $12,000 per year	Deducted as an expense of the period	Inventoriable at $15 per telescope produced using budgeted denominator level of 800 units produced per year

The difference between VC and AC operating incomes is *a matter of timing.* Under VC, FMOH costs are expensed in the period incurred. Under AC, FMOH costs are allocated to output produced and are not expensed until those units are sold.

Be sure that other issues don't distract you from seeing clearly that the difference between variable costing and absorption costing is how fixed manufacturing costs are accounted for. If inventory levels change, operating income will differ between the two methods because of the difference in accounting for fixed manufacturing costs. To see this, let's compare telescope sales of 600, 700, and 800 units by Stassen in 2003, when 800 units were produced. Of the $12,000 total fixed manufacturing costs, the amount expensed in the 2003 income statement would be

Under variable costing, whether

■ sales are 600, or 700, or 800 units	$12,000 expensed

Under absorption costing, when

■ sales are 600 units, inventory is 200 units, and $3,000 ($15 × 200) is included in inventory	$9,000 expensed ($12,000 − $3,000)
■ sales are 700 units, inventory is 100 units, and $1,500 ($15 × 100) is included in inventory	$10,500 expensed ($12,000 − $1,500)
■ sales are 800 units, inventory is 0 units, and $0 ($15 × 0) is included in inventory	$12,000 expensed ($12,000 − $0)

This chapter's appendix describes how the choice of variable costing or absorption costing affects the breakeven quantity of sales.

Sometimes **direct costing** is used to describe the inventory-costing method we call *variable costing*. However, direct costing is not an accurate description for two reasons:

1. Variable costing does not include all direct costs as inventoriable costs. Only direct variable manufacturing costs are included. Any direct fixed manufacturing costs and any direct nonmanufacturing costs are excluded from inventoriable costs.
2. Variable costing includes as inventoriable costs not only direct manufacturing costs but also some indirect costs (indirect variable manufacturing costs).

Note also that *variable costing* is a less than perfect term to describe this inventory-costing method because not all variable costs are inventoriable costs. Only variable manufacturing costs are inventoriable.

EXPLAINING DIFFERENCES IN OPERATING INCOME

Data for Three-Year Example

The Stassen example in Exhibit 9-1 covers one accounting period (a year). We now extend the example to cover three years. In both 2004 and 2005, Stassen has a production-volume

3 Explain differences in operating income under absorption costing

...affected by unit level of production and unit level of sales

and variable costing

...affected only by unit level of sales

variance because telescope production differs from the budgeted level of production of 800 units per year used to calculate the budgeted fixed manufacturing cost per unit. The actual quantities sold for 2004 and 2005 are the same as the sales quantities budgeted for these respective years, given in units in the following table:

	2003	2004	2005
Beginning inventory	0	200	50
Production	800	500	1,000
Sales	600	650	750
Ending inventory	200	50	300

Chapter 8 (pp. 258–260) discusses the computation and interpretation of the production-volume variance (PVV).

All other 2003 data given in the Stassen example earlier still apply for 2004 and 2005.

Comparing Income Statements

Exhibit 9-2 presents the income statement under variable costing, Panel A, and the income statement under absorption costing, Panel B, for 2003, 2004, and 2005. Keep in mind the following points about absorption costing as you study Panel B of both Exhibits 9-1 and 9-2:

1. The $15 fixed manufacturing cost rate is based on a budgeted denominator level of 800 units produced per year ($12,000 ÷ 800 units = $15 per unit). Whenever production—that's the quantity produced not the quantity sold—deviates from the denominator level, there will be a production-volume variance. The amount of the variance here is $15 per unit multiplied by the difference between the actual level of production and the denominator level.

In 2004, production was 500 units, 300 lower than the denominator level of 800 units. The result is an unfavorable production-volume variance of $4,500 ($15 per unit × 300 units). The year 2005 has a favorable production-volume variance of $3,000 ($15 per unit × 200 units), due to production of 1,000 units exceeding the denominator level of 800 units.

Recall how standard costing works. Each time a unit is manufactured, $15 of fixed manufacturing costs is included in the cost of goods manufactured and available for sale. In 2004, when 500 units are manufactured, $7,500 ($15 per unit × 500 units) of fixed costs are included in the cost of goods available for sale (see Exhibit 9-2, Panel B, line 4). Total fixed manufacturing costs for 2004 are $12,000. The production-volume variance of $4,500 U equals the difference between $12,000 and $7,500. In Panel B, note how, for each year, the fixed manufacturing costs included in the cost of goods available for sale plus the production-volume variance always equals $12,000.

2. The production-volume variance, which relates to fixed manufacturing overhead, exists under absorption costing but not under variable costing. Why? Because under variable costing, fixed manufacturing costs of $12,000 are always treated as an expense of the period, regardless of the level of production (and sales).

The PVV is the difference between the lump-sum budgeted FMOH and FMOH allocated to output produced. Because FMOH costs aren't allocated to output produced under VC (FMOH costs are expensed as incurred), there is no PVV under VC.

Here's a summary of the operating income differences for Stassen Company during the 2003–2005 period:

	2003	2004	2005
1. Absorption-costing operating income	$16,800	$14,600	$26,700
2. Variable-costing operating income	13,800	16,850	22,950
3. Difference: (1)−(2)	3,000	(2,250)	3,750
4. Difference as a % of absorption operating income	17.9%	(15.4%)	14.0%

These percentage differences illustrate why managers whose performance is measured by reported income are concerned about the choice between variable costing and absorption costing.

Why do variable costing and absorption costing usually report different income numbers? In general, if the unit level of inventory increases during an accounting period, less operating income will be reported under variable costing than absorption costing. Conversely, if the inventory level decreases, more operating income will be reported under variable costing than absorption costing. The difference in reported operating

EXHIBIT 9-2 **Comparison of Variable Costing and Absorption Costing**
Stassen Company: Telescope Product-Line Income Statements for 2003, 2004, and 2005

PANEL A: VARIABLE COSTING

	2003		2004		2005	
Revenues: $100 × 600; 650; 750 units		$60,000		$65,000		$75,000
Variable costs						
Beginning inventory: $20 × 0; 200; 50 units	$ 0		$ 4,000		$ 1,000	
Variable manufacturing costs:						
$20 × 800; 500; 1,000 units	16,000		10,000		20,000	
Cost of goods available for sale	16,000		14,000		21,000	
Deduct ending inventory: $20 × 200; 50; 300 units	(4,000)		(1,000)		(6,000)	
Variable cost of goods sold	12,000		13,000		15,000	
Variable marketing costs:						
$19 × 600; 650; 750 units	11,400		12,350		14,250	
Adjustment for variable cost variances	0		0		0	
Total variable costs		23,400		25,350		29,250
Contribution margin		36,600		39,650		45,750
Fixed costs						
Fixed manufacturing costs	12,000		12,000		12,000	
Fixed marketing costs	10,800		10,800		10,800	
Adjustment for fixed cost variances	0		0		0	
Total fixed costs		22,800		22,800		22,800
Operating income		$13,800		$16,850		$22,950

PANEL B: ABSORPTION COSTING

	2003		2004		2005	
Revenues: $100 × 600; 650; 750 units		$60,000		$65,000		$75,000
Cost of goods sold						
Beginning inventory: $35 × 0; 200; 50 units	$ 0		$ 7,000		$ 1,750	
Variable manufacturing costs:						
$20 × 800; 500; 1,000 units	16,000		10,000		20,000	
Fixed manufacturing costs:						
$15 × 800; 500; 1,000 units	12,000		7,500		15,000	
Cost of goods available for sale	28,000		24,500		36,750	
Deduct ending inventory: $35 × 200; 50; 300 units	(7,000)		(1,750)		(10,500)	
Adjustment for manufacturing variances[a]	0		4,500 U		(3,000) F	
Cost of goods sold		21,000		27,250		23,250
Gross margin		39,000		37,750		51,750
Operating costs						
Variable marketing costs:						
$19 × 600; 650; 750 units	11,400		12,350		14,250	
Fixed marketing costs	10,800		10,800		10,800	
Adjustment for operating cost variances	0		0		0	
Total operating costs		22,200		23,150		25,050
Operating income		$16,800		$14,600		$26,700

[a]Production-volume variance:
Fixed manufacturing costs per unit × (Denominator level − Actual output units produced)
2003: $15 × (800 − 800) units = $15 × 0 = $0
2004: $15 × (800 − 500) units = $15 × 300 = $4,500 U
2005: $15 × (800 − 1,000) units = $15 × (200) = $3,000 F

income is due solely to (a) moving fixed manufacturing costs into inventories as inventories increase and (b) moving fixed manufacturing costs out of inventories as inventories decrease.

The difference between operating income under absorption costing and variable costing can be computed by Formula 1, which focuses on fixed manufacturing costs in beginning inventory and ending inventory:

Formula 1

Absorption-costing operating income	–	Variables-costing operating income	=	Fixed manufacturing costs in ending inventory under absorption costing	–	Fixed manufacturing costs in beginning inventory under absorption costing
2003: $16,800	–	$13,800	=	($15 per unit × 200 units)	–	($15 per unit × 0 units)
		$3,000	=	$3,000		
2004: $14,600	–	$16,850	=	($15 per unit × 50 units)	–	($15 per unit × 200 units)
	–	$2,250	=	–$2,250		
2005: $26,700	–	$22,950	=	($15 per unit × 300 units	–	($15 per unit × 50 units)
		$3,750	=	$3,750		

Fixed manufacturing costs in ending inventory are deferred to a future period under absorption costing. For example, $3,000 of fixed manufacturing overhead is deferred to 2004 at December 31, 2003. Under variable costing, all $12,000 of fixed manufacturing costs are treated as an expense of 2003.

An alternative formula that highlights the movement of costs between inventory and cost of goods sold is

Formula 2

Absorption-costing operating income	–	Variable-costing operating income	=	Fixed manufacturing costs inventoried in units produced under absorption costing	–	Fixed manufacturing costs in cost of goods sold under absorption costing
2003: $16,800	–	$13,800	=	($15 per unit × 800 units)	–	($15 per unit × 600 units)
		$3,000	=	$3,000		
2004: $14,600	–	$16,850	=	($15 per unit × 500 units)	–	($15 per unit × 650 units)
		–$2,250	=	–$2,250		
2005: $26,700	–	$22,950	=	($15 per unit × 1,000 units)	–	($15 per unit × 750 units)
		$3,750	=	$3,750		

There is increasing pressure on managers to reduce inventory levels. Some companies are achieving steep reductions in inventory levels using policies such as just-in-time production; they are also benefiting from better sharing of information between suppliers and manufacturers about precisely when materials need to be delivered. One consequence is that operating income differences between immaterial costing and variable costing for companies having low inventory levels become immaterial in amount. Looking at this in the extreme: if managers hold zero levels of inventory at the start and end of each accounting period, there will be no difference between the operating income under absorption costing and variable costing.

Effect of Sales and Production on Operating Income

Given a constant contribution margin per unit and constant fixed costs, the period-to-period change in operating income under variable costing is driven solely by changes in the quantity of units actually sold. Consider the variable-costing operating income of Stassen in (a) 2004 versus 2003 and (b) 2005 versus 2004.

Recall that,

Contribution margin per unit	=	Selling price	–	Variable manufacturing cost per unit	–	Variable marketing cost per unit
	=	$100 per unit	–	$20 per unit	–	$19 per unit
	=	$61 per unit				

Change in variable-costing operating income	=	Contribution margin per unit	×	Change in quantity of units sold
(a) 2004 vs. 2003: $16,850 – $13,800	=	$61 per unit	×	(650 units– 600 units)
$3,050	=	$3,050		
(b) 2005 vs. 2004: $22,950 – $16,850	=	$61 per unit	×	(750 units – 650 units)
$6,100	=	$6,100		

Under variable costing, Stassen managers cannot increase operating income by "producing for inventory." Why not? Because, as you can see from the preceding computations, *only the quantity of units sold drives operating income.* We'll explain later in this chapter that absorption costing enables managers to increase operating income by increasing the unit level of sales, as well as by producing more units. Exhibit 9-3 compares the differences between variable costing and absorption costing.

PERFORMANCE MEASURES AND ABSORPTION COSTING

Absorption costing is the required inventory method for external reporting in most countries. Yet, many companies use variable costing for internal reporting to reduce the undesirable incentives to build up inventories that absorption costing can create.

Undesirable Buildup of Inventories

4 Understand how absorption costing can provide undesirable incentives for managers to build up finished goods inventory

...producing more units for inventory absorbs fixed manufacturing costs and increases operating income

Absorption costing enables a manager to increase operating income in a specific period by increasing production—even if there is no customer demand for the additional production! One motivation for this action could be that a manager's bonus is based on reported absorption-costing operating income. Assume that Stassen's managers have such a bonus plan. Exhibit 9-4 shows how Stassen's absorption-costing operating income for 2004 changes as the production level changes. This exhibit assumes that all variances, including the production-volume variance, are written off to cost of goods sold at the end of each year. Beginning inventory of 200 units and sales of 650 units for 2004 are unchanged from the case shown in Exhibit 9-2.

Exhibit 9-4 shows that production of only 450 units meets 2004 sales of 650 units. Operating income at this production level is $13,850. By producing more than 450 units, commonly referred to as *producing for inventory,* Stassen increases absorption-costing operating income. Each unit in 2004 ending inventory will increase operating income by $15. For example, if 800 units are produced, ending inventory will be 350 units and operating income will be $19,100. This amount is $5,250 more than the operating income with zero ending inventory (350 units × $15 per unit = $5,250). Under absorption costing, by

EXHIBIT 9-3 Comparative Income Effects of Variable Costing and Absorption Costing

Question	Variable Costing	Absorption Costing	Comment
Are fixed manufacturing costs inventoried?	No	Yes	Basic theoretical question of when these costs should be expensed
Is there a production-volume variance?	No	Yes	Choice of denominator level affects measurement of operating income under absorption costing only
Are classifications between variable and fixed costs routinely made?	Yes	Infrequently	Absorption costing can be easily modified to obtain subclassifications for variable and fixed costs, if desired (for example, see Exhibit 9-1, Panel B)
How do changes in unit inventory levels affect operating income?[a]			Differences are attributable to the timing of when fixed manufacturing costs are expensed
Production = sales	Equal	Equal	
Production > sales	Lower[b]	Higher[c]	
Production < sales	Higher	Lower	
What are the effects on cost-volume-profit relationship (for a given level of fixed costs and a given contribution margin per unit)?	Driven by unit level of sales	Driven by (a) unit level of sales, (b) unit level of production, and (c) chosen denominator level	Management control benefit: Effects of changes in production level on operating income are easier to understand under variable costing

[a]Assuming that all manufacturing variances are written off as period costs, that no change occurs in work-in-process inventory, and no change occurs in the budgeted fixed manufacturing overhead cost rate between accounting periods.

[b]That is, lower operating income than under absorption costing.

[c]That is, higher operating income than under variable costing.

EXHIBIT 9-4	Effect on Absorption-Costing Operating Income of Different Production Levels Stassen Company: Telescope Product-Line Income Statement for 2004 at Sales of 650 Units				
Unit Data					
Beginning inventory	200	200	200	200	200
Production	450	500	650	800	900
Goods available for sale	650	700	850	1,000	1,100
Sales	650	650	650	650	650
Ending inventory	0	50	200	350	450
Income Statement					
Revenues	$65,000	$65,000	$65,000	$65,000	$65,000
Cost of goods sold					
Beginning inventory	7,000	7,000	7,000	7,000	7,000
Variable manufacturing costs	9,000	10,000	13,000	16,000	18,000
Fixed manufacturing costs	6,750	7,500	9,750	12,000	13,500
Cost of goods available for sale	22,750	24,500	29,750	35,000	38,500
Deduct ending inventory	0	(1,750)	(7,000)	(12,250)	(15,750)
Adjustment for manufacturing variances[a]	5,250 U	4,500 U	2,250 U	0	(1,500) F
Cost of goods sold	28,000	27,250	25,000	22,750	21,250
Gross margin	37,000	37,750	40,000	42,250	43,750
Operating costs					
Marketing costs	23,150	23,150	23,150	23,150	23,150
Adj. for marketing variances	0	0	0	0	0
Total operating costs	23,150	23,150	23,150	23,150	23,150
Operating income	$13,850	$14,600	$16,850	$19,100	$20,600

[a]Production-volume variance:
Fixed manufacturing costs per unit × (Denominator level − Actual output units produced)
$15 × (800 − 450) units = $15 × 350 = $5,250 U
$15 × (800 − 500) units = $15 × 300 = $4,500 U
$15 × (800 − 650) units = $15 × 150 = $2,250 U
$15 × (800 − 800) units = $15 × 0 = $0
$15 × (800 − 900) units = $15 × (100) = $1,500 F

producing 350 units for inventory, $5,250 of fixed manufacturing overhead costs are included in finished goods inventory and so are not expensed in 2004.

The undesirable effects of producing for inventory may be very large, and they can arise in several ways. For example,

1. A plant manager may switch to manufacturing products that absorb the highest amount of fixed manufacturing costs, regardless of the customer demand for these products (called "cherry picking" the production line). Production of items that absorb the least or lower fixed manufacturing costs may be delayed, resulting in failure to meet promised customer delivery dates (which can result in losing customers).

2. A plant manager may accept a particular order to increase production, even though another plant in the same company is better suited to handle that order.

3. To meet increased production, a manager may defer maintenance beyond the current accounting period. Although operating income in this period may increase as a result, future operating income will probably decrease by a larger amount because of increased repairs and less-efficient equipment.

The example in Exhibit 9-4 focuses on only one year (2004). A Stassen manager who built up ending inventories of telescopes to 450 units in 2004 would have to further increase ending inventories in 2005 to increase that year's operating income by producing for inventory. There are limits to how much inventory levels can be increased over time (including due to physical constraints on storage space). Such limits reduce the likelihood of some of absorption costing's undesirable effects occurring.

Proposals for Revising Performance Evaluation

The undesirable effects of absorption costing can be reduced in several ways:

1. Careful budgeting and inventory planning to reduce management's freedom to build up excess inventory. For example, the budgeted monthly balance sheets have estimates of the dollar amount of inventories. If actual inventories exceed these dollar amounts, top management can investigate the inventory buildups.

2. Change the accounting system. Discontinue the use of absorption costing for internal reporting; instead use variable costing. This change will eliminate the incentives of managers to produce for inventory because all fixed manufacturing costs will be expensed.

3. Incorporate a carrying charge for inventory in the internal accounting system. For example, an inventory carrying charge of 1% per month could be assessed for the investment tied up in inventory and for spoilage and obsolescence when evaluating a manager's performance.

4. Change the period used to evaluate performance. Critics of absorption costing give examples in which managers take actions that maximize quarterly or annual income at the potential expense of long-run income. By evaluating performance over a 3- to 5-year period, managers will be less tempted to produce for inventory.

5. Include nonfinancial as well as financial variables in the measures used to evaluate performance (see Concepts in Action, p. 297). Companies are currently using nonfinancial and physical measures, such as the following, to monitor managers' performance in key areas:

$$\text{(a)}\quad \frac{\text{Ending inventory in units this period}}{\text{Ending inventory in units last period}}$$

$$\text{(b)}\quad \frac{\text{Sales in units this period}}{\text{Ending inventory in units this period}}$$

Any buildup of inventory at the end of the year would be signaled by tracking the month-to-month behavior of these two nonfinancial inventory measures. Companies that manufacture or sell several products could report these two measures for each of the products they manufacture and sell.

THROUGHPUT COSTING

Some managers maintain that even variable costing promotes an excessive amount of costs being inventoried. They argue that only direct materials are "truly variable." **Throughput costing,** also called **super-variable costing,** is a method of inventory costing in which only direct material costs are included as inventoriable costs. All other costs are costs of the period in which they are incurred. In particular, variable direct manufacturing labor costs and variable indirect manufacturing costs are regarded as period costs and deducted as expenses of the period.

Exhibit 9-5 on the next page is the throughput-costing income statement for Stassen Company for 2003, 2004, and 2005. *Throughput contribution* equals revenues minus all direct material costs of the goods sold. Compare the operating income amounts reported in Exhibit 9-5 with those for absorption costing and variable costing:

	2003	2004	2005
Absorption-costing operating income	$16,800	$14,600	$26,700
Variable-costing operating income	13,800	16,850	22,950
Throughput-costing operating income	12,000	18,200	20,700

Advocates of throughput costing maintain that, in the short run, manufacturing costs other than direct materials are relatively fixed. They view costs relating to workers, equipment, occupancy, and so on as relatively fixed with respect to providing productive capacity during the period.

Only the $11 direct material cost per unit is inventoriable under throughput costing, compared with $35 per unit for absorption costing and $20 per unit for variable costing. When the production quantity exceeds sales, as in 2003 and 2005, throughput costing results in the largest amount of expenses in the current period's income statement.

EXHIBIT 9-5

Throughput-Costing Stassen Company: Telescope Product-Line Income Statements for 2003, 2004, and 2005

	2003	2004	2005
Revenues: $100 × 600; 650; 750 units	$60,000	$65,000	$75,000
Direct material cost of goods sold			
Beginning inventory: $11 × 0; 200; 50 units	0	2,200	550
Direct material: $11 × 800; 500; 1,000 units	8,800	5,500	11,000
Cost of goods available for sale	8,800	7,700	11,550
Deduct ending inventory: $11 × 200; 50; 300 units	(2,200)	(550)	(3,300)
Total direct material cost of goods sold	6,600	7,150	8,250
Adjustment for variances	0	0	0
Total direct material costs	6,600	7,150	8,250
Throughput contribution[a]	53,400	57,850	66,750
Other costs			
Manufacturing[b]	19,200	16,500	21,000
Marketing[c]	22,200	23,150	25,050
Total other costs	41,400	39,650	46,050
Operating income	$12,000	$18,200	$20,700

[a]Throughput contribution equals revenues minus all direct material cost of goods sold.
[b]Fixed costs + (variable cost per unit × units produced); $12,000 + ($4 + $5) × 800; 500; 1,000 units
[c]Fixed costs + (variable cost per unit × units sold); $10,800 + $19 × 600; 650; 750 units

Advocates of throughput costing say it provides less incentive to produce for inventory than either variable costing or, especially, absorption costing.

CAPSULE COMPARISON OF INVENTORY-COSTING METHODS

For example, a company might use AC based on a standard-costing system for external financial reporting and VC based on a standard-costing system for internal reports.

Variable costing (including throughput costing, an extreme form of variable costing) and absorption costing may be combined with actual, normal, or standard costing. Exhibit 9-6 compares product costing under six alternative inventory-costing systems:

Variable Costing	Absorption Costing
Actual costing	Actual costing
Normal costing	Normal costing
Standard costing	Standard costing

EXHIBIT 9-6 **Comparison of Alternative Inventory-Costing Systems**

			Actual Costing	Normal Costing	Standard Costing
Absorption Costing	Variable Costing	**Variable Direct Manufacturing Costs**	Actual prices × Actual quantity of inputs used	Actual prices × Actual quantity of inputs used	Standard prices × Standard quantity of inputs allowed for actual output achieved
		Variable Indirect Manufacturing Costs	Actual variable indirect rates × Actual quantity of cost-allocation bases used	Budgeted variable indirect rates × Actual quantity of cost-allocation bases used	Standard variable indirect rates × Standard quantity of cost-allocation bases allowed for actual output achieved
		Fixed Direct Manufacturing Costs	Actual prices × Actual quantity of inputs used	Actual prices × Actual quantity of inputs used	Standard prices × Standard quantity of inputs allowed for actual output achieved
		Fixed Indirect Manufacturing Costs	Actual fixed indirect rates × Actual quantity of cost-allocation bases used	Budgeted fixed indirect rates × Actual quantity of cost-allocation bases used	Standard fixed indirect rates × Standard quantity of cost-allocation bases allowed for actual output achieved

CONCEPTS IN ACTION

Yield Improvements and the Production-Volume Variance at Analog Devices

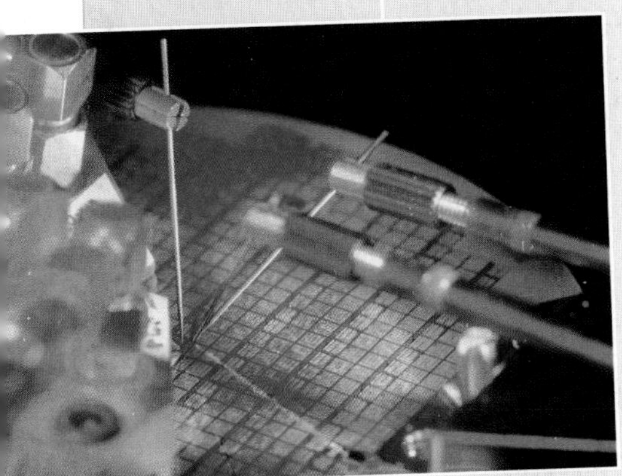

Analog Devices, Inc., (ADI) produces integrated circuits and systems used in computer disc drives, medical instruments, and consumer electronics. As we described on p. 226, improving yield—the quantity of good die produced on a silicon wafer divided by the total number of die that could be printed and produced on the wafer—is critical to delivering high-quality products at low cost.

For internal reporting purposes, ADI uses a variable-costing system. Fixed costs—comprising fixed overhead costs—are allocated to products only for the purposes of external reporting. The denominator used to allocate standard fixed overhead costs to products is practical machine capacity assuming efficient operations—machines working six hours per day, say. However, suppose running the machines only four hours a day, say, is adequate to meet actual demand. The result is an unfavorable production-volume variance because budgeted fixed overhead costs exceed the overhead costs allocated to production.

How do improvements in yield affect the production-volume variance? As yields improve, machines need to be run for even fewer hours to produce the actual output. That's because fewer silicon wafers need to be started to get the desired quantity of good product. Consequently, even fewer of the budgeted fixed overhead costs get allocated to production, the costs in inventory decline, and the unfavorable production-volume variance gets bigger. As the production-volume variance gets written off to cost of goods sold, short-term profit margins decline. Thus, quality improvements can have negative operating-income effects.

The performance evaluation of production planners at ADI was weighted more toward satisfying customer orders than reducing inventory levels. Thus, even as yields improved, planners were reluctant to reduce the number of wafer starts until they were sure that the higher yields would continue. They did not want to be in a position in which ADI lacked inventory to meet customer requests. Building up inventory also improved short-term operating income.

Commenting on the tensions and trade-offs, Ray Stata, ADI's chairman and president, warned, "Unless quality improvement and other more-fundamental performance measures are elevated to the same level of importance as financial measures, when conflicts arise, financial considerations win out." However, believing in the long-run benefits of higher quality, ADI continued to improve yield, and it developed performance measures so production planners and operations managers did not produce more product simply to absorb more fixed overhead costs into inventory.

Source: Analog Devices: The Half-Life System, Harvard Business School case number 9-190-061 and discussions with company management.

Variable costing has been controversial among accountants—not because of disagreement about the need to delineate between variable and fixed costs for internal planning and control, but as it pertains to external reporting (see Surveys of Company Practice, p. 298). Accountants who favor variable costing for external reporting maintain that the fixed portion of manufacturing costs is more closely related to the capacity to produce than to the actual production of specific units. Hence, fixed costs should be expensed, not inventoried.

Accountants who favor VC argue that FMOH costs are incurred to create the capacity to produce units. Once the capacity is created, FMOH costs should be expensed, regardless of how much of that capacity is actually used.

Accountants who support absorption costing maintain that inventories should carry a fixed manufacturing cost component. Why? Because both variable manufacturing costs and fixed manufacturing costs are necessary to produce goods. Therefore, both types of costs should be inventoriable, regardless of their different behavior patterns.

For external reporting to shareholders, companies around the globe tend to follow the generally accepted accounting principle that all manufacturing costs are inventoriable. For tax reporting in the United States, all manufacturing costs plus some product design

SURVEYS OF COMPANY PRACTICE

Usage of Variable Costing by Companies

Surveys of company practice in many countries report that approximately 30% to 50% of companies use variable costing in their internal accounting system:

	United States[a]	Canada[a]	Australia[b]	Japan[b]	Sweden[c]	United Kingdom[b]
Variable costing used	31%	48%	33%	31%	42%	52%
Absorption costing used	65	52	} 67	} 69	} 58	} 48
Other	4	0				

Surveys to date have not examined usage of throughput costing.

Many companies using variable costing for internal reporting also use absorption costing for external reporting or tax reporting. How do companies using variable costing treat fixed manufacturing overhead (MOH) in their internal reporting system?

	Australia[b]	Japan[b]	United Kingdom[b]
Prorate fixed MOH to inventory/cost of goods sold at end of period	41%	39%	25%
Use variable costing for monthly costing, and adjust to absorption costing once a year	11	8	4
Use both variable costing and absorption costing as dual systems	23	33	31
Treat fixed MOH as a period cost	25	3	35
Other	0	17	5

The most common problem reported by companies using variable costing is the difficulty of classifying costs into fixed or variable categories.

[a]Adapted from Inoue, "A Comparative Study."
[b]Adapted from Blayney and Yokoyama, "A Comparative Analysis."
[c]Adapted from Ask and Ax, "A Survey of."
Full citations are given in Appendix A at the end of the book.

VC isn't acceptable for external financial reporting or tax reporting. If a company uses VC, it must be in addition to AC. Surveys show that 30% to 50% of companies use VC for internal reports. These companies have decided that the benefits of VC outweigh its costs.

and administrative costs (such as legal costs) must be included as inventoriable costs.[1] Administrative costs must be allocated between those costs related to manufacturing activities (inventoriable costs) and those not related to manufacturing.

A key issue in absorption costing is the choice of the capacity level used to compute fixed manufacturing cost per unit produced. Part 2 of this chapter discusses this issue.

[1] Section 1.471-11 of the U.S. Internal Revenue Code (Inventories of Manufacturers) states that "both direct and indirect production costs must be taken into account in the computation of inventoriable costs in accordance with the 'full absorption' method of inventory costing . . . Costs are considered to be production costs to the extent that they are incident to and necessary for production or manufacturing operations or processes. Production costs include direct production costs and fixed and variable indirect production costs." Case law is useful to examine when determining the precise boundaries between inventoriable and non-inventoriable costs.

PROBLEM FOR SELF-STUDY

Assume Stassen Company on January 1, 2003, decides to contract with another company to preassemble a large percentage of the components of its telescopes. The revised manufacturing cost structure during the 2003 to 2005 period is

Variable manufacturing cost per unit produced	
Direct material cost	$30.50
Direct manufacturing labor cost	2.00
Indirect manufacturing cost	1.00
Total variable manufacturing cost per unit produced	$33.50
Total fixed manufacturing costs (all indirect)	$1,200

Under the revised cost structure, a larger percentage of Stassen's manufacturing costs are variable with respect to units produced. The denominator level of production used to calculate budgeted fixed manufacturing cost per unit in 2003, 2004, and 2005 is 800 units. Assume no other change from the data underlying Exhibits 9-1 and 9-2. Summary information pertaining to absorption-costing operating income and variable-costing operating income with this revised cost structure is

	2003	2004	2005
Absorption-costing operating income	$16,800	$18,650	$24,000
Variable-costing operating income	16,500	18,875	23,625
Difference	$ 300	$ (225)	$ 375

Required

1. Compute the budgeted fixed manufacturing overhead cost per unit in 2003, 2004, and 2005.
2. Explain the difference between absorption-costing operating income and variable-costing operating income in 2003, 2004, and 2005, focusing on fixed manufacturing costs in beginning and ending inventory.
3. Why are these differences smaller than the differences in Exhibit 9-2?

SOLUTION

1.

$$\text{Budgeted fixed manufacturing overhead cost per unit} = \frac{\text{Budgeted fixed manfacturing overhead costs}}{\text{Budgeted production units}} = \frac{\$1{,}200}{800 \text{ units}} = \$1.50 \text{ per unit}$$

2.

$$\begin{pmatrix}\text{Absorption-costing}\\ \text{operating}\\ \text{income}\end{pmatrix} - \begin{pmatrix}\text{Variable-costing}\\ \text{operating}\\ \text{income}\end{pmatrix} = \begin{pmatrix}\text{Fixed manufacturing}\\ \text{costs in ending inventory}\\ \text{under absorption costing}\end{pmatrix} - \begin{pmatrix}\text{Fixed manufacturing costs}\\ \text{in beginning inventory}\\ \text{under absorption costing}\end{pmatrix}$$

2003: $16,800 − $16,500 = ($1.50 per unit × 200 units) − ($1.50 per unit × 0 units)
$300 = $300

2004: $18,650 − $18,875 = ($1.50 per unit × 50 units) − ($1.50 per unit × 200 units)
−$225 = −$225

2005: $24,000 − $23,625 = ($1.50 per unit × 300 units) − ($1.50 per unit × 50 units)
$375 = $375

3. Subcontracting a large part of manufacturing has greatly reduced the magnitude of fixed manufacturing costs. This reduction, in turn, means differences between absorption costing and variable costing are much smaller than in Exhibits 9-1 and 9-2.

PART TWO: DENOMINATOR-LEVEL CAPACITY CONCEPTS AND FIXED-COST CAPACITY ANALYSIS

Determining the "right" level of capacity is one of the most strategic and difficult decisions managers face. Having too much capacity to produce relative to capacity needed to meet demand means incurring large costs of unused capacity. Having too little capacity to produce means that demand from some customers may be unfilled. These customers may go to other sources of supply and never return. We now consider issues that arise with capacity costs.

6 **Describe the various capacity concepts that can be used in absorption costing**

...theoretical capacity, practical capacity, normal capacity utilization, master-budget capacity utilization

ALTERNATIVE DENOMINATOR-LEVEL CAPACITY CONCEPTS FOR ABSORPTION COSTING

Earlier chapters, especially Chapters 4, 5, and 8, have highlighted how normal-costing systems and standard-costing systems report costs in an ongoing timely manner throughout an accounting period. The choice of the capacity level used to allocate budgeted fixed manufacturing costs to products can greatly affect the operating income reported by a normal-costing system or a standard-costing system and the product cost information available to managers.

Consider Bushells Company, which produces 12-ounce bottles of iced tea at its Sydney bottling plant. The annual fixed manufacturing costs of the bottling plant are \$5,400,000. Bushells currently uses absorption costing with a standard-costing system for external reporting purposes, and it calculates its budgeted fixed manufacturing rate on a per case basis (one case is twenty-four 12-ounce bottles of iced tea). We will now examine four different capacity levels used as the denominator to compute the budgeted fixed manufacturing overhead cost rate: theoretical capacity, practical capacity, normal capacity utilization, and master-budget capacity utilization.

Theoretical Capacity and Practical Capacity

In business and accounting, *capacity* ordinarily means "constraint," an "upper limit." **Theoretical capacity** is the level of capacity based on producing at full efficiency all the time. Bushells can produce 10,000 cases of iced tea per shift when the bottling lines are operating at maximum speed. Assuming 360 days per year, the theoretical annual capacity for three 8-hour shifts per day is

$$10{,}000 \text{ cases per shift} \times 3 \text{ shifts per day} \times 360 \text{ days} = 10{,}800{,}000 \text{ cases}$$

Theoretical capacity is theoretical in the sense that it does not allow for any plant maintenance, interruptions because of bottle breakage on the filling lines, or any other factor. Theoretical capacity represents an ideal goal of capacity usage. Theoretical capacity is unattainable in the real world.

Practical capacity is the level of capacity that reduces theoretical capacity by unavoidable operating interruptions, such as scheduled maintenance time, shutdowns for holidays, and so on. Assume that the practical capacity is the practical production rate of 8,000 cases per shift for three shifts per day for 300 days a year. The practical annual capacity is

$$8{,}000 \text{ cases per shift} \times 3 \text{ shifts per day} \times 300 \text{ days} = 7{,}200{,}000 \text{ cases}$$

Engineering and human resource factors are both important when estimating theoretical or practical capacity. Engineers at the Bushells' plant can provide input on the technical capabilities of machines for filling bottles. Human-safety factors, such as increased injury risk when the line operates at faster speeds, are also necessary considerations in estimating practical capacity.

Normal Capacity Utilization and Master-Budget Capacity Utilization

Both theoretical capacity and practical capacity measure capacity levels in terms of what a plant can *supply*—available capacity. In contrast, normal capacity utilization and master-budget capacity utilization measure capacity levels in terms of *demand* for the output of the plant—the amount of the available capacity that the plant expects to use based on the demand for its products. In many cases, budgeted demand is well below the production capacity available.

Normal capacity utilization is the level of capacity utilization that satisfies average customer demand over a period (say, 2 to 3 years) that includes seasonal, cyclical, and trend factors. **Master-budget capacity utilization** is expected level of capacity utilization for the current budget period, typically one year. These two capacity utilization levels can differ—for example, when an industry has cyclical periods of high and low demand or when management believes that the budgeted production for the coming period is not representative of long-run demand.

Consider Bushells' master budget for 2004, based on production of 4,000,000 cases of tea per year.[2] Despite using this master-budget capacity utilization level of 4,000,000 cases for 2004, top management believes that over the next three years the normal (average) annual production level will be 5,000,000 cases. They view 2004's budgeted production level of 4,000,000 cases to be "abnormally" low. Why? Because a major competitor (Tea-Mania) has been sharply reducing its selling price and spending large amounts on advertising. Bushells expects that the competitor's lower price and advertising blitz will not be a long-run phenomenon and that, in 2005, Bushells' production and sales will be higher.

Effect on Budgeted Fixed Manufacturing Overhead Cost Rate

We now illustrate how each of these four denominator levels affect the budgeted fixed manufacturing overhead cost rate. Bushells has budgeted fixed manufacturing costs of $5,400,000 for 2004. This lump-sum amount is incurred to provide the capacity to bottle iced tea. This lump sum, includes, among other costs, lease costs for bottling equipment and the compensation of the plant manager. The budgeted fixed manufacturing overhead cost rates for 2004 for each of the four capacity-level concepts are

Choosing a denominator level only arises under AC. Both VC and throughput costing expense the lump-sum FMOH costs in the period incurred.

Capacity Concept (1)	Budgeted Fixed Manufacturing Overhead per Year (2)	Budgeted Capacity Level (in Cases) (3)	Budgeted Fixed Manufacturing Overhead Cost per Case (4) = (2) ÷ (3)
Theoretical capacity	$5,400,000	10,800,000	$0.50
Practical capacity	5,400,000	7,200,000	0.75
Normal capacity utilization	5,400,000	5,000,000	1.08
Master-budget capacity utilization	5,400,000	4,000,000	1.35

The budgeted fixed manufacturing overhead cost rate based on master-budget capacity utilization, $1.35 per case, is 170% higher than the cost rate based on theoretical capacity, $0.50 per case. This big difference in cost rates is because theoretical capacity is much larger than the master-budget capacity utilization.

Standard variable manufacturing cost is $5.20 per case. The total standard manufacturing cost per case with alternative capacity-level concepts is

Denominator-Level Capacity Concept (1)	Variable Manufacturing Cost per Case (2)	Fixed Manufacturing Cost per Case (3)	Total Manufacturing Cost per Case (4) = (2) + (3)
Theoretical capacity	$5.20	$0.50	$5.70
Practical capacity	5.20	0.75	5.95
Normal capacity utilization	5.20	1.08	6.28
Master-budget capacity utilization	5.20	1.35	6.55

CHOOSING A CAPACITY LEVEL

7 **Understand the major factors management considers in choosing a capacity level to compute the budgeted fixed overhead cost rate**

...for example, effect on product costing, capacity management, pricing decisions, and financial statements

Which capacity level should a company use to calculate the budgeted fixed manufacturing cost per case? There is no requirement that companies use the same capacity-level concept, say, for management planning and control, external reporting to shareholders, and income tax purposes. In choosing a capacity level, management considers several factors, including

[2] Management plans to run one shift for 300 days in 2004 at a speed of 8,000 cases per shift. A second shift will run for 200 days (in the warmer months) at the same speed of 8,000 cases per shift. Thus, budgeted production for 2004 is (300 days × 8,000 cases/day) + (200 days × 8,000 cases/day) = 4,000,000 cases.

(a) effect on product costing and capacity management, (b) effect on pricing decisions, (c) effect on performance evaluation, (d) effect on financial statements, (e) regulatory requirements, and (f) difficulties in forecasting chosen capacity-level concepts. We now discuss each factor.

Effect on Product Costing and Capacity Management

Cost data from a normal-costing system or a standard-costing system are often used in pricing or product-mix decisions. As the Bushells example illustrates, the use of theoretical capacity results in an unrealistically small fixed manufacturing overhead cost per case because it is based on an idealistic and unattainable level of capacity. Theoretical capacity is rarely used to calculate the budgeted fixed manufacturing cost per case because it departs significantly from the real capacity available to a company.

Many companies favor practical capacity as the denominator to calculate the budgeted fixed manufacturing cost per case. Practical capacity in the Bushells example represents the maximum number of cases (7,200,000) that Bushells intends to produce per year for the $5,400,000 it will spend on capacity each year. If Bushells had consistently planned to produce fewer cases of iced tea, say 4,000,000 cases each year, it would have built a smaller plant and incurred lower costs.

Bushells budgets $0.75 in fixed manufacturing overhead cost per case based on the $5,400,000 it costs to acquire the capacity to produce 7,200,000 cases. This plant capacity is acquired well before Bushells uses the capacity and even before Bushells knows how much of the capacity it will actually use. That is, the budgeted fixed manufacturing cost of $0.75 per case measures the *cost per case of supplying the capacity.*

Demand for Bushells' iced tea in 2004 is expected to be 4,000,000 cases, lower than practical capacity. The cost of *supplying* the capacity needed to make 4,000,000 case is still $0.75 per case. That's because capacity is acquired in "lumpy" amounts, and it costs $5,400,000 per year to acquire the capacity to make 7,200,000 cases. The capacity and its cost are fixed *in the short run;* the capacity supplied cannot be reduced to match the capacity needed in 2004. As a result, not all of the capacity supplied at $0.75 per case will be needed or used in 2004. Using practical capacity, managers can subdivide the cost of resources supplied into used and unused components. At the supply cost of $0.75 per case, manufacturing resources that Bushells will use equal $3,000,000 ($0.75 per case × 4,000,000 cases). Manufacturing resources that Bushells will not use are $2,400,000 [$0.75 per case × (7,200,000 − 4,000,000) cases].

Using practical capacity fixes the cost of capacity at the cost of supplying the capacity, regardless of the demand for the capacity. Highlighting the cost of capacity acquired but not used directs managers' attention to managing unused capacity, perhaps by designing new products to fill unused capacity, leasing out unused capacity to others, or eliminating unused capacity. In contrast, using either of the capacity levels based on the demand for Bushells' iced tea—master-budget capacity utilization or normal capacity utilization—hides the amount of unused capacity. If Bushells had used the master-budget capacity utilization as the capacity level, it would have calculated the budgeted fixed manufacturing cost per case as $1.35 ($5,400,000 ÷ 4,000,000 cases). This calculation does not use data about practical capacity, so it does not separately identify the cost of unused capacity. Note, however, that the cost of $1.35 per case includes a charge for unused capacity—the $0.75 fixed manufacturing resource that would be used to produce each case at practical capacity plus the cost of unused capacity allocated to each case, $0.60 per case ($2,400,000 ÷ 4,000,000 cases).

From the perspective of long-run product costing, which cost of capacity should Bushells use for pricing purposes or for benchmarking its product cost structure against competitors: $0.75 per case based on practical capacity? or $1.35 per case based on master-budget capacity utilization? Probably, the $0.75 per case based on practical capacity. Why? Because $0.75 per case represents the budgeted cost per case of only the capacity used to produce the product and explicitly excludes the cost of any unused capacity. Customers will be willing to pay a price that covers the cost of the capacity actually used but will not want to pay for capacity that is not used to produce the product. Customers expect Bushells to manage its unused capacity or bear the cost of unused capacity, not pass it along to them. Moreover, if Bushells' competitors manage unused capacity more effectively, the cost of capacity in the competitors' cost structures (which guides competitors' pricing decisions) is likely to approach $0.75 per case. In the next section we show how the use of normal capacity utilization or master-budget capacity utilization can result in setting selling prices that are not competitive.

Pricing Decisions and the Downward Demand Spiral

8 **Describe how attempts to recover fixed costs of capacity may lead to price increases and lower demand**

...customers are unwilling to pay for a company's unused capacity

The easiest way to understand the *downward demand spiral* is via an example. Assume Bushells uses master-budget capacity utilization of 4,000,000 cases for product costing in 2004. The resulting manufacturing cost is $6.55 per case ($5.20 variable manufacturing cost per case + $1.35 fixed manufacturing overhead per case). Assume a competitor (Lipton Iced Tea) in December 2003 offers to supply a major customer of Bushells (a customer who was expected to purchase 1,000,000 cases in 2004) iced tea at $6.25 per case. The Bushells manager, not wanting to show a loss on the account and wanting to recoup all costs in the long run, declines to match the competitor's price and the account is lost. The lost account means budgeted fixed manufacturing costs of $5,400,000 will be spread over the remaining master-budget volume of 3,000,000 cases at a rate of $1.80 per case ($5,400,000 ÷ 3,000,000 cases).

Suppose yet another customer of Bushells—also accounting for 1,000,000 cases of budgeted volume—receives a bid from a competitor is price at $6.60 per case. The Bushells manager compares this bid with his revised unit cost of $7.00 ($5.20 + $1.80), declines to match the competition, and the account is lost. The planned output would shrink further to 2,000,000 units. The budgeted fixed manufacturing cost per unit for the remaining 2,000,000 cases now would be $2.70 ($5,400,000 ÷ 2,000,000 cases). The effect of spreading fixed manufacturing costs over a shrinking master-budget capacity utilization amount is

Master-Budget Capacity Utilization Denominator Level (Cases) (1)	Fixed Manufacturing Cost per Case [$5,400,000 ÷ (1)] (2)	Variable Manufacturing Cost per Case (3)	Total Manufacturing Cost per Case (4) = (2) + (3)
4,000,000	$1.35	$5.20	$ 6.55
3,000,000	1.80	5.20	7.00
2,000,000	2.70	5.20	7.90
1,000,000	5.40	5.20	10.60

The **downward demand spiral** for a company is the continuing reduction in the demand for its products that occurs when prices of competitors' products are not met and (as demand drops further) higher and higher unit costs result in more and more reluctance to meet competitors' prices.

The use of practical capacity as the denominator to calculate the budgeted fixed manufacturing cost per case would avoid the recalculation of unit costs when expected demand levels change. That's because the fixed cost rate would be calculated based on the capacity available rather then the capacity used to meet demand. Managers who use reported unit costs in a mechanical way to set prices are less likely to promote a downward demand spiral when they use practical capacity concepts than when they use the normal capacity or master-budget capacity utilization concepts.

Effect on Performance Evaluation

Consider how the choice between normal capacity utilization, master-budget capacity utilization, and practical capacity affects how a marketing manager is evaluated. Normal capacity utilization is often used as a basis for long-run plans. The normal capacity utilization depends on the time span selected and the forecasts made for each year. *However, normal capacity utilization is an average that provides no meaningful feedback to the marketing manager for a particular year.* Using normal capacity utilization as a reference for judging current performance of a marketing manager is an example of misusing a long-run measure for a short-run purpose. The master-budget capacity utilization, rather than normal capacity utilization or practical capacity, is what should be used for evaluating a marketing manager's performance in the current year. That's because the master budget is the principal short-run planning and control tool. Managers feel more obligated to reach the levels specified in the master budget, which should have been carefully set in relation to the maximum opportunities for sales in the current year.

When large differences exist between practical capacity and master-budget capacity utilization, several companies (such as Texas Instruments) classify part of the large difference as *planned unused capacity*. One reason for this approach is performance evaluation. Consider our Bushells iced-tea example. The managers in charge of capacity planning usually do not make pricing decisions. Top management decided to build an iced-tea plant with 7,200,000 cases of practical capacity, focusing on demand over the next five years. But, Bushells' marketing managers, who are mid-level managers, make the pricing decisions. These executives believe they should be held accountable only for the manufacturing overhead costs related to their potential customer base in 2004. The master-budget capacity utilization suggests a customer base in 2004 of 4,000,000 cases ($\frac{5}{9}$ of the 7,200,000 practical capacity). Using responsibility accounting principles (see Chapter 6, pp. 191–193), only $\frac{5}{9}$ of the budgeted total fixed manufacturing costs ($5,400,000 × $\frac{5}{9}$ = $3,000,000) would be attributed to the fixed capacity costs of meeting 2004 demand. The remaining $\frac{4}{9}$ of the numerator ($5,400,000 × $\frac{4}{9}$ = $2,400,000) would be separately shown as the capacity cost of meeting long-run demand increases expected to occur beyond 2004.[3]

9 **Explain how the capacity level chosen to calculate the budgeted fixed overhead cost rate affects the production-volume variance**

...if capacity level is greater (less) than actual production, there is an unfavorable (favorable) production-volume variance

Effect on Financial Statements

The magnitude of the favorable/unfavorable production-volume variance under absorption costing will be affected by the choice of the denominator used to calculate the budgeted fixed manufacturing cost per case. Assume Bushells' actual production in 2004 is 4,400,000 cases of iced tea. Actual sales for 2004 are 4,200,000 cases. Also assume no beginning inventory for 2004 and no price variances, spending variances, or efficiency variances in manufacturing costs. Those assumptions mean budgeted fixed manufacturing overhead costs and actual fixed manufacturing overhead costs are both $5,400,000. The average selling price per case of iced tea is $8.00. Operating costs equal $2,810,000.

The production-volume variance was introduced in Chapter 8 (p. 259):

$$\text{Production-volume variance} = \begin{pmatrix}\text{Budgeted}\\ \text{fixed}\\ \text{overhead}\end{pmatrix} - \begin{pmatrix}\text{Fixed overhead allocated using}\\ \text{budgeted cost per output unit}\\ \text{allowed for actual output produced}\end{pmatrix}$$

The higher the denominator level, (1) the lower the budgeted FMOH cost rate, (2) the lower the amount of FMOH allocated to output produced (because the budgeted FMOH cost rate is lower), and (3) the higher the unfavorable PVV (because the higher the denominator level, the more likely actual output will fall short of that level).

Different capacity-level concepts can be used to compute the budgeted fixed overhead cost rate per unit. Using the data given earlier in the chapter (p. 301), the different capacity-level concepts will result in different amounts of production-volume variance:

Production-volume variance (theoretical capacity) = $5,400,000 − (4,400,000 cases × $0.50 per case)
= $5,400,000 − $2,200,000
= $3,200,000, or $3,200,000 U

Production-volume variance (practical capacity) = $5,400,000 − (4,400,000 cases × $0.75 per case)
= $5,400,000 − $3,300,000
= $2,100,000, or $2,100,000 U

Production-volume variance (normal capacity utilization) = $5,400,000 − (4,400,000 cases × $1.08 per case)
= $5,400,000 − $4,752,000
= $648,000 or $648,000 U

Production-volume variance (master budget capacity utilization) = $5,400,000 − (4,400,000 cases × $1.35 per case)
= $5,400,000 − $5,940,000
= −$540,000 or $540,000 F

[3] For further discussion, see T. Klammer, *Capacity Measurement and Improvement* (Chicago: Irwin, 1996). This research was facilitated by CAM-I, an organization promoting innovative cost management practices. CAM-I's research on capacity costs explores ways in which companies can identify types of capacity costs that can be reduced (or eliminated) without affecting the required output to meet customer demand. An example is improving processes to successfully eliminate the costs of capacity held in anticipation of handling difficulties due to imperfect coordination with suppliers and customers.

How Bushells handles its end-of-period variances will determine the effect these production-volume variances will have on the company's operating income. We now discuss the three alternative approaches Bushells can use to handle the production-volume variance. These approaches were first discussed in Chapter 4 (p. 114–118).

1. *Adjusted allocation-rate approach.* This approach restates all amounts in the general and subsidiary ledgers by using actual rather than budgeted cost rates. Given that actual fixed manufacturing overhead costs are \$5,400,000 and actual production is 4,400,000 cases, the recalculated fixed manufacturing overhead cost is \$1.23 per case (\$5,400, 000 ÷ 4,400,000 cases, rounded up to the nearest cent). The adjusted allocation-rate approach results in the choice of the capacity level used to calculate the budgeted fixed manufacturing overhead cost per case having no effect on end-of-period financial statements. In effect, an actual costing system is adopted at the end of the period.

2. *Proration approach.* The underallocated or overallocated overhead is spread among (a) ending work in process, (b) ending finished goods, and (c) cost of goods sold. The proration restates the ending balances of (a), (b), and (c) to what they would have been if actual cost rates had been used rather than budgeted cost rates. The proration approach also results in the choice of the capacity level used to calculate the budgeted fixed manufacturing overhead cost per case having no effect on end-of-period financial statements.

3. *Write-off variances to cost of goods sold approach.* Exhibit 9-7 shows how use of this approach affects Bushells' operating income for 2004. Recall, Bushells had no beginning inventory, production of 4,400,000 cases, and sales of 4,200,000 cases. Hence, the ending inventory on December 31, 2004, is 200,000 cases. Using master-budget capacity utilization as the denominator results in assigning the highest amount of fixed manufacturing overhead cost per case to the 200,000 cases in ending inventory. Accordingly, operating income is highest using the master-budget capacity utilization concept. The differences in operating income for the four denominator-level concepts in Exhibit 9-7 are due to different amounts of fixed manufacturing overhead being inventoried at the end of 2004:

	Fixed Manufacturing Overhead in Dec. 31, 2004, Inventory
Theoretical capacity	200,000 cases × \$0.50 per case = \$100,000
Practical capacity	200,000 cases × 0.75 per case = 150,000
Normal capacity utilization	200,000 cases × 1.08 per case = 216,000
Master-budget capacity utilization	200,000 cases × 1.35 per case = 270,000

In Exhibit 9-7, the \$54,000 difference (\$3,820,000 − \$3,766,000) in operating income between the master-budget capacity and the normal capacity utilization concepts is due to the difference in fixed manufacturing overhead inventoried (\$270,000 − \$216,000).

Regulatory Requirements

For tax reporting purposes in the United States, the Internal Revenue Service (IRS) requires companies to use practical capacity to calculate budgeted fixed manufacturing cost per case. At year-end, proration of any variances between inventories and cost of goods sold is required (unless the variance is immaterial in amount) to calculate the company's operating income.[4]

Difficulties in Forecasting Chosen Denominator-Level Concept

The practical-capacity concept measures the available supply of capacity. Managers can usually use engineering studies and human resource considerations (such as worker safety) to obtain a reliable estimate of this concept for the budget period. However, it is more difficult to estimate normal utilization reliably. For example, many U.S. steel

Note, practical capacity need not be constant over time. For example, improvements in plant layout and increases in worker efficiency both can result in significant increases in practical capacity for the same plant over time.

[4] U.S. tax reporting requires the use of either the adjusted allocation-rate approach or the proration approach. Section 1.471-11 of the U.S. Internal Revenue Code states: "The proper use of the standard cost method requires that a taxpayer must reallocate to the goods in ending inventory a pro rata portion of any net negative or net positive overhead variances."

EXHIBIT 9-7 **Income Statement Effects of Using Alternative Capacity-Level Concepts Bushells Company for 2004**

	Theoretical Capacity	Practical Capacity	Normal Capacity Utilization	Master-Budget Capacity Utilization
Denominator level in cases	10,800,000	7,200,000	5,000,000	4,000,000
Revenues[a]	$33,600,000	$33,600,000	$33,600,000	$33,600,000
Cost of goods sold				
Beginning inventory	0	0	0	0
Variable manufacturing costs[b]	22,880,000	22,880,000	22,880,000	22,880,000
Fixed manufacturing overhead costs[c]	2,200,000	3,300,000	4,752,000	5,940,000
Cost of goods available for sale	25,080,000	26,180,000	27,632,000	28,820,000
Deduct ending inventory[d]	(1,140,000)	(1,190,000)	(1,256,000)	(1,310,000)
Total COGS (at standard costs)	23,940,000	24,990,000	26,376,000	27,510,000
Adjustment for manufacturing variances[e]	3,200,000 U	2,100,000 U	648,000 U	(540,000) F
Total cost of goods sold	27,140,000	27,090,000	27,024,000	26,970,000
Gross margin	6,460,000	6,510,000	6,576,000	6,630,000
Operating costs	2,810,000	2,810,000	2,810,000	2,810,000
Operating income	$ 3,650,000	$ 3,700,000	$ 3,766,000	$ 3,820,000

[a]$8.00 × 4,200,000 units = $33,600,000
[b]$5.20 × 4,400,000 units = $22,880,000
[c]Fixed manufacturing overhead costs:
$0.50 × 4,400,000 units = $2,200,000
$0.75 × 4,400,000 units = $3,300,000
$1.08 × 4,400,000 units = $4,752,000
$1.35 × 4,400,000 units = $5,940,000

[d]Ending inventory costs:
($5.20 + $0.50) × 200,000 units = $1,140,000
($5.20 + $0.75) × 200,000 units = $1,190,000
($5.20 + $1.08) × 200,000 units = $1,256,000
($5.20 + $1.35) × 200,000 units = $1,310,000
[e]See text (p. 259) for computation of the production-volume variance.

companies in the 1980s believed they were in the downturn of a demand cycle that would have an upturn within two or three years. After all, steel had been a cyclical business in which upturns followed downturns, making the notion of *normal utilization* appear reasonable. Unfortunately, the steel cycle in the 1980s did not turn up; some companies and numerous plants closed. Some marketing managers are prone to overestimate their ability to regain lost sales and market share. Their estimate of "normal" demand for their product may be based on an overly optimistic outlook. Master-budget capacity utilization typically focuses only on the expected capacity utilization for the next year. Master-budget capacity utilization can be more reliably estimated than normal capacity utilization.

CAPACITY COSTS AND DENOMINATOR-LEVEL ISSUES

Let's consider several more factors that affect the planning and control of capacity costs.

1. Costing systems, such as normal costing or standard costing, do not recognize uncertainty in the way managers recognize it. A *single* amount rather than a range of possible amounts is used as the denominator when calculating budgeted fixed manufacturing cost per unit in absorption costing. Yet, managers face uncertainty about demand—they even face uncertainty about their capability to supply. Bushells' plant has estimated practical capacity of 7,200,000 cases. The estimated master-budget capacity utilization for 2004 is 4,000,000 cases. These estimates are uncertain. Managers recognize uncertainty in their capacity planning decisions. Bushells built its current plant with 7,200,000-case practical capacity in part to provide the capability to meet possible demand surges. Even if these demand surges do not occur in a given period, it would be wrong to conclude all capacity not used in a given period is wasted resources. *The gains from meeting sudden demand surges may well require having unused capacity in some periods.*

2. The fixed manufacturing overhead cost rate is based on a numerator—budgeted fixed manufacturing overhead costs—and a denominator—some measure of capacity or capacity utilization. Our discussion so far has emphasized issues concerning the choice of the denominator. Challenging issues also arise in measuring the numerator. For example, deregulation of the U.S. electric utility industry has resulted in many electric utilities becoming unprofitable. This situation has led to write-downs in the values of their plant and equipment. The write-downs reduce the numerator via the depreciation used to compute fixed capacity cost per kilowatt-hour of electricity produced.

3. Capacity costs arise in nonmanufacturing parts of the value chain, as well as with the manufacturing costs emphasized in this chapter. Bushells may acquire a fleet of vehicles capable of distributing the practical capacity of its iced-tea plant. When actual production is below the practical capacity, there will be unused capacity cost issues with the distribution function, as well as with the manufacturing function.

As you saw in Chapter 8, capacity cost issues are prominent in many service-sector companies, such as airlines, hospitals, railroads, and banks, even though these companies carry no inventory and so have no inventory-costing issues. For example, in calculating the fixed overhead cost per patient-day in its obstetrics and gynecology department, a hospital must decide what denominator to use—practical capacity, normal utilization, or master-budget utilization. Its decision may have implications for capacity management, as well as pricing and performance evaluation.

4. For simplicity and to focus on the main ideas about choosing a denominator to calculate a budgeted fixed manufacturing cost rate, our Bushells example assumed that all fixed manufacturing overhead costs had a single cost driver: cases of iced tea produced. As you saw in Chapter 5, activity-based costing systems have multiple overhead cost pools at the output-unit, batch, product-sustaining, and facility-sustaining levels, each with its own cost driver. In calculating the activity cost rates (for setups and material handling, say), management must choose a capacity level for the quantity of the cost driver (setup-hours or loads moved). Should it use practical capacity, normal capacity utilization, or master-budget capacity utilization? For all the reasons described in the chapter (such as pricing and capacity management), most proponents of activity-based costing argue that practical capacity should be used as the denominator to calculate activity cost rates.

PROBLEM FOR SELF-STUDY

Suppose Bushells Company is computing its operating income for 2006. That year's results are identical to the results for 2004, shown in Exhibit 9-7, except that master-budget capacity utilization for 2006 is 6,000,000 cases instead of 4,000,000 cases. Production in 2006 is 4,400,000 cases. There is no beginning inventory on January 1, 2006, and there are no variances other than the production-volume variance. Bushells writes off this variance to cost of goods sold. Sales in 2006 are 4,200,000 cases.

Required

How would the results for Bushells Company in Exhibit 9-7 differ if the year were 2006 rather than 2004? Show your computations.

SOLUTION

The only change in Exhibit 9-7 results would be for the master-budget capacity utilization level. The budgeted fixed manufacturing overhead cost rate for 2006 is

$$\frac{\$5,400,000}{6,000,000 \text{ cases}} = \$0.90 \text{ per case}$$

The manufacturing cost per case is \$6.10 (\$5.20 + \$0.90). So, the production-volume variance for 2006 is

$$(6,000,000 \text{ cases} - 4,400,000 \text{ cases}) \times \$0.90 \text{ per case} = \$1,440,000, \text{ or } \$1,440,000 \text{ U}$$

The income statement for 2006 shows:

Revenues: \$8.00 per case × 4,200,000 cases	$33,600,000
Cost of goods sold	
Beginning inventory	0

Continued

Variable manufacturing costs:	
$5.20 per case × 4,400,000 cases	22,880,000
Fixed manufacturing costs:	
$0.90 per case × 4,400,000 cases	3,960,000
Cost of goods available for sale	26,840,000
Deduct ending inventory:	
$6.10 per case × 200,000 cases	(1,220,000)
Cost of goods sold (at standard costs)	25,620,000
Adjustment for variances	1,440,000 U
Cost of goods sold	27,060,000
Gross margin	6,540,000
Operating costs	2,810,000
Operating income	$ 3,730,000

The higher denominator level used to calculate budgeted fixed manufacturing cost per case in the 2006 master budget means that fewer fixed manufacturing overhead costs are inventoried in 2006 than in 2004, given identical sales and production levels and assuming the production-volume variance is written off to cost of goods sold.

DECISION POINTS SUMMARY

The following question-and-answer format summarizes the chapter's learning objectives. Each decision presents a key question related to a learning objective. The guidelines are the answer to that question.

Decision	Guidelines
1. How does variable costing differ from absorption costing?	Variable costing and absorption costing differ in only one respect: how to account for fixed manufacturing costs. Under variable costing, fixed manufacturing costs are excluded from inventoriable costs and are a cost of the period in which they are incurred. Under absorption costing, fixed manufacturing costs are inventoriable and become a part of cost of goods sold in the period when sales occur.
2. What formats do companies use when preparing income statements under variable costing and absorption costing?	The variable-costing income statement is based on the contribution-margin format. The absorption-costing income statement is based on the gross-margin format.
3. How do level of sales and level of production affect operating income under variable costing and absorption costing?	Under variable costing, operating income is driven by the unit level of sales. Under absorption costing, operating income is driven by the unit level of production, as well as by the unit level of sales.
4. Why might managers build up finished goods inventory if they use absorption costing?	When absorption costing is used, managers can increase current operating income by producing more units for inventory. Producing for inventory absorbs more fixed manufacturing costs into inventory and reduces costs expensed in the period. Critics of absorption costing label this manipulation of income as the major negative consequence of treating fixed manufacturing overhead as an inventoriable cost.
5. How does throughput costing differ from variable costing and absorption costing?	Throughput costing treats all costs except direct materials as costs of the period in which they are incurred. Throughput costing results in a lower amount of manufacturing costs being inventoried than either variable or absorption costing.
6. What are the various capacity levels a company can use to calculate budgeted fixed manufacturing cost rate?	Capacity levels can be measured in terms of what a plant can supply—theoretical capacity or practical capacity. Capacity can also be measured in terms of demand for the output of a plant—normal capacity utilization or master-budget capacity utilization.

7. What are the major factors managers consider in choosing the capacity level to compute the budgeted fixed overhead cost rate?

The major factors managers consider in choosing the capacity level to compute the budgeted fixed manufacturing cost per unit are (a) effect on product costing and capacity management, (b) effect on pricing decisions, (c) effect on performance evaluation, (d) effect on financial statements, (e) regulatory requirements, and (f) difficulties in forecasting chosen capacity-level concepts.

8. Should a company with high fixed costs and unused capacity raise selling prices to fully recoup its costs?

No, companies with high fixed costs and unused capacity may encounter ongoing and increasingly greater reductions in demand if they continue to raise selling prices to fully recoup variable and fixed costs from a declining sales base. This phenomenon is called the downward demand spiral.

9. How does the capacity level chosen to calculate the budgeted fixed overhead cost rate affect the production-volume variance?

When the chosen capacity level exceeds the actual production level, there will be an unfavorable production-volume variance; when the chosen capacity level is less than the actual production level, there will be a favorable production-volume variance.

APPENDIX: BREAKEVEN POINTS IN VARIABLE COSTING AND ABSORPTION COSTING

Chapter 3 introduced cost-volume-profit analysis. If variable costing is used, the breakeven point (that's where operating income is \$0) is computed in the usual manner. There is only one breakeven point in this case, and it depends on (1) fixed costs and (2) contribution margin per unit.

The formula for computing the breakeven point under variable costing is a special case of the more general target operating income formula from Chapter 3 (p. 67):

$$\text{Let } Q = \text{Number of units sold to earn the target operating income}$$

$$\text{Then, } Q = \frac{\text{Total fixed costs} + \text{Target operating income}}{\text{Contribution margin per unit}}$$

Breakeven occurs when the target operating income is \$0. In our Stassen illustration for 2004 (see pp. 289–292):

$$Q = \frac{(\$12{,}000 + \$10{,}800) + \$0}{\$100 - (\$20 + \$19)} = \frac{\$22{,}800}{\$61}$$

$$= 374 \text{ units (rounded up to the nearest unit)}$$

Proof of breakeven point:

Revenues, \$100 × 374 units	\$37,400
Variable costs, \$39 × 374 units	14,586
Contribution margin, \$61 × 374 units	22,814
Fixed costs	22,800
Operating income	\$ 14

Operating income is not \$0 because the breakeven number of units is rounded up to 374 from 373.77.

If absorption costing is used, the required number of units sold to earn a specific target operating income is not unique because of the number of variables involved. The following formula shows the factors that will affect the target operating income under absorption costing:

$$Q = \frac{\text{Total fixed costs} + \text{Target operating income} + \left[\text{Fixed manufacturing cost rate} \times \left(\text{Breakeven sales in units} - \text{Units produced}\right)\right]}{\text{Contribution margin per unit}}$$

Remember, "Total fixed costs" in this formula includes *all* fixed costs (not just FMOH costs).

In this formula, the numerator is the sum of three terms (from the perspective of the two "+" signs), compared with two terms in the numerator of the variable-costing formula stated earlier. The additional term in the numerator under absorption costing is

This formula shows that under AC, there's a unique breakeven point for each different quantity of units produced. Also, there's an inverse relation between the quantity of units produced and the quantity of units needed to be sold to break even. The more units produced, the more FMOH costs allocated to those units, and the fewer units needed to be sold to break even.

$$\left[\text{Fixed manufacturing cost rate} \times \left(\text{Breakeven sales in units} - \text{Units produced}\right)\right]$$

This term reduces the fixed costs that need to be recovered when units produced exceed the breakeven sales quantity. When production exceeds the breakeven sales quantity, some of the fixed manufacturing costs that are expensed under variable costing are not expensed under absorption costing; they are instead included in finished goods inventory.

For Stassen Company in 2004, one breakeven point, Q, under absorption costing for production of 500 units is

$$Q = \frac{(\$12,000+\$10,800)+0+[\$15(Q-500)]}{\$100-(\$20+\$19)}$$
$$= \frac{\$22,800+\$15Q-\$7,500}{\$61}$$
$$\$61Q = \$15,300+\$15Q$$
$$\$46Q = \$15,300$$
$$Q = 333 \text{ (rounded up to the nearest unit)}$$

Proof of breakeven point:

Revenues, $100 × 333 units		$33,300
Cost of goods sold		
Cost of goods sold at standard cost, $35 × 333 units	$11,655	
Production-volume variance, $15 × (800 − 500) units	4,500 U	16,155
Gross margin		17,145
Operating costs		
Variable operating costs, $19 × 333 units	6,327	
Fixed operating costs	10,800	17,127
Operating income		$ 18

Operating income is not $0 because the breakeven number of units is rounded up to 333 from 332.61.

The breakeven point under absorption costing depends on (1) total fixed costs, (2) contribution margin per unit, (3) unit level of production, and (4) the capacity level chosen as the denominator to set the fixed manufacturing overhead cost rate. For Stassen in 2004, a combination of 333 units sold, 500 units produced, and an 800-unit denominator level would result in an operating income of $0. Note, however, that there are many combinations of these four factors that would give an operating income of $0. For example, a combination of 284 units sold, 650 units produced, and an 800-unit denominator level also results in an operating income of $0 under absorption costing.

Proof of breakeven point:

Revenues, $100 × 284 units		$28,400
Cost of goods sold		
Cost of goods sold at standard cost, $35 × 284 units	$ 9,940	
Production-volume variance, $15 × (800 − 650) units	2,250 U	12,190
Gross margin		16,210
Operating costs		
Variable operating costs, $19 × 284 units	5,396	
Fixed operating costs	10,800	16,196
Operating income		$ 14

Operating income is not $0 because the breakeven number of units is rounded up to 284 from 283.70.

Suppose actual production in 2004 were equal to the denominator level, 800 units, and there were no units sold and no fixed operating costs. All the units produced would be placed in inventory, so all the fixed manufacturing overhead would be included in inventory. There would be no production-volume variance. The company could break even with no sales whatsoever! In contrast, under variable costing, the operating loss would be equal to the fixed manufacturing costs of $12,000.

TERMS TO LEARN

This chapter and the Glossary at the end of the book contain definitions of:

absorption costing (287)
direct costing (289)
downward demand spiral (303)
master-budget capacity utilization (301)
normal capacity utilization (300)
practical capacity (300)
super-variable costing (295)
theoretical capacity (300)
throughput costing (295)
variable costing (287)

ASSIGNMENT MATERIAL

Questions

9-1 Differences in operating income between variable costing and absorption costing are due solely to accounting for fixed costs. Do you agree? Explain.

9-2 Why is the term *direct costing* a misnomer?

9-3 Do companies in either the service sector or the merchandising sector make choices about absorption costing versus variable costing?

9-4 Explain the main conceptual issue under variable costing and absorption costing regarding the proper timing for the release of fixed manufacturing overhead as expense.

9-5 "Companies that make no variable-cost/fixed-cost distinctions must use absorption costing, and those that do make variable-cost/fixed-cost distinctions must use variable costing." Do you agree? Explain.

9-6 The main trouble with variable costing is that it ignores the increasing importance of fixed costs in manufacturing companies. Do you agree? Why?

9-7 Give an example of how, under absorption costing, operating income could fall even though the unit sales level rises.

9-8 What are the factors that affect the breakeven point under (a) variable costing and (b) absorption costing?

9-9 Critics of absorption costing have increasingly emphasized its potential for leading to undesirable incentives for managers. Give an example.

9-10 What are two ways of reducing the negative aspects associated with using absorption costing to evaluate the performance of a plant manager?

9-11 What denominator-level capacity concepts emphasize what a plant can supply? What denominator-level capacity concepts emphasize what customers demand for products produced by a plant?

9-12 Describe the downward demand spiral and its implications for pricing decisions.

9-13 Will the financial statements of a company always differ when different choices at the start of the period are made regarding the denominator-level capacity concept?

9-14 What is the IRS's requirement for tax reporting regarding the choice of a denominator-level capacity concept?

9-15 "The difference between practical capacity and master-budget capacity utilization is the best measure of management's ability to balance the costs of having too much capacity and having too little capacity." Do you agree? Explain.

Exercises

9-16 **Variable and absorption costing, explaining operating income differences.** Nascar Motors assembles and sells motor vehicles. Data relating to April and May of 2003 are

	April	May
Unit data		
Beginning inventory	0	150
Production	500	400
Sales	350	520
Variable costs		
Manufacturing cost per unit produced	$ 10,000	$ 10,000
Operating cost per unit sold	3,000	3,000

Fixed costs		
Manufacturing costs	$2,000,000	$2,000,000
Operating costs	600,000	600,000

The selling price per motor vehicle is $24,000.

Required

1. Present income statements for Nascar Motors in April and May of 2003 under (a) variable costing and (b) absorption costing.
2. Prepare a numerical reconciliation and explanation of the difference between operating income for each month under absorption costing and variable costing.

Excel Application For students who wish to practice their spreadsheet skills, the following is a step-by-step approach to creating an Excel spreadsheet to work this problem.

Step-by-Step

(Program your spreadsheet to perform all necessary calculations. Do not "hard-code" any of your calculations.)

1. At the top of a new spreadsheet, create an "Original Data" section for the unit data (add a row with a calculation for ending inventory), selling price, variable cost data, and fixed cost data for April and May in exactly the same format as shown for Nascar Motors.
2. Skip two rows, create a section called "Inventoriable Costs," with rows for "Variable Manufacturing Costs," "Fixed Indirect Manufacturing Costs for April," "Fixed Indirect Manufacturing Costs for May," "Total Inventoriable Costs for April," and "Total Inventoriable Costs for May," and columns for "Variable Costing" and "Absorption Costing." Follow a similar format to the one shown for Stassen Company at the bottom of p. 287. Use data from the Original Data section to compute inventoriable costs under both variable and absorption costing (Hint: Under absorption costing, the fixed indirect manufacturing costs allocated to each unit of inventory should reflect total fixed manufacturing costs divided by the actual level of production, whereas inventoriable costs under variable costing should reflect only variable manufacturing costs.).
3. Skip two rows, create a section called "Problem 1" and a subsection, "Panel A: Variable Costing." Following a format similar to Panel A, Exhibit 9-2, set up an income statement using the contribution-margin format by creating rows for "Revenues," "Beginning Inventory," "Variable Manufacturing Costs," "Cost of Goods Available for Sale," "Ending Inventory," "Variable Cost of Goods Sold," "Variable Operating Costs," "Total Variable Costs," "Contribution Margin," "Fixed Manufacturing Costs," "Fixed Operating Costs," "Total Fixed Costs," and "Operating Income." Create columns for April and May. Complete this income statement using the data you created in steps 1 and 2.
4. Skip two rows, create another subsection, "Panel B: Absorption Costing." Following a format similar to Panel B, Exhibit 9-2, set up an income statement using the gross-margin format by creating rows for "Revenues," "Beginning Inventory," "Variable Manufacturing Costs," "Fixed Manufacturing Costs," "Cost of Goods Available for Sale," "Ending Inventory," "Cost of Goods Sold," "Gross Margin," "Variable Operating Costs," "Fixed Operating Costs," "Total Operating Costs," and "Operating Income." Create columns for April and May. Complete this income statement using data you created in steps 1 and 2.
5. *Verify the accuracy of your spreadsheet:* Go to your Original Data section and change fixed manufacturing costs for April and May from $2,000,000 to $2,500,000. If you programmed your spreadsheet correctly, operating income under absorption costing for April should change to $1,500,000.

9-17 Throughput costing (continuation of Exercise 9-16). The variable manufacturing costs per unit of Nascar Motors are

	April	May
Direct materials	$6,700	$6,700
Direct manufacturing labor	1,500	1,500
Manufacturing overhead	1,800	1,800

Required

1. Present income statements for Nascar Motors in April and May of 2003 under throughput costing.
2. Contrast the results in requirement 1 with those in requirement 1 of Exercise 9-16.
3. Give one motivation for Nascar Motors to adopt throughput costing.

9-18 Variable and absorption costing, explaining operating income differences. BigScreen Corporation manufactures and sells 50-inch television sets. Data relating to January, February, and March of 2004 are

	January	February	March
Unit data			
Beginning inventory	0	300	300
Production	1,000	800	1,250
Sales	700	800	1,500

Variable costs			
Manufacturing cost per unit produced	$ 900	$ 900	$ 900
Operating cost per unit sold	600	600	600
Fixed costs			
Manufacturing costs	$400,000	$400,000	$400,000
Operating costs	140,000	140,000	140,000

The selling price per unit is $2,500.

Required

1. Present income statements for BigScreen in January, February, and March of 2004 under (a) variable costing and (b) absorption costing.
2. Explain differences between (a) and (b) for January, February, and March.

9-19 Throughput costing (continuation of Exercise 9-18). The variable manufacturing costs per unit of BigScreen Corporation are

	January	February	March
Direct materials	$500	$500	$500
Direct manufacturing labor	100	100	100
Manufacturing overhead	300	300	300
	$900	$900	$900

Required

1. Present income statements for BigScreen in January, February, and March of 2004 under throughput costing.
2. Contrast the results in requirement 1 with those in requirement 1 of Exercise 9-18.
3. Give one motivation for BigScreen to adopt throughput costing.

9-20 Variable versus absorption costing. The Zwatch Company manufactures trendy, high-quality moderately priced watches. As Zwatch's senior financial analyst, you are asked to recommend a method of inventory costing. The CFO will use your recommendation to construct Zwatch's 2004 income statement. The following data are for the year ended December 31, 2004:

Beginning inventory, January 1, 2004	85,000 units
Ending inventory, December 31, 2004	34,500 units
2004 sales	345,400 units
Selling price (to distributor)	$22.00 per unit
Variable manufacturing cost per unit, including direct materials	$5.10 per unit
Variable operating cost per unit sold	$1.10 per unit sold
Fixed manufacturing overhead	$1,440,000
Denominator-level machine-hours	6,000
Standard production rate	50 units per machine-hour
Fixed operating costs	$1,080,000

Assume standard costs per unit are the same for units in beginning inventory and units produced during the year. Also, assume no price, spending, or efficiency variances.

Required

1. Prepare income statements under variable and absorption costing for the year ended December 31, 2004.
2. What is Zwatch's operating income under each costing method (in percentage terms)?
3. Explain the difference in operating income between the two methods.
4. Which costing method would you recommend to the CFO? Why?

9-21 Absorption and variable costing. (CMA) Osawa, Inc., planned and actually manufactured 200,000 units of its single product in 2004, its first year of operation. Variable manufacturing cost was $20 per unit produced. Variable operating cost was $10 per unit sold. Planned and actual fixed manufacturing costs were $600,000. Planned and actual fixed operating costs totaled $400,000 in 2004. Osawa sold 120,000 units of product in 2004 at $40 per unit.

Required

1. Osawa's 2004 operating income using absorption costing is (a) $440,000, (b) $200,000, (c) $600,000, (d) $840,000, (e) none of these.
2. Osawa's 2004 operating income using variable costing is (a) $800,000, (b) $440,000, (c) $200,000, (d) $600,000, (e) none of these.

9-22 Absorption versus variable costing. Sonnenheim Bamberger is a German pharmaceutical company that produces a single drug—Mimic™—for the treatment of hair loss in men. Sonnenheim began commercial production of Mimic™ on January 1, 2004. Patients use three pills per day (365 days a year). Sonnenheim marketing analysts estimate 50,000 patients will use Mimic™ in 2004. Production in 2004 is 54,750,000 units (pills). However, only 44,800 patients are prescribed Mimic™ during 2004. Each patient used three pills per day for 365 days a year. The average wholesale selling price (the price Sonnenheim receives from distributors) is $1.20 per pill. Sonnenheim's actual costs are as follows:

Variable cost per unit	
Manufacturing cost *per pill produced*	
Direct materials	$0.05
Direct manufacturing labor	0.04
Manufacturing overhead	0.11
Marketing cost *per pill sold*	0.07
Fixed costs	
Manufacturing costs	$ 7,358,400
R&D	4,905,600
Marketing	19,622,400

Required

1. What is the number of Mimic[TM] pills actually sold in 2004, assuming all patients began using the drug on January 1 and used it through December 31? What is ending inventory on December 31, 2004?
2. Calculate operating income under variable costing and absorption costing for Sonnenheim Bamberger for the year ended December 31, 2004. The allocation base for fixed manufacturing costs under absorption costing is $0.15 per unit (pill) produced. All under- or overabsorbed fixed costs are written off to cost of goods sold.
3. Explain differences in operating income in requirement 2.

9-23 **Comparison of actual-costing methods.** The Rehe Company sells its razors at $3 per unit. The company uses a first-in, first-out actual-costing system. A new fixed manufacturing overhead rate is computed each year by dividing the actual fixed manufacturing overhead cost by the actual production units. The following simplified data are related to its first two years of operation:

	2003	2004
Sales	1,000 units	1,200 units
Production	1,400 units	1,000 units
Costs:		
Variable manufacturing	$ 700	$ 500
Fixed manufacturing	700	700
Variable operating	1,000	1,200
Fixed operating	400	400

Required

1. Prepare income statements based on variable costing for each of the two years.
2. Prepare income statements based on absorption costing for each of the two years.
3. Prepare a numerical reconciliation and explanation of the difference between operating income for each year under absorption costing and variable costing.
4. Critics have claimed that a widely used accounting system has led to undesirable buildups of inventory levels. (a) Is variable costing or absorption costing more likely to lead to such buildups? Why? (b) What can be done to counteract undesirable inventory buildups?

9-24 **Capacity management, denominator-level capacity concepts.** Each of the following items is identified by a number:

1. Should be used for performance evaluation
2. Measures the denominator level in terms of demand for the output of the plant
3. Represents the expected level of capacity utilization for the next budget period
4. Is based on producing at full efficiency all the time
5. Takes into account seasonal, cyclical, and trend factors
6. Measures the denominator level in terms of what a plant can supply
7. Represents an ideal benchmark
8. Highlights the cost of capacity acquired but not used
9. Hides the cost of capacity acquired but not used
10. Should be used for long-term pricing purposes
11. If used as the denominator-level concept, would avoid the restatement of unit costs when expected demand levels change

Required Match each of the items with one or more of the following denominator-level capacity concepts by putting appropriate letter(s) by each number:

a. Theoretical capacity
b. Practical capacity
c. Normal capacity utilization
d. Master-budget capacity utilization

9-25 **Denominator-level problem.** The Spalding Sails company produces the Spalding 26, a very popular 26-foot recreational yacht. Spalding Sails takes pride in the high quality they build into their affordable yachts. The company has been in business for 35 years. Management has recently adopted absorption costing and is debating which denominator-level concept to use. The Spalding 26 sells for an average price of $15,000. Budgeted fixed manufacturing overhead for 2004 is estimated at $3,800,000. Spalding uses subassembly operators that provide component parts. Assume for simplicity that each yacht can be started and completed in a single shift. The following are the denominator-level options that management has been considering:

a. Theoretical capacity—based on two shifts, completion of four boats per shift, and a 360-day year—$2 \times 4 \times 360 = 2{,}880$.
b. Practical capacity—theoretical capacity adjusted for unavoidable interruptions, breakdowns, and so forth—$2 \times 3 \times 300 = 1{,}800$.
c. Normal capacity utilization—based on the Marketing Department's estimate of 1,000 units.
d. Master-budget capacity utilization—the booming stock market and a record number of baby boomers retiring over the coming year has prompted the Marketing Department to issue a special estimate for 2004 of 1,200 units.

Required

1. Calculate the budgeted fixed manufacturing overhead cost rates under the four denominator-level concepts.
2. Why compute fixed costs at the individual product level? Why is this only done under absorption costing?
3. Why would Spalding Sails prefer to use either theoretical or practical capacity?
4. Under a cost-based pricing system, what is the negative aspect of a master-budget denominator level? What may be the positive aspect?

9-26 Variable and absorption costing and breakeven points (chapter appendix). Shasta Hills, a winery in northern California, manufactures a premium cabernet and sells primarily to distributors. Wine is sold in cases of one dozen bottles. In the year ended December 31, 2004, Shasta Hills sold 242,400 cases at an average selling price of $94 per case. The following additional data are for Shasta Hills for the year ended December 31, 2004 (assume constant unit costs and no price, spending, or efficiency variances):

Beginning inventory, January 1, 2004	32,600 cases
Ending inventory, December 31, 2004	24,800 cases
Fixed manufacturing overhead	$3,753,600
Fixed operating costs	$6,568,800
Variable costs	
Direct materials	
Grapes	$16 per case
Bottles, corks, and crates	$10 per case
Direct labor	
Bottling	$6 per case
Winemaking	$14 per case
Aging	$2 per case

On December 31, 2003, the cost per case for ending inventory is $46 for variable costing and $61 for absorption costing.

Required

1. Calculate cases of production for Shasta Hills in 2004.
2. Find the breakeven point (number of cases) in 2004
   a. under variable costing
   b. under absorption costing
3. Grape prices are expected to increase 25% in 2005. Assuming all other data are the same, calculate the minimum number of cases Shasta Hills must sell in 2005 to break even:
   a. under variable costing
   b. under absorption costing

9-27 ABC and capacity usage. Zaynab Bibi Company has identified the following activities and cost drivers for its manufacturing overhead. Zaynab calculates activity cost rates based on cost driver capacity.

Activity	Activity Costs	Cost Driver Capacity
Machine setup	$500,000	5,000 setup-hours
Material handling	200,000	100,000 pounds of material

Zaynab makes only two products: Daska and Kothi. During 2004, Daska required 3,000 machine setup-hours and handling of 40,000 pounds of materials. Kothi's production required 1,500 setup-hours and handling of 50,000 pounds of materials.

Required

1. Calculate the costs allocated to each product from each activity.
2. Compute the cost of unused capacity for each activity.

9-28 ABC and capacity usage. The controller of Harris Corporation has collected the following data for two activities. Harris calculates activity cost rates based on cost driver capacity.

Activity	Cost Driver	Capacity	Cost
Power	Kilowatt hours	50,000 kilowatt hours	$200,000
Quality inspection	Number of inspections	10,000 inspections	300,000

The company makes two products: Tulsa and Okla. For the year just ended, the following consumption of cost drivers was reported:

Product	Kilowatt hours	Quality Inspections
Tulsa	10,000	5,000
Okla	35,000	4,000

Required

1. Compute the costs allocated to each product from each activity.
2. Calculate the cost of unused capacity for each activity.

9-29 **Cost behavior, activity-based costing, capacity usage.** Finn and Sawyer Company employs five individuals for its bill-processing activity. Each of the employees is paid fixed annual salary of $30,000. The budgeted annual activity output of bill processing is 6,000 bills per employee. All other costs in the bill-processing activity are variable and are budgeted at $22,500 for the year. During the year, 26,000 bills were actually processed. There are no price, efficiency, or spending variances for variable costs and there is no spending variance for fixed costs.

Required

1. Calculate the budgeted fixed rate, budgeted variable rate, and the budgeted total rate for bill-processing activity.
2. Compute the total capacity available in bill-processing activity in units.
3. Compute the unused capacity in bill-processing activity in units.
4. For (a) fixed costs and (b) variable costs, calculate the cost of bill-processing activity supplied, the cost of capacity used for the bill-processing activity, and the cost of unused capacity, if any, for the bill-processing activity. Are there any differences between fixed costs and variable costs with respect to unused capacity. Explain.

Problems

9-30 **Variable costing versus absorption costing.** The Mavis Company uses an absorption-costing system based on standard costs. Total variable manufacturing cost, including direct material cost, is $3 per unit; the standard production rate is 10 units per machine-hour. Total budgeted and actual fixed manufacturing overhead costs are $420,000. Fixed manufacturing overhead is allocated at $7 per machine-hour ($420,000 ÷ 60,000 machine-hours of denominator level). Selling price is $5 per unit. Variable operating cost, which is driven by units sold, is $1 per unit. Fixed operating costs are $120,000. Beginning inventory in 2004 is 30,000 units; ending inventory is 40,000 units. Sales in 2004 are 540,000 units. The same standard unit costs persisted throughout 2003 and 2004. For simplicity, assume that there are no price, spending, or efficiency variances.

Required

1. Prepare an income statement for 2004 assuming that all underallocated or overallocated overhead is written off at year-end as an adjustment to Cost of Goods Sold.
2. The president has heard about variable costing. She asks you to recast the 2004 statement as it would appear under variable costing.
3. Explain the difference in operating income as calculated in requirements 1 and 2.
4. Graph how fixed manufacturing overhead is accounted for under absorption costing. That is, there will be two lines: one for the budgeted fixed overhead (which is equal to the actual fixed manufacturing overhead in this case) and one for the fixed overhead allocated. Show how the overallocated or underallocated manufacturing overhead might be indicated on the graph.
5. Critics have claimed that a widely used accounting system has led to undesirable buildups of inventory levels. (a) Is variable costing or absorption costing more likely to lead to such buildups? Why? (b) What can be done to counteract undesirable inventory buildups?

9-31 **Breakeven under absorption costing (chapter appendix).** Refer to Problem 9-30.

Required

1. Compute the breakeven point (in units) under variable costing.
2. Compute the breakeven point (in units) under absorption costing.
3. Suppose that production is exactly equal to the denominator level, but no units are sold. Fixed manufacturing costs are unaffected. Assume, however, that all operating costs are avoided. Compute operating income under (a) variable costing and (b) absorption costing. Explain the difference between your answers.

9-32 **The All-Fixed Company in 2004.** (R. Marple, adapted) It is the end of 2004. The All-Fixed Company began operations in January 2003. The company is so named because it has no variable costs. All its costs are fixed; they do not vary with output.

The All-Fixed Company is located on the bank of a river and has its own hydroelectric plant to supply power, light, and heat. The company manufactures a synthetic fertilizer from air and river water and sells its product at a price that is not expected to change. It has a small staff of employees, all hired on a fixed annual salary. The output of the plant can be increased or decreased by adjusting a few dials on a control panel.

The following data are for the operations of the All-Fixed Company:

	2003	2004[a]
Sales	10,000 tons	10,000 tons
Production	20,000 tons	—
Selling price	$30 per ton	$30 per ton
Costs (all fixed):		
Manufacturing	$280,000	$280,000
Operating	$ 40,000	$ 40,000

[a]Management adopted the policy, effective January 1, 2004, of producing only as much product as needed to fill sales orders. During 2004, sales were the same as for 2003 and were filled entirely from inventory at the start of 2004.

Required

1. Prepare income statements with one column for 2003, one column for 2004, and one column for the two years together, using (a) variable costing and (b) absorption costing.
2. What is the breakeven point under (a) variable costing and (b) absorption costing?
3. What inventory costs would be carried on the balance sheet on December 31, 2003 and 2004, under each method?
4. Assume that the performance of the top manager of the company is evaluated and rewarded largely on the basis of reported operating income. Which costing method would the manager prefer? Why?

9-33 Comparison of variable costing and absorption costing. Consider the following data:

Hinkle Company
Income Statements for the Year Ended December 31, 2003

	Variable Costing	Absorption Costing
Revenues	$7,000,000	$7,000,000
Cost of goods sold (at standard)	3,660,000	4,575,000
Fixed manufacturing overhead	1,000,000	—
Manufacturing variances (all unfavorable):		
Direct materials price and efficiency	50,000	50,000
Direct manufacturing labor price and efficiency	60,000	60,000
Variable manufacturing overhead spending and efficiency	30,000	30,000
Fixed manufacturing overhead:		
Spending	100,000	100,000
Production volume	—	400,000
Total marketing costs (all fixed)	1,000,000	1,000,000
Total administrative costs (all fixed)	500,000	500,000
Total costs	6,400,000	6,715,000
Operating income	$ 600,000	$ 285,000

The inventories, carried at standard costs, were

	Variable Costing	Absorption Costing
December 31, 2002	$1,320,000	$1,650,000
December 31, 2003	60,000	75,000

Required

1. Tim Hinkle, president of Hinkle Company, has asked you to explain why the operating income for 2003 is less than for 2002, even though sales have increased 40% over last year. What will you tell him?
2. At what percentage of denominator level was the plant operating during 2003?
3. Prepare a numerical reconciliation and explanation of the difference between operating income under absorption costing and variable costing.
4. Critics have claimed that a widely used accounting system has led to undesirable buildups of inventory levels. (a) Is variable costing or absorption costing more likely to lead to such buildups? Why? (b) What can be done to counteract undesirable inventory buildups?

9-34 Alternative denominator-level concepts. Lucky Lager recently purchased a brewing plant from a bankrupt company. The brewery is in Austin, Texas. It was constructed only two years ago. The plant has budgeted fixed manufacturing overhead of $42 million ($3.5 million each month) in 2003. Paul Vautin, the controller of the brewery, must decide on the denominator-level concept to use in its absorption costing system for 2003. The options available to him are

a. Theoretical capacity for 2003: 600 barrels an hour for 24 hours per day × 365 days = 5,256,000 barrels

b. Practical capacity for 2003: 500 barrels an hour for 20 hours per day × 350 days = 3,500,000 barrels

c. Normal capacity utilization for 2003: 400 barrels an hour for 20 hours per day × 350 days = 2,800,000 barrels

d. Master-budget capacity utilization for 2003 (separate rates computed for each half-year)

- January–June 2003 budget: 320 barrels an hour for 20 hours a day × 175 days = 1,120,000 barrels
- July–December 2003 budget: 480 barrels an hour for 20 hours a day × 175 days = 1,680,000 barrels

Variable standard manufacturing costs per barrel are $45 (variable direct materials, $32; variable manufacturing labor, $6; and variable manufacturing overhead, $7). The Austin brewery "sells" its output to the sales division of Lucky Lager at a budgeted price of $68 per barrel.

Required

1. Compute the budgeted fixed manufacturing overhead rate using each of the four denominator-level concepts for (a) beer produced in March 2003 and (b) beer produced in September 2003. Explain why any differences arise.
2. Explain why the theoretical capacity and practical capacity concepts are different.
3. Which denominator-level concept would the plant manager of the Austin brewery prefer when senior management of Lucky Lager is judging plant manager performance during 2003? Explain.

9-35 Operating income effects of alternative denominator-level concepts (continuation of Problem 9-34). In 2003, the Austin brewery of Lucky Lager showed these results:

Beginning inventory, January 1, 2003	0 barrels
Production	2,600,000 barrels
Ending inventory, December 31, 2003	200,000 barrels

The Austin brewery had actual costs of:

Variable manufacturing costs	$120,380,000
Fixed manufacturing overhead costs	40,632,000

The sales division of Lucky Lager purchased 2,400,000 barrels in 2003 at the $68 per barrel rate.

All manufacturing variances are written off to cost of goods sold in the period in which they are incurred.

Required

1. Compute the operating income of the Austin brewery using the denominator-level concepts of (a) theoretical capacity, (b) practical capacity, and (c) normal capacity utilization. Explain any differences among (a), (b), and (c).
2. What denominator-level concept would Lucky Lager prefer for U.S. income tax reporting? Explain.
3. Explain the ways in which the IRS might restrict the flexibility of a company like Lucky Lager, which uses absorption costing, to reduce its taxable income.

9-36 Downward demand spiral. Pismo Company manufactures 1 terabyte optical mini-disk systems. The current year's monthly production and sales are budgeted at 10,000 units. Pismo's variable manufacturing cost per unit is $200, and its monthly fixed manufacturing overhead costs total $1,000,000. Pismo sets the selling price of its product by adding a 100% markup to the full product cost per unit. The full product cost per unit includes variable manufacturing cost per unit plus the fixed manufacturing overhead cost per unit based on fully allocating total fixed manufacturing overhead costs to the units produced.

Required

1. Compute Pismo Company's budgeted selling price.
2. Due to intense competition, Pismo had to revise its budgeted monthly production and sales downward to 8,000 units. Compute Pismo Company's revised budgeted selling price.
3. Comment on your results in 1 and 2 above.

9-37 Effects of denominator-level choice. The Wong Company installed standard costs and a flexible budget on January 1, 2003. The president has been pondering how fixed manufacturing overhead should be allocated to products. Machine-hours has been chosen as the allocation base. Her remaining uncertainty is the denominator-level for machine-hours. She decides to wait for the first month's results before making a final choice of what denominator-level should be used from that day forward.

In January 2003, the actual units of output had a standard of 70,000 machine-hours allowed. If the company used practical capacity as the denominator-level, the fixed manufacturing overhead spending variance would be $10,000, unfavorable, and the production-volume variance would be $36,000, unfavorable. If the company used normal capacity utilization as the denominator-level, the production-volume variance would be $20,000, favorable. Budgeted fixed manufacturing overhead was $120,000 for the month.

Required

1. Compute the denominator level, assuming that the normal capacity utilization concept is chosen.
2. Compute the denominator level, assuming that the practical capacity concept is chosen.
3. Suppose you are the executive vice president. You want to maximize your 2003 bonus, which depends on 2003 operating income. Assume that the production-volume variance is added or deducted from operating income at year-end. Which denominator-level would you favor? Why?

9-38 Denominator level, production-volume variance. National Electronics, Inc., acquired plant assets based on forecasts of long-range demand for its products. Its budgeted manufacturing overhead costs for 2004 are $10,500,000. For each of the four alternative denominator-level capacities, National's capacity is

Denominator-Level Capacity	Denominator Level (in machine-hours)
Theoretical capacity	2,100,000
Practical capacity	1,500,000
Normal capacity utilization	1,312,500
Master-budget capacity utilization	1,000,000

Required

1. Calculate budgeted fixed manufacturing overhead rate per machine-hour for each denominator-level capacity.
2. For 2004 actual output, 1,100,000 budgeted machine-hours were allowed. Compute production-volume variance under each of the denominator-level capacity assumptions.

9-39 Cost allocation, downward demand spiral. Western Health Maintenance (WHM) operates a chain of 10 hospitals in the Los Angeles area. For many years, it has operated a central food-catering facility in Santa Monica, which delivers meals to the hospitals. The Santa Monica facility has the capacity to serve 3,650,000 meals a year (10,000 meals a day). In 2004 it budgeted for 2,920,000 meals (8,000 meals a day), based on demand estimates from each hospital controller. The budgeted variable cost per meal in 2004 is $3.80, which includes delivery to the hospital. Budgeted fixed costs for 2004 are $4,380,000.

In July 2004, the new WHM president announces that each hospital is to be a profit center. In addition, the head of each hospital can purchase services from outside WHM, provided those services meet the WHM quality requirements. The president gives catering as an example. Roy Jenkins, the head of the Santa Monica catering facility, is less than pleased. This facility will also become a profit center (it has been a cost center for many years) under the reorganization.

Jenkins charged each hospital $5.30 per meal in 2004—comprising $3.80 variable cost plus $1.50 allocation of budgeted fixed costs. Several hospitals complained about the $5.30 cost, as well as the quality of the food. (Jenkins sarcastically labels the quality complaints as "recycled mystery-meat stories.") Indeed, the cost rose from $4.90 in 2003 to $5.30 in 2004. Jenkins defended the increase, claiming he needed to spread the same fixed costs over a smaller number of patient-days in 2004. WHM experienced negative press on a local TV station in 2003 and early 2004, and local doctors are referring fewer patients to the WHM hospitals.

In October 2004, Jenkins started to prepare the 2005 budget, including the new cost to be charged per meal. He estimated that the total annual demand for meals at all 10 WHM hospitals would be 2,550,000. Then he learned that 3 of the 10 hospitals will use an outside canteen service, which reduces the 2005 budgeted demand at the Santa Monica facility to 2,000,000 meals. No change in total fixed costs or variable cost per meal is expected in 2005.

Required

1. How did Jenkins compute the budgeted fixed cost per meal in 2004?
2. What alternative cost-per-meal figures might Jenkins compute for meals delivered to WHM hospitals in 2005? Which cost figure should Jenkins use? Why?
3. What factors should Jenkins consider in pricing meals the Santa Monica facility prepares for the WHM hospitals?

9-40 Cost allocation, budgeted rates, ethics (continuation of Problem 9-39). The actual meal counts used in 2004 by all of WHM's hospitals were less than the budgeted amounts each hospital controller provided Jenkins at the start of 2004. Jenkins suspects collusion on the part of the hospital controllers. He is concerned that the 2005 budgeted meal counts from the individual hospitals will likewise turn out to be way too optimistic about actual demand.

Required

1. Why might the individual hospital administrators deliberately overestimate the 2004 budgeted meal-count demand?
2. Jenkins decides to approach the WHM corporate controller to discuss his concerns about the individual hospital controllers colluding on budgeted meal-count demand. What evidence should the corporate controller seek to investigate Jenkin's concerns?
3. What steps should the corporate controller take to reduce any incentives individual hospital controllers have to deliberately overestimate meal demand for 2005?

Collaborative Learning Problem

9-41 Absorption, variable and throughput costing. The Waterloo, Ontario, plant of Maple Leaf Motors assembles the Icarus motor vehicle. The standard unit manufacturing cost per vehicle in 2003 is

Direct materials	$6,000
Direct manufacturing labor	1,800
Variable manufacturing overhead	2,000
Fixed manufacturing overhead	?

The Waterloo plant is highly automated. Maximum productive capacity per month is 4,000 vehicles. Variable manufacturing overhead is allocated to vehicles on the basis of assembly time. The standard assembly time per vehicle is 20 hours. Fixed manufacturing overhead in 2003 is allocated on the basis of the standard assembly time for the budgeted normal capacity utilization of the plant. In 2003, the budgeted normal capacity utilization is 3,000 vehicles per month. The budgeted monthly fixed manufacturing overhead is $7,500,000.

On January 1, 2003, there is zero beginning inventory of Icarus vehicles. The actual unit production and sales figures for the first three months of 2003 are

	January	February	March
Production	3,200	2,400	3,800
Sales	2,000	2,900	3,200

Assume no direct materials variances, no direct manufacturing labor variances, and no manufacturing overhead spending or efficiency variances in the first three months of 2003.

Bret Hart, a vice president of Maple Leaf Motors, is the manager of the Waterloo plant. His compensation includes a bonus that is 0.5% of quarterly operating income. Operating income is calculated using absorption costing. Maple Leaf Motors prepares absorption-costing income statements monthly, which includes an adjustment to cost of goods sold for the total manufacturing variances occurring in that month.

The Waterloo plant "sells" each Icarus to Maple Leaf's marketing subsidiary at $16,000 per vehicle. No marketing costs are incurred by the Waterloo plant.

Required

1. Compute (a) the fixed manufacturing overhead cost per unit and (b) the total manufacturing cost per unit.
2. Compute the monthly operating income for January, February, and March under absorption costing. What bonus is paid each month to Bret Hart?
3. How much would use of variable costing change Hart's bonus each month if the same 0.5% figure were applied to variable-costing operating income?
4. Explain the differences in Hart's bonuses in requirements 2 and 3.
5. How much would use of throughput costing change Hart's bonus if the same 0.5% figure were applied to throughput-costing operating income?
6. Outline different approaches Maple Leaf Motors could use to reduce possible undesirable behavior associated with the use of absorption costing at its Waterloo plant.

CHAPTER 9 INTERNET EXERCISE

The Boeing Corporation and Dell Computer Corporation use different methods to allocate fixed manufacturing costs between inventory and cost of goods sold. To better understand the concepts of variable costing and absorption costing, go to www.prenhall.com/horngren, click on *Cost Accounting*, 11th ed., and access the Internet exercise for Chapter 9.

CHAPTER 9 VIDEO CASE

WHEELED COACH: Capacity Analysis

Collins Industries, headquartered in Hutchinson, Kansas, is the largest manufacturer of ambulances in the world. Production takes place at Collins' Wheeled Coach subsidiary, located in Winter Park, Florida. The company can customize its three basic vehicle lines in thousands of ways, so that each vehicle is unique to the customer ordering it. Vehicles range from the economy Type II van-style ambulance to the deluxe Medical Attack Vehicle.

There are nearly 18,000 different inventory items to choose from in designing each vehicle. No vehicle begins production until all required materials are in inventory. Because each of the company's assembly lines aims to roll a completed vehicle off the line each day, tight control over manufacturing capacity and inventory is essential.

The main assembly lines on the production floor are fed daily from subsidiary job shops nearby. Some of the job shops include (1) a complete carpentry shop for all interior cabinetry construction; (2) a metal fabrication shop for creation of the ambulance's metal shell; (3) a paint shop for prepping, painting, and detailing; (4) an electrical shop for wiring; (5) an upholstery shop for interior seat and bench fabrication; and (6) a Plexiglas shop for creating all interior cabinet windows. None of these job shops produces goods to stock; everything is made to order a day or two before it's required for assembly. A detailed "bill of materials" is used to request and release direct materials to the job shops and the assembly line. In this fashion, Wheeled Coach can keep its inventory costs low while maximizing its use of existing production capacity.

QUESTIONS

1. Assume Wheeled Coach has a separate manufacturing facility for each ambulance type. Budgeted annual fixed manufacturing costs for the Medical Attack Vehicle facility are $2,000,000 for 2002 and include such items as plant manager compensation, plant insurance, and equipment depreciation that will be the same regardless of the number of shifts each day or the number of days each week that the plant will be operating. The master budget for 2002 is based on production of four vehicles per four-day workweek. This volume is lower than normal because the plant is closed on Fridays for building and equipment maintenance. The company also has a tradition of closing for two weeks each August for summer holiday. For 2003 and 2004, the company expects to increase production to a more practical level of one vehicle per day, five days a week, with maintenance done in the evenings. Each workday is eight hours. The company anticipates running one shift per day for all budget years.

   If every ambulance produced in this facility takes the same amount of time to complete, what is the 2002 budgeted fixed manufacturing overhead cost rate per ambulance under theoretical capacity, practical capacity, normal capacity utilization, and master-budget capacity utilization?
2. Assume the standard variable manufacturing costs for an individual Medical Attack Vehicle are $40,000. Compute the standard manufacturing cost per vehicle under theoretical capacity, practical capacity, normal capacity utilization, and master-budget capacity utilization.
3. For 2002, Wheeled Coach's master-budget utilization for product costing is 200 units. The company has a major customer that buys 10 Medical Attack Vehicles a year. A new competitor, MedTechnix, has offered this customer a price of $47,000 per vehicle. Using the results from question 2, should Wheeled Coach match the competitor's bid? Why or why not?

CHAPTER 10

Determining How Costs Behave

LEARNING OBJECTIVES

1. Explain the two assumptions frequently used in cost-behavior estimation
2. Describe linear cost functions and three common ways in which they behave
3. Understand various approaches to cost estimation
4. Outline six steps in estimating a cost function on the basis of past cost relationships
5. Describe three criteria used to evaluate and choose cost drivers
6. Explain and give examples of nonlinear cost functions
7. Distinguish the cumulative average-time learning model from the incremental unit-time learning model
8. Be aware of data problems encountered in estimating cost functions

www.prenhall.com/horngren

Have you ever assembled a model airplane from a kit? If so, you had to read and follow instructions, step by step, snap and glue parts together, and carefully paint each part assembled. Putting it all together probably took a lot longer than you expected. If you assembled another model airplane a short time later, did it go faster than the first? Likely it did. That's because you had gained experience and skill from your first assembly. Although you may not have kept track of your time as you assembled each model airplane, you knew you were gaining efficiency and experience. It's the same with large-scale production of real airplanes at Boeing. Managers and workers learn to become more efficient as they produce more units. This "learning-curve effect" leads to a reduction in variable cost per unit and can be significant when those costs are attached to high-priced goods such as commercial aircraft.

Managers must know how costs behave to make strategic decisions and operating decisions, such as: Which of alternative product design choices is most profitable? Should a component part be made or bought? What effect will a 20% increase in units sold have on operating income? Why is the variable overhead efficiency variance so large? How should managers choose cost drivers in an activity-based costing system?

Knowledge of cost behavior is needed to answer these questions. This chapter will focus on how to determine cost-behavior patterns — that is, on understanding how costs change in relation to changes in activity levels, changes in the quantity of products produced, and so on.

GENERAL ISSUES IN ESTIMATING COST FUNCTIONS

Basic Assumptions and Examples of Cost Functions

1 Explain the two assumptions frequently used in cost-behavior estimation
...cost functions are linear and have a single cost driver

Cost behavior is best seen through cost functions. A **cost function** is a mathematical description of how a cost changes with changes in the level of an activity relating to that cost. Examples of activities are preparing setups for production runs and operating machines. Cost functions can be plotted on a graph by measuring the level of an activity, such as number of batches of production or number of machine-hours, on the horizontal axis (called the x-axis) and the amount of total costs corresponding to — or preferably, dependent on — the levels of that activity on the vertical axis (called the y-axis).

Estimating cost functions often relies on two assumptions.

1. Variations in total costs are explained by variations in the level of a single activity related to those costs (the cost driver).
2. Cost behavior is approximated by a linear cost function within the relevant range. For a **linear cost function** represented graphically, total cost versus the level of a single activity related to that cost is a straight line within the relevant range.

2 Describe linear cost functions
...graph of cost function is a straight line

and three common ways in which they behave
...variable, fixed, and mixed

We use these two assumptions throughout most, not all, of this chapter. Not all cost functions are linear and can be explained by a single activity. Later sections will discuss cost functions that do not rely on these assumptions.

To see the role of cost functions in business decisions, consider the negotiations between Cannon Services and World Wide Communications (WWC) for exclusive use of a telephone line between New York and Paris. WWC offers Cannon the choice of any one of three alternative cost structures.

- *Alternative 1*: $5 per phone-minute used. Total cost to Cannon varies with the number of phone-minutes used. That is, the number of phone-minutes used is the only factor whose change causes a change in total cost.

Panel A in Exhibit 10-1 presents this *variable cost* for Cannon Services. Total cost (measured vertically along the y-axis) changes in proportion to the number of phone-minutes used (measured horizontally along the x-axis) within the relevant range. (A relevant range, described in Chapter 2, is the range of the activity in which there is a relationship between total cost and the level of activity.) Under Alternative 1, there is no fixed cost. Total cost simply increases by $5 for every additional phone-minute used. Panel A

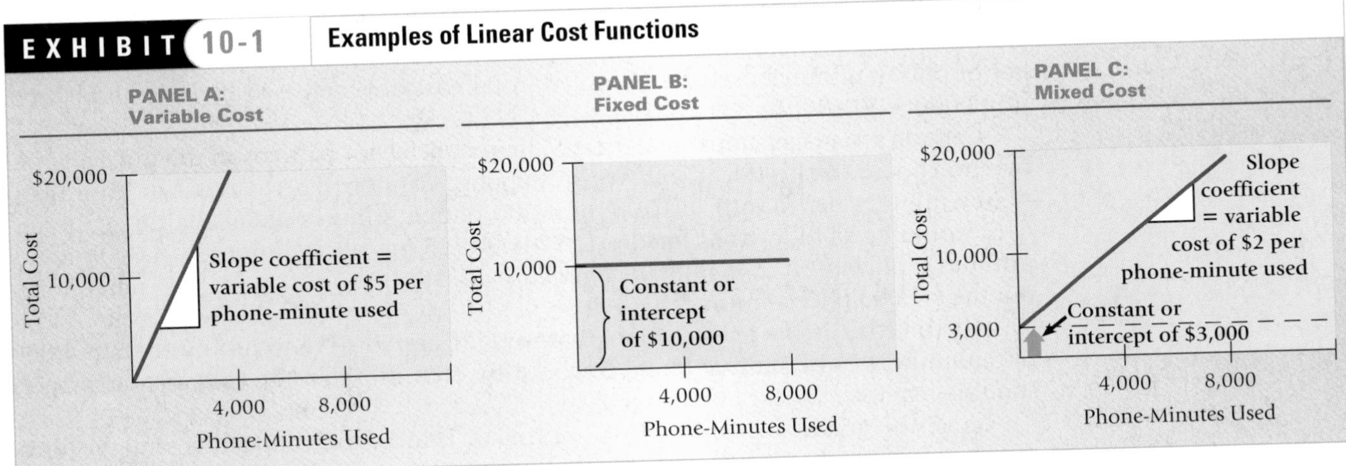

illustrates the $5 **slope coefficient**, the amount by which total cost changes when a one-unit change occurs in the level of activity (one phone-minute in the Cannon example) within the relevant range.

We can write the cost function in Panel A of Exhibit 10-1 as

$$y = \$5X$$

where X measures the actual number of phone-minutes used (on the *x*-axis), and *y* measures the total cost of the phone-minutes used (on the *y*-axis) calculated using the cost function. Throughout the chapter, uppercase letters, such as X, refer to the actual observations, and lowercase letters, such as *y*, represent estimates or calculations made using a cost function.

- *Alternative 2*: $10,000 per month. Total cost will be $10,000 per month, regardless of the number of phone-minutes used. (We use the same activity measure, number of phone-minutes used, to compare cost-behavior patterns under the three alternatives.) With this alternative, the cost is fixed, not variable.

Panel B in Exhibit 10-1 presents this *fixed cost* for Cannon Services. The fixed cost of $10,000 is called a **constant;** it is the component of total cost that, within the relevant range, does not vary with changes in the level of the activity. Under alternative 2, the constant accounts for all the cost because there is no variable cost. Graphically, the slope coefficient of the cost function is zero; this cost function intersects the *y*-axis at the constant value, and hence the *constant* is also called the **intercept.**

We can write the cost function in Panel B as

$$y = \$10,000$$

- *Alternative 3*: $3,000 per month plus $2 per phone-minute used. This is an example of a mixed cost. A **mixed cost**—also called a **semivariable cost**—is a cost that has both fixed and variable elements. Under this alternative, the cost has one component that is fixed regardless of the number of phone-minutes used—a fixed cost of $3,000 per month—and another component that is variable with respect to the number of phone-minutes used—a variable cost of $2 per phone-minute used.

Panel C in Exhibit 10-1 presents this mixed cost for Cannon Services. Unlike the graphs of alternatives 1 and 2, Panel C has both a constant, or intercept, value of $3,000 and a slope coefficient of $2.

We can write the cost function in Panel C of Exhibit 10-1 as

$$y = \$3,000 + \$2X$$

In the case of a mixed cost, total cost in the relevant range increases as the number of phone-minutes used increases. Note, total cost does not vary strictly in proportion to the number of phone-minutes used within the relevant range. For example, when 4,000 phone-minutes are used, the total cost is [$3,000 + ($2 per phone-minute × 4,000 phone-minutes)] = \$11,000, but when 8,000 phone-minutes are used, total cost is [\$3,000 + (\$2 per phone-minute × 8,000 phone-minutes)] = \$19,000. Although the number of phone-minutes used has doubled, total cost has increased by only about 73% [(\$19,000 − \$11,000) ÷ \$11,000].

Cannon's managers must understand the cost-behavior patterns in the three alternatives to choose the best deal with WWC. Suppose Cannon expects to use at least 4,000 phone-minutes per month. Its cost for 4,000 phone-minutes under the three alternatives would be as follows: *alternative 1*, \$20,000 (\$5 per phone-minute × 4,000 phone-minutes); *alternative 2*, \$10,000; *alternative 3*, \$11,000 [\$3,000 + (\$2 per phone-minute × 4,000 phone-minutes)].

Alternative 2 is the least costly. Moreover, if Cannon were to use more than 4,000 phone-minutes, alternatives 1 and 3 would be even more costly. Cannon's managers should, therefore, choose alternative 2.

Note, the graphs in Exhibit 10-1 are linear. That is, they appear as straight lines. Because we know these graphs are straight lines, we do not need to plot multiple points to draw them. We simply need to know the constant, or intercept, amount (commonly designated a) and the slope coefficient (commonly designated b). For any linear cost function based on a single activity (our two assumptions), knowing a and b is sufficient to describe and graphically plot all the values within the relevant range of number of phone-minutes used. We write a general form of this linear cost function as

$$y = a + bX$$

Under alternative 1, a = \$0 and b = \$5 per phone-minute used; under alternative 2, a = \$10,000, b = \$0 per phone-minute used; and under alternative 3, a = \$3,000, b = \$2 per phone-minute used. To plot the mixed cost function in Panel C, we draw a line starting from the point marked \$3,000 on the y-axis and increasing at a rate of \$2 per phone-minute used.

Brief Review of Cost Classification

Let's review briefly Chapter 2's three criteria for classifying a cost into its variable and fixed components.

Choice of cost object A particular cost item could be variable with respect to one cost object and fixed with respect to another cost object. Consider Super Shuttle, an airport transportation company. If the fleet of vans it owns is the cost object, then the annual van registration and license costs would be variable costs with respect to the number of vans owned. But if a particular van is the cost object, then the registration and license costs for that van are fixed costs with respect to the miles driven during a year.

Time horizon Whether a cost is variable or fixed with respect to a particular activity depends on the time horizon being considered in the decision situation. The longer the time horizon, other things being equal, the more likely that the cost will be variable. For example, inspection costs at Boeing Company are typically fixed in the short run with respect to inspection-hours used. But in the long run, Boeing's total inspection costs will vary with the inspection-hours required: More inspectors will be hired if more inspection-hours are needed, and some inspectors will be laid off or reassigned to other tasks if fewer inspection-hours are needed.

Relevant range Never forget that variable and fixed cost-behavior patterns are valid for linear cost functions only within the given relevant range. Outside the relevant range, variable and fixed cost-behavior patterns change, causing costs to become nonlinear (nonlinear means the plot of the relationship on a graph is not a straight line). For example, Exhibit 10-2 plots the relationship over several years between total direct manufacturing labor costs and the number of valves produced each year by AMC, Inc., at its Cleveland plant. In this case, the nonlinearities outside the relevant range occur because of labor and other inefficiencies. Knowing the proper relevant range is essential to properly classify costs.

Cost estimation underlies many topics in cost accounting. Examples include CVP analysis (Ch. 3), flexible budgets and variances (Chs. 7 and 8), and variable costing (Ch. 9).

Cost Estimation

The Cannon Services/WWC example illustrates variable-, fixed-, and mixed-cost functions using information about *future* cost structures proposed to Cannon by WWC. Often, however, cost functions are estimated from *past* cost data. **Cost estimation** is the attempt

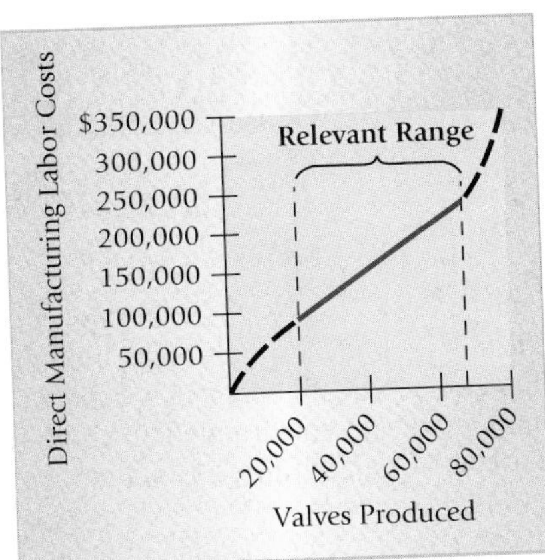

EXHIBIT 10-2

Linearity Within Relevant Range for AMC, Inc.

If you've had a microeconomics course, the cost function in Exhibit 10-2 should look familiar. Below the relevant range, total costs increase at a decreasing rate due to economies of scale. Above the relevant range, diminishing marginal returns cause total costs to increase at an increasing rate.

to measure a past relationship based on data from past costs and the related level of an activity. For example, managers could use cost estimation to understand what causes marketing costs to change from year to year (for example, the number of cars sold or the number of new car models introduced) and the fixed and variable components of these costs (see Surveys of Company Practice, p. 328). Managers are interested in estimating past cost-behavior functions primarily because these estimates can help them make more-accurate **cost predictions**, or forecasts, about future costs. Better cost predictions help managers make more-informed planning and control decisions, such as preparing the budget of marketing costs for next year. But better management decisions, cost predictions, and estimation of cost functions depend on correctly identifying the factors that affect costs.

THE CAUSE-AND-EFFECT CRITERION IN CHOOSING COST DRIVERS

The most important issue in estimating a cost function is determining whether a cause-and-effect relationship exists between the level of an activity and the costs related to that level of activity. Without a cause-and-effect relationship, managers will be unable to estimate or predict costs and, hence, will have difficulty managing those costs. The cause-and-effect relationship might arise as a result of:

1. *A physical relationship between the level of activity and costs.* An example of a physical relationship is when units of production is used as the activity that affects direct material costs. Producing more units requires more direct materials, which results in higher total direct material costs.
2. *A contractual arrangement.* In alternative 1 of the Cannon Services example described earlier, number of phone-minutes used is specified in the contract as the level of activity that affects the telephone line costs.
3. *An implication of logic and knowledge of operations.* An example is when number of parts is used as the activity measure of ordering costs. It seems likely that a product with many parts will incur higher ordering costs than a product with few parts.

Be careful not to interpret a high correlation, or connection, in the relationship between two variables to mean that either variable causes the other. For example, a high correlation between two variables, u and v, indicates merely that *the two variables move together*. It is possible that u may cause v, v may cause u, both may be affected by a third variable z, or the correlation may be due to random chance. No conclusions about cause and effect are warranted by high correlations alone. For example, higher production generally results in higher material costs and higher labor costs. Material costs and labor costs are highly correlated, but neither causes the other.

Consider another example. Over the past 36 years, the New York Stock Exchange index has almost always increased during the year in which an original National Football League team (such as the San Francisco 49ers) has won the Super Bowl, and it has almost always decreased in the year in which an original American Football League team (such as the Denver Broncos) has won. There is, however, no plausible cause-and-effect explanation for this high correlation.

For many years, church attendance and alcohol consumption were positively correlated. However, this was not because attending church increased people's alcohol consumption or because drinking alcohol promoted piety. Rather, it was due to *increasing population* and its independent effects on both church attendance and alcohol consumption. The conclusion: high correlation between two variables does not necessarily mean that a cause-and-effect relationship exists.

SURVEYS OF COMPANY PRACTICE

International Comparison of Cost Classification by Companies

Organizations differ in classifying individual costs. A variable-cost item in one organization can be a fixed-cost item in another organization. Consider labor costs. Home construction companies often classify labor cost as a variable cost. These companies rapidly adjust their labor force in response to changes in the demand for housing construction. In contrast, oil-refining companies often classify labor cost as a fixed cost. The labor force is stable even when sizable changes occur in the volume or type of oil products refined.

Surveys indicate significant differences in the percentage of companies in various countries classifying individual cost categories as variable, fixed, or mixed. A lower percentage of U.S. and Australian companies treat labor costs as a fixed cost compared with Japanese companies.

	U. S. Companies			Japanese Companies			Australian Companies		
Cost Category	**Variable**	**Mixed**	**Fixed**	**Variable**	**Mixed**	**Fixed**	**Variable**	**Mixed**	**Fixed**
Production labor	86%	6%	8%	52%	5%	43%	70%	20%	10%
Setup labor	60	25	15	44	6	50	45	33	22
Materials-handling labor	48	34	18	23	16	61	40	30	30
Quality-control labor	34	36	30	13	12	75	21	27	52
Tooling	32	35	33	31	26	43	25	28	47
Energy	26	45	29	42	31	27	—	—	—
Building occupancy	1	6	93	0	0	100	—	—	—
Depreciation	1	7	92	0	0	100	—	—	—

Source: Adapted from the NAA Tokyo Affiliate, "Management Accounting in the Advanced Manufacturing," and Joye and Blayney, "Cost and Management Accounting." Full citations are in Appendix A at the end of the book.

Only a cause-and-effect relationship (based on, say, a physical relationship, a contract, or logic)—not merely correlation—establishes an economically plausible relationship between the level of an activity and its costs. Economic plausibility is critical because it gives the analyst confidence that the estimated relationship will appear again and again in other sets of data from the same situation.

Recall from Chapter 2 that when a cause-and-effect relationship exists between a change in the level of an activity and a change in the level of total costs, we refer to the activity measure as a cost driver. Because economic plausibility is essential for cost estimation, we use the terms *level of activity* and *level of cost driver* interchangeably when estimating cost functions. To identify cost drivers on the basis of data gathered over time, always use a long time horizon. Why? Because, as our example of inspection costs at Boeing Company illustrates (p. 326), costs may be fixed in the short run (during which time they have no cost driver), but they may be variable and have a cost driver in the long run.

3 Understand various approaches to cost estimation

...for example, the regression analysis method determines the line that best fits the data

COST ESTIMATION METHODS

Four methods of cost estimation are

1. Industrial engineering method
2. Conference method
3. Account analysis method
4. Quantitative analysis methods

These methods differ with respect to (a) how expensive they are to implement, (b) the assumptions they make, and (c) the information they provide about the accuracy of the estimated cost function. They are not mutually exclusive. Many organizations use a combination of these methods.

Industrial Engineering Method

The **industrial engineering method,** also called the **work-measurement method,** estimates cost functions by analyzing the relationship between inputs and outputs in physical terms. Consider a carpet manufacturer that uses inputs of cotton, wool, dyes, direct manufacturing labor, machine time, and power. Production output is square yards of carpet. Time-and-motion studies analyze the time and materials required to perform the various operations to produce the carpet. For example, a time-and-motion study may conclude that to produce 10 square yards of carpet requires one hour of direct manufacturing labor. Standards and budgets transform these physical input measures into costs. The result is an estimated cost function relating direct manufacturing labor costs to the cost driver, square yards of carpet produced.

This method has its roots in studies performed and techniques developed by scientific management pioneers Frank and Lillian Gilbreth in the early twentieth century.

The industrial engineering method can be very time-consuming. Some government contracts mandate its use. Many organizations find it too costly or impractical for analyzing their entire cost structure. For example, physical relationships between inputs and outputs may be difficult to specify for individual cost items, such as R&D and advertising.

Conference Method

The **conference method** estimates cost functions on the basis of analysis and opinions about costs and their drivers gathered from various departments of a company (purchasing, process engineering, manufacturing, employee relations, and so on). The Cooperative Bank in the United Kingdom has a Cost-Estimating Department that develops cost functions for its retail banking products (checking accounts, VISA cards, mortgages, and so on) on the basis of a consensus of estimates from personnel of the particular departments.

The conference method encourages interdepartmental cooperation. The pooling of expert knowledge from each value-chain function gives the conference method credibility. Because the conference method does not require detailed analysis of data, cost functions and cost estimates can be developed quickly. However, the emphasis on opinions rather than systematic estimation means that the accuracy of the cost estimates depends largely on the care and skill of the people providing the inputs.[1]

Account Analysis Method

The **account analysis method** estimates cost functions by classifying cost accounts in the subsidiary ledger as variable, fixed, or mixed with respect to the identified level of activity. Typically, managers use qualitative rather than quantitative analysis when making these cost-classification decisions. The account analysis approach is widely used.

Consider indirect manufacturing labor costs for a small production area (or cell) at Elegant Rugs, which uses state-of-the-art automated weaving machines to produce carpets for homes and offices. These costs include wages paid to indirect manufacturing labor for supervision, maintenance, quality control, and setups. During the most recent 12-week period, Elegant Rugs ran the machines in the cell for a total of 862 hours and incurred total indirect manufacturing labor costs of $12,501. Using qualitative analysis, the manager and the cost analyst determine that indirect manufacturing labor costs are mixed costs. As machine-hours vary, one component of the cost (such as supervision cost) is fixed, whereas another component (such as maintenance cost) is variable. The goal is to use account analysis to estimate a linear cost function for indirect manufacturing labor costs with number of machine-hours as the cost driver. The cost analyst uses experience and judgment to separate total indirect manufacturing labor costs ($12,501) into costs that are fixed ($2,157) and costs that are variable ($10,344) with respect to the number of machine-hours used. Variable cost per machine-hour is $10,344 ÷ 862 machine-hours = $12 per machine-hour. The linear cost equation, $y = a + bX$, in this example is

Indirect manufacting labor costs = $2,157 + ($12 per machine-hour × Number of machine-hours)

The indirect manufacturing labor cost per machine-hour is $12,501 ÷ 862 machine-hours = $14.50 per machine-hour. Management at Elegant Rugs can use the cost function to estimate the indirect manufacturing labor costs of using, say, 950 machine-hours to

[1] The conference method is further described in W. Winchell, *Realistic Cost Estimating for Manufacturing,* 2nd ed. (Dearborn, MI: Society for Manufacturing Engineers, 1989).

EXHIBIT 10-3

Weekly Indirect Manufacturing Labor Costs and Machine-Hours for Elegant Rugs

Week	Indirect Manufacturing Labor Costs (1)	Cost Driver: Machine-Hours (2)
1	$1,190	68
2	1,211	88
3	1,004	62
4	917	72
5	770	60
6	1,456	96
7	1,180	78
8	710	46
9	1,316	82
10	1,032	94
11	752	68
12	963	48

produce carpet in the next 12-week period. Estimated costs equal \$2,157 + (950 machine-hours × \$12 per machine-hour) = \$13,557. The indirect manufacturing labor costs per machine-hour decrease to \$13,557 ÷ 950 machine-hours = \$14.27 per machine-hour, as fixed costs are spread over a greater number of machine-hours.

To obtain reliable estimates of the fixed and variable components of cost, organizations must take care to ensure that individuals thoroughly knowledgeable about the operations make the cost-classification decisions. Supplementing the account analysis method with the conference method improves its credibility.

The industrial engineering, conference, and account analysis methods require less historical data than most quantitative analyses. Consequently, cost estimation for a new product will usually begin with one or more of these three methods. Quantitative analysis may be used for this product later on, after the company collects the necessary historical data.

Quantitative Analysis Methods

Quantitative analysis uses a formal mathematical method to fit cost functions to past data observations. Columns 1 and 2 of Exhibit 10-3 show the breakdown of Elegant Rugs's total indirect manufacturing labor costs of \$12,501 and total 862 machine-hours into weekly data for the most recent 12-week period. Note that the data are paired—for each week there is data for indirect manufacturing labor costs and corresponding data for number of machine-hours. For example, week 12 shows indirect manufacturing labor costs of \$963 and 48 machine-hours. The next section uses the data in Exhibit 10-3 to illustrate how to estimate a cost function using quantitative analysis.

STEPS IN ESTIMATING A COST FUNCTION USING QUANTITATIVE ANALYSIS

4 Outline six steps in estimating a cost function on the basis of past cost relationships

...for example, identifying and collecting data on cost drivers, plotting the data, and estimating the relationship between cost drivers and costs

There are six steps in estimating a cost function using a quantitative analysis of a past cost relationship. One step is choosing a cost driver, which is not always simple. Frequently, the cost analyst, working with a management team, will cycle through the six steps several times, trying alternative economically plausible cost drivers to identify a cost driver that best fits the data.

Step 1: **Choose the Dependent Variable.** Choice of the **dependent variable** (the cost to be predicted) will depend on the cost function being estimated. In the Elegant Rugs example, the dependent variable is indirect manufacturing labor costs. The dependent variable will then include all manufacturing labor costs that are classified as indirect.

Step 2: **Identify the Independent Variable or Cost Driver.** The **independent variable** (level of activity or cost driver) is the factor used to predict the dependent variable (costs). When the cost is an indirect cost, as with Elegant Rugs, the independent variable is also called a cost-allocation base. Although these terms are sometimes used interchangeably, usually we use the term *cost driver* to describe the independent variable.

The chapter focuses on a single independent variable or cost driver. The appendix to this chapter (pp. 351–354) describes how multiple cost drivers can be used to predict a dependent variable or cost.

A cost driver should (a) have an *economically plausible* relationship with the dependent variable and (b) be measurable. Economic plausibility means that the relationship (describing how changes in the cost driver lead to changes in the costs being considered) is based on a physical relationship, a contract, or logic and makes economic sense to the operating manager and the management accountant. All the individual items included in the dependent variable should have the same cost driver. Some dependent-variable cost categories include more than one item of cost, and sometimes these different cost items do not have the same cost driver. When a single relationship does not exist, the cost analyst should investigate the possibility of estimating more than one cost function, one for each cost category/cost driver pair.

As an example, consider several types of fringe benefits paid to employees and the cost drivers of the benefits:

Fringe Benefit	Cost Driver
Health benefits	Number of employees
Cafeteria meals	Number of employees
Pension benefits	Salaries of employees
Life insurance	Salaries of employees

The costs of health benefits and cafeteria meals can be combined into one cost pool because they both have the same cost driver—the number of employees. Pension benefits and life insurance costs have a different cost driver—the salaries of employees—and, therefore, should not be combined with health benefits and cafeteria meals. Instead, pension benefits and life insurance should be combined into a separate cost pool. Using that cost pool, pension benefits and life insurance costs can be estimated using salaries of employees receiving these benefits as the cost driver.

Step 3: **Collect Data on the Dependent Variable and the Cost Driver.** This is usually the most difficult step in cost analysis. Cost analysts obtain data from company documents, from interviews with managers, and through special studies. These data may be time-series data or cross-sectional data.

Time-series data pertain to the same entity (organization, plant, activity, and so on) over successive past periods. Weekly observations of indirect manufacturing labor costs and number of machine-hours at Elegant Rugs are an example of time-series data. The ideal time-series database would contain numerous observations for a company whose operations have not been affected by economic or technological change. A stable economy and technology ensure that data collected during the estimation period represent the same underlying relationship between the cost driver and the dependent variable. Moreover, the periods (for example, daily, weekly, or monthly) used to measure the dependent variable and the cost driver should be consistent throughout the observations.

Cross-sectional data pertain to different entities during the same period. For example, studies of loans processed and the related personnel costs at 50 individual, yet similar branches of a bank during March 2003 would produce cross-sectional data for that month. A later section of this chapter describes problems that arise in data collection.

Step 4: **Plot the Data.** The general relationship between the level of the cost driver and the costs can readily be observed in a graphical representation of the data, which is commonly called a plot of the data. Moreover, the plot highlights extreme observations (observations outside the general pattern) that analysts should check. Was there an error in recording the data or an unusual event, such as a work stoppage, that makes these observations unrepresentative of the normal relationship between the level of the cost driver and the costs? Plotting the data also provides insight into whether the relationship is approximately linear and what the relevant range of the cost function is.

Exhibit 10-4 is a plot of the weekly data from columns 1 and 2 of Exhibit 10-3. This graph provides strong visual evidence of a positive linear relationship between number of machine-hours and indirect manufacturing labor costs (that

EXHIBIT 10-4

Plot of Weekly Indirect Manufacturing Labor Costs and Machine-Hours for Elegant Rugs

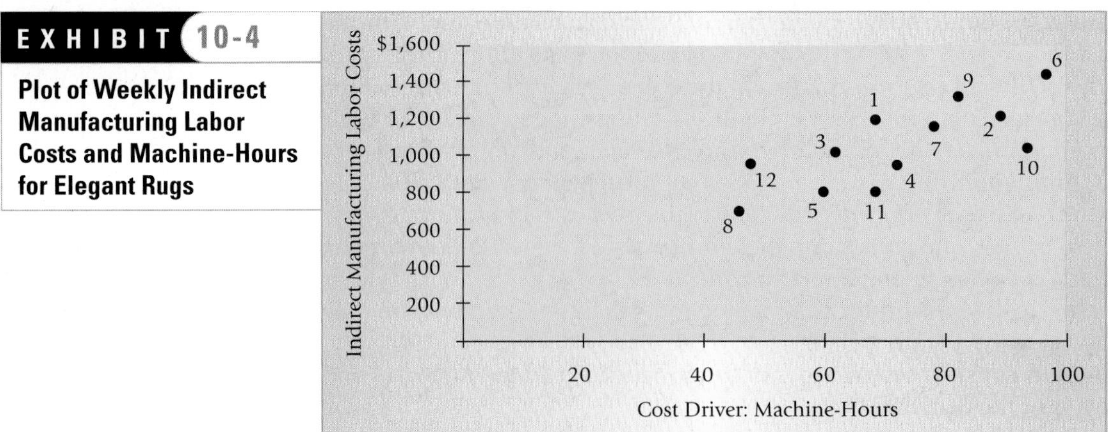

is, when machine-hours go up, so do indirect manufacturing labor costs). There do not appear to be any extreme observations in Exhibit 10-4. The relevant range is from 46 to 96 machine-hours per week (weeks 8 and 6 respectively).

Step 5: **Estimate the Cost Function.** We will show two ways to estimate the cost function for our Elegant Rugs data. One uses the high-low method, and the other uses regression analysis, the two most common forms of quantitative analysis. We show these following Step 6.

Step 6: **Evaluate the Cost Driver of the Estimated Cost Function.** In this step, we describe criteria for evaluating the cost driver of the estimated cost function. We do this after illustrating the high-low method and regression analysis.

High-Low Method

The simplest method of quantitative analysis is the **high-low method**. It uses only the highest and lowest observed values of the cost driver within the relevant range and their respective costs. The cost function is estimated by using these two points to calculate the slope coefficient and the constant or intercept. We illustrate the high-low method using data from Exhibit 10-3.

	Indirect Manufacturing Labor Costs	Cost Driver: Machine-Hours
Highest observation of cost driver (week 6)	$1,456	96
Lowest observation of cost driver (week 8)	710	46
Difference	$ 746	50

The slope coefficient, b, is calculated as:

$$\text{Slope coefficient} = \frac{\text{Difference between costs associated with highest and lowest observations of the cost driver}}{\text{Difference between highest and lowest observations of the cost driver}}$$

$$= \$746 \div 50 \text{ machine-hours} = \$14.92 \text{ per machine-hour}$$

To compute the constant, we can use either the highest or the lowest observation of the cost driver. Both calculations yield the same answer because the solution technique solves two linear equations with two unknowns, the slope coefficient and the constant. Because

$$y = a + bX$$
$$a = y - bX$$

therefore, at the highest observation of the cost driver, the constant, a, is calculated as:

$$\text{Constant} = \$1,456 - (\$14.92 \text{ per machine-hour} \times 96 \text{ machine-hours}) = \$23.68$$

And at the lowest observation of the cost driver,

$$\text{Constant} = \$710 - (\$14.92 \text{ per machine-hour} \times 46 \text{ machine-hours}) = \$23.68$$

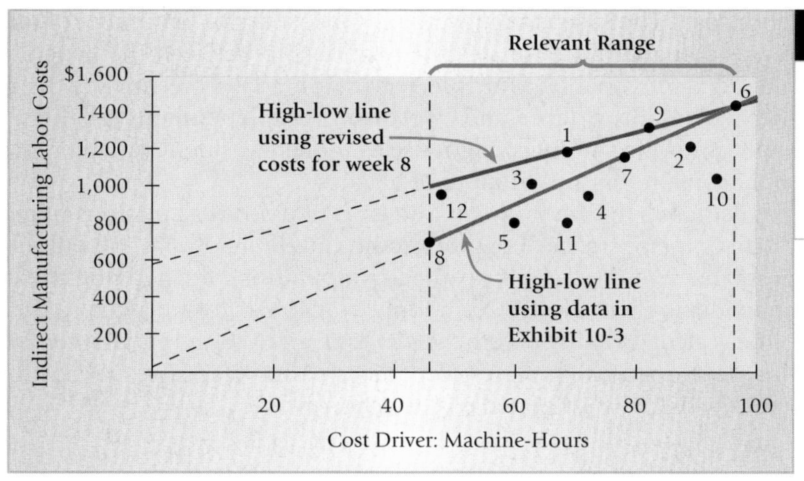

EXHIBIT 10-5

High-Low Method for Weekly Indirect Manufacturing Labor Costs and Machine-Hours for Elegant Rugs

Thus, the high-low estimate of the cost function is

$$y = a + bX$$
$$y = \$23.68 + (\$14.92 \text{ per machine-hour} \times \text{Number of machine-hours})$$

The maroon line in Exhibit 10-5 shows the estimated cost function using the high-low method (based on the data in Exhibit 10-3). The estimated cost function is a straight line joining the observations with the highest and lowest values of the cost driver (machine-hours). The intercept (a = $23.68), the point where the dashed extension of the maroon line meets the y-axis, is the constant component of the equation that provides the best linear approximation of how a cost behaves *within the relevant range* of 46 to 96 machine-hours. The intercept should not be interpreted as an estimate of the fixed costs of Elegant Rugs if no machines were run. That's because running no machines and shutting down the plant—that is, using zero machine-hours—is outside the relevant range.

Suppose indirect manufacturing labor costs in week 6 were $1,280, instead of $1,456, while 96 machine-hours were used. In this case, the highest observation of the cost driver (96 machine-hours in week 6) will not coincide with the newer highest observation of the costs ($1,316 in week 9). How would this change affect our high-low calculation? Given that the cause-and-effect relationship runs *from* the cost driver *to* the costs in a cost function, we choose the highest and lowest observations of the cost driver (the factor that causes the costs to change). The high-low method would estimate the new cost function still using data from weeks 6 (high) and 8 (low).

There is a danger of relying on only two observations to estimate a cost function. Suppose that because a labor contract guarantees certain minimum payments in week 8, indirect manufacturing labor costs in week 8 were inflated to $1,000, instead of $710, when only 46 machine-hours were used. The blue-green line in Exhibit 10-5 shows the cost function that would be estimated by the high-low method using this revised cost. Other than the two points used to draw the line, all other data lie below the line! In this case, picking the highest and lowest observations for machine-hours would result in an estimated cost function that poorly describes the underlying linear cost relationship between number of machine-hours and indirect manufacturing labor costs.

Sometimes the high-low method is modified so that the two observations chosen are a *representative high* and a *representative low*. Managers use this modification to avoid having extreme observations, which arise from abnormal events, affect the cost function. The advantage of the high-low method is that it is simple to compute; the disadvantage is that it ignores information from all but two observations when estimating the cost function.

A representative high (low) could be the average of the observations with, say, the two or three highest (lowest) values of the cost driver.

Regression Analysis Method

The regression analysis method uses all available data to estimate the cost function. **Regression analysis** is a statistical method that measures the average amount of change in the dependent variable associated with a unit change in one or more independent variables. In the Elegant Rugs example, the dependent variable is total indirect manufacturing

If you've had a statistics course, you might not think there is much connection between regression analysis and accounting. But this section shows an important accounting application for regression analysis.

labor costs. The independent variable, or cost driver, is number of machine-hours. **Simple regression** analysis estimates the relationship between the dependent variable and one independent variable. **Multiple regression** analysis estimates the relationship between the dependent variable and two or more independent variables. Multiple regression analysis for Elegant Rugs might use as the independent variables, or cost drivers, number of machine-hours and number of batches.

Because software programs are used to do the calculations of regression analysis, our discussion emphasizes how we should interpret and use the output from those software programs. We do present detailed computations for deriving the regression line in the appendix to this chapter. Commonly available software (such as Excel) on personal computers calculate almost all the statistics referred to in this chapter. Exhibit 10-6 shows the line developed using regression analysis that best fits the data in columns 1 and 2 of Exhibit 10-3. The estimated cost function is

$$y = \$300.98 + \$10.31X$$

The regression line is fitted through a set of observations so that it best represents the underlying relationship or pattern in the observations.

A positive slope of a regression line means that costs are low for small values of the cost driver and costs are higher for higher values of the cost driver.

The regression line in Exhibit 10-6 is derived using the least-squares technique. The regression line minimizes the sum of the squared vertical differences from the data points (the various points on the graph) to the regression line. The vertical difference, called **residual term**, measures the distance between actual cost and the estimated cost for each observation. Exhibit 10-6 shows the residual term for the week 1 data. The line from the observation to the regression line is drawn perpendicular to the horizontal axis, or x-axis. The smaller the residual terms, the better the fit between actual cost observations and estimated costs. *Goodness of fit* indicates the strength of the relationship between the cost driver and costs. The regression line in Exhibit 10-6 rises from left to right. The positive slope of this line and small residual terms indicate that, on average, indirect manufacturing labor costs increase as number of machine-hours increase. The vertical dashed lines in Exhibit 10-6 indicate the relevant range, the range within which the cost function applies.

The estimate of the slope coefficient, b, indicates that indirect manufacturing labor costs vary at the average amount of $10.31 for every machine-hour used within the relevant range. Management can use the regression equation when budgeting for future indirect manufacturing labor costs. For instance, if 90 machine-hours are budgeted for the upcoming week, the predicted indirect manufacturing labor costs would be

$$y = \$300.98 + (\$10.31 \text{ per machine-hour} \times 90 \text{ machine-hours}) = \$1{,}228.88$$

The regression method is more accurate than the high-low method because the regression equation estimates costs using information from all observations, whereas the high-low equation uses information from only two observations. The inaccuracies of the high-low method can mislead managers. Consider the high-low equation in the preceding section, $y = \$23.68 + \$14.92$ per machine-hour. For 90 machine-hours, the predicted weekly cost based on the high-low equation is $23.68 + ($14.92 per machine-hour × 90 machine-hours) = $1,366.48. Suppose that for 7 weeks over the next 12-week period, Elegant Rugs runs its machines for 90 hours each week. Assume average indirect manufacturing labor

EXHIBIT 10-6

Regression Model for Weekly Indirect Manufacturing Labor Costs and Machine-Hours for Elegant Rugs

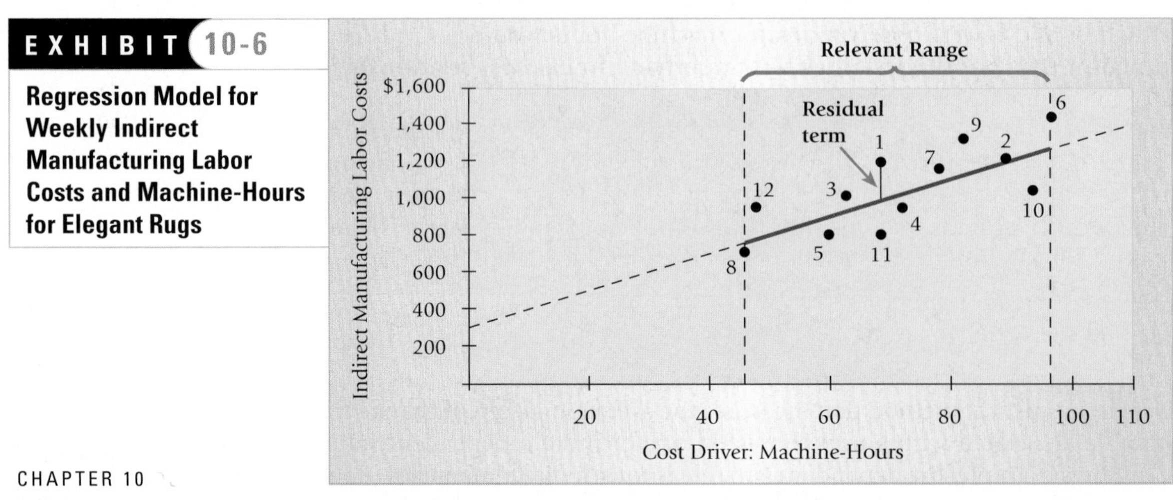

costs for those 7 weeks is $1,300. Based on the high-low prediction of $1,366.48, Elegant Rugs would conclude it has performed well because actual costs are less than predicted costs. But comparing the $1,300 performance with the more accurate $1,228.88 prediction of the regression model tells a much different story and would probably prompt Elegant Rugs to search for ways to improve its cost performance.

Accurate cost estimation helps managers predict future costs and evaluate the success of cost-reduction initiatives. Suppose the manager at Elegant Rugs is interested in evaluating whether recent strategic decisions that led to changes in the production process and resulted in the data in Exhibit 10-3 have reduced indirect manufacturing labor costs, such as supervision, maintenance, and quality control. Using data on number of machine-hours used and indirect manufacturing labor costs of the previous process, the manager estimates the regression equation, $y = \$545.26 + (\$15.86 \text{ per machine-hour} \times \text{number of machine-hours})$. The constant ($300.98 versus $545.26) and the slope coefficient ($10.31 versus $15.86) are both smaller than before. It appears that the new process has decreased indirect manufacturing labor costs.

EVALUATING COST DRIVERS OF THE ESTIMATED COST FUNCTION

How does a company determine the best cost driver when estimating a cost function? In many cases, the choice of a cost driver is aided substantially by understanding operations and cost accounting.

To see why understanding operations is needed, consider the costs to maintain and repair metal cutting machines at Helix Corporation, a manufacturer of filing cabinets. Helix schedules repairs and maintenance at a time that production is at a low level to avoid having to take machines out of service when they are needed most. An analysis of the monthly data will then show high repair costs in months of low production and low repair costs in months of high production. Someone unfamiliar with operations might conclude that there is an inverse relationship between production and repair costs. The engineering link between units of production and repair costs, however, is usually clear-cut. Over time, there is a cause-and-effect relationship: The higher the level of production, the higher the repair costs. To estimate the relationship correctly, operating managers and analysts recognize that repair costs will tend to lag behind periods of high production, and hence, they will use production of the prior period as the cost driver.

In other cases, choosing a cost driver is more subtle and difficult. Consider again indirect manufacturing labor costs at Elegant Rugs. Management believes that both number of machine-hours and number of direct manufacturing labor-hours are plausible cost drivers of indirect manufacturing labor costs. Management is not sure that number of machine-hours is the better cost driver. Exhibit 10-7 presents weekly data on indirect manufacturing labor costs and number of machine-hours for the most recent 12-week

EXHIBIT 10-7

Weekly Indirect Manufacturing Labor Costs, Machine-Hours, and Direct Manufacturing Labor-Hours for Elegant Rugs

Week	Indirect Manufacturing Labor Costs (1)	Cost Driver: Machine-Hours (2)	Alternative Cost Driver: Direct Manufacturing Labor-Hours (3)
1	$1,190	68	30
2	1,211	88	35
3	1,004	62	36
4	917	72	20
5	770	60	47
6	1,456	96	45
7	1,180	78	44
8	710	46	38
9	1,316	82	70
10	1,032	94	30
11	752	68	29
12	963	48	38

period from Exhibit 10-3, together with data on number of direct manufacturing labor-hours for the same period.

What guidance do the different cost-estimation methods provide for choosing among cost drivers? The industrial engineering method relies on analyzing physical relationships between cost drivers and costs, relationships that are difficult to specify in this case. The conference method and the account analysis method use subjective assessments to choose a cost driver and to estimate the fixed and variable components of the cost function. In these cases, managers must rely on their best judgment. Managers cannot use these methods to test and try alternative cost drivers. The major advantage of quantitative methods is that they are objective—a given data set and estimation method results in a unique estimated cost function—and that managers can use these methods to evaluate different cost drivers. We use the regression analysis approach to illustrate how to evaluate different cost drivers.

As in most applications, the cost function in the Elegant Rugs example is not valid at shutdown (x = 0) because that point is outside the relevant range. That is, the y-intercept, $744.67, is not the fixed costs at 0 direct manufacturing labor-hours because at shutdown many costs can be avoided (for example, laying off salaried personnel). In this example, the $744.67 is simply the constant component of the equation that provides the best linear fit of the data.

First, the cost analyst at Elegant Rugs inputs the data in columns 1 and 3 of Exhibit 10-7 into a computer and, using regression analysis software, estimates the following regression equation of indirect manufacturing labor costs based on number of direct manufacturing labor-hours:

$$y = \$744.67 + \$7.72X$$

Exhibit 10-8 shows the data points plotted for indirect manufacturing labor costs based on number of direct manufacturing labor-hours, and the regression line that best fits the data. Exhibit 10-6 shows the corresponding graph when number of machine-hours is the cost driver. To decide which cost driver Elegant Rugs should choose, the analyst compares the machine-hour regression equation and the direct manufacturing labor-hour regression equation. There are three criteria used to make this evaluation.

5 Describe three criteria used to evaluate and choose cost drivers

...economically plausible relationships, good fit, and significant effect of the cost driver on costs

1. *Economic plausibility.* Both cost drivers are economically plausible. However, in the state-of-the-art, highly automated production environment at Elegant Rugs, managers familiar with the operations believe that costs such as machine maintenance are likely to be more closely related to number of machine-hours used than to number of direct manufacturing labor-hours.
2. *Goodness of fit.* Compare Exhibits 10-6 and 10-8. The vertical differences between actual costs and predicted costs are much smaller for the machine-hours regression than for the direct manufacturing labor-hours regression. Number of machine-hours thus has a stronger relationship—or goodness of fit—with indirect manufacturing labor costs.
3. *Significance of independent variable.* Again compare Exhibits 10-6 and 10-8. The machine-hours regression line has a steep slope relative to the slope of the direct manufacturing labor-hours regression line. *For the same (or more) scatter of observations about the line (goodness of fit)*, a flat, or slightly sloped regression line indicates a weak relationship between the cost driver and costs. In our example, changes in direct manufacturing labor-hours appear to have a small effect on indirect manufacturing labor costs.

EXHIBIT 10-8

Regression Model for Weekly Indirect Manufacturing Labor Costs and Direct Manufacturing Labor-Hours for Elegant Rugs

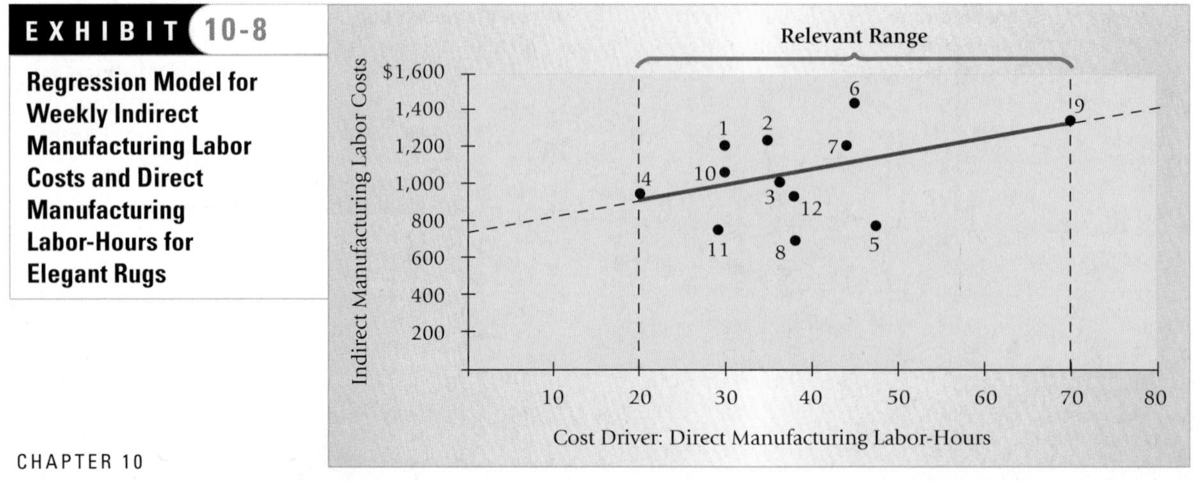

Elegant Rugs should prefer number of machine-hours to number of direct manufacturing labor-hours as the cost driver and use the cost function $y = \$300.98 + (\$10.31$ per machine-hour $\times$ number of machine-hours) to predict future indirect manufacturing labor costs.

Why is choosing the correct cost driver to estimate indirect manufacturing labor costs so important? Consider the following strategic decision that management at Elegant Rugs must make. The company is thinking of introducing a new style of carpet. Sales of 650 square yards of this carpet are expected each week. Management estimates 72 machine-hours and 21 direct manufacturing labor-hours would be required per week to produce the 650 square yards of carpet needed. Using the machine-hour regression equation, Elegant Rugs would predict costs of $y = \$300.98 + (\$10.31$ per machine-hour $\times$ 72 machine-hours) = \$1,043.30. If it used direct manufacturing labor-hours as the cost driver, it would have incorrectly predicted costs of \$744.67 + (\$7.72 per labor-hour × 21 labor-hours) = \$906.79. If Elegant Rugs chooses similarly incorrect cost drivers for other indirect costs as well and systematically underestimates costs, it would conclude that the costs of manufacturing the new style of carpet are low and fixed (fixed because the regression line is nearly flat). But the actual costs driven by number of machine-hours used and other correct cost drivers would be higher. By failing to identify the proper cost drivers, management would be misled into believing the new style of carpet is more profitable than it actually is. It might decide to introduce the new style of carpet, whereas if Elegant had identified the correct cost driver it might have decided not to introduce the new carpet.

Incorrectly estimating the cost function would also have repercussions for cost management and cost control. Suppose number of direct manufacturing labor-hours is used as the cost driver, and actual indirect manufacturing labor costs for the new carpet are \$970. Actual costs would then be higher than the predicted costs of \$906.79. Management would feel compelled to find ways to cut costs. In fact, on the basis of the preferred machine-hour cost driver, the plant would have actual costs lower than the \$1,043.30 predicted costs—a performance that management should seek to replicate, not change!

COST DRIVERS AND ACTIVITY-BASED COSTING

Activity-based costing (ABC) systems focus on individual activities—such as product design, machine setup, material handling, distribution, and customer service—as the fundamental cost objects. To implement ABC systems, managers must identify a cost driver for each activity. For example, using methods described in this chapter, the manager must decide whether the number of loads moved or the weight of loads moved is the cost driver of material-handling costs.

To choose the cost driver and use it to estimate the cost function in our material-handling example, the manager collects data on material-handling costs and the quantities of the two competing cost drivers over a long enough period. Why a long period? Because in the short run, material-handling costs may be fixed and, therefore, will not vary with changes in the level of the cost driver. In the long run, however, there is a clear cause-and-effect relationship between material-handling costs and the cost driver. Suppose number of loads moved is the cost driver of material-handling costs. Increases in the number of loads moved will require more material-handling labor and equipment; decreases will result in equipment being sold and labor being reassigned to other tasks.

ABC systems have a great number and variety of cost drivers and cost pools. That means ABC systems require many cost relationships to be estimated. In estimating the cost function for each cost pool, the manager must pay careful attention to the cost hierarchy. For example, if a cost is a batch-level cost such as setup cost, the manager must only consider batch-level cost drivers like number of setup-hours.

A cost hierarchy categorizes costs into different cost pools on the basis of the different types of cost drivers. A common four-part cost hierarchy is output unit-level costs, batch-level costs, product-sustaining costs, and facility-sustaining costs (see p. 141–142).

As the Concepts in Action (p. 338) indicates, managers implementing ABC systems use a variety of methods—industrial engineering, conference, and regression analysis—to estimate slope coefficients. In making these choices, managers trade off level of detail, accuracy, feasibility, and costs of estimating cost functions.

6 Explain and give examples of nonlinear cost functions

...graph of cost function is not a straight line because of quantity discounts or costs changing in steps

NONLINEARITY AND COST FUNCTIONS

Thus far we have assumed linear cost functions. In practice, cost functions are not always linear. To see what a nonlinear cost function looks like, return to Exhibit 10-2 (p. 327),

CONCEPTS IN ACTION

Activity-Based Costing, Cost Drivers, and Revenue Drivers

Cost estimation in activity-based costing and other systems blends the various methods presented in this chapter. To determine the cost of an activity, ABC systems often rely on expert analyses and opinions gathered from operating personnel (the conference method). For example, Loan Department staff at the Cooperative Bank in the United Kingdom subjectively estimate the costs of the loan processing activity and the cost driver of loan processing costs—the number of loans processed, a batch-level cost driver, rather than the amount of the loans, an output unit-level cost driver—to derive the cost of processing a loan.

ABC systems sometimes use input-output relationships (the industrial engineering method) to identify cost drivers and the cost of an activity. For example, John Deere and Company uses work-measurement methods to identify a batch-level cost driver, the number of standard loads moved, and the cost per load moved within its components plant.

Regression analysis is also used to choose the cost drivers of activities. Consider how heavy equipment manufacturer Caterpillar identifies the cost driver for receiving costs in its ABC system. Three plausible cost drivers are the weight of parts received, the number of parts received, and the number of shipments received. The weight and number of parts are output unit-level cost drivers, whereas the number of shipments is a batch-level cost driver. Caterpillar uses the weight of parts as the basis for cost assignment because a regression analysis showed that it is the primary driver of the costs of receiving material.

Can regression analysis be used to identify the drivers of revenue? For example, when launching new products, how much should pharmaceutical companies spend on hiring sales representatives to visit doctors' offices, on television advertising, and on advertising in medical journals? Using multiple regression analysis, companies such as Novartis can identify which of the different forms of product promotion yield the highest revenues and returns. For the pharmaceutical industry as a whole, research shows that the revenue gains from visits to doctors' offices and advertising in medical journals are greater than the revenue gains from television advertising.

Source: Based on the Cooperative Bank, Harvard Business School Case No. N9-195-196; John Deere Component Works (A), Harvard Business School Case 9-187-107; S. Neshlin, "ROI Analysis of Pharmaceutical Promotion," *Medical Marketing and Media*, 2001, and discussions with the companies.

but now let's expand the relevant range to 0 to 80,000 valves produced from the original relevant range of 20,000 to 65,000. You can see that the cost function over this expanded range is graphically represented by a line that is nonlinear. A **nonlinear cost function**'s total costs based on the level of a single activity, represented graphically, is not a straight line within the relevant range.

Consider another example. Economies of scale in advertising may enable an advertising agency to double the number of advertisements for less than double the costs. Even direct material costs are not always linear variable costs. Consider quantity discounts on direct material purchases. As shown in Exhibit 10-9, Panel A, the total direct material costs rise. But, because of quantity discounts, total direct material costs rise more slowly (as indicated by the slope coefficient) as the units of direct material purchased increase. This cost function has b = \$25 per unit for 1 to 1,000 units purchased, b = \$15 per unit for 1,001 to 2,000 units purchased, and b = \$10 per unit for 2,001 to 3,000 units purchased. The direct material cost per unit falls at each price break—that is, the cost per unit decreases with larger purchase orders. If the relevant range is considered to be from 1 to 3,000 units, the cost function is nonlinear—not a straight line. If, however, the relevant range is defined more narrowly (e.g., from 1 to 1,000 units) the cost function is linear.

Step cost functions are also examples of nonlinear cost functions. A **step cost function** is a cost function in which the cost remains the same over various ranges of the level of activity, but the cost increases by discrete amounts—that is, increases in steps—as the

EXHIBIT 10-9 Effects of Quantity Discounts on Slope of Direct Materials Cost Function

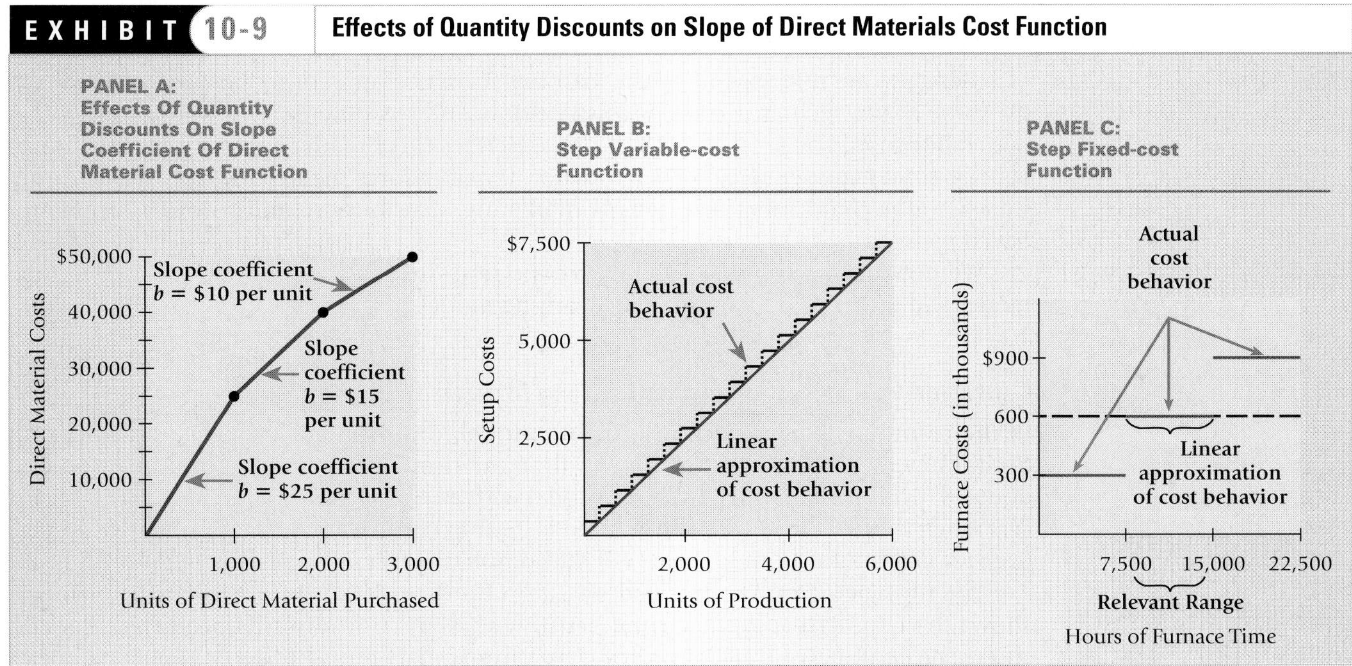

level of activity changes from one range to the next. Panel B in Exhibit 10-9 shows *a step variable-cost function,* a step cost function in which cost remains the same over *narrow* ranges of the level of activity in each relevant range. Exhibit 10-9, Panel B, presents the relationship between units of production and setup costs. The pattern is a step cost function because, as we described in Chapter 5 on activity-based costing, setup costs are related to each production batch started. If the relevant range is considered to be from 0 to 6,000 production units, the cost function is nonlinear. However, as shown by the blue-green line in Exhibit 10-9, Panel B, managers often approximate step variable costs with a continuously variable-cost function. This type of step cost pattern also occurs when inputs such as material-handling labor, supervision, and process engineering labor are acquired in discrete quantities but used in fractional quantities.

Panel C in Exhibit 10-9 shows a *step fixed-cost function* for Crofton Steel, a company that operates large heat-treatment furnaces to harden steel parts. Looking at Panel C and Panel B, you can see that the main difference between a step variable-cost function and a step fixed-cost function is that the cost in a step fixed-cost function remains the same over *wide* ranges of the activity in each relevant range. The ranges indicate the number of furnaces being used (each furnace costs $300,000). The cost increases from one range to the next higher range when the hours of furnace time needed require the use of another furnace. The relevant range of 7,500 to 15,000 hours of furnace time indicates that the company expects to operate with two furnaces at a cost of $600,000. Management considers the cost of operating furnaces as a fixed cost within this relevant range of operation. However, if the relevant range is considered to be from 0 to 22,500 hours, the cost function is nonlinear: The graph in Exhibit 10-9, Panel C, is not a single straight line; it is three broken lines.

A major means of cost management is to utilize a particular level of step fixed costs as fully as possible (that is, on a particular step, operate as far to the right side as feasible). For example, in Panel C, needing 15,000 hours of furnace time will fully utilize two furnaces.

LEARNING CURVES AND NONLINEAR COST FUNCTIONS

Nonlinear cost functions also result from learning curves. A **learning curve** is a function that measures how labor-hours per unit decline as units of production increase because workers are learning and becoming better at their jobs. Managers use learning curves to predict how labor-hours, or labor costs, will increase as more units are produced.

The aircraft-assembly industry first documented the effect that learning has on efficiency. In general, as workers become more familiar with their tasks, their efficiency improves. Managers learn how to improve the scheduling of work shifts. Plant operators learn how best to operate the facility. As a result of improved efficiency, unit costs decrease as productivity increases, and the unit-cost function behaves nonlinearly. These nonlinearities must be considered when estimating and predicting unit costs.

Managers are now extending the learning-curve notion to other business functions in the value chain, such as marketing, distribution, and customer service, and to costs other than labor costs. The term *experience curve* describes this broader application of the learning curve. An **experience curve** is a function that measures the decline in cost per unit in various value-chain functions such as marketing, distribution, and so on, as units produced increase.

We now describe two learning-curve models: the cumulative average-time learning model and the incremental unit-time learning model.

Cumulative Average-Time Learning Model

7 Distinguish the cumulative average-time learning model

...average time per unit declines by constant perentage, as units produced double

from the incremental unit-time learning model

...incremental time to produce last unit declines by constant percentage, as units produced double

Question: Does a higher learning percentage (say, 90% rather than 80%) indicate a faster rate of learning?
Answer: No, a higher learning percentage indicates a *slower* rate of learning. For example, consider in Exhibit 10-11 the line for two cumulative units. Under this 80% learning curve, the cumulative average time per unit is 80 labor-hours. If the rate of learning had been 90%, the cumulative average time per unit would have been 90 labor-hours (100 × 0.90).

In the **cumulative average-time learning model**, the cumulative average time per unit declines by a constant percentage each time the cumulative quantity of units produced doubles. Exhibit 10-10 illustrates this model with an 80% learning curve. The 80% means that when the quantity of units produced is doubled from X to $2X$, the cumulative average time *per unit* for the $2X$ units is 80% of the cumulative average time *per unit* for the X units. Average time per unit has dropped by 20% (100% − 80%). In Exhibit 10-10, Panel A shows the cumulative average time per unit as a function of units produced. Panel B shows the cumulative total labor-hours as a function of units produced. The data points underlying Exhibit 10-10, and the details of their calculation, are shown in Exhibit 10-11. Note, as the number of units produced doubles from 1 to 2, the cumulative average time per unit declines from 100 hours to 80% of 100 hours, or 0.80 × 100 hours = 80 hours. As the number of units doubles from 2 to 4, the cumulative average time per unit declines to 80% of 80 hours = 64 hours, and so on. To obtain the cumulative total time, multiply the cumulative average time per unit by the cumulative number of units produced. For example, to produce 4 cumulative units would require 256 labor-hours (4 units × 64 cumulative average labor-hours per unit).

Incremental Unit-Time Learning Model

In the **incremental unit-time learning model**, the incremental time needed to produce the last unit declines by a constant percentage each time the cumulative quantity of units produced doubles. Exhibit 10-12 illustrates this model with an 80% learning curve. The 80% here means that when the quantity of units produced is doubled from X to $2X$, the time needed to produce the last unit when $2X$ total units are produced is 80% of the time needed to produce the last unit when X total units are produced. In Exhibit 10-12, Panel A shows the cumulative average time per unit as a function of cumulative units produced. Panel B in Exhibit 10-12 shows the cumulative total labor-hours as a function of units produced. The data points underlying Exhibit 10-12, and the details of their calculation, are shown in Exhibit 10-13. Note how when the units produced double from 2 to 4, the time to produce unit 4 (the last unit when 4 units are produced) is 64 hours, which is 80% of the 80 hours needed to produce unit 2 (the last unit when 2 units are produced). We obtain the cumulative total time by summing the individual unit times in column 2. For example, to produce 4 cumulative units would require 314.21 labor-hours (100.00 + 80.00 + 70.21 + 64.00).

The incremental unit-time model predicts a higher cumulative total time to produce two or more units than the cumulative average-time model, assuming the same learning rate for both models. If we compare the results in Exhibit 10-11 with the results in Exhibit 10-13, to produce 4 cumulative units, the 80% incremental unit-time learning model predicts 314.21 labor-hours versus 256.00 labor-hours predicted by the 80% cumulative average-time learning model. That's because under the cumulative average-time learning model the *average labor-hours needed to produce all 4 units* is 64 hours; the labor-hour amount needed to produce unit 4 is much less than 64 hours—it is 45.37 hours (see Exhibit 10-11). Under the incremental unit-time learning model, the labor-hour amount needed to produce unit 4 is 64 hours, and the labor-hours needed to produce the first three units are more than 64 hours, so the average time needed to produce all 4 units is more than 64 hours.

EXHIBIT 10-10

Plots for Cumulative Average-Time Learning Model

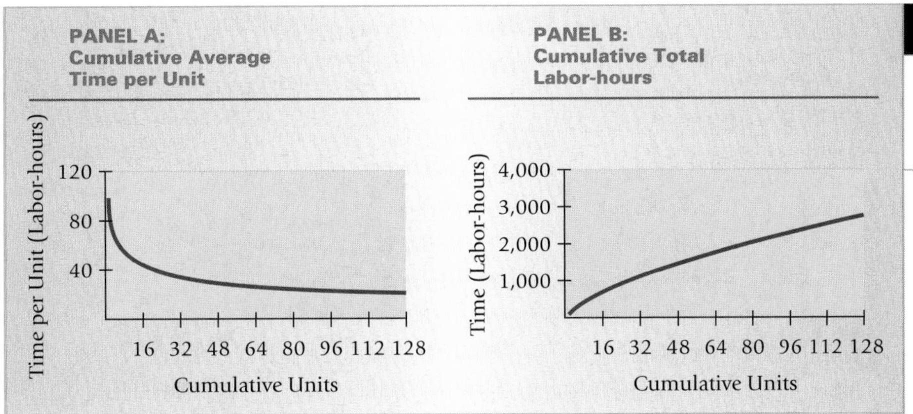

EXHIBIT 10-11

Cumulative Average-Time Learning Model

Cumulative Number of Units (1)	Cumulative Average Time per Unit (y): Labor-Hours (2)	Cumulative Total Time: Labor-Hours (3) = (1) × (2)	Individual Unit Time for Xth Unit: Labor-Hours (4)
1	100.00	100.00	100.00
2	80.00 (100 × 0.8)	160.00	60.00
3	70.21	210.63	50.63
4	64.00 (80 × 0.8)	256.00	45.37
5	59.57	297.85	41.85
6	56.17	337.02	39.17
7	53.45	374.15	37.13
8	51.20 (64 × 0.8)	409.60	35.45
•	•	•	•
•	•	•	•
•	•	•	•
16	40.96 (51.2 × 0.8)	655.36	28.06

Note: The mathematical relationship underlying the cumulative average-time learning model is

$$y = aX^b$$

where
y = Cumulative average time (labor-hours) per unit
X = Cumulative number of unites produced
a = Time (labor-hours) required to produce the first unit
b = Factor used to calculate cumulative average time to produce units

The value of b is calculated as

$$b = \frac{\ln \text{(learning-curve \% in decimal form)}}{\ln 2}$$

For an 80% learning curve,

$$b = \frac{\ln 0.8}{\ln 2} = \frac{-0.2231}{0.6931} = -0.3219$$

As an illustration, when $X = 3$, $a = 100$, and $b = -0.3219$

$$y = 100 \times 3^{-0.3219} = 70.21 \text{ labor-hours}$$

The cumulative total time when $X = 3$ is $70.21 \times 3 = 210.63$ labor-hours.

The individual unit times in column 4 are calculated using the data in column 3. For example, the individual unit time for the third unit is 50.63 labor-hours (210.63 − 160.00).

Which of these two models is preferable? The choice can only be made on a case-by-case basis. For example, if in a particular situation the behavior of manufacturing labor-hour usage as production levels increase follows a pattern like the one predicted by the cumulative average-time learning model, then that model should be used. Engineers, plant managers, and workers are good sources of information on the amount and type of

After collecting data on costs and labor-hours, regression analysis can be used to help managers choose between these two learning curve models.

EXHIBIT 10-12

Plots for Incremental Unit-Time Learning Model

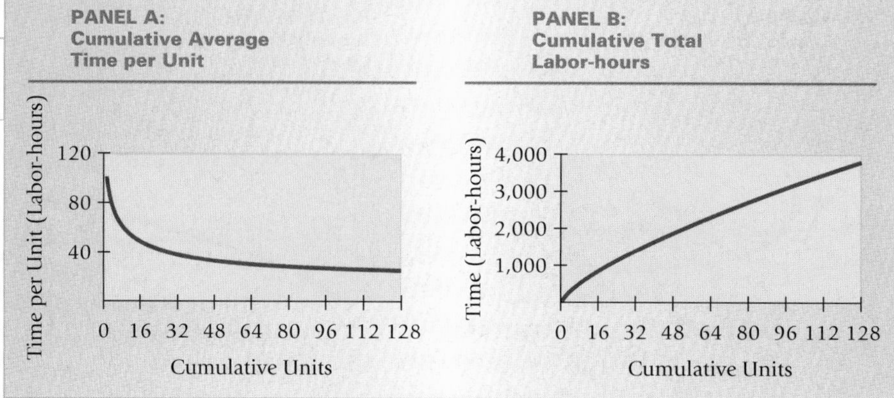

EXHIBIT 10-13

Incremental Unit-Time Learning Model

Cumulative Number of Units (1)	Individual Unit Time for Xth Unit (y): Labor-Hours (2)	Cumulative Total Time: Labor-Hours (3)	Cumulative Average Time per Unit: Labor-Hours (4) = (3) ÷ (1)
1	100.00	100.00	100.00
2	80.00 (100 × 0.8)	180.00	90.00
3	70.21	250.21	83.40
4	64.00 (80 × 0.8)	314.21	78.55
5	59.57	373.78	74.76
6	56.17	429.95	71.66
7	53.45	483.40	69.06
8	51.20 (64 × 0.8)	534.60	66.82
•	•	•	•
•	•	•	•
•	•	•	•
16	40.96 (51.2 × 0.8)	892.00	55.75

Note: The mathematical relationship underlying the incremental unit-time learning model is

$$y = aX^b$$

where y = Time (labor-hours) taken to produce the last single unit
X = Cumulative number of units produced
a = Time (labor-hours) required to produce the first unit
b = Factor used to calculate incremental unit time to produce units

$$b = \frac{\ln(\text{learning-curve\% in decimal form})}{\ln 2}$$

For an 80% learning curve,

$$b = \frac{\ln 0.8}{\ln 2} = \frac{-0.2231}{0.6931} = -0.3219$$

As an illustration, when $X = 3$, $a = 100$, and $b = -0.3219$

$$y = 100 \times 3^{-0.3219} = 70.21 \text{ labor-hours}$$

The cumulative total time when $X = 3$ is $100 + 80 + 70.21 = 250.21$ labor-hours.

learning actually occurring as production increases. Plotting this information is helpful in selecting the appropriate model.[2]

Setting Prices, Budgets, and Standards

How do companies use learning curves? Consider the data in Exhibit 10-11 for the cumulative average-time learning model. Suppose the variable costs subject to learning effects

[2] For details, see C. Bailey, "Learning Curve Estimation of Production Costs and Labor-Hours Using a Free Excel Add-In," *Management Accounting Quarterly*, Summer 2000. Free software for estimating learning curves is available at the Web site (www.bus.ucf.edu/bailey.)

EXHIBIT 10-14

Predicting Costs Using Learning Curves

Cumulative Number of Units	Cumulative Average Time per Unit: Labor-Hours[a]	Cumulative Total Time: Labor-Hours	Cumulative Costs at $50 per Labor-Hour	Additions to Cumulative Costs
1	100.00	100.00	$ 5,000 (100.00 × $50)	$ 5,000
2	80.00	160.00	8,000 (160.00 × $50)	3,000
4	64.00	256.00	12,800 (256.00 × $50)	4,800
8	51.20	409.60	20,480 (409.60 × $50)	7,680
16	40.96	655.36	32,768 (655.36 × $50)	12,288

[a]Based on the cumulative average-time learning model. See Exhibit 10-11 for the computation of these amounts.

consist of direct manufacturing labor, at $20 per hour, and related overhead, at $30 per direct manufacturing labor-hour. Managers should predict the costs shown in Exhibit 10-14.

These data show that the effects of the learning curve could have a major influence on decisions. For example, a company might set an extremely low selling price on its product to generate high demand. As the company's production increases to meet this growing demand, cost per unit drops. The company "rides the product down the learning curve" as it establishes a higher market share. Although the company may have earned little operating income on its first unit sold—it may actually have lost money on that unit—the company earns more operating income per unit as output increases.

Alternatively, subject to legal and other considerations, the company might set a low price on just the final 8 units. After all, the labor and related overhead cost per unit for these final 8 units is predicted to be only $12,288 ($32,768 − $20,480). On these final 8 units, the $1,536 cost per unit ($12,288 ÷ 8 units) is much lower than the $5,000 cost per unit of the first unit produced.

Many companies incorporate learning-curve effects when evaluating performance. For example, the Nissan Motor Company expects its workers to learn and improve on the job and evaluates performance accordingly. It sets assembly-labor efficiency standards for new models of cars after taking into account the learning that will occur as more units are produced.

The learning-curve models examined in Exhibits 10-11 to 10-14 assume that learning is driven by a single variable (production output). Other models of learning have been developed (by companies such as Analog Devices and Yokogowa Hewlett-Packard) that focus on how quality—rather than manufacturing labor-hours—will change over time, rather than as more units are produced. Some recent studies suggest that factors other than production output, such as job rotation and organizing workers into teams, contribute to learning that improves quality.

DATA COLLECTION AND ADJUSTMENT ISSUES

8 Be aware of data problems encountered in estimating cost functions

...for example, unreliable data and poor recordkeeping, extreme observations, treating fixed costs as if they are variable, and a changing relationship between a cost driver and cost

The ideal database for estimating cost functions quantitatively has two characteristics:

1. *The database should contain numerous reliably measured observations of the cost driver (the independent variable) and the costs (the dependent variable).* Errors in measuring the costs and the cost driver are serious. They result in inaccurate estimates of the effect of the cost driver on costs.
2. *The database should consider for the cost driver many values spanning a wide range.* Using only a few values of the cost driver that are grouped closely considers too small a segment of the relevant range and reduces the confidence in the estimates obtained.

Unfortunately, cost analysts typically do not have the advantage of working with a database having both characteristics. This section outlines some frequently encountered data problems and steps the analyst can take to overcome these problems.

1. The time period for measuring the dependent variable (for example, machine-lubricant costs) does not properly match the period for measuring the cost driver. This problem often arises when accounting records are not kept on the accrual basis. Consider a cost function with machine-lubricant costs as the dependent variable and number of machine-hours as the cost driver. Assume that the lubricant is purchased sporadically and stored for later use. Records maintained on the cash basis will indicate little lubricant consumption in many months and large lubricant consumption in other months. These records present an obviously inaccurate picture of what is actually taking place. The analyst should use accrual accounting to measure consumption of machine lubricants to better match costs with the cost driver in this example.

2. Fixed costs are allocated as if they are variable. For example, costs such as depreciation, insurance, or rent may be allocated to products to calculate cost per unit of output. *The danger is to regard these costs as variable rather than as fixed. They seem to be variable because of the allocation methods used.* To avoid this problem, the analyst should distinguish carefully between fixed costs and variable costs and not treat allocated fixed cost per unit as a variable cost.

3. Data are either not available for all observations or are not uniformly reliable. Missing cost observations often arise from a failure to record a cost or from classifying a cost incorrectly. For example, marketing costs may be understated because costs of sales visits to customers may be incorrectly recorded as customer-service costs. Recording data manually rather than electronically tends to result in a higher percentage of missing observations and erroneously entered observations. Errors also arise when data on cost drivers originate outside the internal accounting system. For example, the Accounting Department may obtain data on testing-hours for medical instruments from the company's Manufacturing Department and data on the number of items shipped to customers from the Distribution Department. These departments might not keep accurate records. To minimize these problems, the cost analyst should design data collection reports that regularly and routinely obtain the required data and should follow up immediately whenever data are missing.

4. Extreme values of observations occur from errors in recording costs (for example, a misplaced decimal point); from nonrepresentative periods (for example, from a period in which a major machine breakdown occurred or from a period in which delay in delivery of materials from an international supplier curtailed production); or from observations outside the relevant range. Analysts should adjust or eliminate unusual observations before estimating a cost relationship.

5. There is no homogeneous relationship between the individual cost items in the dependent variable-cost pool and the cost driver. A homogeneous relationship exists when each activity whose costs are included in the dependent variable has the same cost driver. In this case, a single cost function can be estimated. As discussed in step 2 for estimating a cost function using quantitative analysis (p. 330), when the cost driver for each activity is different, separate cost functions, each with its own cost driver, should be estimated for each activity.

6. The relationship between the cost driver and the cost is not stationary. That is, the underlying process that generated the observations has not remained stable over time. For example, the relationship between number of machine-hours and manufacturing overhead costs is unlikely to be stationary when the data cover a period in which new technology was introduced. One way to see if the relationship is stationary is to split the sample into two parts and estimate separate cost relationships—one for the period before the technology was introduced and one for the period after the technology was introduced. Then, if the estimated coefficients for the two periods are similar, the analyst can pool the data to estimate a single cost relationship. When feasible, pooling data provides a larger data set for the estimation, which increases the confidence in the cost predictions being made.

7. Inflation has affected costs, the cost driver, or both. For example, inflation may cause costs to change even when there is no change in the level of the cost driver. To study the underlying cause-and-effect relationship between the level of the cost driver and costs, the analyst should remove purely inflationary price effects from the data by dividing each cost by the price index on the date the cost was incurred.

In many cases, a cost analyst must expend much effort to reduce the effect of these problems before estimating a cost function on the basis of past data.

PROBLEM FOR SELF-STUDY

The Helicopter Division of Aerospatiale is examining helicopter assembly costs at its plant in Marseilles, France. It has received an initial order for eight of its new land-surveying helicopters. Aerospatiale can adopt one of two methods of assembling the helicopters:

	Labor-Intensive Assembly Method	Machine-Intensive Assembly Method
Direct material cost per helicopter	\$40,000	\$36,000
Direct assembly labor time for first helicopter	2,000 labor-hours	800 labor-hours
Learning curve for assembly labor time per helicopter	85% cumulative average time[a]	90% incremental unit time[b]
Direct assembly labor cost	\$30 per hour	\$30 per hour
Equipment-related indirect manufacturing cost	\$12 per direct-assembly labor-hour	\$45 per direct-assembly labor-hour
Material-handling-related indirect manufacturing cost	50% of direct material cost	50% of direct material cost

[a]Using the formula (p. 341), for an 85% learning curve, $b = \frac{\ln 0.85}{\ln 2} = \frac{-0.1625}{0.6931} = -0.2345$

[b]Using the formula (p. 342), for a 90% learning curve, $b = \frac{\ln 0.90}{\ln 2} = \frac{-0.1053}{0.6931} = -0.1520$

Required

1. How many direct-assembly labor-hours are required to assemble the first eight helicopters under (a) the labor-intensive method and (b) the machine-intensive method?
2. What is the cost of assembling the first eight helicopters under (a) the labor-intensive method and (b) the machine-intensive method?

SOLUTION

1a. Labor-intensive assembly method based on an 85% cumulative average-time learning model:

Cumulative Number of Units (1)	Cumulative Average Time per Unit (*y*): Labor-Hours (2)	Cumulative Total Time: Labor-Hours (3) = 1 × (2)	Individual Unit Time for *X*th Unit: Labor-Hours (4)
1	2,000	2,000	2,000
2	1,700 (2,000 × 0.85)	3,400	1,400
3	1,546	4,638	1,238
4	1,445 (1,700 × 0.85)	5,780	1,142
5	1,371	6,855	1,075
6	1,314	7,884	1,029
7	1,267	8,869	985
8	1,228.25 (1,445 × 0.85)	9,826	957

The cumulative average-time per unit for the Xth unit in column 2 is calculated as $y = aX^b$; see Exhibit 10-11 (p. 341). For example, when $X = 3$, $y = 2{,}000 \times 3^{-0.2345} = 1{,}546$ labor-hours.

1b. Machine-intensive assembly method based on a 90% incremental unit-time learning model:

Cumulative Number of Units (1)	Individual Unit Time for *X*th Unit (y): Labor-Hours (2)	Cumulative Total Time: Labor-Hours (3)	Cumulative Average Time per Unit: Labor-Hours (4) = (3) ÷ (1)
1	800	800	800
2	720 (800 × 0.9)	1,520	760
3	677	2,197	732

Continued

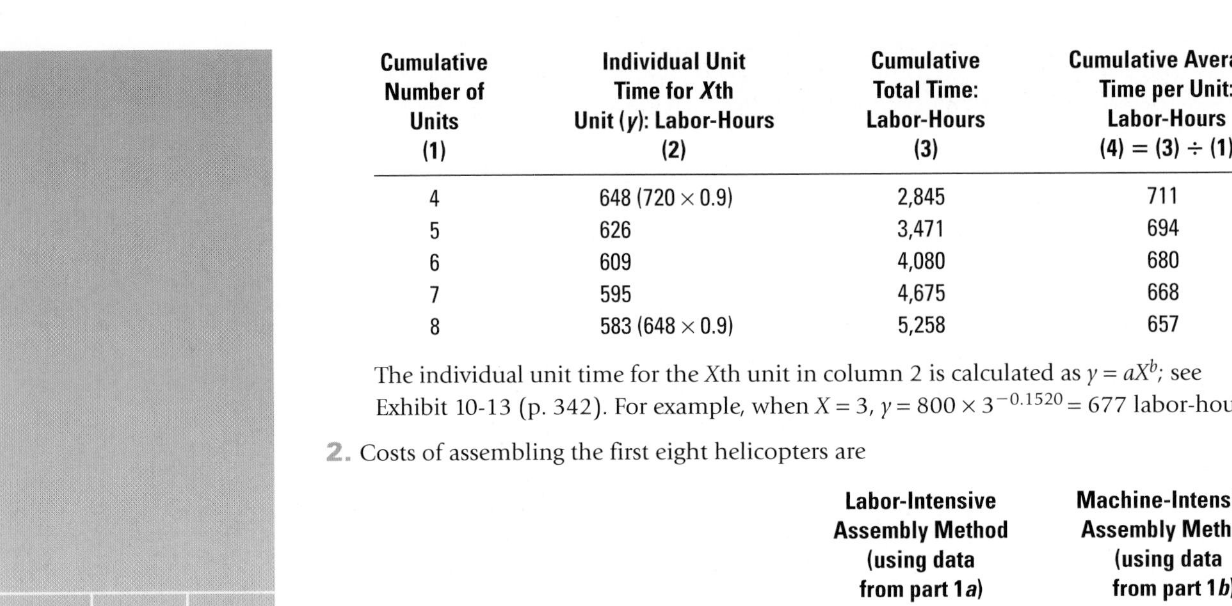

Cumulative Number of Units (1)	Individual Unit Time for *X*th Unit (*y*): Labor-Hours (2)	Cumulative Total Time: Labor-Hours (3)	Cumulative Average Time per Unit: Labor-Hours (4) = (3) ÷ (1)
4	648 (720 × 0.9)	2,845	711
5	626	3,471	694
6	609	4,080	680
7	595	4,675	668
8	583 (648 × 0.9)	5,258	657

The individual unit time for the Xth unit in column 2 is calculated as $y = aX^b$; see Exhibit 10-13 (p. 342). For example, when $X = 3$, $y = 800 \times 3^{-0.1520} = 677$ labor-hours.

2. Costs of assembling the first eight helicopters are

	Labor-Intensive Assembly Method (using data from part 1*a*)	Machine-Intensive Assembly Method (using data from part 1*b*)
Direct materials:		
8 helicopters × \$40,000 per helicopter	\$320,000	
8 helicopters × \$36,000 per helicopter		\$288,000
Direct assembly labor:		
9,826 hrs. × \$30/hr.; 5,258 hrs. × \$30/hr.	294,780	157,740
Indirect manufacturing costs		
Equipment-related:		
9,826 hrs. × \$12/hr.; 5,258 hrs. × \$45/hr.	117,912	236,610
Materials-handling-related:		
0.50 × \$320,000; 0.50 × \$288,000	160,000	144,000
Total assembly costs	\$892,692	\$826,350

The machine-intensive method's assembly costs are \$66,342 lower than the labor-intensive method (\$892,692 − \$826,350).

DECISION POINTS — SUMMARY

The following question-and-answer format summarizes the chapter's learning objectives. Each decision presents a key question related to a learning objective. The guidelines are the answer to that question.

Decision	Guidelines
1. What assumptions are usually made when estimating a cost function?	The two assumptions frequently made in cost-behavior estimation are (a) changes in total costs can be explained by changes in the level of a single activity, and (b) cost behavior can adequately be approximated by a linear function of the activity level within the relevant range.
2. What is a linear cost function and what types of cost behavior can it represent?	A linear cost function is a cost function in which, within the relevant range, the graph of total costs based on the level of a single activity is a straight line. Linear cost functions can be described by a constant, *a*, which represents the estimate of the total cost component that, within the relevant range, does not vary with changes in the level of the activity; and a slope coefficient, *b*, which represents the estimate of the amount by which total costs change for each unit change in the level of the activity within the relevant range. Three types of linear cost functions are variable, fixed, and mixed (or semivariable).

3. What are the different approaches that can be used to estimate a cost function?	Four methods for estimating cost functions are the industrial engineering method, the conference method, the account analysis method, and quantitative analysis methods (the high-low method and the regression analysis method). If possible, the cost analyst should apply more than one method. Each method is a check on the others.
4. What are the steps to estimate a cost function on the basis of an analysis of a past cost relationship?	There are six steps to estimate a cost function on the basis of an analysis of past cost relationships: (a) choose the dependent variable; (b) identify the cost driver; (c) collect data on the dependent variable and the cost driver; (d) plot the data; (e) estimate the cost function; and (f) evaluate the estimated cost function. In most situations, working closely with operations managers, the cost analyst will cycle through these steps several times before identifying an acceptable cost function.
5. How should a company evaluate and choose cost drivers?	Three criteria for evaluating and choosing cost drivers are (a) economic plausibility, (b) goodness of fit, and (c) significance of independent variable.
6. What is a nonlinear cost function and how does it arise?	A nonlinear cost function is a cost function in which the graph of total costs based on the level of a single activity is not a straight line within the relevant range. Nonlinear costs can arise due to quantity discounts, step cost functions, and learning-curve effects.
7. What are the different types of learning curve models a company can use?	The learning curve is an example of a nonlinear cost function. Labor-hours per unit decline as units of production increase. In the cumulative average-time learning model, the cumulative average-time per unit declines by a constant percentage each time the cumulative quantity of units produced doubles. In the incremental unit-time learning model, the incremental unit time (the time needed to produce the last unit) declines by a constant percentage each time the cumulative quantity of units produced doubles.
8. What are the common data problems a company must watch for when estimating costs?	The most difficult task in cost estimation is collecting high-quality, reliably measured data on the costs and the cost driver. Common problems include missing data, extreme values of observations, changes in technology, and distortions resulting from inflation.

APPENDIX: REGRESSION ANALYSIS

This appendix describes the estimation of the regression equation, several commonly used regression statistics, and how to choose among cost functions that have been estimated by regression analysis. We use the data for Elegant Rugs presented in Exhibit 10-3 (p. 330).

Estimating the Regression Line

The least-squares technique for estimating the regression line minimizes the sum of the squares of the vertical deviations from the data points to the estimated regression line (also called *residual term* in Exhibit 10-6, p. 334). The objective is to find the values of a and b in the linear cost function $y = a + bX$, where y is the *predicted* cost value as distinguished from the *observed* cost value, which we denote by Y. We wish to find the numerical values of a and b that minimize $\Sigma(Y - y)^2$, the sum of the squares of the vertical deviations between Y and y. Generally, these computations are done using software packages such as Excel. For the data in our example,[3] $a = \$300.98$ and $b = \$10.31$, so that the equation of the regression line is $y = \$300.98 + \$10.31X$.

Goodness of Fit

Goodness of fit measures how well the predicted values, y, based on the cost driver, X, match actual cost observations, Y. The regression analysis method computes a measure of

[3] The formulae for a and b are

$$a = \frac{(\Sigma Y)(\Sigma X^2) - (\Sigma X)(\Sigma XY)}{n(\Sigma X^2) - (\Sigma X)(\Sigma X)} \quad \text{and} \quad b = \frac{n(\Sigma XY) - (\Sigma X)(\Sigma Y)}{n(\Sigma X^2) - (\Sigma X)(\Sigma X)}$$

where for the Elegant Rugs data in Exhibit 10-3,

Continued

goodness of fit, called the coefficient of determination. The **coefficient of determination, r^2**, measures the percentage of variation in Y explained by X (the independent variable). That is, the coefficient of determination indicates the proportion of the variance of Y that is explained by the independent variable X (where $\overline{Y} = \Sigma Y \div n$). It is more convenient to express the coefficient of determination as 1 minus the proportion of total variance that is *not* explained by the independent variable—that is 1 minus the ratio of unexplained variation to total variation. The unexplained variance arises because of differences between the actual values, Y, and the predicted values, y, which in the Elegant Rugs example is given by[4]

$$r^2 = 1 - \frac{\text{Unexplained variation}}{\text{Total variation}} = 1 - \frac{\Sigma(Y-y)^2}{\Sigma(Y-\overline{Y})^2} = 1 - \frac{290{,}824}{607{,}699} = 0.52$$

The calculations indicate that r^2 increases as the predicted values, y, more closely approximate the actual observations, Y. The range of r^2 is from 0 (implying no explanatory power) to 1 (implying perfect explanatory power). Generally, an r^2 of 0.30 or higher passes the goodness-of-fit test. Do not rely exclusively on goodness of fit. It can lead to the indiscriminate inclusion of independent variables that increase r^2 but have no economic plausibility as cost drivers. Goodness of fit has meaning only if the relationship between the cost drivers and costs is economically plausible.

Significance of Independent Variables

Managers generally find it helpful to consult with a technical expert on regression analysis when obtaining a reliable cost function is crucial to their decisions.

Do changes in the economically plausible independent variable result in significant changes in the dependent variable? Or alternatively stated, is the slope coefficient, b, of the regression line statistically significant (that is, different from \$0)? Recall, for example, that in the regression of number of machine-hours and indirect manufacturing labor costs in the Elegant Rugs illustration, b is estimated from a sample of 12 observations. The estimate b is subject to random factors, as are all sample statistics. That is, a different sample of 12 data points would undoubtedly give a different estimate of b. The **standard error of the estimated coefficient** indicates how much the estimated value b is likely to be affected by random factors. The t-value of the b coefficient measures how large the value of the estimated coefficient is relative to its standard error. With 12 observations and two parameters a and b to be estimated, a cut-off t-value with an absolute value greater than 2.228 suggests that the b coefficient is significantly different from \$0.[5] In other

---

n = number of data points = 12

ΣX = sum of the given X values = $68 + 88 + \cdots + 48 = 862$

ΣX^2 = sum of squares of the X values = $(68)^2 + (88)^2 + \cdots + (48)^2 = 4{,}624 + 7{,}744 + \cdots + 2{,}304 = 64{,}900$

ΣY = sum of given Y values = $1{,}190 + 1{,}211 + \cdots + 963 = 12{,}501$

ΣXY = sum of the amounts obtained by multiplying each of the given X values by the associated observed Y value = $(68)(1{,}190) + (88)(1{,}211) + \cdots + (48)(963)$ $= 80{,}920 + 106{,}568 + \cdots + 46{,}224 = 928{,}716$

$$a = \frac{(12{,}501)(64{,}900) - (862)(928{,}716)}{12(64{,}900) - (862)(862)} = \$300.98$$

$$b = \frac{12(928{,}716) - (862)(12{,}501)}{12(64{,}900) - (862)(862)} = \$10.31$$

[4]From footnote 3, $\Sigma Y = 12{,}501$ and $\overline{Y} = 12{,}501 \div 12 = 1{,}041.75$.

$$\Sigma(Y-\overline{Y})^2 = (1{,}190 - 1{,}041.75)^2 + (1{,}211 - 1{,}041.75)^2 + \cdots + (963 - 1{,}041.75)^2 = 607{,}699$$

Each value of X generates a predicted value of y. For example, in week 1, $y = \$300.98 + (\$10.31 \times 68) = \$1002.06$; in week 2, $y = \$300.98 + (\$10.31 \times 88) = \$1{,}208.26$; and in week 12, $y = \$300.98 + (\$10.31 \times 48) = \$795.86$.

$$\Sigma(Y-y)^2 = (1{,}190 - 1{,}002.06)^2 + (1{,}211 - 1{,}208.26)^2 + \cdots + (963 - 795.86)^2 = 290{,}824$$

[5]The cut-off t-value for inferring that a b coefficient is significantly different from 0 is a function of the number of degrees of freedom in regression analysis. The number of degrees of freedom is calculated as the sample size

Simple Regression Results with Indirect Manufacturing Labor Costs as Dependent Variable and Machine-Hours as Independent Variable (Cost Driver) for Elegant Rugs

Variable	Coefficient (1)	Standard Error (2)	*t*-Value (3) = (1) ÷ (2)
Constant	\$300.98	\$229.75	1.31
Independent variable 1: Machine-hours	\$10.31	\$3.12	3.30
$r^2 = 0.52$; Durbin-Watson statistic = 2.05			

words, a relationship exists between the independent variable and the dependent variable that cannot be attributed to random chance alone.

Exhibit 10-15 shows a convenient format for summarizing the regression results for number of machine-hours and indirect manufacturing labor costs. The *t*-value for the slope coefficient *b* is \$10.31 ÷ \$3.12 = 3.30, which exceeds the cut-off *t*-value of 2.228. Therefore, the coefficient of the machine-hours variable is significantly different from \$0—that is, the probability is low (less than 5%) that random factors could have caused the coefficient *b* to be positive. Alternatively, we can restate our conclusion in terms of a *confidence interval*: There is less than a 5% chance that the true value of the machine-hours coefficient lies outside the range \$10.31 ± (2.228 × \$3.12), or \$10.31 ± \$6.95, or from \$3.36 to \$17.26. Therefore, we can conclude that changes in number of machine-hours do affect indirect manufacturing labor costs. Similarly, using data from Exhibit 10-15, the *t*-value for the constant term *a* is \$300.98 ÷ \$229.75 = 1.31, which is less than 2.228. This *t*-value indicates that, within the relevant range, the constant term is *not* significantly different from zero. The only statistic not discussed in Exhibit 10-15, the Durbin-Watson statistic, will be discussed in the following section.

Specification Analysis of Estimation Assumptions

Specification analysis is the testing of the assumptions of regression analysis. If the assumptions of (1) linearity within the relevant range, (2) constant variance of residuals, (3) independence of residuals, and (4) normality of residuals all hold, then the simple regression procedures give reliable estimates of coefficient values. This section provides a brief overview of specification analysis. When these assumptions are not satisfied, more-complex regression procedures are necessary to obtain the best estimates.[6]

1. *Linearity within the relevant range.* A common assumption—and one that appears to be reasonable in many business applications—is that a linear relationship exists between the independent variable *X* and the dependent variable *Y* within the relevant range. If a linear regression model is used to estimate a nonlinear relationship, however, the coefficient estimates obtained will be inaccurate.

   When there is only one independent variable, the easiest way to check for linearity is to study the data plotted on a scatter diagram, a step that often is unwisely skipped. Exhibit 10-6 (p. 334) presents a scatter diagram for the indirect manufacturing labor costs and machine-hours variables of Elegant Rugs shown in Exhibit 10-3 (p. 330). The scatter diagram reveals that linearity appears to be a reasonable assumption for these data.

   The learning-curve models discussed in this chapter (pp. 339–343) are examples of nonlinear cost functions. Costs increase when the level of production increases, but by lesser amounts than would occur with a linear cost function. In this case, the analyst should estimate a nonlinear cost function that incorporates learning effects.

2. *Constant variance of residuals.* The vertical deviation of the observed value *Y* from the regression line estimate *y* is called the *residual term, disturbance term,* or *error term,* $u = Y - y$. The assumption of constant variance implies that the residual terms are unaffected by

minus the number of parameters (in this example, two, *a* and *b*) estimated in the regression. The cut-off *t*-value of 2.00 assumes 60 degrees of freedom. The smaller the sample size, the greater is the cut-off *t*-value. For 10 degrees of freedom, the cut-off *t*-value is 2.228.

[6] For details see, for example, W. H. Greene, *Econometric Analysis*, 4th ed. (Upper Saddle River, NJ: Prentice Hall, 2000).

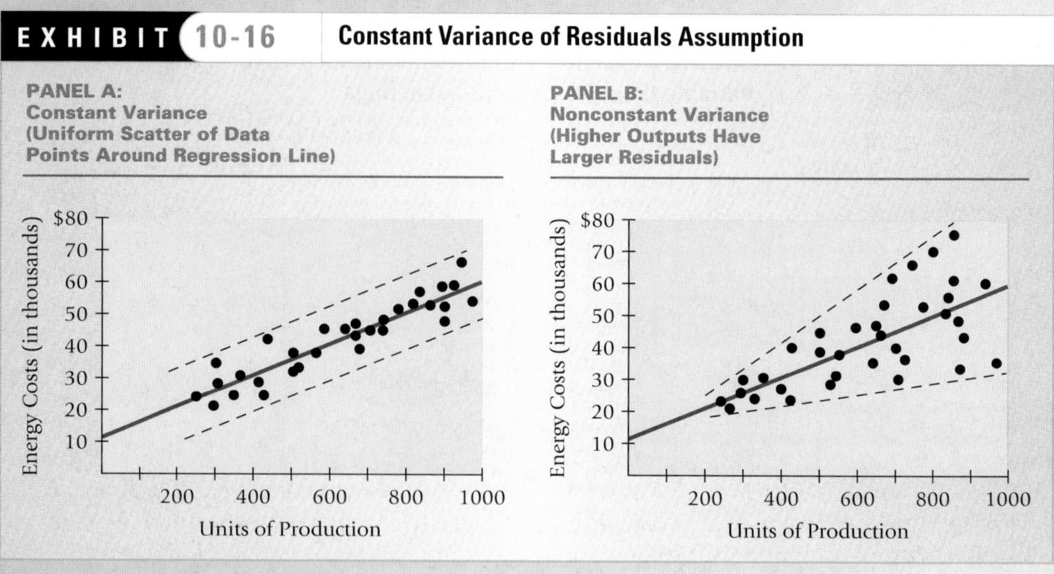

the level of the cost driver. The assumption also implies that there is a uniform scatter, or dispersion, of the data points about the regression line. The scatter diagram is the easiest way to check for constant variance. This assumption holds for Panel A, but not for Panel B, of Exhibit 10-16. Constant variance is also known as *homoscedasticity*. Violation of this assumption is called *heteroscedasticity*.

Heteroscedasticity does not affect the accuracy of the regression estimates a and b. It does, however, reduce the reliability of the estimates of the standard errors, and thus affects the precision with which inferences can be drawn.

3. *Independence of residuals*. The assumption of independence of residuals is that the residual term for any one observation is not related to the residual term for any other observation. The problem of *serial correlation* in the residuals (also called *autocorrelation*) arises when there is a systematic pattern in the sequence of residuals such that the residual in observation n conveys information about the residuals in observations $n + 1$, $n + 2$, and so on. The scatter diagram helps in identifying autocorrelation. Autocorrelation does not exist in Panel A, but it does in Panel B of Exhibit 10-17. Observe the systematic pattern of the residuals in Panel B—positive residuals for extreme (high and low) quantities of direct materials used and negative residuals for moderate quantities of direct materials used. No such pattern exists in Panel A.

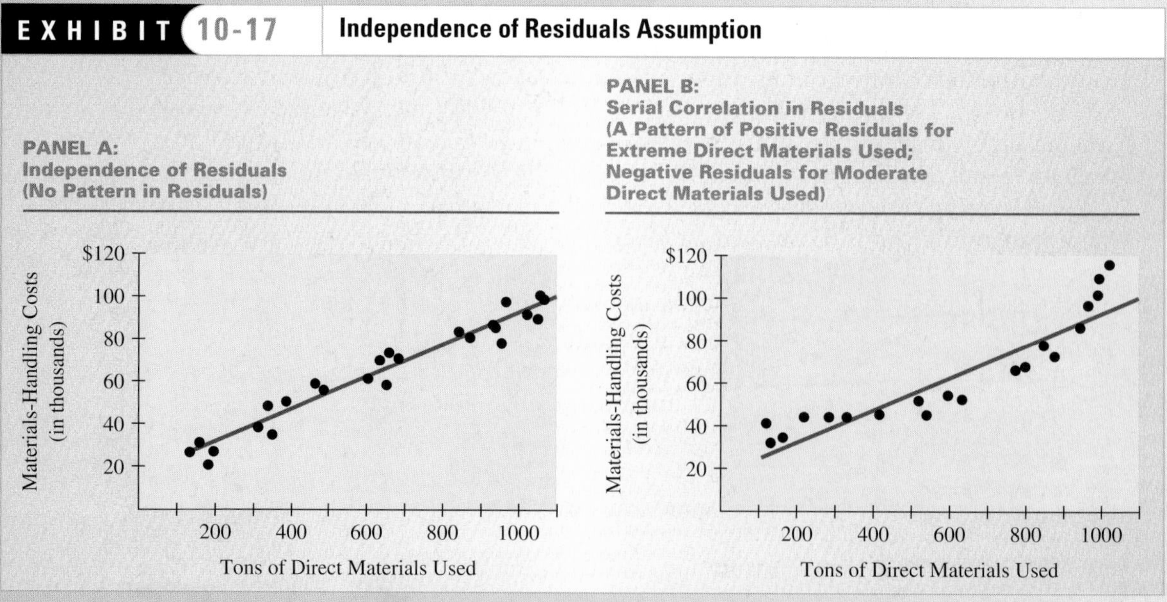

Like nonconstant variance of residuals, serial correlation does not affect the accuracy of the regression estimates a and b. It does, however, affect the standard errors of the coefficients, which in turn affect the precision with which inferences about the population parameters can be drawn from the regression estimates.

The Durbin-Watson statistic is one measure of serial correlation in the estimated residuals. For samples of 10 to 20 observations, a Durbin-Watson statistic in the 1.10 – 2.90 range indicates that the residuals are independent. The Durbin-Watson statistic for the regression results of Elegant Rugs in Exhibit 10-15 is 2.05. Therefore, an assumption of independence in the estimated residuals is reasonable for this regression model.

4. *Normality of residuals.* The normality of residuals assumption means that the residuals are distributed normally around the regression line. This assumption is necessary for making inferences about y, a, and b.

Using Regression Output to Choose Cost Drivers of Cost Functions

Consider the two choices of cost drivers we described earlier in this chapter for indirect manufacturing labor costs (y):

$$y = a + (b \times \text{Number of machine-hours})$$
$$y = a + (b \times \text{Number of direct manufacturing labor-hours})$$

Exhibits 10-6 and 10-8 show plots of the data for the two regressions. Exhibit 10-15 reports regression results for the cost function using number of machine-hours as the independent variable. Exhibit 10-18 presents comparable regression results for the cost function using number of direct manufacturing labor-hours as the independent variable.

On the basis of the material presented in this appendix, which regression is better? Exhibit 10-19 compares these two cost functions in a systematic way. For several criteria, the cost function based on machine-hours is preferable to the cost function based on direct manufacturing labor-hours. The economic plausibility criterion is especially important.

Do not always assume that any one cost function will perfectly satisfy all the criteria in Exhibit 10-19. A cost analyst must often make a choice among "imperfect" cost functions, in the sense that the data of any particular cost function will not perfectly meet one or more of the assumptions underlying regression analysis. For example, both of the cost functions in Exhibit 10-19 are imperfect because, as stated in the section on specification analysis of estimation assumptions, inferences drawn from only 12 observations are not reliable.

Multiple Regression and Cost Hierarchies

In some cases, a satisfactory estimation of a cost function may be based on only one independent variable, such as number of machine-hours. In many cases, however, basing the estimation on more than one independent variable (that is, multiple regression) is more economically plausible and improves accuracy. The most widely used equations to express relationships between two or more independent variables and a dependent variable are linear in the form

$$Y = a + b_1X_1 + b_2X_2 + \cdots + u$$

Simple Regression Results with Indirect Manufacturing Labor Costs as Dependent Variable and Direct Manufacturing Labor-Hours as Independent Variable (Cost Driver) for Elegant Rugs

Variable	Coefficient (1)	Standard Error (2)	*t*-Value (3) = (1) ÷ (2)
Constant	\$744.67	\$217.61	3.42
Independent variable 1: Direct manufacturing labor-hours	\$7.72	\$5.40	1.43
$r^2 = 0.17$; Durbin-Watson statistic = 2.26			

EXHIBIT 10-19

Comparison of Alternative Cost Functions for Indirect Manufacturing Labor Costs Estimated with Simple Regression for Elegant Rugs

Criterion	Cost Function 1: Machine-Hours as Independent Variable	Cost Function 2: Direct Manufacturing Labor-Hours as Independent Variable
Economic plausibility	A positive relationship between indirect manufacturing labor costs (technical support labor) and machine hours is economically plausible in Elegant Rugs' highly automated plant.	A positive relationship between indirect manufacturing labor costs and direct manufacturing labor-hours is economically plausible, but less so than machine-hours in Elegant Rugs' highly automated plant on a week-to-week basis.
Goodness of fit[a]	$r^2 = 0.52$ Excellent goodness of fit.	$r^2 = 0.17$ Poor goodness of fit.
Significance of independent variable(s)	The t-value of 3.30 is significant.	The t-value of 1.43 is not significant.
Specification analysis of estimation assumptions	Plot of the data indicates that assumptions of linearity, constant variance, independence of residuals, (Durbin-Watson statistic = 2.05), and normality of residuals hold, but inferences drawn from only 12 observations are not reliable.	Plot of the data indicates that assumptions of linearity, constant variance, independence of residuals (Durbin-Watson statistic = 2.26) and normality of residuals hold, but inferences drawn from only 12 observations are not reliable.

[a]If the number of observations available to estimate the machine-hour regression differs from the number of observations available to estimate the direct manufacturing labor-hours regression, an *adjusted* r^2 can be calculated to take this difference (in degrees of freedom) into account. Programs such as Excel calculate and present *adjusted* r^2.

where

Y = Cost to be predicted
$X_1, X_2, \cdots$ = Independent variables on which the prediction is to be based
$a, b_1, b_2, \cdots$ = Estimated coefficients of the regression model
u = Residual term that includes the net effect of other factors not in the model as well as measurement errors in the dependent and independent variables

Multiple regression analysis is useful for estimating total costs when different levels of the cost hierarchy are involved. This example uses number of machine-hours (an output unit-level cost driver) and number of production batches (a batch-level cost driver).

Example Consider the Elegant Rugs data in Exhibit 10-20 (p. 353). The company's ABC analysis indicates that indirect manufacturing labor costs include large costs incurred for setup and changeover costs when a new batch of carpets is started. Management believes that in addition to number of machine-hours (an output unit-level cost driver), indirect manufacturing labor costs are also affected by the number of production batches of carpet manufactured during each week (a batch-level driver). Elegant Rugs estimates the relationship between two independent variables, number of machine-hours and number of production batches of carpet manufactured during the week, and indirect manufacturing labor costs.

Exhibit 10-21 presents results for the following multiple regression model, using data in columns 1, 2, and 4 of Exhibit 10-20:

$$y = \$42.58 + \$7.60X_1 + \$37.77X_2$$

where X_1 is the number of machine-hours and X_2 is the number of production batches. It is economically plausible that both number of machine-hours and number of production batches would help explain variations in indirect manufacturing labor costs at Elegant Rugs. The r^2 of 0.52 for the simple regression using number of machine-hours (Exhibit 10-16) increases to 0.72 with the multiple regression in Exhibit 10-21. The t-values suggest that the independent variable coefficients of both number of machine-hours and number of production batches are significantly different from zero ($t = 2.74$ is the coefficient for

Week	Indirect Manufacturing Labor Costs (1)	Machine-Hours (2)	Direct Manufacturing Labor-Hours (3)	Number of Production Batches (4)
1	$1,190	68	30	12
2	1,211	88	35	15
3	1,004	62	36	13
4	917	72	20	11
5	770	60	47	10
6	1,456	96	45	12
7	1,180	78	44	17
8	710	46	38	7
9	1,316	82	70	14
10	1,032	94	30	12
11	752	68	29	7
12	963	48	38	14

EXHIBIT 10-20

Weekly Indirect Manufacturing Labor Costs, Machine-Hours, Direct Manufacturing Labor-Hours, and Number of Production Batches for Elegant Rugs

number of machine-hours, and $t = 2.48$ is the coefficient for number of production batches). The multiple regression model in Exhibit 10-21 satisfies both economic plausibility and statistical criteria, and it explains much greater variation (that is, r^2 of 0.72 versus r^2 of 0.52) in indirect manufacturing labor costs than the simple regression model using only number of machine-hours as the independent variable. Number of machine-hours and number of production batches are important cost drivers of indirect manufacturing labor costs at Elegant Rugs.

In Exhibit 10-21, the slope coefficients—\$7.60 for number of machine-hours and \$37.77 for number of production batches—measure the change in indirect manufacturing labor costs associated with a unit change in an independent variable (assuming that the other independent variable is held constant). For example, indirect manufacturing labor costs increase by \$37.77 when one more production batch is added, assuming that the number of machine-hours is held constant.

An alternative approach would create two separate cost pools—one for costs related to number of machine-hours and another for costs related to number of production batches. Elegant Rugs would then estimate the relationship between the cost driver and the costs in each cost pool. The difficult task under this approach would be properly dividing the indirect manufacturing labor costs into the two cost pools.

Multicollinearity

A major concern that arises with multiple regression is multicollinearity. **Multicollinearity** exists when two or more independent variables are highly correlated with each other. Generally, users of regression analysis believe that a coefficient of correlation between independent variables greater than 0.70 indicates multicollinearity. Multicollinearity increases the standard errors of the coefficients of the individual

EXHIBIT 10-21 **Multiple Regression Results with Indirect Manufacturing Labor Costs and Two Independent Variables or Cost Drivers (Machine-Hours and Production Batches) for Elegant Rugs**

Variable	Coefficient (1)	Standard Error (2)	*t*-Value (3) = (1) ÷ (2)
Constant	$42.58	$213.91	0.20
Independent variable 1:			
Machine-hours	$7.60	$2.77	2.74
Independent variable 2:			
Number of production batches	$37.77	$15.25	2.48
$r^2 = 0.72$; Durbin-Watson statistic = 2.49			

variables. That is, variables that are economically and statistically significant will appear not to be significantly different from zero.

The coefficients of correlation between the potential independent variables for Elegant Rugs in Exhibit 10-20 are

Combinations of Pairs of Independent Variables	Coefficient of Correlation
Machine-hours and direct manufacturing labor-hours	0.12
Machine-hours and production batches	0.40
Direct manufacturing labor-hours and production batches	0.31

These results indicate that multiple regressions using any pair of the independent variables in Exhibit 10-21 are not likely to encounter multicollinearity problems.

When multicollinearity exists, try to obtain new data that do not suffer from multicollinearity problems. Do not drop an independent variable (cost driver) that should be included in a model because it is correlated with another independent variable. Omitting such a variable will cause the estimated coefficient of the independent variable included in the model to be biased away from its true value.

TERMS TO LEARN

This chapter and the Glossary at the end of this book contain definitions of:

account analysis method (p. 329)
coefficient of determination (r^2) (348)
conference method (329)
constant (325)
cost estimation (326)
cost function (324)
cost predictions (327)
cumulative average-time learning model (340)
dependent variable (330)
experience curve (340)
high-low method (332)
incremental unit-time learning model (340)
independent variable (330)
industrial engineering method (329)
intercept (325)
learning curve (339)
linear cost function (324)
mixed cost (325)
multicollinearity (353)
multiple regression (334)
nonlinear cost function (338)
regression analysis (333)
residual term (334)
semivariable cost (325)
simple regression (334)
slope coefficient (325)
specification analysis (349)
standard error of the estimated coefficient (348)
step cost function (338)
work-measurement method (329)

ASSIGNMENT MATERIAL

Questions

10-1 What two assumptions are frequently made when estimating a cost function?

10-2 Describe three alternative linear cost functions.

10-3 What is the difference between a linear and a nonlinear cost function? Give an example of each type of cost function.

10-4 "High correlation between two variables means that one is the cause and the other is the effect." Do you agree? Explain.

10-5 Name four approaches to estimating a cost function.

10-6 Describe the conference method for estimating a cost function. What are two advantages of this method?

10-7 Describe the account analysis method for estimating a cost function.

10-8 List the six steps in estimating a cost function on the basis of an analysis of a past cost relationship. Which step is typically the most difficult for the cost analyst?

10-9 When using the high-low method, should you base the high and low observations on the dependent variable or on the cost driver?

10-10 Describe three criteria for evaluating cost functions and choosing cost drivers.

10-11 Define learning curve. Outline two models that can be used when incorporating learning into the estimation of cost functions.

10-12 Discuss four frequently encountered problems when collecting cost data on variables included in a cost function.

10-13 What are the four key assumptions examined in specification analysis in the case of simple regression?

10-14 "All the independent variables in a cost function estimated with regression analysis are cost drivers." Do you agree? Explain.

10-15 "Multicollinearity exists when the dependent variable and the independent variable are highly correlated." Do you agree? Explain.

Exercises

10-16 Estimating a cost function. The controller of the Ijiri Company wants you to estimate a cost function from the following two observations in a general ledger account called Maintenance:

Month	Machine-Hours	Maintenance Costs Incurred
January	4,000	$3,000
February	7,000	3,900

Required

1. Estimate the cost function for maintenance.
2. Can the constant in the cost function be used as an estimate of fixed maintenance cost per month? Explain.

10-17 Identifying variable-, fixed-, and mixed-cost functions. The Pacific Corporation operates car rental agencies at more than 20 airports. Customers can choose from one of three contracts for car rentals of one day or less:

- Contract 1: $50 for the day
- Contract 2: $30 for the day plus $0.20 per mile traveled
- Contract 3: $1 per mile traveled

Required

1. Plot separate graphs for each of the three contracts, with costs on the vertical axis and miles traveled on the horizontal axis.
2. Express each contract as a linear cost function of the form $y = a + bX$.
3. Identify each contract as a variable-, fixed-, or mixed-cost function.

10-18 Various cost-behavior patterns. (CPA, adapted) Select the graph that matches the numbered manufacturing cost data. Indicate by letter which graph best fits the situation or item described.

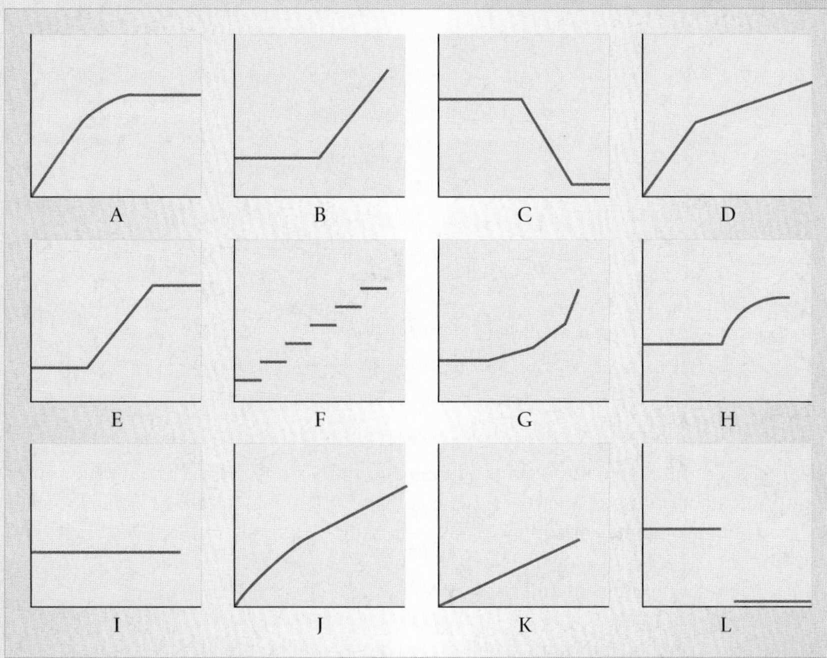

The vertical axes of the graphs represent total cost, and the horizontal axes represent units produced during a calendar year. In each case, the zero point of dollars and production is at the intersection of the two axes. The graphs may be used more than once.

1. Annual depreciation of equipment, where the amount of depreciation charged is computed by the machine-hours method.
2. Electricity bill—a flat fixed charge, plus a variable cost after a certain number of kilowatt-hours are used, in which the quantity of kilowatt-hours used varies proportionately with quantity of units produced.
3. City water bill, which is computed as follows:

First 1,000,000 gallons or less	$1,000 flat fee
Next 10,000 gallons	$0.003 per gallon used
Next 10,000 gallons	$0.006 per gallon used
Next 10,000 gallons	$0.009 per gallon used
and so on	and so on

   The gallons of water used vary proportionately with the quantity of production output.
4. Cost of direct materials, where direct material cost per unit produced decreases with each pound of material used (for example, if 1 pound is used, the cost is $10; if 2 pounds are used, the cost is $19.98; if 3 pounds are used, the cost is $29.94), with a minimum cost per unit of $9.20.
5. Annual depreciation of equipment, where the amount is computed by the straight-line method. When the depreciation schedule was prepared, it was anticipated that the obsolescence factor would be greater than the wear-and-tear factor.
6. Rent on a manufacturing plant donated by the city, where the agreement calls for a fixed-fee payment unless 200,000 labor-hours are worked, in which case no rent is paid.
7. Salaries of repair personnel, where one person is needed for every 1,000 machine-hours or less (that is, 0–1,000 hours requires one person, 1,001–2,000 hours requires two people, and so on).
8. Cost of direct materials used (assume no quantity discounts).
9. Rent on a manufacturing plant donated by the county, where the agreement calls for rent of $100,000 to be reduced by $1 for each direct manufacturing labor-hour worked in excess of 200,000 hours, but a minimum rental fee of $20,000 must be paid.

10-19 Matching graphs with descriptions of cost and revenue behavior. (D. Green, adapted) Given below are a number of graphs.

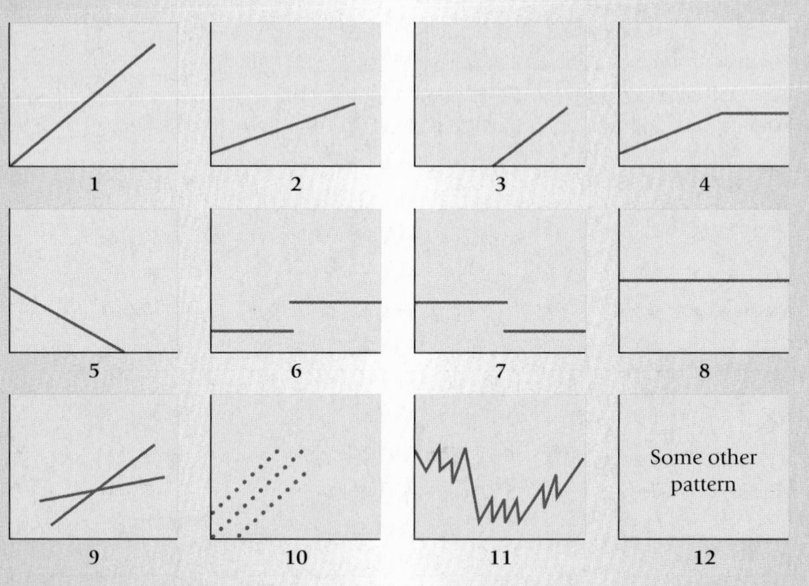

If the horizontal axis represents the units produced over the year and the vertical axis represents *total* cost or revenue, indicate by number which graph best fits the situation or item described. Some graphs may be used more than once; some may not apply to any of the situations.

a. Direct materials costs
b. Supervisors' salaries for one shift and two shifts
c. A cost-volume-profit graph
d. Mixed costs—for example, car rental fixed charge plus variable rate for miles driven
e. Depreciation of plant, computed on a straight-line basis
f. Data supporting the use of a variable-cost rate, such as manufacturing labor cost of $14 per unit produced
g. Incentive bonus plan that pays managers $0.10 for every unit produced above some level of production
h. Interest expense on $2 million borrowed at a fixed rate of interest

10-20 Account analysis method. Lorenzo operates a car wash. Incoming cars are put on an automatic conveyor belt. Cars are washed as the conveyor belt carries the car from the start station to the finish station. After the car moves off the conveyor belt, the car is dried manually. Workers then clean and vacuum the inside of the car. Lorenzo serviced 80,000 cars in 2004. Lorenzo reports the following costs for 2004.

Account Description	Costs
Car wash labor	$240,000
Soap, cloth, and supplies	32,000
Water	28,000
Electric power to move conveyor belt	72,000
Depreciation	64,000
Salaries	46,000

Required

1. Classify each account as variable or fixed with respect to the number of cars washed. Explain.
2. Lorenzo expects to wash 90,000 cars in 2005. Use the cost classification you developed in requirement 1 to estimate Lorenzo's total costs in 2005. Depreciation is computed on a straight-line basis.

10-21 Account analysis method. Gower, Inc., a manufacturer of plastic products, reports the following manufacturing costs and account analysis classification for the year ended December 31, 2004.

Account	Classification	Amount
Direct materials	All variable	$300,000
Direct manufacturing labor	All variable	225,000
Power	All variable	37,500
Supervision labor	20% variable	56,250
Materials-handling labor	50% variable	60,000
Maintenance labor	40% variable	75,000
Depreciation	0% variable	95,000
Rent, property taxes, and administration	0% variable	100,000

Gower, Inc., produced 75,000 units of product in 2004. Gower's management is estimating costs for 2005 on the basis of 2004 numbers. The following additional information is available for 2005.

a. Direct materials prices in 2005 are expected to increase by 5% compared with 2004.
b. Under the terms of the labor contract, direct manufacturing labor wage rates are expected to increase by 10% in 2005 compared with 2004.
c. Power rates and wage rates for supervision, materials handling, and maintenance are not expected to change from 2004 to 2005.
d. Depreciation costs are expected to increase by 5%, and rent, property taxes, and administration costs are expected to increase by 7%.
e. Gower, Inc., expects to manufacture and sell 80,000 units in 2005.

Required

1. Prepare a schedule of variable, fixed, and total manufacturing costs for each account category in 2005. Estimate total manufacturing costs for 2005.
2. Calculate Gower's total manufacturing cost per unit in 2004, and estimate total manufacturing cost per unit in 2005.
3. How can you obtain better estimates of fixed and variable costs? Why would these better estimates be useful to Gower?

10-22 Estimating a cost function, high-low method. Laurie Daley is examining customer-service costs in the Southern Region of Capitol Products. Capitol Products has more than 200 separate electrical products that are sold with a 6-month guarantee of full repair or replacement with a new product. When a product is returned by a customer, a service report is prepared. This service report includes details of the problem and the time and cost of resolving the problem. Weekly data for the most recent 10-week period are

Week	Customer-Service Department Costs	Number of Service Reports
1	$13,845	201
2	20,624	276
3	12,941	122
4	18,452	386
5	14,843	274
6	21,890	436
7	16,831	321
8	21,429	328
9	18,267	243
10	16,832	161

Required

1. Plot the relationship between customer-service costs and number of service reports. Is the relationship economically plausible?
2. Use the high-low method to compute the cost function, relating customer-service costs to the number of service reports.
3. What variables, in addition to number of service reports, might be cost drivers of monthly customer-service costs of Capitol Products?

10-23 **Linear cost approximation.** Terry Lawler, managing director of the Memphis Consulting Group, is examining how overhead costs behave with changes in monthly professional labor-hours billed to clients. Assume the following historical data:

Total Overhead Costs	Professional Labor-Hours Billed to Clients
$340,000	3,000
400,000	4,000
435,000	5,000
477,000	6,000
529,000	7,000
587,000	8,000

Required

1. Compute the linear cost function, relating total overhead cost to professional labor-hours, using the representative observations of 4,000 and 7,000 hours. Plot the linear cost function. Does the constant component of the cost function represent the fixed overhead costs of the Memphis Consulting Group? Why?
2. What would be the predicted total overhead costs for (a) 5,000 hours and (b) 8,000 hours using the cost function estimated in requirement 1? Plot the predicted costs and actual costs for 5,000 and 8,000 hours.
3. Lawler had a chance to accept a special job that would have boosted professional labor-hours from 4,000 to 5,000 hours. Suppose Lawler, guided by the linear cost function, rejected this job because it would have brought a total increase in contribution margin of $38,000, before deducting the predicted increase in total overhead cost, $43,000. What is the total contribution margin actually forgone?

10-24 **Cost-volume-profit and regression analysis.** Garvin Corporation manufactures a children's bicycle, model CT8. Garvin currently manufactures the bicycle frame. During 2002, Garvin made 30,000 frames at a total cost of $900,000. Ryan Corporation has offered to supply as many frames as Garvin wants at a cost of $28.50 per frame. Garvin anticipates needing 36,000 frames each year for the next few years.

Required

1. a. What is the average cost of manufacturing a bicycle frame in 2002? How does it compare to Ryan's offer?
   b. Can Garvin use the answer in requirement 1a to determine the cost of manufacturing 36,000 bicycle frames? Explain.
2. Garvin's cost analyst uses annual data from past years to estimate the following regression equation with total manufacturing costs of the bicycle frame as the dependent variable and bicycle frames produced as the independent variable

$$y = \$432{,}000 + \$15X$$

   During the years used to estimate the regression equation, the production of bicycle frames had varied from 28,000 to 36,000. Using this equation, estimate how much it would cost Garvin to manufacture 36,000 bicycle frames. How much more or less costly is it to manufacture the frames rather than to acquire them from Ryan?
3. What other information would you need in order to be confident that the equation in requirement 2 accurately predicts the cost of manufacturing bicycle frames?

10-25 **Regression analysis, service company.** (CMA, adapted) Bob Jones owns a catering company that prepares banquets and parties. For a standard cocktail party the cost on a per-person basis is

Food and beverages	$15
Labor (0.5 hour × $10 per hour)	5
Overhead (0.5 hour × $14 per hour)	7
Total cost per person	$27

Jones is quite certain about his estimates of the food, beverages, and labor costs but is not as comfortable with the overhead estimate. The overhead estimate was based on the actual data for the past 12 months presented below. These data indicate that overhead costs vary with the direct labor-hours used. The $14 estimate was determined by dividing total overhead costs for the 12 months by total labor-hours.

Month	Labor-Hours	Overhead Costs
January	2,500	$ 55,000
February	2,700	59,000
March	3,000	60,000
April	4,200	64,000
May	7,500	77,000
June	5,500	71,000
July	6,500	74,000
August	4,500	67,000
September	7,000	75,000
October	4,500	68,000
November	3,100	62,000
December	6,500	73,000
Total	57,500	$805,000

Jones has recently become aware of regression analysis. He estimated the following regression equation with overhead costs as the dependent variable and labor-hours as the independent variable.

$$y = \$48,271 + \$3.93X$$

Required

1. Plot the relationship between overhead costs and labor-hours. Draw the regression line and evaluate it using the criteria of economic plausibility, goodness of fit, and slope of the regression line.
2. Using data from the regression analysis, what is the variable cost per person for a cocktail party?
3. Bob Jones has been asked to prepare a bid for a 200-person cocktail party to be given next month. Determine the minimum bid price that Jones would be willing to submit to recoup variable costs.

Excel Application For students who wish to practice their spreadsheet skills, the following is a step-by-step approach to creating an Excel spreadsheet to work this problem.

Step-by-Step:

1. At the top of a new spreadsheet, create an "Original Data" section for the data provided for Bob Jones Catering. Create columns for "Month," "Labor-Hours," and "Overhead Costs" in the same format as the table of monthly labor hours and overhead costs shown for Bob Jones Catering above.
2. Skip two rows, create a section, "Regression Output."
3. Skip two more rows, create a section "Regression Diagram."
4. Estimate the regression equation with overhead costs as the dependent variable and labor hours as the independent variable by carrying out the following steps: (a) click on the tools menu and choose the "Data Analysis" option; (b) in the "Data Analysis" dialog box, click on "Regression" and click "OK"; (c) click in the "Input y Range" box so the cursor is in this box, then use your mouse to highlight the cells in the "Overhead Costs" column; (d) click in the "Input x Range" box so the cursor is in this box, then use your mouse to highlight the cells in the "Labor-Hours" column; (e) under "Output options" select "Output Range" and click in the "Output Range" box so the cursor is in this box, then use your mouse to highlight a cell in the "Regression Output" section you created in step 2; (f) click "OK" to close the regression dialog box.
5. After completing step 4, you will have a variety of regression statistics in your "Regression Output" section. In this output, there is a column, "Coefficients," and two rows, "Intercept" and "X Variable 1." The number in the intercept row of the coefficients column is your estimate of the intercept; the number in the x variable row of the coefficients column is your estimate of the slope.
6. Use the chart wizard to create a scatterplot of the relationship between overhead costs and labor-hours. Draw the regression line through these points by doing the following: (a) place the pointer on one of the data points on the graph and right click on your mouse and choose "Add Trendline"; (b) in the "Add Trendline" dialog box, choose "Linear" and click "OK."
7. After completing step 6, Excel will draw the regression line you calculated in step 6, through the data points. Use the resulting regression output and plot to answer question 1, and use the slope coefficient that you calculated in steps 4 and 5 to answer question 2.

10-26 Regression analysis, activity-based costing, choosing cost drivers. Jill Flaherty collects the following data to identify cost drivers of distribution costs at Saratoga Corporation. Distribution costs include the costs of organizing shipments and moving packaged units. Flaherty thinks that because the product is heavy, the number of units moved will affect distribution costs significantly, but she is uncertain.

Month	Distribution Costs	Number of Packaged Units Moved	Number of Shipments Made
January	$ 28,000	51,000	200
February	20,000	43,000	210
March	17,000	28,000	185
April	32,000	67,000	315
May	40,000	73,000	335
June	24,000	54,000	225
July	22,000	37,000	190
August	35,000	72,000	390
September	42,000	71,000	280
October	23,000	56,000	360
November	33,000	52,000	380
December	22,000	45,000	270
Total	$338,000	649,000	3,340

Flaherty estimates the following regression equations:

$$y = \$1,349 + (\$0.496 \times \text{Number of packaged units moved})$$
$$y = \$10,417 + (\$63.77 \times \text{Number of shipments made})$$

Required

1. Plot the monthly data and the regression lines for each of the following cost functions:
   a. Distribution costs = $a + (b \times$ Number of packaged units moved)
   b. Distribution costs = $a + (b \times$ Number of shipments made)
   Which cost driver for distribution costs would you choose? Explain briefly.
2. Flaherty anticipates moving 40,000 units in 220 shipments next month. Using the preferable cost function, what amount of distribution costs should Flaherty budget?

10-27 Learning curve, cumulative average-time learning model. Global Defense manufactures radar systems. It has just completed the manufacture of its first newly designed system, RS-32. It took 3,000 direct manufacturing labor-hours (DMLH) to produce this one unit. Global believes that a 90% cumulative average-time learning model for direct manufacturing labor-hours applies to RS-32. (A 90% learning curve means $b = -0.1520$). The variable costs of producing RS-32 are

Direct material costs	$80,000 per unit of RS-32
Direct manufacturing labor costs	$25 per DMLH
Variable manufacturing overhead costs	$15 per DMLH

Required Calculate the total variable costs of producing 2, 4, and 8 units.

10-28 Learning curve, incremental unit-time learning model. Assume the same information for Global Defense as in Exercise 10-27, except that Global Defense uses a 90% incremental unit-time learning model as a basis for predicting direct manufacturing labor-hours. (A 90% learning curve means $b = -0.1520$.)

Required

1. Calculate the total variable costs of producing 2, 3, and 4 units.
2. If you solved Exercise 10-27, compare your cost predictions in the two exercises for 2 and 4 units. Why are the predictions different?

Problems

10-29 High-low method. Ken Howard, financial analyst at JVR Corporation, is examining the behavior of quarterly maintenance costs for budgeting purposes. Howard collects the following data on machine-hours worked and maintenance costs for the past 12 quarters:

Quarter	Machine-Hours	Maintenance Costs
1	90,000	$185,000
2	110,000	220,000
3	100,000	200,000
4	120,000	240,000
5	85,000	170,000
6	105,000	215,000
7	95,000	195,000
8	115,000	235,000
9	95,000	190,000
10	115,000	225,000
11	105,000	180,000
12	125,000	250,000

1. Estimate the cost function for the quarterly data using the high-low method.
2. Plot and comment on the estimated cost function.
3. Howard anticipates that JVR will operate machines for 90,000 hours in quarter 13. Calculate the predicted maintenance costs in quarter 13 using the cost function estimated in requirement 1.

Required

10-30 High-low method; regression analysis. (CIMA, adapted) Anna Martinez, the financial manager at the Casa Real restaurant, is checking if there is any relationship between newspaper advertising and sales revenues at the restaurant. She obtains the following monthly data for the past 10 months:

Month	Revenues	Advertising Costs
March	$50,000	$2,000
April	70,000	3,000
May	55,000	1,500
June	65,000	3,500
July	55,000	1,000
August	65,000	2,000
September	45,000	1,500
October	80,000	4,000
November	55,000	2,500
December	60,000	2,500

They estimate the following regression equation:

$$\text{Monthly revenues} = \$39{,}502 + (8.723 \times \text{Advertising costs})$$

1. Plot the relationship between advertising costs and revenues.
2. Draw the regression line and evaluate it using the criteria of economic plausibility, goodness of fit, and slope of the regression line.
3. Use the high-low method to compute the cost function, relating advertising costs and revenues.
4. Using (a) the regression equation and (b) the high-low equation, what is the increase in revenues for each $1,000 spent on advertising within the relevant range? Which method should Martinez use to predict the effect of advertising costs on revenues? Explain briefly.

Required

10-31 Regression analysis, activity-based costing, choosing cost drivers. Larry Chu, the plant controller at Rohan Plastics, wants to identify cost drivers for support overhead costs. Indirect support consists of skilled staff responsible for the efficient functioning of all aspects (setup, production, maintenance, and quality control) of the plastic injection molding facility. In talking to the support staff, Chu has the impression that the staff spends a sizable portion of their time ensuring that the equipment is set up correctly and checking that the first units of production in each batch are of good quality.

Chu has collected the following data for the past 12 months:

Month	Support Overhead	Machine-Hours	Number of Batches
January	$ 84,000	2,250	309
February	41,000	2,400	128
March	63,000	2,850	249
April	44,000	2,100	159
May	44,000	2,700	216
June	48,000	2,250	174
July	66,000	3,800	264
August	46,000	3,600	162
September	33,000	1,850	147
October	66,000	3,300	219
November	81,000	3,750	303
December	57,000	2,000	106
Total	$673,000	32,850	2,436

Chu estimates the following two regression equations:

$$y = \$28.089 + (\$10.23 \times \text{Machine-hours})$$
$$y = \$16{,}031 + (\$197.30 \times \text{Number of batches})$$

where y is the monthly support overhead.

1. Plot the monthly data and the regression lines for each of the following cost functions:
   a. Support overhead costs $= a + (b \times \text{Machine-hours})$
   b. Support overhead costs $= a + (b \times \text{Number of batches})$
   Which cost driver for support overhead costs would you choose? Explain.

Required

2. Chu anticipates 2,600 machine-hours and 300 batches for next month. Using the cost driver you chose in requirement 1, what amount of support overhead costs should Chu budget?
3. Chu adds 20% to costs to determine target revenues (and hence prices). Costs other than support overhead are expected to equal $125,000 next month. Compare the target revenue numbers obtained if the cost driver is (i) machine-hours or (ii) number of batches. What would happen if Chu picked the cost driver you did not choose in requirement 1 to set target revenues and prices. Describe any other implications of choosing the "other" cost driver and cost function.

10-32 Time lag consideration in interpreting regression results. Aza Company manufactures apparel for young adults. It has four peak-load periods, one each for manufacturing the clothing suitable for spring, summer, fall, and winter. Each of these periods lasts for two months. In off-peak periods, Aza schedules equipment maintenance and runs advertising campaigns to introduce new lines of clothing.

Aza wanted to study the cost-behavior pattern of its equipment maintenance costs and the relationship between its sales and advertising costs. Using monthly data and linear regression analysis, the following results were obtained:

Maintenance costs = $38,000 – ($1.20 per Machine-hour × Number of machine-hours)
Sales revenue = $250,000 – (2.10 × Advertising costs)

Required Interpret the regression results.

10-33 Cost estimation, cumulative average-time learning curve. The Nautilus Company, which is under contract to the U.S. Navy, assembles troop deployment boats. As part of its research program, it completes the assembly of the first of a new model (PT109) of deployment boats. The Navy is impressed with the PT109. It requests that Nautilus submit a proposal on the cost of producing another seven PT109s.

Nautilus reports the following cost information for the first PT109 assembled by Nautilus:

Direct materials	$100,000
Direct manufacturing labor (10,000 labor-hours × $30)	300,000
Tooling cost[a]	50,000
Variable manufacturing overhead[b]	200,000
Other manufacturing overhead[c]	75,000
	$725,000

[a]Tooling can be reused at no extra cost, because all of its cost has been assigned to the first deployment boat.
[b]Variable manufacturing overhead is proportional to direct manufacturing labor-hours; a rate of $20 per hour is used for purposes of bidding on contracts.
[c]Other manufacturing overhead is allocated at a flat rate of 25% of direct manufacturing labor costs for purposes of bidding on contracts.

Nautilus uses an 85% cumulative average-time learning model as a basis for forecasting direct manufacturing labor-hours on its assembling operations. (An 85% learning curve means $b = -0.2345$.)

Required

1. Calculate predicted total costs of producing seven PT109s for the Navy. (Nautilus will keep the first deployment boat assembled, costed at $725,000, as a demonstration model for potential customers.)
2. What is the dollar amount of difference between (a) the predicted total costs for producing the seven PT109s in requirement 1, and (b) the predicted total costs for producing the seven PT109s assuming that there is no learning curve for direct manufacturing labor? That is, for (b) assume a linear function for units produced and direct manufacturing labor-hours.

10-34 Cost estimation, incremental unit-time learning model. Assume the same information for the Nautilus Company as in Problem 10-33 with one exception. This exception is that Nautilus uses an 85% incremental unit-time learning model as a basis for predicting direct manufacturing labor-hours on its assembling operations. (An 85% learning curve means $b = -0.2345$.)

Required

1. Prepare a prediction of the total costs for producing the seven PT109s for the Navy.
2. If you solved requirement 1 of Problem 10-33, compare your cost prediction there with the one you made here. Why are the predictions different?

10-35 Evaluating alternative simple regression models, nonprofit. (Chapter Appendix) Kathy Hanks, executive assistant to the president of Southwestern University, is concerned about the overhead costs at her university. Cost pressures are severe, so controlling and reducing overhead costs are very important. Hanks believes overhead costs incurred are generally a function of the number of different academic programs (including different specializations, degrees, and majors) that the university offers and the number of enrolled students. Both have grown significantly over the years. She collects the following data:

Year	Overhead Costs (in thousands)	Number of Academic Programs	Number of Enrolled Students
1	$13,500	29	3,400
2	19,200	36	5,000
3	16,800	49	2,600
4	20,100	53	4,700
5	19,500	54	3,900
6	23,100	58	4,900
7	23,700	88	5,700
8	20,100	72	3,900
9	22,800	83	3,500
10	29,700	73	3,700
11	31,200	101	5,600
12	38,100	103	7,600

She finds the following results for two separate simple regression models:

Regression 1: Overhead costs = $a + (b \times$ Number of academic programs)

Variable	Coefficient	Standard Error	*t*-Value
Constant	$7,127.75	$3,335.34	2.14
Independent variable 1:			
Number of academic programs	$240.64	$47.33	5.08

$r^2 = 0.72$; Durbin-Watson statistic = 1.81

Regression 2: Overhead costs = $a + (b \times$ Number of enrolled students)

Variable	Coefficient	Standard Error	*t*-Value
Constant	$5,991.75	$5,067.88	1.18
Independent variable 1:			
Number of enrolled students	$3.78	$1.07	3.53

$r^2 = 0.55$; Durbin-Watson statistic = 0.77

Required

1. Plot the relationship between overhead costs and each of the following variables: (a) number of academic programs and (b) number of enrolled students.
2. Evaluate the two regression models estimated by Hanks. Use the format in Exhibit 10-19 (p. 352).
3. What insights do the analyses provide about controlling overhead costs at the university?

10-36 Evaluating multiple regression models, nonprofit (continuation of Problem 10-35). (Chapter Appendix)

Required

1. Given your findings in Problem 10-35, should Hanks use multiple regression analysis to better understand the cost drivers of overhead costs? Explain.
2. Hanks decides that the simple regression analysis in Problem 10-35 should be extended to a multiple regression analysis. She finds the following result:

Regression 3: Overhead costs = $a + (b_1 \times$ Number of academic programs) + $(b_2 \times$ Number of enrolled students)

Variable	Coefficient	Standard Error	*t*-Value
Constant	$2,779.62	$3,620.05	0.77
Independent variable 1:			
Number of academic programs	$178.37	$51.54	3.46
Independent variable 2:			
Number of enrolled students	$1.87	$0.92	2.03

$r^2 = 0.81$; Durbin-Watson statistic = 1.84

The coefficient of correlation between number of academic programs and number of students is 0.60. Use the format in Exhibit 10-19 (p. 352) to evaluate the multiple regression model. (Assume linearity, constant variance and normality of residuals.) Should Hanks choose the multiple regression model instead of the two simple regression models of Problem 10-35?

3. How might Southwestern's president use these regression results to manage overhead costs?

10-37 Purchasing Department cost drivers, activity-based costing, simple regression analysis. (Chapter Appendix) Fashion Flair operates a chain of 10 retail department stores. Each department store makes its own purchasing decisions. Barry Lee, assistant to the president of Fashion Flair, is interested in better understanding the drivers of Purchasing Department costs. For many years, Fashion Flair has allocated Purchasing Department costs to products on the basis of the dollar value of merchandise purchased. A $100 item is allocated 10 times as many overhead costs associated with the Purchasing Department as a $10 item.

Lee recently attended a seminar titled "Cost Drivers in the Retail Industry." In a presentation at the seminar, Couture Fabrics, a leading competitor that has implemented activity-based costing, reported number of purchase orders and number of suppliers to be the two most important cost drivers of Purchasing Department costs. The dollar value of merchandise purchased in each purchase order was not found to be a significant cost driver. Lee interviewed several members of the Purchasing Department at the Fashion Flair store in Miami. They believed that Couture Fabric's conclusions also applied to their Purchasing Department.

Lee collects the following data for the most recent year for Fashion Flair's 10 retail department stores:

Department Store	Purchasing Department Costs (PDC)	Dollar Value of Merchandise Purchased (MP$)	Number of Purchase Orders (No. of PO's)	Number of Suppliers (No. of S's)
Baltimore	$1,523,000	$ 68,315,000	4,357	132
Chicago	1,100,000	33,456,000	2,550	222
Los Angeles	547,000	121,160,000	1,433	11
Miami	2,049,000	119,566,000	5,944	190
New York	1,056,000	33,505,000	2,793	23
Phoenix	529,000	29,854,000	1,327	33
Seattle	1,538,000	102,875,000	7,586	104
St. Louis	1,754,000	38,674,000	3,617	119
Toronto	1,612,000	139,312,000	1,707	208
Vancouver	1,257,000	130,944,000	4,731	201

Lee decides to use simple regression analysis to examine whether one or more of three variables (the last three columns in the table) are cost drivers of Purchasing Department costs. Summary results for these regressions are as follows:

Regression 1: PDC = $a + (b \times$ MP$)

Variable	Coefficient	Standard Error	*t*-Value
Constant	$1,039,061	$343,439	3.03
Independent variable 1: MP$	0.0031	0.0037	0.84
$r^2 = 0.08$; Durbin-Watson statistic = 2.41			

Regression 2: PDC = $a + (b \times$ No. of PO's)

Variable	Coefficient	Standard Error	*t*-Value
Constant	$730,716	$265,419	2.75
Independent variable 1: No. of PO's	$ 156.97	$ 64.69	2.43
$r^2 = 0.42$; Durbin-Watson statistic = 1.98			

Regression 3: PDC = $a + (b \times$ No. of S's)

Variable	Coefficient	Standard Error	*t*-Value
Constant	$814,862	$247,821	3.29
Independent variable 1: No. of S's	$3,875	$1,697	2.28
$r^2 = 0.39$; Durbin-Watson statistic = 1.97			

Required

1. Compare and evaluate the three simple regression models estimated by Lee. Graph each one. Also, use the format employed in Exhibit 10-19 (p. 352) to evaluate the information.
2. Do the regression results support the Couture Fabrics presentation about Purchasing Department cost drivers? Which of these cost drivers would you recommend in designing an ABC system?
3. How might Lee gain additional evidence on drivers of Purchasing Department costs at each of Fashion Flair's stores?

10-38 Purchasing Department cost drivers, multiple regression analysis (continuation of 10-37). (Chapter Appendix) Barry Lee decides that the simple regression analysis used in Problem 10-37 could be extended to a multiple regression analysis. He finds the following results for several multiple regressions:

Regression 4: PDC = $a + (b_1 \times$ No. of PO's) $+ (b_2 \times$ No. of S's)

Variable	Coefficient	Standard Error	*t*-Value
Constant	$485,384	$257,477	1.89
Independent variable 1: No. of PO's	$123.22	$57.69	2.14
Independent variable 2: No. of S's	$2,952	$1,476	2.00
$r^2 = 0.63$; Durbin-Watson statistic = 1.90			

Regression 5: PDC = $a + (b_1 \times$ No. of PO's$) + (b_2 \times$ No. of S's$) + (b_3 \times$ MP$)

Variable	Coefficient	Standard Error	*t*-Value
Constant	$494,684	$310,205	1.59
Independent variable 1: No. of PO's	$124.05	$63.49	1.95
Independent variable 2: No. of S's	$2,984	$1,622	1.84
Independent variable 3: MP$	−0.0002	0.0030	−0.07

$r^2 = 0.63$; Durbin-Watson statistic = 1.90

The coefficients of correlation between pairwise combinations of the variables are

	PDC	MP$	No. of PO's
MP$	0.29		
No. of PO's	0.65	0.27	
No. of S's	0.63	0.34	0.29

Required

1. Evaluate regression 4 using the criteria of economic plausibility, goodness of fit, significance of independent variables and specification analysis. Compare regression 4 with regressions 2 and 3 in Problem 10-37. Which model would you recommend that Lee use? Why?
2. Compare regression 5 with regression 4. Which model would you recommend that Lee use? Why?
3. Lee estimates the following data for the Baltimore store for next year: dollar value of merchandise purchased, $75,000,000; number of purchase orders, 3,900; number of suppliers, 110. How much should Lee budget for Purchasing Department costs for the Baltimore store for next year?
4. What difficulties do not arise in simple regression analysis that may arise in multiple regression analysis? Is there evidence of such difficulties in either of the multiple regressions presented in this problem? Explain.
5. Give two examples of decisions in which the regression results reported here (and in Problem 10-37) could be informative.

10-39 Regression computations, ethics. (Chapter Appendix) Cleveland Engineering manufactures small electric motors. Data on manufacturing labor costs and units produced for the last four quarters follow:

Quarter	Manufacturing Labor Costs	Units Produced
1	$176,000	9,000
2	174,000	10,000
3	165,000	9,000
4	205,000	12,000
Total	$720,000	40,000

The bonus paid to Peter Smith, the manufacturing manager, depends on how manufacturing labor costs in a quarter compare with average manufacturing labor costs in the previous four quarters. In the recently concluded quarter 5, Cleveland Engineering produced 12,000 motors and incurred manufacturing labor costs of $208,000. Smith is very happy with the results. Over the previous four quarters, the average manufacturing labor cost per unit is $18 ($720,000 ÷ 40,000 units), resulting in a benchmark for quarter 5 of $18 × 12,000 = $216,000. Just as Smith is thinking about his bonus, Allison Hart, the plant controller, knocks on his door.

Allison Hart: "I am sorry that we couldn't beat the benchmark over the last four quarters."

Peter Smith: "What do you mean we didn't beat the benchmark? Here are the numbers I just calculated. Against a benchmark of $216,000, we achieved $208,000."

Allison Hart: "No, that's not how the calculations are done. Some of the labor costs are fixed and others vary with production. My analysis separates the fixed from the variable components. My calculations show that our quarter 5 performance was worse than the previous four quarters.

Peter Smith: "Please review your calculations. You can report a better benchmark! Your regression approach is subject to estimation error. You should make some adjustment for that. If we don't show senior management that we are reducing labor costs, they might shut us down because they don't believe we can be competitive. I am sure that no one in this plant wants that to happen."

Required

1. Verify, by either using the formulas given in the chapter appendix or a software program that performs regression analysis, that the regression equation is given by

$$y = \$65{,}000 + (\$11.50 \times \text{Units produced})$$

with an $r^2 = 0.88$.

2. What is the benchmark for quarter 5 that Allison Hart had calculated?

3. Why is there a difference between the benchmark calculated by Peter Smith and the benchmark calculated in requirement 2? Which benchmark do you prefer? Explain your answer.
4. Identify the steps that Allison Hart should follow in attempting to resolve the situation created by Peter Smith's comment about adjusting the benchmark.

Collaborative Learning Problem

10-40 High-low method, alternative regression functions, accrual accounting adjustments. Trevor Kennedy, the cost analyst at a can manufacturing plant of United Packaging, is examining the relationship between total engineering support costs reported in the plant records and machine-hours. These costs have two components: (1) labor, which is paid monthly, and (2) materials and parts, which are purchased from an outside vendor every three months. After further discussion with the operating manager, Kennedy discovers that the materials and parts numbers reported in the monthly records are on an "as purchased," or cash accounting basis and not on an "as used," or accrual accounting basis. By examining materials and parts usage records, Kennedy is able to restate the materials and parts costs to an "as used" basis. (No restatement of the labor costs was necessary.) The reported and restated costs are as as follows:

Month	Labor: Reported Costs (1)	Materials and Parts: Reported Costs (2)	Materials and Parts: Restated Costs (3)	Total Engineering Support: Reported Costs (4) = (1) + (2)	Total Engineering Support: Restated Costs (5) = (1) + (3)	Machine-Hours (6)
March	$347	$847	$182	$1,194	$529	30
April	521	0	411	521	932	63
May	398	0	268	398	666	49
June	355	961	228	1,316	583	38
July	473	0	348	473	821	57
August	617	0	349	617	966	73
September	245	821	125	1,066	370	19
October	487	0	364	487	851	53
November	431	0	290	431	721	42

The regression results for total engineering support reported costs as the dependent variable, are
Regression 1: Engineering support reported costs = $a + (b \times$ Machine-hours)

Variable	Coefficient	Standard Error	t-Value
Constant	$1,393.20	$305.68	4.56
Independent variable 1: Machine-hours	−$14.23	$6.15	−2.31

$r^2 = 0.43$; Durbin-Watson statistic = 2.26

The regression results for total engineering support restated costs as the dependent variable, are
Regression 2: Engineering support restated costs = $a + (b \times$ Machine-hours)

Variable	Coefficient	Standard Error	t-Value
Constant	$176.38	$53.99	3.27
Independent variable 1: Machine-hours	$11.44	$1.08	10.59

$r^2 = 0.94$; Durbin-Watson statistic = 1.31

Required

1. Plot the cost functions relating (i) the *reported costs* for total engineering support to machine-hours and (ii) the *restated costs* for total engineering support to machine-hours. Comment on the plots.
2. Use the high-low method to compute estimates of the cost functions $y = a + bX$ for (a) reported engineering support costs and machine-hours and (b) restated engineering support costs and machine-hours.
3. Contrast and evaluate the cost function estimated with regression using restated data for materials and parts with the cost function estimated with regression using the data reported in the plant records. Use the comparison format employed in Exhibit 10-19 (p. 352).
4. Of all the cost functions estimated in requirements 2 and 3, which one would you choose to best represent the relationship between engineering support costs and machine-hours? Why?
5. What problems might Kennedy encounter when restating the materials and parts costs recorded to an "as used," or accrual accounting basis?
6. Why is it important for Kennedy to pick the correct cost function? That is, illustrate two potential problems Kennedy could encounter by choosing a cost function other than the one you chose in requirement 4.

CHAPTER 10 INTERNET EXERCISE

Knowing how costs vary by identifying cost drivers and distinguishing fixed costs from variable costs is frequently the key to making good management decisions. To better understand how costs behave, go to www.prenhall.com/horngren, click on *Cost Accounting,* 11th ed. and access the Internet exercise for Chapter 10.

CHAPTER 10 CASE

U.S. BREWING INDUSTRY: Cost Estimation

Hobie Leland, Jr., has been assigned to a project to estimate the cost-volume relationship of Ace Brewing Company. Hobie first analyzes Ace's internal records and discovers that since 1982, Ace has been a single-line-of-business company. Prior to 1982, it also owned a soft-drink company (Hoff Beverage Company), and the accounting records did not separately report the costs associated with the brewing and soft-drink operations. Hobie decides to base his analysis on the 1982 to 2000 period and collects the data in Exhibit 10-22.

EXHIBIT 10-22 Ace Brewing Company: 1982–2000

Year	Cost of Goods Sold (in millions)	Barrels Sold (in millions)	Wholesale Price Index of Beer
1982	$166.943	5.844	0.533
1983	184.981	6.672	0.533
1984	206.666	7.444	0.535
1985	229.200	8.219	0.536
1986	252.122	9.047	0.540
1987	285.380	10.123	0.552
1988	313.070	10.910	0.557
1989	305.044	10.225	0.570
1990	324.391	10.517	0.596
1991	367.779	11.797	0.611
1992	395.559	12.600	0.612
1993	431.398	13.128	0.623
1994	530.769	14.297	0.719
1995	630.160	15.669	0.759
1996	696.039	17.037	0.769
1997	688.045	16.003	0.794
1998	720.258	15.367	0.848
1999	765.303	15.115	0.933
2000	832.018	15.091	1.000

QUESTIONS

1. Estimate the following linear relationship between cost of sales (C_t) and barrels of beer sold (V_t) from 1982–2000 using (a) the high-low method and (b) regression analysis. Evaluate the results.
2. One problem in using time series data to estimate cost-volume relationships arises from inflation. One technique proposed to handle this problem is to deflate the dependent variable by a price index (P_t). The "Wholesale Price Index of Beer" from 1982 to 2000 is presented in Exhibit 10-22. Estimate the following linear relationship using regression analysis:

$$\frac{C_t}{P_t} = \alpha + \beta \cdot V_t$$

Evaluate the results.

3. Hobie remembered a warning from his college days: serial correlation in the residuals is frequently encountered in regressions using time series data. A common approach to serial correlation of the residuals is to estimate the model in the first differences of the variables, rather than in the levels of the variables:

$$\left(\frac{C_t}{P_t} - \frac{C_{t-1}}{P_{t-1}}\right) = \alpha + \beta\,(V_t - V_{t-1})$$

Estimate this relationship for Ace using regression anlaysis. Is serial correlation in the residuals less of a problem than with the model estimated in 2 above?

4. Which regression equation would you choose to estimate the cost-volume relationship of Ace? Explain briefly.

CHAPTER 11

Decision Making and Relevant Information

LEARNING OBJECTIVES

1. Use the five-step decision process to make decisions
2. Differentiate relevant from irrelevant costs and revenues in decision situations
3. Distinguish between quantitative and qualitative factors in decision making
4. Beware of two potential problems in relevant-cost analysis
5. Explain the opportunity-cost concept and why it is used in decision making
6. Know how to choose which products to produce when there are capacity constraints
7. Discuss factors managers must consider when adding or discontinuing customers and segments
8. Explain why book value of equipment is irrelevant in equipment-replacement decisions
9. Explain how conflicts can arise between the decision model used by a manager and the performance evaluation model used to evaluate the manager

www.prenhall.com/horngren

We make decisions every day. Some are simple: what to wear or what to have for breakfast. Some are not simple: whether to take a summer internship, take classes in summer school, volunteer at a youth camp, or travel. Yet they all have something in common: a basic, logical decision process that involves gathering information, considering future costs and benefits, making a choice, acting on the choice, and evaluating the results. Organizations use the same process to make decisions. Each manager of a Store 24 convenience store must regularly make decisions about allocation of shelf space, what types of gooods to purchase, and how to best staff the store for efficiency and profitability. Opportunity costs, relevant costs, and relevant revenues for every option should be considered in the decision process.

We now explore the decision-making process and focus on specific decisions, such as accepting or rejecting a one-time-only special order, insourcing or outsourcing products or services, and replacing or keeping equipment. We're going to look closely at distinguishing *relevant* items from *irrelevant* items in making these decisions.

INFORMATION AND THE DECISION PROCESS

Shareholders want managers to make decisions that are in the shareholders' best interest.

Managers usually follow a *decision model* for choosing among different courses of action. A **decision model** is a formal method of making a choice, often involving both quantitative and qualitative analyses. Management accountants work with managers by analyzing and presenting relevant data to guide decisions.

Consider a strategic decision facing Home Appliances, a manufacturer of vacuum cleaners: Should it reorganize its manufacturing operations to reduce manufacturing labor costs? Assume there are only two alternatives: "do not reorganize" or "reorganize."

The reorganization will eliminate all manual handling of materials. The current manufacturing line uses 20 workers — 15 workers operate machines, and 5 workers handle materials. The 5 materials-handling workers have been hired on contracts that permit layoffs without additional payments. Each worker puts in 2,000 hours annually. The cost of reorganization (consisting mostly of equipment leases) is predicted to be $90,000 each year. The predicted production output of 25,000 units will be unaffected by the decision. Also unaffected are the predicted selling price of $250, the direct material cost per unit of $50, manufacturing overhead of $750,000, and marketing costs of $2,000,000.

1 Use the five-step decision process to make decisions

...obtain information, make predictions, choose an alternative, implement the decision, and evaluate perfomance

Managers typically use the five-step decision process described in Exhibit 11-1 to make decisions such as "do not reorganize" or "reorganize." In this exhibit, note the sequence of the steps and how step 5 evaluates performance to provide feedback about actions taken in the previous steps. This feedback might affect future predictions, the prediction method itself, the decision model, or the implementation of the decision.

THE CONCEPT OF RELEVANCE

2 Differentiate relevant from irrelevant costs and revenues in decision situations

...only costs and revenues that are expected to occur in the future and differ among alternative courses of action are relevant

Relevant Costs and Relevant Revenues

Much of this chapter focuses on step 3 in Exhibit 11-1 and on the concepts of relevant costs and relevant revenues when choosing among alternatives. **Relevant costs** are *expected future costs* and **relevant revenues** are *expected future revenues* that differ among the alternative courses of action being considered. Be sure you understand that to be relevant costs and relevant revenues they *must*

It's essential to understand the concept of relevance; it is used extensively in this chapter and many to follow.

a. *Occur in the future* — every decision deals with selecting a course of action based on its expected future results — and
b. *Differ among the alternative courses of action* — costs and revenues that do not differ will not matter and, hence, will have no bearing on the decision being made.

The question is always, What difference will an action make?

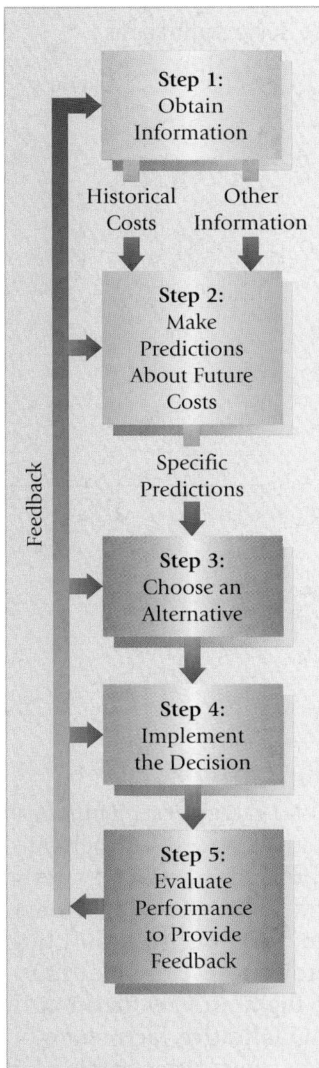

Historical labor costs are $14 per hour. A recently negotiated increase in employee benefits of $2 per hour will increase labor costs to $16 per hour in the future. The reorganization of manufacturing operations is expected to reduce the number of workers from 20 to 15 by eliminating all 5 workers who handle materials.

Use the information from step 1 together with an assessment of probability as a basis for predicting the future labor costs. Under the existing "do not reorganize" alternative, costs are predicted to be $640,000 (20 workers × 2,000 hours per worker × $16 per hour), and under the "reorganize" alternative, costs are predicted to be $480,000 (15 workers × 2,000 hours per worker × $16 per hour). The reorganization is predicted to cost $90,000 per year.

The predicted benefits of the different alternatives in step 2 are compared (savings from eliminating materials-handling labor costs, 5 workers × 2,000 hours per worker × $16 per hour = $160,000) and are related to the cost of the reorganization ($90,000) along with other considerations (such as likely effects on employee morale). Management chooses the reorganize alternative.

The manager implements the decision reached in step 3 by reorganizing manufacturing operations.

Evaluating performance of the decision implemented in step 4 provides the feedback as the five-step sequence is then repeated in whole or in part. Actual results show that the new manufacturing labor costs are $540,000, rather than the predicted $480,000, due to lower-than-expected manufacturing labor productivity. This historical information can help managers in making better subsequent predictions that allow for more learning time. Alternatively, managers may improve implementation through, for example, employee training or better supervision.

EXHIBIT 11-1

Five-Step Decision Process for Home Appliances

Exhibit 11-2 presents the financial data underlying the choice between the "do not reorganize" and the "reorganize" alternatives for Home Appliances. The first two columns present *all data*. The last two columns present only relevant costs—the $640,000 and $480,000 expected future manufacturing labor costs and the $90,000 expected future reorganization costs that differ between the two alternatives. The revenues, direct materials, manufacturing overhead, and marketing items can be ignored because they do not differ between the alternatives and are irrelevant.

Note, the past manufacturing labor cost of $14 per hour and total past manufacturing labor costs of $560,000 (20 workers × 2,000 hours per worker × $14 per hour) do not appear in Exhibit 11-2. *Although they may be a useful basis for making informed predictions of the expected future manufacturing labor costs of $640,000 and $480,000, historical costs themselves are past costs that are irrelevant to decision making.* Past costs are also called **sunk costs** because they are unavoidable and cannot be changed no matter what action is taken.

The data in Exhibit 11-2 indicate that reorganizing the manufacturing operations will increase predicted operating income by $70,000 each year. Note, we reach the same conclusion whether we use "all data" or include only "relevant data" in the analysis. By confining the analysis to only the relevant data, managers can clear away the clutter of potentially confusing irrelevant data. Focusing on the relevant data is especially helpful when all the information needed to prepare a detailed income statement is unavailable. Understanding which costs are relevant and which are irrelevant helps the decision maker concentrate on obtaining only the pertinent data and saves time.

EXHIBIT 11-2 Determining Relevant Revenues and Relevant Costs for Home Appliances

	All Data		Relevant Data	
	Alternative 1: Do Not Reorganize	Alternative 2: Reorganize	Alternative 1: Do Not Reorganize	Alternative 2: Reorganize
Revenues[a]	$6,250,000	$6,250,000	—	—
Costs:				
Direct materials[b]	1,250,000	1,250,000	—	—
Manufacturing labor	640,000[c]	480,000[d]	$ 640,000[c]	$ 480,000[d]
Manufacturing overhead	750,000	750,000	—	—
Marketing	2,000,000	2,000,000	—	—
Reorganization costs	—	90,000	—	90,000
Total costs	4,640,000	4,570,000	640,000	570,000
Operating income	$1,610,000	$1,680,000	$(640,000)	$(570,000)
	$70,000 Difference		$70,000 Difference	

[a]25,000 units × $250 per unit = $6,250,000
[b]25,000 units × $50 per unit = $1,250,000
[c]20 workers × 2,000 hours per worker × $16 per hour = $640,000
[d]15 workers × 2,000 hours per worker × $16 per hour = $480,000

Some managers may prefer to focus only on relevant revenues and relevant costs (for example, the rightmost two columns in Exhibit 11-2). That is, managers reduce their information load by excluding irrelevant data. Research has shown that when inundated with data, people tend to (1) make poorer decisions, (2) take longer to decide, but tend to (3) be more confident in their decisions.

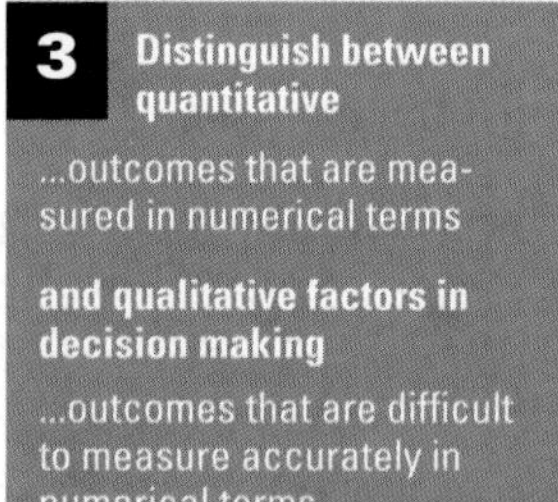

Qualitative and Quantitative Relevant Information

We divide the outcomes of alternatives into two broad categories: *quantitative* and *qualitative*. **Quantitative factors** are outcomes that are measured in numerical terms. Some quantitative factors are financial; they can be expressed in monetary terms. Examples include the costs of direct materials, direct manufacturing labor, and marketing. Other quantitative factors are nonfinancial; they can be measured numerically, but they are not expressed in monetary terms. Reduction in new product-development time for a manufacturing company and the percentage of on-time flight arrivals for an airline company are examples of quantitative nonfinancial factors. **Qualitative factors** are outcomes that are difficult to measure accurately in numerical terms. Employee morale is an example.

Relevant cost analysis generally emphasizes quantitative factors that can be expressed in financial terms. But just because qualitative factors and quantitative nonfinancial factors cannot be measured easily in financial terms does not make them unimportant. In fact, managers must at times give more weight to these factors. For example, Home Appliances would want to carefully consider the negative effect on employee morale of laying off materials-handling workers, a qualitative factor, before choosing the "reorganize" alternative. Trading off nonfinancial and financial considerations is seldom easy.

Exhibit 11-3 summarizes the key features of relevant information.

AN ILLUSTRATION OF RELEVANCE: CHOOSING OUTPUT LEVELS

The concept of relevance applies to all decision situations. In this and the following several sections, we present some of these decision situations. We start by considering decisions

EXHIBIT 11-3

Key Features of Relevant Information

- Past (historical) costs may be helpful as a basis for making predictions. However, past costs themselves are always irrelevant when making decisions.
- Different alternatives can be compared by examining differences in expected total future revenues and costs.
- Not all expected future revenues and costs are relevant. Expected future revenues and costs that do not differ among alternatives are irrelevant and, hence, can be eliminated from the analysis. The key question is always, What difference will it make?
- Appropriate weight must be given to qualitative factors and quantitative nonfinancial factors.

	Total	Per Unit
Revenues (30,000 towels × $20 per towel)	$600,000	$20
Cost of goods sold (manufacturing costs)	360,000	12
Marketing costs	210,000	7
Full costs of the product	570,000	19
Operating income	$ 30,000	$ 1

EXHIBIT 11-4

Budgeted Income Statement for August, Absorption-Costing Format for Fancy Fabrics

that affect output levels. For example, managers must choose whether to introduce a new product or try to sell more units of an existing product. Managers are interested in the effect changes in output levels will have on the company and on operating income.

One-Time-Only Special Orders

One type of decision that affects output levels is accepting or rejecting special orders when there is idle production capacity and the special orders have no long-run implications. We use the term **one-time-only special order** to describe these conditions.

Example 1: *Fancy Fabrics manufactures quality bath towels at its highly automated Burlington, North Carolina, plant. The plant has a production capacity of 48,000 towels each month. Current monthly production is 30,000 towels. Retail department stores account for all existing sales. Expected results for the coming month (August) are shown in Exhibit 11-4. (These amounts are predictions.) We assume all costs can be classified as either variable with respect to a single driver (units of output) or fixed. The manufacturing cost of $12 per unit consists of:*

	Variable Cost per Unit	*Fixed Cost per Unit*	*Total Cost per Unit*
Direct material	*$6.00*	—	*$ 6.00*
Direct manufacturing labor	*0.50*	*$1.50*	*2.00*
Manufacturing overhead	*1.00*	*3.00*	*4.00*
Manufacturing costs	*$7.50*	*$4.50*	*$12.00*

The marketing cost per unit is $7 ($5 of which is variable). Fancy Fabrics incurs no R&D costs, product-design costs, distribution costs, or customer-service costs.

As a result of a strike at its existing towel supplier, a luxury hotel chain has offered to buy 5,000 towels from Fancy Fabrics in August at $11 per towel. No subsequent sales to this hotel chain are anticipated. Fixed manufacturing costs are tied to the 48,000-towel production capacity. That is, fixed manufacturing costs relate to the production capacity available, regardless of the capacity used. If Fancy Fabrics accepts the special order, it will use existing idle capacity to produce the 5,000 towels, and fixed manufacturing costs will not change. No marketing costs will be necessary for the 5,000-unit one-time-only special order. Accepting this special order is not expected to affect the selling price or the quantity of towels sold to regular customers. Should Fancy Fabrics accept the hotel chain's offer?

Exhibit 11-4 presents data for this example on an absorption-costing basis. In this exhibit, the manufacturing cost of $12 per unit and the marketing cost of $7 per unit include both variable and fixed costs. The sum of all costs (variable and fixed) in a particular business function in the value chain, such as manufacturing costs or marketing costs, are called **business function costs. Full costs of the product,** in this case $19 per unit, are the sum of all variable and fixed costs in all business functions in the value chain (R&D, design, production, marketing, distribution, and customer service). For Fancy Fabrics, full costs of the product consist of costs in manufacturing and marketing because these are the only business functions. No marketing costs are necessary for the special order, so the manager of Fancy Fabrics will focus only on manufacturing costs. Based on the manufacturing cost per unit of $12—which is greater than the $11 per unit price offered by the hotel chain—the manager might reject the offer.

Exhibit 11-5 separates manufacturing and marketing costs into their variable- and fixed-cost components and presents data in the format of a contribution income statement. The relevant revenues and costs are the expected future revenues and costs that differ as a result of accepting the special offer—revenues of $55,000 ($11 per unit × 5,000 units) and variable manufacturing costs of $37,500 ($7.50 per unit × 5,000 units). The

EXHIBIT 11-5

One-Time-Only Special-Order Decision for Fancy Fabrics: Comparative Contribution Income Statements

	Per unit (1)	Without the Special Order, 30,000 Units To Be Sold: Total (2) = (1) × 30,000	With the Special Order, 35,000 Units To Be Sold: Total (3)	Difference: Relevant Amounts for the 5,000 Units Special Order (4)
Revenues	$20.00	$600,000	$655,000	$55,000[c]
Variable costs:				
Manufacturing	7.50[a]	225,000	262,500	37,500[d]
Marketing	5.00	150,000	150,000	—[e]
Total variable costs	12.50	375,000	412,500	37,500
Contribution margin	7.50	225,000	242,500	17,500
Fixed Costs:				
Manufacturing	4.50[b]	135,000	135,000	—[f]
Marketing	2.00	60,000	60,000	—[f]
Total fixed costs	6.50	195,000	195,000	—
Operating income	$ 1.00	$ 30,000	$ 47,500	$17,500

[a]Variable manufacturing costs = Direct materials, $6 + Direct manufacturing labor, $0.50 + Manufacturing overhead, $1 = $7.50.
[b]Fixed manufacturing costs = Direct manufacturing labor, $1.50 + Manufacturing overhead, $3 = $4.50.
[c]5,000 units × $11.00 per unit = $55,000.
[d]5,000 units × $7.50 per unit = $37,500.
[e]No variable marketing costs would be incurred for the 5,000-unit one-time-only special order.
[f]Fixed manufacturing costs and fixed marketing costs also would be unaffected by the special order.

Exhibit 11-5 illustrates two keys to analyzing relevant costs and relevant revenues for decisions: (1) distinguish relevant costs and revenues from irrelevant ones and (2) use the contribution income statement to focus on whether each variable cost and each fixed cost is affected by the alternatives under consideration. The contribution income statement groups costs into their variable-cost and fixed-cost components to highlight contribution margin. The contribution income statement is most useful for short-run decisions because, in the long run, costs are not fixed.

fixed manufacturing costs and all marketing costs *(including variable marketing costs)* are irrelevant in this case. That's because these costs will not change in total whether or not the special order is accepted. Fancy Fabrics would gain an additional $17,500 (relevant revenues, $55,000 – relevant costs, $37,500) in operating income by accepting the special order. In this example, comparing total amounts for 30,000 units versus 35,000 units in Exhibit 11-5, or focusing only on the relevant amounts in the difference column in Exhibit 11-5, avoids a misleading implication—the implication that would result from comparing the $11 per unit selling price against the manufacturing cost per unit of $12 (Exhibit 11-4), which includes both variable and fixed manufacturing costs.

Question: In the example, is it reasonable to expect that the special order will not affect Fancy Fabrics' regular business? *Answer:* Unless Fancy Fabrics has effectively segmented the market, the special order may affect its regular business. But a hotel chain is an entirely different class of customer than retail department-store chains, so Fancy Fabrics' market may be sufficiently segmented. The phrase "one-time-only special order" highlights the point that special orders are assumed to be short-run business that do not affect regular business.

The assumption of no long-run or strategic implications is crucial to our analysis of the one-time-only special-order decision. Suppose Fancy Fabrics concludes that the retail department stores (its regular customers) will demand a lower price if it sells towels at $11 apiece to the luxury hotel chain. In this case, revenues from regular customers will become relevant. Why? Because the future revenues from regular customers if the special order is accepted or rejected will differ. The relevant-revenue and relevant-cost analysis of the luxury hotel chain order would have to be modified to consider both the short-run benefits from accepting the order and the long-run consequences on profitability if prices were lowered to all regular customers.

4 Beware of two potential problems in relevant-cost analysis

...(1) incorrect general assumptions, such as all variable costs are relevant and all fixed costs are irrelevant, and (2) using unit costs

Potential Problems in Relevant-Cost Analysis

Two potential problems should be avoided in relevant-cost analysis. First, watch out for incorrect general assumptions, such as all variable costs are relevant and all fixed costs are irrelevant. In the Fancy Fabrics example, the variable marketing cost of $5 per unit is irrelevant because Fancy Fabrics will incur no extra marketing costs by accepting the special order. Similarly, fixed manufacturing costs could be relevant. Consider again the Fancy Fabrics example. The extra production of 5,000 towels per month does not affect fixed manufacturing costs because we assumed that the relevant range is from 30,000 to 48,000 towels per month. In some cases, producing the extra 5,000 towels might increase fixed manufacturing costs. Suppose Fancy Fabrics would need to run three shifts of 16,000 towels per shift to achieve full capacity of 48,000 towels per month. Increasing the monthly production from 30,000 to 35,000 would require a partial third shift because two shifts could produce only 32,000 towels. The extra shift would increase fixed manufacturing costs, thereby making any additional fixed manufacturing costs relevant for this decision.

Second, unit-cost data can potentially mislead decision makers in two ways:

1. *When irrelevant costs are included.* Consider the $4.50 of fixed direct manufacturing labor and manufacturing overhead cost included in the $12 per unit manufacturing cost in the one-time-only special-order decision (see Exhibits 11-4 and 11-5). This $4.50 per unit cost is irrelevant, given the assumptions in our example, so it should be excluded.
2. *When the same unit costs are used at different output levels.* Generally, use total costs rather than unit costs. Then, if desired, the total costs can be unitized. In the illustration, total fixed manufacturing costs remain at $135,000 even if Fancy Fabrics accepts the special order and produces 35,000 towels. Including the fixed manufacturing cost per unit of $4.50 as a cost of the special order would lead to the erroneous conclusion that total fixed manufacturing costs would increase to $157,500 ($4.50 per towel × 35,000 towels).

The best way to avoid these two potential problems is to keep focusing on (a) total revenues and total costs (rather than unit revenue and unit cost) and (b) the relevance concept. Always require each item included in the analysis to be expected *total* future revenues and expected *total* future costs that differ among the alternatives.

INSOURCING-VERSUS-OUTSOURCING AND MAKE-VERSUS-BUY DECISIONS

We now apply the concept of relevance to another strategic decision: whether a company should make a part or buy it from a supplier. We again assume idle capacity.

Outsourcing and Idle Facilities

Outsourcing is purchasing goods and services from outside vendors rather than **insourcing,** which is producing the same goods or providing the same services within the organization. For example, Kodak prefers to manufacture its own films (insourcing), but it has IBM do its data processing (outsourcing). Toyota relies on outside vendors to supply some parts and components but chooses to manufacture other parts internally.

Decisions about whether a producer of goods or services will insource or outsource are also called **make-or-buy decisions.** Sometimes qualitative factors dictate management's make-or-buy decision. For example, Dell Computer buys the Pentium chip for its personal computers from Intel because Dell does not have the know-how and technology to make the chip itself. Coca-Cola does not outsource the manufacture of its concentrate to maintain the secrecy of its formula. Surveys of companies indicate they consider the most important factors in the make-or-buy decision to be quality, dependability of suppliers, and cost.

Example 2: The El Cerrito Company manufactures thermostats—consisting of relays, switches, and valves—for home and industrial use. El Cerrito makes its own switches. Columns 1 and 2 of the following table show the current costs for HDS, its heavy-duty switch, based on an analysis of its various manufacturing activities:

	Total Current Costs of Producing 10,000 Units in 25 Batches (1)	*Current Cost per Unit (2) = (1) ÷ 10,000*	*Expected Total Costs of Producing 10,000 Units in 50 Batches Next Year (3)*	*Expected Cost per Unit (4) = (3) ÷ 10,000*
Direct materials	*$ 80,000*	*$ 8.00*	*$ 80,000*	*$ 8.00*
Direct manufacturing labor	*10,000*	*1.00*	*10,000*	*1.00*
Variable manufacturing overhead costs for power and utilities	*40,000*	*4.00*	*40,000*	*4.00*
Mixed (variable and fixed) manufacturing overhead costs of materials handling and setup	*17,500*	*1.75*	*20,000*	*2.00*
Fixed manufacturing overhead costs of plant lease, insurance, and administration	*30,000*	*3.00*	*30,000*	*3.00*
Total manufacturing costs	*$177,500*	*$17.75*	*$180,000*	*$18.00*

Materials-handling and setup activities occur each time a batch of HDS is made. El Cerrito produces the 10,000 units of HDS in 25 batches, with 400 units in each batch. The number of batches is the cost driver for these cost. Total materials-handling costs and setup costs equal fixed costs of $5,000 plus variable cost of $500 per batch [$5,000 + (25 batches × $500 per batch) = $17,500]. El Cerrito starts production only after it receives an order. The company's customers want to lower their inventory levels, so they are pressuring El Cerrito to supply thermostats in smaller batch sizes. El Cerrito anticipates producing the 10,000 units of HDS next year in 50 batches of 200 units per batch. Through continuous improvement, the company expects to reduce variable cost for materials handling and setup to $300 per batch. No other changes in variable cost per unit or fixed costs are anticipated.

Another manufacturer offers to sell El Cerrito 10,000 units of HDS next year for $16 per unit on whatever delivery schedule El Cerrito wants. Assume that financial factors dominate in this make-or-buy decision. Should El Cerrito make or buy HDS?

Columns 3 and 4 of the preceding table indicate the expected total costs and expected cost per unit of producing 10,000 units of HDS next year. Direct material costs, direct manufacturing labor costs, and variable manufacturing overhead costs that vary with units produced are not expected to change because El Cerrito plans to continue to produce 10,000 units next year at the same variable cost per unit as this year. Materials-handling and setup costs are expected to increase, even with no change in total production quantity. That's because these costs will vary with the number of batches, not the number of units produced. Expected total materials-handling costs and setup costs are $20,000 [$5,000 + (50 batches × the cost per batch of $300)]. El Cerrito expects fixed manufacturing overhead costs to remain the same as this year. The expected manufacturing cost per units for next year is $18. It appears that the company should buy HDS because the expected $18 per unit cost of making the part is more than the $16 per unit to buy it. But, a make-or-buy decision is often not obvious. To make a decision, management needs to answer the question: What is the difference in relevant costs between the alternatives?

For the moment, suppose (a) the capacity now used to make HDS will become idle next year if HDS is purchased and (b) the $30,000 of fixed manufacturing overhead will continue to be incurred next year, regardless of the decision made. Assume the $5,000 in fixed salaries to support materials handling and setup will not be incurred if the manufacture of HDS is completely shut down next year.

Exhibit 11-6 presents the relevant-cost computations. El Cerrito will save $10,000 by making HDS rather than buying it from the outside supplier. Making HDS is the preferred alternative.

Note how the key concepts of relevance presented in Exhibit 11-3 apply here:

1. Current-cost data in Example 2, columns 1 and 2 (p. xxx), play no role in the analysis in Exhibit 11-6 because for next year's make-or-buy decision these costs are past costs and, hence, irrelevant. They only help in predicting future costs.

EXHIBIT 11-6

Relevant (Incremental) Items for Make-or-Buy Decision for HDS at the El Cerrito Company

Relevant Items	Total Relevant Costs		Relevant Cost Per Unit	
	Make	Buy	Make	Buy
Outside purchase of parts		$160,000		$16
Direct materials	$ 80,000		$ 8	
Direct manufacturing labor	10,000		1	
Variable manufacturing overhead	40,000		4	
Mixed (variable and fixed) materials-handling and setup overhead	20,000		2	
Total relevant costs[a]	$150,000	$160,000	$15	$16
Difference in favor of making HDS	$ 10,000		$1	

[a]Additionally, the $30,000 of plant lease, plant insurance, and plant administration costs could be included under both alternatives. But these costs are irrelevant to the decision.

2. Exhibit 11-6 shows $20,000 of future materials-handling and setup costs under the make alternative but not under the buy alternative. Why? Because buying HDS and not manufacturing it will save $20,000 in future variable costs per batch and avoidable fixed costs. The $20,000 represents future costs that differ between the alternatives and so is relevant to the make-or-buy decision.
3. Exhibit 11-6 excludes the $30,000 of plant lease, insurance, and administration costs under both alternatives. Why? Because these future costs will not differ between the alternatives, so they are irrelevant.

A common term in decision making is *incremental cost.* An **incremental cost** is the additional total cost incurred for an activity. In Exhibit 11-6, the incremental cost of making HDS is the additional total cost of $150,000 that El Cerrito will incur if it decides to make HDS. The $30,000 of fixed manufacturing overhead is not an incremental cost because El Cerrito will incur these costs whether or not it makes HDS. Similarly, the incremental cost of buying HDS from an outside supplier is the additional total cost of $160,000 that El Cerrito will incur if it decides to buy HDS. A **differential cost** is the difference in total cost between two alternatives. In Exhibit 11-6, the differential cost between make-HDS and buy-HDS alternatives is $10,000 ($160,000 – $150,000). Note that *incremental cost* and *differential cost* are sometimes used interchangeably in practice. When faced with these terms, always be sure what they mean.

We define *incremental revenue* and *differential revenue* similarly to incremental cost and differential cost. **Incremental revenue** is the additional total revenue from an activity. **Differential revenue** is the difference in total revenue between two alternatives.

Using resources that would have been idle can increase profitability or decrease unprofitability. Consider Beijing Engineering, at which the *China Daily* noted that workers were "busy producing electric plaster-spraying machines" even though the unit cost of 1,230 yuan exceeded the selling price of 985 yuan, resulting in a loss of 245 yuan per sprayer. Still, to meet market demand, the plant continued to produce sprayers. The fixed labor and equipment costs were 759 yuan per sprayer. In the short run, the production of sprayers, even at a loss, actually reduced the company's operating loss (from 759 yuan per sprayer to 245 yuan per sprayer).

Strategic and Qualitative Factors

Strategic and qualitative factors affect outsourcing decisions. For example, El Cerrito may prefer to manufacture HDS in-house to retain control over the design, quality, reliability, and delivery schedules of the switches it uses in its thermostats. Conversely, despite the cost advantages documented in Exhibit 11-6, El Cerrito may prefer to outsource, become a smaller and leaner organization, and focus on areas of its core competencies—the manufacture and sale of thermostats. As an example of focus, advertising companies, like J. Walter Thompson, only do the creative and planning aspects of advertising (their core competencies) and outsource production activities, such as film, photographs, and illustrations.

Outsourcing is not without risks. As a company's dependence on its suppliers increases, suppliers could increase prices and let quality and delivery performance slip. To minimize these risks, companies generally enter into long-run contracts specifying costs, quality, and delivery schedules with their suppliers. Intelligent managers build close partnerships or alliances with a few key suppliers. Toyota goes so far as to send its own engineers to improve suppliers' processes. Suppliers of companies such as Ford, Hyundai, Panasonic, and Sony have researched and developed innovative products, met demands for increased quantities, maintained quality and on-time delivery, and lowered costs—actions that the companies themselves would not have had the competencies to achieve. The Concepts in Action (p. 378) describes how Volkswagen has outsourced the entire manufacturing of its trucks and buses at its Resende, Brazil, plant to its suppliers.

5 Explain the opportunity-cost concept and why it is used in decision making

... in all decisions, it is important to consider the contribution to income forgone by choosing a particular alternative and rejecting others

OPPORTUNITY COSTS, OUTSOURCING, AND CAPACITY CONSTRAINTS

The calculations in Exhibit 11-6 assumed that the capacity currently used to make HDS will remain idle if El Cerrito purchases the parts from the outside manufacturer. More

CONCEPTS IN ACTION

VW Takes Outsourcing to the Limit

Volkswagen's bus and truck plant in Resende, Brazil, is a virtual plant: VW has completely outsourced manufacturing to a team of carefully selected supplier-partners in a radical experiment in production operations. At Resende, VW is transformed from manufacturer to general contractor, overseeing assembly operations performed by seven German, U.S., Brazilian, and Japanese components suppliers, with not one VW employee so much as turning a screw. Only 200 of the total 1,000 Resende workers are actual VW employees.

When designing the Resende plant, VW asked suppliers to bid for the opportunity to own one of seven major modules required to build a car, such as axles and brakes or engine and transmission. Suppliers have invested $50 million to build, equip, and stock their areas. VW's contract with suppliers is for 10- to 15-year periods, with the conditions that suppliers must achieve specified cost and performance targets and maintain cutting-edge technologies.

The plant is divided into seven zones, demarcated by yellow floor stripes. Within the boundaries of its zone, each supplier assembles its component from subcomponents sourced from 400 minor suppliers. In parallel with subcomponent assembly, final assembly occurs as the chassis (the vehicle platform) passes through the zones, and each company adds its respective component-module until the finished VW rolls off the line. Following each vehicle through the line is a single VW employee—a master craftsman assigned to track the vehicle and solve problems on the spot. Suppliers are paid for each completed vehicle that passes final inspection.

Despite representing seven different companies, the suppliers operate as a tightly integrated team, wearing the same uniforms and receiving the same pay. The assembly line is highly cross-functional, with representatives from each supplier meeting each morning to plan the day's production and each evening to address issues and solve any problems. Each supplier has visibility of the entire production process, which stimulates ideas for simplification, streamlining, and product and process changes.

The specialization and component knowledge of each supplier, combined with the close interaction among suppliers, improves quality and efficiency. Locating the major component and final assemblies together at the same plant improves production flow and compresses total assembly time. It also simplifies logistics and reduces materials-handling, production control, manufacturing engineering, and coordination costs.

Although the plant has made some adjustments that make its operations more conventional, preliminary results look promising. Resende employs 1,500 manufacturing workers, instead of 2,500 at a comparable older VW plant. The time to assemble a truck has been reduced from 52 to 35 hours. These improvements have enabled VW to quickly earn more than a 20% share in the Brazilian truck and bus markets.

Source: D. J. Schemo, "Is VW's New Plant Lean, or Just Mean?" *The New York Times* (November 19, 1996); J. Friedland; "VW Puts Suppliers on Production Line," *The Wall Street Journal* (February 15, 1996); L. Goering, "Revolution at Plant X," *Chicago Tribune* (April 13, 1997); D. Sedgwick, "Just What Does an Automaker Make?" *Automotive News International* (September 1, 2000); "Mercedes and VW Fight From Factory Floor Up," *Gazeta Mercantil Online* (April 4, 2001).

generally though, the released capacity can be used for other, more profitable purposes. The choice then is not whether to make or buy but how best to use available production capacity.

Example 3: *Suppose El Cerrito buys HDS from the outside supplier. Then, El Cerrito's best use of the capacity that becomes available is to produce 5,000 units of RS, a regular switch, for Terrence Corporation. John Marquez, the accountant at El Cerrito, estimates the following future revenues and costs if RS is manufactured and sold:*

EXHIBIT 11-7 **Total-Alternatives Approach and Opportunity-Cost Approach to Make-or-Buy Decisions for El Cerrito**

	Alternatives for El Cerrito		
Relevant Items	**1. Make HDS and Do Not Make RS**	**2. Buy HDS and Do Not Make RS**	**3. Buy HDS and Make RS**
PANEL A: TOTAL-ALTERNATIVES APPROACH TO MAKE-OR-BUY DECISIONS			
Total incremental future costs of making/buying HDS (from Exhibit 11-6)	$150,000	$160,000	$160,000
Deduct excess of future revenues over future costs from RS	0	0	(25,000)
Total relevant costs under total-alternatives approach	$150,000	$160,000	$135,000
PANEL B: OPPORTUNITY-COST APPROACH TO MAKE-OR-BUY DECISIONS			
Total incremental future costs of making/buying HDS (from Exhibit 11-6)	$150,000	$160,000	$160,000
Opportunity cost: Profit contribution forgone because capacity will not be used to make RS, the next-best alternative	25,000	25,000	0
Total relevant costs under opportunity-cost approach	$175,000	$185,000	$160,000

Note that the differences in costs across the columns in Panels A and B are the same—the cost of alternative 3 is $15,000 less than the cost of alternative 1 and $25,000 less than the cost of alternative 2.

Incremental future revenues		*$80,000*
Incremental future costs		
Direct materials	*$30,000*	
Direct manufacturing labor	*5,000*	
Variable overhead (power, utilities)	*15,000*	
Materials-handling and setup overheads	*5,000*	
Total incremental future costs		*55,000*
Incremental future operating income		*$25,000*

Because of capacity constraints, El Cerrito can make either HDS or RS, but not both. Which of the following three alternatives should El Cerrito choose?

1. *Make HDS and do not make RS for Terrence*
2. *Buy HDS and do not make RS for Terrence*
3. *Buy HDS and make RS for Terrence*

Exhibit 11-7, Panel A, summarizes the "total-alternatives" approach—the future costs and revenues for *all* alternatives. Alternative 3, buying HDS and using the available capacity to make and sell RS, is the preferred alternative. The future incremental costs of buying HDS from an outside supplier ($160,000) are more than the future incremental costs of making HDS in-house ($150,000). But El Cerrito can use the capacity freed up by buying HDS to gain $25,000 in operating income (additional future revenues of $80,000 minus additional future costs of $55,000) by making and selling RS to Terrence. The *net relevant costs* of buying HDS and making and selling RS are $160,000 – $25,000 = $135,000.

You probably will find the total-alternatives approach easier to understand. To use it, merely analyze the cash flows into and out of the company. We suggest you use the total-alternatives approach until you are sufficiently comfortable with the concept of opportunity cost to use the opportunity-cost approach.

Deciding to use a resource in a particular way causes a manager to give up the opportunity to use the resource in alternative ways. This lost opportunity is a cost that the manager must take into consideration when making a decision. **Opportunity cost** is the contribution to income that is forgone or rejected by not using a limited resource in its next-best alternative use. For example, the (relevant) cost of going to school for an MBA degree is not only the cost of tuition, books, lodging, and food, but also the income forgone (opportunity cost) by studying rather than working. Presumably the estimated

The opportunity-cost concept is from economics.

future benefits of obtaining an MBA (for example, a higher paying career) will exceed these costs.

Exhibit 11-7, Panel B, displays the opportunity-cost approach for analyzing the alternatives faced by El Cerrito. When using the opportunity-cost approach, focus on the costs of making or buying HDS.

Consider alternative 1, make HDS and do not make RS, and ask, What are all the costs of making HDS under this alternative? Certainly, El Cerrito will incur $150,000 of incremental costs to make HDS. But is this the entire cost? No, because by deciding to use limited manufacturing resources to make HDS, El Cerrito will give up the opportunity to earn $25,000 from not using these resources to make RS. Therefore, the relevant costs of making HDS are the incremental costs of $150,000 *plus* the opportunity cost of $25,000.

Next consider alternative 2, buy HDS and do not make RS. The incremental cost of buying HDS will be $160,000. But there is also an opportunity cost of $25,000 as a result of deciding not to make RS.

Finally consider alternative 3, buy HDS and make RS. The incremental cost of buying HDS will be $160,000. The opportunity cost is zero. Why? Because by choosing this alternative, El Cerrito will not forgo the profit it can earn from making and selling RS.

Panel B leads management to the same conclusion as Panel A—buying HDS and making RS is the preferred alternative.

Panels A and B of Exhibit 11-7 describe two consistent approaches to decision making with capacity constraints. The total-alternatives approach in Panel A includes all future incremental costs and revenues. For example, under alternative 3, the additional future operating income from *using capacity to make and sell RS* is subtracted from the future incremental cost of buying HDS. The opportunity-cost analysis in Panel B takes the opposite approach. It focuses on HDS. *Whenever capacity is not going to be used to make and sell RS*, the future forgone operating income is added as an opportunity cost of making or buying HDS, as in alternatives 1 and 2. (Note, when RS is made, as in alternative 3, there is "no opportunity cost of not making RS.") Thus, whereas Panel A *subtracts* $25,000 under alternative 3, Panel B *adds* $25,000 under alternative 1 and also under alternative 2. Panel B highlights the idea that when capacity is constrained, the relevant revenues and costs of any alternative equal the incremental future revenues and costs plus the opportunity cost. However, when more than two alternatives are being considered simultaneously, it is generally easier to use the total-alternatives approach.

Opportunity costs are not incorporated into formal financial accounting records. Why? Because historical record keeping is limited to transactions involving alternatives that were *actually selected,* rather than alternatives that were rejected. Rejected alternatives do not produce transactions and so they are not recorded. If El Cerrito makes HDS, it would not make RS, and it would not record any accounting entries for RS. Yet the opportunity cost of making HDS, which equals the operating income that El Cerrito forgoes by not making RS, is a crucial input into the make-versus-buy decision. Consider again Exhibit 11-7, Panel B. On the basis of only the incremental costs systematically recorded in the accounting system, it is less costly for El Cerrito to make rather than buy HDS. Recognizing the opportunity cost of $25,000 leads to the different conclusion that it is preferable to buy HDS.

Suppose El Cerrito has sufficient capacity to make RS even if it makes HDS. In this case, El Cerrito has a fourth alternative, Make HDS and Make RS. For this alternative, the opportunity cost of making HDS is $0 because El Cerrito does not give up the $25,000 operating income from making RS even if it chooses to manufacture HDS. The relevant costs are $150,000 (incremental costs of $150,000 plus opportunity cost of $0). It follows that, under these conditions, El Cerrito would prefer to make HDS rather than buy it, and make RS as well.

Besides quantitative considerations, the final make-or-buy decision should consider strategic factors and qualitative factors as well. If El Cerrito decides to buy HDS from an outside supplier, it should consider factors such as the supplier's reputation for quality and timely delivery. El Cerrito would also want to consider the consequences of selling RS to Terrence, if Terrence uses RS to produce thermostats that compete with El Cerrito.

CONCEPTS IN ACTION

American Airlines, the Internet, and Opportunity Costs

What are the relevant costs for American Airlines to fly a customer on a round-trip flight from Dallas to San Francisco, leaving on Friday, May 31, 2002, and returning on Monday, June 3, 2002? The incremental costs are very small—mainly food costs of, say, $20—because the other costs are fixed—the plane, pilots, ticket agents, and baggage handlers. The question is, What are the opportunity costs? To determine the opportunity costs, American Airlines must assess what profit it has forgone by selling a seat to a particular customer. The profit forgone depends on whether the flight is full—meaning the aircraft is operating at capacity. American would normally charge $400 for this round-trip ticket. If seats are available, the opportunity cost is zero. If the flight is full, the opportunity cost is $380 ($400 − $20), the profit American would make by selling the same seat to another customer. The relevant cost is $400—the incremental cost of $20 plus the opportunity cost of $380.

If a customer calls to purchase the ticket in early May 2002, American computes the relevant costs to be $400 because it expects that its flight will be full. But what if on Wednesday, May 29, 2002, American finds that the plane will not be full? The relevant cost for each remaining seat on the flight will be only the $20 incremental cost, and American can lower its prices well below $400—to, say, $100—and still make a profit. Waiting until the last minute and recognizing that opportunity costs are zero enables American to lower its prices drastically in the hopes of attracting more customers while still earning a profit.

The Internet makes it possible for American to tell its potential customers cheaply and quickly about these lowered fares. Using what is called "push" technology, American broadcasts information about all flights on which seats are available to subscribers who have registered free of charge on American Airlines' home page www.aa.com. Every Wednesday morning, an e-mail is sent to each subscriber indicating departure and arrival cities for which cheap fares, often around $100, are available. The requirement? Travel must start on Friday or Saturday and end before the following Monday. By waiting until Wednesday to announce the fares, American can be certain that unfilled seats are available and that the opportunity costs for the fares it offers are therefore zero. The Internet allows information to be disseminated to a large audience quickly and at virtually no cost. American Airlines' low-fare subscription service is a good example of how a company that has a good understanding of relevant costs can take advantage of its low variable-cost structure using the Internet.

Carrying Costs of Inventory

To see another example of an opportunity cost, consider the following data for El Cerrito.

Annual estimated HDS requirements for next year	10,000 units
Cost per unit when each purchase is of 1,000 units	$16.00
Cost per unit when each purchase is equal to or greater than 10,000 units; $16 minus 1% discount	$15.84
Cost of a purchase order	$100.00
Alternatives under consideration:	
A. Make 10 purchases of 1,000 units each during next year	
B. Make 1 purchase of 10,000 units at the start of next year	
Average investment in inventory:	
A. (1,000 units × $16.00 per unit) ÷ 2[a]	$8,000
B. (10,000 units × $15.84 per unit) ÷ 2[a]	$79,200
Annual interest rate for investment in government Treasury bill	6%

[a]The example assumes that HDS purchases will be used up uniformly throughout the year. The average investment in inventory during the year is the cost of the inventory when a purchase is received plus the cost of inventory just before the next purchase is delivered (in our example, zero) divided by 2.

El Cerrito will pay cash for the HDS it buys. Which purchasing alternative is more economical for El Cerrito? The following table presents the two alternatives.

	Alternative A: Make 10 Purchases of 1,000 Units Each During the Year (1)	Alternative B: Make 1 Purchase of 10,000 Units at Beginning of Year (2)	Difference (3) = (1) − (2)
Annual purchase-order costs (10 purch. orders ¥ $100/ purch. order; 1 purch. order ¥ $100/ purch. order)	$ 1,000	$ 100	$ 900
Annual purchase costs (10,000 units ¥ $16.00/unit; 10,000 units ¥ $15.84/unit)	160,000	158,400	1,600
Annual interest income that could be earned if investment in inventory were invested in 6% government Treasury bills (opportunity cost)(0.06 ¥ $8,000; 0.06 ¥ $79,200)	480	4,752	(4,272)
Relevant costs	$161,480	$163,252	$(1,772)

The opportunity cost of holding inventory is the income forgone by tying up money in inventory and not investing it elsewhere. The opportunity cost would not be recorded in the accounting system because, once the alternative of investing money elsewhere is rejected, there are no transactions related to this alternative to record. Column 3 indicates that, consistent with the trends toward holding smaller inventories, purchasing smaller quantities of 1,000 units throughout the year is preferred to purchasing all 10,000 units at the beginning of the year. Why? Because the lower opportunity cost of holding smaller inventory exceeds the higher purchase and ordering costs. If the opportunity cost of money tied up in inventory were greater than 6% per year, or if other incremental benefits of holding lower inventory were considered—such as lower insurance, material-handling, storage, obsolescence, and breakage costs—making 10 purchases would be even more preferable.

6 Know how to choose which products to produce when there are capacity constraints

...select the product with the highest contribution margin per unit of the limiting resource

PRODUCT-MIX DECISIONS UNDER CAPACITY CONSTRAINTS

We now examine how the concept of relevance applies to **product-mix decisions**—the decisions by a company about which products to sell and in what quantities. These decisions usually have only a short-run focus because the level of capacity can be expanded in the long run. For example, BMW, the German car manufacturer, must continually adapt the mix of its different models of cars (e.g., 325i, 525i, and 740i) to short-run fluctuations in material costs, selling prices, and demand. To determine product mix, a company maximizes operating income, given the constraints the company faces, such as capacity and demand. Throughout this section, we assume that as short-run changes in product mix occur, the only costs that change are costs that are variable with respect to the number of units produced (and sold). Under this assumption, the analysis of individual product contribution margins provides insight into the product mix that maximizes operating income.

Example 4: *Power Recreation assembles two engines—a snowmobile engine and a boat engine—at its Lexington, Kentucky, plant.*

	Snowmobile Engine	*Boat Engine*
Selling price	*$800*	*$1,000*
Variable cost per unit	*560*	*625*
Contribution margin per unit	*$240*	*$ 375*
Contribution margin percentage ($240 ÷ $800; $375 ÷ $1,000)	*30%*	*37.5%*

Assume that only 600 machine-hours are available daily for assembling engines. Additional capacity cannot be obtained in the short run. Power Recreation can sell as many engines as it produces. The constraining resource, then, is machine-hours. It takes two machine-hours to produce one snowmobile engine and five machine-hours to produce one boat engine. What product mix should Power Recreation choose to maximize its operating income?

FIRST-YEAR RESULTS: ACCRUAL ACCOUNTING

	Keep		Replace	
Revenues		$1,100,000		$1,100,000
Operating costs				
Cash-operating costs	$800,000		$460,000	
Depreciation	200,000		300,000	
Loss on disposal	—		360,000	
Total operating costs		1,000,000		1,120,000
Operating income (loss)		$ 100,000		$ (20,000)

Even if top management's goals encompass the two-year period (consistent with the decision model), the manager will focus on first-year results if his or her evaluation is based on short-run measures such as first-year operating income.

Resolving the conflict between the decision model and the performance evaluation model is frequently a baffling problem in practice. In theory, resolving the difficulty seems obvious—design consistent models. Consider our replacement example. Year-by-year effects on operating income of replacement can be budgeted for the two-year planning horizon. The manager would be evaluated on the understanding that the first year would be expected to be poor and the next year much better.

The practical difficulty is that accounting systems rarely track each decision separately. Performance evaluation focuses on responsibility centers for a specific period, not on projects or individual items of equipment over their useful lives. Thus, the impacts of many different decisions are combined in a single performance report. Top management, through the reporting system, is rarely aware of particular desirable alternatives that were not chosen by subordinate managers.

Consider another conflict between the decision model and the performance evaluation model. Suppose a manager buys a particular machine only to discover shortly thereafter that a better machine could have been purchased instead. The decision model may suggest replacing the machine that was just bought with the better machine, but will the manager do so? Probably not. Why not? Because replacing the machine so soon after its purchase may reflect badly on the manager's capabilities and performance. If the manager's bosses have no knowledge of the better machine, the manager may prefer to keep the recently purchased machine rather than alert them to the better machine.

PROBLEM FOR SELF-STUDY

Wally Lewis is manager of the engineering development division of Goldcoast Products, Inc. Lewis has just received a proposal signed by all 10 of his engineers to replace the workstations with networked personal computers (networked PCs). Lewis is not enthusiastic about the proposal.

Data on the workstation and networked PC machines are

	Workstations	Networked PCs
Original cost	$300,000	$135,000
Useful life	5 years	3 years
Current age	2 years	0 years
Remaining useful life	3 years	3 years
Accumulated depreciation	$120,000	Not acquired yet
Current book value	$180,000	Not acquired yet
Current disposal value (in cash)	$95,000	Not acquired yet
Terminal disposal value (in cash 3 years from now)	$0	$0
Annual computer-related cash operating costs	$40,000	$10,000
Annual revenues	$1,000,000	$1,000,000
Annual non-computer-related operating costs	$880,000	$880,000

Lewis's annual bonus includes a component based on division operating income. He has a promotion possibility next year that would make him a group vice president of Goldcoast Products.

Continued

Required

1. Compare the costs of the workstation and networked PC options. Consider the cumulative results for the three years together, ignoring time value of money and income taxes.
2. Why might Lewis be reluctant to purchase the networked PCs?

SOLUTION

1. The following table considers all cost items when comparing future costs of the workstation and networked PC options:

	Three Years Together		
All Items	**Workstations (1)**	**Networked PCs (2)**	**Difference (3) = (1) − (2)**
Revenues	$3,000,000	$3,000,000	—
Operating costs			
Noncomputer-related operating costs	2,640,000	2,640,000	—
Computer-related cash operating costs	120,000	30,000	$ 90,000
Workstations' book value			
Periodic write-off as depreciation or	180,000	—	
Lump-sum write-off	—	180,000	—
Current disposal value of workstations	—	(95,000)	95,000
Networked PCs, written off periodically as depreciation	—	135,000	(135,000)
Total operating costs	2,940,000	2,890,000	50,000
Operating income	$ 60,000	$ 110,000	$(50,000)

Alternatively, the analysis could focus on only those items in the preceding table that differ between the alternatives.

	Three Years Together		
Relevant Items	**Workstations**	**Networked PCs**	**Difference**
Computer-related cash operating costs	$120,000	$ 30,000	$ 90,000
Current disposal value of workstations	—	(95,000)	95,000
Networked PCs, written off periodically as depreciation	—	135,000	(135,000)
Total relevant costs	$120,000	$ 70,000	$ 50,000

The analysis suggests that it is cost-effective to replace the workstations with the networked PCs.

2. The accrual accounting operating incomes for the first year under the "keep workstations" versus the "buy networked PCs" alternatives are

	Keep Workstations		Buy Networked PCs	
Revenues		$1,000,000		$1,000,000
Operating costs				
Noncomputer-related operating costs	$880,000		$880,000	
Computer-related cash operating costs	40,000		10,000	
Depreciation	60,000		45,000	
Loss on disposal of workstations	—		85,000[a]	
Total operating costs		980,000		1,020,000
Operating income		$ 20,000		$ (20,000)

[a]$85,000 = Book value of workstations, $180,000 − Current disposal price, $95,000

Lewis would be far less happy with the expected operating loss of $20,000 if the networked PCs are purchased than he would be with the expected operating income of $20,000 if the workstations are kept. The decision would eliminate the component of his bonus based on operating income. He might also perceive the $20,000 operating loss as reducing his chances of being promoted to a group vice president.

DECISION POINTS — SUMMARY

The following question-and-answer format summarizes the chapter's learning objectives. Each decision presents a key question related to a learning objective. The guidelines are the answer to that question.

Decision	Guidelines
1. What is the five-step process that can be used to make decisions?	The five-step decision process is (a) obtain information, (b) make predictions, (c) choose an alternative, (d) implement the decision, and (e) evaluate performance to provide feedback.
2. When is a revenue or cost relevant for a particular decision?	To be relevant for a particular decision, a revenue or cost must meet two criteria: (a) it must be an expected future revenue or expected future cost, and (b) it must differ among alternative courses of action.
3. Should both quantitative and qualitative factors be considered in making decisions?	Yes, the outcomes of alternative actions can be quantitative and qualitative. Quantitative outcomes are measured in numerical terms. Some quantitative outcomes can be expressed in financial terms, others cannot. Qualitative factors, such as employee morale, are difficult to measure accurately in numerical terms. Consideration must be given to both quantitative and qualitative factors in making decisions.
4. What potential problems should be avoided in relevant-cost analysis?	Two potential problems to avoid in relevant-cost analysis are (a) making incorrect general assumptions—such as all variable costs are relevant and all fixed costs are irrelevant—and (b) losing sight of grand totals, focusing instead on unit amounts.
5. What is an opportunity cost and why should it be included when making decisions?	Opportunity cost is the contribution to income that is forgone or rejected by not using a limited resource in its next-best alternative use. Opportunity cost is included in decision making because it represents the best alternative way in which an organization may have used its resources had it not made the decision it did.
6. When resources are constrained, how should managers choose which of multiple products to produce and sell?	Under these conditions, managers should select the product that yields the highest contribution margin per unit of the constraining or limiting resource (factor).
7. In deciding to discontinue or add customers, branches, or segments, how should managers take into account allocated overhead costs?	Managers should ignore allocated overhead costs when making decisions about discontinuing and adding customers, branches, and segments. They should focus instead on how total costs differ among alternatives.
8. Is book value of existing equipment relevant in equipment-replacement decisions?	Book value of existing equipment is a past, or historical, cost and, therefore, is irrelevant in equipment-replacement decisions.
9. How can conflicts arise between the decision model and the performance evaluation model used to evaluate the manager?	Top management faces a persistent challenge—that is, making sure that the performance evaluation model of subordinate managers is consistent with the decision model. A common inconsistency is to tell subordinate managers to take a multiple-year view in their decision making but then judge their performance only on the basis of the current year's operating income.

APPENDIX: LINEAR PROGRAMMING

In this chapter's Power Recreation example (p. 382), suppose both the snowmobile and boat engines must be tested on a very expensive machine before shipping to customers. The available machine-hours for testing is limited. Production data are

Department	Available Daily Capacity in Hours	Use of Capacity in Hours per Unit of Product		Daily Maximum Production in Units	
		Snowmobile Engine	Boat Engine	Snowmobile Engine	Boat Engine
Assembly	600 machine-hours	2.0 machine-hours	5.0 machine-hours	300[a] snow engines	120 boat engines
Testing	120 testing-hours	1.0 machine-hour	0.5 machine-hour	120 snow engines	240 boat engines

[a]For example, 600 machine-hours ÷ 2.0 machine-hours per snowmobile engine = 300, the maximum number of snowmobile engines that the Assembly Department can make if it works exclusively on snowmobile engines.

EXHIBIT 11-13

Operating Data for Power Recreation

	Department Capacity (per Day) In Product Units				
	Assembly	**Testing**	**Selling Price**	**Variable Cost per Unit**	**Contribution Margin per Unit**
Only snowmobile engines	300	120	$ 800	$560	$240
Only boat engines	120	240	$1,000	$625	$375

Exhibit 11-13 summarizes these and other relevant data. Furthermore, as a result of material shortages for boat engines, Power Recreation cannot produce more than 110 boat engines per day. How many engines of each type should Power Recreation produce and sell daily to maximize operating income?

Because there are multiple constraints, a technique called *linear programming* can be used to determine the number of engines Power Recreation should produce. LP models typically assume that all costs are either variable or fixed with respect to a single driver (units of output). As we shall see, LP models also require certain other linear assumptions to hold. When these assumptions fail, other decision models should be considered.[3]

Steps in Solving an LP Problem

Being an accounting student, you probably are pleased to see an accounting application of linear programming, a technique taught in courses such as operations management, management science, or quantitative analysis for business decisions.

We use the data in Exhibit 11-13 to illustrate the three steps in solving an LP problem. Throughout this discussion, S equals the number of units of snowmobile engines produced, and B equals the number of units of boat engines produced.

Step 1: Determine the Objective Function. The **objective function** of a linear program expresses the objective or goal to be maximized (say, operating income) or minimized (say, operating costs). In our example, the objective is to find the combination of engines that maximizes total contribution margin. Fixed costs remain the same regardless of the product-mix decision and are irrelevant. The linear function expressing the objective for the total contribution margin *(TCM)* is:

$$TCM = \$240S + \$375B$$

S and B in the objective function and in the constraints always appear in linear form—that is, they never appear as S^2 or B^2 or $\sqrt{S}$ or $\sqrt{B}$, etc. As you see in Exhibit 11-14, the plot of the objective function and the constraints are linear—they appear as straight lines. It is this linear form of the optimization program that leads to the name *linear programming.*

Step 2: Specify the Constraints. A **constraint** is a mathematical inequality or equality that must be satisfied by the variables in a mathematical model. The following linear inequalities express the relationships in our example:

Assembly Department constraint	$2S + 5B \leq 600$
Testing Department constraint	$1S + 0.5B \leq 120$
Material shortage constraint for boat engines	$B \leq 110$
Negative production is impossible	$S \geq 0$ and $B \geq 0$

The three solid lines on the graph in Exhibit 11-14 show the existing constraints for Assembly and Testing and the material shortage constraint.[4] The feasible or technically possible alternatives are those combinations of quantities of snowmobile and boat engines that satisfy all the constraining resources or factors. The shaded "area of feasible solutions" in Exhibit 11-14 shows the boundaries of those product combinations that are feasible.

[3]Other decision models are described in G. Eppen, F. Gould, C. Schmidt, J. Moore, and L. Weatherford, *Introductory Management Science: Decision Modeling with Spreadsheets,* 5th ed. (Upper Saddle River, NJ: Prentice Hall, 1998); and S. Nahmias, *Production and Operations Analysis,* 4th ed. (New York: McGraw-Hill/Irwin, 2001).

[4]As an example of how the lines are plotted in Exhibit 11-14, use equal signs instead of inequality signs and assume for the Assembly Department that $B = 0$; then $S = 300$ (600 machine-hours ÷ 2 machine-hours per snowmobile engine). Assume that $S = 0$; then $B = 120$ (600 machine-hours ÷ 5 machine-hours per boat engine). Connect those two points with a straight line.

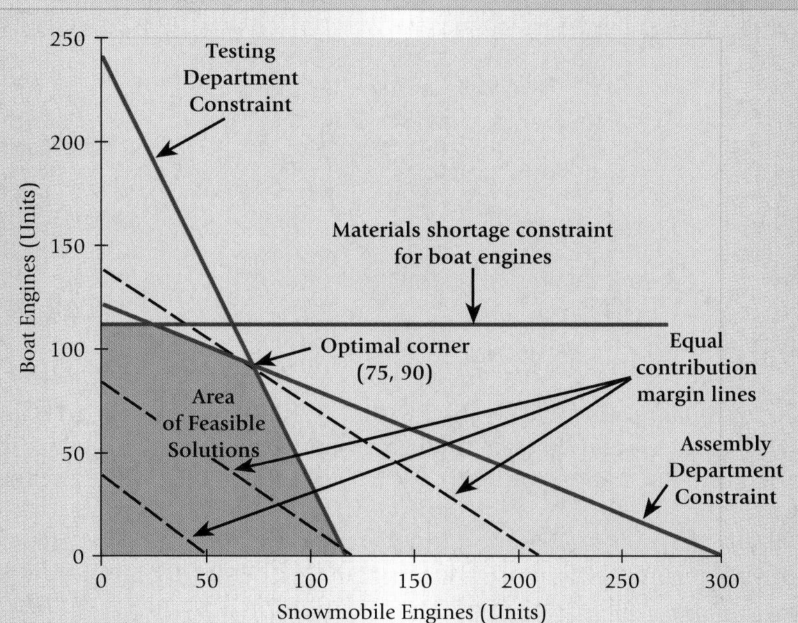

EXHIBIT 11-14

Linear Programming: Graphic Solution for Power Recreation

Step 3: Compute the Optimal Solution. Linear programming (LP) is an optimization technique used to maximize the *objective function* when there are multiple *constraints.* We present two approaches for finding the optimal solution using LP: trial-and-error approach and graphic approach. These approaches are easy to use in our example because there are only two variables in the objective function and a small number of constraints. Understanding these approaches provides insight into LP. In most real-world LP applications, managers use computer software packages to calculate the optimal solution.[5]

Trial-and-error approach The optimal solution can be found by trial and error, by working with coordinates of the corners of the area of feasible solutions.

First, select any set of corner points and compute the total contribution margin. Five corner points appear in Exhibit 11-14. It is helpful to use simultaneous equations to obtain the exact coordinates on the graph. To illustrate, the corner point ($S = 75$, $B = 90$) can be derived by solving the two pertinent constraint inequalities as simultaneous equations:

	$2S + 5B = 600$	(1)
	$1S + 0.5B = 120$	(2)
Multiplying (2) by 2.0:	$2S + 1B = 240$	(3)
Subtracting (3) from (1):	$4B = 360$	
Therefore,	$B = 360 \div 4 = 90$	
Substituting for B in (2):	$1S + 0.5(90) = 120$	
	$S = 120 - 45 = 75$	

Given $S = 75$ snowmobile engines and $B = 90$ boat engines, TCM = (\$240 per snowmobile engine × 75 snowmobile engines) + (\$375 per boat engine × 90 boat engines) = \$51,750.

[5]Although the trial-and-error and graphic approaches can be useful for two or possibly three variables, they are impractical when many variables exist. Standard computer software packages rely on the simplex method. The *simplex method* is an iterative step-by-step procedure for determining the optimal solution to an LP problem. It starts with a specific feasible solution and then tests it by substitution to see whether the result can be improved. These substitutions continue until no further improvement is possible and the optimal solution is obtained.

Second, move from corner point to corner point and compute the total contribution margin at each corner point.

Trial	Corner Point (S, B)	Snowmobile Engines (S)	Boat Engines (B)	Total Contribution Margin
1	(0, 0)	0	0	\$240(0) + \$375(0) = \$0
2	(0, 110)	0	110	\$240(0) + \$375(110) = \$41,250
3	(25, 110)	25	110	\$240(25) + \$375(110) = \$47,250
4	(75, 90)	75	90	\$240(75) + \$375(90) = \$51,750[a]
5	(120, 0)	120	0	\$240(120) + \$375(0) = \$28,800

[a]The optimal solution.

The optimal product mix is the mix that yields the highest total contribution: 75 snowmobile engines and 90 boat engines. To understand the solution, consider what happens when moving from the point (25, 110) to (75, 90). Power Recreation gives up \$7,500 [\$375 × (110 – 90)] in contribution margin from boat engines while gaining \$12,000 [\$240 × (75 – 25)] in contribution margin from snowmobile engines. This results in a net increase in contribution margin of \$4,500 (\$12,000 – \$7,500), from \$47,250 to \$51,750.

Graphic approach Consider all possible combinations that will produce the same total contribution margin of, say, \$12,000. That is,

$$\$240S + \$375B = \$12,000$$

The set of \$24,000 contribution margins is a line through ($S = 100$, $B = 0$) and ($S = 0$; $B = 64$), which is parallel to the line representing the set of \$12,000 contribution margins.

This set of \$12,000 contribution margins is a straight dashed line through [$S = 50$ (\$12,000 ÷ \$240); $B = 0$)] and [$S = 0$, $B = 32$ (\$12,000 ÷ \$375)] in Exhibit 11-14. Other equal total contribution margins can be represented by lines parallel to this one. In Exhibit 11-14, we show three dashed lines. Lines drawn farther from the origin represent more sales of both products and higher amounts of equal contribution margins.

The optimal line is the one farthest from the origin but still passing through a point in the area of feasible solutions. This line represents the highest total contribution margin. The optimal solution—the number of snowmobile engines and boat engines that will maximize the objective function, total contribution margin—is the corner point ($S = 75$, $B = 90$). This solution will become apparent if you put a straight-edge ruler on the graph and move it outward from the origin and parallel with the \$12,000 line. Move the ruler as far away from the origin as possible—that is, increase the total contribution margin—without leaving the area of feasible solutions. In general, the optimal solution in a maximization problem lies at the corner where the dashed line intersects an extreme point of the area of feasible solutions. Moving the ruler out any farther puts it outside the feasible region.

Sensitivity Analysis

Large changes in contribution margin per unit of products may not affect the optimal product mix if there are no other nearby corner points.

What are the implications of uncertainty about the accounting or technical coefficients used in the objective function (such as the contribution margin per unit of snowmobile engines or boat engines) or the constraints (such as the number of machine-hours it takes to make a snowmobile engine or a boat engine)? Consider how a change in the contribution margin of snowmobile engines from \$240 to \$300 per unit would affect the optimal solution. Assume the contribution margin for boat engines remains unchanged at \$375 per unit. The revised objective function will be

$$TCM = \$300S + \$375B$$

Using the trial-and-error approach to calculate the total contribution margin for each of the five corner points described in the previous table, the optimal solution is still ($S = 75$, $B = 90$). What if the contribution margin of snowmobile engines falls to \$160? The optimal solution remains the same ($S = 75$, $B = 90$). Thus, big changes in the contribution margin per unit of snowmobile engines have no effect on the optimal solution in this case. That's because, although the slopes of the equal contribution margin lines in Exhibit 11-14 change as the contribution margin of snowmobile engines changes from \$240 to \$300 to \$160 per unit, the farthest point at which the equal contribution margin lines intersect the area of feasible solutions is still ($S = 75$, $B = 90$).

TERMS TO LEARN

book value (p. 386)
business function costs (373)
constraint (392)
decision model (370)
differential cost (377)
differential revenue (377)
full costs of the product (373)
incremental cost (377)
incremental revenue (377)
insourcing (375)
linear programming (LP) (393)
make-or-buy decisions (375)
objective function (392)
one-time-only special order (373)
opportunity cost (379)
outsourcing (375)
product-mix decisions (382)
qualitative factors (372)
quantitative factors (372)
relevant costs (370)
relevant revenues (370)
sunk costs (371)

ASSIGNMENT MATERIAL

Questions

11-1 Outline the five-step sequence in a decision process.

11-2 Define *relevant costs.* Why are historical costs irrelevant?

11-3 "All future costs are relevant." Do you agree? Why?

11-4 Distinguish between quantitative and qualitative factors in decision making.

11-5 Describe two potential problems that should be avoided in relevant-cost analysis.

11-6 "Variable costs are always relevant, and fixed costs are always irrelevant." Do you agree? Why?

11-7 "A component part should be purchased whenever the purchase price is less than its total manufacturing cost per unit." Do you agree? Why?

11-8 Define *opportunity cost.*

11-9 "Managers should always buy inventory in quantities that result in the lowest purchase cost per unit." Do you agree? Why?

11-10 "Management should always maximize sales of the product with the highest contribution margin per unit." Do you agree? Why?

11-11 "A branch or business segment that shows negative operating income should be shut down." Do you agree? Explain briefly.

11-12 "Cost written off as depreciation on equipment already purchased is always irrelevant." Do you agree? Why?

11-13 "Managers will always choose the alternative that maximizes operating income or minimizes costs in the decision model." Do you agree? Why?

11-14 Describe the three steps in solving a linear programming problem.

11-15 How might the optimal solution of a linear programming problem be determined?

Exercises

11-16 Disposal of assets. Answer the following questions.

1. A company has an inventory of 1,000 assorted parts for a line of missiles that has been discontinued. The inventory cost is \$80,000. The parts can be either (a) remachined at total additional costs of \$30,000 and then sold for \$35,000 or (b) sold as scrap for \$2,000. Which action is more profitable? Show your calculations.

2. A truck, costing $100,000 and uninsured, is wrecked its first day in use. It can be either (a) disposed of for $10,000 cash and replaced with a similar truck costing $102,000 or (b) rebuilt for $85,000, and thus be brand-new as far as operating characteristics and looks are concerned. Which action is less costly? Show your calculations.

11-17 The careening personal computer. (W. A. Paton) An employee in the Accounting Department of a company was moving a personal computer from one room to another. As he came alongside an open stairway, he slipped and the computer got away from him. It careened down the stairs with a great racket and wound up at the bottom, completely destroyed. Hearing the crash, the office manager came rushing out and turned rather pale when he saw what had happened. "Someone tell me quickly," the manager yelled, "if that is one of our fully depreciated items." A check of the accounting records showed that the smashed computer was, indeed, one of those items that had been written off. "Thank God!" exclaimed the manager.

Required Explain and comment on the point of this anecdote.

11-18 Multiple choice. (CPA) Choose the best answer.

1. The Woody Company manufactures slippers and sells them at $10 a pair. Variable manufacturing cost is $4.50 a pair, and allocated fixed manufacturing cost is $1.50 a pair. It has enough idle capacity available to accept a one-time-only special order of 20,000 pairs of slippers at $6 a pair. Woody will not incur any marketing costs as a result of the special order. What would the effect on operating income be if the special order could be accepted without affecting normal sales? (a) $0, (b) $30,000 increase, (c) $90,000 increase, or (d) $120,000 increase.
2. The Reno Company manufactures Part No. 498 for use in its production line. The manufacturing cost per unit for 20,000 units of Part No. 498 is as follows:

Direct material	$ 6
Direct manufacturing labor	30
Variable manufacturing overhead	12
Fixed manufacturing overhead allocated	16
Total manufacturing cost per unit	$64

The Tray Company has offered to sell 20,000 units of Part No. 498 to Reno for $60 per unit. Reno will make the decision to buy the part from Tray if there is an overall savings of at least $25,000 for Reno. If Reno accepts Tray's offer, $9 per unit of the fixed overhead allocated would be eliminated. Furthermore, Reno has determined that the released facilities could be used to save relevant costs in the manufacture of Part No. 575. For Reno to achieve an overall savings of $25,000, the amount of relevant costs that would have to be saved by using the released facilities in the manufacture of Part No. 575 would be (a) $80,000, (b) $85,000, (c) $125,000, or (d) $140,000.

11-19 Special order, activity-based costing. (CMA, adapted) The Award Plus Company manufactures medals for winners of athletic events and other contests. Its manufacturing plant has the capacity to produce 10,000 medals each month. Current production and sales are 7,500 medals per month. The company normally charges $150 per medal. Cost information for the current activity level is as follows:

Variable costs that vary with number of units produced	
Direct materials	$ 262,500
Direct manufacturing labor	300,000
Variable costs (for setups, materials handling, quality control, and so on) that vary with number of batches, 150 batches × $500 per batch	75,000
Fixed manufacturing costs	275,000
Fixed marketing costs	175,000
Total costs	$1,087,500

Award Plus has just received a special one-time-only order for 2,500 medals at $100 per medal. Accepting the special order would not affect the company's regular business. Award Plus makes medals for its existing customers in batch sizes of 50 medals (150 batches × 50 medals per batch = 7,500 medals). The special order requires Award Plus to make the medals in 25 batches of 100 each.

Required

1. Should Award Plus accept this special order? Show your calculations.
2. Suppose plant capacity were only 9,000 medals instead of 10,000 medals each month. The special order must either be taken in full or rejected completely. Should Award Plus accept the special order? Show your calculations.
3. As in requirement 1, assume that monthly capacity is 10,000 medals. Award Plus is concerned that if it accepts the special order, its existing customers will immediately demand a price discount of $10 in the month in which the special order is being filled. They would argue that Award Plus's capacity costs are now being spread over more units and that existing customers should get the benefit of these lower costs. Should Award Plus accept the special order under these conditions? Show your calculations.

11-20 Make versus buy, activity-based costing. The Svenson Corporation manufactures cellular modems. It manufactures its own cellular modem circuit boards (CMCB), an important part of the cellular modem. It reports the following cost information about the costs of making CMCBs in 2003 and the expected costs in 2004:

	Current Costs in 2003	Expected Costs in 2004
Variable manufacturing costs		
Direct material cost per CMCB	$ 180	$ 170
Direct manufacturing labor cost per CMCB	50	45
Variable manufacturing cost per batch for setups, material handling, and quality control	1,600	1,500
Fixed manufacturing cost		
Fixed manufacturing overhead costs that can be avoided if CMCBs are not made	320,000	320,000
Fixed manufacturing overhead costs of plant depreciation, insurance, and administration that cannot be avoided even if CMCBs are not made	800,000	800,000

Svenson manufactured 8,000 CMCBs in 2003 in 40 batches of 200 each. In 2004, Svenson anticipates needing 10,000 CMCBs. The CMCBs would be needed in 80 batches of 125 each.

The Minton Corporation has approached Svenson about supplying CMCBs to Svenson in 2004 at $300 per CMCB on whatever delivery schedule Svenson wants.

Required

1. Calculate the total expected manufacturing cost per unit of making CMCBs in 2004.
2. Suppose the capacity currently used to make CMCBs will become idle if Svenson purchases CMCBs from Minton. On the basis of financial considerations alone, should Svenson make CMCBs or buy them from Minton? Show your calculations.
3. Now suppose that if Svenson purchases CMCBs from Minton, its best alternative use of the capacity currently used for CMCBs is to make and sell special circuit boards (CB3s) to the Essex Corporation. Svenson estimates the following incremental revenues and costs from CB3s:

Total expected incremental future revenues	$2,000,000
Total expected incremental future costs	$2,150,000

On the basis of financial considerations alone, should Svenson make CMCBs or buy them from Minton? Show your calculations.

11-21 Inventory decision, opportunity costs. Lawnox, a manufacturer of lawn mowers, predicts that 240,000 spark plugs will have to be purchased next year. Lawnox estimates that 20,000 spark plugs will be required each month. A supplier quotes a price of $8 per spark plug. The supplier also offers a special discount option: If all 240,000 spark plugs are purchased at the start of the year, a discount of 5% off the $8 price will be given. Lawnox can invest its cash at 8% per year. It costs Lawnox $200 to place each purchase order.

Required

1. What is the opportunity cost of interest forgone from purchasing all 240,000 units at the start of the year instead of in 12 monthly purchases of 20,000 units per order?
2. Would this opportunity cost ordinarily be recorded in the accounting system? Why?
3. Should Lawnox purchase 240,000 units at the start of the year or 20,000 units each month? Show your calculations.

11-22 Relevant costs, contribution margin, product emphasis. The Beach Comber is a take-out food store at a popular beach resort. Susan Sexton, owner of the Beach Comber, is deciding how much refrigerator space to devote to four different drinks. Pertinent data on these four drinks are as follows:

	Cola	Lemonade	Punch	Natural Orange Juice
Selling price per case	$18.00	$19.20	$26.40	$38.40
Variable cost per case	$13.50	$15.20	$20.10	$30.20
Cases sold per foot of shelf space per day	25	24	4	5

Sexton has a maximum front shelf space of 12 feet to devote to the four drinks. She wants a minimum of 1 foot and a maximum of 6 feet of front shelf space for each drink.

Required

1. Compute the contribution margin per case of each type of drink?
2. A co-worker of Sexton's recommends that she maximize the shelf space devoted to those drinks with the highest contribution margin per case. Evaluate this recommendation.
3. What shelf-space allocation for the four drinks would you recommend for the Beach Comber? Show your calculations.

11-23 Selection of most profitable product. Body-Builders, Inc., produces two basic types of weight-lifting equipment, Model 9 and Model 14. Pertinent data are as follows:

	Per Unit	
	Model 9	Model 14
Selling price	$100.00	$70.00
Costs		
Direct material	28.00	13.00
Direct manufacturing labor	15.00	25.00
Variable manufacturing overhead*	25.00	12.50
Fixed manufacturing overhead*	10.00	5.00
Marketing (all variable)	14.00	10.00
Total cost	92.00	65.50
Operating income	$ 8.00	$ 4.50

*Allocated on the basis of machine-hours.

The weight-lifting craze is such that enough of either Model 9 or Model 14 can be sold to keep the plant operating at full capacity. Both products are processed through the same production departments.

Required Which products should be produced? Briefly explain your answer.

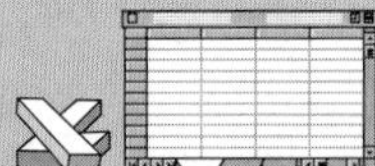

Excel Application For students who wish to practice their spreadsheet skills, the following is a step-by-step approach to creating an Excel spreadsheet to work this problem.

Step-by-Step

1. Open a new spreadsheet. At top, create an "Original Data" section for the data provided by Body-Builders, Inc. Create rows for the per unit data on selling price, costs, and operating income in exactly the same format as presented by Body-Builders, Inc., above.

(Program your spreadsheet to perform all necessary calculations. Do not "hard-code" any amounts, such as contribution margin, requiring addition, subtraction, multiplication, or division operations.)

2. Skip two rows and create a "Product Mix Analysis" section. Create columns for Model 9 and Model 14 and rows for "Selling Price, Variable Cost per Unit, Contribution Margin per Unit, Relative Use of Machine-Hours per Unit of Product," and "Contribution Margin per Machine-Hour." Use the data from your Original Data section to enter selling price, and to calculate variable cost per unit, and contribution margin per unit for each model.
3. In the "Relative Use of Machine-Hours per Unit of Product" row, enter the *relative* use of machine-hours per unit of product for Models 9 and 14, respectively. (*Hint:* Variable and fixed manufacturing overhead are allocated on the basis of machine-hours, and the variable and fixed manufacturing overhead cost per unit for Model 9 are twice as high as for Model 14.)
4. Enter calculations for contribution margin per machine-hour for Models 9 and 14 by multiplying contribution margin per unit by the relative use of machine-hours per unit of product.
5. *Check the accuracy of your spreadsheet.* Go to your Original Data section and change the selling price of Model 14 from $70 to $69 per unit. If you programmed your spreadsheet correctly, contribution margin per machine-hour for Model 14 should change to $17.

11-24 Which base to close, relevant-cost analysis, opportunity costs. The U.S. Defense Department has the difficult decision of deciding which military bases to shut down. Military and political factors obviously matter, but cost savings are also an important factor. Consider two naval bases located on the West Coast—one in Alameda, California, and the other in Everett, Washington. The Navy has decided that it needs only one of those two bases permanently, so one must be shut down. The decision regarding which base to shut down will be made on cost considerations alone. The following information is available:

a. The Alameda base was built at a cost of $100 million. The operating costs of the base are $400 million per year. The base is built on land owned by the Navy, so the Navy pays nothing for the use of the property. If the base is closed, the land will be sold to developers for $500 million.
b. The Everett base was built at a cost of $150 million on land leased by the Navy from private citizens. The Navy can choose to lease the land permanently for a lease payment of $3 million per year. If it decides to keep the Everett base open, the Navy plans to invest $60 million in a fixed income note, which at 5% interest will earn the $3 million the government needs for the lease payments. The land and buildings will immediately revert back to the owner if the base is closed. The operating costs of the base, excluding lease payments, are $300 million per year.
c. If the Alameda base is shut down, the Navy will have to transfer some personnel to the Everett facility. As a result, the yearly operating costs at Everett will increase by $100 million per year. If the Everett facility is closed down, no extra costs will be incurred to operate the Alameda facility.

The California delegation in Congress argues that it is cheaper to shut down the Everett base for two reasons: (1) It would save $100 million per year in additional costs required to operate the Everett base, and (2) it would save the lease payment of $3 million per year. (Recall that the Alameda base requires no cash payments for use of the land because the land is owned by the Navy.) Do you agree with the California delegation's arguments and conclusions? In your answer, identify and explain all costs that you consider relevant and all costs that you consider irrelevant for the base-closing decision.

Required

11-25 Closing and opening stores. Sanchez Corporation runs two convenience stores, one in Connecticut and one in Rhode Island. Operating income for each store in 2004 is as follows:

	Connecticut Store	Rhode Island Store
Revenues	$1,070,000	$860,000
Operating costs		
Cost of goods sold	750,000	660,000
Lease rent (renewable each year)	90,000	75,000
Labor costs (paid on an hourly basis)	42,000	42,000
Depreciation of equipment	25,000	22,000
Utilities (electricity, heating)	43,000	46,000
Allocated corporate overhead	50,000	40,000
Total operating costs	1,000,000	885,000
Operating income (loss)	$ 70,000	$ (25,000)

The equipment has a zero disposal value. In a senior management meeting, Maria Lopez, the management accountant at Sanchez Corporation, makes the following comment, "Sanchez can increase its profitability by closing down the Rhode Island store or by adding another store like it."

Required

1. By closing down the Rhode Island store, Sanchez can reduce overall corporate overhead costs by $44,000. Calculate Sanchez's operating income if it closes the Rhode Island store. Is Maria Lopez's statement about the effect of closing the Rhode Island store correct? Explain.
2. Calculate Sanchez's operating income if it keeps the Rhode Island store open and opens another store with revenues and costs identical to the Rhode Island store (including a cost of $22,000 to acquire equipment with a one-year useful life and zero disposal value). Opening this store will increase corporate overhead costs by $4,000. Is Maria Lopez's statement about the effect of adding another store like the Rhode Island store correct? Explain.

11-26 Choosing customers. Broadway Printers operates a printing press with a monthly capacity of 2,000 machine-hours. Broadway has two main customers, Taylor Corporation and Kelly Corporation. Data on each customer for January follows:

	Taylor Corporation	Kelly Corporation	Total
Revenues	$120,000	$80,000	$200,000
Variable costs	42,000	48,000	90,000
Contribution margin	78,000	32,000	110,000
Fixed costs (allocated)	60,000	40,000	100,000
Operating income	$ 18,000	$(8,000)	$ 10,000
Machine-hours required	1,500 hours	500 hours	2,000 hours

Kelly Corporation indicates that it wants Broadway to do an *additional* $80,000 worth of printing jobs during February. These jobs are identical to the existing business Broadway did for Kelly in January in terms of variable costs and machine-hours required. Broadway anticipates that the business from Taylor Corporation in February would be the same as that in January. Broadway can choose to accept as much of the Taylor and Kelly business for February as its capacity allows. Assume that total machine-hours and fixed costs for February will be the same as in January.

Required

What action should Broadway take to maximize its operating income? Show your calculations.

11-27 Relevance of equipment costs. The Auto Wash Company has just today paid for and installed a special machine for polishing cars at one of its several outlets. It is the first day of the company's fiscal year. The machine cost $20,000. Its annual cash operating costs total $15,000. The machine will have a four-year useful life and a zero terminal disposal value.

After the machine has been used for only one day, a salesperson offers a different machine that promises to do the same job at annual cash operating costs of $9,000. The new machine will cost $24,000 cash, installed. The "old" machine is unique and can be sold outright for only $10,000, minus $2,000 removal cost. The new machine, like the old one, will have a four-year useful life and zero terminal disposal value.

Revenues, all in cash, will be $150,000 annually, and other cash costs will be $110,000 annually, regardless of this decision.

For simplicity, ignore income taxes and the time value of money.

Required

1. **a.** Prepare a statement of cash receipts and disbursements for each of the four years under each alternative. What is the cumulative difference in cash flow for the four years taken together?
   b. Prepare income statements for each of the four years under each alternative. Assume straight-line depreciation. What is the cumulative difference in operating income for the four years taken together?
   c. What are the irrelevant items in your presentations in requirements a and b? Why are they irrelevant?
2. Suppose the cost of the "old" machine was $1 million rather than $20,000. Nevertheless, the old machine can be sold outright for only $10,000, minus $2,000 removal cost. Would the net differences in requirements 1a and 1b change? Explain.
3. Is there any conflict between the decision model and the incentives of the manager who has just purchased the "old" machine and is considering replacing it a day later?

11-28 Equipment upgrade versus replacement. (A. Spero, adapted) The Pacifica Corporation makes steel table lamps. It is considering either upgrading its existing production line or replacing it. The production equipment was purchased two years ago for $600,000. It has an expected useful life of five years, a terminal disposal value of $0, and is depreciated on a straight-line basis at the rate of $120,000 per year. The equipment has a current book value of $360,000 and a current disposal value of $90,000. The following table presents expected costs under the upgrade and replace alternatives:

	Upgrade	**Replace**
Expected one-time-only equipment costs	$300,000	$750,000
Variable manufacturing cost per lamp	$12	$9
Expected production and sales of lamps per year	60,000 units	60,000 units
Selling price of lamps	$25	$25

The expected useful life after the machine is upgraded or replaced is three years, and the expected terminal disposal value is $0. If the machine is upgraded, the $300,000 would be added to the current book value of $360,000 and depreciated on a straight-line basis. The new equipment, if purchased, will also be depreciated on a straight-line basis.

For simplicity, ignore income taxes and the time value of money.

Required

1. Should Pacifica upgrade its production line or replace it? Show your calculations.
2. **a.** Now suppose the capital expenditure needed to replace the production line is not known. All other data are as given previously. What is the maximum price that Pacifica would be willing to pay for the new line to prefer replacing the existing line to upgrading it?
   b. Assume that the capital expenditure needed to replace the production line is $750,000. Now suppose the expected production and sales quantity is not known. For what production and sales quantity would Pacifica prefer to (i) replace the line or (ii) upgrade the line?
3. Consider again the basic information given in this exercise. Suppose John Azinger, the manager of the Pacifica Corporation, is evaluated on operating income. The coming year's operating income is crucial to Azinger's bonus. What alternative would Azinger choose? Explain.

Problems

11-29 Contribution approach, relevant costs. Air Frisco has leased a single jet aircraft that it operates between San Francisco and the Fijian Islands. Only tourist-class seats are available on its planes. An analyst has collected the following information:

Seating capacity per plane	360 passengers
Average number of passengers per flight	200 passengers
Average one-way fare	$500
Variable fuel costs	$14,000 per flight
Food and beverage service costs (no charge to passenger)	$20 per passenger
Commission to travel agents paid by Air Frisco (all tickets are booked by travel agents)	8% of fare
Fixed annual lease costs allocated to each flight	$53,000 per flight
Fixed ground-services (maintenance, check in, baggage handling) costs allocated to each flight	$7,000 per flight
Fixed flight-crew salaries allocated to each flight	$4,000 per flight

For simplicity, assume that fuel costs are unaffected by the actual number of passengers on a flight.

Required

1. Calculate the total contribution margin from passengers that Air Frisco earns on each one-way flight between San Francisco and Fiji.
2. The Market Research Department of Air Frisco indicates that lowering the average one-way fare to $480 will increase the average number of passengers per flight to 212. On the basis of financial considerations alone, should Air Frisco lower its fare? Show your calculations.
3. Travel International, a tour operator, approaches Air Frisco on the possibility of chartering its aircraft. The terms of charter are as follows: (a) For each one way flight, Travel International will pay Air Frisco $74,500 to charter the plane and to use its flight crew and ground-service staff; (b) Travel International will pay for fuel costs; and (c) Travel International will pay for all food costs. On the basis of financial considerations alone, should Air Frisco accept Travel International's offer? Show your calculations. What other factors should Air Frisco consider in deciding whether to charter its plane to Travel International?

11-30 Relevant costs, opportunity costs. Larry Miller, the general manager of Basil Software, must decide when to release the new version of Basil's spreadsheet package, Easyspread 2.0. Development of Easyspread 2.0 is complete; however, the diskettes, compact discs, and user manuals have not yet been produced. The product can be shipped starting July 1, 2003.

The key problem is that Basil has overstocked the previous version of its spreadsheet package, Easyspread 1.0. Miller knows that once Easyspread 2.0 is introduced, Basil will not be able to sell any more units of Easyspread 1.0. Rather than just throwing away the inventory of Easyspread 1.0, Miller is wondering if it might be better to continue to sell Easyspread 1.0 for the next three months and introduce Easyspread 2.0 on October 1, 2003, when the inventory of Easyspread 1.0 will be sold out.

The following information is available.

	Easyspread 1.0	Easyspread 2.0
Selling price	$150	$185
Variable cost per unit of diskettes, compact discs, user manuals	20	25
Development cost per unit	65	95
Marketing and administrative cost per unit	35	40
Total cost per unit	120	160
Operating income per unit	$ 30	$ 25

Development cost per unit for each product equals the total costs of developing the software product divided by the anticipated unit sales over the life of the product. Marketing and administrative costs are fixed costs in 2003, incurred to support all marketing and administrative activities of Basil Software. Marketing and administrative costs are allocated to products on the basis of the budgeted revenues of each product. The preceding unit costs assume Easyspread 2.0 will be introduced on October 1, 2003.

Required

1. On the basis of financial considerations alone, should Miller introduce Easyspread 2.0 on July 1, 2003, or wait until October 1, 2003? Show your calculations, clearly identifying relevant and irrelevant revenues and costs.
2. What other factors might Larry Miller consider in making a decision?

11-31 Opportunity costs. (H. Schaefer) The Wolverine Corporation is working at full production capacity producing 10,000 units of a unique product, Rosebo. Manufacturing cost per unit for Rosebo is as follows:

Direct material	$ 2
Direct manufacturing labor	3
Manufacturing overhead	5
Total manufacturing cost	$10

Manufacturing overhead cost per unit is based on variable cost per unit of $2 and fixed costs of $30,000 (at full capacity of 10,000 units). Marketing cost, all variable, is $4 per unit, and the selling price is $20.

A customer, the Miami Company, has asked Wolverine to produce 2,000 units of Orangebo, a modification of Rosebo. Orangebo would require the same manufacturing processes as Rosebo. Miami has offered to pay Wolverine $15 for a unit of Orangebo and half the marketing cost per unit.

Required

1. What is the opportunity cost to Wolverine of producing the 2,000 units of Orangebo? (Assume that no overtime is worked.)
2. The Buckeye Corporation has offered to produce 2,000 units of Rosebo for Wolverine so that Wolverine may accept the Miami offer. That is, if Wolverine accepts the Buckeye offer, Wolverine would manufacture 8,000 units of Rosebo and 2,000 units of Orangebo and purchase 2,000 units of Rosebo from Buckeye. Buckeye would charge Wolverine $14 per unit to manufacture Rosebo. On the basis of financial considerations alone, should Wolverine accept the Buckeye offer? Show your calculations.
3. Suppose Wolverine had been working at less than full capacity, producing 8,000 units of Rosebo at the time the Miami offer was made. Calculate the minimum price Wolverine should accept for Orangebo under these conditions. (Ignore the previous $15 selling price.)

11-32 Product mix, relevant costs. (N. Melumad, adapted) Pendleton Engineering makes cutting tools for metalworking operations. It makes two types of tools: R3, a regular cutting tool, and HP6, a high-precision cutting tool. R3 is manufactured on a regular machine, but HP6 must be manufactured on both the regular machine and a high-precision machine. The following information is available.

	R3	HP6
Selling price	$100	$150
Variable manufacturing cost per unit	$ 60	$100
Variable marketing cost per unit	$15	$35
Budgeted total fixed overhead costs	$350,000	$550,000
Hours required to produce 1 unit on the regular machine	1.0	0.5

Additional information includes:

a. Pendleton faces a capacity constraint on the regular machine of 50,000 hours per year.
b. The capacity of the high-precision machine is not a constraint.
c. Of the $550,000 budgeted fixed overhead costs of HP6, $300,000 are lease payments for the high-precision machine. This cost is charged entirely to HP6 because Pendleton uses the machine exclusively to produce HP6. The lease agreement for the high-precision machine can be canceled at any time without penalties.
d. All other overhead costs are fixed and cannot be changed.

Required

1. What product mix—that is, how many units of R3 and HP6—will maximize Pendleton's operating income?
2. Suppose Pendleton can increase the annual capacity of regular machines by 15,000 machine-hours at a cost of $150,000. Should Pendleton increase the capacity of regular machines by 15,000 machine-hours? By how much will Pendleton's operating income increase? Show your calculations.
3. Suppose that the capacity of the regular machines has been increased to 65,000 hours. Pendleton has been approached by Carter Corporation to supply 20,000 units of another cutting tool, S3, for $120 per unit. Pendleton must either accept the order for all 20,000 units or reject it totally. S3 is exactly like R3 except that its variable manufacturing costs are $70 per unit. (It takes one hour to produce one unit of S3 on the regular machine, and variable marketing costs equal $15 per unit.) What product mix should Pendleton choose to maximize operating income? Show your calculations.

11-33 Discontinuing a product line, selling more units. The Northern Division of Grossman Corporation makes and sells tables and beds. The following estimated revenue and cost information from the division's activity-based costing system is available for 2002.

	4,000 Tables	5,000 Beds	Total
Revenues ($125 × 4,000; $200 × 5,000)	$500,000	$1,000,000	$1,500,000
Variable direct materials and direct manufacturing labor costs ($75 × 4,000; $105 × 5,000)	300,000	525,000	825,000
Depreciation on equipment used exclusively by each product line	42,000	58,000	100,000
Marketing and distribution costs			
$40,000 (fixed) + $750 per shipment × 40 shipments	70,000		205,000
$60,000 (fixed) + $750 per shipment × 100 shipments		135,000	
Fixed general administration costs of the division allocated to product lines on the basis of revenues	110,000	220,000	330,000
Allocated corporate-office costs allocated to product lines on the basis of revenues	50,000	100,000	150,000
Total costs	572,000	1,038,000	1,610,000
Operating income (loss)	$(72,000)	$ (38,000)	$ (110,000)

Additional information includes:

a. On January 1, 2002, the equipment has a book value of $100,000 and zero disposal value. Any equipment not used will remain idle.
b. Fixed marketing and distribution costs of a product line can be avoided if the line is discontinued.
c. Fixed general administration costs of the division and corporate-office costs will not change if sales of individual product lines are increased or decreased or if product lines are added or dropped.

Required

1. On the basis of financial considerations alone, should the Northern Division discontinue the tables product line, assuming the released facilities remain idle? Show your calculations.
2. What would be the effect on Northern Division's operating income if it were to sell 4,000 more tables? Assume that to do so the division would have to acquire additional equipment costing $42,000 with a one-year useful life and zero terminal disposal value. Assume further that the fixed marketing and distribution costs would not change but that the number of shipments would double. Show your calculations.

11-34 Discontinuing or adding division (continuation of 11-33). Refer to the information presented in Problem 11-33.

Required

1. Given the Northern Division's expected operating loss of $110,000, should Grossman Corporation shut it down? Assume that shutting down the Northern Division will have no effect on corporate-office costs but will lead to savings of all general administration costs of the division. Show your calculations.
2. Suppose the manager at corporate headquarters responsible for making the decision of whether to shut down the Northern Division will be evaluated in 2002 on the Northern Division's operating income after allocating corporate-office costs. Will the manager prefer to shut down the division? Show your calculations. Is the decision model consistent with the performance evaluation model? Explain.
3. Suppose Grossman Corporation has the opportunity to open another division, the Southern Division, whose revenues and costs are expected to be identical to the Northern Division's revenues and costs (including a cost of $100,000 to acquire equipment with a one-year useful life and zero terminal disposal value). Opening the new division will have no effect on corporate-office costs. Should Grossman open the Southern Division? Show your calculations.

11-35 Make or buy, unknown level of volume. (A. Atkinson) Oxford Engineering manufactures small engines. The engines are sold to manufacturers who install them in such products as lawn mowers. The company currently manufactures all the parts used in these engines but is considering a proposal from an external supplier who wishes to supply the starter assemblies used in these engines.

The starter assemblies are currently manufactured in Division 3 of Oxford Engineering. The costs relating to the starter assemblies for the past 12 months were as follows:

Direct materials	$200,000
Direct manufacturing labor	150,000
Manufacturing overhead	400,000
Total	$750,000

Over the past year, Division 3 manufactured 150,000 starter assemblies. The average cost for each starter assembly is $5 ($750,000 ÷ 150,000).

Further analysis of manufacturing overhead revealed the following information. Of the total manufacturing overhead, only 25% is considered variable. Of the fixed portion, $150,000 is an allocation of general overhead that would remain unchanged for the company as a whole if production of the starter assemblies is discontinued. A further $100,000 of the fixed overhead is avoidable if production of the starter assemblies is discontinued. The balance of the current fixed overhead, $50,000, is the division manager's salary. If production of the starter assemblies is discontinued, the manager of Division 3 will be transferred to Division 2 at the same salary. This move will allow the company to save the $40,000 salary that would otherwise be paid to attract an outsider to this position.

Required

1. Tidnish Electronics, a reliable supplier, has offered to supply starter-assembly units at $4 per unit. Because this price is less than the current average cost of $5 per unit, the vice president of manufacturing is eager to accept this offer. On the basis of financial considerations alone, should the outside offer be accepted? Show your calculations. (*Hint:* Production output in the coming year may be different from production output in the last year.)
2. How, if at all, would your response to requirement 1 change if the company could use the vacated plant space for storage and, in so doing, avoid $50,000 of outside storage charges currently incurred? Why is this information relevant or irrelevant?

11-36 Make versus buy, activity-based costing, opportunity costs. (N. Melumad and S. Reichelstein, adapted) The Ace Company produces bicycles. This year's expected production is 10,000 units. Currently, Ace makes the chains for its bicycles. Ace's management accountant reports the following costs for making the 10,000 bicycle chains:

	Cost per Unit	Costs for 10,000 Units
Direct materials	$4.00	$ 40,000
Direct manufacturing labor	2.00	20,000
Variable manufacturing overhead (power and utilities)	1.50	15,000
Inspection, setup, materials handling		2,000
Machine rent		3,000
Allocated fixed costs of plant administration, taxes, and insurance		30,000
Total costs		$110,000

Ace has received an offer from an outside vendor to supply any number of chains Ace requires at $8.20 per chain. The following additional information is available:

a. Inspection, setup, and materials-handling costs vary with the number of batches in which the chains are produced. Ace produces chains in batch sizes of 1,000 units. Ace estimates that it will produce the 10,000 units in 10 batches.

b. Ace rents the machine used to make the chains. If Ace buys all of its chains from the outside vendor, it does not need to pay rent on this machine.

Required

1. Assume that if Ace purchases the chains from the outside supplier, the facility where the chains are currently made will remain idle. On the basis of financial considerations alone, should Ace accept the outside supplier's offer at the anticipated production (and sales) volume of 10,000 units? Show your calculations.
2. For this question, assume that if the chains are purchased outside, the facilities where the chains are currently made will be used to upgrade the bicycles by adding mud flaps and reflectors. As a consequence, the selling price of bicycles will be raised by \$20. The variable cost per unit of the upgrade would be \$18, and additional tooling costs of \$16,000 would be incurred. On the basis of financial considerations alone, should Ace make or buy the chains, assuming that 10,000 units are produced (and sold)? Show your calculations.
3. The sales manager at Ace is concerned that the estimate of 10,000 units may be high and believes that only 6,200 units will be sold. Production will be cut back, freeing up work space. This space can be used to add the mud flaps and reflectors whether Ace goes outside for the chains or makes them in-house. At this lower output, Ace will produce the chains in eight batches of 775 units each. On the basis of financial considerations alone, should Ace purchase the chains from the outside vendor? Show your calculations.

11-37 Multiple choice, comprehensive problem on relevant costs. The following are the Class Company's unit cost of manufacturing and marketing a high-style pen at an output level of 20,000 units per month:

Manufacturing cost	
Direct material	\$1.00
Direct manufacturing labor	1.20
Variable manufacturing indirect cost	0.80
Fixed manufacturing indirect cost	0.50
Marketing cost	
Variable	1.50
Fixed	0.90

Required

The following situations refer only to the preceding data; there is *no connection* between the situations. Unless stated otherwise, assume a regular selling price of \$6 per unit. Choose the best answer to each question. Show your calculations.

1. In an inventory of 10,000 units of the high-style pen presented in the balance sheet, the appropriate unit cost to use is (a) \$3.00, (b) \$3.50, (c) \$5.00, (d) \$2.20, or (e) \$5.90.
2. The pen is usually produced and sold at the rate of 240,000 units per year (an average of 20,000 per month). The selling price is \$6 per unit, which yields total annual revenues of \$1,440,000. Total costs are \$1,416,000, and operating income is \$24,000, or \$0.10 per unit. Market research estimates that unit sales could be increased by 10% if prices were cut to \$5.80. Assuming the implied cost-behavior patterns continue, this action, if taken, would
   a. Decrease operating income by \$7,200.
   b. Decrease operating income by \$0.20 per unit (\$48,000) but increase operating income by 10% of revenues (\$144,000), for a net increase of \$96,000.
   c. Decrease fixed cost per unit by 10%, or \$0.14, per unit, and thus decrease operating income by \$0.06 (\$0.20 – \$0.14) per unit.
   d. Increase unit sales to 264,000 units, which at the \$5.80 price would give total revenues of \$1,531,200 and lead to costs of \$5.90 per unit for 264,000 units, which would equal \$1,557,600, and result in an operating loss of \$26,400.
   e. None of these.
3. A contract with the government for 5,000 units of the pens calls for the reimbursement of all manufacturing costs plus a fixed fee of \$1,000. No variable marketing costs are incurred on the government contract. You are asked to compare the following two alternatives:

Sales Each Month to	Alternative A	Alternative B
Regular customers	15,000 units	15,000 units
Government	0 units	5,000 units

   Operating income under alternative B is greater than that under alternative A by (a) \$1,000, (b) \$2,500, (c) \$3,500, (d) \$300, or (e) none of these.

4. Assume the same data with respect to the government contract as in requirement 3 except that the two alternatives to be compared are

Sales Each Month to	Alternative A	Alternative B
Regular customers	20,000 units	15,000 units
Government	0 units	5,000 units

Operating income under alternative B relative to that under alternative A is (a) $4,000 less, (b) $3,000 greater, (c) $6,500 less, (d) $500 greater, or (e) none of these.

5. The company wants to enter a foreign market in which price competition is keen. The company seeks a one-time-only special order for 10,000 units on a minimum-unit-price basis. It expects that shipping costs for this order will amount to only $0.75 per unit, but the fixed costs of obtaining the contract will be $4,000. The company incurs no variable marketing costs other than shipping costs. Domestic business will be unaffected. The selling price to break even is (a) $3.50, (b) $4.15, (c) $4.25, (d) $3.00, or (e) $5.00.
6. The company has an inventory of 1,000 units of pens that must be sold immediately at reduced prices. Otherwise, the inventory will be worthless. The unit cost that is relevant for establishing the minimum selling price is (a) $4.50, (b) $4.00, (c) $3.00, (d) $5.90, or (e) $1.50.
7. A proposal is received from an outside supplier who will make and ship these high-style pens directly to the Class Company's customers as sales orders are forwarded from Class's sales staff. Class's fixed marketing costs will be unaffected, but its variable marketing costs will be slashed by 20%. Class's plant will be idle, but its fixed manufacturing overhead will continue at 50% of present levels. How much per unit would the company be able to pay the supplier without decreasing operating income? (a) $4.75, (b) $3.95, (c) $2.95, (d) $5.35, or (e) none of these.

11-38 Make or buy (continuation of 11-37). Assume that, as in requirement 7 of Problem 11-37, a proposal is received from an outside supplier who will make and ship high-style pens directly to the Class Company's customers as sales orders are forwarded from Class's sales staff. If the supplier's offer is accepted, the present plant facilities will be used to make a new pen whose unit costs will be

Variable manufacturing cost	$5.00
Fixed manufacturing cost	1.00
Variable marketing cost	2.00
Fixed marketing cost	0.50

Total fixed manufacturing overhead will be unchanged from the original level given at the beginning of Problem 11-37. Fixed marketing costs for the new pens are over and above the fixed marketing costs incurred for marketing the high-style pens at the beginning of Problem 11-37. The new pen will sell for $9. The minimum desired operating income on the two pens taken together is $50,000 per year.

Required

What is the maximum purchase cost per unit that the Class Company would be willing to pay for subcontracting the production of the high-style pens?

11-39 Optimal production plan, computer manufacturer. (Chapter Appendix) Information Technology, Inc., assembles and sells two products: printers and desktop computers. Customers can purchase either (a) a computer or (b) a computer plus a printer. The printers are *not* sold without the computer. The result is that the quantity of printers sold is equal to or less than the quantity of desktop computers sold. The contribution margins are $200 per printer and $100 per computer.

Each printer requires 6 assembly-hours on production line 1 and 10 assembly-hours on production line 2. Each computer requires 4 assembly-hours on production line 1 only. (Many of the components for each computer are preassembled by external vendors.) Production line 1 has 24 assembly-hours available per day. Production line 2 has 20 assembly-hours available per day.

Let X represent units of printers and Y represent units of desktop computers. The production manager must decide on the optimal mix of printers and computers to manufacture.

Required

1. Formulate the production manager's problem in an LP format.
2. Calculate the combination of printers and computers that will maximize the operating income of Information Technology. Use both the trial-and-error and graphic approaches. Show your work.

11-40 Optimal product mix. (CMA adapted, Chapter Appendix) Della Simpson, Inc., sells two popular brands of cookies, Della's Delight and Cathy's Chocolate Chip. Both cookies go through the Mixing and Baking Departments, but Della's Delight is also dipped in chocolate in the Coating Department.

Michael Sesnowitz, vice president for sales, believes that Della Simpson can sell all of its daily production of Cathy's Chocolate Chips and Della's Delights. Both cookies are made in batches of 300 cookies. The batch times (in minutes) for producing each type of cookie and the minutes available per day are as follows:

	Mixing	Baking	Dipping
Della's Delight (in minutes)	30	10	20
Cathy's Chocolate Chip (in minutes)	15	15	0
Minutes available per day	600	300	320

Revenue and cost data for each type of cookie are

	Della's Delight	Cathy's Chocolate Chip
Revenue per batch	$ 525	$ 335
Variable cost per batch	175	85
Monthly fixed costs (allocated to each product)	20,350	16,650

Required

1. Formulate the decision facing Michael Sesnowitz as an LP model. Use *D* to represent the quantity of Della's Delights made and sold and *C* to represent the quantity of Cathy's Chocolate Chips made and sold.
2. Compute the optimal quantities of Della's Delights and Cathy's Chocolate Chips that Della Simpson should make and sell.

11-41 Make versus buy, ethics. (CMA, adapted) Lynn Hardt, a management accountant with the Paibec Corporation, is evaluating whether a component MTR-2000 should continue to be manufactured by Paibec or purchased from Marley Company. Marley has submitted a bid to manufacture and supply the 32,000 units of MTR-2000 that Paibec will need for 2002 at a selling price of $17.30.

Hardt has gathered the following information regarding Paibec's costs to manufacture 30,000 units of MTR-2000 in 2001:

Direct materials	$195,000
Direct manufacturing labor	120,000
Plant space rental	84,000
Equipment leasing	36,000
Other manufacturing overhead	225,000
Total manufacturing costs	$660,000

Hardt has also collected the following information related to manufacturing MTR-2000:

- Prices of direct materials used in the production of MTR-2000 are expected to increase by 8% in 2002.
- Paibec's direct manufacturing labor contract calls for a 5% increase in 2002.
- Paibec can withdraw from the plant space rental agreement without any penalty. Paibec will have no need for this space if MTR-2000 is not manufactured.
- The equipment lease can be terminated by paying $6,000.
- 40% of the other manufacturing overhead is considered variable. Variable overhead changes proportionately with the number of units produced. The fixed component of other manufacturing overhead costs is expected to remain the same whether or not MTR-2000 is manufactured.

John Porter, plant manager at Paibec Corporation, indicates to Hardt that the current performance of the plant can be significantly improved and that the cost increases she is assuming are unlikely to occur. Hence, the analysis should be done assuming costs will be considerably below current levels. Hardt knows that Porter is concerned about outsourcing MTR-2000 because it will mean that some of his close friends will be laid off.

Hardt believes that it is unlikely that the plant will achieve the lower costs Porter describes. She is very confident about the accuracy of the information she has collected, but she is also unhappy about laying off employees.

Required

1. On the basis of the financial information Hardt has obtained, should Paibec make MTR-2000 or buy it in 2002? Show your calculations.
2. What other factors should Paibec consider before making a decision?
3. What should Lynn Hardt do in response to John Porter's comments?

Collaborative Learning Problem

11-42 Optimal product mix. (CMA, adapted) OmniSport's Plastics Department is currently manufacturing 5,000 pairs of skates annually, making full use of its machine capacity. The selling price and total cost per unit associated with OmniSport's skates are

Selling price per pair of skates		$98
Cost per pair of skates		
Direct material	$20	
Variable machine operating cost ($16 per machine-hour)	24	
Manufacturing overhead cost	18	
Marketing and administrative cost	21	83
Operating income per pair of skates		$15

OmniSport believes it could sell 8,000 pairs of skates annually if it had sufficient manufacturing capacity. Colcott, Inc., has offered to provide up to 6,000 pairs of skates per year at a price of $75 per pair delivered to OmniSport's facility.

Jack Petrone, OmniSport's product manager, has suggested that the company can make better use of its Plastics Department by manufacturing snowboard bindings. Petrone believes that OmniSport could expect to sell up to 12,000 snowboard bindings annually. Petrone's estimate of the selling price and total cost per unit to manufacture 12,000 snowboard bindings are

Selling price per snowboard binding		$60
Cost per snowboard binding		
Direct material	$20	
Variable machine operating cost ($16 per machine-hour)	8	
Manufacturing overhead cost	6	
Marketing and administrative cost	10	44
Operating income per snowboard binding		$16

Other information pertinent to OmniSport's operations includes the following:

- In the Plastics Department, OmniSport uses machine-hours as the allocation base for manufacturing overhead costs. The fixed manufacturing overhead component of these costs for the current year is the $30,000 of fixed plantwide manufacturing overhead that has been allocated to the Plastics Department. These costs will not be affected by the product-mix decision.
- Variable marketing and administrative cost per unit for the various products are as follows:

Manufactured in-line skates	$9
Purchased in-line skates	4
Manufactured snowboard bindings	8

Fixed marketing and administrative costs of $60,000 are not affected by the product-mix decision.

Required

Calculate the quantity of each product that OmniSport should manufacture and/or purchase to maximize operating income. Show your calculations.

CHAPTER 11 INTERNET EXERCISE

An important first step in the decision-making process is identifying relevant information. CCH offers an excellent on-line tool kit to assist small business owners in identifying relevant information for making capital-budgeting decisions. To learn more, go to www.prenhall.com/horngren, click on *Cost Accounting*, 11th ed., and access the Internet exercise for Chapter 11.

CHAPTER 11 VIDEO CASE

STORE 24: Decision Making and Relevant Information

As purveyors of primarily commodity convenience products, the convenience store industry faces lots of competitive pressure. Gas stations are encroaching on convenience store territory with new mini-mart stores. And neighborhood drugstores are expanding their turf by charging less for products that used to be the exclusive domain of the convenience store—products like cigarettes, food service, packaged beverages, candy, snacks, and milk products. Convenience stores are battling back by offering a deeper selection of products. Because drugstore chains, in particular, must maintain a certain amount of square footage for pharmacy and nonfood items, they can't always carry the latest, coolest items.

Store 24, based in Waltham, Massachusetts, is all too familiar with these industry trends. The company has responded by offering speedy service—in and out in under 30 seconds—redesigned layouts to put the best-selling items within easy reach, and updated product offerings. The 34-year-old company's 82 stores operate throughout the northeastern United States, in both urban and suburban locations.

One recent day, President and CEO Bob Gordon met with CFO Paul Doucette to discuss a proposal from a new vendor to stock its line of fruit-flavored waters in Store 24's refrigerated cases. The water comes in 16-ounce, single-serve clear plastic bottles. There are three flavors available: Mandarin-Tangerine, Very Cherry Berry, and Citrus-Melon. Although product-inventory ordering decisions are generally left to individual store managers, this decision is being considered by headquarters staff because it's a new vendor who must pass approval before Store 24 puts the company on its approved vendor list. If the vendor is approved, the flavored waters will displace another company's product in the refrigerated beverage case in each store because there is a fixed amount of space in those cases.

Although layouts vary among Store 24 locations, each store has nine refrigerated beverage cases, with eight shelves per case. The current cold-beverage product mix is

Dairy (milk and related beverages)	1 case
Gatorade and sports drinks	1 case
Juice products	1 case
Beer	2 cases
Sodas	3 cases
Water (plain and sparkling)	1 case

As it turns out, the only place Store 24 could stock the new flavored waters is in the case that currently holds plain and sparkling water products. All other cases are dedicated to the products they carry through contractual arrangements with those vendors. The water case holds four shelves of 24-ounce, single-serve plain water bottles, and four shelves of 24-ounce, single-serve sparkling water bottles. Each shelf is 36 inches wide and 12 inches deep. The fixed costs of operating each refrigerated case are $2,000 annually for depreciation and $600 annually for utilities and maintenance.

As for the products, a 24-ounce, round plastic bottle occupies 3 inches of shelf space; a 16-ounce, round plastic bottle occupies 2 inches of shelf space. Products can't be stacked. The selling price of a single 24-ounce plain water bottle is $1.25, with a variable cost per unit of $0.813. The selling price of a single 24-ounce sparkling water is $1.75, with a variable cost per unit of $1.225. The suggested selling price of the 16-ounce flavored water bottle is $1.50, with a variable cost per unit of $1.125.

Industry data source: Convenience Store News, May 28, 2001, issue.

QUESTIONS

1. Using Exhibit 11–1 (p. 371), describe Store 24's five-step decision process for deciding whether to carry the new fruit-flavored water.
2. What is the contribution margin per bottle of product? What is the contribution margin ratio per product? What is the contribution margin per square foot of shelf space for each product (16-ounce flavored water, 24-ounce plain water, 24-ounce sparkling water)?
3. What is the constraining resource?
4. On the basis of financial considerations alone, should Store 24 stock the new flavored waters in place of some of the plain and sparkling water products? Explain briefly.
5. What factors should Store 24 consider in deciding how much of shelf space it should devote to each of the three water products—plain, sparkling, and flavored.

CHAPTER 12

Pricing Decisions and Cost Management

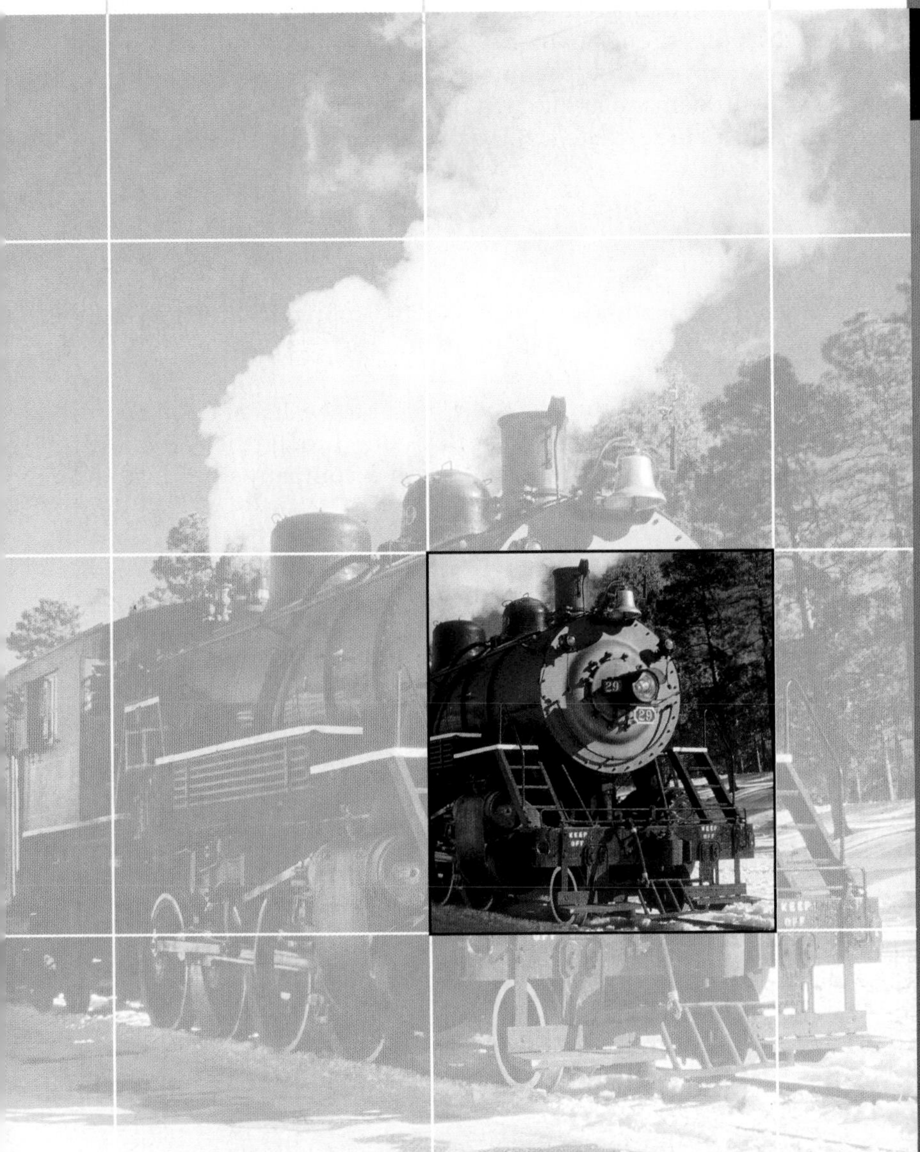

LEARNING OBJECTIVES

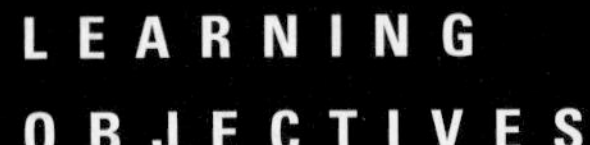

1. Discuss the three major influences on prices
2. Distinguish short-run from long-run pricing decisions
3. Price products using the target-costing approach
4. Apply the concepts of cost incurrence and locked-in costs
5. Price products using the cost-plus approach
6. Use life-cycle budgeting and costing when making pricing decisions
7. Describe two pricing practices in which noncost factors are important when setting prices
8. Explain the effects of antitrust laws on pricing

www.prenhall.com/horngren

What price would you pay to go back in time? That's just one question managers at the Grand Canyon Railway try to answer as they price tickets for rides on their restored classic train. The train travels from a historic depot in Williams, Arizona, to the South Rim of the Grand Canyon and back, giving travelers a chance to experience what it must have been like to journey to the canyon around the turn of the 20th century.

The train has three classes of service: basic coach, upgraded "bar" car service, and first class. Pricing for each level takes into consideration customer demand, competitive forces, and of course, costs. The railway faces considerable fixed costs, including train restoration, maintenance of track and cars, the reservation center, and fuel, among many others. Managers know that if they set ticket prices too high, empty seats will translate into lost revenues.

Pricing decisions are management decisions about what to charge for products and services. These are strategic decisions affecting the quantity produced and sold and, therefore, revenues and costs. To maximize operating income, companies should produce and sell units so long as the revenue from an additional unit exceeds the cost of producing it. Product costs, however, are calculated differently for different time horizons and different contexts. To measure the costs of a product, you need to understand cost-behavior patterns, cost drivers, and the concept of relevance introduced in Chapter 11. This chapter describes how managers evaluate demand at different prices and manage costs across the value chain and over the product's life cycle to achieve profitability.

1 Discuss the three major influences on prices
...customers, competitors, and costs

This framework is consistent with economics courses.

MAJOR INFLUENCES ON PRICING DECISIONS

Customers, Competitors, and Costs

The price of a product or service depends on the demand and supply for it. Three influences on demand and supply are customers, competitors, and costs.

Customers Customers influence price through their effect on the demand for a product or service. Companies must always examine pricing decisions through the eyes of their customers. Too high a price may cause customers to reject a company's product and choose a competing or substitute product.

Competitors No business operates in a vacuum. Companies must always be aware of the actions of competitors. At one extreme, alternative or substitute products of competitors can affect demand and force a company to lower its prices. At the other extreme, a company without a competitor can set higher prices. When there are competitors, knowledge of rivals' technology, plant capacity, and operating policies enable a company to estimate its competitors' costs—valuable information in setting its own prices.

Suppose the yen weakens from \$1 = 110 yen in 2002 to \$1 = 120 yen in 2003. Then a product that costs 1,320 yen can be purchased for \$12 (1,320 yen/110 yen per \$1) in 2002 and for \$11 (1,320 yen/120 yen per \$1) in 2003.

Because competition spans international borders, costs and pricing decisions are also affected by fluctuations in the exchange rates between different countries' currencies. For example, if the yen weakens against the U.S. dollar, Japanese products become cheaper for American consumers and, consequently, more competitive in U.S. markets.

Costs Costs influence prices because they affect supply. The lower the cost of producing a product relative to the price customers pay for it, the greater the quantity of product the company is willing to supply. Managers who understand the cost of producing their companies' products set prices that make the products attractive to customers while maximizing their companies' operating incomes. In computing the relevant costs for a pricing decision, the manager must consider relevant costs in all value-chain business functions, from R&D to customer service.

Because there are many competitors and many customers, any one company or any one customer cannot influence the price.

Surveys of how managers make pricing decisions reveal that companies weigh customers, competitors, and costs differently. Companies selling similar commodity-type products, such as wheat, rice, and soybeans, in highly competitive markets have no control over setting prices and must accept the price determined by a market consisting of many participants. Cost information only helps the company decide on the output level that maximizes its operating income. In less competitive markets, such as for cameras and cellular phones, products are differentiated and all three factors affect prices; the value customers place on a product and the prices charged for competing products affect demand, and the costs of producing and delivering the product influence supply. As competition lessens even more, the key factor affecting pricing decisions is the customers' willingness to pay, not costs or competitors.

As competition lessens and there are fewer competitors, each selling a somewhat different product, a company can charge a price for its product that is different from other companies' prices.

Time Horizon of Pricing Decisions

Short-run pricing decisions typically have a time horizon of less than one year and include decisions such as (a) pricing a *one-time-only special order* with no long-run implications, and (b) adjusting product mix and output volume in a competitive market.

Long-run pricing decisions involve a time horizon of one year or longer and include pricing a product in a major market where there is some leeway in setting price. Two key differences affect pricing for the long run versus the short run: Costs that are often irrelevant for short-run pricing decisions, such as fixed costs that cannot be changed, are generally relevant in the long run because costs can be altered in the long run; and profit margins in long-run pricing decisions are often set to earn a reasonable return on investment. Short-run pricing is more opportunistic—prices are decreased when demand is weak and increased when demand is strong.

2 Distinguish short run

... less than one year with mostly incremental costs being relevant

from long run pricing decisions

... more than one year with all product costs being relevant

COSTING AND PRICING FOR THE SHORT RUN

Example: *The National Tea Corporation (NTC) operates a plant with a monthly capacity of 1 million cases of iced tea (240 cans per case). Current production and sales are 600,000 cases per month. The selling price is $90 per case. R&D, product and process design costs, and customer-service costs are negligible. All variable costs vary with respect to output units (cases), and output units equal sales units. The variable cost per case and the fixed cost per case, based on a production quantity of 600,000 cases per month, are*

	Variable Cost per Case	*Fixed Cost per Case*	*Variable and Fixed Cost per Case*
Manufacturing costs			
Direct material costs	$ 7	—	$ 7
Packaging costs	18	—	18
Direct manufacturing labor costs	4	—	4
Manufacturing overhead costs	6	$13	19
Manufacturing costs	35	13	48
Marketing costs	5	16	21
Distribution costs	9	8	17
Full cost of the product	$49	$37	$86

The $48 cost per case under absorption costing is appropriate for external financial reporting, but not for pricing. The $86 full product cost per case is relevant for long-run pricing because in the long run all costs, both fixed and variable costs from all parts of the value chain, must be recovered to continue in business.

Calico Tea (CT) has asked NTC to bid on supplying 250,000 cases each month for the next four months only. After this period, CT will manufacture and sell its own tea. CT is unlikely to place any future sales orders with NTC. Whether NTC accepts or rejects this order will not affect NTC's revenues—neither the units sold nor the selling price—from existing sales outlets.

The variable manufacturing costs of the iced tea for CT are identical to the variable manufacturing costs of the tea currently made by NTC. If NTC makes the extra 250,000 cases, NTC would continue to incur the same total fixed manufacturing overhead, $7,800,000 per month. NTC would incur a further $300,000 in monthly fixed manufacturing overhead—$100,000 in material procurement costs and $200,000 in process-changeover costs. No additional costs will be required for R&D, design, marketing, distribution, or customer service. NTC knows that a price above $45 per case probably will not be competitive because one of its competitors, with a highly efficient plant, has sizable idle capacity and is eager to win the CT contract. What price per case should NTC bid for the 250,000-case contract?

For some decisions, it's erroneous to assume that variable costs are relevant and fixed costs are irrelevant. The NTC example shows that some variable costs are irrelevant (marketing, distribution), whereas the special order would generate some incremental batch-level fixed costs that are relevant (material procurement, process changeover).

Relevant Costs for Pricing a Special Order

Exhibit 12-1 presents an analysis of the monthly relevant costs, using concepts developed in Chapter 11. Relevant costs include all manufacturing costs that will change in total by accepting the special order: *all direct and indirect variable manufacturing costs plus material procurement costs and process-changeover costs related to the special order.* Existing fixed

EXHIBIT 12-1

Monthly Relevant Costs for NTC: The 250,000-Case Short-Run Special Order

Direct materials (250,000 cases × $7 per case)		$1,750,000
Packaging (250,000 cases × $18 per case)		4,500,000
Direct manufacturing labor (250,000 cases × $4 per case)		1,000,000
Variable manufacturing overhead (250,000 cases × $6 per case)		1,500,000
Incremental fixed manufacturing overhead		
Material procurement	$100,000	
Process changeover	200,000	
Total incremental fixed manufacturing overhead		300,000
Total relevant costs		$9,050,000
Relevant cost per case: $9,050,000 ÷ 250,000 cases = $36.20		

manufacturing overhead costs are irrelevant because these costs will not change if the special order is accepted. But, the *additional* material procurement and process-changeover costs of $300,000 per month for the special order are relevant because they will be incurred only if the special order is accepted. All nonmanufacturing costs will be unaffected by accepting the special order, so they are irrelevant.

Exhibit 12-1 shows total incremental costs for the 250,000-case special order of $9,050,000, or $36.20 per case. Therefore, accepting any bid above $36.20 per case will improve its profitability in the short run. For example, a successful bid of $40 per case will increase NTC's monthly operating income by $950,000 [($40 per case – $36.20 per case) × 250,000 cases].

Note again how unit cost can mislead. The table on p. 411 reports total manufacturing cost to be $48 per case. The $48 per case cost might erroneously suggest that a bid of $40 per case for the CT special order will result in NTC sustaining an $8 per case loss. Why is this conclusion erroneous? Because total manufacturing costs per case include $13 of fixed manufacturing cost per case that will not be incurred on the 250,000-case special order. These costs are irrelevant for the special-order bid.

Strategic and Other Factors in Pricing a Special Order

Cost data, although necessary information in NTC's decision on the price to bid, are not the only inputs for the decision. NTC must be strategic and consider the likely bids of competitors. If NTC knows its rival plans to bid $39 per case, NTC could bid $38 per case instead of $40 per case. This lower price will increase operating income by $450,000 [($38 per case – $36.20 per case) × 250,000 cases]. NTC's strategy is to bid as high a price above $36.20 as possible while remaining lower than competing bids.

Now suppose NTC believes CT will sell the iced tea purchased from NTC in NTC's current markets—and at a lower price than NTC. Suppose further that customers will not have a brand or taste preference for either tea (the teas are, after all, identical) and will make their purchase decision based on price alone. If NTC has to lower prices in these markets just to compete with CT, should the relevant costs of the bidding decision include revenues lost on sales to some existing customers? Yes, if supplying tea to CT will cause NTC to charge lower prices than it otherwise would have charged. NTC should bid a price that at least covers both the incremental cost of $36.20 per case and the revenues that will be lost on existing sales if prices are lowered. But what if CT can purchase the tea from another supplier at the same low price it can buy from NTC and, as a result, can force NTC to lower prices to some of its existing customers? In this case, NTC's potential loss in revenues from regular customers should not be considered relevant to the bidding decision. That's because the revenues would be lost whether or not NTC wins the bid and, therefore, are irrelevant to the pricing decision.

Our NTC example assumes that (a) NTC has idle capacity and (b) a competing bidder with an efficient plant and sizable idle capacity will also bid for the CT order. That's why our short-run pricing decision focuses on identifying the minimum price for NTC to break even on the CT order. In other cases, companies might experience strong demand in the short run and have limited capacity. In these cases, companies will strategically increase prices in the short run to as much as the market will bear. We observe such high short-run prices in the case of new products—for example, microprocessors, computer chips, or software.

COSTING AND PRICING FOR THE LONG RUN

Short-run pricing decisions are responses to short-run demand and supply conditions, but they cannot form the basis of a long-run relationship with customers. Long-run pricing is a strategic decision. Buyers—whether a person buying a box of Wheaties, Bechtel Corporation buying a fleet of tractors, or General Foods Corporation buying audit services—typically prefer stable and predictable prices over a long time horizon. A stable price reduces the need for continuous monitoring of suppliers' prices, improves planning, and builds long-run buyer-seller relationships. But to charge a stable price and earn the desired long-run return, a company must know and manage its costs, over the long run, of supplying product to customers.

Calculating Product Costs

Consider Astel Computer Corporation. Astel manufactures two brands of personal computers (PCs): Deskpoint and Provalue. Deskpoint is Astel's top-of-the-line product, a Pentium 4 chip-based PC. Our analysis focuses on pricing Provalue, a less-powerful Pentium chip-based machine.

The manufacturing cost of Provalue is calculated using activity-based costing (ABC), described in Chapter 5. Astel has three direct manufacturing cost categories—direct materials, direct manufacturing labor, and direct machining costs—and three indirect manufacturing cost pools—ordering and receiving, testing and inspection, and rework—in its accounting system. Astel treats machining costs as a direct cost of Provalue because it is manufactured on machines that are dedicated to the production of Provalue.[1] The following table summarizes the activity cost pools, the cost driver for each activity, and the cost per unit of each cost driver for each indirect manufacturing cost pool.

Manufacturing Activity	Description of Activity	Cost Driver	Cost per Unit of Cost Driver
Ordering and receiving	Placing orders and receiving components	Number of orders	$80 per order
Testing and inspection	Testing components and final product	Testing-hours	$2 per testing-hour
Rework	Correcting and fixing errors and defects	Rework-hours	$40 per rework-hour

Astel uses a long-run time horizon to price Provalue. Over this horizon, Astel's management regards

1. Direct material costs as varying with the units of Provalue produced;
2. Direct manufacturing labor costs as varying with direct manufacturing labor-hours; and
3. Ordering and receiving, testing and inspection, and rework costs as varying with their respective cost drivers.

For example, ordering and receiving costs vary with the number of orders. Staff members responsible for placing orders can be reassigned or laid off in the long run if fewer orders need to be placed, or the number of staff members can be increased in the long run to process more orders. Direct machining costs, such as rental charges, do not vary with machine-hours over this time horizon, so they are fixed in the long run.

Astel has no beginning or ending inventory of Provalue in 2004 and manufactures and sells 150,000 units during the year. How does Astel calculate Provalue's manufacturing costs? It uses the following information, which indicates the resources used to manufacture Provalue in 2004:

[1] If Deskpoint and Provalue had shared the same machines, we could allocate machining costs on the basis of the budgeted machine-hours used to manufacture Provalue and treat this cost as an indirect fixed cost. The basic analysis would be exactly as described in the chapter except that machining costs would appear as indirect rather than direct fixed costs.

1. Direct material cost per unit of Provalue is $460.
2. Direct manufacturing labor-hours required to manufacture Provalue equal 480,000 (3.20 direct manufacturing labor-hours per unit of Provalue × 150,000 units) at a cost of $20 per direct manufacturing labor-hour.
3. Direct fixed costs of machines used exclusively for the manufacture of Provalue total $11,400,000, representing a capacity of 300,000 machine-hours at a cost of $38 per hour. Each unit of Provalue requires 2 machine-hours. Hence, the entire machining capacity is used to manufacture Provalue (2 machine-hours per unit × 150,000 units = 300,000 machine-hours).
4. Number of orders placed to purchase components required for the manufacture of Provalue is 22,500 at a cost of $80 per order. (We assume Provalue has 450 components supplied by different suppliers, and 50 orders are placed for each component).
5. Number of testing-hours used for Provalue is 4,500,000 (150,000 Provalue units are tested for 30 hours per unit) at a cost of $2 per testing-hour.
6. Number of units of Provalue reworked during the year is 12,000 (8% of the 150,000 units manufactured). Each of these units requires 2.5 hours of rework for a total of 30,000 hours (12,000 units × 2.5 hours per unit) at a rate of $40 per rework-hour.

Exhibit 12-2 indicates total cost of manufacturing Provalue of $102 million and manufacturing cost per unit of $680. Manufacturing, however, is just one business function in the value chain. To set long-run prices, Astel calculates the *full cost* of producing and selling Provalue.

For its nonmanufacturing value-chain functions, Astel identifies direct costs and chooses cost drivers and cost pools for indirect costs that measure cause-and-effect relationships. Astel allocates costs to Provalue based on the quantity of cost driver units that Provalue uses. Exhibit 12-3 summarizes the operating income for Provalue for 2004 based on an activity-based analysis of cost in all value-chain functions. (For brevity, supporting calculations for nonmanufacturing value-chain functions are not given.) Astel earns $15 million from Provalue, or $100 per unit sold in 2004.

Alternative Long-Run Pricing Approaches

How do companies use product cost information to make long-run pricing decisions? Two different starting points for pricing decisions are

1. Market-based
2. Cost-based, also called cost-plus

EXHIBIT 12-2

Manufacturing Costs of Provalue for 2004 Using Activity-Based Costing

	Total Manufacturing Costs for 150,000 Units (1)	Manufacturing Cost per Unit (2) = (1) ÷ 150,000
Direct manufacturing costs		
Direct material costs		
(150,000 units × $460 per unit)	$ 69,000,000	$460
Direct manufacturing labor costs		
(480,000 hours × $20 per hour)	9,600,000	64
Direct machining costs		
(300,000 machine-hours × $38 per machine-hour)	11,400,000	76
Direct manufacturing costs	90,000,000	600
Indirect manufacturing costs		
Ordering and receiving costs		
(22,500 orders × $80 per order)	1,800,000	12
Testing and inspection costs		
(4,500,000 hours × $2 per hour)	9,000,000	60
Rework costs (30,000 hours × $40 per hour)	1,200,000	8
Indirect manufacturing costs	12,000,000	80
Total manufacturing costs	$102,000,000	$680

EXHIBIT 12-3

Product Profitability of Provalue for 2004 Using Value-Chain Activity-Based Costing

	Total Amounts for 150,000 Units (1)	Per Unit (2) = (1) ÷ 150,000
Revenues	$150,000,000	$1,000
Cost of goods sold[a] (from Exhibit 12-2)		
Direct material costs	69,000,000	460
Direct manufacturing labor costs	9,600,000	64
Direct machining costs	11,400,000	76
Indirect manufacturing overhead costs	12,000,000	80
Cost of goods sold	102,000,000	680
Operating costs		
R&D costs	5,400,000	36
Design costs of products and processes	6,000,000	40
Marketing costs	15,000,000	100
Distribution costs	3,600,000	24
Customer-service costs	3,000,000	20
Operating costs	33,000,000	220
Full cost of the product	135,000,000	900
Operating income	$ 15,000,000	$ 100

[a]Cost of goods sold = Total manufacturing costs, because there is no beginning or ending inventory of Provalue in 2004.

The market-based approach to pricing starts by asking, Given what our customers want and how our competitors will react to what we do, what price should we charge? The cost-based approach to pricing starts by asking, Given what it costs us to make this product, what price should we charge that will recoup our costs and achieve a required return on investment?

Companies operating in markets that are competitive (for example, commodities such as oil and natural gas) use the market-based approach. The items produced or services provided by one company are very similar to items produced or provided by others. Companies in these markets must accept the prices set by the market.

In industries in which there is product differentiation (for example, automobiles, management consulting, and legal services), companies use market-based or cost-based approaches as the starting point for pricing decisions. Some companies first look at costs and then consider customers or competitors—the cost-based approach. Others start by considering customers and competitors and then look at costs—the market-based approach. Both approaches consider customers, competitors, and costs. Only their *starting points* differ. Always keep in mind market forces, regardless of which pricing technique is used. Consider first the market-based approach.

TARGET COSTING FOR TARGET PRICING

3 Price products using the target-costing approach

...identify an estimated price customers are willing to pay and then compute a target cost to earn the desiered profit

One form of market-based pricing is target pricing. A **target price** is the estimated price for a product or service that potential customers will pay. This estimate is based on an understanding of customers' perceived value for a product and how competitors will price competing products. A company's sales and marketing organization, through close contact and interaction with customers, is usually in the best position to identify customers' needs and their perceived value for a product. Companies also conduct market research studies about product features that customers want and the prices they are willing to pay for those features. Understanding what customers value is a key aspect of being customer focused.

Market-based pricing is becoming more popular as more companies adopt a customer-driven focus.

A company has less access to its competitors. To gauge how competitors might react, a company needs to understand competitors' technologies, products, costs, and financial conditions. For example, knowing competitors' technologies and products helps a company to (a) evaluate how distinctive its own products will be in the market and (b) determine the prices it might be able to charge as a result of being distinctive.

Where does a company obtain information about its competitors? Usually from customers, suppliers, and employees of competitors. Another source of information is *reverse engineering*—that's disassembling and analyzing competitors' products to determine product designs and materials and becoming acquainted with the technologies used by competitors. Many companies, including Ford, General Motors, and PPG Industries, have departments whose sole job is to analyze competitors with respect to these considerations.

Target price, calculated using information from customers and competitors, forms the basis for calculating target cost. *Target cost per unit* is the target price minus *target operating income per unit.* **Target operating income per unit** is the operating income that a company aims to earn per unit of a product or service sold. **Target cost per unit** is the estimated long-run cost per unit of a product or service that enables the company to achieve its target operating income per unit when selling at the target price.[2]

What relevant costs should we include in the target-cost calculations? We include *all* future costs, both variable and fixed, because in the long run, a company's prices and revenues must recover all its costs. If all costs are not recovered, the company's best alternative is to shut down—an action that results in forgoing all future revenues and saving all future costs, whether fixed or variable.

Target cost per unit is often lower than the existing *full cost per unit of the product.* Target cost per unit is really just that—a target—something the company must aim for. To achieve target cost per unit and target operating income per unit, the company must reduce the cost of making its products. Target costing is used in different industries around the world. Examples of companies that use target pricing and target costing include DaimlerChrysler, Ford, General Motors, Toyota, and Daihatsu in the automobile industry; Matsushita, Panasonic, and Sharp in the electronics industry; and Compaq and Toshiba in the personal computer industry.

Implementing Target Pricing and Target Costing

There are four steps in developing target prices and target costs. We illustrate these steps using our Provalue example.

Step 1: Develop a Product That Satisfies the Needs of Potential Customers. Astel is planning design modifications for Provalue. Astel's market research indicates that customers do not value Provalue's extra features, such as special audio features and designs that accommodate upgrades that can make the PC run faster and perform calculations more quickly. They want Astel to redesign Provalue into a no-frills PC and sell it at a much lower price.

Step 2: Choose a Target Price. Astel expects its competitors to lower the prices of PCs that compete against Provalue by 15%. Astel's management wants to respond aggressively by reducing Provalue's price by 20%, from $1,000 to $800 per unit. At this lower price, Astel's marketing manager forecasts an increase in annual sales from 150,000 to 200,000 units.

Step 3: Derive a Target Cost per Unit by Subtracting Target Operating Income per Unit from the Target Price. Astel's management wants a 10% target operating income on sales revenues.

Total target revenues	= \$800 per unit × 200,000 units = \$160,000,000
Total target operating income (10%)	= 0.10 × \$160,000,000 = \$16,000,000
Target operating income per unit	= \$16,000,000 ÷ 200,000 units = \$80 per unit
Target cost per unit	= Target price – Target operating income per unit
	= \$800 per unit – \$80 per unit = \$720 per unit
Total current full costs of Provalue	= \$135,000,000 (from Exhibit 12-3)
Current full cost per unit of Provalue	= \$135,000,000 ÷ 150,000 units = \$900 per unit

[2]For a more detailed discussion of target costing, see S. Ansari, J. Bell, and The CAM-I Target Cost Core Group, *Target Costing: The Next Frontier in Strategic Cost Management* (Homewood, IL: Irwin, 1996).

Provalue's $720 target cost per unit is well below its existing $900 unit cost. Astel's goal is to reduce its unit cost by $180. Cost reduction efforts need to extend to all parts of the value chain — from R&D to customer service — including seeking lower prices from suppliers for materials and components.

Step 4: Perform Value Engineering to Achieve Target Cost. **Value engineering** is a systematic evaluation of all aspects of the value-chain business functions, with the objective of reducing costs while satisfying customer needs. As we describe next, value engineering can result in improvements in product designs, changes in materials specifications, or modifications in process methods.

Value Engineering, Cost Incurrence, and Locked-In Costs

Managers implementing value engineering find it useful to distinguish value-added activities and costs from nonvalue-added activities and costs in producing a product or service. A **value-added cost** is a cost that, if eliminated, would reduce the actual or perceived value or utility (usefulness) customers obtain from using the product or service. Examples are costs of specific product features and attributes desired by customers, such as fast response time, adequate memory, preloaded software, clear images on the monitor, and prompt customer service. A **nonvalue-added cost** is a cost that, if eliminated, would not reduce the actual or perceived value or utility (usefulness) customers obtain from using the product or service. It is a cost that the customer is unwilling to pay for. Examples of nonvalue-added costs are costs of reworking and repairing products.

Traditional cost accounting systems don't classify costs as value-added or nonvalue-added. To obtain this information, management accountants must work closely with production and marketing personnel.

Activities and their costs do not always fall neatly into value-added or nonvalue-added categories. Some costs, such as materials handling and inspection, fall in the gray area in between because they include both value-added and nonvalue-added aspects. Despite these troublesome gray areas, attempts to distinguish value-added from nonvalue-added costs provide a useful overall framework for value engineering.

Some material-handling and inspection costs are needed to move the product through the manufacturing process and to ensure its quality. But beyond a point, these activities do not add value to the customer. Companies implementing JIT and TQM practices seek to improve product design and the manufacturing process while reducing material-handling and inspection costs.

In the Provalue example, direct materials, direct manufacturing labor, and direct machining costs are value-added costs. Ordering, receiving, testing, and inspection costs fall in the gray area — customers perceive some portion but not all of these costs as necessary for adding value. Rework costs, including costs of delivering reworked products, are nonvalue-added costs.

Value engineering aims to reduce nonvalue-added costs by reducing the quantity of cost drivers of nonvalue-added activities. For example, to reduce rework costs, Astel must reduce rework-hours. Value engineering also seeks to reduce value-added costs by achieving greater efficiency in value-added activities. For example, to reduce direct manufacturing labor costs, Astel must reduce the direct manufacturing labor-hours needed to make Provalue. But how should Astel reduce rework-hours and direct manufacturing labor-hours?

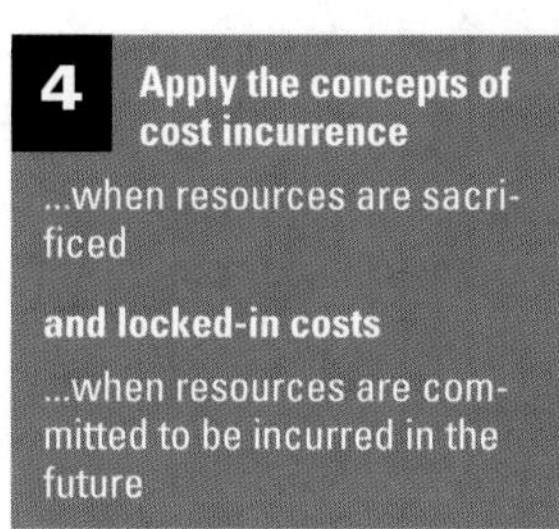

Astel needs to distinguish when costs are incurred from when costs are locked in. **Cost incurrence** describes when a resource is consumed (or benefit forgone) to meet a specific objective. Costing systems emphasize cost incurrence. For example, Astel's costing system recognizes direct material costs of Provalue as each unit of Provalue is assembled and sold. But Provalue's direct material cost per unit is *locked in*, or *designed in*, much earlier, when product designers choose the components that will go into Provalue. **Locked-in costs (designed-in costs)** are costs that have not yet been incurred but, based on decisions that have already been made, will be incurred in the future.

Why is it necessary to distinguish when costs are locked in from when costs are incurred? Because it is difficult to alter or reduce costs that are already locked in. If Astel experiences quality problems during manufacturing, its ability to improve quality and reduce scrap may be limited by Provalue's design. Scrap and rework costs are incurred during manufacturing, but they may be locked in much earlier in the value chain by faulty design. Similarly, in the software industry, costs of developing software are often locked in at the design and analysis stage. Costly and difficult-to-fix errors that appear during coding and testing are frequently locked in by bad designs.

Here are some examples of how Provalue's design decisions affect value-added and nonvalue-added costs in various value-chain functions:

1. Designing Provalue so that various parts snap-fit together, rather than solder together, decreases value-added direct manufacturing labor-hours and the related costs.

2. Simplifying the Provalue design and using fewer components decreases ordering and receiving costs and also decreases testing and inspection costs.
3. Designing Provalue to be lighter and smaller reduces value-added distribution and packaging costs.
4. Designing Provalue to reduce repairs and the related costs at customer sites reduces nonvalue-added customer-service costs.

Exhibit 12-4 illustrates how the locked-in cost curve and the cost-incurrence curve might appear in the case of Provalue. The bottom curve, graphically representing cost incurrence, uses information from Exhibit 12-3 to plot the cumulative cost per unit incurred in different business functions of the value chain. The top curve plots how cumulative costs are locked in. (The specific numbers underlying this curve are assumed.) Total cumulative cost per unit for both curves is $900. *However, the graph emphasizes the wide divergence between the time when costs are locked in and when they are incurred.* For example, once the product is designed and the operations to manufacture, market, distribute, and support the product are determined, more than 86% ($780 ÷ $900) of the unit cost of Provalue is locked in. Costs such as direct materials, direct manufacturing labor, and many manufacturing, marketing, distribution, and customer-service costs are all locked in at the end of the design stage, when only about 8% ($76 ÷ $900) of the unit cost is actually incurred!

In some companies, every worker makes suggestions for improvement. Much of the cost reduction occurs gradually via many small improvements. Also, because direct material is often a significant cost, many manufacturers work closely with their suppliers to achieve the target direct material cost.

To reduce costs, Astel focuses on the design stage. The company organizes a cross-functional value-engineering team consisting of marketing managers, product designers, manufacturing engineers, purchasing managers, suppliers, and management accountants. The team evaluates the impact of design innovations and modifications on all value-chain functions. To interact knowledgeably with team members, the management accountant must develop a solid understanding of the technical and business aspects of the entire value chain. The goal is to estimate cost savings and to explain the cost implications of alternative design choices to the team.

Do not assume that costs are always locked in at the design stage. In some industries, such as legal and consulting, costs are locked in and incurred at about the same time. If costs are not locked in early, cost reduction can be achieved right up to the time when costs are incurred. In these cases, costs are lowered through improved operating efficiency and productivity, rather than better design.

EXHIBIT 12-4

Pattern of Cost Incurrence and Locked-in Costs for Provalue

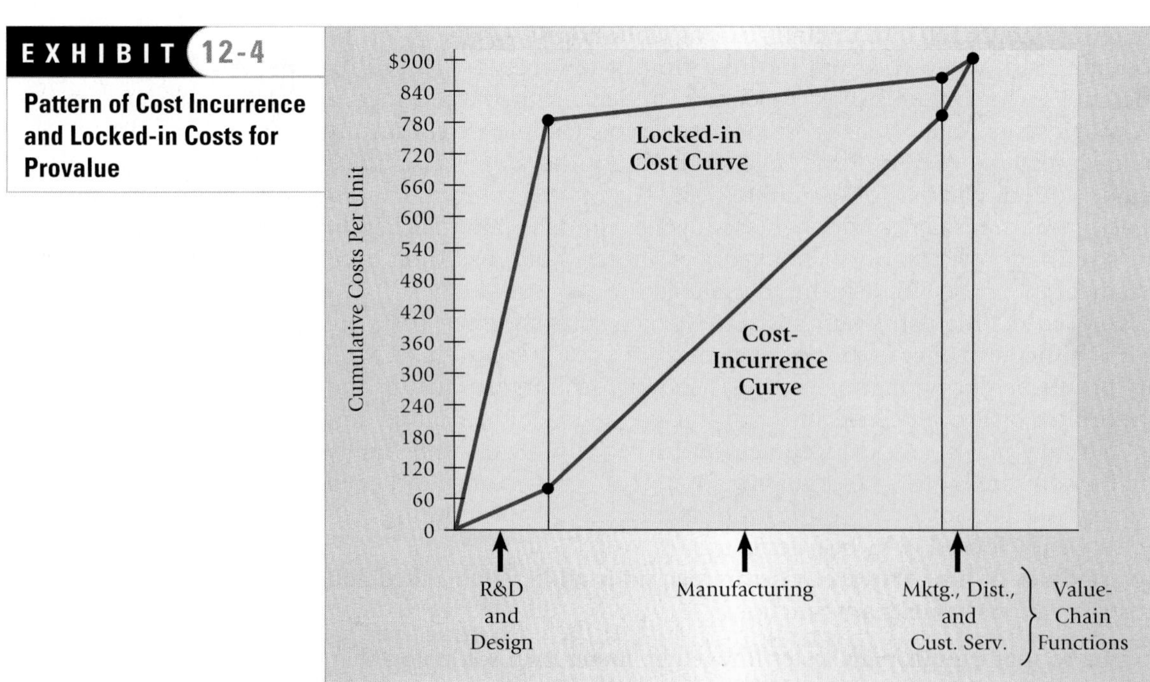

ACHIEVING THE TARGET COST PER UNIT FOR PROVALUE

Value engineering often has strategic implications. For example, value engineering leads Astel to consider discontinuing Provalue and replacing it by introducing Provalue II. Provalue II is a high-quality, highly reliable, no-frills machine that has fewer features and meets customers' price expectations. Provalue II has fewer components and is easier to manufacture and test. In place of the 150,000 Provalue units manufactured and sold in 2004, Astel expects to make and sell 200,000 Provalue II units in 2005. The following tables use an activity-based approach to compare cost-driver quantities and rates for Provalue and Provalue II.

		Provalue (Exhibit 12-2)		Provalue II		
Cost Category	Cost Driver	Quantity of Cost Driver for 150,000 Units	Cost per Unit of Cost Driver	Quantity of Cost Driver for 200,000 Units	Cost per Unit of Cost Driver	Explanation of Cost Drivers and Costs for Provalue II
DIRECT COSTS						
Direct materials	Units produced	150,000	$460	200,000	$385	The Provalue II design will use a simplified main printed circuit board and fewer components.
Direct manufacturing labor	Direct manu-facturing labor-hours	480,000	20	530,000	20	Provalue II will require 2.65 direct manufacturing labor-hours per unit compared with 3.20 direct manufacturing labor-hours per unit for Provalue. Total direct manufacturing labor-hours for Provalue II equal 530,000 (2.65 labor-hours × 200,000 units).
Direct machining	Machine-hours	300,000	38	300,000	38	The new design will require 1.5 machine-hours per unit of Provalue II, compared with 2 machine-hours per unit for Provalue. Astel will use the entire 300,000 machine-hours of capacity to produce 200,000 units of Provalue II (1.5 machine-hours × 200,000 units = 300,000 machine-hours).
INDIRECT MANUFACTURING COSTS						
Ordering	Number of orders	22,500	80	21,250	80	Astel will place 50 orders for each of the 425 components in Provalue II. Total orders for Provalue II will be 21,250 (425 × 50).
Testing	Testing-hours	4,500,000	2	3,000,000	2	Provalue II is easier to test and will require 15 testing-hours per unit. Total testing-hours for Provalue II will be 3,000,000 (15 × 200,000 units).
Reworking	Rework-hours	30,000	40	32,500	40	Provalue II will have a lower rework rate of 6.5% because it is easier to manufacture. Total units reworked will be 13,000 (6.5% × 200,000). It will still take 2.5 hours to rework a unit, for a total of 32,500 hours (13,000 × 2.5).

Note how value engineering reduces both value-added costs (by designing Provalue II to use less costly direct materials and fewer direct manufacturing labor-hours) and non-value-added costs (by simplifying Provalue II's design to reduce rework-hours). For simplicity, we assume that value engineering will not reduce the $80 cost per order, the $2 cost per testing-hour, or the $40 cost per rework-hour. By making these activities more efficient, value engineering can also reduce costs by reducing these cost-driver rates (see the Problem for Self-Study, p. 430).

The only total costs that value engineering cannot reduce are the total fixed machining costs. Whether or not Astel uses all 300,000 machine-hours of capacity available to it for manufacturing Provalue II, Astel will incur machining costs of $11,400,000 (300,000 machine-hours × $38 per machine-hour). But Astel uses value engineering to reduce the machining-hours required to make Provalue II to 1.5 hours per unit. This reduction allows Astel to use the available machine capacity to make and sell more units of Provalue II (200,000 units versus 150,000 units for Provalue), thereby reducing the machining cost per unit.

Exhibit 12-5 presents the target manufacturing costs of Provalue II, using data for the quantity of the cost-driver and the cost-driver rate from the Provalue II columns in the preceding table. For comparison, Exhibit 12-5 also shows the manufacturing cost per unit of Provalue from Exhibit 12-2. The new design is expected to reduce the manufacturing cost per unit by $140 (from $680 to $540) at the expected sales quantity of 200,000 units. Using an analysis similar to the one used in manufacturing, Astel estimates the expected effect of the new design on costs in other business functions of the value chain. Exhibit 12-6 shows that the estimated full unit cost of the product equals $720—the target cost per unit for Provalue II. Astel's goals are to sell Provalue II at the target price, achieve target cost, and earn the target operating income.[3]

To attain target costs, many companies combine *kaizen*, or *continuous improvement* methods, which are aimed at improving productivity and eliminating waste, with value engineering and better designs. After actual costs are known, companies compare actual and target costs to gain insights about improvements that can be made in subsequent target-costing efforts.

Unless managed properly, value engineering and target costing can have undesired effects:

- The cross-functional team may add too many features, such as a faster microprocessor or more memory than customers want, just to accommodate the different wishes of team members.
- A product may be in development for a long time as alternative designs are evaluated over and over.

EXHIBIT 12-5 Target Manufacturing Costs of Provalue II for 2005

	PROVALUE II		PROVALUE
	Estimated Manufacturing Costs for 200,000 Units (1)	Estimated Manufacturing Cost per Unit (2) = (1) ÷ 200,000	Manufacturing Cost per Unit (Exhibit 12-2, Column 2) (3)
Direct manufacturing costs			
Direct material costs (200,000 units × $385 per unit)	$ 77,000,000	$385.00	$460.00
Direct manufacturing labor costs (530,000 hours × $20 per hour)	10,600,000	53.00	64.00
Direct machining costs (300,000 machine-hours × $38 per machine-hour)	11,400,000	57.00	76.00
Direct manufacturing costs	99,000,000	495.00	600.00
Indirect manufacturing costs			
Ordering and receiving costs (21,250 orders × $80 per order)	1,700,000	8.50	12.00
Testing and inspection costs (3,000,000 hours × $2 per hour)	6,000,000	30.00	60.00
Rework costs (32,500 hours × $40 per hour)	1,300,000	6.50	8.00
Indirect manufacturing costs	9,000,000	45.00	80.00
Total manufacturing costs	$108,000,000	$540.00	$680.00

[3]For more details, see R. Cooper and R. Slagmulder, *Target Costing and Value Engineering*, (Portland, OR: Productivity Press, 1997).

EXHIBIT 12-6

Target Product Profitability of Provalue II for 2005

	Estimated Total Costs for 200,000 Units (1)	Estimated Total Cost per Unit (2) = (1) ÷ 200,000
Revenues	$160,000,000	$800
Cost of goods sold[a] (from Exhibit 12-5)		
Direct material costs	77,000,000	385
Direct manufacturing labor costs	10,600,000	53
Direct machining costs	11,400,000	57
Indirect manufacturing costs	9,000,000	45
Cost of goods sold	108,000,000	540
Operating costs		
R&D costs	4,000,000	20
Design costs of products and processes	6,000,000	30
Marketing costs	18,000,000	90
Distribution costs	4,400,000	22
Customer-service costs	3,600,000	18
Operating costs	36,000,000	180
Full cost of the product	144,000,000	720
Operating income	$ 16,000,000	$ 80

[a]Cost of goods sold = Total manufacturing costs, because there is no beginning or ending inventory for Provalue II in 2005.

- Organizational conflicts may develop as the burden of cutting costs falls unequally on different business functions in the company's value chain, for example, more on manufacturing than on marketing.

To avoid these pitfalls, target-costing efforts should always (a) focus on the customer, (b) pay attention to schedules, and (c) build a culture of teamwork and cooperation across business functions.

COST-PLUS PRICING

5 Price products using the cost-plus approach

...some measure of cost plus a markup

Instead of using the external market-based approach for their long-run pricing decisions, managers sometimes use a cost-based approach. The general formula for setting a cost-based price adds a markup component to the cost base:

Cost base	$ X
Markup component	Y
Prospective selling price	$\$X + Y$

Managers use the cost-plus pricing formula only as a starting point for pricing decisions. The markup component is rarely a rigid number. Instead, it is flexible, depending on the behavior of customers and competitors. The markup component is ultimately determined by the market.[4]

Cost-Plus Target Rate of Return on Investment

Consider a cost-based pricing formula that Astel could use. Assume Astel's engineers have redesigned Provalue into Provalue II and that Astel uses a 12% markup on the full unit cost of the product in developing the prospective selling price.

Cost base (full unit cost of Provalue II, Exhibit 12-6)	$720.00
Markup component 12% (0.12 × $720)	86.40
Prospective selling price	$806.40

Obviously, accurate product cost data are critical to companies that use cost-plus pricing. Accurate product cost data are also important for value engineering and cost management in companies that use target costing. These observations help explain the popularity of ABC systems.

[4]Exceptions are pricing of electricity and natural gas in many countries, where prices are set on the basis of costs plus a return on invested capital. Chapter 15 discusses the use of costs to set prices in the defense-contracting industry. In these situations, in which products are not subject to competitive forces, cost accounting techniques substitute for markets as the basis for setting prices.

How is the markup percentage of 12% determined? One way is to choose a markup to earn a *target rate of return on investment*. The **target rate of return on investment** is the target annual operating income that an organization aims to achieve divided by invested capital. Invested capital can be defined in many ways. In this chapter, we define invested capital as total assets—that is, long-term assets plus current assets. Suppose Astel's (pretax) target rate of return on investment is 18% and Provalue II's capital investment is $96 million. The target annual operating income for Provalue II is

Invested capital	$96,000,000
Target rate of return on investment	18%
Target annual operating income (0.18 × $96,000,000)	$17,280,000
Target operating income per unit of Provalue II ($17,280,000 ÷ 200,000 units)	$86.40

This calculation indicates that Astel needs to earn a target operating income of $86.40 on each unit of Provalue II. What markup does the $86.40 represent? Expressed as a percentage of the full product cost per unit of $720, the markup is 12% ($86.40 ÷ $720).

Do not confuse the 18% target rate of return on investment with the 12% markup percentage.

- The 18% target rate of return on investment expresses Astel's expected annual operating income as a percentage of investment.
- The 12% markup expresses operating income per unit as a percentage of the full product cost per unit.

Astel first calculates target rate of return on investment and then determines markup percentage.

Alternative Cost-Plus Methods

Companies sometimes find it difficult to determine the specific amount of capital they invested to support a specific product. That's because computing the specific amount of invested capital requires knowing, for example, the allocations of investments in equipment and buildings to produce individual products—a difficult and somewhat arbitrary task. Some companies prefer to use alternative cost bases and markup percentages that still earn a return on invested capital but do not require explicit calculations of invested capital to set price.

We illustrate these alternatives using the Astel example. Exhibit 12-7 separates the cost per unit for each business function of the value chain into its variable- and fixed-cost components (without providing details of the calculations). The following table illustrates some alternative cost bases for Provalue II using assumed markup percentages.

EXHIBIT 12-7

Estimated Cost Structure of Provalue II for 2005

Business Function	Estimated Variable Cost per Unit	Estimated Fixed Cost per Unit[a]	Business Function Cost per Unit
R&D	$ 8	$ 12	$ 20
Design of product/process	10	20	30
Manufacturing	483	57	540
Marketing	25	65	90
Distribution	15	10	25
Customer service	6	9	15
Total	$547	$173	$720
	↑ Per unit variable cost of the product	↑ Per unit fixed cost of the product	↑ Per unit full cost of the product

[a]Based on budgeted annual production of 200,000 units.

Cost Base	Estimated Cost per Unit (1)	Markup Percentage (2)	Markup Component (3) = (1) × (2)	Prospective Selling Price (4) = (1) + (3)
Variable manufacturing cost	$483.00	65%	$313.95	$796.95
Variable cost of the product	547.00	45	246.15	793.15
Manufacturing cost	540.00	50	270.00	810.00
Full cost of the product	720.00	12	86.40	806.40

The different cost bases and markup percentages give four prospective selling prices that are close to each other. In practice, a company will choose a cost base that it regards as reliable and a markup percentage that is based on its experience in pricing products to recover its costs and earn a required return on investment. For example, a company may choose the full cost of the product as a base if it is unsure about distinguishing variable from fixed costs.

The markup percentages in the preceding table vary a great deal, from a high of 65% on variable manufacturing cost to a low of 12% on full cost of the product. Why the wide variation? Because cost bases that include fewer costs have a higher markup percentage to compensate for the costs excluded from the base. The precise markup percentage also depends on the extent of competition in the marketplace. Markups and profit margins tend to be lower in more-competitive markets.

Surveys indicate that most managers use the full cost of the product for their cost-based pricing decisions (see Surveys of Company Practice on p. 424)—that is, they include both fixed and variable costs when calculating the cost per unit. Managers cite the following advantages for including fixed cost per unit in the cost base for pricing decisions:

1. *Full recovery of all costs of the product.* For long-run pricing decisions, full cost of the product informs managers of the minimum cost they need to recover to continue in business. Using variable cost as a base does not give managers this information. There is then a temptation to engage in excessive long-run price cutting as long as prices provide a positive contribution margin. Long-run price cutting, however, will result in losses if long-run revenues are less than the long-run full cost of the product.
2. *Price stability.* Managers believe that basing prices on the full cost of the product promotes price stability, because it limits the ability of salespersons to cut prices. Managers prefer price stability because it facilitates forecasting and planning.
3. *Simplicity.* A full-cost formula for pricing does not require a detailed analysis of cost-behavior patterns to separate costs into fixed and variable components for each product. Many costs—for example, testing, inspection, and setups—have both variable- and fixed-cost components. Determining the variable cost of each activity and product is not straightforward.

Suppose the full cost of a product based on sales of 1,000 units is

Variable cost per unit	$30
Fixed cost per unit (avoidable if product is discontinued)	20
Full cost per unit	$50

A manager may be tempted to cut price to, say, $35 because the product still gives a positive contribution margin. However, if sales are only 1,000 units, the $5,000 of contribution margin will not recover the $20,000 ($20 per unit × 1,000 units) of fixed costs, and the product will not be profitable. Using full cost per unit measures the costs that must be recovered over the longer run if the product is to be profitable.

Including the fixed cost per unit in the cost base for pricing is not without problems. Allocating fixed costs to products can be arbitrary. Also, calculating the fixed cost per unit requires a denominator that is likely only an estimate of capacity or expected units of future sales. Errors in these estimates will cause the actual full cost per unit of the product to differ from the estimated amount.

Cost-Plus Pricing and Target Pricing

The selling prices computed under cost-plus pricing are *prospective* prices. Suppose Astel's initial product design results in a $750 cost for Provalue II. Assuming a 12% markup, Astel sets a prospective price of $840 [$750 + (0.12 × $750)]. In the competitive personal computer market, customer and competitor reactions to this price may force Astel to reduce the markup percentage and lower the price to, say, $800. Astel may then want to redesign Provalue II to reduce the cost to $720 per unit, as in our example, and achieve a markup close to 12% while keeping the price at $800. The eventual design and cost-plus price chosen must balance the trade-offs among costs, markup, and customer reactions.

The target pricing approach reduces the need to go back and forth among prospective cost-plus prices, customer reactions, and design modifications. The target-pricing approach first determines product characteristics and target price on the basis of customer preferences and expected competitor responses. Market considerations and target

SURVEYS OF COMPANY PRACTICE

Differences in Pricing Practices and Cost Management Methods in Various Countries

Surveys of financial officers of the largest industrial companies in several countries indicate similarities and differences in pricing practices around the globe. The use of cost-based pricing appears to be more prevalent in the United States than in Ireland, Japan, and the United Kingdom. Japanese survey data indicate that market-based target pricing practices vary considerably among industries. Although a majority of Japanese companies in assembly-type operations (for example, electronics and automobiles) use target costing for pricing, it is far less prevalent in Japanese process-type industries (for example, chemicals, oil, and steel).

Ranking of factors primarily used as a starting point to price products (1 is most important):

	United States	Japan	Ireland	United Kingdom
Market-based	2	1	1	1
Cost-based	1	2	2	2

Compared with the other countries surveyed, Japanese companies use value engineering more frequently and involve designers more often when estimating costs.

Use of value engineering and designers in cost management:

	Australia	Japan	United Kingdom
Percentage of companies that use value engineering or analysis for cost reduction	24%	58%	29%
Percentage of companies in which designers are involved in estimating costs	25%	46%	32%

When costs are used for pricing decisions, the pattern is consistent—overwhelmingly, companies around the globe use full costs of the product rather than variable costs.

Ranking of cost methods used in pricing decisions (1 is most important):

	United States	United Kingdom	Ireland
Based on full costs of the product	1	1	1
Based on variable costs of the product	2	2	2

Source: Adapted from Management Accounting Research Group, "Investigation"; Blayney and Yokoyama, "Comparative Analysis"; Grant Thornton, "Survey"; Cornick, Cooper, and Wilson, "How Do Companies"; Mills and Sweeting, "Pricing Decisions"; and Drury, Braund, Osborne, and Tayles, "A Survey." Full citations are in Appendix A at the end of the book.

price then serve to focus and motivate managers to reduce costs—also referred to as "cost down"—and achieve target cost and target operating income. Sometimes target cost is not achieved. Managers must then redesign the product or work with a smaller profit margin.

To attract new clients, public accounting firms often deliberately bid less than their expected full cost on first-time audits, a practice called *low-balling,* in anticipation that profits from future audits will more than make up for the initial shortfall.

Suppliers who provide unique products and services—accountants and management consultants, for example—usually use cost-plus pricing. Professional service firms set prices based on hourly cost-plus billing rates of partners, managers, and associates. These prices are, however, reduced in competitive situations. Professional service firms also take a multiple-year client perspective when deciding prices. Certified public accountants, for example, sometimes charge a client a low price initially and a higher price later.

LIFE-CYCLE PRODUCT BUDGETING AND COSTING

6 Use life-cycle budgeting and costing when making pricing decisions

...accumulate all costs of a product for all years from initial R&D to final customer service

Companies sometimes need to consider how to cost and price a product over a multiple-year product life cycle. The **product life cycle** spans the time from initial R&D on a product to when customer servicing and support is no longer offered for that product. For motor vehicles, this time span may range from 12 to 15 years. For pharmaceutical products, the time span may be 15 to 20 years.

Using **life-cycle budgeting,** managers estimate the revenues and individual value-chain costs attributable to each product from its initial R&D to its final customer servicing and support. **Life-cycle costing** tracks and accumulates individual value-chain costs attributable to each product from its initial R&D to its final customer servicing and support.

Life-cycle costing can be implemented by coding revenues and costs by product as well as by functional account (for example, R&D, advertising, etc.) in journal entries. Data can then be compiled for each product.

Life-Cycle Budgeting and Pricing Decisions

Budgeted life-cycle costs can provide information needed for strategically evaluating pricing decisions. Consider Insight, Inc., a computer software company, developing a new accounting package, "General Ledger." Assume the following budgeted amounts for General Ledger over a six-year product life cycle:

Years 1 and 2

R&D costs	$240,000
Design costs	160,000

Product life cycles are shortening, which makes it more desirable to use life-cycle budgeting and life-cycle costing.

Years 3 to 6

	One-Time Setup Costs	Variable Cost per Package
Production costs	$100,000	$25
Marketing costs	70,000	24
Distribution costs	50,000	16
Customer-service costs	80,000	30

To be profitable, Insight must generate revenues to recover costs of all six business functions taken together and, in particular, its high nonproduction costs. Exhibit 12-8 presents the life-cycle budget for General Ledger for three alternative selling price/sales-quantity combinations.

Several features make life-cycle budgeting particularly important:

1. Nonproduction costs are large. Production costs are commonly visible by product in most accounting systems. However, costs associated with R&D, design, marketing, distribution, and customer service are less visible on a product-by-product basis. When nonproduction costs are significant, as in the General Ledger example, identifying these costs by product is essential for target pricing, target costing, value engineering, and cost management.
2. The development period for R&D and design is long and costly. In the General Ledger example, R&D and design span two years and constitute more than 30% of total costs for each of the three combinations of selling price and predicted sales quantity. When a high percentage of total life-cycle costs are incurred before any production begins and before any revenues are received, the company needs accurate revenue and cost predictions for the product. It uses this information to decide whether to begin the costly R&D and design activities.
3. Many costs are locked in at R&D and design stages—even if R&D and design costs themselves are small. In our General Ledger example, a poorly designed software accounting package that is difficult to install and use would result in higher marketing, distribution, and customer-service costs. These costs would be even higher if the product failed to meet promised quality-performance levels. A life-cycle revenue and cost budget prevents these relationships among business function costs from being overlooked in decision making. Life-cycle budgeting highlights costs throughout the product's life cycle and so facilitates value engineering at the design stage before costs are locked in. The amounts presented in Exhibit 12-8 are the outcome of value engineering.

At the beginning of a product's life-cycle, it's difficult to determine how successful the product will be. The earlier costs are locked in (before there is much information on the probability that the product will succeed), the riskier the product.

Insight decides to sell the General Ledger package for $480 per package because this price maximizes life-cycle operating income. Exhibit 12-8 assumes that the selling price

EXHIBIT 12-8

Budgeted Life-Cycle Revenues and Costs for "General Ledger" Software Package of Insight, Inc.[a]

	Alternative Selling Price/ Sales-Quantity Combinations		
	A	**B**	**C**
Selling price per package	$400	$480	$600
Sales quantity in units	5,000	4,000	2,500
Life-cycle revenues			
($400 × 5,000; $480 × 4,000; $600 × 2,500)	$2,000,000	$1,920,000	$1,500,000
Life-cycle costs			
R&D costs	240,000	240,000	240,000
Design costs of product/process	160,000	160,000	160,000
Production costs			
$100,000 + ($25 × 5,000); $100,000 + ($25 × 4,000); $100,000 + ($25 × 2,500)	225,000	200,000	162,500
Marketing costs			
$70,000 + ($24 × 5,000); $70,000 + ($24 × 4,000); $70,000 + ($24 × 2,500)	190,000	166,000	130,000
Distribution costs			
$50,000 + ($16 × 5,000); $50,000 + ($16 × 4,000); $50,000 + ($16 × 2,500)	130,000	114,000	90,000
Customer-service costs			
$80,000 + ($30 × 5,000); $80,000 + ($30 × 4,000); $80,000 + ($30 × 2,500)	230,000	200,000	155,000
Total life-cycle costs	1,175,000	1,080,000	937,500
Life-cycle operating income	$ 825,000	$ 840,000	$ 562,500

[a]This exhibit does not take into consideration the time value of money when computing life-cycle revenues or life-cycle costs. Chapter 21 outlines how this important factor can be incorporated into such calculations.

per package is the same over the entire life cycle. For strategic reasons, however, Insight may decide to skim the market—charging higher prices to customers eager to try General Ledger when it first comes out (just as you would skim cream from milk) and lowering prices later. The life-cycle budget will then incorporate this strategy.

Most accounting systems, including financial statements issued under generally accepted accounting principles, report results on a calendar basis—monthly, quarterly, and annually. In contrast, product life-cycle reporting does not have this calendar-based focus. Developing life-cycle reports for each of a company's products requires tracking costs and revenues on a product-by-product basis over several calendar periods. When costs of the business functions of the value chain are tracked over the entire life cycle, the total magnitude of these costs for each individual product can be computed and analyzed. Comparing actual costs incurred to life-cycle budgets provides feedback and learning that can be applied to subsequent products.

Uses of Life-Cycle Budgeting and Costing

Hewlett-Packard (H-P) has a substantial share of the computer printer market. To maintain market share, H-P "cuts short" a printer's product life by bringing a newer version to market while the "old" version still has substantial market share. Why do they "cannibalize" their own products? Because, in the computer industry, being first to market helps gain market share.

Life-cycle budgeting is closely related to target pricing and target costing. Consider the automobile industry. Products have long life cycles, and a large portion of total life-cycle costs are locked in at the design stage. Design decisions affect costs over several years. Companies such as DaimlerChrysler, Ford, General Motors, Nissan, and Toyota determine target prices and target costs for their car models using life-cycle budgets that estimate revenues and costs over a multiple-year horizon.

Management of environmental costs provides another example of life-cycle costing and value engineering. Environmental laws—for example, the U.S. Clean Air Act and the U.S. Superfund Amendment and Reauthorization Act—have introduced tougher environmental standards, imposed stringent cleanup requirements, and introduced severe penalties for polluting the air and contaminating subsurface soil and groundwater. Environmental costs are often locked in at the product and process design stage. To avoid environmental liabilities, companies in industries such as oil refining and chemical processing do value engineering and design products and the processes to manufacture the products to prevent and reduce pollution over the product's life cycle. Laptop computer manufacturers — for example, Compaq and Apple — have introduced costly recycling programs to ensure that nickel-cadmium batteries that can leak hazardous chemicals into the soil are disposed of in an environmentally safe way at the end of the batteries' life.

A different notion of life-cycle costs is customer life-cycle costs. **Customer life-cycle costs** focus on the total costs incurred by a customer to acquire and use a product or service until it is replaced. Customer life-cycle costs for a car include the cost of the car itself plus the costs of operating and maintaining the car minus the disposal value of the car. Customer life-cycle costs can be an important consideration in the pricing decision. For example, Ford's goal is to design cars that require minimal maintenance for 100,000 miles. Ford expects to charge a higher price and/or to gain greater market share by selling cars designed to meet these goals. Similarly, manufacturers of washing machines, dryers, and dishwashers charge higher prices for models that save electricity and have low maintenance costs.

CONSIDERATIONS OTHER THAN COSTS IN PRICING DECISIONS

7 Describe two pricing practices in which noncost factors are important when setting prices

...price discrimination— charging different customers different prices for the same product; and peak-load pricing—charging higher prices when demand approaches capacity

In some cases, cost is *not* a major factor in setting prices. Consider the prices airlines charge for a round-trip flight from San Francisco to Cleveland. A coach-class ticket for the flight with 21-day advance purchase is $350 if the passenger stays in Cleveland over a Saturday night. It is $1,600 if the passenger returns without staying over a Saturday night. Can this price difference be explained by the difference in the cost to the airline of these round-trip flights? No; it costs the airline the same amount to transport the passenger from San Francisco to Cleveland and back, whether or not the passenger stays in Cleveland over a Saturday night. To explain this difference in price, we must recognize the potential for price discrimination.

Price discrimination is the practice of charging different customers different prices for the same product or service. How does price discrimination work in our airline example? The demand for airline tickets comes from two main sources: business travelers and pleasure travelers. Business travelers must travel to conduct business for their companies, so their demand for air travel is relatively insensitive to price. Insensitivity of demand to price changes is called *demand inelasticity*. Airlines can earn higher operating income by charging business travelers higher prices because higher prices have little effect on their demand for air travel. Also, business travelers generally travel to their destinations, complete their work, and return home within the same week.

Pleasure travelers not only don't usually need to return home during the week, but they prefer to spend weekends at their destinations. Because they pay for their tickets themselves, they are much more sensitive to price than business travelers — pleasure travelers' demand is more price-elastic. It is profitable for the airlines to charge low fares to stimulate demand among pleasure travelers.

How can airlines keep fares high for business travelers while, at the same time, keeping fares low for pleasure travelers? Requiring a Saturday night stay discriminates between the two customer segments. The airline price-discriminates to take advantage of different sensitivities to prices exhibited by business travelers and pleasure travelers. Price differences exist even though there is no cost difference in serving the two segments.

What if business conditions weaken such that business travelers become more sensitive to price? The airlines may then need to lower the prices paid by business travelers. In late 2001, to stimulate business travel, some airlines started offering discounted fares on certain routes without requiring a Saturday night stay.

For the 2002 Winter Olympics in Salt Lake City, hotels initially charged very high rates and required multiple-night stays. Airlines also charged high fares for flights into and out of many cities in the region for roughly a month around the Games. Given that demand was expected to far exceed capacity, the hospitality industry and airlines employed peak-load pricing to increase their profits.

In addition to price discrimination, pricing decisions also consider other noncost considerations such as capacity constraints. **Peak-load pricing** is the practice of charging a higher price for the same product or service when the demand for it approaches the physical limit of the capacity to produce that product or service. Prices charged during periods when demand on the production capacity is high represent what customers are willing to pay for the product or service. These prices are greater than the prices charged when slack or excess capacity is available. Peak-load pricing occurs in the telephone, telecommunications, hotel, car rental, and electric utility industries. Consider the daily rental rates charged by Avis Corporation in November 2001 for mid-sized cars rented at Boston Airport:

Monday through Thursday	$69 per day
Friday through Sunday	$22 per day

Avis's actual daily costs of renting a car are the same whether the car is rented on a weekday or on a weekend. Why the difference in prices? One explanation is that there is a greater demand for cars on weekdays because of business activity. Faced with capacity limits, Avis charges peak-load prices at levels the market will bear.

Concepts in Action in Chapter 11 (p. 381) discusses American Airlines' Internet pricing of seats on flights with excess capacity (flights with unsold seats)—an example of price discrimination and nonpeak-load pricing.

A second explanation is that the rental rates are a form of price discrimination. On weekdays, the demand for cars comes largely from business travelers, who need to rent cars to conduct their business and who are insensitive to prices. Higher rental rates on weekdays is profitable because it has little effect on demand. Weekend rental demand comes from pleasure travelers, who are price-sensitive. Lower rates stimulate demand from these individuals and increase Avis's operating income. Under either explanation, the pricing decision is not driven by cost considerations.

Another example of considerations other than costs affecting prices occurs when the same product is sold in different countries. Consider software, books, and medicines produced in one country and sold globally. The prices charged in each country vary much more than the costs of delivering the product to each country. These price differences arise because of differences in the purchasing power of consumers in different countries and government restrictions that may limit the prices that can be charged.

8 Explain the effects of antitrust laws on pricing

...pricing below costs to drive out competitors or fixing prices artificially high to harm consumers is illegal

EFFECTS OF ANTITRUST LAWS ON PRICING

Legal considerations affect pricing decisions. Companies are not always free to charge whatever they like. For example, under the U.S. Robinson-Patman Act, a manufacturer cannot price-discriminate between two customers if the intent is to lessen or prevent competition for customers. Three key features of price-discrimination laws are

1. They apply to manufacturers, not service providers;
2. Price discrimination is permissible if differences in prices can be justified by differences in costs; and
3. Price discrimination is illegal only if the intent is to destroy competition.

Price discrimination by airlines and car rental companies described earlier is legal both because these companies are service companies and because their practices do not hinder competition.

To comply with U.S. antitrust laws, such as the Sherman Act, the Clayton Act, the Federal Trade Commission Act, and the Robinson-Patman Act, pricing must not be predatory.[5] A company engages in **predatory pricing** when it deliberately prices below its costs in an effort to drive out competitors and restrict supply and then raises prices rather than enlarge demand.[6]

The U.S. Supreme Court established the following conditions to prove that predatory pricing has occurred:

1. The predator company charges a price below an appropriate measure of its costs, and
2. The predator company has a reasonable prospect of recovering in the future, through larger market share or higher prices, the money it lost by pricing below cost.

The Supreme Court has not specified the "appropriate measure of costs."[7]

Most courts in the United States have defined the "appropriate measure of costs" as the short-run marginal or average variable costs.[8] In *Adjustor's Replace-a-Car v. Agency*

[5]Discussion of the Sherman Act and the Clayton Act is in A. Barkman and J. Jolley, "Cost Defenses for Antitrust Cases," *Management Accounting* 67 (no. 10): 37–40.

[6]For more details, see W. Viscusi, J. Vernon, and J. Harrington, *Economics of Regulation and Antitrust*, 2nd *ed.* (Cambridge, MA: MIT Press, 1995); and J. L. Goldstein, "Single Firm Predatory Pricing in Antitrust Law: The Rose Acre Recoupment Test and the Search for an Appropriate Judicial Standard," *Columbia Law Review* 91 (1991): 1557–1592.

[7]*Brooke Group v. Brown & Williamson Tobacco*, 113 S. Ct. (1993); T. J. Trujillo, "Predatory Pricing Standards Under Recent Supreme Court Decisions and Their Failure to Recognize Strategic Behavior as a Barrier to Entry," *Iowa Journal of Corporation Law* (Summer 1994): 809–831.

[8]An exception is *McGahee v. Northern Propane Gas Co.* [858 F, 2d 1487 (1988)], in which the Eleventh Circuit Court held that prices below average total cost constitute evidence of predatory intent. For more discussion,

Rent-a-Car,[9] Adjuster's (the plaintiff) claimed that it was forced to withdraw from the Austin and San Antonio, Texas, markets because Agency had engaged in predatory pricing. To prove predatory pricing, Adjuster pointed to "the net loss from operations" in Agency's income statement, calculated after allocating Agency's headquarters overhead. The judge, however, ruled that Agency had not engaged in predatory pricing because the price it charged for a rental car never dropped below its average variable costs.

It would be wise for companies that have concerns about their conformance with antitrust laws to have accounting systems that incorporate the following procedures:

1. Collect data and keep detailed records of variable costs for all value-chain business functions.
2. Review all proposed prices below variable costs in advance, with a presumption that claims of predatory intent will occur.

The Supreme Court decision in *Brooke Group v. Brown & Williamson Tobacco (BWT)* increased the difficulty of proving predatory pricing. The Court ruled that pricing below average variable costs is not predatory if the company does not have a reasonable chance of later increasing prices or market share to recover its losses.[10] The defendant, BWT, a cigarette manufacturer, sold "brand name" cigarettes and had 12% of the cigarette market. The introduction of generic cigarettes threatened BWT's market share. BWT responded by introducing its own version of generics priced below average variable cost, thereby making it difficult for generic manufacturers to continue in business. The Supreme Court ruled that BWT's action was a competitive response and not predatory pricing. That's because, given BWT's current small 12% market share and the existing competition within the industry, it would be unable to later charge a monopoly price to recoup its losses.

Closely related to predatory pricing is dumping. Under U.S. laws, **dumping** occurs when a non-U.S. company sells a product in the United States at a price below the market value in the country where it is produced, and this lower price materially injures or threatens to materially injure an industry in the United States. If dumping is proven, an antidumping duty can be imposed under U.S. tariff laws equal to the amount by which the foreign price exceeds the U.S. price. Cases related to dumping have occurred in the cement, computer, steel, semiconductor, and sweater industries. In 2001, the U.S. International Trade Commission ruled that companies from Argentina and South Africa had dumped hot-rolled steel in the U.S. market. The commission levied antidumping tariffs on the prices charged by these companies.

The World Trade Organization (WTO) is playing an increasing role in resolving trade disputes among member countries. The WTO is an international institution created with the goal of promoting and regulating trade practices among countries by lowering import duties and tariffs. In August 2000, a WTO panel found that WTO antidumping rules override U.S. antidumping laws. In contrast to U.S. laws, WTO rules do not allow for triple damages, and they require a finding of material injury to an industry before any antidumping tariff can be levied.[11]

Another violation of antitrust laws is collusive pricing. **Collusive pricing** occurs when companies in an industry conspire in their pricing and production decisions to achieve a price above the competitive price and so restrain trade. In 1996, the Justice Department fined Archer-Daniels-Midland (ADM) $100 million for collusive pricing of citric acid and lysine. In 2000, ADM was also fined by the European Commission. In 1999, the Justice Department levied $862 million in fines for collusive pricing by five vitamin manufacturers: Hoffman La Roche, BASF, Eisaid, Daiichi Pharmaceuticals, and Takeda Chemical Industries. Collusive pricing is also a concern in Internet-based electronic marketplaces that operate in industries such as chemicals, plastics, and electronics. (See Concepts in Action, p. 430)

---

see P. Areeda and D. Turner, "Predatory Pricing and Related Practices under Section 2 of Sherman Act," *Harvard Law Review* 88 (1975): 697–733. For an overview of case law, see W. Viscusi, J. Vernon, and J. Harrington, *Economics of Regulation and Antitrust,* 2nd ed. (Cambridge, MA: MIT Press, 1995). See also the "Legal Developments" section of the *Journal of Marketing* for summaries of court cases.

[9] *Adjustor's Replace-a-Car, Inc. v. Agency Rent-a-Car,* 735 2d 884 (1984).

[10] *Brooke Group v. Brown & Williamson Tobacco,* 113 S. Ct. (1993).

[11] See Bagley, C., *Managers and the Legal Environment: Strategies for the 21st Century,* 4th ed. (Cincinnati, OH: Southwestern Publishing, 2002).

CONCEPTS IN ACTION

Pricing and the Internet

The Internet offers many opportunities for creative pricing strategies. The airlines example in Chapter 11 illustrates the advantages the Internet provides to convey information to buyers rapidly and to conclude transactions efficiently when costs are largely fixed and there is unused capacity that must be used quickly or otherwise lost. A similar situation exists for international telephone companies who may have temporary excess capacity they may want to sell. Companies such as Band-X match those in need of capacity with those with excess capacity.

For long-run pricing decisions, companies such as Dell Computer customize products and prices to individual customers. Dell sets prices for different configurations of its computer (memory, hard drive space, size of monitor, etc.) and allows customers to choose the configuration they want. CISCO Systems, a supplier of telecommunications equipment, also customizes products and prices. CISCO's Web-based ordering and pricing tool also checks customer orders for accuracy. If a customer orders a product that is incorrectly configured, the system flags the discrepancy and suggests alternative configurations.

Search engines such as Yahoo! do personalized pricing. If a user searches for a Web site about skiing, say, the user will be shown a list of skiing sites along with advertisements about skiing-related products. Yahoo! charges advertisers 50% more for showing advertisements to targeted customers because such customers are more interested in and, therefore, more likely to buy, the advertised products.

The Internet has also created opportunities for buyers and sellers to meet to transact business, in what are called business-to-business (B2B) exchanges. On the one hand, the free flow of information and the large number of buyers and sellers suggest that these exchanges will have competitive prices. On the other hand, suppliers could engage in "coordinated action," or collusion, to keep prices high. Government regulators are keeping a close eye on B2B exchanges for antitrust violations. No charges for collusive pricing have as yet been brought.

Source: C. Bagley, *Managers and the Legal Environment: Strategies for the 21st Century*, 4th ed. (Southwestern Publishing, Cincinnati: 2002); C. Shapiro and H. Varian, *Information Rules* (Harvard Business School Press, Boston: 2000); and discussions with companies.

PROBLEM FOR SELF-STUDY

Reconsider the Astel Computer example (pp. 419–421). Astel's marketing manager realizes that a further reduction in price is necessary to sell 200,000 units of Provalue II. To maintain a target profitability of \$16 million, or \$80 per unit on Provalue II (the same amounts shown in Exhibit 12-6), Astel will need to reduce costs of Provalue II by \$6 million, or \$30 per unit. Astel targets a reduction of \$4 million, or \$20 per unit, in manufacturing costs, and \$2 million, or \$10 per unit, in marketing, distribution, and customer-service costs. The cross-functional team assigned to this task proposes the following changes to manufacture Provalue II:

1. Purchase more subassembled components that combine the functions performed by individual components. This change will not affect Provalue II's quality or performance but will reduce direct materials costs from \$385 to \$375 per unit.
2. Reengineer the way ordering and receiving is done to reduce ordering and receiving costs per order from \$80 to \$60. Using component subassemblies will reduce from 425 to 400 the number of purchased components in Provalue II. As in the chapter example, Astel will place 50 orders per year for each component.
3. Reduce the labor and power required per hour of testing. This action will decrease testing and inspection costs for Provalue II from \$2 to \$1.70 per testing-hour. Under the new proposal, each Provalue II will be tested for 14 hours, a 1-hour reduction.
4. Develop new rework procedures that will reduce the rework costs from \$40 to \$32 per hour. It is expected that 13,000 units (6.5% of 200,000) of Provalue II will be reworked and that it will take 2.5 hours to rework each unit.

No changes are proposed in direct manufacturing labor costs per unit and in total machining costs.

Required

Will the proposed changes achieve Astel's targeted reduction of $4 million, or $20 per unit, in manufacturing costs? Show your computations.

SOLUTION

Exhibit 12-9 presents the manufacturing costs for Provalue II based on the proposed changes. Manufacturing costs will decline from $108 million, or $540 per unit (Exhibit 12-5), to $104 million, or $520 per unit (Exhibit 12-9), and will achieve the target reduction of $4 million, or $20 per unit.

EXHIBIT 12-9 Target Manufacturing Cost of Provalue II for 2005 Based on Proposed Changes

	Estimated Manufacturing Costs for 200,000 Units (1)	Estimated Manufacturing Cost per Unit (2) = (1) ÷ 200,000
Direct manufacturing costs		
Direct material costs (200,000 units × $375 per unit)	$ 75,000,000	$375.00
Direct manufacturing labor costs (530,000 hours × $20 per hour)	10,600,000	53.00
Direct machining costs		
(300,000 machine-hours × $38 per machine-hour)	11,400,000	57.00
Direct manufacturing costs	97,000,000	485.00
Indirect manufacturing costs		
Ordering and receiving costs (20,000[a] orders × $60 per order)	1,200,000	6.00
Testing and inspection costs (2,800,000[b] hours × $1.70 per hour)	4,760,000	23.80
Rework costs (32,500[c] hours × $32 per hour)	1,040,000	5.20
Indirect manufacturing costs	7,000,000	35.00
Total manufacturing cost	$104,000,000	$520.00

[a]400 components × 50 orders per component = 20,000 orders.
[b]200,000 units × 14 testing-hours per unit = 2,800,000 testing-hours.
[c]13,000 units × 2.5 rework-hours per unit = 32,500 rework-hours.

DECISION POINTS SUMMARY

The following question-and-answer format summarizes the chapter's learning objectives. Each decision presents a key question related to a learning objective. The guidelines are the answers to that question.

Decision	Guidelines
1. What are the three major influences on pricing decisions?	Customers, competitors, and costs influence prices through their effects on demand and supply—customers and competitors affect demand, and costs affect supply.
2. How do short-run pricing decisions differ from long-run pricing decisions?	Short-run pricing decisions focus on a period of less than one year and have no long-run implications. Long-run pricing decisions focus on a time horizon of one year or longer. The time horizon appropriate to a decision on pricing dictates which costs are relevant, how costs are managed, and the profit that needs to be earned.
3. How do companies price products using target costing?	One approach to long-run pricing is to use a target price. Target price is the estimated price that potential customers are willing to pay for a product or service. Target operating income per unit is subtracted from the target price to determine target cost per unit. Target cost per unit is the estimated long-run cost of a product or service that when sold enables the company to achieve target operating income per unit. The challenge for the organization is to make the cost improvements necessary through value-engineering methods to achieve the target cost.

Continued

4. Why is it important to distinguish cost incurrence from locked-in costs?	Cost incurrence describes when a resource is sacrificed. Locked-in costs are costs not yet incurred but which, based on decisions that have already been made, will be incurred in the future. To reduce costs, techniques such as value engineering are most effective *before* costs are locked in.
5. How do companies price products using the cost-plus approach?	The cost-plus approach to pricing adds a markup component to a cost base as the starting point for pricing decisions. Many different costs, such as full cost of the product or manufacturing cost, can serve as the cost base in applying the cost-plus formula. Prices are then modified on the basis of customers' reactions and competitors' responses. Therefore, the size of the "plus" is determined by the market.
6. What is life-cycle budgeting and life-cycle costing and when should companies use them?	Life-cycle budgeting estimates and life-cycle costing tracks and accumulates the costs (and revenues) attributable to a product from its initial R&D to its final customer servicing and support. These life-cycle concepts are particularly important when (a) nonproduction costs are large, (b) a high percentage of total life-cycle costs are incurred before production begins and before any revenues are earned, and (c) a high fraction of the life-cycle costs are locked in at the R&D and design stages.
7. What are price discrimination and peak-load pricing?	Price discrimination is charging some customers a higher price for a given product or service than other customers. Peak-load pricing is charging a higher price for the same product or service when demand approaches physical capacity limits. Under price discrimination and peak-load pricing, prices differ among market segments even though the cost of providing the product or service is approximately the same.
8. How do the antitrust laws affect pricing?	To comply with antitrust laws, a company must not engage in predatory pricing, dumping, or collusive pricing, which lessen competition, put another company at a competitive disadvantage, or harm consumers.

TERMS TO LEARN

The chapter and the Glossary at the end of the book contain definitions of:

collusive pricing (p. 429)
cost incurrence (417)
customer life-cycle costs (427)
designed-in costs (417)
dumping (429)
life-cycle budgeting (425)
life-cycle costing (425)
locked-in costs (417)
nonvalue-added cost (417)
peak-load pricing (427)
predatory pricing (428)
price discrimination (427)
product life cycle (425)
target cost per unit (416)
target operating income per unit (416)
target price (415)
target rate of return on investment (422)
value-added cost (417)
value engineering (417)

ASSIGNMENT MATERIAL

Questions

12-1 What are the three major influences on pricing decisions?

12-2 "Relevant costs for pricing decisions are full costs of the product." Do you agree? Explain.

12-3 Give two examples of pricing decisions with a short-run focus.

12-4 How is activity-based costing useful for pricing decisions?

12-5 Describe two alternative approaches to long-run pricing decisions.

12-6 What is a *target cost per unit*?

12-7 Describe value engineering and its role in target costing.

12-8 Give two examples of a value-added cost and two examples of a nonvalue-added cost.

12-9 "It is not important for a company to distinguish between cost incurrence and locked-in costs." Do you agree? Explain.

12-10 What is *cost-plus pricing*?

12-11 Describe three alternative cost-plus pricing methods.

12-12 Give two examples in which the difference in the costs of two products or services is much smaller than the difference in their prices.

12-13 What is *life-cycle budgeting*?

12-14 What are three benefits of using a product life-cycle reporting format?

12-15 Define *predatory pricing, dumping*, and *collusive pricing*.

Exercises

12-16 Relevant-cost approach to pricing decisions, special order. The following financial data apply to the videotape production plant of the Dill Company for October 2003:

	Budgeted Manufacturing Cost per Video Tape
Direct material	$1.50
Direct manufacturing labor	0.80
Variable manufacturing overhead	0.70
Fixed manufacturing overhead	1.00
Total manufacturing cost	$4.00

Variable manufacturing overhead varies with the number of units produced. Fixed manufacturing overhead of $1 per tape is based on budgeted fixed manufacturing overhead of $150,000 per month and budgeted production of 150,000 tapes per month. The Dill Company sells each tape for $5.

Marketing costs have two components:

- Variable marketing costs (sales commissions) of 5% of revenues
- Fixed monthly costs of $65,000

During October 2003, Lyn Randell, a Dill Company salesperson, asked the president for permission to sell 1,000 tapes at $3.80 per tape to a customer not in Dill's normal marketing channels. The president refused this special order because the selling price was below the total budgeted manufacturing cost.

Required

1. What would have been the effect on monthly operating income of accepting the special order?
2. Comment on the president's "below manufacturing costs" reasoning for rejecting the special order.
3. What other factors should the president consider before accepting or rejecting the special order?

12-17 Relevant-cost approach to short-run pricing decisions. The San Carlos Company is an electronics business with eight product lines. Income data for one of the products (XT-107) for June 2004 are

Revenues, 200,000 units at average price of $100		$20,000,000
Variable costs		
Direct materials at $35 per unit	$ 7,000,000	
Direct manufacturing labor at $10 per unit	2,000,000	
Variable manufacturing overhead at $5 per unit	1,000,000	
Sales commissions at 15% of revenues	3,000,000	
Other variable costs at $5 per unit	1,000,000	
Total variable costs		14,000,000
Contribution margin		6,000,000
Fixed costs		5,000,000
Operating income		$ 1,000,000

Abrams, Inc., an instruments company, has a problem with its preferred supplier of XT-107 components. This supplier has had a three-week labor strike. Abrams approaches the sales representative, Sarah Holtz, of the San Carlos Company about providing 3,000 units of XT-107 at a price of $80 per unit. Holtz informs the XT-107 product manager, Jim McMahon, that she would accept a flat commission of $6,000 rather than the usual 15% of revenues if this special order were accepted. San Carlos has the capacity to produce 300,000 units of XT-107 each month, but demand has not exceeded 200,000 units in any month in the past year.

Required

1. If the 3,000-unit order from Abrams is accepted, how much will operating income increase or decrease? (Assume the same cost structure as in June 2004.)
2. McMahon ponders whether to accept the 3,000-unit special order. He is afraid of the precedent that might be set by cutting the price. He says, "The price is below our full cost of $95 per unit. I think we should quote a full price, or Abrams will expect favored treatment again and again if we continue to do business with them." Do you agree with McMahon? Explain.

12-18 Short-run pricing, capacity constraints. Boutique Chemicals makes a specialized chemical product, Bolzene, from a specially imported material, Pyrone. To make 1 kilogram of Bolzene requires 1.5 kilograms of Pyrone. Bolzene has a contribution margin of $6 per kilogram. Boutique has just received a request to manufacture 3,000 kilograms of Seltium, which also requires Pyrone as the material input. An analyst at Boutique calculates the following costs of making 1 kilogram of Seltium:

Pyrone (2 kilograms × $4 per kilogram)	$ 8
Direct manufacturing labor	4
Variable manufacturing overhead cost	3
Fixed manufacturing overhead cost allocated	5
Total manufacturing cost	$20

Boutique has adequate unused plant capacity to make Seltium.

Required

1. Suppose Boutique has adequate Pyrone available to make Seltium. What is the minimum price per kilogram that Boutique should charge to manufacture Seltium?
2. Now suppose Pyrone is in short supply. The Pyrone used to make Seltium will reduce the Bolzene that Boutique can make and sell. What is the minimum price per kilogram that Boutique should charge to manufacture Seltium?

12-19 **Value-added, nonvalue-added costs.** The Marino Repair Shop repairs and services machine tools. A summary of its costs (by activity) for 2004 is as follows:

a. Materials and labor for servicing machine tools	$800,000
b. Rework costs	75,000
c. Expediting costs caused by work delays	60,000
d. Materials-handling costs	50,000
e. Materials procurement and inspection costs	35,000
f. Preventive maintenance of equipment	15,000
g. Breakdown maintenance of equipment	55,000

Required

1. Classify each cost as value-added, nonvalue-added, or in the gray area in between.
2. For any cost classified in the gray area, assume 65% of it is value-added and 35% is nonvalue-added. How much of the total of all seven costs is value-added and how much is nonvalue-added?
3. Marino is considering the following changes: (a) introducing quality improvement programs whose net effect will be to reduce rework and expediting costs by 75% and materials and labor costs for servicing machine tools by 5%; (b) working with suppliers to reduce materials procurement and inspection costs by 20% and materials-handling costs by 25%; and (c) increasing preventive maintenance costs by 50% to reduce breakdown maintenance costs by 40%. Calculate the effect of programs (a), (b), and (c) on value-added costs, nonvalue-added costs, and total costs? Comment briefly.

12-20 **Target operating income, value-added costs, service company**. Carasco Associates prepares architectural drawings to conform to local structural safety codes. Its income statement for 2004 is

Revenues	$680,000
Salaries of professional staff (8,000 hours × $50 per hour)	400,000
Travel	18,000
Administrative and support costs	160,000
Total costs	578,000
Operating income	$102,000

Following is the percentage of time spent by professional staff on various activities:

Doing calculations and preparing drawings for clients	75%
Checking calculations and drawings	4
Correcting errors found in drawings (not billed to clients)	7
Making changes in response to client requests (billed to clients)	6
Correcting own errors regarding building codes (not billed to clients)	8
Total	100%

Assume administrative and support costs vary with professional labor costs.

Required

Consider each requirement independently.

1. How much of the total costs in 2004 are value-added, nonvalue-added, or in the gray area in between? Explain your answers briefly. What actions can Carasco take to reduce its costs?
2. Suppose Carasco could eliminate all errors so that it did not need to spend any time making corrections and, as a result, could proportionately reduce professional labor costs. Calculate Carasco's operating income.
3. Now suppose Carasco could take on as much business as it could get done, but it could not add more professional staff. Assume Carasco could eliminate all errors so that it does not need to spend any time correcting errors. Assume Carasco could use the time saved to increase revenues proportionately. Assume travel costs will remain at $18,000. Calculate Carasco's operating income.

12-21 **Target prices, target costs, activity-based costing.** Snappy Tiles is a small distributor of marble tiles. Snappy identifies its three major activities and cost pools as ordering, receiving and storage, and shipping, and reports the following details for 2003:

Activity	Cost Driver	Quantity of Cost Driver	Cost per Unit of Cost Driver
1. Placing and paying for orders of marble tiles	Number of orders	500	$50 per order
2. Receiving and storage	Loads moved	4,000	$30 per load
3. Shipping of marble tiles to retailers	Number of shipments	1,500	$40 per shipment

Snappy buys 250,000 marble tiles at an average cost of $3 per tile and sells them to retailers at an average price of $4 per tile. Assume Snappy has no fixed costs.

Required

1. Calculate Snappy's operating income for 2003.
2. For 2004, retailers are demanding a 5% discount off the 2003 price. Snappy's suppliers are only willing to give a 4% discount. Snappy expects to sell the same quantity of marble tiles in 2004 as in 2003. If all other costs and cost-driver information remain the same, calculate Snappy's operating income for 2004.
3. Suppose further that Snappy decides to make changes in its ordering and receiving and storing practices. By placing long-run orders with its key suppliers, Snappy expects to reduce the number of orders to 200 and the cost per order to $25 per order. By redesigning the layout of the warehouse and reconfiguring the crates in which the marble tiles are moved, Snappy expects to reduce the number of loads moved to 3,125 and the cost per load moved to $28. Will Snappy achieve its target operating income of $0.30 per tile in 2004? Show your calculations.

12-22 Target costs, effect of product-design changes on product costs. Medical Instruments uses a manufacturing costing system with one direct-cost category (direct materials) and three indirect-cost categories:

a. Setup, production order, and materials-handling costs that vary with the number of batches
b. Manufacturing operations costs that vary with machine-hours
c. Costs of engineering changes that vary with the number of engineering changes made

In response to competitive pressures at the end of 2003, Medical Instruments employed value engineering techniques to reduce manufacturing costs. Actual information for 2003 and 2004 are

	2003	2004
Setup, production-order, and materials-handling cost per batch	$ 8,000	$ 7,500
Total manufacturing operating cost per machine-hour	$55	$50
Cost per engineering change	$12,000	$10,000

The management of Medical Instruments wants to evaluate whether value engineering has succeeded in reducing the target manufacturing cost per unit of one of its products, HJ6, by 10%. Actual results for 2003 and 2004 for HJ6 are

	Actual Results for 2003	Actual Results for 2004
Units of HJ6 produced	3,500	4,000
Direct material cost per unit of HJ6	$1,200	$1,100
Total number of batches required to produce HJ6	70	80
Total machine-hours required to produce HJ6	21,000	22,000
Number of engineering changes made	14	10

Required

1. Calculate the manufacturing cost per unit of HJ6 in 2003.
2. Calculate the manufacturing cost per unit of HJ6 in 2004.
3. Did Medical Instruments achieve the target manufacturing cost per unit for HJ6 in 2004? Explain.
4. Explain how Medical Instruments reduced the manufacturing cost per unit of HJ6 in 2004.

12-23 Cost-plus target return on investment pricing. John Beck is the managing partner of a business that has just finished building a 60-room motel. Beck anticipates that he will rent these rooms for 16,000 nights next year (or 16,000 room-nights). All rooms are similar and will rent for the same price. Beck estimates the following operating costs for next year:

Variable operating costs	$3 per room-night	
Fixed costs		
Salaries and wages		$175,000
Maintenance of building and pool		37,000
Other operating and administration costs		140,000
Total fixed costs		$352,000

The capital invested in the motel is $960,000. The partnership's target return on investment is 25%. Beck expects demand for rooms to be uniform throughout the year. He plans to price the rooms at full cost plus a markup on full cost to earn the target return on investment.

Required

1. What price should Beck charge for a room-night? What is the markup as a percentage of the full cost of a room-night?
2. Beck's market research indicates that if the price of a room-night determined in requirement 1 is reduced by 10%, the expected number of room-nights Beck could rent would increase by 10%. Should Beck reduce prices by 10%? Show your calculations.

12-24 Cost-plus and target pricing. (S. Sridhar, adapted) Waterford, Inc., manufactures and sells 15,000 units of a raft, RF17, in 2004. The full cost per unit is $200. Waterford earns a 20% return on an investment of $1,800,000 in 2004.

Required

1. Calculate the selling price and the markup percentage on the full cost per unit of RF17 in 2004.
2. If the selling price in requirement 1 represents a markup percentage of 40% on variable cost per unit, calculate the variable cost per unit of RF17 in 2004.
3. Calculate Waterford's operating income if it had increased the selling price to $230. At this price Waterford would have sold 13,500 units of RF17. Assume no change in total fixed costs. Should Waterford increase the selling price of RF17 to $230?
4. In response to competitive pressures, Waterford must reduce the price of RF17 to $210 in 2005, in order to achieve sales of 15,000 units. Waterford plans to reduce its investment to $1,650,000. If Waterford wants to maintain a 20% return on investment, what is the target cost per unit in 2005?

12-25 Life-cycle product costing, activity-based costing. Destin Products makes digital watches. Destin is preparing a product life-cycle budget for a new watch, MX3. Development on the new watch is to start shortly. Estimates for MX3 are as follows:

Life-cycle units manufactured and sold	400,000
Selling price per watch	$40
Life-cycle costs	
R&D and design costs	$1,000,000
Manufacturing	
Variable cost per watch	$15
Variable cost per batch	$600
Watches per batch	500
Fixed costs	$1,800,000
Marketing	
Variable cost per watch	$3.20
Fixed costs	$1,000,000
Distribution	
Variable cost per batch	$280
Watches per batch	160
Fixed costs	$720,000
Customer-service cost per watch	$1.50

Ignore the time value of money.

Required

1. Calculate the budgeted life-cycle operating income for the new watch.
2. What percentage of the budgeted total product life-cycle costs will be *incurred* by the end of the R&D and design stages?
3. An analysis reveals that 80% of the budgeted total product life-cycle costs of the new watch will be *locked in* at the R&D and design stage. What are the implications for managing MX3's costs?
4. Destin's Market Research Department estimates that reducing MX3's price by $3 will increase life-cycle unit sales by 10%. If unit sales increase by 10%, Destin plans to increase manufacturing and distribution batch sizes by 10% as well. Assume that all variable costs per watch, variable costs per batch, and fixed costs will remain the same. Should Destin reduce MX3's price by $3? Show your calculations.

12-26 Considerations other than cost in pricing. Examples of prices charged per minute by AT&T for long-distance state-to-state telephone calls within the United States at different times of the day and week are

Peak period (8 a.m. to 5 p.m., Monday through Friday)	$0.30
Evenings (5 p.m. to 11 p.m., Monday through Friday)	$0.25
Nights and weekends	$0.16

Required

1. Are there differences in incremental costs per minute to AT&T for telephone calls made during peak hours compared with telephone calls made at other times of the day?
2. Why do you think AT&T charges different prices per minute for telephone calls made during peak hours compared with telephone calls made at other times of the day?

Problems

12-27 Relevant-cost approach to pricing decisions. Stardom, Inc., cans peaches for sale to food distributors. All costs are classified as either manufacturing or marketing. Stardom prepares monthly budgets. The March 2004 budgeted absorption-costing income statement is as follows:

Revenues (1,000 crates × $100 a crate)	$100,000
Cost of goods sold	60,000
Gross margin	40,000
Marketing costs	30,000
Operating income	$ 10,000
Normal markup percentage:	
$40,000 ÷ $60,000 = 66.7% of absorption cost	

Monthly costs are classified as fixed or variable (with respect to the number of crates produced for manufacturing costs and with respect to the number of crates sold for marketing costs):

	Fixed	Variable
Manufacturing	$20,000	$40,000
Marketing	16,000	14,000

Stardom has the capacity to can 1,500 crates per month. The relevant range in which monthly fixed manufacturing costs will be "fixed" is from 500 to 1,500 crates per month.

Required

1. Calculate the markup percentage based on total variable costs.
2. Assume that a new customer approaches Stardom to buy 200 crates at $55 per crate for cash. The customer does not require additional marketing effort. Additional manufacturing costs of $2,000 (for special packaging) will be required. Stardom believes that this is a one-time-only special order because the customer is discontinuing business in six weeks' time. Stardom is reluctant to accept this 200-crate special order because the $55 per crate price is below the $60 per crate absorption cost. Do you agree with this reasoning? Explain.
3. Assume that the new customer decides to remain in business. How would this longevity affect your willingness to accept the $55 per crate offer? Explain.

12-28 Cost-plus and market-based pricing. California Temps, a large labor contractor, supplies contract labor to building construction companies. For 2004, California Temps has budgeted to supply 80,000 hours of contract labor. Its variable costs are $12 per hour, and its fixed costs are $240,000. Roger Mason, the general manager, has proposed a cost-plus approach for pricing labor at full cost plus 20%.

Required

1. Calculate the price per hour that California Temps should charge based on Mason's proposal.
2. The marketing manager supplies the following information on demand levels at different prices:

Price per Hour	Demand (Hours)
$16	120,000
17	100,000
18	80,000
19	70,000
20	60,000

   California Temps can meet any of these demand levels. Fixed costs will remain unchanged for all the demand levels. On the basis of this additional information, calculate the price per hour that California Temps should charge.
3. Comment on your answers to requirements 1 and 2. Why are they the same or different?

12-29 Cost-plus and market-based pricing. (CMA, adapted) Best Test Laboratories evaluates the reaction of materials to extreme increases in temperature. Much of the company's early growth was attributable to government contracts. Recent growth has come from diversification and expansion into commercial markets. Environmental testing at Best Test now includes:

Heat testing	(HTT)	Arctic condition testing	(ACT)
Air turbulence testing	(ATT)	Aquatic testing	(AQT)
Stress testing	(SST)		

Currently, all of the budgeted operating costs are collected in a single overhead pool. All of the estimated testing hours are also collected in a single pool. One rate per test-hour is used for all five types of testing. This hourly rate is marked up by 45% to recover administrative costs, taxes, and profit in the selling price.

Rick Shaw, Best Test's controller, believes that there is enough variation in the test procedures and cost structure to establish separate costing and billing rates. He also believes that the inflexible rate structure currently being used is inadequate in today's competitive environment. After analyzing the following data, he has recommended new rates for Best Test's upcoming fiscal year.

The budgeted total test laboratory costs for the coming year are

Test pool labor (10 employees)	$ 420,000
Supervision	72,000
Equipment depreciation	178,460
Heat	170,000
Electricity	124,000
Water	74,000
Setup	58,000
Indirect materials	104,000
Operating supplies	62,000
Total test lab costs	$1,262,460
Total estimated test-hours	106,000

Shaw has determined the resource usage by test type in the following table:

	HTT	ATT	SST	ACT	AQT
Test pool labor employees	3	2	2	1	2
Supervision	40%	15%	15%	15%	15%
Depreciation	$48,230	$22,000	$39,230	$32,000	$37,000
Heat	50%	5%	5%	30%	10%
Electricity	30%	10%	10%	40%	10%
Water	—	—	20%	20%	60%
Setup	20%	15%	30%	15%	20%
Indirect materials	15%	15%	30%	20%	20%
Operating supplies	10%	10%	25%	20%	35%
Test-hours	29,680	12,720	27,560	22,260	13,780
Competitors' hourly billing rates	$17.50	$19.00	$15.50	$16.00	$20.00

Required

1. Compute the single pool hourly cost and hourly billing rate for Best Test Laboratories.
2. Compute the five separate hourly billing rates for Best Test Laboratories.
3. Discuss what effect the new cost-plus method will have on the pricing structure for each of the five test types. Given the competitors' hourly billing rates, how might Best Test modify its pricing?
4. In general, identify at least three other internal or external factors that influence pricing structure.

12-30 **Product costs, activity-based costing**. Executive Power (EP) manufactures and sells computers and computer peripherals to several nationwide retail chains. John Farnham is the manager of the printer division. Its two best-selling printers are P-41 and P-63.

The manufacturing cost of each printer is calculated using EP's activity-based costing system. EP has one direct-manufacturing cost category (direct materials) and the following five indirect-manufacturing cost pools:

Indirect-Manufacturing Cost Pool	Quantity of Allocation Base	Allocation Rate
1. Materials handling	Number of parts	$1.20 per part
2. Assembly management	Hours of assembly time	$40 per hour of assembly time
3. Machine insertion of parts	Number of machine-inserted parts	$0.70 per machine-inserted part
4. Manual insertion of parts	Number of manually inserted parts	$2.10 per manually inserted part
5. Quality testing	Hours of quality testing time	$25 per testing-hour

Product characteristics of P-41 and P-63 are as follows:

	P-41	P-63
Direct material costs	$407.50	$292.10
Number of parts	85 parts	46 parts
Hours of assembly time	3.2 hours	1.9 hours
Number of machine-inserted parts	49 parts	31 parts
Number of manually inserted parts	36 parts	15 parts
Hours of quality testing	1.4 hours	1.1 hours

Required What is the manufacturing cost of P-41? Of P-63?

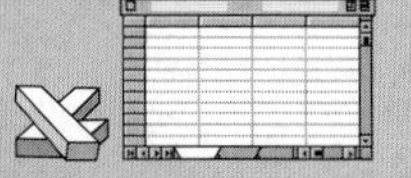

Excel Application For students who wish to practice their spreadsheet skills, the following is a step-by-step approach to creating an Excel spreadsheet to work this problem.

Step-by-Step

1. Open a new spreadsheet. At top, create an "Original Data" section for the data provided by Executive Power. Create rows for the indirect manufacturing cost pools of "Materials Handling, Assembly Management, Machine-insertion of Parts, Manual-insertion of Parts," and "Quality Testing" and create a column for allocation rate in the same format presented by Executive Power on page 438.
2. Skip two rows and enter the data on product characteristics by creating columns for each of the products (P-41 and P-63) and rows for "Direct Material Costs, Number of Parts, Hours of Assembly Time, Number of Machine-inserted Parts, Number of Manually inserted Parts," and "Hours of Quality Testing" in the same format presented by Executive Power on page 438.

(Program your spreadsheet to perform all necessary calculations. Do not "hard-code" any amounts, such as materials-handling cost, requiring addition, subtraction, multiplication, or division operations.)

3. Skip two rows and create a "Manufacturing Cost Calculations" section. Create columns for each of the products (P-41 and P-63) and rows for each of the cost categories including: "Direct Materials, Materials Handling, Assembly Management, Machine-insertion of Parts, Manual-insertion of Parts," and "Quality Testing." Enter calculations for these costs using data from the Original Data section.
4. Include calculations for total *indirect* manufacturing product costs (that is, excluding direct material cost) and total manufacturing product costs on separate rows in this section.
5. *Verify the accuracy of your spreadsheet*: Go to your Original Data section and change the allocation rate for the materials-handling cost pool from $1.20 to $1.50 per part. If you programmed your spreadsheet correctly, total manufacturing product costs for P-41 should change to $807.90.

12-31 **Target cost, activity-based costing (continuation of 12-30).** Assume all the information in Problem 12-30. A foreign competitor has introduced products very similar to P-41 and P-63. Given their announced selling prices, Farnham estimates the P-41 clone to have a manufacturing cost of approximately $680 and the P-63 clone to have a manufacturing cost of approximately $390. He calls a meeting of product designers and manufacturing personnel. They all agree to use the $680 and $390 figures as target costs for redesigned versions of EP's P-41 and P-63, respectively. Product designers examine alternative ways of designing printers with comparable performance but lower cost. They come up with the following revised designs for P-41 and P-63 (called P-41 REV and P-63 REV, respectively):

	P-41 REV	P-63 REV
Direct material costs	$381.20	$263.10
Number of parts	71 parts	39 parts
Hours of assembly time	2.1 hours	1.6 hours
Number of machine-inserted parts	59 parts	29 parts
Number of manually inserted parts	12 parts	10 parts
Hours of quality testing	1.2 hours	0.9 hours

Required

1. What is a target cost per unit?
2. Using the activity-based costing system outlined in Problem 12-30, compute the manufacturing costs of P-41 REV and P-63 REV. How do these costs compare with the $680 and $390 target costs per unit?
3. Explain the differences between P-41 and P-41 REV and between P-63 and P-63 REV.
4. Assume now that John Farnham has achieved major cost reductions in one activity. As a result, the allocation rate in the assembly-management activity will be reduced from $40 to $28 per assembly-hour. How will this activity-cost reduction affect the manufacturing costs of P-41 REV and P-63 REV? Comment on the results.

12-32 **Target prices, target costs, value engineering, cost incurrence, locked-in costs, activity-based costing.** Cutler Electronics makes a radio-cassette player, CE100, which has 80 components. Cutler sells 7,000 units each month for $70 each. The costs of manufacturing CE100 are $45 per unit, or $315,000 per month. Monthly manufacturing costs incurred are

Direct material costs	$182,000
Direct manufacturing labor costs	28,000
Machining costs (fixed)	31,500
Testing costs	35,000
Rework costs	14,000
Ordering costs	3,360
Engineering costs (fixed)	21,140
Total manufacturing costs	$315,000

Cutler's management identifies the activity cost pools, the cost drivers for each activity, and the cost per unit of the cost driver for each overhead cost pool as follows:

Manufacturing Activity	Description of Activity	Cost Driver	Cost per Unit of Cost Driver
1. Machining costs	Machining components	Machine-hours of capacity	\$4.50 per machine-hour
2. Testing costs	Testing components and final product (Each unit of CE100 is tested individually.)	Testing-hours	\$2 per testing-hour
3. Rework costs	Correcting and fixing errors and defects	Units of CE100 reworked	\$20 per unit
4. Ordering costs	Ordering of components	Number of orders	\$21 per order
5. Engineering costs	Designing and managing of products and processes	Capacity of engineering-hours	\$35 per engineering-hour

Cutler's management views direct material costs and direct manufacturing labor costs as variable with respect to the units of CE100 manufactured. Over a long-run horizon, each of the overhead costs described in the preceding table varies, as described, with the chosen cost drivers.

The following additional information describes the existing design:

a. Testing and inspection time per unit is 2.5 hours.
b. 10% of the CE100s manufactured are reworked.
c. Cutler places two orders with each component supplier each month. Each component is supplied by a different supplier.
d. It currently takes 1 hour to manufacture each unit of CE100.

In response to competitive pressures, Cutler must reduce its price to \$62 per unit and its costs by \$8 per unit. No additional sales are anticipated at this lower price. However, Cutler stands to lose significant sales if it does not reduce its price. Manufacturing has been asked to reduce its costs by \$6 per unit. Improvements in manufacturing efficiency are expected to yield a net savings of \$1.50 per radio-cassette player, but that is not enough. The chief engineer has proposed a new modular design that reduces the number of components to 50 and also simplifies testing. The newly designed radio-cassette player, called "New CE100" will replace CE100.

The expected effects of the new design are as follows:

a. Direct material costs for the New CE100 are expected to be lower by \$2.20 per unit.
b. Direct manufacturing labor costs for the New CE100 are expected to be lower by \$0.50 per unit.
c. Machining time required to manufacture the New CE100 is expected to be 20% less, but machine-hour capacity will not be reduced.
d. Time required for testing the New CE100 is expected to be lower by 20%.
e. Rework is expected to decline to 4% of New CE100s manufactured.
f. Engineering-hours capacity will remain the same.

Assume that the cost per unit of each cost driver for CE100 continues to apply to New CE100.

Required

1. Calculate Cutler's manufacturing cost per unit of New CE100.
2. Will the new design achieve the per unit cost reduction targets that have been set for the manufacturing costs of New CE100? Show your calculations.
3. The problem describes two strategies to reduce costs: (a) improving manufacturing efficiency and (b) modifying the design. Which strategy has a bigger impact on Cutler's costs? Why? Explain briefly.

12-33 Cost-plus pricing. (CMA, adapted) Hall Company specializes in packaging bulk drugs. Wyant Memorial Hospital has asked Hall to bid on the packaging of one million doses of medication at full cost plus a return on full cost of no more than 9% after income taxes. Wyant defines cost as including all variable costs of performing the service, a reasonable amount of fixed overhead, and incremental administrative costs. The hospital will supply all packaging materials and ingredients. Wyant has indicated that any bid over \$0.07 per dose will be rejected.

Don Greenway, director of cost accounting at the Hall Company, has accumulated the following information prior to the preparation of the bid:

Variable direct manufacturing labor cost	\$16.00/direct manufacturing labor-hour
Variable overhead cost	\$9.00/direct manufacturing labor-hour
Fixed overhead cost	\$30.00/direct manufacturing labor-hour
Incremental administrative costs	\$5,000 for the order
Production rate	1,000 doses/direct manufacturing labor-hour

Hall Company is subject to an income tax rate of 40%.

Required

1. Calculate the minimum price per dose that Hall could bid for the Wyant job without changing Hall's net income.
2. Calculate Hall's bid price per dose using the full-cost criterion and the maximum allowable return specified by Wyant.

3. Without considering your answer to requirement 2, assume that the price per dose that Hall calculated using the cost-plus criterion specified by Wyant is greater than the maximum bid of $0.07 per dose allowed by Wyant. Discuss the factors that Hall should consider before deciding whether to submit a bid at the maximum price of $0.07 per dose.

12-34 Life-cycle product costing, product mix. Decision Support Systems (DSS) is examining the profitability and pricing policies of three of its recent engineering software packages:

- EE-46: package for electrical engineers
- ME-83: package for mechanical engineers
- IE-17: package for industrial engineers

Summary details on each package over their two-year "cradle-to-grave" product lives are as follows:

Package	Selling Price	Number of Units Sold Year 1	Year 2
EE-46	$250	2,000	8,000
ME-83	300	2,000	3,000
IE-17	200	5,000	3,000

Assume that no inventory remains on hand at the end of Year 2.

DSS is deciding which product lines to emphasize. In the past two years, profitability has been mediocre. DSS is particularly concerned with the increase in R&D costs. An analyst pointed out that for one of its most recent packages (IE-17), major efforts had been made to reduce R&D costs.

Nancy Sullivan, the engineering software manager, decides to collect the following life-cycle revenue and cost information for the EE-46, ME-83, and IE-17 packages:

	EE-46		ME-83		IE-17	
	Year 1	Year 2	Year 1	Year 2	Year 1	Year 2
Revenues	$500,000	$2,000,000	$600,000	$900,000	$1,000,000	$600,000
Costs						
R&D	700,000	0	450,000	0	240,000	0
Design of product	185,000	15,000	110,000	10,000	80,000	16,000
Manufacturing	75,000	225,000	105,000	105,000	143,000	65,000
Marketing	140,000	360,000	120,000	150,000	240,000	208,000
Distribution	15,000	60,000	24,000	36,000	60,000	36,000
Customer service	50,000	325,000	45,000	105,000	220,000	388,000

Required

1. How does a product life-cycle income statement differ from a conventional income statement? What are the benefits of using a product life-cycle reporting format?
2. Present a product life-cycle income statement for each software package. Which package is the most profitable, and which is the least profitable? Ignore the time value of money.
3. How do the three software packages differ in their cost structure (the percentage of total costs in each cost category)?

12-35 Considerations other than cost in pricing. In an advertisement in a San Francisco newspaper, three hotel chains published their weekend and weekday daily room rates for various cities in California.

Hotel	City	Daily Rate Weekend	Weekday
Westin	Palo Alto	$149	$319
Westin	Santa Clara	89	239
Sheraton	San Francisco (airport)	109	219
Sheraton	Sunnyvale	89	209
Four Points	Pleasanton	75	169
Four Points	Sunnyvale	89	209

Weekend rates required Friday and/or Saturday night stay.

Required

1. Explain the reason(s) why the hotels charge lower rates for Friday and Saturday nights.
2. In the same advertisement, two hotels published their room rates for Anaheim (where Disneyland is located), and one hotel published its room rate for Fisherman's Wharf in San Francisco (a popular tourist attraction). Interestingly, the weekend rates in each of these three cases were the same as weekday rates. Explain how this situation differs from the one in requirement 1.

12-36 Airline pricing, considerations other than cost in pricing. Air Americo, about to introduce a daily round-trip flight from New York to Los Angeles, is determining how it should price its round-trip tickets.

The market research group at Air Americo segments the market into business and pleasure travelers. It provides the following information on the effect of two different prices on the number of seats expected to be sold and the variable cost per ticket, including the commission paid to the travel agent:

Price Charged	Variable Cost per Ticket	Number of Seats Expected to be Sold	
		Business	Pleasure
$ 500	$ 80	200	100
2,000	180	190	20

Pleasure travelers start their travel during one week, spend at least one weekend at their destination, and return the following week or thereafter. Business travelers usually start and complete their travel within the same week. They do not stay over weekends.

Assume that round-trip fuel costs are fixed costs of $24,000, and that fixed costs allocated to the round-trip flight for airplane lease costs, ground services, and flight crew salaries total $188,000.

Required

1. If you could charge different prices to business travelers and pleasure travelers, would you? Show your computations.
2. Explain the key factor (or factors) for your answer in requirement 1.
3. How might Air Americo implement price discrimination? That is, what plan could the airline formulate so that business travelers and pleasure travelers each pay the price desired by the airline?

12-37 **Ethics and pricing.** Baker, Inc., is preparing to submit a bid for a ball-bearings order. Greg Lazarus, controller of the Bearings Division of Baker, has asked John Decker, the cost analyst, to prepare the bid. To determine price, Baker's policy is to mark up the full costs of the product by 10%. Lazarus tells Decker that he is keen on winning the bid and that the price he calculates should be competitive.

Decker prepares the following costs for the bid:

Direct materials		$40,000
Direct manufacturing labor		10,000
Overhead costs		
Design and parts administration	$4,000	
Production-order	5,000	
Setup	5,500	
Materials-handling	6,500	
General and administration	9,000	
Total overhead costs		30,000
Full product costs		$80,000

All direct costs and 30% of overhead costs are incremental costs of the order.

Lazarus reviews the numbers and says, "Your costs are way too high. You have allocated too much overhead costs to this job. You know our fixed overhead is not going to change if we win this order and manufacture the bearings. Rework your numbers. You have got to make the costs lower."

Decker verifies his numbers are correct. He knows that Lazarus wants this order because the additional revenues from the order would lead to a big bonus for Lazarus and the senior division managers. Decker knows that if he does not come up with a lower bid, Lazarus will be very upset.

Required

1. Using Baker's pricing policy and based on Decker's estimates, calculate the price Baker should bid for the ball-bearings order.
2. Calculate the incremental costs of the ball-bearing order. Why do you think Baker uses full costs of the product rather than incremental costs in its pricing decisions?
3. Evaluate whether Lazarus' suggestion to Decker to use lower cost numbers is unethical. Would it be unethical for Decker to change his analysis so that a lower cost can be calculated? What steps should Decker take to resolve this situation?

Collaborative Learning Problem

12-38 **Target prices, target costs, value engineering.** Avery, Inc., manufactures component parts. One product, Tvez, has annual sales of 50,000 units and sells for $40.60 per unit. Avery includes all R&D and design costs in engineering costs. Avery has no marketing, distribution, or customer-service costs.

Direct costs of Tvez including long-run fixed cost of machine capacity dedicated to Tvez are

Direct material costs (variable)	$850,000
Direct manufacturing labor costs (variable)	300,000
Direct machining costs (fixed, 50,000 hrs. × $3/hr.)	150,000

Avery's management identifies the following activity cost pools, cost drivers for each activity, and the cost per unit of each cost driver:

Activity	Cost Driver	Cost per Unit of Cost Driver
Setup	Setup-hours	$25 per setup-hour
Testing	Testing-hours	$2 per testing-hour
Engineering	Complexity of product and process	Costs assigned to products by special study

Over a long-run horizon, management views indirect costs as variable with respect to their chosen cost drivers. For example, setup costs vary with the number of setup-hours. Additional data for Tvez are

Production batch size	500 units
Setup time per batch	12 hours
Testing and inspection time per unit of product produced	2.5 hours
Engineering costs incurred on Tvez	$170,000

Facing competitive pressures, Avery wants to reduce the price of Tvez to $34.80, well below its current price of $40.60. The reduction in price will allow Avery to maintain its current unit sales. If Avery does not reduce price, it will lose sales. The challenge for Avery is to reduce the cost of Tvez. Avery's engineers have proposed product design and process improvements for the "New Tvez" to replace Tvez.

The expected effects of the new design relative to Tvez are as follows:

a. Direct material costs for New Tvez are expected to decrease by $3.00 per unit.
b. Direct manufacturing labor costs for New Tvez are expected to decrease by $0.75 per unit.
c. New Tvez will take 6 setup-hours for each setup.
d. Time required for testing each unit of New Tvez is expected to be reduced by 0.5 hour.
e. Engineering costs will be unchanged.

Assume that the batch sizes are the same for New Tvez as for Tvez. If Avery requires additional resources to implement the new design, it can acquire these resources in the quantities needed. Further assume the cost per unit of each cost driver for the New Tvez is the same as for Tvez.

Required

1. Calculate the full cost per unit for Tvez using activity-based costing.
2. What is the markup percentage on the full cost per unit for Tvez?
3. What is Avery's target cost per unit for New Tvez if it is to maintain the same markup percentage on the full cost per unit as for Tvez?
4. Will the New Tvez design achieve the target cost calculated in requirement 3? Explain.
5. What price will Avery charge for New Tvez if it uses the same markup percentage on the full cost per unit for New Tvez as for Tvez?

CHAPTER 12 INTERNET EXERCISE

Understanding the distinction between fixed costs and variable costs is critical when making pricing decisions. This is certainly true for the airline industry with its high fixed costs and unsold seats. To better understand these concepts, go to www.prenhall.com/horngren, click on *Cost Accounting,* 11th ed., and access the Internet exercise for Chapter 12.

CHAPTER 12 VIDEO CASE

GRAND CANYON RAILWAY: Pricing

In the high mountain country of Arizona, you can travel back to a time when the West was wild. The Grand Canyon Railway offers visitors a chance to relive history aboard its vintage trains that run between Williams, Arizona and the South Rim of the Grand Canyon.

Riders have a choice of three classes of service: Coach class, which features travel in fully restored 1923 Harriman coaches; the Club Car, which includes bar service; and the Chief Car, offering elegant first-class service. Because capacity in each railcar is fixed, managers rely on a wide range of information to determine the best mix of prices to charge in filling seats. For instance, data are gathered about operating costs of fuel, labor, food and beverage, and maintenance. Indirect costs, such as costs of administration and the reservations center, also are recorded. Peak-load pricing is practiced during the summer season (April to September), when demand for travel approaches capacity.

Continued

The railway's cost structure is heavily weighted toward fixed costs, such as depreciation on railroad tracks, engines, physical facilities, and administrative salaries. Pricing must cover variable costs to make a contribution toward recouping these fixed costs. Costs can be driven by a number of factors. For example, passenger-driven unit costs include food and beverage; trip-driven unit costs include fuel, engineers, and entertainment; and facility-sustaining costs include advertising and railroad-track costs.

In addition to historical costs and sales data, managers rely on monthly reports of future bookings and past travel patterns for estimating future operating income. Managers look at demographic data to determine where customers come from. They also analyze data on pricing promotions to determine which ones are best received and most profitable. Based on this information, managers recently reduced the number of discounts offered to travelers. Although the number of passengers decreased by 12% in a recent year, profitability increased 67%.

QUESTIONS

1. What environmental and market factors might affect the Grand Canyon Railway's pricing decisions?
2. What are the implications of the Grand Canyon Railway's cost structure?
3. Because capacity on the railway is fixed each trip, how might managers try to fill empty seats in the Club and Chief cars on the day of departure?
4. How does offering fewer pricing discounts affect Grand Canyon Railway's costs?
5. Why might it make sense for Grand Canyon Railway to attempt to increase revenues through booking tour packages, including train transport, hotels, and meals?

CHAPTER 13

Strategy, Balanced Scorecard, and Strategic Profitability Analysis

LEARNING OBJECTIVES

1. Recognize which of two generic strategies a company is using
2. Identify what comprises reengineering
3. Present the four perspectives of the balanced scorecard
4. Analyze changes in operating income to evaluate strategy
5. Distinguish engineered from discretionary costs
6. Identify unused capacity and how to manage it

www.prenhall.com/horngren

Scorekeeping is standard for tracking performance in games, sporting events, and even beauty contests. But now many organizations are starting to track corporate performance. McDonald's, the world's largest fast-food restaurant, keeps score along three dimensions: financial, customer satisfaction, and employee satisfaction. By providing managers just these three categories of performance at its corporate-owned stores, the company helps direct their attention to the areas of greatest strategic importance. And it's not enough to perform well in one area. Managers must focus on all three areas to be sure they are balancing their efforts appropriately. It may seem like a game to some, but let's face it: Whether for fun or profit, everyone wants to play to win.

This chapter focuses on how management accounting information is useful in the implementation and evaluation of an organization's strategy. Strategy drives the operations of a company and guides managers' short-run and long-run decisions. We will describe the balanced scorecard approach to implementing strategy and how to analyze operating income for purposes of evaluating strategy. We also show how management accounting information helps strategic initiatives, such as productivity improvement, reengineering, and downsizing.

WHAT IS STRATEGY?

In today's fast-changing business environment, the management accountant must have a clear understanding of where the company is headed and how all functions of the value chain work together.

Strategy specifies how an organization matches its own capabilities with the opportunities in the marketplace to accomplish its objectives. In formulating its strategy, an organization must thoroughly understand the industry in which it operates. Industry analysis focuses on five forces: (1) competitors, (2) potential entrants into the market, (3) equivalent products, (4) bargaining power of customers, and (5) bargaining power of input suppliers.[1] The collective effect of these forces shapes an organization's profit potential. In general, profit potential decreases with greater competition, stronger potential entrants, products that are similar, and more-demanding customers and suppliers.

To illustrate these five forces, we'll consider Chipset, Inc., a manufacturer of linear integrated circuit devices (LICDs) used in modems and communication networks. Chipset produces a single specialized product, CX1. This standard, high-performance microchip can be used in multiple applications that require instant processing of real-time data. CX1 was designed with extensive input from customers.

Competitors Chipset has many growth opportunities — and many small competitors. Companies in the industry have high fixed costs. There is steady pressure to use capacity fully, and even more pressure on selling prices. Reducing prices of products is critical for growth because it allows LICDs to be incorporated into mass-market modems. CX1 enjoys a reputation of having superior product features relative to competitive products; nevertheless, competition is severe with respect to price, timely delivery, and quality. Quality is important because LICD failure disrupts the communication network.

Potential entrants into the market This industry is not attractive to potential new entrants. Competition keeps profit margins small, and lots of capital is needed to set up a new manufacturing facility. Companies that have been making LICDs are further down the learning curve, so they know how to lower costs. Existing companies also have the advantage of close relationships with customers.

Equivalent products Chipset employs a technology that allows its customers to use CX1 as needed to best meet their needs. The flexible design of CX1 and the fact that it is closely integrated into end-products made by Chipset's customers reduce the potential for

[1] M. Porter, *Competitive Strategy* (New York: Free Press, 1980); M. Porter, *Competitive Advantage* (New York: Free Press, 1985); M. Porter, "What Is Strategy," *Harvard Business Review* (November-December 1996).

equivalent products or new technologies to replace CX1 during the next few years. This risk is reduced even further if Chipset continuously improves CX1's design and processes to decrease production costs.

Bargaining power of customers Customers have bargaining power because each buys large quantities of product. Customers can also obtain microchips from other suppliers. Signing contracts to deliver microchips is important to Chipset. Customers recognize this, so they negotiate hard with Chipset to keep prices down.

Bargaining power of input suppliers Chipset purchases high-quality materials, such as silicon wafers, pins for connectivity, and plastic or ceramic packaging from its suppliers. Chipset also uses skilled engineers, technicians, and manufacturing labor. Materials suppliers and employees have some bargaining power to demand higher prices and wages.

In summary, strong competition and the bargaining powers of customers and suppliers put significant pressure on prices. Chipset is considering responding to these challenges by adopting one of two basic strategies: *differentiating its product* or *achieving cost leadership.*

1 Recognize which of two generic strategies a company is using

...product differentiation or cost leadership

Product differentiation is an organization's ability to offer products or services perceived by its customers to be superior and unique relative to the products or services of its competitors. Hewlett-Packard has successfully differentiated its products in the electronics industry, as have Merck in the pharmaceutical industry and Coca-Cola in the soft drink industry. Through innovative product R&D, carefully cultivating their brands, and bringing products to market rapidly, these companies have been able to provide better and differentiated products. This differentiation increases brand loyalty and the prices customers are willing to pay.

Cost leadership is an organization's ability to achieve lower costs relative to competitors through productivity and efficiency improvements, elimination of waste, and tight cost control. Some cost leaders in their respective industries are Home Depot (building products), Texas Instruments (consumer electronics), and Emerson Electric (electric motors). These companies all provide products and services that are similar to—not differentiated from—those of their competitors, but at a lower cost to the customer. Lower selling prices, rather than unique products or services, provide a competitive advantage for these cost leaders.

When the only computers were mainframes, IBM was able to differentiate its product through superior service. When the PC was introduced, selling price to the end-user (and therefore, cost leadership) became much more important as the product changed to one with many more potential customers (both businesses and individuals).

What strategy should Chipset follow? CX1 is already somewhat differentiated from competing products. Differentiating CX1 further will be costly, but it may allow Chipset to charge a higher price. Conversely, reducing the cost of CX1 will allow the company to reduce price and spur growth. The CX1 technology allows Chipset's customers to achieve different performance levels by simply altering the number of CX1 units in their products. This solution is more cost effective than designing new customized microchips for different applications. Customers want Chipset to keep the current design of CX1 but lower its price. Chipset's current engineering staff is also more skilled at making product and process improvements than in creatively designing brand-new products and technologies. Chipset concludes that it should follow a cost leadership strategy. Of course, successful cost leadership will also increase Chipset's market share and help the company grow. Chipset's next challenge is to effectively implement its cost leadership strategy.

IMPLEMENTATION OF STRATEGY AND THE BALANCED SCORECARD

As scorekeeper (p. 8), the management accountant designs reports to help managers track progress in implementing strategy. Many organizations have introduced a *balanced scorecard* approach to manage the implementation of their strategies.

The Balanced Scorecard

The **balanced scorecard** translates an organization's mission and strategy into a set of performance measures that provides the framework for implementing the strategy.[2] The

[2]See R. S. Kaplan and D. P. Norton, *The Balanced Scorecard* (Harvard Business School Press, 1996).

balanced scorecard does not focus solely on achieving financial objectives. It also highlights the nonfinancial objectives that an organization must achieve to meet its financial objectives. The scorecard measures an organization's performance from four perspectives: (1) financial, (2) customer, (3) internal business processes, and (4) learning and growth. A company's strategy influences the measures it uses to track performance in each of these perspectives.

It's called the balanced scorecard because it balances the use of financial and nonfinancial performance measures to evaluate short-run and long-run performance in a single report. The balanced scorecard reduces managers' emphasis on short-run financial performance, such as quarterly earnings. That's because the nonfinancial and operational indicators, such as product quality and customer satisfaction, measure changes that a company is making for the long run. The financial benefits of these long-run changes may not appear immediately in short-run earnings, but strong improvement in nonfinancial measures is an indicator of economic value creation in the future. For example, an increase in customer satisfaction, as measured by customer surveys and repeat purchases, is a signal of higher sales and income in the future. By balancing the mix of financial and nonfinancial measures, the balanced scorecard broadens management's attention to short-run and long-run performance.

Performance measures in the balanced scorecard must be closely linked with the company's strategy. When the measures are linked (assuming a sound strategy), the company focuses on what it needs to do to be successful.

We illustrate the four perspectives of the balanced scorecard using the Chipset example. To understand the measures Chipset uses to monitor progress under each perspective, we must recognize the actions Chipset plans to take to further its cost leadership strategy: improve quality and reengineer processes. As a result of these actions, Chipset expects to reduce costs and downsize, eliminating capacity in excess of the capacity needed to support future growth. However, it does not want to cut personnel to the extent that it would adversely affect employee morale and hinder future growth.

2 Identify what comprises reengineering

...redesign business processes to improve performance by reducing cost and improving quality

Quality Improvement and Reengineering at Chipset

To improve quality—that is, reduce defects and improve yields in its manufacturing process—Chipset needs to obtain real-time data about manufacturing process parameters, such as temperature and pressure, and to implement more-effective process control methods. The goal is to maintain process parameters within tight ranges. Chipset must also train its workers in quality management techniques to help them identify the causes of defects and ways to prevent them. Following this training, Chipset needs to empower its workers to use their own initiative to make decisions and take actions that will improve quality, such as maintaining process parameters within tight ranges.

Real-time data means instantaneous and continuous data about process parameters.

Reengineering is closely related to value engineering (Chapter 12, p. 417). Reengineering focuses on redesigning business processes to improve performance and satisfy customers. Value engineering relies on product design modifications, changes in material specifications, and the like to improve performance and satisfy customers.

A second element of Chipset's strategy to reduce costs is reengineering its order delivery process. **Reengineering** is the fundamental rethinking and redesign of business processes to achieve improvements in critical measures of performance, such as cost, quality, service, speed, and customer satisfaction.[3] To illustrate reengineering, consider the order delivery system at Chipset in 2002. When Chipset receives a purchase order from a customer, a copy is sent to manufacturing, where a production scheduler begins the planning for manufacturing the ordered items. Frequently, there is a long wait before production begins. After manufacturing is complete, the CX1 chips are sent to the Shipping Department, which matches the quantities of CX1 to be shipped against customer purchase orders. Often, the completed CX1 chips are held in inventory until a truck is available for shipment to the customer. If the quantity shipped does not match the number of chips requested by the customer, a special shipment is scheduled. The shipping documents are sent to the Billing Department for issuing invoices. Special staff in the Accounting Department follow up with customers for payments.

Successful reengineering projects involve an entire process, which cuts across functional lines of the company. The gains arise from the integration of effort and the elimination of unnecessary steps and waiting time.

The many transfers of CX1 chips and/or information about them across departments (sales, manufacturing, shipping, billing, and accounting) to satisfy a customer order have slowed down the process and created delays. Furthermore, no single individual has been responsible for fulfilling each customer order. A multifunction team from the various

[3]See M. Hammer and J. Champy, *Reengineering the Corporation: A Manifesto for Business Revolution* (New York: Harper, 1993); E. Ruhli, C. Treichler, and S. Schmidt, "From Business Reengineering to Management Reengineering—A European Study," *Management International Review* (1995): 361–371; G. Hall, J. Rosenthal, and J. Wade, "How to Make Reengineering Really Work," *Harvard Business Review* (November-December 1993): 119–131.

departments has reengineered the order delivery process for 2003. The goal is to make the entire organization more customer-focused and reduce delays by eliminating the number of interdepartment transfers. Under the new system, a customer relationship manager will be responsible for each customer and the customer's orders. Chipset and its customers will enter into long-term contracts specifying quantities and prices. The customer relationship manager will work closely with the customer and with manufacturing to specify delivery schedules for CX1 one month in advance. The schedule of customer orders will be sent electronically to manufacturing. Completed chips will be shipped directly from the manufacturing plant to customer sites. Each shipment will automatically trigger an invoice that will be sent electronically to the customer. Customers will transfer funds electronically to Chipset's bank.

The experiences of many companies, such as AT&T, Banca di America e di Italia, Cigna Insurance, Ford Motor, Hewlett-Packard, and Siemens Nixdorf, indicate that the benefits from reengineering are most significant when it cuts across functional lines to focus on an entire business process (as in the Chipset example). Reengineering only the shipping or invoicing activity at Chipset rather than the entire order delivery process would not be particularly beneficial. Successful reengineering efforts involve changing roles and responsibilities, eliminating unnecessary activities and tasks, using information technology, and developing employee skills. Chipset's balanced scorecard for 2003 must track Chipset's progress in reengineering its order delivery process from both the nonfinancial and financial perspectives.

The Four Perspectives of the Balanced Scorecard

3 Present the four perspectives of the balanced scorecard

...financial, customer, internal business process, learning and growth

Exhibit 13-1 presents Chipset's balanced scorecard. It highlights the four perspectives of performance: financial, customer, internal business process, and learning and growth. At the beginning of 2003, the company specifies the objectives, measures, initiatives, and actions it must take to achieve the objectives and target performance (the first four columns of Exhibit 13-1). The target performance levels for nonfinancial measures are based on competitor benchmarks. They indicate the performance levels necessary to meet customer needs, compete effectively, and achieve financial goals. The fifth column, which describes actual performance, is completed at the end of 2003. This column shows how well Chipset has performed relative to its target performance.

In setting the target performance in a balanced scorecard, the company shouldn't just aim to be better than it has been in the past. It must strive to be among the "best in class" in comparison with its competitors.

Financial perspective This perspective evaluates the profitability of the strategy. Because cost reduction relative to competitors' costs and sales growth are Chipset's key strategic initiatives, the financial perspective focuses on how much of operating income and return on capital results from reducing costs and selling more units of CX1.

Customer perspective This perspective identifies the targeted market segments and measures the company's success in these segments. To monitor its growth objectives, Chipset uses measures such as market share in the communication networks segment, number of new customers, and customer satisfaction.

Internal business process perspective This perspective focuses on internal operations that further the customer perspective by creating value for customers and further the financial perspective by increasing shareholder value. Chipset determines internal business process improvement targets after benchmarking against its main competitors. We discussed in Chapter 12 that there are different sources of competitor cost analysis—published financial statements, prevailing prices, customers, suppliers, former employees, industry experts, and financial analysts. Chipset also physically disassembles competitors' products to compare them with its own products and designs. This activity helps Chipset estimate competitors' costs. The internal business process perspective comprises three subprocesses:

1. The *innovation process:* Creating products, services, and processes that will meet the needs of customers. Chipset is aiming to lower costs and promote growth by improving the technology of its manufacturing.
2. The *operations process:* Producing and delivering existing products and services that will meet the needs of customers. Chipset's strategic initiatives are (a) improving

EXHIBIT 13-1 The Balanced Scorecard for Chipset, Inc., for 2003

Objectives	Measures	Initiatives	Target Performance	Actual Performance
Financial Perspective				
Increase shareholder value	Operating income from productivity gain	Manage costs and unused capacity	$2,000,000	$2,100,000
	Operating income from growth	Build strong customer relationships	$3,000,000	$3,420,000
	Revenue growth	Build strong customer relationships	6%	$6.48%[a]
Customer Perspective				
Increase market share	Market share in communication networks segment	Identify future needs of customers	6%	7%
Increase customer satisfaction	New customers	Identify new target customer segments	1	1[b]
	Customer satisfaction survey	Increase customer focus of sales organization	90% of customers give top two ratings	87% of customers give top two ratings
Internal Business Process Perspective				
Improve manufacturing quality and productivity	Yield	Identify root causes of problems and improve quality	78%	79.3%
Reduce delivery time to customers	Order delivery time	Reengineer order delivery process	30 days	30 days
Meet specified delivery dates	On-time delivery	Reengineer order delivery process	92%	90%
Improve processes	Number of major improvements in manufacturing and business processes	Organize R & D teams from manufacturing and sales to modify processes	5	5
Improve manufacturing capability	Percentage of processes with advanced controls	Organize R & D/manufacturing teams to implement advanced controls	75%	75%
Learning and Growth Perspective				
Align employee and organization goals	Employee satisfaction survey	Employee participation and suggestions program to build teamwork	80% of employees give top two ratings	88% of employees give top two ratings
Develop process skill	Percentage of employees trained in process and quality management	Employee training programs	90%	92%
Empower workforce	Percentage of line workers empowered to manage processes	Have supervisors act as coaches rather than decision makers	85%	90%
Enhance information system capabilities	Percentage of manufacturing processes with real-time feedback	Improve on-line and off-line data gathering	80%	80%

[a](Revenues in 2003 − Revenues in 2002) ÷ Revenues in 2002 = ($28,750,000 − $27,000,000 ÷ $27,000,000 = 6.48%.
[b]Number of customers increased from seven to eight in 2003.

manufacturing quality, (b) reducing delivery time to customers, and (c) meeting specified delivery dates.

3. *Postsales service:* Providing service and support to the customer after the sale of a product or service. Although customers do not require much post sales service, CX1 monitors how quickly and accurately CX1 is responding to customer service requests.

Learning and growth perspective This perspective identifies the capabilities the organization must excel at to achieve superior internal processes that create value for customers and shareholders. Chipset's learning and growth perspective emphasizes three capabilities: (1) employee capabilities, measured using employee education and skill levels; (2) information system capabilities, measured by percentage of manufacturing processes with real-time feedback; and (3) motivation, measured by employee satisfaction and percentage of manufacturing and sales employees (line employees) empowered to manage processes.

The arrows in Exhibit 13-1 indicate the cause-and-effect linkages—how gains in the learning and growth perspective lead to improvements in internal business processes, which in turn lead to higher customer satisfaction and market share, and finally lead to superior financial performance. Note how the scorecard describes elements of Chipset's strategy implementation. Worker empowerment, training, and information systems improve employee satisfaction and lead to manufacturing and business process improvements that in turn improve quality and reduce delivery time. The result is increased customer satisfaction and higher market share. These initiatives have been successful from a financial perspective. Chipset has earned significant operating income from its cost leadership strategy, which has also led to growth.

In Exhibit 13-1, note how each of the four perspectives focuses management on different elements of the business, with different measures, initiatives, and target performance goals. All four perspectives are linked to the company's strategy and are expected to positively affect financial performance over time.

Aligning the Balanced Scorecard to Strategy

Different strategies call for different scorecards. Suppose Visilog, another company in the microchip industry, follows a product differentiation strategy in designing custom chips for modems and communication networks. Visilog designs its balanced scorecard to fit its strategy. For example, in the financial perspective, Visilog evaluates how much of its operating income comes from charging premium prices for its products. In the customer perspective, Visilog measures the percentage of its revenues from new products and new customers. In the internal business process perspective, Visilog measures the development of advanced manufacturing capabilities to produce custom chips. In the learning and growth perspective, Visilog measures new product development time. Of course, Visilog uses some of the measures described in the balanced scorecard in Exhibit 13-1. For example, revenue growth, customer satisfaction ratings, order delivery time, on-time delivery, percentage of frontline workers empowered to manage processes, and employee satisfaction ratings are also important measures under the product differentiation strategy. The point is to align the balanced scorecard with company strategy.[4] Exhibit 13-2 presents some common measures found on company scorecards.

Implementing a Balanced Scorecard

To successfully implement a balanced scorecard requires commitment and leadership from top management. At Chipset, the team building the balanced scorecard (headed by the vice president of strategic planning) conducted interviews with senior managers, probed executives about customers, competitors, and technological developments, and sought proposals for balanced scorecard objectives across the four perspectives. The team then met to discuss the responses and build a prioritized list of objectives.

In a meeting with all senior managers, the team sought to achieve consensus on the scorecard objectives and to establish a cause-and-effect linkage across the chosen objectives. Senior management was then divided into four groups, with each group responsible for one of the perspectives. In addition, representatives from the next

Employees quickly learn that "the aspects of their performance that are measured are what's important." That is, the act of collecting and reporting various numbers can be a powerful way to motivate employees. The company needs to choose these performance measures with care and think through their implications for employee behavior.

[4]For simplicity, we have presented the balanced scorecard in the context of companies that have followed either a cost leadership or a product differentiation strategy. Of course, a company may have some products for which cost leadership is critical and other products for which product differentiation is important. The company will then develop separate scorecards to implement the different product strategies. In still other contexts, product differentiation may be of primary importance, but some cost leadership must also be achieved. The balanced scorecard measures would then be linked in a cause-and-effect way to this strategy.

EXHIBIT 13-2 Frequently Cited Balanced Scorecard Measures

Financial Perspective

Operating income, revenue growth, revenues from new products, gross margin percentage, cost reductions in key areas, economic value added[a] (EVA®), return on investment[a]

Customer Perspective

Market share, customer satisfaction, customer retention percentage, time taken to fulfill customers' requests, number of customer complaints

Internal Business Process Perspective

Innovation Process: Manufacturing capabilities, number of new products or services, new product development times, and number of new patents

Operations Process: Yield, defect rates, time taken to deliver product to customers, percentage of on-time deliveries, average time taken to manufacture orders, setup time, manufacturing downtime

Postsales Service: Time taken to replace or repair defective products, hours of customer training for using the product

Learning and Growth Perspective

Employee education and skill levels, employee satisfaction scores, employee turnover rates, information system availability, percentage of processes with advanced controls, percentage of employee suggestions implemented, percentage of compensation based on individual and team incentives

[a]These measures are described in Chapter 23.

lower levels of management and key functional managers were included in each group to broaden the base of inputs. The groups identified measures for each objective and the sources of information for each measure. The groups then met to finalize scorecard objectives, measures, targets, and the initiatives to achieve the targets. The final balanced scorecard was communicated and used to evaluate the performance of managers throughout the company.

Features of a Good Balanced Scorecard

A well-designed balanced scorecard has several features:

1. It tells the story of a company's strategy, articulating a sequence of cause-and-effect relationships—the links among the various perspectives that describe how strategy will be implemented. Each measure in the scorecard is part of a cause-and-effect chain, from strategy formulation to financial outcomes.

2. It helps to communicate the strategy to all members of the organization by translating the strategy into a coherent and linked set of understandable and measurable operational targets. Guided by the scorecard, managers and employees take actions and make decisions to achieve the company's strategy. To focus these actions, some companies, such as Mobil and Citigroup, have pushed down and developed scorecards at the division and department levels.

In contrast to for-profit companies, nonprofit organizations have primary objectives such as number of people served and other service goals.

3. In for-profit companies, the balanced scorecard places strong emphasis on financial objectives and measures. Managers sometimes tend to focus too much on innovation, quality, and customer satisfaction as ends in themselves, even if they do not lead to tangible payoffs. A balanced scorecard emphasizes nonfinancial measures as a part of a program to achieve future financial performance. When financial and nonfinancial performance measures are properly linked, most, if not all, of the nonfinancial measures serve as indicators of future financial performance. In the Chipset example, the improvements in nonfinancial factors have, in fact, already led to improvements in financial factors.

Are you surprised by the limited number of performance measures in a balanced scorecard?

4. The balanced scorecard limits the number of measures, identifying only the most critical ones. The purpose is to focus managers' attention on measures that most affect the implementation of strategy.

5. The balanced scorecard highlights less-than-optimal tradeoffs that managers may make when they fail to consider operational and financial measures together. For example, a company whose strategy is innovation and product differentiation could achieve superior short-run financial performance by reducing spending on R&D. A good balanced scorecard would signal that the short-run financial performance might have been achieved by taking actions that hurt future financial performance because a leading indicator of that performance, R&D spending and R&D output, has declined.

Well, individuals' limits on processing information and perceiving trade-offs among various measures translate into the idea that "fewer is better." That is, management needs to specify only the critical measures so that employees focus their efforts on improving items that will make a difference in achieving the company's strategic goals.

Pitfalls in Implementing a Balanced Scorecard

Pitfalls to avoid in implementing a balanced scorecard include the following:

1. Don't assume the cause-and-effect linkages are precise. They are merely hypotheses. Over time, a company must gather evidence of the strength and speed of the linkages among the nonfinancial and financial measures. With experience, organizations should alter their scorecards to include those nonfinancial objectives and measures that are the best leading indicators of financial performance (a lagging indicator). Understanding that the scorecard evolves over time helps to avoid unproductively trying to design the "perfect" scorecard at the outset.

2. Don't seek improvements across all of the measures all of the time. Trade-offs may need to be made across various strategic goals. For example, strive for quality and on-time performance but not beyond a point at which further improvement in these objectives may be inconsistent with long-run profit maximization.

3. Don't use only objective measures in the balanced scorecard. Chipset's balanced scorecard includes both objective measures (such as operating income from cost leadership, market share, and manufacturing yield) and subjective measures (such as customer and employee satisfaction ratings). When using subjective measures, though, management must be careful to trade off the benefits of the richer information these measures provide against the imprecision and potential for manipulation.

4. Don't fail to consider both costs and benefits of initiatives such as spending on information technology and R&D before including these objectives in the balanced scorecard. Otherwise, management may focus the organization on measures that will not result in overall long-run financial benefits.

A company does not need to get its balanced scorecard perfect the first time. Expect it to evolve over time as better measures are found and the company better understands the linkages between processes and profits. As the environment and strategy change over time, the items in the scorecard also will need to change.

5. Don't ignore nonfinancial measures when evaluating managers and employees. Managers tend to focus on what their performance is measured by. Excluding nonfinancial measures when evaluating performance will reduce the significance and importance that managers give to nonfinancial measures (see Surveys of Company Practice, p. 454).

6. Don't use too many measures. It clutters the balanced scorecard and takes attention away from the measures that are critical for implementing strategy.

EVALUATING THE SUCCESS OF A STRATEGY

4 **Analyze changes in operating income to evaluate strategy**

...growth, price recovery, and productivity

To evaluate how successfully it has implemented its strategy, Chipset compares the target and actual performance columns of its balanced scorecard in Exhibit 13-1. Chipset met most targets set on the basis of competitor benchmarks. Meeting these targets suggests that the strategic initiatives that Chipset identified and measured for learning and growth resulted in improvements in internal business processes, customer measures, and financial performance. The financial measures show that Chipset achieved targeted cost savings and growth. Note, the financial measures isolate specific sources of operating income changes rather than the aggregate changes in operating income.

Some companies might be tempted to gauge the success of their strategies by measuring the change in their operating incomes from one year to the next. This approach is inadequate because operating income can increase simply because entire markets are expanding, not because a company's specific strategy has been successful. Also, changes in operating income might be caused by factors outside the strategy. For example, a company such as Chipset that has chosen a cost leadership strategy may find that its operating income increase has instead resulted incidentally from, say, some degree of product differentiation. Managers and accountants need to evaluate the success of a strategy by linking the sources of operating income increases to the strategy.

SURVEYS OF COMPANY PRACTICE

Widening the Performance Measurement Lens Using the Balanced Scorecard[a]

A survey[a] of 100 large U.S. companies indicates that 60% use some variation of the balanced scorecard. Of these adopters, more than 80% are either using or planning to use the scorecard or variations of it for incentive compensation purposes.

As the following table shows, companies adopting the scorecard cite the broadening of the performance measures as the most important reason for adopting it.

Reason	Percentage Citing as Highly Important
Combines operational and financial measures	88%
Minimizes reliance on a single measure	67%
Shows if improvement in one area adversely affects another	35%

Surveys[b] also indicate that the balanced scorecard helps in designing performance measures that communicate strategy and in identifying key financial performance measures. Despite the broadening of performance measures, companies continue to assign more weight to financial results in performance evaluation.

Performance Measure Category	Average Relative Weight
Financial perspective	55%
Customer perspective	19%
Internal business process perspective	12%
Learning and growth perspective	14%

The survey results indicate some problems and challenges in implementing the balanced scorecard. These include (1) difficulty in evaluating the relative importance of different measures, (2) problems in measuring and quantifying important qualitative data, (3) lack of clarity resulting from a large number of measures, and (4) the time and expense necessary for designing and maintaining the scorecard. Despite these challenges, the survey indicates that executives find the scorecard effective and useful. Balanced scorecards are also being implemented in other countries around the globe — for example, in Canada, Finland, Portugal, and Scandinavia.[c]

[a]Adapted from "CompScan Report," Towers Perrin. Full citations are in Appendix A at the end of the book.
[b]Frigo, "2001 CMG Survey."
[c]Ax and Bjornenak, "The Building," Malmi, "Balanced Scorecard," and Rodrigues and Sousa, "The Use of."

To evaluate the success of its strategy, a company can subdivide changes in operating income into components that can be identified with product differentiation, cost leadership, and growth. Why growth? Because successful cost leadership or product differentiation generally increases market share and helps a company to grow. Subdividing the change in operating income to evaluate the success of a company's strategy is conceptually similar to variance analysis, discussed in Chapters 7 and 8, although some of the details differ. One difference is comparing actual operating performance over two different periods rather than comparing actual to budgeted numbers in the same time period. A company is successful in implementing its strategy when the amounts of the product differentiation, cost leadership, and growth components of operating income changes align closely with its strategy.

This section is difficult but important. This strategic analysis is an example of how the management accountant can add significant insight and value for the management team in assessing the effectiveness of implementing their strategy.

STRATEGIC ANALYSIS OF OPERATING INCOME

The following illustration explains how to subdivide the change in operating income from one year to the next into components that describe how successful a company has been with regard to cost leadership, product differentiation, and growth.[5]

[5]For other details, see R. Banker, S. Datar, and R. Kaplan, "Productivity Measurement and Management Accounting," *Journal of Accounting, Auditing and Finance* (1989): 528–554.

Chipset presents the following data for 2002 and 2003.

	2002	2003
1. Units of CX1 produced and sold	1,000,000	1,150,000
2. Selling price	$27	$25
3. Direct materials (square centimeters of silicon wafers)	3,000,000	2,900,000
4. Direct material cost per square centimeter	$1.40	$1.50
5. Manufacturing processing capacity (in square centimeters of silicon wafer)	3,750,000	3,500,000
6. Conversion costs	$16,050,000	$15,225,000
7. Conversion cost per unit of capacity (Row 6 ÷ Row 5)	$4.28	$4.35
8. R&D employees	40	39
9. R&D costs	$4,000,000	$3,900,000
10. R&D cost per employee (Row 9 ÷ Row 8)	$100,000	$100,000

Chipset provides the following additional information.

1. *Conversion costs* are all manufacturing costs other than direct materials. Conversion costs for each year depend on production capacity defined in terms of the square centimeters of silicon wafers that can be processed. Such costs do not vary with the actual quantity of silicon wafers processed. (Because direct manufacturing labor costs are small, and tied to capacity, Chipset includes these costs with other manufacturing costs as part of conversion costs rather than as a separate cost category.) To reduce conversion costs, management would have to reduce capacity by selling some of the manufacturing equipment and reassigning to other tasks or laying off some manufacturing personnel.

2. At the start of each year, management uses its discretion to determine the amount of R&D work to be done. The amount of R&D work is independent of the actual quantity of CX1 produced and sold or silicon wafers processed.

3. Chipset's marketing and sales costs are small relative to the other costs and so are included in the other cost categories. Chipset has fewer than 10 customers, each purchasing roughly the same quantities of CX1. Because of the highly technical nature of the product, Chipsets uses a multifunction team approach for its marketing and sales activities. Engineers from R&D work closely with customers to understand their needs regarding upgrades of CX1 and to market CX1 to them. Once a contract to supply chips is signed, the customer relationship manager located in the manufacturing area is responsible for ensuring that quality products are delivered as and when agreed. This cross-functional team approach ensures that, although marketing and sales costs are small, the entire Chipset organization remains focused on increasing customer satisfaction and market share. (The Problem for Self-Study at the end of this chapter describes a situation in which marketing, sales, and customer-service costs are significant.)

4. Chipset's asset structure is not materially different in 2002 and 2003. Operating income for each year is as follows.

	2002	2003
Revenues		
($27 per unit × 1,000,000 units; $25 per unit × 1,150,000 units)	$27,000,000	$28,750,000
Costs		
Direct material costs		
($1.40/sq.cm. × 3,000,000 sq. cm.; $1.50/sq. cm. × 2,900,000 sq. cm.)	4,200,000	4,350,000
Conversion costs		
($ 4.28/sq. cm. × 3,750,000 sq. cm.; $4.35/sq. cm. × 3,500,000 sq. cm.)	16,050,000	15,225,000
R&D costs	4,000,000	3,900,000
Total costs	24,250,000	23,475,000
Operating income	$ 2,750,000	$ 5,275,000
Increase in operating income	$2,525,000	

Our goal is to evaluate how much of the $2,525,000 increase in operating income was caused by the successful implementation of the company's cost leadership strategy. To do this, we analyze three main components: growth, price recovery, and productivity.

The **growth component** measures the change in operating income attributable solely to the change in the quantity of output sold between 2002 and 2003. The calculations for the growth component are similar to the sales-volume variance introduced in Chapter 7.

The **price-recovery component** measures the change in operating income attributable solely to changes in Chipset's prices of inputs and outputs between 2002 and 2003. The calculations for the price-recovery component are similar to the selling-price variance and the price and spending variances for materials, labor, and overhead introduced in Chapters 7 and 8. The price-recovery component measures the change in output price compared with the changes in input prices. A company that has successfully pursued a strategy of product differentiation will be able to increase its output price faster than the increase in its input prices, boosting profit margins and operating income: It will show a large positive price-recovery component.

The **productivity component** measures the change in costs attributable to a change in the quantity of inputs used in 2003 relative to the quantity of inputs that would have been used in 2002 to produce the 2003 output. The calculations for the productivity component are similar to the efficiency variances introduced in Chapters 7 and 8. The productivity component measures the amount by which operating income increases by using inputs productively to lower costs. A company that has successfully pursued a strategy of cost leadership will be able to produce a given quantity of output with fewer inputs: It will show a large positive productivity component. Given Chipset's strategy of cost leadership, we expect the increase in operating income to be attributable to the productivity and growth components, but not price recovery. We now examine these three components in detail.

Growth Component

The growth component measures the increase in revenues minus the increase in costs from selling more units of CX1 in 2003 (1,150,000 units) than in 2002 (1,000,000 units), assuming nothing else has changed. That is, this calculation assumes that the output prices, input prices, efficiencies, and capacities of 2002 are the same in 2003.

Revenue effect of growth

$$\text{Revenue effect of growth component} = \left(\text{Actual units of output sold in 2003} - \text{Actual units of output sold in 2002}\right) \times \text{Output price in 2002}$$

$$= (1{,}150{,}000 \text{ units} - 1{,}000{,}000 \text{ units}) \times \$27 \text{ per unit}$$

$$= \$4{,}050{,}000 \text{ F}$$

This component is favorable (F) because it increases operating income. Decreases in operating income are unfavorable (U).

We keep the 2002 price of CX1 unchanged and focus only on the increase in output sold between 2002 and 2003. That's because the objective of the revenue effect of the growth component is to isolate the increase in revenues between 2002 and 2003 due solely to the change in the quantity sold, *assuming* the 2002 selling price continues into 2003.

Cost effect of growth Of course, to produce the higher output sold in 2003, more inputs are needed. The cost effect of growth measures the amount by which costs in 2003 would have increased (1) if the 2002 relationship between inputs and outputs continued in 2003 and (2) if prices of inputs in 2002 continued in 2003.

$$\text{Cost effect of growth component} = \left(\begin{array}{c}\text{Actual units of input or}\\ \text{capacity that would}\\ \text{have been used to produce}\\ \text{2003 output assuming}\\ \text{the same input-output}\\ \text{relationship that existed in 2002}\end{array} - \begin{array}{c}\text{Actual units of}\\ \text{inputs or capacity}\\ \text{to produce}\\ \text{2002 output}\end{array}\right) \times \begin{array}{c}\text{Input}\\ \text{price}\\ \text{in 2002}\end{array}$$

We use 2002 input–output relationships and 2002 input prices because the goal is to isolate the increase in costs caused solely by the growth in the units of CX1 sold between 2002 and 2003. The actual units of input or capacity to produce the 2002 output is given in the basic data for Chipset (p. 455). A brief explanation of the individual calculations for the actual units of input or capacity that would have been used to produce 2003 output, assuming the same 2002 input-output relationship, follows.

Direct materials. To produce 1,150,000 units of CX1 in 2003, compared with the 1,000,000 units produced in 2002 (15% more), Chipset would require a proportionate increase in the 3,000,000 square centimeters of direct materials used in 2002. That is, the quantity of direct materials required equals 3,450,000 square centimeters (3,000,000 × 1,150,000/1,000,000).

Conversion costs. Our example assumes conversion costs are fixed costs at any given level of capacity. Chipset has manufacturing capacity to process 3,750,000 square centimeters of silicon wafers in 2002 at a cost of $16,050,000. To produce the higher 2003 output of 1,150,000 units of CX1 in 2002, assuming the same 2002 input–output relationship, Chipset would need to process 3,450,000 square centimeters of silicon wafers as calculated in the previous paragraph. Chipset already has capacity to process 3,750,000 square centimeters of silicon wafers. Therefore, Chipset would not need any additional capacity.

R&D costs. R&D costs are fixed costs unless management decides to change the level of costs. R&D costs would not change in 2002 if Chipset had to produce and sell the higher 2003 volume in 2002. R&D costs are adequate to support the higher output of CX1; they do not depend on either the quantity of CX1 produced or silicon wafers processed.

The cost effect of the growth component is

Direct material costs	(3,450,000 sq. cm. – 3,000,000 sq. cm.) × $1.40/sq. cm. =	$630,000 U
Conversion costs	(3,750,000 sq. cm. – 3,750,000 sq. cm.) × $4.28/sq. cm. =	0
R&D costs	(40 employees – 40 employees) × $100,000/empl. =	0
Total cost effect of the growth component		$630,000 U

In summary, the net increase in operating income as a result of growth equals:

Revenue effect of the growth component	$4,050,000 F
Cost effect of the growth component	630,000 U
Increase in operating income due to the growth component	$3,420,000 F

Price-Recovery Component

The price-recovery component of operating income measures the changes in revenues and costs to produce the 1,150,000 units of CX1 manufactured in 2003 caused solely by the changes in the price of CX1 and in the prices of inputs required to make CX1 between 2002 and 2003, assuming that the 2002 relationship between inputs and outputs continued in 2003.

Revenue effect of price recovery

$$\text{Revenue effect of price-recovery component} = \left(\text{Output price in 2003} - \text{Output price in 2002}\right) \times \text{Actual units of output sold in 2003}$$

$$= (\$25 \text{ per unit} - \$27 \text{ per unit}) \times 1{,}150{,}000 \text{ units}$$

$$= \$2{,}300{,}000 \text{ U}$$

The calculation focuses on price changes in CX1 between 2002 and 2003. Why? Because the objective of the revenue effect of price recovery is to isolate the change in revenues between 2002 and 2003 due solely to the change in selling prices.

Cost effect of price recovery

$$\text{Cost effect of price-recovery component} = \left(\text{Input price 2003} - \text{Input price 2002}\right) \times \text{Actual units of inputs or capacity that would have been used to produce 2003 output assuming the same input-output relationship that existed in 2002}$$

Direct material costs	($1.50 per sq. cm. – $1.40 per sq. cm.)	× 3,450,000 sq. cm.	=	$345,000 U
Conversion costs	($4.35 per sq. cm. – $4.28 per sq. cm.)	× 3,750,000 sq. cm.	=	262,500 U
R&D costs	($100,000/empl. – $100,000/empl.)	× 40 employees	=	0
Total cost effect of price-recovery component				$607,500 U

Note, the quantity of inputs needed to produce the output in 2003 (using the 2002 input-output relationship) has already been determined when calculating the cost effect of growth. The calculation focuses on the change in costs caused solely by the change in the input prices between 2002 and 2003.[6]

In summary, the net decrease in operating income attributable to price recovery (measured by the change in output prices relative to the change in input prices) is

Revenue effect of the price-recovery component	$2,300,000 U
Cost effect of the price-recovery component	607,500 U
Decrease in operating income due to the price-recovery component	$2,907,500 U

The price-recovery analysis indicates that, even as the prices of its inputs increased, Chipset could not pass these increases on to its customers via higher prices of CX1.

Productivity Component

The productivity component of operating income uses 2003 input prices to measure how costs have decreased as a result of using fewer inputs, a better mix of inputs, and/or less capacity to produce 2003 output, compared with the inputs and capacity that would have been used based on the input–output relationship that existed in 2002.

$$\text{Productivity component} = \left(\begin{array}{c}\text{Actual units of}\\ \text{inputs or capacity}\\ \text{used to produce}\\ \text{2003 output}\end{array} - \begin{array}{c}\text{Actual units of}\\ \text{inputs or capacity that}\\ \text{would have been used}\\ \text{to produce 2003}\\ \text{output assuming the same}\\ \text{input-output relationship}\\ \text{that existed in 2002}\end{array}\right) \times \begin{array}{c}\text{Input}\\ \text{price in}\\ \text{2003}\end{array}$$

The calculations use 2003 prices and output. That's because the productivity component isolates the change in costs between 2002 and 2003 caused solely by the change in the quantities, mix, and/or capacities of inputs.[7]

The actual units of capacity that would have been used to produce 2003 output, assuming the same 2002 input-output relationship, have already been calculated for the growth component (pp. 456–457). The actual units of inputs or capacity to produce 2003 output is given in the basic data for Chipset on p. 455.

The productivity component of cost changes is

Direct material costs	(2,900,000 sq. cm. – 3,450,000 sq. cm.)	× $1.50/sq. cm.	=	$ 825,000 F
Conversion costs	(3,500,000 sq. cm. – 3,750,000 sq. cm.)	× $4.35/sq. cm.	=	1,087,500 F
R&D costs	(39 employees – 40 employees)	× $100,000/empl.	=	100,000 F
Increase in operating income due to the productivity component				$2,012,500 F

We comment briefly on the individual items of the productivity component.

[6]Do not try to draw strict parallels between the calculations here and those for variances in Chapters 7 and 8. For example, the price-recovery component calculation takes the difference in input prices and multiplies it by the actual quantity of inputs that would have been used in 2003, assuming the 2002 input-output relationship. In Chapters 7 and 8, we multiplied the difference between actual and budgeted input prices by the actual quantity of inputs used in 2003. The Chapter 13 calculations are based on the production function in 2002, not 2003. Why? Because Chipset wants to isolate the effect on operating income of changes in input prices alone.

[7]Note that the productivity component calculation uses actual 2003 input prices, whereas its counterpart, the efficiency variance in Chapters 7 and 8, uses budgeted prices. (In effect, the budgeted prices correspond to 2002 prices). Year 2003 prices are used in the productivity calculation because Chipset wants its managers to choose input quantities to minimize costs in 2003 based on currently prevailing prices. If 2002 prices had been used in the productivity calculation, managers would choose input quantities based on irrelevant input prices that prevailed a year ago! Using budgeted prices in Chapters 7 and 8 does not pose a similar problem. Why? Because, unlike 2002 prices that describe what happened a year ago, budgeted prices represent prices that are expected to prevail in the current period. Moreover, budgeted prices can be changed, if necessary, to bring them in line with actual current period prices.

Direct materials. At the 2002 quality levels, Chipset would have required 3,450,000 (3,000,000 × 1,150,000/1,000,000) square centimeters of silicon wafers to produce 1,150,000 units of CX1 in 2003. As a result of quality and yield improvements, Chipset processes 2,900,000 square centimeters of silicon wafers in 2003.

Conversion costs. These are fixed costs that change only if management takes actions to alter manufacturing capacity. Because of the reengineered processes and quality improvements, Chipset needs to process only 2,900,000 square centimeters of silicon wafers to produce 1,150,000 units of CX1 in 2003. In 2002, Chipset had the capacity to process 3,750,000 square centimeters of silicon wafers. To reduce costs, Chipset's management decreases capacity to a level that can process only 3,500,000 square centimeters of silicon wafers by selling old equipment and laying off some workers.

Note that productivity improvements do not occur automatically for fixed costs. When the company needs less capacity, the only way to save some of these costs is for management to reduce capacity (in either equipment/facilities and/or personnel).

R&D costs. These are also fixed costs that change only if management takes actions to reduce the number of R&D employees. Chipset ended 2003 with 39 research engineers, but it started with 40 engineers. Chipset's management did not replace an engineer who quit.

The productivity component indicates that Chipset was able to increase operating income by improving quality and productivity, eliminating capacity, and reducing costs. The appendix to this chapter examines partial and total factor productivity changes between 2002 and 2003 and describes how the management accountant can obtain a deeper understanding of Chipset's cost leadership strategy. Note that the productivity component focuses exclusively on costs, so there is no revenue effect for this component.

Exhibit 13-3 summarizes the growth, price-recovery, and productivity components of the changes in operating income. At a basic level, companies that have been successful at cost leadership will show large favorable productivity and growth components. Companies that have successfully differentiated their products will show large favorable price-recovery and growth components. In Chipset's case, productivity contributed $2,012,500 to the increase in operating income, and growth contributed $3,420,000. Operating income suffered because Chipset was unable to pass along increases in input prices. Had Chipset been able to differentiate its product, the price-recovery effects might have been less unfavorable or perhaps even favorable.

The further analysis described in this section gives management more strategic information to evaluate its policies. By analyzing the effect of the market growth rate in the industry, Chipset's managers can isolate the effect of what they have accomplished (with either cost leadership or product differentiation) versus what resulted from changes in the marketplace.

Further Analysis of Growth, Price-Recovery, and Productivity Components

As in all variance and profit analysis, the analyst will want to examine the sources of operating income more closely. In the Chipset example, growth might have been helped by an increase in industry market size. Therefore, at least part of the increase in operating income may be attributable to favorable economic conditions in the industry rather than to any successful implementation of strategy. Some of the growth might also have come as a result of a management decision at Chipset to take advantage of its productivity gains by

EXHIBIT 13-3 Strategic Analysis of Profitability

	Income Statement Amounts in 2002 (1)	Revenue and Cost Effects of Growth Component in 2003 (2)	Revenue and Cost Effects of Price-Recovery Component in 2003 (3)	Cost Effect of Productivity Component in 2003 (4)	Income Statement Amounts in 2003 (5) = (1) + (2) + (3) + (4)
Revenues	$27,000,000	$4,050,000 F	$2,300,000 U	—	$28,750,000
Costs	24,250,000	630,000 U	607,500 U	$2,012,500 F	23,475,000
Operating income	$ 2,750,000	$3,420,000 F	$2,907,500 U	$2,012,500 F	$ 5,275,000
			$2,525,000 F		

Change in operating income

decreasing prices. In this case, the increase in operating income from cost leadership equals the productivity gain plus any increase in operating income from growth in market share attributable to productivity improvements minus any decrease in operating income from a strategic decision to lower prices.

To illustrate these ideas, consider again the Chipset example and the following additional information.

- The market growth rate in the industry is 10% in 2003. Of the 150,000 (1,150,000 – 1,000,000) units of increase in sales of CX1 between 2002 and 2003, 100,000 (0.10 × 1,000,000) units are due to an increase in industry market size (which Chipset should have benefited from regardless of its productivity gains), and the remaining 50,000 units are due to an increase in market share.
- During 2003, Chipset experiences a $1.35, or 5%, decline in the price of CX1 (0.05 × $27 = $1.35). Taking advantage of productivity gains, management reduces the price of CX1 by an additional $0.65, which leads to the 50,000 unit increase in market share. [Recall that the total decrease in the price of CX1 is $2 ($1.35 + $0.65).]

The effect of the industry-market size factor on operating income (rather than any specific strategic actions) is

Increase in operating income due to growth in industry market size	
$\$3,420,000 \text{ (Exhibit 13-3, column 2)} \times \frac{100,000}{150,000}$	$2,280,000 F

Lacking a differentiated product, Chipset experiences a $1.35 decline in output prices even while the prices of its inputs increase.

The effect of product differentiation on operating income is

Decrease in operating income due to a decline in the selling price of CX1 (other than the strategic reduction in price included as part of the cost leadership component) $1.35 × 1,150,000	$1,552,500 U
Increase in prices of inputs (cost effect of price recovery)	607,500 U
Decrease in operating income due to product differentiation	$2,160,000 U

The effect of cost leadership on operating income is

Productivity component	$2,012,500 F
Effect of strategic decision to reduce price ($0.65/unit × 1,150,000 units)	747,500 U
Growth in market share due to productivity improvement and strategic decision to reduce prices	
$\$3,420,000 \text{ (Exhibit 13-3, column 2)} \times \frac{50,000 \text{ units}}{150,000 \text{ units}}$	1,140,000 F
Increase in operating income due to cost leadership	$2,405,000 F

A summary of the change in operating income between 2002 and 2003 follows

Change due to industry market size	$2,280,000 F
Change due to product differentiation	2,160,000 U
Change due to cost leadership	2,405,000 F
Change in operating income	$2,525,000 F

Under different assumptions of how the change in selling price affects the quantity of CX1 sold, the analyst will attribute different amounts to different strategies. The point to understand here is that, consistent with its cost leadership strategy, the productivity gains of $2,012,500 Chipset made in 2003 were a big part of the operating income increases in 2003. The Problem for Self-Study describes the analysis of the growth, price-recovery, and productivity components for a company following a product differentiation strategy. The Concepts in Action (p. 461) describes the problems of dot-com companies that emphasized growth and did not achieve cost leadership or product differentiation.

DOWNSIZING AND THE MANAGEMENT OF CAPACITY

As we saw in our discussion of the productivity component, fixed costs are tied to capacity. Unlike variable costs, fixed costs do not change automatically with changes in activity level (such as silicon wafers started into production in the case of manufacturing over-

CONCEPTS IN ACTION

Growth Versus Profitability Choices of Dot-com Companies

Competitive advantage comes from product differentiation or cost leadership. Successful implementation of these strategies helps a company be profitable and grow. During the dot-com boom, many dot-com companies pursued a strategy of short-run growth to gain brand recognition and market share, with the goal of later translating such growth into higher prices (via product differentiation) or lower costs (via cost leadership). The most spectacular failures of dot-com companies occurred in companies that followed the "get big fast" model but then failed to differentiate their products or reduce their costs.

One such example was Webvan. At Webvan, customers ordered groceries online. Webvan then delivered these groceries to customers' houses. The benefit to customers was that they avoided the hassle of driving, parking, and standing in line at the supermarket. Webvan's model was to get big fast. *The New York Times* noted that "long before it began to get the bugs out of its initial 100,000 square-foot distribution center in Oakland, California, Webvan began a three-year program to replicate the facility in 26 cities nationwide, at a cost of $35 million each." Webvan also spent large amounts of money on marketing to establish its brand. The operational challenges of an online grocery business are immense. Webvan never generated anywhere near the sales volume it was expecting. The low margins of the retail grocery business, perishable inventory, and large amounts of unused capacity led to heavy losses. In July 2001, Webvan filed for bankruptcy, having spent almost all of the $1.2 billion of its invested capital.

Webvan could not become profitable because its cost structure was higher than the bricks-and-mortar grocery stores it competed against. Lower costs due to productivity increases or economies of scale did not materialize. Despite brand recognition, Webvan did not have a favorable price-recovery component of operating income because customers were unwilling to pay a substantially higher price for the convenience of online grocery shopping. Without a cost or product differentiation advantage, the growth component of operating income was unfavorable because costs exceeded revenues. The more Webvan sold, the more money it lost, leading to its eventual bankruptcy. Long-term success rests on gaining cost leadership or product differentiation, which Webvan never achieved.

Source: New York Times (July 10, 2001, and July 20, 2001); The Wall Street Journal (August 9, 1999); and Webvan's 2000 10K filings.

head costs). How then can managers reduce capacity-based fixed costs? By measuring and managing unused capacity. **Unused capacity** is the amount of productive capacity available over and above the productive capacity employed to meet consumer demand in the current period. To understand unused capacity, it is necessary to distinguish *engineered costs* from *discretionary costs.*

> **5** **Distinguish engineered costs**
> ...when a cause-and-effect relationship exists between output produced and costs incurred
> **from discretionary costs**
> ... when no cause-and-effect relationship exists between output produced and costs incurred

Engineered costs result from a cause-and-effect relationship between the cost driver — output — and the (direct or indirect) resources used to produce that output. In the Chipset example, direct material costs are *direct engineered costs*. Conversion costs are an example of *indirect engineered costs*. Consider the year 2003. The output of 1,150,000 units of CX1 and the efficiency with which inputs are converted into outputs result in 2,900,000 square centimeters of silicon wafers being started into production. Manufacturing conversion cost resources used to produce 1,150,000 units of CX1 equal $12,615,000 ($4.35 per sq. cm. × 2,900,000 sq. cm.), assuming that the cost of resources used increases proportionately with the number of square centimeters of silicon wafers processed. Of course, conversion costs are higher ($15,225,000) because these costs relate to the manufacturing capacity to process 3,500,000 square centimeters of silicon wafer ($4.35 per sq. cm. × 3,500,000 sq. cm. = $15,225,000). Although these costs are fixed in the short run, over the longer run there is a cause-and-effect relationship between output and manufacturing capacity required (and conversion costs needed). Thus, engineered costs can be variable or fixed in the short run.

Discretionary costs have two important features to consider: (1) They arise from periodic (usually annual) decisions regarding the maximum amount to be incurred, and (2) they have no measurable cause-and-effect relationship between output and resources used. There is often a delay between when a resource is acquired and when it is used. Examples of discretionary costs include advertising, executive training, R&D, health care, and corporate-staff department costs such as legal, human resources, and public relations. The most noteworthy aspect of discretionary costs is that managers are seldom confident that the "correct" amounts are being spent. The founder of Lever Brothers, an international consumer-products company, once noted, "Half the money I spend on advertising is wasted; the trouble is, I don't know which half!" In the Chipset example, R&D costs are discretionary costs because there is no measurable cause-and-effect relationship between output of 1,150,000 units produced and R&D resources needed or used.[8]

Relationships Between Inputs and Outputs

Engineered costs differ from discretionary costs in two ways: the type of process and the level of uncertainty represented in a cost. Engineered costs pertain to processes that are detailed, physically observable, and repetitive, such as manufacturing or customer-service activities. Discretionary costs are associated with processes such as advertising, public relations, and management training that are sometimes called *black boxes,* because they are less precise in terms of the relationship between output produced and resources used.

Uncertainty refers to the possibility that an actual amount will deviate from an expected amount. The higher the level of uncertainty about the relationship between outputs and resources used, the less likely a cause-and-effect relationship will exist, leading the cost to be classified as a discretionary cost. R&D costs have an uncertain effect on output because of the nature of the task—whether the R&D effort will be successful and lead to output is not known when the R&D is started—and because other factors such as overall market conditions, competitors' R&D investments, and new product introductions also affect the level of output produced. In contrast, there is a low level of uncertainty about the effect on output of manufacturing conversion resources used because the nature of the task—using more manufacturing conversion resources results in more output—and other factors do not affect this relationship. Exhibit 13-4 summarizes these key distinctions between engineered and discretionary costs.

EXHIBIT 13-4 Differences Between Engineered and Discretionary Costs

	Engineered Costs	Discretionary Costs
Process or activity	**a.** Detailed and physically observable **b.** Repetitive	**a.** Black box (knowledge of process is sketchy or unavailable) **b.** Nonrepetitive or nonroutine
Level of uncertainty	Moderate or small (for example, shipping or manufacturing settings)	Large (for example, R&D or advertising settings)

Source: This exhibit is a modification of one suggested by H. Itami.

[8]Managers also describe some costs as *infrastructure costs*—costs that arise from having property, plant, and equipment and a functioning organization. Examples are depreciation, long-run lease rental, and the acquisition of long-run technical capabilities. These costs are generally fixed costs because they are committed to and acquired before they are used. Infrastructure costs can be engineered or discretionary. For instance, manufacturing overhead cost incurred at Chipset to acquire manufacturing capacity is an infrastructure cost that is an example of an engineered cost. In the long run, there is a cause-and-effect relationship between output and manufacturing overhead costs needed to produce that output. R&D cost incurred to acquire technical capability is an infrastructure cost that is an example of a discretionary cost. There is no measurable cause-and-effect relationship between output and R&D cost incurred.

Identifying Unused Capacity for Engineered and Discretionary Overhead Costs

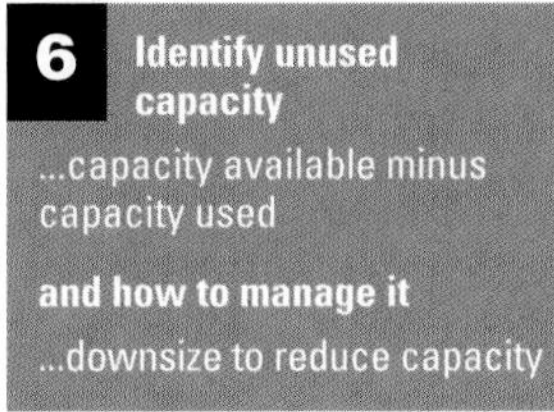

How does the distinction between engineered and discretionary costs help a manager understand and manage unused capacity? Actually, the different types of costs have very different relationships to capacity. Consider first the engineered conversion costs. Chipset management indicates that manufacturing capacity can be added or reduced in increments to process 250,000 square centimeters of silicon wafers. Adding or reducing capacity takes time. Conversion costs change in steps, as shown in Exhibit 13-5. At each level, conversion costs are fixed. For example, conversion costs are fixed at $13,050,000 if Chipset wants enough capacity to process between 2,750,001 and 3,000,000 square centimeters of silicon wafers. If Chipset wants to process more than 3,000,000, say, 3,100,000, it would need to increase its capacity to 3,250,000 square centimeters, an increase of 250,000 square centimeters of capacity at a cost of $1,087,500.

At the start of 2003, Chipset has capacity to process 3,750,000 square centimeters of silicon wafers. Quality and productivity improvements made during 2003 enable Chipset to produce 1,150,000 units of CX1 by processing 2,900,000 square centimeters of silicon wafers. Chipset calculates its unused manufacturing capacity as 850,000 (3,750,000 – 2,900,000) square centimeters of silicon wafer processing capacity at the beginning of 2003, which corresponds to conversion costs of $3,697,500 ($4.35 per sq. cm. × 850,000 sq. cm.). As shown in Exhibit 13-5, this unused capacity of $3,697,500 can also be calculated as $16,312,500 (manufacturing overhead costs to process 3,750,000 sq. cm. of silicon wafers) minus $12,615,000 ($4.35 per sq. cm. × 2,900,000, the manufacturing resources used to process 2,900,000 sq. cm. of silicon wafers).

The absence of a cause-and-effect relationship makes identifying unused capacity for discretionary costs difficult. Management cannot determine the R&D resources used for the actual output produced to compare to R&D capacity. And without a measure of capacity used, it is not possible to compute unused capacity (as it is possible to do for engineered conversion costs).

EXHIBIT 13-5 Engineered Costs and Unused Capacity at Chipset, Inc., in 2003

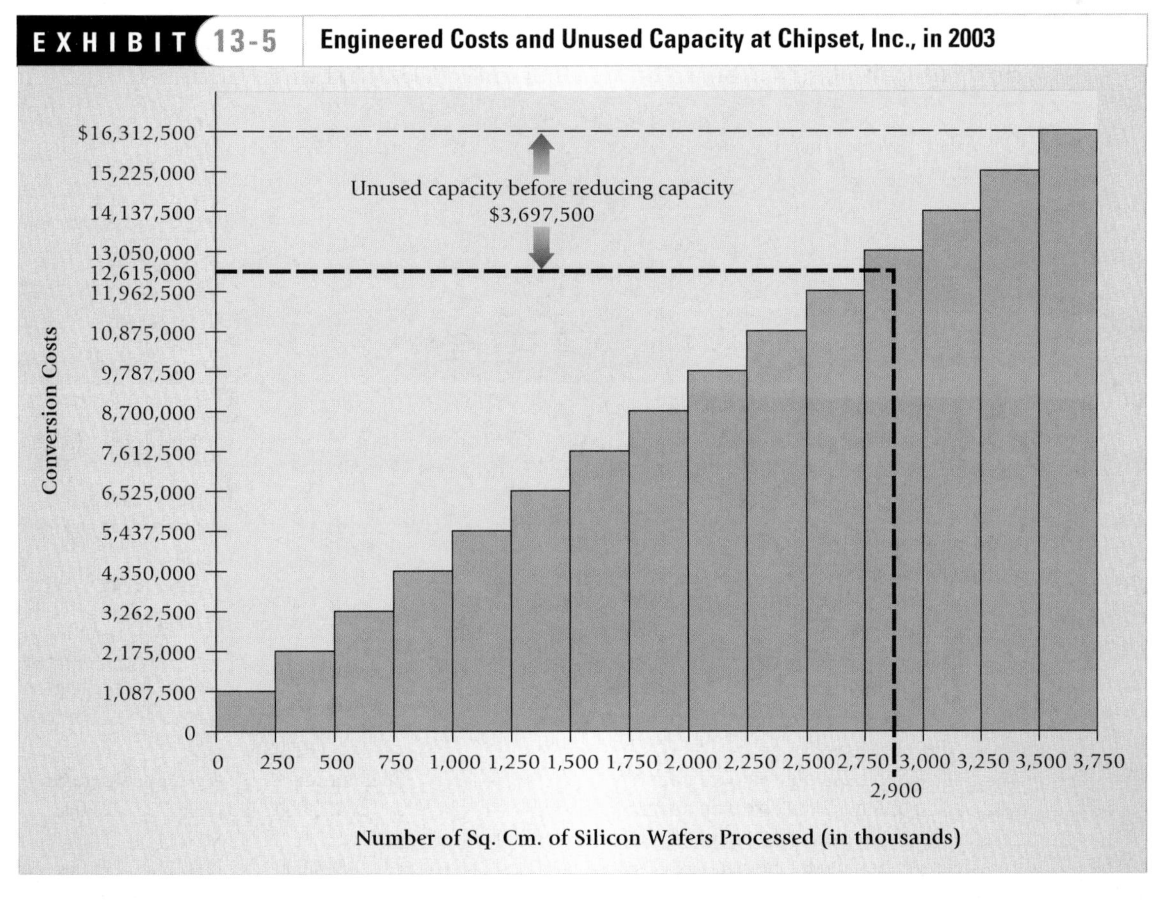

Managing Unused Capacity

What actions can Chipset management take when it identifies unused capacity? In general, it has two options: It can attempt to eliminate the unused capacity, or it can attempt to grow output by utilizing the unused capacity.

In recent years, many companies have *downsized* in an attempt to eliminate their unused capacity. **Downsizing** (also called **rightsizing**) is an integrated approach of configuring processes, products, and people to match costs to the activities that need to be performed to operate effectively and efficiently in the present and future. Companies such as AT&T, Delta Airlines, General Motors, IBM, and Scott Paper have downsized to focus on their core businesses and have instituted organization changes to increase efficiency, reduce costs, and improve quality. However, downsizing often means eliminating jobs, which can have an adverse effect on employee morale and the culture of a company. Downsizing is best done in the context of a company's overall strategy and by retaining individuals who have better management, leadership, and technical skills and experience.

Consider Chipset's options with respect to its unused manufacturing capacity. Because it needs to process 2,900,000 square centimeters of silicon wafers in 2003, it could reduce capacity to 3,000,000 square centimeters (recall, manufacturing capacity can be added or reduced only in increments of 250,000 sq. cm.), resulting in cost savings of $3,262,500 [(3,750,000 sq. cm. – 3,000,000 sq. cm.) × $4.35 per sq. cm.]. Chipset's strategy, however, is not only to reduce costs but also to grow its business. So early in 2003, Chipset reduces its manufacturing capacity by only 250,000 square centimeters—from 3,750,000 square centimeters to 3,500,000 square centimeters—saving $1,087,500 ($4.35 per sq. cm. × 250,000 sq. cm.). It retains some unused capacity for future growth. By avoiding greater reductions in capacity, it also maintains the morale of its skilled and capable workforce. The success of this strategy will depend on Chipset achieving the future growth it has projected.

Because identifying unused capacity for discretionary costs is difficult, downsizing or otherwise, managing this unused capacity is also difficult. Chipset's management uses judgment and discretion to reduce R&D costs by $100,000 in 2003. Its rationale is to reduce R&D costs without significantly affecting the output of the R&D activity. Greater reductions in R&D costs could harm the business by slowing down needed product and process improvements. Chipset must balance the need for cost reductions without compromising quality, continuous improvement, and future growth. Not balancing these factors led Delta Airlines' board of directors to replace the airline's CEO in 1997. Even though aggressive cost cutting had restored Delta to profitability, the board felt that those cuts had compromised customer satisfaction, a key to the company's future success and growth.

PROBLEM FOR SELF-STUDY

Following a strategy of product differentiation, Westwood Corporation makes a high-end kitchen range hood, KE8. Here's Westwood's data for 2002 and 2003.

	2002	2003
1. Units of KE8 produced and sold	40,000	42,000
2. Selling price	$100	$110
3. Direct materials (square feet)	120,000	123,000
4. Direct material costs per square foot	$10	$11
5. Manufacturing capacity for KE8	50,000 units	50,000 units
6. Conversion costs	$1,000,000	$1,100,000
7. Conversion costs per unit of capacity (Row 6 ÷ Row 5)	$20	$22
8. Selling and customer-service capacity	30 customers	29 customers
9. Selling and customer-service costs	$720,000	$725,000
10. Cost per customer of selling and customer-service capacity (Row 9 ÷ Row 8)	$24,000	$25,000

Westwood produced no defective units and reduced direct material usage per unit of KE8 in 2003. Conversion costs in each year are tied to manufacturing capacity. Selling and customer-service costs are related to the number of customers that the selling and service functions are designed to support. Westwood has 23 customers in 2002 and 25 customers in 2003.

Required

1. Describe briefly the elements you would include in Westwood's balanced scorecard.
2. Calculate the growth, price-recovery, and productivity components that explain the change in operating income from 2002 to 2003.
3. Suppose during 2003, the market for high-end kitchen range hoods grew at 3% in terms of number of units and all increases in market share (that is, increases in the number of units sold greater than 3%) are due to Westwood's product differentiation strategy. Calculate how much of the change in operating income from 2002 to 2003 is due to the industry-market-size factor, cost leadership, and product differentiation.
4. How successful has Westwood been in implementing its strategy? Explain.

SOLUTION

1. The balanced scorecard should describe Westwood's product differentiation strategy. The elements that should be included in its balanced scorecard are
   - *Financial perspective* Increase in operating income from higher margins on KE8 and growth
   - *Customer perspective* Market share in high-end market and customer satisfaction
   - *Internal business perspective* Manufacturing quality, order delivery time, on-time delivery, and new product features added
   - *Learning and growth perspective* Development time for new products and improvements in manufacturing processes
2. Operating income for each year is

	2002	2003
Revenues		
($100 per unit × 40,000 units; $110 per unit × 42,000 units)	$4,000,000	$4,620,000
Costs		
Direct material costs		
($10 per sq. ft. × 120,000 sq. ft.; $11 per sq. ft. × 123,000 sq. ft.)	1,200,000	1,353,000
Conversion costs		
($20 per unit × 50,000 units; $22 per unit × 50,000 units)	1,000,000	1,100,000
Selling and customer-service costs		
($24,000 per customer × 30 customers; $25,000 per customer × 29 customers)	720,000	725,000
Total costs	2,920,000	3,178,000
Operating income	$1,080,000	$1,442,000
Change in operating income	$362,000 F	

Growth Component

$$\text{Revenue effect of growth component} = \left(\begin{array}{c}\text{Actual units of}\\ \text{output sold}\\ \text{in 2003}\end{array} - \begin{array}{c}\text{Actual units of}\\ \text{output sold in}\\ \text{2002}\end{array}\right) \times \begin{array}{c}\text{Output}\\ \text{price}\\ \text{in 2002}\end{array}$$

$$= (42{,}000 \text{ units} - 40{,}000 \text{ units}) \times \$100 \text{ per unit}$$

$$= \$200{,}000 \text{ F}$$

$$\text{Cost effect of growth component} = \left(\begin{array}{c}\text{Actual units of input or}\\ \text{capacity that would}\\ \text{have been used to produce}\\ \text{2003 output assuming}\\ \text{the same input-output}\\ \text{relationship that existed in 2002}\end{array} - \begin{array}{c}\text{Actual units of}\\ \text{inputs or capacity}\\ \text{to produce}\\ \text{2002 output}\end{array}\right) \times \begin{array}{c}\text{Input}\\ \text{price}\\ \text{in 2002}\end{array}$$

Direct material costs that would be required in 2003 to produce 42,000 units instead of the 40,000 units produced in 2002, assuming the 2002 input-output relationship continued into 2003 can be calculated as follows:

Continued

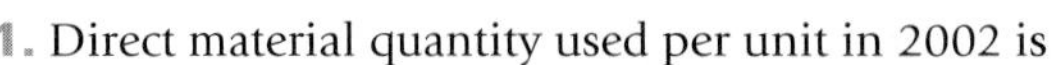

1. Direct material quantity used per unit in 2002 is

$$120{,}000 \text{ sq. ft.} \div 40{,}000 \text{ units} = 3 \text{ sq. ft. per unit}$$

2. Direct materials quantity used in 2003, assuming the 2002 input–output relationship is

$$3 \text{ sq. ft. per unit} \times 42{,}000 \text{ units} = 126{,}000 \text{ sq. ft.}$$

Conversion costs and selling and customer-service costs will not change because adequate capacity already exists in 2002 to support 2003 output and customers.

The cost effect of growth component are

Direct material cost	(126,000 sq. ft. – 120,000 sq. ft.) × \$10 per sq. ft. =	\$60,000 U
Conversion costs	(50,000 units – 50,000 units) × \$20 per unit =	0
Selling and customer-service costs	(30 cust. – 30 cust.) × \$25,000 per customer =	0
Cost effect of the growth component		\$60,000 U

In summary, the net increase in operating income as a result of the growth component equals:

Revenue effect of the growth component	\$200,000 F
Cost effect of the growth component	60,000 U
Increase in operating income due to the growth component	\$140,000 F

Price-Recovery Component

$$\begin{aligned}\text{Revenue effect of price-recovery component} &= \left(\text{Output price in 2003} - \text{Output price in 2002}\right) \times \text{Actual units of output sold in 2003}\\ &= (\$110 \text{ per unit} - \$100 \text{ per unit}) \times 42{,}000 \text{ units}\\ &= \$420{,}000 \text{ F}\end{aligned}$$

$$\text{Cost effect of price-recovery component} = \left(\text{Input price in 2003} - \text{Input price in 2002}\right) \times \begin{matrix}\text{Actual units of inputs or capacity}\\ \text{that would have been used}\\ \text{to produce 2003 output}\\ \text{assuming the same input-output}\\ \text{relationship that}\\ \text{existed in 2002}\end{matrix}$$

Direct material costs	(\$11 per sq. ft. – \$10 per sq. ft.) × 126,000 sq. ft. =	\$126,000 U
Conversion costs	(\$22 per unit – \$20 per unit) × 50,000 units =	100,000 U
Selling and cust.-service costs	(\$25,000 per cust. – \$24,000 per cust.) × 30 customers =	30,000 U
Total cost effect of the price-recovery component		\$256,000 U

In summary, the net increase in operating income as a result of the price-recovery component equals

Revenue effect of the price-recovery component	\$420,000 F
Cost effect of the price-recovery component	256,000 U
Increase in operating income due to the price-recovery component	\$164,000 F

Productivity Component

$$\text{Productivity component} = \left(\begin{matrix}\text{Actual units of}\\ \text{inputs or capacity}\\ \text{used to produce}\\ \text{2003 output}\end{matrix} - \begin{matrix}\text{Actual units of}\\ \text{inputs or capacity that}\\ \text{would have been used}\\ \text{to produce 2003}\\ \text{output assuming the same}\\ \text{input-output relationship}\\ \text{that existed in 2002}\end{matrix}\right) \times \begin{matrix}\text{Input}\\ \text{price in}\\ \text{2003}\end{matrix}$$

The productivity component of cost changes is

Direct material costs	(123,000 sq. ft. – 126,000 sq. ft.) × \$11 per sq. ft. =	\$33,000 F
Conversion costs	(50,000 units – 50,000 units) × \$20 per unit =	0
Selling and customer-service costs	(29 cust. – 30 per cust.) × \$25,000/cust. =	25,000 F
Increase in operating income due to the productivity component		\$58,000 F

A summary of the change in operating income between 2002 and 2003 follows:

	Income Statement Amounts in 2002 (1)	Revenue and Cost Effects of Growth Component in 2003 (2)	Revenue and Cost Effects of Price-Recovery Component in 2003 (3)	Cost Effect of Productivity Component in 2003 (4)	Income Statement Amounts in 2003 (5) = (1) = (2) + (3) + (4)
Revenue	$4,000,000	$200,000 F	$420,000 F	—	$4,620,000
Costs	2,920,000	60,000 U	256,000 U	$58,000 F	3,178,000
Operating income	$1,080,000	$140,000 F	$164,000 F	$58,000 F	$1,442,000

$362,000 F

Change in operating income

3. *Effect of the industry-market-size factor on operating income*

Of the increase in sales from 40,000 to 42,000 units, 3% or 1,200 units (0.03 × 40,000) is due to growth in market size, and 800 units (2,000 − 1,200) is due to an increase in market share. The increase in Westwood's operating income from the industry-market-size factor rather than specific strategic actions is

$\$140{,}000 \text{ (column 2 of preceding table)} \times \frac{1{,}200}{2{,}000}$ — 84,000 F

Effect of product differentiation on operating income

Increase in the selling price of KE8 (revenue effect of the price-recovery component)	$420,000 F
Increase in prices of inputs (cost effect of the price-recovery component)	256,000 U
Growth in market share due to product differentiation	
$\$140{,}000 \text{ (column 2 of preceding table)} \times \frac{800}{2{,}000}$	56,000 F
Increase in operating income due to product differentiation	$220,000 F

Effect of cost leadership on operating income

Productivity component	$58,000 F

A summary of the change in operating income from 2002 to 2003 follows:

Change due to the industry-market-size factor	$ 84,000 F
Change due to product differentiation	220,000 F
Change due to cost leadership	58,000 F
Change in operating income	$362,000 F

4. The analysis of operating income indicates that a significant amount of the increase in operating income resulted from Westwood's successful implementation of its product differentiation strategy. The company was able to continue to charge a premium price for KE8 and increase market share. Westwood was also able to earn additional operating income from improving its productivity.

DECISION POINTS SUMMARY

The following question-and-answer format summarizes the chapter's learning objectives. Each decision presents a key question related to a learning objective. The guidelines are the answer to that question.

Decision	**Guidelines**
1. What are two generic strategies a company can use?	Two generic strategies are product differentiation and cost leadership. Product differentiation is offering products and services that are perceived by customers as being superior and unique. Cost leadership is achieving low costs relative to competitors.

Continued

2. What is reengineering?	Reengineering is the rethinking of business processes, such as the order delivery process, to improve critical performance measures such as cost, quality, and customer satisfaction.
3. How can an organization translate its strategy into a set of performance measures?	It can do so by developing a balanced scorecard that provides the framework for a strategic measurement and management system. The balanced scorecard measures performance from four perspectives: (1) financial, (2) customer, (3) internal business processes, and (4) learning and growth.
4. How can a company analyze changes in operating income to evaluate the success of its strategy?	To evaluate the success of its strategy, a company can subdivide the change in operating income into growth, price-recovery, and productivity components. The growth component measures the change in revenues and costs from selling more or less units, assuming no changes in prices, efficiencies, or capacities. The price-recovery component measures changes in revenues and costs as a result solely of changes in the prices of outputs and inputs. The productivity component measures the decrease in costs from using fewer inputs and from reducing capacity. A company is considered successful in implementing its strategy when changes in operating income align closely with that strategy.
5. How can a company distinguish engineered costs from discretionary costs?	Engineered costs result from a cause-and-effect relationship between output and the resources needed to produce that output. Discretionary costs arise from periodic (usually annual) decisions regarding the maximum amount to be incurred. They are not tied to a cause-and-effect relationship between inputs and outputs.
6. Can a company identify unused capacity and if so, how can unused capacity be managed?	Identifying unused capacity is easier for engineered costs than for discretionary costs. Downsizing is an approach to managing unused apacity by matching costs to the activities that need to be performed.

APPENDIX: PRODUCTIVITY MEASUREMENT

Productivity measures the relationship between actual inputs used (both quantities and costs) and actual outputs produced. The lower the inputs for a given quantity of outputs or the higher the outputs for a given quantity of inputs, the higher the productivity. Measuring productivity improvements over time highlights the specific input-output relationships that contribute to cost leadership.

Partial Productivity Measures

Partial productivity, the most frequently used productivity measure, compares the quantity of output produced with the quantity of an individual input used. In its most common form, partial productivity is expressed as a ratio:

$$\text{Partial productivity} = \frac{\text{Quantity of output produced}}{\text{Quantity of input used}}$$

The higher the ratio, the greater the productivity.

Consider direct materials productivity at Chipset in 2003.

$$\begin{aligned}\begin{array}{c}\text{Direct materials}\\ \text{partial productivity}\end{array} &= \frac{\text{Quantity of CX1 units produced during 2003}}{\text{Direct materials quantity used to produce CX1 in 2003}}\\ &= \frac{\text{1,150,000 units of CX1}}{\text{2,900,000 sq. cms. of direct materials}}\\ &= \text{0.400 units of CX1 per sq. cm. of direct materials}\end{aligned}$$

Partial productivity (PP) measures are partial in the sense that they measure the amount of output produced per unit of a single input. PP measures are in terms of physical inputs and outputs and do not use input prices.

Note that the direct materials partial productivity ignores Chipset's other inputs, manufacturing conversion capacity, and R&D. Partial productivity measures become more meaningful when comparisons are made that examine productivity changes over time, either across different facilities or relative to a benchmark. Exhibit 13-6 presents partial productivity measures for Chipset's inputs for 2003 and the comparable 2002 inputs that would have been used to produce 2003 output, using information from the productivity component calculations on p. 458. These measures compare the actual inputs used in 2003 to produce 1,150,000 units of CX1 with the inputs that would have been used in 2003 had the input-output relationship from 2002 continued in 2003.

Evaluating Changes in Partial Productivities

We need to distinguish between the partial productivity effects of variable-cost components and fixed-cost components. That's because for variable-cost elements, such as direct materials, productivity improvements automatically result in using fewer input resources. Chipset's improvements in direct materials productivity in 2003 resulted in 2,900,000 square centimeters of direct materials being acquired and used, rather than the 3,450,000 square centimeters that would have been required to produce 1,150,000 units of output in 2003 at the 2002 productivity level. For fixed-cost elements, such as conversion costs, using less of the available fixed-capacity resources will not lead automatically to lowering the cost of these resources. To improve partial productivity in these cases, management must release workers or reduce capacity. These actions are often more difficult to implement and, as shown in Exhibit 13-6, they result in lower partial productivity gains for fixed-cost categories than for variable-cost categories.

Consider partial productivity for manufacturing conversion capacity. At the 2002 productivity levels, Chipset would need to start into production 3,450,000 square centimeters of silicon wafers to manufacture 1,150,000 units. Chipset has the capacity to process 3,750,000 square centimeters of silicon wafers. Efficiency improvements result in Chipset having to process 2,900,000 square centimeters in 2003. Reducing the square centimeters of silicon wafers processed does not automatically lead to a decrease in manufacturing conversion capacity. Partial productivity increases because Chipset's managers release workers and reduce manufacturing conversion capacity to 3,500,000 square centimeters of processing capacity.

A manufacturer could measure word-processing productivity by using the number of pages processed as the output (even though this output is not sold to outside customers).

An advantage of partial productivity measures is that they focus on a single input. As a result, they are simple to calculate and easily understood by operations personnel. Managers and operators examine these numbers to understand the reasons underlying productivity changes from one period to the next. For example, Chipset's managers will evaluate whether lower defect rates (which led management to reduce capacity and increase manufacturing conversion partial productivity from 2002 to 2003) were caused by better training of workers, lower labor turnover, better incentives, improved methods, or substitution of materials for labor. Isolating the relevant factors helps Chipset implement and sustain these practices in the future. Chipset can then set targets for gains in manufacturing conversion productivity and monitor planned productivity improvements.

For all their advantages, partial productivity measures also have some serious drawbacks. Because partial productivity focuses on only one input at a time rather than on all inputs simultaneously, managers cannot evaluate the effect of input substitutions on overall productivity. Suppose partial productivity for manufacturing conversion capacity increases from one period to the next while direct materials partial productivity decreases. Partial productivity measures cannot evaluate whether the increase in manufacturing conversion partial productivity offsets the decrease in direct materials partial productivity.

EXHIBIT 13-6

Comparing Chipset's Partial Productivities in 2002 and 2003

Input (1)	Partial Productivity in 2003 (2)	Comparable Partial Productivity Based on 2002 Input-Output Relationships (3)	Percentage Change from 2002 to 2003 (4)
Direct materials	$\frac{1,150,000}{2,900,000} = 0.400$	$\frac{1,150,000}{3,450,000} = 0.333$	$\frac{0.400 - 0.333}{0.333} = 20.0\%$
Manufacturing conversion capacity	$\frac{1,150,000}{3,500,000} = 0.329$	$\frac{1,150,000}{3,750,000} = 0.307$	$\frac{0.329 - 0.307}{0.307} = 7.1\%$
R&D	$\frac{1,150,000}{39} = 29,487$	$\frac{1,150,000}{40} = 28,750$	$\frac{29,487 - 28,750}{28,750} = 2.6\%$

Total factor productivity (TFP), or total productivity, is a measure of productivity that considers all inputs simultaneously.

Total Factor Productivity

Total factor productivity (TFP) is the ratio of the quantity of output produced to the costs of all inputs used based on current period prices.

$$\text{Total factor productivity} = \frac{\text{Quantity of output poduced}}{\text{Cost of all inputs used}}$$

TFP considers all inputs simultaneously and the tradeoffs across inputs based on current input prices. Do not think of all productivity measures as physical measures lacking financial content—how many units of output are produced per unit of input. TFP is intricately tied to minimizing total cost—a financial objective.

Calculating and Comparing Total Factor Productivity

We first calculate Chipset's TFP in 2003, using 2003 prices and 1,150,000 units of output produced (based on information from the first part of the productivity component calculations on p. 458).

$$\begin{aligned}
\begin{array}{c}\text{Total factor}\\ \text{productivity}\\ \text{for 2003}\\ \text{using}\\ \text{2003 prices}\end{array} &= \frac{\text{Quantity of output produced in 2003}}{\text{Cost of inputs used in 2003 based on 2003 prices}}\\
&= \frac{1{,}150{,}000}{(2{,}900{,}000 \times \$1.50) + (3{,}500{,}000 \times \$4.35) + (39 \times \$100{,}000)}\\
&= \frac{1{,}150{,}000}{\$23{,}475{,}000}\\
&= 0.048988 \text{ units of output per dollar of input cost}
\end{aligned}$$

By itself, the 2003 TFP of 0.048988 units of CX1 per dollar of input costs is not particularly helpful. We need something to compare the 2003 TFP against. One alternative is to compare TFPs of other similar companies in 2003. However, finding similar companies and obtaining accurate comparable data are often difficult. Companies, therefore, usually compare their own TFPs over time. In the Chipset example, we use as a benchmark, TFP calculated using the inputs that Chipset would have used in 2002 to produce 1,150,000 units of CX1 at 2003 prices (that is, we use the costs calculated from the second part of the productivity component calculations on p. 458). Why do we use 2003 prices? Because using the current year's prices in both calculations controls for input-price differences and focuses the analysis on the adjustments the manager made in the quantities of inputs in response to changes in prices.

$$\begin{aligned}
\begin{array}{c}\text{Benchmark}\\ \text{TFP}\end{array} &= \frac{\text{Quantity of output produced in 2003}}{\begin{array}{c}\text{Cost of inputs that would have been used in 2002}\\ \text{to produce 2003 output}\end{array}}\\
&= \frac{1{,}150{,}000}{(3{,}450{,}000 \times \$1.50) + (3{,}750{,}000 \times \$4.35) + (40 \times \$100{,}000)}\\
&= \frac{1{,}150{,}000}{\$25{,}487{,}500}\\
&= 0.045120 \text{ units of output per dollar of input cost}
\end{aligned}$$

Using 2003 prices, TFP increased 8.6% [(0.048988 – 0.045120) ÷ 0.045120 = 0.086, or 8.6%] from 2002 to 2003. Note that the 8.6% increase in TFP also equals the $2,012,500 gain (Exhibit 13-3, column 4) divided by the $23,475,000 of actual costs incurred in 2003. (Exhibit 13-3, column 5). Total factor productivity increased because Chipset produced more output per dollar of input costs in 2003 relative to 2002, measured in both years using 2003 prices. The gain in TFP occurs because Chipset increases the partial productivities of individual inputs and, consistent with its strategy, seeks the least expensive combination of inputs to produce CX1. Note that increases in TFP cannot be due to differences in input prices because we used 2003 prices to evaluate both the inputs that Chipset would have used in 2002 to produce 1,150,000 units of CX1 and the inputs actually used in 2003.

Be aware of the intuition underlying the benchmark TFP calculation. We want to assess whether employees, in producing this period's outputs, used a combination of inputs that is more cost-effective than simply continuing last period's combination. Our goal is to see if the current period combination of inputs (at current period prices) is more cost-effective than simply continuing (at current period prices) the input combination used in the prior period.

Using Partial and Total Factor Productivity Measures

A major advantage of TFP is that it measures the combined productivity of all inputs used to produce output and explicitly considers gains from using fewer physical inputs as well as substitution among inputs. Managers can analyze these numbers to understand the reasons for changes in TFP. Chipset's managers will evaluate whether TFP increased from 2002 to 2003 due to better human resource management practices, higher quality of materials, or improved manufacturing methods. Chipset will adopt the most successful practices and use TFP measures to implement and evaluate strategy by setting targets and monitoring trends.

Although TFP measures are comprehensive, operations personnel find financial TFP measures more difficult to understand and less useful than physical partial productivity measures in performing their tasks. Physical measures of manufacturing labor partial productivity, for example, provide direct feedback to workers about output produced per labor-hour worked by focusing on factors within the workers' control. Manufacturing labor partial productivity also has the advantage that it can be easily compared across periods because it uses physical inputs rather than inputs that are weighted by the prices prevailing in different periods. Workers, therefore, often prefer to tie productivity-based bonuses to gains in manufacturing labor partial productivity. Unfortunately, this situation creates incentives for workers to substitute materials (and capital) for labor, which improves their own productivity measure, while possibly decreasing the overall productivity of the company as measured by TFP. To overcome the possible incentive problems of partial productivity measures, some companies—for example, TRW, Eaton, and Whirlpool—explicitly adjust bonuses based on manufacturing labor partial productivity for the effects of other factors such as investments in new equipment and higher levels of scrap. That is, they combine partial productivity with TFP-like measures.

Many companies such as Behlen Manufacturing, a steel fabricator, and Motorola, a microchip manufacturer, use both partial productivity and total factor productivity to evaluate performance. *Partial productivity and TFP measures work best together because the strengths of one offset weaknesses in the other.*

TERMS TO LEARN

This chapter and the Glossary at the end of the book contain definitions of:

balanced scorecard (p. 447)
cost leadership (447)
discretionary costs (462)
downsizing (464)
engineered costs (461)
growth component (455)
partial productivity (468)
price-recovery component (456)
product differentiation (447)
productivity (468)
productivity component (456)
reengineering (448)
rightsizing (464)
total factor productivity (TFP) (470)
unused capacity (461)

ASSIGNMENT MATERIAL

Questions

13-1 Define *strategy*.

13-2 Describe the five key forces to consider when analyzing an industry.

13-3 Describe two generic strategies.

13-4 What are the four key perspectives in the balanced scorecard?

13-5 What is *reengineering?*

13-6 Describe three features of a good balanced scorecard.

13-7 What are three important pitfalls to avoid when implementing a balanced scorecard?

13-8 Describe three key components in doing a strategic analysis of operating income.

13-9 Why might an analyst incorporate the industry-market-size factor and the interrelationships among the growth, price-recovery, and productivity components into a strategic analysis of operating income?

13-10 How does an engineered cost differ from a discretionary cost?

13-11 "The distinction between engineered and discretionary costs is irrelevant when identifying unused capacity." Do you agree? Comment briefly.

13-12 What is *downsizing?*

13-13 What is a partial productivity measure?

13-14 What is *total factor productivity?*

13-15 "We are already measuring total factor productivity. Measuring partial productivities would be of no value." Do you agree? Comment briefly.

Exercises

13-16 **Balanced scorecard.** La Quinta Corporation manufactures corrugated cardboard boxes. It competes and plans to grow by producing high-quality boxes at a low cost and by delivering them to customers in a timely manner. There are many other manufacturers who produce similar boxes. La Quinta believes that continuously improving its manufacturing processes and having satisfied employees are critical to implementing its strategy in 2004.

Required

1. Is La Quinta's 2004 strategy one of product differentiation or cost leadership? Explain briefly.
2. Indicate two measures you would expect to see under each perspective in La Quinta's balanced scorecard for 2004. Explain your answer briefly.

13-17 **Analysis of growth, price-recovery, and productivity components (continuation of 13-16).** An analysis of La Quinta's operating income changes between 2003 and 2004 shows the following:

Operating income for 2003	$1,600,000
Add growth component	60,000
Deduct price-recovery component	(50,000)
Add productivity component	180,000
Operating income for 2004	$1,790,000

The industry market size for corrugated boxes did not grow in 2004, input prices did not change, and La Quinta reduced the prices of its boxes.

Required

1. Was La Quinta's gain in operating income in 2004 consistent with the strategy you identified in requirement 1 of Exercise 13-16?
2. Explain the productivity component. In general, does it represent savings in only variable costs, only fixed costs, or both variable and fixed costs?

13-18 **Balanced scorecard.** Below is a random-order listing of perspectives, strategic objectives, and performance measures for the balanced scorecard.

Perspectives

Internal business process
Customer
Learning and growth
Financial

Strategic Objectives

Acquire new customers
Increase shareholder value
Retain customers
Improve manufacturing quality
Develop profitable customers
Increase proprietary products
Increase information system capabilities
Enhance employee skills
On-time delivery by suppliers
Increase profit generated by each salesperson
Introduce new products
Minimize invoice error rate

Performance Measures

Percentage of defective product units
Return on assets
Number of patents
Employee turnover rate
Net income
Customer profitability
Percentage of processes with real-time feedback
Return on sales
Average job-related training-hours per employee
Return on equity
Percentage of on-time deliveries by suppliers
Product cost per unit
Profit per salesperson
Percentage of error-free invoices
Customer cost per unit
Earnings per share
Number of new customers
Percentage of customers retained

For each perspective, select those strategic objectives from the list that best relate to it. For each strategic objective, select the most appropriate performance measure(s) from the list. **Required**

13-19 Growth, price-recovery, and productivity components. Oceano T-Shirt Company sells a variety of T-shirts. Oceano presents the following data for its first two years of operations, 2003 and 2004. For simplicity, assume that all purchasing and selling costs are included in the average cost per T-shirt and that each customer buys one T-shirt.

	2003	2004
Number of T-shirts purchased	20,000	30,000
Number of T-shirts lost	400	300
Number of T-shirts sold	19,600	29,700
Average selling price	$15	$14
Average cost per T-shirt	$10	$9
Administrative capacity in terms of number of customers that can be served	40,000	36,000
Administrative costs	$80,000	$68,400
Administrative cost per customer	$2	$1.90

Administrative costs depend on the number of customers that Oceano has created capacity to support, not the actual number of customers served.

Required

1. Calculate the growth, price-recovery, and productivity components of changes in operating income between 2003 and 2004.
2. Comment on your results in requirement 1.

13-20 Strategy, balanced scorecard. Meredith Corporation makes a special-purpose machine, D4H, used in the textile industry. Meredith has designed the D4H machine for 2003 to be distinct from its competitors. It has been generally regarded as a superior machine. Meredith presents the following data for 2002 and 2003.

	2002	2003
1. Units of D4H produced and sold	200	210
2. Selling price	$40,000	$42,000
3. Direct materials (kilograms)	300,000	310,000
4. Direct material cost per kilogram	$8	$8.50
5. Manufacturing capacity in units of D4H	250	250
6. Total conversion costs	$2,000,000	$2,025,000
7. Conversion cost per unit of capacity	$8,000	$8,100
8. Selling and customer-service capacity	100 customers	95 customers
9. Total selling and customer-service costs	$1,000,000	$940,500
10. Selling and customer-service capacity cost per customer	$10,000	$9,900
11. Design staff	12	12
12. Total design costs	$1,200,000	$1,212,000
13. Design cost per employee	$100,000	$101,000

Meredith produces no defective machines, but it wants to reduce direct materials usage per D4H machine in 2003. Conversion costs in each year depend on production capacity defined in terms of D4H units that can be produced, not the actual units produced. Selling and customer-service costs depend on the number of customers that Meredith can support, not the actual number of customers it serves. Meredith has 75 customers in 2002 and 80 customers in 2003. At the start of each year, management uses its discretion to determine the number of design staff for the year. The design staff and its costs have no direct relationship with the quantity of D4H produced or the number of customers to whom D4H is sold.

Required

1. Is Meredith's strategy one of product differentiation or cost leadership? Explain briefly.
2. Describe briefly key elements that you would include in Meredith's balanced scorecard and the reasons for doing so.

13-21 Strategic analysis of operating income (continuation of 13-20). Refer to Exercise 13-20.

Required

1. Calculate the operating income of Meredith Corporation in 2002 and 2003.

2. Calculate the growth, price-recovery, and productivity components that explain the change in operating income from 2002 to 2003.
3. Comment on your answer in requirement 2. What do these components indicate?

13-22 Analysis of growth, price-recovery, and productivity components (continuation of 13-21). Suppose that during 2003, the market for Meredith's special-purpose machines grew by 3% All increases in market share (that is sales increases greater than 3%) are due to Meredith's product differentiation strategy.

Required

Calculate how much of the change in operating income from 2002 to 2003 is due to the industry-market-size factor, cost leadership, and product differentiation. How successful has Meredith been in implementing its strategy? Explain.

13-23 Identifying and managing unused capacity (continuation of 13-20). Refer to the Meredith Corporation information in Exercise 13-20.

Required

1. Where possible, calculate the amount and cost of unused capacity for (a) manufacturing, (b) selling and customer service, and (c) design at the beginning of 2003 based on 2003 production. If you could not calculate the amount and cost of unused capacity, indicate why not.
2. Suppose Meredith can add or reduce its manufacturing capacity in increments of 30 units. What is the maximum amount of costs that Meredith could save in 2003 by downsizing manufacturing capacity?
3. Meredith, in fact, does not eliminate any of its unused manufacturing capacity. Why might Meredith not downsize?

13-24 Strategy, balanced scorecard, service company. Snyder Corporation is a small information systems consulting firm that specializes in helping companies implement sales management software. The market for Snyder's products is very competitive. To compete, Snyder must deliver quality service at a low cost. Snyder bills clients in terms of units of work performed, which depends on the size and complexity of the sales management system. Snyder presents the following data for 2002 and 2003.

	2002	2003
1. Units of work performed	60	70
2. Selling price	$50,000	$48,000
3. Software implementation labor-hours	30,000	32,000
4. Cost per software implementation labor-hour	$60	$63
5. Software implementation support capacity (in units of work)	90	90
6. Total cost of software implementation support	$360,000	$369,000
7. Software implementation support capacity cost per unit of work	$4,000	$4,100
8. Number of employees doing software development	3	3
9. Total software development costs	$375,000	$390,000
10. Software development cost per employee	$125,000	$130,000

Software implementation labor-hour costs are variable costs. Software implementation support costs for each year depend on the software implementation support capacity (defined in terms of units of work) that Snyder chooses to maintain each year. It does not vary with the actual units of work performed that year. At the start of each year, management uses its discretion to determine the number of software development employees. The software development staff and costs have no direct relationship with the number of units of work performed.

Required

1. Is Snyder Corporation's strategy one of product differentiation or cost leadership? Explain briefly.
2. Describe key elements you would include in Snyder's balanced scorecard and your reasons for doing so.

13-25 Strategic analysis of operating income (continuation of 13-24). Refer to the information in Exercise 13-24.

Required

1. Calculate the operating income of Snyder Corporation in 2002 and 2003.
2. Calculate the growth, price-recovery, and productivity components that explain the change in operating income from 2002 to 2003.
3. Comment on your answer in requirement 2. What do these components indicate?

13-26 Analysis of growth, price-recovery, and productivity components (continuation of 13-25). Suppose that during 2003 the market for implementing sales management software increases by 5% and that Snyder experiences a 1% decline in selling prices. Assume that any further decreases in selling price and increases in market share are strategic choices by Snyder's management to implement their cost leadership strategy.

Required

Calculate how much of the change in operating income from 2002 to 2003 is due to the industry-market-size factor, cost leadership, and product differentiation. How successful has Snyder been in implementing its strategy? Explain.

13-27 Identifying and managing unused capacity (continuation of 13-24). Refer to the Snyder Corporation information in Exercise 13-24.

Required

1. Where possible, calculate the amount and cost of unused capacity for (a) software implementation support and (b) software development at the beginning of 2003, based on units of work performed in 2003. If you could not calculate the amount and cost of unused capacity, indicate why not.
2. Suppose Snyder can add or reduce its software implementation support capacity in increments of 15 units. What is the maximum amount of costs that Snyder could save in 2003 by downsizing software implementation support capacity?
3. Snyder, in fact, does not eliminate any of its unused software implementation support capacity. Why might Snyder not downsize?

Problems

13-28 Balanced scorecard. (R. Kaplan, adapted). Caltex, Inc., refines gasoline and sells it through its own Caltex Gas Stations. On the basis of market research, Caltex determines that 60% of the overall gasoline market consists of "service-oriented customers," medium- to high-income individuals who are willing to pay a higher price for gas if the gas stations can provide excellent customer service, such as a clean facility, a convenience store, friendly employees, a quick turnaround, the ability to pay by credit card, and high-octane premium fuel. The remaining 40% of the overall market are "price shoppers" who look to buy the cheapest gasoline available. Caltex's strategy is to focus on the 60% of service-oriented customers. Caltex's balanced scorecard for 2004 follows. For brevity, the initiatives taken under each objective are omitted.

Objectives	Measures	Target Performance	Actual Performance
Financial Perspective			
Increase shareholder value	Operating income changes from price recovery	$90,000,000	$95,000,000
	Operating income changes from growth	$65,000,000	$67,000,000
Customer Perspective			
Increase market share	Market share of overall gasoline market	10%	9.8%
Internal Business Process Perspective			
Improve gasoline quality	Quality index	94 points	95 points
Improve refinery performance	Refinery reliability index (%)	91%	91%
Ensure gasoline availability	Product availability index (%)	99%	100%
Learning and Growth Perspective			
Increase refinery process capability	Percentage of refinery processes with advanced controls	88%	90%

Required

1. Was Caltex successful in implementing its strategy in 2004? Explain your answer.
2. Would you have included some measure of employee satisfaction and employee training in the learning and growth perspective? Are these objectives critical to Caltex for implementing its strategy? Why or why not? Explain briefly.
3. Explain how Caltex did not achieve its target market share in the total gasoline market but still exceeded its financial targets. Is "market share of overall gasoline market" the correct measure of market share? Explain briefly.
4. Is there a cause-and-effect linkage between improvements in the measures in the internal business process perspective and the measures in the customer perspective? That is, would you add other measures to the internal business process perspective or the customer perspective? Why or why not? Explain briefly.
5. Do you agree with Caltex's decision not to include measures of changes in operating income from productivity improvements under the financial perspective of the balanced scorecard? Explain briefly.

13-29 Balanced scorecard. Lee Corporation manufactures various types of color laser printers in a highly automated facility with high fixed costs. The market for laser printers is competitive. The various color laser printers on the market are comparable in terms of features and price. Lee believes that satisfying customers with products of high quality at low costs is key to achieving its target profitability. For 2004, Lee plans to achieve higher quality and lower costs by improving yields and reducing defects in its manufacturing operations. Lee will train workers and encourage and empower them to take the necessary actions. Currently, a significant amount of Lee's capacity is used to produce products that are defective and cannot be sold. Lee expects that higher yields will reduce the capacity that Lee needs to manufacture products. Lee does not anticipate that improving manufacturing will automatically lead to lower costs because Lee has high fixed costs. To reduce fixed costs per unit, Lee could lay off employees and sell equipment or use the capacity to produce and sell more of its current products or improved models of its current products.

Lee's balanced scorecard (intiatives omitted) for the just-completed accounting year 2004 follows.

Objectives	Measures	Target Performance	Actual Performance
Financial Perspective			
Increase shareholder value	Operating income changes from productivity	$1,000,000	$400,000
	Operating income changes from growth	$1,500,000	$600,000
Customer Perspective			
Increase market share	Market share in color laser printers	5%	4.6%
Internal Business Process Perspective			
Improve manufacturing quality	Yield	82%	85%
Reduce delivery time to customers	Order delivery time	25 days	22 days
Learning and Growth Perspective			
Develop process skills	Percentage of employees trained in process and quality management	90%	92%
Enhance information system capabilities	Percentage of manufacturing processes with real-time feedback	85%	87%

Required

1. Was Lee successful in implementing its strategy in 2004? Explain.
2. Is Lee Corporation's balanced scorecard useful in helping Lee understand why it did not reach its target market share in 2004? If it is, explain why. If it is not, explain what other measures you might want to add under the customer perspective and why.
3. Would you have included some measure of employee satisfaction in the learning and growth perspective and new product development in the internal business process perspective? That is, do you think employee satisfaction and development of new products are critical to Lee for implementing its strategy? Why or why not? Explain briefly.
4. What problems, if any, do you see in Lee improving quality and significantly downsizing to eliminate unused capacity?

13-30 Strategic analysis of operating income. Halsey Company sells women's clothing. Halsey's strategy is to offer a wide selection of clothes and excellent customer service and to charge a premium price. Halsey presents the following data for 2004 and 2005. For simplicity, assume that each customer purchases one piece of clothing.

	2004	2005
1. Pieces of clothing purchased and sold	40,000	40,000
2. Average selling price	$60	$59
3. Average cost per piece of clothing	$40	$41
4. Selling and customer-service capacity	51,000 customers	43,000 customers
5. Selling and customer-service costs	$357,000	$296,700
6. Selling and customer-service capacity cost per customer (Line 5 ÷ Line 4)	$7 per customer	$6.90 per customer
7. Purchasing and administrative capacity	980	850
8. Purchasing and administrative costs	$245,000	$204,000
9. Purchasing and administrative capacity cost per distinct design	$250 per design	$240 per design

EXHIBIT 14-1 Purposes of Cost Allocation

Purpose	Illustrations
1. To provide information for economic decisions	To decide whether to add a new airline flight To decide whether to manufacture a component part of a television set or to purchase it from another manufacturer To decide on the selling price for a customized product or service To evaluate how much of available capacity is being used to support different products
2. To motivate managers and employees	To encourage the design of products that are simpler to manufacture or less costly to service To encourage sales representatives to push high-margin products or services
3. To justify costs or compute reimbursement	To cost products at a "fair" price, often required by government defense contracts To compute reimbursement for a consulting firm that is based on a percentage of the cost savings resulting from the implementation of its recommendations
4. To measure income and assets for reporting to external parties	To cost inventories for financial reporting. (Under generally accepted accounting principles, inventoriable costs include manufacturing costs but exclude research and development, marketing, distribution, and customer-service costs.) To cost inventories for reporting to tax authorities

Cost allocations can be used to motivate managers to consume less or more of the company's resources. To *discourage* use, the cost of a department's services could be allocated according to the amount of services used. To *encourage* use of a department's services (for example, internal audit), top management might (1) not allocate any of the cost of that department's services or (2) allocate a fixed amount of the cost of that department to other departments regardless of how much of those services are used by those other departments (the other departments may feel obligated to use the services to get their "money's worth").

- may or may not be allocated to a government contract to satisfy purpose 3 (cost reimbursement, in which the terms of the contract will guide the allocation decision), and
- cannot be allocated to inventory under generally accepted accounting principles (GAAP) to satisfy purpose 4 (income and asset measurement for reporting to external parties).

Different costs are appropriate for different purposes. Consider costs of a product in terms of the business functions in the value chain.

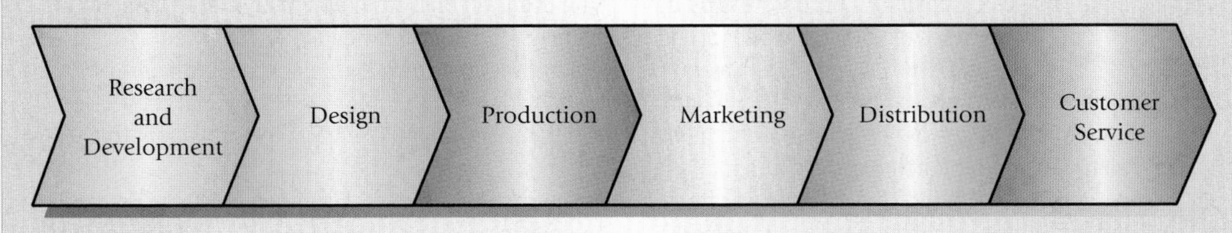

The same set of costs in these six business functions typically will not satisfy each of the four purposes in Exhibit 14-1.

For some decisions related to the economic-decision purpose (for example, long-run product pricing), the costs in all six functions should be included.

For the motivation purpose, costs from more than one business function are often included to emphasize to managers how costs in different functions are related to each other. For example, product designers in some Japanese companies incorporate costs of other functions in the value chain—such as production, distribution, and customer service—into their product-cost estimates. The aim is to focus attention on how different product design options affect total costs.

For the cost-reimbursement purpose, the particular contract will often stipulate whether all six of the business functions or only a subset of them are to be reimbursed. For instance, cost-reimbursement rules for U.S. government contracts explicitly exclude marketing costs.

For the purpose of income and asset measurement for reporting to external parties, inventoriable costs under GAAP include only manufacturing costs (and product design costs in some cases). In the United States, R&D costs in most industries are a period cost when they are incurred,[1] as are marketing, distribution, and customer-service costs.

2 Guide cost-allocation decisions using appropriate criteria

...such as identifying factors that cause resources to be consumed

Using the cause-and-effect criterion to choose a cost-allocation base means the base is a cost driver of the indirect-cost pool.

CRITERIA TO GUIDE COST-ALLOCATION DECISIONS

Role of Dominant Criteria

Exhibit 14-2 presents four criteria used to guide cost-allocation decisions. These decisions affect both the number of indirect-cost pools and the cost-allocation base for each indirect-cost pool. Managers must first identify the purpose for a particular cost allocation and then select the criteria to allocate costs. We emphasize the superiority of the cause-and-effect and the benefits-received criteria, especially when the purpose of cost allocation is economic decisions or motivation.[2]

Fairness and ability to bear are less frequently used criteria than cause and effect or benefits received. Fairness is a difficult criterion on which to obtain agreement. What one party views as fair, another party may view as unfair.[3] For example, a university may view allocating a share of general administrative costs to government contracts as fair because general administrative costs are incurred to support all activities of the university. The government may view the allocation of such costs as unfair because the general administrative costs would have been incurred by the university whether or not the government contract had been signed. To get a sense of the ability-to-bear criterion, consider a product that consumes a large amount of indirect costs but whose selling price is currently below its direct costs. This product has no ability to bear any of the indirect costs it uses. If the indirect costs it consumes are allocated to other products, these other products are effectively subsidizing the product that is losing money.

The cause-and-effect criterion is the primary one used in activity-based costing (ABC) applications. ABC systems use the concept of a cost hierarchy to identify the cost drivers that best demonstrate the cause-and-effect relationship between each

EXHIBIT 14-2

Criteria for Cost-Allocation Decisions

1. Cause and Effect. Using this criterion, managers identify the variables that cause resources to be consumed. For example, managers may use hours of testing as the variable when allocating the costs of a quality-testing area to products. Cost allocations based on the cause-and-effect criterion are likely to be the most credible to operating personnel.

2. Benefits Received. Using this criterion, managers identify the beneficiaries of the outputs of the cost object. The costs of the cost object are allocated among the beneficiaries in proportion to the benefits each receives. Consider a corporatewide advertising program that promotes the general image of the corporation rather than any individual product. The costs of this program may be allocated on the basis of division revenues; the higher the revenues, the higher the division's allocated cost of the advertising program. The rationale behind this allocation is that divisions with higher revenues apparently benefited from the advertising more than divisions with lower revenues and, therefore, ought to be allocated more of the advertising costs.

3. Fairness or Equity. This criterion is often cited in government contracts when cost allocations are the basis for establishing a price satisfactory to the government and its suppliers. Cost allocation here is viewed as a "reasonable" or "fair" means of establishing a selling price in the minds of the contracting parties. For most allocation decisions, fairness is a difficult-to-achieve objective rather than an operational criterion.

4. Ability to Bear. This criterion advocates allocating costs in proportion to the cost object's ability to bear costs allocated to it. An example is the allocation of corporate executive salaries on the basis of division operating income. The presumption is that the more-profitable divisions have a greater ability to absorb corporate headquarters' costs.

The following sequential outline gives the "big picture" of cost allocation:

1. Determine the purpose of the allocation, because the purpose defines *what costs* will be allocated.
2. Decide *how* to allocate the costs from step 1. To do so,
   a. Decide *how many indirect-cost pools* to form, and then
   b. Identify an *allocation base* (preferably a cost driver) *for each cost pool.*

[1] In some industries (such as software), U.S.-based companies can capitalize R&D costs when certain criteria are met (such as the R&D leads to a product that is believed to be commercially viable).

[2] The Federal Accounting Standards Advisory Board (which sets standards for management accounting for U.S. government departments and agencies) recommends: "Cost assignments should be performed by: (a) directly tracing costs whenever feasible and economically practicable, (b) assigning costs on a cause-and-effect basis, (c) allocating costs on a reasonable and consistent basis." (FASAB, 1995, p. 12).

[3] Kaplow and Shavell, for example, in a review of the legal literature, note that "notions of fairness are many and varied. They are analyzed and rationalized by different writers in different ways, and they also typically depend upon the circumstances under consideration. Accordingly, it is not possible to identify, a consensus view on these notions...." See L. Kaplow and S. Shavell, "Fairness Versus Welfare," *Harvard Law Review*, February 2001.

activity and the costs in the related cost pool. The cost drivers are then chosen as cost-allocation bases.

Cost-Benefit Approach

Companies place great importance on the cost-benefit approach when designing and implementing their cost allocations. Companies incur costs not only in collecting data but also in taking the time to educate managers about cost allocations. In general, the more-complex the cost allocations, the higher these education costs.

The costs of designing and implementing complex cost allocations are highly visible. The benefits from using well-designed cost allocations — enabling managers to make better-informed sourcing decisions, pricing decisions, cost-control decisions, and so on — are difficult to measure. Still, when making cost allocations, managers should consider the benefits as well as the costs.

Spurred by rapid reductions in the costs of collecting and processing information, companies today are moving toward more-detailed cost allocations. Many companies have now developed manufacturing or distribution overhead costing systems that use multiple (in some cases more than 10) cost-allocation bases. Also, some businesses have state-of-the-art-information technology already in place for operating their plants or distribution networks. Applying this existing technology to allocate costs is less expensive — and more inviting — than developing cost allocations from scratch.

COST ALLOCATION AND COSTING SYSTEMS

In this section, we focus on the first purpose of cost allocation, to provide information for economic decisions such as pricing, by measuring the full costs of delivering products based on an ABC system.

Chapter 5 described how ABC systems define activity-cost pools and use activity-cost drivers as allocation bases to assign costs of activity-cost pools to products. In this section, we focus on how costs are assigned to the activity-cost pools.

We will use Consumer Appliances, Inc. (CAI), to illustrate how costs incurred in different parts of a company can be assigned, and then reassigned, for costing products, services,

EXHIBIT 14-3 Division Activity-Cost Pools and Cost-Allocation Bases, CAI, Inc., for Refrigerator Division (R) and Clothes Dryer Division (CD)

Activity	Example of Costs	Amount	Cost Hierarchy Category	Cost-Allocation Base	Cause-and-Effect Relationship That Motivates the Choice of Allocation Base
Design	Design engineering salaries	(R) $6,000,000 (CD) 4,250,000	Product sustaining	Parts times cubic feet	Complex products (more parts and larger size) require greater design resources.
Setups of machines	Setup labor and equipment cost	(R) $3,000,000 (CD) 2,400,000	Batch level	Setup-hours	Overhead costs of the setup activity increase as setup-hours increase.
Manufacturing operations	Plant and equipment, energy	(R) $25,000,000 (CD) 18,750,000	Output unit level	Machine-hours	Manufacturing operations overhead costs support machines and, hence, increase with machine usage.
Distribution	Shipping labor and equipment	(R) $8,000,000 (CD) 5,500,000	Output unit level	Cubic feet	Distribution overhead costs increase with cubic feet of product shipped.
Administration	Division executive salaries	(R) $1,000,000 (CD) 800,000	Facility sustaining	Revenues	Weak relationship between division executive salaries and revenues, but justified by CAI on a benefits-received basis.
Facility	Annual building and space costs	(R) $4,500,000 (CD) 3,500,000	All	Square-feet	Facility costs increase with square feet of space.

customers, or contracts. CAI has two divisions and each has its own manufacturing plant—the Refrigerator Division with a plant in Minneapolis and the Clothes Dryer Division with a plant in St. Paul. CAI's headquarters is in a separate location in Minneapolis. In each division, CAI manufactures and sells multiple products that differ in size and complexity.

CAI collects costs at the following levels:

1. *Corporate costs*—there are three major categories of corporate costs:
   - Treasury costs—interest of $900,000 on debt used to finance the construction of new assembly equipment in the two divisions. Cost of new assembly equipment is $5,200,000 in the Refrigerator Division and $3,800,000 in the Clothes Dryer Division.
   - Human resource management costs—recruitment and ongoing employee training and development, $1,600,000.
   - Corporate administration costs—executive salaries, rent, and general administration costs, $5,400,000.
2. *Division costs*—there are two direct-cost categories (direct materials and direct manufacturing labor) and six indirect-cost categories. Exhibit 14-3 presents the division activity-cost pools and cost-allocation bases. CAI identifies the cost hierarchy category for each cost pool—output unit-level, batch level, product-sustaining level, and facility-sustaining level (as described in Chapter 5, pp. 143–144).

"Overhead costs" here encompasses manufacturing overhead costs, corporate overhead costs, and design and distribution overhead costs.

In practice, costing systems are usually much more complex than most textbook examples. Although we use simplified examples to aid learning, the underlying concepts apply equally in more-complex, real-world costing systems.

Exhibit 14-4 presents an overview diagram of the allocation of corporate and division overhead costs to products for CAI. Look first at the middle row of the exhibit, where you see "Division Indirect Costs," and scan the lower half. It is similar to Exhibit 5-3, Panel A (p. 146), which illustrates ABC systems using activity-cost pools and cost drivers. The only additional feature in the lower half of Exhibit 14-4 is that CAI has a cost pool called Facility Costs (far right, middle row), which accumulates all annual costs of buildings and furnishings (such as depreciation) incurred in the division. The arrows in the exhibit indicate that CAI allocates these costs to the other activity-cost pools using the square feet area required for the different activities (design, setup, manufacturing, distribution, and administration). The activity-cost pools then include the costs of the building and facilities needed to perform the various activities.

The activity-cost pools are allocated to products on the basis of cost drivers described in Exhibit 14-3. These cost drivers are chosen as the cost-allocation bases because there is a cause-and-effect relationship between the cost drivers and the costs in the activity-cost pool. A cost rate per unit is calculated for each cost-allocation base. Indirect costs are allocated to products on the basis of the total quantity of the cost-allocation base for each activity used by the product.

Next focus on the upper half of Exhibit 14-4: how corporate costs are allocated to divisions and then to activity-cost pools. Before getting into the details of the allocations, let's first consider some broader choices that CAI faces regarding the allocation of corporate costs.

3 Discuss decisions faced when collecting costs in indirect-cost pools

...determining the number of cost pools and the costs to be included in each cost pool

Allocating Corporate Costs to Divisions and Products

CAI has several choices to make when accumulating and allocating corporate costs to divisions.

1. Which corporate cost categories should be included in the indirect costs of the divisions? Should CAI allocate all corporate costs or only a subset of them?

a. Some companies allocate all corporate costs to divisions. They believe that corporate costs are incurred to support division activities. Allocating all corporate costs motivates division managers to examine how corporate costs are planned and controlled. Also, companies that want to calculate the full cost of products must allocate corporate costs to activity-cost pools of divisions.

b. Other companies do not allocate corporate costs to divisions. They believe that these costs are not controllable by division managers.

c. Still other companies allocate only those corporate costs, such as corporate human resources, that are widely perceived as either causally related to division activities or provide explicit benefits to divisions. These companies exclude corporate costs such as

EXHIBIT 14-4 **Overview Diagram of Allocation of Corporate Overhead and Division Overhead Costs to Products, CAI, Inc.**

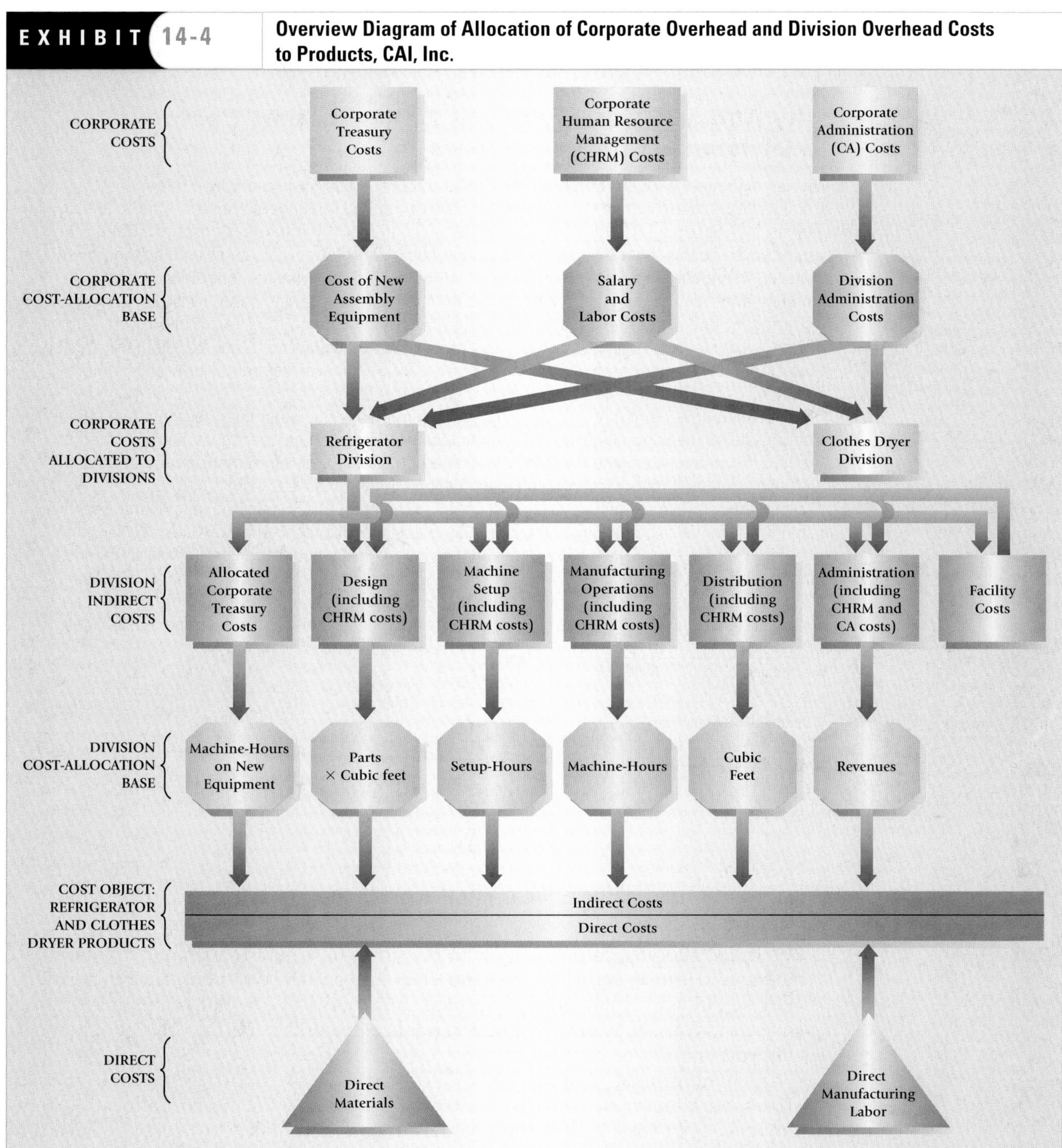

corporate donations to charitable foundations because division managers often have no say in making these decisions and because the benefits to the divisions are less evident or too remote (see Surveys of Company Practice, p. 488).

For some decision purposes, allocating some but not all corporate costs to divisions may be the preferred alternative. Consider the performance evaluation of division managers. The controllability notion (see pp. 192–193) is frequently used to justify excluding some corporate costs from division reports. For example, the salaries of the top management at corporate headquarters are often excluded from responsibility accounting reports of division managers. Although divisions tend to benefit from these corporate costs, division managers argue they have no say in ("are not responsible for") how much of these corporate resources they use or how much they cost. The contrary

SURVEYS OF COMPANY PRACTICE

Why Allocate Corporate and Other Support Costs to Divisions and Departments

Why do managers allocate corporate and other support costs to divisions and departments? A broad set of reasons is given in surveys. One survey of U.S. managers[a] reported the following (ranked by frequency): (1) to remind profit-center managers that indirect costs exist and that profit-center income must be adequate to cover some share of corporate, as well as their own, costs; (2) to encourage use of central services that would otherwise be underutilized; and (3) to stimulate profit-center managers to put pressure on other managers to control service costs.

Canadian executives[b] cited the following objectives, ranked in order of importance, for allocating costs to divisions and departments: (1) to determine costs; (2) to evaluate profit centers; (3) to fix accountability; (4) to allocate cost per unit of usage; (5) to promote more-effective resource usage; and (6) to foster cost awareness.

These executives encountered the following difficulties in implementing their cost-allocation programs: allocations resulting in profit-center losses, friction among managers, unstable market prices, allocations perceived as arbitrary, usage hard to monitor, agreement on the allocation method difficult to obtain, and time-consuming allocation process.

Similar surveys were conducted among Australian[c] and United Kingdom[d] managers. Both sets of managers gave the same ranking of the following reasons for allocating corporate costs to divisions (in order of importance): (1) to acknowledge that divisions would incur such costs if they were independent units or if the services were not provided internally; (2) to make division managers aware that corporate costs exist; (3) to stimulate division managers to put pressure on corporate managers to control costs; and (4) to stimulate division managers to economize in usage of corporate services.

[a]Fremgen and Liao, "The Allocation."
[b]Atkinson, "Intra-firm Cost."
[c]Ramadan, "The Rationale."
[d]Dean, Joye, and Blayney, "Strategic Management."
Full citations are in Appendix A at the end of the book.

argument is that full allocation is justified because the divisions receive benefits from all corporate costs.

2. If CAI allocates corporate costs to divisions, how many cost pools should it use? One extreme is to aggregate all corporate costs into a single cost pool. The other extreme is to have numerous individual corporate cost pools. A variety of factors may prompt managers to consider using multiple cost pools. A major factor is the concept of homogeneous cost pools.

In a **homogeneous cost pool,** all of the costs in the cost pool have the same or a similar cause-and-effect or benefits-received relationship with the cost-allocation base. Homogeneity of costs is important because creating homogeneous cost pools leads to more-accurate costs of a given cost object. If a homogeneous cost pool exists, the cost allocations using that pool will be the same as they would be if costs of each individual activity in that pool were allocated separately. The greater the degree of homogeneity, the fewer the number of cost pools required to explain accurately the differences in how divisions or products use resources of the company.

For example, when allocating corporate costs to divisions, CAI can combine corporate administration costs and corporate human resource management costs into a single cost pool if both cost categories have the same or a similar cause-and-effect relationship with the same cost-allocation base (say, number of employees in each division). If, however, each cost category has a cause-and-effect relationship with a different cost-allocation base (for example, number of employees in each division affects corporate human resource management costs, whereas revenues of each division affect corporate administration costs), CAI will prefer to maintain separate cost pools for each of these costs. Determining homogeneous cost pools requires judgment and should be revisited on a regular basis to evaluate whether the cause-and-effect relationship between the cost-allocation base and the different cost categories in a cost pool has changed.

Another factor in deciding on the number of cost pools is the views of managers. Do they believe that aggregating corporate costs into a single cost pool ignores important differences in how divisions use corporate resources? A final factor is the costs of implementing a multiple cost-pool system. Improvements in information-gathering technology are enhancing the capability of companies and reducing the cost of using multiple cost pools.

3. If CAI allocates corporate costs to divisions, which allocation bases should it use? *Generally, the ones that have the best cause-and-effect relationship with costs.*

Implementing Corporate Cost Allocations

We illustrate the allocation of corporate costs to divisions in CAI's ABC system. CAI chooses to allocate all corporate costs to divisions. It could have chosen the option of not allocating some corporate costs to divisions and, hence, to products. Not allocating some costs would result in total company profitability being less than the sum of individual division and product profitabilities.

This section links the cost-allocation material in this chapter with the ABC material in Chapter 5.

The demands for corporate resources by the Refrigerator Division and the Clothes Dryer Division depend on the demand that each division's products place on these resources. Exhibit 14-4 graphically represents the allocations.

1. CAI allocates treasury costs to each division on the basis of the cost of new assembly equipment installed in each division (the cost driver of treasury costs). It allocates the \$900,000 of treasury costs as follows (using information from p. 486):

$$\text{Refrigerator Division:} \quad 900{,}000 \times \frac{\$5{,}200{,}000}{\$5{,}200{,}000 + \$3{,}800{,}000} = \$520{,}000$$

$$\text{Clothes Dryer Division:} \quad \$900{,}000 \times \frac{\$3{,}800{,}000}{\$5{,}200{,}000 + \$3{,}800{,}000} = \$380{,}000$$

Each division then creates a separate cost pool consisting of the allocated corporate treasury costs and reallocates these costs to products on the basis of machine-hours used on the new equipment. Treasury costs are an output unit-level cost because they represent resources sacrificed on activities performed on each individual unit of a product.

2. CAI's analysis indicates that the demand for corporate human resource management (CHRM) costs for recruitment and training varies with total salary and labor costs. As a result, these costs are allocated to divisions on the basis of the total salary and labor costs incurred in each division. Suppose salary and labor costs are \$44,000,000 in the Refrigerator Division and \$36,000,000 in the Clothes Dryer Division. Then CHRM costs are allocated to the divisions as follows:

$$\text{Refrigerator Division:} \quad \$1{,}600{,}000 \times \frac{\$44{,}000{,}000}{\$44{,}000{,}000 + \$36{,}000{,}000} = \$880{,}000$$

$$\text{Clothes Dryer Division:} \quad \$1{,}600{,}000 \times \frac{\$36{,}000{,}000}{\$44{,}000{,}000 + \$36{,}000{,}000} = \$720{,}000$$

Each division reallocates the CHRM costs allocated to it to the indirect-cost pools of design, machine setup, manufacturing operations, distribution, and division administration on the basis of the total salary and labor costs incurred for each of these activities. CHRM costs are added to the indirect-cost pools in each division and allocated to products using the cost driver for each cost pool. Thus, CHRM costs are product-sustaining costs (for the portion of CHRM costs allocated to the design cost pool), batch-level costs (for the portion of CHRM costs allocated to the machine setup cost pool), output unit-level costs (for the portions of CHRM costs allocated to the manufacturing operations and distribution cost pools), and facility-sustaining costs (for the portion of CHRM costs allocated to the division administration cost pool).

3. CAI allocates corporate administration costs to each division on the basis of division administration costs (see Exhibit 14-3) because corporate administration's main role is to support division management.

$$\text{Refrigerator Division:} \quad \$5{,}400{,}000 \times \frac{\$1{,}000{,}000}{\$1{,}000{,}000 + \$800{,}000} = \$3{,}000{,}000$$

$$\text{Clothes Dryer Division:} \quad \$5{,}400{,}000 \times \frac{\$800{,}000}{\$1{,}000{,}000 + \$800{,}000} = \$2{,}400{,}000$$

Each division adds the allocated corporate administration costs to the division administration cost pool. The costs in this cost pool are facility-sustaining costs and do not have a cause-and-effect relationship with individual products produced and sold by each division. CAI's policy, however, is to allocate all costs to products so that CAI's division managers become aware of all costs incurred at CAI in their pricing and other decisions. It allocates the division administration costs (including allocated corporate administration costs) to products on the basis of product revenues (a benefits-received criterion).

Exhibit 14-4 highlights the different ways CAI allocates corporate overhead costs to divisions and then to products. The company

- Establishes a separate activity-cost pool at the division level to allocate corporate treasury costs to products.
- Allocates CHRM costs to divisions on the basis of division salary and labor costs and then reallocates the CHRM costs allocated to divisions to multiple activity-cost pools on the basis of the total salary and labor costs in each cost pool. Thus, the activity-cost pools of each division include an allocation of CHRM costs, as shown in Exhibit 14-4.
- Allocates corporate administration costs to divisions on the basis of division administration costs and adds these costs to a single activity-cost pool (division administration) as shown in Exhibit 14-4.

As we described in Chapter 5, focusing on activities and the hierarchy of costs promotes cost management. The set of activities and the actions necessary to manage costs are different if a cost is an output unit-level cost, a batch-level cost, a product-sustaining cost, or a facility-sustaining cost. For example, to manage setup cost, which is a batch-level cost, CAI must focus on batch-level activities, such as ways to reduce setup-hours and the cost per setup-hour.

Exhibit 14-4 also reinforces the idea that costing systems have multiple cost objects, such as corporate headquarters, divisions, departments, and products. An individual cost item can be simultaneously a direct cost of one cost object and an indirect cost of another cost object. Consider the salary of the manager of CHRM at CAI. Her salary is a direct cost of the Corporate Human Resource Management group at CAI's corporate office. It is then allocated as an indirect cost to each of CAI's divisions and reallocated as an indirect cost of the products in each division.

The issues discussed in this section regarding divisions and products apply nearly identically to customers, as we shall show next. *Instructors and students who, at this point, want to explore more-detailed issues in cost allocation rather than customer issues can skip ahead to Chapter 15.*

CUSTOMER REVENUES AND CUSTOMER COSTS

Customer-profitability analysis is the reporting and analysis of revenues earned from customers and the costs incurred to earn those revenues. An analysis of customer differences in revenues and costs can provide insight into why differences exist in the operating incomes earned from different customers. With this information, managers can ensure that customers making large contributions to the operating income of a company receive a level of attention from the company matching their contribution to the company's profitability.

Customer-profitability analysis is management accounting's response to the notion that "the customer is priority one" from marketing and management courses. In particular, this section shows how accounting can provide marketing personnel with useful information.

Consider Spring Distribution Company, which sells bottled water. It has two distribution channels: (1) a wholesale distribution channel that sells to supermarkets, drugstores, and other stores and (2) a retail distribution channel for a small number of business customers. We focus mainly on customer-profitability analysis in Spring's retail distribution channel. The list selling price in this channel is \$14.40 per case (24 bottles). The full cost to Spring is \$12 per case. If every case is sold at list price in this distribution channel, Spring would earn a gross margin of \$2.40 per case.

Customer Revenue Analysis

Consider revenues from 4 of Spring's 10 retail customers in June 2004:

	CUSTOMER			
	A	B	G	J
1. Cases sold	42,000	33,000	2,900	2,500
2. List selling price	$14.40	$14.40	$14.40	$14.40
3. Discount	$0.96	$0.24	$1.20	$0.00
4. Invoice price	$13.44	$14.16	$13.20	$14.40
5. Revenues (1 × 4)	$564,480	$467,280	$38,280	$36,000

4 **Discuss why a company's revenues can differ across customers purchasing the same product**

...differences in the quantity purchased and the price discounts given

Two variables explain revenue differences across these four customers: (1) the number of cases they purchased and (2) the magnitude of price discounting.

Price discounting is the reduction of selling prices below list selling prices to encourage increases in customer purchases. Companies that record only the final invoice price in their information system cannot readily track the magnitude of their price discounting.[4]

Price discounts are a function of multiple factors, including the volume of product purchased (higher-volume customers receive higher discounts) and the desire to sell to a customer who might help promote other sales. Discounts could also be due to poor negotiating by a salesperson or the unwanted effect of an incentive plan based only on revenues.

Tracking discounts by customer and by salesperson helps improve customer profitability. For example, Spring Distribution may decide to strictly enforce its volume-based price discounting policy. It may also require its salespeople to obtain approval for giving large discounts to customers who do not normally qualify for such discounts. In addition, Spring could track the future sales of customers who its salespeople argue warrant a sizable price discount due to their predicted "high growth potential." For example, Spring should track future sales to customer G to see if the $1.20 per case discount translates into higher future sales. Training in sales forecasting should be given to salespeople who have difficulty accurately predicting the future growth in sales of customers.

Customer revenues are one element of customer profitability. The other element is customer costs.

Customer Cost Analysis

5 **Apply the concept of cost hierarchy to customer costing**

...such as assigning some costs to individual customers and other costs to distribution channels or to corporate-wide efforts

We apply to customers the cost hierarchy discussed in Chapter 5 and the previous section. A **customer cost hierarchy** categorizes costs related to customers into different cost pools on the basis of different types of cost drivers, or cost-allocation bases, or different degrees of difficulty in determining cause-and-effect or benefits-received relationships. Spring's ABC system focuses on customers rather than products. It has one direct cost—the cost of bottled water—and multiple indirect-cost pools. Spring identifies five categories of indirect costs in its customer cost hierarchy:

- *Customer output unit-level costs*—costs of activities to sell each unit (case) to a customer. An example is product-handling costs of each case sold.
- *Customer batch-level costs*—costs of activities that are related to a group of units (cases) sold to a customer. Examples are costs incurred to process orders or to make deliveries.
- *Customer-sustaining costs*—costs of activities to support individual customers, regardless of the number of units or batches of product delivered to the customer. Examples are costs of visits to customers or costs of displays at customer sites.
- *Distribution-channel costs*—costs of activities related to a particular distribution channel rather than to each unit of product, each batch of product, or specific customers. An example is the salary of the manager of Spring's retail distribution channel.

[4] Further analysis of customer revenues could distinguish gross revenues from net revenues. This approach highlights differences across customers in sales returns. Additional discussion of ways to analyze revenue differences across customers is in R. S. Kaplan and R. Cooper, *Cost and Effect* (Boston, MA: Harvard Business School Press, 1998, Chapter 10).

- *Corporate-sustaining costs*—costs of activities that cannot be traced to individual customers or distribution channels. Examples are top management and general administration costs.

Note from these descriptions that four of the five levels of Spring's cost hierarchy closely parallel the cost hierarchy described in Chapter 5, except that Spring focuses on customers whereas the cost hierarchy in Chapter 5 focused on products. Spring has one additional cost hierarchy category, distribution channel costs, for the costs it incurs to support its wholesale and retail distribution channels.

6 Discuss why customer-level costs differ across customers

...different customers place different demands on a company's resources

Customer-Level Costs

Spring is particularly interested in analyzing customer-level indirect costs that are incurred in the first three categories of the customer cost hierarchy: customer output unit-level costs, customer batch-level costs, and customer-sustaining costs. Spring believes that it can work with customers to influence these costs. It believes that customer actions will have less impact on distribution-channel and corporate-sustaining costs. The following table shows five activities (in addition to cost of goods sold) that Spring identifies as resulting in customer-level costs. The table indicates the cost drivers and cost-driver rates for each activity, as well as the cost-hierarchy category for each activity.

Activity Area	Cost Driver and Rate	Cost-Hierarchy Category
Product handling	$0.50 per case sold	Customer output unit-level costs
Order taking	$100 per purchase order	Customer batch-level costs
Delivery vehicles	$2 per delivery mile traveled	Customer batch-level costs
Rushed deliveries	$300 per expedited delivery	Customer batch-level costs
Visits to customers	$80 per sales visit	Customer-sustaining costs

Information on the quantity of cost drivers used by each of four customers are

	CUSTOMER			
	A	B	G	J
Number of purchase orders	30	25	15	10
Number of deliveries	60	30	20	15
Miles traveled per delivery	5	12	20	6
Number of rushed deliveries	1	0	2	0
Number of visits to customers	6	5	4	3

Exhibit 14-5 shows a customer-profitability analysis for the four retail customers using information on customer revenues previously presented (p. 491) and customer-level costs from the ABC system.

Spring Distribution can use the information in Exhibit 14-5 to work with customers to reduce the quantity of activities needed to support them. Consider a comparison of Customer G and Customer A. Customer G purchases only 7% of the cases that customer A purchases (2,900 versus 42,000). Yet, compared to Customer A, Customer G uses half as many purchase orders, two-thirds as many visits to customers, a third as many deliveries, and twice as many rushed deliveries. By implementing charges for each of these services, Spring might be able to induce Customer G to make fewer purchase orders, customer visits, deliveries and rushed deliveries while looking to increase sales in the future.

The ABC system also highlights a second opportunity for cost reduction: Spring can seek to reduce costs of each activity. For example, improving the efficiency of the ordering process (such as by having customers order electronically) can reduce costs even if customers place the same number of orders (see Concepts in Action, p. 493).

Exhibit 14-6 shows the monthly operating income for Spring. The customer-level operating income of customers A and B in Exhibit 14-5 are shown in columns 8 and 9 of Exhibit 14-6. The format of Exhibit 14-6 is structured on Spring's cost hierarchy. All costs incurred to serve customers are not allocated in Exhibit 14-6. For example, distribution-channel costs such as the salary of the manager of the retail distribution channel are not allocated to customers. That's because changes in customer behavior will not affect distribution-channel costs. Distribution-channel costs will be affected by decisions

EXHIBIT 14-5 **Customer-Profitability Analysis for Four Retail Channel Customers of Spring Distribution for June 2004**

	CUSTOMER			
	A	B	G	J
Revenues at list prices				
$14.40 × 42,000; 33,000; 2,900; 2,500	$604,800	$475,200	$ 41,760	$36,000
Discount				
$0.96 × 42,000; $0.24 × 33,000; $1.20 × 2,900; $0 × 2,500	40,320	7,920	3,480	0
Revenues (at actual prices)	564,480	467,280	38,280	36,000
Cost of goods sold				
$12 × 42,000; 33,000; 2,900; 2,500	504,000	396,000	34,800	30,000
Gross margin	60,480	71,280	3,480	6,000
Customer-level operating costs				
Product handling $0.50 × 42,000; 33,000; 2,900; 2,500	21,000	16,500	1,450	1,250
Order taking $100 × 30; 25; 15; 10	3,000	2,500	1,500	1,000
Delivery vehicles $2 × (5 × 60); (12 × 30); (20 × 20); (6 × 15)	600	720	800	180
Rushed deliveries $300 × 1; 0; 2; 0	300	0	600	0
Visits to customers $80 × 6; 5; 4; 3	480	400	320	240
Total customer-level operating costs	25,380	20,120	4,670	2,670
Customer-level operating income	$ 35,100	$ 51,160	$ (1,190)	$ 3,330

CONCEPTS IN ACTION

Customer Profitability at PHH and Federal Express

PHH, a vehicle management company, leases vehicles to corporations and individuals and offers a broad range of related services, such as vehicle management, vehicle maintenance, and accident-related support. PHH uses an ABC system to price new business and to calculate customer profitability.

The costs of serving different customers vary. Some customers want quick vehicle deliveries, whereas others give PHH relatively long lead times. To satisfy orders with short delivery times, PHH purchases vehicles at a higher cost from a dealer rather than a manufacturer. Customers differ in their accident rates and the costs of vehicle repairs and maintenance. Some customers are satisfied with PHH's standardized reports; other customers demand customized reports. Some customers lease a small range of vehicles; other customers lease a more-diverse set of vehicles that costs PHH more to manage and maintain. PHH uses its customer profitability analysis to charge customers for different vehicle/service combinations. The goal is to achieve a "more consistent and disciplined approach to pricing."

Federal Express, the largest express delivery company in the world, also calculates customer profitability. The costs to serve a customer vary with "the service selected (how fast a package has to be delivered), destination city, weight, size, and whether the shipment was picked up by a Federal Express courier or dropped off by the customer at one of Federal Express' locations." Federal Express uses these same parameters to set prices. The goal is to achieve profitability across all of its customers, offering volume discounts to customers who use its services heavily.

To reduce customer costs, Federal Express uses "a comprehensive Internet strategy." Its Web site enables customers to "accomplish all of the tasks they could otherwise accomplish by phone or in person," including preparing shipping labels, arranging for pickups, finding drop-off locations, and tracking and tracing packages. The Web site also calculates shipping charges, invoices the customer daily, and produces customized reports. By the early 2000s, more than 70% of Federal Express' total transactions were handled electronically, resulting in 20,000 fewer employees being hired.

Source: Conversations with PHH management and with D. Swenson of the University of Idaho; Federal Express 2000 10K; E. Turban et. al., *Electronic Commerce* (Prentice Hall, 2000); and stock-analyst reports by Schroder (3/3/99), Morgan Stanley (4/16/99), and Salomon Smith Barney (6/22/99).

EXHIBIT 14-6 Income Statement of Spring Distribution for June 2004

	CUSTOMER DISTRIBUTION CHANNELS										
		Wholesale Customers					Retail Customers				
	Total (1) = (2) + (7)	Total (2)	A1 (3)	A2 (4)	• (5)	• (6)	Total (7)	A[a] (8)	B[a] (9)	• (10)	• (11)
Revenues (at actual prices)	$12,138,120	$10,107,720	$1,946,000	$1,476,000			$2,030,400	$564,480	$467,280		
Customer-level costs	11,633,760	9,737,280	1,868,000	1,416,000			1,896,480	529,380	416,120		
Customer-level operating income	504,360	370,440	$ 78,000	$ 60,000			133,920	$ 35,100	$ 51,160		
Distribution-channel costs	160,500	102,500					58,000				
Distribution-channel-level operating income	343,860	$ 267,940					$ 75,920				
Corporate-sustaining costs	263,000										
Operating income	$ 80,860										

[a]Full details are presented in Exhibit 14-5.

pertaining to the whole channel, such as a decision to discontinue retail distribution. Another reason for not allocating distribution-channel costs to customers is motivation. Salespersons responsible for managing individual customer accounts would be demotivated if their bonuses were affected by the allocation to customers of distribution-channel costs over which they had minimal influence.

Next, consider corporate-sustaining costs such as top management and general administration costs. These costs are common to individual customers and distribution channels. However, they are not clearly or practically allocable. That's because there is no cause-and-effect or benefits-received relationship between any cost-allocation base and corporate-sustaining costs. Allocation of corporate-sustaining costs serves no useful purpose in decision making, performance evaluation, or motivation. For example, if retail distribution were discontinued, corporate-sustaining costs would mostly be unaffected. Allocating corporate-sustaining costs to distribution channels could give the misleading impression that the potential cost savings from discontinuing a distribution channel would be greater than the likely amount.

Some managers and cost accountants fully allocate all costs to customers and distribution channels so that (1) the sum of operating incomes of all customers in a distribution channel (segment) equals the operating income of the distribution channel and (2) the sum of the distribution-channel operating incomes equals companywide operating income. These managers argue that customers and products must eventually be profitable on a full cost basis. In the previous example, CAI allocated all corporate and division-level costs to its refrigerator and clothes dryer products (see pp. 485 – 490). For some decisions, such as pricing, allocating all costs ensures that prices are set at a level to cover the cost of all resources used to produce and sell products. Nevertheless, the value of the hierarchical format in Exhibit 14-6 is that it distinguishes among various degrees of objectivity when allocating costs, and it dovetails with the different levels at which decisions are made and performance is evaluated. The issue of when and what costs to allocate is another example of the "different costs for different purposes" theme emphasized throughout the book.

CUSTOMER-PROFITABILITY PROFILES

Customer-profitability profiles are a useful tool for managers. Exhibit 14-7 ranks Spring's 10 retail customers on customer-level operating income. (Four of these customers are analyzed in Exhibit 14-5.)

Column 4, computed by adding the individual amounts in column 1, shows the cumulative customer-level operating income. For example, row 3 for customer C has a cumulative income of $107,330 in column 4. This $107,330 is the sum of $51,160 for customer B, $35,100 for customer A, and $21,070 for customer C.

EXHIBIT 14-7 Customer-Profitability Analysis for Retail Channel Customers: Spring Distribution, June 2004

Customers Ranked on Customer-Level Operating Income

Customer Code	Customer-Level Operating Income (1)	Customer Revenue (2)	Customer-Level Operating Income Divided by Revenue (3) = (1) ÷ (2)	Cumulative Customer-Level Operating Income (4)	Cumulative Customer-Level Operating Income as a % of Total Customer-Level Operating Income (5) = (4) ÷ $133,920
B	$ 51,160	$ 467,280	10.9 %	$ 51,160	38%
A	35,100	564,480	6.2	86,260	64
C	21,070	255,640	8.2	107,330	80
D	17,580	277,000	6.3	124,910	93
F	7,504	123,500	6.1	132,414	99
J	3,330	36,000	9.3	135,744	101
E	3,176	193,000	1.6	138,920	104
G	–1,190	38,280	–3.1	137,730	103
H	–1,690	38,220	–4.4	136,040	102
I	–2,120	37,000	–5.7	133,920	100
	$133,920	$2,030,400			

Column 5 shows what percentage the $107,330 cumulative total for customers A, B, and C is of the total customer-level operating income of $133,920 earned in the retail distribution channel from all 10 customers. The three most profitable customers contribute 80% of total customer-level operating income. This high percentage of operating income contributed by a small number of customers is a common finding in many studies. It highlights how vital a small set of customers is to Spring's retail profitability. These customers should receive the highest service and priority. Microsoft uses the phrase "not all revenue dollars are endowed equally in profitability" to stress this point.

Column 3 shows the profitability per dollar of revenue by customer. This measure of customer profitability indicates that, although customer A contributes the second-highest operating income, the profitability per dollar of revenue is lower because of high price discounts. Spring should work to increase profit margins on Customer A by decreasing the discounts or saving customer-level costs while maintaining sales. Customer J has a higher 9.3% profit margin but has lower total sales. Spring's challenge with Customer J is to maintain margins while increasing sales.

Managers often find the bar chart presentation in Exhibit 14-8 to be the most intuitive way to visualize customer profitability. The highly profitable customers clearly stand out. Moreover, the number of loss-causing customers and the magnitude of their losses are apparent. Spring's managers must explore ways to make "loss category" customers profitable.

The "80-20 rule"also applies to customers: 80% of a company's profits often come from 20% of its customers. Customer-profitability information can help marketing and customer-service personnel (1) to focus on maintaining the best-possible relations with those 20% of customers and (2) to transform the other 80% into more-profitable customers.

Assessing Customer Value

Exhibits 14-5 to 14-8 emphasize short-run customer profitability. Other factors managers should consider in deciding how to allocate resources across customers include:

1. *Likelihood of customer retention.* The more likely a customer will continue to do business with a company, the more valuable the customer. Customers differ in their loyalty and their willingness to frequently "shop their business."
2. *Potential for customer growth.* The higher the likely growth of the customer's industry and the customer's sales (due to, say, the ability to develop new products), the more valuable the customer. Customers to whom a company can cross-sell one or more of the company's other products are more desirable.
3. *Long-run customer profitability.* This factor will be influenced by the first two factors specified and the resources likely to be required to retain customer accounts.

EXHIBIT 14-8

Bar Chart of Customer-Level Operating Income for Spring Distribution's Retail Channel Customers in June 2004

The idea that "a picture is worth a thousand words" is supported by research findings. Graphs and charts help managers make faster and better-informed decisions. PC-based graphics software makes it easier for management accountants to provide information in pictorial form.

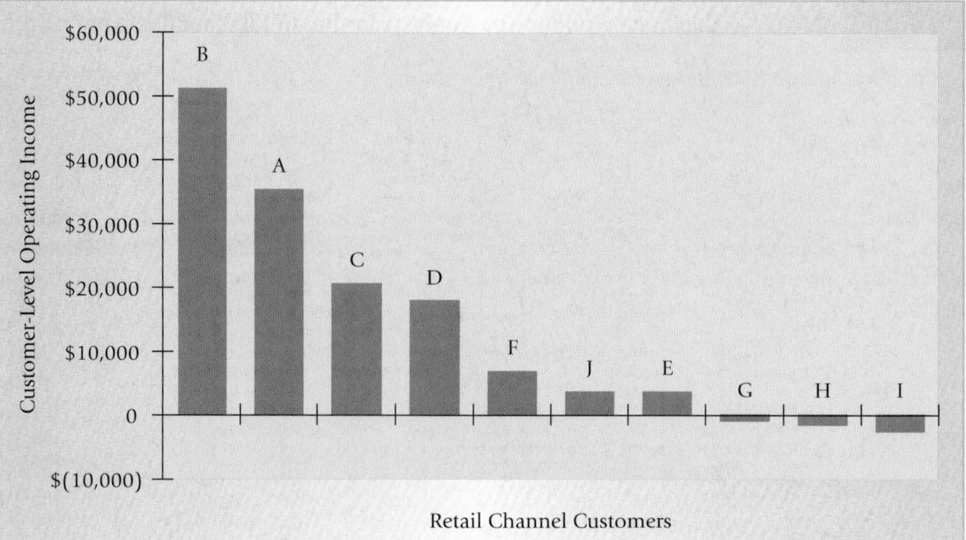

4. *Increases in overall demand from having well-known customers.* Some customers with established reputations help generate sales from other customers. Some customers are valuable because they provide product endorsements.
5. *Ability to learn from customers.* Customers who provide ideas about new products or ways to improve existing products are especially valuable.

Managers should be cautious when deciding to discontinue customers. The long-run unprofitability of a customer may provide misleading signals about a customer's short-run profitability. Not all costs assigned to a customer are variable in the short run. Discontinuing a currently unprofitable customer will not necessarily eliminate all the costs assigned to that customer in the short run.

SALES VARIANCES

The customer-profitability analysis in the previous section focused on the actual profitability of individual customers within a distribution channel (retail, for example) and their impact on Spring's profitability in June 2004. At a more strategic level, however, Spring operates in two different markets: wholesale and retail. The operating margins in the retail market are much higher than the operating margins in the wholesale market. In June 2004, Spring had budgeted to sell 80% of its cases to wholesalers and 20% to retailers. It actually sold more cases in total than it had budgeted, but its actual sales mix (in cases) was 84% to wholesalers and 16% to retailers. Regardless of the profitability of sales to individual customers within each of the retail and wholesale channels, Spring's actual operating income, relative to the budget, is likely to be positively affected by the higher sales of cases and negatively affected by the shift in mix away from retail customers. That's because retail customers are more profitable than wholesale customers. The sales-quantity and sales-mix variances identify the effect of each of these factors on Spring's profitability.

Spring classifies all customer-level costs as variable costs and distribution-channel and corporate-sustaining costs as fixed costs. To simplify the sales-variances analysis and calculations, we make two assumptions: All customer batch-level costs vary in proportion to output units, and all customer-sustaining costs vary in proportion to output units. The assumption for customer batch-level costs means that average customer batch sizes remain the same as the total cases sold vary. The assumptions imply that all variable costs can be thought of as being variable with respect to units (cases) sold. If these assumptions did not hold, the analysis would become more complex and would have to be done using the ABC-variance analysis approach described in Chapter 7, pp. 232–234. The basic insights, however, would not change.

Budgeted and actual operating data for June 2004 are

"Unit" in the column headings refers to a case of 24 bottles.

Budget for June 2004

	Selling Price per Unit (1)	Variable Cost per Unit (2)	Contribution Margin per Unit (3) = (1) − (2)	Sales Volume in Units (4)	Sales Mix (Based on Units) (5)	Contribution Margin (6) = (3) × (4)
Wholesale channel	$13.37	$12.88	$0.49	712,000	80%[a]	$348,880
Retail channel	14.10	13.12	0.98	178,000	20	174,440
Total				890,000	100%	$523,320

[a]For example, percentage of unit sales to wholesale channel = 712,000 units ÷ 890,000 total units = 80%.

Actual Results for June 2004

	Selling Price per Unit (1)	Variable Cost per Unit (2)	Contribution Margin per Units (3) = (1) − (2)	Sales Volume in Units (4)	Sales Mix (Based on Units) (5)	Contribution Margin (6) = (3) × (4)
Wholesale channel	$13.37	$12.88	$0.49	756,000	84%	$370,440
Retail channel	14.10	13.17	0.93	144,000	16	133,920
Total				900,000	100%	$504,360

The budgeted and actual fixed distribution-channel costs and corporate-sustaining costs are $160,500 and $263,000, respectively (see Exhibit 14-6, p. 494).

The levels of detail introduced in Chapter 7 included the static-budget variance (Level 1), the flexible-budget variance (Level 2), and the sales-volume variance (Level 2). The sales-quantity and sales-mix variances are Level 3 variances that subdivide the sales-volume variance.[5]

Static-Budget Variance

The *static-budget variance* is the difference between an actual result and the corresponding budgeted amount in the static budget. Our analysis focuses on the difference between the actual and budgeted contribution margins. The total static-budget variance is $18,960 U (actual contribution margin of $504,360 − budgeted contribution margin of $523,320). Exhibit 14-9 (columns 1 and 3) uses the columnar format introduced in Chapter 7 to show detailed calculations of the static-budget variance. More insight about the static-budget variance can be gained by subdividing it into the flexible-budget variance and the sales-volume variance.

Flexible-Budget Variance and Sales-Volume Variance

The *flexible-budget variance* is the difference between an actual result and the corresponding flexible-budget amount based on the actual output level in the budget period. The flexible-budget contribution margin is equal to the budgeted contribution margin per unit times the actual unit volume sold. Exhibit 14-9, Column 2 shows the flexible-budget calculations. The flexible budget measures the contribution margin that Spring would have budgeted for the actual quantities of cases sold. The flexible-budget variance is the difference between columns 1 and 2 in Exhibit 14-9. The only difference between columns 1 and 2 is that the actual units sold is multiplied by actual contribution margin per unit in column 1 and budgeted contribution margin per unit in column 2. The $7,200 unfavorable total flexible-budget variance arises because the actual contribution margin on retail sales of $0.93 per case is lower than the budgeted amount of $0.98 per case.

The *sales-volume variance* is the difference between a flexible-budget amount and the corresponding static-budget amount. In Exhibit 14-9, the sales-volume variance shows

[5] The presentation of the variances in this chapter and the appendix draws on teaching notes prepared by J. K. Harris.

EXHIBIT 14-9 Flexible-Budget and Sales-Volume Variance Analysis of Spring Distribution for June 2004

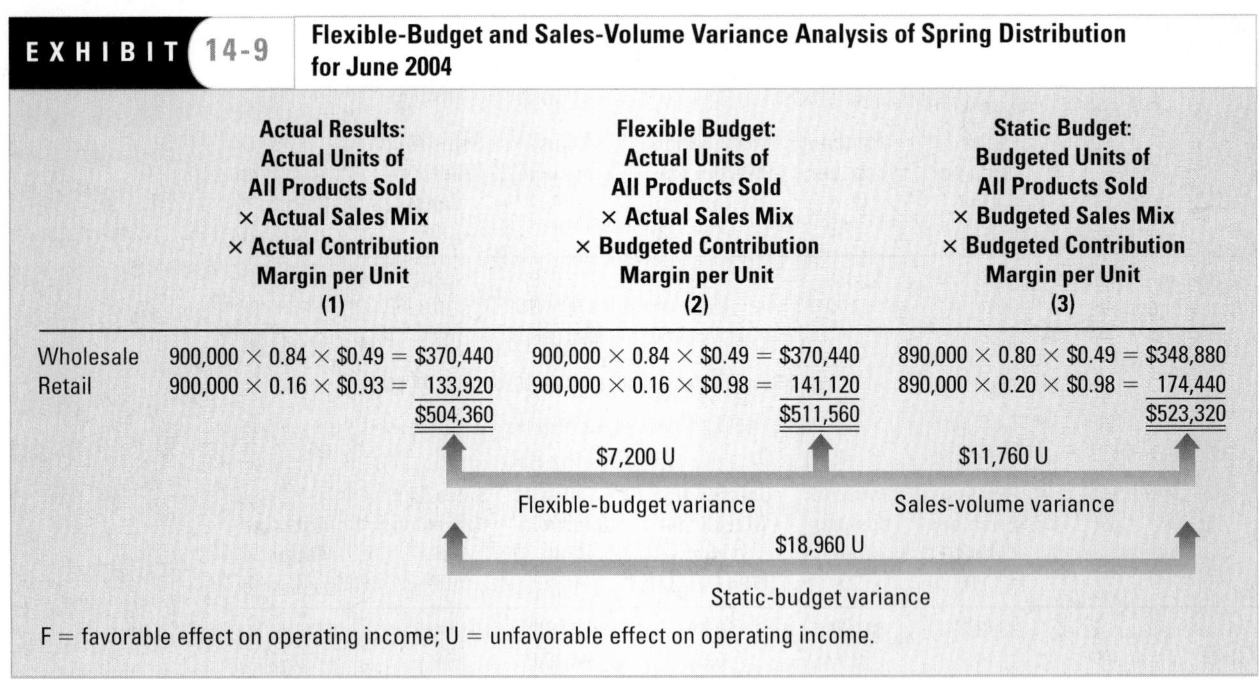

	Actual Results: Actual Units of All Products Sold × Actual Sales Mix × Actual Contribution Margin per Unit (1)	Flexible Budget: Actual Units of All Products Sold × Actual Sales Mix × Budgeted Contribution Margin per Unit (2)	Static Budget: Budgeted Units of All Products Sold × Budgeted Sales Mix × Budgeted Contribution Margin per Unit (3)
Wholesale	900,000 × 0.84 × \$0.49 = \$370,440	900,000 × 0.84 × \$0.49 = \$370,440	890,000 × 0.80 × \$0.49 = \$348,880
Retail	900,000 × 0.16 × \$0.93 = 133,920	900,000 × 0.16 × \$0.98 = 141,120	890,000 × 0.20 × \$0.98 = 174,440
	\$504,360	\$511,560	\$523,320

F = favorable effect on operating income; U = unfavorable effect on operating income.

the effect on budgeted contribution margin of the difference between the actual quantity and the budgeted quantity of units sold. The sales-volume variance is the difference between columns 2 and 3 in Exhibit 14-9. The \$11,760 U sales-volume variance plus the \$7,200 flexible-budget variance equals the \$18,960 U static-budget variance. Managers can gain additional insight into sales-volume changes by separating the sales-volume variance into a sales-mix variance and a sales-quantity variance.

7 Provide additional information about the sales-volume variance by calculating the sales-mix variance

...actual sales-mix differs from budgeted sales mix

and the sales-quantity variance

...actual total unit sales differs from budgeted total unit sales

The variances described here—sales-mix variance, sales-quantity variance, market-share variance, and market-size variance—provide information on why sales differed from expectations, which is especially helpful to marketing managers in planning and controlling their activities.

SALES-MIX AND SALES-QUANTITY VARIANCES

Exhibit 14-10 uses the columnar approach to calculate the sales-mix variance and the sales-quantity variance. Refer to this exhibit when reading the following discussion of these two variances.

Sales-Mix Variance

The **sales-mix variance** is the difference between (1) the budgeted contribution margin for the *actual sales mix* and (2) the budgeted contribution margin for the *budgeted sales mix*. The formula and computations (using data from p. 497) are

	Actual Units of All Products Sold	×	(Actual Sales-Mix Percentage	−	Budgeted Sales-Mix Percentage)	×	Budgeted Contribution Margin per Unit	=	Sales-Mix Variance
Wholesale	900,000 units	×	(0.84	−	0.80)	×	\$0.49 per unit	=	\$17,640F
Retail	900,000 units	×	(0.16	−	0.20)	×	\$0.98 per unit	=	35,280U
Sales-mix variance									\$17,640U

A favorable sales-mix variance arises for the wholesale channel because the 84% actual sales-mix percentage exceeds the 80% budgeted sales-mix percentage. In contrast, the retail channel has an unfavorable variance because the 16% actual sales-mix percentage is less than the 20% budgeted sales-mix percentage. The sales-mix variance is unfavorable because the actual sales mix shifted toward the less-profitable wholesale channel relative to the budgeted sales mix.

The concept underlying the sales-mix variance is best explained in terms of the budgeted contribution margin per composite unit of the sales mix. A **composite unit** is a hypothetical unit with weights based on the mix of individual units. For the actual mix,

0.80 (50% of 1.6) ton of Latoms at $70 per ton	$ 56.00
0.48 (30% of 1.6) ton of Caltoms at $80 per ton	38.40
0.32 (20% of 1.6) ton of Flotoms at $90 per ton	28.80
Total budgeted cost of 1.6 tons of tomatoes	$123.20

Budgeted average cost per ton of tomatoes is $123.20 ÷ 1.60 tons = $77 per ton.

Because Delpino uses fresh tomatoes to make ketchup, no inventories of tomatoes are kept. Purchases are made as needed, so all price variances relate to tomatoes purchased and used. Actual results for June 2003 show that a total of 6,500 tons of tomatoes were used to produce 4,000 tons of ketchup:

3,250	tons of Latoms at actual cost of $70 per ton	$227,500
2,275	tons of Caltoms at actual cost of $82 per ton	186,550
975	tons of Flotoms at actual cost of $96 per ton	93,600
6,500	tons of tomatoes	507,650
Budgeted cost of 4,000 tons of ketchup at $123.20 per ton		492,800
Flexible-budget variance for direct materials		$ 14,850 U

Given the standard ratio of 1.60 tons of tomatoes to 1 ton of ketchup, 6,400 tons of tomatoes should be used to produce 4,000 tons of ketchup. At the standard mix, the quantities of each type of tomato required are

Latoms 0.50 × 6,400 = 3,200 tons
Caltoms 0.30 × 6,400 = 1,920 tons
Flotoms 0.20 × 6,400 = 1,280 tons

Direct Materials Price and Efficiency Variances

Exhibit 14-13 presents in columnar form the analysis of the flexible-budget variance for direct materials discussed in Chapter 7. The materials price and efficiency variances are calculated separately for each input material and then added together. The variance analysis prompts Delpino to investigate the unfavorable price and efficiency variances. Why did they pay more for the tomatoes and use greater quantities than they had budgeted for? Were the actual market prices of tomatoes higher, in general, or could the Purchasing Department have negotiated lower prices? Did the inefficiencies result from inferior tomatoes or from problems in processing?

Direct Materials Mix and Direct Materials Yield Variances

Managers sometimes have discretion to substitute one material for another. The manager of Delpino's ketchup plant has some leeway in combining Latoms, Caltoms, and Flotoms

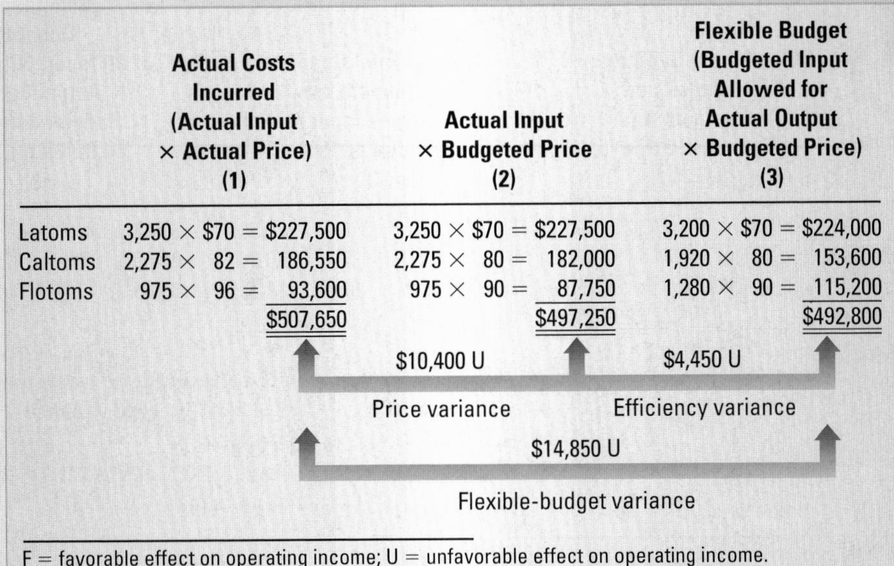

	Actual Costs Incurred (Actual Input × Actual Price) (1)	Actual Input × Budgeted Price (2)	Flexible Budget (Budgeted Input Allowed for Actual Output × Budgeted Price) (3)
Latoms	3,250 × $70 = $227,500	3,250 × $70 = $227,500	3,200 × $70 = $224,000
Caltoms	2,275 × 82 = 186,550	2,275 × 80 = 182,000	1,920 × 80 = 153,600
Flotoms	975 × 96 = 93,600	975 × 90 = 87,750	1,280 × 90 = 115,200
	$507,650	$497,250	$492,800

F = favorable effect on operating income; U = unfavorable effect on operating income.

EXHIBIT 14-13

Direct Materials Price and Efficiency Variances for the Delpino Corporation for June 2004

without affecting quality. We will assume that to maintain quality, the mix percentages of each type of tomato can only vary up to 5% from the standard mix. For example, the percentage of Caltoms in the mix can vary between 25% and 35% (30% ± 5%). When inputs are substitutable, direct materials efficiency improvement relative to budgeted costs can come from two sources: (1) using a cheaper mix to produce a given quantity of output, measured by the direct materials mix variance, and (2) using less input to achieve a given quantity of output, measured by the direct materials yield variance.

Holding the actual total quantity of all direct materials inputs used constant, the total **direct materials mix variance** is the difference between (1) the budgeted cost for the actual mix of the actual total quantity of direct materials used and (2) the budgeted cost of the budgeted mix of the actual total quantity of direct materials used. Holding the budgeted input mix constant, the **direct materials yield variance** is the difference between (1) the budgeted cost of direct materials based on the actual total quantity of direct materials used and (2) the flexible-budget cost of direct materials based on the budgeted total quantity of direct materials allowed for the actual output produced. Exhibit 14-14 presents the direct materials mix and yield variances for the Delpino Corporation.

Direct materials mix variance The direct materials mix variance is the sum of the direct materials mix variances for each input:

$$\begin{array}{c}\text{Direct}\\\text{materials}\\\text{mix variance}\\\text{for each}\\\text{input}\end{array} = \begin{array}{c}\text{Actual total}\\\text{quantity of all}\\\text{direct materials}\\\text{inputs used}\end{array} \times \left(\begin{array}{c}\text{Actual}\\\text{direct materials}\\\text{input mix}\\\text{percentage}\end{array} - \begin{array}{c}\text{Budgeted}\\\text{direct materials}\\\text{input mix}\\\text{percentage}\end{array}\right) \times \begin{array}{c}\text{Budgeted}\\\text{price of}\\\text{direct material}\\\text{input}\end{array}$$

The direct materials mix variances are

Latoms	6,500 tons × (0.50 – 0.50) × $70 per ton	=	6,500 ×	0.00 ×	$70	=	$ 0
Caltoms	6,500 tons × (0.35 – 0.30) × $80 per ton	=	6,500 ×	0.05 ×	$80	=	26,000 U
Flotoms	6,500 tons × (0.15 – 0.20) × $90 per ton	=	6,500 ×	–0.05 ×	$90	=	29,250 F
Total direct materials mix variance							$ 3,250 F

The direct materials mix variance is favorable because relative to the budgeted mix, Delpino substitutes 5% of the cheaper Caltoms for 5% of the more-expensive Flotoms.

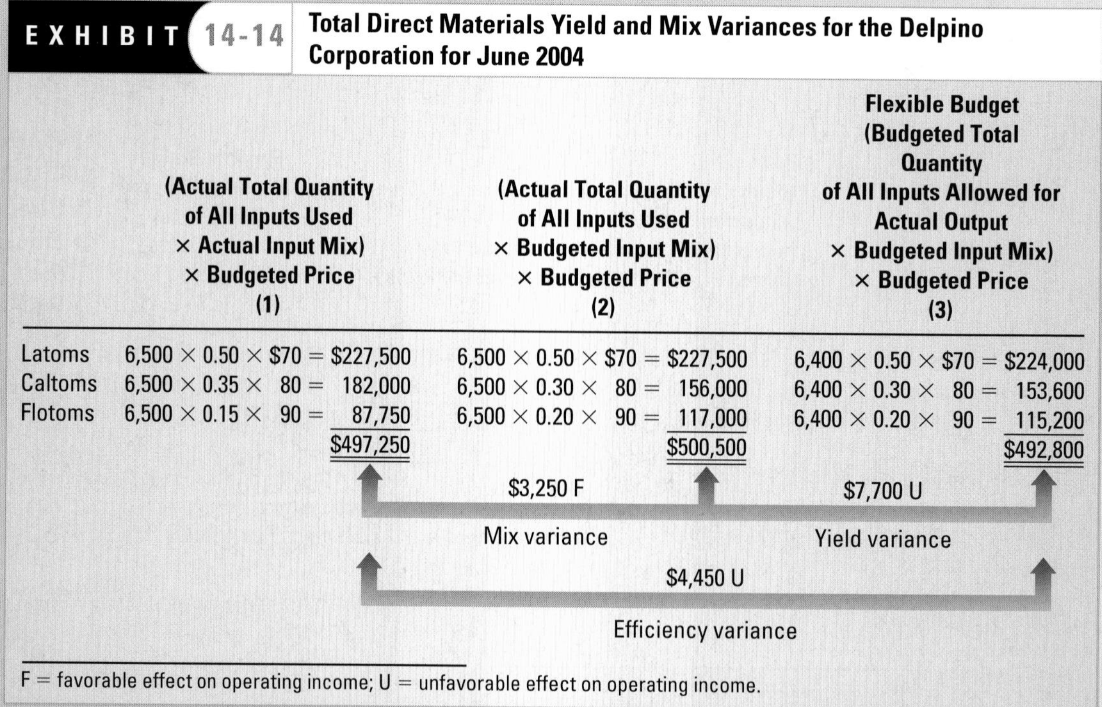

EXHIBIT 14-14 Total Direct Materials Yield and Mix Variances for the Delpino Corporation for June 2004

	(Actual Total Quantity of All Inputs Used × Actual Input Mix) × Budgeted Price (1)	(Actual Total Quantity of All Inputs Used × Budgeted Input Mix) × Budgeted Price (2)	Flexible Budget (Budgeted Total Quantity of All Inputs Allowed for Actual Output × Budgeted Input Mix) × Budgeted Price (3)
Latoms	6,500 × 0.50 × $70 = $227,500	6,500 × 0.50 × $70 = $227,500	6,400 × 0.50 × $70 = $224,000
Caltoms	6,500 × 0.35 × 80 = 182,000	6,500 × 0.30 × 80 = 156,000	6,400 × 0.30 × 80 = 153,600
Flotoms	6,500 × 0.15 × 90 = 87,750	6,500 × 0.20 × 90 = 117,000	6,400 × 0.20 × 90 = 115,200
	$497,250	$500,500	$492,800

F = favorable effect on operating income; U = unfavorable effect on operating income.

Direct Materials Yield Variance The direct materials yield variance is the sum of the direct materials yield variances for each input:

Budgeted price per unit of each type of material (or labor) is used to calculate the mix and yield variances. Keeping prices constant at budgeted amounts allows us to compare for an input category (1) the actual quantity used with the budgeted quantity allowed and (2) the actual mix with the budgeted mix.

$$\text{Direct materials yield variance for each input} = \left(\text{Actual total quantity of all direct materials inputs used} - \text{Budgeted total quantity of all direct materials inputs allowed for actual output}\right) \times \text{Budgeted direct materials input mix percentage} \times \text{Budgeted price of direct materials input}$$

The direct materials yield variances are

Latoms	(6,500 − 6,400) tons × 0.50 × $70 per ton	= 100 × 0.50 × $70 =	$3,500 U
Caltoms	(6,500 − 6,400) tons × 0.30 × $80 per ton	= 100 × 0.30 × $80 =	2,400 U
Flotoms	(6,500 − 6,400) tons × 0.20 × $90 per ton	= 100 × 0.20 × $90 =	1,800 U
Direct materials yield variance			$7,700 U

The direct materials yield variance is unfavorable because Delpino used 6,500 tons of tomatoes rather than the 6,400 tons that it should have used to produce 4,000 tons of ketchup. Holding the budgeted mix and budgeted prices of tomatoes constant, the budgeted cost per ton of tomatoes in the budgeted mix is $77 per ton. The unfavorable yield variance represents the budgeted cost of using 100 more tons of tomatoes, (6,500 − 6,400) tons × $77 per ton = $7,700 U. Delpino would want to investigate reasons for the unfavorable yield variances. For example, did the substitution of the cheaper Caltoms for Flotoms that resulted in the favorable mix variance also cause the unfavorable yield variance?

The direct materials variances computed in Exhibits 14-13 and 14-14 can be summarized as follows:

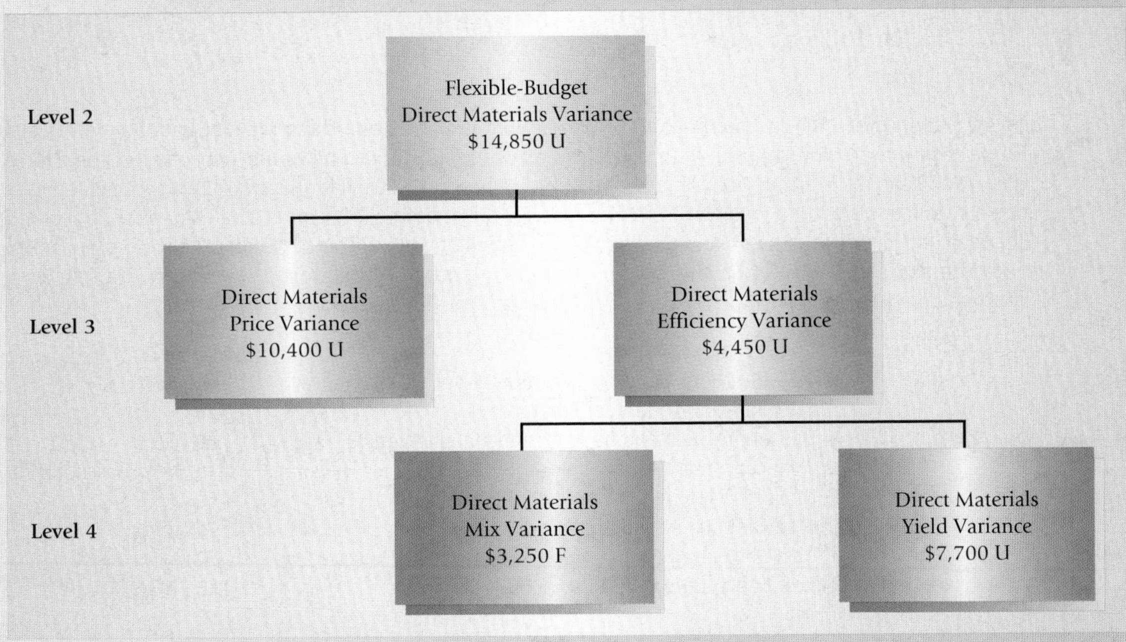

TERMS TO LEARN

This chapter and the Glossary at the end of the book contain definitions of:

composite unit (p. 498)
customer cost hierarchy (491)
customer-profitability analysis (490)
direct materials mix variance (506)
direct materials yield variance (506)
homogeneous cost pool (488)
market-share variance (500)
market-size variance (501)
price discounting (491)
sales-mix variance (498)
sales-quantity variance (499)

Questions

14-1 "I am going to focus on the customers of my business and leave cost-allocation issues to my accountant." Do you agree with this comment by a division president? Why?

14-2 How can an individual cost item, such as the salary of a plant security guard, be both a direct cost and an indirect cost?

14-3 A given cost may be allocated for one or more purposes. List four purposes.

14-4 What criteria might be used to guide cost-allocation decisions? Which are the dominant criteria?

14-5 Show how managers can gain insight into the causes of a sales-volume variance by drilling down into the components of this variance.

14-6 How can the concept of a composite unit be used to explain why an unfavorable total sales-mix variance of contribution margin occurs?

14-7 Explain why a favorable sales-quantity variance occurs.

14-8 Distinguish between a market-share variance and a market-size variance.

14-9 Why might some companies not compute market-size and market-share variances?

14-10 Why is customer-profitability analysis a vitally important topic to managers?

14-11 How can the extent of price discounting be tracked on a customer-by-customer basis?

14-12 Why should "A customer-profitability profile highlights those customers who should be dropped to improve profitability." Do you agree? Explain.

14-13 Give examples of three different levels of costs in a customer-cost hierarchy.

14-14 Distinguish between processes in which the inputs are and are not substitutable.

14-15 Explain how the direct materials mix and yield variances provide additional information about the direct materials efficiency variance.

Exercises

14-16 Cost allocation in hospitals, alternative allocation criteria. Dave Meltzer vacationed at Lake Tahoe last winter. Unfortunately, he broke his ankle while skiing and spent two days at the Sierra University Hospital. Meltzer's insurance company received a $4,800 bill for his two-day stay. One item that caught Meltzer's attention was an $11.52 charge for a roll of cotton. Meltzer is a salesman for Johnson & Johnson and knows that the cost to the hospital of the roll of cotton is in the $2.20 to 3.00 range. He asked for a breakdown of the $11.52 charge. The accounting office of the hospital sent him the following information:

a. Invoiced cost of cotton roll	$ 2.40
b. Cost of processing of paperwork for purchase	0.60
c. Supplies-room management fee	0.70
d. Operating-room and patient-room handling costs	1.60
e. Administrative hospital costs	1.10
f. University teaching-related costs	.60
g. Malpractice insurance costs	1.20
h. Cost of treating uninsured patients	2.72
i. Profit component	0.60
Total	$11.52

Meltzer believes the overhead charge is obscene. He comments, "There was nothing I could do about it. When they come in and dab your stitches, it's not as if you can say, 'Keep your cotton roll. I brought my own.'"

Required

1. Compute the overhead rate Sierra University Hospital charged on the cotton roll.
2. What criteria might Sierra use to justify allocation of the overhead items b through i in the preceding list? Examine each item separately and use the allocation criteria listed in Exhibit 14-2 (p. 484) in your answer.
3. What should Meltzer do about the $11.52 charge for the cotton roll?

14-17 Cost allocation and motivation. Environ Petroleum Company is engaged in all phases of exploring, refining, and marketing of oil and petrochemical products. To ensure full compliance with all applicable laws, the company has a legal department staffed by lawyers who have expertise in a variety of legal areas. The top management of Environ wants to motivate all operating managers to seek legal counsel from the in-house lawyers whenever necessary to avoid violation of any laws during the course of its operations.

Currently, users of the Legal Department are allocated cost at a $400 standard hourly rate based on actual usage. The chief financial officer has suggested that department managers would make more use of the Legal Department services, and thus avoid potential legal pitfalls, if the service was provided free of cost to their departments.

Comment on the proposal of the chief financial officer. Do you have any alternative suggestion(s)? **Required**

14-18 Cost allocation to divisions. Rembrandt Hotel & Casino is situated on beautiful Lake Tahoe in Nevada. The complex includes a 300-room hotel, a casino, and a restaurant. As Rembrandt's new controller, you are asked to recommend the basis to be used for allocating fixed overhead costs to the three divisions in 2004. You are presented with the following income statement information for 2003:

	Hotel	Restaurant	Casino
Revenues	$16,425,000	$5,256,000	$12,340,000
Direct costs	9,819,260	3,749,172	4,248,768
Segment margin	$ 6,605,740	$1,506,828	$ 8,091,232

You are also given the following data on the three segments:

	Hotel	Restaurant	Casino
Floor space (square feet)	80,000	16,000	64,000
Number of employees	200	50	250

You may choose to allocate indirect costs based on direct costs, square feet, or the number of employees. Total fixed overhead for 2003 was $14,550,000.

Required

1. Calculate segment margins in percentage terms prior to allocating fixed overhead costs.
2. Allocate indirect costs to the three divisions using each of the three allocation bases suggested. Calculate segment margins in dollar and percentage terms with each allocation base.
3. Discuss the results. How would you decide how to allocate indirect costs to the divisions? Why?
4. Would you recommend closing any of the three divisions (and possibly reallocating resources to other divisions) as a result of your analysis? If so, which division would you close and why?

14-19 Cost allocation to divisions. Lenzig Corporation has three divisions: Fibers, Paper, and Pulp. As Lenzig's new controller, you are reviewing the basis to be used for allocating fixed overhead costs to the three divisions in 2004. The following information is available for 2003:

	Pulp	Paper	Fibers
Revenue	$8,500,000	$17,500,000	$24,000,000
Administrative costs	$1,200,000	$1,800,000	$3,000,000
Number of employees	300	250	450
Floor space (square feet)	30,000	24,000	66,000
Segment margin	$3,200,000	$7,100,000	$9,700,000

In the past, Lenzig has allocated fixed overhead costs to the division using segment margin percentages. A review of the fixed overhead costs indicates that they consist of the following:

Human resource management	$1,800,000
Facility	2,700,000
Corporate administration	4,500,000
Total	$9,000,000

After considering the nature of the fixed-cost items, you decide to make the allocations in 2004 using the following bases:

Human resource management	Number of employees
Facility	Floor space
Corporate administration	Divisional administrative costs

Required

1. Allocate 2003 indirect costs to the three divisions using segment margin percentages.
2. Allocate 2003 indirect costs to the three divisions using the bases you have selected.
3. Discuss the reason(s) why your approach is preferable.

14-20 Customer profitability, service company. Instant Service (IS) is a repair-service company specializing in the rapid repair of photocopying machines. Each of its 10 clients pays a fixed monthly service fee (based on the type of photocopying machines owned by that client and the number of employees at that site). IS keeps records of the time technicians spend at each client's location and the cost of the equipment used to repair each photocopying machine. IS recently decided to compute the profitability of each customer. The following data (in thousands) pertain to May 2003:

	Customer Revenues	Customer Costs
Avery Group	$260	$182
Duran Systems	180	184
Retail Systems	163	178
Wizard Partners	322	225
Santa Clara College	235	308
Grainger Services	80	74
Software Partners	174	100
Problem Solvers	76	108
Business Systems	137	110
Okie Enterprises	373	231

Required

1. Compute the operating income of each customer. Prepare exhibits for Instant Service that are patterned after Exhibits 14-7 and 14-8. Comment on the results.
2. What options regarding individual customers should Instant Service consider in light of your customer-profitability analysis in requirement 1?
3. What problems might Instant Service encounter in accurately estimating the operating costs of each customer?

14-21 Customer profitability, distribution. Figure Four is a distributor of pharmaceutical products. Its ABC system has five activities:

Activity Area	Cost Driver Rate in 2003
1. Order processing	$40 per order
2. Line-item ordering	$3 per line item
3. Store deliveries	$50 per store delivery
4. Carton deliveries	$1 per carton
5. Shelf-stocking	$16 per stocking-hour

Rick Flair, the controller of Figure Four, wants to use this ABC system to examine individual customer profitability within each distribution market. He focuses first on the Ma and Pa single-store distribution market. Two customers are used to exemplify the insights available with the ABC approach. Data pertaining to these two customers in August 2003 are as follows:

	Charleston Pharmacy	Chapel Hill Pharmacy
Total orders	12	10
Average line items per order	10	18
Total store deliveries	6	10
Average cartons shipped per store delivery	24	20
Average hours of shelf stocking per store delivery	0	0.5
Average revenue per delivery	$2,400	$1,800
Average cost of goods sold per delivery	$2,100	$1,650

Required

1. Use the ABC information to compute the operating income of each customer in August 2003. Comment on the results.
2. Flair ranks the individual customers in the Ma and Pa single-store distribution market on the basis of monthly operating income. The cumulative operating income of the top 20% of customers is $55,680. Figure Four reports negative operating income of $21,247 for the bottom 40% of its customers. Make four recommendations that you think Figure Four should consider in light of this new customer-profitability information.

14-22 Variance analysis, multiple products. The Detroit Penguins play in the American Ice Hockey League. The Penguins play in the Downtown Arena (owned and managed by the City of Detroit), which has a capacity of 15,000 seats (5,000 lower-tier seats and 10,000 upper-tier seats). The Downtown Arena charges the Penguins a per ticket charge for use of their facility. All tickets are sold by the Reservation Network, which charges the Penguins' a reservation fee per ticket. The Penguins' budgeted contribution margin for each type of ticket in 2004 is computed as follows:

	Lower-Tier Tickets	Upper-Tier Tickets
Selling price	$35	$14
Downtown Arena fee	10	6
Reservation Network fee	5	3
Contribution margin per ticket	$20	$ 5

The budgeted and actual average attendance figures per game in the 2004 season are

	Budgeted Seats Sold	Actual Seats Sold
Lower tier	4,000	3,300
Upper tier	6,000	7,700
Total	10,000	11,000

There was no difference between the budgeted and actual contribution margin for lower-tier or upper-tier seats.

The manager of the Penguins was delighted that actual attendance was 10% above budgeted attendance per game, especially given the depressed state of the local economy in the past six months.

Required

1. Compute the sales-volume variance for each type of ticket and in total for the Detroit Penguins in 2004. (Calculate all variances in terms of contribution margins.)
2. Compute the sales-quantity and sales-mix variances for each type of ticket and in total in 2004.
3. Present a summary of the variances in requirements 1 and 2. Comment on the results.

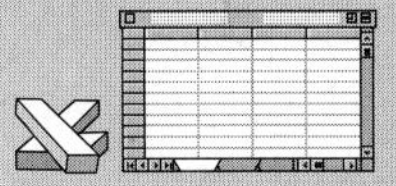

Excel Application For students who wish to practice their spreadsheet skills, the following is a step-by-step approach to creating an Excel spreadsheet to work this problem.

Step-by-Step

1. Open up a new spreadsheet. At top, create an "Original Data" section for the data provided by the Detroit Penguins in the same format as shown above. Create columns for each type of ticket ("Lower tier" and "Upper tier") and rows for "Selling Price, Downtown Arena Fee, Reservation Network Fee", and "Contribution Margin per Ticket." Skip two rows, and create rows for each type of ticket, a "Total" row, and columns for "Budgeted Seats Sold" and "Actual Seats Sold."

(Program your spreadsheet to perform all necessary calculations. Do not "hard-code" any amounts, such as sales-mix variance, requiring addition, subtraction, multiplication, or division operations.)

2. Skip two rows and create a new section, "Problem 1—Sales volume variance calculations." Create rows for "Lower-tier Tickets, Upper-tier Tickets," and "All Tickets." Using the data in your Original Data section, enter calculations for sales-volume variances for each ticket type and total sales-volume variance for all tickets.
3. Skip two rows and create a section, "Problem 2." Create a subsection, "Sales-mix percentages." In this subsection, create rows for each ticket type and columns for "Budgeted" and "Actual." Enter calculations for the budgeted and actual sales-mix percentages for each ticket type.
4. Skip two rows and create another subsection, "Sales-quantity variance calculations." The format for this section should be the same as the one you used in step 2. Using the data from your Original Data section and the sales-mix percentages from step 3, enter calculations for sales-quantity variances for each ticket type and total sales-quantity variance for all tickets.
5. Skip two rows and create another subsection, "Sales-mix variance calculations." The format for this section should be the same as the one you used in step 2. Using the data from your Original Data section and the sales-mix percentages from step 3, enter calculations for sales-mix variances for each ticket type and total sales-mix variance for all tickets.
6. *Check the accuracy of your spreadsheet:* Go to your Original Data section and change the reservation network fee for lower-tier tickets from $5 to $6. If your spreadsheet is programmed correctly, sales-volume variance should change to $4,800 unfavorable.

14-23 Variance analysis, working backward. The Jinwa Corporation sells two brands of wine glasses: Plain and Chic. Jinwa provides the following information for sales in the month of June 2003:

Static-budget total contribution margin	$5,600
Budgeted units to be sold of all glasses in June 2003	2,000 units
Budgeted contribution margin per unit of Plain	$2 per unit
Budgeted contribution margin per unit of Chic	$6 per unit
Total sales-quantity variance	$1,400 U
Actual sales-mix percentage of Plain	60%

All variances are to be computed in contribution-margin terms.

Required

1. Calculate the sales-quantity variances for each product for June 2003.
2. Calculate the individual product and total sales-mix variances for June 2003. Calculate the individual product and total sales-volume variances for June 2003.
3. Briefly describe the conclusions you would draw from the variances.

14-24 **Variance analysis, multiple products.** Soda-King manufactures and sells three soft drinks: Kola, Limor, and Orlem. Budgeted and actual results for 2003 (all in U.S. dollars) are as follows:

	BUDGET FOR 2003			ACTUAL FOR 2003		
Product	**Selling Price per Carton**	**Variable Cost per Carton**	**Cartons Sold**	**Selling Price per Carton**	**Variable Cost per Carton**	**Cartons Sold**
Kola	$6.00	$4.00	400,000	$6.20	$4.50	480,000
Limor	$4.00	$2.80	600,000	$4.25	$2.75	900,000
Orlem	$7.00	$4.50	1,500,000	$6.80	$4.60	1,620,000

Required

1. Compute the total sales-volume variance, the total sales-mix variance, and the total sales-quantity variance. (Calculate all variances in terms of contribution margin). Show results for each product in your computations.
2. What inferences can you draw from the variances computed in requirement 1?

14-25 **Market-share and market-size variances (continuation of 14-24).** Soda-King prepared the budget for 2003 assuming a 10% market share based on total sales in the Western region of the United States. The total soft drinks market was estimated to reach sales of 25 million cartons in the region. However, actual total sales volume in the Western region was 24 million cartons.

Required Calculate the market-share and market-size variances for Soda-King in 2003. (Report all variances in terms of contribution margin.) Comment on the results.

Problems

14-26 **Allocation of central corporate costs to divisions.** Dusty Rhodes, the corporate controller of Richfield Oil Company, is about to make a presentation to the senior corporate executives and the top managers of its four divisions. These divisions are

- Oil & Gas Upstream (the exploration, production, and transportation of oil and gas)
- Oil & Gas Downstream (the refining and marketing of oil and gas)
- Chemical Products
- Copper Mining

Under the existing internal accounting system, costs incurred at central corporate headquarters are collected in a single pool and allocated to each division on the basis of its actual revenues. The central corporate costs (in millions) for the most recent year are

Interest on debt	$2,000
Corporate salaries	100
Accounting and control	100
General marketing	100
Legal	100
Research and development	200
Public affairs	208
Personnel and payroll	192
	$3,000

Public affairs includes the public relations staff, the lobbyists, and the sizable donations Richfield makes to numerous charities and nonprofit institutions.

Summary data (dollar amounts in millions) related to the four divisions for the most recent year are

	Oil & Gas Upstream	Oil & Gas Downstream	Chemical Products	Copper Mining	Total
Revenues	$7,000	$16,000	$4,000	$3,000	$30,000
Operating costs	$3,000	$15,000	$3,800	$3,200	$25,000
Operating income	$4,000	$1,000	$200	$(200)	$5,000
Identifiable assets	$14,000	$6,000	$3,000	$2,000	$25,000
Number of employees	9,000	12,000	6,000	3,000	30,000

The top managers of each division share in a divisional-income bonus pool. Divisional income is defined as operating income less allocated central corporate costs.

Rhodes is about to propose a change in the method used to allocate central corporate costs. He favors collecting these costs in four separate pools:

- *Cost Pool 1—Interest on debt.* Allocated using identifiable assets of divisions
- *Cost Pool 2—Corporate salaries, accounting and control, general marketing, legal, and research and development.* Allocated using revenues of divisions
- *Cost Pool 3—Public affairs.* Allocated using operating income (if positive) of divisions, with only divisions with positive operating income included in the allocation base
- *Cost Pool 4—Personnel and payroll.* Allocated using number of employees in divisions

Required

1. What purposes might be served by the allocation of central corporate costs to each division at Richfield Oil?
2. Compute the operating income of each division when all central corporate costs are allocated using revenues of each division.
3. Compute the operating income of each division when central corporate costs are allocated using the four cost pools.
4. What are the strengths and weaknesses of Rhodes' proposal relative to the existing single cost-pool method?

14-27 Allocation of central corporate costs to divisions. Legarde has four geographically dispersed divisions:

- Book publishing
- Broadcasting
- Print Media
- Multimedia

Under the current allocation system, costs incurred at Legarde corporate headquarters are collected in a single pool and allocated to each division on the basis of its revenues. The central corporate costs for 2003 are

Interest on debt	$ 10,000,000
Human resource management	150,000,000
Corporate administration	50,000,000
Research and development	100,000,000
Advertising	200,000,000
	$510,000,000

Summary data (in millions of U.S. dollars) related to the divisions for 2003 are

	Multimedia	Broadcasting	Print Media	Book Publishing
Revenues	$1,400	$4,500	$2,500	$1,600
Direct costs	750	3,500	2,000	1,000
Segment margin	$ 650	$1,000	$ 500	$ 600

The following information on the four divisions is also available.

	Multimedia	Broadcasting	Print Media	Book Publishing
Floor space (square feet)	40,000	160,000	200,000	100,000
Number of employees	1,000	3,000	2,500	1,500
Divisional administrative costs (in millions of U.S. dollars)	$150	$400	$250	$200

A review of the central corporate costs for divisions reveals the following:

- Out of the total $10 million interest on debt, $6.5 million is for the debt to purchase a building for the Broadcasting division. The remaining $3.5 million interest cost is on the borrowings for the purchase of equipment for the Multimedia division.
- No research and development work is done for the Print Media division. The director of research and development estimates that 40% of the work in her responsibility area is done for the Multimedia division, and the remaining 60% is done equally for the Broadcasting and Book Publishing divisions.
- Advertising campaigns sponsored at the central corporate level are to boost the overall corporate image. It is assumed that the benefits to the divisions are in proportion to their revenues.
- The resources expended by human resource management on recruiting, training, and so forth for the divisions are approximately in proportion to the number of employees.
- To support divisional managers, the corporate management works very closely with them. The divisional administrative costs are a good indicator of the relative size of each division's management team.

Required Allocate the central corporate costs to divisions that are consistent with cause-and-effect or benefits-received criteria.

14-28 Customer-profitability analysis, customer-cost hierarchy. Zoot's Suits is a ready-to-wear suit manufacturer. Zoot's has four customers: two wholesale-channel customers and two retail-channel customers:

- April Wholesalers
- Madison Brothers Wholesale Company
- Suitors Men's Store
- Design Clothing Store

Zoot's owner and CEO, Al Sims, has developed the following ABC system:

Activity	Cost Driver	Rate in 2004
Order Processing	Number of purchase orders	$245 per order
Sales Visits	Number of customer visits	$1,430 per visit
Delivery—Regular	Number of regular deliveries	$300 per delivery
Delivery—Rushed	Number of rushed deliveries	$850 per delivery

List selling price per suit is $200, and average cost per suit is $110. Sims wants to evaluate the profitability of each of the four customers in 2003 to explore opportunities for increasing the profitability of his company in 2004. The following data are available for 2003:

	WHOLESALE CUSTOMERS		RETAIL CUSTOMERS	
Item	**April**	**Madison**	**Suitors**	**Design**
Total number of orders	44	62	212	250
Total number of sale visits	8	12	22	20
Regular deliveries	41	48	166	190
Rush deliveries	3	14	46	60
Average number of suits per order	400	200	30	25
Average selling price per suit	$140	$160	$170	$180

Required

1. Calculate the customer-level operating income in 2003 using the format in Exhibit 14-5.
2. What do you recommend Al Sims to do to increase the company's operating income in 2004.?
3. Assume Zoot's distribution-channel costs are $350,000 for its wholesale customers and $210,000 for the retail customers. Also assume that its corporate-sustaining costs are $250,000. Prepare a customer cost hierarchy report for Zoot's using the format in Exhibit 14-6.

14-29 Customer profitability, distribution. Spring Distribution has decided to analyze the profitability of five new customers (see p. 490–496). It buys bottled water at $12 per case and sells to retail customers at a list price of $14.40 per case. Data pertaining to five customers are

	CUSTOMER				
	P	**Q**	**R**	**S**	**T**
Cases sold	2,080	8,750	60,800	31,800	3,900
List selling price	$14.40	$14.40	$14.40	$14.40	$14.40
Actual selling price	$14.40	$14.16	$13.20	$13.92	$12.96
Number of purchase orders	15	25	30	25	30
Number of customer visits	2	3	6	2	3
Number of deliveries	10	30	60	40	20
Miles traveled per delivery	14	4	3	8	40
Number of expedited deliveries	0	0	0	0	1

Its five activities and their cost drivers are

Activity	Cost Driver Rate
Order taking	$100 per purchase order
Customer visits	$80 per customer visit
Deliveries	$2 per delivery mile traveled
Product handling	$0.50 per case sold
Expedited deliveries	$300 per expedited delivery

Required

1. Compute the customer-level operating income of each of the five retail customers now being examined (P, Q, R, S, and T). Comment on the results.

2. What insights are gained by reporting both the list selling price and the actual selling price for each customer?
3. What factors should Spring Distribution consider in deciding whether to drop one or more of the five customers?

14-30 Customer loyalty clubs and profitability analysis. The Sherriton Hotels chain embarked on a new customer loyalty program in 2003. The 2003 year-end data have been collected, and it is now time for you to determine whether the loyalty program should be continued, discontinued, or perhaps altered to improve loyalty and profitability levels at Sherriton.

Sherriton's loyalty program consists of three different customer loyalty levels. All new customers can sign up for the Sherriton Bronze Card. This card provides guests with a complimentary bottle of wine per night (cost to the chain is $5 per bottle) and $20 in restaurant coupons each night (cost to the chain is $10). Bronze customers also receive a 10% discount off the nightly rate. The program enables the chain to track a member's stays and activities. Once customers have stayed and paid for 20 nights at any of the chain's locations worldwide, they are upgraded to Silver Customer status. Silver benefits include the bottle of wine (cost to the chain is $5 per bottle per night), $30 in restaurant coupons per night (cost to the chain is $15), and a 20% off every night from the 21st night on. A customer who reaches the 50-night level is upgraded to Gold Customer status. Gold status increases the nightly discount to 30% and replaces the $5 bottle of wine with a bottle of champagne per night (cost to the chain is $20 per bottle). As well, $40 in restaurant coupons per night are granted (cost to the chain is $20). Assume all bottles and coupons offered are used.

The average full price for one night's stay is $200. The chain incurs variable costs of $65 per night, exclusive of loyalty program costs. Total fixed costs for the chain are $140,580,000. Sherriton operates 10 hotels, with, on average, 500 rooms each. All hotels are open for business 365 days a year, and approximate average occupancy rates are around 80%. Following are some loyalty program characteristics:

Loyalty Program	Number of Customers	Average Number of Nights per Customer
Gold	2,430	60
Silver	8,340	35
Bronze	80,300	10
No program	219,000	1

Note that a Gold Customer would have received the 10% discount for his or her first 20 stays, received the 20% discount for the next 30 stays, and the 30% discount only for the last 10 nights. Assume that all program members signed on to the program the first time they stayed with one of the chain's hotels. Also, assume the restaurants are managed by a 100%-owned subsidiary of Sherriton.

Required

1. Calculate the program contribution margin for each of the three programs, as well as for the customers not subscribing to the loyalty program. Which of the programs is the most profitable? Which is the least profitable? Do not allocate fixed costs to individual rooms or specific loyalty programs.
2. Prepare an income statement for Sherriton for the year ended December 31, 2003.
3. What is the average room rate per night? What are average variable costs per night inclusive of the loyalty program?
4. Explain what drives the profitability (or lack thereof) of Sherriton's loyalty program.

14-31 Customer profitability, customer cost hierarchy. Ramish Electronics has two retail customers and two wholesale customers. Pertinent information relating to each customer for 2004 follows (all amounts are in thousands of U.S. dollars):

	WHOLESALE		RETAIL	
	North America Wholesaler	South America Wholesaler	Big Sam Stereo	World Market
Cost of goods sold	$325,000	$490,000	$112,000	$ 92,000
Delivery costs:				
Regular	300	450	150	80
Expedited	120	200	10	5
Order processing	800	1,000	200	130
Product handling	5,000	6,000	800	900
Sales visits	480	550	240	165
Revenues at list prices	400,000	600,000	130,000	100,000
Discounts from list prices	30,000	50,000	7,000	0

Ramish's distribution-channel costs are $30 million for wholesale customers and $10 million for retail customers. Its corporate-sustaining costs are $60 million.

Required

1. Calculate customer-level operating income using the format in Exhibit 14-5.
2. Prepare a customer cost hierarchy report, using the format in Exhibit 14-6.

14-32 Variance analysis, sales-mix and sales-quantity variances. Aussie Infonautics, Inc., produces handheld Windows CE™–compatible organizers. Aussie Infonautics markets three different handheld models. PalmPro is a souped-up version for the executive on the go; PalmCE is a consumer-oriented version; and PalmKid is a stripped-down version for the young adult market. You are Aussie Infonautics' senior vice president of marketing. The CEO has discovered that the total contribution margin came in lower than budget, and it is your responsibility to explain to him why actual results are different from the budget. Budgeted and actual operating data for the company's third quarter (2004) are as follows:

Budgeted Operating Data, Third Quarter 2004

	Selling Price	Variable Cost per Unit	Contribution Margin per Unit	Sales Volume in Units
PalmPro	$379	$182	$197	12,500
PalmCE	269	98	171	37,500
PalmKid	149	65	84	50,000
				100,000

Actual Operating Data, Third Quarter 2004

	Selling Price	Variable Cost per Unit	Contribution Margin per Unit	Sales Volume in Units
PalmPro	$349	$178	$171	11,000
PalmCE	285	92	193	44,000
PalmKid	102	73	29	55,000
				110,000

Required

1. Compute the actual and budgeted contribution margins in dollars for each product and in total.
2. Calculate the actual and budgeted sales mixes for the three products.
3. Calculate total sales-volume, sales-mix, and sales-quantity variances for the third quarter of 2004.
4. Given that your CEO is known to have temper tantrums, you want to be well prepared for this meeting. In order to prepare, write a paragraph or two explaining why actual results were not as good as the budgeted amounts.

14-33 Market-share and market-size variances (continuation of 14-32). Aussie Infonautics' senior vice president of marketing prepared his budget at the beginning of the third quarter assuming a 25% market share based on total sales. The total handheld-organizer market was estimated by Foolinstead Research to reach sales of 400,000 units worldwide in the third quarter. However, actual sales were 500,000 units.

Required

1. Calculate the market-share and market-size variances for Aussie Infonautics in the third quarter of 2004 (report all variances in terms of contribution margins).
2. Explain what happened based on the market-share and market-size variances.
3. Calculate the actual market size, in units, that would have led to no market-size variance (again using budgeted contribution margin per unit). Use this market-size figure to find the actual market share that would have led to a zero market-share variance.

14-34 Variance analysis, multiple products. Debbie's Delight, Inc., operates a chain of cookie stores. Budgeted and actual operating data of its three Chicago stores for August 2003 are as follows:

Budget for August 2003

	Selling Price per Pound	Variable Cost per Pound	Contribution Margin per Pound	Sales Volume in Pounds
Chocolate chip	$4.50	$2.50	$2.00	45,000
Oatmeal raisin	5.00	2.70	2.30	25,000
Coconut	5.50	2.90	2.60	10,000

Budget for August 2003 *(continued)*

	Selling Price per Pound	Variable Cost per Pound	Contribution Margin per Pound	Sales Volume in Pounds
White chocolate	6.00	3.00	3.00	5,000
Macadamia nut	6.50	3.40	3.10	15,000
				100,000

Actual for August 2003

	Selling Price per Pound	Variable Cost per Pound	Contribution Margin per Pound	Sales Volume in Pounds
Chocolate chip	$4.50	$2.60	$1.90	57,600
Oatmeal raisin	5.20	2.90	2.30	18,000
Coconut	5.50	2.80	2.70	9,600
White chocolate	6.00	3.40	2.60	13,200
Macadamia nut	7.00	4.00	3.00	21,600
				120,000

Debbie's Delight focuses on contribution margin in its variance analysis.

Required

1. Compute the total sales-volume variance for August 2003.
2. Compute the total sales-mix variance for August 2003.
3. Compute the total sales-quantity variance for August 2003.
4. Comment on your results in requirements 1, 2, and 3.

14-35 Market-share and market-size variances (continuation of 14-34). Debbie's Delight attains a 10% market share based on total sales of the Chicago market. The total Chicago market is expected to be 1,000,000 pounds in sales volume for August 2003. The actual total Chicago market for August 2003 was 960,000 pounds in sales volume.

Required

Compute the market-share and market-size variances for Debbie's Delight in August 2003. Report all variances in contribution-margin terms. Comment on the results.

14-36 Direct materials efficiency, mix, and yield variances. (Chapter Appendix, CMA adapted) The Energy Products Company produces a gasoline additive, Gas Gain, that increases engine efficiency and improves gasoline mileage. The actual and budgeted quantities (in gallons) of materials required to produce Gas Gain and the budgeted prices of materials in August 2003 are as follows:

Chemical	Actual Quantity	Budgeted Quantity	Budgeted Price
Echol	24,080	25,200	$0.20
Protex	15,480	16,800	0.45
Benz	36,120	33,600	0.15
CT-40	10,320	8,400	0.30

Required

1. Calculate the total direct materials efficiency variance for August 2003.
2. Calculate the total direct materials mix and yield variances for August 2003.
3. What conclusions would you draw from the variance analysis?

14-37 Direct materials price, efficiency, mix and yield variances. (Chapter Appendix) Greenwood, Inc., manufactures apple products such as apple jelly and applesauce. It makes applesauce by blending Tolman, Golden Delicious, and Ribston apples. Budgeted costs to produce 100,000 pounds of applesauce in November 2003 are as follows:

45,000 pounds of Tolman apples at $0.30 per pound	$13,500
180,000 pounds of Golden Delicious apples at $0.26 per pound	46,800
75,000 pounds of Ribston apples at $0.22 per pound	16,500

Actual costs in November 2003 are

62,000 pounds of Tolman apples at $0.28 per pound	$17,360
155,000 pounds of Golden Delicious apples at $0.26 per pound	40,300
93,000 pounds of Ribston apples at $0.20 per pound	18,600

Required

1. Calculate the total direct materials price and efficiency variances for November 2003.
2. Calculate the total direct materials mix and yield variances for November 2003.
3. Comment on your results in requirements 1 and 2.

14-38 Customer profitability, responsibility for environmental cleanup, ethics. Industrial Fluids, Inc. (IF), manufactures and sells fluids used by metal-cutting plants. These fluids enable metal cutting to be done more accurately and more safely.

IF has more than 1,000 customers. It is currently undertaking a customer-profitability analysis. Ariana Papandopolis, a newly hired MBA, is put in charge of the project. One issue in this analysis is IF's liability for its customers' fluid disposal.

Papandopolis discovers that IF may have a responsibility under U.S. environmental legislation for the disposal of toxic waste by its customers. Moreover, she visits 10 customer sites and finds dramatic differences in their toxic-waste-handling procedures. She describes one site owned by Acme Metal as an "environmental nightmare about to become a reality." She tells the IF controller that even if they have only one-half of the responsibility for the cleanup at Acme's site, they will still be facing very high damages. He is displeased that Acme Metal has not paid its account to IF for the past three months and has formally sought protection from its creditors. He cautions Papandopolis to be careful in her written report. He notes that, "IF does not want any smoking guns in its files in case of subsequent litigation."

Required

1. As Papandopolis prepares IF's customer-profitability analysis, how should she handle any estimates of litigation and cleanup costs that IF may be held responsible for?
2. How should Papandopolis handle the Acme Metal situation when she prepares a profitability report for that customer?

Collaborative Learning Problem

14-39 Customer profitability, credit-card operations. The Freedom Card is a credit card that competes with national credit cards such as Visa and Master Card. Freedom Card is marketed by the Bay Bank. Mario Verdolini is manager of the Freedom Card division. He is seeking to develop a customer-profitability reporting system. He collects the following information on four users of the Freedom Card during 2003:

	A	B	C	D
Annual purchases at retail merchants	$80,000	$26,000	$34,000	$8,000
Customer transactions at retail merchant	800	520	272	200
Annual fee	$50	$0	$50	$0
Average annual outstanding balance on credit card on which interest is paid to Bay Bank	$6,000	$0	$2,000	$100
Inquiries to Bay Bank	6	12	8	2
Credit-card replacement due to loss or theft	0	2	1	0

Customer B pays no membership fee because his card was issued under a special "lifetime promotion program," in which annual fees are waived as long as the card is used at least once a year. Customer D is a student. Bay Bank does not charge an annual fee to student credit-card holders at select universities.

Bay Bank has an ABC system that Verdolini can use in his analysis. The following data apply to 2003:

a. Each customer transaction with a retail merchant costs Bay Bank $0.50 to process.
b. Each customer inquiry to Bay Bank costs $5.
c. Replacing a lost card costs $120.
d. Annual cost to Bay Bank of maintaining a credit-card account is $108 (includes sending out monthly statements).

Bay Bank receives 2.0% of the purchase amount from retail merchants when the Freedom Card is used. Bad debts of the Freedom Card in 2003 were 0.5% of the total purchases at retail merchants. Thus, Bay Bank nets 1.5% of the total purchases made using the Freedom Card.

Bay Bank had an interest spread of 9% in 2003 on the average outstanding balances on which interest is paid by its credit-card holders. An interest spread is the difference between what Bay Bank receives from card holders on outstanding balances and what it pays to obtain the funds so used. Thus, on a $500 average annual outstanding balance in 2003, Bay Bank would receive $45 in interest revenues (9% × $500).

Required

1. Compute the customer profitability of the four representative credit-card users of the Freedom Card for 2003.
2. Develop profiles of (a) profitable card holders and (b) unprofitable card holders for Bay Bank.
3. Should Bay Bank charge its card holders for making inquiries (such as outstanding balances or disputed charges) or for replacing lost or stolen cards?
4. Verdolini has an internal proposal that Bay Bank discontinue a sizable number of the low-volume credit-card customers. What factors should he consider in evaluating and responding to this proposal?
5. Verdolini seeks your group's advice on an ethical issue he is facing. A chain of gambling casinos (Lucky Roller) has offered to provide Freedom Card holders with money advances of up to $500 at its casinos. Verdolini observes that from a strictly financial perspective, providing money advances to its customers would be highly profitable. Should Freedom Card holders be able to obtain money advances at Lucky Roller gambling casinos? Explain.

CHAPTER 14 INTERNET EXERCISE

Cost allocation is an inescapable problem facing nearly every organization and arising in nearly every facet of accounting. It played an important role in Hewlett-Packard's spin-off of its test and measurement business, Agilent Technologies. To take a look at the cost allocation challenge that Hewlett-Packard faced, go to www.prenhall.com/horngren, click on *Cost Accounting,* 11th ed. and access the Internet exercise for Chapter 14.

CHAPTER 14 VIDEO CASE

NANTUCKET NECTARS: Cost Allocation

Tom First and Tom Scott knew they didn't want corporate "suit and tie" jobs when they graduated from Brown University. Both were fond of summers spent on Nantucket Island, off the coast of Massachusetts, and enjoyed the laid-back atmosphere of the resort community. To earn living expenses, the pair operated a boat in the harbor to service the grocery and sanitation needs of visiting vessels. Back at school, Tom First suggested they concoct a peach juice beverage reminiscent of one he had sampled in Spain on a recent trip. One blender and lots of peaches later, the two Toms emerged with their first "Nantucket Nectar" beverage, named after their beloved harbor home.

Sales the following summer were encouraging and, as graduation loomed, the two started seriously considering opening their own juice beverage company rather than working for a large corporation. In 1989, Tom and Tom graduated and began in earnest their new full-time jobs as founders of the Nantucket Nectars beverage company. Today, their Cambridge, Massachusetts–based, privately held company makes close to 50 flavors of juice drinks, ranging from best-selling Orange Mango to "Super Nectars" such as Mama Calcium and Protein Smooth. Sales hover around the $70 million mark annually. Ocean Spray, the large cranberry juice cooperative based in the Northeast, is a major shareholder.

The company partners with a number of juice bottlers, called "co-packers," to produce the juice. Recipes are created in the company's central test kitchen, with detailed specifications for winning flavors communicated to both the internal Purchasing function and each co-packer. Several new juice flavors are created each year, with less-popular flavors retired from the product lines. Direct materials are sourced from a variety of vendors, ranging from cane sugar producers and fruit growers to glass bottle makers and label printers.

The ingredients are combined at the plant in 5,000-gallon batches. Each batch feeds the production line, which is set to fill 550 bottles per minute. As bottles come off the line, they are packed into cases of 20 bottles each. Cases are shrink-wrapped and stacked onto pallets. Full pallets are transported via forklift to trucks waiting to travel to distributor warehouses. Distributors pull product from the warehouses for delivery to retail outlets such as restaurants and grocery stores.

Ninety sales representatives are scattered throughout four regions of the country: Central, Pacific Northwest, East, and Northeast. Each region is supplied by its own set of co-packers. Each region's sales representatives have responsibility for opening new customer accounts and securing local distributors for the company's single-serve juice bottles and cans, and multi-serve juice cartons. To help boost sales in their regions, regional managers can request promotional support from headquarters' Mobile Juice Guy Team. This team of four full-time employees roves the United States, from region to region as requested by regional managers, in a dedicated full-size van to help promote Nantucket Nectars at charitable events, local festivals, community sports events, and so on. The mobile team takes banners, display tables, and plenty of coupons and product for sampling by a crowd. Regional managers expect to see a boost in new customer accounts and sales as a result of incurring the expense to bring in the team.

Back at company headquarters in Cambridge, the company has installed an enterprise-resource planning (ERP) system to help managers get a better handle on all costs associated with running the business. With the design and implementation of the new system, managers had to rethink cost allocation and the types of reports they would be able to generate from the detailed information being gathered. Previously, the Mobile Team costs were not allocated, but with the new system's capabilities, top management is interested in allocating these costs in the most appropriate manner and charging sales and regional managers for the services of the Mobile Juice Guy Team.

QUESTIONS

1. The first purpose of cost allocation is to provide information for economic decisions. What types of economic decisions that involve cost allocation might Nantucket Nectars face with respect to the Mobile Juice Guy Team?
2. The second purpose of cost allocation is to motivate managers and other employees. Give an example of how cost allocation can help motivate managers to use the Mobile Juice Guy Team.
3. The third purpose of cost allocation is to justify costs or compute reimbursement. Give an example of this role of cost allocation for the Mobile Juice Guy Team.
4. The fourth purpose of cost allocation is to measure income and assets for reporting to external parties. Give examples of these allocations at Nantucket Nectars.

CHAPTER 15

Allocation of Support Department Costs, Common Costs, and Revenues

LEARNING OBJECTIVES

1. Differentiate the single-rate from the dual-rate cost-allocation method
2. Understand how the uncertainty user managers face is affected by the choice between budgeted and actual cost-allocation rates
3. Allocate support department costs using the direct, step-down, and reciprocal methods
4. Allocate common costs using either the stand-alone or the incremental method
5. Explain the importance of explicit agreement between contracting parties when reimbursement is based on costs incurred
6. Understand how bundling of products gives rise to revenue-allocation issues
7. Allocate the revenues of a bundled package to the individual products in that package

www.prenhall.com/horngren

M*any universities, for example, Harvard, MIT, and Stanford, do research that is funded by the U.S. government. Government support for university research has led to major advances in scientific fields such as particle physics and genetics. The government reimburses universities for the full costs of doing the research. Full costs include indirect costs of the research—such as a share of the costs the university incurs for general administration, libraries, and operations and maintenance. Which indirect costs to allocate and how much of these costs should be allocated to government-sponsored research is often not clear cut. In the early 1990s, the U.S. Department of Defense and Stanford University were locked in a dispute regarding the amount of indirect costs Stanford had claimed on government-sponsored research.*

Our discussion of cost allocation in Chapter 14 emphasized choice of cost pools and allocation bases, and which costs to allocate. This chapter focuses on several other issues that arise in cost allocations:

1. Should different methods of allocation be used for fixed and variable costs?
2. Should budgeted or actual rates be used?
3. Should budgeted or actual quantities be used?

We illustrate these issues in the context of allocating costs from a support department (such as a computer facility) to an operating division (such as manufacturing). We also consider allocation of costs when support departments provide reciprocal support to each other, as well as support to operating divisions. Similar issues arise when allocating costs from one cost pool to another cost pool within a division or from activity-cost pools to products.

We also examine the allocation of common costs—costs of an activity that are shared by two or more users. A final section of this chapter examines revenue-allocation issues that arise when companies sell a single bundle of multiple products or services.

ALLOCATING COSTS OF A SUPPORT DEPARTMENT TO OPERATING DIVISIONS

Single-Rate and Dual-Rate Methods

1 Differentiate the single-rate cost-allocation method
...one rate for allocating costs in a cost pool
from the dual-rate cost-allocation method
...two rates for allocating costs in a cost pool—one for variable costs and one for fixed costs

The **single-rate cost-allocation method** allocates costs in each cost pool to cost objects using the same rate per unit of the single allocation base. No distinction is made between fixed and variable costs in the cost pool. The **dual-rate cost-allocation method** classifies costs in each cost pool into two pools—a variable-cost pool and a fixed-cost pool—with each pool using a different cost-allocation base.

Consider Sand Hill Company's (SHC's) Central Computer Department. This department has only two users: the Microcomputer Division and the Peripheral Equipment Division. The following data apply to the 2004 budget:

Fixed costs of operating the computer facility in the 6,000-hour to 18,750-hour relevant range	$3,000,000
Practical capacity	18,750 hours
Budgeted long-run usage (quantity) in hours:	
Microcomputer Division	8,000 hours
Peripheral Equipment Division	4,000 hours
Total	12,000 hours
Budgeted variable cost per hour in the 6,000-hour to 18,750-hour relevant range	$200 per hour used

The demand for computer services could occur as a result of output unit-level, batch-level or product-sustaining activities in the user divisions.

Chapter 9 (pp. 300–301) described alternative denominator choices—normal capacity utilization and master-budget capacity utilization as measures of capacity demanded, and theoretical capacity and practical capacity as measures of capacity supplied—for allocating manufacturing costs to products. Similar issues arise when allocating costs of a support department to user divisions.

Consider first the allocation of computer facility costs based on the *demand for or usage of* computer services. Under the single-rate method, the costs of the Central Computer Department in 2004 would be allocated at the following budgeted rate:

Budgeted usage	12,000 hours
Budgeted total cost pool: \$3,000,000 + (12,000 hours × \$200/hour)	\$5,400,000
Budgeted total rate per hour: \$5,400,000 ÷ 12,000 hours	\$450 per hour used
Allocation rate for Microcomputer Division	\$450 per hour used
Allocation rate for Peripheral Equipment Division	\$450 per hour used

The budgeted rate of \$450 per hour significantly differs from the \$200 budgeted variable cost per hour. The \$450 rate includes an allocated amount of \$250 per hour (budgeted fixed costs, \$3,000,000, ÷ budgeted usage, 12,000 hours) for the fixed costs of operating the facility. These fixed costs will be incurred whether the computer runs at its practical capacity of 18,750 hours, or, say, at its 12,000-hour budgeted usage.

Using the single-rate method transforms the \$250 fixed cost per hour of the Central Computer Department (and SHC) into a variable cost to users of that facility. Seeing what are fixed costs charged to them as variable costs could lead internal users to purchase computer time outside the company—if the option exists. Consider an external vendor that charges less than \$450 per hour but more than \$200 per hour. A division of SHC that uses this vendor rather than the Central Computer Department will decrease its own division costs—but, the overall costs to SHC will increase! Suppose the Microcomputer Division uses an external vendor that charges \$340 per hour when the Central Computer Department has unused capacity. In the short run, SHC incurs an extra \$140 per hour—\$340 external purchase price per hour minus the savings of \$200 in internal variable cost per hour from not using the in-house facility—because the fixed costs of the Computer Department will remain the same.

When the dual-rate method is used, allocation bases must be chosen for both the variable and fixed cost pools. Assume that budgeted rates are used. The allocation quantities chosen are *budgeted usage for fixed costs* and *actual usage for variable costs.* The total budgeted usage of 12,000 hours comprises 8,000 hours for the Microcomputer Division and 4,000 hours for the Peripheral Equipment Division. The budgeted fixed cost rate is \$250 per hour (\$3,000,000 ÷ 12,000 hours). The costs allocated to the Microcomputer Division in 2004 would be

Fixed costs: \$250 per hour × 8,000 hours	\$2,000,000
Variable costs	\$200 per hour used

The costs allocated to the Peripheral Equipment Division in 2004 would be

Fixed costs: \$250 per hour × 4,000 hours	\$1,000,000
Variable costs	\$ 200 per hour used

Assume now that during 2004, the Microcomputer Division actually uses 9,000 hours, and the Peripheral Equipment Division actually uses 3,000 hours. The costs allocated to these two divisions are computed as:

Under the single-rate method

Microcomputer Division: 9,000 hours × \$450 per hour	\$4,050,000
Peripheral Equipment Division: 3,000 hours × \$450 per hour	\$1,350,000

Under the dual-rate method

Microcomputer Division: \$2,000,000 + (9,000 hours × \$200 per hour)	\$3,800,000
Peripheral Equipment Division: \$1,000,000 + (3,000 hours × \$200 per hour)	\$1,600,000

An alternative method is to allocate fixed costs of the computer facility based on the *supply* of capacity. We illustrate this approach using the 18,750 hours of practical capacity of the Central Computer Department.

Budgeted fixed-cost rate per hour, \$3,000,000 ÷ 18,750 hours	\$160 per hour
Budgeted variable-cost rate per hour	200 per hour
Budgeted total-cost rate per hour	\$360 per hour

The costs are allocated to the two divisions as follows:

Under the single-rate method

Microcomputer Division: 9,000 hours × \$360 per hour	\$3,240,000
Peripheral Equipment Division: 3,000 hours × \$360 per hour	1,080,000
Fixed costs of unused computer capacity: 6,750[a] hours × \$160 per hour	1,080,000

[a]6,750 hours = Practical capacity of 18,750 hours − 9,000 hours used by Microcomputer Division − 3,000 hours used by Peripheral Equipment Division.

Under the dual-rate method

Microcomputer Division: 8,000 × \$160 (fixed costs) + 9,000 × \$200	\$3,080,000
Peripheral Equipment Division: 4,000 × \$160 (fixed costs) + 3,000 × \$200	1,240,000
Fixed costs of unused computer capacity: 6,750[b] hours × \$160 per hour	1,080,000

[b]6,750 hours = Practical capacity of 18,750 hours − 8,000 hours budgeted to be used by Microcomputer Division − 4,000 hours budgeted to be used by Peripheral Equipment Division.

Note that the difference between the single-rate and dual-rate methods arises because the single-rate method allocates fixed costs based on actual usage of computer resources by the user divisions, whereas the dual-rate method allocates fixed costs based on *budgeted* usage. Both the single-rate and the dual-rate methods allocate only the actual fixed-cost resources used or budgeted fixed-cost resources to be used by the Microcomputer and Peripheral Equipment divisions. Unused Computer Department resources are highlighted but not allocated to the divisions. The advantage of using practical capacity is that it focuses management's attention on managing the unused capacity (described in Chapter 9, p. 302). Using practical capacity also avoids burdening the user divisions with the cost of unused capacity of the Computer Department. When costs are allocated on the basis of budgeted or actual usage, all \$3,000,000 of fixed costs, including cost of unused capacity, are allocated to user divisions. If costs are used as a basis for pricing, then charging user divisions for unused capacity could result in the downward demand spiral (see p. 303).

Regardless of the denominator level used to allocate costs to user divisions, there are benefits and costs of both the single-rate and dual-rate methods. One obvious benefit of the single-rate method is the low cost to implement it. The single-rate method avoids the often expensive analysis necessary to classify the individual cost items of a department into fixed and variable categories. However, the single-rate method may lead division managers to make outsourcing decisions that are in their own best interest but are not in the best interest of the organization as a whole.

A big benefit of the dual-rate method is that it signals to division managers how variable costs and fixed costs behave differently. This information would guide division managers to make decisions that benefit the organization as a whole, as well as each division. For example, using a third-party computer provider who charges more than \$200 per hour results in SHC and each division being worse off than using its own Central Computer Department, which has a variable cost of \$200 per hour. That's because, in any event, fixed costs would be charged to each division, regardless of whether a division bought the service inside or outside the company.

2 **Understand how the uncertainty user managers face is affected by the choice between budgeted cost-allocation rates**

...no uncertainty because users know rates at start of period

and actual cost-allocation rates

...uncertainty because users don't know rates until end of period

Budgeted Versus Actual Rates

The decision whether to use budgeted or actual cost rates affects the level of uncertainty user divisions face. When cost allocations are made using budgeted rates, managers of divisions to which costs are allocated face no uncertainty about the rates to be used in that budget period. Users can then determine the amount of the service to request and—if the option exists—whether to use the internal department source or an external vendor. In contrast, when actual rates are used for cost allocation, the user departments will not know the rates to be used until the end of the budget period.

Budgeted rates also help motivate the manager of the supplier (support) department (for example, the Central Computer Department) to improve efficiency. During the budget period, the supplier department, not the user divisions, bears the risk of any unfavorable cost variances. Why? Because the user divisions do not pay for any costs that exceed the budgeted rates. The manager of the supplier department likely would view the budgeted rates negatively, especially when unfavorable cost variances occur due to price increases outside of his or her control. Of course, if top management is able to identify these uncontrollable factors, the manager may be absolved of responsibility for these variances. Using budgeted rates also ensures that user divisions do not pay for any inefficiencies of the supplier department.

If the costs of the supplier department's inefficiency were passed to the user divisions, the supplier department would have no incentive to work efficiently.

Some organizations recognize it may not always be best to impose the risks of variances from budgeted amounts completely on the supplier department (as when costs are allocated using budgeted rates) or completely on the user divisions (as when costs are allocated using actual rates). For example, the supplier department and the user division may agree to share the risk (through an explicit formula) of a large uncontrollable increase in the price of materials used by the support department.

Budgeted Usage, Actual Usage, and Capacity-Level Allocation Bases

Under the dual-rate method, the choice between actual usage and budgeted usage for allocating fixed costs also can affect a manager's behavior. Consider the budget of $3,000,000 fixed costs at the Central Computer Department of SHC. Assume that the actual fixed costs and budgeted fixed costs are equal and that the actual usage by the Microcomputer Division is always equal to the budgeted usage. We now look at the effect on allocating the $3,000,000 in total fixed costs based on actual usage, when actual usage by the Peripheral Equipment Division equals (Case 1), is greater than (Case 2), and is less than (Case 3) the budgeted usage. Recall that the budgeted usage is 8,000 hours for the Microcomputer Division and 4,000 hours for the Peripheral Equipment Division. Exhibit 15-1, column 3, presents the allocation of total fixed costs of $3,000,000 to each division for these three cases.

In Case 1, the fixed-cost allocation equals the expected amount. In Case 2, the fixed-cost allocation is $400,000 less to the Microcomputer Division than expected ($1,600,000 vs. $2,000,000). In Case 3, the fixed-cost allocation is $400,000 more than expected ($2,400,000 vs. $2,000,000). Why this increase of $400,000 to the Microcomputer Division in Case 3, even though its actual usage equals its budgeted usage? Because fixed costs are spread over fewer hours of actual usage. That is, variations in usage in the Peripheral Equipment Division affect the fixed costs allocated to the Microcomputer Division. When actual usage is the allocation base, user divisions will not know how much cost is allocated to them until the end of the budget period.

Question: Under the dual-rate method, why shouldn't fixed costs be allocated according to divisions' actual usage?
Answer: Because (1) fixed costs would be treated as if they were variable costs, so (2) the allocation wouldn't capture the cause and effect of cost incurrence (fixed costs are "caused" by long-run expected usage), and (3) changes in one division's usage would affect another division's allocation (illustrated in Exhibit 15-1).

When budgeted usage is the allocation base, user divisions will know in advance their allocated costs regardless of actual usage (Exhibit 15-1, column 2). This information helps the user divisions with both short-run and long-run planning. Companies commit to infrastructure costs (such as the fixed costs of a support department) on the basis of a long-run planning horizon; budgeted usage measures the long-run demands of the user divisions for support department services.

Allocating fixed costs on the basis of budgeted long-run usage may tempt some managers to underestimate their planned usage. Underestimating will result in their divisions bearing a lower percentage of fixed costs (assuming all other managers do not similarly

EXHIBIT 15-1 Effect of Variations in Actual Usage on Departmental Cost Allocations

	(1) Actual Usage		(2) Budgeted Usage as Allocation Base		(3) Actual Usage as Allocation Base		(4) Practical Capacity-Based Allocations	
Case	Micro. Div.	Perif. Div.	Micro. Div.	Perif. Div.	Micro. Div.	Perif. Div.	Micro. Div.	Perif. Div.
1	8,000 hours	4,000 hours	$2,000,000[a]	$1,000,000[b]	$2,000,000[a]	$1,000,000[b]	$1,280,000[g]	$ 640,000[h]
2	8,000 hours	7,000 hours	$2,000,000[a]	$1,000,000[b]	$1,600,000[c]	$1,400,000[d]	$1,280,000[g]	$1,120,000[i]
3	8,000 hours	2,000 hours	$2,000,000[a]	$1,000,000[b]	$2,400,000[e]	$ 600,000[f]	$1,280,000[g]	$ 320,000[j]

[a] $\frac{8,000}{(8,000 + 4,000)} \times \$3,000,000$ [c] $\frac{8,000}{(8,000 + 7,000)} \times \$3,000,000$ [e] $\frac{8,000}{(8,000 + 2,000)} \times \$3,000,000$ [g] 8,000 × $160 [i] 7,000 × $160

[b] $\frac{4,000}{(8,000 + 4,000)} \times \$3,000,000$ [d] $\frac{7,000}{(8,000 + 7,000)} \times \$3,000,000$ [f] $\frac{2,000}{(8,000 + 2,000)} \times \$3,000,000$ [h] 4,000 × $160 [j] 2,000 × $160

underestimate their usage). To discourage such underestimates, some companies offer rewards and bonuses — the carrot approach — to managers who make accurate forecasts of long-run usage. Other companies impose cost penalties — the stick approach—for underestimating long-run usage. For instance, a higher cost rate is charged after a division exceeds its budgeted usage.

As we have seen, an alternative to using measures of capacity demanded — budgeted usage or actual usage — is to allocate fixed costs of the Central Computer Department on the basis of the practical capacity supplied. The budgeted fixed cost rate is $160 per hour (budgeted fixed costs, $3,000,000, ÷ practical capacity, 18,750 hours). Exhibit 15-1, column 4, shows the fixed costs allocated to the Microcomputer and Peripheral Equipment divisions using this approach.

There are three features of this approach: (1) Each division is only charged for the computer facility services it actually uses; (2) variations in actual usage in one division (the Peripheral Equipment Division) do not affect the costs allocated to the other division (the Microcomputer Division is allocated $1,280,000 in all three cases); and (3) the costs of unused capacity of the computer facility are highlighted and not allocated to user divisions. In all three cases, the total amount of fixed costs allocated to the user divisions is less than the $3,000,000 fixed costs of the Central Computer Department.

The SHC example highlights general issues that arise when allocating costs from one or more departments (divisions) to others. We next examine the special case in which two or more of the departments whose costs are being allocated provide reciprocal support to each other as well as to operating departments.

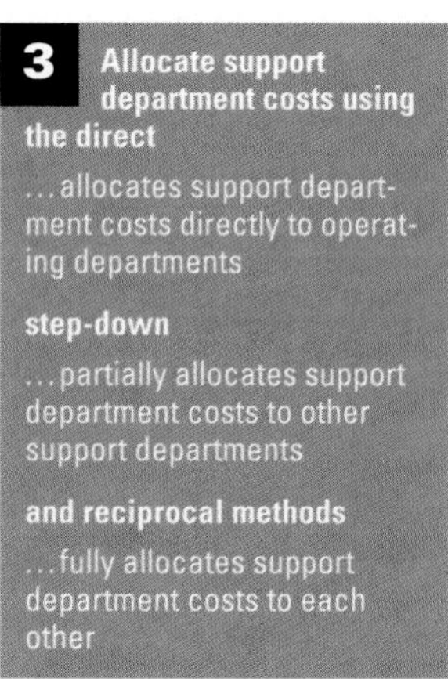

ALLOCATING COSTS OF MULTIPLE SUPPORT DEPARTMENTS

Operating and Support Departments

Companies distinguish operating departments from support departments. An **operating department,** also called a **production department** in manufacturing companies, directly adds value to a product or service. A **support department,** also called a **service department,** provides the services that assist other internal departments (operating departments and other support departments) in the company. Support departments create special cost-allocation problems when they provide reciprocal support to each other as well as support to operating departments. An example of reciprocal support is a Corporate Human Resource (HR) Department providing services to a Corporate Legal Department (such as advice about hiring attorneys) while the Corporate Legal Department provides services to the HR department (such as advice on compliance with labor laws). More-accurate support department cost allocations result in more-accurate product, service, and customer costs.

Reciprocal support department allocations can also arise when there are two or more central support departments and two or more operating divisions. Sand Hill Company in the previous section could have a Central Computer Department and a Central Human Resource Department supporting the two operating divisions—the Microcomputer Division and the Peripheral Equipment Division.

Consider Castleford Engineering, which operates at practical capacity to manufacture engines used in electric power generating plants. Castleford has two support departments and two operating departments in its manufacturing facility:

Support Departments	Operating Departments
Plant (and equipment) maintenance	Machining
Information systems	Assembly

The two support departments at Castleford provide reciprocal support to each other as well as support to the two operating departments. Costs are accumulated in each department for planning and control purposes. Exhibit 15-2 displays the data for our example. We explain the percentages in this exhibit using the Plant Maintenance Department. This support department provides a total of 8,000 hours of support work: 20% (1,600 ÷ 8,000 = 0.20) for the Information Systems Department, 30% (2,400 ÷ 8,000 = 0.30) for the Machining Department, and 50% (4,000 ÷ 8,000 = 0.50) for the Assembly Department.

We now examine three methods of allocating the costs of support departments: *direct, step-down,* and *reciprocal.* To focus on concepts, we use the single-rate method to allocate the costs of each support department. (This chapter's Problem for Self-Study illustrates the dual-rate method for allocating support department costs.)

EXHIBIT 15-2 Data for Allocating Support Department Costs at Castleford Engineering for 2004

	SUPPORT DEPARTMENTS		OPERATING DEPARTMENTS		
	Plant Maintenance	Information Systems	Machining	Assembly	Total
Budgeted manufacturing overhead costs before any interdepartment cost allocations	$600,000	$116,000	$400,000	$200,000	$1,316,000
Support work furnished:					
By Plant Maintenance					
Budgeted labor-hours	—	1,600	2,400	4,000	8,000
Percentage	—	20%	30%	50%	100%
By Information Systems					
Budgeted computer time	200	—	1,600	200	2,000
Percentage	10%	—	80%	10%	100%

Direct Allocation Method

The **direct allocation method,** or simply the **direct method,** is the most widely used method of allocating support department costs. The direct method allocates each support department's costs directly to the operating departments. Exhibit 15-3 illustrates this method using the data in Exhibit 15-2. The base used to allocate Plant Maintenance costs to the operating departments is the budgeted total maintenance labor-hours worked in the operating departments: 2,400 + 4,000 = 6,400 hours. This amount

In terms of computational detail, the direct allocation method is the simplest, the step-down allocation method adds complexity, and the reciprocal allocation method is the most complex.

EXHIBIT 15-3 Direct Method of Allocating Support Department Costs for 2004 at Castleford Engineering

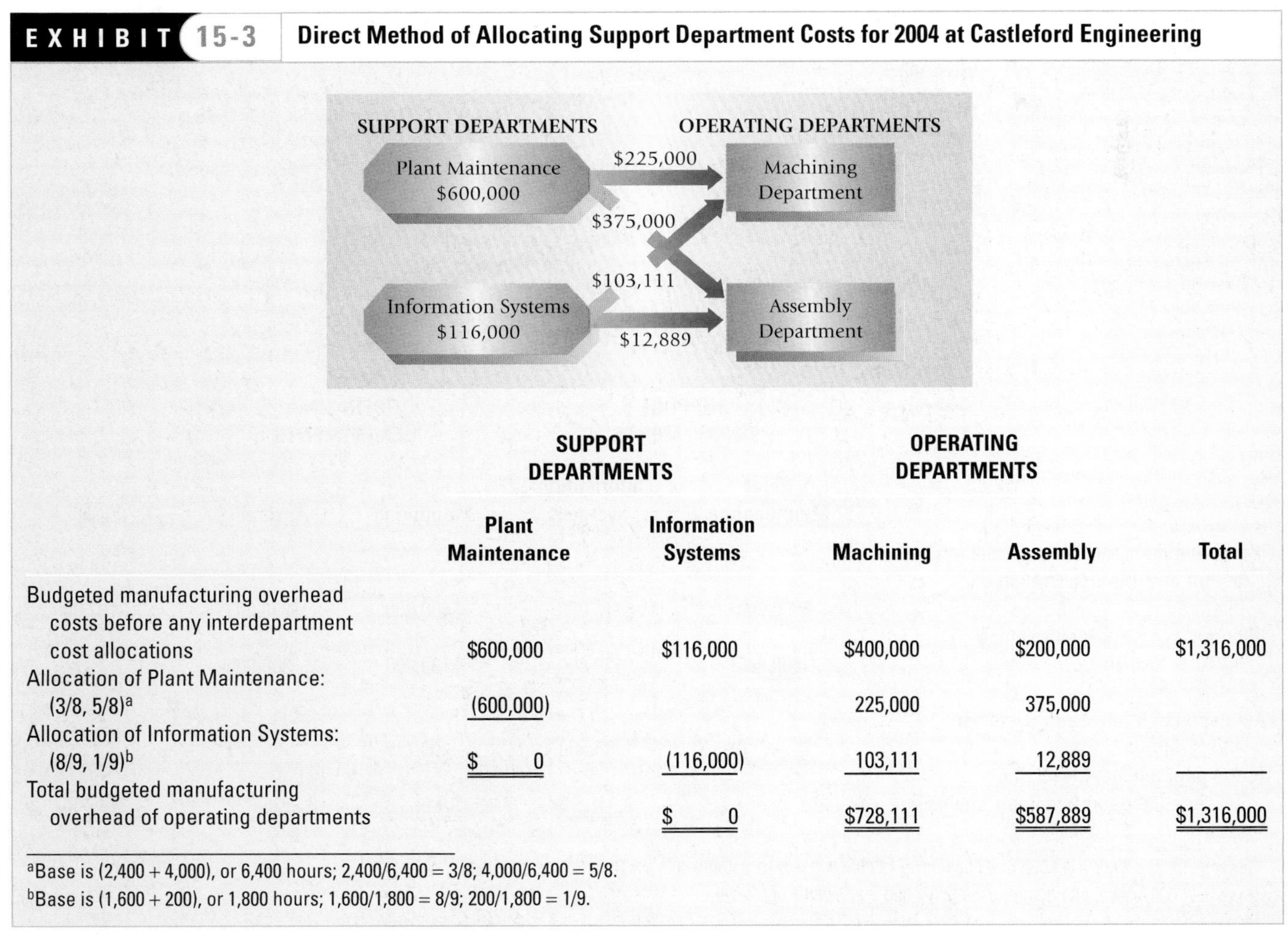

	SUPPORT DEPARTMENTS		OPERATING DEPARTMENTS		
	Plant Maintenance	Information Systems	Machining	Assembly	Total
Budgeted manufacturing overhead costs before any interdepartment cost allocations	$600,000	$116,000	$400,000	$200,000	$1,316,000
Allocation of Plant Maintenance: (3/8, 5/8)[a]	(600,000)		225,000	375,000	
Allocation of Information Systems: (8/9, 1/9)[b]	$ 0	(116,000)	103,111	12,889	
Total budgeted manufacturing overhead of operating departments		$ 0	$728,111	$587,889	$1,316,000

[a]Base is (2,400 + 4,000), or 6,400 hours; 2,400/6,400 = 3/8; 4,000/6,400 = 5/8.
[b]Base is (1,600 + 200), or 1,800 hours; 1,600/1,800 = 8/9; 200/1,800 = 1/9.

excludes the 1,600 hours of support time provided by Plant Maintenance to Information Systems. Similarly, the base used for allocation of Information Systems costs to the operating departments is 1,600 + 200 = 1,800 hours of computer time, which excludes the 200 hours of support time provided by Information Systems to Plant Maintenance.

The benefit of the direct method is simplicity. There is no need to predict the usage of support department services by other support departments. A disadvantage of the direct method is its failure to recognize reciprocal services provided among support departments. We now examine a straightforward approach to partially recognize the services provided among support departments.

Step-Down Allocation Method

Some organizations use the **step-down allocation method,** also called the **sequential allocation method,** which allows for *partial* recognition of the services provided by support departments to other support departments.

Exhibit 15-4 shows the step-down method. The Plant Maintenance cost of $600,000 is allocated first. Exhibit 15-2 shows that Plant Maintenance provides 20% of its services to Information Systems, 30% to Machining, and 50% to Assembly. Therefore, $120,000 is allocated to Information Systems (20% of $600,000), $180,000 to Machining (30% of $600,000), and $300,000 to Assembly (50% of $600,000). The Information Systems costs now total $236,000: budgeted overhead costs of the Information Systems Department before any interdepartmental cost allocations (from Exhibit 15-2), $116,000, plus $120,000 from the allocation of Plant Maintenance costs to the Information Systems Department. The $236,000 is then only allocated between the two operating departments based on the proportion of the Information Systems Department services provided to Machining and Assembly. From Exhibit 15-2, the Information

EXHIBIT 15-4 Step-down Method of Allocating Support Department Costs for 2004 at Castleford Engineering

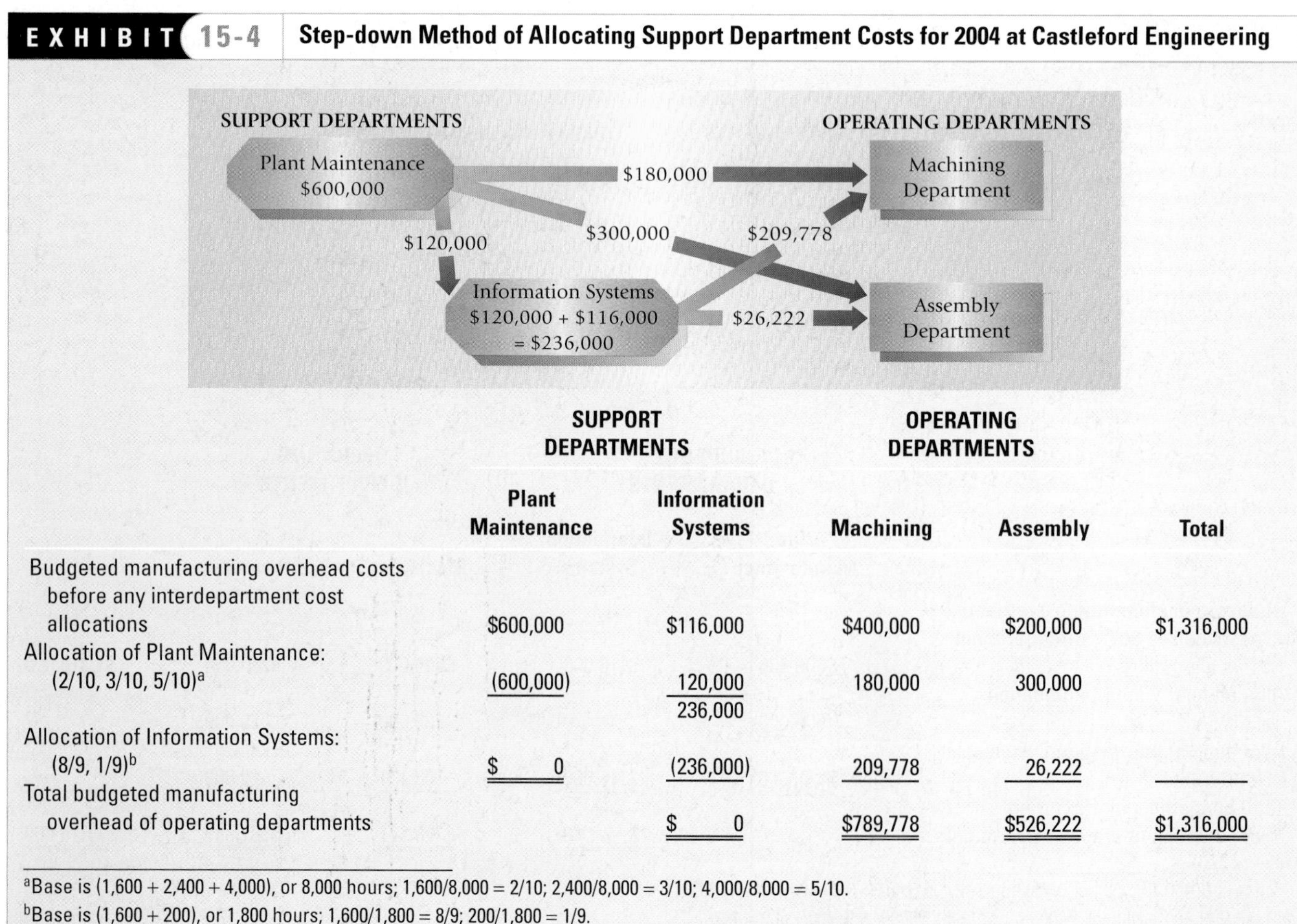

	SUPPORT DEPARTMENTS		OPERATING DEPARTMENTS		
	Plant Maintenance	Information Systems	Machining	Assembly	Total
Budgeted manufacturing overhead costs before any interdepartment cost allocations	$600,000	$116,000	$400,000	$200,000	$1,316,000
Allocation of Plant Maintenance: (2/10, 3/10, 5/10)[a]	(600,000)	120,000	180,000	300,000	
		236,000			
Allocation of Information Systems: (8/9, 1/9)[b]	$ 0	(236,000)	209,778	26,222	
Total budgeted manufacturing overhead of operating departments		$ 0	$789,778	$526,222	$1,316,000

[a]Base is (1,600 + 2,400 + 4,000), or 8,000 hours; 1,600/8,000 = 2/10; 2,400/8,000 = 3/10; 4,000/8,000 = 5/10.
[b]Base is (1,600 + 200), or 1,800 hours; 1,600/1,800 = 8/9; 200/1,800 = 1/9.

Systems Department provides 80% of its services to Machining and 10% to Assembly, so \$209,778 (8/9 × \$236,000) is allocated to Machining and \$26,222 (1/9 × \$236,000) is allocated to Assembly.

Note that this method requires the support departments to be ranked (sequenced) in the order that the step-down allocation is to proceed. In our example, the costs of the Plant Maintenance Department were allocated first to all other departments, including the Information Systems Department. The costs of the Information Systems support department were allocated second but only to the two operating departments. Different sequences will result in different allocations of support department costs to operating departments—for example, if the Information Systems Department costs had been allocated first and the Plant Maintenance Department costs second. A popular step-down sequence begins with the support department that renders the highest percentage of its total services to *other support departments.* The sequence continues with the department that renders the next-highest percentage, and so on, ending with the support department that renders the lowest percentage.[1] In our example, costs of the Plant Maintenance Department were allocated first because it provides 20% of its services to the Information Systems Department, whereas the Information Systems Department provides only 10% of its services to the Plant Maintenance Department (see Exhibit 15-2).

Under the step-down method, once a support department's costs have been allocated, no subsequent support department costs are allocated back to it. Once the Plant Maintenance Department costs are allocated, it receives no further allocation from other (lower-ranked) support departments. The result is that the step-down method does not recognize the total services that support departments provide to each other. The reciprocal method fully recognizes all such services, as you will see next.

Reciprocal Allocation Method

The **reciprocal allocation method** allocates costs by explicitly including the mutual services provided among all support departments. For example, the Plant Maintenance Department maintains all the computer equipment in the Information Systems Department. Similarly, Information Systems provides database support for Plant Maintenance. The reciprocal allocation method fully incorporates interdepartmental relationships into the support department cost allocations.

Exhibit 15-5 presents a simple way to understand the reciprocal method. First, Plant Maintenance (PM) costs are allocated to all other departments, including the Information System (IS) support department (IS, 20%; Machining, 30%; Assembly, 50%). The costs in IS then total \$236,000 (\$116,000 + \$120,000 from the first-round allocation), as in Exhibit 15-4. The \$236,000 is then allocated to all other departments, including the PM support department, that the IS department supports—PM, 10%; Machining, 80%; Assembly, 10% (see Exhibit 15-2). The PM costs that had been brought down to \$0 now again have \$23,600 from the IS Department allocation. These costs are again reallocated to all other departments, including IS, in the same ratio that the PM costs were previously allocated. Now the IS Department costs that had been brought down to \$0 have \$4,720 from the PM Department allocations. These costs are again reallocated in the same ratio that the IS costs were previously allocated. Successive rounds result in smaller and smaller amounts being allocated to and reallocated from the support departments until eventually all costs are allocated to the operating departments.

An alternative way to implement reciprocal allocation is to formulate and solve linear equations. This requires three steps.

Step 1: Express Support Department Costs and Support Department Reciprocal Relationships in the Form of Linear Equations. Let *PM* be the *complete reciprocated costs* of Plant Maintenance and *IS* be the complete reciprocated costs of Information Systems. We then express the data in Exhibit 15-2 as follows:

$$PM = \$600{,}000 + 0.1IS \qquad (1)$$

$$IS = \$116{,}000 + 0.2PM \qquad (2)$$

[1]An alternative approach to selecting the sequence of allocations is to begin with the support department that renders the highest dollar amount of services to other support departments. The sequence ends with the allocation of the costs of the department that renders the lowest dollar amount of services to other support departments.

EXHIBIT 15-5 Reciprocal Method of Allocating Support Department Costs for 2004 at Castleford Engineering Using Repeated Iterations

	SUPPORT DEPARTMENTS		OPERATING DEPARTMENTS		
	Plant Maintenance	Information Systems	Machining	Assembly	Total
Budgeted manufacturing overhead costs before any interdepartmental cost allocations	$600,000	$116,000	$400,000	$200,000	$1,316,000
1st Allocation of Plant Maintenance: (2/10, 3/10, 5/10)[a]	(600,000)	120,000	180,000	300,000	
		236,000			
1st Allocation of Information Systems (1/10, 8/10, 1/10)[b]	23,600	(236,000)	188,800	23,600	
2nd Allocation of Plant Maintenance: (2/10, 3/10, 5/10)[a]	(23,600)	4,720	7,080	11,800	
2nd Allocation of Information Systems: (1/10, 8/10, 1/10)[b]	472	(4,720)	3,776	472	
3rd Allocation of Plant Maintenance: (2/10, 3/10, 5/10)[a]	(472)	94	142	236	
3rd Allocation of Information Systems: (1/10, 8/10, 1/10)[b]	9	(94)	75	10	
4th Allocation of Plant Maintenance: (2/10, 3/10, 5/10)[a]	(9)	2	2	5	
4th Allocation of Information Systems: (1/10, 8/10, 1/10)[b]	0	(2)	2	0	
Total budgeted manufacturing overhead of operating departments	$ 0	$ 0	$779,877	$536,123	$1,316,000

Total support department amounts allocated and reallocated (the numbers in parentheses in first two columns)
Plant Maintenance: $600,000 + $23,600 + $472 + $9 = $624,081
Information Systems: $236,000 + $4,720 + $94 + $2 = $240,816

[a]Base is (1,600 + 2,400 + 4,000) or 8,000 hours; 1,600 ÷ 8,000 = 2/10; 2,400 ÷ 8,000 = 3/10; 4,000 ÷ 8,000 = 5/10.
[b]Base is (200 + 1,600 + 200) or 2,000 hours; 200 ÷ 2,000 = 1/10; 1,600 ÷ 2,000 = 8/10; 200 ÷ 2,000 = 1/10.

The $0.1IS$ term in equation (1) is the percentage of the Information Systems services *used by* Plant Maintenance. The $0.2PM$ term in equation (2) is the percentage of the Plant Maintenance services *used by* Information Systems. By **complete reciprocated costs** in equations (1) and (2), we mean the support department's own costs plus any interdepartmental cost allocations. This complete reciprocated costs figure is sometimes called the **artificial costs** of the support department.

Step 2: Solve the Set of Linear Equations to Obtain the Complete Reciprocated Costs of Each Support Department. Substituting equation (2) into (1):

$$PM = \$600{,}000 + [0.1(\$116{,}000 + 0.2PM)]$$
$$PM = \$600{,}000 + \$11{,}600 + 0.02PM$$
$$0.98PM = \$611{,}600$$
$$PM = \$624{,}082$$

Substituting into equation (2):

$$IS = \$116{,}000 + 0.2(\$624{,}082)$$
$$IS = \$116{,}000 + \$124{,}816 = \$240{,}816$$

When there are more than two support departments with reciprocal relationships, computer software such as Excel can be used to calculate the complete reciprocated costs of each support department. The complete reciprocated cost figures also appear at the bottom of Exhibit 15-5 as the total amounts allocated and reallocated (subject to minor rounding differences).

Step 3: Allocate the Complete Reciprocated Costs of Each Support Department to All Other Departments (Both Support Departments and Operating Departments) on the Basis of the Usage Percentages (Based on Total Units of Service

Provided to All Departments). Consider the Information Systems Department. The complete reciprocated costs of $240,816 are allocated as follows:

To Plant Maintenance (1/10) × $240,816	=	$ 24,082
To Machining (8/10) × $240,816	=	192,652
To Assembly (1/10) × $240,816	=	24,082
Total		$240,816

Exhibit 15-6 presents summary data pertaining to the reciprocal method.

One source of confusion to some managers using the reciprocal cost-allocation method is why the $864,898 complete reciprocated costs of the support departments exceeds the budgeted amount of $716,000.

Support Department	Complete Reciprocated Costs	Budgeted Costs	Difference
Plant Maintenance	$624,082	$600,000	$ 24,082
Information Systems	240,816	116,000	124,816
Total	$864,898	$716,000	$148,898

Differences among the three methods' allocations increase (1) as the magnitude of the reciprocal services increases and (2) as the differences across operating departments' usage of each support department's services increase.

Each support department's complete reciprocated cost is greater than the budgeted amount to take into account that the allocation of support costs will be to all departments using its services and not just to operating departments. It is this step that ensures that the reciprocal method fully recognizes all the interrelationships among support departments, as well as relationships between support and operating departments. The difference between the

EXHIBIT 15-6 Reciprocal Method of Allocating Support Department Costs for 2004 at Castleford Engineering Using Linear Equations

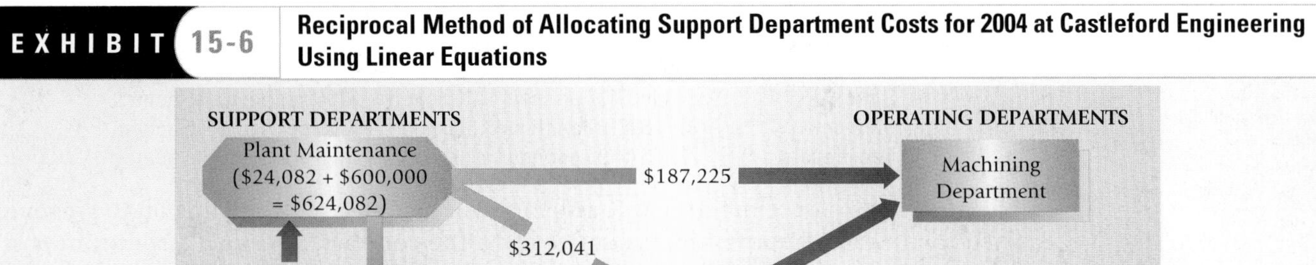

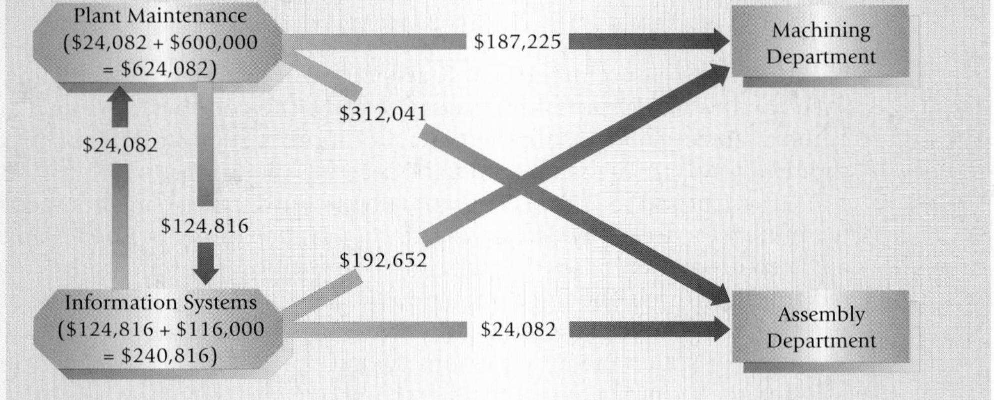

	SUPPORT DEPARTMENTS		OPERATING DEPARTMENTS		
	Plant Maintenance	Information Systems	Machining	Assembly	Total
Budgeted manufacturing overhead costs before any interdepartment cost allocations	$600,000	$116,000	$400,000	$200,000	$1,316,000
Allocation of Plant Maintenance: (2/10, 3/10, 5/10)[a]	(624,082)	124,816	187,225	312,041	
Allocation of Information Systems: (1/10, 8/10, 1/10)[b]	24,082	(240,816)	192,652	24,082	
Total budgeted manufacturing overhead of operating departments	$ 0	$ 0	$779,877	$536,123	$1,316,000

[a]Base is (1,600 + 2,400 + 4,000), or 8,000 hours; 1,600 ÷ 8,000 = 2/10; 2,400 ÷ 8,000 = 3/10; 4,000 ÷ 8,000 = 5/10.
[b]Base is (200 + 1,600 + 200), or 2,000 hours; 200 ÷ 2,000 = 1/10; 1,600 ÷ 2,000 = 8/10; 200 ÷ 2,000 = 1/10.

complete reciprocated costs and the budgeted costs for each support department is the total costs that are allocated among support departments. The total costs allocated to the operating departments under the reciprocal allocation method are still only $716,000.

Overview of Methods

Assume that Castleford reallocates the total budgeted overhead costs of each operating department in Exhibits 15-3 through 15-6 to individual products on the basis of budgeted machine-hours for the Machining Department (4,000 hours) and budgeted labor-hours for the Assembly Department (3,000 hours). The budgeted overhead allocation rates (to the nearest dollar) for each support department by allocation method are

Support Department Cost-Allocation Method	Total Budgeted Overhead Costs After Allocation of All Support Department Costs		Budgeted Overhead Rate per Hour for Product-Costing Purposes	
	Machining	Assembly	Machining (4,000 machine-hours)	Assembly (3,000 labor-hours)
Direct	$728,111	$587,889	$182	$196
Step-down	789,778	526,222	197	175
Reciprocal	779,877	536,123	195	179

These differences in budgeted overhead rates with alternative support department cost-allocation methods can, for example, affect the amount of costs Castleford is reimbursed for engines it manufactures under cost-reimbursement contracts. Consider a cost-reimbursement contract that uses 100 machine-hours in the Machining Department and 15 labor-hours in the Assembly Department. The support department costs allocated to this contract under the three methods would be

Direct:	$21,140 ($182 per hour × 100 hours + $196 per hour × 15 hours)
Step-down:	22,325 ($197 per hour × 100 hours + $175 per hour × 15 hours)
Reciprocal:	22,185 ($195 per hour × 100 hours + $179 per hour × 15 hours)

The amount of cost reimbursed to Castleford will be different depending on the method used to allocate support department costs to the contract. To avoid disputes in cost-reimbursement contracts that require allocation of support department costs, managers should always clarify the method to be used for allocation.

The reciprocal method is conceptually the most precise method because it considers the mutual services provided among all support departments. The advantage of the direct and step-down methods is that they are simple to compute and understand relative to the reciprocal method. The direct method is widely used (see Surveys of Company Practice, p. 533). However, as computing power to do repeated iterations (as in Exhibit 15-5) or to solve sets of simultaneous equations (as on pp. 529 – 530) increases, more companies will find the reciprocal method easier to implement.

Another advantage of the reciprocal method is that it highlights the complete reciprocated costs of support departments and how these costs differ from the budgeted or actual costs of the departments. Knowing the complete reciprocated costs of a support department is a key input for decisions about whether to outsource all the services that the support department provides.

Suppose all of Castleford's support department costs are variable over the period of a possible outsourcing contract. Consider a third party's bid to provide, say, all the information systems services currently provided by Castleford's Information Systems Department. Do not compare the bid to the $116,000 costs reported for the Information Systems Department. The complete reciprocated costs of the Information Systems Department, which include the services the Plant Maintenance Department provides the Information Systems Department, are $240,816 to deliver 2,000 hours of computer time to all other departments at Castleford. The complete reciprocated costs for computer time are $120,408 per hour ($240,816 ÷ 2,000 hours). Other things being equal, a third party's bid to provide the same information services as Castleford's internal department at less than $240,816, or $120.408 per hour (even if much greater than $116,000) would improve Castleford's operating income. To see this point, note that the relevant savings from shutting down the Information Systems Department are

SURVEYS OF COMPANY PRACTICE

Allocation of Support Department Costs

Use of the direct method of allocating support department costs is widespread. Systematic surveys of support department cost-allocation methods are available for Australia, Japan, and the United Kingdom.

Support Department Cost-Allocation Method	Australia	Japan	United Kingdom
1. Direct method	43%	58%	64%
2. Step-down method	3	27	6
3. Reciprocal method	5	10	14
4. Other method	15	1	8
5. Not allocated	34	4	8
	100%	100%	100%

Source: From Blayney and Yokoyama, "Comparative Analysis." Full citation is in Appendix A at the end of the book.

$116,000 of Information Systems Department costs *plus* $124,816 of Plant Maintenance Department costs. By closing down the Information Systems Department, Castleford will no longer incur the 20% of Plant Maintenance Department costs (equal to $124,816) that were incurred to support the Information Systems Department. Hence the total relevant-cost savings are $240,816 ($116,000 + $124,816).[2] Neither the direct nor the step-down allocation methods can provide this relevant information for outsourcing decisions.

We now consider common costs, another special class of costs for which cost accountants have developed specific allocation methods.

ALLOCATING COMMON COSTS

4 **Allocate common costs using either the stand-alone method**

... uses cost information of each user as a separate entity to allocate common costs in a more balanced way

or the incremental method

... allocates common costs primarily to one user, as if it were the only user, and remaining costs to other users

A **common cost** is a cost of operating a facility, activity, or like cost object that is shared by two or more users. Consider Jason Stevens, a graduating senior in Seattle who has been invited to a job interview with an employer in Albany. The round-trip Seattle–Albany airfare costs $1,200. A week later, Stevens is also invited to an interview with an employer in Chicago. The Seattle–Chicago round-trip airfare costs $800. Stevens decides to combine the two recruiting trips into a Seattle–Albany– Chicago–Seattle trip that will cost $1,500 in airfare. The $1,500 is a common cost that benefits both prospective employers. Two methods of allocating this common cost between the two prospective employers are the stand-alone method and the incremental method.

Stand-Alone Cost-Allocation Method

The **stand-alone cost-allocation method** uses information pertaining to each user of a cost object as a separate entity to determine the cost-allocation weights. For the common-cost airfare of $1,500, information about the separate (stand-alone) round-trip airfares ($1,200 and $800) is used to determine the allocation weights:

$$\text{Albany employer:} \quad \frac{\$1,200}{\$1,200 + \$800} \times \$1,500 = 0.60 \times \$1,500 = \$900$$

$$\text{Chicago employer:} \quad \frac{\$800}{\$800 + \$1,200} \times \$1,500 = 0.40 \times \$1,500 = \$600$$

[2]Technical issues when using the reciprocal method in outsourcing decisions are discussed in R. S. Kaplan and A. A. Atkinson, *Advanced Management Accounting*, 3rd ed. (Upper Saddle River, NJ: Prentice Hall, 1998, pp. 73–81).

Advocates of this method often emphasize the fairness or equity criterion described in Exhibit 14-2 (p. 484). The method is viewed as fair because each employer bears a proportionate share of total costs in relation to the individual stand-alone costs.

Incremental Cost-Allocation Method

The incremental cost-allocation method creates the incentive for users of the cost object to not want to be the first-ranked user. That's because the first-ranked user has more costs allocated to it.

The **incremental cost-allocation method** ranks the individual users of a cost object in the order of users most responsible for the common costs and then uses this ranking to allocate costs among those users. The first-ranked user of the cost object is the *primary user* and is allocated costs up to the costs of the primary user as a stand-alone user. The second-ranked user is the *first incremental user* and is allocated the additional cost that arises from two users instead of only the primary user. The third-ranked user is the *second incremental user* and is allocated the additional cost that arises from three users instead of two users, and so on.

To see how this method works, consider again Jason Stevens and his $1,500 airfare cost. Assume the Albany employer is viewed as the primary party. Stevens' rationale is that he had already committed to go to Albany before accepting the invitation to interview in Chicago. The cost allocations would be

Party	Costs Allocated	Costs Remaining to be Allocated to Other Parties
Albany (primary)	$1,200	$300 ($1,500 – $1,200)
Chicago (incremental)	300	0

The Albany employer is allocated the full Seattle–Albany airfare. The unallocated part of the total airfare is then allocated to the Chicago employer. If the Chicago employer had been chosen as the primary party, the cost allocations would have been Chicago $800 (the stand-alone round-trip Seattle–Chicago airfare) and Albany $700 ($1,500 – $800). When there are more than two parties, this method requires them to be ranked from first to last (say, based on the date on which each employer invited the candidate to interview).

Under the incremental method, the primary party typically receives the highest allocation of the common costs. No surprise that most users in common-cost situations propose themselves as an incremental party! In some cases, the incremental users are newly formed companies or a company's new subunits, such as a new product line or a new sales territory. Chances for their short-run survival may be enhanced if they bear a low allocation of the common costs.

When both parties are viewed as primary parties, there is no incremental party. If there is a large common cost that has to be incurred, using the incremental method can cause the parties to dispute who is the incremental party! One approach in such situations is to use the stand-alone cost-allocation method.[3]

A caution regarding Stevens' cost-allocation options: His chosen method must be acceptable to each prospective employer. Some prospective employers may have guidelines for recruiting costs. For example, the Albany employer may have a policy that the maximum reimbursable airfare is a seven-day advance booking price in economy class. If this amount is less than the amount that Stevens would receive under, say, the stand-alone method, then the employer's upper-limit guideline would govern how much could be allocated to that employer. Stevens should obtain approval before he purchases his ticket about what cost-allocation method(s) each prospective employer views as acceptable.

Disputes over how to allocate common costs are often encountered. The next section discusses the role of cost data in various types of contracts. This is also an area in which disputes about cost allocation frequently arise.

[3]Another approach is to use the Shapley value that considers each party as first the primary party and then the incremental party. From the calculations shown on this page, the Albany employer is allocated $1,200 as the primary party and $700 as the incremental party for an average of $950 [($1,200 + $700) ÷ 2]. The Chicago employer is allocated $800 as the primary party and $300 as the incremental party for an average of $550 [($800 + 300) ÷ 2]. The Shapley value approach would allocate $950 to the Albany employer and $550 to the Chicago employer. For further discussion, see J. Demski, "Cost Allocation Games," in S. Moriarity (Ed.), *Joint Cost Allocations* (University of Oklahoma Center for Economic and Management Research, 1981).

COST ALLOCATIONS AND CONTRACTS

5 Explain the importance of explicit agreement between contracting parties when reimbursement is based on costs incurred

...to avoid disputes on allowable cost items and how indirect costs should be allocated

Many commercial contracts include clauses based on cost accounting information. For example:

1. A contract between the Department of Defense and a company designing and assembling a new fighter plane specifies that the price paid for the plane is to be based on the contractor's costs plus a fixed fee.
2. A research contract between a university and a government agency specifies that the university is to be reimbursed its direct costs plus an overhead rate that is a percentage of direct costs.
3. A contract between an energy-consulting firm and a hospital specifies that the consulting firm is to receive a fixed fee plus a share of the energy-cost savings arising from implementing the consulting firm's recommendations.

Contract disputes arise often, usually with respect to cost allocation. The areas of dispute between the contracting parties can be reduced by making the "rules of the game" explicit and in writing at the time the contract is signed. Such "rules of the game" include the definition of cost items allowed; the definitions of terms used, such as what constitutes direct labor; the permissible cost-allocation bases; and how differences between budgeted and actual costs are to be accounted for.

Contracting with the U.S. Government

The U.S. government reimburses most contractors in either of two main ways:

1. The *contractor is paid a set price without analysis of actual contract cost data*. This approach is used, for example, when there is competitive bidding, when there is adequate price competition, or when there is an established catalog with prices quoted for items sold in substantial quantities to the general public.
2. The *contractor is paid after analysis of actual contract cost data*. In some cases, the contract will explicitly state that reimbursement is based on actual allowable costs plus a fixed fee.[4] This arrangement is called a *cost-plus contract*.

Hughes Aircraft builds standard planes for commercial customers and specialized fighter planes for the U.S. armed services. Hughes has fixed-price contracts with commercial customers and cost-plus contracts with the U.S. armed services. If Hughes could shift indirect costs away from (fixed-price) commercial customers and to the cost-plus contracts, Hughes would increase its revenues. Such situations are one reason why the U.S. government employs cost accountants—to check the accounting records of defense contractors.

All contracts with U.S. government agencies must comply with cost accounting standards issued by the **Cost Accounting Standards Board (CASB).** For government contracts, the CASB has the exclusive authority to make, put into effect, amend, and rescind cost accounting standards and interpretations. The standards are designed to achieve *uniformity and consistency* in regard to measurement, assignment, and allocation of costs to contracts within the United States.[5]

In government contracting, there is a complex interplay of political considerations and accounting principles. Terms such as "fairness" and "equity," as well as cause and effect and benefits received, are often used in government contracts.

Fairness of Pricing

In many defense contracts involving new weapons and equipment, the uncertainty is high about what it would cost to produce the weapon or equipment. Such contracts are rarely subject to competitive bidding. That's because no contractor is willing to assume all the

[4]The Federal Acquisition Regulation (FAR) includes the following definition of "allocability" (in FAR 31.201-4):

> A cost [is] allocable if it is assignable or chargeable to one or more cost objectives in accordance with the relative benefits received or other equitable relationship. Subject to the foregoing, a cost is allocable to a government contract if it:
> - Is incurred specifically for the contract;
> - Benefits both the contract and other work,... and can be distributed to them in reasonable proportion to the benefits received; or
> - Is necessary to the overall operation of the business, although a direct relationship to any particular cost objective cannot be shown.

F. Alston, M. Worthington, and L. Goldsman, *Contracting with the Federal Government*, 3rd ed. (New York: Wiley, 1993, p. 136). This book contains extensive discussion of the use of cost data in government contracting.

[5]Details on the Cost Accounting Standards Board are available from its Web site: www.fedmarket.com. The CASB is part of the Office of Federal Procurement Policy, U.S. Office of Management and Budget.

risk of receiving a fixed price for the contract and subsequently incurring high costs to fulfill the contract. Hence, setting a market-based fixed price for the contract fails to attract contractors, or the contract price is too high from the government's standpoint. Therefore, the government assumes a major share of the risk of the potentially high costs of completing the contract. It negotiates contracts by using *costs plus a fixed fee* as a substitute for selling prices as ordinarily set by suppliers in the marketplace. In costs-plus-fixed-fee contracts, which often involve billions of dollars, a cost allocation may be difficult to defend on the basis of any cause-and-effect reasoning. Nonetheless, the contracting parties may still view it as a "reasonable" or "fair" means to help establish a contract amount.

Cost-based prices are one way of setting prices for products when no market price exists. One problem with a cost-plus contract is that the producer has less incentive to control costs because cost increases can be passed on to the buyer. Cost-reimbursement contracts must be specific and, if possible, should include incentives to prevent such abuses.

Some costs become "allowable"; others are "unallowable." An **allowable cost** is a cost that the contract parties agree to include in the costs to be reimbursed. Some contracts specify how allowable costs are to be determined. For example, only economy-class airfares are allowable in many U.S. government contracts. Other contracts identify cost categories that are unallowable. For example, the costs of lobbying activities and alcoholic

CONCEPTS IN ACTION

Contract Disputes over Reimbursable Costs for U.S. Government Agencies

Allegations about a contractor overcharging a government agency invariably make interesting copy for the media. The following four examples are from cases in which contractors "settled with the government without admitting liability with respect to the charges." The names of the companies are disguised. These examples illustrate several types of cost disputes that arise in practice:

- XYZ, Inc., agreed to pay $4.5 million to settle allegations that they illegally overcharged the Navy for labor costs on contracts. It was alleged that managers at XYZ directed their employees to overcharge labor time to a number of military contracts even though management knew the employees did not devote as much time to the contract as was charged to the government. Note that when labor-hours are used to allocate overhead costs to a contract, overstating labor-hours will result in both direct costs and indirect costs being overcharged. This form of overcharging is sometimes referred to as *double-bilking.*

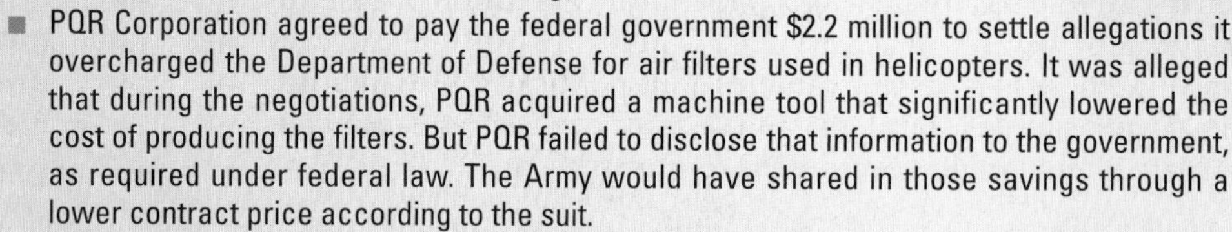

- PQR Corporation agreed to pay the federal government $2.2 million to settle allegations it overcharged the Department of Defense for air filters used in helicopters. It was alleged that during the negotiations, PQR acquired a machine tool that significantly lowered the cost of producing the filters. But PQR failed to disclose that information to the government, as required under federal law. The Army would have shared in those savings through a lower contract price according to the suit.
- STV paid $228,705 in damages to the U.S. government to settle a lawsuit alleging overcharging the Army for tank ammunition. The allegations centered on the prices STV told the government it would pay for two components ($39.89 and $40.95). It was alleged that STV actually paid lower prices ($39.00 and $39.35) as part of a multi-year contract with its suppliers.
- MNP Corporation agreed to pay $175 million to the federal government to settle charges that it overcharged the Department of Health and Human Services for Medicare reimbursements. MNP provided nursing home care for both Medicare and non-Medicare patients. The government reimbursed MNP on the basis of the amount of time that MNP's nurses spent with Medicare patients. The government claimed that MNP routinely created time sheets that allocated more nursing time and costs to Medicare than were actually spent on Medicare patients. According to the government, MNP had an incentive to do this because Medicare reimbursement rates were higher than the rates paid by the other patients the company served. The $175 million settlement equaled MNP's earnings over the previous five years.

Source: Articles in *Defense Daily* and *Defense Weekly* and press releases from the Department of Justice and U.S. Department of Health and Human Services.

beverages are not allowable costs in U.S. government contracts. However, what costs are allowable are not always clear cut. Contract disputes and allegations about overcharging the government arise from time to time (see Concepts in Action, p. 536).

REVENUE ALLOCATION AND BUNDLED PRODUCTS

Allocation issues can also arise when revenues from multiple products (for example, different software programs) are bundled together and sold at a single price. The methods for revenue allocation parallel those described for common-cost allocations.

Revenues are inflows of assets (almost always cash or accounts receivable) received for products or services provided to customers. Analogous to cost allocation, **revenue allocation** occurs when revenues are related to a particular *revenue object* but cannot be traced to it in an economically feasible (cost-effective) way. A **revenue object** is anything for which a separate measurement of revenue is desired. Examples of revenue objects include products, customers, and divisions. We illustrate revenue-allocation issues for Supersoft, which develops, sells, and supports three software packages:

> **6** **Understand how bundling of products**
> ...two or more products sold for a single price
> **gives rise to revenue-allocation issues**
> ...allocating revenues to each product in the bundle to evaluate managers of individual products

1. WordMaster, a word-processing program—current version is WordMaster 5.0 released 36 months ago (January 2001).
2. SpreadMaster, a spreadsheet program—current version is SpreadMaster 3.0, released 18 months ago (July 2002).
3. FinanceMaster, a budgeting and cash management program—current version is FinanceMaster 1.0, released 6 months ago (July 2003) with a lot of favorable media attention.

When a manager is deciding whether to keep or discontinue a product line, the product line is both the revenue object and the cost object.

Supersoft sells these three products individually and as bundled products.

A **bundled product** is a package of two or more products (or services) that is sold for a single price, but individual components of the bundle also may be sold as separate items at their own "stand-alone" prices. The price of a bundled product is typically less than the sum of the prices of the individual products sold separately. For example, banks often provide individual customers with a bundle of services from different departments (checking, safety deposit box, and investment advisory) for a single fee. A resort hotel may offer, for a single amount per customer, a weekend package that includes services from its Lodging (the room), Food (the restaurant), and Recreational (golf and tennis) departments. When department managers have revenue or profit responsibilities for individual products, the bundled revenue must be allocated among the individual products in the bundle.[6]

Supersoft allocates revenues from its bundled product sales (called "suite sales") to individual products. Individual product-profitability is used to compensate software engineers, outside developers, and product managers responsible for developing and managing each product.

REVENUE-ALLOCATION METHODS

> **7** **Allocate revenues of a bundled package to the individual products in that package**
> ...using stand-alone method, incremental method, or management judgment

How should Supersoft allocate suite revenues to individual products? Here is information pertaining to the three "stand-alone" and "suite" selling prices in 2003:

	Selling Price
Stand-alone	
WordMaster	$125
SpreadMaster	150
FinanceMaster	225
Suite	
Word + Spread	$220
Word + Finance	280
Word + Spread + Finance	380

[6]Revenue-allocation issues also arise in external reporting. Statement of Position 97-2 (Software Revenue Recognition) states that with bundled products, revenue allocation "based on vendor-specific objective evidence of fair value" is required. The "price charged when the element is sold separately" is said to be "objective evidence of fair value." See *Journal of Accountancy* (January 1998, p. 106).

The manufacturing cost per unit of each software product is WordMaster, \$18; SpreadMaster, \$20; and FinanceMaster, \$25.

Just as we saw in the section on common-cost allocations, the two main revenue-allocation methods are the stand-alone method and the incremental method.

Conceptually, it is preferable to allocate common revenues based on unit revenues or stand-alone revenues because they best reflect customers' willingness to pay for the different products. If the products are never sold separately, however, individual selling prices and revenues are unavailable, so revenues are allocated based on unit costs (which should be available in the company's accounting records) or on number of units.

Using unit costs will make the different products appear equally profitable in terms of gross margin %. In the Supersoft example:

	Word	Finance
Revenues	\$118	\$162
Mfg. cost	18	25
Gross margin	\$100	\$137
Gross margin%	84.7%	84.6%

Using physical units is most appropriate when the values of the individual products in the bundle are approximately equal. For example, this method would be inappropriate for a bundle that includes a washing machine and a box of detergent. It would be nonsense to allocate half of the revenue to the box of detergent.

Stand-Alone Revenue-Allocation Method

The **stand-alone revenue-allocation method** uses product-specific information on the products in the bundle as weights for allocating the bundled revenues to the individual products. The term *stand-alone* refers to the product as a separate (nonsuite) item. Consider the Word + Finance suite, which sells for \$280. Four types of weights for the stand-alone method are as follows:

1. *Selling prices.* Using the individual selling prices of \$125 for WordMaster and \$225 for FinanceMaster, the weights for allocating the \$280 costs between the products are

$$\text{WordMaster:}\quad \frac{\$125}{\$125+\$225}\times\$280 = 0.357\times\$280 = \$100$$

$$\text{FinanceMaster:}\quad \frac{\$225}{\$125+\$225}\times\$280 = 0.643\times\$280 = \$180$$

2. *Unit costs.* This method uses the costs of the individual products (in this case, manufacturing cost per unit) to determine the weights for the revenue allocations.

$$\text{WordMaster:}\quad \frac{\$18}{\$18+\$25}\times\$280 = 0.419\times\$280 = \$117$$

$$\text{FinanceMaster:}\quad \frac{\$25}{\$18+\$25}\times\$280 = 0.581\times\$280 = \$163$$

3. *Physical units.* This method gives each product unit in the suite the same weight when allocating suite revenue to individual products. Thus, with two products in the Word + Finance suite, each product is allocated 50% of the suite revenues.

$$\text{WordMaster:}\quad \frac{1}{1+1}\times\$280 = 0.50\times\$280 = \$140$$

$$\text{FinanceMaster:}\quad \frac{1}{1+1}\times\$280 = 0.50\times\$280 = \$140$$

4. *Stand-alone product revenues.* Stand-alone product revenues will capture the quantity of each product sold as well as their selling prices. Assume the stand-alone revenues in 2003 are WordMaster, \$27 milllion; SpreadMaster, \$15 million; and FinanceMaster, \$9 million. The weights for the Word + Finance suite would be

$$\text{WordMaster:}\quad \frac{\$27\text{ million}}{\$27\text{ million}+\$9\text{ million}}\times\$280 = 0.75\times\$280 = \$210$$

$$\text{FinanceMaster:}\quad \frac{\$9\text{ million}}{\$27\text{ million}+\$9\text{ million}}\times\$280 = 0.25\times\$280 = \$70$$

The lower revenue allocation to FinanceMaster is, in part, due to it only being released partway through 2003 (July 2003).

These four approaches to determining weights for the stand-alone method result in very different revenue allocations to the individual products:

Revenue-Allocation Weights	WordMaster	FinanceMaster
Selling prices	\$100	\$180
Unit costs	117	163
Physical units	140	140
Stand-alone product revenues	210	70

Which method is preferred? The selling price and stand-alone product revenue weights explicitly consider the price customers are willing to pay for the individual products. Weighting approaches that use revenue information better capture "benefits received" by customers than unit costs or physical units. Allocating on the basis of stand-alone product revenues also has the advantage of giving more weight to the product that generates more revenues and that probably drives the sales of the bundled product. The physical units revenue-allocation method is used when any of the other methods cannot be used (such as when selling prices are unstable or unit costs are difficult to calculate for individual products).

Incremental Revenue-Allocation Method

The **incremental revenue-allocation method** ranks individual products in a bundle according to criteria determined by management—such as the product in the bundle with the most sales—and then uses this ranking to allocate bundled revenues to individual products. The first-ranked product is the *primary product* in the bundle. The second-ranked product is the *first incremental product*, the third-ranked product is the *second incremental product*, and so on.

Under the incremental revenue-allocation method, all users of the revenue object want to be the first-ranked user, because the first-ranked user will be allocated a larger portion of the revenues.

How do companies decide on product ranking under the incremental revenue-allocation method? One way is to survey customers on how important each of the individual products was in their decisions to purchase the bundled products. Another way is to use data on recent stand-alone sales performance of the individual products in the bundle. A third way is for top managers to use their knowledge or intuition to decide the rankings.

Consider again the Word + Finance suite of Supersoft. Assume FinanceMaster is designated as the primary product. If the suite selling price exceeds the stand-alone price of the primary product, the primary product is allocated 100% of its stand-alone revenue. Because the suite price of $280 exceeds the stand-alone price of $225 for FinanceMaster, FinanceMaster is allocated revenues of $225, with the remaining revenue of $55 ($280 – $225) allocated to WordMaster:

Product	Revenue Allocated	Revenue Remaining to Be Allocated to Other Products
FinanceMaster	$225	$55 ($280 – $225)
WordMaster	55	0
Total revenue allocated	$280	

If the suite price is less than or equal to the stand-alone price of the primary product, the primary product is allocated 100% of the suite revenue. All other products in the suite receive no allocation of revenue.

When there are more than two products in the suite, the suite revenue is allocated sequentially. Assume FinanceMaster is the primary product in Supersoft's three-product suite (Finance + Spread + Word). SpreadMaster is the first incremental product, and WordMaster is the second incremental product. This suite sells for $380. The allocation of the $380 suite revenues proceeds as follows:

Product	Revenue Allocated	Revenue Remaining to Be Allocated to Other Products
FinanceMaster	$225	$155 ($380 – $225)
SpreadMaster	150	5 ($155 – $150)
WordMaster	5	0 ($5 – $5)
Total revenue allocated	$380	

Now suppose FinanceMaster is the primary product, WordMaster is the first incremental product, and SpreadMaster is the second incremental product.

Product	Revenue Allocated	Revenue Remaining to Be Allocated to Other Products
FinanceMaster	$225	$155 ($380 – $225)
WordMaster	125	30 ($155 – $125)
SpreadMaster	30	0 ($30 – $30)
Total revenue allocated	$380	

The ranking of the individual products in the suite determines the revenues allocated to them. Product managers at Supersoft likely would differ on how they believe their individual products contribute to sales of the suite products. It is possible that each product manager would claim to be responsible for the primary product in the

Word + Spread + Finance suite![7] Because the stand-alone revenue-allocation method does not require rankings of individual products in the suite, this method is less likely to cause acrimonious debates among product managers.

Other Revenue-Allocation Methods

Management judgment not explicitly based on a specific formula is another method of revenue allocation. In one case, the president of a software company decided to issue a set of revenue-allocation weights after the managers of the three products in a bundled suite could not agree among themselves on a set of weights. The weights chosen by the president were 45% for product A, 45% for product B, and 10% for product C. The factors the president considered included stand-alone selling prices (all three were very similar), stand-alone unit sales (A and B were over 10 times more than C), product ratings by independent experts, and consumer awareness. The product C manager complained that his 10% weighting drastically shortchanged the contribution of product C to suite revenues. The president responded that its inclusion in the suite greatly increased consumer exposure to product C, with the result that product C's total revenues would be far larger (even with only 10% of suite revenues) than if it had not been included in the suite.

[7]Calculating the Shapley value will mitigate this problem because each product will be considered as a primary, first-incremental, and second-incremental product. The revenue allocated to each product is an average of the revenues calculated for each product under these different assumptions: FinanceMaster, $185; WordMaster, $85; SpreadMaster, $110.

Order			Revenues Allocated to Each Product		
Primary	First Incremental	Second Incremental	FinanceMaster	WordMaster	SpreadMaster
FinanceMaster	WordMaster	SpreadMaster	$ 225	$125	$ 30 ($380 – $225 – $125)
FinanceMaster	SpreadMaster	WordMaster	225	5 ($380 – $225 – $150)	150
Word Master	FinanceMaster	SpreadMaster	225	125	30 ($380 – $125 – $225)
WordMaster	SpreadMaster	FinanceMaster	105 ($380 – $125 – $150)	125	150
SpreadMaster	FinanceMaster	WordMaster	225	5 ($380 – $150 – $225)	150
SpreadMaster	Word Master	FinanceMaster	105 ($380 – $150 – $125)	125	150
Total:			$1,110	$510	$660
Average Revenue Allocated:			$1,110 ÷ 6 = $185	$510 ÷ 6 = $85	$660 ÷ 6 = $110

PROBLEM FOR SELF-STUDY

This problem illustrates how support department cost-allocation methods can be used in a setting different from the example examined in the chapter (Exhibits 15-2 through 15-6). In this problem, the cost of central corporate support departments are allocated to operating divisions. The corporate departments provide services to each other as well as to the operating divisions. Also, this problem illustrates the use of the dual-rate method of allocating support departments' costs. (The dual-rate method can also be used in manufacturing support department cost allocations).

Computer Horizons budgets the following amounts for its two central corporate support departments (legal and personnel) in supporting each other and the two manufacturing divisions, the Laptop Division (LTD) and the Work Station Division (WSD):

	Budgeted Usage by				
To Be Supplied By	Legal	Personnel	LTD	WSD	Total
Legal (hours)	—	250	1,500	750	2,500
(percentages)	—	10%	60%	30%	100%
Personnel (hours)	2,500	—	22,500	25,000	50,000
(percentages)	5%	—	45%	50%	100%

Details on actual usage are

To Be Supplied By	Legal	Personnel	LTD	WSD	Total
		Actual Usage by			
Legal (hours)	—	400	400	1,200	2,000
(percentages)	—	20%	20 %	60 %	100%
Personnel (hours)	2,000	—	26,600	11,400	40,000
(percentages)	5%	—	66.5%	28.5%	100%

The actual costs were

	Legal	Personnel
Fixed	$360,000	$475,000
Variable	$200,000	$600,000

Fixed costs are allocated on the basis of budgeted capacity. Variable costs are allocated on the basis of actual usage.

Required

What amount of support department costs for legal and personnel will be allocated to LTD and WSD using (a) the direct method, (b) the step-down method (allocating the Legal Department costs first), and (c) the reciprocal method using linear equations?

SOLUTION

Exhibit 15-7 presents the computations for allocating the fixed and variable support department costs. A summary of these costs follows:

	Laptop Division (LTD)	Work Station Division (WSD)
(a) Direct Method		
Fixed costs	$465,000	$370,000
Variable costs	470,000	330,000
	$935,000	$700,000
(b) Step-Down Method		
Fixed costs	$458,053	$376,947
Variable costs	488,000	312,000
	$946,053	$688,947
(c) Reciprocal Method		
Fixed costs	$462,513	$372,487
Variable costs	476,364	323,636
	$938,877	$696,123

EXHIBIT 15-7 Alternative Methods of Allocating Corporate Support Department Costs to Operating Divisions of Computer Horizons: Dual-Rate Method

Allocation Method	Legal (Corporate Support Department)	Personnel (Corporate Support Department)	LTD (Manufacturing Divisions)	WSD (Manufacturing Divisions)	Total
A. Direct Method					
Fixed Costs	$360,000	$ 475,000			
Legal (1,500 ÷ 2,250; 750 ÷ 2,250)	(360,000)		$240,000	$120,000	
Personnel (22,500 ÷ 47,500; 25,000 ÷ 47,500)	$ 0	(475,000)	225,000	250,000	
		$ 0	$465,000	$370,000	$835,000
Variable Costs	$200,000	$ 600,000			
Legal (400 ÷ 1,600; 1,200 ÷ 1,600)	(200,000)		$ 50,000	$150,000	
Personnel (26,600 ÷ 38,000; 11,400 ÷ 38,000)	$ 0	(600,000)	420,000	180,000	
		$ 0	$470,000	$330,000	$800,000

(*Continued*)

B. Step-Down Method

(Legal Department First)					
Fixed Costs	$360,000	$475,000			
Legal (250 ÷ 2,500; 1,500 ÷ 2,500; 750 ÷ 2,500)	(360,000)	36,000	$216,000	$108,000	
Personnel (22,500 ÷ 47,500; 25,000 ÷ 47,500)	$ 0	(511,000)	242,053	268,947	
		$ 0	$458,053	$376,947	$835,000
Variable Costs	$200,000	$600,000			
Legal (400 ÷ 2,000; 400 ÷ 2,000; 1,200 ÷ 2,000)	(200,000)	40,000	$ 40,000	$120,000	
Personnel (26,600 ÷ 38,000; 11,400 ÷ 38,000)	$ 0	(640,000)	448,000	192,000	
		$ 0	$488,000	$312,000	$800,000

C. Reciprocal Method

Fixed Costs	$360,000	$475,000			
Legal (250 ÷ 2,500; 1,500 ÷ 2,500; 750 ÷ 2,500)	(385,678)[a]	38,568	$231,407	$115,703	
Personnel (2,500 ÷ 50,000; 22,500 ÷ 50,000; 25,000 ÷ 50,000)	25,678	(513,568)[a]	231,106	256,784	
	$ 0	$ 0	$462,513	$372,487	$835,000
Variable Costs	$200,000	$600,000			
Legal (400 ÷ 2,000; 400 ÷ 2,000; 1,200 ÷ 2,000)	(232,323)[b]	46,465	$ 46,465	$139,393	
Personnel (2,000 ÷ 40,000; 26,600 ÷ 40,000; 11,400 ÷ 40,000)	32,323	(646,465)[b]	429,899	184,243	
	$ 0	$ 0	$476,364	$323,636	$800,000

[a]FIXED COSTS

Letting LF= Legal Department Fixed Costs, and PF= Personnel Department Fixed Costs, the simultaneous equations for the reciprocal method for fixed costs are

$$
\begin{aligned}
LF &= \$360{,}000 + 0.05\,PF\\
PF &= \$475{,}000 + 0.10\,LF\\
LF &= \$360{,}000 + 0.05\,(\$475{,}000 + 0.10LF)\\
LF &= \$385{,}678\\
PF &= \$475{,}000 + 0.10\,(\$385{,}678) = \$513{,}568
\end{aligned}
$$

[b]VARIABLE COSTS

Letting LV= Legal Department Variable Costs, and PV= Personnel Department Variable Costs, the simultaneous equations for the reciprocal method for variable costs are

$$
\begin{aligned}
LV &= \$200{,}000 + 0.05\,PV\\
PV &= \$600{,}000 + 0.20\,LV\\
LV &= \$200{,}000 + 0.05\,(\$600{,}000 + 0.20LV)\\
LV &= \$232{,}323\\
PV &= \$600{,}000 + 0.20\,(\$232{,}323) = \$646{,}465
\end{aligned}
$$

DECISION POINTS

SUMMARY

The following question-and-answer format summarizes the chapter's learning objectives. Each decision presents a key question related to a learning objective. The guidelines are the answer to that question.

Decision	Guidelines
1. Should a manager use the single-rate or the dual-rate cost allocation method?	The single-rate cost-allocation method allocates costs in each cost pool to cost objects using the same rate per unit of the single allocation base. In the dual-rate method, costs are grouped into a variable cost pool and a fixed cost pool; each pool uses a different cost-allocation base. If costs can be easily separated into variable and fixed costs, the dual-rate cost-allocation method should be used because it provides better information for making decisions.

2. What factors should a manager consider when deciding whether to use budgeted or actual cost-allocation rates?

When cost allocations are made using budgeted rates, managers of divisions to which costs are allocated face no uncertainty about the rates to be used in that budget period. In contrast, when actual rates are used for cost allocation, managers do not know the rates to be used until the end of the budget period. If actual rates are used, the efficiency of the supplier department affects the costs allocated to the user department.

3. What methods can a manager use to allocate costs of multiple support departments to operating departments?

The three methods are direct, step-down, and reciprocal. The direct method ignores any reciprocal services provided among support departments and allocates support department costs directly to operating departments. The step-down method allows for partial recognition of services provided among support departments. The reciprocal method provides full recognition of those services, but it is more complex than the direct or step-down methods.

4. What methods can a manager use to allocate common costs to two or more users?

Common costs are the costs of a cost object (such as operating a facility or performing an activity) that are shared by two or more users. The stand-alone cost-allocation method uses information pertaining to each user of the cost object to determine cost-allocation weights. The incremental cost-allocation method ranks individual users of the cost object and allocates common costs first to the primary user and then to the other incremental users.

5. How can contract disputes over reimbursements based on costs be reduced?

Make the cost-assignment rules as explicit as possible (and in writing). These rules should include details such as the allowable cost items, the acceptable cost-allocation bases, and how differences between budgeted and actual costs are to be accounted for.

6. What is product bundling and why does it give rise to revenue-allocation issues?

Bundling occurs when a package of two or more products (or services) is sold for a single price. Revenue allocation of the bundled price is required when managers of the individual products in the bundle are evaluated on product revenues or product operating incomes.

7. What methods can a manager use to allocate revenues of a bundled package to individual products in the package?

Revenues can be allocated for a bundled product using the stand-alone method, the incremental method, or management judgment.

TERMS TO LEARN

This chapter and the Glossary at the end of the book contain definitions of:

allowable cost (p. 536)
artificial cost (530)
bundled product (537)
common cost (533)
complete reciprocated costs (530)
Cost Accounting Standards Board (CASB) (535)
direct allocation method (527)
direct method (527)
dual-rate cost-allocation method (522)
incremental cost-allocation method (534)
incremental revenue-allocation method (539)
operating department (526)
production department (526)
reciprocal allocation method (529)
revenue allocation (537)
revenue object (537)
service department (526)
single-rate cost-allocation method (522)
sequential allocation method (528)
stand-alone cost-allocation method (533)
stand-alone revenue-allocation method (538)
step-down allocation method (528)
support department (526)

ASSIGNMENT MATERIAL

Questions

15-1 Distinguish between the single-rate and the dual-rate cost-allocation methods.

15-2 Describe how the dual-rate method is useful to division managers in decision making.

15-3 How do budgeted cost rates motivate the manager of the support department to improve efficiency?

15-4 Give examples of bases used to allocate support department cost pools to operating departments.

15-5 Why might a manager prefer that budgeted rather than actual indirect cost-allocation rates be used for costs being allocated to her department from another department?

15-6 "To ensure unbiased cost allocations, fixed indirect costs should be allocated on the basis of estimated long-run use by user department managers." Do you agree? Why?

15-7 Distinguish among the three methods of allocating the costs of support departments to operating departments.

15-8 What is conceptually the most defensible method for allocating support department costs? Why?

15-9 Distinguish between two methods of allocating common costs.

15-10 What role does the Cost Accounting Standards Board play when companies contract with the U.S. government?

15-11 What is one key way to reduce cost-allocation disputes that arise with government contracts?

15-12 Describe how companies are increasingly facing revenue-allocation decisions.

15-13 Distinguish between the stand-alone and the incremental revenue-allocation methods.

15-14 Identify and discuss arguments individual product managers may put forward to support their preferred revenue-allocation method.

15-15 How might a dispute over the allocation of revenues of a bundled product be resolved?

Exercises

15-16 **Single-rate versus dual-rate allocation methods, support department.** The Chicago power plant that services all manufacturing departments of MidWest Engineering has a budget for the coming year. This budget has been expressed in the following terms on a monthly basis:

Manufacturing Department	Needed at Practical Capacity Production Level (Kilowatt-Hours)	Average Expected Monthly Usage (Kilowatt-Hours)
Rockford	10,000	8,000
Peoria	20,000	9,000
Hammond	12,000	7,000
Kankakee	8,000	6,000
Totals	50,000	30,000

The expected monthly costs for operating the power plant during the budget year are $15,000: $6,000 variable and $9,000 fixed.

Required

1. Assume that a single cost pool is used for the power plant costs. What amounts will be allocated to each manufacturing department if (a) the rate is calculated based on practical capacity and costs are allocated based on practical capacity and (b) the rate is calculated based on expected monthly usage and costs are allocated based on expected monthly usage.
2. Assume the dual-rate method is used with separate cost pools for the variable and fixed costs. Variable costs are allocated on the basis of expected monthly usage. Fixed costs are allocated on the basis of practical capacity. What dollar amounts will be allocated to each manufacturing department? Why might you prefer the dual-rate method?

15-17 **Single-rate cost-allocation method, budgeted versus actual costs and quantities.** Fruit Juice, Inc., processes orange juice at its East Miami plant (part of the Orange Juice Division) and grapefruit juice at its West Miami plant (part of the Grapefruit Juice Division). It purchases oranges and grapefruit from growers' cooperatives in the Orlando area. It owns its own trucking fleet. Each Miami plant is the same distance from Orlando. The trucking fleet is operated as a cost center. Each Miami plant is billed for the direct and indirect costs of each round-trip.

The trucking fleet costs include direct costs (labor costs of drivers, fuel, and toll charges) and indirect costs. Indirect costs include depreciation on tires and the vehicle, insurance, and state registration fees.

At the start of 2004, the Orange Juice Division budgeted for 150 round-trips from Orlando to East Miami, and the Grapefruit Juice Division budgeted for 100 round-trips from Orlando to West Miami. Based on these 250 budgeted trips (equal to the practical capacity of the trucking fleet), the budgeted indirect costs of the trucking fleet were $575,000. The following actual results occurred:

Trucking fleet indirect costs	$483,750
Number of round-trips, Orlando–East Miami plant	150
Number of round-trips Orlando–West Miami plant	75

The trucking fleet division uses the single-rate method when allocating indirect trucking costs.

1. What is the indirect cost rate per round-trip when (a) budgeted costs and budgeted round-trips are used and (b) when actual costs and actual round-trips are used? **Required**
2. What are the effects of using the rate based on budgeted costs/budgeted round-trips rather than the rate based on actual costs/actual round-trips to allocate costs to the Orenge Juice Division using the actual number of round trips.

15-18 Dual-rate cost-allocation method, budgeted versus actual costs, and practical capacity versus actual quantities (continuation of 15-17). Fruit Juice, Inc., decides to examine the effect of using the dual-rate method for allocating indirect trucking costs to each round-trip. At the start of 2004, the budgeted indirect costs were

Variable indirect cost per round-trip	$1,500
Fixed indirect costs	$200,000

The actual results for the 225 round-trips made in 2004 were

Variable indirect costs	$303,750
Fixed indirect costs	180,000
	$483,750

Assume all other information to be the same as in Exercise 15-17.

1. What is the indirect cost rate per round-trip with the dual-rate method when budgeted costs and budgeted round-trips are used? Total costs are computed using budgeted rate times actual usage (trips) for variable costs and budgeted rate times practical capacity usage for fixed costs. **Required**
2. From the viewpoint of the Orange Juice Division, what are the effects of using the dual-rate method rather than the single-rate methods?

15-19 Support department cost allocation; direct and step-down methods. Phoenix Consulting provides outsourcing services and advice to both government and corporate clients. For costing purposes, Phoenix classifies its departments into two support departments (Administrative/Human Resources and Information Systems) and two operating departments (Government Consulting and Corporate Consulting). For the first quarter of 2003, Phoenix incurs the following costs in its four departments:

Administrative/Human Resources (A/H)	$ 600,000
Information Systems (IS)	2,400,000
Government Clients (GOVT)	8,756,000
Corporate Clients (CORP)	12,452,000

The actual level of support relationships among the four departments for the first quarter of 2003 was

	Used By			
Supplied By	**A/H**	**IS**	**GOVT**	**CORP**
A/H	—	25%	40%	35%
IS	10%	—	30%	60%

The Administrative/Human Resources support percentages are based on head count. The Information Systems support percentages are based on actual computer time used.

1. Allocate the two support department costs to the two operating departments using the following methods: **Required**
   a. Direct method
   b. Step-down method (allocate A/H first)
   c. Step-down method (allocate IS first)
2. Compare and explain differences in the support department costs allocated to each operating department.
3. What approaches might be used to decide the sequence in which to allocate support departments when using the step-down method? What approach would you recommend Phoenix use if, on government consulting jobs, it is required to use the step-down method?

15-20 Support department cost allocation, reciprocal method (continuation of 15-19). Refer to the data given in Exercise 15-19.

1. Allocate the two support department costs to the two operating departments using the reciprocal method. Use (a) linear equations and (b) repeated iterations. **Required**
2. Compare and explain differences in requirement 1 with those in requirement 1 of Exercise 15-19. Which method do you prefer? Why?

Excel Application For students who wish to practice their spreadsheet skills, the following is a step-by-step approach to creating an Excel spreadsheet to use repeated iterations to work problem 1b.

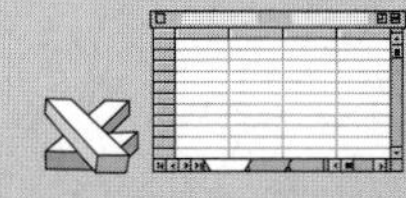

Step-by-Step

1. Open up a new spreadsheet. At top, create an "Original Data" section for the department-cost and support-relationship data provided by Phoenix Consulting. Enter the department costs for A/H, IS, GOVT, and CORP and the level of support relationships (expressed in %) among these departments in exactly the same format as presented on page 545.

(Program your spreadsheet to perform all necessary calculations. Do not "hard-code" any amounts, such as your cost allocations, requiring addition, subtraction, multiplication, or division operations.)

2. Skip two rows and create a section "Cost Allocation—Reciprocal Method" using a similar format to Exhibit 15-5. Create columns for the support departments (A/H and IS), the operating departments (GOVT and CORP), and for "Totals." Create rows for "Department Costs Before Cost Allocations, 1st Allocation of A/H Costs, 1st Allocation of IS Costs, 2nd Allocation of A/H Costs," and "2nd Allocation of IS Costs." You will add more rows as more iterations are needed.
3. Use the department cost data from your Original Data section to fill in the row for Department Costs Before Cost Allocations. Next, use the data on the level of support relationships among the departments from your Original Data section to calculate the 1st and 2nd allocations of A/H and IS costs. Continue to add rows for further iterations of cost allocations until the costs remaining to be allocated are sufficiently close to zero at which time allocate any costs remaining in a support department to CORP. When done, include calculations on separate rows for "Total Costs of Operating Departments" and "Total Support Department Costs Allocated to Operating Departments."
4. *Check the accuracy of your spreadsheet:* Go to your Original Data section and change the level of support relationships between the A/H department and the IS, GOVT, and CORP departments from 25%, 40%, 35% to 25%, 50%, 25%. If you programmed your spreadsheet correctly, total costs (after all cost allocations) in the GOVT department should change to $9,971,385.

15-21 Direct and step-down allocation. *e-books* is an online book retailer. The company has four departments. The two revenue-producing departments are Corporate Sales and Consumer Sales. The two support departments are Administrative (human resources, accounting, and so on), and Information Systems. Each of the sales departments conducts merchandising and marketing operations independently.

The following data are available for September 2004:

Departments	Revenues	Number of Employees	Processing Time Used (in minutes)
Corporate Sales	$1,334,200	42	1,920
Consumer Sales	667,100	28	1,600
Administrative	—	14	320
Information Systems	—	21	1,120

Costs incurred in each of the four departments for September 2004 are as follows:

Corporate Sales	$998,270
Consumer Sales	489,860
Administrative	72,700
Information Systems	234,400

Use number of employees to allocate Administrative costs and processing time used to allocate Information Systems costs.

Required

1. Allocate the support department costs to the revenue-producing departments using the direct method.
2. Rank the support departments based on the percentage of their services rendered to other support departments. Use this ranking to allocate support costs based on the step-down allocation method.
3. How could you have ranked the support departments differently?

15-22 Reciprocal cost allocation (continuation 15-21). Consider *e-books* again. The controller of *e-books* reads a widely used text that states that "the reciprocal method is conceptually the most defensible." He seeks your assistance.

Required

1. Describe the key features of the reciprocal allocation method.
2. Allocate the support department costs (Administrative and Information Systems) to the two revenue-producing departments using the reciprocal allocation method.
3. Under what condition is the reciprocal method more accurate than the direct and step-down methods? In the case presented in this exercise, which method would you recommend? Why?

15-23 Allocation of common costs. Sam, Sarah, and Tony work as skilled machinists at Bedford Engineering. They share a penthouse apartment that has a lounge room with the latest 50-inch TV. Tony owns the apartment, its furniture, and the TV. He can subscribe to a cable television company that has the following packages available:

Package	Per Month
A. Basic news	$32
B. Premium movies	25
C. Premium sports	30
D. Basic news + Premium movies	50
E. Basic news + Premium sports	54
F. Premium movies + Premium sports	48
G. Basic news + Premium Movies + Premium sports	70

Sam is a TV news junkie who has average interest in movies and zero interest in sports ("they are overpaid jocks"). Sarah is a movie buff, likes sports, and avoids the news ("it's all depressing anyway"). Tony is into sports in a big way, has average interest in news, and zero interest in movies ("he always falls asleep before the end"). They all agree that the purchase of the $70 total package is a "win-win-win" situation.

Each of the roommates works on a different eight-hour shift at Bedford, so conflicts in viewing are minimal.

Required

1. What criteria might be used to guide the choice about how to allocate the $70 monthly cable fee among Sam, Sarah, and Tony?
2. Outline two methods of allocating the $70 among Sam, Sarah, and Tony.

15-24 Allocation of common costs. Joan Ernst, a graduating senior at a university near Sacramento, received an invitation to visit a prospective employer in Baltimore. A few days later, she received an invitation from a prospective employer in Chicago. She decided to combine her visits, traveling from Sacramento to Baltimore, Baltimore to Chicago, and Chicago to Sacramento.

Ernst received job offers from both companies. Upon her return, she decided to accept the offer in Chicago. She is puzzled over how to allocate her travel costs between the two employers. She has collected the following data for regular round-trip fares with no stopovers:

Sacramento to Baltimore	$1,400
Sacramento to Chicago	$1,100

Ernst paid $1,800 for her three-leg flight (Sacramento–Baltimore, Baltimore–Chicago, Chicago–Sacramento). In addition, she paid $30 each way for limousines from her home to Sacramento Airport and back when she returned.

Required

1. How should Ernst allocate the $1,800 airfare between the employers in Baltimore and Chicago using (a) the stand-alone cost-allocation method and (b) the incremental cost-allocation method?
2. Which method would you recommend Ernst use and why?
3. How should Ernst allocate the $60 limousine charges between the employers in Baltimore and Chicago?

15-25 Revenue allocation, bundled products. Pebble Resorts operates a five-star hotel with a world-recognized championship golf course. It has a decentralized management structure. There are three divisions:

- Lodging (rooms, conference facilities)
- Food (restaurants and in-room service)
- Recreation (golf course, tennis courts, and so on)

Starting next month, Pebble will offer a two-day, two-person "getaway package" deal for $700. This deal includes:

- Two nights' stay for two in an ocean-view room—separately priced at $640 ($320 per night for two).
- Two rounds of golf separately priced at $300 ($150 per round). One person can do two rounds, or two people can do one round each.
- Candlelight dinner for two at the exclusive Pebble Pacific Restaurant—separately priced at $80 per person.

Samantha Lee, president of the Recreation Division, recently asked the CEO of Pebble Resorts how her division would share in the $700 revenue from the package. The golf course was operating at 100% capacity (and then some). Under the "getaway package" rules, participants who booked one week in advance were guaranteed access to the golf course. Lee noted that every "getaway" booking would displace a $150 booking. She stressed that the high demand reflected the devotion of her team to keeping the golf course rated in the "Best 10 Courses in the World" listings in *Golf Monthly*. As an aside, she also noted that the Lodging and Food divisions only had to turn away customers on "peak-season events such as the New Year's period."

Required

1. With selling prices as the weights, allocate the $700 "getaway package" revenue to the three divisions using:
   a. The stand-alone revenue-allocation method
   b. The incremental revenue-allocation method (with Recreation first, then Lodging, and then Food)
2. What are the pros and cons of *a* and *b* in requirement 1?

15-26 Revenue allocation, bundled products, additional complexities (continuation of 15-25). The individual items in the "getaway package" deal at Pebble Resorts are not fully used by each guest. Assume that 10% of the "getaway package" users in its first month do not use the golfing option, and 5% do not use the food option. The lodging option has a 100% usage rate.

Required How should Pebble Resorts recognize this nonuse factor in its revenue sharing of the $700 package across the Lodging, Food, and Recreation divisions? Explain.

Problems

15-27 Single-rate, dual-rate, and practical capacity allocation. Patrick's Department Store has a free gift-wrapping service for the customers who want to get their purchases gift wrapped. Patrick's has a monthly practical capacity to gift wrap 8,000 items that it allocates among its different departments. Monthly fixed practical capacity costs of the gift-wrapping service are $6,000. Average budgeted variable cost to gift wrap an item is $0.60. Though the service is free to the customers, the department where the customer made the purchase is allocated gift-wrapping service costs.

Various departments' actual use of the gift-wrapping service during the current month and their respective needs at practical capacity follow.

Department	Actual Number of Gifts Wrapped	Number of Gifts That Can Be Wrapped at Practical Capacity
Gifts	2,200	2,800
Men's Wear	750	1,000
Women's Wear	1,600	2,100
Footwear	450	700
China	650	900
Linen	350	500

Required

1. Allocate the costs for the gift-wrapping service to each department using a single-rate method based on actual number of gifts wrapped.
2. Compute the amount allocated to each department using the dual-rate method when fixed costs are allocated based on practical capacity and variable costs are allocated using actual usage.
3. Comment on your results in requirements 1 and 2.

15-28 Single-rate versus dual-rate cost-allocation methods. (W. Crum, adapted) Carolina Company has designed and built a power plant to serve its three factories. Data for 2003 are as follows:

	USAGE IN KILOWATT-HOURS		
Factory	Needed at Practical Capacity Production Level	Budgeted Usage	Actual Usage
Durham	100,000	80,000	85,000
Charlotte	60,000	50,000	40,000
Raleigh	40,000	30,000	35,000
Total	200,000	160,000	160,000

Budgeted fixed costs of the power plant were $1 million in 2003; budgeted variable costs, $2 million.

Required

1. Allocate the power plant's costs to Durham, Charlotte, and Raleigh using the single-rate method in which the budgeted rate is calculated using practical capacity but costs are allocated to Durham, Charlotte, and Raleigh based on actual usage.
2. Allocate the power plant's costs to Durham, Charlotte, and Raleigh using the single-rate method in which the budgeted rate is based on budgeted usage and costs are allocated to Durham, Charlotte, and Raleigh based on actual usage.
3. Allocate the power plant's costs to Durham, Charlotte, and Raleigh using the dual-rate method in which the budgeted fixed-cost rate is calculated using practical capacity and fixed costs are allocated to Durham, Charlotte, and Raleigh based on practical capacity. The budgeted variable-cost rate is calculated using budgeted usage and variable costs are allocated to Durham, Charlotte, and Raleigh based on actual usage.
4. Allocate the power plant's costs to Durham, Charlotte, and Raleigh using the dual-rate method in which the budgeted fixed-cost rate is calculated using budgeted usage and fixed costs are allocated to Durham, Charlotte, and Raleigh based on budgeted usage. The budgeted variable-cost rate is calculated using budgeted usage and variable costs are allocated to Durham, Charlotte, and Raleigh based on actual usage.

15-29 Single-rate, dual-rate, and practical capacity allocations. Raymond, Inc., has its own power plant, which has two users, Cutting Department and Welding Department. When the plans were prepared for the power plant, top management decided that its practical capacity should be 150,000 machine-hours (MH). Annual budgeted practical capacity fixed costs are $450,000, and budgeted variable costs are $2.00 per machine-hour. The following data are available:

	Cutting Department	Welding Department	Total
Actual usage in 2004 (MH)	60,000	40,000	100,000
Practical capacity for each department (MH)	90,000	60,000	150,000

Required

1. Allocate the power plant's costs to the Cutting and the Welding departments using a single-rate method in which the budgeted rate is calculated using practical capacity and costs are allocated based on actual usage.
2. Allocate the power plant's costs to the Cutting and Welding departments using the dual-rate method in which the fixed costs are allocated based on practical capacity and variable costs are allocated based on actual usage.
3. Allocate the power plant's costs to the Cutting and Welding departments using the dual-rate method in which the fixed-cost rate is calculated using practical capacity but fixed costs are allocated to the Cutting and Welding departments based on actual usage. Variable costs are allocated based on actual usage.
4. Comment on your results in requirements 1, 2, and 3.

15-30 Cost allocation, actual versus budgeted usage. (CMA, revised) Bulldog, Inc., is a large manufacturing company that runs its own electrical power plant from the excess steam produced in its manufacturing process. Power is provided to two production departments: Department A and Department B. The capacity of the power plant was originally determined by the expected peak demands of the two production departments. The expected normal usages are, respectively, 60% and 60,000,000 kilowatt-hours (kWh) for Department A, and 40% and 40,000,000 kWh for Department B.

The budgeted monthly costs of producing power, based on normal usage of 100,000,000 kWh, are $30,000,000 in fixed costs and $7,500,000 in variable costs. For November, the actual kilowatt-hours used were 60,000,000 by Department A and 20,000,000 by Department B. Actual fixed costs were $30,000,000, and actual variable costs were $7,500,000.

Terry Lamb, the controller, prepared the following monthly report:

Bulldog Inc.
Monthly Allocation Report
November 2003

Power plant usage	80,000,000 kWh
Actual costs:	
Variable	$ 7,500,000
Fixed	30,000,000
Total	$37,500,000
Rate per kWh ($37,500,000 ÷ 80,000,000 kWh)	$0.46875
Allocations:	
To Department A (60,000,000 kWh × $0.46875)	$28,125,000
To Department B (20,000,000 kWh × $0.46875)	9,375,000
Total allocated	$37,500,000

Lamb fully allocated all power plant costs on the basis of actual kilowatt-hours used by each production department. This report will be submitted to the two production-department operating managers.

Required

1. Discuss at least two problems with the monthly allocation report prepared by Lamb for November 2003.
2. Prepare a revised monthly allocation report for November 2003 using a flexible-budget approach. Use budgeted rates times actual usage for variable costs and budgeted rates assuming budgeted (normal) usage for fixed costs.
3. Discuss the behavioral implication of Lamb's monthly allocation report for November 2003 on the production manager of Department B.

15-31 Allocating costs of support departments; step-down and direct methods. The Central Valley Company has prepared department overhead budgets for normal-volume levels before allocations as follows:

Support departments:		
Building and grounds	$10,000	
Personnel	1,000	
General factory administration	26,090	
Cafeteria: operating loss	1,640	
Storeroom	2,670	
Total		$ 41,400
Operating departments:		
Machining	$34,700	
Assembly	48,900	
Total		83,600
Total for support and operating departments		$125,000

Management has decided that the most appropriate inventory costs are achieved by using individual department overhead rates. These rates are developed after support department costs are allocated to operating departments.

Bases for allocation are to be selected from the following:

Department	Direct Manufacturing Labor-Hours	Number of Employees	Square Feet of Floor Space Occupied	Manufacturing Labor-Hours	Number of Requisitions
Building and grounds	0	0	0	0	0
Personnel[a]	0	0	2,000	0	0
General plant administration	0	35	7,000	0	0
Cafeteria: operating loss	0	10	4,000	1,000	0
Storeroom	0	5	7,000	1,000	0
Machining	5,000	50	30,000	8,000	2,000
Assembly	15,000	100	50,000	17,000	1,000
Total	20,000	200	100,000	27,000	3,000

[a]Basis used is number of employees.

Required

1. Using a worksheet, allocate support department costs by the step-down method. Develop overhead rates per direct manufacturing labor-hour for machining and assembly. Allocate the costs of the support departments in the order given in this problem. Use the allocation base for each support department you think is most appropriate.
2. Using the direct method, rework requirement 1.
3. Based on the following information about two jobs, determine the total overhead costs for each job by using rates developed in (a) requirement 1 and (b) requirement 2.

	Direct Manufacturing Labor-Hours	
	Machining	**Assembly**
Job 88	18	2
Job 89	3	17

4. The company evaluates performance of operating departments' managers on the basis of how well they managed their total costs, including allocated costs. As the manager of the Machining Department, which allocation method would you prefer from the results obtained in requirements 1 and 2? Explain.

15-32 Support department cost allocations; single-department cost pools; direct, step-down, and reciprocal methods. The Manes Company has two products. Product 1 is manufactured entirely in Department X. Product 2 is manufactured entirely in Department Y. To produce these two products, the Manes Company has two support departments: A (a materials-handling department) and B (a power-generating department).

An analysis of the work done by departments A and B in a typical period follows:

	Used By			
Supplied By	**A**	**B**	**X**	**Y**
A	—	100	250	150
B	500	—	100	400

The work done in Department A is measured by the direct labor-hours of materials-handling time. The work done in Department B is measured by the kilowatt-hours of power.

The budgeted costs of the support departments for the coming year are

	Department A	Department B
Variable indirect labor and indirect materials costs	$ 70,000	$10,000
Supervision	10,000	10,000
Depreciation	20,000	20,000
	$100,000	$40,000
	+ Power costs	+ Materials-handling costs

The budgeted costs of the operating departments for the coming year are $1,500,000 for Department X and $800,000 for Department Y.

Supervisory costs are salary costs. Depreciation in B is the straight-line depreciation of power-generation equipment in its nineteenth year of an estimated 25-year useful life; it is old but well-maintained equipment.

Required

1. What are the allocations of costs of support departments A and B to operating departments X and Y using (a) the direct method, (b) the step-down method (allocate Department A first), (c) the step-down method (allocate Department B first), and (d) the reciprocal method?
2. The power company has offered to supply all the power needed by the Manes Company and to provide all the services of the present power department. The cost of this service will be $40 per kilowatt-hour of power. Should Manes accept? Explain.

15-33 Common costs. Jason Miller and Eric Jackson would like to lease an office building to open their separate law offices. The building has a total of 1,500 square feet of office space. Miller and Jackson need 900 square feet and 600 square feet, respectively. If each rents the space on his own, the rent will be $1 per square foot. If they rent the space together, the rent will decrease to $0.80 per square foot.

Required

1. Calculate Miller and Jackson's respective share of the rent under the stand-alone cost-allocation method.
2. Do requirement 1 using the incremental cost-allocation method. Assume Miller to be the primary party.
3. What method would you recommend Miller and Jackson use to share the rent?

15-34 Revenue allocation, bundled products. Pétale Parfum (PP) manufactures and sells upscale perfumes. In recent months, PP has started selling its products in bundled form, as well as in individual form. Sales in 2003 of three products that have been sold individually are as follows:

	Retail Price	Units Sold
Stand-alone		
Fraîche	$100	20,000
Désarmer	80	37,500
Innocence	250	20,000
Suite		
Fraîche + Désarmer	150	
Fraîche + Innocence	280	

Each of the products is manufactured by a separate division.

Required

1. Compute the weights for allocating revenues to each division for each of the bundled products using:
   a. The stand-alone revenue-allocation method based on total revenues of individual products
   b. The incremental revenue-allocation method, with Innocence ranked 1; Désarmer, 2; and Fraîche, 3; based on retail prices of individual products. According to this ranking, the primary product in a suite has the highest rank, and so on.
2. What method would you recommend for allocating revenues to each division for each of the bundled products?

15-35 Overhead disputes. (Suggested by Howard Wright) The Azure Ship Company works on U.S. Navy vessels and commercial vessels. General yard overhead (for example, the cost of the Purchasing Department) is allocated to the jobs on the basis of direct labor costs.

In 2004, Azure's total $150 million of direct labor costs consisted of $50 million Navy and $100 million commercial. The general yard overhead was $30 million.

Navy auditors periodically examine the records of defense contractors. The auditors investigated a nuclear submarine contract, which was based on cost-plus-fixed-fee pricing. The auditors claimed that the Navy was entitled to a refund because of double-counting of overhead in 2004.

The government contract included the following provision:

Par. 15-202. Direct Costs

(a) A direct cost is any cost that can be identified specifically with a particular cost object. Direct costs are not limited to items that are incorporated in the end product such as material or labor. Costs identified specifically with the contract are direct costs of the contract and are to be charged directly thereto. Costs identified specifically with other work of the contractor are direct costs of that work and are not to be charged to the contract directly or indirectly. When items ordinarily chargeable as indirect costs are charged to the contract as direct costs, the cost of like items applicable to other work must be eliminated from indirect costs allocated to the contract.

Azure formed a special expediting purchasing group, the SE group, to join with the central purchasing group to obtain materials solely for the nuclear submarine. Their direct costs, $5 million, were included as direct labor of the nuclear work. Accordingly, overhead was allocated to the contracts in the usual manner. The SE cost of $5 million was not included in the general yard overhead. The auditors claimed that no overhead should have been allocated to these SE costs.

Required

1. Compute the amount of the refund that the Navy would claim.
2. Suppose the Navy also discovered that $4 million of general yard overhead was devoted exclusively to commercial engine-room purchasing activities. Compute the additional refund that the Navy would claim. (Note: This $4 million was never classified as direct labor. Furthermore, the Navy would claim that it should be reclassified as a direct cost but not as direct labor.)

Collaborative Learning Exercise

15-36 Allocating costs of support departments; dual rates; direct, step-down, and reciprocal methods. Magnum T.A., Inc., specializes in the assembly and installation of high-quality security systems for the home and business segments of the market. The four departments at its highly automated state-of-the-art assembly plant are

Service Departments	Assembly Departments
Engineering Support	Home Security Systems
Information Systems Support	Business Security Systems

The budgeted level of service relationships, which is at practical capacity, for 2004 is

	Used By			
Supplied By	Engineering Support	Information Systems Support	Home Security Systems	Business Security Systems
Engineering Support	—	0.10	0.40	0.50
Information Systems Support	0.20	—	0.30	0.50

The actual level of service relationships for 2004 is

	Used By			
Supplied By	Engineering Support	Information Systems Support	Home Security Systems	Business Security Systems
Engineering Support	—	0.15	0.30	0.55
Information Systems Support	0.25	—	0.15	0.60

Magnum collects fixed costs and variable costs for each department in separate cost pools. The actual costs in each pool for 2004 are

	Fixed-Cost Pool	Variable-Cost Pool
Engineering Support	$2,700,000	$8,500,000
Information Systems Support	8,000,000	3,750,000

Fixed costs are allocated on the basis of budgeted level of service. Variable costs are allocated on the basis of the actual level of service.

COST ACCOUNTING

A MANAGERIAL EMPHASIS, 11th ed.

HORNGREN • DATAR • FOSTER

Why will all Students learn better from Horngren/Datar/Foster?

- ***NEW*** **Decision Points** at the end of each chapter summarize the key management implications of chapter content.
- ***NEW*** **Step-by-Step Excel Application Problems** enable students to see how to build their own Excel Spreadsheets to solve cost accounting problems.
- ***NEW*** An **Internet Exercise** appears at the end of each chapter so students gain experience using the Internet to solve cost accounting problems.
- ***NEW*** **Margin Notes** are designed to emphasize key points, provide greater relevance, and improve overall readability.
- ***NEW*** **Streaming Videos** (from www.prenhall.com/horngren) are linked with the Chapter-Opening Vignettes. Students can see how real companies face real cost accounting issues; these set the stage for the chapter content to be introduced.
- ***NEW*** **Student CD-ROM** contains a rich assortment of tools (PowerPoints, spreadsheets, and videos) to aid students in learning cost accounting topics.
- ***Companion Web Site*** This site at www.prenhall.com/horngren provides students with online quizzes, tutorial assistance, current events, links to key accounting sites, writing resources, research center, study tips, downloads, and much more.

Horngren/Datar/Foster is the #1 most complete, up-to-date, and best-selling cost accounting text in the world. Students will learn from the best available resource!

The support department costs allocated to each assembly department are allocated to products on the basis of units assembled. The units assembled in each department during 2004 are

Home Security Systems	7,950 units
Business Security Systems	3,750 units

Required

1. Allocate the support department costs to the assembly departments using the dual-rate method and (a) the direct method, (b) the step-down method (allocate Information Systems Support first), (c) the step-down method (allocate Engineering Support first), (d) the reciprocal method (use linear equations), and (e) the reciprocal method (use repeated iterations). Present results in a format similar to Exhibit 15-7.
2. Compare the support department costs allocated to each Home Security Systems unit assembled and each Business Security Systems unit assembled under (a), (b), (c), (d), and (e) in requirement 1.
3. What factors might explain why the reciprocal method is not more widely used in practice?
4. Refer to the results obtained in requirements 1 and 2. Which alternative would be preferred by the manager of Home Security Systems? Explain.

CHAPTER 15 INTERNET EXERCISE

In recent years states have begun to deregulate electricity markets and are offering consumers the ability to choose their electricity provider. This involves unbundling electricity generation, transmission, and distribution services and gives rise to many contentious cost allocation issues. To better understand the cost allocation issues facing state regulators, go to www.prenhall.com/horngren, click on *Cost Accounting*, 11th ed., and access the Internet problem for Chapter 15.

CHAPTER 15 CASE

STANFORD UNIVERSITY[1]: Indirect-Cost Allocation, Indirect-Cost Recovery

In 1990, an extensive audit was conducted on Stanford University's cost allocations for federally funded research. The federal government follows a policy of reimbursing universities for the full costs of conducting federally sponsored research. In a statement to investigators, Stanford President Donald Kennedy provided some historical perspective:

> *After WWII, the United States made the decision to convert its wartime research efforts into a greatly expanded basic research program located in our universities, where the training of the next generation of scientists takes place. Originally, federal support of basic research in universities developed along the lines of an "assistance model"; academic scientists wanted to work on fundamental problems and the government (in the first instance, the Office of Naval Research) wanted to get it done.... Federal support for university research has made possible an extraordinarily broad array of valuable advances in fields from microbiology to engineering, from particle physics to genetics. At Stanford, federal research support has played a critical role in stunning advances, including such non-invasive technologies as magnetic resonance imaging; the discovery of the first reliable cure for Hodgkin's disease;...and a series of basic discoveries essential to modern genetic engineering.*[2]

Indirect Cost Recovery

Specific governmental guidelines existed for determination of costs eligible for indirect-cost recovery for research activities. Office of Management and Budget (OMB) Circular A-21, titled "Cost Principles for Educational Institutions," establishes:

> *...principles for determining the costs applicable to research and development, training, and other sponsored work performed by colleges and universities under grants, contracts and other agreements with the federal government. The cost of a sponsored agreement is comprised of the allowable direct costs incident to its performance, plus the allocable portion of the allowable indirect costs of the institution.*
>
> *Direct costs are those costs that can be identified specifically with a particular sponsored project, an instructional activity, or any other institutional activity; or that can be directly assigned to such activities relatively easily with a high degree of accuracy. Indirect costs are those that are incurred for common or joint objectives and therefore cannot be identified readily and specifically with a particular sponsored project. Identification with the sponsored work rather than the nature of the goods or services involved is the determining factor in distinguishing direct from indirect costs of sponsored agreement. At educational institutions, such [indirect] costs normally are classified under the following indirect cost categories: depreciation and use allowances, general administration and general expenses, sponsored projects administration expenses, operations and maintenance expenses, library expenses, departmental administration expenses, and student administration and services.*
>
> *A cost is allocable to a particular cost objective . . . if the goods or services involved are chargeable or assignable to such cost objective in accordance with relative benefits received or other equitable relationship. The test of allowability of costs under these principles are: (a) they must be reasonable; (b) they must be allocable to sponsored agreements under the principles and methods provided herein; (c) they must be given consistent treatment through application of those generally accepted accounting principles appropriate to the circumstances; and (d) they must conform to any limitations or exclusions set forth in these principles or in the sponsored agreement as to types or amounts of cost items.*[3]

Unless a university and its cognizant government agency agree on a different method of cost determination, the methodology in the circular applies. Indirect-cost rates are negotiated each year between universities and their cognizant federal agencies, such as the National Institutes of Health and the National Science Foundation. The agencies are also responsible for auditing university contracts. The Department of Defense (DoD) is the cognizant agency for Stanford, with its Office of Naval Research (ONR) negotiating cost rates and the Defense Contract Audit Agency (DCAA) conducting audits.

Stanford's 1988–1989 operating expenses were about $355 million. In that year, Stanford received $78 million in indirect-cost reimbursement from the government. Some of the indirect cost pools included for reimbursement were economy-class air travel related to a specific research project; depreciation on the university's yacht *Victoria;* alcoholic beverages and entertainment costs; advertising; organized fund-raising costs; costs of books and periodicals purchased for campus libraries; alumni activities; investment management; operation, renovation, and depreciation of university-owned houses; and public relations.

Stanford deducted a certain percentage (say, 20%) from the indirect cost pools to adjust for the amounts included in the cost pools that are unallowable or unallocable to government contracts. It then allocated the remaining amount in the indirect cost pool to government-sponsored research contracts on the basis of its agreement with the government.

QUESTIONS

1. Why does the federal government engage in cost-plus contracting rather than seek competitive bids for sponsored research?
2. During the audit, there was a review of the costs that fall under Circular A-21. As defined in this case, distinguish between:
   a. Direct and indirect costs
   b. Allocable and unallocable costs
3. There are four possible combinations of the terms above (e.g., indirect, allocable costs). Use the table column layout below to categorize the costs given in the next to last paragraph in the case.

Example	Direct or Indirect	Allocable or Unallocable	Explanation

4. Why does the federal government pay indirect costs of sponsored research?

[1]Case summary prepared from the entire case on Stanford University by Steven Huddart, copyright 1992 by the Board of Trustees of the Leland Stanford Junior University.

[2]Donald Kennedy, in a statement to the Subcommittee on Oversight and Investigations (March 13, 1991).

[3]Excerpts from OMB Circular A-21, "Cost Principles for Educational Institutions" (March, 1979).

CHAPTER

16

Cost Allocation: Joint Products and Byproducts

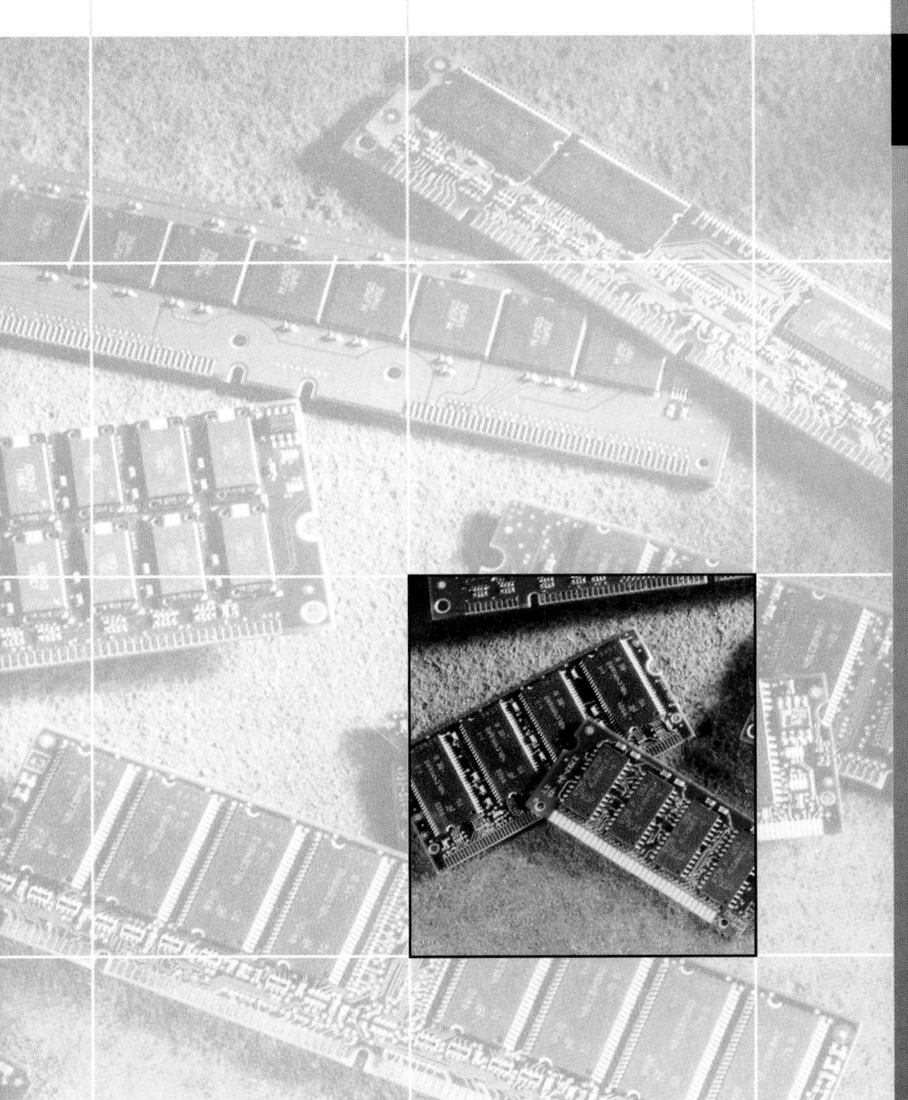

LEARNING OBJECTIVES

1. Identify the splitoff point in a joint-cost situation
2. Distinguish joint products from byproducts
3. Explain why joint costs are allocated to individual products
4. Allocate joint costs using four different methods
5. Explain why the sales value at splitoff method is preferred when allocating joint costs
6. Explain why joint costs are irrelevant in a sell-or-process-further decision
7. Account for byproducts using two different methods

www.prenhall.com/horngren

You're not alone if you don't know who manufactured the memory chips in your computer. Computer memory chips are produced by a few companies in a very competitive industry. Name-brand memory chips don't help sell personal computers, but a low price does. Buyers such as Compaq, Dell, and IBM seek the lowest-price suppliers to help their finished products be price-competitive. Memory chips also are used for items such as home appliances, palm-size organizers, and cellular phones. Chip producers make chips for different devices in a joint production process. The issue for chip producers is accurate allocation of costs to different types of chips. That's where joint-cost-allocation techniques come in.

Preceding chapters have emphasized costing for companies that produce only a single product or companies that produce several products in separate processes. We now consider the more-complex case in which companies produce two or more products simultaneously in the same process(es). For example, a pineapple-processing plant produces multiple products (such as rings, juice, and crushed pineapple) from each pineapple processed. This chapter examines methods for allocating costs to joint products. Some of the topics discussed in this chapter are related to issues covered in Chapters 14 and 15. We also examine how cost numbers appropriate for one purpose, such as external reporting, may not be appropriate for other purposes, such as decisions about the further processing of joint products. This chapter provides yet another illustration of using different costs for different purposes—a theme that underlies cost accounting.

JOINT-COST BASICS

1 Identify the splitoff point in a joint-cost situation

...when two or more products become separately identifiable

Allocating joint costs is particularly troublesome because it isn't feasible to apply the cause-and-effect criterion.

Joint costs are the costs of a production process that yields multiple products simultaneously. Consider the distillation of coal, which yields coke, natural gas, and other products. The cost of this distillation is called a joint cost. The **splitoff point** is the juncture in a joint production process when two or more products become separately identifiable. An example is the point at which coal becomes coke, natural gas, and other products. **Separable costs** are all costs—manufacturing, marketing, distribution, and so on—incurred beyond the splitoff point that are assignable to each of the specific products identified at the splitoff point. At or beyond the splitoff point, decisions relating to sale or further processing of each identifiable product can be made independently of decisions about the other products.

Industries abound in which a production process simultaneously yields two or more products, either at the splitoff point or after further processing. Exhibit 16-1 presents examples of joint-cost situations in diverse industries. In each of these examples, no individual product can be produced without the accompanying products appearing, although in some cases the proportions can be varied. A refinery cannot only produce gasoline from crude oil; it also simultaneously produces kerosene, benzene and naphtha. The focus of joint costing is on assigning costs to individual products at the splitoff point. The focus here contrasts with the focus in preceding chapters, which emphasized assigning costs to individual products as assembly occurs.

2 Distinguish joint products

...products with high sales values

from byproducts

...products with low sales values

The outputs of a joint production process can be classified into two general categories: outputs with a positive sales value and outputs with a zero sales value. The term **product** describes any output that has a positive sales value (or an output that enables an organization to avoid incurring costs). The sales value can be high or low. When a joint production process yields only one product with a high sales value, compared with the sales values of the other products of the process, that product is called a **main product.** When a joint production process yields two or more products with high sales values compared with the sales values of the other products, those products are called **joint products.** The other products of a joint production process that have low sales values compared with the sales value of the main product or joint products are called **byproducts.** For example, if timber (logs) is processed into standard lumber and wood chips, the standard lumber is a main product and the wood chips are the byproduct. That's because the standard lumber has a high sales value com-

Industry	Separable Products at the Splitoff Point
Agriculture and Food Processing	
Cocoa beans	Cocoa butter, cocoa powder, cocoa drink mix, tanning cream
Lamb	Lamb cuts, tripe, hides, bones, fat
Hogs	Bacon, ham, spare ribs, pork roast
Raw milk	Cream, liquid skim
Lumber	Lumber of varying grades and shapes
Turkeys	Breast, wings, thighs, drumsticks, digest, feather meal, and poultry meal
Extractive Industries	
Coal	Coke, gas, benzol, tar, ammonia
Copper ore	Copper, silver, lead, zinc
Petroleum	Crude oil, natural gas, raw LPG
Salt	Hydrogen, chlorine, caustic soda
Chemical Industries	
Raw LPG (liquefied petroleum gas)	Butane, ethane, propane
Semiconductor Industry	
Fabrication of silicon-wafer chips	Memory chips of different quality (as to capacity), speed, life expectancy, and temperature tolerance

EXHIBIT 16-1

Examples of Joint-Cost Situations

pared with the wood chips. If, on the other hand, logs are processed into fine-grade lumber, standard lumber, and wood chips, the fine-grade lumber and standard lumber are joint products, and the wood chips are the byproduct. That's because both the fine-grade lumber and the standard lumber have high sales values compared with the wood chips.

Some outputs of the joint production process have zero sales value. For example, the offshore processing of hydrocarbons to obtain oil and gas also yields water that has zero sales value and is recycled back into the ocean. Similarly, the processing of mineral ore to obtain gold and silver also yields dirt that has zero sales value and is recycled back into the ground. No journal entries are made in the accounting system to record the processing of outputs with zero sales value, because there is no value to record. Exhibit 16-2 presents an overview of the key terms introduced in this section.[1]

The distinctions represented graphically in Exhibit 16-2 are not so definite in practice. For example, some companies may classify the kerosene obtained when refining crude oil as a byproduct because they believe kerosene has low sales value relative to the sales values of gasoline and other products. Other companies may classify kerosene as a joint product because they believe kerosene has high sales value relative to the sales values of gasoline and other products. Moreover, the classification of products—main, joint, or

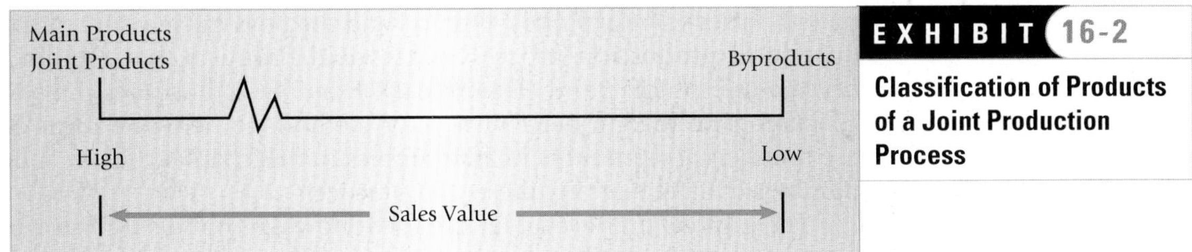

EXHIBIT 16-2

Classification of Products of a Joint Production Process

[1]Some outputs of a joint production process have "negative" revenue when their disposal costs (such as the costs of handling nonsaleable toxic substances that require special disposal procedures) are considered. These disposal costs should be added to the joint production costs that are allocated to joint or main products.

byproduct—can change over time, especially for products such as lower-grade semiconductor chips whose market prices can increase or decrease by, say, 30% or more in any one year. When prices of lower-grade chips are high, they are considered joint products together with higher-grade chips; when prices of lower-grade chips fall, the chips are considered byproducts. Be sure you understand how terms are used and how products are classified by the company you are dealing with.

3 Explain why joint costs are allocated to individual products

...to calculate cost of goods sold and inventory, and for reimbursements under cost-plus contracts and other claims

Why Allocate Joint Costs?

Here are some of the contexts that require joint costs to be allocated to individual products or services:

1. Computation of inventoriable costs and cost of goods sold for financial accounting purposes and reports for income tax authorities.
2. Computation of inventoriable costs and cost of goods sold for internal reporting purposes. Such reports are used in division profitability analysis and affect evaluation of division managers' performance.
3. Cost reimbursement under contracts for companies that have a few, but not all, of their products or services reimbursed under cost-plus contracts with, say, a government agency.
4. Insurance-settlement computations for damage claims made on the basis of cost information by businesses having joint products, main products, or byproducts.
5. Rate regulation for one or more of the jointly produced products or services that are subject to price regulation.[2]
6. Litigation in which costs of joint products are key inputs.

These six contexts highlight reasons why joint costs must be allocated.

4 Allocate joint costs using four different methods

...sales value at splitoff, physical measure, net realizable value (NRV), constant gross-margin percentage NRV

APPROACHES TO ALLOCATING JOINT COSTS

Two approaches are used to allocate joint costs.

- *Approach 1.* Allocate joint costs using *market-based* data such as revenues. This chapter illustrates three methods that use this approach:
  a. Sales value at splitoff method
  b. Net realizable value (NRV) method
  c. Constant gross-margin percentage NRV method
- *Approach 2.* Allocate joint costs using *physical measures,* such as the weight (in, say, kilograms) or volume (in, say, cubic feet) of the joint products.

In preceding chapters, we used the cause-and-effect and benefits-received criteria for guiding cost-allocation decisions (see Exhibit 14-2, p. 484). Joint costs do not have a cause-and-effect relationship with individual products; that's because the production process simultaneously yields multiple products. Using the benefits-received criterion leads to a preference for methods under approach 1. Revenues are, in general, a better indicator of benefits received than physical measures. Mining companies, for example, receive more benefits from 1 ton of gold than they do from 10 tons of coal.

In the simplest joint production process, the joint products are sold at the splitoff point without further processing. We begin with the simplest case (Example 1) to illustrate the sales value at splitoff method and the physical-measure method. Then we introduce joint production processes that yield products that require further processing beyond the splitoff point (Example 2). Example 2 illustrates the NRV method and the constant-gross margin percentage NRV method. To help you focus on key concepts, we use numbers and amounts in all examples in this chapter that are much smaller than the numbers that are typically present in practice.

The exhibits in this chapter use the following symbols to distinguish a joint or main product from a byproduct:

[2]See J. Crespi and J. Harris, "Joint Cost Allocation Under the Natural Gas Act: An Historical Review," *Journal of Extractive Industries Accounting* 2 (2): 133–142.

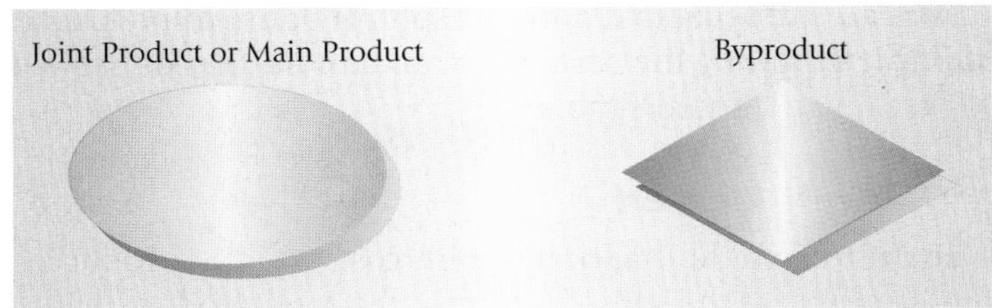

To facilitate comparisons across the methods described earlier, we report gross-margin percentages for individual products under each method.

Example 1: Farmers' Dairy purchases raw milk from individual farms and processes it until the splitoff point, when two products—cream and liquid skim—emerge. These two products are sold to an independent company, which markets and distributes them to supermarkets and other retail outlets.

Summary data for May 2004 are

- Raw milk processed, 110,000 gallons; 10,000 gallons are lost in the production process due to evaporation, spillage, and the like, yielding 25,000 gallons of cream and 75,000 gallons of liquid skim.

	Production	Sales
■ Cream	25,000 gallons	20,000 gallons at $8 per gallon
■ Liquid skim	75,000 gallons	30,000 gallons at $4 per gallon

- Inventories

	Beginning Inventory	Ending Inventory
Raw milk	0 gallons	0 gallons
Cream	0 gallons	5,000 gallons
Liquid skim	0 gallons	45,000 gallons

- Cost of purchasing 110,000 gallons of raw milk and processing it until the splitoff point to yield cream and liquid skim, $400,000.

Exhibit 16-3 depicts the basic relationships in this example.

How much of the $400,000 joint costs should be allocated to the cost of goods sold of 20,000 gallons of cream and 30,000 gallons of liquid skim, and how much should be allocated to the ending inventory of 5,000 gallons of cream and 45,000 gallons of liquid skim? The joint production costs of $400,000 cannot be traced to either product. That's

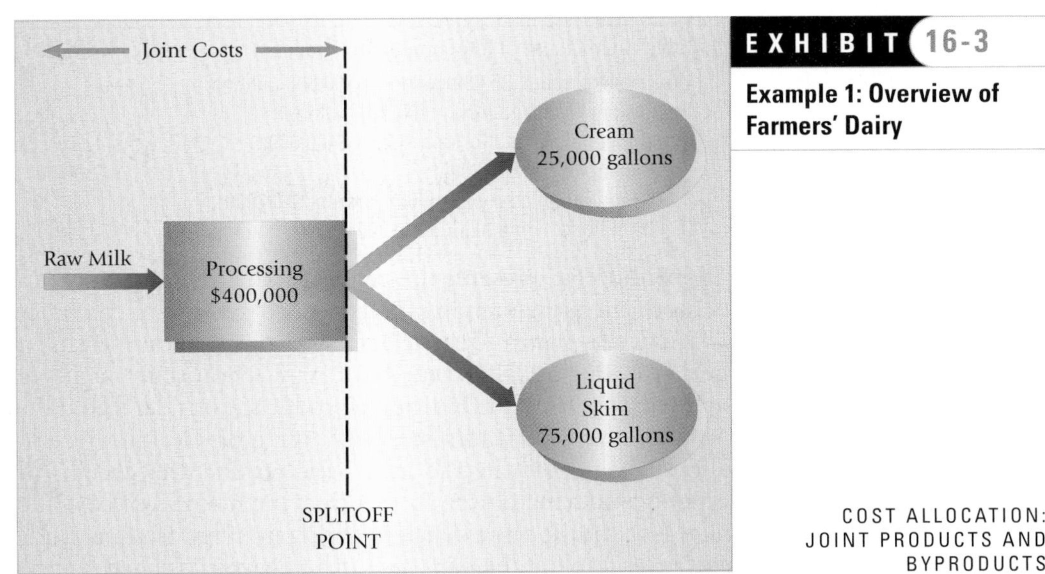

EXHIBIT 16-3

Example 1: Overview of Farmers' Dairy

because the products are not separated until the splitoff point. Joint-cost-allocation methods can be used for determining the costs of cream and liquid skim sold and for costing the inventories of cream and liquid skim.

Sales Value at Splitoff Method

The **sales value at splitoff method** allocates joint costs to joint products on the basis of the relative total sales value at the splitoff point of the total production of these products during the accounting period. We illustrate the allocation of joint costs to individual products in proportion to total sales value at splitoff for Example 1:

	Cream	Liquid Skim	Total
1. Sales value of total production at splitoff point (cream, 25,000 gallons × \$8/gallon; liquid skim, 75,000 gallons × \$4/gallon)	\$200,000	\$300,000	\$500,000
2. Weighting (\$200,000 ÷ \$500,000; \$300,000 ÷ \$500,000)	0.40	0.60	
3. Joint costs allocated (cream, 0.40 × \$400,000; liquid skim, 0.60 × \$400,000)	\$160,000	\$240,000	\$400,000
4. Joint production cost per gallon (cream, \$160,000 ÷ 25,000 gallons; liquid skim, \$240,000 ÷ 75,000 gallons)	\$6.40/gal.	\$3.20/gal.	

The equality of the gross-margin percentages for the individual products always occurs under the sales value at splitoff method when there are no beginning inventories and all products are sold at the splitoff point.

This method uses the sales value of the *entire production of the accounting period.* The reason is that the joint costs were incurred on all units produced, not just the portion sold during the current period. Exhibit 16-4 presents the product-line income statement using the sales value at splitoff method. Both cream and liquid skim have gross-margin percentages of 20%.

You can now see why the sales value at splitoff method follows the benefits-received criterion of cost allocation: Costs are allocated to products in proportion to their expected revenues. This method is both straightforward and intuitive. The cost-allocation base (total sales value at splitoff) is expressed in terms of a common denominator (the amount of revenues) that is systematically recorded in the accounting system. To use this method, a company needs the market selling prices for all products at the splitoff point.

Physical-Measure Method

The **physical-measure method** allocates joint costs to joint products on the basis of the relative weight, volume, or other physical measure at the splitoff point of the total production of these products during the accounting period. In Example 1, the \$400,000 joint costs produced 25,000 gallons of cream and 75,000 gallons of liquid skim. Using the number of gallons produced as the physical measure, joint costs are allocated as follows:

	Cream	Liquid Skim	Total
1. Physical measure of total production (gallons)	25,000	75,000	100,000
2. Weighting (cream, 25,000 gallons ÷ 100,000 gallons; liquid skim 75,000 gallons ÷ 100,000 gallons)	0.25	0.75	
3. Joint costs allocated (cream, 0.25 × \$400,000; liquid skim, 0.75 × \$400,000)	\$100,000	\$300,000	\$400,000
4. Joint production cost per gallon (cream, \$100,000 ÷ 25,000 gallons; liquid skim, \$300,000 ÷ 75,000 gallons)	\$4/gal.	\$4/gal.	

Exhibit 16-5 presents the product-line income statement using the physical-measure method. The gross-margin percentages are 50% for cream and 0% for liquid skim.

Under the benefits-received criterion, the physical-measure method is less preferred than the sales value at splitoff method. Why? Because it has no relationship to the revenue-producing power of the individual products. Consider a gold mine that extracts ore containing gold, silver, and lead. Use of a common physical measure (tons) would result in almost all costs being allocated to lead—the product that weighs the most but has the lowest revenue-producing power. In this case, the method of cost allocation is inconsistent with the reason for the mine owner incurring mining costs—to find gold and silver, not lead. As another example, if the joint costs of a hog were assigned to its various products on the basis

	Cream	Liquid Skim	Total
Revenues (cream, 20,000 gal. × $8/gal.; liquid skim, 30,000 gal. × $4/gal.)	$160,000	$120,000	$280,000
Costs of goods sold (joint costs)			
Production costs (cream, 0.40 × $400,000; liquid skim, 0.60 × $400,000)	160,000	240,000	400,000
Deduct ending inventory (cream, 5,000 gal. × $6.40/gal.; liquid skim, 45,000 gal. × $3.20/gal.)	32,000	144,000	176,000
Cost of goods sold (joint costs)	128,000	96,000	224,000
Gross margin	$ 32,000	$ 24,000	$ 56,000
Gross-margin percentage	20%	20%	20%

EXHIBIT 16-4

Joint Costs Allocated Using Sales Value at Splitoff Method: Farmers' Dairy Product-Line Income Statement for May 2004

of weight, center-cut pork chops would have the same cost per pound as pigs feet, lard, bacon, ham, bones, and so forth—when, in fact, costs are incurred for the revenue-generating benefits of the products. In a product-line income statement, the pork products that have a high sales value per pound—for example, center-cut pork chops—would show a big "profit," and products that have a low sales value per pound—for example, bones—would show sizable losses.

The physical-measure method doesn't meet any of the cost-allocation criteria—cause and effect, benefits received, fairness, and ability to bear described in Exhibit 14-2, p. 484.

Obtaining comparable physical measures for all products is not always straightforward. Consider the joint costs of producing oil and gas; oil is a liquid and gas is a vapor. To use a physical measure, such as barrels, in this context requires technical assistance from petroleum engineers on how to convert the vapor into a measure that can be added to barrels of oil. For example, gas could be converted to barrels of oil based on the energy equivalent of the gas and oil. Technical personnel outside of accounting may be required when using some physical measures to allocate joint costs.

Determining which products of a joint process to include in a physical-measure computation can greatly affect the allocations between or among those products. Outputs with no sales value (such as dirt in gold mining) are always excluded. Although many more tons of dirt than gold are produced, costs are not incurred to produce outputs that have zero sales value. Byproducts with low sales values relative to the joint products or the main product also are often excluded from the denominator used in the physical-measure method. The general guideline for the physical-measure method is to include only the joint-product outputs in the weighting computations.

Net Realizable Value (NRV) Method

In many cases, products are processed beyond the splitoff point to bring them to a marketable form or to increase their value above their selling price at the splitoff point. To illustrate, let's extend the Farmers' Dairy example.

	Cream	Liquid Skim	Total
Revenues (cream, 20,000 gal. × $8/gal.; liquid skim, 30,000 gal. × $4/gal.)	$160,000	$120,000	$280,000
Costs of goods sold (joint costs)			
Production costs (cream, 0.25 × $400,000; liquid skim, 0.75 × $400,000)	100,000	300,000	400,000
Deduct ending inventory (cream, 5,000 gal. × $4/gal.; liquid skim, 45,000 gal. × $4/gal.)	20,000	180,000	200,000
Cost of goods sold (joint costs)	80,000	120,000	200,000
Gross margin	$ 80,000	$ 0	$ 80,000
Gross-margin percentage	50%	0%	28.6%

EXHIBIT 16-5

Joint Costs Allocated Using Physical-Measure Method: Farmers' Dairy Product-Line Income Statement for May 2004

EXHIBIT 16-6

Example 2: Overview of Farmers' Dairy

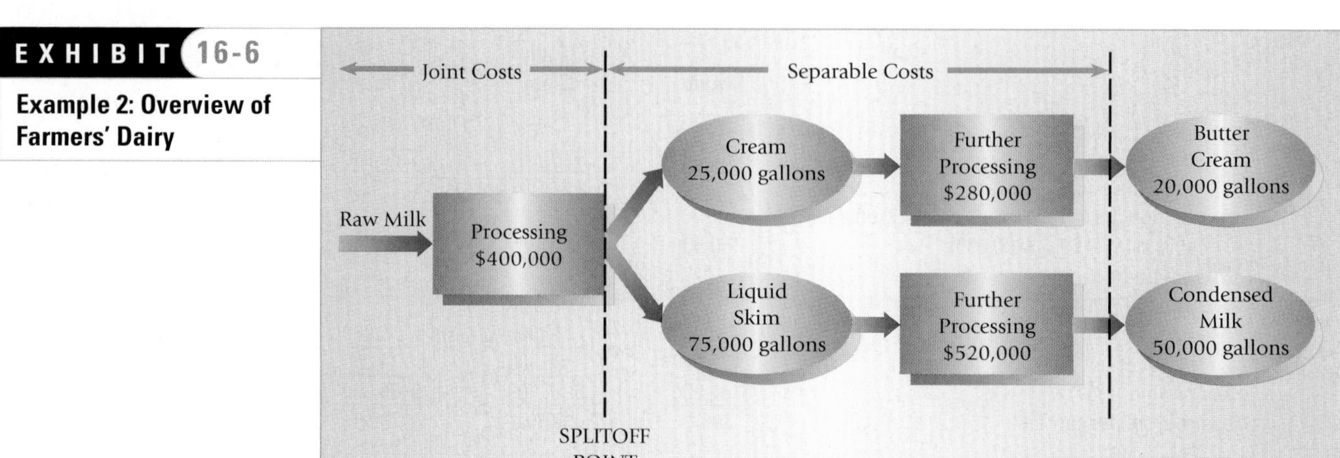

Example 2: Assume the same data as in Example 1 except that here both cream and liquid skim can be processed further:

- Cream→Buttercream: 25,000 gallons of cream are further processed to yield 20,000 gallons of buttercream at additional processing costs of $280,000. Buttercream, which sells for $25 per gallon, is used in the manufacture of butter-based products.
- Liquid Skim→Condensed Milk: 75,000 gallons of liquid skim are further processed to yield 50,000 gallons of condensed milk at additional processing costs of $520,000. Condensed milk sells for $22 per gallon.

Sales during the accounting period were 12,000 gallons of buttercream and 45,000 gallons of condensed milk. Exhibit 16-6 depicts the basic relationships of how raw milk is converted into cream and liquid skim in a joint production process, and how the cream is separately processed into buttercream and the liquid skim is separately processed into condensed milk. Inventory information follows:

	Beginning Inventory	Ending Inventory
Raw milk	0 gallons	0 gallons
Cream	0 gallons	0 gallons
Liquid skim	0 gallons	0 gallons
Buttercream	0 gallons	8,000 gallons
Condensed milk	0 gallons	5,000 gallons

The NRV method is often used for joint products that have no market value at splitoff. This method, however, requires assumptions about events occurring beyond splitoff. In what quantities will products be produced? What will be the selling prices? How much will be the separable costs?

The **net realizable value (NRV) method** allocates joint costs to joint products on the basis of the relative NRV—the final sales value minus the separable costs—of the total production of the joint products during the accounting period. The NRV method is typically used in preference to the sales value at splitoff method only when we don't know the market selling prices for one or more products at splitoff. Joint costs in this example are allocated as follows:

	Buttercream	Condensed Milk	Total
1. Final sales value of total production (buttercream, 20,000 gallons × $25/gallon; condensed milk, 50,000 gallons × $22/gallon)	$500,000	$1,100,000	$1,600,000
2. Deduct separable costs to complete and sell	280,000	520,000	800,000
3. Net realizable value at splitoff point	$220,000	$ 580,000	$ 800,000
4. Weighting ($220,000 ÷ $800,000; $580,000 ÷ $800,000)	0.275	0.725	
5. Joint costs allocated (buttercream, 0.275 × $400,000; condensed milk, 0.725 × $400,000)	$110,000	$ 290,000	$ 400,000
6. Production cost per gallon (buttercream, [$110,000 + $280,000] ÷ 20,000 gallons; condensed milk, [$290,000 + $520,000] ÷ 50,000 gallons)	$19.50/gal.	$16.20/gal.	

	Buttercream	Condensed Milk	Total
Revenues (buttercream, 12,000 gal. × $25/gal.; condensed milk, 45,000 gal. × $22/gal.)	$300,000	$990,000	$1,290,000
Cost of goods sold			
Joint costs (buttercream, 0.275 × $400,000; condensed milk, 0.725 × $400,000)	110,000	290,000	400,000
Separable costs	280,000	520,000	800,000
Cost of goods available for sale	390,000	810,000	1,200,000
Deduct ending inventory (buttercream, 8,000 gal. × $19.50/gal.; condensed milk, 5,000 gal. × $16.20/gal.)	156,000	81,000	237,000
Cost of goods sold	234,000	729,000	963,000
Gross margin	$ 66,000	$261,000	$ 327,000
Gross-margin percentage	22.0%	26.4%	25.3%

EXHIBIT 16-7

Joint Costs Allocated Using NRV Method: Farmers' Dairy Product-Line Income Statement for May 2004

Exhibit 16-7 presents the product-line income statement using the estimated NRV method. The gross-margin percentages are 22.0% for buttercream and 26.4% for condensed milk.

The NRV method is often implemented using simplifying assumptions. For example, companies that frequently change the number of processing steps beyond the splitoff point often assume a specific set of such steps. Also, if the selling prices of joint products vary frequently, a given set of selling prices may be consistently used throughout the accounting period.[3]

Because the sales value at splitoff method does not require knowledge of the processing steps beyond the splitoff point, it is less complex than the NRV method. However, using the sales value at splitoff method is not always feasible. That's because there may not be market prices for at least one of the products at the splitoff point. Market prices may only be available after processing occurs beyond the splitoff point.

Constant Gross-Margin Percentage NRV Method

The **constant gross-margin percentage NRV method** allocates joint costs to joint products in such a way that the overall gross-margin percentage is identical for the individual products. This method entails three steps. Exhibit 16-8 on the next page shows these three steps for allocating the $400,000 joint costs between buttercream and condensed milk in the Farmers' Dairy example. As we describe each step, refer to Exhibit 16-8 for an illustration of the step.

- *Step 1:* Compute the overall gross-margin percentage for all joint products together. Note, Exhibit 16-8 uses the final sales value of the *total production* during the accounting period, $1,600,000, *not the total sales* of the period, to calculate the overall gross margin percentage of 25%.
- *Step 2:* Multiply the overall gross-margin percentage and the final sales values of each product to calculate the gross margin for each product. Subtract the gross margin for each product from the final sales value of each product to obtain the total costs that each product will bear.
- *Step 3:* Deduct the separable costs from the total costs that each product will bear to obtain the joint-cost allocation.

The joint costs allocated to a product can be negative under this method. Some products may receive negative allocations of joint costs to bring their gross-margin percentages up to the overall average. Exhibit 16-9 presents the product-line income statement for the constant gross-margin percentage NRV method.

The constant gross-margin percentage NRV method works backward. For each product, the gross margin (based on the overall gross-margin percentage) and separable costs are deducted from final sales value of units produced. The resulting dollar amount for each product is its allocation of joint costs.

Under the constant gross-margin NRV method, the gross-margin percentage for each product is the same, regardless of its separable costs. This method, in effect, "subsidizes" products with relatively high separable costs by assigning less joint costs to them. That's why the product, buttercream, has a 25% gross margin under the constant gross-margin percentage NRV method (in Exhibit 16-9) but has a 22% gross-margin percentage under the NRV method (in Exhibit 16-7).

[3] One extension of the NRV method is to include in the separable costs an imputed interest cost on assets used beyond the splitoff point. This extension raises issues of valuation of those assets and the computation of the imputed interest cost (see Chapter 23, p. 789).

EXHIBIT 16-8

Joint Costs Allocated Using Constant Gross-Margin Percentage NRV Method: Farmers' Dairy for May 2004

Step 1

Final sales value of total production during the accounting period:	
(20,000 gal. × \$25/gal.) + (50,000 gal. × \$22/gal.)	\$1,600,000
Deduct joint and separable costs (\$400,000 + \$280,000 + \$520,000)	1,200,000
Gross margin	\$ 400,000
Gross-margin percentage (\$400,000 ÷ \$1,600,000)	25%

Step 2

	Buttercream	Condensed Milk	Total
Final sales value of total production during the accounting period: (buttercream, 20,000 gal. × \$25/gal.; condensed milk, 50,000 gal. × \$22/gal.)	\$500,000	\$1,100,000	\$1,600,000
Deduct gross margin, using overall gross-margin percentage (25%)	125,000	275,000	400,000
Cost of goods available for sale	375,000	825,000	1,200,000
Step 3			
Deduct separable costs to complete and sell	280,000	520,000	800,000
Joint costs allocated	\$ 95,000	\$ 305,000	\$ 400,000

The constant gross-margin percentage NRV method is different in one fundamental way from the two other market-based joint-cost-allocation methods described earlier. The sales value at splitoff method and the NRV method allocate only the joint costs to the joint products. Neither method takes account of profits earned either before or after the splitoff point when allocating the joint costs. In contrast, the constant gross-margin percentage NRV method is both a joint-cost method and a profit-allocation method. The total difference between the sales value of production of all products and the separable cost of all products includes both (a) the joint costs and (b) the total gross margin. Gross margin is allocated to the joint products under the constant gross-margin method to determine the joint-cost allocations so that each product has the same gross-margin percentage.

5 **Explain why the sales value at splitoff method is preferred when allocating joint costs**

...objectively measures the benefits received by each product

Choosing a Method

Which method of allocating joint costs should be used? Use the sales value at splitoff method when selling-price data are available (even if further processing is done). Reasons for using the sales value at splitoff method include:

EXHIBIT 16-9

Farmers' Dairy Product-Line Income Statement for May 2004: Joint Costs Allocated Using Constant Gross-Margin Percentage NRV Method

	Buttercream	Condensed Milk	Total
Revenues (buttercream, 12,000 gal. × \$25/gal.; condensed milk, 45,000 gal. × \$22/gal.)	\$300,000	\$990,000	\$1,290,000
Cost of goods sold			
Joint costs (from Exhibit 16-8)	95,000	305,000	400,000
Separable costs	280,000	520,000	800,000
Cost of goods available for sale	375,000	825,000	1,200,000
Deduct ending inventory (buttercream, 8,000 gal. × \$18.75/gal.;[a] condensed milk, 5,000 gal. × \$16.50/gal.)[b]	150,000	82,500	232,500
Cost of goods sold	225,000	742,500	967,500
Gross margin	\$ 75,000	\$247,500	\$ 322,500
Gross-margin percentage	25%	25%	25%

[a] \$375,000 ÷ 20,000 gallons = \$18.75/gallon.
[b] \$825,000 ÷ 50,000 gallons = \$16.50/gallon.

1. *It measures the value of the joint product immediately at the end of the joint process.* The sales value at splitoff is the best measure of the benefits received as a result of joint processing relative to all the other methods of allocating joint costs.
2. *No anticipation of subsequent management decisions.* The sales value at splitoff method does not require information on the processing steps after splitoff, if there is further processing. In contrast, the NRV method and constant gross-margin percentage NRV method require information on (a) the specific sequence of further processing decisions (b) the separable costs of further processing, and (c) the point at which individual products are sold.
3. *Availability of a meaningful basis to allocate joint costs to products.* The sales value at splitoff method and the other market-based methods have a meaningful basis to allocate joint costs to products, which is revenues. In contrast, the physical-measure method may lack a meaningful basis that can be used to allocate joint costs to individual products.
4. *Simplicity.* The sales value at splitoff method is simple. In contrast, the NRV and constant gross-margin percentage NRV methods can be complex for processing operations having multiple products and multiple splitoff points. This complexity is increased when management makes frequent changes in the specific sequence of postsplitoff processing decisions or in the point at which individual products are sold.

When selling prices of all products at the splitoff point are not available, other joint-cost-allocation methods are used. The NRV method attempts to approximate the sales value at splitoff by subtracting separable costs incurred after the splitoff point on each product from selling prices. The NRV method assumes that all the markup or profit margin is attributable to the joint process and none of the markup is attributable to the separable costs. Profit, however, is attributable to all phases of production and marketing, not just the joint process. Despite its complexities, the NRV method is used when selling prices at splitoff are not available. It is a better measure of benefits received compared with the constant gross-margin percentage NRV method and the physical-measure method (see Surveys of Company Practice, p. 566).

The main advantage of the constant gross-margin percentage NRV method is that it is easy to implement. This method treats the joint products as though they comprise a single product by calculating an aggregate gross-margin percentage. The method then applies this gross-margin percentage to each product and backs into the joint costs allocated to each product. This method avoids the complexities inherent in the NRV method to measure the benefits received by each of the joint products at the splitoff point. The main issue with the constant gross-margin percentage NRV method is the assumption that all the products have the same ratio of cost to sales value. A constant ratio of cost to sales value across products is very uncommon in companies that produce multiple products that do not involve joint costs.

Although there are difficulties in using the physical-measure method—the lack of congruence with the benefits-received criterion and the possible lack of a meaningful common denominator for allocating the joint costs—there are instances when it may be preferred. Consider rate regulation. Market-based measures are difficult to use in the context of rate or price regulation. It is circular reasoning to use selling prices as a basis for setting prices (rates) and at the same time use selling prices to allocate the costs on which prices (rates) are based. To avoid this circular reasoning, the physical-measure method may be used in rate regulation.

Not Allocating Joint Costs

The preceding methods for allocating joint costs to individual products are all somewhat arbitrary, so some companies do not allocate joint costs to products. Instead, they carry their inventories at NRV. Income on each product is recognized when production is completed. Industries that use variations of this no-allocation approach include meatpacking, canning, and mining.

Accountants do not ordinarily carry inventories at NRV. That's because by carrying inventory at NRV, income is recognized *before* sales are made. In response, some companies using this no-allocation approach carry their inventories at NRV minus an estimated operating income margin. The result is that in the year of production, all of the joint costs of that accounting period are matched against the estimated revenues from the

SURVEYS OF COMPANY PRACTICE

Joint-Cost Allocation in the Oil Patch

The petroleum industry, one of the largest in the world, is an example of an industry with joint costs. Petroleum mining and processing starts with hydrocarbons being extracted from either onshore or offshore fields. Petroleum companies obtain multiple products, such as crude oil, natural gas, and raw LPG (liquefied petroleum gas). The LPG is often further processed into butane, ethane, and propane. How should these joint refining costs be allocated to the separate marketable products produced at the refinery? These costs include the costs of hydrocarbons put into the refinery and the processing costs at the refinery.

One survey focused on the joint-cost-allocation methods chosen by refiners for external reporting purposes:

Market-based measures	
NRV	46%
Other	20
Physical-based measures	
Volume (barrels, gallons, or cubic feet)	27
Mass (weight or molecular mass)	2
Other	5
	100%

Market-based measures are preferred for joint-cost allocation, with the NRV method the predominant choice. The most common other market-based measure reported in the survey was a variation of the NRV method in which the final sales value of each product is used as the allocation base without any deduction for the expected separable costs of production and marketing. This variation illustrates how companies make adjustments to the basic methods described in this chapter, often on the grounds of a perceived cost-benefit basis.

Source: Adapted from Koester and Barnett, "Petroleum Refinery Joint Cost Allocation." See Appendix A for full citation.

production of that accounting period. When any end-of-period inventories are sold in the next period, the cost of goods sold will be the NRV minus the estimated operating income margin shown for the ending inventory of the previous accounting period.

IRRELEVANCE OF JOINT COSTS FOR DECISION MAKING

Should the joint costs allocated to the joint products be used in making pricing decisions for each joint product? No. Why not? Because all joint-cost allocations to products are somewhat arbitrary. There is no cause-and-effect relationship that identifies the resources demanded by each joint product that can then be used as a basis for pricing. The way it is in much of joint-costing, selling prices drive joint-cost allocations; cost allocations do not drive pricing.

6 Explain why joint costs are irrelevant in a sell-or-process-further decision

...joint costs are the same whether or not further processing occurs

Let's consider further the irrelevance of joint costs for decision making. Many manufacturing companies constantly face the decision of whether to further process a joint product. For example, Farmers' Dairy can sell the joint products, cream and liquid skim, at the splitoff point, or further process them into buttercream and condensed milk. In the petroleum-refining industry, the refiner must decide whether to sell raw liquefied petroleum gas as a product or process it further into butane, ethane, and propane.

Chapter 11 introduced the concepts of *relevant revenues*—expected future revenues that differ among alternative courses of action — and *relevant costs*—expected future costs that differ among alternative courses of action. These concepts have important implications for decisions on whether a joint product or main product should be sold at the splitoff point or processed further. Joint costs incurred up to the splitoff point are irrelevant because these costs will be incurred whether the product is sold at the splitoff point or processed further. Moreover, the decision whether to process further should not be influenced by the total amount of the joint costs; nor should the decision to process further be influenced by the portion of the joint costs allocated to individual products.

Sell or Process Further

The decision to incur additional costs for further processing should be based on the incremental operating income attainable beyond the splitoff point. Example 2 assumed it was profitable for both cream and liquid skim to be further processed, respectively, into buttercream and condensed milk. The incremental analysis for these decisions to process further is

Further Processing Cream into Buttercream

Incremental revenues	
($25/gallon × 20,000 gallons) – ($8/gallon × 25,000 gallons)	$300,000
Deduct incremental processing costs	280,000
Increase in operating income from buttercream	$ 20,000

Further Processing Liquid Skim into Condensed Milk

Incremental revenues	
($22/gallon × 50,000 gallons) – ($4/gallon × 75,000 gallons)	$800,000
Deduct incremental processing costs	520,000
Increase in operating income from condensed milk	$280,000

In this example, operating income increases for both products, so the manager should process cream into buttercream and liquid skim into condensed milk. *The $400,000 joint costs incurred up to splitoff—and how they are allocated—are irrelevant in deciding whether to process further.* Why irrelevant? Because the joint costs of $400,000 are the same whether or not further processing occurs.

Incremental costs are the additional costs incurred for an activity, such as process further. *Do not assume all separable costs in joint-cost allocations are always incremental costs.* Some separable costs may be fixed costs, such as lease costs on buildings where the further processing is done; some separable costs may be sunk costs, such as depreciation on the equipment that converts cream into buttercream; some separable costs may be allocated costs, such as corporate costs allocated to the condensed milk operations. None of these costs will differ between the alternatives of selling products at the splitoff point or processing further.

Joint-Cost Allocation and Performance Evaluation

The potential conflict between cost concepts used for decision making and cost concepts used for evaluating the performance of managers could also arise in sell-or-process-further decisions. To see how, let's continue with Example 2. Suppose allocated fixed costs of further processing cream into buttercream equal $45,000 and that these costs will only be charged to buttercream and to the manager's product-line income statement if buttercream is produced. How might this affect the decision to process further?

As we have seen, on the basis of incremental revenues and incremental costs, Farmers' Dairy's operating income will increase by $20,000 by processing the cream into buttercream. However, producing the buttercream also results in an additional charge for allocated fixed costs of $45,000. If the manager is evaluated on a full-cost basis (that is, after allocating all costs), processing cream into buttercream will lead to the manager's performance-evaluation measure being lower by $25,000 (incremental operating income, $20,000, – allocated fixed costs, $45,000). Therefore, the manager may be tempted to sell cream directly and not process it into buttercream.

A similar conflict can also arise with respect to production of joint products. Consider again Example 1. Suppose Farmers' Dairy has the option of selling raw milk at a profit of $20,000. From a decision-making standpoint, Farmers should process raw milk into cream and liquid skim because the total revenues from selling both joint products ($500,000, p. 560) exceed the joint costs ($400,000, p. 560) by $100,000 (which is greater than the $20,000 Farmers' Dairy would make if it did not process). Suppose, however, the cream and liquid skim product lines are managed by different managers, each of whom is evaluated based on a product-line income statement. If the physical-measure method of joint-cost allocation is used and the selling price per gallon of liquid skim falls below $4.00 per gallon, the liquid skim product line will show a loss (from Exhibit 16-5, p. 561, revenues will be less than $120,000, but cost of goods sold will be unchanged at $120,000). The manager of the liquid skim line will prefer, from his performance-evaluation standpoint, to not produce the liquid skim and sell the raw milk instead.

This conflict between decision making and performance evaluation is less severe if Farmers' uses any of the market-based methods of joint-cost allocations—sales value at splitoff, NRV, or constant gross-margin percentage NRV. That's because each of these methods allocates costs on the basis of revenues that generally lead to positive incomes for each joint product.

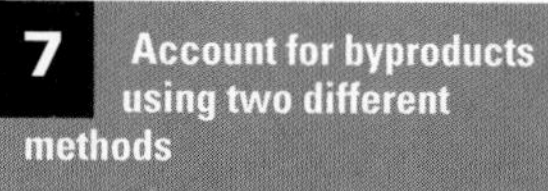

ACCOUNTING FOR BYPRODUCTS

Joint production processes may yield not only joint products and main products but byproducts as well. Although byproducts have much lower sales values than the sales values of joint or main products, the presence of byproducts in a joint production process can affect the allocation of joint costs. Let's consider a two-product example consisting of a main product and a byproduct.

Distinguishing joint products from byproducts is based on the relative magnitude of their revenues, but this can be a gray area requiring judgment.

Example 3: The Meatworks Group processes meat from slaughterhouses. One of its departments cuts lamb shoulders and generates two products:

- Shoulder meat (the main product)—sold for $60 per pack
- Hock meat (the byproduct)—sold for $4 per pack (net of any selling costs)

Data under each column indicate the number of packs for this department in July 2004 are

	Production	Sales	Beginning Inventory	Ending Inventory
Shoulder meat	5,000	4,000	0	1,000
Hock meat	1,000	300	0	700

The joint manufacturing costs of these products in July 2004 were $250,000, comprising $150,000 for direct materials and $100,000 for conversion costs. Both products are sold at the splitoff point without further processing, as Exhibit 16-10 shows.

Two byproduct accounting methods are presented. Method A, the production method, recognizes byproducts in the financial statements at the time production is completed. Method B, the sale method, delays recognition of byproducts until the time of sale. Recognition of byproducts at the time of production is conceptually correct. Recognition at the time of sales often occurs in practice when the dollar amounts of byproducts are immaterial.[4] Exhibit 16-11 presents the income statement of the Meatworks Group under both methods.

EXHIBIT 16-10

Example 3: Overview of Meatworks Group

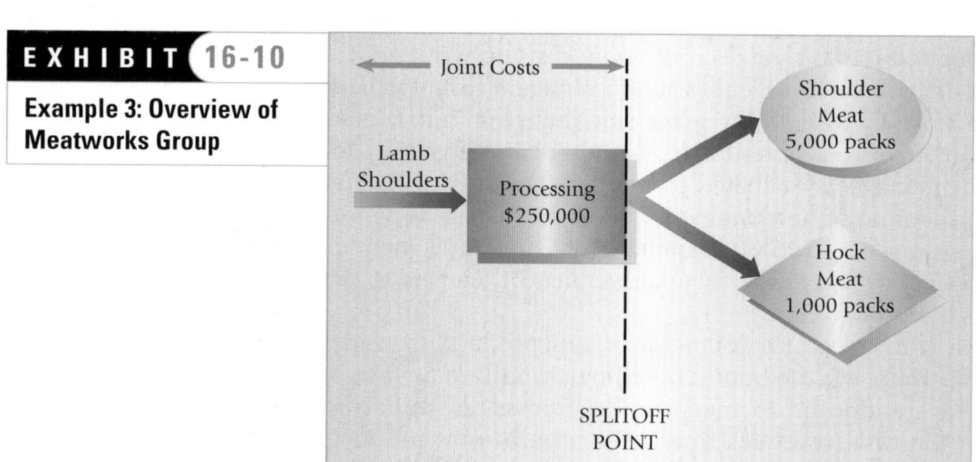

[4]Further discussion on byproduct accounting methods is in C. Cheatham and M. Green, "Teaching Accounting for Byproducts," *Management Accounting News & Views* (Spring, 1988): 14–15; and D. Stout and D. Wygal, "Making Byproducts a Main Product of Discussion: A Challenge to Accounting Educators," *Journal of Accounting Education* (1989): 219–233.

EXHIBIT 16-11

Income Statement of Meatworks Group For July 2004

	BYPRODUCT ACCOUNTING METHOD	
	Method A: Recognized at Production	Method B: Recognized at Sale
Revenues		
Main product: shoulder meat (4,000 packs × $60/pack)	$240,000	$240,000
Byproduct: Hock meat (300 packs × $4/pack)	—	1,200
Total revenues	240,000	241,200
Cost of goods sold		
Total manufacturing costs	250,000	250,000
Deduct byproduct revenue (1,000 packs × $4/pack)	4,000	—
Net manufacturing costs	246,000	250,000
Deduct main-product inventory	49,200 [a]	50,000 [b]
Cost of goods sold	196,800	200,000
Gross margin	$ 43,200	$ 41,200
Gross-margin percentage	18.00%	17.08%
Inventoriable costs (end of period):		
Main product: Shoulder meat	$ 49,200	$ 50,000
Byproduct: Hock meat (700 packs × $4/pack)[c]	2,800	0

[a](1,000 ÷ 5,000) × net manufacturing cost = (1,000 ÷ 5,000) × $246,000 = $49,200.
[b](1,000 ÷ 5,000) × total manufacturing cost = (1,000 ÷ 5,000) × $250,000 = $50,000.
[c]Recorded at selling prices.

Method A: Byproducts Recognized at Time Production Is Completed

This method recognizes the byproduct in the financial statements—the 1,000 packs of hock meat—in the month it is produced, July 2004. The NRV from the byproduct produced is offset against the costs of the main product (see Concepts in Action, p. 570). The following journal entries illustrate this method:

1. Work in Process	150,000	
Accounts Payable		150,000
To record direct materials purchased and used in production during July.		
2. Work in Process	100,000	
Various accounts		100,000
To record conversion costs in the production process during July; examples include energy, manufacturing supplies, all manufacturing labor, and plant depreciation.		
3. Byproduct Inventory—Hock Meat (1,000 packs × $4/pack)	4,000	
Finished Goods—Shoulder Meat ($250,000 – $4,000)	246,000	
Work in Process ($150,000 + $100,000)		250,000
To record cost of goods completed during July.		
4. a. Cost of Goods Sold [(4,000 packs ÷ 5,000 packs) × $246,000]	196,800	
Finished Goods—Shoulder Meat		196,800
To record the cost of the main product sold during July.		
b. Cash or Accounts Receivable (4,000 packs × $60/pack)	240,000	
Revenues—Shoulder Meat		240,000
To record the sales of the main product during July.		
5. Cash or Accounts Receivable (300 packs × $4/pack)	1,200	
Byproduct Inventory—Hock Meat		1,200
To record the sales of the byproduct during July.		

This method reports the byproduct inventory of hock meat in the balance sheet at its $4 per pack selling price [(1,000 packs – 300 packs) × $4/pack = $2,800].

One variation of this method would be to report byproduct inventory at its NRV reduced by a normal profit margin.[5] When the byproduct inventory is sold in a

CONCEPTS IN ACTION

Chicken Processing: Costing of Joint Products and Byproducts

Chicken processing operations provide examples in which joint and byproduct costing issues can arise. White breast meat, the highest revenue-generating product, is obtained from the front end of the bird; dark meat from the back end. Other edible products include chicken wings and giblets. There are many nonedible products that have a diverse set of uses. For example, poultry feathers are used in bedding and sporting goods.

Poultry companies use individual-product cost information for several purposes. One purpose is in customer-profitability analysis. Customers (such as supermarkets and fast-food restaurants) differ greatly in the mix of products they purchase. Individual-product cost data enable companies to determine differences in individual customer profitability. A subset of products is placed into frozen storage, which creates a demand for individual-product cost information for inventory valuation.

Companies differ in how they cost individual products. Consider two of the largest U.S. companies: Southern Poultry and Golden State Poultry (disguised names).

Southern Poultry classifies white breast meat as the single main product in its costing system. All other products are classified as byproducts. Selling prices of the many byproducts are used to reduce the chicken processing costs that are allocated to the main product. The white breast meat is often further processed into many individual products (such as trimmed chicken and marinated chicken). The separable cost of this further processing is added to the cost per pound of deboned white breast meat to obtain the cost of further-processed products.

Golden State Poultry classifies any product sold to a retail outlet as a joint product. Such products include breast fillets, half-breasts, thighs, and whole legs. All other products are classified as byproducts. Revenue that will be earned from byproducts is offset against the chicken processing cost before that cost is allocated among the joint products. The average selling prices of products sold to its retail outlets are used to allocate the net chicken processing cost to the individual joint products. The distribution costs of transporting the chicken products from the processing plants to retail outlets are not taken into account when determining the weights for joint-cost allocation.

Source: Adapted from conversations with executives of Southern Poultry and Golden State Poultry.

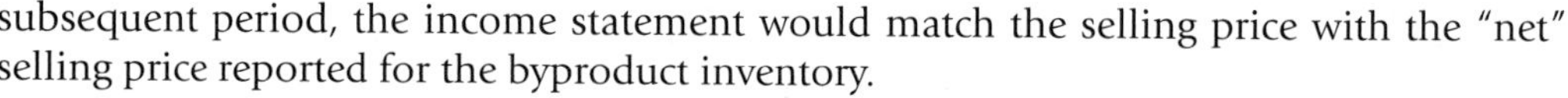
subsequent period, the income statement would match the selling price with the "net" selling price reported for the byproduct inventory.

Method B: Byproducts Recognized at Time of Sale

This method makes no journal entries until sale of the byproduct occurs. Revenues of the byproduct are reported as a revenue item in the income statement at the time of sale. These revenues are either grouped with other sales, included as other income, or deducted from cost of goods sold. In the Meatworks Group example, byproduct revenues in July 2004 are $1,200 (300 packs × $4/pack) because only 300 packs of the hock meat are sold in July (of the 1,000 packs produced). The journal entries are

You may find that contrasting the journal entries under the two methods of accounting for byproducts is helpful in understanding the differences between the methods.

1. and 2. Same as for method A.

3.	Finished Goods—Shoulder Meat	250,000	
	Work in Process		250,000
	To record cost of goods completed during July.		

[5]One approach would be to assume all products have the same "normal" profit margin like the constant gross-margin percentage NRV method. Alternatively, the company might allow products to have different profit margins based on an analysis of the margins earned by other companies who sell them as individual products.

4. a.	Cost of Goods Sold [(4,000 packs ÷ 5,000 packs) × $250,000]	200,000	
	Finished Goods—Shoulder Meat		200,000
	To record the cost of the main product sold during July.		
b.	Same as for method A.		
5.	Cash or Accounts Receivable	1,200	
	Revenues—Shoulder Meat		1,200
	To record the sales of the byproduct during July.		

Method B is used in practice primarily on the grounds that the dollar amounts of byproducts are immaterial. However, this method permits managers to "manage" reported earnings by timing when they sell byproducts. Managers may store byproducts for several periods and give revenues and income a "small boost" by selling byproducts accumulated over several periods when revenues and profits from the main product or joint products are low.

Technically, both methods of accounting for byproducts violate generally accepted accounting principles (GAAP). Method A recognizes byproduct revenues at the time products are produced, but GAAP wouldn't recognize revenues until sale occurs. Method B violates GAAP because it doesn't recognize byproduct inventory as an asset. These technical violations are permissible because the dollar amounts of byproducts are (by definition) immaterial.

PROBLEM FOR SELF-STUDY

Inorganic Chemicals purchases salt and processes it into products such as caustic soda, chlorine, and PVC (polyvinyl chloride). In July 2003, Inorganic Chemicals purchased salt for $40,000. Conversion costs of $60,000 were incurred up to the splitoff point, at which time two salable products were produced: caustic soda and chlorine. Chlorine can be further processed into PVC.

The July 2003 production and sales information is:

	Production	Sales	Selling Price per Ton
Caustic soda	1,200 tons	1,200 tons	$ 50 per ton
Chlorine	800 tons		
PVC	500 tons	500 tons	200 per ton

All 800 tons of chlorine were further processed, at an incremental cost of $20,000, to yield 500 tons of PVC. There were no beginning or ending inventories of caustic soda, chlorine, or PVC in July.

There is an active market for chlorine. Inorganic Chemicals could have sold all of its July production of chlorine at $75 a ton.

Required

1. Allocate the joint costs of $100,000 between caustic soda and chlorine under the (a) sales value at splitoff method, (b) physical-measure (tons) method, and (c) NRV method.
2. What is the gross-margin percentage of (a) caustic soda and (b) PVC under the three allocation methods in 1?
3. Lifetime Swimming Pool Products offers to purchase 800 tons of chlorine in August 2003 at $75 a ton. This sale would mean that no PVC would be produced in August. How would accepting this offer affect Inorganic's August 2003 operating income?

SOLUTION

1. a. Sales value at splitoff method

	Caustic Soda	Chlorine	Total
1. Sales value at splitoff (caustic soda, 1,200 tons × $50/ton; chlorine, 800 tons × $75/ton)	$60,000	$60,000	$120,000
2. Weighting ($60,000 ÷ $120,000; $60,000 ÷ $120,000)	0.5	0.5	
3. Joint costs allocated ($40,000 + $60,000) (caustic soda, 0.5 × $100,000; chlorine, 0.5 × $100,000)	$50,000	$50,000	$100,000

Continued

b. Physical-measure method

	Caustic Soda	Chlorine	Total
1. Physical measure (tons)	1,200	800	2,000
2. Weighting (1,200 tons ÷ 2,000 tons; 800 tons ÷ 2,000 tons)	0.6	0.4	
3. Joint costs allocated (caustic soda, 0.6 × $100,000; chlorine, 0.4 × $100,000)	$60,000	$40,000	$100,000

c. NRV method

	Caustic Soda	Chlorine	Total
1. Final sales value of production (caustic soda, 1,200 tons × $50/ton; PVC from chlorine, 500 tons × $200/ton)	$60,000	$100,000	$160,000
2. Deduct separable costs	0	20,000	20,000
3. NRV at splitoff point	$60,000	$ 80,000	$140,000
4. Weighting ($60,000 ÷ $140,000; $80,000 ÷ $140,000)	3/7	4/7	
5. Joint costs allocated (caustic soda 3/7 × $100,000; chlorine, 4/7 × $100,000)	$42,857	$ 57,143	$100,000

2. a. Caustic soda

	Sales Value at Splitoff Point	Physical Measure	NRV
Sales	$60,000	$60,000	$60,000
Deduct joint costs	50,000	60,000	42,857
Gross margin	$10,000	$ 0	$17,143
Gross-margin percentage	16.7%	0%	28.6%

b. PVC

	Sales Value at Splitoff Point	Physical Measure	NRV
Sales	$100,000	$100,000	$100,000
Deduct joint costs	50,000	40,000	57,143
Deduct separable costs	20,000	20,000	20,000
Gross margin	$ 30,000	$ 40,000	$ 22,857
Gross-margin percentage	30.0%	40.0%	22.9%

3. Incremental revenues from further processing of chlorine into PVC:

(500 tons × $200/ton) – (800 tons × $75/ton)	$40,000
Incremental costs of further processing chlorine into PVC	20,000
Incremental operating income from further processing	$20,000

The operating income would be reduced by $20,000 if Inorganic sold 800 tons of chlorine to Lifetime Swimming Pool Products instead of further processing the chlorine into PVC.

DECISION POINTS

SUMMARY

The following question-and-answer format summarizes the chapter's learning objectives. Each decision presents a key question related to a learning objective. The guidelines are the answer to that question.

Decision	Guidelines
1. What are a joint cost and a split off point?	A joint cost is the cost of a single production process that yields multiple products simultaneously. The splitoff point is the juncture in a joint production process when the products become separately identifiable.
2. How do joint products differ from byproducts?	Joint products have high total sales value at the splitoff point. A byproduct has a low total sales value at the splitoff point compared with the sales value of a joint or main product. Products can change from byproducts to joint products when their total sales values significantly increase or change from joint products to byproducts when their total sales values significantly decrease.
3. Why are joint costs allocated to individual products?	The purposes for allocating joint costs to products include inventory costing for financial accounting and internal reporting, cost reimbursement, insurance settlements, rate regulation, and product-cost litigation.
4. What methods can be used to allocate joint costs to individual products?	The methods available to allocate joint costs to products are sales value at splitoff, NRV, constant gross-margin percentage NRV, and physical measure.
5. Which is the preferred method for allocating joint costs to individual products?	The sales value at splitoff method is used when market prices exist at splitoff because using revenues is consistent with the benefits-received criterion, it does not anticipate subsequent management decisions on further processing, and it is simple.
6. Are joint costs relevant in a sell-or-process-further analysis?	No, joint costs and how they are allocated are irrelevant in deciding whether to process further because joint costs are the same whether or not further processing occurs.
7. What methods can be used to account for byproducts?	Byproduct accounting methods differ on whether byproducts are recognized in financial statements at the time of production or at the time of sale. Recognition at the time of production is conceptually correct. Recognition at the time of sale is often used in practice because dollar amounts of byproducts are immaterial.

TERMS TO LEARN

This chapter and the Glossary at the end of the book contain definitions of:

byproducts (p. 556)
constant gross-margin percentage NRV method (563)
joint costs (556)
joint products (556)
main product (556)
net realizable value (NRV) method (562)
physical-measure method (560)
product (556)
sales value at splitoff method (560)
separable costs (556)
splitoff point (556)

ASSIGNMENT MATERIAL

Questions

16-1 Give two examples of industries in which joint costs are found. For each example, what are the individual products at the splitoff point?

16-2 What is a joint cost? What is a separable cost?

16-3 Distinguish between a joint product and a byproduct.

16-4 Why might the number of products in a joint-cost situation differ from the number of outputs? Give an example.

16-5 Provide three reasons for allocating joint costs to individual products or services.

16-6 Why does the sales value at splitoff method use the sales value of the total production in the accounting period and not just the sales value of the products sold?

16-7 Describe a situation in which the sales value at splitoff method cannot be used but the NRV method can be used for joint-cost allocation.

16-8 Distinguish between the sales value at splitoff method and the NRV method.

16-9 Give two limitations of the physical-measure method of joint-cost allocation.

16-10 How might a company simplify its use of the NRV method when final selling prices can vary sizably in an accounting period and management frequently changes the point at which it sells individual products?

16-11 Why is the constant gross-margin percentage NRV method sometimes called a "joint-cost and a profit-allocation" method?

16-12 "Managers must decide whether a product should be sold at splitoff or processed further. The sales value at splitoff method of joint-cost allocation is the best method for generating the information managers need." Do you agree? Explain.

16-13 "Managers should consider only additional revenues and separable costs when making decisions about selling at splitoff or processing further." Do you agree? Explain.

16-14 Describe two major methods to account for byproducts.

16-15 Why might managers seeking a monthly bonus based on attaining a target operating income prefer a byproduct accounting method that recognizes byproducts at the time of sale rather than at the time of production?

Exercises

16-16 **Joint-cost allocation, insurance settlement.** Chicken Little grows and processes chickens. Each chicken is disassembled into five main parts. Information pertaining to production in July 2004 is

Parts	Pounds of Product	Wholesale Selling Price per Pound When Production Is Complete
Breasts	100	$1.10
Wings	20	0.40
Thighs	40	0.70
Bones	80	0.20
Feathers	10	0.10

Joint cost of production in July 2004 was $100.

A special shipment of 20 pounds of breasts and 10 pounds of wings has been destroyed in a fire. Chicken Little's insurance policy provides for reimbursement for the cost of the items destroyed. The insurance company permits Chicken Little to use a joint-cost-allocation method. The splitoff point is assumed to be at the end of the production line.

Required

1. Compute the cost of the special shipment destroyed using
   a. Sales value at splitoff method
   b. Physical-measure method (pounds of finished product)
2. What joint-cost-allocation method would you recommend Chicken Little use? Explain.

16-17 **Joint products and byproducts (continuation of 16-16).** Chicken Little is computing the ending inventory values for its July 31, 2004, balance sheet. Ending inventory amounts on July 31 are 10 pounds of breasts, 4 pounds of wings, 3 pounds of thighs, 5 pounds of bones, and 2 pounds of feathers.

Chicken Little's management wants to use the sales value at splitoff point method. However, they want you to explore the effect on ending inventory values of classifying one or more products as a byproduct rather than a joint product.

Required

1. Assume Chicken Little classifies all five products as joint products. What are the ending inventory values of each product on July 31, 2004?
2. Assume Chicken Little uses a byproduct method that recognizes byproducts in the financial statements at the time production is completed. The total revenues to be received from the sale of byproducts produced that period are offset against the joint cost of production of the joint products. What are the ending inventory values for each joint product on July 31, 2004, assuming breasts and thighs are the joint products and wings, bones, and feathers are byproducts?
3. Comment on differences in the results in requirements 1 and 2.

16-18 Net realizable value method. Illawara, Inc., produces two joint products, cooking oil and soap oil, from a single vegetable-oil refining process. In July 2004, the joint costs of this process were $24,000,000. Separable processing costs beyond the splitoff point were cooking oil, $30,000,000, and soap oil, $7,500,000. Cooking oil sells for $50 per drum. Soap oil sells for $25 per drum. Illawara produced and sold 1,000,000 drums of cooking oil and 500,000 drums of soap oil. There are no beginning or ending inventories of cooking oil or soap oil.

Allocate the $24,000,000 joint costs using the NRV method. **Required**

Excel Application For students who wish to practice their spreadsheet skills, the following is a step-by-step approach to creating an Excel spreadsheet to work this problem.

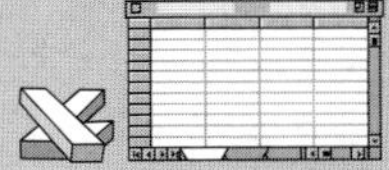

Step-by-Step

1. Open a new spreadsheet. At top, create an "Original Data" section for the data provided by Illawara, Inc. Create a row for "Joint Costs" and enter the joint costs of the refining process in this row. Skip two rows, create columns for "Cooking Oil" and "Soap Oil" and create rows for "Separable Costs, Selling Price," and "Sales Volume" and enter the data for Illawara.

(Program your spreadsheet to perform all necessary calculations. Do not "hard-code" any amounts, such as the weighting for the joint-cost allocation, requiring addition, subtraction, multiplication, or division operations.)

2. Skip two rows, create a new section, "Joint-Cost Allocation." Create a table in the same format as shown at the bottom of page 562, with columns for "Cooking Oil, Soap Oil, " and "Total," and rows labeled "Final Sales Value of Total Production," "Deduct Separable Costs to Complete and Sell," "NRV at Splitoff Point," "Weighting," and "Joint Costs Allocated."
3. Using the data from your Original Data section, enter the calculations for Final Sales Value of Total Production, Separable Costs to Complete and Sell, and NRV at Splitoff Point for Cooking Oil, Soap Oil, and Total.
4. Use the NRVs at Splitoff Point for Cooking Oil, Soap Oil, and Total from step 3 to calculate the weights on cooking oil and soap oil to be used in the joint-cost allocation. Use these weights to allocate joint costs to cooking oil and soap oil.
5. *Check the accuracy of your spreadsheet:* Go to your Original Data section and change the selling price of cooking oil from $50 per drum to $45 per drum. If your spreadsheet is programmed correctly, joint costs allocated to cooking oil and soap oil should change to $18,000,000 and $6,000,000, respectively.

16-19 Alternative joint-cost-allocation methods, further-process decision. The Wood Spirits Company produces two products, turpentine and methanol (wood alcohol), by a joint process. Joint costs amount to $120,000 per batch of output. Each batch totals 10,000 gallons: 25% methanol and 75% turpentine. Both products are processed further without gain or loss in volume. Separable processing costs are methanol, $3 per gallon; turpentine, $2 per gallon. Methanol sells for $21 per gallon. Turpentine sells for $14 per gallon.

Required

1. How much joint costs per batch should be allocated to turpentine and to methanol, assuming that joint costs are allocated on a physical-measure (number of gallons at splitoff point) basis?
2. If joint costs are to be assigned on an NRV basis, how much joint cost should be assigned to turpentine and to methanol?
3. Prepare product-line income statements per batch for requirements 1 and 2. Assume no beginning or ending inventories.
4. The company has discovered an additional process by which the methanol (wood alcohol) can be made into a pleasant-tasting alcoholic beverage. The selling price of this beverage would be $60 a gallon. Additional processing would increase separable costs $9 per gallon (in addition to the $3 per gallon separable cost required to yield methanol). The company would have to pay excise taxes of 20% on the selling price of the beverage. Assuming no other changes in cost, what is the joint cost applicable to the wood alcohol (using the NRV method)? Should the company produce the alcoholic beverage? Show your computations.

16-20 Alternative methods of joint-cost allocation, ending inventories. The Darl Company operates a simple chemical process to convert a single material into three separate items, referred to here as X, Y, and Z. All three end products are separated simultaneously at a single splitoff point.

Products X and Y are ready for sale immediately upon splitoff without further processing or any other additional costs. Product Z, however, is processed further before being sold. There is no available market price for Z at the splitoff point.

The selling prices quoted here are expected to remain the same in the coming year. During 2004, the selling prices of the items and the total amounts sold were

- X—120 tons sold for $1,500 per ton
- Y—340 tons sold for $1,000 per ton
- Z—475 tons sold for $700 per ton

The total joint manufacturing costs for the year were $400,000. An additional $200,000 was spent to finish product Z.

There were no beginning inventories of X, Y, or Z. At the end of the year, the following inventories of completed units were on hand: X, 180 tons; Y, 60 tons; Z, 25 tons. There was no beginning or ending work in process.

Required

1. Compute the cost of inventories of X, Y, and Z for balance sheet purposes and the cost of goods sold for income statement purposes as of December 31, 2004, using
   a. NRV method of joint-cost allocation
   b. Constant gross-margin percentage NRV method of joint-cost allocation
2. Compare the gross-margin percentages for X, Y, and Z using the two methods given in requirement 1.

16-21 Joint-cost allocation, process further. Sinclair Refining Company (SRC) is a 100%-owned subsidiary of Sinclair Oil & Gas. SRC operates a refinery that processes hydrocarbons sold to it by Sinclair Production Company, another 100%-subsidiary of Sinclair Oil & Gas. SRC's refinery has three outputs from its processing of hydrocarbons: crude oil, natural gas liquids, and gas. The first two outputs are liquids, whereas gas is a vapor. However, gas can be converted into a liquid equivalent using a standard industry conversion factor. For costing purposes, SRC assumes all three outputs are jointly produced until a single splitoff point, at which each output appears separately and is then further processed individually.

For August 2003, the following data apply (the numbers are small to keep the focus on key concepts):

- Crude oil—150 barrels produced and sold at $18 per barrel. Separable costs beyond the splitoff point are $175.
- Natural gas liquids—50 barrels produced and sold at $15 per barrel. Separable costs beyond the splitoff point are $105.
- Gas—800 equivalent barrels produced and sold at $1.30 per equivalent barrel. Separable costs beyond the splitoff point are $210.

SRC paid Sinclair Production Company $1,400 for hydrocarbons delivered to it from its offshore platform in August 2003. The cost of operating the refinery in August up to the splitoff point was $400, including $100 of gas charges from Deadhorse Utilities, an independent utility company. Deadhorse signed a long-term contract with SRC several years ago when gas prices were much lower than in 2003.

A new federal law has recently been passed that taxes crude oil at 30% of operating income. No new tax is to be paid on natural gas liquid or natural gas. Starting August 2003, SRC must report a separate product-line income statement for crude oil. One challenge facing SRC is how to allocate the joint cost of producing the three separate salable outputs. Assume no beginning or ending inventory.

Required

1. Draw a diagram showing the joint-cost situation for SRC.
2. Allocate the August 2003 joint cost among the three salable products using
   a. Physical-measures method
   b. NRV method
3. Show the operating income for each product using the methods in requirement 2.
4. Discuss the pros and cons of the two methods to Sinclair Oil & Gas for product emphasis decisions.
5. Draft a letter to the taxation authorities on behalf of Sinclair Oil & Gas that justifies the joint-cost-allocation method you recommend Sinclair use.

16-22 Joint-cost allocation, physical-measures method (continuation of 16-21). Assume that SRC is not able to sell its gas output. The refinery is located in a remote area, and a terrorist group has just destroyed major sections of the gas pipeline used to transport the gas to market. The pipeline that carries the crude oil and natural gas liquid is still operational. Sinclair Production Company must now reinject the gas into the offshore field. The costs of the hydrocarbons to SRC will not be reduced, but Sinclair Production (not SRC) will bear the cost of gas reinjection. No separable costs of gas production beyond the splitoff point will now be incurred.

Required

1. Assume the same data for all three outputs for August 2003 apply to the new set of facts. Show the operating income for each salable product using the NRV method of joint-cost allocation.
2. Assume the taxation authorities argue that for crude oil income tax determination the physical-measures method should be used to allocate joint costs and that all outputs (including gas, whether sold or reinjected) should be used in deciding the cost-allocation weights. Draft a letter to the taxation authorities on behalf of Sinclair Oil & Gas. Be specific when possible.

16-23 Process further or sell. (R. Capettini, adapted) Henley Company produces joint products A, B, and C, from a single joint process with a fixed cost of $5,000 and a variable cost of $2.00 per input unit. Each product can be either processed further or, at the splitoff point, it can be sold or disposed of at a cost. Out of each input unit, Henley Company produces one unit of product A, three units of product B, and two units of product C.

Required

1. Use the following data to decide whether Henley Company should process each product further or dispose of it (or sell it) at the splitoff point if Henley inputs 5,000 units. For each product, show how much better off Henley would be if it followed your advice versus making the alternative decision. Assume that if Henley does not further process a product, it does not incur any of the further processing costs.

Product	Selling Price per Unit at Splitoff Point	Cost per Unit to Dispose of Product at Splitoff Point	Further Processing Costs		Selling Price per Unit After Further Processing
			Fixed	Variable per unit	
A	—	$0.20	$ 6,000	$0.90	$1.50
B	$0.50	—	1,000	1.00	1.50
C	—	0.90	10,000	1.10	5.40

2. What is Henley Company's gross margin at the 5,000-unit input level?

16-24 **Accounting for a main product and a byproduct.** (Cheatham and Green, adapted) Bill Dundee is the owner and operator of Louisiana Bottling, a bulk soft-drink producer. A single production process yields two bulk soft drinks: Rainbow Dew (the main product) and Resi-Dew (the byproduct). Both products are fully processed at the splitoff point, and there are no separable costs.

For September 2003, the cost of the soft-drink operations is $120,000. Production and sales data are as follows:

	Production (in Gallons)	Sales (in Gallons)	Selling Price per Gallon
Main product: Rainbow Dew	10,000	8,000	$20
Byproduct: Resi-Dew	2,000	1,400	2

There were no beginning inventories on September 1, 2003. An overview of operations follows:

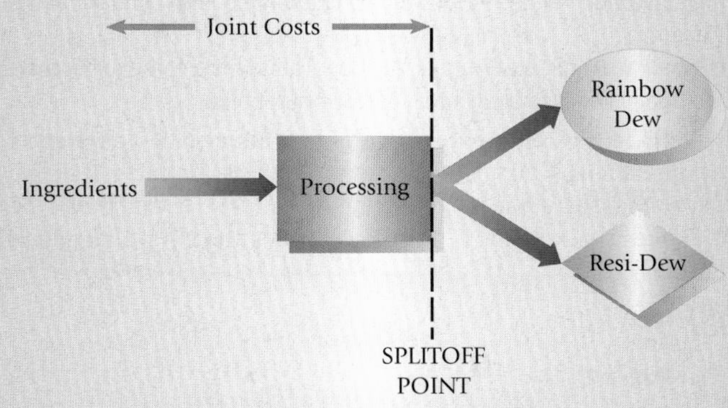

Required

1. What is the gross margin for Louisiana Bottling under methods A and B of byproduct accounting described on pp. 568–571 of this chapter?
2. What are the inventory costs reported in the balance sheet on September 30, 2003, for Rainbow Dew and Resi-Dew under the two methods of byproduct accounting in requirement 1?

16-25 **Joint costs and byproducts.** (W. Crum) Caldwell Company processes an ore in Department 1, from which comes three products, L, W, and X. Product L is processed further in Department 2. Product W is sold without further processing. Product X is considered a byproduct and is processed further in Department 3. Costs in Department 1 are $800,000, Department 2 costs are $100,000, and Department 3 costs are $50,000. Processing 600,000 pounds in Department 1 results in 50,000 pounds of product L, 300,000 pounds of product W, and 100,000 pounds of product X.

Product L sells for $10 per pound. Product W sells for $2 per pound. Product X sells for $3 per pound. The company wants to make a gross margin of 10% of revenues on product X and needs to allow 25% of revenues for marketing costs on product X.

Required

1. Compute unit costs per pound for products L, W, and X, treating X as a byproduct. Use the NRV method for allocating joint costs. Deduct the NRV of the byproduct produced from the joint cost of products L and W.
2. Compute unit costs per pound for products L, W, and X, treating all three as joint products and allocating costs by the NRV method.

Problems

16-26 **Alternative methods of joint-cost allocation, product-mix decision.** Pacific Lumber processes lumber products for sale to lumber wholesalers. Its most popular line is oak products. Oak tree growers sell Pacific Lumber whole trees. These trees are jointly processed up to the splitoff point at which raw select oak, raw white oak, and raw knotty oak become separable products. Each raw product is then separately further processed by Pacific Lumber into finished products (select oak, white oak, and knotty oak) that are sold to lumber wholesalers. Data for August 2004 are

a. Joint processing costs (including cost of oak trees)—$300,000

b. Separable product at splitoff point
- Raw select oak, 30,000 board-feet
- Raw white oak, 50,000 board-feet
- Raw knotty oak, 20,000 board-feet

c. Final product produced and sold
- Select oak, 25,000 board feet at $16 per board-foot
- White oak, 40,000 board feet at $9 per board-foot
- Knotty oak, 15,000 board feet at $7 per board-foot

d. Separable processing costs
- For select oak, $60,000
- For white oak, $90,000
- For knotty oak, $15,000

There is an active market for raw oak products. Selling prices available in August 2004 were raw select oak, $8 per board-foot; raw white oak, $4 per board-foot; and raw knotty oak, $3 per board-foot.

There were no beginning or ending inventories for August 2004.

Required

1. Allocate the joint costs to the three products using
   a. Sales value at splitoff method
   b. Physical-measures method
   c. NRV method
2. Assume that not all final products produced in August 2004 were sold. Ending inventory for August 2004 was select oak, 1,000 board-feet; white oak, 2,000 board-feet; and knotty oak, 500 board-feet. What would be the ending inventory values in the August 30 balance sheet under each product for the three methods in requirement 1?
3. Is Pacific Lumber maximizing its total August 2004 operating income by fully processing each raw oak product into its finished product form? Show your computations.

16-27 **Alternative methods of joint-cost allocation, product-mix decisions.** The Sunshine Oil Company buys crude vegetable oil. Refining this oil results in four products at the splitoff point: A, B, C, and D. Product C is fully processed at the splitoff point. Products A, B, and D can individually be further refined into Super A, Super B, and Super D. In the most recent month (December), the output at the splitoff point was

- Product A, 300,000 gallons
- Product B, 100,000 gallons
- Product C, 50,000 gallons
- Product D, 50,000 gallons

The joint costs of purchasing and processing the crude vegetable oil were $100,000. Sunshine had no beginning or ending inventories. Sales of product C in December were $50,000. Products A, B, and D were further refined and then sold. Data related to December are

	Separable Processing Costs to Make Super Products	Revenues
Super A	$200,000	$300,000
Super B	80,000	100,000
Super D	90,000	120,000

Sunshine had the option of selling products A, B, and D at the splitoff point. This alternative would have yielded the following revenues for the December production:

- Product A, $50,000
- Product B, $30,000
- Product D, $70,000

Required

1. Compute the gross-margin percentage for each product sold in December, using the following methods for allocating the $100,000 joint costs:
   a. Sales value at splitoff
   b. Physical measure
   c. NRV
2. Could Sunshine have increased its December operating income by making different decisions about the further processing of products A, B, or D? Show the effect on operating income of any changes you recommend.

16-28 **Comparison of alternative joint-cost-allocation methods, further-processing decision, chocolate products.** Roundtree Chocolates manufactures and distributes chocolate products. It purchases cocoa beans and processes them into two intermediate products:

- Chocolate-powder liquor base
- Milk-chocolate liquor base

These two intermediate products become separately identifiable at a single splitoff point. Every 500 pounds of cocoa beans yields 20 gallons of chocolate-powder liquor base and 30 gallons of milk-chocolate liquor base.

The chocolate-powder liquor base is further processed into chocolate powder. Every 20 gallons of chocolate-powder liquor base yield 200 pounds of chocolate powder. The milk-chocolate liquor base is further processed into milk chocolate. Every 30 gallons of milk-chocolate liquor base yield 340 pounds of milk chocolate.

An overview of the manufacturing operations at Roundtree Chocolates follows:

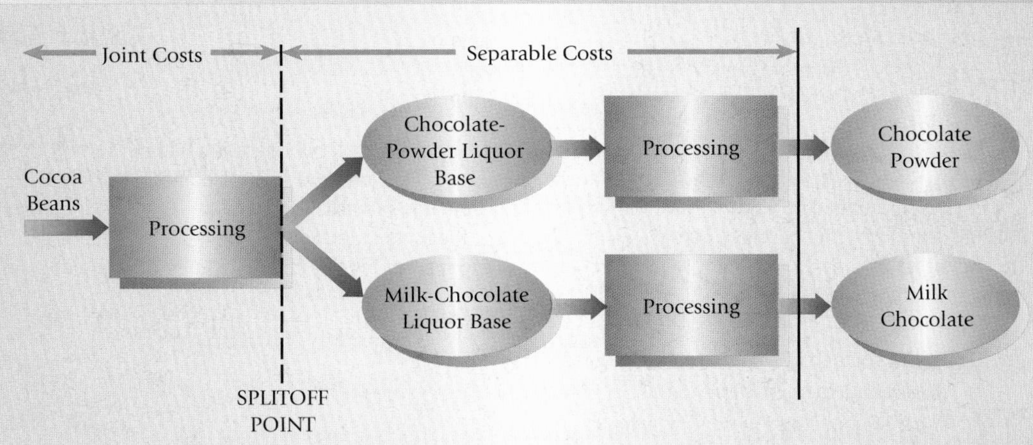

Production and sales data for August 2003 are

- Cocoa beans processed, 5,000 pounds
- Costs of processing cocoa beans to splitoff point (including purchase of beans) = $10,000

	Production	Sales	Selling Price
Chocolate powder	2,000 pounds	2,000 pounds	$4 per pound
Milk chocolate	3,400 pounds	3,400 pounds	$5 per pound

The August 2003 separable costs of processing chocolate-powder liquor base into chocolate powder are $4,250. The August 2003 separable costs of processing milk-chocolate liquor base into milk chocolate are $8,750.

Roundtree fully processes both of its intermediate products into chocolate powder or milk chocolate. There is an active market for these intermediate products. In August 2003, Roundtree could have sold the chocolate-powder liquor base for $21 a gallon and the milk-chocolate liquor base for $26 a gallon.

Required

1. Calculate how the joint costs of $10,000 would be allocated between the chocolate-powder and milk-chocolate liquor bases under the following methods:
   a. Sales value at splitoff
   b. Physical measure (gallons)
   c. NRV
   d. Constant gross-margin percentage NRV
2. What are the gross-margin percentages of the chocolate-powder and milk-chocolate liquor bases under each of the methods in requirement 1?
3. Could Roundtree Chocolates have increased its operating income by a change in its decision to fully process both of its intermediate products? Show your computations.

16-29 Joint-cost allocation, process further or sell. (CMA, adapted) Sonimad Sawmill, Inc. (SSI), purchases logs from independent timber contractors and processes the logs into three types of lumber products:

- Studs for residential building (walls, ceilings)
- Decorative pieces (fireplace mantels, beams for cathedral ceilings)
- Posts used as support braces (mine support braces, braces for exterior fences around ranch properties)

These products are the result of a joint sawmill process that involves removal of bark from the logs, cutting the logs into a workable size (ranging from 8 to 16 feet in length), and then cutting the individual products from the logs, depending on the type of wood (pine, oak, walnut, or maple) and the size (diameter) of the log.

The joint process results in the following costs and outputs of products for a typical month:

Direct materials (rough timber logs)	$ 500,000
Debarking (labor and overhead)	50,000
Sizing (labor and overhead)	200,000
Product cutting (labor and overhead)	250,000
Total joint costs	$1,000,000

Product yields and average sales values on a per unit basis from the joint process are as follows:

Product	Monthly Output of Materials at Splitoff Point	Fully Processed Selling Price
Studs	75,000 units	$ 8
Decorative pieces	5,000 units	100
Posts	20,000 units	20

The studs are sold as rough-cut lumber after emerging from the sawmill operation without further processing by SSI. Also, the posts require no further processing beyond the splitoff point. The decorative pieces must be planed and further sized after emerging from the sawmill. This additional processing costs $100,000 per month and normally results in a loss of 10% of the units entering the process. Without this planing and sizing process, there is still an active intermediate market for the unfinished decorative pieces in which the selling price averages $60 per unit.

Required

1. Based on the information given for Sonimad Sawmill, Inc., allocate the joint processing costs of $1,000,000 to each of the three product lines using:
   a. Sales value at splitoff method
   b. Physical-measures method (volume in units)
   c. NRV method
2. Prepare an analysis for Sonimad Sawmill, Inc., that compares processing the decorative pieces further, as they currently do, with selling them as a rough-cut product immediately at splitoff.
3. Assume Sonimad Sawmill announced that in six months it will sell the rough-cut product at splitoff due to increasing competitive pressure. Identify at least three types of likely behavior that will be demonstrated by the skilled labor in the planing and sizing process as a result of this announcement. Include in your discussion how this behavior could be improved by management.

16-30 Joint-cost allocation, relevant costs. (R. Capettini, adapted) Consider the following scenario. Each day a butcher buys a 200-pound pig for $300. The pig can be processed to yield the following three products:

	Selling Price per Pound	Weight (Pounds)
Pork chops	$4.00	30
Ham	$3.00	50
Bacon	$1.20	120
		200

Day 1 The butcher buys a pig. The $300 joint cost of the pig is allocated to individual products based on the relative weights of the products.

	Selling Price	Weight (Pounds)	Revenues	–	Joint Costs Allocated	=	Operating Income
Pork chops	$4.00	30	$120	–	$ 45.00	=	$ 75.00
Ham	3.00	50	150	–	75.00	=	75.00
Bacon	1.20	120	144	–	180.00	=	(36.00)
			$414	–	$300.00	=	$114.00

Day 2 The butcher buys an identical pig and throws out the bacon because it has been shown to lose money. She now has 80 pounds of "good output."

	Selling Price	Weight (Pounds)	Revenues	–	Joint Costs Allocated	=	Operating Income
Pork chops	$4.00	30	$120	–	$112.50	=	$ 7.50
Ham	3.00	50	150	–	187.50	=	(37.50)
			$270	–	$300.00	=	$(30.00)

Day 3 The butcher buys an identical pig and throws out the ham and the bacon because they have been shown to lose money. She now has 30 pounds of "good output."

	Selling Price	Weight (Pounds)	Revenues	–	Joint Costs Allocated	=	Operating Income
Pork chops	$4.00	30	$120	–	$300.00	=	$(180.00)
			$120	–	$300.00	=	$(180.00)

Day 4 The butcher buys an identical pig and throws out the whole pig because each product has been shown to lose money. Therefore, she loses $300.

Required

1. Comment on the preceding series of decisions.
2. How would the joint costs be allocated to all three products using the sales value at splitoff method?
3. Should the operating income numbers from requirement 2 be used to determine if the butcher is better off by selling or not selling individual products? Explain briefly.

16-31 Joint and byproducts, NRV method. (CPA) The Harrison Corporation produces three products: Alpha, Beta, and Gamma. Alpha and Gamma are joint products, and Beta is a byproduct of Alpha. No joint costs are to be allocated to the byproduct. The production processes for a given year are as follows:

a. In Department 1, 110,000 pounds of direct material, Rho, are processed at a total cost of $120,000. After processing in Department 1, 60% of the units are transferred to Department 2, and 40% of the units (now Gamma) are transferred to Department 3.
b. In Department 2, the material is further processed at a total additional cost of $38,000. Then 70% of the units (now Alpha) are transferred to Department 4; and 30% emerge as Beta, the byproduct, to be sold at $1.20 per pound. Separable marketing costs for Beta are $8,100.
c. In Department 4, Alpha is processed at a total additional cost of $23,660. After this processing, Alpha is ready for sale at $5 per pound.
d. In Department 3, Gamma is processed at a total additional cost of $165,000. In this department, a normal loss of units of Gamma occurs, which equals 10% of the good units of output. The remaining good units of output are then sold for $12 per pound.

Required

1. Prepare a schedule showing the allocation of the $120,000 joint costs between Alpha and Gamma using the NRV method. The NRV of Beta should be treated as an addition to the sales value of Alpha.
2. Independent of your answer to requirement 1, assume that $102,000 of total joint costs were appropriately allocated to Alpha. Assume also that there were 48,000 pounds of Alpha and 20,000 pounds of Beta available to sell. Prepare an income statement through the gross-margin line item for Alpha using the following facts:
   a. During the year, sales of Alpha were 80% of the pounds available for sale. There was no beginning inventory.
   b. The NRV of Beta available for sale is to be deducted from the cost of producing Alpha. The ending inventory of Alpha is to be based on the net costs of production.
   c. All other cost and selling-price data are listed in A through D above.

16-32 NRV method, byproducts. (CMA, adapted) Princess Corporation grows, processes, packages, and sells three joint apple products: (a) sliced apples that are used in frozen pies, (b) applesauce, and (c) apple juice. The outside skin of the apple, processed as animal feed, is treated as a byproduct. Princess uses the NRV method to allocate costs of the joint process to its joint products. The byproduct is inventoried at its estimated selling price when produced. The NRV of the byproduct is used to reduce the joint production costs before the splitoff point. The following details of Princess production process are available:

- The apples are washed and the outside skin is removed in the Cutting Department. The apples are then cored and trimmed for slicing. The three joint products and the byproduct are recognizable after processing in the Cutting Department. Each product is then transferred to a separate department for final processing.
- The trimmed apples are moved to the Slicing Department, where they are sliced and frozen. Any juice generated during the slicing operation is frozen with the slices.
- The pieces of apple trimmed from the fruit are processed into applesauce in the Crushing Department. The juice generated during this operation is used in the applesauce.
- The core and any surplus apple pieces generated from the Cutting Department are pulverized into a liquid in the Juicing Department. There is a loss equal to 8% of the weight of the good output produced in this department.
- The outside skin is chopped into animal feed and packaged in the Feed Department. It can be kept in cold storage until needed.

A total of 270,000 pounds of apples were processed in the Cutting Department during November. The following schedule shows the costs incurred in each department, the proportion by weight transferred to the four final-processing departments, and the selling price of each end product:

Processing Data and Costs
November 2003

Department	Costs Incurred	Proportion of Product by Weight Transferred to Departments	Selling Price per Pound of Final Product
Cutting	$60,000		
Slicing	11,280	33%	$0.80
Crushing	8,550	30	0.55
Juicing	3,000	27	0.40
Feed	700	10	0.10
Total	$83,530	100%	

Required

1. For the month of November 2003, calculate:
   - **a.** The output of apple slices, applesauce, apple juice, and animal feed, in pounds
   - **b.** The NRV at the splitoff point of each joint product
   - **c.** The amount of Cutting Department costs assigned to each joint product and the amount assigned to the byproduct following Princess' cost-allocation method described above
   - **d.** The gross margin in dollars for each joint product
2. Comment on the significance to management of the gross-margin dollar information by joint product for planning and control purposes, as distinguished from inventory-costing purposes.

16-33 Process further or sell, byproduct. (CMA, adapted) Newcastle Mining Company (NMC) produces and sells bulk raw coal to other coal companies and exporters. NMC mines and stockpiles the coal. The coal is then passed through a one-step crushing process before being loaded onto river barges for shipment to customers. The annual output of 10 million tons, which is expected to remain stable, has an average cost of $20 per ton with an average selling price of $27 per ton.

Management is currently evaluating the possibility of further processing the coal by sizing and cleaning to expand markets and enhance product revenues. Management has rejected the possibility of constructing a large sizing and cleaning plant because of the significant long-term capital investment required.

Bill Rolland, controller of NMC, asks Amy Kimbell, mining engineer, to develop cost and revenue projections for further processing the coal using a variety of contractual arrangements. After extensive discussions with vendors and contractors, Kimbell prepares the following projections of incremental costs of sizing and cleaning NMC's annual output:

Newcastle Mining Company
Sizing and Cleaning Processes

	Incremental Costs
Direct labor	$600,000 per year
Supervisory personnel	$100,000 per year
Heavy equipment rental, operating, and maintenance costs	$25,000 per month
Contract sizing and cleaning	$3.50 per ton
Outbound rail freight (per 60-ton rail car)	$240 per car

In addition to the preceding cost information, market samples obtained by Kimbell show that electrical utilities enter into contracts for sized and cleaned coal similar to that mined by Newcastle at an expected average price of $36 per ton.

Kimbell has learned that 5% of the raw bulk output that enters the sizing and cleaning process will be lost as a primary product. Normally, 75% of this product loss can be salvaged as coal fines, which are small pieces ranging from dustlike particles up to pieces two inches in diameter. Coal fines are too small for use by electrical utilities but are frequently sold to steel manufacturers for use in blast furnaces.

Unfortunately, the price for coal fines frequently fluctuates between $14 and $24 per ton (F.O.B. shipping point), and the timing of market volume is erratic. Although companies generally sell all their coal fines during a year, it is not unusual to stockpile this product for several months before making any significant sales.

Required

1. Prepare an analysis that shows whether it is more profitable for Newcastle Mining Company to continue to sell the raw bulk coal or to process it further through sizing and cleaning. (*Note:* Ignore any value related to the coal fines in your analysis.)
2. Now consider the potential value of the coal fines and prepare an addendum that shows how their value affects the results of your analysis prepared in requirement 1.

3. What other factors should be considered in evaluating a sell-or-process-further decision?

16-34 Byproduct, disposal costs, ethics. Enrique Chemicals, Inc., is a multinational company. One of its subsidiaries is located in a small East European country. The country has only a few environmental protection laws, and even those are not enforced so as "to encourage rapid industrialization." The subsidiary's three major products emerge at splitoff point from a common input. The joint costs are allocated to each product using the sales values at splitoff method. In addition to the three joint products, another product that emerges at splitoff point is a hazardous material. The hazardous material can be dumped into the Gulf at zero cost to the company. Alternatively, it can be processed further and sold as a cleaning liquid.

The cost accountant responsible for joint-cost allocation presented the following comparative analysis to you, the controller:

	Alternatives	
	Dump into the Gulf	**Process Further**
Revenue	$0	$ 500,000
Costs:		
Further processing	0	300,000
Allocated joint costs	0	250,000
Marketing and distribution	0	50,000
Total costs	0	600,000
Net realizable value	$0	$(100,000)

Required

1. Comment on the comparative analysis prepared by the cost accountant purely from a financial perspective. Show any supporting computations.
2. Assume, regardless of your conclusions in requirement 1, that adopting the process-further alternative would lead to a decrease in the company's operating income. Disposal of the hazardous waste in a manner different than dumping it into the Gulf would also be costly. Discuss the legal and ethical implications of dumping the hazardous material into the Gulf.

Collaborative Learning Exercise

16-35 Joint-cost allocation, process further or sell. (CMA, adapted) Goodson Pharmaceutical Company manufactures three joint products from a joint process: Altox, Lorex, and Hycol. Data regarding these products for the fiscal year ended May 31, 2003, are as follows:

	Altox	Lorex	Hycol
Units produced	170,000	500,000	330,000
Selling price per unit at splitoff	$3.50	—	$2.00
Separable costs	—	$1,400,000	—
Final selling price per unit	—	$5.00	—

The joint production cost up to the splitoff point at which Altox, Lorex, and Hycol become separable products is $1,800,000.

The president of Goodson, Arlene Franklin, is reviewing an opportunity to change the way in which these three products are processed and sold. Proposed changes for each product are as follows:

- Altox is currently sold at the splitoff point to a manufacturer of vitamins. Altox can also be processed into a blood pressure medication. However, this additional processing causes a loss of 20,000 units of Altox. The separable costs to further process Altox are estimated to be $250,000 annually. The blood pressure medication sells for $5.50 per unit.
- Lorex is currently processed further after the splitoff point and is sold by Goodson as a cold remedy. The company has received an offer from another pharmaceutical company to purchase Lorex at the splitoff point for $2.25 per unit.
- Hycol is an oil produced from the joint process and is currently sold at the splitoff point to a cosmetics manufacturer. Goodson's Research Department has suggested that the company process this product further and sell it as an ointment to relieve muscle pain. The additional processing would cost $75,000 annually and would result in 25% more units of product. The ointment sells for $1.80 per unit.

Required

1. Allocate the $1,800,000 joint production cost to Altox, Lorex, and Hycol using the NRV method.
2. Identify which of the three joint products Goodson Pharmaceutical Company should sell at the splitoff point in the future and which of the three the company should process further to maximize operating income. Support your decisions with appropriate computations.

CHAPTER 16 INTERNET EXERCISE

A thorough understanding of a product process is essential to properly allocate joint and separable costs. To gain a better understanding of the challenges involved with allocating joint product costs, take a tour of a Tyson Food's chicken processing plant. To take the tour go to www.prenhall.com/horngren, click on *Cost Accounting,* 11th ed., and access the Internet exercise for Chapter 16.

CHAPTER 16 CASE

MEMORY MANUFACTURING COMPANY: Joint-Cost Allocation

The Memory Manufacturing Company (MMC) produces and markets many different kinds of memory modules for high-priced and low-priced end products in the computer industry. Memory modules are the output from two basic manufacturing processes: chip fabrication and testing, and module assembly and testing.

Raw silicon wafer is the input in the chip fabrication process. Each batch of wafers yield two grades of chips—a "standard" chip and a "deluxe" chip—from a single process consisting of 200 different manufacturing operations. The finished chips in each batch are tested and classified as standard and deluxe on the basis of their density (the number of memory bits on each chip) and their speed (the time required to access the bits). It costs $24,000 to process each batch. Because the two grades of chips are produced simultaneously, the cost incurred to produce each type of chip cannot be identified.

In the module assembly and testing process, each batch of standard chips is converted into standard memory modules at a separately identified cost of $1,000, and each batch of deluxe chips is converted into deluxe memory modules at a separately identified cost of $1,500. The following table shows production, cost, and price data for a batch of standard and deluxe memory modules.

	Standard Memory Modules	Deluxe Memory Modules
Quantity produced per batch	500	500
Number of bits produced per batch	250,000	500,000
Separable assembly and testing costs per batch	$1,000	$1,500
Market price per batch	$8,500	$25,000

QUESTIONS

1. Should MMC account for the standard memory module as a byproduct or a joint product?
2. Chips represent the major cost of the memory modules, yet different grades of chips result from a single manufacturing process. Calculate the production cost per unit of the deluxe chip and the standard chip using (a) the NRV method, (b) the constant gross-margin percentage NRV method, and (c) the physical-measure method, based on the number of bits produced.
3. Which of the cost-allocation methods described in 2 should MMC use to allocate joint costs?
4. MMC is evaluating whether to process further the 500 standard memory modules manufactured in each batch to yield 400 modules of a new memory module called DRAM. The total additional costs of converting 500 standard memory modules into 400 DRAMs would be $1,600, and the selling price per DRAM module would be $26. Suppose MMC uses the physical-measure method and allocates joint costs to the deluxe and standard memory modules on the basis of the number of bits produced. Should MMC sell the standard memory modules or the DRAM modules?

CHAPTER

17

Process Costing

LEARNING OBJECTIVES

1. Identify the situations in which process-costing systems are appropriate
2. Describe the five steps in process costing
3. Calculate equivalent units and understand how to use them
4. Prepare journal entries for process-costing systems
5. Use the weighted-average method of process costing
6. Use the first-in, first-out (FIFO) method of process costing
7. Incorporate standard costs into a process-costing system
8. Apply process-costing methods to cases with transferred-in costs

www.prenhall.com/horngren

Orange Mango. Watermelon Strawberry. Pink Lemonade. A few of the all-natural juice beverages the "juice guys" of Nantucket Nectars create each day at their beverage bottling plants. For nearly 16 hours each day, raw ingredients for juice flavors are blended and then poured into glass bottles as they speed along a timed conveyer system. Regardless of juice flavor, the production process is the same, relying on an exact series of standard production steps. At Nantucket's largest bottler, nearly 400,000 single-serve bottles of juice are produced daily.

Because each bottle of juice is almost identical to the others, a process-costing system is used by the bottling plant to calculate the cost per bottle. This information is helpful to the plant managers as they control the costs of daily operations and plan for the introduction of new juice blends in the production schedule. Numerous control checkpoints throughout the bottling process not only help managers assure top quality in the finished product but also during production help identify possible problems, such as incorrect acidity levels that require an entire production run be discarded or faulty labeling that requires halting production until the label-attaching machinery is adjusted or repaired. These inefficiencies introduce costs that, unlike the sweet beverages being produced, leave a bitter taste on profits.

1 Identify the situations in which process-costing systems are appropriate
...when masses of identical or similar units are produced

Our study of product costing so far has emphasized job costing. The cost object in a job-costing system is a job that constitutes a distinctly identifiable product or service. In this chapter and the next, we consider products such as chemicals, pharmaceuticals, and semiconductors. Companies producing such products use process costing, in which each individual process forms the basis of the costing system.

Costing systems described in Chapters 4 and 5 serve three functions: (a) determining the costs of products or services that aid in planning decisions such as pricing and product mix, (b) valuing inventory and cost of goods sold for external reporting, and (c) managing costs and evaluating performance. As we examine process costing in this chapter, we will emphasize the first two functions. We will be concerned only incidentally with the third function—cost management and performance evaluation—which is discussed in other chapters (see, for example, Chapters 6, 7, and 8). The ideas described there apply to process-costing systems as well.

ILLUSTRATING PROCESS COSTING

In a *process-costing system,* the unit cost of a product or service is obtained by assigning total costs to many identical or similar units. In a manufacturing process-costing setting, each unit receives the same or similar amounts of direct material costs, direct manufacturing labor costs, and indirect manufacturing costs (manufacturing overhead). Unit costs are then computed by dividing total costs incurred by the number of units of output from the production process.

The main difference between process costing and job costing is the *extent of averaging* used to compute unit costs of products or services. In a job-costing system, individual jobs use different quantities of production resources; so it would be incorrect to cost each job at the same average production cost. In contrast, when identical or similar units of products or services are mass-produced, not processed as individual jobs, process costing is used to calculate an average production cost for all units produced (see *Surveys of Company Practice,* p. 587).

Consider the following illustration of process costing.

Example: *Global Defense, Inc., manufactures thousands of components for missiles and military equipment. These components are assembled in the Assembly Department. Upon completion, the units are transferred to the Testing Department. We focus on the Assembly Department process for one component, DG-19. All units are identical and meet a set of demanding performance specifications. The process-costing system for DG-19 in the Assembly Department has a single direct-cost category—direct materials—and a single indirect-cost category—conversion costs. Conversion costs are all manufacturing costs other than direct material costs and include manufacturing labor, energy, plant depreciation, and so on. Direct materials are added at the beginning of the process in Assembly. Conversion costs are added evenly during assembly.*

SURVEYS OF COMPANY PRACTICE

Process Costing in Different Industries

A survey of cost accounting practices in Australian manufacturing companies indicates the widespread use of process-costing systems for product costing across a variety of industries. The reported percentages exceed 100% because several companies surveyed use more than one product-costing system.

Primary	Food	Textiles	Metals	Chemicals	Refining
Process costing	96%	91%	92%	75%	100%
Job-order costing	4	18	25	25	25
Other	—	—	8	12	—

	Printing and Publishing	Furniture and Fixtures	Machinery and Computers	Electronics
Process costing	20%	38%	43%	55%
Job-order costing	73	63	65	58
Other	13	—	9	10

The survey data indicate that the use of process costing varies considerably among industries. Process costing is widely used in mass-production industries that manufacture homogeneous products, such as, food, textiles, primary metals, chemicals, and refining. In contrast, as we move across the spectrum to industries that produce many distinct and different products, job-order costing is favored over process costing, for example, in industries such as printing and publishing, furniture and fixtures, machinery and computers, and electronics.

Source: Adapted from Joye and Blayney, "Cost and Management Accounting Practices." Full citation is in Appendix A at the end of the book.

The following diagram represents these facts:

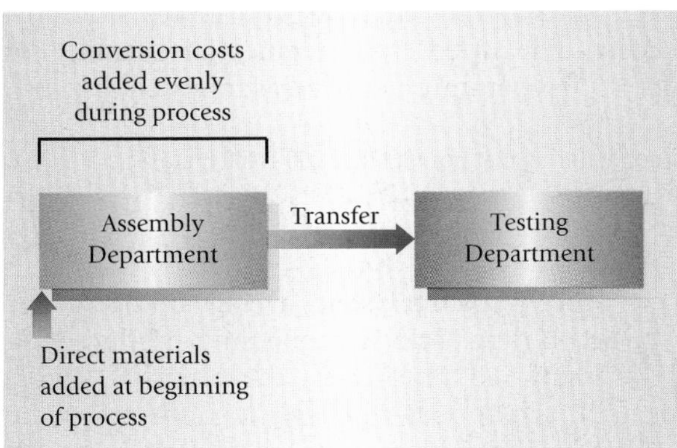

Process-costing systems separate costs into cost categories according to when costs are introduced into the process. Often, as in our Global Defense example, only two cost classifications, direct materials and conversion costs, are necessary to assign costs to products. Why only two? Because *all* direct materials are added to the process at one time and *all* conversion costs are generally added to the process evenly through time. If, however, two different direct materials were added to the process at different points in time, two different direct materials categories would be needed to assign these costs to products. Similarly, if manufacturing labor were added to the process at a different time than when the other conversion costs were added, an additional cost category—direct manufacturing labor costs—would be needed to separately assign these costs to products.

We will use the production of the DG-19 component in the Assembly Department to illustrate process costing in three cases, starting with the simplest case and introducing additional complexities in subsequent cases:

Cases 1 and 2 do not need to consider weighted average versus FIFO because beginning work in process is zero. Differences between weighted average and FIFO arise only when there is beginning work in process *and* manufacturing cost per unit changes from period to period.

- *Case 1*—Process costing with zero beginning and zero ending work-in-process inventory of DG-19 (all units are started and fully completed within the accounting period). *This case presents the most basic concepts of process costing and illustrates the feature of averaging of costs.*
- *Case 2*—Process costing with zero beginning work-in-process inventory but some ending work-in-process inventory of DG-19 (some units of DG-19 started during the accounting period are incomplete at the end of the period). *This case introduces the concept of equivalent units.*
- *Case 3*—Process costing with both some beginning and some ending work-in-process inventory of DG-19. *This case adds more complexities and describes the effect of weighted-average and first-in, first-out (FIFO) cost flow assumptions on cost of units completed and cost of work-in-process inventory.*

CASE 1: PROCESS COSTING WITH ZERO BEGINNING AND ZERO ENDING WORK-IN-PROCESS INVENTORY

On January 1, 2004, there was no beginning inventory of DG-19 units in the Assembly Department. During January 2004, Global Defense started, completed assembly of, and transferred out to the Testing Department 400 units.

Data for the Assembly Department for January 2004 are

Physical Units for January 2004

Work in process, beginning inventory (January 1)	0 units
Started during January	400 units
Completed and transferred out during January	400 units
Work in process, ending inventory (January 31)	0 units

Total Costs for January 2004

Direct material costs added during January	$32,000
Conversion costs added during January	24,000
Total Assembly Department costs added during January	$56,000

Global Defense records direct material costs and conversion costs in the Assembly Department as these costs are incurred. By averaging, the assembly cost per unit of DG-19 is $56,000 ÷ 400 units = $140 per unit, itemized as follows:

Direct material cost per unit ($32,000 ÷ 400 units)	$ 80
Conversion cost per unit ($24,000 ÷ 400 units)	60
Assembly Department cost per unit	$140

This case shows that in a process-costing system, average unit costs are calculated by dividing total costs in a given accounting period by total units produced in that period. Because each unit is identical, we assume all units receive the same amount of direct materials and conversion costs. This approach applies whenever a company produces a homogeneous product or service but has no incomplete units when each accounting period ends. This situation is common in service-sector organizations. For example, a bank can adopt this process-costing approach to compute the unit cost of processing 100,000 customer deposits, each similar to the other, made in a month.

CASE 2: PROCESS COSTING WITH ZERO BEGINNING BUT SOME ENDING WORK-IN-PROCESS INVENTORY

In February 2004, Global Defense places another 400 units of DG-19 into production. Because all units placed into production in January were completely assembled, there is no beginning inventory of partially completed units in the Assembly Department on February 1. Some customers ordered late, so not all units started in February were completed by the end of the month. Only 175 units are completed and transferred to the Testing Department.

Data for the Assembly Department for February 2004 are

Physical Units for February 2004	
Work in process, beginning inventory (February 1)	0 units
Started during February	400 units
Completed and transferred out	175 units
Work in process, ending inventory (February 29)	225 units

The 225 partially assembled units as of February 29, 2004, are fully processed with respect to direct materials. That's because all direct materials in the Assembly Department are added at the beginning of the assembly process. Conversion costs, however, are added evenly during assembly. Based on the work completed relative to the total work required to complete the DG-19 units still in the process, an Assembly Department supervisor estimates that the partially assembled units are, on average, 60% complete from the perspective of conversion costs.

Total Costs for February 2004	
Direct material costs added during February	$32,000
Conversion costs added during February	18,600
Total Assembly Department costs added during February	$50,600

The accuracy of product costs in process-costing systems hinges on the accuracy of the estimate of percentage of completion, particularly when work in process is large.

How accurate the completion estimate is with respect to conversion costs depends on the care, skill, and experience of the estimator and the nature of the conversion process. Estimating the degree of completion is usually easier for direct material costs than for conversion costs. That's because the quantity of direct materials needed for a completed unit and the quantity of direct materials for a partially completed unit can be measured more accurately. In contrast, the conversion sequence usually consists of a number of basic operations for a specified number of hours, days, or weeks, for various steps in assembly, testing, and so forth. The degree of completion for conversion costs depends on what proportion of the total conversion costs needed to complete one unit or one batch of production has been devoted to units still in process. This estimate is more difficult to make accurately. Because of these difficulties, department supervisors and line managers—individuals most familiar with the process—often make these estimates. Still, in some industries, such as semiconductor manufacturing, no exact estimate is possible or, as in the textile industry, vast quantities in process make the task of making estimates costly. In these cases, all work in process in every department is assumed to be complete to some degree with respect to conversion costs (for example, one-third, one-half, or two-thirds complete).

2 Describe the five steps in process costing

...to assign total costs to units completed and to units in work in process

The point to understand here is that a partially assembled unit is not the same as a fully assembled unit. Faced with some fully assembled units and some partially assembled units, Global Defense calculates in five steps (1) the cost of fully assembled units in February 2004 and (2) the cost of the partially assembled units still in process at the end of that month:

- *Step 1*—Summarize the flow of physical units of output.
- *Step 2*—Compute output in terms of equivalent units.
- *Step 3*—Compute equivalent unit costs.
- *Step 4*—Summarize total costs to account for.
- *Step 5*—Assign total costs to units completed and to units in ending work in process.

3 Calculate equivalent units

...output units adjusted for incomplete units

and understand how to use them

...to assign costs to units completed and to units in ending work in process

Physical Units and Equivalent Units (Steps 1 and 2)

Step 1 tracks the physical units of output—the number of output units, whether complete or incomplete. Where did they come from? Where did they go? The physical units column of Exhibit 17-1 tracks where the physical units came from (400 units started) and where they went (175 units completed and transferred out, and 225 units in ending inventory).

Step 2 measures the output for February (175 fully assembled units plus 225 partially assembled units). Because all 400 physical units are not uniformly completed, output in step 2 is computed in *equivalent units,* not in physical units.

EXHIBIT 17-1

Steps 1 and 2: Summarize Output in Physical Units and Compute Equivalent Units Assembly Department of Global Defense, Inc., for February 2004

Flow of Production	(Step 1) Physical Units	(Step 2) Equivalent Units Direct Materials	Conversion Costs
Work in process, beginning	0		
Started during current period	400		
To account for	400		
Completed and transferred out during current period	175	175	175
Work in process, ending[a]	225		
(225 × 100%; 225 × 60%)	—	225	135
Accounted for	400	—	—
Work done in current period only		400	310

[a]Degree of completion in this department: direct materials, 100%; conversion costs, 60%.

To see what we mean by equivalent units, let's say that during a month, 50 physical units were started but not completed by the end of the month. These 50 units in ending inventory are estimated to be 70% complete with respect to conversion costs. Let's look at those units from the perspective of the conversion costs incurred to get the units to be 70% complete. Suppose we put all the conversion costs represented in the 70% into making fully completed units. How many units could have been 100% complete by the end of the month? The answer: 35 units. Why? Because 70% conversion costs incurred on 50 incomplete units could have been incurred to make 35 (0.70 × 50) complete units by the end of the month. That is, if all the conversion-cost input in the 50 units in inventory were used to make completed output units, the company would have been able to make 35 completed units (also called *equivalent units*) of output.

Equivalent units is a derived amount of output units that (a) takes the quantity of each input (factor of production) in units completed or in incomplete units of work in process and (b) converts the quantity of input into the amount of completed output units that could be made with that quantity of input. Note, equivalent units are calculated separately for each input (cost category). This chapter focuses on equivalent-unit calculations in manufacturing settings. Equivalent-unit concepts are also found in nonmanufacturing settings. For example, universities convert their part-time student enrollments into "full-time student equivalents."

Whenever a factor of production is added at a different stage in the production process, a separate equivalent-unit computation is required. In the Global Defense example, suppose steel is added at the beginning of Assembly and electronics are added 75% of the way through Assembly. Ending work in process that is 60% complete would have had 100% steel added but 0% electronics added. Thus, we need separate equivalent-unit calculations for steel and electronics—even though both are elements of direct materials.

When calculating equivalent units in step 2, focus on quantities. Disregard dollar amounts until after equivalent units are computed. In the Global Defense example, all 400 physical units—the 175 fully assembled units and the 225 partially assembled units—are 100% complete with respect to direct materials because all direct materials are added in the Assembly Department at the start of the process. Therefore, Exhibit 17-1 shows output as 400 *equivalent* units for direct materials: 175 equivalent units for the 175 physical units assembled and transferred out, and 225 equivalent units for the 225 physical units in ending work-in-process inventory, because all the complete and the incomplete units are 100% complete with respect to direct materials.

The 175 fully assembled units are completely processed with respect to conversion costs. The partially assembled units in ending work in process are 60% complete (on average). Therefore, the conversion costs in the 225 partially assembled units are *equivalent* to conversion costs in 135 (60% of 225) fully assembled units. Hence, Exhibit 17-1 shows output as 310 *equivalent units* with respect to conversion costs: 175 equivalent units for the 175 physical units assembled and transferred out and 135 equivalent units for the 225 physical units in ending work-in-process inventory.

Calculation of Product Costs (Steps 3, 4, and 5)

Exhibit 17-2 shows steps 3, 4, and 5. Together, they are called the *production cost worksheet.* Step 3 calculates equivalent-unit costs by dividing the sum of direct material costs and conversion costs added during February by the related quantity of equivalent units of work done in February (as calculated in Exhibit 17-1).

		Total Production Costs	Direct Materials		Conversion Costs
(Step 3)	Costs added during February	$50,600	$32,000		$18,600
	Divide by equivalent units of work done in current period (Exhibit 17-1)		÷ 400		÷ 310
	Cost per equivalent unit		$ 80		$ 60
(Step 4)	Total costs to account for	$50,600			
(Step 5)	Assignment of costs:				
	Completed and transferred out (175 units)	$24,500	($175^a \times$ \$80)	+	($175^a \times$ \$60)
	Work in process, ending (225 units):				
	Direct materials	18,000	$225^b \times$ \$80		
	Conversion costs	8,100			$135^b \times$ \$60
	Total work in process	26,100			
	Total costs accounted for	$50,600			

[a]Equivalent units completed and transferred out from Exhibit 17-1, step 2.
[b]Equivalent units in ending work in process from Exhibit 17-1, step 2.

EXHIBIT 17-2

Steps 3, 4, and 5: Compute Equivalent-Unit Costs, Summarize Total Costs to Account For, and Assign Costs to Units Completed and to Units in Ending Work in Process Assembly Department of Global Defense, Inc., for February 2004

To see the importance of using equivalent units in unit-cost calculations, compare conversion costs for January and February 2004. Total conversion costs of $18,600 for the 400 units worked on during February are lower than the conversion costs of $24,000 for the 400 units worked on in January. However, the conversion costs to fully assemble a unit are $60 in both January and February. Total conversion costs are lower in February because fewer equivalent units of conversion-costs work were completed in February (310) than in January (400). Using physical units instead of equivalent units in the per unit calculation would have led to the erroneous conclusion that conversion costs per unit declined from $60 in January to $46.50 ($18,600 ÷ 400 units) in February. This incorrect costing might have prompted Global Defense, for example, to lower the price of DG-19 when, in fact, costs have not declined.

If you remember where the units go in step 1, there is no need to memorize where the costs go in step 5, because the costs attach to the units. In Exhibits 17-1 and 17-2, the costs are attached (1) to units completed and transferred out of Assembly and (2) to units in ending work in process.

Step 4 in Exhibit 17-2 summarizes total costs to account for. Because the beginning balance of the work-in-process inventory is zero, total costs to account for (that is, the total charges or debits to the Work in Process—Assembly account) consist only of the costs added during February: direct materials of $32,000 and conversion costs of $18,600, for a total of $50,600.

Step 5 in Exhibit 17-2 assigns these costs to units completed and transferred out and to units still in process at the end of February 2004. *The idea is to attach dollar amounts to the equivalent output units for direct materials and conversion costs of (a) units completed and (b) ending work in process, as calculated in Exhibit 17-1, step 2. The equivalent output units for each input are multiplied by the cost per equivalent unit, as calculated in step 3 of Exhibit 17-2.* For example, the costs assigned to the 225 physical units in ending work in process are

To see the big picture in process costing, be sure to tie the numbers in the production cost report (Exhibit 17-2) to the related Work in Process T-account (Exhibit 17-3).

Direct material costs of 225 equivalent units (Exhibit 17-1, step 2) × $80 cost per equivalent unit of direct materials calculated in step 3	$18,000
Conversion costs of 135 equivalent units (Exhibit 17-1, step 2) × $60 cost per equivalent unit of conversion costs calculated in step 3	8,100
Total cost of ending work in process	$26,100

Note also that total costs to account for of $50,600 (step 4) equal total costs accounted for (step 5).

Journal Entries

Journal entries in process-costing systems are similar to the entries made in job-costing systems with respect to direct materials and conversion costs. The main difference is that, in process costing, there is one Work-in-Process account for each process—in our example, Work in Process—Assembly and Work in Process—Testing. Global Defense purchases

4 Prepare journal entries for process-costing systems

...similar to job costing, but separate entries are made for each department

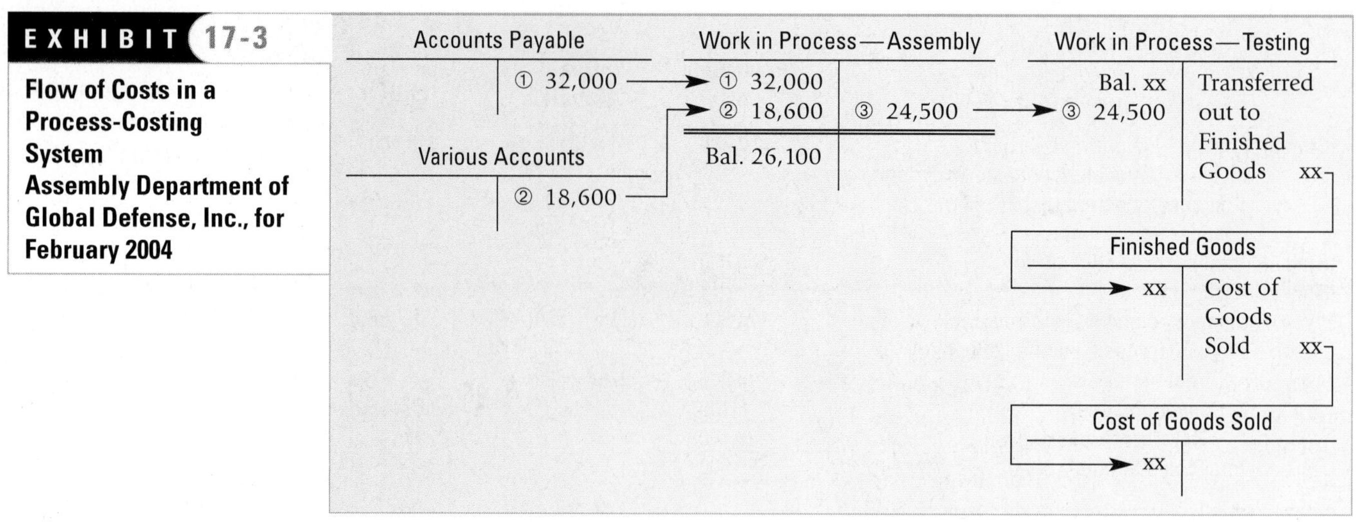

direct materials as needed. These materials are delivered directly to the Assembly Department. Using amounts from Exhibit 17-2, summary journal entries for February are

1. Work in Process—Assembly	32,000	
Accounts Payable Control		32,000
To record direct materials purchased and used in production during February.		
2. Work in Process—Assembly	18,600	
Various accounts		18,600
To record Assembly Department conversion costs for February; examples include energy, manufacturing supplies, all manufacturing labor, and plant depreciation.		
3. Work in Process—Testing	24,500	
Work in Process—Assembly		24,500
To record cost of goods completed and transferred from Assembly to Testing during February.		

Exhibit 17-3 shows a general framework for the flow of costs through the T-accounts. Notice how entry 3 for \$24,500 follows the physical transfer of goods from Assembly to the Testing Department. The T-account, Work in Process—Assembly, shows February 2004's ending balance of \$26,100, which is the beginning balance of Work in Process—Assembly in March 2004.

CASE 3: PROCESS COSTING WITH SOME BEGINNING AND SOME ENDING WORK-IN-PROCESS INVENTORY

At the beginning of March 2004, Global Defense had 225 partially assembled DG-19 units in the Assembly Department. It started production of another 275 units in March 2004. Data for the Assembly Department for March are

Physical Units for March 2004

Work in process, beginning inventory (March 1)	225 units
Direct materials (100% complete)	
Conversion costs (60% complete)	
Started during March	275 units
Completed and transferred out during March	400 units
Work in process, ending inventory (March 31)	100 units
Direct materials (100% complete)	
Conversion costs (50% complete)	

Total Costs for March 2004

Work in process, beginning inventory		
Direct materials (225 equivalent units × \$80 per unit)	\$18,000	
Conversion costs (135 equivalent units × \$60 per unit)	8,100	\$26,100
Direct material costs added during March		19,800
Conversion costs added during March		16,380
Total costs to account for		\$62,280

Global Defense now has incomplete units in both beginning work-in-process inventory and ending work-in-process inventory for March 2004. We use the five steps described earlier to calculate (1) the cost of units completed and transferred out and (2) the cost of ending work in process. To assign costs to each of these categories, however, we need to choose an inventory cost-flow method. We first describe the five-step approach for the weighted-average method and then for the first-in, first-out method. The different cost-flow methods produce different amounts for cost of units completed and for ending work in process because unit costs of inputs tend to change from one period to the next.

WEIGHTED-AVERAGE METHOD

5 **Use the weighted-average method of process costing**

...assigns costs based on total costs and equivalent units completed to date

The **weighted-average process-costing method** calculates the equivalent-unit cost of all the *work done to date* (regardless of the accounting period in which it was done) and assigns this cost to equivalent units completed and transferred out of the process and to equivalent units in ending work-in-process inventory. The weighted-average cost is the total of all costs entering the Work in Process account (whether they are from beginning work in process or from work started during the period) divided by total equivalent units of work done to date. We now describe the weighted-average method using the five-step procedure introduced in Case 2.

Step 1: **Summarize the Flow of Physical Units.** The physical units column of Exhibit 17-4 shows where the units came from—225 units from beginning inventory and 275 units started during the current period—and where they went—400 units completed and transferred out and 100 units in ending inventory. These data for March were given on page 592.

Step 2: **Compute Output in Terms of Equivalent Units.** As we saw in Case 2, partially assembled units are complete in terms of direct materials because direct materials are introduced at the beginning of the process. For conversion costs, the fully assembled physical units transferred out are, of course, fully completed. The Assembly Department supervisor estimates the partially assembled physical units in March 31 work in process to be 50% complete (on average).

The equivalent-units columns in Exhibit 17-4 show the equivalent units of work done to date: equivalent units completed and transferred out and equivalent units in ending work in process (500 equivalent units of direct materials and 450 equivalent units of conversion costs). The equivalent units of work done to date *also* equal the equivalent units in beginning inventory (work done in the previous period) plus the equivalent units of work done in the current period, because:

$$\begin{array}{c}\text{Equivalent units}\\\text{in beginning}\\\text{work in process}\end{array} + \begin{array}{c}\text{Equivalent units}\\\text{of work done in}\\\text{current period}\end{array} = \begin{array}{c}\text{Equivalent units}\\\text{completed and}\\\text{transferred out}\\\text{in current period}\end{array} + \begin{array}{c}\text{Equivalent units}\\\text{in ending}\\\text{work in process}\end{array}$$

The equivalent-unit calculation in the weighted-average method is only concerned with total equivalent units of *work done to date,* regardless of whether (1) the work was done during the previous period and is part of beginning work in process or (2) it was done during the current period. That is, the weighted-average method *merges* equivalent units in beginning inventory (work done before March) with equivalent units of work done in the

EXHIBIT 17-4

Steps 1 and 2: Summarize Output in Physical Units and Compute Equivalent Units Weighted-Average Method of Process Costing Assembly Department of Global Defense, Inc., for March 2004

Flow of Production	(Step 1) Physical Units (given p. 592)	(Step 2) Equivalent Units Direct Materials	Conversion Costs
Work in process, beginning	225		
Started during current period	275		
To account for	500		
Completed and transferred out during current period	400	400	400
Work in process, ending[a]	100		
(100 × 100%; 100 × 50%)		100	50
Accounted for	500		
Work done to date		500	450

[a]Degree of completion in this department: direct materials, 100%; conversion costs, 50%.

current period (March). *Thus, the stage of completion of the current-period beginning work in process is irrelevant and not used in the computation.*

Step 3: Compute Equivalent-Unit Costs. Exhibit 17-5, step 3, shows the computation of equivalent-unit costs for direct materials and conversion costs. The weighted-average cost per equivalent unit is obtained by dividing the sum of costs for beginning work in process plus the costs for work done in the current period by total equivalent units of work done to date. When calculating the weighted-average conversion cost per equivalent unit in Exhibit 17-5, for example, we divide total conversion costs, $24,480 (beginning work in process, $8,100, plus work done in current period, $16,380), by total equivalent units, 450 (equivalent units of conversion costs in beginning work in process and in work done in current period), to get a weighted-average cost per equivalent unit of $54.40.

Step 4: Summarize Total Costs to Account For. The total costs to account for in March 2004 are described in the example data on page 593: beginning work in process, $26,100 (direct materials, $18,000, plus conversion costs, $8,100), plus costs added during March, $36,180 (direct materials, $19,800, plus conversion costs, $16,380). The total of these costs is $62,280.

Step 5: Assign Costs to Units Completed and to Units in Ending Work in Process. This step costs all work done to date: (1) the cost of units completed and transferred out of the process and (2) the cost of ending work in process. Step 5 in Exhibit 17-5 takes the equivalent units completed and transferred out and equivalent units in ending work in process calculated in Exhibit 17-4, step 2, and attaches dollar amounts to them. These amounts are the weighted-average cost per equivalent unit for direct materials and the weighted-average cost per equivalent unit for conversion costs calculated in step 3. For example, the total costs of the 100 physical units in ending work in process are

Direct materials:	
100 equivalent units × weighted-average cost per equivalent unit of $75.60	$ 7,560
Conversion costs:	
50 equivalent units × weighted-average cost per equivalent unit of $54.40	2,720
Total costs of ending work in process	$10,280

The following table summarizes the total costs to account for ($62,280) and how they are accounted for in Exhibit 17-5. The arrows indicate that costs of units completed and transferred out and in ending work in process are calculated using weighted-average total costs obtained after merging costs of beginning work in process and costs added in the current period.

EXHIBIT 17-5

Steps 3, 4, and 5: Compute Equivalent-Unit Costs, Summarize Total Costs to Account For, and Assign Costs to Units Completed and to Units in Ending Work in Process Weighted-Average Method of Process Costing Assembly Department of Global Defense, Inc., for March 2004

		Total Production Costs	Direct Materials	Conversion Costs
(Step 3)	Work in process, beginning (given, p. 593)	$26,100	$18,000	$ 8,100
	Costs added in current period (given, p. 593)	36,180	19,800	16,380
	Costs incurred to date		$37,800	$24,480
	Divide by equivalent units of work done to date (Exhibit 17-4)		÷ 500	÷ 450
	Cost per equivalent unit of work done to date		$ 75.60	$ 54.40
(Step 4)	Total costs to account for	$62,280		
(Step 5)	Assignment of costs:			
	Completed and transferred out (400 units)	$52,000	(400[a] × $75.60) +	(400[a] × $54.40)
	Work in process, ending (100 units):			
	Direct materials	7,560	100[b] × $75.60	
	Conversion costs	2,720		50[b] × $54.40
	Total work in process	10,280		
	Total costs accounted for	$62,280		

[a]Equivalent units completed and transferred out from Exhibit 17-4, step 2.
[b]Equivalent units in ending work in process from Exhibit 17-4, step 2.

Costs to Account For	
Beginning work in process	$26,100
Costs added in current period	36,180
Total costs to account for	$62,280

Costs Accounted for Calculated at Weighted-Average Cost	
Completed and transferred out	$52,000
Ending work in process	10,280
Total costs accounted for	$62,280

Before proceeding, review Exhibits 17-4 and 17-5 to check your understanding of the weighted-average method. Note: Exhibit 17-4 deals only with physical and equivalent units, not costs. Exhibit 17-5 shows the cost amounts.

The purpose of Exhibits 17-4 and 17-5 (weighted average), 17-6 and 17-7 (FIFO), and 17-8 and 17-9 (standard costing) is to calculate the costs of the units completed and transferred out during March 2004 in order to record the journal entry debiting Work in Process—Testing and crediting Work in Process—Assembly.

Using amounts from Exhibit 17-5, summary journal entries under the weighted-average method for March 2004 at Global Defense, are

1. Work in Process—Assembly	19,800	
Accounts Payable Control		19,800
To record direct materials purchased and used in production during March.		
2. Work in Process—Assembly	16,380	
Various accounts		16,380
To record Assembly Department conversion costs for March; examples include energy, manufacturing supplies, all manufacturing labor, and plant depreciation.		
3. Work in Process—Testing	52,000	
Work in Process—Assembly		52,000
To record cost of goods completed and transferred from Assembly to Testing during March.		

The T-account, Work in Process—Assembly, under the weighted-average method shows:

Work in Process—Assembly

Beginning inventory, March 1	26,100	③ Completed and transferred out to Work in Process—Testing	52,000
① Direct materials	19,800		
② Conversion costs	16,380		
Ending inventory, March 31	10,280		

6 Use the first-in, first-out (FIFO) method of process costing

...assigns costs based on costs and equivalent units of work done in current period

FIRST-IN, FIRST-OUT METHOD

The **first-in, first-out (FIFO) process-costing method** (a) assigns the cost of the *previous* accounting period's equivalent units in beginning work-in-process inventory to the first units completed and transferred out of the process; and (b) assigns the cost of equivalent units worked on during the *current* period first to complete beginning inventory, next to start and complete new units, and finally to units in ending work-in-process inventory. The FIFO method assumes that the earliest equivalent units in work in process are completed first.

A distinct feature of the FIFO process-costing method is that work done on beginning inventory before the current period is kept separate from work done in the current period. Costs incurred in the current period and units produced in the current period are used to calculate costs per equivalent unit of work done in the current period. In contrast, equivalent-unit and cost-per-equivalent-unit calculations under the weighted-average method merge the units and costs in beginning inventory with units and costs of work done in the current period.

We now describe the FIFO method using the five-step procedure introduced in Case 2.

Step 1: Summarize the Flow of Physical Units. Exhibit 17-6, step 1, traces the flow of physical units of production. The following observations help explain the calculation of physical units under the FIFO method for Global Defense.

- The first physical units assumed to be completed and transferred out during the period are 225 units from the beginning work-in-process inventory.
- The March data on page 592 indicate that 400 physical units were completed during March. The FIFO method assumes that the first 225 of these units were from beginning inventory; thus, 175 (400 – 225) of the 275 physical units started must have been completed during March.
- Ending work-in-process inventory consists of 100 physical units—the 275 physical units started minus the 175 of these units that were completed.
- The physical units "to account for" equal the physical units "accounted for" (500 units).

Step 2: Compute Output in Terms of Equivalent Units. Exhibit 17-6 also presents the computations for step 2 under the FIFO method. *The equivalent-unit calculations for each cost category focus on the equivalent units of work done in the current period (March) only.*

EXHIBIT 17-6

Steps 1 and 2: Summarize Output in Physical Units and Compute Equivalent Units FIFO Method of Process Costing Assembly Department of Global Defense, Inc., for March 2004

During March 2004, beginning work in process had 0% direct materials and 40% conversion costs added to it. That's because at the start of March, beginning work in process was 100% complete with respect to direct materials and 60% complete with respect to conversion costs. This same concept applies to Exhibits 17-8 and 17-13.

Flow of Production	(Step 1) Physical Units	(Step 2) Equivalent Units Direct Materials	Conversion Costs
Work in process, beginning (given, p. 592)	225	(work done before current period)	
Started during current period (given, p. 592)	275		
To account for	500		
Completed and transferred out during current period:			
From beginning work in process[a]	225		
[225 × (100% – 100%); 225 × (100% – 60%)]		0	90
Started and completed	175[b]		
(175 × 100%, 175 × 100%)		175	175
Work in process, ending[c] (given, p. 592)	100		
(100 × 100%; 100 × 50%)		100	50
Accounted for	500		
Work done in current period only		275	315

[a]Degree of completion in this department: direct materials, 100%; conversion costs, 60%.
[b]400 physical units completed and transferred out minus 225 physical units completed and transferred out from beginning work-in-process inventory.
[c]Degree of completion in this department: direct materials, 100%; conversion costs, 50%.

Under the FIFO method, the equivalent units of work done in March on the beginning work-in-process inventory equal the 225 physical units times *the percentage of work remaining to be done in March to complete these units:* 0% for direct materials, because beginning work in process is 100% complete with respect to direct materials, and 40% for conversion costs, because beginning work in process is 60% complete with respect to conversion costs. The results are 0 (0% × 225) equivalent units of work for direct materials and 90 (40% × 225) equivalent units of work for conversion costs.

The equivalent units of work done on the 175 physical units started and completed equals 175 units times 100% for both direct materials and conversion costs, because all work on these units is done in the current period.

The equivalent units of work done on the 100 units of ending work in process equal 100 physical units times 100% for direct materials (because all direct materials for these units are added in the current period) and 50% for conversion costs (because 50% of conversion-costs work on these units is done in the current period).

Step 3: **Compute Equivalent-Unit Costs.** Exhibit 17-7 shows the step 3 computation of equivalent-unit costs for *work done in the current period only* for direct materials and conversion costs. For example, the conversion cost per equivalent unit of $52 is obtained by dividing current-period conversion costs of $16,380 by current-period conversion-costs equivalent units of 315.

Step 4: **Summarize Total Costs to Account For.** The total production costs column in Exhibit 17-7 presents step 4 and summarizes the total costs to account for in March 2004 (beginning work in process and costs added in the current period) of $62,280, as described in the example data (p. 593).

Step 5: **Assign Costs to Units Completed and to Units in Ending Work in Process.** Exhibit 17-7 shows the assignment of costs under the FIFO method. The costs of

EXHIBIT 17-7

Steps 3, 4, and 5: Compute Equivalent-Unit Costs, Summarize Total Costs to Account For, and Assign Costs to Units Completed and to Units in Ending Work in Process
FIFO Method of Process Costing
Assembly Department of Global Defense, Inc., for March 2004

	Total Production Costs	Direct Materials	Conversion Costs
Work in process, beginning (given, p. 593)	$26,100	(costs of work done before current period)	
(Step 3) Costs added in current period (given, p. 593)	36,180	$19,800	$16,380
Divide by equivalent units of work done in current period (Exhibit 17-6)		÷ 275	÷ 315
Cost per equivalent unit of work done in current period		$ 72	$ 52
(Step 4) Total costs to account for	$62,280		
(Step 5) Assignment of costs:			
Completed and transferred out (400 units):			
Work in process, beginning (225 units)	$26,100		
Direct materials added in current period	0	$0^{a} \times \$72$	
Conversion costs added in current period	4,680		$90^{a} \times \$52$
Total from beginning inventory	30,780		
Started and completed (175 units)	21,700	$(175^{b} \times \$72)$ +	$(175^{b} \times \$52)$
Total costs of units completed and transferred out	52,480		
Work in process, ending (100 units):			
Direct materials	7,200	$100^{c} \times \$72$	
Conversion costs	2,600		$50^{c} \times \$52$
Total work in process, ending	9,800		
Total costs accounted for	$62,280		

[a]Equivalent units used to complete beginning work in process from Exhibit 17-6, step 2.
[b]Equivalent units started and completed from Exhibit 17-6, step 2.
[c]Equivalent units in ending work in process from Exhibit 17-6, step 2.

work done in the current period are assigned (1) first to the additional work done to complete the beginning work in process, then (2) to the work done on units started and completed during the current period, and finally (3) to the ending work in process. *Step 5 takes each of the equivalent units calculated in Exhibit 17-6, step 2, and attaches dollar amounts to them (using the cost-per-equivalent-unit calculations in step 3).* The goal is to determine the total cost of all units completed from beginning inventory and from work started and completed in the current period, and the costs of ending work in process done in the current period.

Of the 400 completed units, 225 units are from beginning inventory and 175 units are started and completed during March. The FIFO method starts by assigning the costs of the beginning work-in-process inventory of $26,100 to the first units completed and transferred out. As we saw in step 2, an additional 90 equivalent units of conversion costs are needed to complete these units in the current period. The current-period conversion cost per equivalent unit is $52, so $4,680 (90 equivalent units × $52 per equivalent unit) of additional costs are incurred to complete the beginning inventory. The total production costs for the units in beginning inventory are $26,100 + $4,680 = $30,780. The 175 units started and completed in the current period consist of 175 equivalent units of direct materials and 175 equivalent units of conversion costs. These units are costed at the cost per equivalent unit in the current period (direct materials, $72, and conversion costs, $52) for a total production cost of $21,700 [(175 equivalent units × $72 per unit) + (175 equivalent units × $52 per unit)].

Under FIFO, ending work-in-process inventory comes from units that were started but not fully completed during the current period. The total costs of the 100 partially assembled physical units in ending work in process are

Direct materials:	
100 equivalent units × $72 cost per equivalent unit in March	$7,200
Conversion costs:	
50 equivalent units × $52 cost per equivalent unit in March	2,600
Total cost of work in process on March 31	$9,800

The following table summarizes the total costs to account for and the costs accounted for of $62,280 in Exhibit 17-7. Notice, under the FIFO method, the layers of beginning work in process and costs added in the current period are kept separate. The arrows indicate where the costs in each layer go—that is, to units completed and transferred out or to ending work in process. Be sure to include the costs of beginning work in process ($26,100) when calculating the costs of units completed from beginning inventory.

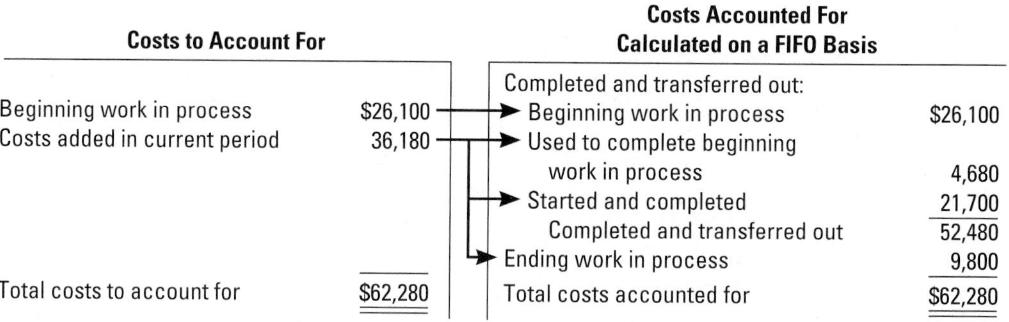

Costs to Account For		Costs Accounted For Calculated on a FIFO Basis	
		Completed and transferred out:	
Beginning work in process	$26,100	→ Beginning work in process	$26,100
Costs added in current period	36,180	→ Used to complete beginning work in process	4,680
		→ Started and completed	21,700
		Completed and transferred out	52,480
		→ Ending work in process	9,800
Total costs to account for	$62,280	Total costs accounted for	$62,280

Before proceeding, review Exhibits 17-6 and 17-7 to check your understanding of the FIFO method. Note: Exhibit 17-6 deals only with physical and equivalent units, not costs. Exhibit 17-7 shows the cost amounts.

The journal entries under the FIFO method are identical to the journal entries under the weighted-average method except for one difference. The entry to record the cost of goods completed and transferred out would be $52,480 under the FIFO method instead of $52,000 under the weighted-average method.

Only rarely is an application of pure FIFO ever encountered in process costing. That's because FIFO is applied within a department to compile the cost of units *transferred out*, but as a practical matter, the units *transferred in* during a given period usually are carried at a single average unit cost. For example, the average cost of units transferred out of the Assembly Department is $52,480 ÷ 400 units = $131.20 per DG-19 unit. The Assembly

Department uses FIFO to distinguish between monthly batches of production. The succeeding department, Testing, however, costs these units (which consist of costs incurred in both February and March) at one average unit cost ($131.20 in this illustration). If this averaging were not done, the attempt to track costs on a pure FIFO basis throughout a series of processes would be cumbersome. As a result, the FIFO method should really be called a *modified* or *department* FIFO method.

COMPARISON OF WEIGHTED-AVERAGE AND FIFO METHODS

Here's the summary of the costs assigned to units completed and to units still in process under the weighted-average and FIFO process-costing methods in our example for March 2004:

	Weighted Average (from Exhibit 17-5)	FIFO (from Exhibit 17-7)	Difference
Cost of units completed and transferred out	$52,000	$52,480	+$480
Work in process, ending	10,280	9,800	−$480
Total costs accounted for	$62,280	$62,280	

The weighted-average ending inventory is higher than the FIFO ending inventory by $480, or 4.9% ($480 ÷ $9,800 = 0.049, or 4.9%). This would be a significant difference when aggregated over the many thousands of products that Global Defense makes. The weighted-average method in our example results in lower cost of goods sold and, hence, higher operating income and higher income taxes than the FIFO method. To see why, recall from the data on page 593 that direct material cost per equivalent unit in beginning work-in-process inventory is $80, and conversion cost per equivalent unit in beginning work-in-process inventory is $60. These costs are greater, respectively, than the $72 direct materials cost and the $52 conversion cost per equivalent unit of work done during the current period. These costs could be lower due to a decline in the prices of direct materials and conversion-cost inputs, and/or they could be lower as a result of Global Defense becoming more efficient in its processes by using smaller quantities of inputs per unit of output.

For the Assembly Department, FIFO assumes that (a) all the higher-cost units from the previous period in beginning work in process are the first to be completed and transferred out of the process and (b) ending work in process consists of only the lower-cost current-period units. The weighted-average method, however, smooths out cost per equivalent unit by assuming that (a) more of the lower-cost units are completed and transferred out and (b) some of the higher-cost units are placed in ending work in process. The decline in the current-period cost per equivalent unit results in a lower cost of units completed and transferred out and a higher ending work-in-process inventory under the weighted-average method compared with FIFO.

Cost of units completed and, hence, operating income can differ materially between the weighted-average and FIFO methods when (1) the direct material or conversion cost per unit varies significantly from period to period and (2) the physical inventory levels of work in process are large in relation to the total number of units transferred out of the process. As companies move toward long-term procurement contracts that reduce differences in unit costs from period to period and reduce inventory levels, the difference in the cost of units completed under the weighted-average and FIFO methods will decrease.[1]

Managers use information from process-costing systems to aid them in pricing and product-mix decisions and to provide them with feedback about their performance. FIFO provides managers with information about changes in the costs per unit from one period to

[1]For example, suppose beginning work-in-process inventory for March was 125 physical units (instead of 225), and suppose costs per equivalent unit of work done in the current period (March) were direct materials, $75, and conversion costs, $55. Assume all other data for March are the same as in our example. In this case, the cost of units completed and transferred out would be $52,833 under the weighted-average method and $53,000 under the FIFO method. The work-in-process ending inventory would be $10,417 under the weighted-average method and $10,250 under the FIFO method (calculations not shown). These differences are much smaller than in the chapter example. The weighted-average ending inventory is higher than the FIFO ending inventory by only $167 ($10,417 − $10,250), or 1.6% ($167 ÷ $10,250 = 0.016, or 1.6%), compared with 4.9% higher in the chapter example.

the next. Managers can use this information to adjust prices (for example, based on the $72 direct materials cost and $52 conversion cost in March) and to evaluate performance in the current period compared with a budget or relative to performance in the previous period. By focusing on work done and the costs of work done during the current period, the FIFO method provides useful information for these planning and control purposes.

The weighted-average method merges unit costs from different accounting periods, obscuring period-to-period comparisons. For example, the weighted-average method would lead managers at Global Defense to make decisions based on the $75.60 direct materials and $54.40 conversion costs, rather than the costs of $72 and $52 prevailing in March. The advantages of the weighted-average method, however, are its computational simplicity and its reporting of a more-representative average unit cost when input prices fluctuate markedly from month to month.

How is activity-based costing related to process costing? Each process—assembly, testing, and so on—can be considered a different (production) activity. However, no additional activities need to be identified within each process. That's because products are homogeneous and use resources of each process in a uniform way.

7 **Incorporate standard costs into a process-costing system**

...use standard costs as the cost per equivalent unit

STANDARD-COSTING METHOD OF PROCESS COSTING

This section assumes that you have already studied Chapters 7 and 8. If you have not, skip to the next major section, Transferred-In Costs in Process Costing, page 603.

Companies that use process-costing systems produce masses of identical or similar units of output. Setting standards for quantities of inputs needed to produce output can be straightforward in such companies. Standard costs per input unit may then be assigned to input quantity standards to develop the standard cost per output unit.

The weighted-average and FIFO methods become very complicated when used in process industries that produce a wide variety of similar products. For example, a steel-rolling mill uses various steel alloys and produces sheets of various sizes and finishes. Both the items of direct materials and the operations performed are few; but used in various combinations, they yield a wide variety of products. In these cases, if the broad averaging procedure of actual process costing were used, the result would be inaccurate costs for each product. Similarly, complex conditions are frequently found, for example, in plants that manufacture rubber products, textiles, ceramics, paints, and packaged food products. The standard-costing method of process costing is especially useful in these situations.

One reason for standard costing's popularity is it simplifies record keeping.

Under the standard-costing method, teams of design and process engineers, operations personnel, and management accountants work together to determine *separate* standard or equivalent-unit costs on the basis of the different technical processing specifications for each product. Identifying standard costs for each product overcomes the disadvantage of costing all products at a single average amount, as under actual costing.

Computations Under Standard Costing

We return to the Assembly Department of Global Defense, Inc., but this time we assign standard costs to the process. Assume the same standard costs apply in February and March of 2004:

Direct materials	$ 74 per unit
Conversion costs	54 per unit
Total standard manufacturing costs	$128 per unit

Data for the Assembly Department are

Physical Units for March 2004	
Work in process, beginning inventory (March 1)	225 units
Direct materials (100% complete)	
Conversion costs (60% complete)	
Started during March	275 units
Completed and transferred out during March	400 units
Work in process, ending inventory (March 31)	100 units
Direct materials (100% complete)	
Conversion costs (50% complete)	

Total Costs for March 2004

Work in process, beginning inventory at standard costs		
Direct materials: 225 equivalent units × $74 per unit	$16,650	
Conversion costs: 135 equivalent units × $54 per unit	7,290	$23,940
Actual direct material cost added during March		19,800
Actual conversion costs added during March		16,380

We illustrate the standard-costing method of process costing using the five-step procedure introduced earlier (p. xxx).

Exhibit 17-8 on the next page presents steps 1 and 2. These steps are identical to the steps described for the FIFO method in Exhibit 17-6. Work done in the current period equals direct materials (275 equivalent units) plus conversion costs (315 equivalent units).

Exhibit 17-9 on the next page describes steps 3, 4, and 5. Step 3, the computation of equivalent-unit costs, is easier under the standard-costing method than under either the weighted-average method or the FIFO method. The costs per equivalent unit are the standard costs: direct materials, $74, and conversion costs, $54. The equivalent-unit costs do not have to be computed in the same manner as they were calculated for the weighted-average and FIFO methods.

The total costs to account for in Exhibit 17-9, step 4 (that is, the total debits to Work in Process—Assembly) differ from the total debits to Work in Process—Assembly under the actual cost-based weighted-average and FIFO methods. That's because, as in all standard-costing systems, the debits to the Work-in-Process account are at standard costs, rather than actual costs. These standard costs total $61,300 in Exhibit 17-9.

Exhibit 17-9, step 5, assigns total costs to units completed and transferred out and to units in ending work-in-process inventory, as in the FIFO method. Step 5 attaches amounts of standard costs to the equivalent units calculated in Exhibit 17-8. These costs are assigned (a) first to complete beginning work-in-process inventory, (b) next to start and complete new units, and (c) finally to start new units that are in ending work-in-process inventory. Note how the $61,300 total costs accounted for in step 5 of Exhibit 17-9 equal the total costs to account for.

Accounting for Variances

Process-costing systems using standard costs usually accumulate actual costs incurred separately from the inventory accounts. The following is an example. The actual costs are recorded in the first two entries. Recall, Global Defense purchases direct materials as needed, and these materials are delivered directly to the Assembly Department. The total variances are recorded in the next two entries. The final entry transfers out the completed goods at standard costs.

For control purposes, variances for direct materials and conversion costs should be based on work done *in the current period only.*

1. Assembly Department Direct Materials Control (at actual costs)	19,800	
Accounts Payable Control		19,800
To record direct materials purchased and used in production during March. This cost control account is debited with actual costs and immediately credited with standard costs assigned to the units worked on (entry 3 below).		
2. Assembly Department Conversion Costs Control (at actual costs)	16,380	
Various accounts		16,380
To record Assembly Department conversion costs for March.		

Entries 3, 4, and 5 use standard cost amounts from Exhibit 17-9.

3. Work in Process—Assembly (at standard costs)	20,350	
Direct Materials Variances		550
Assembly Department Direct Materials Control		19,800
To record actual direct materials used and total direct materials variances.		

Continued on page 603

EXHIBIT 17-8

Steps 1 and 2: Summarize Output in Physical Units and Compute Equivalent Units
Use of Standard Costs in Process Costing
Assembly Department of Global Defense, Inc., for March 2004

Flow of Production	(Step 1) Physical Units	(Step 2) Equivalent Units Direct Materials	Conversion Costs
Work in process, beginning (given, p. 592)	225		
Started during current period (given, p. 592)	275		
To account for	500		
Completed and transferred out during current period:			
From beginning work in process[a]	225		
[225 × (100% – 100%); 225 × (100% – 60%)]		0	90
Started and completed	175[b]		
(175 × 100%, 175 × 100%)		175	175
Work in process, ending[c] (given, p. 592)	100		
(100 × 100%; 100 × 50%)		100	50
Accounted for	500		
Work done in current period only		275	315

[a]Degree of completion in this department: direct materials, 100%; conversion costs, 60%.
[b]400 physical units completed and transferred out minus 225 physical units completed and transferred out from beginning work-in-process inventory.
[c]Degree of completion in this department: direct materials, 100%; conversion costs, 50%.

EXHIBIT 17-9

Steps 3, 4, and 5: Compute Equivalent-Unit Costs, Summarize Total Costs to Account For, and Assign Costs to Units Completed and to Units in Ending Work in Process
Use of Standard Costs in Process Costing
Assembly Department of Global Defense, Inc., for March 2004

		Total Production Costs	Direct Materials		Conversion Costs
(Step 3)	Standard cost per equivalent unit (given, p. 600)		$ 74		$ 54
	Work in process, beginning (given, p. 601)				
	Direct materials, 225 × $74; Conversion costs, 135 × $54	$23,940			
	Costs added in current period at standard costs				
	Direct materials, 275 × $74; Conversion costs, 315 × $54	37,360	20,350		17,010
(Step 4)	Costs to account for	$61,300			
(Step 5)	Assignment of costs at standard costs:				
	Completed and transferred out (400 units):				
	Work in process, beginning (225 units)	$23,940			
	Direct materials added in current period	0	0[a] × $74		
	Conversion costs added in current period	4,860			90[a] × $54
	Total from beginning inventory	28,800			
	Started and completed (175 units)	22,400	(175[b] × $74)	+	(175[b] × $54)
	Total costs of units completed and transferred out	51,200			
	Work in process, ending (100 units):				
	Direct materials	7,400	100[c] × $74		
	Conversion costs	2,700			50[c] × $54
	Total work in process, ending	10,100			
	Total costs accounted for	$61,300			
Summary of variances for current performance					
Costs added in current period at standard costs (see step 3 above)			$20,350		$17,010
Actual costs incurred (given p. 593)			19,800		16,380
Variance			$ 550 F		$ 630 F

[a]Equivalent units to complete beginning work in process from Exhibit 17-8, step 2.
[b]Equivalent units started and completed from Exhibit 17-8, step 2.
[c]Equivalent units in ending work in process from Exhibit 17-8, step 2.

4. Work in Process—Assembly (at standard costs)	17,010	
Conversion Costs Variances		630
Assembly Department Conversion Costs Control		16,380
To record actual conversion costs and total conversion costs variances.		
5. Work in Process—Testing (at standard costs)	51,200	
Work in Process—Assembly (at standard costs)		51,200
To record costs of units completed and transferred out at standard cost from Assembly to Testing.		

Variances arise under the standard-costing method, as in entries 3 and 4. That's because the standard costs assigned to products on the basis of work done in the current period do not equal the actual costs incurred in the current period. Variances can be measured and analyzed in little or great detail for planning and control purposes, as described in Chapters 7 and 8. Exhibit 17-10 shows how the standard costs flow through the accounts.

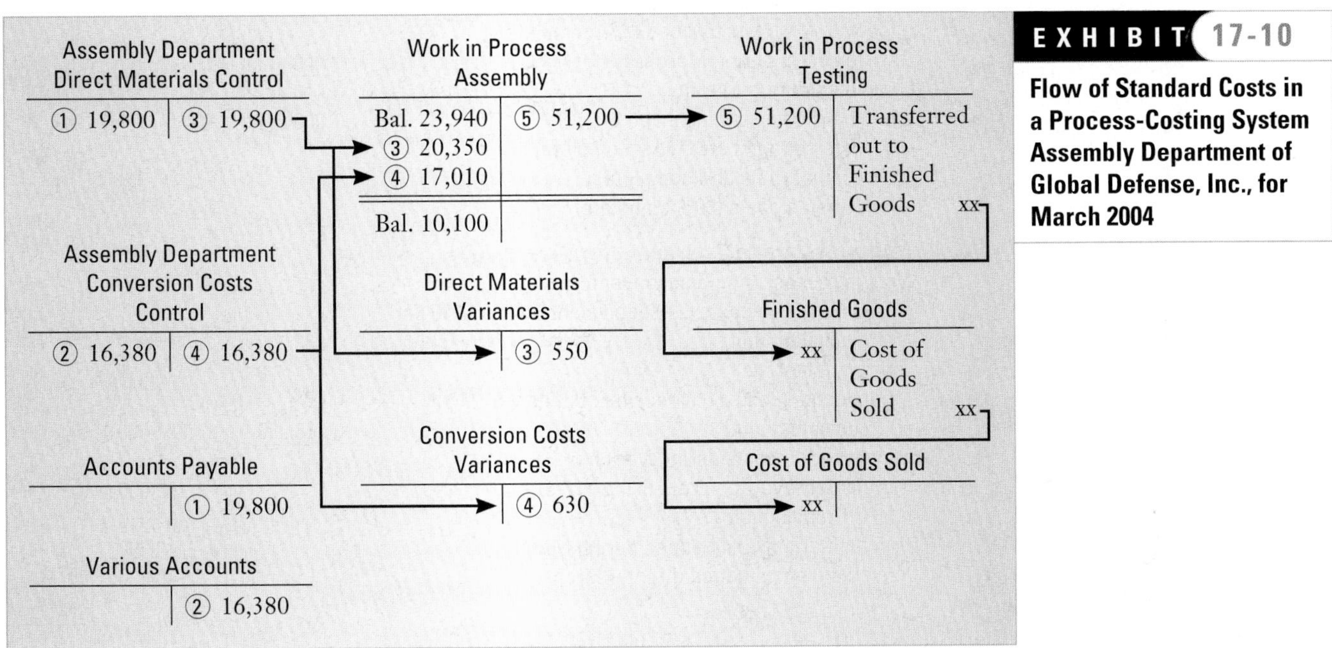

EXHIBIT 17-10

Flow of Standard Costs in a Process-Costing System Assembly Department of Global Defense, Inc., for March 2004

TRANSFERRED-IN COSTS IN PROCESS COSTING

8 Apply process-costing methods to cases with transferred-in costs

...using weighted-average and FIFO methods

Many process-costing systems have two or more departments or processes in the production cycle. As units move from department to department, the related costs are also transferred by monthly journal entries. If standard costs are used, accounting for such transfers is simple. However, if the weighted-average or FIFO method is used, the accounting can become more complex. We now extend our Global Defense, Inc., example to the Testing Department. As the assembly process is completed, the Assembly Department of Global Defense immediately transfers DG-19 units to its Testing Department. Here the units receive additional direct materials at the *end* of the process, such as crating and other packing materials to prepare the units for shipment. Conversion costs are added evenly during the Testing Department's process. As units are completed in Testing, they are immediately transferred to Finished Goods.

The following diagram (on p. 604) graphically represents these facts:

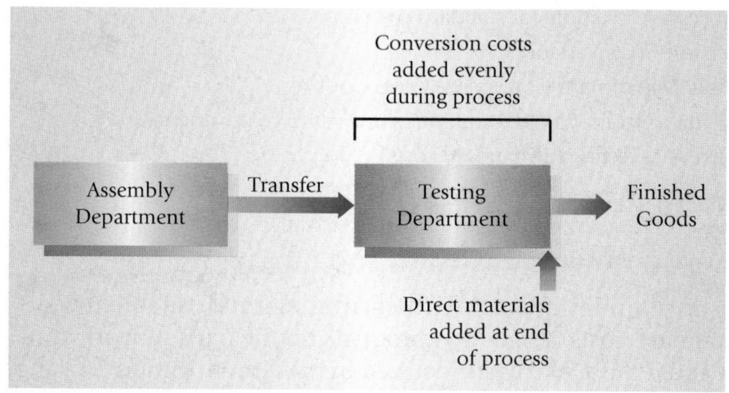

Data for the Testing Department for March 2004 are

Physical Units for March 2004		
Work in process, beginning inventory (March 1)	240 units	
Transferred-in costs (100% complete)		
Direct materials (0% complete)		
Conversion costs (5/8 or 62.5% complete)		
Transferred-in during March	400 units	
Completed during March	440 units	
Work in process, ending inventory (March 31)	200 units	
Transferred-in costs (100% complete)		
Direct materials (0% complete)		
Conversion costs (80% complete)		
Costs of Testing Department for March 2004		
Work in process, beginning inventory[2]		
Transferred-in costs (240 equivalent units × $140 per equivalent unit)	$33,600	
Direct materials	0	
Conversion costs (150 equivalent units × $120 per equivalent unit)	18,000	$51,600
Transferred-in costs during March		
Weighted-average (from Exhibit 17-5)		52,000
FIFO (from Exhibit 17-7)		52,480
Direct materials costs added during March		13,200
Conversion costs added during March		48,600

Transferred-in costs (also called **previous department costs**) are the costs incurred in previous departments that are carried forward as the product's cost when it moves to a subsequent process in the production cycle. That is, as the units move from one department to the next, their costs are transferred with them. Computations of Testing Department costs consist of transferred-in costs, as well as the direct materials and conversion costs added in Testing.

Transferred-in costs are treated as if they are a separate type of direct material added at the beginning of the process. When successive departments are involved, transferred units from one department become all or a part of the direct materials of the next department; however, they are called transferred-in costs, not direct materials costs.

Transferred-In Costs and the Weighted-Average Method

To examine the weighted-average process-costing method with transferred-in costs, we use the five-step procedure described earlier (p. 589) to assign costs of the Testing Department to units completed and transferred out and to units in ending work in process.

[2]The beginning work-in-process inventory is the same under both the weighted-average and FIFO inventory methods because we assume costs per equivalent unit to be the same in both January and February. If the cost per equivalent unit had been different in the two months, the work-in-process inventory at the end of February (beginning of March) would be costed differently under the weighted-average and FIFO methods. If this were the case, the basic approach to process costing with transferred-in costs would still be the same as what we describe in this section. Only the beginning balances of work in process would be different.

EXHIBIT 17-11

Steps 1 and 2: Summarize Output in Physical Units and Compute Equivalent Units
Weighted-Average Method of Process Costing
Testing Department of Global Defense, Inc., for March 2004

Flow of Production	(Step 1) Physical Units (given p. 604)	(Step 2) Equivalent Units Transferred-In Costs	Direct Materials	Conversion Costs
Work in process, beginning	240			
Transferred in during current period	400			
To account for	640			
Completed and transferred out during current period	440	440	440	440
Work in process, ending[a]	200			
(200 × 100%; 200 × 0%; 200 × 80%)		200	0	160
Accounted for	640			
Work done to date		640	440	600

[a]Degree of completion in this department: transferred-in costs, 100%; direct materials, 0%; conversion costs, 80%.

Exhibit 17-11 shows steps 1 and 2. The computations are the same as the calculations of equivalent units under the weighted-average method for the Assembly Department in Exhibit 17-4, but here we also have transferred-in costs as another input. The units, of course, are fully completed as to transferred-in costs carried forward from the previous process. Note, direct material costs have a zero degree of completion in both the beginning and ending work-in-process inventories because, in Testing, direct materials are introduced at the *end* of the process.

Exhibit 17-12 describes steps 3, 4, and 5 for the weighted-average method. Beginning work in process and work done in the current period are combined for purposes of computing equivalent-unit costs for transferred-in costs, direct material costs, and conversion costs.

The journal entry for the transfer from Testing to Finished Goods (see Exhibit 17-12) is shown at the top of page 606.

EXHIBIT 17-12

Steps 3, 4, and 5: Compute Equivalent-Unit Costs, Summarize Total Costs to Account For, and Assign Costs to Units Completed and to Units in Ending Work in Process
Weighted-Average Method of Process Costing
Testing Department of Global Defense, Inc., for March 2004

		Total Production Costs	Transferred-In Costs		Direct Materials		Conversion Costs
(Step 3)	Work in process, beginning (given, p. 604)	$ 51,600	$33,600		$ 0		$18,000
	Costs added in current period (given, p. 604)	113,800	52,000		13,200		48,600
	Costs incurred to date		$85,600		$13,200		$66,600
	Divide by equivalent units of work done to date (Exhibit 17-11)		÷ 640		÷ 440		÷ 600
	Equipment-unit costs of work done to date		$133.75		$ 30		$ 111
(Step 4)	Total costs to account for	$165,400					
(Step 5)	Assignment of costs:						
	Completed and transferred out (440 units)	$120,890	(440[a] × $133.75)	+	(440[a] × $30)	+	(440[a] × $111)
	Work in process, ending (200 units):						
	Transferred-in costs	26,750	200[b] × $133.75				
	Direct materials	0			0[b] × $30		
	Conversion costs	17,760					160[b] × $111
	Total work in process, ending	44,510					
	Total costs accounted for	$165,400					

[a]Equivalent units completed and transferred out from Exhibit 17-11, step 2.
[b]Equivalent units in ending work in process from Exhibit 17-11, step 2.

Finished Goods Control	120,890	
Work in Process—Testing		120,890

To record cost of goods completed and transferred from Testing to Finished Goods.

Because of the many details involved in computations for process costing, it's easy to lose sight of the big picture. The goal is to calculate the costs of the units completed. Complications arise from two sources: (1) When costs change from period to period, we choose a cost-flow assumption—weighted average, FIFO, or standard costing; and (2) when there are incomplete units, we calculate equivalent units.

Entries in the Work in Process—Testing account (see Exhibit 17-12) are

Work in Process—Testing

Beginning inventory, March 1	51,600	Transferred out	120,890
Transferred-in costs	52,000		
Direct materials	13,200		
Conversion costs	48,600		
Ending inventory, March 31	44,510		

Transferred-In Costs and the FIFO Method

To examine the FIFO process-costing method with transferred-in costs, we again use the five-step procedure. Exhibit 17-13 shows steps 1 and 2. Other than considering transferred-in costs, the computations of equivalent units are the same as under the FIFO method for the Assembly Department shown in Exhibit 17-6.

Exhibit 17-14 describes steps 3, 4, and 5. The cost per equivalent unit for the current period in step 3 is only calculated on the basis of costs transferred in and work done in the current period. In steps 4 and 5, the total costs to account for and accounted for of $165,880 under the FIFO method differ from the corresponding amounts under the weighted-average method of $165,400. That's because of the different costs of completed units transferred in from the Assembly Department under the two methods—$52,480 under FIFO and $52,000 under weighted average.

The journal entry for the transfer from Testing to Finished Goods (see Exhibit 17-14) is

Finished Goods Control	122,360	
Work in Process—Testing		122,360

To record cost of goods completed and transferred from Testing to Finished Goods.

EXHIBIT 17-13 Steps 1 and 2: Summarize Output in Physical Units and Compute Equivalent Units FIFO Method of Process Costing Testing Department of Global Defense, Inc., for March 2004

Flow of Production	(Step 1) Physical Units	(Step 2) Equivalent Units Transferred-In Costs	Direct Materials	Conversion Costs
Work in process, beginning (given, p. 604)	240	(work done before current period)		
Transferred in during current period (given, p. 604)	400			
To account for	640			
Completed and transferred out during current period:				
From beginning work in process[a]	240			
[240 × (100% – 100%); 240 × (100% – 0%); 240 × (100% – 62.5%)]		0	240	90
Started and completed	200[b]			
(200 × 100%; 200 × 100%; 200 × 100%)		200	200	200
Work in process, ending[c] (given, p. 604)	200			
(200 × 100%; 200 × 0%; 200 × 80%)		200	0	160
Accounted for	640			
Work done in current period only		400	440	450

[a]Degree of completion in this department: Transferred-in costs, 100%; direct materials, 0%; conversion costs, 62.5%.

[b]440 physical units completed and transferred out minus 240 physical units completed and transferred out from beginning work-in-process inventory.

[c]Degree of completion in this department: transferred-in costs, 100%; direct materials, 0%; conversion costs, 80%.

Entries in the Work in Process—Testing account (see Exhibit 17-14) are

Work in Process—Testing

Beginning inventory, March 1,	51,600	Transferred out	122,360
Transferred-in costs	52,480		
Direct materials	13,200		
Conversion costs	48,600		
Ending inventory, March 31	43,520		

Remember that in a series of interdepartmental transfers, each department is regarded as separate and distinct for accounting purposes. All costs transferred in during a given accounting period are carried at the same unit cost, as described when discussing modified FIFO (pp. 598–599), whether previous departments used the weighted-average method or the FIFO.

Points to Remember about Transferred-In Costs

Here are some points to remember when accounting for transferred-in costs:

1. Be sure to include transferred-in costs from previous departments in your calculations.
2. In calculating costs to be transferred on a FIFO basis, do not overlook the costs assigned in the previous period to units that were in process at the beginning of the current period but are now included in the units transferred. For example, do not overlook the $51,600 in Exhibit 17-14.

EXHIBIT 17-14 **Steps 3, 4, and 5: Compute Equivalent-Unit Costs, Summarize Total Costs to Account For, and Assign Costs to Units Completed and to Units in Ending Work in Process FIFO Method of Process Costing Testing Department of Global Defense, Inc., for March 2004**

		Total Production Costs	Transferred-In Costs	Direct Materials	Conversion Costs
	Work in process, beginning (given, p. 604)	$ 51,600	(costs of work done before current period)		
(Step 3)	Costs added in current period (given, p. 604)	114,280	$52,480	$13,200	$48,600
	Divide by equivalent units of work done in current period (Exhibit 17-13)		÷ 400	÷ 440	÷ 450
	Cost per equivalent unit of work done in current period		$131.20	$ 30	$ 108
(Step 4)	Total costs to account for	$165,880			
(Step 5)	Assignment of costs:				
	Completed and transferred out (440 units):				
	Work in process, beginning (240 units)	$ 51,600			
	Transferred-in costs added in current period	0	0[a] × $131.20		
	Direct materials added in current period	7,200		240[a] × $30	
	Conversion costs added in current period	9,720			90[a] × $108
	Total from beginning inventory	68,520			
	Started and completed (200 units)	53,840	(200[b] × $131.20) +	(200[b] × $30) +	(200[b] × $108)
	Total costs of units completed and transferred out	122,360			
	Work in process, ending (200 units):				
	Transferred-in costs	26,240	200[c] × $131.20		
	Direct materials	0		0[c] × $30	
	Conversion costs	17,280			160[c] × $108
	Total work in process, ending	43,520			
	Total costs accounted for	$165,880			

[a]Equivalent units used to complete beginning work in process from Exhibit 17-13, step 2.
[b]Equivalent units started and completed from Exhibit 17-13, step 2.
[c]Equivalent units in ending work in process from Exhibit 17-13, step 2.

CONCEPTS IN ACTION

Hybrid Costing for Customized Products at Levi Strauss

Levi Strauss, the company that invented blue jeans more than a century ago, is now able to produce individually customized jeans by means of computer-controlled technology. A computer graphic designer in Boston, Sung Park, came to Levi Strauss with the idea. He realized that a pattern for a piece of clothing is just a big computer graphic, except that the lines of the graphic image are cut instead of drawn. He also realized that, whereas the sizing of men's jeans is fairly straightforward—based on simple waist and inseam dimensions—the sizing of women's jeans is much more complicated—a function not only of waist size and inseam, but also hip size and the variance in the difference between waist and hip sizes. His female friends complained about the frustration they experienced from not being able to find off-the-shelf jeans that fit them well.

Today there are a number of Levi Strauss stores where women—and men—can get custom-fit, "Original Spin" jeans. The process works roughly as follows. The customer selects a fabric. A salesperson takes the customer's measurements and enters them into a computer; or, in a few stores, the customer can step into a body-scanning booth that records the measurements. The data is then sent via modem to the company's factory in Texas, where a robot cuts out the needed pieces of fabric. Finally, employees sew the pieces together. The custom-fit jeans cost only about $10 more than jeans bought off-the-shelf.

Historically, costs associated with individually customized products have generally fallen into the domain of job costing. Levi Strauss uses a hybrid-costing system—job costing for the fabric that customers choose, but process costing to account for conversion costs. Even though each pair is cut differently, the cost of cutting and sewing each pair is the same. The cost of making each pair of jeans is calculated by accumulating all the conversion costs and dividing by the number of jeans made.

This combination of customization with certain features of mass production is called *mass customization.* It is the consequence of being able to digitize information that individual customers indicate is important to them. Various products that companies are now able to customize within a mass production setting (e.g., personal computers, windows, bicycles) still require a lot of human intervention and job costing of materials. But as manufacturing systems become flexible, process costing is used to account for the standardized conversion costs.

Source: Copley News Service (2/14/00), *Boston Globe* (1/4/95), and Levi Strauss annual reports.

3. Unit costs may fluctuate between periods. Therefore, transferred units may contain batches accumulated at different unit costs. For example, the 400 units transferred in at $52,480 in Exhibit 17-14 using the FIFO method consist of units that have different unit costs of direct materials and conversion costs when these units were worked on in the Assembly Department (see Exhibit 17-7). Remember, however, that when these units are transferred to the Testing Department, they are costed at *one* average unit cost of $131.20 ($52,480 ÷ 400 units), as in Exhibit 17-14.
4. Units may be measured in different denominations in different departments. Consider each department separately. For example, unit costs could be based on kilograms in the first department and liters in the second department. Accordingly, as units are received in the second department, their measurements must be converted to liters.

HYBRID-COSTING SYSTEMS

Product-costing systems do not always fall neatly into either job-costing or process-costing categories. Consider Ford Motor Company. Automobiles may be manufactured in a continuous flow (suited to process costing), but individual units may be customized with a special combination of engine size, transmission, music system, and so on (which requires job costing).

A **hybrid-costing system** blends characteristics from both job-costing and process-costing systems. Job-costing and process-costing systems are best viewed as the ends of a continuum:

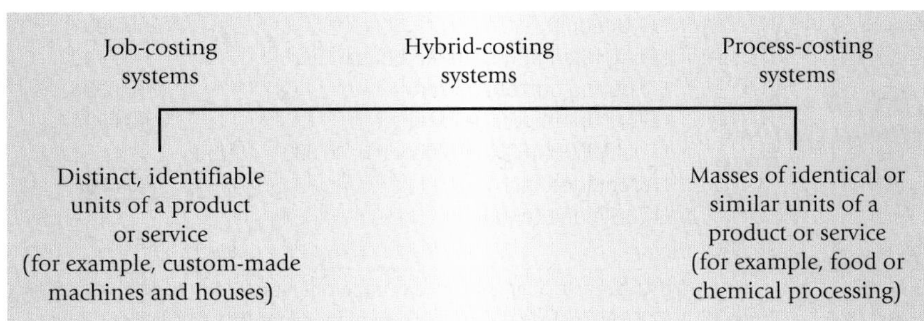

Product-costing systems must often be designed to fit the particular characteristics of different production systems. Many production systems are a hybrid—they have some features of custom-order manufacturing and other features of mass-production manufacturing. Manufacturers of a relatively wide variety of closely related standardized products (for example, televisions, dishwashers, and washing machines) tend to use a hybrid-costing system. The Concepts in Action (p. 608) describes a hybrid-costing system. The appendix to this chapter explains *operation costing,* a common type of hybrid-costing system.

PROBLEM FOR SELF-STUDY

Allied Chemicals operates a thermo-assembly process as the second of three processes at its plastics plant. Direct materials in thermo-assembly are added at the end of the process. Conversion costs are added evenly during the process. The following data pertain to the Thermo-Assembly Department for June 2004:

Work in process, beginning inventory	50,000 units
Transferred-in costs (100% complete)	
Direct materials (0% complete)	
Conversion costs (80% complete)	
Transferred in during current period	200,000 units
Completed and transferred out during current period	210,000 units
Work in process, ending inventory	? units
Transferred-in costs (100% complete)	
Direct materials (0% complete)	
Conversion costs (40% complete)	

Required

Compute equivalent units under (1) the weighted-average method and (2) the FIFO method.

SOLUTION

1. The weighted-average method uses equivalent units of work done to date to compute equivalent-unit costs. The calculations follow:

(Continued)

Flow of Production	(Step 1) Physical Units (given)	(Step 2) Equivalent Units Transferred-In Costs	Direct Materials	Conversion Costs
Work in process, beginning	50,000			
Transferred in during current period	200,000			
To account for	250,000			
Completed and transferred out during current period	210,000	210,000	210,000	210,000
Work in process, ending[a]	40,000[b]			
(40,000 × 100%; 40,000 × 0%; 40,000 × 40%)		40,000	0	16,000
Accounted for	250,000			
Work done to date		250,000	210,000	226,000

[a]Degree of completion in this department: transferred-in costs, 100%; direct materials, 0%; conversion costs, 40%.

[b]250,000 physical units to account for minus 210,000 physical units completed and transferred out.

2. The FIFO method uses equivalent units of work done in current period only when computing equivalent-unit costs. The calculations follow:

Flow of Production	(Step 1) Physical Units	(Step 2) Equivalent Units Transferred-In Costs	Direct Materials	Conversion Costs
Work in process, beginning (given)	50,000			
Transferred in during current period (given)	200,000			
To account for	250,000			
Completed and transferred out during current period				
From beginning work in process[a]	50,000			
[50,000 × (100% – 100%); 50,000 × (100% – 0%); 50,000 × (100% – 80%)]		0	50,000	10,000
Started and completed	160,000[b]			
(160,000 × 100%; 160,000 × 100%; 160,000 × 100%)		160,000	160,000	160,000
Work in process, ending[c] (given)	40,000			
(40,000 × 100%; 40,000 × 0%; 40,000 × 40%)		40,000	0	16,000
Accounted for	250,000			
Work done in current period only		200,000	210,000	186,000

[a]Degree of completion in this department: transferred-in costs, 100%; direct materials, 0%; conversion costs, 80%.

[b]210,000 physical units completed and transferred out minus 50,000 physical units completed and transferred out from beginning work-in-process inventory.

[c]Degree of completion in this department: transferred-in costs, 100%; direct materials, 0%; conversion costs, 40%.

DECISION POINTS — SUMMARY

The following question-and-answer format summarizes the chapter's learning objectives. Each decision presents a key question related to a learning objective. The guidelines are the answer to that question.

Decision	Guidelines
1. Under what conditions is a process-costing system used?	A process-costing system is used to determine the cost of a product or service when masses of identical or similar units are produced. Industries using process-costing systems include food, textiles, and oil refining.
2. What are the five steps in a process-costing system to assign costs to units completed and to units in ending work in process?	The five steps in a process-costing system are (a) summarize the flow of physical units of output, (b) compute output in terms of equivalent units, (c) compute equivalent-unit costs, (d) summarize total costs to account for, and (e) assign total costs to units completed and to units in ending work in process.
3. What are equivalent units and why is it necessary to calculate them?	Equivalent units is a derived amount of output units that (a) takes the quantity of each input (factor of production) in units completed or in incomplete units in work in process and (b) converts the quantity of input into the amount of completed output units that could be made with that quantity of input. Equivalent-unit calculations are necessary when all physical units of output are not uniformly completed during an accounting period.
4. Are journal entries in process-costing systems similar to journal entries in job-costing systems?	Journal entries in a process-costing system are similar to journal entries in a job-costing system. The main difference is that in a process-costing system, there is a separate Work-in-Process account for each department.
5. What is the weighted-average method of process costing?	The weighted-average method computes unit costs by dividing the total costs incurred to date by the total equivalent units completed to date, and assigns this average cost to units completed and to units in ending work-in-process inventory.
6. What is the first-in, first-out method of process costing?	The first-in, first-out (FIFO) method computes unit costs based on costs incurred during the period and equivalent units of work done in the current period. It assigns the costs of the beginning work-in-process inventory to the first units completed, and it assigns the costs of the equivalent units worked on during the current period first to complete beginning inventory, next to start and complete new units, and finally to units in ending work-in-process inventory.
7. How does the standard-costing method simplify process costing?	Under this method, standard costs serve as the cost per equivalent unit when assigning cost to units completed and to units in ending work-in-process inventory.
8. How are the weighted-average and FIFO process-costing methods applied to transferred-in costs?	The weighted-average process-costing method computes transferred-in costs per unit by dividing total transferred-in costs to date by the total equivalent transferred-in units completed to date, and assigns this average cost to units completed and to units in ending work-in-process inventory. The FIFO process-costing method computes transferred-in costs per unit based on costs transferred in during the period and equivalent units of transferred-in costs of work done in the current period. The FIFO method assigns transferred-in costs in beginning work in process to units completed and the costs transferred in during the current period first to complete beginning inventory (if needed), next to start and complete new units, and finally to units in ending work-in-process inventory.

APPENDIX: OPERATION COSTING

This appendix describes operation costing and illustrates operation costing through an example using calculations and journal entries.

Overview of Operation-Costing Systems

An **operation** is a standardized method or technique that is performed repetitively, often on different materials, resulting in different finished goods. Multiple operations are usually conducted within a department. For instance, a suit maker may have a cutting operation and a hemming operation within a single department. The term *operation*, however, is often used loosely. It may be a synonym for a department or process. For example, some companies may call their finishing department a finishing process or a finishing operation.

An **operation-costing system** is a hybrid-costing system applied to batches of similar, but not identical, products. Each batch of products is often a variation of a single design, and it proceeds through a sequence of operations; but each batch does not necessarily move through the same operations as other batches. Within each operation, all product units are treated exactly alike, using identical amounts of the operation's resources. Batches are also called production runs.

Units that do not pass through an operation are not allocated any costs of that operation.

Consider a company that makes suits. Management may select a single basic design for every suit to be made. Depending on specifications, each batch of suits varies somewhat from other batches. One batch may use wool; another batch, cotton. One batch may require special hand stitching; another batch, machine stitching. Other products manufactured in batches are semiconductors, textiles, and shoes.

An operation-costing system uses work orders that specify the needed direct materials and step-by-step operations. Product costs are compiled for each work order. Direct materials that are unique to different work orders are specifically identified with the appropriate work order, as in job-costing systems. Each unit uses an identical amount of conversion costs for a given operation. For each operation, a single average conversion cost per unit is calculated, as in process costing, by dividing total conversion costs by all units passing through that operation. The average conversion cost is assigned to each unit passing through a given operation. Our examples in the chapter assume only two cost categories, direct materials and conversion costs, but operation costing can have more than two cost categories. The costs in each category are identified with specific work orders using job-costing or process-costing methods as appropriate.

Managers find operation costing useful in cost management because operation costing focuses on the control of physical processes, or operations, of a given production system. For example, in clothing manufacturing, managers are concerned with fabric waste, the number of fabric layers that can be cut at one time, and so on. Operation costing measures in financial terms how well managers have controlled physical processes.

Illustration of an Operation-Costing System

Baltimore Company, a clothing manufacturer, produces two lines of blazers for department stores. Wool blazers use better-quality materials and undergo more operations than polyester blazers. Operations information on work order 423 for 50 wool blazers and work order 424 for 100 polyester blazers follows:

	Work Order 423	Work Order 424
Direct materials	Wool	Polyester
	Satin full lining	Rayon partial lining
	Bone Buttons	Plastic buttons
Operations		
1. Cutting cloth	Use	Use
2. Checking edges	Use	Do not use
3. Sewing body	Use	Use
4. Checking seams	Use	Do not use
5. Machine sewing of collars and lapels	Do not use	Use
6. Hand sewing of collars and lapels	Use	Do not use

Cost data for these work orders, started and completed in March 2003, follow:

	Work Order 423	Work Order 424
Number of blazers	50	100
Direct material costs	$ 6,000	$3,000
Conversion costs allocated:		
Operation 1	580	1,160
Operation 2	400	—
Operation 3	1,900	3,800
Operation 4	500	—
Operation 5	—	875
Operation 6	700	—
Total manufacturing costs	$10,080	$8,835

As in process costing, all product units in any work order are assumed to consume identical amounts of conversion costs of a particular operation. Baltimore's operation-costing system uses a budgeted rate to calculate the conversion costs of each operation. The budgeted rate for Operation 1 (amounts assumed) is

$$\text{Operation 1 budgeted conversion-cost rate in 2003} = \frac{\text{Operation 1 budgeted conversion costs in 2003}}{\text{Operation 1 budgeted product units in 2003}}$$

$$= \frac{\$232{,}000}{20{,}000 \text{ units}}$$

$$= \$11.60 \text{ per unit}$$

In this example, the 20,000-unit denominator is the sum of wool jackets and polyester jackets expected to be processed in Operation 1. It's appropriate to use this sum of the two different types of jackets because each jacket requires the same amount of conversion costs.

The budgeted conversion costs of Operation 1 include labor, power, repairs, supplies, depreciation, and other overhead of this operation. If some units have not been completed (so all units in Operation 1 have not received the same amounts of conversion costs), the conversion-cost rate is computed by dividing budgeted conversion costs by the *equivalent units* of conversion costs, as in process costing.

As goods are manufactured, conversion costs are allocated to the work orders processed in Operation 1 by multiplying the $11.60 conversion cost per unit by the number of product units processed. The conversion costs of Operation 1 for 50 wool blazers (work order 423) are $11.60 per blazer × 50 blazers = $580; and for 100 polyester blazers (work order 424) are $11.60 per blazer × 100 blazers = $1,160. If work order 424 had contained 75 blazers, its total costs in Operation 1 would be $870 ($11.60 per blazer × 75 blazers). When equivalent units are used to calculate the conversion-cost rate, costs are allocated to work orders by multiplying the conversion cost per equivalent unit by the number of equivalent units in the work order. Direct material costs of $6,000 for the 50 wool blazers (work order 423) and $3,000 for the 100 polyester blazers (work order 424) are specifically identified with each order, as in a job-costing system. Operation unit costs are assumed to be the same regardless of the work order, but direct material costs vary across orders because the materials for each work order vary.

Journal Entries

Actual conversion costs for Operation 1 in March 2003—assumed to be $24,400, of which $580 are on work order 423 and $1,160 are on work order 424—are entered into a Conversion Costs Control account:

1. Conversion Costs Control	24,400	
Various accounts (such as Wages Payable Control and Accumulated Depreciation)		24,400

Summary journal entries for assigning costs to the polyester blazers (work order 424) follow. Entries for the wool blazers would be similar. Of the $3,000 of direct materials for work order 424, $2,975 are used in Operation 1. The journal entry to record the use of direct materials for the 100 polyester blazers in March is

2. Work in Process, Operation 1 — 2,975
   Materials Inventory Control — 2,975

	Debit	Credit
2. Work in Process, Operation 1	2,975	
Materials Inventory Control		2,975

The journal entry to record the allocation of conversion costs to products uses the budgeted rate of $11.60 per blazer times the 100 polyester blazers processed, or $1,160:

	Debit	Credit
3. Work in Process, Operation 1	1,160	
Conversion Costs Allocated		1,160

The journal entry to record the transfer of the 100 polyester blazers from Operation 1 to Operation 3 (polyester blazers do not go through Operation 2) is

	Debit	Credit
4. Work in Process, Operation 3	4,135	
Work in Process, Operation 1		4,135

After posting, the Work in Process, Operation 1, account appears as follows:

Work in Process, Operation 1

② Direct materials	2,975	④ Transferred to Operation 3	4,135
③ Conversion costs allocated	1,160		

The costs of the blazers are transferred through the operations in which the blazers are worked on and then to finished goods in the usual manner. Costs are added throughout the year in the Conversion Costs Control account and the Conversion Costs Allocated account. Any overallocation or underallocation of conversion costs is disposed of in the same way as overallocated or underallocated manufacturing overhead in a job-costing system. (See pp. 114 – 118 for more details.)

TERMS TO LEARN

This chapter and the Glossary at the end of the book contain definitions of:

equivalent units (p. 590)
first-in, first-out (FIFO) process-costing method (p. 596)
hybrid-costing system (p. 609)
operation (p. 612)
operation-costing system (p. 612)
previous department costs (p. 604)
transferred-in costs (p. 604)
weighted-average process-costing method (p. 593)

ASSIGNMENT MATERIAL

Questions

17-1 Give three examples of industries that generally use process-costing systems.

17-2 In process costing, why are costs often divided into two main classifications?

17-3 Explain equivalent units. Why are equivalent-unit calculations necessary in process costing?

17-4 What problems might arise in estimating the degree of completion of an aircraft blade in a machine shop?

17-5 Name the five key steps in process costing when equivalent units are computed.

17-6 Name the three inventory methods commonly associated with process costing.

17-7 Describe the distinctive characteristic of weighted-average computations in assigning costs to units completed and to units in ending work in process.

17-8 Describe the distinctive characteristic of FIFO computations in assigning costs to units completed and to units in ending work in process.

17-9 Why should the FIFO method be called a modified or department FIFO method?

17-10 Identify a major advantage of the FIFO method for purposes of planning and control.

17-11 Identify the main difference between journal entries in process costing and job costing.

17-12 "Standard-costing methods are particularly applicable to process-costing situations." Do you agree? Why?

17-13 Why should the accountant distinguish between transferred-in costs and additional direct materials costs for each subsequent department in a process-costing system?

17-14 "Transferred-in costs are those incurred in the preceding accounting period." Do you agree? Explain.

17-15 "There's no reason for me to get excited about the choice between the weighted-average and FIFO methods in my process-costing system. I have long-term contracts with my materials suppliers at fixed prices." State the conditions under which you would (a) agree and (b) disagree with this statement made by a plant controller. Explain.

Exercises

17-16 Equivalent units, zero beginning inventory. International Electronics manufactures microchips in large quantities. Each microchip undergoes assembly and testing. The total assembly costs during January 2004 were

Direct materials used	$ 720,000
Conversion costs	760,000
Total manufacturing costs	$1,480,000

Required

1. Assume there was no beginning inventory on January 1, 2004. During January, 10,000 microchips were placed into production and all 10,000 were fully completed at the end of the month. What is the unit cost of an assembled microchip in January?
2. Assume that during February 10,000 microchips are placed into production. Further assume the same total assembly costs for January are also incurred in February, but only 9,000 microchips are fully completed at the end of the month. All direct materials have been added to the remaining 1,000 microchips. However, on average, these remaining 1,000 microchips are only 50% complete as to conversion costs. (a) What are the equivalent units for direct materials and conversion costs and their respective equivalent-unit costs for February? (b) What is the unit cost of an assembled microchip in February 2004?
3. Explain the difference in your answers to requirements 1 and 2.

17-17 Journal entries (continuation of 17-16). Refer to requirement 2 of Exercise 17-16.

Required

Prepare summary journal entries for the use of direct materials and incurrence of conversion costs. Also prepare a journal entry to transfer out the cost of goods completed. Show the postings to the Work-in-Process account.

17-18 Zero beginning inventory, materials introduced in middle of process. Vaasa Chemicals has a Mixing Department and a Refining Department. Its process-costing system in the Mixing Department has two direct materials cost categories (Chemical P and Chemical Q) and one conversion costs pool. The following data pertain to the Mixing Department for July 2004:

Units	
Work in process, July 1	0
Units started	50,000
Completed and transferred to Refining Department	35,000
Costs	
Chemical P	$250,000
Chemical Q	70,000
Conversion costs	135,000

Chemical P is introduced at the start of operations in the Mixing Department, and chemical Q is added when the product is three-fourths completed in the Mixing Department. Conversion costs are added evenly during the process. The ending work in process in the Mixing Department is two-thirds complete.

Required

1. Compute the equivalent units in the Mixing Department for July 2004 for each cost category.
2. Compute (a) the cost of goods completed and transferred to the Refining Department during July and (b) the cost of work in process as of July 31, 2004.

17-19 Weighted-average method, equivalent units. Consider the following data for the Satellite Assembly Division of Aerospatiale:

The Satellite Assembly Division uses the weighted-average method of process costing.

	Physical Units (Satellites)	Direct Materials	Conversion Costs
Beginning work in process (May 1)[a]	8	$ 4,933,600	$ 910,400
Started in May 2004	50		
Completed during May 2004	46		

Continued

	Physical Units (Satellites)	Direct Materials	Conversion Costs
Ending work in process (May 31)[b]	12		
Costs added during May 2004		$32,200,000	$13,920,000

[a]Degree of completion: direct materials, 90%; conversion costs, 40%.
[b]Degree of completion: direct materials, 60%; conversion costs, 30%.

Required Compute equivalent units for direct materials and conversion costs. Show physical units in the first column of your schedule.

17-20 Weighted-average method, assigning costs (continuation of 17-19).

Required For the data in Exercise 17-19, calculate cost per equivalent unit for direct materials and conversion costs, summarize total costs to account for, and assign these costs to units completed and transferred out and to units in ending work in process.

17-21 FIFO method, equivalent units. Refer to the information in Exercise 17-19. Suppose the Satellite Assembly Division uses the FIFO method of process costing instead of the weighted-average method.

Required Compute equivalent units for direct materials and conversion costs. Show physical units in the first column of your schedule.

17-22 FIFO method, assigning costs (continuation of 17-21).

Required For the data in Exercise 17-19, use the FIFO method to calculate cost per equivalent unit for direct materials and conversion costs, summarize total costs to account for, and assign these costs to units completed and transferred out and to units in ending work in process.

17-23 Standard-costing method, assigning costs. Refer to the information in Exercise 17-19. Suppose the Satellite Assembly Division uses the standard-costing method of process costing. Suppose further that the Satellite Assembly Division determines standard costs of $695,000 per equivalent unit for direct materials and $295,000 per equivalent unit for conversion costs for both beginning work in process and work done in the current period.

Required

1. Compute equivalent units for direct materials and conversion costs. Show physical units in the first column of your schedule.
2. Summarize total costs to account for, and assign these costs to units completed and transferred out and to units in ending work in process.
3. Compute the total direct materials and conversion costs variances for May 2004.

17-24 Weighted-average method, assigning costs. The Chatham Company makes a water-treatment chemical in a single processing department. Direct materials are added at the start of the process. Conversion costs are added evenly during the process. Chatham uses the weighted-average method of process costing. The following information for July 2004 is available.

		Equivalent Units	
	Physical Units	Direct Materials	Conversion Costs
Work in process, July 1	10,000[a]	10,000	7,000
Started during July	40,000		
Completed and transferred out during July	34,000	34,000	34,000
Work in process, July 31	16,000[b]	16,000	8,000

[a]Degree of completion: direct materials, 100%; conversion costs, 70%.
[b]Degree of completion: direct materials, 100%; conversion costs, 50%.

Total Costs for July 2004		
Work in process, beginning		
Direct materials	$60,000	
Conversion costs	70,000	$130,000
Direct materials added during July		280,000
Conversion costs added during July		371,000
Total costs to account for		$781,000

Required

1. Calculate cost per equivalent unit for direct materials and conversion costs.
2. Summarize total costs to account for, and assign these costs to units completed (and transferred out) and to units in ending work in process.

17-25 FIFO method, assigning costs.

Do Exercise 17-24 using the FIFO method. Note that you first need to calculate the equivalent units of work done in the current period (for direct materials and conversion costs) to complete beginning work in process, to start and complete new units, and to produce ending work in process. Required

17-26 Standard-costing method, assigning costs. Refer to the information in Exercise 17-24. Suppose Chatham determines standard costs of $6.50 per equivalent unit for direct materials and $10.30 per equivalent unit for conversion costs for both beginning work in process and work done in the current period.

Required

1. Do Exercise 17-24 using the standard-costing method. Note that you first need to calculate the equivalent units of work done in the current period (for direct materials and conversion costs) to complete beginning work in process, to start and complete new units, and to produce ending work in process.
2. Compute the total direct materials and conversion costs variances for July 2004.

17-27 Transferred-in costs, weighted-average method. Hideo Chemicals manufactures an industrial solvent in two departments: mixing and cooking. This question focuses on the Cooking Department. During June 2004, 90 tons of solvent were completed and transferred out from the Cooking Department. Direct materials are added at the end of the process. Conversion costs are added evenly during the process. Hideo Chemicals uses the weighted-average method of process costing. The following information for June 2004 is available.

		Equivalent Units (Tons)		
	Physical Units (Tons)	Transferred-In Costs	Direct Materials	Conversion Costs
Work in process, June 1[a]	40	40	0	30
Transferred in during June	80			
Completed and transferred out during June	90	90	90	90
Work in process, June 30[b]	30	30	0	15

[a]Degree of completion: transferred-in costs, 100%; direct materials, 0%; conversion costs, 75%.
[b]Degree of completion: transferred-in costs, 100%; direct materials, 0%; conversion costs, 50%.

Total Costs for June, 2004		
Work in process, beginning		
Transferred-in costs	$40,000	
Direct materials	0	
Conversion costs	18,000	$ 58,000
Transferred-in costs added during June		87,200
Direct materials added during June		36,000
Conversion costs added during June		49,725
Total costs to account for		$230,925

Required

1. Calculate cost per equivalent unit for transferred-in costs, direct materials, and conversion costs.
2. Summarize total costs to account for, and assign these costs to units completed (and transferred out) and to units in ending work in process.

17-28 Transferred-in costs, FIFO method. Refer to the information in Exercise 17-27. Suppose that Hideo uses the FIFO method instead of the weighted-average method in all its departments. The only changes under the FIFO method are that the total transferred-in costs of beginning work in process are $39,200 and that the transferred-in costs added during June are $85,600.

Do Exercise 17-27 using the FIFO method. Note that you first need to calculate equivalent units of work done in the current period (for transferred-in costs, direct materials, and conversion costs) to complete beginning work in process, to start and complete new units, and to produce ending work in process. Required

17-29 Operation Costing (Chapter Appendix). Feather Light Shoe Company manufactures two styles of men's shoes: Designer and Regular. Designer style is made from leather, and Regular style uses synthetic materials. Three operations—cutting, sewing and packing—are common to both styles, but only Designer style passes through a lining operation. The conversion cost rates for 2004 are

	Cutting	Sewing	Lining	Packing
Rate per unit (pair)	$10	$15	$8	$2

Details of two work orders processed in August are

	Work Order 815	Work Order 831
Number of units (pairs)	1,000	5,000
Direct materials costs	$30,000	$50,000
Style	Designer	Regular

Required Calculate the total costs and the total cost per unit of work order 815 and work order 831.

Problems

17-30 Weighted-average method. Global Defense, Inc., is a manufacturer of military equipment. Its Santa Fe plant manufactures the Interceptor Missile under contract to the U.S. government and friendly countries. All Interceptors go through an identical manufacturing process. Every effort is made to ensure that all Interceptors are identical and meet many demanding performance specifications. The process-costing system at the Santa Fe plant has a single direct-cost category (direct materials) and a single indirect-cost category (conversion costs). Each Interceptor passes through two departments: the Assembly Department and the Testing Department. Direct materials are added at the beginning of the process in Assembly. Conversion costs are added evenly during the Assembly Department's process. When the Assembly Department finishes work on each Interceptor, it is immediately transferred to Testing.

Global Defense uses the weighted-average method of process costing. Data for the Assembly Department for October 2004 are

	Physical Units (Missiles)	Direct Materials	Conversion Costs
Work in process, October 1[a]	20	$ 460,000	$120,000
Started during October 2004	80		
Completed during October 2004	90		
Work in process, October 31[b]	10		
Costs added during October 2004		$2,000,000	$935,000

[a]Degree of completion: direct materials, ?%; conversion costs, 60%.
[b]Degree of completion: direct materials, ?%; conversion costs, 70%.

Required

1. For each cost element, compute equivalent units in the Assembly Department. Show physical units in the first column of your schedule.
2. For each cost element, calculate costs per equivalent unit.
3. Summarize total Assembly Department costs for October 2004, and assign these costs to units completed and transferred out and to units in ending work in process.

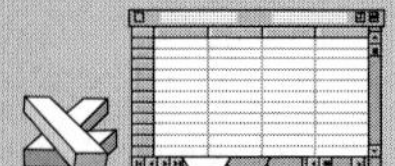

Excel Application For students who wish to practice their spreadsheet skills, the following is a step-by-step approach to creating an Excel spreadsheet to work this problem.

Step-by-Step

1. Open up a new spreadsheet. At top, create an "Original Data" section for the Assembly Department data provided by Global Defense. Enter the "Physical Units, Direct Materials," and "Conversion Cost" data in exactly the same format as presented above.

(Program your spreadsheet to perform all necessary calculations. Do not "hard-code" any amounts, such as equivalent-unit costs, requiring addition, subtraction, multiplication, or division.)

2. Skip two rows and create a section, "Problem 1," in exactly the same format as in Exhibit 17-4. Create columns for "Physical Units, Equivalent Units of Direct Materials" and "Equivalent Units of Conversion Costs" and rows for each of the items in Exhibit 17-4 (e.g., first row, "Work in Process, Beginning," and the last row, "Work Done to Date"). Use the data from your Original Data section to complete this section.
3. Skip two rows and create a section, "Problem 2," in the same format as Step 3 of Exhibit 17-5. Create columns for "Total Production Costs," "Direct Materials" and "Conversion Costs."
4. Next, enter a calculation for the "Cost per Equivalent Unit of Work Done to Date" for "Direct Materials" and "Conversion Costs."
5. Skip two rows and create a section, "Problem 3" in the same format as Steps 4 and 5 of Exhibit 17-5 (using columns for "Total Production Costs," "Direct Materials," and "Conversion Costs" created in Step 3).
6. Use the data you created in steps 1 to 4 to complete your "Problem 3" section.
7. *Check the accuracy of your spreadsheet:* Go to your Original Data section and change direct materials costs added for October from $2,000,000 to $2,500,000. If you programmed your spreadsheet correctly, the cost per equivalent unit of work done to date for direct materials in problem 2 should change to $29,600.

17-31 Journal entries (continuation of 17-30).

Prepare a set of summarized journal entries for all October 2004 transactions affecting Work in Process—Assembly. Set up a T-account for Work in Process—Assembly, and post your entries to it. **Required**

17-32 FIFO method (continuation of 17-30 and 17-31).

Do Problem 17-30 using the FIFO method of process costing. Explain any difference between the costs per equivalent unit in the Assembly Department under the weighted-average method and the FIFO method. **Required**

17-33 Transferred-in costs, weighted average method (related to 17-30 to 17-32). Global Defense, Inc., as you know, manufactures the Interceptor Missile at its Santa Fe plant. It has two departments: Assembly Department and Testing Department. This problem focuses on the Testing Department. (Problems 17-30 to 17-32 focused on the Assembly Department.) Direct materials are added when the Testing Department process is 90% complete. Conversion costs are added evenly during the Testing Department's process. As work in Assembly is completed, each unit is immediately transferred to Testing. As each unit is completed in Testing, it is immediately transferred to Finished Goods.

Global Defense uses the weighted-average method of process costing. Data for the Testing Department for October 2004 are

	Physical Units (Missiles)	Transferred-In Costs	Direct Materials	Conversion Costs
Work in process, October 1[a]	30	$ 985,800	$ 0	$ 331,800
Transferred-in during October 2004	?			
Completed during October 2004	105			
Work in process October 31[b]	15			
Costs added during October 2004		$3,192,866	$3,885,000	$1,581,000

[a]Degree of completion: transferred-in costs, ?%; direct materials, ?%; conversion costs, 70%.

[b]Degree of completion: transferred-in costs, ?%; direct materials, ?%; conversion costs, 60%.

Required

1. What is the percentage of completion for (a) transferred-in costs and direct materials in beginning work-in-process inventory, and (b) transferred-in costs and direct materials in ending work-in-process inventory?
2. For each cost category, compute equivalent units in the Testing Department. Show physical units in the first column of your schedule.
3. For each cost category, calculate the cost per equivalent unit, summarize total Testing Department costs for October 2004, and assign these costs to units completed (and transferred out) and to units in ending work in process.
4. Prepare journal entries for October transfers from the Assembly Department to the Testing Department and from the Testing Department to Finished Goods.

17-34 Transferred-in costs, FIFO method (continuation of 17-33).

Using the FIFO process-costing method, do the requirements of Problem 17-33. Under the FIFO method, the transferred-in costs for the beginning work in process in the Testing Department on October 1 are $980,060, and costs transferred in during October to the Testing Department are $3,188,000. All other data are unchanged. **Required**

17-35 Weighted-average method. Star Toys manufactures one type of wooden toy figure. It buys wood as its direct material for the Forming Department of its Madison plant. The toys are transferred to the Finishing Department, where they are hand-shaped and metal is added to them. The process-costing system at Star Toys has a single direct-cost category (direct materials) and a single indirect-cost category (conversion costs). Direct materials are added when the Forming Department process is 10% complete. Conversion costs are added evenly during the Forming Department's process.

Star Toys uses the weighted-average method of process costing. Consider the following data for the Forming Department in April 2004:

	Physical Units (Toys)	Direct Materials	Conversion Costs
Work in process, April 1[a]	300	$ 7,500	$ 2,125
Started during April 2004	2,200		
Completed during April 2004	2,000		
Work in process, April 30[b]	500		
Costs added during April 2004		$70,000	$42,500

[a]Degree of completion: direct materials, 100%; conversion costs, 40%.

[b]Degree of completion: direct materials, 100%; conversion costs, 25%.

Summarize total Forming Department costs for April 2004, and assign these costs to units completed (and transferred out) and to units in ending work in process. **Required**

17-36 Journal entries (continuation of 17-35).

Required

Prepare a set of summarized journal entries for all April transactions affecting Work in Process—Forming. Set up a T-account for Work in Process—Forming, and post your entries to it.

17-37 FIFO method (continuation of 17-35).

Required

Do Problem 17-35 using FIFO and three decimal places for unit costs. If you did (the original) Problem 17-35, explain any difference between the cost of work completed and transferred out and the cost of ending work in process in the Forming Department under the weighted-average method and the FIFO method.

17-38 Transferred-in costs, weighted-average method (related to 17-35 through 17-37). Star Toys, as you know, manufactures one type of wooden toy figure at its Madison plant. It has two departments: a Forming Department and a Finishing Department. (Problems 17-35 through 17-37 focused on the Forming Department.) Consider now the Finishing Department, which processes the formed toys through hand-shaping and the addition of metal. All additional direct materials are added when the Finishing Department process is 80% complete. Conversion costs are added evenly during finishing operations. When the Finishing Department completes work on each toy, it is immediately transferred to Finished Goods.

Star Toys uses the weighted-average method of process costing. The following is a summary of the April 2004 operations in the Finishing Department:

	Physical Units (Toys)	Transferred-In Costs	Direct Materials	Conversion Costs
Work in process, April 1[a]	500	$ 17,750	$ 0	$ 7,250
Transferred in during April 2004	2,000			
Completed during April 2004	2,100			
Work in process, April 30[b]	400			
Costs added during April 2004		$104,000	$23,100	$38,400

[a]Degree of completion: transferred-in costs, 100%; direct materials, 0%; conversion costs, 60%.
[b]Degree of completion: transferred-in costs, 100%; direct materials, 0%; conversion costs, 30%.

Required

1. Summarize total Finishing Department costs for April 2004, and assign these costs to units completed (and transferred out) and to units in ending work in process.
2. Prepare journal entries for April transfers from the Forming Department to the Finishing Department and from the Finishing Department to Finished Goods.

17-39 Transferred-in costs, FIFO method (continuation of 17-38).

Required

1. Using the FIFO process-costing method, do Problem 17-38. Under FIFO, the transferred-in costs for the beginning work in process in the Finishing Department on April 1 are $17,520, and the costs transferred in during April are $103,566. All other data are unchanged.
2. If you did Problem 17-38, explain any difference between the cost of work completed and transferred out and the cost of ending work in process in the Finishing Department under the weighted-average method and the FIFO method.

17-40 Transferred-in costs, weighted-average and FIFO methods. Frito-Lay, Inc., manufactures convenience foods, including potato chips and corn chips. Production of corn chips occurs in four departments: cleaning, mixing, cooking, and drying and packaging. Consider the Drying and Packaging Department, where direct materials (packaging) are added at the end of the process. Conversion costs are added evenly during the process. The accounting records of a Frito-Lay plant provide the following information for corn chips in its Drying and Packaging Department during a weekly period (week 37):

	Physical Units (Cases)	Transferred-In Costs	Direct Materials	Conversion Costs
Beginning work in process[a]	1,250	$29,000	$ 0	$ 9,060
Transferred-in during week 37 from Cooking Department	5,000			
Completed during week 37	5,250			
Ending work in process, week 37[b]	1,000			
Costs added during week 37		$96,000	$25,200	$38,400

[a]Degree of completion: transferred-in costs, 100%; direct materials, ?%; conversion costs, 80%.
[b]Degree of completion: transferred-in costs, 100%; direct materials, ?%; conversion costs, 40%.

Required

1. Using the weighted-average method, summarize the total Drying and Packaging Department costs for week 37, and assign these costs to units completed (and transferred out) and to units in ending work in process.

2. Assume that the FIFO method is used for the Drying and Packaging Department. Under FIFO, the transferred-in costs for work-in-process beginning inventory in week 37 are $28,920, and the transferred-in costs during week 37 from the Cooking Department are $94,000. All other data are unchanged. Summarize the total Drying and Packaging Department costs for week 37, and assign these costs to units completed and transferred out and to units in ending work in process using the FIFO method.

17-41 Standard costing with beginning and ending work in process. The Victoria Corporation uses the standard-costing method for its process-costing system. Standard costs for the Cooking Process are $6 per equivalent unit for direct materials and $3 per equivalent unit for conversion costs. All direct materials are introduced at the beginning of the process, and conversion costs are added evenly during the process. The operating summary for May 2004 include the following data for the Cooking Process.

Work-in-process inventories:
May 1, 3,000 units[a]
(direct materials, $18,000; conversion costs, $5,400)
May 31, 5,000 units[b]
Units started in May, 20,000
Units completed and transferred out of cooking in May: 18,000
Additional actual costs incurred for cooking during May:
Direct materials, $125,000
Conversion costs, $57,000

[a]Degree of completion: direct materials, 100%; conversion costs, 60%.
[b]Degree of completion: direct materials, 100%; conversion costs, 50%.

Required

1. Compute the total standard costs of units transferred out in May and the total standard costs of the May 31 inventory of work in process.
2. Compute the total May variances for direct materials and conversion costs.

17-42 Operation costing, equivalent units. (Chapter Appendix, CMA, adapted) Gregg Industries manufactures plastic molded chairs. The three models of molded chairs, all variations of the same design, are Standard, Deluxe, and Executive. The company uses an operation-costing system.

Gregg has extrusion, form, trim, and finish operations. Plastic sheets are produced by the extrusion operation. During the forming operation, the plastic sheets are molded into chair seats and the legs are added. The Standard model is sold after this operation. During the trim operation, the arms are added to the Deluxe and Executive models and the chair edges are smoothed. Only the Executive model enters the finish operation, in which padding is added. All of the units produced receive the same steps within each operation.

The May units of production and direct materials costs incurred are as follows:

	Units Produced	Extrusion Materials	Form Materials	Trim Materials	Finish Materials
Standard model	6,000	$ 72,000	$24,000	$ 0	$ 0
Deluxe model	3,000	36,000	12,000	9,000	0
Executive model	2,000	24,000	8,000	6,000	12,000
	11,000	$132,000	$44,000	$15,000	$12,000

The total conversion costs for the month of May are

	Extrusion Operation	Form Operation	Trim Operation	Finish Operation
Total conversion costs	$269,500	$132,000	$69,000	$42,000

Required

1. For each product produced by Gregg Industries during May, determine (a) the unit cost and (b) the total cost. Support your answer with appropriate calculations.
2. Now consider the following information for June. All unit costs in June are identical to the May unit costs calculated in 1(a). At the end of June, 1,000 units of the Deluxe model remained in work in process. These units were 100% complete as to materials costs and 60% complete in the trim operation. Determine the cost of the Deluxe model work-in-process inventory at the end of June.

17-43 Equivalent-unit computations, benchmarking, ethics. Margaret Major is the corporate controller of Leisure Suits. Leisure Suits has 20 plants that manufacture suits for retail stores. Each plant uses a process-costing system. At the end of each month, each plant manager submits a production report and a production-cost report. The production report includes the plant manager's estimate of the percentage of completion of the ending work in process as to direct materials and conversion costs. Major uses these estimates to compute the equivalent units of work done in each plant and the cost per equivalent unit of work done for both direct materials and conversion costs in each month. Plants are ranked from 1 to 20 in terms of (a) cost per equivalent unit of direct materials and (b) cost per equivalent unit of conversion costs. The three top-ranked plants in each category receive a bonus and are written up as the best in their class in the company newsletter.

Major has been pleased with the success of her benchmarking program. However, she has just received some unsigned letters stating that two plant managers have been manipulating their monthly estimates of percentage of completion in an attempt to obtain best-in-class status.

Required

1. How and why might plant managers "manipulate" their monthly estimates of percentage of completion?
2. Major's first reaction is to contact each plant controller and discuss the problem raised by the unsigned letters. Is that a good idea?
3. Assume that the plant controller's primary reporting responsibility is to the plant manager and that each plant controller receives the phone call from Major mentioned in 2. What is the ethical responsibility of each plant controller (a) to Margaret Major and (b) to Leisure Suits in relation to the equivalent-unit information each plant provides?
4. How might Major gain some insight into whether the equivalent-unit figures provided by particular plants are being manipulated?

Collaborative Learning Problem

17-44 **Transferred-in costs, equivalent-unit costs, working backward.** Lennox Plastics has two processes: extrusion and thermo-assembly. Consider the June 2004 data for physical units in the thermo-assembly process: beginning work in process, 15,000 units; transferred in from the Extruding Department during June, 9,000; ending work in process, 5,000. Direct materials are added when the process in the Thermo-assembly Department is 80% complete. Conversion costs are added evenly during the process. Lennox Plastics uses the FIFO method of process costing. The following information is available.

	Transferred-In Costs	Direct Materials	Conversion Costs
Beginning work in process	$90,000	—	$45,000
Percentage completion of beginning work in process	100%	—	60%
Costs added in current period	$58,500	$57,000	$57,200
Cost per equivalent unit of work done in current period	$6.50	$3	$5.20

Required

1. For each cost category, compute equivalent units of work done in the current period.
2. For each cost category, compute separately the equivalent units of work done to complete beginning work-in-process inventory, to start and complete new units, and to produce ending work in process.
3. For each cost category, calculate the percentage of completion of ending work-in-process inventory.
4. Summarize total costs to account for, and assign these costs to units completed (and transferred out) and to units in ending work in process.

CHAPTER 17 INTERNET EXERCISE

Perhaps the best way to understand the flow of costs in a process costing system is to take a plant tour. To tour the world's largest fully integrated cheese plant, go to www.prenhall.com/horngren, click on *Cost Accounting* 11th ed., and access the Internet Problem for Chapter 17.

NANTUCKET NECTARS: Process Costing

"Juice Guys" Tom First and Tom Scott started Nantucket Nectars in 1989 with a blender and the idea for a peach nectar drink. With a booming summer business servicing boats visiting the harbor off Nantucket Island, the two founders knew they wanted to find a way to keep their connection to the island after college graduation. What they didn't know was how big their simple juice-drink idea would become. Today, Nantucket Nectars makes close to 50 different juice drinks and flavored teas with all-natural ingredients and no preservatives. There must be something to those beverages, because sales in a recent year topped $70 million.

The process of converting fruit into juice blends starts with a recipe. The company's test kitchen develops the specifications for each drink and then gives those details to the company's buyers. The buyers secure the necessary quantities of ingredients, such as cane sugar and fruit juice concentrates, for delivery to one of five bottling plants around the country. The bottling plants, called "co-packers," are expert at producing large batches of bottled beverages, and they play a role in finalizing the specifications for each new drink recipe.

Inside the plant, beverage production is scheduled to achieve maximum efficiency. Ingredients are timed to arrive by the first of the month. Some materials, such as single-serve glass bottles, arrive throughout the day at the plant. The ingredients are mixed in 5,000-gallon batches, according to recipe specifications. Each batch makes about 36,000 bottles of finished juice. Every blended-juice batch is checked for quality to be sure the correct levels of acidity and sweetness are present before the batch is released to the production line.

From ingredient batching, the juice is pumped into storage tanks that feed the production line. The tank contents are heated to 190 degrees to inhibit bacteria growth. Empty glass bottles are removed from their shipping pallets and travel by automated conveyer through a 220-degree steam bath that tempers the glass before filling. Without this step, the cold glass would shatter when filled with hot juice. The conveyer line speed is set to fill 550 bottles per minute. The entire line shuts down if there is a problem at any point.

Once bottles are filled, they are capped and sprayed with ID codes on both cap and bottle shoulder. The codes contain bottling plant ID, date, and time. Then the bottles travel through a large cooling tunnel. The tunnel draws a vacuum in each bottle by lowering the liquid temperature to 100 to 105 degrees. This quick-cooling process also helps maintain juice color because there are no preservatives added for this purpose. The conveyer then moves through a check station to verify that each bottle has sealed properly and has cooled to the correct temperature. Each bottle will also pass by an electronic eye that checks to be sure it is filled to the right level. Those bottles that don't pass are mechanically kicked off the line.

After this stage, the juice bottles are ready for labeling. An automated labeling machine glues a label to each bottle, and then the bottles are moved via conveyer to a final quality checkpoint. Here, the bottles are inspected for proper labeling and spray codes. If problems are detected, the production line is halted until the problem is corrected. After passing inspection, the bottles are ready for tray packaging. Each full tray is called a "case," and it holds 20 bottles. Trays are inspected to be sure the correct amount of glue holds the ends securely so cases don't break later. As full trays come off the production line, they are shrink-wrapped and bundled into pallets of 60 cases each. The pallets are wrapped in plastic and prepared for transport to a distribution warehouse. From there, distributors pick up their orders and deliver the juices to retail outlets for customer sale. About 20,000 cases, or 400,000 bottles, come off the production line each day.

QUESTIONS

1. Why is process costing an appropriate system of accounting for the costs of Nantucket Nectars' juice-beverage production?
2. What are the direct material costs associated with the production of the juices, and when would those costs be added to the production process (beginning, middle, or end)?
3. What items would be considered "conversion costs"?
4. Think about the production process and the daily production of juice. How important are equivalent-unit calculations for costing units in ending inventory? Would you expect there to be significant differences in the inventory costs under the weighted-average and FIFO methods?

CHAPTER

18

Spoilage, Rework, and Scrap

LEARNING OBJECTIVES

1. Distinguish among spoilage, rework, and scrap
2. Describe the accounting procedures for normal and abnormal spoilage
3. Account for spoilage in process costing using the weighted-average method
4. Account for spoilage in process costing using the first-in, first-out (FIFO) method
5. Account for spoilage in process costing using the standard-costing method
6. Account for spoilage in job costing
7. Account for rework in job costing
8. Account for scrap

www.prenhall.com/horngren

What's your reaction when a professor gives back your homework and tells you to do it over? Disappointment? Managers feel the same way when they learn the products they produce are defective. Progress and productivity halt when finished work has to be redone. And the rework is costly. In addition to rework cost are costs of spoilage and scrap that result from some manufacturing activities, such as glass manufacturing.

Managers are focusing increasingly on improving the quality of and reducing the defects in their products, services, and activities. A rate of defects regarded as normal in the past is no longer tolerable. Managers know that reducing defects reduces costs and makes their company more competitive. Jack Welch, the former chairman and chief executive officer of General Electric (GE), considers emphasis on reducing defects in all of GE's operations as one of the reasons for the company's success. Welch describes GE's quality efforts as "the most challenging and potentially rewarding initiative we have ever undertaken." Highlighting and recording the costs of defects as they occur help managers better determine what to do about defects and their costs.

In this chapter, we focus on three types of costs that arise as a result of defects—spoilage, rework, and scrap—and ways to account for them. And we describe how to determine (a) the cost of products, (b) the cost of goods sold, and (c) inventory valuation when there are spoilage, rework, and scrap.

TERMINOLOGY

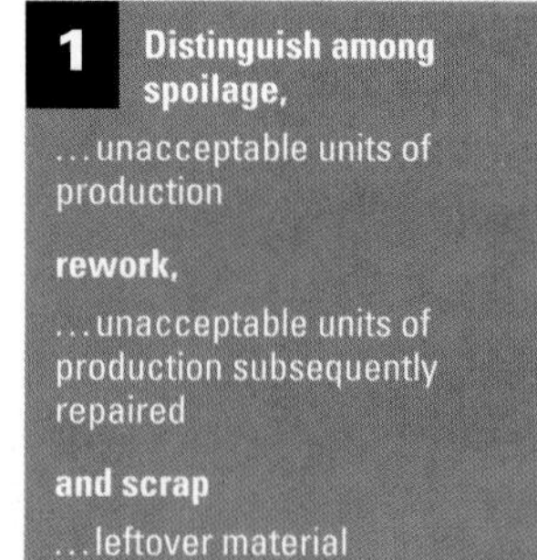
1 Distinguish among spoilage,
...unacceptable units of production
rework,
...unacceptable units of production subsequently repaired
and scrap
...leftover material

The terms used in this chapter may seem familiar, but be sure you understand them in the context of management accounting.

Spoilage is units of production—whether fully or partially completed—that do not meet the standards required by customers for good units and that are discarded or sold for reduced prices. Examples of spoilage are defective shirts, jeans, shoes, and carpeting sold as "seconds," and defective aluminum cans sold to aluminum manufacturers for remelting in the production of aluminum foils.

Rework is units of production that do not meet the standards required by customers for finished units that are subsequently repaired and sold as acceptable finished units. For example, defective units of products (such as pagers, computers, and telephones) detected during or after production but before units are shipped to customers can sometimes be reworked and sold as good products.

Spoilage, rework, and scrap can often be controlled in the value chain's R&D and product-design functions, when the products and production processes are developed.

Scrap is material left over when making a product. It has low sales value compared with the sales value of the product. Examples are short lengths from woodworking operations, edges from plastic molding operations, and frayed cloth and end cuts from suit-making operations.

It is difficult to motivate managers to reduce spoilage, rework, and scrap unless these costs are visible.

Some amounts of spoilage, rework, or scrap are inherent in many production processes. For example, semiconductor manufacturing is so complex and delicate that some spoiled units are commonly produced; and usually, the spoiled units cannot be reworked. An example of spoilage and rework occurs in the manufacture of high-precision machine tools built to exact tolerances; spoiled units can be reworked to meet standards, but only at a considerable cost. And in the mining industry, companies process ore that contains varying amounts of valuable metals and rock. Some amount of rock, which is scrap, is inevitable, but its volume can often be decreased. The Surveys of Company Practice, p. 627, describes spoilage (rejects), rework, and scrap in the U.S. electronics industry.

DIFFERENT TYPES OF SPOILAGE

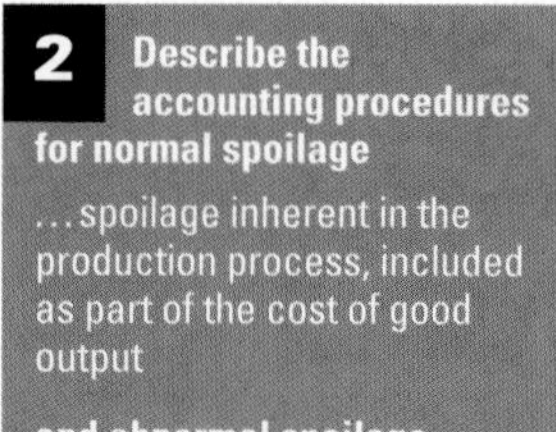
2 Describe the accounting procedures for normal spoilage
...spoilage inherent in the production process, included as part of the cost of good output
and abnormal spoilage
...spoilage that should not arise, recorded as a loss of the period

Accounting for spoilage aims to determine the magnitude of spoilage costs and to distinguish between costs of normal and abnormal spoilage.[1] To manage, control, and reduce spoilage costs, companies need to highlight these costs, not bury them as an unidentified part of the costs of good units manufactured.

[1]The helpful suggestions of Samuel Laimon, University of Saskatchewan, are gratefully acknowledged.

SURVEYS OF COMPANY PRACTICE

Rejection in the Electronics Industry

From country to country and from industry to industry, the rates of rejected and reworked units vary tremendously. The data in the following table focus on different segments of the U.S. electronics industry. The data reported are median numbers drawn from companies that are members of the American Electronics Association. The reject rate is rejects as a percentage of items checked by quality control. The rework rate is reworked items as a percentage of rejects and returns. The scrap rate reports scrap as a percentage of all materials and products purchased. Also reported is the operating-income-to-revenues figure for each segment of the electronics industry.

Segment of Electronics Industry	Reject Rate (% rejects)	Rework Rate (% rework)	Scrap Rate (% scrap)	Operating Income to Revenues
1. Computers and office equipment (includes mainframes, minicomputers, microcomputers, printers, and point-of-sale equipment)	2.6%	6.5%	0.6%	5.3%
2. Electronic components and accessories (includes printed circuit boards and semiconductors)	1.6	2.0	1.6	4.5
3. Specialized production equipment (includes semiconductor production equipment)	7.5	10.0	0.4	5.7
4. Telecommunications equipment (includes telephone, radio, and TV apparatus)	1.0	2.0	1.3	4.7
5. Aerospace, nautical, and military equipment (includes aircraft manufacture and guided missiles)	—	1.5	0.5	6.5
6. Laboratory and measurement devices (includes optical instruments and process-control equipment)	4.9	3.3	0.7	3.9
7. Prepackaged software	1.0	0.8	0.1	4.0
8. Computer-related services (includes data processing and computer systems design)	5.0	N/A	N/A	7.8

The reject rate for specialized production equipment is five times greater than the reject rate for electronic components and semiconductors. Electronic components and semiconductors show a low percentage of rework (in part because rework is not always possible when defects arise). Scrap rates are reasonably small across all industry segments. The operating-income-to-revenues ratio ranges from 3.9% for laboratory and measurement devices to 6.5% for aerospace, nautical, and military equipment. Given these profitability percentages, reductions in reject and rework rates can markedly increase the profitability of many companies in the electronics industry.

Source: Adapted from American Electronics Association, Operating Ratios Survey. Full citation is in Appendix A at the end of the book.

To illustrate normal and abnormal spoilage, consider Mendonza Plastics, which makes plastic casings for the iMac computer using plastic injection molding. In October 2002, Mendonza incurs costs of $615,000 to produce 20,500 units but produces 20,000 good units and 500 spoiled units. Mendonza has no beginning inventory and no ending inventory that month. Of the 500 spoiled units, 400 units are spoiled because of the inability of the injection molding machines to manufacture 100% good casings all the time. That is, these units are spoiled despite running the machines carefully and efficiently. The remaining 100 units are spoiled because of machine breakdowns and operator errors.

Normal Spoilage

Normal spoilage is spoilage inherent in a particular production process that arises even under efficient operating conditions. Depending on the production process, management decides the spoilage it considers normal. At Mendonza Plastics, the 400 units spoiled because of the limitations of injection molding machines and despite efficient operating conditions are normal spoilage. Costs of normal spoilage are typically included as a component of the costs of good units manufactured because good units cannot be made without also making some units that are spoiled. At Mendonza, the cost per unit manufactured is $30 ($615,000 ÷ 20,500 units). The cost of normal spoilage is $12,000 ($30 per unit × 400 units). The cost of good units manufactured is $612,000—the cost of the good units themselves, $600,000 ($30 per unit × 20,000 good units), plus $12,000, the cost of normal spoilage. The cost per good unit is $30.60 ($612,000 ÷ 20,000 units).

Normal spoilage rates are computed by dividing units of normal spoilage by total *good units completed,* not total *actual units started* in production. (At Mendonza Plastics, the normal spoilage rate is 400 ÷ 20,000 = 0.02, or 2%, not 400 ÷ 20,500 = 0.0195, or 1.95%.) Why? Because normal spoilage is the spoilage related to the good units produced.

Abnormal Spoilage

Abnormal spoilage is spoilage that would not arise under efficient operating conditions. It is not inherent in a particular production process. At Mendonza, the 100 units spoiled because of machine breakdowns and operator errors are abnormal spoilage. Abnormal spoilage is usually regarded as avoidable and controllable. Line operators and other plant personnel can generally decrease or eliminate abnormal spoilage by identifying reasons for machine breakdowns, accidents, and the like, and taking steps to prevent their recurrence. To highlight the effect of abnormal spoilage costs, companies calculate the units of abnormal spoilage and record the cost of abnormal spoilage in a Loss from Abnormal Spoilage account, which appears as a separate line item in the income statement. At Mendonza, the loss from abnormal spoilage is $3,000 ($30 per unit × 100 units).

Many companies, such as Toyota, think of their production processes strategically. They do not take their production processes as given. Instead, they constantly redesign products and improve processes to drive normal spoilage downward. Toyota seeks a perfection standard as part of their emphasis on total quality control. Their goal is zero defects, which means they treat all spoilage as abnormal.

Issues about accounting for spoilage arise in both process-costing and job-costing systems. We first present the accounting for spoilage in process-costing systems because it is an extension of the discussion of process costing in Chapter 17.

PROCESS COSTING AND SPOILAGE

How do process-costing systems account for spoiled units? We have already said that units of abnormal spoilage should be counted and recorded separately. But what about units of normal spoilage? These units can either be counted (approach A) or not counted (approach B) when computing output units—physical or equivalent—in a process-costing system. The following example and discussion illustrate the superiority of approach A over approach B.

Count All Spoilage

Example 1: Chipmakers, Inc., manufactures computer chips for television sets. All direct materials are added at the beginning of the production process. To highlight issues that arise with normal spoilage, we assume no beginning inventory and focus only on direct materials costs. In May 2003, $270,000 in direct materials were introduced into production. Production data for May indicate that 10,000 units were started, 5,000 good units were completed, and 1,000 units were spoiled (all normal spoilage).[2] Ending work in process was 4,000 units—each unit 100% complete as to direct material costs. Spoilage is detected upon completion of the process.

An **inspection point** is the stage of the production cycle at which products are examined to determine whether they are acceptable or unacceptable units. Spoilage is typically assumed to occur at the stage of completion where inspection takes place. That's because spoilage is not detected until inspection. In our example, spoilage is assumed to occur at the end of the process. As a result, the spoiled units are assumed to be 100% complete with respect to direct materials.

Exhibit 18-1 computes and assigns direct materials unit costs using approach A and approach B. Approach A shows 10,000 equivalent units of output: 5,000 equivalent units in good units completed [5,000 physical units × 1.00 (that is, 100%)], 4,000 units in ending work in process (4,000 physical units × 100%), and 1,000 equivalent units in normal spoilage (1,000 physical units × 100%). Approach B shows 9,000 equivalent units of output: 5,000 equivalent units in good units completed and 4,000 equivalent units in ending work in process. Not counting the equivalent units for normal spoilage (approach B) decreases equivalent units, resulting in a higher cost of each good unit. A $30 equivalent-unit cost in approach B, by not counting spoiled units, instead of a $27 equivalent-unit cost in approach A, by counting spoiled units, is assigned to work in process that has not reached the inspection point. The direct materials costs assigned to good units completed, which include the costs of normal spoilage, are understated by $12,000—$150,000 instead of $162,000. The 4,000 units in ending work in process contain costs of spoilage of $12,000 ($120,000 – $108,000) that do not pertain to the 4,000 units in ending work in process because they have not yet been inspected. That $12,000 belongs with the good units completed and transferred out. The 4,000 units in ending work in process undoubtedly include some units that will be detected as spoiled when they are inspected upon completion in the subsequent accounting period. Under approach B, the ending work in process is being charged for spoilage in the current period, and it will be charged again in the next period when inspection occurs as the units are completed. That is, under approach B, these units will be charged twice for spoilage. Such cost distortions do not occur under approach A when spoiled units are recognized in the computation of equivalent units, because the costs of normal spoilage are assigned

Because the inspection point in this example is at the end of the process, normal spoilage costs would be allocated only to units that are 100% complete, the units completed and transferred out.

EXHIBIT 18-1

Effect of Recognizing Equivalent Units in Spoilage for Direct Material Costs Chipmakers, Inc., for May 2003

	Approach A: Recognizing Spoiled Units When Computing Output in Equivalent Units	Approach B: Not Counting Spoiled Units When Computing Output in Equivalent Units
Costs to account for	$270,000	$270,000
Divide by equivalent units	÷ 10,000	÷ 9,000
Cost per equivalent unit	$ 27	$ 30
Assignment of costs		
Good units completed: (5,000 × $27; 5,000 × $30)	$135,000	$150,000
Add normal spoilage: (1,000 × $27)	27,000	0
Costs of good units transferred out	$162,000	$150,000
Work in process, ending:		
(4,000 × $27; 4,000 × $30)	108,000	120,000
Costs accounted for	$270,000	$270,000

[2]For simplicity, we assume all spoilage (normal and abnormal) has zero net disposal value. If spoiled units have positive disposal value, the costs of normal and abnormal spoilage would be reduced by this amount. The section on "Job Costing and Spoilage" later in this chapter presents the accounting for this case.

only to the good units produced. Approach A has a further advantage. It highlights the cost of normal spoilage as $27,000, compared with approach B, which shows no cost for normal spoilage (see Exhibit 18-1). The $27,000 cost focuses management's attention on reducing spoilage. Therefore, we will use approach A to present process costing with spoilage.

The Five-Step Procedure for Process Costing with Spoilage

Example 2: *Anzio Company manufactures a wooden recycling container in its Forming Department. Direct materials for this product are added at the beginning of the production cycle. Conversion costs are added evenly during production. Some units of this product are spoiled as a result of defects, which are detectable only upon inspection of finished units. Normally, spoiled units are 10% of the finished output of good units. That is, for every 10 good units produced, there is 1 unit of normal spoilage. Summary data for July 2003 are*

Physical Units for July 2003

Work in process, beginning inventory (July 1)	*1,500 units*
Direct materials (100% complete)	
Conversion costs (60% complete)	
Started during July	*8,500 units*
Completed and transferred out in July	*7,000 good units*
Work in process, ending inventory (July 31)	*2,000 units*
Direct materials (100% complete)	
Conversion costs (50% complete)	

Total Costs for July 2003

Work in process, beginning inventory		
Direct materials (1,500 equivalent units × $8/unit)	*$12,000*	
Conversion costs (900 equivalent units × $10/unit)	*9,000*	*$ 21,000*
Direct materials costs added during July		*76,500*
Conversion costs added during July		*89,100*
Total costs to account for		*$186,600*

The five-step procedure for process costing used in Chapter 17 needs only slight modification to accommodate spoilage.

Step 1: Summarize the Flow of Physical Units of Output. Identify units of both normal and abnormal spoilage.

$$\text{Total Spoilage} = \left(\text{Beginning units} + \text{Units started}\right) - \left(\text{Goods units transferred out} + \text{Ending units}\right)$$
$$= (1{,}500 + 8{,}500) - (7{,}000 + 2{,}000)$$
$$= 10{,}000 - 9{,}000$$
$$= 1{,}000 \text{ units}$$

Normal spoilage is 10% of the 7,000 units of *good* output, or 700 units.

$$\text{Abnormal spoilage} = \text{Total spoilage} - \text{Normal spoilage}$$
$$= 1{,}000 - 700$$
$$= 300 \text{ units}$$

Step 2: Compute Output in Terms of Equivalent Units. Compute equivalent units for spoilage in the same way we compute equivalent units for good units. Following approach A, all spoiled units are included in the computation of output units. Because Anzio's inspection point is at the completion of production, the same amount of work will have been done on each spoiled and each completed good unit.

Step 3: Compute Equivalent-Unit Costs. This step is similar to step 3 in Chapter 17.

Step 4: Summarize Total Costs to Account For. The total costs to account for are all the costs debited to Work in Process. The details for this step are similar to step 4 in Chapter 17.

Step 5: **Assign Total Costs to Units Completed, to Spoiled Units, and to Units in Ending Work in Process.** This step now includes computation of the cost of spoiled units and the cost of good units.

We illustrate these five steps of process costing for each inventory-costing method: weighted-average, FIFO, and standard costing.

Weighted-Average Method and Spoilage

Exhibit 18-2, Panel A, presents steps 1 and 2 to calculate equivalent units of work done to date and includes calculations of equivalent units of normal and abnormal spoilage. Exhibit 18-2, Panel B, presents steps 3, 4, and 5 (together called the production cost worksheet).

Step 3 presents the equivalent-unit cost calculations using the weighted-average method. Note how, for each cost category, the costs of beginning work in process and costs of work done in the current period are totaled and divided by the equivalent units of all work done to date to calculate the weighted-average cost. Step 4 summarizes the total costs to account for. Step 5 assigns costs to completed units, normal and abnormal spoiled units, and ending inventory by multiplying the equivalent units calculated in step 2 by the cost per equivalent unit calculated in step 3. Note, the $13,825 costs of normal spoilage are added to the costs of the related good units. The cost per good unit completed and transferred out of the process equals the total costs transferred out, including the costs of normal spoilage, divided by the number of good units produced, $152,075 ÷ 7,000 good units = $21.725 per good unit. This amount is not equal to $19.75 per good unit, the sum of the $8.85 cost per equivalent unit of direct materials plus the $10.90 cost per equivalent unit of conversion costs. The cost per good unit equals the total cost of direct materials and conversion costs per equivalent unit, $19.75, plus a share of the normal spoilage $1.975 ($13,825 ÷ 7,000 good units) = $21.725 per good unit. The $5,925 costs of abnormal spoilage are assigned to the Loss from Abnormal Spoilage account and do not appear in the good-unit costs.[3]

3 **Account for spoilage in process costing using the weighted-average method**

...spoilage cost based on total costs and equivalent units completed to date

In Panel B, Exhibit 18-2, total costs to account for in step 3 represent the debits to the Work in Process account. Step 5 represents the credits to the Work in Process account, with debits (1) to the Loss from Abnormal Spoilage account for $5,925 and (2) to Finished Goods for $152,075 (the cost of units completed and transferred out). Step 5 also shows the ending balance of work in process, $28,600.

FIFO Method and Spoilage

Exhibit 18-3, Panel A, presents steps 1 and 2 using the FIFO method, which focuses on equivalent units of work done in the current period. Exhibit 18-3, Panel B, presents steps 3, 4, and 5. Note how when assigning costs, the FIFO method keeps the costs of the beginning work in process separate and distinct from the costs of work done in the current period. All spoilage costs are assumed to be related to units completed during this period, using the unit costs of the current period.[4]

4 **Account for spoilage in process costing using the first-in, first-out method**

...spoilage cost based on costs and equivalent units of work done in current period

To simplify calculations under FIFO, spoiled units are accounted for *as if* they were started in the current period. Although some of the beginning work in process probably did spoil, all spoilage is treated as if it came from current production.

Standard-Costing Method and Spoilage

This section assumes you have studied Chapters 7 and 8 and the standard-costing method in Chapter 17 (pp. 600–603). *If not, skip to the next section.* The standard-costing method simplifies the computations for normal and abnormal spoilage. Suppose Anzio Company develops the following standard costs per unit for work done in the Forming Department in July 2003:

Direct materials	$ 8.50
Conversion costs	10.50
Total manufacturing cost	$19.00

5 **Account for spoilage in process costing using the standard-costing method**

...spoilage cost based on standard costs as the costs per equivalent unit

[3]The actual costs of spoilage (and rework) are often greater than the costs recorded in the accounting system because opportunity costs of disruption of the production line, storage, and lost contribution margins are not recorded in accounting systems. Chapter 19 discusses these opportunity costs from the perspective of cost management.

[4]If the FIFO method were used in its purest form, normal spoilage costs would be split between the units started and completed during the current period and the units completed from beginning work in process—using the appropriate unit costs of the period in which the units were worked on. The simpler, modified FIFO method, as illustrated in Exhibit 18-3, in effect uses the unit costs of the current period for assigning normal spoilage costs to the goods completed from beginning work in process. This modified FIFO method assumes that all normal spoilage traceable to the beginning work in process was started and completed during the current period.

Weighted-Average Method of Process Costing with Spoilage Forming Department of the Anzio Company for July 2003

PANEL A: Steps 1 and 2—Summarize Output in Physical Units and Compute Equivalent Units

Flow of Production	(Step 1) Physical Units (given, p. 630)	(Step 2) Equivalent Units Direct Materials	Conversion Costs
Work in process, beginning	1,500		
Started during current period	8,500		
To account for	10,000		
Good units completed and transferred out during current period	7,000	7,000	7,000
Normal spoilage[a]	700		
(700 × 100%; 700 × 100%)		700	700
Abnormal spoilage[b]	300		
(300 × 100%; 300 × 100%)		300	300
Work in process, ending[c]	2,000		
(2,000 × 100%; 2,000 × 50%)		2,000	1,000
Accounted for	10,000		
Work done to date		10,000	9,000

[a]Normal spoilage is 10% of good units transferred out: 10% × 7,000 = 700 units. Degree of completion of normal spoilage in this department: direct materials, 100%; conversion costs, 100%.

[b]Abnormal spoilage = Total spoilage − Normal spoilage = 1,000 − 700 = 300 units. Degree of completion of abnormal spoilage in this department: direct materials, 100%; conversion costs, 100%.

[c]Degree of completion in this department: direct materials, 100%; conversion costs, 50%.

PANEL B: Steps 3, 4, and 5—Compute Equivalent-Unit Costs, Summarize Total Costs to Account for, and Assign Costs to Units Completed, to Spoilage Units, and to Units in Ending Work in Process

		Total Production Costs	Direct Materials		Conversion Costs
(Step 3)	Work in process, beginning (given, p. 630)	$ 21,000	$12,000		$ 9,000
	Costs added in current period (given, p. 630)	165,600	76,500		89,100
	Costs incurred to date		88,500		98,100
	Divide by equivalent units of work done to date		÷ 10,000		÷ 9,000
	Equivalent-unit costs of work done to date		$ 8.85		$ 10.90
(Step 4)	Total costs to account for	$186,600			
(Step 5)	Assignment of costs				
	Good units completed and transferred out (7,000 units)				
	Costs before adding normal spoilage	$138,250	(7,000[d] × $8.85)	+	(7,000[d] × $10.90)
	Normal spoilage (700 units)	13,825	(700[d] × $8.85)	+	(700[d] × $10.90)
(A)	Total cost of good units completed & transferred out	152,075			
(B)	Abnormal spoilage (300 units)	5,925	(300[d] × $8.85)	+	(300[d] × $10.90)
	Work in process, ending (2,000 units)				
	Direct materials	17,700	2,000[d] × $8.85		
	Conversion costs	10,900			1,000[d] × $10.90
(C)	Total work in process, ending	28,600			
(A) + (B) + (C)	Total costs accounted for	$186,600			

[d]Equivalent units of direct materials and conversion costs calculated in step 2 in Panel A.

EXHIBIT 18-3 First-In, First-Out (FIFO) Method of Process Costing with Spoilage Forming Department of the Anzio Company for July 2003

PANEL A: Steps 1 and 2—Summarize Output in Physical Units and Compute Equivalent Units

Flow of Production	(Step 1) Physical Units	(Step 2) Equivalent Units Direct Materials	Conversion Costs
Work in process, beginning (given, p. 630)	1,500		
Started during current period (given, p. 630)	8,500		
To account for	10,000		
Good units completed and transferred out during current period:			
From beginning work in process[a]	1,500		
[1,500 × (100% – 100%); 1,500 × (100% – 60%)]		0	600
Started and completed	5,500[b]		
(5,500 × 100%; 5,500 × 100%)		5,500	5,500
Normal spoilage[c]	700		
(700 × 100%; 700 × 100%)		700	700
Abnormal spoilage[d]	300		
(300 × 100%; 300 × 100%)		300	300
Work in process, ending[e]	2,000		
(2,000 × 100%; 2,000 × 50%)		2,000	1,000
Accounted for	10,000		
Work done in current period only		8,500	8,100

[a]Degree of completion in this department: direct materials, 100%; conversion costs, 60%.
[b]7,000 physical units completed and transferred out minus 1,500 physical units completed and transferred out from beginning work-in-process inventory.
[c]Normal spoilage is 10% of good units transferred out: 10% × 7,000 = 700 units. Degree of completion of normal spoilage in this department: direct materials, 100%; conversion costs, 100%.
[d]Abnormal spoilage = Actual spoilage – Normal spoilage = 1,000 – 700 = 300 units. Degree of completion of abnormal spoilage in this department: direct materials, 100%; conversion costs, 100%.
[e]Degree of completion in this department: direct materials, 100%; conversion costs, 50%.

PANEL B: Steps 3, 4, and 5—Compute Equivalent-Unit Costs, Summarize Total Costs to Account for, and Assign Costs to Units Completed, to Spoilage Units, and to Units in Ending Work in Process

		Total Production Costs	Direct Materials		Conversion Costs
(Step 3)	Work in process, beginning (given, p. 630)	$ 21,000			
	Costs added in current period (given, p. 630)	165,600	$76,500		$89,100
	Divide by equivalent units of work done in current period		÷ 8,500		÷ 8,100
	Equivalent-unit costs of work done in current period		$ 9		$ 11
(Step 4)	Total costs to account for	$186,600			
(Step 5)	Assignment of costs:				
	Good units completed and transferred out (7,000 units)				
	Work in process, beginning (1,500 units)	$ 21,000			
	Direct materials added in current period	0	0[f] × $9		
	Conversion costs added in current period	6,600			600[f] × $11
	Total from beginning inventory before normal spoilage	27,600			
	Started and completed before normal spoilage (5,500 units)	110,000	(5,500[f] × $9)	+	(5,500[f] × $11)
	Normal spoilage (700 units)	14,000	(700[f] × $9)	+	(700[f] × $11)
(A)	Total cost of good units transferred out	151,600			
(B)	Abnormal spoilage (300 units)	6,000	(300[f] × $9)	+	(300[f] × $11)
	Work in process, ending (2,000 units)				
	Direct materials	18,000	2,000[f] × $9		
	Conversion costs	11,000			1,000[f] × $11
(C)	Total work in process, ending	29,000			
(A) + (B) + (C)	Total costs accounted for	$186,600			

[f]Equivalent units of direct materials and conversion costs calculated in step 2 in Panel A.

Assume the same standard cost per unit also applies to the beginning inventory: 1,500 equivalent units of direct materials and 900 equivalent units of conversion costs. Hence, the beginning inventory at standard costs is

Direct materials, 1,500 units × \$8.50/unit	\$12,750
Conversion costs, 900 units × \$10.50/unit	9,450
Total manufacturing costs	\$22,200

Exhibit 18-4, Panel A, presents steps 1 and 2 for calculating physical and equivalent units. These steps are the same as for the FIFO method described in Exhibit 18-3. Exhibit 18-4, Panel B, presents steps 3, 4, and 5.

In Step 3, the cost per equivalent unit is simply the standard cost: \$8.50 per unit for direct materials, and \$10.50 per unit for conversion costs. The standard-costing method makes calculating equivalent-unit costs unnecessary and so simplifies process costing. The costs to account for in step 4 are at standard costs and, hence, they differ from the costs to account for under the weighted-average and FIFO methods, which are at actual costs. Step 5 assigns standard costs to units completed (including normal spoilage), to abnormal spoilage, and to ending work in process inventory by multiplying the equivalent units calculated in step 2 by the standard cost per equivalent unit presented in step 3. Variances can be measured and analyzed in the manner described in Chapter 17 (p. 601).[5]

Journal Entries

The information from Panel B in Exhibits 18-2, 18-3, and 18-4 supports the following journal entries for the transfer of good units completed to finished goods and to recognize the loss from abnormal spoilage.

	Weighted Average		FIFO		Standard Costs	
Finished Goods	152,075		151,600		146,300	
Work in Process—Forming		152,075		151,600		146,300
To transfer good units completed in July.						
Loss from Abnormal Spoilage	5,925		6,000		5,700	
Work in Process—Forming		5,925		6,000		5,700
To recognize abnormal spoilage detected in July.						

Inspection Points and Allocating Costs of Normal Spoilage

Our Anzio Company illustration assumes inspection upon completion of the units. However, spoilage might actually occur at various stages of the production cycle, although it is typically detected only at one or more inspection points. The cost of spoiled units is assumed to be all costs incurred by spoiled units prior to inspection. When spoiled goods have a disposal value (for example, carpeting sold as "seconds"), the net cost of spoilage is computed by deducting disposal value from the costs of the spoiled goods accumulated to the inspection point. The unit costs of normal and abnormal spoilage are the same when the two are detected at the same inspection point. However, situations might arise when abnormal spoilage is detected at a different point than normal spoilage. Consider shirt manufacturing. Normal spoilage in the form of defective shirts is identified upon inspection at the end of the production process. Now suppose a defective machine causes many defective shirts to be produced in the middle of the production process. These defective shirts would be abnormal spoilage and would occur at a different point in the production process than normal spoilage. In such cases, the unit cost of abnormal spoilage, which is based on costs incurred up to the middle of the production process, would differ from the unit cost of normal spoilage, which is based on costs incurred through the end of the production process.

Consider another example of how abnormal spoilage may occur at other than the inspection point. If a foreman at a glass plant discovers a furnace has been contaminated with foreign matter, abnormal spoilage is detected and recorded in the accounting system at that time—well before completed glass products are inspected.

Costs of abnormal spoilage are separately accounted for as losses of the accounting period in which they are detected. However, recall that normal spoilage costs are added to costs of good units, which raises an additional issue: Should normal spoilage costs be

[5]For example, from Exhibit 18-4, Panel B, the standard costs for July are direct materials used, \$72,250, and conversion costs, \$85,050. From p. 630, the actual costs added during July are direct materials, \$76,500, and conversion costs, \$89,100, resulting in a direct materials variance of \$72,250 − \$76,500 = \$4,250 U and a conversion costs variance of \$85,050 − \$89,100 = \$4,050 U. These variances could then be subdivided further as in Chapters 7 and 8; the abnormal spoilage would be part of the efficiency variance.

EXHIBIT 18-4 **Use of Standard Costs in Process Costing with Spoilage Forming Department of the Anzio Company for July 2003**

PANEL A: Steps 1 and 2—Summarize Output in Physical Units and Compute Equivalent Units

Flow of Production	(Step 1) Physical Units	(Step 2) Equivalent Units Direct Materials	Conversion Costs
Work in process, beginning (given, p. 630)	1,500		
Started during current period (given, p. 630)	8,500		
To account for	10,000		
Good units completed and transferred out during current period:			
From beginning work in process[a]	1,500		
[1,500 × (100% – 100%); 1,500 × (100% – 60%)]		0	600
Started and completed	5,500[b]		
(5,500 × 100%; 5,500 × 100%)		5,500	5,500
Normal spoilage[c]	700		
(700 × 100%; 700 × 100%)		700	700
Abnormal spoilage[d]	300		
(300 × 100%; 300 × 100%)		300	300
Work in process, ending[e]	2,000		
(2,000 × 100%; 2,000 × 50%)		2,000	1,000
Accounted for	10,000		
Work done in current period only		8,500	8,100

[a]Degree of completion in this department: direct materials, 100%; conversion costs, 60%.

[b]7,000 physical units completed and transferred out minus 1,500 physical units completed and transferred out from beginning work-in-process inventory.

[c]Normal spoilage is 10% of good units transferred out: 10% × 7,000 = 700 units. Degree of completion of normal spoilage in this department: direct materials, 100%; conversion costs, 100%.

[d]Abnormal spoilage = Actual spoilage – Normal spoilage = 1,000 – 700 = 300 units. Degree of completion of abnormal spoilage in this department: direct materials, 100%; conversion costs, 100%.

[e]Degree of completion in this department: direct materials, 100%; conversion costs, 50%.

PANEL B: Steps 3, 4, and 5—Compute Equivalent-Unit Costs, Summarize Total Costs to Account for, and Assign Costs to Units Completed, to Spoilage Units, and to Units in Ending Work in Process

		Total Production Costs	Direct Materials		Conversion Costs
(Step 3)	Standard cost per equivalent unit (given, p. 631)	$ 19.00	$ 8.50		$ 10.50
	Work in process, beginning (given, p. 634)	$ 22,200			
	Costs added in current period at standard prices				
	Direct materials, 8,500 × $8.50; conversion costs, 8,100 × $10.50	157,300	72,250		85,050
(Step 4)	Costs to account for	$179,500			
(Step 5)	Assignment of costs at standard costs:				
	Good units completed and transferred out (7,000 units)				
	Work in process, beginning (1,500 units)	$ 22,200			
	Direct materials added in current period	0	0[f] × $8.50		
	Conversion costs added in current period	6,300			600[f] × $10.50
	Total from beginning inventory before normal spoilage	28,500			
	Started and completed before normal spoilage (5,500 units)	104,500	(5,500[f] × $8.50)	+	(5,500[f] × $10.50)
	Normal spoilage (700 units)	13,300	(700[f] × $8.50)	+	(700[f] × $10.50)
(A)	Total cost of good units transferred out	146,300			
(B)	Abnormal spoilage (300 units)	5,700	(300[f] × $8.50)	+	(300[f] × $10.50)
	Work in process, ending (2,000 units)				
	Direct materials	17,000	2,000[f] × $8.50		
	Conversion costs	10,500			1,000[f] × $10.50
(C)	Total work in process, ending	27,500			
(A) + (B) + (C)	Total costs accounted for	$179,500			

[f]Equivalent units of direct materials and conversion costs calculated in step 2 in Panel A.

allocated between completed units and ending work-in-process inventory? *The common approach is to presume that normal spoilage occurs at the inspection point in the production cycle and to allocate its cost over all units that have passed that point during the accounting period.* In the Anzio Company example, spoilage is assumed to occur when units are inspected at the end of the production cycle, so no costs of normal spoilage are allocated to ending work in process.

The costs of normal spoilage are allocated to units in ending work in process—in addition to completed units—if the units in ending work in process have passed the inspection point. For example, if the inspection point is at the halfway stage of production, then any work in process that is at least 50% complete would be allocated a full measure of normal spoilage costs, and those spoilage costs would be calculated on the basis of all costs incurred prior to the inspection point. But if work in process is less than 50% complete, no normal spoilage costs would be allocated to it. The appendix to this chapter contains a discussion of spoilage when units are inspected at different points in the production cycle.

Early and frequent inspections prevent any further direct materials and conversion costs being wasted on units that are already spoiled. If inspection can occur when units are 80% (rather than 100%) complete as to conversion costs, and spoilage occurs prior to the 80% point, a company can avoid incurring the final 20% of conversion costs on the spoiled units.

6 Account for spoilage in job costing

...normal spoilage assigned directly or indirectly to job; abnormal spoilage written off as a loss of the period

JOB COSTING AND SPOILAGE

The concepts of normal and abnormal spoilage also apply to job-costing systems. Abnormal spoilage is separately identified with the goal of eliminating it altogether. Costs of abnormal spoilage are not considered to be inventoriable costs and are written off as costs of the period during which the abnormal spoilage is detected. Normal spoilage costs in job-costing systems—just as in process-costing systems—are inventoriable costs, although increasingly companies are tolerating only small amounts of spoilage as normal. When assigning costs, job-costing systems generally distinguish *normal spoilage attributable to a specific job* from *normal spoilage common to all jobs.*

We describe accounting for spoilage in job costing using the following example.

Although not the focus of this example, Hull calculates the $2,000 cost per part based on its inventory costing method (weighted average, FIFO, or standard costing).

Example 3: *In the Hull Machine Shop, 5 aircraft parts out of a job lot of 50 aircraft parts are spoiled. Costs assigned prior to the inspection point are $2,000 per part. Our presentation here and in subsequent sections focuses on how the $2,000 cost per part is accounted for. When the spoilage is detected, the spoiled goods are inventoried at $600 per part, the net disposal value.*

Normal spoilage attributable to a specific job When normal spoilage occurs because of the specifications of a particular job, that job bears the cost of the spoilage reduced by the disposal value of the spoilage. The journal entry to recognize disposal value (items in parentheses indicate subsidiary ledger postings) is

Materials Control (spoiled goods at current net disposal value): 5 units × $600/unit	3,000	
Work-in-Process Control (specific job): 5 units × $600/unit		3,000

Because the costs of normally spoiled units attributable to a specific job are in that job's Work in Process account, the cost of both good units and normally spoiled units will be spread over the good units, which increases the cost per unit of the good units. No journal entry is necessary for normal spoilage, except to reduce (credit) the job's Work in Process account for any disposal value of the normal spoilage.

Note, the Work-in-Process Control (specific job) has already been debited (charged) $10,000 for the spoiled parts (5 spoiled parts × $2,000 per part). The effect of the $3,000 entry is to make the net cost of normal spoilage, $7,000 ($10,000 – $3,000), an additional cost of the 45 (50 – 5) good units produced. The total cost of the 45 good units is $97,000, comprising $90,000 (45 units × $2,000 per unit) incurred to produce the good units plus the $7,000 net cost of normal spoilage. The cost per good unit is $2,155.56 ($97,000 ÷ 45 good units).

Normal spoilage common to all jobs In some cases, spoilage may be considered a normal characteristic of a given production cycle. The spoilage inherent in production will, of course, occur when a specific job is being worked on. But the spoilage is not attributable to, and hence is not charged to, the specific job. Instead, the spoilage is costed as manufacturing overhead. The journal entry is

Materials Control (spoiled goods at current disposal value): 5 units × $600/unit	3,000	
Manufacturing Overhead Control (normal spoilage): ($10,000 – $3,000)	7,000	
Work-in-Process Control (specific job): 5 units × $2,000/unit		10,000

When normal spoilage is common to all jobs, the budgeted manufacturing overhead rate includes a provision for normal spoilage cost. Normal spoilage cost is spread, through overhead allocation, over all jobs rather than loaded on specific jobs.[6] For example, if Hull produced 140 good units across all jobs in a given month, the $7,000 of normal spoilage overhead costs would be allocated at the rate of $7,000 ÷ 140 good units = $50 per good unit. Normal spoilage overhead costs allocated to the 45 good units in the job would be $2,250 ($50 × 45 good units). The total cost of the 45 good units is $92,250: $90,000 (45 units × $2,000 per unit) incurred to produce the good units plus $2,250 of normal spoilage overhead costs. The cost per good unit is $2,050 ($92,250 ÷ 45 good units).

Abnormal spoilage If the spoilage is abnormal, the net loss is charged to an abnormal loss account. Unlike normal spoilage costs, abnormal spoilage costs are not included as a part of the cost of good units produced. The total cost of the 45 good units is $90,000 (45 units × $2,000 per unit). The cost per good unit is $2,000 ($90,000 ÷ 45 good units).

Materials Control (spoiled goods at current disposal value):		
5 units × $600/unit	3,000	
Loss from Abnormal Spoilage: ($10,000 – $3,000)	7,000	
Work-in-Process Control (specific job): 5 units × $2,000/unit		10,000

Even though, for external reporting purposes, abnormal spoilage costs are written off in the period and are not linked to specific jobs or units, companies often identify the particular reasons for abnormal spoilage, and, when appropriate, link abnormal spoilage with specific jobs or units for cost management purposes.

REWORK

7 Account for rework in job costing

...normal rework assigned directly or indirectly to job; abnormal rework written off as a loss of the period

Rework is units of production that are inspected, determined to be unacceptable, repaired, and sold as acceptable finished goods. We again distinguish (1) normal rework attributable to a specific job, (2) normal rework common to all jobs, and (3) abnormal rework.

Consider the Hull Machine Shop data in Example 3 on page 636. Assume the five spoiled parts are reworked. The journal entry for the $10,000 of total costs (the details of these costs are assumed) assigned to the five spoiled units before considering rework costs is:

Work-in-Process Control (specific job)	10,000	
Materials Control		4,000
Wages Payable Control		4,000
Manufacturing Overhead Allocated		2,000

Assume the rework costs equal $3,800 (comprising $800 direct materials, $2,000 direct manufacturing labor, and $1,000 manufacturing overhead).

Normal rework attributable to a specific job If the rework is normal but occurs because of the requirements of a specific job, the rework costs are charged to that job. The journal entry is

Work-in-Process Control (specific job)	3,800	
Materials Control		800
Wages Payable Control		2,000
Manufacturing Overhead Allocated		1,000

Normal rework common to all jobs When rework is normal and not attributable to a specific job, the costs of rework are charged to manufacturing overhead and spread, through overhead allocation, over all jobs.

[6]Note that costs *already assigned to products* are charged back to Manufacturing Overhead Control, which generally accumulates only *costs incurred*, not both costs incurred and costs already assigned.

Question: Why are both MOH Control and MOH Allocated in the same journal entry?
Answer: MOH Control is debited because the normal rework is common to all jobs (rather than attributable to a specific job). In such cases, the additional MOH costs incurred to rework the units (such as electricity and materials handling) are spread over all jobs by including an allowance for estimated rework in the budgeted MOH (accounted for by the credit to MOH Allocated).

Manufacturing Overhead Control (rework costs)	3,800	
Materials Control		800
Wages Payable Control		2,000
Manufacturing Overhead Allocated		1,000

Abnormal rework If the rework is abnormal, it is recorded by charging abnormal rework to a loss account.

Loss from Abnormal Rework	3,800	
Materials Control		800
Wages Payable Control		2,000
Manufacturing Overhead Allocated		1,000

Accounting for rework in a process-costing system also requires abnormal rework to be distinguished from normal rework. A process-costing system accounts for abnormal rework in the same way as a job-costing system. Accounting for normal rework follows the accounting described for normal rework common to all jobs (units) because masses of identical or similar units are being manufactured.

Costing rework focuses managers on the resources wasted on activities that would not have to be undertaken if the product were made correctly. The cost of rework prompts managers to seek ways to reduce rework, for example, by designing new products or processes, training workers, or investing in new machines. To eliminate rework and to simplify the accounting, some companies set a standard of zero rework. All rework is then treated as abnormal and written off as a cost of the current period.

ACCOUNTING FOR SCRAP

8 Account for scrap
...reduces cost of job either at time of sale or at time of production

Scrap is material left over when making a product; it has low sales value compared with the sales value of the product. No distinction is made between normal and abnormal scrap because no cost is attached to scrap. The only distinction made is between scrap attributable to a specific job and scrap common to all jobs.

There are two aspects of accounting for scrap:

1. Planning and control, including physical tracking
2. Inventory costing, including when and how it affects operating income

Initial entries to scrap records are commonly in physical terms. In various industries, items such as stamped-out metal sheets or edges of molded plastic parts are quantified by weighing, counting, or some other expedient means. Scrap records not only help measure efficiency, but they also help keep track of scrap and so reduce the chances of theft. Scrap reports are prepared as source documents for periodic summaries of the amount of actual scrap compared with the budgeted or standard amounts. Scrap is either sold or disposed of quickly, or stored for later sale, disposal, or reuse.

Careful tracking of scrap often extends into the accounting records. Surveys indicate that 60% of companies maintain a distinct account for scrap costs somewhere in their accounting system. The issues here are similar to Chapter 16's issues regarding the accounting for byproducts:

1. When should the value of scrap be recognized in the accounting records—at the time scrap is produced or at the time scrap is sold?
2. How should revenues from scrap be accounted for?

To illustrate, we extend our Hull example. Assume the manufacture of aircraft parts generates scrap and that the scrap from a job has a net sales value of $900.

Rework costs are recorded in the accounts when incurred because they tend to be material in amount. Because scrap is immaterial in amount, it may not be recorded in the accounts until the time of sale (rather than at the time of production).

Recognizing Scrap at the Time of Its Sale

When the dollar amount of scrap is immaterial, the simplest accounting is to make a notation of the quantity of scrap returned to the storeroom and to regard scrap sales as a separate line item of other revenues in the income statement. The only journal entry is

Sale of scrap:	Cash or Accounts Receivable	900	
	Scrap Revenues		900

When the dollar amount of scrap is material and the scrap is sold quickly after it is produced, the accounting depends on whether the scrap is attributable to a specific job or common to all jobs.

Scrap attributable to a specific job Job-costing systems sometimes trace the scrap revenues to the jobs that yielded the scrap. This method is used only when the tracing can be done in an economically feasible way. For example, the Hull Machine Shop and particular customers, such as the U.S. Department of Defense, may reach an agreement that provides for charging specific jobs with all rework or spoilage costs and for crediting these jobs with all scrap revenues that arise from the jobs. The journal entry is

Scrap returned to storeroom:	No journal entry. [Notation of quantity received and related job is entered in the inventory record]		
Sale of scrap:	Cash or Accounts Receivable	900	
	Work-in-Process Control		900
	Posting made to specific job cost record.		

Unlike spoilage and rework, there is no cost attached to the scrap, and hence no distinction is made between normal and abnormal scrap. All scrap revenues, whatever the amount, are credited to the specific job. Scrap revenues reduce the costs of the job.

Scrap common to all jobs The journal entry in this case is

Scrap returned to storeroom:	No journal entry. [Notation of quantity received and related job is entered in the inventory record]		
Sale of scrap:	Cash or Accounts Receivable	900	
	Manufacturing Overhead Control		900
	Posting made to subsidiary ledger—"Sales of Scrap" column on department cost record.		

This method does not link scrap with any particular job or product. Instead, all products bear production costs without any credit for scrap revenues except in an indirect manner: The expected scrap revenues are considered when setting the budgeted manufacturing overhead rate. Thus, the budgeted overhead rate is lower than it would be if the overhead budget had not been reduced by the expected scrap revenues. This accounting for scrap is used in both job-costing and process-costing systems.

Recognizing Scrap at the Time of Its Production

Our preceding illustrations assume that scrap returned to the storeroom is sold quickly and hence is not assigned an inventory cost figure. Sometimes, as in the case with edges of molded plastic parts, the value of scrap is not immaterial, and the time between storing it and selling or reusing it can be long. In these situations, the company inventories scrap at a conservative estimate of its net realizable value so that production costs and related scrap revenues are recognized in the same accounting period. Some companies tend to delay sales of scrap until its market price is considered attractive. Volatile price fluctuations are typical for scrap metal. In these cases, it's not easy to determine some "reasonable inventory value."

Scrap attributable to a specific job The journal entry in the Hull example is

Scrap returned to storeroom:	Materials Control	900	
	Work-in-Process Control		900

Scrap common to all jobs The journal entry in this case is

Scrap returned to storeroom:	Materials Control	900	
	Manufacturing Overhead Control		900

In job costing, the cost of scrap is already in the Work in Process account of the job generating the scrap. If the scrap is attributable to that job, the costs are where they should be and no journal entry is necessary; when the scrap is sold, then that particular job's Work in Process account is credited to reduce the cost of the job by the amount of the scrap's disposal value.

Observe that Materials Control account is debited in place of Cash or Accounts Receivable. When the scrap is sold, the journal entry is

Sale of scrap:	Cash or Accounts Receivable	900	
	Materials Control		900

Scrap is sometimes reused as direct materials rather than sold as scrap. In this case, Materials Control is debited at its estimated net realizable value and then credited when the scrap is reused. For example, the entries when the scrap generated is common to all jobs are

Scrap returned to storeroom:	Materials Control	900	
	Manufacturing Overhead Control		900
Reuse of scrap:	Work-in-Process Control	900	
	Materials Control		900

The accounting for scrap under process costing is like the accounting under job costing when scrap is common to all jobs because process costing applies to the manufacture of masses of identical or similar units.

CONCEPTS IN ACTION

Managing Waste and Environmental Costs at the DuPont Corporation

The DuPont Corporation manufactures a wide range of chemicals and chemical products. DuPont uses the term *waste* to describe the spoilage and scrap it generates. Besides the cost of lost materials, chemical waste is a particular problem because of its impact on the environment. Strict environmental laws require that chemical waste be disposed of in an environmentally safe way, further adding to the cost of generating waste.

DuPont calculates the full costs of waste to include: (1) the costs of materials lost in the chemical process minus their disposal value; (2) the full costs of semi-finished and finished products spoiled; (3) the full costs of disposing of or treating the waste, such as site charges for hazardous waste or costs of scrubbers and biotreatment plants to treat the waste; and (4) the costs of any solvents used to clean plant and equipment as a result of generating waste.

DuPont believes business profits do not have to be gained at the expense of the environment and seeks to reduce the "environmental impact" of all its businesses. Consistent with the Environmental Protection Agency's (EPA's) recommendations, DuPont focuses on source reduction (the avoidance of waste altogether, rather than disposal or treatment of waste) as the best way to achieve profitability and environmental performance. DuPont calculates the total cost of waste to highlight to managers the operational and environmental costs of waste, and it rewards managers for reducing waste. This approach motivates individual plants to take actions, such as redesigning products, reconfiguring processes, or investing in capital equipment to reduce waste altogether. For example, DuPont increased its material yield in its $2 billion Lycra business from 75% in 1990 to more than 90% in 1999.

The company's new process for Terathane®—developed by a Dupont team with members from LaPorte, Texas; Niagara Falls, New York; Deepwater, New Jersey; and Wilmington, Delaware—is a good example of how DuPont reduces waste costs. The new process significantly reduces environmental emissions and energy use. Relative to the old technology, the new technology reduced air emissions by 200,000 pounds, solid waste by 25 million pounds, aqueous waste by 500 million pounds, and steam use by more than 150 million pounds, while generating cost savings of more than $5 million a year.

Source: Adapted from Environmental Respect Awards, DuPont Corporation, and based on discussions with Dale Martin, manager, Environmental Effectiveness; C. Holliday, "Sustainable Growth, the DuPont Way," *Harvard Business Review*, September 2001, pp. 129–134.

Managers focus their attention on ways to reduce scrap and to use it more profitably, especially when the cost of scrap is high (see Concepts in Action, p. 640). General Motors Corporation has redesigned its plastic injection molding processes to reduce the scrap plastic that must be broken away from its molded products. General Motors also regrinds and reuses the plastic scrap as direct material, saving substantial input costs.

PROBLEM FOR SELF-STUDY

Burlington Textiles has some spoiled goods that had an assigned cost of $40,000 and zero net disposal value.

Required

Prepare a journal entry for each of the following conditions under (a) process costing (Department A) and (b) job costing:

1. Abnormal spoilage of $40,000
2. Normal spoilage of $40,000 regarded as common to all operations
3. Normal spoilage of $40,000 regarded as attributable to specifications of a particular job

SOLUTION

(a) Process Costing			(b) Job Costing		
1. Loss from Abnormal Spoilage	40,000		Loss from Abnormal Spoilage	40,000	
Work in Process—Dept. A		40,000	Work-in-Process Control (specific job)		40,000
2. No entry until units are completed and transferred out. Then the normal spoilage costs are transferred as part of the cost of good units.			Manufacturing Overhead Control	40,000	
			Work-in-Process Control (specific job)		40,000
Work in Process—Dept. B	40,000				
Work in Process—Dept. A		40,000			
3. Not applicable			No entry. Normal spoilage cost remains in Work-in-Process Control (specific job).		

DECISION POINTS

SUMMARY

The following question-and-answer format summarizes the chapter's learning objectives. Each decision presents a key question related to a learning objective. The guidelines are the answer to that question.

Decision	Guidelines
1. What are spoilage, rework, and scrap?	Spoilage is units of production that do not meet the standards required by customers for good units, and that are discarded or sold for reduced prices. Rework is unacceptable units that are subsequently repaired and sold as acceptable finished goods. Scrap is material left over when making a product; it has low sales value compared with the sales value of the product.
2. What are normal and abnormal spoilage and how are they accounted for?	Normal spoilage is inherent in a particular production process and arises even under efficient operating conditions. Abnormal spoilage would not arise under efficient operating conditions. Generally, accounting systems explicitly recognize both types of spoilage when computing the number of output units. Normal spoilage is typically included in the cost of good output units; abnormal spoilage is recorded as a loss for the accounting period in which it is detected.

Continued

3. How does the weighted-average method of process costing calculate the costs of good units and spoilage?	The weighted-average method combines costs in beginning inventory with costs of the current period when determining the costs of good units (which include a normal spoilage amount) and the costs of abnormal spoilage.
4. How does the FIFO method of process costing calculate the costs of good units and spoilage?	The FIFO method keeps separate the costs in beginning inventory from the costs of the current period when determining the costs of good units (which include a normal spoilage amount) and the costs of abnormal spoilage.
5. How does the standard-costing method of process costing calculate the costs of good units and spoilage?	The standard-costing method uses standard costs to determine the costs of good units (which include a normal spoilage amount) and the costs of abnormal spoilage.
6. How do job-costing systems account for spoilage?	Normal spoilage specific to a job is assigned to that job, or when common to all jobs, it is allocated as part of manufacturing overhead. Loss from abnormal spoilage is recorded as a cost of the accounting period in which it is detected.
7. How do job-costing systems account for rework?	Completed reworked units should be indistinguishable from non-reworked good units. Normal rework can be assigned to a specific job, or when common to all jobs, as part of manufacturing overhead. Abnormal rework is written off as a cost of the accounting period in which it is detected.
8. How is scrap accounted for?	Scrap is recognized in the accounting records either at the time of its sale or at the time of its production. Sale of scrap, if immaterial, is often recognized as other revenue. If material, the sale of scrap or its net realizable value reduces the cost of a specific job or, when common to all jobs, reduces manufacturing overhead.

APPENDIX: INSPECTION AND SPOILAGE AT INTERMEDIATE STAGES OF COMPLETION IN PROCESS COSTING

Consider how inspection at various stages of completion affects the amount of normal and abnormal spoilage. Assume that normal spoilage is 10% of the good units passing inspection in the Forging Department of Dana Corporation, a manufacturer of automobile parts. Direct materials are added at the start of production in the Forging Department. Conversion costs are added evenly during the process.

Consider three different cases: Inspection occurs at (1) the 20%, (2) the 50%, or (3) the 100% completion stage. A total of 8,000 units are spoiled in all three cases. Normal spoilage is computed on the basis of the number of *good units* that pass the inspection point *during the current period*. The following data are for October. Note how the number of units of normal and abnormal spoilage change, depending on when inspection occurs.

	Physical Units: Inspection at Stage of Completion		
Flow of Production	**At 20%**	**At 50%**	**At 100%**
Work in process, beginning (25%)[a]	11,000	11,000	11,000
Started during October	74,000	74,000	74,000
To account for	85,000	85,000	85,000
Good units completed and transferred out (85,000 − 8,000 spoiled − 16,000 ending)	61,000	61,000	61,000
Normal spoilage	6,600[b]	7,700[c]	6,100[d]
Abnormal spoilage (8,000 − normal spoilage)	1,400	300	1,900
Work in process, ending (75%)[a]	16,000	16,000	16,000
Accounted for	85,000	85,000	85,000

[a]Degree of completion for conversion costs in this department at the dates of the work-in-process inventories.

[b]10% × (74,000 units started − 8,000 units spoiled), because only the units started passed the 20% completion inspection point in the current period. Beginning work in process is excluded from this calculation because, being 25% complete at the start of the period, it passed the inspection point in the previous period.

[c]10% × (85,000 units − 8,000 units spoiled), because *all* units passed the 50% completion inspection point in the current period.

[d]10% × 61,000, because 61,000 units are fully completed and inspected in the current period.

The following diagram shows the flow of physical units for October and illustrates the normal spoilage numbers in the table. Note that 61,000 good units are completed and transferred out — 11,000 from beginning work in process and 50,000 started and completed during the period — and 16,000 units are in ending work in process.

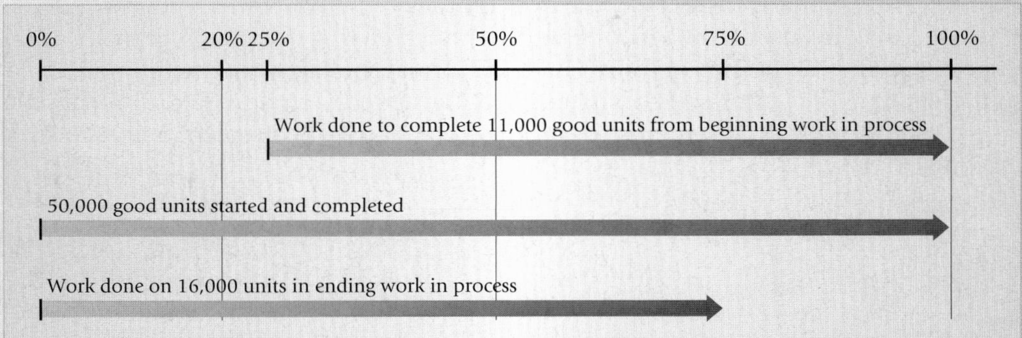

This time line is helpful in calculating the amount of normal spoilage in the current period.

To see the number of units passing each inspection point, consider in the diagram the vertical lines at the 20%, 50%, and 100% inspection points. Note, the vertical line at 20% cuts two horizontal lines, 50,000 good units started and completed and 16,000 units in ending work in process, for a total of 66,000 good units. (The 20% vertical line does not cut the line representing work done on the 11,000 good units completed from beginning work in process because these units are already 25% complete at the start of the period and, hence, are not inspected this period.) Normal spoilage equals 10% of 66,000 = 6,600 units. Similarly, the vertical line at the 50% point cuts all three horizontal lines, indicating that 11,000 + 50,000 + 16,000 = 77,000 good units pass this point. Normal spoilage in this case is 10% of 77,000 = 7,700 units. At the 100% point, normal spoilage = 10% of (11,000 + 50,000) = 6,100 units.

Exhibit 18-5 shows the computation of equivalent units under the weighted-average method, assuming inspection at the 50% completion stage. The calculations depend on the direct materials and conversion costs incurred to get the units to this inspection point. The spoiled units have a full measure of direct materials and a 50% measure of conversion costs. The computations of equivalent-unit costs and the assignment of total costs to units completed and to ending work in process are similar to the computations in previous illustrations in this chapter. Because ending work in process has passed the inspection point in this example, these units bear normal spoilage costs, just like the units that have been completed and transferred out. For example, conversion costs for units completed and

Question: If ending work in process is 70% complete, should it get a "full dose" of normal spoilage when inspection is at the 50% completion point?
Answer: Yes, because spoilage is recognized at the inspection point. Even though these units are only 70% of the way through the production cycle, they are nevertheless complete in terms of normal spoilage at the 50% completion point.

EXHIBIT 18-5

Steps 1 and 2: Computing Equivalent Units with Spoilage Weighted-Average Method of Process Costing Forging Department of the Dana Corporation for October

Flow of Production	(Step 1) Physical Units	(Step 2) Equivalent Units Direct Materials	Conversion Costs
Work in process, beginning[a]	11,000		
Started during current period	74,000		
To account for	85,000		
Good units completed and transferred out	61,000	61,000	61,000
Normal spoilage	7,700		
(7,700 × 100%; 7,700 × 50%)		7,700	3,850
Abnormal spoilage	300		
(300 × 100%; 300 × 50%)		300	150
Work in process, ending[b]	16,000		
(16,000 × 100%; 16,000 × 75%)		16,000	12,000
Accounted for	85,000		
Total work done to date		85,000	77,000

[a]Degree of completion: direct materials, 100%; conversion costs, 25%.
[b]Degree of completion: direct materials, 100%; conversion costs, 75%.

transferred out include conversion costs for 61,000 good units produced plus 50% × (10% × 61,000) = 0.50 × 6,100 = 3,050 equivalent units of normal spoilage. We multiply by 50% to obtain equivalent units of normal spoilage because conversion costs are only 50% complete at the inspection point. Conversion costs of equivalent units in ending work in process include conversion costs of 75% of 16,000 = 12,000 equivalent good units plus 50% × (10% × 16,000) = 0.50 × 1,600 = 800 equivalent units of normal spoilage. We take 10% of 16,000 because 16,000 good units currently in ending work in process passed the inspection point. Thus, the equivalent units of normal spoilage accounted for are 3,050 equivalent units related to units completed and transferred out plus 800 equivalent units related to units in ending work in process for a total of 3,850 equivalent units shown in Exhibit 18-5.

TERMS TO LEARN

abnormal spoilage (p. 628)
inspection point (629)
normal spoilage (628)
rework (626)
scrap (626)
spoilage (626)

ASSIGNMENT MATERIAL

Questions

18-1 Why is there an unmistakable trend in manufacturing to improve quality?

18-2 Distinguish among spoilage, rework, and scrap.

18-3 "Normal spoilage is planned spoilage." Discuss.

18-4 "Costs of abnormal spoilage are losses." Explain.

18-5 "What has been regarded as normal spoilage in the past is not necessarily acceptable as normal spoilage in the present or future." Explain.

18-6 "Units of abnormal spoilage are inferred rather than identified." Explain.

18-7 "In accounting for spoiled units, we are dealing with cost assignment rather than cost incurrence." Explain.

18-8 "Total input includes abnormal as well as normal spoilage and is, therefore, inappropriate as a basis for computing normal spoilage." Do you agree? Explain.

18-9 "The inspection point is the key to the allocation of spoilage costs." Do you agree? Explain.

18-10 "The unit cost of normal spoilage is the same as the unit cost of abnormal spoilage." Do you agree? Explain.

18-11 "In job costing, the costs of normal spoilage that occur while a specific job is being done are charged to the specific job." Do you agree? Explain.

18-12 "The costs of rework are always charged to the specific jobs in which the defects were originally discovered." Do you agree? Explain.

18-13 "Abnormal rework costs should be charged to a loss account, not to manufacturing overhead." Do you agree? Explain.

18-14 When is a company justified in inventorying scrap?

18-15 How do managers use information about scrap?

Exercises

18-16 **Normal and abnormal spoilage in units.** The following data, in physical units, describe a grinding process for January:

Work in process, beginning	19,000
Started during current period	150,000
To account for	169,000
Spoiled units	12,000
Good units completed and transferred out	132,000
Work in process, ending	25,000
Accounted for	169,000

Inspection occurs at the 100% completion stage. Normal spoilage is 5% of the good units passing inspection.

1. Compute the normal and abnormal spoilage in units. **Required**
2. Assume that the equivalent-unit cost of a spoiled unit is $10. Compute the amount of potential savings if all spoilage were eliminated, assuming that all other costs would be unaffected. Comment on your answer.

18-17 Weighted-average method, spoilage, equivalent units. (CMA, adapted) Consider the following data for November 2003 from Gray Manufacturing Company, which makes silk pennants and uses a process-costing system. All direct materials are added at the beginning of the process, and conversion costs are added evenly during the process. Spoilage is detected upon inspection at the completion of the process. Spoiled units are disposed of at zero net disposal value. Gray Manufacturing Company uses the weighted-average method of process costing.

	Physical Units (Pennants)	Direct Materials	Conversion Costs
Work in process, November 1[a]	1,000	$ 1,423	$ 1,110
Started in November 2003	?		
Good units completed and transferred out during November 2003	9,000		
Normal spoilage	100		
Abnormal spoilage	50		
Work in process, November 30[b]	2,000		
Costs added during November 2003		$12,180	$27,750

[a]Degree of completion: direct materials, 100%; conversion costs, 50%.
[b]Degree of completion: direct materials, 100%; conversion costs, 30%.

Compute equivalent units for direct materials and conversion costs. Show physical units in the first column of your schedule. **Required**

18-18 Weighted-average method, assigning costs (continuation of 18-17).
For the data in Exercise 18-17, calculate the cost per equivalent unit for direct materials and conversion costs, summarize total costs to account for, and assign these costs to units completed and transferred out (including normal spoilage), to abnormal spoilage, and to units in ending work in process. **Required**

18-19 FIFO method, spoilage, equivalent units. Refer to the information in Exercise 18-17. Suppose Gray Manufacturing Company uses the FIFO method of process costing instead of the weighted-average method.
Compute equivalent units for direct materials and conversion costs. Show physical units in the first column of your schedule. **Required**

18-20 FIFO method, assigning costs (continuation of 18-19).
For the data in Exercise 18-17, use the FIFO method to calculate the cost per equivalent unit for direct materials and conversion costs, summarize total costs to account for, and assign these costs to units completed and transferred out (including normal spoilage), to abnormal spoilage, and to units in ending work in process. **Required**

18-21 Weighted-average method, spoilage. Wang Manufacturing Company uses the weighted-average method of process costing. All direct materials are added at the beginning of the process, and conversion costs are added evenly during the process. Spoiled units are detected upon inspection at the end of the process and are disposed of at zero net disposal value. Summary data for March 2004 are

	Physical Units	Direct Materials	Conversion Costs
Work in process, March 1[a]	30,000	$240,000	$180,000
Started in March 2004	50,000		
Good units completed and transferred out during March 2004	40,000		
Normal spoilage	6,000		
Abnormal spoilage	2,000		
Work in process, March 31[b]	32,000		
Costs added during March 2004		$420,000	$583,200

[a]Degree of completion: direct materials, 100%; conversion costs, 60%.
[b]Degree of completion: direct materials, 100%; conversion costs, 75%.

1. For each cost category, compute equivalent units. Show physical units in the first column of your schedule. **Required**
2. For each cost category, calculate cost per equivalent unit.
3. Summarize total costs to account for, and assign these costs to units completed and transferred out (including normal spoilage), to abnormal spoilage, and to units in ending work in process.

18-22 FIFO method, spoilage. Refer to the information in 18-21.

Required Do Exercise 18-21 using the FIFO method. Note that you first need to calculate the equivalent units of work done in the current period (for direct materials and conversion costs) to complete beginning work in process, to start and complete new units, for normal and abnormal spoilage units, and to produce ending work in process.

18-23 Standard-costing method, spoilage. Refer to the information in Exercise 18-21. Suppose Wang determines standard costs of $8 per equivalent unit for direct materials and $10 per equivalent unit for conversion costs for both beginning work in process and work done in the current period.

Required Do Exercise 18-21 using the standard-costing method. Note that you first need to calculate the equivalent units of work done in the current period (for direct materials and conversion costs) to complete beginning work in process, to start and complete new units, for normal and abnormal spoilage units, and to produce ending work in process.

18-24 Weighted-average method, spoilage. Superchip specializes in the manufacture of microchips for aircraft. Direct materials are added at the start of the production process. Conversion costs are added evenly during the process. Some units of this product are spoiled as a result of defects not detectable before inspection of finished goods. Normally, the spoiled units are 15% of the good units transferred out. Spoiled units are disposed of at zero net disposal value. Superchip uses the weighted-average method of process costing.

Summary data for September 2003 are

	Physical Units (Microchips)	Direct Materials	Conversion Costs
Work in process, September 1[a]	400	$ 64,000	$ 10,200
Started in September 2003	1,700		
Good units completed and transferred out during September 2003	1,400		
Work in process, September 30[b]	300		
Costs added during September 2003		$378,000	$153,600

[a]Degree of completion: direct materials, 100%; conversion costs, 30%.

[b]Degree of completion: direct materials, 100%; conversion costs, 40%.

Required

1. For each cost category, compute equivalent units. Show physical units in the first column of your schedule.
2. For each cost category, calculate cost per equivalent unit.
3. Summarize total costs to account for, and assign these costs to units completed and transferred out (including normal spoilage), to abnormal spoilage, and to units in ending work in process.

Required **18-25 FIFO method, spoilage.** Refer to the information in Exercise 18-24.

Do Exercise 18-24 using the FIFO method of process costing.

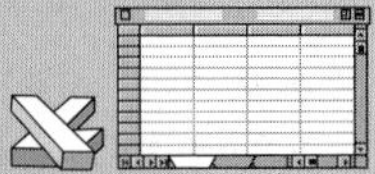

Excel Application For students who wish to practice their spreadsheet skills, the following is a step-by-step approach to creating an Excel spreadsheet to work this problem.

Step-by-Step

1. Open a new spreadsheet. At top, create an "Original Data" section for the Assembly Department data provided by Superchip. Enter the data for "Physical Units, Direct Materials, " and "Conversion Costs" in exactly the same format as above.

(Program your spreadsheet to perform all necessary calculations. Do not "hard-code" any amounts—such as equivalent-unit costs—requiring addition, subtraction, multiplication, or division operations.)

2. Skip two rows and create a section, "Problem 1," in the same format as in Panel A of Exhibit 18-3. Create columns for "Physical Units, Equivalent Units of Direct Materials" and "Equivalent Units of Conversion Costs" and rows for each of the items shown in Exhibit 18-3 (that is, the first row will be "Work in Process, Beginning" and the last row will be "Work Done in Current Period Only."). Use the data from your Original Data section to complete this section.
3. Skip two rows and create a section, "Problem 2," in the same format as Step 3 of Exhibit 18-3, Panel B. Create columns for "Total Production Costs," "Direct Materials" and "Conversion Costs."
4. Next, enter a calculation for the "Cost per Equivalent Unit of Work Done in the Current Period" for Direct Materials and Conversion Costs.
5. Skip two rows and create a section, "Problem 3," in the same format as Steps 4 and 5 of Exhibit 18-3, Panel B (using columns for "Total Production Costs," Direct Materials," and "Conversion Costs" created in Step 3).
6. Use the data you created in steps 1 to 4 to complete your "Problem 3" section.

7. *Verify the accuracy of your spreadsheet:* Go to your Original Data section and change Direct Material Costs Added for September 2003 from $378,000 to $400,000. If you programmed your spreadsheet correctly, the cost per equivalent unit of work done in the current period only for direct materials in problem 2 should change to $235.29.

18-26 Standard-costing method, spoilage. Refer to the information in Exercise 18-24. Suppose Superchip determines standard costs of $205 per equivalent unit for direct materials and $80 per (equivalent) unit for conversion costs for both beginning work in process and work done in the current period.

Required

Do Exercise 18-24 using the standard-costing method.

18-27 Spoilage and job costing. (L. Bamber) Bamber Kitchens produces a variety of items in accordance with special job orders from hospitals, plant cafeterias, and university dormitories. An order for 2,500 cases of mixed vegetables costs $6 per case: direct materials, $3; direct manufacturing labor, $2; and manufacturing overhead allocated, $1. The manufacturing overhead rate includes a provision for normal spoilage. Consider each requirement independently.

Required

1. Assume that a laborer dropped 200 cases. Suppose part of the 200 cases could be sold to a nearby prison for $200 cash. Prepare a journal entry to record this event. Calculate and explain briefly the unit cost of the remaining 2,300 cases.
2. Refer to the original data. Tasters at the company reject 200 of the 2,500 cases. The 200 cases are disposed of for $400. Assume that this rejection rate is considered normal. Prepare a journal entry to record this event, and calculate the unit cost if
   a. The rejection is attributable to exacting specifications of this particular job.
   b. The rejection is characteristic of the production process and is not attributable to this specific job.
   c. Are unit costs the same in requirements 2a and 2b? Explain your reasoning briefly.
3. Refer to the original data. Tasters rejected 200 cases that had insufficient salt. The product can be placed in a vat, salt can be added, and the product can be reprocessed into jars. This operation, which is considered normal, will cost $200. Prepare a journal entry to record this event and calculate the unit cost of all the cases if
   a. This additional cost was incurred because of the exacting specifications of this particular job.
   b. This additional cost occurs regularly because of difficulty in seasoning.
   c. Are unit costs the same in requirements 3a and 3b? Explain your reasoning briefly.

18-28 Reworked units, costs of rework. White Goods assembles washing machines at its Auburn plant. In February 2004, 60 tumbler units that cost $44 each (from a new supplier who subsequently went bankrupt) were defective and had to be disposed of at zero disposal value. White Goods was able to rework all 60 washing machines by substituting new tumbler units purchased from one of its existing suppliers. Each replacement tumbler cost $50.

Required

1. What alternative approaches are there to account for the material costs of reworked units?
2. Should White Goods use the $44 tumbler or $50 tumbler to calculate the costs of materials reworked? Explain.
3. What other costs might White Goods include in its analysis of the total costs of rework due to the tumbler units purchased from the (now) bankrupt supplier?

18-29 Scrap, job costing. The Mendoza Company has an extensive job-costing facility that uses a variety of metals. Consider each requirement independently.

Required

1. Job 372 uses a particular metal alloy that is not used for any other job. Assume that scrap is material in amount and sold quickly after it is produced. The scrap is sold for $490. Prepare the journal entry.
2. The scrap from Job 372 consists of a metal used by many other jobs. No record is maintained of the scrap generated by individual jobs. Assume that scrap is accounted for at the time of sale of scrap. Scrap totaling $4,000 is sold. Prepare two alternative journal entries that could be used to account for the sale of scrap.
3. Suppose the scrap generated in requirement 2 is returned to the storeroom for future use and a journal entry is made to record the scrap. A month later, the scrap is reused as direct material on a subsequent job. Prepare the journal entries to record these transactions.

Problems

18-30 Weighted-average method, spoilage. The Alston Company operates under the weighted-average method of process costing. It has two departments, Cleaning and Milling. For both departments, conversion costs are added evenly during the processes. Direct materials are added at the beginning of the process in the Cleaning Department, and additional direct materials are added at the end of the milling process. The costs and unit-production statistics for May follow. All unfinished work at the end of May is 25% complete as to conversion costs. The beginning inventory (May 1) was 80% complete as to conversion costs as of May 1. All completed work is transferred to the next department.

	Cleaning	Milling
Beginning Inventories		
Cleaning: $1,000 direct materials, $800 conversion costs	$1,800	
Milling: $6,450 transferred-in costs and $2,450 conversion costs		$8,900
Costs Added During Current Period		
Direct materials	$9,000	$640
Conversion costs	$8,000	$4,950
Physical Units		
Units in beginning inventory	1,000	3,000
Units started this month	9,000	7,400
Good units completed and transferred out	7,400	6,000
Normal spoilage	740[a]	300[b]
Abnormal spoilage	260	100

[a]Normal spoilage in Cleaning Department is 10% of good units completed and transferred out.
[b]Normal spoilage in Milling Department is 5% of good units completed and transferred out.

Additional Information

1. Spoilage is assumed to occur at the end of each of the two processes, when the units are inspected. Spoiled units are disposed of at zero net disposal value.
2. Assume that there is no shrinkage, evaporation, or abnormal spoilage other than that indicated in the information given.
3. Carry unit-cost calculations to four decimal places when necessary. Calculate final totals to the nearest dollar.

Required For the Cleaning Department, summarize total costs to account for, and assign these costs to units completed and transferred out (including normal spoilage), to abnormal spoilage, and to units in ending work in process. (Problem 18-32 explores additional facets of this problem.)

18-31 FIFO method, spoilage. Refer to the information in Problem 18-30.

Required Do Problem 18-30 using the FIFO method of process costing. (Problem 18-33 explores additional facets of this problem.)

18-32 Weighted-average method, Milling Department (continuation of 18-30). Refer to the information in Problem 18-30.

Required For the Milling Department, summarize total costs to account for, and assign these costs to units completed and transferred out (including normal spoilage), to abnormal spoilage, and to units in ending work in process.

18-33 FIFO method, Milling Department (continuation of 18-31). Refer to the information in Problem 18-30.

Required For the Milling Department, use the FIFO method to summarize total costs to account for, and assign these costs to units completed and transferred out (including normal spoilage), to abnormal spoilage, and to units in ending work in process.

18-34 Job-costing spoilage and scrap. (F. Mayne) Santa Cruz Metal Fabricators, Inc., has a large job, No. 2734, that calls for producing various ore bins, chutes, and metal boxes for enlarging a copper concentrator. The following charges were made to the job in November 2004:

Direct materials	$26,951
Direct manufacturing labor	15,076
Manufacturing overhead	7,538

The contract with the customer called for the total price to be based on a cost-plus approach. The contract defined cost to include direct materials, direct manufacturing labor costs, and manufacturing overhead to be allocated at 50% of direct manufacturing labor costs. The contract also provided that the total costs of all work spoiled were to be removed from the billable cost of the job and that the benefits from scrap sales were to reduce the billable cost of the job.

Required

1. In accordance with the stated terms of the contract, prepare journal entries for the following two items:
   a. A cutting error was made in production. The up-to-date job cost record for this batch of work showed materials of $650, direct manufacturing labor of $500, and allocated overhead of $250. Because fairly large pieces of metal were recoverable, the company believed that the scrap value was $600 and that the materials recovered could be used on other jobs. The spoiled work was sent to the warehouse.

b. Small pieces of metal cuttings and scrap in November 2004 amounted to $1,250, which was the price quoted by a scrap dealer. No journal entries were made with regard to the scrap until the price was quoted by the scrap dealer. The scrap dealer's offer was immediately accepted.

2. Consider normal and abnormal spoilage. Suppose the contract described above had contained the clause "a normal spoilage allowance of 1% of the job costs will be included in the billable costs of the job."
   a. Is this clause specific enough to define exactly how much spoilage is normal and how much is abnormal? Explain.
   b. Repeat requirement 1a with this "normal spoilage of 1%" clause in mind. You should be able to provide two slightly different journal entries.

18-35 Job costing, rework. Bristol Corporation manufactures two brands of motors, SM-5 and RW-8. The costs of manufacturing each SM-5 motor, excluding rework costs, are direct materials, $300; direct manufacturing labor, $60; and manufacturing overhead, $190. Defective units are sent to a separate rework area. Rework costs per SM-5 motor are direct materials, $60; direct manufacturing labor, $45; and manufacturing overhead, $75.

In February 2004, Bristol manufactured 1,000 SM-5 and 500 RW-8 motors. Eighty of the SM-5 motors and none of the RW-8 motors required rework. Bristol classifies 50 of the SM-5 motors reworked as normal rework caused by inherent problems in its production process that only coincidentally occurred during the production of SM-5. Hence the rework costs for these 50 SM-5 motors are normal rework costs not specifically attributable to the SM-5 product. Bristol classifies the remaining 30 units of SM-5 motors reworked as abnormal rework. Bristol allocates manufacturing overhead on the basis of machine-hours required to manufacture SM-5 and RW-8. Each SM-5 and RW-8 motor requires the same number of machine-hours.

Required

1. Prepare journal entries to record the accounting for the cost of the spoiled motors and for rework.
2. What were the total rework costs charged to SM-5 motors in February 2004?

18-36 Job costing, scrap. Wong Corporation makes two different types of hubcaps for cars: models HM3 and JB4. Circular pieces of metal are stamped out of steel sheets (leaving the edges as scrap), formed, and finished. The stamping operation is identical for both types of hubcaps. During March, Wong manufactured 20,000 units of HM3 and 10,000 units of JB4. In March, manufacturing costs per unit of HM3 and JB4 before accounting for the scrap were as follows:

	HM3	JB4
Direct materials	$10	$15
Direct manufacturing labor	3	4
Materials-related manufacturing overhead (materials handling, storage, etc.)	2	3
Other manufacturing overhead	6	8
Manufacturing costs per unit	$21	$30

Materials-related manufacturing costs are allocated to products at 20% of direct materials costs. Other manufacturing overhead is allocated to products at 200% of direct manufacturing labor costs. Because the same metal sheets are used to make both types of hubcaps, Wong maintains no records of the scrap generated by individual products. Scrap generated during manufacturing is accounted for at the time it is returned to the storeroom as an offset to materials-related manufacturing overhead. The value of scrap generated during March and returned to the storeroom was $7,000.

Required

1. Prepare a journal entry to summarize the accounting for scrap during March.
2. Suppose the scrap generated in March is sold in April for $7,000. Prepare a journal entry to account for this transaction.
3. Do you agree with the manufacturing costs per unit of $21 for HM3 and $30 for JB4? What adjustments, if any, would you make? Explain your answer briefly.

18-37 Physical units, inspection at various stages of completion. (Chapter Appendix) Normal spoilage is 6% of the good units passing inspection in a forging process. In March, a total of 10,000 units were spoiled. Other data include units started during March, 120,000; work in process, beginning, 14,000 units (20% completed for conversion costs); and work in process, ending, 11,000 units (70% completed for conversion costs).

Required

In columnar form, compute the normal and abnormal spoilage in units, assuming the inspection point is at (a) 15% stage of completion, (b) 40% stage of completion, and (c) 100% of stage of completion.

18-38 Weighted-average method, inspection at 80% completion. (A. Atkinson) (Chapter Appendix) Ottawa Manufacturing produces a plastic toy in a two-stage molding and finishing operation. The company uses the weighted-average method of process costing. During June, the following data were recorded for the Finishing Department:

Units of beginning inventory	10,000
Percentage completion of beginning units	25%
Cost of direct materials in beginning work in process	$0
Units started	70,000
Units completed	50,000
Units in ending inventory	20,000
Percentage completion of ending units	95%
Spoiled units	10,000
Costs added during current period:	
Direct materials	$655,200
Direct manufacturing labor	$635,600
Manufacturing overhead	$616,000
Work in process, beginning:	
Transferred-in costs	$82,900
Conversion costs	$42,000
Cost of units transferred in during current period	$647,500

Conversion costs are incurred evenly during the process. Direct materials costs are incurred when production is 90% complete. The inspection point is at the 80% stage of production. Normal spoilage is 10% of all good units that pass inspection. Spoiled units are disposed of at zero net disposal value.

Required For June, summarize total costs to account for, and assign these costs to units completed and transferred out (including normal spoilage), to abnormal spoilage, and to units in ending work in process.

18-39 Job costing, spoilage, ethics. (CMA, adapted) Richport Company manufactures products that often require specification changes or modifications to meet its customers' needs. Still, Richport has been able to establish a normal spoilage rate of 2.5% of normal input. Normal spoilage is recognized during the budgeting process and classified as a component of manufacturing overhead when determining the overhead rate.

Rose Duncan, one of Richport's inspection managers, obtains the following information for Job No. N1192-122, which was recently completed, just before the end of Richport's current accounting year. The units will be delivered early in the next accounting year. A total of 122,000 units were started, and 5,000 spoiled units were rejected at final inspection, yielding 117,000 good units. Rejected units were sold at $7 per unit. Duncan indicates that all rejects were related to this specific job.

The total costs for all 122,000 units of Job No. N1192-122 follow. The job has been completed, but the costs are yet to be transferred to Finished Goods.

Direct materials	$2,196,000
Direct manufacturing labor	1,830,000
Manufacturing overhead	2,928,000
Total manufacturing costs	$6,954,000

Required

1. Calculate the unit quantities of normal and abnormal spoilage.
2. Prepare the journal entry (or entries) to account for Job No. N1192-122, including spoilage, disposal of spoiled units, and transfer of costs to the Finished Goods account.
3. Richport Company has small profit margins and is anticipating very low operating income for the year. The controller, Thomas Rutherford, tells Martha Gonzales, the management accountant responsible for Job No. N1192-122, the following, "This was an unusual job. I think all 5,000 spoiled units should be considered normal." Gonzales knows that Richport's normal spoilage rate has been a good measure of normal spoilage levels on similar jobs in the past and that the spoilage levels for Job N1192-122 were much greater. She feels Rutherford made these comments because he wants to show higher operating income for the year.
   a. Prepare the journal entry (or entries), similar to the journal entry (or entries) prepared in requirement 2, to account for Job No. N1192-122 if all spoilage were considered normal. By how much will Richport's operating income be affected if all spoilage is considered normal?
   b. What should Martha Gonzales do?

Collaborative Learning Problem

18-40 FIFO method, spoilage, working backward. The Cooking Department of Spicer, Inc., uses a process-costing system. Direct materials are added at the beginning of the cooking process. Conversion costs are added evenly during the cooking process. Consider the following data for the Cooking Department for January:

	Physical Units	Direct Materials	Conversion Costs
Work in process, January 1[a]	10,000	$220,000	$30,000
Started in January	74,000		
Good units completed and transferred out during January	61,000		
Spoiled units	8,000		
Work in process, January 31	15,000		
Costs added during January		$1,480,000	$942,000
Cost per equivalent unit of work done in January		$20	$12

[a]Degree of completion: direct materials, 100%; conversion costs, 25%.

Spicer uses the FIFO method of process costing. Inspection occurs when production is 100% complete. Normal spoilage is 11% of good units completed and transferred out during the current period.

Required

1. For each cost category, compute equivalent units of work done in the current period (January).
2. For each cost category, compute separately the equivalent units of work done to complete beginning work-in-process inventory, to start and complete new units, for normal and abnormal spoilage, and to produce ending work-in-process inventory.
3. For each cost category, calculate the percentage of completion of ending work-in-process inventory.
4. Summarize total costs to account for, and assign these costs to units completed and transferred out (including normal spoilage), to abnormal spoilage, and to units in ending work in process.

CHAPTER 18 INTERNET EXERCISE

In addition to improving product quality and reducing costs, efforts to reduce spoilage, rework, and scrap can play an important role in improving the environment. Interface Inc., the world's largest commercial carpet manufacturer is a leader in sustainable manufacturing. To learn more about its war on waste and sustainable manufacturing program, go to www.prenhall.com/horngren, click on *Cost Accounting* 11th ed., and access the Internet exercise for Chapter 18.

CHAPTER 18 CASE

THE UNITED LIBBEY–NIPPON PLANT: Responsibility and Accounting for Scrap

Libbey-Owens-Ford Co., (L-O-F), is a major producer of glass products in the United States. Its newest plant, United L/N, is a joint venture between L-O-F and a Japanese company, Nippon Sheet Glass.

The management of the United L/N plant is evaluated on the basis of its ability to meet profit goals established by the board of directors. The production process is fully automated, requiring no human intervention from beginning to end. High quality and minimal scrap are expected to be the norm.

Steps in the fabrication process are **(1)** Direct material for the United L/N plant is raw glass obtained from the Rossford plant of L-O-F; the raw glass is cut to the basic shape of the "lite" it will become (a lite is a unit such as a rear window, called a "back lite," or a side window, a "side lite"); **(2)** the cut pattern is edged; **(3)** the edged pattern goes through a furnace where it is formed (bent to shape) and tempered; **(4)** the final product is inspected, packed, and shipped. A small team of operators monitors all steps in the process, performs regular preventive maintenance, changes the computer settings for different lites, and makes unscheduled repairs as needed.

United L/N's costs consist of short-term fixed operating costs, labor costs of the operating teams, and the price of raw glass from the Rossford plant based on the standard manufacturing cost of the raw glass. Because the entire process is automated, the feed rate is constant across all subprocesses for each individual lite being fabricated. The costing system accumulates conversion costs in one large cost pool, assigns conversion costs to units based on standard feed rates, and traces direct materials costs based on standard input prices. The system allows for standard levels of downtime and anticipated yields.

"We began experiencing problems with our yields at United L/N," commented Ken Marvin, planning and control director. "One problem was keeping the furnaces on the two production lines working efficiently. Each furnace was designed to work perfectly when a certain number of glass pieces were being fired, a certain number were on the threshold entering the furnace, and a certain number were leaving it. In our traditional plants, we stockpile pieces in front of the furnaces so that we can keep them filled to their optimal levels when forming and tempering. However, the United L/N production lines were designed such that inventories did not have to be maintained in front of the furnaces to keep the furnaces running efficiently at all times. Unfortunately, for reasons such as problems during pattern cutting or edging, there might be gaps in the lines as they enter the furnaces. Partly because of these gaps and the resulting inefficient furnace operations, we have had unacceptably high scrap rates. Of course, scrap decreases the plant's yield. Furthermore, the plant incurs the opportunity costs associated both with having an empty tempering furnace and with having to rest the furnace after it has been empty during periods of time when it was programmed to be full."

"From the United L/N point of view, the problem with scrap is caused by imperfections in the raw glass rather than by problems with the process," Marvin said. "The plant's management, therefore, believes that the scrap costs (the price paid for the raw glass plus United L/N's manufacturing costs) should be charged to the Rossford Plant. Rossford plant managers believe that the charge-back cost, even if appropriate (which remains an issue), is much too high. United L/N's costing system costs every piece as if it goes through the entire process even if scrap occurs, for example, at the pattern cutting or edging stages."

QUESTIONS

1. As a member of the Rossford team, what would be your position regarding the treatment of the United L/N scrap cost?
2. As a member of the United L/N team, what would be your position regarding the treatment of the United L/N scrap?
3. How could United L/N's management determine the specific causes of defects (for example, bad glass or defective cutting, edging, or tempering operations) in units that are scrapped? What are the implications for the process-costing system?
4. What could be done to solve the problems of furnace inefficiency and ineffectiveness?

CHAPTER 19

Quality, Time, and the Theory of Constraints

LEARNING OBJECTIVES

1. Explain the four cost categories in a costs-of-quality program
2. Use three methods to identify quality problems
3. Identify the relevant costs and benefits of quality improvements
4. Provide examples of nonfinancial quality measures of customer satisfaction and internal performance
5. Describe the benefits of financial and nonfinancial measures of quality
6. Describe customer-response time and explain why delays happen and their costs
7. Apply the three measures in the theory of constraints
8. Manage bottlenecks

www.prenhall.com/horngren

"Quality"—achieving it is hard work. Companies the world over say they strive to make "quality" products or provide "quality" services. Some companies deliver a higher level of quality than others. The Ritz-Carlton Hotel is the first hotel company to win the Malcolm Baldridge National Quality Award. The Ritz-Carlton's ongoing commitment to furthering its quality is evident in every department, from housekeeping to room service. Inefficiencies, breakdowns, and variations from expected levels are tracked. Anything that misses target service standards is analyzed and discussed at weekly staff meetings to be sure it doesn't happen again. All staff, from the general manager to the newest front-desk clerk, realize that a failure to meet a guest's quality expectations could mean the guest will check out, not come back, and inform others of his or her dissatifaction.

Customers are becoming more intolerant of poor quality and long delivery times. To satisfy customers, managers need to find cost-effective ways to continuously improve the quality of their products and to shorten delivery times. This chapter describes how managers can identify what constrains an organization from producing higher-quality products and what gets in the way of making products faster, as well as how to remove these constraints. We'll explain how management accountants can help managers to take strategic initiatives toward improving quality and reducing delays and to make decisions when faced with multiple constraints.

QUALITY AS A COMPETITIVE TOOL

The American Society for Quality Control defines *quality* as the total features and characteristics of a product or a service made or performed according to specifications to satisfy customers at the time of purchase and during use. Many companies throughout the world—for example, Hewlett-Packard and Ford Motor Company in the United States and Canada, British Telecom in the United Kingdom, Fujitsu and Toyota in Japan, Crysel in Mexico, and Samsung in South Korea—have emphasized quality as an important strategic dimension. That's because a quality focus reduces costs and increases customer satisfaction. Several high-profile awards—the Malcolm Baldridge Quality Award in the United States, the Deming Prize in Japan, and the Premio Nacional de Calidad in Mexico—are given to companies that have produced high-quality products.

International quality standards have emerged. ISO 9000, developed by the International Organization for Standardization, is a set of five international standards for quality management adopted by more than 85 countries. ISO 9000 enables companies to effectively document and certify the elements of their production processes that lead to quality. To ensure that their suppliers deliver high-quality products at competitive costs, companies such as DuPont and General Electric require their suppliers to obtain ISO 9000 certification. Documenting evidence of quality through ISO 9000 has become a condition for competing in the global marketplace.

Focusing on the quality of a product will generally build expertise in producing it, lower costs of making it, create higher satisfaction for customers using it, and generate higher future revenues for the company selling it. Dell Computer's quality initiatives increased customer satisfaction and fueled its 5,740% increase in revenues, 7,963% increase in profits, and 7,762% increase in stock price for the 10 years ending September 2001. In some cases, the benefit of better quality, as in memory chips, is in preserving revenues, not generating higher revenues. A company that does not invest in quality improvement while competitors are doing so will likely suffer a decline in its market share, revenues, and profits.

As corporations' responsibilities toward the environment grow, managers are applying the ideas of quality management to find cost-effective ways to reduce the environmental and economic costs of air pollution, waste water, oil spills, and hazardous waste disposal. Under the U.S. Clean Air Act, costs of environmental damage can be extremely high. Exxon paid $125 million in fines and restitution on top of $1 billion in civil payments for the Exxon Valdez oil spill, which harmed the Alaskan coast. An environmental management standard, ISO 14000, encourages organizations to pursue environmental goals vigorously by developing (1) environmental management systems to reduce environmental costs and (2) environmental auditing and performance-evaluation systems to review and provide feedback on environmental goals.

We focus on two basic aspects of quality: *quality of design* and *conformance quality*.

Quality of design refers to how closely the characteristics of a product or service meet the needs and wants of customers. Suppose customers of photocopying machines want copiers that combine copying, faxing, scanning, and electronic printing. Photocopying machines that fail to meet these customer needs fail in the quality of their designs. If customers of a bank want online banking services, then not providing these services would be a quality-of-design failure.

Conformance quality refers to the performance of a product or service relative to its design and product specifications. For example, if a photocopying machine mishandles paper or breaks down, it fails to satisfy conformance quality. A bank that deposits a customer's check into the wrong account fails on conformance quality.

Even if a product meets manufacturing specifications (good conformance quality), it can still be of poor overall quality if it fails to satisfy customer needs and wants (poor design quality).

To ensure that performance will achieve customer satisfaction, companies must first design products to satisfy customers through quality of design. They must then meet design specifications through conformance quality. The following diagram illustrates that actual performance can fall short of customer satisfaction because of quality-of-design failure and because of conformance-quality failure.

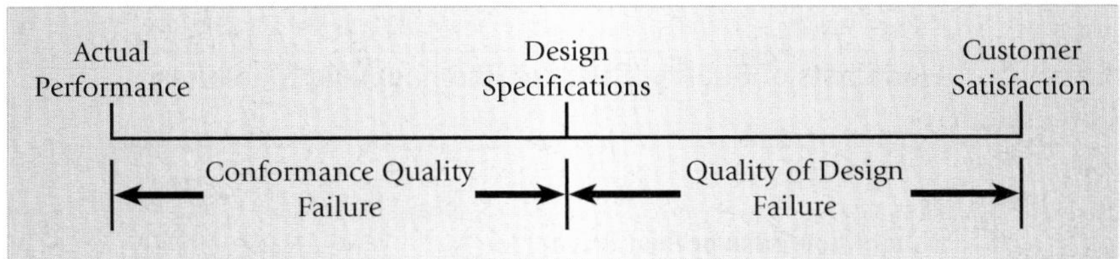

What we have to determine is how to measure the costs of quality. Consider first the case of conformance quality; it is easier to explain.

COSTS OF QUALITY

1 Explain the four cost categories in a costs-of-quality program

...prevention, appraisal, internal failure, and external failure

The **costs of quality (COQ)** refer to the costs incurred to prevent, or the costs arising as a result of, producing a low-quality product. Costs of quality are classified into four categories; examples for each category are listed in Exhibit 19-1.

1. **Prevention costs**—costs incurred to preclude the production of products that do not conform to specifications.
2. **Appraisal costs**—costs incurred to detect which of the individual units of products do not conform to specifications.
3. **Internal failure costs**—costs incurred on a defective product before it is shipped to customers.
4. **External failure costs**—costs incurred on a defective product after it is shipped to customers.

EXHIBIT 19-1

Items Pertaining to Costs-of-Quality Reports

Prevention Costs	Appraisal Costs	Internal Failure Costs	External Failure Costs
Design engineering Process engineering Supplier evaluations Preventive equipment maintenance Quality training New materials used to manufacture products	Inspection Online product manufacturing and process inspection Product testing	Spoilage Rework Scrap Breakdown maintenance Manufacturing/process engineering on internal failure	Customer support Manufacturing/process engineering for external failures Warranty repair costs Liability claims

The items in Exhibit 19-1 come from all business functions of the value chain, and they are broader than the internal failure costs of spoilage, rework, and scrap in manufacturing considered in Chapter 18.

An important role of management accounting is to prepare costs-of-quality (COQ) reports for managers (see Exhibit 19-2).

We illustrate the issues in managing quality—computing the costs of quality, identifying quality problems, and taking actions to improve quality—using Photon Corporation. Photon makes many products. We'll focus on Photon's photocopying machines, which earned an operating income of $24 million on revenues of $300 million (from sales of 20,000 copiers) in 2003. Photon determines the costs of quality of its photocopying machines by adapting the seven-step activity-based costing approach described in Chapter 5.

Step 1: **Identify the Chosen Product.** The product is the 20,000 photocopying machines that Photon made and sold. Photon's goal is to calculate the total costs of quality of these machines.

In this example, all costs of quality—prevention, appraisal, internal failure, and external failure—are indirect costs of the photocopying machines.

Step 2: **Identify the Product's Direct Costs of Quality.** The photocopying machines have no direct costs of quality.

Step 3: **Select the Cost-Allocation Bases to Use for Allocating Indirect Costs of Quality to the Product.** Column 1 of Exhibit 19-2, Panel A, classifies activities that result in prevention, appraisal, internal failure, and external failure costs, and indicates in parentheses the business functions of the value chain in which these costs

EXHIBIT 19-2 **Analysis of Activity-Based Costs of Quality (COQ) for Photocopying Machines at Photon Corporation**

PANEL A: COQ REPORT

Cost of Quality and Value-Chain Category (1)	Allocation Base or Cost Driver: Rate[a] (2)	Allocation Base or Cost Driver: Quantity (3)	Total Costs (4) = (2) × (3)	Percentage of Revenues (5) = (4) ÷ $300,000,000
Prevention costs				
Design engineering (R&D/Design)	$80 per hour	40,000 hours	$ 3,200,000	1.1%
Process engineering (R&D)/Design)	$60 per hour	45,000 hours	2,700,000	0.9
Total prevention costs			5,900,000	2.0
Appraisal costs				
Inspection (Manufacturing)	$40 per hour	240,000 hours	9,600,000	3.2
Total appraisal costs			9,600,000	3.2
Internal failure costs				
Rework (Manufacturing)	$100 per hour	100,000 hours	10,000,000	3.3
Total internal failure costs			10,000,000	3.3
External failure costs				
Customer support (Marketing)	$50 per hour	12,000 hours	600,000	0.2
Transportation (Distribution)	$240 per load	3,000 loads	720,000	0.2
Warranty repair (Customer service)	$110 per hour	120,000 hours	13,200,000	4.4
Total external failure costs			14,520,000	4.8
Total costs of quality			$40,020,000	13.3%

[a]Amounts assumed.

PANEL B: OPPORTUNITY COST ANALYSIS

Costs-of-Quality Category (1)	Total Estimated Contribution Margin Lost (2)	Percentage of Sales (3) = (2) ÷ $300,000,000
External failure costs		
Estimated forgone contribution margin and income on lost sales	$12,000,000[b]	4.0%
Total external failure costs	$12,000,000	4.0%

[b]Calculated as total revenues minus all variable costs (whether output-unit, batch, product-sustaining, or facility-sustaining) on lost sales in 2003. If poor quality causes Photon to lose sales in subsequent years as well, the opportunity costs will be even larger.

occur. For example, the inspection activity results in appraisal costs and occurs in the manufacturing function. Photon identifies the number of inspection-hours as the cost-allocation base for the inspection activity. To avoid details not needed to explain the concepts here, we do not provide information on the total quantities of each cost-allocation base.

Step 4: Identify the Indirect Costs of Quality Associated with Each Cost-Allocation Base. These are the total costs (variable and fixed) incurred on each of the costs-of-quality activities, such as inspections, in all of Photon's operations. To avoid details not needed to understand the points described here, we do not provide information about these total costs.

Step 5: Compute the Rate per Unit of Each Cost-Allocation Base Used to Allocate Indirect Costs of Quality to the Product. For each activity, the total costs (calculated in step 4) are divided by the total quantity of the cost-allocation base (calculated in step 3) to compute the rate per unit of each cost-allocation base. Column 2 of Exhibit 19-2, Panel A, shows these rates (without supporting calculations), including the $40 per hour for the inspection activity.

Step 6: Compute the Indirect Costs of Quality Allocated to the Product. Photon first determines the quantities of each of the cost-allocation bases used by the photocopying machines (column 3 of Panel A). For example, photocopying machines use 240,000 inspection-hours. The indirect costs of quality of the photocopying machines, shown in column 4, Panel A, equal the total quantity of the cost-allocation base used by the photocopying machines for each activity multiplied by the cost-allocation rate from step 5. For example, quality-related inspection costs for the photocopying machines are $9,600,000 ($40 per hour × 240,000 inspection-hours).

Step 7: Compute the Total Costs of Quality by Adding All Direct and Indirect Costs of Quality Assigned to the Product. Photon's total cost of quality in the COQ report for photocopying machines is $40.02 million, or 13.3% of current revenues, as you see at the bottom of the fourth and fifth columns in Panel A.

The total costs of quality typically shown in COQ reports exclude costs-of-quality items, such as the opportunity cost of the contribution margin and income forgone from lost sales, lost production, or lower prices as a result of poor quality. Why are opportunity costs excluded? Because they are not recorded in financial accounting systems and are difficult to estimate. Photon's Market Research Department estimates lost sales of 2,000 photocopying machines in 2003 because of external failures. The forgone contribution margin and operating income of $12 million (Exhibit 19-2, Panel B) measures the financial costs of estimated sales lost because of quality problems. Total costs of quality, including opportunity costs, equal $52.02 million ($40.02 million in Panel A + $12 million in Panel B), or 17.3% of current revenues. Opportunity costs account for 23% ($12 million ÷ $52.02 million) of Photon's total costs of quality.

Spoilage and rework in Chapter 18 covered only appraisal costs and internal failure costs. You can see in Exhibit 19-2 that these costs are just the tip of the iceberg—38% ($19.60 ÷ $52.02)—of Photon's total COQ, including the opportunity costs in Panel B.

The COQ report and the opportunity-cost analysis highlight Photon's high internal and external failure costs. To reduce costs of quality, Photon must identify and reduce failures caused by quality problems.

TECHNIQUES USED TO ANALYZE QUALITY PROBLEMS

2 Use three methods to identify quality problems

...control charts, Pareto diagrams, and cause-and-effect diagrams

Three techniques for identifying and analyzing quality problems are control charts, Pareto diagrams, and cause-and-effect diagrams.

Control Charts

Statistical quality control (SQC), also called statistical process control (SPC), is a formal means of distinguishing between random and nonrandom variations in an operating process. Random variations occur, for example, when power surges or chance fluctuations in temperature cause defective products to be produced in a chemical process. Nonrandom variations occur when defective products are produced as a result of a systematic problem such as inaccurate temperature readings. A **control chart,** one of the tools in SQC, is a graph of a series of successive observations of a particular step, procedure, or operation taken at

EXHIBIT 19-3 **Statistical Quality Control Charts: Daily Defect Rate for Photocopying Machines at the Photon Corporation**

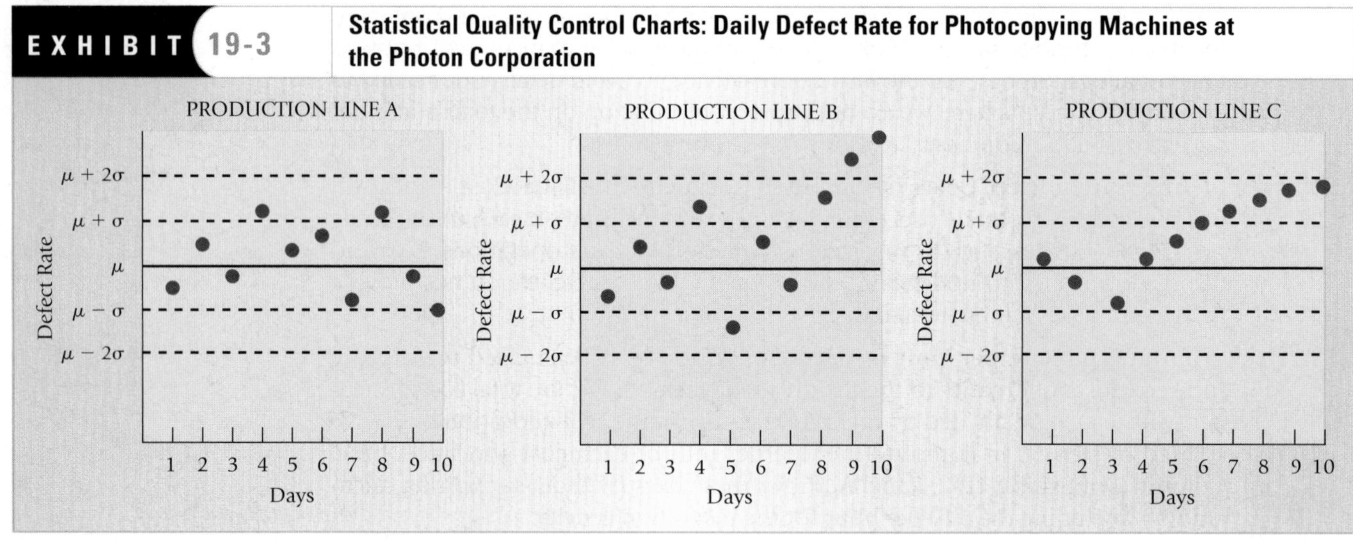

regular intervals of time. Each observation is plotted relative to specified ranges that represent the limits within which the observations are expected to fall. Only those observations outside the control limits are ordinarily regarded as nonrandom and worth investigating.

The arithmetic mean is the sum of the observations divided by the number of observations. The standard deviation measures how much the observations differ from the mean. If the observations are clustered around the mean, the standard deviation is small. If the observations are widely dispersed around the mean, the standard deviation is large.

If you have had a statistics course, you will understand the meaning of the 2-sigma rule in the control charts. If the defect rates are normally distributed and the production process is "in control," then a defect rate of more than 2-sigma from the mean is due to random variations only about 5% of the time.

Exhibit 19-3 presents control charts for the daily defect rates observed at Photon's three photocopying machine production lines. Defect rates in the prior 60 days for each production line were assumed to provide a good basis from which to calculate the distribution of daily defect rates. The arithmetic mean (μ, read mu) and standard deviation (σ, read sigma) are the two parameters of the distribution that are used in the control charts in Exhibit 19-3. On the basis of experience, the company decides that any observation outside the $\mu \pm 2\sigma$ range should be investigated.

For production line A, all observations are within the range of $\pm 2\sigma$ from the mean, so management believes no investigation is necessary. For production line B, the last two observations signal that an out-of-control occurrence is highly likely. Given the $\pm 2\sigma$ rule, both observations would be investigated. Production line C illustrates a process that would not prompt an investigation under the $\pm 2\sigma$ rule but that may well be out of control. That's because the last eight observations show a clear direction, and the last six are getting further and further away from the mean. Statistical procedures have been developed using the trend as well as the variation to evaluate whether a process is out of control.

Pareto Diagrams

Observations outside control limits serve as inputs for *Pareto diagrams*. A **Pareto diagram** is a chart that indicates how frequently each type of defect occurs, ordered from the most

EXHIBIT 19-4

Pareto Diagram for Photocopying Machines at Photon Corporation

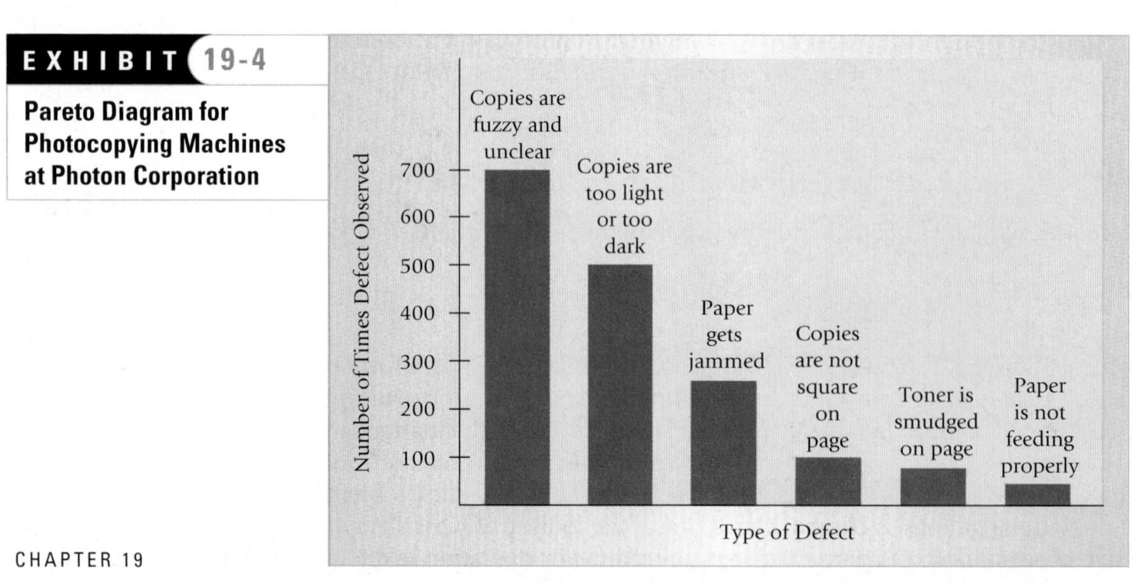

frequent to the least frequent. Exhibit 19-4 presents a Pareto diagram of quality problems with respect to Photon's photocopying machines. Fuzzy and unclear copies are the most frequently recurring problem.

Fuzzy and unclear copies result in high rework costs. Sometimes fuzzy and unclear copies occur at customer sites and result in high warranty and repair costs.

Cause-and-Effect Diagrams

The most frequently recurring and costly problems identified by the Pareto diagram are analyzed using *cause-and-effect diagrams*. A **cause-and-effect diagram** identifies potential causes of defects. Exhibit 19-5 presents the cause-and-effect diagram describing potential reasons why fuzzy and unclear copies occur. The exhibit identifies four categories of potential causes of failure: human factors, methods and design factors, machine-related factors, and materials and components factors. As additional arrows are added providing more-detailed reasons for each cause of defect, this diagram begins to resemble the bone structure of a fish (hence, cause-and-effect diagrams are also called *fishbone diagrams*).[1] The analysis of quality problems is facilitated by automated equipment and computers recording the number and types of defects and the operating conditions that existed at the time the defects occurred. Using these inputs, computer programs simultaneously prepare the control charts, Pareto diagrams, and fishbone diagrams.

Combinations of methods can help identify quality problems. Photon's management first used the Pareto diagram to identify the most frequently encountered defect (fuzzy and unclear copies) and then used the cause-and-effect diagram to identify specific causes of the defect.

RELEVANT COSTS AND BENEFITS OF QUALITY IMPROVEMENT

3 Identify the relevant costs

...incremental costs

and benefits of quality improvements

...cost savings and increase in contribution margin

Analysis of Photon's cause-and-effect diagram reveals that the steel frame (or chassis) of the copier is often mishandled as it travels from a supplier's warehouse to Photon's plant. The frame must be produced to within very precise specifications, or else copier components (such as drums, mirrors, and lenses) will not fit exactly on the frame. Mishandling during transport causes the frame to vary from manufacturing specifications, causing the copier to produce fuzzy and unclear copies.

EXHIBIT 19-5 Cause-and-Effect Diagram for Fuzzy and Unclear Photocopies at Photon Corporation

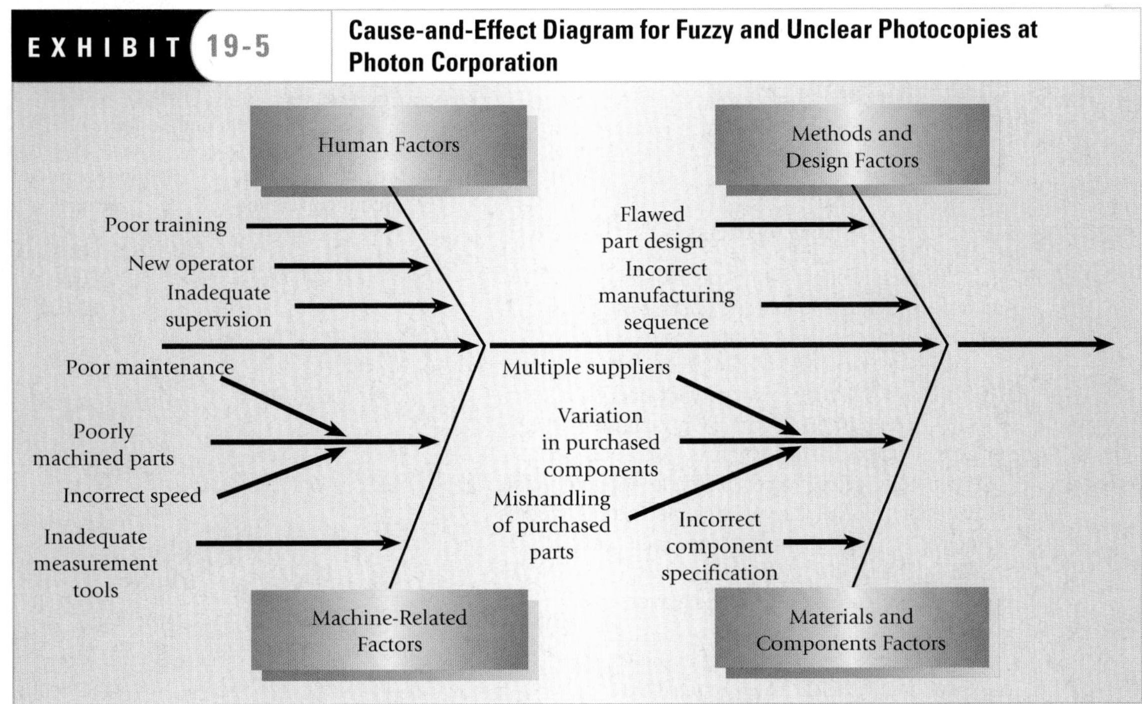

[1]Managers in U.S. electronics companies consider the following factors (ranked in order of importance with 1 = most important) as contributing to improvements in quality: (1) better product design, (2) improved process design, (3) improved training of operators, (4) improved products from suppliers, and (5) investments in technology and equipment. See G. Foster and L. Sjoblom, "Survey of Quality Practices in the U.S. Electronics Industry," *Journal of Management Accounting Research* 8 (1996), 55–86.

The team of engineers working to solve this problem offers two solutions: (1) further inspect the frames immediately upon delivery or (2) redesign and strengthen the frames and the containers used to transport them to better withstand mishandling during transportation.

To evaluate each alternative versus the status quo, management identifies the relevant costs and benefits for each solution. Remember, relevant-cost and relevant-revenue analysis ignores allocated amounts, as explained in Chapter 11. The key question is *how total costs and total revenues will change under each solution.*

Photon considers only a one-year time horizon over which to analyze each solution because it plans to introduce a completely new line of copiers at the end of the year. The new line is so different that the choice of either the inspection or the redesign alternative will have no effect on the sales of copiers in future years.

Exhibit 19-6 shows the relevant costs and benefits for each alternative.

1. *Estimated incremental costs:* $400,000 for the inspection alternative; $460,000 for the redesign alternative.

2. *Cost savings from less rework, customer support, and repairs.* Exhibit 19-6, column 1, shows that reducing rework results in savings of $40 per hour. Exhibit 19-2, Panel A, column 2, shows total rework cost per hour of $100. Why the difference? Because Photon concludes that as it improves quality, it will only save the $40 variable cost per rework-hour, not the $60 fixed cost per rework-hour.

Exhibit 19-6, column 2, shows the inspection alternative is expected to eliminate 24,000 rework-hours and to save variable costs of $960,000 ($40 per hour × 24,000 rework-hours). The redesign alternative is expected to eliminate 32,000 rework-hours and to save variable costs of $1,280,000 ($40 per rework-hour × 32,000 rework-hours). Exhibit 19-6 also shows expected variable-cost savings in customer support, transportation, and warranty repair for the two alternatives.

3. *Increased contribution margin from higher sales as a result of building a reputation for quality and performance*: $1,500,000 for 250 copiers under the inspection alternative and $1,800,000 for 300 copiers under the redesign alternative. This benefit is important. Quality improvements cannot always be translated into lower costs. For example, laying off workers to reduce costs would adversely affect the morale of employees and hurt future quality initiatives. Management should always look for opportunities to generate higher revenues from quality improvements.

EXHIBIT 19-6

Estimated Effect of Quality-Improvement Actions on Costs of Quality for Photocopying Machines at Photon Corporation

The largest single COQ item in this exhibit is contribution margin from additional sales generated by improved quality.

	Relevant Costs and Benefits of	
Relevant Items	**Further Inspecting Incoming Frames (2)**	**Redesigning Frames (3)**
Additional design engineering costs	—	$ 160,000
Additional process engineering costs	—	300,000
Additional inspection and testing costs	$ 400,000	—
Saving in rework costs		
$40 per hour × 24,000 fewer rework-hours	(960,000)	—
$40 per hour × 32,000 fewer rework-hours		(1,280,000)
Savings in customer-support costs		
$20 per hour × 2,000 fewer customer-support hours	(40,000)	
$20 per hour × 2,800 fewer customer-support hours		(56,000)
Savings in transportation costs for repair parts		
$180 per load × 500 fewer loads moved	(90,000)	
$180 per load × 700 fewer loads moved		(126,000)
Savings in warranty repair costs		
$45 per hour × 20,000 fewer repair-hours	(900,000)	
$45 per hour × 28,000 fewer repair-hours		(1,260,000)
Total contribution margin from sales of		
250 additional copiers	(1,500,000)	
300 additional copiers		(1,800,000)
Net cost savings and additional contribution margin	$(3,090,000)	$(4,062,000)
Difference in favor of redesigning frame	$972,000	

Exhibit 19-6 shows that both the inspection and the redesign alternatives yield net benefits relative to the status quo. However, the net benefits from the redesign alternative are expected to be $972,000 greater.

Photon can use its COQ report to examine how incurring quality-related costs in one category affects quality-related costs in other catagories. In our example, redesigning the frame increases prevention costs (design and process engineering), decreases internal failure costs (rework), and decreases external failure costs (warranty repairs). COQ reports give more insight when managers compare trends over time. In successful quality programs, the costs of quality as a percentage of revenues and the sum of internal and external failure costs as a percentage of total costs of quality decrease over time. Many companies—for example, Compaq and Toyota—believe they should eliminate all failure costs and have zero defects.

COSTS OF DESIGN QUALITY

So far we have focused on measuring the cost of conformance quality and the methods, including design modifications, that companies use to reduce defects and costs of quality. In addition to conformance quality, companies must also pay attention to quality of design by designing products that satisfy customer needs—for example, by producing photocopying machines that combine faxing, scanning, and electronic printing, if that is what customers desire. These costs are mainly in the form of the opportunity cost of sales lost from not producing a product that customers want. Many of the costs of design quality are very difficult to measure objectively. For this reason, most companies do not measure the financial costs of design quality. Instead, companies rely on nonfinancial measures.

NONFINANCIAL MEASURES OF QUALITY AND CUSTOMER SATISFACTION

4 Provide examples of nonfinancial quality measures of customer satisfaction

...customer complaints, on-time delivery

and internal performance

...product defects, process yield

To evaluate how well their actual performance satisfies customer needs and wants (see diagram, p. 655), companies supplement financial measures with nonfinancial measures of quality of design and conformance quality. Nonfinancial measures indicate the future needs and preferences of customers, as well as specific areas that need improvement. In this sense, nonfinancial measures of quality are leading indicators of future long-run performance, unlike financial measures of quality that focus on the short run. Management accountants usually maintain and present these nonfinancial measures.

We focus first on nonfinancial measures of customer satisfaction, including nonfinancial measures of quality of design and external failure, and then we look at internal performance measures, including nonfinancial measures of prevention, appraisal, and internal failure.

Nonfinancial Measures of Customer Satisfaction

To evaluate how well they are doing, companies such as Dell (see Concepts in Action, p. 662), Federal Express, and General Electric measure customer satisfaction over time. Some measures are

- Market research information on customer preferences and customer satisfaction with specific product features
- Number of defective units shipped to customers as a percentage of total units shipped
- Number of customer complaints (Companies estimate that for every customer who actually complains, there are 10 to 20 others who have had bad experiences with the product or service but did not complain.)
- Percentage of products that fail soon or often
- Delivery delays (the difference between the scheduled delivery date and the date requested by the customer)
- On-time delivery rate (the percentage of shipments made on or before the scheduled delivery date)

Management monitors whether these numbers improve or deteriorate over time. If improvement occurs, management can be more confident about operating income being strong in future years. If these numbers deteriorate, operating income will likely be weak in the future.

In addition to these routine nonfinancial measures, many companies such as DaimlerChrysler and Toyota conduct surveys to measure customer satisfaction. Surveys provide a deeper perspective into customer experiences and preferences about products. They also provide a glimpse of features that customers would like in future products.

Nonfinancial Measures of Internal Performance

To satisfy their customers, managers must constantly improve the quality of work done inside their company. Most companies use nonfinancial measures of internal quality to supplement financial measures, such as prevention, appraisal, and internal failure costs. For example, Analog Devices, a semiconductor manufacturer, follows trends in these gauges of quality:

- Number of defects for each product line
- Process yield (ratio of good output to total output)
- Employee turnover (ratio of number of employees who leave the company to the average total number of employees)

CONCEPTS IN ACTION

Dell Computer's QUEST

What was behind Dell Computer's phenomenal 7,762% increase in stock price, 5,740% growth in revenues, and 7,963% increase in profits for the 10 years ending September 2001? Certainly not a high gross margin; Dell's was a modest 22% of revenues. What was responsible for those numbers is QUEST—Quality Underlies Every Single Task—an employee-oriented initiative of total quality management. QUEST is the bedrock of Dell's execution and innovation, leading to superb product quality, speedy manufacturing, and responsive postsales customer service.

Under the QUEST approach, workers are organized into teams of salespersons, assemblers, testers, technicians, shippers, and maintenance personnel. A QUEST team starts to work on manufacturing a computer only after a salesperson has received an order. Only one person, the assembler, builds the system from start to finish. Testers rigorously test the product for reliability and performance, often for more than 24 hours. Technicians then install customized and proprietary software, and shippers ship the product directly to customers. Dell does not sell its computers through retailers.

Dell's success is built around customer satisfaction. *Fortune* magazine ranked Dell as one of the top two computer manufacturers in customer satisfaction. Customers cited hardware quality and reliability, performance and speed, and service and support as the reasons for their satisfaction. How does Dell achieve such high customer-satisfaction ratings?

- *By helping customers to configure their products to meet customers' requirements and specifications.* As a result, all hardware and software are designed to be compatible with and seamlessly integrated into existing systems.
- *By manufacturing a high-quality product.* During the manufacturing process, operators receive immediate feedback about the product. If the product fails a test, operators troubleshoot to correct the problem. Dell takes no chances with respect to performance in its testing procedures. Its notebook computers, for example, must survive intense shaking on a vibrating table, exposure to extreme temperatures, and a series of drop tests.
- *By providing excellent technical support after delivering products to its customers.* When customers call with questions, the technical support staff responds promptly with high-quality advice.

Source: Adapted from K. Chambers, "Inside the Cell," *Dell Insider* (May–June 1997); and Dell Computer Annual Report, 2000. For more information, visit the Dell Computer Web site at www.dell.com.

Many companies go further and try to understand the factors that lead to better internal quality (see Chapter 13, p. 447–453, on the balanced scorecard). For example, some companies measure employee empowerment and employee satisfaction as drivers of internal quality.

- A measure of employee empowerment is the ratio of the number of processes in which employees have the right to make decisions without consulting supervisors to the total number of processes.
- A measure of employee satisfaction is the ratio of employees indicating high satisfaction ratings to the total number of employees surveyed.

For a single reporting period, nonfinancial measures of quality may not mean much, but they are informative when managers examine trends over time as they seek to improve performance. To provide information on trends, the management accountant must review the nonfinancial measures for accuracy and consistency.

EVALUATING QUALITY PERFORMANCE

5 Describe the benefits of financial measures of quality
...evaluate trade-offs among different categories of costs of quality
and nonfinancial measures of quality
...identify problem areas, highlight leading indicators of future performance

Financial and nonfinancial measures of quality have different advantages.

Advantages of COQ Measures

1. Consistent with the attention-directing role of management accounting, COQ focuses managers' attention on the costs of poor quality.
2. Financial COQ measures assist in problem solving by comparing costs and benefits of different quality-improvement programs and setting priorities for cost reduction.
3. COQ provides a single, summary measure of quality performance for evaluating trade-offs among prevention costs, appraisal costs, internal failure costs, and external failure costs.

Advantages of Nonfinancial Measures of Quality

1. Nonfinancial measures of quality are often easy to quantify and understand.
2. Nonfinancial measures direct attention to physical processes, such as process yield, hence focusing attention on the precise problem areas that need improvement.
3. Nonfinancial measures, such as number of defects, provide immediate short-run feedback on whether quality-improvement efforts have succeeded.
4. Nonfinancial measures, such as measures of customer satisfaction, are useful indicators of future long-run performance.

COQ measures and nonfinancial measures supplement each other. Most organizations use both types of measures to gauge quality performance. Some corporations, such as McDonald's, evaluate employees and individual franchisees on multiple measures of quality and customer satisfaction. A mystery shopper—an outside party contracted by McDonald's to evaluate restaurant performance—scores each restaurant on quality, cleanliness, and service. Each restaurant's performance on these dimensions is evaluated over time and against other restaurants.

TIME AS A COMPETITIVE TOOL

Companies increasingly view time as a driver of strategy.[2] Doing necessary things correctly and quickly helps increase revenues and decrease costs. A moving company such as United Van Lines will be able to generate more revenues if it can move goods in good condition from one place to another faster and on time. Companies such as AT&T, General Electric, and Wal-Mart attribute not only higher revenues but also lower costs to doing things faster and on time. They cite, for example, the need to carry less inventory because of their ability to respond rapidly to customer demands.

[2]See G. Stalk and T. Hout, *Competing Against Time* (New York: Free Press, 1990).

EXHIBIT 19-7

Components of Customer-Response Time

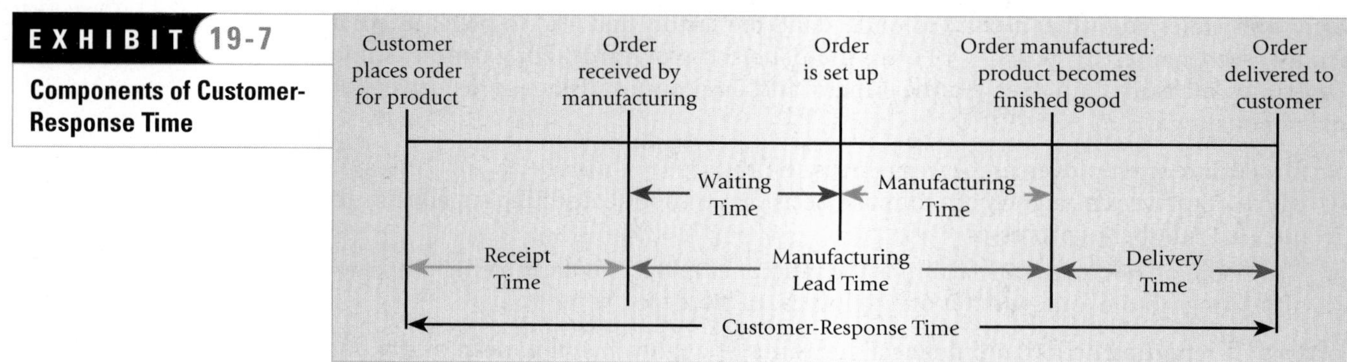

Companies need to measure time to manage it properly. In this chapter, we focus on *operational measures of time,* which reveal how quickly companies respond to customers' demands for their products and services and their reliability in meeting scheduled delivery dates. Two common operational measures of time are customer-response time and on-time performance.

Customer-Response Time

6 Describe customer-response time

...time between customer order and product delivery

and explain why delays happen and their costs

...uncertainty about customer orders and limited capacity lead to lower revenues and higher inventory carrying costs

Customer-response time is the duration from the time a customer places an order for a product or service to the time the product or service is delivered to the customer. Fast responses to customers are of strategic importance in industries such as construction, banking, car rental, and fast food. Some companies, such as Boeing, have to pay penalties to compensate their airline customers for lost revenues and profits (from being unable to schedule flights) as a result of delays in delivering airplanes to them on time.

Exhibit 19-7 describes the components of customer-response time. In the case of Boeing, *receipt time* is how long it takes the Marketing Department to specify to Manufacturing the exact requirements in the customer's order. **Manufacturing lead time** (also called **manufacturing cycle time**) is the duration between the time an order is received by Manufacturing to the time it becomes a finished good. Manufacturing lead time is the sum of waiting time and manufacturing time for an order. An aircraft order received by Boeing may need to wait because the required equipment is busy processing earlier orders. *Delivery time* is how long it takes to deliver a completed order to the customer.

Customer-response time is particularly important in mail-order catalog companies. To compete more effectively with stores (as well as with other mail-order companies), mail-order companies promise delivery of their products in a week or less. Second-day express delivery is standard for companies such as Neiman Marcus. Many companies believe their customers are willing to pay a higher price for faster delivery.

Several companies have adopted manufacturing lead time as the base for allocating indirect manufacturing costs to products. They believe that using manufacturing lead time as a cost-allocation base motivates managers to reduce the time it takes to manufacture products. Over time, total overhead costs decrease and operating income rises.

On-Time Performance

On-time performance refers to situations in which the product or service is actually delivered by the time it was scheduled to be delivered. Consider Federal Express, which specifies a price per package and a next-day delivery time of 10:30 A.M. for its overnight courier service. Federal Express measures on-time performance by how often it meets its stated delivery time of 10:30 A.M. On-time performance increases customer satisfaction. Commercial airlines gain loyal passengers as a result of consistent on-time service. But there is a trade-off between customer-response time and on-time performance. Deliberately scheduling longer customer-response times, such as airlines lengthening scheduled arrival times, makes achieving on-time performance easier—but it could displease customers!

TIME DRIVERS AND COSTS OF TIME

Managing customer-response time and on-time performance requires understanding the causes and costs of delays. Delays can occur, for example, at a machine in manufacturing or at a check-out counter in a store.

Uncertainty and Bottlenecks as Drivers of Time

A **time driver** is any factor in which a change in the factor causes a change in the speed of an activity. Two time drivers we consider are

- Uncertainty about when customers will order products or services. For example, the more randomly Boeing receives orders for its airplanes, the more likely queues will form and delays will occur.
- Bottlenecks due to limited capacity. A **bottleneck** occurs in an operation when the work to be performed approaches or exceeds the capacity available to do it. For example, a bottleneck results and causes delays when products that need to be processed at a particular machine arrive while the machine is being used to process other products. Bottlenecks also occur when many people try to view the same information at a company's Web site (see Concepts in Action below).

Consider Falcon Works (FW), which uses one turning machine to convert steel bars into a special gear for pumps. FW makes this gear only after customers have ordered it. To focus on manufacturing lead time, we assume FW's receipt time and delivery time are minimal.

FW expects it will receive 30 orders for gears, but it could receive 10, 30, or 50 orders. Each order is for 1,000 units and will take 100 hours of manufacturing time (8 hours of setup time to clean and prepare the machine, and 92 hours of processing time). The annual capacity of the machine is 4,000 hours. If FW receives the 30 orders it expects, the total amount of manufacturing time required on the machine will be 3,000 hours (100 hours per order × 30 orders), which is within the available machine capacity of 4,000 hours. Even though expected capacity utilization is not strained, queues and

CONCEPTS IN ACTION

Overcoming Bottlenecks on the Internet

Many companies are using the Internet to buy and sell their products and services and to provide customers with needed information. As a company's dependency on the Internet increases, the inability of a company to handle all the traffic to its Internet site can become a serious problem. As the chief financial officer of a company said, one hour of network downtime can mean "eight million dollars of commerce that didn't happen." A study conducted in 1999 found that more than 40% of online shoppers abandoned a transaction because the site they were dealing with was too slow in responding.

Reasons for the slow response include faulty software and electrical power failures. But one of the big reasons is bottlenecks: too many people trying to view the same information on a computer server at the same time. To relieve the bottleneck, companies—such as EMC, Hitachi, and others—have developed technology called *remote mirroring*, which allows a company to copy, or "mirror," huge databases in many different geographically remote locations.

The basic ideas for this technology were developed in the early 1990s and were called "redundant arrays of inexpensive disks" (or RAID). RAID technology equips a computer with two separate storage disks. New data is recorded simultaneously on both disks (one of which is normally "redundant"). The result, however, is that if one disk "crashes," the other can take over almost immediately.

The blossoming of e-commerce in the late 1990s stimulated an adaptation of RAID technology in the form of remote mirroring: Databases were copied, via the Internet, on computer-storage devices located quite far from each other. The extra copy serves as a backup in the event of system crashes, but it also relieves the problem of traffic congestion on the Internet. Exodus Communications, which manages the Web sites of many companies, uses remote mirroring technology to instantly reroute Web traffic around trouble spots on the network to data sites that have much less traffic and faster response times. Remote mirroring allows companies to efficiently relieve bottleneck constraints, increase capacity, and improve customer-response time.

Source: *Risk Management* (May 2001); *Wall Street Journal* (March 20, 2001); *Business Wire* (October 4, 1999); and a poll conducted by www.esearch.com in 1999.

delays can still occur. That's because uncertainty about when FW's customers will place their orders can cause an order to be received while the machine is processing an order received earlier.

In the single-product case, under certain assumptions about the pattern of customer orders and how orders will be processed,[3] **average waiting time,** the average amount of time that an order will wait in line before it is set up and processed, equals:

$$\frac{\text{Annual average number of orders for gears} \times \left(\text{Manufacturing time per order for gears}\right)^2}{2 \times \left[\text{Annual machine capacity} - \left(\text{Annual average number of orders for gears} \times \text{Manufacturing time per order for gears}\right)\right]}$$

$$= \frac{30 \times (100)^2}{2 \times [4{,}000 - (30 \times 100)]} = \frac{30 \times 10{,}000}{2 \times (4{,}000 - 3{,}000)} = \frac{300{,}000}{2 \times 1{,}000} = \frac{300{,}000}{2{,}000} = 150 \text{ hours per order}$$

Manufacturing time per order enters the numerator in the formula as a squared term. It indicates the disproportionately large impact manufacturing times have on waiting time. The longer the manufacturing time, the much greater the chance that the machine will be in use when an order arrives, and the longer will be the delays. The denominator in this formula is a measure of the unused capacity, or cushion. The smaller the unused capacity, the greater the chance that the machine is processing an order received earlier, and the greater the delays.

Our formula describes only the *average* waiting time. A particular order might arrive when the machine is free, in which case manufacturing will start immediately. In other situations, FW may receive an order while two other orders are waiting to be processed, and that means the delay will be longer than 150 hours. Average manufacturing lead time for an order is 250 hours (150 hours of average waiting time + 100 hours of manufacturing time).

Now suppose FW is considering whether to introduce a new product, a piston for pumps. FW expects to receive 10 orders for pistons, each order for 800 units, in the coming year. Each order will take 50 hours of manufacturing time, comprising 3 hours for setup and 47 hours of processing. The expected demand for FW's gears will be unaffected by whether FW introduces piston products.

Average waiting time *before* an order is set up and processed is given by the following formula, which is an extension of the preceding formula for the single-product case.

$$\frac{\left[\text{Annual average number of orders for gears} \times \left(\text{Manufacturing time per order for gears}\right)^2\right] + \left[\text{Annual average number of orders for pistons} \times \left(\text{Manufacturing time per order for pistons}\right)^2\right]}{2 \times \left[\text{Annual machine capacity} - \left(\text{Annual average number of orders for gears} \times \text{Manufacturing time per order for gears}\right) - \left(\text{Annual average number of orders for pistons} \times \text{Manufacturing time per order for pistons}\right)\right]}$$

$$= \frac{[30 \times (100)^2] + [10 \times (50)^2]}{2 \times [4{,}000 - (30 \times 100) - (10 \times 50)]} = \frac{(30 \times 10{,}000) + (10 \times 2{,}500)}{2 \times (4{,}000 - 3{,}000 - 500)}$$

$$= \frac{300{,}000 + 25{,}000}{2 \times 500} = \frac{325{,}000}{1{,}000} = 325 \text{ hours per order}$$

The introduction of pistons (1) cuts the unused capacity cushion in half (from 1,000 to 500 hours), which doubles the average waiting time by halving the denominator; and (2) increases the demands on the process (the numerator) by 25,000 hours, which further increases average waiting time. The total effect of introducing pistons is to increase average waiting time by 117% [(325 – 150) ÷ 150].

Introducing pistons causes average waiting time for an order to more than double, from 150 hours to 325 hours. That's because introducing pistons causes unused capacity to shrink, increasing the probability that, at any point in time, new orders will arrive while current orders are being manufactured or waiting to be manufactured. Average waiting time is very sensitive to the shrinking of unused capacity.

Average manufacturing lead time for a gear order is 425 hours (325 hours of average waiting time + 100 hours of manufacturing time), and for a piston order it is 375 hours (325 hours of average waiting time + 50 hours of manufacturing time). Note, a piston

[3]The technical assumptions are (a) that customer orders for the product follow a Poisson distribution with a mean equal to the expected number of orders (30 in our example), and (b) that orders are processed on a first-in, first-out (FIFO) basis. The Poisson arrival pattern for customer orders has been found to be reasonable in many real-world settings. The FIFO assumption can be modified. Under the modified assumptions, the basic queuing and delay effects will still occur, but the precise formulas will be different.

order spends 86.7% (325 ÷ 375) of its manufacturing lead time just waiting for manufacturing to start!

Given the anticipated effects on manufacturing lead time of adding pistons, should FW introduce pistons? The management accountant likely would be asked to evaluate the profitability of a new product, given capacity constraints. FW's management accountant needs to identify and analyze the relevant revenues and costs of adding the piston product and, in particular, to evaluate the cost effects of the resulting delays on all products.

Relevant Revenues and Costs of Time

To determine the relevant revenues and costs of adding pistons, consider the following additional information:

Product	Annual Average Number of Orders	Average Selling Price per Order If Average Manufacturing Lead Time per Order Is: Less Than 300 Hours	More Than 300 Hours	Direct Materials Cost per Order	Inventory Carrying Cost per Order per Hour
Gears	30	$22,000	$21,500	$16,000	$1.00
Pistons	10	10,000	9,600	8,000	0.50

Manufacturing lead times affect both revenues and costs in our example. Revenues are affected because customers are willing to pay a higher price for faster delivery. On the cost side, direct materials costs and inventory carrying costs are the only costs that will be affected by introducing pistons (all other costs are unaffected, hence irrelevant). Direct materials inventory carrying costs usually consist of the opportunity costs of investment tied up in inventory (see Chapter 11, p. 380–382) and the relevant costs of storage, such as space rental, spoilage, deterioration, and materials handling. Companies usually calculate inventory carrying costs on a per unit per year basis. To simplify computations, we express inventory carrying costs on a per order per hour basis. As in most companies, we assume FW acquires direct materials at the time the order is received by manufacturing, and, therefore, incurs inventory carrying costs for the duration of the manufacturing lead time.

FW acquires direct materials when it receives an order, rather than waiting until just before manufacturing is scheduled to start. That's because FW is uncertain about (1) how long it will take to obtain materials from suppliers and (2) when manufacturing will start.

Exhibit 19-8 presents relevant revenues and costs for the "introduce pistons" and "do not introduce pistons" alternatives. The decision is to not introduce pistons. This is the case despite pistons having a positive contribution margin of $1,600 ($9,600 – $8,000) per order. Also, FW has the capacity to process pistons (even if it produces pistons, FW will, on average, use only 3,500 of the available 4,000 machine-hours). So why is FW

EXHIBIT 19-8

Determining Expected Relevant Revenues and Costs for Falcon Works' Decision to Introduce Pistons

Relevant Items	Alternative 1: Introduce Pistons (1)	Alternative 2: Do Not Introduce Pistons (2)	Difference (3) = (1) – (2)
Expected revenues	$741,000[a]	$660,000[b]	$81,000
Expected variable costs	560,000[c]	480,000[d]	(80,000)
Expected inventory carrying costs	14,625[e]	7,500[f]	(7,125)
Expected total costs	574,625	487,500	(87,125)
Expected revenues minus expected costs	$166,375	$172,500	$(6,125)

[a]($21,500 × 30) + ($9,600 × 10) = $741,000; average manufacturing lead time will be more than 300 hours.

[b]($22,000 × 30) = $660,000; average manufacturing lead time will be less than 300 hours.

[c]($16,000 × 30) + ($8,000 × 10) = $560,000.

[d]$16,000 × 30 = $480,000.

[e](Average manufacturing lead time for gears × Unit carrying costs per order for gears × Expected number of orders for gears) + (Average manufacturing lead time for pistons × Unit carrying costs per order for pistons × Expected number of orders for pistons) = (425 × $1.00 × 30) + (375 × $0.50 × 10) = $12,750 + $1,875 = $14,625.

[f]Average manufacturing lead time for gears × Unit carrying costs per order for gears × Expected number of orders for gears = 250 × $1.00 × 30 = $7,500.

better off to not produce pistons? *Because of the negative effects that producing pistons will have on the existing product, gears.* The following table presents the *costs of time*—that is, the expected loss in revenues and expected increase in costs as a result of delays caused by using machine capacity to manufacture pistons.

	Effect of Increasing Average Manufacturing Lead Time		Expected Loss in Revenues Plus Expected Increase in Costs of Introducing Pistons
Product	Expected Loss in Revenues for Gears (1)	Expected Increase in Carrying Costs for All Products (2)	(3) = (1) + (2)
Gears	$15,000[a]	$5,250[b]	$20,250
Pistons	—	1,875[c]	1,875
Total	$15,000	$7,125	$22,125

[a]($22,000 – $21,500) per order × 30 expected orders = $15,000.
[b](425 – 250) hours per order × $1.00 per hour × 30 expected orders = $5,250.
[c](375 – 0) hours per order × $0.50 per hour × 10 expected orders = $1,875.

Introducing pistons causes the average manufacturing lead time of gears to increase from 250 hours to 425 hours. The cost of longer manufacturing lead times is an increase in inventory carrying costs of gears and a decrease in gear revenues (caused by average manufacturing lead time for gears exceeding 300 hours). The expected costs of longer lead times from introducing pistons, $22,125, exceeds the expected contribution margin of $16,000 ($1,600 per order × 10 expected orders) from selling pistons by $6,125 (the difference calculated in Exhibit 19-8).

This example illustrates that excess capacity at the bottleneck is desirable when there is randomness or variability in the arrival of orders. The unused capacity acts as a cushion to absorb some of the variability in the receipt of orders, which reduces average waiting time.

Our simple setting[4] illustrates that when demand uncertainty is high, some unused capacity is desirable. Increasing the capacity of a bottleneck resource reduces manufacturing lead times and delays. One way to increase capacity is to reduce the time required for setups and processing via more-efficient setups and processing. Another way to increase capacity is to invest in new equipment, such as flexible manufacturing systems that can be programmed to switch quickly from producing one product to producing another. Delays can also be reduced through careful scheduling of orders on machines—for example, by batching similar jobs together for processing.

To monitor performance on delays, many companies use nonfinancial measures. Some measures, such as customer-response time and on-time performance, focus on customer satisfaction. Other measures, such as manufacturing time and waiting time, emphasize internal performance. Nonfinancial measures of time help companies identify areas in need of improvement.

7 Apply the three measures in the theory of constraints

...throughput contribution, investments, and operating costs

THEORY OF CONSTRAINTS AND THROUGHPUT CONTRIBUTION ANALYSIS

In this section, we consider products that are made from multiple parts and processed on many machines. With multiple parts and machines, dependencies arise among operations—some operations cannot be started until parts from a previous operation are available. Furthermore, some operations are bottlenecks, and others are not.

You may have studied the theory of constraints (developed by Eli Goldratt) in operations management or production courses.

The **theory of constraints (TOC)** describes methods to maximize operating income when faced with some bottleneck and some nonbottleneck operations.[5] The TOC defines three measurements:

1. **Throughput contribution** equals revenues minus the direct materials cost of the goods sold.

[4]Other complexities, such as analyzing a network of machines, priority scheduling, and allowing for uncertainty in processing times, are beyond the scope of this book. In these cases, the basic queuing and delay effects persist, but the precise formulas are more complex.

[5]See E. Goldratt and J. Cox, *The Goal* (New York: North River Press, 1986); E. Goldratt, *The Theory of Constraints* (New York: North River Press, 1990); E. Noreen, D. Smith, and J. Mackey, *The Theory of Constraints and Its Implications for Management Accounting* (New York: North River Press, 1995).

2. *Investments* equal the sum of materials costs in direct materials, work-in-process, and finished goods inventories; R&D costs; and costs of equipment and buildings.
3. *Operating costs* equal all costs of operations (other than direct materials) incurred to earn throughput contribution. Operating costs include salaries and wages, rent, utilities, and depreciation.

The objective of TOC is to increase throughput contribution while decreasing investments and operating costs. *TOC considers a short-run time horizon and assumes that operating costs are fixed costs.* The steps in managing bottleneck operations are

8 Manage bottlenecks ...keep bottlenecks busy and increase bottleneck efficiency and capacity

Step 1: Recognize that the bottleneck operation determines throughput contribution of the entire system.

Step 2: Find the bottleneck operation by identifying operations with large quantities of inventory waiting to be worked on.

Step 3: Keep the bottleneck operation busy and subordinate all nonbottleneck operations to the bottleneck operation. That is, the needs of the bottleneck operation determine the production schedule of nonbottleneck operations.

Step 3 echoes one of the concepts described in Chapter 11: To maximize operating income, the plant must maximize contribution margin (in this case, throughput contribution) of the constrained or bottleneck resource (see pp. 382–383). For this reason, step 3 suggests that the bottleneck machine must always be kept running. It should not be waiting for jobs. To achieve this objective, companies often maintain a small buffer inventory of jobs waiting for the bottleneck machine. The bottleneck machine sets the pace for all nonbottleneck machines. For example, workers at nonbottleneck machines are instructed to not produce more output than can be processed by the bottleneck machine. Producing more nonbottleneck output only creates excess inventory; it does not increase throughput contribution.

Step 4: Take actions to increase the efficiency and capacity of the bottleneck operation: The objective is to increase the difference between throughput contribution and the incremental costs of increasing efficiency and capacity. The management accountant's role in step 4 is calculating throughput contribution, identifying relevant and irrelevant costs, and doing cost-benefit analyses of alternative actions.

We illustrate step 4 using data from Cardinal Industries (CI). CI manufactures car doors in two operations: stamping and pressing.

	Stamping	Pressing
Capacity per hour	20 units	15 units
Annual capacity (6,000 hours of capacity available in each operation; 6,000 hours × 20 units/hour; 6,000 hours × 15 units/hour)	120,000 units	90,000 units
Annual production and sales	90,000 units	90,000 units
Other fixed operating costs (excluding direct materials)	$720,000	$1,080,000
Other fixed operating costs per unit produced ($720,000 ÷ 90,000 units; $1,080,000 ÷ 90,000 units)	$8 per unit	$12 per unit

Each door sells for $100 and has direct materials costs of $40. Variable costs in other functions of the value chain—R&D, design of products and processes, marketing, distribution, and customer service—are negligible. CI's output is constrained by the capacity of 90,000 units in the pressing operation. What can CI do to relieve the bottleneck constraint of the pressing operation? Desirable actions include:

a. *Eliminate idle time (time when the pressing machine is neither being set up to process products nor actually processing products) at the bottleneck operation.* CI is considering permanently positioning two workers at the pressing operation to unload finished units as soon as one batch of units is processed and to set up the machine to process the next batch. Suppose the annual cost of this action is $48,000 and the effect is to increase bottleneck output by 1,000 doors per year. Should CI incur the additional costs? Yes, because CI's relevant throughput contribution increases by $60,000 [(selling price per door, $100, – direct materials cost per door, $40) × 1,000 doors], which exceeds the additional cost of $48,000. All other costs are irrelevant.

b. *Process only those parts or products that increase throughput contribution, not parts or products that will remain in finished goods or spare parts inventories.* Manufacturing products that remain in inventory does not increase throughput contribution.

c. *Shift products that do not have to be made on the bottleneck machine to nonbottleneck machines or to outside processing facilities.* Suppose the Spartan Corporation, an outside contractor, offers to press 1,500 doors at $15 per door from stamped parts that CI supplies. Spartan's quoted price is greater than CI's own operating costs in the Pressing Department of $12 per door. Should CI accept the offer? Yes, because pressing is the bottleneck operation. Getting additional doors pressed by Spartan increases throughput contribution by $90,000 [($100 – $40) per door × 1,500 doors], while relevant costs increase by $22,500 ($15 per door × 1,500 doors). The fact that CI's unit cost is less than Spartan's quoted price plays no role in the analysis.

Suppose Gemini Industries, another outside contractor, offers to stamp 2,000 doors from direct materials that CI supplies at $6 per door. Gemini's price is lower than CI's operating cost of $8 per door in the Stamping Department. Should CI accept the offer? No, because other operating costs are fixed costs. CI will not save any costs by subcontracting the stamping operations. Total costs will be greater by $12,000 ($6 per door × 2,000 doors) under the subcontracting alternative. Stamping more doors will not increase throughput contribution, which is constrained by pressing capacity.

The opportunity cost of lost throughput contribution arising from quality problems at the bottleneck is an internal failure cost.

d. *Reduce setup time and processing time at bottleneck operations (for example, by simplifying the design or reducing the number of parts in the product).* Suppose CI can reduce setup time at the pressing operation by incurring additional costs of $55,000 a year. Suppose further that reducing setup time enables CI to press 2,500 more doors a year. Should CI incur the costs to reduce setup time? Yes, because throughput contribution increases by $150,000 [($100 – $40 per door) × 2,500 doors], which exceeds the additional costs incurred of $55,000. Will CI find it worthwhile to incur costs to reduce machining time at the nonbottleneck stamping operation? No. Other operating costs will increase, but throughput contribution will remain unchanged because the bottleneck has not been relieved.

e. *Improve the quality of parts or products manufactured at the bottleneck operation.* Poor quality is often more costly at a bottleneck operation than it is at a nonbottleneck operation. The cost of poor quality at a nonbottleneck operation is the cost of materials wasted. If CI produces 1,000 defective doors at the stamping operation, the cost of poor quality is $40,000 (direct materials cost per door, $40, × 1,000 doors). No throughput contribution is forgone because stamping has unused capacity. Despite the defective production, stamping can produce and transfer 90,000 good-quality doors to the pressing operation. At a bottleneck operation, the cost of poor quality is the cost of materials wasted *plus* the opportunity cost of lost throughput contribution. Bottleneck capacity not wasted in producing defective units could be used to generate additional throughput contribution. If CI produces 1,000 defective units at the pressing operation, the cost of poor quality is $100,000: direct materials costs of $40,000 (direct materials cost per door, $40, × 1,000 doors) plus forgone throughput contribution of $60,000 [($100 – $40) per door × 1,000 doors].

The high costs of poor quality at the bottleneck operation mean that bottleneck time should not be wasted processing units that are defective. That is, inspection should be done before processing parts at the bottleneck operation to ensure that only good-quality units are transferred to the bottleneck operation. Furthermore, quality-improvement programs should place special emphasis on minimizing defects at bottleneck machines.

If the actions in step 4 are successful, the capacity of the pressing operation will increase and eventually exceed the capacity of the stamping operation. The bottleneck will then shift to the stamping operation. CI would then focus continuous-improvement actions on increasing stamping efficiency and capacity. For example, the contract with Gemini Industries to stamp 2,000 doors at $6 per door from direct materials supplied by CI becomes attractive now. Why? Because throughput contribution increases by ($100 –

$40) per door × 2,000 doors = $120,000, while costs increase by $12,000 ($6 per door × 2,000 doors).

The theory of constraints emphasizes the management of bottleneck operations as the key to improving the performance of production operations as a whole. It focuses on the short-run maximization of throughput contribution—revenues minus direct materials costs. Because TOC regards operating costs as difficult to change in the short run, it does not identify individual activities and drivers of costs. TOC is, therefore, less useful for the long-run management of costs. Activity-based costing (ABC) systems, on the other hand, have a longer-run perspective focused on improving processes by eliminating non-value-added activities and reducing the costs of performing value-added activities. ABC systems are, therefore, more useful for long-run pricing, long-run cost control and profit planning, and capacity management. The short-run TOC emphasis on maximizing throughput contribution by managing bottlenecks complements the long-run strategic cost management focus of ABC.[6]

[6]For an excellent evaluation of TOC, operations management, cost accounting, and the relationship between TOC and activity-based costing, see A. Atkinson, *"Cost Accounting, the Theory of Constraints, and Costing ,"* (Issue Paper, CMA Canada, December 2000).

PROBLEM FOR SELF-STUDY

The Sloan Moving Corporation transports household goods from one city to another within the continental United States. It measures quality of service in terms of (a) time required to transport goods, (b) on-time delivery (within two days of agreed-upon delivery date), and (c) number of lost or damaged shipments. Sloan is considering investing in a new scheduling and tracking system costing $160,000 per year, which should help it improve performance with respect to items (b) and (c). The following information describes Sloan's current performance and the expected performance if the new system is implemented:

	Current Performance	Expected Future Performance
On-time delivery performance	85%	95%
Variable cost per carton lost or damaged	$60	$60
Fixed cost per carton lost or damaged	$40	$40
Number of cartons lost or damaged per year	3,000 cartons	1,000 cartons

Sloan expects each percentage point increase in on-time performance will result in revenue increases of $20,000 per year. Sloan's contribution margin percentage is 45%.

Required

1. Should Sloan acquire the new system? Show your calculations.
2. Calculate the minimum amount of revenue increase needed for the benefits from the new system to equal the costs.

SOLUTION

1. Additional costs of the new scheduling and tracking system are $160,000 per year. Additional annual benefits of the new scheduling and tracking system are

Additional annual revenues from a 10% improvement in on-time performance, from 85% to 95%, $20,000 per 1% × 10 percentage points	$200,000
45% contribution margin from additional annual revenues (0. 45 × $200,000)	$ 90,000
Decrease in costs per year from fewer cartons lost or damaged (only variable costs are relevant) [$60 per carton × (3,000 – 1,000) cartons]	120,000
Total additional benefits	$210,000

Continued

Because the expected benefits of $210,000 exceed the costs of $160,000, Sloan should invest in the new system.

2. As long as Sloan earns a contribution margin of $40,000 (to cover incremental costs of $160,000 minus relevant variable-cost savings of $120,000) from additional annual sales, investing in the new system is beneficial. This contribution margin corresponds to additional sales of $40,000 ÷ 0.45 = $88,889.

DECISION POINTS — SUMMARY

The following question-and-answer format summarizes the chapter's learning objectives. Each decision presents a key question related to a learning objective. The guidelines are the answer to that question.

Decision	Guidelines
1. What are the four cost categories of a costs-of-quality program?	Four cost categories in a costs-of-quality program are prevention costs (costs incurred to preclude the production of products that do not conform to specifications), appraisal costs (costs incurred to detect which of the individual units of products do not conform to specifications), internal failure costs (costs incurred by a nonconforming product before it is shipped to customers), and external failure costs (costs incurred by a nonconforming product after it is shipped to customers).
2. What methods can managers use to identify quality problems and improve quality?	Three methods to identify quality problems and to improve quality are (a) control charts, to distinguish random from nonrandom variations in an operating process; (b) Pareto diagrams, which indicate how frequently each type of failure occurs; and (c) cause-and-effect diagrams, which identify potential causes of failure.
3. How do managers identify the relevant costs and benefits of quality improvements?	The relevant costs of quality improvement are the incremental costs to implement the quality program. The relevant benefits are the cost savings and the estimated increase in contribution margin from the higher sales due to quality improvements.
4. What nonfinancial measures of customer satisfaction and internal performance can managers use?	Nonfinancial measures of customer satisfaction include number of customer complaints and on-time delivery rate. Nonfinancial measures of internal quality performance include product defect levels and process yields.
5. Why should managers use both financial and nonfinancial measures of quality?	Financial measures are helpful to evaluate trade-offs among prevention costs, appraisal costs, and failure costs. Nonfinancial measures identify problem areas that need improvement and serve as indicators of future long-run performance.
6. What is customer-response time? What are the reasons for and the costs of delays?	Customer-response time is the duration between the time a customer places an order for a product or service to the time the product or service is delivered to the customer. Delays occur because of (a) uncertainty about when customers will order products or services and (b) bottlenecks due to limited capacity. Bottlenecks are operations at which the work to be performed approaches or exceeds the available capacity. The costs of delays include lower revenues and increased inventory carrying costs.
7. What three measures do managers need to implement the theory of constraints?	The three measures in the theory of constraints are (a) throughput contribution (equal to revenues minus direct materials cost of the goods sold); (b) investments (equal to the sum of materials costs in direct materials, work-in-process, and finished goods inventories, R&D costs, and costs of equipment and buildings); and (c) operating costs (equal to all operating costs, other than direct materials costs, incurred to earn throughput contribution).
8. What are the steps managers can take to manage bottlenecks?	The four steps in managing bottlenecks are (a) recognize that the bottleneck operation determines throughput contribution, (b) find the bottleneck, (c) keep the bottleneck busy and subordinate all nonbottleneck operations to the bottleneck operation, and (d) increase bottleneck efficiency and capacity.

TERMS TO LEARN

This chapter and the Glossary at the end of the book contain definitions of:

appraisal costs (p. 655)
average waiting time (666)
bottleneck (665)
cause-and-effect diagram (659)
conformance quality (655)
control chart (657)
costs of quality (COQ) (655)
customer-response time (664)
external failure costs (655)
internal failure costs (655)
manufacturing cycle time (664)
manufacturing lead time (664)
on-time performance (664)
Pareto diagram (658)
prevention costs (655)
quality of design (655)
theory of constraints (TOC) (668)
throughput contribution (668)
time driver (665)

ASSIGNMENT MATERIAL

Questions

19-1 Describe two benefits of improving quality.

19-2 How does conformance quality differ from quality of design? Explain.

19-3 Name two items classified as prevention costs.

19-4 Distinguish between internal failure costs and external failure costs.

19-5 Describe three methods that companies use to identify quality problems.

19-6 "Companies should focus on financial measures of quality because these are the only measures of quality that can be linked to bottom-line performance." Do you agree? Explain.

19-7 Give two examples of nonfinancial measures of customer satisfaction.

19-8 Give two examples of nonfinancial measures of internal performance.

19-9 Distinguish between customer-response time and manufacturing lead time.

19-10 "There is no trade-off between customer-response time and on-time performance." Do you agree? Explain.

19-11 Give two reasons why delays occur.

19-12 "Companies should always make and sell all products whose selling prices exceed variable costs." Assuming fixed costs are irrelevant, do you agree? Explain.

19-13 Describe the three main measures used in the theory of constraints.

19-14 Describe the four key steps in managing bottleneck operations.

19-15 Describe three ways to improve the performance of a bottleneck operation.

Exercises

19-16 **Costs of quality.** (CMA, adapted) Bergen, Inc., produces telephone equipment. Jerry Holman, Bergen's president, decided to devote more resources to the improvement of product quality after learning that his company's products had been ranked fourth in product quality in a 2002 survey of telephone equipment users. Bergen's quality-improvement program has now been in operation for two years, and the cost report shown below has recently been issued.

Semi-annual Costs of Quality Report, Bergen, Inc. (in thousands)

	6/30/2003	12/31/2003	6/30/2004	12/31/2004
Prevention costs				
Machine maintenance	$ 215	$ 215	$ 190	$ 160
Training suppliers	5	45	20	15
Design reviews	20	102	100	95
Total prevention costs	240	362	310	270
Appraisal costs				
Incoming inspection	45	53	36	22
Final testing	160	160	140	94
Total appraisal costs	205	213	176	116

Continued

	6/30/2003	12/31/2003	6/30/2004	12/31/2004
Internal failure costs				
Rework	120	106	88	62
Scrap	68	64	42	40
Total internal failure costs	188	170	130	102
External failure costs				
Warranty repairs	69	31	25	23
Customer returns	262	251	116	80
Total external failure costs	331	282	141	103
Total quality costs	$ 964	$1,027	$ 757	$ 591
Total production and revenues	$4,120	$4,540	$4,650	$4,510

Required

1. Calculate the ratio of each COQ category to revenues for each period. Has Bergen's quality-improvement program been successful? Explain.
2. Jerry Holman believed that a quality-improvement program was essential and that Bergen, Inc., could no longer afford to ignore the importance of product quality. Discuss how Bergen could measure the opportunity cost of not implementing the quality-improvement program.

19-17 Costs of quality analysis, nonfinancial quality measures. The Hartono Corporation manufactures and sells industrial grinders. The following table presents financial information pertaining to quality in 2004 and 2005 (in thousands):

	2005	2004
Revenues	$12,500	$10,000
Inspection of production	85	110
Scrap	200	250
Design engineering	240	100
Cost of returned goods	145	60
Product-testing equipment	50	50
Customer support	30	40
Rework costs	135	160
Preventive equipment maintenance	90	35
Product liability claims	100	200
Incoming materials inspection	40	20
Breakdown maintenance	40	90
Product-testing labor	75	220
Training	120	45
Warranty repair	200	300
Supplier evaluation	50	20

Required

1. Classify the cost items in the table into prevention, appraisal, internal failure, or external failure categories.
2. Calculate the ratio of each COQ category to revenues in 2004 and 2005. Comment on the trends in costs of quality between 2004 and 2005.
3. Give two examples of nonfinancial quality measures that Hartono Corporation could monitor as part of a total quality-control effort.

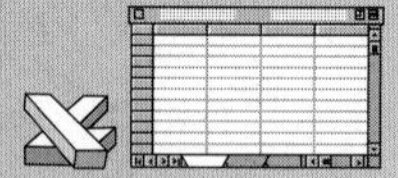

Excel Application For students who wish to practice their spreadsheet skills, the following is a step-by-step approach to creating an Excel spreadsheet to work this problem.

Step-by-Step

1. Open a new spreadsheet. Create a row for "Revenues" and columns for "2005" and "2004."

(Program your spreadsheet to perform all necessary calculations. Do not "hard-code" any amounts, such as prevention costs as a percentage of sales, requiring addition, subtraction, multiplication, or division operations.)

2. Skip two rows and create columns for "Cost" and "Cost as a Percentage of Revenues" for 2005. Create two more columns right next to these columns for "Cost" and "Cost as a Percentage of Revenues" for 2004. Create rows for each item of prevention costs (for example, "Preventive Maintenance") and "Total Prevention Costs"; each item of appraisal costs and "Total Appraisal Costs"; each item of internal failure costs and "Total Internal Failure Costs" each item of external failure costs and "Total External Failure Costs." Finally, create a row for "Total Costs of Quality."
3. Enter calculations for total cost of a Percentage of Revenues of each Cost of Quality category (for example, total prevention costs) and Total Costs of Quality in 2004 and 2005.

4. Skip two rows and create a section, "COQ Trend Analysis," with rows for "Prevention Costs, Appraisal Costs, Internal Failure Costs, External Failure Costs", and "Total Costs of Quality" and columns for "Percent of Sales in 2005" and "Percent of Sales in 2004." Fill in this section using the data you created in steps 2 and 3.
5. Create a bar chart to compare each of the categories and total costs of quality in 2005 and 2004 by highlighting the "Percent of Sales in 2005" and "Percent of Sales in 2004" columns and clicking the chart wizard icon. Choose "Column" under chart type. Format as necessary and click on "Finish."
6. *Verify the accuracy of your spreadsheet:* Change revenues in 2005 from $12,500 to $9,500. If you programmed your spreadsheet correctly, total prevention costs as a percentage of revenues for 2005 should change to 5.3%.

19-18 Costs-of-quality analysis, nonfinancial quality measures. Ontario Industries manufactures two types of refrigerators, Olivia and Solta. Information on each refrigerator is as follows:

	Olivia	Solta
Units manufactured and sold	10,000 units	5,000 units
Selling price	$2,000	$1,500
Variable costs per unit	$1,200	$800
Hours spent on design	6,000	1,000
Testing and inspection hours per unit	1	0.5
Percentage of units reworked in plant	5%	10%
Rework costs per refrigerator	$500	$400
Percentage of units repaired at customer site	4%	8%
Repair costs per refrigerator	$600	$450
Estimated lost sales from poor quality	—	300 units

The labor rates per hour for two activities are as follows:

- Design — $75 per hour
- Testing and inspection — $40 per hour

Required

1. Calculate the costs of quality for Olivia and Solta, classified into prevention, appraisal, internal failure, and external failure categories.
2. For each type of refrigerator, calculate the ratio of each COQ category as a percentage of revenues. Compare and comment on the costs of quality for Olivia and Solta.
3. Give two examples of nonfinancial quality measures that Ontario Industries could monitor as part of a total quality-control program.

19-19 Nonfinancial measures of quality and time. (CMA, adapted) Eastern Switching Co. (ESC) produces telecommunications equipment. Charles Laurant, ESC's president, believes that product quality is the key to gaining competitive advantage. Laurant implemented a total quality management (TQM) program with an emphasis on customer satisfaction. The following information is available for the first year (2004) of the TQM program compared with the previous year.

	2003	2004
Total number of units produced and sold	10,000	11,000
Units delivered before scheduled delivery date	8,500	9,900
Number of defective units shipped	400	330
Number of customer complaints other than for defective units	500	517
Average time from when customer places order for a unit to when unit is delivered to the customer	30 days	25 days
Number of units reworked during production	600	627
Manufacturing lead time	20 days	16 days
Direct and indirect manufacturing labor-hours	90,000	110,000

Required

1. For each of the years 2003 and 2004, calculate
   a. Percentage of defective units shipped
   b. On-time delivery rate
   c. Customer complaints as a percentage of units shipped
   d. Percentage of units reworked during production
2. On the basis of your calculations in requirement 1, has ESC's performance on quality and timeliness improved?
3. Philip Larkin, a member of ESC's board of directors, comments that regardless of the effect that the program has had on quality, the output per labor-hour has declined between 2003 and 2004. Larkin believes that lower output per labor-hour will lead to an increase in costs and lower operating income.

a. How did Larkin conclude that output per labor-hour declined in 2004 relative to 2003?
b. Why might output per labor-hour decline in 2004?
c. Do you think that a lower output per labor-hour will decrease operating income in 2004? Explain briefly.

19-20 Quality improvement, relevant costs, and relevant revenues. The Photon Corporation manufactures and sells 20,000 copiers each year. The variable and fixed costs of rework and repair are as follows:

	Variable Costs	Fixed Costs	Total Costs
Rework costs per hour	$ 40	$60	$100
Repair costs			
Customer-support costs per hour	20	30	50
Transportation costs per load	180	60	240
Warranty repair costs per hour	45	65	110

Photon's engineers are currently working to solve the problem of copies being too light or too dark. They propose changing the lens of the copier. The new lens will cost $50 more than the old lens. Each copier uses one lens. Photon uses a one-year time horizon for this decision, because it plans to introduce a new copier at the end of the year. Photon believes that even as it improves quality, it will not be able to save any of the fixed costs of rework or repair.

By changing the lens, Photon expects that it will (1) save 12,000 hours of rework, (2) save 800 hours of customer support, (3) move 200 fewer loads, (4) save 8,000 hours of repair, and (5) sell 100 additional copiers for a total contribution margin of $600,000.

Required

Should Photon change to the new lens? Show your calculations.

19-21 Customer-response time, on-time delivery. Pizzafest, Inc., makes and delivers pizzas to homes and offices in the Boston area. Fast, on-time delivery is one of Pizzafest's key strategies. Pizzafest provides the following information for 2004 about its customer-response time—the amount of time from when a customer calls to place an order to when the pizza is delivered.

	January–June	July–December
Pizzas delivered in 30 minutes or less	100,000	150,000
Pizzas delivered in between 31 and 45 minutes	200,000	260,000
Pizzas delivered in between 46 and 60 minutes	80,000	70,000
Pizzas delivered in between 61 and 75 minutes	20,000	20,000
Total pizzas delivered	400,000	500,000

Required

1. For January–June and July–December 2004, calculate the percentage of pizzas delivered in each of the four time intervals (30 minutes or less, 31–45 minutes, 46–60 minutes, and 61–75 minutes). On the basis of these calculations, has customer-response time improved in July–December compared with January–June?
2. When customers call Pizzafest, they often ask how long it will take for the pizza to be delivered to their homes or offices. If Pizzafest quotes a long time interval, customers often will not place the order. If Pizzafest quotes too short a time interval and the pizza is not delivered on time, customers get upset and Pizzafest will lose repeat business. Based on the January–June 2004 data, what customer-response time should Pizzafest quote to its customers if
   a. It wants to have an on-time delivery performance of 75%?
   b. It wants to have an on-time delivery performance of 95%?
3. If Pizzafest had quoted the customer-response times you calculated in requirements 2a and 2b, would it have met its on-time delivery performance targets of 75% and 95%, respectively, for July–December 2004? Explain.
4. Pizzafest is considering giving an on-time guarantee for January–June 2005. If the pizza is not delivered within 60 minutes of placing the order, the customer gets the pizza free. Pizzafest estimates that it will make additional sales of 20,000 pizzas as a result of giving this guarantee. It estimates that it will fail to deliver a total of 15,000 pizzas on time. The average price of a pizza is $13, and the variable cost of a pizza is $7.
   a. What is the effect on Pizzafest's operating income of making this offer?
   b. What nonfinancial and qualitative factors should Pizzafest consider before making this offer?
   c. What actions can Pizzafest take to reduce customer-response time?

19-22 Waiting time, banks. Regal Bank has a small branch in Orillia, Canada. The counter is staffed by one teller. The counter is open for five hours (300 minutes) each day (the operational capacity). It takes 5 minutes to serve a customer (service time). The Orillia branch expects to serve 40 customers each day. (Note that the number of customers corresponds to the number of orders in the chapter discussion.)

Required

1. Using the formula on p. 666, calculate how long, on average, a customer will wait in line before being served.
2. How long, on average, will a customer wait in line if the branch expects to serve 50 customers each day?

3. The bank is considering ways to reduce waiting time. How long will customers have to wait, on average, if the time to serve a customer is reduced to four minutes and the bank expects to serve 50 customers each day?

19-23 Waiting time, relevant costs, and relevant revenues. The Orillia branch of Regal Bank is thinking of offering additional services to its customers. Its counter is open for five hours (300 minutes) each day (the operational capacity). If it introduces the new services, the bank expects to serve an average of 60 customers each day, instead of the 40 customers it currently averages. It will take 4 minutes to serve each customer (service time), regardless of whether the new services are offered. (Note that the number of customers corresponds to the number of orders in the chapter discussion.)

Required

1. Using the formula on p. 666, calculate how long, on average, a customer will wait in line before being served.
2. Regal Bank's policy is that the average waiting time in the line should not exceed 5 minutes. The bank cannot reduce the time to serve a customer below 4 minutes without negatively affecting quality. To reduce average waiting time for the 60 customers it expects to serve each day, the bank decides to keep the counter open for 336 minutes each day. Verify that by keeping the counter open for 336 minutes, the bank will be able to achieve its goal of an average waiting time of 5 minutes or less.
3. The bank expects to generate, on average, $30 in additional operating income each day as a result of offering the new services. The teller is paid $10 per hour and is employed in increments of an hour (that is, the teller can be employed for 5, 6, or 7 hours, and so on, but not for a fraction of an hour). If the bank wants average waiting time to be no more than 5 minutes, should the bank offer the new services?

19-24 Theory of constraints, throughput contribution, relevant costs. The Mayfield Corporation manufactures filing cabinets in two operations: machining and finishing. It provides the following information.

	Machining	Finishing
Annual capacity	100,000 units	80,000 units
Annual production	80,000 units	80,000 units
Fixed operating costs (excluding direct materials)	$640,000	$400,000
Fixed operating costs per unit produced ($640,000 ÷ 80,000; $400,000 ÷ 80,000)	$8 per unit	$5 per unit

Each cabinet sells for $72 and has direct materials costs of $32 incurred at the start of the machining operation. Mayfield has no other variable costs. Mayfield can sell whatever output it produces. The following requirements refer only to the preceding data. There is no connection between the requirements.

Required

1. Mayfield is considering using some modern jigs and tools in the finishing operation that would increase annual finishing output by 1,000 units. The annual cost of these jigs and tools is $30,000. Should Mayfield acquire these tools? Show your calculations.
2. The production manager of the Machining Department has submitted a proposal to do faster setups that would increase the annual capacity of the Machining Department by 10,000 units and cost $5,000 per year. Should Mayfield implement the change? Show your calculations.

19-25 Theory of constraints, throughput contribution, relevant costs. Refer to the information in Exercise 19-24 in answering the following requirements. There is no connection between the requirements.

Required

1. An outside contractor offers to do the finishing operation for 12,000 units at $10 per unit, double the $5 per unit that it costs Mayfield to do the finishing in-house. Should Mayfield accept the subcontractor's offer? Show your calculations.
2. The Hunt Corporation offers to machine 4,000 units at $4 per unit, half the $8 per unit that it costs Mayfield to do the machining in-house. Should Mayfield accept the subcontractor's offer? Show your calculations.

19-26 Theory of constraints, throughput contribution, quality. Refer to the information in Exercise 19-24 in answering the following requirements. There is no connection between the requirements.

Required

1. Mayfield produces 2,000 defective units at the machining operation. What is the cost to Mayfield of the defective items produced? Explain your answer briefly.
2. Mayfield produces 2,000 defective units at the finishing operation. What is the cost to Mayfield of the defective items produced? Explain your answer briefly.

Problems

19-27 Quality improvement, relevant costs, and relevant revenues. The Thomas Corporation sells 300,000 V262 valves to the automobile and truck industry. Thomas has a capacity of 110,000 machine-hours and can produce 3 valves per machine-hour. V262's contribution margin per unit is $8. Thomas sells only 300,000 valves because 30,000 valves (10% of the good valves) need to be reworked. It takes 1 machine-hour to rework 3 valves, so 10,000 hours of capacity are used in the rework process. Thomas's rework costs are $210,000. Rework costs consist of:

- Direct materials and direct rework labor (variable costs): $3 per unit
- Fixed costs of equipment, rent, and overhead allocation: $4 per unit

Thomas's process designers have developed a modification that would maintain the speed of the process and ensure 100% quality and no rework. The new process would cost $315,000 per year. The following additional information is available:

- The demand for Thomas's V262 valves is 370,000 per year.
- The Jackson Corporation has asked Thomas to supply 22,000 T971 valves (another product) if Thomas implements the new design. The contribution margin per T971 valve is $10. Thomas can make two T971 valves per machine-hour with 100% quality and no rework.

Required

1. Suppose Thomas's designers implement the new design. Should Thomas accept Jackson's order for 22,000 T971 valves? Show your calculations.
2. Should Thomas implement the new design? Show your calculations.
3. What nonfinancial and qualitative factors should Thomas consider in deciding whether to implement the new design?

19-28 Quality improvement, relevant costs, and relevant revenues. The Tan Corporation uses multicolor molding to make plastic lamps. The molding operation has a capacity of 200,000 units per year. The demand for lamps is very strong. Tan will be able to sell whatever output quantities it can produce at $40 per lamp.

Tan can start only 200,000 units into production in the Molding Department because of capacity constraints on the molding machines. If a defective unit is produced at the molding operation, it must be scrapped, and the net disposal value of scrap is zero. Of the 200,000 units started at the molding operation, 30,000 units (15%) are scrapped. Scrap costs, based on total (fixed and variable) manufacturing costs incurred up to the molding operation equal $25 per unit as follows:

Direct materials (variable)	$16 per unit
Direct manufacturing labor, setup labor, and materials-handling labor (variable)	3 per unit
Equipment, rent, and other allocated overhead, including inspection and testing costs on scrapped parts (fixed)	6 per unit
Total	$25 per unit

Tan's designers have determined that adding a different type of material to the existing direct materials would reduce scrap to zero, but it would increase the variable costs by $4 per lamp in the Molding Department.

Required

1. Should Tan use the new material? Show your calculations.
2. What nonfinancial and qualitative factors should Tan consider in making the decision?

19-29 Statistical quality control, airline operations. Peoples Skyway operates daily round-trip flights on the London–New York route using a fleet of three 747s; the Spirit of Birmingham, the Spirit of Glasgow, and the Spirit of Manchester. The budgeted quantity of fuel for each round-trip flight is the mean (average) fuel usage. Over the past 12 months, the average fuel usage per round-trip is 100 gallon-units, with a standard deviation of 10 gallon-units. A gallon-unit is 1,000 gallons.

Cilla Black, the operations manager of Peoples Skyway, uses a statistical quality-control (SQC) approach in deciding whether to investigate fuel usage per round-trip flight. She investigates those flights with fuel usage greater than two standard deviations from the mean.

In October, Black receives the following report for round-trip fuel usage by the three planes operating on the London–New York route:

Flight	Spirit of Birmingham (gallon-units)	Spirit of Glasgow (gallon-units)	Spirit of Manchester (gallon-units)
1	104	103	97
2	94	94	104
3	97	96	111
4	101	107	104
5	105	92	122
6	107	113	118
7	111	99	126
8	112	106	114
9	115	101	117
10	119	93	123

Required

1. Using the $\pm 2\sigma$ rule, what variance investigation decisions would be made?
2. Present SQC charts for round-trip fuel usage for each of the three 747s in October. What inferences can you draw from the charts?

3. Some managers propose that Peoples Skyway present its SQC charts in monetary terms rather than in physical-quantity terms (gallon-units). What are the advantages and disadvantages of using monetary fuel costs rather than gallon-units in the SQC charts?

19-30 Compensation linked with profitability, on-time delivery, and external quality performance measures. Pacific-Dunlop supplies tires to major automotive companies. It has two tire plants in North America, in Detroit and Los Angeles. The quarterly bonus plan for each plant manager has three components:

a. *Profitability performance.* Add 2% of operating income.
b. *On-time delivery performance.* Add $10,000 if on-time delivery performance to the 10 most important customers is 98% or better. If on-time performance to these customers is below 98%, add nothing.
c. *Product quality performance.* Deduct 50% of cost of sales returns from the 10 most important customers.

Quarterly data for 2004 for the Detroit and Los Angeles plants are as follows:

	January–March	April–June	July–September	October–December
Detroit				
Operating income	$800,000	$850,000	$7,00,000	$900,000
On-time delivery rate[a]	98.4%	98.6%	97.1%	97.9%
Cost of sales returns[a]	$18,000	$26,000	$10,000	$25,000
Los Angeles				
Operating income	$1,600,000	$1,500,000	$1,800,000	$1,900,000
On-time delivery rate[a]	95.6%	97.1%	97.9%	98.4%
Cost of sales returns[a]	$35,000	$34,000	$28,000	$22,000

[a]For the 10 most important customers.

Required

1. Compute the bonuses paid in each quarter of 2004 to the plant managers of the Detroit and Los Angeles plants.
2. Discuss the three components of the bonus plan as measures of profitability, on-time delivery, and product quality.
3. Why would you want to evaluate plant managers on the basis of both operating income and on-time delivery rate?
4. Give one example of what might happen if on-time delivery rate were dropped as a performance-evaluation measure.

19-31 Waiting times, manufacturing lead times. The SRG Corporation uses an injection molding machine to make a plastic product, Z39. SRG makes products only after receiving firm orders from its customers. SRG estimates that it will receive 50 orders for Z39 (each order is for 1,000 units) during the coming year. Each order of Z39 will take 80 hours of machine time. The annual capacity of the machine is 5,000 hours.

Required

1. Calculate (a) the average amount of time that an order for Z39 will wait in line before it is processed and (b) the average manufacturing lead time per order for Z39.
2. SRG is considering introducing a new product, Y28. SRG estimates that, on average, it will receive 25 orders of Y28 (each order for 200 units) in the coming year. Each order of Y28 will take 20 hours of machine time. The average demand for Z39 will be unaffected by the introduction of Y28. Calculate (a) the average waiting time for an order received and (b) the average manufacturing lead time per order for each product, if SRG introduces Y28.

19-32 Waiting times, relevant revenues, and relevant costs (continuation of 19-31). SRG is still deciding whether it should introduce Y28. The following table provides information on selling prices, variable costs, and inventory carrying costs for Z39 and Y28. SRG will incur additional variable costs and inventory carrying costs for Y28 only if it introduces Y28. Fixed costs equal to 40% of variable costs are allocated to all products produced and sold during the year.

Product	Annual Average Number of Orders	Average Selling Price per Order If Average Manufacturing Lead Time per Order Is: Less Than 320 Hours	More Than 320 Hours	Variable Cost per Order	Inventory Carrying Cost per Order per Hour
Z39	50	$27,000	$26,500	$15,000	$0.75
Y28	25	8,400	8,000	5,000	0.25

Required

1. Should SRG manufacture and sell Y28? Show your calculations.

2. Should SRG manufacture and sell Y28 if the data in problem 19-31 is changed as follows: average selling price per order is $6,400 instead of $8,400, if average manufacturing lead time per order is less than 320 hours; and $6,000 instead of $8,000, if average manufacturing lead time per order is more than 320 hours? All other data for Y28 are the same.

19-33 Manufacturing lead times, relevant revenues, and relevant costs. The Brandt Corporation makes wire harnesses for the aircraft industry. Brandt is uncertain about when and how many customer orders will be received. The company makes harnesses only after receiving firm orders from its customers. Brandt has recently purchased a new machine to make two types of wire harnesses, one for Boeing airplanes (B7) and the other for Airbus Industries airplanes (A3). The annual capacity of the new machine is 6,000 hours. The following information is available for next year.

Customer	Annual Average Number of Orders	Manufacturing Time Required	Average Selling Price per Order If Average Manufacturing Lead Time Is Less Than 200 Hours	More Than 200 Hours	Variable Costs per Order	Inventory Carrying Costs per Order per Hour
B7	125	40 hours	$15,000	$14,400	$10,000	$0.50
A3	10	50 hours	13,500	12,960	9,000	0.45

Required

1. Calculate the average manufacturing lead times per order (a) if Brandt manufactures only B7 and (b) if Brandt manufactures both B7 and A3.
2. Even though A3 has a positive contribution margin, Brandt's managers are evaluating whether Brandt should (a) make and sell only B7 or (b) make and sell both B7 and A3. Which alternative will maximize Brandt's operating income? Show your calculations.
3. What other factors should Brandt consider in choosing between the alternatives in requirement 2?

19-34 Theory of constraints, throughput contribution, relevant costs. Colorado Industries manufactures electronic testing equipment. Colorado also installs the equipment at customers' sites and ensures that it functions smoothly. Additional information on the Manufacturing and Installation departments is as follows (capacities are expressed in terms of the number of units of electronic testing equipment):

	Equipment Manufactured	Equipment Installed
Annual capacity	400 units per year	300 units per year
Equipment manufactured and installed	300 units per year	300 units per year

Colorado manufactures only 300 units per year because the Installation Department has only enough capacity to install 300 units. The equipment sells for $40,000 per unit (installed) and has direct materials costs of $15,000. All costs other than direct materials costs are fixed. The following requirements refer only to the preceding data. There is no connection between the requirements.

Required

1. Colorado's engineers have found a way to reduce equipment manufacturing time. The new method would cost an additional $50 per unit and would allow Colorado to manufacture 20 additional units a year. Should Colorado implement the new method? Show your calculations.
2. Colorado's designers have proposed a change in direct materials that would increase direct materials costs by $2,000 per unit. This change would enable Colorado to install 320 units of equipment each year. If Colorado makes the change, it will implement the new design on all equipment sold. Should Colorado use the new design? Show your calculations.
3. A new installation technique has been developed that will enable Colorado's engineers to install 10 additional units of equipment a year. The new method will increase installation costs by $50,000 each year. Should Colorado implement the new technique? Show your calculations.
4. Colorado is considering how to motivate workers to improve their productivity (output per hour). One proposal is to evaluate and compensate workers in the Manufacturing and Installation departments on the basis of their productivities. Do you think the new proposal is a good idea? Explain briefly.

19-35 Theory of constraints, throughput contribution, quality, relevant costs. Aardee Industries manufactures pharmaceutical products in two departments: Mixing and Tablet-Making. Additional information on the two departments follows. Each tablet contains 0.5 gram of direct materials.

	Mixing	Tablet Making
Capacity per hour	150 grams	200 tablets
Monthly capacity (2,000 hours available in each of mixing and tablet making)	300,000 grams	400,000 tablets
Monthly production	200,000 grams	390,000 tablets
Fixed operating costs (excluding direct materials)	$16,000	$39,000
Fixed operating costs per tablet ($16,000 ÷ 200,000; $39,000 ÷ 390,000)	$0.08 per gram	$0.10 per tablet

The Mixing Department makes 200,000 grams of direct materials mixture (enough to make 400,000 tablets) because the Tablet-Making Department has only enough capacity to process 400,000 tablets. All direct materials costs are incurred in the Mixing Department. Aardee incurs $156,000 in direct materials costs. The Tablet-Making Department manufactures only 390,000 tablets from the 200,000 grams of mixture processed; 2.5% of the direct materials mixture is lost in the tablet-making process. Each tablet sells for $1. All costs other than direct materials costs are fixed costs. The following requirements refer only to the preceding data. There is no connection between the requirements.

Required

1. An outside contractor makes the following offer: If Aardee will supply the contractor with 10,000 grams of mixture, the contractor will manufacture 19,500 tablets for Aardee (allowing for the normal 2.5% loss during the tablet-making process) at $0.12 per tablet. Should Aardee accept the contractor's offer? Show your calculations.
2. Another company offers to prepare 20,000 grams of mixture a month from direct materials Aardee supplies. The company will charge $0.07 per gram of mixture. Should Aardee accept the company's offer? Show your calculations.
3. Aardee's engineers have devised a method that would improve quality in the tablet-making operation. They estimate that the 10,000 tablets currently being lost would be saved. The modification would cost $7,000 a month. Should Aardee implement the new method? Show your calculations.
4. Suppose that Aardee also loses 10,000 grams of mixture in its mixing operation. These losses can be reduced to zero if the company is willing to spend $9,000 per month in quality-improvement methods. Should Aardee adopt the quality-improvement method? Show your calculations.
5. What are the benefits of improving quality at the mixing operation compared with improving quality at the tablet-making operation?

19-36 Quality improvement, Pareto diagram, cause-and-effect diagram. The Murray Corporation manufactures, sells, and installs photocopying machines. Murray has placed heavy emphasis on reducing defects and failures in its production operations. Murray wants to apply the same total quality management principles to manage its accounts receivable.

Required

1. On the basis of your knowledge and experience, what would you classify as failures in accounts receivable?
2. Give examples of prevention activities that could reduce failures in accounts receivable.
3. Draw a Pareto diagram of the types of failures in accounts receivable and cause-and-effect diagram of possible causes of one type of failure in accounts receivable.

19-37 Ethics and quality. Information from a quality report for 2004 prepared by Lindsey Williams, assistant controller of Citocell, a manufacturer of electric motors, is as follows:

Revenues	$10,000,000
Inspection of production	90,000
Warranty liability	260,000
Product testing	210,000
Scrap	230,000
Design engineering	200,000
Percentage of customer complaints	5%
On-time delivery rate	93%

Davey Evans, the plant manager of Citocell, is eligible for a bonus if the total costs of quality as a percentage of revenues are less than 10%, the percentage of customer complaints is less than 4%, and the on-time delivery rate exceeds 92%. Evans is unhappy about the customer complaints of 5% because, when preparing her report, Williams actually surveyed customers regarding customer satisfaction. Evans expected Williams to be less proactive and wait for customers to complain. Evans's concern with Williams's approach is that it introduces subjectivity into the results and also fails to capture the seriousness of customers' concerns. "When you wait for a customer to complain, you know they are complaining because it is something important. When you do customer surveys, customers mention whatever is on their mind, even if it is not terribly important."

John Roche, the controller, asks Williams to see him. He tells her about Evans's concerns. "I think Davey has a point. See what you can do." Williams is confident that the customer complaints are genuine and that customers are concerned about quality and service. She believes it is important for Citocell to be proactive and obtain systematic and quick customer feedback, and then to use this information to make improvements. She is also well aware that Citocell has not done customer surveys in the past, and except for her surveys, Evans would probably be eligible for the bonus. She is confused about how to handle Roche's request.

Required

1. Calculate the ratio of each cost-of-quality category (prevention, appraisal, internal failure, and external failure) to revenues in 2004. Are the total costs of quality as a percentage of revenues less than 10%?
2. Would it be unethical for Williams to modify her analysis? What steps should Williams take to resolve this situation?

Collaborative Learning Problem

19-38 Quality improvement, theory of constraints. The Wellesley Corporation makes printed cloth in two operations, weaving and printing. Direct materials costs are Wellesley's only variable costs. The demand for Wellesley's cloth is very strong. Wellesley can sell whatever output quantities it produces at $1,250 per roll to a distributor who markets, distributes, and provides customer service for the product.

	Weaving	Printing
Monthly capacity	10,000 rolls	15,000 rolls
Monthly production	9,500 rolls	8,550 rolls
Direct materials costs per roll of cloth processed at each operation	$500	$100
Fixed operating costs	$2,850,000	$427,500
Fixed operating costs per roll ($2,850,000 ÷ 9,500; $427,500 ÷ 8,550)	$300 per roll	$50 per roll

Wellesley can start only 10,000 rolls of cloth in the Weaving Department because of capacity constraints of the weaving machines. If the weaving operation produces defective cloth, the cloth must be scrapped and yields zero net disposal value. Of the 10,000 rolls of cloth started at the weaving operation, 500 rolls (5%) are scrapped. Scrap costs per roll, based on total (fixed and variable) manufacturing costs per roll incurred up to the end of the weaving operation, equal $785 per roll as follows:

Direct materials costs per roll (variable)	$500
Fixed operating costs per roll ($2,850,000 ÷ 10,000 rolls)	285
Total manufacturing costs per roll in Weaving Department	$785

The good rolls from the Weaving Department (called gray cloth) are sent to the Printing Department. Of the 9,500 good rolls started at the printing operation, 950 rolls (10%) are scrapped and yield zero net disposal value. Scrap costs, based on total (fixed and variable) manufacturing costs per unit incurred up to the end of the printing operation, equal $930 per roll calculated as follows:

Total manufacturing costs per roll in Weaving Department		$785
Printing Department manufacturing costs		
Direct materials costs per roll (variable)	$100	
Fixed operating costs per roll ($427,500 ÷ 9,500 rolls)	45	
Total manufacturing costs per roll in Printing Department		145
Total manufacturing costs per roll		$930

The Wellesley Corporation's total monthly sales of printed cloth equal the Printing Department's output.

Required Each requirement refers only to the preceding data. There is no connection between the requirements.

1. The Printing Department is considering buying 5,000 additional rolls of gray cloth from an outside supplier at $900 per roll. The Printing Department manager is concerned that the cost of purchasing the gray cloth is much higher than Wellesley's cost of manufacturing it. The quality of the gray cloth acquired from outside is very similar to that manufactured in-house. The Printing Department expects that 10% of the rolls obtained from the outside supplier will be scrapped. Should the Printing Department buy the gray cloth from the outside supplier? Show your calculations.
2. Wellesley's engineers have developed a method that would lower the Printing Department's scrap rate to 6% at the printing operation. Implementing the new method would cost $350,000 per month. Should Wellesley implement the change? Show your calculations.
3. The design engineering team has proposed a modification that would lower the Weaving Department's scrap rate to 3%. The modification would cost the company $175,000 per month. Should Wellesley implement the change? Show your calculations.

CHAPTER 19 INTERNET EXERCISE

In today's competitive manufacturing environment, margins are thinner than ever, and customers are demanding ever-higher levels of quality. But rather than costing money, quality improvement programs can actually produce significant savings and improve profitability. To learn how, go to www.prenhall.com/horngren, click on *Cost Accounting,* 11th ed., and access the Internet exercise for Chapter 19.

CHAPTER 19 VIDEO CASE

RITZ-CARLTON HOTEL COMPANY: Managing Quality

If you have only heard or read the name "The Ritz-Carlton," you are probably thinking of luxury and quality. That's what the managers at their 31 hotels and resorts want you to think. As managers at the first hotel company ever to win the Malcolm Baldrige National Quality Award, they see quality as a daily commitment to meeting customer expectations and making sure each hotel is free of any deficiency in fulfilling those expectations. In the hotel industry, quality can be hard to quantify. Ritz-Carlton guests do not purchase a product, they buy an experience. So creating the right combination of elements to make the experience outstanding to guests is the challenge and the goal of every employee, from maintenance to management.

Before applying for consideration for the Baldridge Award, company management undertook a rigorous self-examination of its operations in an attempt to measure and quantify quality. Nineteen processes were studied, including room service, guest reservation and registration, message delivery, and breakfast service. This period of self-study included statistical measurement of process work flows and cycle times for areas ranging from room-service delivery times and reservations to valet parking and housekeeping efficiency. Each hotel focused on one of the 19 areas for a year. The results were used to develop benchmarks against which future performance could be measured.

With specific, quantifiable targets in place, managers at the Ritz-Carlton now focus on continuous improvement. The goal is 100% customer satisfaction. Each hotel and resort property is run as an independent business, so the general manager at each location takes ownership for monitoring quality and taking action to prevent problems from arising or affecting a guest. Performance is reviewed at daily and weekly management meetings, and results are communicated back to employees. After all, if a guest's experience does not meet expectations, the company risks losing that guest to the competition.

One way the company has put more meaning behind its quality efforts is to organize its employees into "self-directed" work teams. The teams are formed within each functional area of the hotel, such as guest services, valet services, food and beverages, housekeeping, and maintenance. Managers no longer operate in command-and-control mode, in which orders are dictated and expected to be carried out. Instead, the employee teams determine employee work scheduling, what work needs to be done, and what to do about quality problems in their areas. Managers are expected to become facilitators and resources for helping the teams achieve their quality goals. Employees are also given the opportunity to take additional training on how the hotel is run, so they can see the relationship of their specific area's efforts to the overall goals of the hotel. Training topics range from budgets and purchasing to payroll and controllable costs. Employees are then tested and compensated for successful completion of training. The Ritz-Carlton expects that a more-educated and informed employee will be in a better position to make decisions that are in the best interest of guests and the organization.

QUESTIONS

1. In what ways could the Ritz-Carlton monitor its success at achieving quality?
2. Many companies say their goal is to provide quality products or services. What actions might you expect from a company that intends "quality" to be more than a slogan?
3. How does lack of quality, or missing a quality goal, affect Ritz-Carlton's contribution margin?
4. Why might it cost the Ritz-Carlton less to "do things right" first time?
5. How could control charts, Pareto diagrams, and cause-and-effect diagrams be used to identify quality problems?
6. What are some nonfinancial measures of customer satisfaction that might be used by the Ritz-Carlton?

CHAPTER

20

Inventory Management, Just-in-Time, and Backflush Costing

LEARNING OBJECTIVES

1. Identify five categories of costs associated with goods for sale
2. Balance ordering costs with carrying costs using the economic-order-quantity (EOQ) decision model
3. Identify and reduce conflicts that can arise between the EOQ decision model and models used for performance evaluation
4. Use a supply-chain approach to inventory management
5. Distinguish materials requirements planning (MRP) systems from just-in-time (JIT) systems for manufacturing
6. Identify the features of a just-in-time production system
7. Use backflush costing
8. Describe different ways backflush costing can simplify traditional job-costing systems

www.prenhall.com/horngren

Have you ever had to step past others already seated to get into your seat just as a movie was about to start? Do you regularly get to your classes with seconds to spare? If so, arriving just in time in the social world may not be regarded very well. But, in the world of inventory management, materials that arrive "just in time" for use in production are not only planned, they're desirable! At Regal Marine, storage space for direct materials waiting to be used in the production of power boats is costly, so big-ticket items such as wood products, engines, and upholstery fabrics arrive at the plant just at the time they're needed in production. This way, Regal Marine doesn't incur storage costs and avoids tying up investment dollars in direct materials inventory. Good inventory management helps keep Regal Marine afloat!

Inventory management is a big part of profit planning for manufacturing and merchandising companies. Materials costs often account for more than 40% of total costs of manufacturing companies and more than 70% of total costs in merchandising companies. Accounting information can play a key role in inventory management. We first consider retail organizations and then manufacturing companies.

INVENTORY MANAGEMENT IN RETAIL ORGANIZATIONS

Management accounting is not a synonym for manufacturing accounting. This point is illustrated by the coverage of retail companies in this chapter.

Inventory management is the planning, coordinating, and controlling activities related to the flow of inventory into, through, and out of an organization. Consider this breakdown of operations for three major retailers for which cost of goods sold constitutes their largest cost item.

	Kroger	Safeway	Wal-Mart
Revenues	100.0%	100.0%	100.0%
Deduct costs:			
Cost of goods sold	76.8	70.4	78.4
Selling and administration costs	18.3	22.5	16.0
Other costs, interest, and taxes	3.5	4.4	2.7
Total costs	98.6	97.3	97.1
Net income	1.4%	2.7%	2.9%

The percentages of net income to revenues are low. This means that better decisions regarding the purchasing and managing of goods for sale can cause dramatic percentage increases in net income.

Costs Associated with Goods for Sale

1 Identify five categories of costs associated with goods for sale

...purchasing, ordering, carrying, stockout, and quality costs

Managing inventories to increase net income requires effectively managing costs that fall into the following five categories:

Toyota works with suppliers to reduce purchasing costs. It sends teams of manufacturing experts to help suppliers streamline their production processes, which helps them meet Toyota's expected annual price reductions and its demands for high quality and on-time delivery.

1. **Purchasing costs** — The cost of goods acquired from suppliers, including incoming freight or transportation costs. These costs usually make up the largest cost category of goods for sale. Discounts for different purchase-order sizes and supplier credit terms affect purchasing costs.
2. **Ordering costs** — The costs of preparing and issuing purchase orders, receiving and inspecting the items included in the orders, and matching invoices received, purchase orders, and delivery records to make payments. Ordering costs include the cost of obtaining purchase approvals, as well as other special processing costs.
3. **Carrying costs** — The costs that arise while holding inventory of goods for sale. Carrying costs include the opportunity cost of the investment tied up in inventory (see Chapter 11, pp. 380–382) and the costs associated with storage, such as space rental, insurance, obsolescence, and spoilage.

Costs associated with goods for resale include opportunity costs that aren't recorded in the financial accounting system.

4. **Stockout costs** — These are costs that result when a company runs out of a particular item for which there is customer demand — a stockout — and the company must act quickly to meet that demand or suffer the costs of not meeting it. A company may respond to a stockout by expediting an order from a supplier. Expediting costs of a stockout include the additional ordering costs plus any associated transportation costs. Or the company may lose sales due to the stockout. In this case, the opportunity cost of the

stockout includes the lost contribution margin on the sale not made due to the item not being in stock, plus any contribution margin lost on future sales due to customer ill will caused by the stockout.

5. **Quality costs**—These are the costs that result when features and characteristics of a product or service are not in conformance with customer specifications. There are four categories of quality costs—prevention costs, appraisal costs, internal failure costs, and external failure costs—described in Chapter 19.

Looking through these five cost categories, you should realize that not all the relevant costs for managing goods for sale are available in existing financial accounting systems. Opportunity costs, which are not typically recorded in those systems, are a significant component in several of these cost categories.

Information-gathering technology increases the reliability and timeliness of inventory information and reduces costs in the five cost categories. For example, bar-coding technology allows a scanner to record purchases and sales of individual units. As soon as a unit is scanned, an instantaneous record of inventory movements is created that helps in the management of purchasing, carrying, and stockout costs.

Economic-Order-Quantity Decision Model

2 Balance ordering costs with carrying costs using the economic-order-quantity (EOQ) decision model

...choose the inventory quantity per order to minimize costs

The first decision in managing goods for sale is how much to order of a given product. The **economic order quantity (EOQ)** is a decision model that calculates the optimal quantity of inventory to order under a set of assumptions. The simplest version of an EOQ model assumes there are only ordering and carrying costs, and it also assumes:

1. The same quantity is ordered at each reorder point.
2. Demand, ordering costs, and carrying costs are known with certainty. The **purchase-order lead time**—the time between placing an order and its delivery—is also known with certainty.
3. Purchasing costs per unit are unaffected by the quantity ordered. This assumption makes purchasing costs irrelevant to determining EOQ because purchasing costs of all units acquired will be the same, regardless of the order size in which the units are ordered.
4. No stockouts occur. The basis for this assumption is that the costs of stockouts are so high that managers maintain adequate inventory to prevent them.
5. In deciding the size of a purchase order, managers consider costs of quality only to the extent that these costs affect ordering or carrying costs.

Given these assumptions, EOQ analysis ignores purchasing costs, stockout costs, and quality costs. EOQ is the order quantity that minimizes the relevant ordering and carrying costs (that is, the ordering and carrying costs affected by the quantity of inventory ordered):

Relevant total costs = Relevant ordering costs + Relevent carrying costs

Example: Video Galore, a video rental store, also sells blank videotapes. It purchases videotapes from Sontek at $14 a package. Sontek pays for all incoming freight. No incoming inspection is necessary because Sontek has a reputation for delivering quality merchandise. Video Galore's annual demand is 13,000 packages, at a rate of 250 packages per week. Video Galore requires a 15% annual return on investment. The purchase-order lead time is two weeks. Relevant ordering costs per purchase order are $200.

Relevant carrying costs per package per year are

Required annual return on investment, 0.15 × $14	*$2.10*
Relevant insurance, materials handling, breakage, and so on, per year	*3.10*
Total	*$5.20*

What is the EOQ of packages of videotapes?

You may be familiar with EOQ, reorder point, and safety stock from finance or production courses. In those courses, costs are assumed. Accountants help (1) decide what costs to include in these calculations and (2) estimate the amounts of these costs.

Carrying costs are higher than you may think. In many companies, average annual carrying costs exceed 30% of purchasing costs. Video Galore's annual carrying costs are 37% ($5.20 ÷ $14.00).

The formula for the EOQ model is

$$EOQ = \sqrt{\frac{2DP}{C}}$$

where

D = Demand in units for a specified period (one year in this example)
P = Relevant ordering costs per purchase order
C = Relevant carrying costs of one unit in stock for the time period used for D (one year)

The formula indicates that EOQ increases with demand and ordering costs and decreases with carrying costs.

For Video Galore:

$$\text{EOQ} = \sqrt{\frac{2 \times 13{,}000 \times \$200}{\$5.20}} = \sqrt{1{,}000{,}000} = 1{,}000 \text{ packages}$$

Purchasing 1,000 packages per order minimizes total ordering and carrying costs.

The annual relevant total costs (RTC) for any order quantity, Q, can be calculated as follows:

$$\text{RTC} = \begin{matrix}\text{Annual}\\ \text{relevant ordering}\\ \text{costs}\end{matrix} + \begin{matrix}\text{Annual}\\ \text{relevant carrying}\\ \text{costs}\end{matrix}$$

$$= \left(\begin{matrix}\text{Number of}\\ \text{purchase orders}\\ \text{per year}\end{matrix} \times \begin{matrix}\text{Relevant ordering}\\ \text{cost per}\\ \text{purchase order}\end{matrix}\right) + \left(\begin{matrix}\text{Average inventory}\\ \text{in units}\end{matrix} \times \begin{matrix}\text{Annual}\\ \text{relevant carrying}\\ \text{costs of one unit}\end{matrix}\right)$$

$$\text{RTC} = \left(\frac{D}{Q} \times P\right) + \left(\frac{Q}{2} \times C\right)$$
$$= \frac{DP}{Q} + \frac{QC}{2}$$

In this formula, Q can be any order quantity, not just the EOQ.

When Q = 1,000 units,

$$\text{RTC} = \frac{13{,}000 \times \$200}{1{,}000} + \frac{1{,}000 \times \$5.20}{2}$$
$$= \$2{,}600 + \$2{,}600 = \$5{,}200$$

The number of deliveries each period (one year in this example) is

$$\frac{D}{\text{EOQ}} = \frac{13{,}000}{1{,}000} = 13 \text{ deliveries}$$

Exhibit 20-1 graphs the annual relevant total costs of ordering (DP/Q) and carrying inventory ($QC/2$) under various order sizes (Q), and it illustrates the trade-off between these two types of costs. The larger the order quantity, the lower the annual relevant ordering costs, but the higher the annual relevant carrying costs. *Annual relevant total costs are at a minimum at the EOQ at which the relevant ordering and carrying costs are equal.*

When to Order, Assuming Certainty

The second decision in managing goods for sale is when to order a given product. The **reorder point** is the quantity level of the inventory on hand that triggers a new purchase order. The reorder point is simplest to compute when both demand and purchase-order lead time are known with certainty:

$$\text{Reorder point} = \begin{matrix}\text{Number of units sold}\\ \text{per unit of time}\end{matrix} \times \begin{matrix}\text{Purchase-order}\\ \text{lead time}\end{matrix}$$

In our Video Galore example, we choose one week as the unit of time in the reorder point formula:

The intuition behind the reorder-point formula is that we need to reorder when the inventory on hand falls to the level at which it equals the amount needed for sales that will occur during the purchase-order lead time.

Economic order quantity	1,000 packages
Number of units sold per week	250 packages per week
Purchase-order lead time	2 weeks

Reorder point = 250 packages per week × 2 weeks = 500 packages

EXHIBIT 20-1 Graphic Analysis of Ordering Costs and Carrying Costs for Video Galore

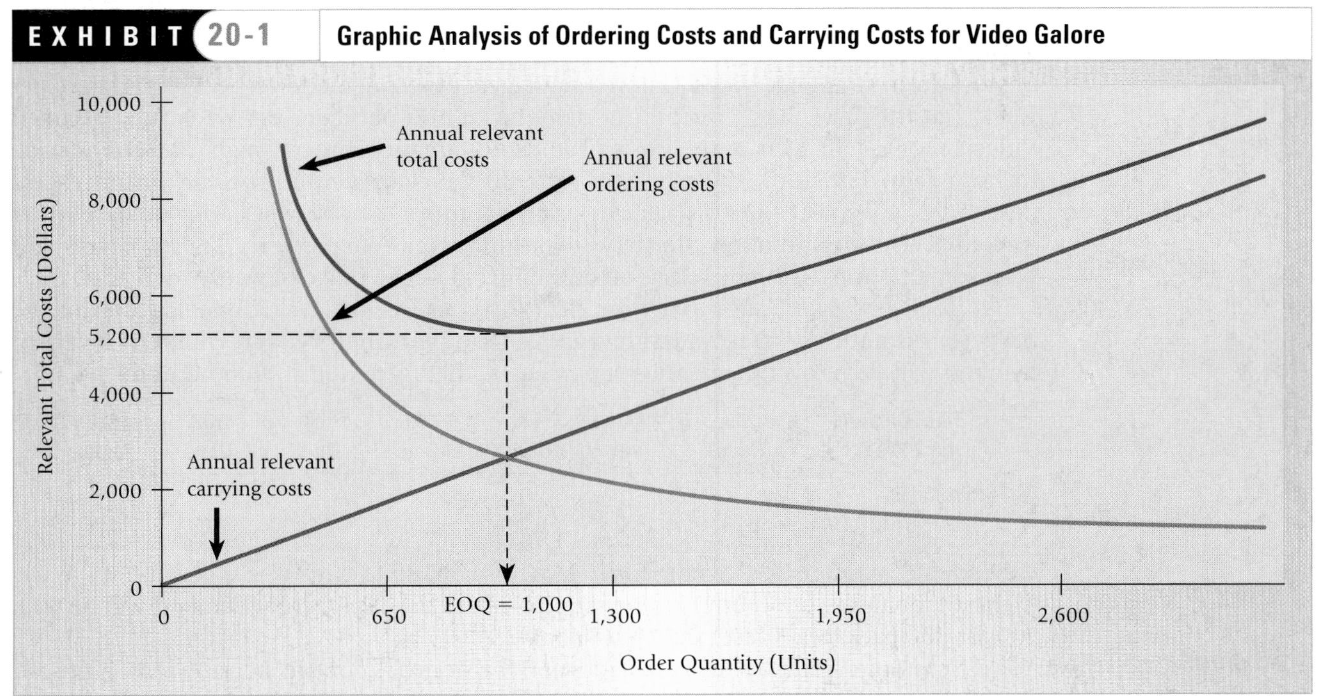

Video Galore will order 1,000 packages each time inventory stock falls to 500 packages. The graph in Exhibit 20-2 shows the behavior of the inventory level of tape packages, assuming demand occurs uniformly during each week.[1] If the purchase-order lead time is two weeks, a new order will be placed when the inventory level falls to 500 packages, so the 1,000 packages ordered will be received at the precise time that inventory reaches zero.

Particularly for low-cost items, companies often use simple signals—such as stock falling below painted lines in bins—to indicate it's time to reorder.

Safety Stock

We have assumed that demand and purchase-order lead time are known with certainty. Retailers who are uncertain about demand, lead time, or the quantity that suppliers can provide, hold safety stock. **Safety stock** is inventory held at all times regardless of the

EXHIBIT 20-2 Inventory Level of Tape Packages for Video Galore[a]

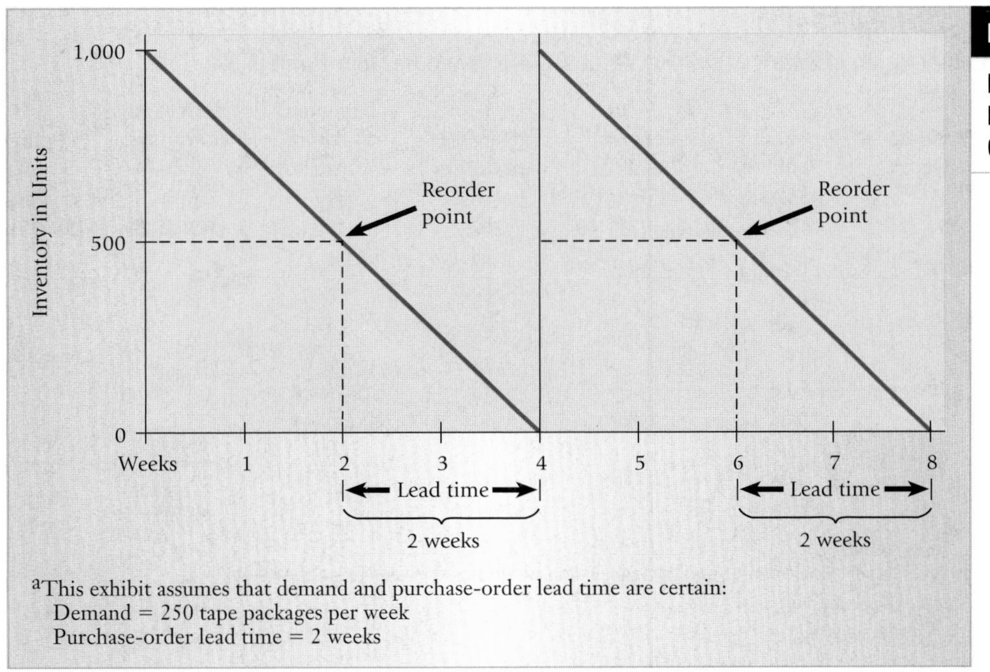

[a]This exhibit assumes that demand and purchase-order lead time are certain:
Demand = 250 tape packages per week
Purchase-order lead time = 2 weeks

[1]This handy but special formula does not apply when the receipt of the order fails to increase inventory to the reorder-point quantity (for example, when the lead time is three weeks and the order is a one-week supply). In these cases, orders will overlap.

quantity of inventory ordered using the EOQ model. Safety stock is used as a buffer against unexpected increases in demand, uncertainty about lead time, and unavailability of stock from suppliers. Video Galore's managers expect demand to be 250 packages per week, but they feel that a maximum demand of 400 packages per week may occur. If Video Galore's managers decide costs of stockouts are prohibitively high, they may decide to hold safety stock of 300 packages. The 300 packages equal the maximum excess demand of 150 (400 – 250) packages per week times the two weeks of purchase-order lead time. The computation of safety stock hinges on demand forecasts. Managers will have some notion—usually based on experience—of the range of weekly demand.

A frequency distribution based on prior daily or weekly levels of demand forms the basis for computing safety stock levels. Assume that one of seven different levels of demand will occur over the two-week purchase-order lead time at Video Galore.

Total Demand for 2 Weeks	**200 Units**	**300 Units**	**400 Units**	**500 Units**	**600 Units**	**700 Units**	**800 Units**
Probability (sums to 1.00)	0.06	0.09	0.20	0.30	0.20	0.09	0.06

We see that 500 units is the most likely level of demand for two weeks because it has the highest probability of occurrence. We see also a 0.35 probability that demand will be 600, 700, or 800 packages (0.20 + 0.09 + 0.06 = 0.35).

In the Video Galore example, stockout costs include only the cost of rush orders, because rush orders are assumed to fully satisfy customer demand. However, stockouts can result in opportunity costs—lost contribution margin on lost current sales and lost future sales.

If a customer wants to buy videotapes and the store has none in stock, Video Galore can "rush" them to the customer at an additional cost to Video Galore of $4 per package. The relevant stockout costs in this case are $4 per package. The optimal safety stock level is the quantity of safety stock that minimizes the sum of the annual relevant stockout and carrying costs. Recall, the relevant carrying costs for Video Galore are $5.20 per unit per year.

Exhibit 20-3 tabulates the total annual relevant stockout and carrying costs when the reorder point is 500 units. We need only consider safety stock levels of 0, 100, 200, and 300 units, because demand will exceed the 500 units of stock available at reordering by 0 if demand is 500, by 100 if demand is 600, by 200 if demand is 700, and by 300 if demand is 800. As Exhibit 20-3 shows, the annual relevant total stockout and carrying costs would be minimized at $1,352, when a safety stock of 200 packages is maintained. Consider the 200 units of safety stock as extra stock that Video Galore maintains. For example, Video Galore's total inventory of tapes at the time of reordering its EOQ of 1,000 units would be 700 units (the reorder point of 500 units plus the safety stock of 200 units).

In calculating safety stock, the trade-off is between stockout costs and carrying costs. Columns 7 and 8 in Exhibit 20-3 show this trade-off.

EXHIBIT 20-3 Computation of Safety Stock For Video Galore When Reorder Point Is 500 Units

Safety Stock Level in Units (1)	Demand Levels Resulting in Stockouts (2)	Stockout in Units[a] (3) = (2) – 500 – (1)	Probability of Stockout (4)	Relevant Stockout Costs[b] (5) = (3) × $4	Number of Orders per Year[c] (6)	Expected Stockout Costs[d] (7) = (4) × (5) × (6)	Relevant Carrying Costs[e] (8) = (1) × $5.20	Relevant Total Costs (9) = (7) + (8)
0	600	100	0.20	$ 400	13	$1,040		
	700	200	0.09	800	13	936		
	800	300	0.06	1,200	13	936		
						$2,912	$ 0	$2,912
100	700	100	0.09	400	13	$ 468		
	800	200	0.06	800	13	624		
						$1,092	$ 520	$1,612
200	800	100	0.06	400	13	$ 312	$1,040	$1,352
300	—	—	—	—	—	$ 0[f]	$1,560	$1,560

[a]Demand level resulting in stockouts – Inventory available during lead time (excluding safety stock), 500 units – Safety stock.
[b]Stockout units × Relevant stockout costs of $4.00 per unit.
[c]Annual demand, 13,000, ÷ 1,000 EOQ = 13 orders per year.
[d]Probability of stockout × Relevant stockout costs × Number of orders per year.
[e]Safety stock × Annual relevant carrying costs of $5.20 per unit (assumes that safety stock is on hand at all times and that there is no overstocking caused by decreases in expected usage).
[f]At a safety stock level of 300 units, no stockouts will occur and, hence, expected stockout costs = $0.

ESTIMATING INVENTORY-RELATED COSTS AND THEIR EFFECTS

As in earlier chapters, you need to determine which costs are relevant when making and evaluating decisions. Here, we need to determine relevant costs for inventory decisions.

Considerations in Obtaining Estimates of Relevant Costs

Implementing the EOQ decision model requires accurate estimates of the annual relevant carrying costs of inventory. Relevant inventory carrying costs consist of the *relevant incremental costs* plus the *relevant opportunity cost of capital.*

What are the *relevant incremental costs* of carrying inventory? Only those costs of the purchasing company—for example, warehouse salaries and rent, costs of obsolescence, and costs of breakage—that change with the quantity of inventory held. Consider the salaries paid to clerks, storekeepers, and materials handlers. These costs are irrelevant if they are unaffected by changes in inventory levels. Suppose, however, that as inventories decrease, total salary costs decrease as the clerks, storekeepers, and materials handlers are transferred to other activities or laid off. In this case, the salaries paid are relevant costs of carrying inventory. Similarly, the costs of storage space owned that cannot be used for other profitable purposes when inventories decrease are irrelevant. But if the space has other profitable uses, or if total rental cost is tied to the amount of space occupied, storage costs are relevant costs of carrying inventory.

What is the *relevant opportunity cost of capital*? It is the return forgone by investing capital in inventory rather than elsewhere. It is calculated as the required rate of return multiplied by those per unit costs that (a) vary with the number of units purchased and (b) are incurred at the time the units are received. (Examples of these per unit costs are the price of units purchased, incoming freight, and incoming inspection.) Opportunity costs are not computed on investments (say, in buildings) if these investments are unaffected by changes in inventory levels.

Finance courses explain how to estimate the cost of capital.

In the case of stockouts, calculating the relevant opportunity cost requires an estimate of the lost contribution margin on the sales lost due to a stockout, as well as the lost contribution margin on future sales lost because of customer ill will resulting from the stockout.

Cost of a Prediction Error

Predicting relevant costs is difficult and seldom flawless, which raises the question, What is the cost when actual relevant costs differ from the estimated relevant costs used for decision making?

Revisit Video Galore. Suppose relevant ordering costs per purchase order are \$100, instead of the \$200 estimate we used earlier. We can calculate the cost of this "prediction" error using a three-step approach.

Step 1: Compute the Monetary Outcome from the Best Action That Could Be Taken, Given the Actual Amount of the Cost Input. Using $D = 13{,}000$ units, $P = \$100$, and $C = \$5.20$,

$$\begin{aligned} \text{EOQ} &= \sqrt{\frac{2DP}{C}} \\ &= \sqrt{\frac{2 \times 13{,}000 \times \$100}{\$5.20}} = \sqrt{500{,}000} \\ &= 707 \text{ packages (rounded)} \end{aligned}$$

The annual relevant total cost when EOQ = 707 packages is

$$\begin{aligned} \text{RTC} &= \frac{DP}{Q} + \frac{QC}{2} \\ &= \frac{13{,}000 \times \$100}{707} + \frac{707 \times \$5.20}{2} \\ &= \$1{,}839 + \$1{,}838 = \$3{,}677 \end{aligned}$$

Step 2: Compute the Monetary Outcome from the Best Action Based on the Incorrect Amount of the Predicted Cost Input. The planned action when the relevant ordering costs per purchase order are predicted to be \$200 is to purchase 1,000 packages in each order (p. 688). The annual relevant total costs using this order quantity when $D = 13{,}000$ units, $P = \$100$, and $C = \$5.20$ are

$$\begin{aligned} \text{RTC} &= \frac{13{,}000 \times \$100}{1{,}000} + \frac{1{,}000 \times \$5.20}{2} \\ &= \$1{,}300 + \$2{,}600 = \$3{,}900 \end{aligned}$$

Step 3: Compute the Difference Between the Monetary Outcomes from Step 1 and Step 2.

	Monetary Outcome
Step 1	$3,677
Step 2	3,900
Difference	$ (223)

The cost of the prediction error, $223, is less than 7% of relevant total costs. The annual relevant total costs curve in Exhibit 20-1 is somewhat flat over the range of order quantities from 650 to 1,300 units. *The square root in the EOQ model reduces the sensitivity of the ordering decision to errors in predicting its parameters.*

3 Identify and reduce conflicts that can arise between the EOQ decision model and models used for performance evaluation

...so managers take actions in the best interest of the company

Evaluating Managers and Goal-Congruence Issues

What happens if the order quantity chosen based on the EOQ decision model is not the same as the order quantity that managers implementing the inventory management decision would choose to make their own performance look best? For example, because there are no opportunity costs recorded in financial accounting systems, there is the possibility of a conflict between the EOQ model's optimal order quantity and the order quantity that the purchasing manager (who is evaluated on financial accounting numbers) will regard as optimal. If the opportunity costs of investments tied up in inventory are excluded from annual carrying costs when evaluating managers' performance, they will be inclined to purchase larger lot sizes of materials. Companies such as Coca-Cola and Wal-Mart resolve this conflict by evaluating performance so that carrying costs, *including a required return on investment,* are charged to the manager responsible for managing inventory levels. To reduce opportunity costs of the investments tied up in inventory, managers have an incentive to reduce inventory levels.

JUST-IN-TIME PURCHASING

Just-in-time (JIT) purchasing is the purchase of materials (or goods) so that they are delivered just as needed for production (or sales). Consider JIT purchasing for Hewlett-Packard's (HP's) manufacture of its computer products. HP has long-term agreements with suppliers for the major components of this product line. Each supplier is required to make frequent deliveries of small orders directly to the production floor, based on the production schedule that HP shares with its suppliers. Because HP holds very little inventory, a supplier who does not deliver components on time, or who delivers components that fail to meet agreed-upon quality standards, can cause an HP assembly plant to not meet its own scheduled deliveries for computer products.

JIT Purchasing and EOQ Model Parameters

Companies moving toward JIT purchasing to reduce their costs of carrying inventories (parameter C in the EOQ model) say that, in the past, those costs have actually been much greater than estimated because costs of warehousing, handling, shrinkage, and capital have not been properly identified. At the same time, the cost of placing a purchase order (parameter P in the EOQ model) is decreasing because:

- Companies are establishing long-term purchasing agreements defining price and quality terms over an extended period. Individual purchase orders covered by those agreements require no additional negotiation regarding price or quality.
- Companies are using electronic links, such as the Internet, to place purchase orders. The cost of placing orders on the Internet is estimated to be a small fraction of the cost of placing orders by telephone or by mail.

- Companies are using purchase-order cards (similar to consumer credit cards such as VISA and MasterCard). As long as purchasing personnel stay within preset total and individual-transaction dollar limits, traditional labor-intensive procurement approval mechanisms are not required.

Exhibit 20-4 tabulates the sensitivity of Video Galore's EOQ (p. 688) to changes in carrying and ordering costs. Exhibit 20-4 supports JIT purchasing: EOQ decreases and ordering frequency increases as relevant carrying costs increase and relevant ordering costs per purchase order decrease.

Relevant Benefits and Relevant Costs of JIT Purchasing

JIT purchasing is not guided solely by the EOQ model. The EOQ model is designed only to emphasize the trade-off between carrying and ordering costs. However, inventory management also includes purchasing costs, stockout costs, and quality costs. Acquiring quality materials and goods, receiving timely deliveries and avoiding stockouts is important in JIT purchasing.

Suppose Video Galore has recently established an Internet business-to-business purchase-order link with Sontek. Video Galore triggers a purchase order for tapes by a single computer entry. Payments are made electronically for batches of deliveries, rather than for each individual delivery. These changes reduce ordering costs from $200 to only $2 per purchase order! Video Galore will use the Internet purchase-order link whether or not it shifts to JIT purchasing. Video Galore is negotiating to have Sontek deliver 100 packages of videotapes 130 times per year (5 times every 2 weeks), instead of delivering 1,000 packages 13 times per year as calculated in Exhibit 20-1. Sontek is willing to make these frequent deliveries, but it would add a small additional amount of $0.02 to the price per package of tapes. Video Galore's required return on investment remains at 15%. Assume annual relevant costs of insurance, materials handling, breakage, and the like remain at $3.10 per package per year.

Also assume that Video Galore incurs no stockout costs under its current purchasing policy, because demand and purchase-order lead times during each four-week period are known with certainty. Video Galore is concerned that lower inventory levels from implementing JIT purchasing will lead to more stockouts because demand variations and delays in supplying tapes are more likely in the short time intervals between orders delivered under JIT purchasing. Despite Sontek's flexible manufacturing processes that enable it to respond rapidly to changing demand patterns, Video Galore expects to incur stockout costs on 150 tape packages per year under a JIT purchasing policy. In the event of a stockout, Video Galore will have to rush-order tape packages from another supplier at an additional cost of $4 per package. Should Video Galore implement the JIT purchasing option of 130 deliveries per year?

Exhibit 20-5 compares Video Galore's relevant costs under the current purchasing policy and the JIT policy, and it shows net cost savings of $1,245.85 per year by shifting to a JIT purchasing policy.

In evaluating and choosing suppliers, quality and on-time delivery become increasingly important as the emphasis shifts away from minimizing purchasing costs to minimizing costs across the entire value chain.

Supplier Evaluation and Relevant Costs of Quality and Timely Deliveries

Companies that implement JIT purchasing choose their suppliers carefully and pay special attention to developing long-run supplier partnerships. Some suppliers are well

EXHIBIT 20-4

Sensitivity of EOQ to Variations in Relevant Ordering and Carrying Costs for Video Galore[a]

Relevant Carrying Costs per Package per Year	Relevant Ordering Costs per Purchase Order			
	$200	$150	$100	$30
$ 5.20	EOQ = 1,000	EOQ = 866	EOQ = 707	EOQ = 387
7.00	862	746	609	334
10.00	721	624	510	279
15.00	589	510	416	228

[a]Assuming annual demand is always 13,000 packages.

EXHIBIT 20-5

Annual Relevant Costs of Current Purchasing Policy and JIT Purchasing Policy for Video Galore

Relevant Item	Relevant Costs Under Current Purchasing Policy	Relevant Costs Under JIT Purchasing Policy
Purchasing costs		
$14 per unit × 13,000 units per year	$182,000.00	
$14.02 per unit × 13,000 units per year		$182,260.00
Ordering costs		
$2 per order × 13 orders per year	26.00	
$2 per order × 130 orders per year		260.00
Opportunity carrying costs, required return on investment		
0.15 per year × $14 cost per unit × 500[a] units of average inventory per year	1,050.00	
0.15 per year × $14.02 cost per unit × 50[b] units of average inventory per year		105.15
Other carrying costs (insurance, materials handling, breakage, and so on)		
$3.10 per unit per year × 500[a] units of average inventory per year	1,550.00	
$3.10 per unit per year × 50[b] units of average inventory per year		155.00
Stockout costs		
No stockouts	0	
$4 per unit × 150 units per year		600.00
Total annual relevant costs	$184,626.00	$183,380.15
Annual difference in favor of JIT purchasing	$1,245.85	

[a]Order quantity ÷ 2 = 1,000 ÷ 2 = 500.
[b]Order quantity ÷ 2 = 100 ÷ 2 = 50.

positioned to support JIT purchasing. Frito-Lay, a supplier of potato chips and other snack foods, makes more-frequent deliveries to retail outlets than many of its competitors. The company's corporate strategy emphasizes service to retailers and consistency, freshness, and quality of the delivered products.

What are the relevant costs when choosing suppliers? Consider again Video Galore. Denton Corporation, another supplier of videotapes, offers to supply all of Video Galore's videotape needs at a price of $13.80 per package—less than Sontek's price of $14.02—under the same JIT delivery terms that Sontek offers. Denton proposes an Internet purchase-order link identical to Sontek's link, making Video Galore's ordering costs $2 per purchase order. Video Galore's relevant costs of insurance, materials handling, breakage, and the like would be $3.00 per package per year if it purchases from Denton, versus $3.10 if it purchases from Sontek. Should Video Galore buy from Denton? To answer, we need to consider the relevant costs of quality and delivery performance.

Video Galore has used Sontek in the past and knows that Sontek will deliver quality tapes on time. Video Galore does not inspect the tape packages that Sontek supplies. Denton, however, does not enjoy such a sterling reputation for quality. Video Galore anticipates the following negative aspects of using Denton:

- Inspection costs of $0.05 per package.
- Average stockouts of 360 tape packages per year requiring rush orders at an additional cost of $4 per package.
- Product returns of 2.5% of all packages sold due to poor tape quality. Video Galore estimates additional costs of $10 to handle each returned package.

Exhibit 20-6 shows the relevant costs of purchasing from Sontek and Denton. Even though Denton is offering a lower price per package, there is a net cost savings of $1,873.35 per year by purchasing tapes from Sontek. Selling high-quality merchandise also has nonfinancial benefits. Selling Sontek's high-quality tapes enhances Video Galore's reputation and increases customer goodwill, which may lead to higher future profitability.

EXHIBIT 20-6

Annual Relevant Costs of Purchasing from Sontek and Denton

Relevant Item	Relevant Costs of Purchasing from Sontek	Denton
Purchasing costs		
$14.02 per unit × 13,000 units per year	$182,260.00	
$13.80 per unit × 13,000 units per year		$179,400.00
Ordering costs		
$2 per order × 130 orders per year	260.00	
$2 per order × 130 orders per year		260.00
Inspection costs		
No inspection necessary	0	
$0.05 per unit × 13,000 units		650.00
Opportunity carrying costs, required return on investment		
0.15 per year × $14.02 × 50[a] units of average inventory per year	105.15	
0.15 per year × $13.80 × 50[a] units of average inventory per year		103.50
Other carrying costs (insurance, materials handling, breakage, and so on)		
$3.10 per unit per year × 50[a] units of average inventory per year	155.00	
$3.00 per unit per year × 50[a] units of average inventory per year		150.00
Stockout costs		
$4 per unit × 150 units per year	600.00	
$4 per unit × 360 units per year		1,440.00
Customer returns costs		
No customer returns	0	
$10 per unit returned × 2.5% × 13,000 units returned		3,250.00
Total annual relevant costs	$183,380.15	$185,253.50
Annual difference in favor of Sontek	$1,873.35	

[a]Order quantity ÷ 2 = 100 ÷ 2 = 50.

INVENTORY MANAGEMENT AND SUPPLY-CHAIN ANALYSIS

4 Use a supply-chain approach to inventory management

...coordinating flow of inventory and information from initial sources of materials to delivery of products to consumers

The levels of inventories held by retailers are influenced by the demand patterns of their customers and supply relationships with their distributors and manufacturers, the suppliers to their manufacturers, and so on. *Supply chain* describes the flow of goods, services, and information from the initial sources of materials and services to the delivery of products to consumers, regardless of whether those activities occur in the same organization or in other organizations. Research shows that there are significant gains to companies in the supply chain from coordinating their activities and sharing information.

Procter and Gamble's (P&G) experience with its Pampers product illustrates the gains from supply-chain coordination. Despite babies using diapers at a steady rate, retailers selling Pampers encountered variability in weekly demand caused by randomness in when families actually purchased disposable diapers. Anticipating even more demand variability and lacking information about inventory available with manufacturers, retailers' orders to the manufacturer (P&G) became more variable. This order variability was made worse by trade promotions that caused retailers to take advantage of lower prices to stock up for the future. Similarly, high variability of orders at P&G translated to more variability of orders to P&G's suppliers.

This higher variability of quantities demanded at suppliers compared with manufacturers and at manufacturers compared with retailers is called the "bullwhip effect" or the "whiplash effect."[2] A consequence of the bullwhip effect is that high levels of inventory are held at all stages in the supply chain.

Companies in a supply chain can benefit by coordinating their activities and sharing information. Suppose that all retailers share daily sales information about Pampers with P&G and P&G's suppliers. Those sales data reduce the level of uncertainty of manufacturers

[2]See H. Lee, V. Padmanabhan, and S. Whang, "The Bullwhip Effect in Supply Chains," *Sloan Management Review* (Spring 1997). These authors discuss four major causes of the bullwhip effect: (1) demand forecasting, (2) order batching, (3) price fluctuation, and (4) rationing and shortage gaming.

SURVEYS OF COMPANY PRACTICE

Challenges In Obtaining the Benefits from a Supply-Chain Analysis

Supply-chain studies reported in the business press frequently cite a wide range of benefits to both manufacturers and retailers. These benefits include fewer stockouts, reduced manufacture of items not subsequently demanded at the retail level, a reduction in rushed manufacturing orders, and lower inventory levels. A survey of 220 retailers and manufacturers highlights some key issues that companies adopting a supply-chain approach to inventory management must address to achieve the full extent of these benefits.

One issue is deciding the information to exchange among companies in the supply chain. Manufacturers gave the following rankings (in terms of importance) about the information they would like to receive from retailers stocking their products:

1. Retail sales forecasts for the products
2. Sales data on the products (such as daily sales at each retail outlet)
3. Pricing and advertising strategies by the retailer
4. Inventory levels at each retail outlet

A second issue is reducing the obstacles to manufacturers and retailers achieving the benefits of a supply-chain approach. Respondents cited the following obstacles:

1. Communication obstacles—including the unwillingness of some parties to share information
2. Trust obstacles—including the concern that all parties will not meet their agreed-upon commitments
3. Information system obstacles—including problems due to the information systems of different parties not being technically compatible
4. Limited resources—including problems due to the people and financial resources given to support a supply-chain initiative not being adequate

Adopting a supply-chain approach requires diverse organizations to cooperate and communicate on a broad set of issues. Respondents emphasized this challenge was not always successfully met. Not surprisingly, not all supply-chain initiatives have delivered the initially projected financial and operating benefits.

Source: Research Incorporated, "Synchronizing the Supply Chain Through Collaborative Design." Full citations are in Appendix A at the end of the book.

---

and suppliers to manufacturers about retail demand for Pampers. This reduction in demand uncertainty combined with sharing inventory data throughout the supply chain leads to (a) fewer stockouts at the retail level, (b) reduced manufacture of Pampers not immediately needed by retailers, (c) fewer manufacturing orders that have to be "rushed" or "expedited," and (d) lower inventories held by each company in the supply chain. The benefits of coordination at P&G have been so great that retailers such as Wal-Mart have gone so far as to contract with P&G to manage Wal-Mart's retail inventories. This practice is called *supplier- or vendor-managed inventory.* Supply chain management, however, is not without its challenges (see Surveys of Company Practice above).

Managers at manufacturing companies have also developed numerous systems to plan and implement production and inventory activities within their plants. We now consider two widely used types of systems: materials requirements planning (MRP) and just-in-time (JIT) production.

5 Distinguish materials requirements planning (MRP) systems
...manufacturing products based on demand forecasts
from just-in-time (JIT) systems for manufacturing
...manufacturing products only upon receiving customer orders

INVENTORY MANAGEMENT AND MRP

Materials requirements planning (MRP) is a "push-through" system that manufactures finished goods for inventory on the basis of demand forecasts. MRP uses (1) demand forecasts for final products; (2) a bill of materials detailing the materials, components, and subassemblies for each final product; and (3) the quantities of materials, components, and product inventories to determine the necessary outputs at each stage of production. Taking into account the lead time required to purchase materials and to manufacture components and finished products, a master production schedule specifies the quantity and timing of each item to be produced. Once production starts as scheduled, the output of each department is pushed through the production line whether or not it is needed. This "push through" can sometimes result in an accumulation of inventory as workstations receive work the workstations are not yet ready to process.

Inventory management is a challenge in an MRP system. One reason for unsuccessful attempts to implement MRP systems has been a failure to collect and update inventory records. The management accountant can aid in MRP by maintaining accurate records of inventory and its costs. For example, after becoming aware of the full costs of carrying finished goods inventory, National Semiconductor contracted with Federal Express to airfreight its microchips from a central location in Singapore to customer sites worldwide, instead of storing products at multiple (and geographically dispersed) warehouses. The change enabled National to move products from plant to customer in 4 days rather than 45 days and to reduce distribution costs from 2.6% to 1.9% of revenues. These benefits subsequently led National to outsource all its shipping activities to Federal Express, including shipments between its own plants in the United States, Scotland, and Malaysia.

The management accountant can also help estimate setup costs and downtime costs for production runs. *Costs of setting up a production run are analogous to ordering costs in the EOQ model.* When the costs of setting up machines are high — as in the case of a blast furnace in a steel mill — processing larger batches of materials and incurring larger inventory carrying costs is cheaper because it reduces the number of setups that must be made. Similarly, when the costs of downtime are high, there are sizable benefits from maintaining continuous production.

MRP is a push-through approach. We now consider JIT production, a "demand-pull" approach.

INVENTORY MANAGEMENT AND JIT PRODUCTION

6 Identify the features of a just-in-time production system

...for example, organizing work in manufacturing cells, improving quality, reducing manufacturing lead time

Just-in-time (JIT) production, also called **lean production,** is a demand-pull manufacturing system because each component in a production line is produced as soon as and only when needed by the next step in the production line. In a JIT production line, manufacturing activity at any particular workstation is prompted by the need for that workstation's output at the following workstation. Demand triggers each step of the production process, starting with customer demand for a finished product at the end of the process and working all the way back to the demand for direct materials at the beginning of the process. In this way, demand pulls an order through the production line. The demand-pull feature of JIT production systems achieves close coordination among workstations. It smoothes the flow of goods, despite low quantities of inventory. JIT production systems aim to simultaneously (1) meet customer demand in a timely way, (2) with high-quality products and (3) at the lowest possible total cost.

A JIT production system has these features:

- Organizes production in **manufacturing cells,** a grouping of all the different types of equipment used to make a given product. Materials move from one machine to another, and various operations are performed in sequence. Materials-handling costs are minimized.
- Hires and trains workers to be multiskilled and capable of performing a variety of operations and tasks, including minor repairs and routine maintenance of equipment.
- Aggressively eliminates defects. Because of the tight links between workstations in the production line and the minimal inventories at each workstation, defects arising at one workstation quickly affect other workstations in the line. JIT creates an urgency for solving problems immediately and eliminating the root causes of defects as quickly as possible. Low levels of inventories allow managers to trace problems back to earlier workstations in the production process where the problems may have originated.
- Reduces *setup time* — the time required to get equipment, tools, and materials ready to start the production of a component or product — and reduces *manufacturing lead time,* the time from when an order is received by manufacturing until it becomes a finished

CONCEPTS IN ACTION

Writing a Book Is as Easy as Making a Cup of Latté

Just-in-time production and supply-chain management have enabled many businesses to reduce their total inventory costs. Recent developments in digital technology, however, are carrying these management techniques one step further. They are making possible perhaps the most extreme form of demand-pull manufacturing via the use of technology that allows publishers to print actual, full-length books *on demand*, in a few minutes.

Book publishing and book retailing have long been hampered by serious inefficiencies in the management of inventory. Consumer tastes for books vary a great deal, and bookstores try to stock as large a selection as possible, with the result that inventory turnover in bookstores tends to be very slow. That makes the carrying costs of inventory high. If stores don't carry books that customers want, however, they incur stockout costs. Book publishers, for their part, have long been stymied by purchasing costs. For decades, books have been printed on bulky offset machines that typically require printing at least 1,000 copies at a time to be economically feasible. That means many books get to be considered out of print (and thus made largely unavailable) because the demand for them isn't large enough.

Enter "print-on-demand" technology. This technology allows companies to scan a book into a digital file so it can be available for printing on a supercharged laser printer whenever there is a demand for it. Because the setup costs for each printing are minimal, printing even a single copy at a time is economically feasible. In the late 1990s and early 2000s, a number of companies, including Ingram and Baker & Taylor (two of the largest book wholesalers in the U.S.), established print-on-demand subsidiaries called, respectively, Lightning Source and Replica Books. One entrepreneur who was hoping to eventually place print-on-demand machines in retail stores said that, in his view of the future, "making a book will be no more difficult than making a latté at Starbucks."

There are, of course, a few limitations to this technology. It is meant to support slow-selling books, not "bestsellers" (which can sell several thousand copies a day). In addition, it is geared to paperback books consisting mostly of text, in one color. It is not usable for printing hardcover books with a lot of color.

The benefits of this technology are lower carrying costs (because books would, in most circumstances, be sold *immediately* after being produced) and lower stockout costs (because the publisher and retailer would always realize sales). On the other hand, there would be additional costs of scanning books into digital files and storing them on servers. What about quality? Although the quality of books produced via print-on-demand technology is very good, it is not of the same quality as books printed on traditional equipment.

Source: New York Times (12/18/00), *Wall Street Journal* (6/1/99), and conversation with publishers.

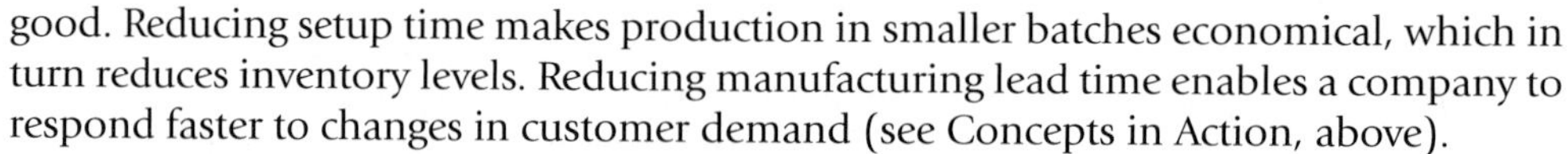

good. Reducing setup time makes production in smaller batches economical, which in turn reduces inventory levels. Reducing manufacturing lead time enables a company to respond faster to changes in customer demand (see Concepts in Action, above).

- Selects only suppliers capable of delivering quality materials in a timely manner. Most companies implementing *JIT production* also implement *JIT purchasing*. JIT plants expect JIT suppliers to make timely deliveries of high-quality goods directly to the production floor.

Enterprise Resource Planning (ERP) Systems[3]

The success of a JIT system hinges on the speed of information flows from customers to manufacturers to suppliers. Information flows is a problem for large companies that have fragmented information systems (for sales, manufacturing, and purchasing) spread over dozens of unlinked computer systems. The Enterprise Resource Planning (ERP) system

[3]For an excellent review, see T. H. Davenport, "Putting the Enterprise into the Enterprise System," *Harvard Business Review*, July–August, 1998.

comprises a single database that collects data and feeds it into applications supporting all of a company's business activities. For example, using an ERP system, a salesperson can generate a contract for a customer in Germany, verify the customer's credit limits, and place a production order. The system schedules manufacturing in, say, Brazil, requisitions materials from inventory, orders components from suppliers, and schedules shipment. It also credits sales commissions to the salesperson and records all the costing and financial accounting information.

ERP systems give low-level managers, workers, customers, and suppliers access to operating information. This benefit, coupled with tight coordination across business functions, enables ERP systems to rapidly shift manufacturing and distribution plans in response to changes in supply and demand. Companies believe that an ERP system is essential to support JIT initiatives because of the effect it has on lead times. Using an ERP system, Autodesk, a maker of computer-aided design software, reduced order lead times from 2 weeks to 1 day; Fujitsu reduced lead times from 18 to 1.5 days. ERP systems also help in forecasting demand and doing materials requirements planning as part of their operations and logistics modules.

Although the tight coupling of systems throughout a business streamlines administrative and financial processes and saves costs, it can also make the system large and unwieldy. Because of its complexity, suppliers of ERP systems such as SAP, Baan, Peoplesoft, and Oracle provide software packages that are standard, but that can be customized, although at considerable cost. Without some customization, unique and distinctive features that confer strategic advantage will not be available. The challenge when implementing ERP systems is to strike the right balance between systems that are common across all of a company's business and geographical locations and systems that for strategic reasons are designed to be unique.

Financial Benefits of JIT and Relevant Costs

Early advocates saw the benefit of JIT production as lower carrying costs of inventory. *But there are other benefits of lower inventories: greater transparency of the production process, heightened emphasis on eliminating the specific causes of rework, scrap, and waste, and lower manufacturing lead times.* In computing the relevant benefits and costs of reducing inventories in JIT production systems, the cost analyst should take into account all benefits.

Consider Hudson Corporation, a manufacturer of brass fittings. Hudson is considering implementing a JIT production system. To implement JIT production, Hudson must incur $100,000 in annual tooling costs to reduce setup times. Hudson expects that JIT will reduce average inventory by $500,000 and that relevant costs of insurance, storage, materials handling, and setup will decline by $30,000 per year. The company's required rate of return on inventory investments is 10% per year. Should Hudson implement a JIT production system? On the basis of the numbers provided, we would be tempted to say no. That's because annual relevant cost savings in carrying costs amount to $80,000 [(10% of $500,000) + $30,000)], which is less than the additional annual tooling costs of $100,000.

Our analysis, however, is incomplete. We have not considered other benefits of lower inventories in JIT production. For example, Hudson estimates that implementing JIT will improve quality and reduce rework on 500 units each year, resulting in savings of $50 per unit. Also, better quality and faster delivery will allow Hudson to charge $2 more per unit on the 20,000 units that it sells each year. The annual relevant quality and delivery benefits from JIT and lower inventory levels equal $65,000 (rework savings, $50/unit, × 500 units + additional contribution margin, $2/unit, × 20,000 units). Total annual relevant benefits and cost savings equal $145,000 ($80,000 + $65,000), which exceeds annual JIT implementation costs of $100,000. Therefore, Hudson should implement a JIT production system.

Performance Measures and Control in JIT Production

In addition to personal observation, the following list describes measures managers use to evaluate and control JIT production and how these measures are expected to be affected.

Personal observation is often more effective in JIT plants than in traditional plants. That's because the production layout in a JIT plant is streamlined and operations aren't obscured by piles of inventory or rework.

1. Financial performance measures, such as inventory turnover ratio (cost of goods sold ÷ inventory), which is expected to decrease

2. Nonfinancial performance measures of time, inventory, and quality, such as:
   - Manufacturing lead time, expected to decrease
   - Units produced per hour, expected to increase
   - Number of days of inventory on hand, expected to decrease
   - $\frac{\text{Total setup time for machines}}{\text{Total manufacturing time}}$, expected to decrease
   - $\frac{\text{Number of units requiring rework or scrap}}{\text{Total number of units started and completed}}$, expected to decrease

Personal observation and nonfinancial performance measures provide the most timely, intuitive, and easy to understand measures of plant performance. Rapid, meaningful feedback is critical because the lack of inventories in a demand-pull system makes it urgent to detect and solve problems quickly.

JIT's Effect on Costing Systems

By reducing materials handling, warehousing, and inspection, JIT systems reduce overhead costs. JIT systems also facilitate direct tracing of some costs usually classified as indirect. For example, the use of manufacturing cells makes it cost effective to trace materials handling and machine operating costs to specific products or product families made in these cells. These costs then become direct costs of those products. Also, the use of multiskilled workers in these cells allows the costs of setup, maintenance, and quality inspection to be traced as direct costs.

The next section discusses *backflush costing*, which is a job-costing system that dovetails with JIT production and is less costly to operate than most traditional costing systems described in Chapters 4, 7, 8, and 9.

BACKFLUSH COSTING

Organizing manufacturing in cells, reducing defects and manufacturing lead time, and ensuring timely delivery of materials, enables purchasing, production, and sales to occur in quick succession with minimal inventories. The absence of inventories makes choices about cost-flow assumptions (such as weighted-average or first-in, first-out) or inventory-costing methods (such as absorption or variable costing) unimportant: All manufacturing costs of the accounting period flow directly into cost of goods sold. The rapid conversion of direct materials into finished goods that are immediately sold greatly simplifies job costing.

Simplified Normal or Standard Job Costing

Traditional normal and standard-costing systems (Chapters 4, 7, and 8) use **sequential tracking,** which is any product-costing method in which recording of the journal entries occurs in the same order as actual purchases and progress in production. Costs are tracked sequentially as products pass through these four stages in a cycle from purchase of direct materials to sale of finished goods:

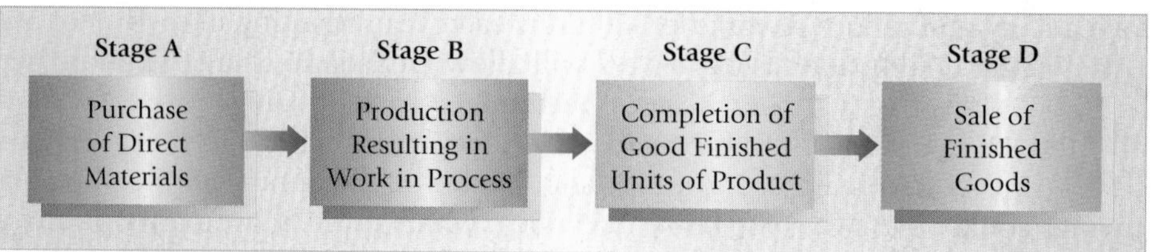

A sequential tracking costing system has four *trigger points,* corresponding to stages A, B, C, and D. **Trigger point** refers to a stage in the cycle from purchase of direct materials (stage A) to sale of finished goods (stage D) at which journal entries are made in the accounting system.

An alternative approach to sequential tracking is backflush costing. **Backflush costing** is a costing system that omits recording some or all of the journal entries relating to the cycle from purchase of direct materials to the sale of finished goods. When journal entries for one or more stages in the cycle are omitted, the journal entries for a subsequent stage use normal or standard costs to work backward to "flush out" the costs in the cycle for which journal entries were *not* made.

The following examples illustrate backflush costing. They differ in the number and placement of trigger points:

8 Discuss different ways backflush costing can simplify traditional job-costing systems

...for example, by not recording journal entries for work in process, purchase of materials, or production of finished goods.

	Number of Journal Entry Trigger Points	Location in Cycle When Journal Entries Are Made
Example 1	3	Stage A. Purchase of direct materials Stage C. Completion of good finished units of product Stage D. Sale of finished goods
Example 2	2	Stage A. Purchase of direct materials Stage D. Sale of finished goods
Example 3	2	Stage C. Completion of good finished units of product Stage D. Sale of finished goods

In all three examples, there are no journal entries in the accounting system for work in process (stage B) because JIT production leads to large reductions in work in process.

We illustrate backflush costing using data from Silicon Valley Computer (SVC), which produces keyboards for personal computers. For April, there are no beginning inventories of direct materials. Moreover, there is zero beginning and ending work in process.

SVC has only one direct manufacturing cost category (direct materials) and one indirect manufacturing cost category (conversion costs). All manufacturing labor costs are included in conversion costs. From its bill of materials and an operations list (description of operations to be undergone), SVC determines that the standard direct materials cost per keyboard unit is $19 and the standard conversion cost is $12 for April.

SVC purchases $1,950,000 of direct materials in April. To focus on the basic concepts, we assume SVC has no direct materials variances in April. Actual conversion costs incurred in April equal $1,260,000. SVC produces 100,000 good keyboard units in April and sells 99,000 units. Any underallocated or overallocated conversion costs are written off to cost of goods sold at the end of April.

Example 1: Trigger points at purchase of direct materials (Stage A), completion of good finished units of product (Stage C), and sale of finished goods (Stage D)

In this example, SVC has two inventory accounts:

Type	Account Title
Combined materials inventory and materials in work in process	Inventory: Materials and In-Process Control
Finished goods	Finished Goods Control

Trigger point 1 occurs when materials are purchased. These costs are charged to Inventory: Materials and In-Process Control. Actual conversion costs are recorded as incurred under backflush costing, just as in other costing systems, and charged to Conversion Costs Control. Conversion costs are allocated to products at trigger point 2—the transfer of units to Finished Goods Control. Trigger point 3 occurs at the time finished goods are sold.

SVC uses the following steps to assign costs to units sold and to inventories.

Step 1: Record Direct Materials Purchased During the Accounting Period.

This flow of costs is analogous to job costing in Chapter 4, except backflush costing bypasses the Work-in-Process account.

Entry (a)	Inventory: Materials and In-Process Control	1,950,000	
	Accounts Payable Control		1,950,000

Step 2: Record Conversion Costs Incurred During the Accounting Period.

Entry (b)	Conversion Costs Control	1,260,000	
	Various accounts (such as Wages Payable)		1,260,000

Step 3: Determine the Number of Good Finished Units Manufactured During the Accounting Period. 100,000 good units were manufactured in April.

Step 4: Compute the Normal or Standard Costs per Finished Unit. The standard cost is $31 ($19 direct materials + $12 conversion costs) per unit.

Step 5: Record the Cost of Good Finished Goods Completed During the Accounting Period. 100,000 units × ($19 + $12) = $3,100,000.

Entry (c)	Finished Goods Control	3,100,000	
	Inventory: Materials and In-Process Control		1,900,000
	Conversion Costs Allocated		1,200,000

This fifth step gives backflush costing its name. Note, costs have not been recorded sequentially with the flow of product along its production route through work in process and finished goods. Instead, the output trigger point reaches back and pulls the standard direct materials costs from Inventory: Materials and In-Process and the standard conversion costs for manufacturing the finished goods.

Step 6: Record the Standard Cost of Goods Sold During the Accounting Period. Standard cost of 99,000 units sold in April (99,000 units × $31 per unit = $3,069,000):

Entry (d)	Cost of Goods Sold	3,069,000	
	Finished Goods Control		3,069,000

Step 7: Record Underallocated or Overallocated Conversion Costs. Actual conversion costs may be underallocated or overallocated in an accounting period. Chapter 4 (pp. 115–117) discussed various ways to dispose of underallocated or overallocated manufacturing overhead costs. Companies that use backflush costing typically have low inventories, so proration of underallocated or overallocated conversion costs between finished goods and cost of goods sold is often not necessary. Many companies write off underallocated or overallocated conversion costs to cost of goods sold only at year-end. Other companies, like SVC, do so monthly. The journal entry to dispose of the difference between actual conversion costs incurred and standard conversion costs allocated is

Entry (e)	Conversion Costs Allocated	1,200,000	
	Cost of Goods Sold	60,000	
	Conversion Costs Control		1,260,000

The April ending inventory balances are

Inventory: Materials and In-Process Control ($1,950,000 – $1,900,000)	$50,000
Finished Goods Control, 1,000 units × $31/unit ($3,100,000 – $3,069,000)	31,000
Total	$81,000

Exhibit 20-7, Panel A (p. 704), summarizes the journal entries for this example. Exhibit 20-8, Panel A (p. 705), provides a general-ledger overview of this version of backflush costing. The elimination of the typical Work-in-Process account reduces the amount of detail in the accounting system. Units on the production line may still be tracked in physical terms, but there is "no assignment of costs" to specific work orders while they are in the production cycle. In fact, there are no work orders or labor time records in the accounting system. Champion International uses a method similar to Example 1 in its specialty papers plant.

When SVC has minimal work-in-process inventory, the three trigger points to make journal entries in Example 1 will lead SVC's backflush costing system to report costs that are similar to the costs reported under sequential tracking. In Example 1, any inventories of direct materials or finished goods are recognized in SVC's backflush costing system when they first appear (as would be done in a costing system using sequential tracking).

Accounting for Variances

The accounting for variances between actual and standard costs is basically the same under all standard-costing systems. The procedures are described in Chapters 7 and 8. In Example 1, if SVC had an unfavorable direct materials price variance of $42,000, entry (a) would be

Inventory: Materials and In-Process Control	1,950,000	
Direct Materials Price Variance	42,000	
Accounts Payable Control		1,992,000

Direct materials costs are often a large proportion of total manufacturing costs, sometimes well over 60%. Consequently, many companies will at least measure the direct materials efficiency variance in total by physically comparing what remains in direct materials inventory against what should remain based on the output of finished goods for the accounting period. In our example, suppose that such a comparison showed an unfavorable materials efficiency variance of $90,000. The journal entry would be

Direct Materials Efficiency Variance	90,000	
Inventory: Materials and In-Process Control		90,000

The underallocated or overallocated manufacturing overhead costs may be split into various overhead variances (spending variance, efficiency variance, and production-volume variance) as explained in Chapter 8 and then closed to cost of goods sold, if immaterial in amount.

Example 2: Trigger points are purchase of direct materials (Stage A) and sale of finished goods (Stage D)

This example uses the SVC data to illustrate a backflush costing system that is more different from a sequential tracking costing system than the backflush costing system in Example 1. This example and Example 1 have the same first trigger point, purchase of direct materials. But the second trigger point in Example 2 is the sale, not the completion, of finished units. Toyota's cost accounting system at its Kentucky plant is similar to this example. There are two justifications for this accounting system:

- To remove the incentive for managers to produce for inventory. If the finished goods inventory includes conversion costs, managers can bolster operating income by producing more units than are sold. Having trigger point 2 as the sale instead of the completion of production eliminates a manager's incentive to produce for inventory by recording conversion costs as period costs instead of inventoriable costs.
- To get managers more focused on selling units.

In this example, there is only one inventory account: direct materials, whether they are in storerooms, in process, or in finished goods.

Type	Account Title
Combines direct materials inventory and any direct materials in work-in-process and finished goods inventories	Inventory Control

Exhibit 20-7, Panel B, presents the journal entries for Example 2. The two trigger points are represented by transactions (a) and (d). Entry (a) is prompted by the same trigger point 1 as in Example 1, the purchase of direct materials. Entry (b) for the conversion costs incurred is recorded in the same way as in Example 1. Trigger point 2 is the sale of finished goods (not the production of finished units, as in Example 1), so there is no entry corresponding to entry (c) of Example 1. The cost of finished units is computed only when finished goods are sold [which corresponds to entry (d) of Example 1]: 99,000 units sold × $31 per unit = $3,069,000, which is comprised of direct materials costs (99,000 units × $19 per unit = $1,881,000) and conversion costs allocated (99,000 units × $12 per unit = $1,188,000).

EXHIBIT 20-7 Journal Entries In Backflush Costing

PANEL A, EXAMPLE 1: Three Trigger Points—Purchase of Direct Materials, Completion of Finished Goods, and Sale of Finished Goods

Transactions			
(a) Purchase of direct materials[a]	Inventory: Materials and In-Process Control	1,950,000	
	Accounts Payable Control		1,950,000
(b) Incur conversion costs	Conversion Costs Control	1,260,000	
	Various Accounts		1,260,000
(c) Completion of finished goods[a]	Finished Goods Control	3,100,000	
	Inventory: Materials and In-Process Control		1,900,000
	Conversion Costs Allocated		1,200,000
(d) Sale of finished goods[a]	Cost of Goods Sold	3,069,000	
	Finished Goods Control		3,069,000
(e) Underallocated or overallocated conversion costs	Conversion Costs Allocated	1,200,000	
	Cost of Goods Sold	60,000	
	Conversion Costs Control		1,260,000

PANEL B, EXAMPLE 2: Two Trigger Points—Purchase of Direct Materials and Sale of Finished Goods

Transactions			
(a) Purchase of direct materials[a]	Inventory Control	1,950,000	
	Accounts Payable Control		1,950,000
(b) Incur conversion costs	Conversion Costs Control	1,260,000	
	Various Accounts		1,260,000
(c) Completion of finished goods	No entry		
(d) Sale of finished goods[a]	Cost of Goods Sold	3,069,000	
	Inventory Control		1,881,000
	Conversion Costs Allocated		1,188,000
(e) Underallocated or overallocated conversion costs	Conversion Costs Allocated	1,188,000	
	Cost of Goods Sold	72,000	
	Conversion Costs Control		1,260,000

PANEL C, EXAMPLE 3: Two Trigger Points—Completion of Finished Goods and Sale of Finished Goods

Transactions			
(a) Purchase of direct materials	No entry		
(b) Incur conversion costs	Conversion Costs Control	1,260,000	
	Various Accounts		1,260,000
(c) Completion of finished goods[a]	Finished Goods Control	3,100,000	
	Accounts Payable Control		1,900,000
	Conversion Costs Allocated		1,200,000
(d) Sale of finished goods[a]	Cost of Goods Sold	3,069,000	
	Finished Goods Control		3,069,000
(e) Underallocated or overallocated conversion costs	Conversion Costs Allocated	1,200,000	
	Cost of Goods Sold	60,000	
	Conversion Costs Control		1,260,000

[a]A trigger point.

No conversion costs are inventoried. That is, compared with Example 1, Example 2 does not assign $12,000 ($12 per unit × 1,000 units) of conversion costs to finished goods inventory. Hence, Example 2 allocates $12,000 less in conversion costs to inventory relative to the conversion costs allocated to inventory in Example 1. Of the $1,260,000 in conversion costs, $1,188,000 is allocated at standard cost to the units sold. The remaining $72,000 ($1,260,000 – $1,188,000) of conversion costs is underallocated. Entry (e) in Exhibit 20-7, Panel B, presents the journal entry if SVC, like many companies, writes off these underallocated costs monthly as additions to cost of goods sold.

EXHIBIT 20-8 General-Ledger Overview of Backflush Costing

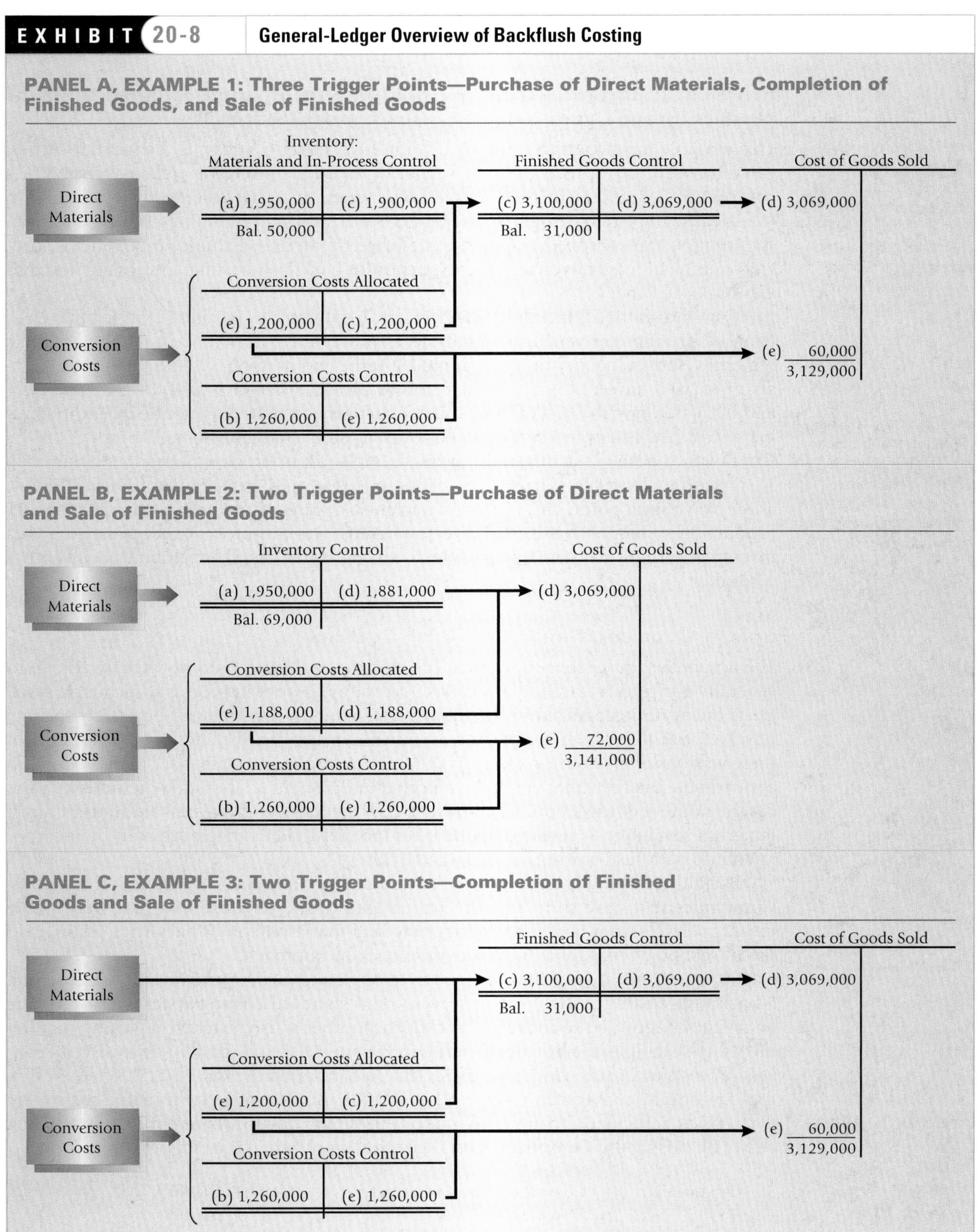

The April ending balance of Inventory Control is $69,000 ($50,000 direct materials still on hand + $19,000 direct materials embodied in the 1,000 units manufactured but not sold during the period). Exhibit 20-8, Panel B, provides a general-ledger overview of this version of backflush costing. Entries are keyed to Exhibit 20-7, Panel B. The approach described in Example 2 closely approximates the costs computed using sequential tracking when a company holds minimal work-in-process and finished goods inventories.

Example 3: Trigger points are completion of good finished units of product (Stage C) and sale of finished goods (Stage D)

Question: Are the only journal entries in backflush costing the ones for the trigger points? *Answer*: No, in addition to the trigger-point entries, journal entries must be made for conversion costs incurred and for disposing of underallocated or overallocated conversion costs.

Example 3 doesn't record Accounts Payable for direct materials until the products being manufactured are completely through the production process! This version of backflush costing is feasible only if there's a short lag between receipt of direct materials and completion of production.

This example has two trigger points. Exhibit 20-7, Panel C, presents the journal entries. In contrast to Example 2, the first trigger point in Example 3 is delayed until SVC's completion of good finished units of product. It is represented by transaction (c). Because the purchase of direct materials is not a trigger point, there is no entry corresponding to transaction (a)—purchases of direct materials. Exhibit 20-8, Panel C, provides a general-ledger overview of this version of backflush costing. Entries are keyed to Exhibit 20-7, Panel C.

Compare entry (c) in Exhibit 20-7, Panel C, with entries (a) and (c) in Exhibit 20-7, Panel A. The simpler version in Example 3 ignores the $1,950,000 purchases of direct materials [shown in entry (a) of Example 1]. At the end of April, $50,000 of direct materials purchased have not yet been placed into production ($1,950,000 – $1,900,000 = $50,000), nor have the cost of those direct materials been entered into the inventory-costing system. The Example 3 version of backflush costing is suitable for a JIT production system in which both direct materials inventory and work-in-process inventory are minimal.

Extending Example 3, backflush costing systems could use the sale of finished goods as the only trigger point. This version of backflush costing would be most suitable for a JIT production system with minimal direct materials, work-in-process, and finished goods inventories. That's because this backflush costing system would maintain no inventory accounts.

Special Consideration in Backflush Costing

The accounting procedures illustrated in Examples 1, 2, and 3 do not strictly adhere to generally accepted accounting principles. For example, work in process, which is an asset, exists but is not recognized in the financial statements. Advocates of backflush costing, however, cite the generally accepted accounting principle of materiality in support of these versions of backflush costing. As the three examples illustrate, backflush costing can approximate the costs that would be reported under sequential costing methods by varying the number of trigger points and where they are located. If material amounts of direct materials inventory or finished goods inventory exist, adjusting entries can be incorporated into backflush costing (as explained below).

Backflush costing is not restricted to companies adopting JIT production methods. Companies that have short manufacturing lead times, or those that have very stable inventory levels from period to period, may find that a version of backflush costing will report cost numbers similar to a sequential tracking approach.

Suppose there are material differences in operating income and inventories based on a backflush costing system and a conventional standard-costing system. An adjusting entry can be recorded to make the backflush number satisfy external reporting requirements. For example, the backflush entries in Example 2 would result in expensing all conversion costs to Cost of Goods Sold ($1,188,000 at standard costs + $72,000 write-off of underallocated conversion costs = $1,260,000). But suppose conversion costs were regarded as sufficiently material in amount to be included in Inventory Control. Then entry (e), closing the Conversion Costs accounts, would change as follows:

Original entry (e)	Conversion Costs Allocated	1,188,000	
	Cost of Goods Sold	72,000	
	Conversion Costs Control		1,260,000
Revised entry (e)	Conversion Costs Allocated	1,188,000	
	Inventory Control (1,000 units × $12)	12,000	
	Cost of Goods Sold	60,000	
	Conversion Costs Control		1,260,000

Critics say backflush costing leaves no audit trails—the ability of the accounting system to pinpoint the uses of resources at each step of the production process. The absence of large amounts of materials inventory and work-in-process inventory means managers can keep track of operations by personal observations, computer monitoring, and nonfinancial measures.

What are the implications of JIT and backflush costing systems for activity-based costing (ABC) systems? Simplifying the production process, as in a JIT system, makes more of the costs direct and reduces the extent of overhead cost allocations. Simplified ABC systems are often adequate for companies implementing JIT. But even these simpler ABC systems can enhance backflush costing. Costs from ABC systems yield more-accurate budgeted conversion costs per unit for different products in the backflush costing system. The activity-based cost data are also useful for product costing, decision making, and cost management.

PROBLEMS FOR SELF-STUDY

PROBLEM 1:

Lee Company has a Singapore plant that manufactures transistor radios. One component is an XT transistor. Expected demand is for 5,200 of these transistors in March 2003. Lee estimates the ordering cost per purchase order to be $250. The carrying cost for one unit of XT in stock is $5.

Required

1. Compute the EOQ for the XT transistor.
2. Compute the number of deliveries of XT in April 2003.

SOLUTION

1. $\text{EOQ} = \sqrt{\dfrac{2 \times 5{,}200 \times \$250}{\$5}}$

   $= 721$ transistors (rounded)

2. Number of deliveries $= \dfrac{5{,}200}{721}$

   $= 7.2$ (rounded up to 8 deliveries in March 2003)

PROBLEM 2:

Littlefield Company uses a backflush costing system with three trigger points:

- Purchase of direct materials
- Completion of good finished units of product
- Sale of finished goods

There are no beginning inventories. Data for April 2003 are

Direct materials purchased	$880,000	Conversion costs allocated	$ 400,000
Direct materials used	850,000	Costs transferred to finished goods	1,250,000
Conversion costs incurred	422,000	Costs of goods sold	1,190,000

Required

1. Prepare summary journal entries for April (without disposing of underallocated or overallocated conversion costs). Assume no direct materials variances.
2. Under an ideal JIT production system, how would the amounts in your journal entries differ from the journal entries in requirement 1?

SOLUTION

1. Journal entries for April are

Entry (a)	Inventory: Materials and In-Process Control	880,000	
	Accounts Payable Control		880,000
	(direct materials purchased)		

Continued

Entry (b)	Conversion Costs Control	422,000	
	Various accounts (such as Wages Payable Control)		422,000
	(conversion costs incurred)		
Entry (c)	Finished Goods Control	1,250,000	
	Inventory: Materials and In-Process Control		850,000
	Conversion Costs Allocated		400,000
	(standard cost of finished goods completed)		
Entry (d)	Cost of Goods Sold	1,190,000	
	Finished Goods Control		1,190,000
	(standard costs of finished goods sold)		

2. Under an ideal JIT production system, if the manufacturing lead time per unit is very short, there could be zero inventories at the end of each day. Entry (c) would be $1,190,000 finished goods production [to match finished goods sold in entry (d)], not $1,250,000. If the Marketing Department could only sell goods costing $1,190,000, the JIT production system would call for direct materials purchases and conversion costs of lower than $880,000 and $422,000, respectively, in entries (a) and (b).

DECISION POINTS

SUMMARY

The following question-and-answer format summarizes the chapter's learning objectives. Each decision presents a key question related to a learning objective. The guidelines are the answer to that question.

Decision	Guidelines
1. What are the five categories of costs associated with goods for sale?	These categories are purchasing costs (costs of goods acquired from suppliers), ordering costs (costs of preparing a purchase order and receiving goods), carrying costs (costs of holding inventory of goods for sale), stockout costs (costs arising when a customer demands a unit of product and that unit is not on hand), and quality costs (prevention, appraisal, internal failure, and external failure costs).
2. How do managers use the EOQ model?	The economic-order-quantity (EOQ) decision model calculates the optimal quantity of inventory to order by balancing ordering and carrying costs. The larger the order quantity, the higher the annual carrying costs and the lower the annual ordering costs. The EOQ model includes both costs recorded in the financial accounting system and opportunity costs not recorded in the financial accounting system.
3. How can companies reduce the conflict between the EOQ decision model and the models used for performance evaluation?	The opportunity cost of investment tied up in inventory is a key input in the EOQ decision model. Some companies include opportunity costs when evaluating managers so that the EOQ decision model is consistent with the performance evaluation model.
4. What is a supply chain, and what is the benefit of supply-chain analysis?	The supply chain describes the flow of goods, services, and information from the initial sources of materials and services to the delivery of products to consumers, regardless of whether those activities occur in the same organization or in other organizations. Utilizing supply-chain analysis allows companies to coordinate their activities and reduce inventories throughout the supply chain.
5. How do materials requirements planning (MRP) systems differ from just-in-time (JIT) production systems?	Materials requirements planning (MRP) systems use a "push-through" approach that manufactures finished goods for inventory on the basis of demand forecasts. Just-in-time (JIT) production systems use a "demand-pull" approach in which goods are only manufactured to satisfy customer orders.
6. What are the features of a JIT production system?	Five features of a JIT production system are (a) organizing production in manufacturing cells, (b) hiring and training multiskilled workers, (c) emphasizing total quality management, (d) reducing manufacturing lead time and setup time, and (e) building strong supplier relationships.

7. What is backflush costing?	Backflush costing delays recording some of the journal entries relating to the cycle from purchase of direct materials to the sale of finished goods.
8. How does backflush costing simplify job costing?	Traditional job-costing systems use sequential tracking, in which recording of the journal entries occurs in the same order as actual purchases and progress in production. Most backflush costing systems do not record journal entries for the work-in-process stage of production. Some backflush costing systems also do not record entries for either the purchase of direct materials or the completion of finished goods.

TERMS TO LEARN

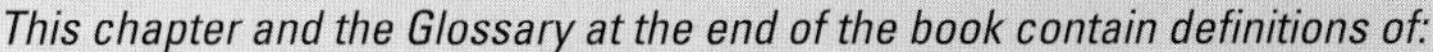

This chapter and the Glossary at the end of the book contain definitions of:

backflush costing (p. 700)
carrying costs (686)
economic order quantity (EOQ) (687)
inventory management (686)
just-in-time (JIT) production (697)
just-in-time (JIT) purchasing (692)
lean production (697)
manufacturing cells (697)
materials requirements planning (MRP) (696)
ordering costs (686)
purchasing costs (686)
purchase-order lead time (687)
quality costs (687)
reorder point (688)
safety stock (689)
sequential tracking (700)
stockout costs (686)
trigger point (700)

ASSIGNMENT MATERIAL

Questions

20-1 Why do better decisions regarding the purchasing and managing of goods for sale frequently cause dramatic percentage increases in net income?

20-2 Name five cost categories that are important in managing goods for sale in a retail organization.

20-3 What assumptions are made when using the simplest version of the economic-order-quantity (EOQ) decision model?

20-4 Give examples of costs included in annual carrying costs of inventory when using the EOQ decision model.

20-5 Give three examples of opportunity costs that typically are not recorded in accounting systems, although they are relevant to the EOQ model.

20-6 What are the steps in computing the cost of a prediction error when using the EOQ decision model?

20-7 Why might goal-congruence issues arise when an EOQ model is used to guide decisions on how much to order?

20-8 Describe JIT purchasing and its benefits.

20-9 What are three factors causing reductions in the cost to place purchase orders of materials?

20-10 Describe how the Internet can be used to reduce the costs of placing purchase orders.

20-11 What is supply-chain analysis, and how can it benefit manufacturers and retailers?

20-12 What are some obstacles to companies adopting a supply-chain approach?

20-13 What are the main features in a JIT production system?

20-14 Distinguish job-costing systems using sequential tracking from backflush costing.

20-15 Describe three different versions of backflush costing.

Exercises

20-16 **Economic order quantity for retailer.** Football World (FW) operates a megastore featuring sports merchandise. It uses an EOQ decision model to make inventory decisions. It is now considering inventory decisions for its San Francisco 49ers jerseys product line. This is a highly popular item. Data for 2004 are

- Expected annual demand for 49ers jerseys: 10,000
- Ordering costs for purchase order: $225
- Carrying costs per year: $10 per jersey

Each jersey costs FW $40 and sells for $75. The $10 carrying cost per jersey per year comprises the required return on investment of $4.80 (12% × $40 purchase price) plus $5.20 in relevant insurance, handling, and theft-related costs. The purchasing lead time is 7 days. FW is open 365 days a year.

Required

1. Calculate the EOQ.
2. Calculate the number of orders that will be placed each year.
3. Calculate the reorder point.

20-17 Economic order quantity, effect of parameter changes (continuation of 20-16). Athletic Products (AP) manufactures the 49ers jerseys that Football World (FW) sells to its customers. AP has recently installed computer software that enables its customers to conduct "one-stop" purchasing using state-of-the-art Web site technology developed by Cisco Systems. FW's ordering cost per purchase order will be $20 using this new technology.

Required

1. Calculate the EOQ for the 49ers jerseys using the revised ordering cost of $20 per purchase order. Assume all other data from Exercise 20-16 are the same. Comment on the result.
2. Suppose AP proposes to "assist" FW. AP will allow FW's customers to order directly from the AP Web site. AP would ship directly to these customers. AP would pay $10 to FW for every 49ers jersey purchased by one of FW's customers. How would this offer affect inventory management at FW? Should FW accept AP's proposal? Explain.

20-18 EOQ for a retailer. The Cloth Center buys and sells fabrics to a wide range of industrial and consumer users. One of the products it carries is denim cloth, used in the manufacture of jeans and carrying bags. The supplier for the denim cloth pays all incoming freight. No incoming inspection of the denim is necessary because the supplier has a track record of delivering high-quality merchandise. The purchasing officer of the Cloth Center has collected the following information:

Annual demand for denim cloth	20,000 yards
Ordering costs per purchase order	$160
Carrying costs per year	20% of purchase costs
Safety stock requirements	None
Cost of denim cloth	$8 per yard

The purchasing lead time is 2 weeks. The Cloth Center is open 250 days a year (50 weeks for 5 days a week).

Required

1. Calculate the EOQ for denim cloth.
2. Calculate the number of orders that will be placed each year.
3. Calculate the reorder point for denim cloth.

20-19 EOQ for manufacturer. Beaumont Corporation makes air conditioners. It purchases 12,000 units of a particular type of compressor part, CU29, each year at a cost of $50 per unit. Beaumont requires a 12% rate of return on investment. In addition, relevant carrying costs (for insurance, materials handling, breakage, and so on) are $2 per unit per year. Relevant costs per purchase order are $120.

Required

1. Calculate Beaumont's EOQ for CU29.
2. Calculate Beaumont's total relevant ordering and carrying costs.
3. Assume that demand is uniform throughout the year and is known with certainty. The purchasing lead time is half a month. Calculate Beaumont's reorder point for CU29.

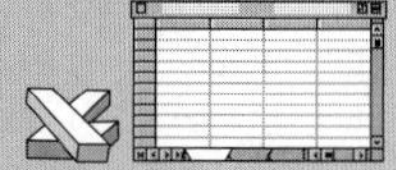

Excel Application For students who wish to practice their spreadsheet skills, the following is a step-by-step approach to creating an Excel spreadsheet to work this problem.

Step-by-Step

1. Open a new spreadsheet. At the top, create an "Original Data" section for the data provided by Beaumont Corporation, with rows for "Annual Demand, Purchase Cost per Unit, Required Return on Investment (%)" and "Relevant Ordering Costs per Purchase Order."

(Program your spreadsheet to perform all necessary calculations. Do not "hard-code" any amounts, such as economic order quantity, requiring addition, subtraction, multiplication, or division operations.)

2. Skip two rows, create a "Relevant Carrying Cost per Unit per Year" section in a format similar to the bottom of page 687. Create rows and enter calculations for "Required Annual Return on Investment," "Relevant Insurance, Materials Handling, and Breakage Costs per Year," and "Total Carrying Costs per Unit per Year."
3. Skip two rows, create a "Problem 1" section, with rows for each of the inputs into the EOQ formula: *D*, *P*, and *C*. Include a calculation for the "Economic Order Quantity" on a separate row.

4. Skip two rows, create a "Problem 2" section. Create rows and enter calculations for "Annual Relevant Ordering Costs" and "Annual Relevant Carrying Costs"and "Relevant Total Costs".
5. Skip two rows, create a "Problem 3" section. Create rows and enter calculations for "Monthly Demand" and "Purchasing Lead Time (in months)", and the "Reorder Point".
6. *Check the accuracy of your spreadsheet*: Go to your Original Data section and change the required return on investment from 12% to 15%. If you programmed your spreadsheet correctly, total carrying cost per unit per year should *increase* to $10, and your economic order quantity should *decrease* to 551 units.

20-20 Sensitivity of EOQ to changes in relevant ordering and carrying costs. Alyia Company's annual demand for Model X253 is 10,000 units. Alyia is unsure about the relevant carrying cost per unit per year and the relevant ordering cost per purchase order. This table presents six possible combinations of carrying and ordering costs.

Relevant Carrying Cost per Unit per Year	Relevant Ordering Cost per Purchase Order
$10	$300
$10	$200
$15	$300
$15	$200
$20	$300
$20	$200

Required

1. Determine EOQ for Alyia for each of the relevant ordering and carrying-cost alternatives.
2. How does your answer to requirement 1 give insight into the impact on EOQ of changes in relevant ordering and carrying costs.

20-21 Purchase-order size for retailer, EOQ, just-in-time purchasing. The 24-Hour Mart operates a chain of supermarkets. Its best-selling soft drink is Fruitslice. Demand (*D*) in April for Fruitslice at its Memphis supermarket is estimated to be 6,000 cases (24 cans in each case). In March, the Memphis supermarket estimated the ordering costs per purchase order (*P*) for Fruitslice to be $30. The carrying costs (*C*) of each case of Fruitslice in inventory for a month were estimated to be $1. At the end of March, the Memphis 24-Hour Mart reestimated its carrying costs to be $1.50 per case per month to take into account an increase in warehouse-related costs.

During March, 24-Hour Mart restructured its relationship with suppliers. It reduced the number of suppliers from 600 to 180. Long-term contracts were signed only with those suppliers that agreed to make product-quality checks before shipping. Each purchase order will now be made by linking into the suppliers' computer network. The Memphis 24-Hour Mart estimated that these changes will reduce the ordering costs per purchase order to $5. The 24-Hour Mart is open 30 days in April.

Required

1. Calculate the EOQ in April for Fruitslice. Assume in turn:

   a. $D = 6{,}000$; $P = \$30$; $C = \$1$
   b. $D = 6{,}000$; $P = \$30$; $C = \$1.50$
   c. $D = 6{,}000$; $P = \$5$; $C = \$1.50$

2. How does your answer to requirement 1 give insight into the retailer's movement toward JIT purchasing policies?

20-22 JIT production, relevant benefits, relevant costs. The Evans Corporation manufactures wireless telephones. Evans is deciding whether to implement a JIT production system, which would require annual tooling costs of $150,000. Evans estimates that the following annual benefits would arise from JIT production.

a. Average inventory would decline by $700,000, from $900,000 to $200,000.
b. Insurance, space, materials-handling, and setup costs, which currently total $200,000, would decline by 30%.
c. The emphasis on quality inherent in JIT systems would reduce rework costs by 20%. Evans currently incurs $350,000 on rework.
d. Better quality would enable Evans to raise the selling prices of its products by $3 per unit. Evans sells 30,000 units each year.

Evans's required rate of return on inventory investment is 12% per year.

Required

1. Calculate the net benefit or cost to the Evans Corporation from implementing a JIT production system.
2. What other nonfinancial and qualitative factors should Evans consider before deciding whether it should implement a JIT system?
3. Suppose Evans implements JIT production. (a) Give examples of performance measures Evans could use to evaluate and control JIT production. (b) What is the benefit to Evans of implementing an enterprise resource planning (ERP) system?

20-23 Backflush costing and JIT production. Road Warrior Corporation assembles handheld computers that have scaled-down capabilities of laptop computers. Each handheld computer takes 6 hours to assemble. Road Warrior uses a JIT production system and a backflush costing system with three trigger points:

- Purchase of direct (raw) materials
- Completion of good finished units of product
- Sale of finished goods

There are no beginning inventories of materials or finished goods. The following data are for August 2003:

Direct (raw) materials purchased	$2,754,000	Conversion costs incurred	$723,600
Direct (raw) materials used	2,733,600	Conversion costs allocated	750,400

Road Warrior records direct materials purchased and conversion costs incurred at actual costs. When finished goods are sold, the backflush costing system "pulls through" standard direct materials costs ($102 per unit) and standard conversion costs ($28 per unit). Road Warrior produced 26,800 finished units in August 2003 and sold 26,400 units. The actual direct materials cost per unit in August 2003 was $102, and the actual conversion cost per unit was $27.

Required

1. Prepare summary journal entries for August 2003 (without disposing of under- or overallocated conversion costs).
2. Post the entries in requirement 1 to T-accounts for applicable Inventory: Direct and In-Process, Conversion Costs Control, Conversion Costs Allocated, and Cost of Goods Sold.
3. Under an ideal JIT production system, how would the amounts in your journal entries differ from those in requirement 1?

20-24 Backflush costing, two trigger points, materials purchase and sale (continuation of 20-23). Assume the same facts as in Exercise 20-23, except that Road Warrior now uses a backflush costing system with the following two trigger points:

- Purchase of direct (raw) materials
- Sale of finished goods

The Inventory Control account will include direct materials purchased but not yet in production, materials in work in process, and materials in finished goods but not sold. No conversion costs are inventoried. Any under- or overallocated conversion costs are written off monthly to Cost of Goods Sold.

Required

1. Prepare summary journal entries for August, including the disposition of under- or overallocated conversion costs.
2. Post the entries in requirement 1 to T-accounts for Inventory Control, Conversion Costs Control, Conversion Costs Allocated, and Cost of Goods Sold.

20-25 Backflush costing, two trigger points, completion of production and sale (continuation of 20-23). Assume the same facts as in Exercise 20-23, except now Road Warrior uses only two trigger points, the completion of good finished units of product and the sale of finished goods. Any under- or overallocated conversion costs are written off monthly to Cost of Goods Sold.

Required

1. Prepare summary journal entries for August, including the disposition of under- or overallocated conversion costs.
2. Post the entries in requirement 1 to T-accounts for Finished Goods Control, Conversion Cost Control, Conversion Costs Allocated, and Cost of Goods Sold.

Problems

20-26 Effect of different order quantities on ordering costs and carrying costs, EOQ. Koala Blue retails a broad line of Australian merchandise at its Santa Monica store. It sells 26,000 Ken Done linen bedroom packages (two sheets and two pillow cases) each year. Koala Blue pays Ken Done Merchandise, Inc., $104 per package. Its ordering costs per purchase order are $72. The carrying costs per package are $10.40 per year.

Liv Carrol, manager of the Santa Monica store, seeks your advice on how ordering and carrying costs vary with different order quantities. Ken Done Merchandise guarantees the $104 purchase cost per package for the 26,000 units budgeted to be purchased in the coming year.

Required

1. Compute the annual ordering costs, the annual carrying costs, and their sum for purchase-order quantities of 300, 500, 600, 700, and 900. What is the EOQ? Comment on your results.
2. Assume that Ken Done Merchandise introduces a computerized ordering network for its customers. Liv Carrol estimates that Koala Blue's ordering costs will be reduced to $40 per purchase order. How will this reduction in ordering costs affect the EOQ for Koala Blue on their linen bedroom packages?

20-27 EOQ, uncertainty, safety stock, reorder point. (CMA adapted) The Starr Company distributes a wide range of electrical products. One of its best-selling items is a standard electric motor. The management of the Starr Company uses the EOQ decision model to determine the optimal number of motors to order. Management now wants to determine how much safety stock to hold.

The Starr Company estimates annual demand (300 working days) to be 30,000 electric motors. Using the EOQ decision model, the company orders 3,000 motors at a time. The lead time for an order is 5 days. The annual carrying costs of one motor in safety stock are $10. Management has also estimated that the additional stockout costs are $20 for each motor they are short.

The Starr Company has analyzed the demand during 200 past reorder periods. The records indicate the following patterns:

Demand During Lead Time	Number of Times Quantity Was Demanded
440	6
460	12
480	16
500	130
520	20
540	10
560	6
	200

Required

1. Determine the level of safety stock for electric motors that the Starr Company should maintain in order to minimize expected stockout costs and carrying costs. When computing carrying costs, assume that the safety stock is on hand at all times and that there is no overstocking caused by decreases in expected demand. (Consider safety stock levels of 0, 20, 40, and 60 units.)
2. What would be the Starr Company's new reorder point?
3. What factors should the Starr Company have considered in estimating the stockout costs?

20-28 EOQ, cost of prediction error. Ralph Menard is the owner of a truck repair shop. He uses an EOQ model for each of his truck parts. He initially predicts the annual demand for heavy-duty tires to be 2,000. Each tire has a purchase price of $50. The incremental ordering costs per purchase order are $40. The incremental carrying costs per year are $4 per tire plus 10% of the supplier's purchase price per tire.

Required

1. Calculate the EOQ for tires, along with the sum of annual relevant ordering costs and relevant carrying costs.
2. Suppose Menard is correct in all his predictions except the purchase price. If he had been a faultless predictor, he would have foreseen that the purchase price would drop to $30. What is the cost of the prediction error?

20-29 JIT purchasing, relevant benefits, relevant costs. (CMA adapted) The Margro Corporation is an automotive supplier that uses automatic turning machines to manufacture precision parts from steel bars. Margro's inventory of raw steel averages $600,000. John Oates, president of Margro, and Helen Gorman, Margro's controller, are concerned about the costs of carrying inventory. The steel supplier is willing to supply steel in smaller lots at no additional charge. Helen Gorman identified the following effects of adopting a JIT inventory program to virtually eliminate steel inventory:

- Without scheduling any overtime, lost sales due to stockouts would increase by 35,000 units per year. However, by incurring overtime premiums of $40,000 per year, the increase in lost sales could be reduced to 20,000 units. This would be the maximum amount of overtime that would be feasible for Margro.
- Two warehouses currently used for steel bar storage would no longer be needed. Margro rents one warehouse from another company under a cancelable leasing arrangement at an annual cost of $60,000. The other warehouse is owned by Margro and contains 12,000 square feet. Three-fourths of the space in the owned warehouse could be rented for $1.50 per square foot per year. Insurance and property tax costs totaling $14,000 per year would be eliminated.

Long-term capital investments by Margro are expected to produce an annual rate of return of 20%. Margro Corporation Budgeted Income Statement for the Year Ending December 31, 2003, (in thousands) is as follows:

Revenues (900,000 units)		$10,800
Cost of goods sold		
Variable costs	$4,050	
Fixed costs	1,450	
Total costs of goods sold		5,500
Gross margin		5,300
Marketing and distribution costs		
Variable costs	$ 900	
Fixed costs	1,500	
Total marketing and distribution costs		2,400
Operating income		$ 2,900

Required

1. Calculate the estimated dollar savings (loss) for the Margro Corporation that would result in 2003 from the adoption of the JIT inventory-control method.

2. Identify and explain other factors that Margro should consider before deciding whether to install a JIT system.

20-30 Relevant benefits and costs of JIT purchasing. Hardesty Medical Instruments is considering JIT implementation in 2003. Hardesty's annual demand for product XJ-200, a surgical scalpel, is 20,000 units. If Hardesty implements JIT, the purchase price of the scalpel is expected to increase from $10 to $10.05 because of frequent deliveries by Morrison Manufacturing, Inc. Morrison enjoys a sterling reputation for quality and reliability. Ordering costs will remain at $5 per order. However, the annual number of orders placed will be 200 instead of the current 20. As a result of frequent ordering, Hardesty's order size will decrease proportionally. Hardesty's required rate of return on investment is 20%. Other carrying costs (insurance, materials handling, and so on) will remain at $4.50 per unit. Currently Hardesty has no stockout costs. Lower inventory levels from implementing JIT will lead to $3 per unit stockout costs on 100 units during the year.

Required

1. Calculate the estimated dollar savings (loss) for Hardesty Medical Instruments from the adoption of JIT purchasing using the format of Exhibit 20-5.
2. Under what conditions would it be beneficial for Hardesty to have Morrison manage all inventories in the supply chain?

20-31 Supplier evaluation and relevant costs of quality and timely deliveries (continuation of 20-30) Hardesty Medical Instruments installed a JIT purchasing system in 2003 and selected Morrison Manufacturing, Inc., as its supplier. Herriott Manufacturing Corporation also manufactures XJ-200. It offers to supply all of Hardesty's XJ-200 needs at a price of $9.75 per unit (less than Morrison's price of $10.05) under the same JIT delivery terms that Morrison offers. Hardesty's relevant carrying costs of insurance, material handling, and so on would be $4.40 per unit per year if it purchases from Herriott. Due to the lower quality of Herriott's product, Hardesty anticipates the following negative consequences of purchasing from Herriott:

- Hardesty would incur inspection costs of $0.08 per unit.
- Average stockouts of 800 units per year would occur from late deliveries, requiring rush orders at a cost of $3 per unit.
- Customers would likely return 10% of all units sold due to poor quality of the product. Hardesty estimates its additional costs to handle each returned unit are $6.

Required Calculate the relevant costs of purchasing (1) from Morrison and (2) from Herriott using the format of Exhibit 20-6. From whom should Hardesty buy XJ-200?

20-32 Supplier evaluation and relevant costs of quality and timely deliveries. Copeland Sporting Goods is evaluating two suppliers of footballs, Big Red and Quality Sports. Pertinent information about each potential supplier follows:

Relevant Item	Big Red	Quality Sports
Purchase price per unit (case)	$50	$51
Ordering costs per order	$6	$6
Inspection costs per unit	$.02	0
Insurance, material handling, and so on per unit per year	$4.00	$4.50
Annual demand	12,000 units	12,000 units
Average quantity of inventory held during the year	100 units	100 units
Required return on investment	15%	15%
Stockout costs per unit	$20	$10
Stockouts per year	350 units	60 units
Customer returns	300 units	25 units
Customer-return costs per unit	$25	$25

Required Calculate the relevant costs of purchasing (1) from Big Red and (2) from Quality Sports using the format of Exhibit 20-6. From whom should Copeland buy footballs?

20-33 Backflush costing and JIT production. The Acton Corporation manufactures electrical meters. For August, there were no beginning inventories of direct materials and no beginning or ending work in process. Acton uses a JIT production system and backflush costing with three trigger points for making entries in the accounting system:

- Purchase of direct materials—debited to Inventory: Direct and In-Process Control
- Completion of good finished units of product—debited to Finished Goods Control
- Sale of finished goods

Acton's August standard cost per meter is direct materials, $25; and conversion costs, $20. The following data apply to August manufacturing:

Direct materials purchased	$550,000	Number of finished units manufactured	21,000
Conversion costs incurred	$440,000	Number of finished units sold	20,000

1. Prepare summary journal entries for August (without disposing of under- or overallocated conversion costs). Assume no direct materials variances.
2. Post the entries in requirement 1 to T-accounts for Inventory: Direct and In-Process Control, Conversion Costs Control, Conversion Costs Allocated, and Cost of Goods Sold.

Required

20-34 Backflush, two trigger points, materials purchase and sale (continuation of 20-33). Assume that the second trigger point for Acton Corporation is the sale—rather than the production—of finished goods. Also, the inventory account is confined solely to direct materials, whether these materials are in a storeroom, in work in process, or in finished goods. No conversion costs are inventoried. They are allocated to the units sold at standard costs. Any under- or overallocated conversion costs are written off monthly to Cost of Goods Sold.

1. Prepare summary journal entries for August, including the disposition of under- or overallocated conversion costs. Assume no direct materials variances.
2. Post the entries in requirement 1 to T-accounts for Inventory Control, Conversion Costs Control, Conversion Costs Allocated, and Cost of Goods Sold.

Required

20-35 Backflush, two trigger points, completion of production and sale (continuation of 20-33). Assume the same facts as in Problem 20-33 except now there are only two trigger points: the completion of good finished units of product and the sale of finished goods.

1. Prepare summary journal entries for August, including the disposition of under- or overallocated conversion costs. Assume no direct materials variances.
2. Post the entries in requirement 1 to T-accounts for Finished Goods Control, Conversion Costs Control, Conversion Costs Allocated, and Cost of Goods Sold.

Required

20-36 Backflush costing, income manipulation, ethics. Carol Brown, the chief financial officer of Silicon Valley Computer is an enthusiastic advocate of JIT production. The SVC Keyboard Division, which produces keyboards for personal computers, has made dramatic improvements in its operations with a highly successful JIT implementation. The Keyboard Division president now wants to adopt backflush costing.

Brown discusses the backflush costing proposal with Ralph Strong, the controller of SVC. Strong is totally opposed to backflush costing. He argues that it will open up "Pandora's box," by allowing division managers to manipulate reported division operating income. A member of Strong's group outlines the three possible variations of backflush costing shown in Exhibit 20-8 (p. 705). Strong notes that none of these three methods tracks work in process. He asserts that this omission would allow managers to "artificially change" reported operating income by manipulating work-in-process levels. He is especially scathing about the backflush costing in which no entries are made until a sale occurs.

"Suppose the division has already met its target operating income and wants to shift some of this year's income to next year," he says. "Under backflush costing with sale of finished goods as the trigger point, the division will have an incentive to not make sales this year of goods produced this year. This is a bizzare incentive. I rest my case about why we should stay with a job-costing system using sequential tracking."

Strong concludes that as long as reported accounting numbers are central to SVC's performance and bonus reviews, backflush costing should never be adopted.

1. What factors should SVC consider in deciding whether to adopt a version of backflush costing?
2. Are Strong's concerns about income manipulation sufficiently important for SVC to not adopt backflush costing?
3. What other ways does SVC have to motivate managers to not "artificially change" reported income?

Required

Collaborative Learning Problem

20-37 Backflushing. The following conversation occurred between Brian Richardson, plant manager at Glendale Engineering, and Charles Cheng, plant controller. Glendale manufactures automotive component parts, such as gears and crankshafts, for automobile manufacturers. Richardson has been very enthusiastic about implementing JIT and about simplifying and streamlining production and other business processes.

"Charles," Richardson began, "I would like to substantially simplify our accounting in the new JIT environment. Can't we just record one accounting entry at the time we ship products to our customers? I don't want to have our staff spending time tracking inventory from one stage to the next, when we have as little inventory as we do."

"Brian," Cheng said, "I think you are right about simplifying the accounting, but we still have a fair amount of direct materials and finished goods inventory that varies from period to period, depending on the demand for specific products. Doing away with all inventory accounting may be a problem."

"Well," Richardson replied, "you know my desire to simplify, simplify, simplify. I know that there are some costs of oversimplifying, but I believe that, in the long run, simplification pays dividends. Why don't you and your staff study the issues involved, and I will put it on the agenda for our next senior plant management meeting."

Required

1. What version of backflush costing would you recommend that Cheng adopt? Remember Richardson's desire to simplify the accounting as much as possible. Develop support for your recommendation.
2. Think about the three examples of backflush costing shown in Exhibit 20-8 (p. 705). These examples differ with respect to the number and types of trigger points used. Suppose your goal of implementing backflush costing is to simplify the accounting, but only if it closely matches the sequential tracking approach. Which version of backflush costing would you propose if:
   - **a.** Glendale had no direct materials and no work-in-process inventories but did have finished goods inventory?
   - **b.** Glendale had no work in process and no finished goods inventories but did have direct materials inventory?
   - **c.** Glendale had no direct materials, no work in process, and no finished goods inventories?
3. Backflush costing has its critics. In an article in the magazine *Management Accounting,* titled "Beware of the New Accounting Myths," R. Calvasina, E. Calvasina, and G. Calvasina state:

   > *The periodic (backflush) system has never been reflective of the reporting needs of a manufacturing system. In the highly standardized operating environments of the present JIT era, the appropriate system to be used is a perpetual accounting system based on an up-to-date, realistic set of standard costs. For management accountants to backflush on an actual cost basis is to return to the days of the outdoor privy (toilet).*

   Comment on this statement.

CHAPTER 20 INTERNET EXERCISE

Although accountants include inventory on the balance sheet as an asset, one might argue that it's a liability. Slow-moving inventory can depress gross profit margins, increase operating expenses, and reduce cash flows. To understand how, go to www.prenhall.com/horngren, click on *Cost Accounting* 11th ed., and access the Internet exercise for Chapter 20.

CHAPTER 20 VIDEO CASE

REGAL MARINE: Supply-Chain Management

Like most manufacturers, a big portion of Regal Marine's costs is tied up in purchase of the materials used in the production of its various luxury-boat models. With such a large amount of capital flowing out of the company on a regular basis, Regal Marine is trying to reduce costs by implementing a supply-chain management approach.

Supply-chain management is more than just seeking the lowest-cost provider of direct materials inputs. Regal Marine is working closely with suppliers to promote innovation, quality, and timely delivery of component parts.

The manufacture of a power boat starts with the fiberglass-and-gelcoat-covered hull and deck. Separate fabrication units off to the side of the main assembly floor produce the upholstered seats, cabinetry, and wiring panels for instrumentation. As boats move through the assembly process, each specially fabricated component is installed. The boats are then shrink-wrapped and loaded onto delivery trucks for shipment to distributors and showrooms.

To strengthen its upstream supply-chain relationship, Regal Marine is partnering with major suppliers of materials, such as windshields, engines, and gelcoatings, to drive innovation at reasonable costs. Key vendors are invited to participate in the product design process so that new materials may be tested and designed into future production boat models.

The company also has joined with about 15 other boat manufacturers to form a purchasing association. The association helps members to negotiate better price discounts with materials suppliers. Association members also share noncompetitive information about industrywide materials changes.

For some components, such as snaps and fasteners, Regal Marine is working with local suppliers to provide direct replenishment on the assembly floor on a just-in-time basis. Suppliers are responsible for maintaining the inventory, and Regal Marine benefits by not having to place orders for restocking. Suppliers make sure no stockouts occur, and they don't charge Regal Marine for the components stocked until they are used in production. This helps Regal Marine drive down its inventory costs.

QUESTIONS

1. Comment on the supply-chain management approaches that Regal Marine uses?
2. What role might Regal Marine's retail distributors play in the company's supply-chain management efforts? What obstacles might Regal Marine and its retail partners face?

CHAPTER 21

Capital Budgeting and Cost Analysis

LEARNING OBJECTIVES

1. Recognize the multiyear focus of capital budgeting
2. Understand the six stages of capital budgeting for a project
3. Use and evaluate the two main discounted cash flow (DCF) methods: the net present value (NPV) method and the internal rate-of-return (IRR) method
4. Use and evaluate the payback method
5. Use and evaluate the accrual accounting rate-of-return (AARR) method
6. Identify and reduce conflicts from using DCF for capital budgeting decisions and accrual accounting for performance evaluation
7. Identify relevant cash inflows and outflows for capital budgeting decisions

www.prenhall.com/horngren

Deer Valley Resort, one of the United States' premier ski resorts, has a unique approach to assuring skiers have an enjoyable, crowd-free experience on their mountain in Utah. They limit lift ticket sales each day so lift lines remain short and skier satisfaction is high. Although the owners limit ticket sales, they don't want to cap their growth and earnings potential, so each year, managers at the resort put together building and renovation plans to improve and expand their facilities.

Throughout each ski season, department managers put together requests for capital improvements. Both financial and nonfinancial costs and benefits are prepared. The plans, which can range from remodeling a dining room to building an entirely new ski lodge, are evaluated, prioritized, and placed in the rolling 10-year capital budget, and funds are secured to pursue the most urgent projects. This commitment to careful planning and skier enjoyment may be part of the reason Deer Valley was selected to host several key events during the 2002 Winter Olympic Games.

Finance courses cover some of the same (and some different) topics that are in this chapter.

Managers continually face the challenge of balancing long-run and short-run factors. We describe how managers incorporate financial and nonfinancial considerations into their long-run planning decisions. We introduce capital budgeting methods, so-called because they deal with how an organization selects projects that are intended to increase its "capital" (meaning the monetary value) of the organization. These methods assist managers in analyzing projects that span multiple years.

Prior to describing specific capital budgeting methods, we highlight how cost analysis for the project-by-project dimension of capital budgeting differs from cost analysis for the period-by-period dimension found in much of accounting.

1 Recognize the multiyear focus of capital budgeting
...because projects last longer than a year

TWO DIMENSIONS OF COST ANALYSIS

Exhibit 21-1 illustrates two different dimensions of cost analysis: (1) horizontally across, as a project dimension, and (2) vertically upward, as an accounting-period dimension. Each project is represented as a horizontal rectangle across time, distinct from other horizontal rectangles. Each project starts and ends at different times, over different time spans longer than one year. Capital budgeting often focuses on an analysis of each project over its entire lifespan by considering *all* the cash flows or cash savings from investing in it. The vertical rectangle for the 2004 accounting period represents the dimension of income determination and routine planning and control that cuts across all projects.

The accounting system that corresponds to the project dimension in Exhibit 21-1 considers life-cycle revenues and costs (described in Chapter 12). For example, a life-cycle analysis for a new-car project at Ford Motor Company could encompass a seven-year period. It would accumulate revenues from the new car as well as costs for all business functions in the value chain, from R&D to customer service incurred on the project.

EXHIBIT 21-1

The Project and Time Dimensions of Capital Budgeting

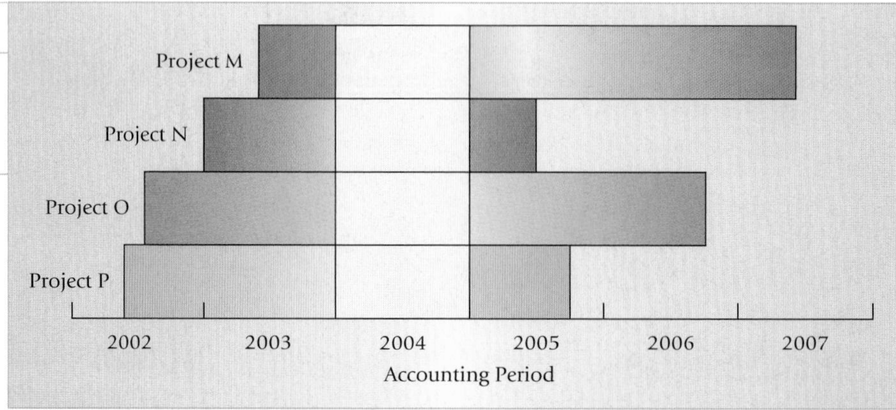

STAGES OF CAPITAL BUDGETING

2 **Understand the six stages of capital budgeting for a project**

...identification, search, information-acquisition, selection, financing, and implementation and control

Capital budgeting is making long-run planning decisions for investments in projects. Capital budgeting is a decision-making and control tool that spans multiple years. There are six stages to capital budgeting:

Step 1: **Identification Stage** *Distinguish which types of capital expenditure projects are necessary to accomplish organization objectives and strategies.* For example, a strategy of product differentiation to increase profitability could be promoted by projects that develop new products, new customers, or new markets. Or, a strategy of cost leadership could be promoted by projects that improve productivity and efficiency. Identifying which types of capital projects to invest in is largely the responsibility of line management and should always be guided by organization objectives and strategy.

Step 2: **Search Stage** *Explore alternative capital investments that will achieve organization objectives.* Cross-functional teams from all parts of the value chain evaluate alternative technologies, machines, and projects. Some alternatives are rejected early. Others are thoroughly evaluated in the next stage, the information-acquisition stage.

Step 3: **Information-Acquisition Stage** *Consider the expected costs and benefits of alternative capital investments.* These costs and benefits can be quantitative or qualitative. Capital budgeting emphasizes quantitative financial factors, but the effects of nonfinancial quantitative and qualitative factors are also considered.

Step 4: **Selection Stage** *Choose projects for implementation.* Organizations choose projects whose expected benefits exceed expected costs by the greatest amounts. The formal quantitative analysis uses decision models based on expected financial costs and benefits. Managers reevaluate the conclusions reached on the basis of the formal analysis, using their judgment to take into account nonfinancial factors.

Step 5: **Financing Stage** *Obtain project funding.* Sources of financing include internally generated (within the organization) cash flow and equity and debt securities sold in the capital markets. Financing is the responsibility of the treasury function, which is overseen by the chief financial officer of the organization.

Step 6: **Implementation and Control Stage** *Get projects under way and monitor their performance.* When a project is implemented, the company evaluates if capital investments are on schedule and within budget. As the project generates cash inflows, monitoring and control include a postinvestment audit comparing projections made at the time the project was selected to the actual results.

We use information from Lifetime Care Hospital, a for-profit taxable company, to illustrate capital budgeting. One of Lifetime Care's goals is to improve the productivity of its X-Ray Department. As a first step to achieve this goal, the manager of Lifetime Care *identifies* a new state-of-the-art X-ray machine as a possible replacement for the existing X-ray machine. The *search* stage yields several alternative models, but the hospital's technical staff focuses on one machine as particularly suitable—XCAM8. The manager next *acquires information* to do a more-detailed evaluation of XCAM8. Quantitative financial information for the formal analysis follows:

Revenues will be unchanged regardless of whether the new X-ray machine is acquired. Lifetime Care charges a fixed rate for a particular diagnosis, regardless of the number of X-rays taken. The only relevant financial benefit in purchasing the new X-ray machine is the cash savings in operating costs.

The existing X-ray machine can operate for five years and will have a $0 terminal disposal value at the end of that time. The required net after-tax initial investment for the new machine is $379,100, computed as follows:

Cost of new machine	*$390,000*
Investment in working capital (supplies and spare parts for new machine)	*9,000*
After-tax cash flow from disposing of existing machine	*(19,900)*
Net after-tax initial investment for new machine	*$379,100*

Most capital budgeting projects require a working-capital increase—a cash outlay (usually at the project's start) that will be recovered at the end of the project.

The manager expects the new machine to have a five-year useful life and a $0 terminal disposal value at the end of that time. The new machine is faster and easier to operate and has the ability to X-ray a larger area. These improvements will decrease labor costs and reduce the average number of X-rays taken per patient. The manager expects the investment to result in annual after-tax cash savings in operating costs of $100,000 for each of the first four years and $91,000 in year 5. These savings generally occur uniformly throughout the year. To simplify computations, all operating cash flows are assumed to occur at the end of the year. *The additional working capital investment of $9,000 is expected to be recovered in full at the end of year 5.*

The manager at Lifetime Care also identifies the following nonfinancial quantitative and qualitative benefits of investing in the new X-ray machine.

1. Higher quality of X-rays leading to improved diagnoses and better patient treatment.
2. Improved safety of technicians and patients. The greater efficiency of the new machine would mean that X-ray technicians and patients would be less exposed to the possible harmful effects of radiation.

These nonfinancial quantitative and qualitative benefits are not considered in the formal financial analysis.

In the *selection* stage, the manager decides whether to purchase the new X-ray machine. This chapter discusses the following capital budgeting methods to analyze financial information:

1. Net present value (NPV)
2. Internal rate of return (IRR)
3. Payback
4. Accrual accounting rate of return (AARR)

Both the NPV and IRR methods use discounted cash flows.

3 **Use and evaluate the two main discounted cash flow (DCF) methods: the net present value (NPV) method and the internal rate-of-return (IRR) method**

...that explicitly consider all project cash flows and the time value of money

Management accountants usually ignore the time value of money in short-run analyses because the amount of interest forgone is insignificant.

DISCOUNTED CASH FLOW

Discounted cash flow (DCF) methods measure all expected future cash inflows and outflows of a project as if they occurred at a single point in time. The key feature of DCF methods is the time value of money. The **time value of money** takes into account that a dollar (or any other monetary unit) received today is worth more than a dollar received at any future time. The reason is that $1 received today can be invested at, say, 10% per year so that it grows to $1.10 at the end of one year. The time value of money is the opportunity cost (the return of $0.10 forgone per year) from not having the money today. Similiarly $1 received one year from now is worth $1 ÷ 1.10 = $0.9091 today. In this way, discounted cash flow methods explicitly weight cash flows by the time value of money. So $100 received one year from now will be weighted by 0.9091 to yield a discounted cash flow of $90.91, which is today's value of that $100 next year. DCF focuses on cash inflows and outflows rather than on operating income as determined by accrual accounting.

The compound interest tables and formulas used in DCF analysis are in Appendix C, pp. 828–831. If you are unfamiliar with compound interest, do not proceed until you have studied Appendix C. The tables in Appendix C will be used frequently in this chapter.

The two DCF methods we describe are the net present value (NPV) method and the internal rate-of-return (IRR) method. DCF methods use the **required rate of return (RRR),** which is the minimum acceptable annual rate of return on an investment. The RRR is the return that an organization could expect to receive elsewhere for an investment of comparable risk. The RRR is also called the **discount rate, hurdle rate, cost of capital** or **opportunity cost of capital.** Assume that the required rate of return for Lifetime Care's X-ray machine project is 8% per year.

Net Present Value Method

The **net present value (NPV) method** calculates the expected monetary gain or loss from a project by discounting all expected future cash inflows and outflows to the present point in time, using the required rate of return. Only projects with a zero or positive NPV are acceptable. That's because the return from these projects equals or exceeds the cost of cap-

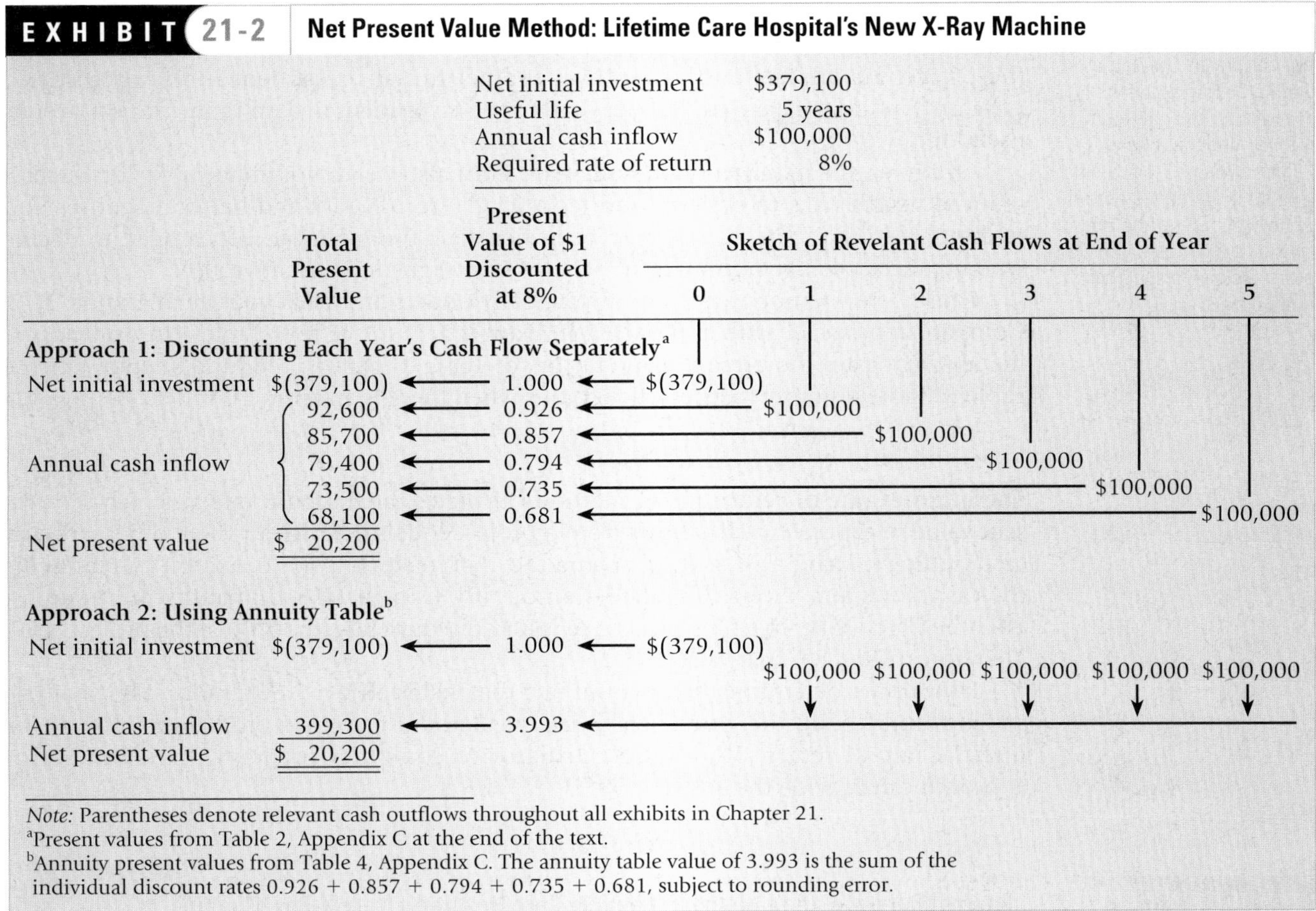

EXHIBIT 21-2 Net Present Value Method: Lifetime Care Hospital's New X-Ray Machine

Net initial investment	$379,100
Useful life	5 years
Annual cash inflow	$100,000
Required rate of return	8%

	Total Present Value	Present Value of $1 Discounted at 8%	Sketch of Revelant Cash Flows at End of Year 0	1	2	3	4	5
Approach 1: Discounting Each Year's Cash Flow Separately[a]								
Net initial investment	$(379,100)	1.000	$(379,100)					
Annual cash inflow	92,600	0.926		$100,000				
	85,700	0.857			$100,000			
	79,400	0.794				$100,000		
	73,500	0.735					$100,000	
	68,100	0.681						$100,000
Net present value	$ 20,200							
Approach 2: Using Annuity Table[b]								
Net initial investment	$(379,100)	1.000	$(379,100)					
				$100,000	$100,000	$100,000	$100,000	$100,000
Annual cash inflow	399,300	3.993						
Net present value	$ 20,200							

Note: Parentheses denote relevant cash outflows throughout all exhibits in Chapter 21.
[a]Present values from Table 2, Appendix C at the end of the text.
[b]Annuity present values from Table 4, Appendix C. The annuity table value of 3.993 is the sum of the individual discount rates 0.926 + 0.857 + 0.794 + 0.735 + 0.681, subject to rounding error.

ital—the return available by investing the capital elsewhere. If all other things are equal, the higher the NPV, the better. To use the NPV method, apply the following three steps:

Step 1: Draw a Sketch of Relevant Cash Inflows and Outflows. The right side of Exhibit 21-2 shows arrows that depict the cash flows. Outflows appear in parentheses. The sketch helps the decision maker visualize and organize the data in a systematic way. Note, Exhibit 21-2 includes the outflow for the acquisition of the new machine at the start of year 1 (also referred to as end of year 0). The NPV method specifies cash flows regardless of the source of the cash flows, such as from operations, purchase or sale of equipment, or investment or recovery of working capital. Do not inject accrual accounting concepts such as sales made on credit or non-cash expenses into the determination of cash inflows and outflows.

Step 2: Choose the Correct Compound Interest Table from Appendix C. In our example, we can discount each year's cash flow separately using Table 2, or we can compute the present value of an annuity, a series of equal cash flows at equal-time intervals, using Table 4, both in Appendix C. If we use Table 2, we find the discount factors for periods 1–5 under the 8% column. Approach 1 in Exhibit 21-2 uses the five discount factors. Because the investment produces an annuity, we may use Table 4. We find the discount factor for five periods under the 8% column. Approach 2 shows that this discount factor is 3.993, which is the sum of the five discount factors used in approach 1. To obtain the present value amount, multiply each discount factor by the amount represented by each arrow on the right in Exhibit 21-2.

Step 3: Sum the Present Value Figures to Determine Net Present Value. If NPV is zero or positive, the project should be accepted; its expected rate of return equals or exceeds the required rate of return. If NPV is negative, the project should be rejected; its expected rate of return is below the required rate of return.

Calculators usually give different results from the results using factors in the tables in Appendix C. That's because (1) the factors in the tables have only three decimal places versus eight (or more) for calculators, and (2) the tables assume cash flow occurs at the end of the period, whereas some calculators assume cash flows are continuous.

Exhibit 21-2 indicates an NPV of $20,200 at the required rate of return of 8% per year. The project is desirable based on quantifiable financial information. The cash flows from the project are adequate to (1) recover the net initial investment in the project and (2) earn a return greater than 8% per year on the investment tied up in the project over its useful life.

Of course, the manager of Lifetime Care must also weigh nonfinancial factors such as reduced health risks to patients and technicians from X-rays and better diagnoses and treatments for patients. If NPV had been negative, the manager would need to decide whether these positive nonfinancial benefits outweighed the negative NPV.

Pause here. Do not proceed until you really understand what you see in Exhibit 21-2. Compare approach 1 with approach 2 in Exhibit 21-2 to see how Table 4 in Appendix C merely aggregates the present value factors of Table 2. That is, the fundamental table is Table 2. Table 4 simply reduces calculations when there is an annuity.

Internal Rate-of-Return Method

The **internal rate-of-return (IRR) method** calculates the discount rate at which the present value of expected cash inflows from a project equals the present value of its expected cash outflows. That is, IRR is the discount rate that makes NPV = $0. Exhibit 21-3 presents the cash flows and shows the calculation of NPV using a 10% annual discount rate for Lifetime Care's X-ray machine project. At a 10% discount rate, the NPV of the project is $0. Therefore, IRR is 10% per year.

How do we determine the discount rate that yields NPV = $0? In most cases, analysts solving capital budgeting problems have a calculator or computer program to provide the internal rate of return. Without a calculator or computer program, a trial-and-error approach can provide the answer.

EXHIBIT 21-3 Internal Rate-of-Return Method:[a] Lifetime Care Hospital's New X-Ray Machine

Net initial investment	$379,100
Useful life	5 years
Annual cash inflow	$100,000
Discount rate	10%

	Total Present Value	Present Value of $1 Discounted at 10%	0	1	2	3	4	5
			Sketch of Revelant Cash Flows at End of Year					
Approach 1: Discounting Each Year's Cash Flow Separately[b]								
Net initial investment	$(379,100) ←	1.000 ←	$(379,100)					
Annual cash inflow	90,900 ←	0.909 ←		$100,000				
	82,600 ←	0.826 ←			$100,000			
	75,100 ←	0.751 ←				$100,000		
	68,300 ←	0.683 ←					$100,000	
	62,100 ←	0.621 ←						$100,000
Net present value[c] (the zero difference proves that the internal rate of return is 10%)	$ 0							
Approach 2: Using Annuity Table								
Net initial investment	$(379,100) ←	1.000 ←	$(379,100)					
				$100,000	$100,000	$100,000	$100,000	$100,000
Annual cash inflow	379,100 ←	3.791[d] ←		↓	↓	↓	↓	↓
Net present value	$ 0							

[a]The internal rate of return is computed by methods explained on pp. 000–000.
[b]Present values from Table 2, Appendix C at the end of the book.
[c]Sum is $(100) due to rounding errors. We round to $0.
[d]Annuity present values from Table 4, Appendix C. The annuity table value of 3.791 is the sum of the individual discount rates 0.909 + 0.826 + 0.751 + 0.683 + 0.621, subject to rounding error.

- *Step 1*: Try a discount rate and calculate the project's NPV using that discount rate.
- *Step 2*: If the calculated NPV is less than zero, try a lower discount rate. (A lower discount rate will increase NPV. Remember that we are trying to find a discount rate for which NPV = \$0.) If NPV is greater than zero, try a higher discount rate to lower NPV. Keep adjusting the discount rate until NPV = \$0. In the Lifetime Care example, a discount rate of 8% yields an NPV of +\$20,200 (see Exhibit 21-2). A discount rate of 12% yields an NPV of –\$18,600 (3.605, the present value annuity factor from Table 4, × \$100,000 minus \$379,100). Therefore, the discount rate that makes NPV = \$0 must lie between 8% and 12%. We try 10% and get NPV = \$0. Hence, the IRR is 10% per year.

The step-by-step computations of internal rate of return are easier when the cash inflows are equal, as in our example. Information from Exhibit 21-3 can be expressed by:

$$\$379{,}100 = \text{Present value of annuity of } \$100{,}000 \text{ at } X\% \text{ per year for 5 years}$$

Or, what factor F in Table 4 (Appendix C) will satisfy this equation?

$$\$379{,}100 = \$100{,}000F$$
$$F = \$379{,}100 \div \$100{,}000 = 3.791$$

On the five-period line of Table 4, find the percentage column that is closest to 3.791. It is exactly 10%. If the factor (F) falls between the factors in two columns, straight-line interpolation is used to approximate IRR. This interpolation is illustrated in the Problem for Self-Study (p. 736).

A project is accepted only if IRR equals or exceeds required rate of return (RRR). In the Lifetime Care example, the X-ray machine has an IRR of 10%, which is greater than the RRR of 8%. On the basis of financial factors, Lifetime Care should invest in the new machine. In general, the NPV and IRR decision rules result in consistent project acceptance and rejection decisions. If IRR exceeds RRR, then the project has a positive NPV (favoring acceptance). If IRR equals RRR, NPV = \$0. If IRR is less than RRR, the NPV is negative (favoring rejection). Obviously, managers prefer projects with higher IRRs to projects with lower IRRs, if all other things are equal. The IRR of 10% means the cash inflows from the project are adequate to (1) recover the net initial investment in the project and (2) earn a return of exactly 10% on the investment tied up in the project over its useful life.

Comparison of Net Present Value and Internal Rate-of-Return Methods

One big advantage of the NPV method is that it expresses computations in dollars, not in percent. Therefore, we can sum NPVs of individual projects to calculate NPV of a combination of projects. In contrast, IRRs of individual projects cannot be added or averaged to represent IRR of a combination of projects.

Surveys of Company Practice (see p. 727), however, report wide use of the IRR method. Why? Probably because managers find the IRR method easier to understand and because, in most instances, their decisions would be unaffected by using one method or the other. In some cases, however, as when comparing two projects with unequal lines or unequal investments, the two methods will not indicate the same decision.

Managers using the IRR method assume that the discount rate is equal to rate of return earned on the project. Such investment opportunities may not be available. Managers using the NPV method assume the funds obtainable from competing projects can be reinvested at the company's RRR. The NPV method is generally regarded as a better method than the IRR method. Refer to corporate finance texts for more details on these issues.

Another advantage of the NPV method is it can be used when the RRR varies over the life of a project. Suppose the X-ray machine considered by Lifetime Care has a RRR of 9% per year in years 1 and 2 and 12% per year in years 3, 4, and 5. Total present value of the cash inflows can be calculated as \$378,100 (computations not shown).

Given the net initial investment of \$379,100, NPV calculations indicate that the project is undesirable: NPV is –\$1,000 (\$378,100 – \$379,100). It is not possible to use the IRR method in this case. Different RRRs in different years (9% annually for years 1 and

2 versus 12% annually for years 3, 4, and 5) mean there is not a single RRR that the IRR (a single figure) can be compared against to decide if the project should be accepted or rejected.

SENSITIVITY ANALYSIS

To present the basics of the NPV and IRR methods, we have assumed that the expected values of cash flows will occur for certain. Obviously, such predictions are not certain. To examine how a result will change if the predicted financial outcomes are not achieved or if an underlying assumption changes, managers can use *sensitivity analysis,* a "what-if" technique introduced in Chapter 3.

Sensitivity analysis can take various forms. Suppose the Lifetime Care manager believes forecasted savings are difficult to predict. She asks, "What is the minimum annual cash savings that makes investment in the new X-ray machine worthwhile—that is, leads to NPV = $0?" For the data in Exhibit 21-2, let A = Annual cash flow and let NPV = $0. Net initial investment is $379,100, and the present value factor at the 8% required annual rate of return for a five-year annuity of $1 is 3.993. Then:

$$\begin{aligned} NPV &= \$0 \\ (3.993A) - \$379{,}100 &= \$0 \\ 3.993A &= \$379{,}100 \\ A &= \$94{,}941 \end{aligned}$$

At the discount rate of 8% per year, annual cash flow can decrease to $94,941 (a decline of $100,000 − $94,941 = $5,059) before the NPV falls to $0. If the manager believes she can attain annual cash savings of at least $94,941, she can justify investing in the new X-ray machine on financial grounds.

Given the rapid pace of technological change, estimating a project's useful life can be one of the most challenging aspects of capital budgeting.

Exhibit 21-4 shows that variations in (1) the annual cash inflows and (2) the RRR significantly affect NPV of the X-ray machine project. NPVs can also vary with different useful lives of a project. Sensitivity analysis helps managers focus on decisions that are most sensitive to different assumptions and worry less about decisions that are not so sensitive.

4 Use and evaluate the payback method
...the time it takes to recoup the investment

PAYBACK METHOD

We now consider the third method for analyzing the financial aspects of projects. **Payback** measures the time it will take to recoup, in the form of expected future cash flows, the net initial investment in a project. Like NPV and IRR, the payback method does not distinguish among the sources of cash flows, such as from operations, purchase or sale of equipment, or investment or recovery of working capital. Payback is simplest to calculate when a project has uniform cash flows. We consider this case first.

Uniform Cash Flows

In the Lifetime Care example, the X-ray machine costs $379,100, has a five-year expected useful life, and generates a $100,000 *uniform* cash flow each year. The payback is

$$\text{Payback} = \frac{\text{Net initial investment}}{\text{Uniform increase in annual future cash flows}} = \frac{\$379{,}100}{\$100{,}000} = 3.8 \text{ years}^{1}$$

The payback method highlights liquidity, a factor that often plays a role in capital budgeting decisions. Managers prefer projects with shorter paybacks (projects that are more liquid) to projects with longer paybacks, if all other things are equal. Projects with shorter paybacks give an organization more flexibility because funds for other projects

[1]Cash savings from the new X-ray machine occur uniformly *throughout* the year, but for simplicity in calculating NPV and IRR, we assume they occur at the *end* of each year. A literal interpretation of this assumption would imply a payback of 4 years because Lifetime Care will only recover its investment when cash inflows occur at the end of year 4. The calculations shown in the chapter, however, better approximate Lifetime Care's payback on the basis of uniform cash flows throughout the year.

Required Rate of Return	Annual Cash Inflows $80,000	$90,000	$100,000	$110,000	$120,000
6%	$(42,140)	$ (20)	$42,100	$84,220	$126,340
8%	$(59,660)	$(19,730)	$20,200	$60,130	$100,060
10%	$(75,820)	$(37,910)	$ 0	$37,910	$ 75,820

[a]All entries in cells assume the project's useful life is five years.

EXHIBIT 21-4

Net Present Value Calculations for Lifetime Care Hospital Under Different Assumptions of Annual Cash Inflows and Required Rate of Return[a]

become available sooner. Also, managers are less confident about cash flow predictions that stretch far into the future.

Under the payback method, organizations choose a cutoff period for a project. The greater the risks of a project, the shorter the cutoff period. Japanese companies favor the payback method over other methods (see Surveys of Company Practice, p. 727) and use cutoff periods ranging from three to five years. Projects with a payback period that is less than the cutoff period are accepted, and those with a payback period that is longer than the cutoff period are rejected. If Lifetime Care's cutoff period under the payback method is three years, it will reject the new machine.

The payback method is easy to understand. Like the DCF methods, the payback method is not affected by accrual accounting conventions such as depreciation. Payback is a useful measure when (1) preliminary screening of many proposals is necessary and (2) the expected cash flows in later years of a project are highly uncertain.

Companies often use the payback method in conjunction with DCF analyses and select those positive NPV projects that also have an acceptably short payback period. Management is likely to emphasize a shorter payback when the future is uncertain (and they don't want to commit cash for long periods) and when interest rates are high.

Two weaknesses of the payback method are that (1) it fails to incorporate the time value of money and (2) it does not consider a project's cash flows after the payback period. Consider an alternative to the $379,100 X-ray machine. Another X-ray machine, with a three-year useful life and $0 terminal disposal value, requires only a $300,000 net initial investment and will also result in cash inflows of $100,000 per year. First, compare the payback periods:

$$\text{Machine 1} = \frac{\$379{,}100}{\$100{,}000} = 3.8 \text{ years}$$

$$\text{Machine 2} = \frac{\$300{,}000}{\$100{,}000} = 3.0 \text{ years}$$

The payback criterion favors machine 2, with the shorter payback. If the cutoff period is three years, machine 1 would fail to meet the payback criterion.

Consider next NPV of the two investment options using Lifetime Care's 8% required rate of return for the X-ray machine investment. At a discount rate of 8%, the NPV of machine 2 is –$42,300 (2.577, the present value annuity factor for three years at 8% per year from Table 4, times $100,000 = $257,700 minus net initial investment of $300,000). Machine 1, as we know, has a positive NPV of $20,200 (from Exhibit 21-2). The NPV criterion suggests Lifetime Care should acquire machine 1. Machine 2, with a negative NPV, would fail to meet the NPV criterion.

The payback method gives a different answer than the NPV method in this example because the payback method ignores cash flows after the payback period and ignores the time value of money. Another problem with the payback method is that choosing too short a cutoff period for project acceptance may promote the selection of only short-lived projects. An organization will tend to reject long-run, positive-NPV projects.

Nonuniform Cash Flows

When cash flows are not uniform, the payback computation takes a cumulative form: The years' cash flows are accumulated until the amount of net initial investment is recovered. Assume that Venture Law Group is considering the purchase of video conferencing equipment for $150,000. The equipment is expected to provide a total cash savings of $380,000 over the next five years, due to reduced travel costs and more-effective use of executive time. The cash savings occur uniformly throughout each year, but nonuniformly across years. Payback occurs during the third year:

Year	Cash Savings	Cumulative Cash Savings	Net Initial Investment Yet to Be Recovered at End of Year
0	—	—	$150,000
1	$ 50,000	$ 50,000	100,000
2	60,000	110,000	40,000
3	80,000	190,000	—
4	90,000	280,000	—
5	100,000	380,000	—

Straight-line interpolation within the third year reveals that the final $40,000 needed to recover the $150,000 investment (that is, $150,000 – $110,000 recovered by the end of year 2) will be achieved halfway through year 3 (in which $80,000 of cash savings occur):

$$\text{Payback} = 2 \text{ years} + \left(\frac{\$40{,}000}{\$80{,}000} \times 1 \text{ year}\right) = 2.5 \text{ years}$$

The video conferencing example has a single cash outflow of $150,000 in year 0. When a project has multiple cash outflows occurring at different points in time, these outflows are added to obtain a total cash outflow figure for the project. No adjustment is made for time value of money when adding these cash outflows in computing the payback period.

5 Use and evaluate the accrual accounting rate-of-return (AARR) method

...after-tax operating income divided by investment

ACCRUAL ACCOUNTING RATE-OF-RETURN METHOD

We now consider a fourth method for analyzing the financial aspects of capital budgeting projects. The **accrual accounting rate of return (AARR)** divides an accrual accounting measure of average annual income of a project by an accrual accounting measure of its investment. It is also called the **accounting rate of return.** We illustrate AARR for the Lifetime Care example using the project's net initial investment as the amount in the denominator:

$$\text{Accrual accounting rate of return} = \frac{\text{Increase in expected average annual after-tax operating income}}{\text{Net initial investment}}$$

The numerator is sometimes "increase in expected average annual operating income," and the denominator is sometimes "average investment per year."

If Lifetime Care purchases the new X-ray machine, the increase in expected average after-tax annual savings in operating costs will be $98,200. This amount is the after-tax total operating savings of $491,000 ($100,000 for four years and $91,000 in year 5) ÷ 5 years. Because the new machine has a $0 terminal disposal value, straight-line depreciation on the new machine is $78,000 per year ($390,000 ÷ 5 years). The net initial investment is $379,100. The AARR on net initial investment is equal to:

$$\text{AARR} = \frac{\$98{,}200 - \$78{,}000}{\$379{,}100} = \frac{\$20{,}200 \text{ per year}}{\$379{,}100} = 0.053, \text{ or } 5.3\% \text{ per year}$$

The AARR of 5.3% per year indicates the rate at which a dollar of investment generates after-tax operating income. AARR on the new X-ray machine is low for two reasons: (1) using the initial investment amount makes the denominator larger, and (2) the annual depreciation must be deducted from the annual operating income in the numerator. Projects whose AARR exceeds a specified accrual accounting required rate of return are considered acceptable (the higher the AARR, the better the project is considered to be).

The AARR method is similar to the IRR method in that both methods calculate a rate-of-return percentage. The AARR calculates return using operating income numbers after considering accruals and taxes, whereas the IRR method calculates return on the basis of after-tax cash flows and the time value of money. Because cash flows and the time value of money are central to capital budgeting decisions, the IRR method is regarded as better than the AARR method.

NPV, IRR, and payback are all based on *cash flows;* AARR is based on *accrual accounting.*

AARR computations are easy to understand, and they use numbers reported in the financial statements. Unlike the payback method, which ignores cash flows after the payback period, the AARR method considers income earned throughout a project's expected useful life. Unlike the NPV method, the AARR method uses accrual accounting income numbers. It does not track cash flows, and it ignores the time value of money. Critics cite these arguments as drawbacks of the AARR method.

SURVEYS OF COMPANY PRACTICE

International Comparison of Capital Budgeting Methods

What methods do companies around the world use for analyzing capital investment decisions? The percentages in the following table indicate how frequently particular capital budgeting methods are used in eight countries. The reported percentages exceed 100% because many companies surveyed use more than one method.

	United States[a,h]	Australia[b]	Canada[c]	Ireland[d]	Japan[b]	Scotland[e]	South Korea[f]	United Kingdom[g]
Payback	59%	61%	50%	84%	52%	78%	75%	76%
IRR	52%	37%	62% }	84% (IRR and NPV combined)	4%	58%	75%	39%
NPV	28%	45%	41% }		6%	48%	60%	38%
AARR	13%	24%	17%	24%	36%	31%	68%	28%
Other	44%	7%	8%	—	5%	—	—	7%

Some observations on these surveys:

1. Companies in the United States, Australia, Canada, Ireland, Scotland, South Korea, and the United Kingdom tend to use two methods, on average, to evaluate capital investments. (The sum of the capital budgeting percentages in the columns for each of these countries is approximately 200%.)
2. Japanese companies tend to use one method. (The sum of the capital budgeting percentages for Japan is approximately 100%.)
3. The payback method is a popular method among companies in all countries. Japanese companies use the payback method as their primary method of analysis in their capital budgeting decisions. Companies in the United States, Australia, Canada, Ireland, Scotland, South Korea, and the United Kingdom use discounted cash flow (DCF) methods (IRR and NPV) extensively.
4. The AARR method lags behind DCF methods in the United States, Australia, Canada, Ireland, Scotland, and the United Kingdom. It is on par with DCF methods in South Korea, and it is very much preferred to DCF methods in Japan.
5. Smaller companies often use DCF methods less than larger companies. One survey of small U.S. companies (revenues less than $5 million) found that the payback method was the primary method for 43% of companies, AARR for 22%, IRR for 16%, NPV for 11%, and other methods for 8%. Reasons given for the preference for payback was its emphasis on liquidity, the difficulty of small companies having access to capital, and simplicity.

[a]Adapted from Smith and Sullivan, "Survey of Cost." [b]Blayney and Yokoyama, "Comparative Analysis." [c]Jog and Srivastava, "Corporate Financial." [d]Clarke and O'Dea, "Management Accounting." [e]Sangster, "Capital Investment. " [f]Kim and Song, "Accounting Practices." [g]Block, "Capital Budgeting." [h]Bruner, Eades, Harris and Higgins, "Best Practices."
Full citations are in Appendix A at the end of the book.

EVALUATING MANAGERS AND GOAL-CONGRUENCE ISSUES

6 Identify and reduce conflicts from using DCF for capital budgeting decisions and accrual accounting for performance evaluation

...good investment decisions can decrease operating income in the project's early years

A manager who uses DCF methods to make capital budgeting decisions can make decisions that are not consistent with decisions that would be made if AARR were used for performance evaluation. Consider the manager of the X-Ray Department at Lifetime Care. The NPV method indicates that the manager should purchase the new X-ray machine because it has a positive NPV of $20,200.

Suppose top management of Lifetime Care uses AARR for judging performance. The manager of the X-Ray Department may reject purchasing the new X-ray machine if the AARR of 5.3% on the investment reduces the AARR of the entire X-ray Department and negatively affects the department's reported performance.

Obviously, there is an inconsistency between using the NPV method as best for capital budgeting decisions and then using a different method to evaluate performance over short time horizons. Managers are tempted to make capital budgeting decisions on the basis of short-run accrual accounting results, even though these decisions, in terms of DCF, are not in the best long-run interest of the organization. Such temptations become more pronounced if managers are frequently transferred (or promoted), or if their bonuses are affected by the level of year-to-year accrual income.[2]

7 Identify relevant cash inflows and outflows for capital budgeting decisions

...differences in expected future cash flows resulting from the investment

RELEVANT CASH FLOWS IN DISCOUNTED CASH FLOW ANALYSIS

One of the biggest challenges in capital budgeting, particularly DCF analysis, is determining which cash flows are relevant in making an investment selection. Relevant cash flows are the differences in expected future cash flows as a result of making the investment. At Lifetime Care, the relevant cash flows are the differences in expected future cash flows between continuing to use the old machine and purchasing the new one. *When reading this section, focus on identifying expected future cash flows and the differences in expected future cash flows.*

To illustrate relevant cash flow analysis, consider the Lifetime Care example and these additional assumptions:

Some entire courses deal with income tax laws; this chapter illustrates a general approach for incorporating income taxes into capital budgeting decisions.

1. Lifetime Care is a profitable company. The income tax rate is 40% of operating income each year.
2. The operating cash savings from the new X-ray machine are $120,000 in years 1 – 4 and $105,000 in year 5.
3. Lifetime uses the straight-line depreciation method, which means an equal amount of depreciation is taken each year.
4. Gains or losses on the sale of depreciable assets are taxed at the same rate as ordinary income.
5. The tax effects of cash inflows and outflows occur at the same time that the cash inflows and outflows occur.
6. Lifetime Care uses an 8% required rate of return for discounting after-tax cash flows.

Summary data for the X-ray machines are

	Old X-Ray Machine	New X-Ray Machine
Purchase price	—	$390,000
Current book value	$40,000	—
Current disposal value	6,500	Not applicable
Terminal disposal value 5 years from now	0	0
Annual depreciation	8,000[a]	78,000[b]
Working capital required	6,000	15,000

[a] $40,000 ÷ 5 years = $8,000 annual depreciation.
[b] $390,000 ÷ 5 years = $78,000 annual depreciation.

[2]Managers are often interested in how accepting a project will affect a bonus plan that is based on reported annual accrual accounting numbers. Do not assume that the AARR computed by the formula on p. 726 is the appropriate number to use in examining the effect that adoption of a project will have on a manager's bonus plan. It is necessary to examine on a year-by-year basis how the AARR is computed when determining bonuses. For example, the numerator in the formula is the "increase in expected average annual after-tax operating income." This average increase need not be the same each year during a project. Assume the president of Lifetime Care receives an annual $50,000 lump-sum bonus if the AARR on assets exceeds 8% in that year. Project A has an AARR over its five-year life of 10% and a net present value of $20,000. Project B has an AARR over its five-year life of 9% and a net present value of $18,000. Project A has cash inflows in years 1 and 5 but zero cash inflows in years 2, 3 and 4. Project B has equal cash inflows in years 1 – 5. It could well be that the president would receive higher bonuses with project B — the project with a lower NPV.

EXHIBIT 21-5

Effect on Cash Flow from Operations, Net of Income Taxes, in Year 1 for Lifetime Care's Investment in the New X-Ray Machine

PANEL A: TWO METHODS BASED ON THE INCOME STATEMENT

(*S*)	Savings in cash costs	$120,000
(*D*)	Additional depreciation deductions	70,000
(*OI*)	Increase in operating income	50,000
(*T*)	Income taxes (Income tax rate $t \times OI$) = 40% × $50,000	20,000
(*NI*)	Increase in net income	$ 30,000
	Increase in cash flow from operations, net of income taxes	
	Method 1: $S - T$ = $120,000 – $20,000 = $100,000 or	
	Method 2: $NI + D$ = $30,000 + $70,000 = $100,000	

PANEL B: ITEM-BY-ITEM METHOD

	Effect of cash operating flows	
(*S*)	Savings in cash costs	$120,000
($t \times S$)	Deduct income tax cash outflow at 40%	48,000
$S - t \times S = (1 - t) \times S$	After-tax cash flow from operations (excluding depreciation effects)	72,000
	Effect of depreciation	
(*D*)	Additional depreciation deductions, $70,000	
($t \times D$)	Income tax cash savings from additional depreciation deductions at 40% × $70,000	28,000
$(1 - t) \times S + (t \times D) = S - (t \times S) + (t \times D)$	Cash flow from operations, net of income taxes	$100,000

Relevant After-Tax Flows

We use the *differential approach* to decision making introduced in Chapter 11. We compare (1) the cash outflows as a result of replacing the old machine with (2) the savings in future cash outflows by using the new machine rather than the old machine.

It is important to first understand how income taxes affect cash flows in each year. Income taxes are a fact of life for most corporations and individuals. As Benjamin Franklin said, "Two things in life are certain: death and taxes." Exhibit 21-5 shows how investing in the new machine will affect Lifetime Care's cash flow from operations and its income taxes in year 1. Recall that Lifetime Care will save $120,000 in before-tax cash operating outflows by investing in the new machine (p. 728), but it will record additional depreciation of $70,000 ($78,000 – $8,000).

Panel A shows that the year 1 cash flow from operations, net of income taxes, equals $100,000, using two methods based on the income statement. The first method focuses on cash items only, the $120,000 cash savings minus income taxes of $20,000. The second method starts with the $30,000 increase in net income (calculated after deducting additional depreciation deductions for income tax purposes) and adds back additional depreciation deductions of $70,000, because depreciation is an operating cost that reduces net income but does not reduce cash outflow.

Panel B of Exhibit 21-5 describes a third method that we will use frequently to compute cash flow from operations, net of income taxes. The easiest way to interpret the third method is to think of the government as a 40% (equal to the tax rate) partner in Lifetime Care. Each time Lifetime Care obtains cost savings, *S*, (or revenues in excess of cash costs), its income is higher by *S*, so it will pay 40% of the cash savings (0.40*S*) in taxes. This results in after-tax cash operating flows of *S* – 0.40*S*, which in this example is $120,000 – (0.40 × $120,000) = $72,000, or $120,000 × (1 – 0.40) = $72,000.

To achieve the higher cash savings, *S*, Lifetime Care incurred higher depreciation charges, *D*, from investing in the new machine. Depreciation cost itself does not affect cash flow because depreciation is a noncash cost, but higher depreciation cost *lowers* Lifetime Care's taxable income by *D*, saving income tax cash outflows of 0.40*D*, which in this example is 0.40 × $70,000 = $28,000.

Letting *t* = tax rate, cash flow from operations, net of income taxes, in this example equals the cash savings, *S*, minus the tax payments on these savings, $t \times S$, plus the tax

EXHIBIT 21-6 Relevant Cash Inflows and Outflows for Lifetime Care Hospital's New X-Ray Machine

	Sketch of Relevant Cash Flows at End of Year					
	0	1	2	3	4	5
1a. Initial machine investment	$(390,000)					
1b. Initial working-capital investment	(9,000)					
1c. After-tax cash flow from current disposal of old machine	19,900					
Net after-tax initial investment	(379,100)					
2a. Annual after-tax cash flow from operations (excluding depreciation effects)		$ 72,000	$ 72,000	$ 72,000	$ 72,000	$ 63,000
2b. Income tax cash savings from annual depreciation deductions		28,000	28,000	28,000	28,000	28,000
3a. After-tax cash flow from terminal disposal of machine						0
3b. After-tax cash flow from recovery of working capital						9,000
Total relevant cash flows, as shown in Exhibits 21-2 and 21-3	$(379,100)	$100,000	$100,000	$100,000	$100,000	$100,000

savings on depreciation deductions, $t \times D$: $\$120{,}000 - (0.40 \times \$120{,}000) + (0.40 \times \$70{,}000) = \$120{,}000 - \$48{,}000 + \$28{,}000 = \$100{,}000$.

By the same logic, each time Lifetime Care shows a gain on sale of assets, *G*, it will show tax outflows, $t \times G$; and each time it shows a loss on sale of assets, *L*, it will show tax benefits or savings, $t \times L$.

A capital investment project typically has three categories of cash flows: (1) net initial investment in the project, which includes the acquisition of a new asset and required additions to working capital, minus the cash flow from current disposal of an existing asset; (2) after-tax cash flow from operations (including income tax cash savings from annual depreciation deductions); and (3) after-tax cash flow from terminal disposal of an asset and recovery of working capital. We use the Lifetime Care example to discuss these three categories.

As you work through the cash flows in each of the three categories, refer to Exhibit 21-6. This exhibit sketches the relevant cash inflows and outflows for Lifetime Care's decision to purchase the new machine as described in items 1 through 3 below. Note, the total relevant cash flows for each year equal the relevant cash flows used in Exhibits 21-2 and 21-3 to illustrate the NPV and IRR methods.

1. Net Initial Investment Three components of net initial investment cash flows are (a) cash outflow to purchase the machine, (b) working-capital cash outflow, and (c) cash inflow from current disposal of the old machine.

1a. *Initial machine investment.* These outflows, made for purchasing plant and equipment, occur at the beginning of the project's life and include cash outflows for transporting and installing the item. In the Lifetime Care example, the $390,000 cost (including transportation and installation) of the X-ray machine is an outflow in year 0. These cash flows are relevant to the capital budgeting decision because they will be incurred only if Lifetime decides to purchase the new machine.

1b. *Initial working-capital investment.* Initial investments in plant and equipment are usually accompanied by incremental initial investments in working capital. These incremental investments take the form of current assets, such as accounts receivable and inventories, minus current liabilities, such as accounts payable. Working-capital investments are similar to plant and equipment investments in that they require cash.

The Lifetime Care example assumes a $9,000 incremental initial investment in working capital (for supplies and spare parts inventory) if the new machine is acquired. The incremental working-capital investment is the difference between the working capital required to operate the new machine ($15,000) and the working-capital investment required to operate the old machine ($6,000). The $9,000 additional investment in working capital is a cash outflow in year 0.

1c. *After-tax cash flow from current disposal of old machine.* Any cash received from disposal of the old machine is a relevant cash inflow (in year 0). It's relevant because it is an expected future cash flow that differs between the alternatives of investing and not investing in the new machine. If Lifetime Care invests in the new X-ray machine, it will dispose of its old machine for $6,500. Recall that the book value (which is original cost minus accumulated depreciation) of the old equipment is irrelevant to the decision (Chapter 11, p. 386). It is a past or sunk cost. Nothing can change what has already been spent.

To calculate the tax consequences of disposing of the old machine, we compute the gain or loss on disposal:

Current disposal value of old machine (given, p. 728)	$ 6,500
Deduct current book value of old machine (given, p. 728)	40,000
Loss on disposal of machine	$(33,500)

Any loss on sale of assets lowers taxable income and results in tax savings. The after-tax cash flow from disposal of the old machine equals:

Current disposal value of old machine (given, p. 728)	$ 6,500
Tax savings on loss (0.40 × $33,500)	13,400
After-tax cash inflow from current disposal of old machine	$19,900

Question: Why is book value of old equipment always irrelevant in capital budgeting decisions? *Answer*: Book value is not associated with any current cash flows. It's the difference between the equipment's original cost and its accumulated depreciation under accrual accounting.

We assume Lifetime Care has sufficient positive taxable income so that the full amount of the loss on disposal of the old machine is a tax deduction in year 0.

If Lifetime Care were a nonprofit organization, not subject to income taxes, the tax consequences of disposal would be $0.

The sum of items **1a, 1b,** and **1c** appears in Exhibit 21-6 as the year 0 net initial investment for the new X-ray machine equal to $379,100 (the initial machine investment, $390,000; plus the additional working-capital investment, $9,000; minus the after-tax cash inflow from current disposal of the old machine, $19,900).

2. Cash Flow from Operations This category includes the difference between each year's cash flow from operations under the two alternatives. Organizations make capital investments to generate cash inflows in the future. These inflows may result from producing and selling additional goods or services, or, as for Lifetime Care, from savings in cash operating costs. Annual cash flow from operations can be net outflows in some years. For example, oil production may require large expenditures every, say, five years to improve oil extraction rates. Always focus on cash flow from operations, not on revenues and expenses under accrual accounting.

The savings in operating cash flows (for labor and materials)—$120,000 in each of the first four years and $105,000 in the fifth year—are relevant because they are expected future cash flows that will differ between the alternatives of investing and not investing in the new machine. The after-tax effects of these cash flows follow.

2a. *Annual after-tax cash flow from operations (excluding depreciation effects).* The 40% tax rate reduces the benefit of the $120,000 operating cash flow savings for years 1–4 with the new X-ray machine. After-tax cash flow (excluding depreciation effects) is

Annual cash flow from operations with new machine	$120,000
Deduct income tax payments (0.40 × $120,000)	48,000
Annual after-tax cash flow from operations	$ 72,000

For year 5, the after-tax cash flow (excluding depreciation effects) is

Annual cash flow from operations with new machine	$105,000
Deduct income tax payments (0.40 × $105,000)	42,000
Annual after-tax cash flow from operations	$ 63,000

Exhibit 21-6, item **2a,** shows the $72,000 amounts for each of the years 1–4 and $63,000 for year 5.

To reinforce the idea about focusing on cash flows, consider the following additional fact about the Lifetime Care example. Suppose total X-Ray Department overhead costs will not change whether the new machine is purchased or the old machine is kept. X-Ray Department overhead costs are allocated to individual X-ray machines—Lifetime has several—on the basis of the labor costs for operating each machine. Because the new X-ray machine would have lower labor costs, overhead costs allocated to it would be $30,000 less than the amount allocated to the machine it would replace. How should Lifetime Care incorporate the decrease in allocated overhead costs of $30,000 in the relevant cash flow analysis?

To answer that question, we need to ask, "Do *total* overhead costs of the X-Ray Department decrease as a result of acquiring the new machine?" In our example, they do not. Total overhead costs of the X-Ray Department remain the same whether or not the new machine is acquired. Only the overhead cost allocated to individual machines changes. The overhead costs allocated to the new machine are $30,000 less than the amount allocated to the machine it would replace. This $30,000 difference in overhead will be allocated to *other* machines in the department. No cash flow savings in total overhead occur. Therefore, the $30,000 should not be included as part of annual cash savings from operations.

Next consider the effects of depreciation. *The depreciation line item is itself irrelevant in DCF analysis.* It is a noncash allocation of costs, whereas DCF is based on inflows and outflows of *cash.* In DCF methods, the initial cost of equipment is regarded as a *lump-sum* outflow of cash in year 0. Deducting depreciation expenses from operating cash inflows would result in counting the lump-sum amount twice. *However, depreciation results in income tax cash savings. These tax savings are a relevant cash flow.*

2b. *Income tax cash savings from annual depreciation deductions.* Depreciation tax deductions, in effect, partially offset the cost of acquiring the new X-ray machine. The following table calculates the income tax cash savings from the additional depreciation deductions each year as a result of acquiring the new machine.

Be clear on how depreciation affects cash flow. Depreciation expense is deductible for income tax purposes, so it reduces the company's tax payment from what it otherwise would have been, which actually *increases* the company's net cash flows.

Year	Depreciation Deduction on New X-Ray Machine (p. 728)	Depreciation Deduction on Old X-Ray Machine (p. 728)	Difference in Depreciation Deduction	Income Tax Rate	Increase in Income Tax Cash Savings from Depreciation Deductions with New X-Ray Machine
1	$78,000	$8,000	$70,000	40%	$28,000
2	78,000	8,000	70,000	40%	28,000
3	78,000	8,000	70,000	40%	28,000
4	78,000	8,000	70,000	40%	28,000
5	78,000	8,000	70,000	40%	28,000

Exhibit 21-6, item **2b,** shows these $28,000 amounts for years 1 – 5.[3]

For economic policy reasons, usually to encourage (or in some cases, discourage) investments, government tax laws specify which depreciation methods and which depreciable lives will be allowed. Suppose the government, under U.S. income tax laws, permitted accelerated depreciation to be used. This provision would result in higher depreciation deductions in earlier years. If it could, should Lifetime Care use accelerated depreciation? Yes, because there is a general rule in tax planning for profitable companies: When there is a legal choice, take the depreciation (or any other deduction) sooner rather than later. That's because income tax savings occur earlier, causing an increase in NPVs.

3. Terminal Disposal of Investment The disposal of the investment generally increases cash inflow when the project terminates. Errors in forecasting the terminal disposal value are seldom critical for long-duration projects because the present value of amounts to be received in the distant future is usually small. Two components of the ter-

[3]If Lifetime Care were a nonprofit hospital not subject to income taxes, cash flow from operations would equal $120,000 in years 1 – 4 and $105,000 in year 5. The operating cash savings would not be reduced by 40%, and there would also be no income tax cash savings from depreciation deductions.

minal disposal value of an investment are (a) the after-tax cash flow from terminal disposal of machines and (b) the after-tax cash flow from recovery of working capital.

3a. *After-tax cash flow from terminal disposal of machines.* At the end of the useful life of the project, the machine's terminal disposal value may be \$0 or an amount considerably less than the net initial investment. The relevant cash inflow is the difference in expected after-tax terminal disposal values at the end of five years under the two alternatives of purchasing the new machine or keeping the old machine.

Both the existing and the new X-ray machines have zero terminal disposal values in year 5. Hence, the difference in after-tax terminal disposal values is also \$0. The general approach for computing the relevant amounts (illustrated for the new machine) is

Terminal disposal value of new machine at end of year 5	\$0
Deduct book value of new machine at end of year 5	0
Gain (or loss) on disposal of new machine	\$0
Terminal disposal value of new machine at end of year 5	\$0
Deduct taxes paid on gain (add taxes saved on loss), 0.40 × \$0	0
After-tax cash inflow from terminal disposal of new machine	\$0

3b. *After-tax cash flow from recovery of working capital.* The initial investment in working capital is usually fully recouped when the project is terminated. At that time, inventories and accounts receivable necessary to support the project are no longer needed. Lifetime Care receives cash equal to the book value of its working capital. Thus, there is no gain or loss on working capital and, hence, no tax consequences. The relevant cash inflow is the difference in the expected working capital recovered under the two alternatives. At the end of year 5, Lifetime recovers \$15,000 cash from working capital if it invests in the new X-ray machine versus \$6,000 if it continues to use the old machine. The relevant cash inflow in year 5 if Lifetime invests in the new machine is \$9,000 (\$15,000 – \$6,000).

Some capital investment projects *reduce* working capital. Assume that a computer-integrated manufacturing (CIM) project with a seven-year life will reduce inventories and, hence, working capital by \$20 million from, say, \$50 million to \$30 million. This reduction will be represented as a \$20 million cash *inflow* for the project in year 0. At the end of seven years, the recovery of working capital will show a relevant incremental cash *outflow* of \$20 million. That's because the company recovers only \$30 million of working capital under CIM, rather than the \$50 million of working capital it would have recovered had it not implemented CIM.

Exhibit 21-6 shows items **3a** and **3b** under the year 5 column. The relevant cash flows in Exhibit 21-6 serve as inputs for the capital budgeting methods described earlier in the chapter.

A project that *decreases* working capital (WC) at the beginning of the project (say, replacing an old machine with a new one) means that an *increase* in WC is required at the end of the project. The relevant WC cash flows are the differences between the WC needs of the new machine and the WC needs of the old machine at the beginning and end of the project.

MANAGING THE PROJECT

Stage 6 of capital budgeting—implementation and control—is managing the project. We'll now look at two aspects of managing a project: management control of the investment activity itself and management control of the project as a whole.

Management Control of Investment Activity

Capital budgeting projects, such as purchasing an X-ray machine or video conferencing equipment, are easy to implement. Other projects, such as building shopping malls or new manufacturing plants, are complex and take much time. In the latter case, monitoring and controlling the investment schedules and budgets is critical to the success of the overall project.

Management Control of the Project—Postinvestment Audit

A postinvestment audit provides management with feedback about the performance of a project, so that management can compare actual results to the costs and benefits expected at the time the project was selected. Suppose actual outcomes (such as operating cash savings from the new X-ray machine in the Lifetime Care example) are much lower than expected. Management must then investigate to determine if this result occurred because the original estimates were overly optimistic or because of implementation problems. Either of these explanations is a concern.

Postinvestment audits of capital projects require information on the costs and benefits attributable to the project. But it can be difficult to disentangle those cash flows from the company's overall cash flows.

Optimistic estimates may result in the acceptance of a project that should have been rejected. To discourage optimistic estimates, companies such as DuPont maintain records comparing actual results with the estimates made by individual managers when seeking approval for capital investments. Postinvestment audits discourage unrealistic forecasts. Implementation problems are a concern because the returns from the project are inadequate. Postinvestment audits can point to areas of implementation that need corrective action.

Postinvestment audits require thoughtfulness and care. They should be done only after project outcomes have stabilized. Doing the audits early may give misleading feedback. Obtaining actual results to compare against estimates is often not easy. For example, actual labor cost savings from the new X-ray machine may not be comparable to the estimated savings because the actual number and types of X-rays taken may be different from the quantities assumed during the selection stage. Other benefits, such as the impact on patient treatment, may be difficult to quantify.

STRATEGIC CONSIDERATIONS IN CAPITAL BUDGETING

A company's strategy is the source of its strategic capital budgeting decisions. Strategic decisions by United Airlines, Westin Hotels, Federal Express, and Pizza Hut to expand in Europe and Asia required capital investments to be made in several countries. The strategic decision by Barnes and Nobles to support book sales over the Internet required capital investments creating BarnesandNoble.com and an Internet infrastructure. General Electric's decision to enter the television industry resulted in a big investment to acquire NBC. Merck's decision to develop a new cholesterol-reducing drug led to major investments in R&D and marketing. General Motors' decision to build a new line of cars led to major investments in its Saturn project.

The strategy underlying some capital investment decisions is leadership in technology. Many companies, for example automobile companies, have invested in computer-integrated manufacturing (CIM) technology to improve quality, shorten lead times, and increase flexibility (for example, being able to quickly switch equipment to manufacture two-door instead of four-door cars). In CIM plants, computers give instructions that quickly and automatically set up and run equipment to manufacture many different products. Computers monitor the products and directly control the process to ensure defect-free, high-quality output. The role of manufacturing labor is largely restricted to computer programming, engineering support, and maintenance of robotic machinery.

Capital investment decisions that are strategic in nature require managers to consider a broad range of factors that may be difficult to estimate. Some strategic investments are made to avoid putting a company at a competitive disadvantage. For example, as cellular telephone companies add features that allow customers to connect to the Internet and send and receive e-mail messages, a company that does not provide these features could suffer a decline in market share. The benefit of capital investments in this case is not higher revenues but the prevention of a decline in revenues and profits. Such benefits may be difficult to quantify.

Consider some of the difficulties of justifying investments in CIM technology. To quantify the benefit of efficiently manufacturing many different products in response to changes in consumer preferences requires some notion of consumer-demand changes that may occur many years in the future. Another benefit of investing in CIM technology is that it increases worker knowledge of and experience with automation. The benefit of this knowledge and experience is difficult to measure. The Concepts in Action (p. 735) describes measurement issues that arise when justifying investments in pollution control equipment.

Intangible Assets and Capital Budgeting

Companies make strategic investments in intangible assets such as brand names, customer bases, and the intellectual capital of employees. Top management can use a capital budgeting tool, such as NPV, to evaluate a company's intangible assets.

CONCEPTS IN ACTION

Capital Budgeting for Pollution Prevention

In response to concerns about the environment, the government has passed many laws to restrict companies' impacts on the environment. Many companies have viewed these laws as imposing costs on them, but attitudes are changing. Companies are increasingly shifting their focus away from pollution control (dealing with the control of environmentally harmful substances) to pollution prevention (minimizing the creation of pollution in the first place, through increased efficiency in the use of materials, energy, water, and other resources). Intelligent use of capital budgeting methods is a key part of this effort.

Suppose a company invests in new manufacturing equipment that allows it to use a less costly and nontoxic direct material. Annual cost savings directly associated with the use of the new equipment include savings in direct material costs and toxic waste disposal. If the capital budgeting analysis ended at this point, however, the investment might show a negative NPV, and the company would, on purely financial grounds, reject the project.

But companies such as DuPont consider other financial benefits. These benefits include cost savings in pollution control activities such as monitoring and testing, permit requirements, and legal compliance reporting. These costs are "hidden" in that they are included in general overhead accounts but typically not identified with specific manufacturing processes. There can also be "hidden" impacts on a company's revenues. For example, the periodic training of employees in pollution control activities adds to costs, and, when there is no idle time, results in lost revenues as a result of having to shut down the plant for a few hours each time a training session is conducted.

Another form of cost savings is the reduction or elimination of various fines or penalties that a company might experience because of noncompliance or accidents. Estimating these costs is more difficult and is generally based on statistical analysis of historical data for the particular company or industry, probability calculations, and professional judgment. Many companies believe an uncertain monetary estimate is probably better than ignoring the potential environmental liability altogether.

Finally, there are more-intangible financial benefits, such as higher revenues from being a more environmentally responsible company. Home Depot, the largest retailer of home improvement products in the United States, buys its lumber products only from a list of "preferred vendors" that it knows to conduct environmentally responsible practices.

Source: D. Jacque Grinnell and Herbert G. Hunt, "Capital Budgeting for Pollution Prevention," *Journal of Cost Management* (July/August 1999); Environmental Protection Agency, "Valuing Potential Environmental Liabilities for Managerial Decision Making" (December 1996); conversations with consulting firm SmithObrien and company managements.

Consider the customer base as an intangible asset. NPV analysis highlights the long-term value of customers. Potato Supreme produces potato products for sale to retail outlets. It is currently analyzing two of its customers, Shine Stores and Always Open. Potato Supreme predicts the following net cash inflows (in thousands) from each customer account for the next five years:

To remain viable, any company needs to keep profitable customers (and gain new ones).

	2003	2004	2005	2006	2007
Shine Stores	$1,450	$1,305	$1,175	$1,058	$ 950
Always Open	690	1,160	1,900	2,950	4,160

Which customer is more valuable to Potato Supreme? Looking at only the current period, 2003, Shine Stores provides more than 200% higher net cash inflows than Always Open ($1,450 versus $690). A different picture emerges when looking over the entire five-year horizon. Using Potato Supreme's 10% RRR, the NPV of the Always Open customer is $7,610, compared with $4,591 for Shine Stores (computations not shown). Note how NPV captures in its estimate of customer value, the future growth of Always Open. Managers can use this information when allocating resources, such as adding salespersons

These NPV amounts are calculated using the 10% present value discount factors in Table 2 of Appendix C. For example, year 1 has a present value of $1,318 ($1,450 × 0.909) for Shine Stores and $627 ($690 × 0.909) for Always Open.

to service individual customers. Potato Supreme can also use NPV calculations to examine the effects of alternative ways of increasing customer loyalty and retention, such as by introducing frequent-purchaser cards.

A comparison of year-to-year changes in customer NPV estimates highlights whether managers have been successful in maintaining long-run profitable relationships with their customers. Suppose the NPV of Potato Supreme's customer base declines 15% in one year. Management can then examine the reasons for the decline, such as aggressive price discounting by salespersons or aggressive pricing by competitors, and devise suitable strategies for the future.

Capital One, a financial services company, uses NPV to estimate the value of different credit-card customers. Cellular telephone companies such as Cellular One and Verizon attempt to sign up customers for multiple years of service. The objective is to prevent "customer churn," customers switching frequently from one company to another. The higher the probability of customer churn, the lower the NPV of the customer to the telecommunications company.

PROBLEM FOR SELF-STUDY

PART A

Returning to the Lifetime Care X-ray machine project, assume Lifetime is a nonprofit organization; the expected annual cash inflows from the operating cost savings are $130,000 in years 1 through 4 and $121,000 in year 5. All other facts are unchanged: a $379,100 net initial investment, a five-year useful life, a $0 terminal disposal value, and an 8% RRR. Year 5 cash inflows are $130,000, which includes $9,000 recovery of working capital.

Required

Compute the following:

1. Net present value
2. Internal rate of return
3. Payback period
4. Accrual accounting rate of return on net initial investment

SOLUTION

1. $NPV = (\$130{,}000 \times 3.993) - \$379{,}100$
   $= \$519{,}090 - \$379{,}100 = \$139{,}990$

2. There are several approaches to computing IRR. One is to use a calculator with an IRR function. This approach gives an IRR of 21.2%. Another approach is to use Table 4 in Appendix C at the end of the text:

$$\$379{,}100 = \$130{,}000F$$
$$F = \frac{\$379{,}100}{\$130{,}000} = 2.916$$

On the five-period line of Table 4, the column closest to 2.916 is 22%. To obtain a more accurate number, use straight-line interpolation:

	Present Value	Factors
20%	2.991	2.991
IRR	—	2.916
22%	2.864	—
Difference	0.127	0.075

$$IRR = 20\% + \frac{0.075}{0.127}(2\%) = 21.2\% \text{ per year}$$

3. $\text{Payback} = \dfrac{\text{Net initial investment}}{\text{Uniform increase in annual future cash flows}}$
   $= \$379{,}100 \div \$130{,}000 = 2.9 \text{ years}$

4.

$$AARR = \frac{\text{Increase in expected average annual operating income}}{\text{Net initial investment}}$$

$$\text{Increase in expected average annual cash operating savings} = [(\$130{,}000 \times 4) + \$121{,}000] \div 5 \text{ years}$$

$$= \$641{,}000 \div 5 = \$128{,}200$$

$$\text{Average annual depreciation} = \$390{,}000 \div 5 \text{ years} = \$78{,}000$$

$$\text{Increase in expected average annual operating income} = \$128{,}200 - \$78{,}000 = \$50{,}200$$

$$AARR = \frac{\$50{,}200}{\$379{,}100} = 13.2\% \text{ per year}$$

PART B

Assume that Lifetime Care is subject to income tax at a 40% rate. All other information from Part A is unchanged. Compute NPV of the new X-ray machine project.

SOLUTION

Exhibit 21-7 shows the computations using a format slightly different from the format used in this chapter. Item 2a. is where the new $130,000 cash flow assumption affects the NPV analysis

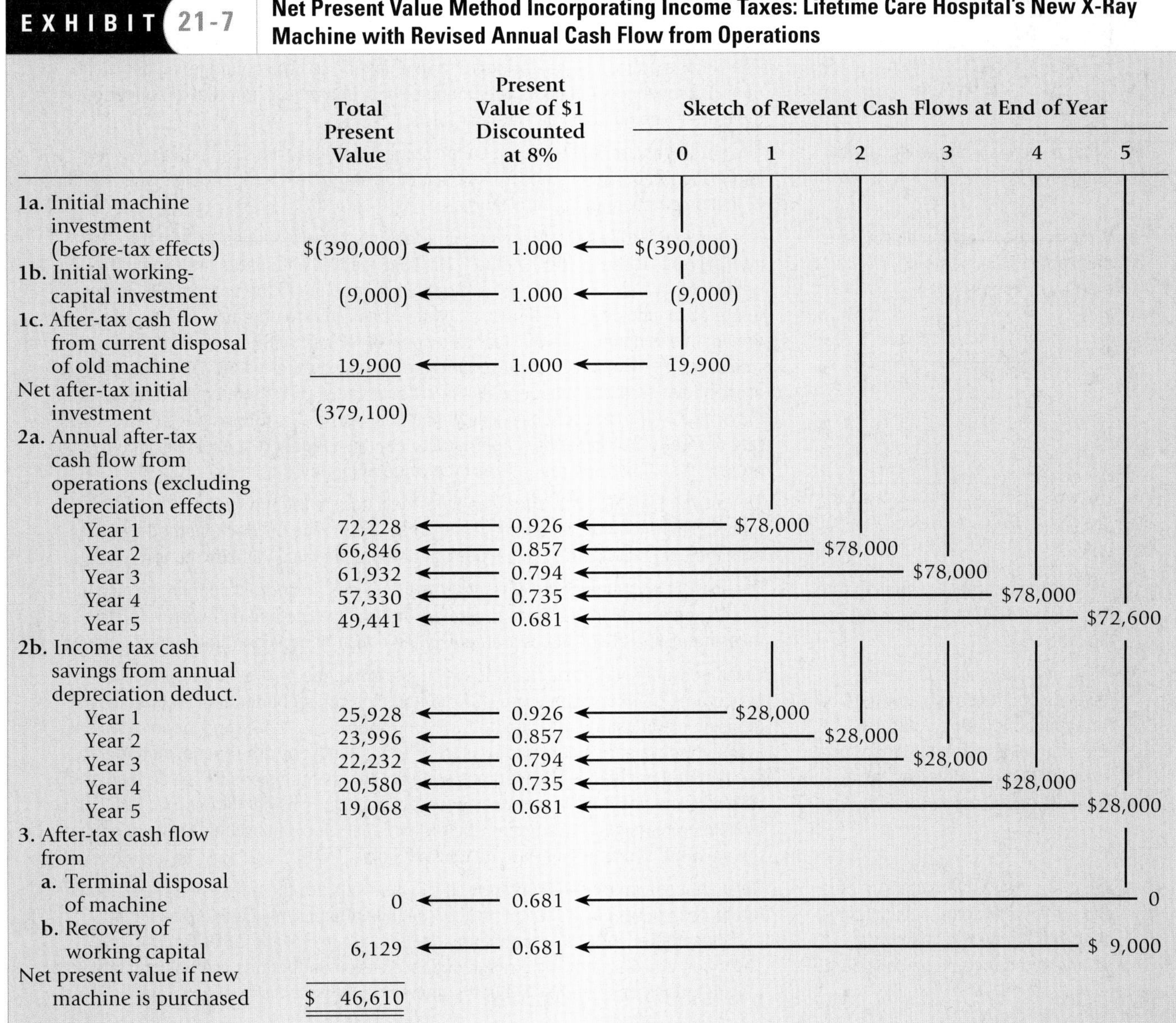

EXHIBIT 21-7 Net Present Value Method Incorporating Income Taxes: Lifetime Care Hospital's New X-Ray Machine with Revised Annual Cash Flow from Operations

	Total Present Value	Present Value of $1 Discounted at 8%	Sketch of Revelant Cash Flows at End of Year 0	1	2	3	4	5
1a. Initial machine investment (before-tax effects)	$(390,000)	1.000	$(390,000)					
1b. Initial working-capital investment	(9,000)	1.000	(9,000)					
1c. After-tax cash flow from current disposal of old machine	19,900	1.000	19,900					
Net after-tax initial investment	(379,100)							
2a. Annual after-tax cash flow from operations (excluding depreciation effects)								
Year 1	72,228	0.926		$78,000				
Year 2	66,846	0.857			$78,000			
Year 3	61,932	0.794				$78,000		
Year 4	57,330	0.735					$78,000	
Year 5	49,441	0.681						$72,600
2b. Income tax cash savings from annual depreciation deduct.								
Year 1	25,928	0.926		$28,000				
Year 2	23,996	0.857			$28,000			
Year 3	22,232	0.794				$28,000		
Year 4	20,580	0.735					$28,000	
Year 5	19,068	0.681						$28,000
3. After-tax cash flow from								
a. Terminal disposal of machine	0	0.681						0
b. Recovery of working capital	6,129	0.681						$ 9,000
Net present value if new machine is purchased	$ 46,610							

(compared to Exhibit 21-6). For years 1 through 4, the after-tax flow (excluding depreciation effects) is

Annual cash flow from operations with new machine	$130,000
Deduct income tax payments (0.40 × $130,000)	52,000
Annual after-tax cash flow from operations	$ 78,000

For year 5, the after-tax flow (excluding depreciation effects) is

Annual cash flow from operations with new machine	$121,000
Deduct income tax payments (0.40 × $121,000)	48,400
Annual after-tax cash flow from operations	$ 72,600

NPV in Exhibit 21-7 is $46,610. As computed in Part A, NPV when there are no income taxes is $139,990.

DECISION POINTS — SUMMARY

The following question-and-answer format summarizes the chapter's learning objectives. Each decision presents a key question related to a learning objective. The guidelines are the answer to that question.

Decision	Guidelines
1. Over what time horizon is capital budgeting done?	Capital budgeting is a long-term planning process for proposed capital projects. The life of a project is usually longer than one year, so capital budgeting decisions consider revenues and costs over long periods. In contrast, accrual accounting measures income on a year-by-year basis.
2. What are the six stages of capital budgeting?	The six stages are (a) the identification stage, (b) the search stage, (c) the information-acquisition stage, (d) the selection stage, (e) the financing stage, and the (f) implementation and control stage.
3. What are the two main discounted cash flow (DCF) methods? What are their advantages?	The two main DCF methods are the net present value (NPV) method and the internal rate-of-return (IRR) method. The NPV method calculates the expected net monetary gain or loss from a project by discounting to the present all expected future cash inflows and outflows, using the required rate of return. A project is acceptable in financial terms if it has a positive NPV. The IRR method computes the rate of return (also called the discount rate) at which the present value of expected cash inflows from a project equals the present value of expected cash outflows from the project. A project is acceptable in financial terms if its IRR exceeds the required rate of return. DCF is the best approach to capital budgeting. It explicitly includes all project cash flows and recognizes time value of money.
4. What is the payback method? What is its limitation?	The payback method measures the time it will take to recoup, in the form of cash inflows, the total cash amount invested in a project. The payback method neglects both the cash flows after the payback period and the time value of money.
5. What is the accrual accounting rate of return (AARR) method? What is its limitation?	The accrual accounting rate of return (AARR) divides an accrual accounting measure of average annual income of a project by an accrual accounting measure of its investment. AARR considers profitability but does not consider time value of money.
6. What conflicts can arise between using discounted cash flow methods for capital budgeting decisions and accrual accounting for performance evaluation? How can these conflicts be reduced?	Using accrual accounting to evaluate the performance of a manager or division may create conflicts with using DCF methods for capital budgeting. Frequently, the decision made using a DCF method will not report good "operating income" results in the project's early years under accrual accounting. For this reason, managers are tempted to not use DCF methods even though the decisions based on them would be the best for the company over the long run. This conflict can be reduced by evaluating managers on a project-by-project basis, looking at their ability to achieve the amounts and timing of forecasted cash flows.
7. What are the relevant cash inflows and outflows for capital budgeting decisions? How should accrual accounting concepts be considered?	Relevant cash inflows and outflows in DCF analysis are the differences in expected future cash flows as a result of making the investment. Only cash inflows and outflows matter; accrual accounting concepts are irrelevant for DCF methods. The income taxes saved as a result of depreciation deductions are relevant because they decrease cash outflows, but the depreciation itself is a noncash item.

APPENDIX: CAPITAL BUDGETING AND INFLATION

The Lifetime Care example (Exhibits 21-2 to 21-6) does not include adjustments for inflation in the relevant revenues and costs. **Inflation** is the decline in the general purchasing power of the monetary unit. An inflation rate of 10% per year means that what you could buy with $100 at the beginning of the year will cost you $110 at the end of the year.

Because of inflation, the cash inflows to be received in future periods will be measured in dollars that have less value than the dollars invested in the project in year 0. Failure to account for inflation will make the project appear more attractive than it really is.

Why is it important to account for inflation in capital budgeting? Because declines in the general purchasing power of the monetary unit, such as dollars, will inflate future cash flows above what they would have been in the absence of inflation. These inflated cash flows will cause the project to look better than it really is, unless the analyst recognizes that the inflated cash flows are measured in dollars that have less purchasing power than the dollars that were initially invested.

When analyzing inflation, distinguish real rate of return from nominal rate of return:

- **Real rate of return** is the rate of return demanded to cover investment risk if there were no inflation. The real rate is made up of two elements: (a) a risk-free element (that's the pure rate of return on risk-free long-term government bonds when there is no expected inflation) and (b) a business-risk element (that's the risk premium demanded for bearing risk).
- **Nominal rate of return** is the rate of return demanded to cover investment risk and the decline in general purchasing power of the monetary unit as a result of expected inflation. The nominal rate is made up of three elements: (a) a risk-free element when there is no expected inflation, (b) a business-risk element, and (c) an inflation element. Items (a) and (b) make up the real rate of return to cover investment risk. The inflation element is the premium above the real rate. The rates of return earned in the financial markets are nominal rates, because investors want to be compensated both for the investment risks they take and for the expected decline in the general purchasing power, as a result of inflation, of the money they get back.

Assume the real rate of return for investments in high-risk cellular data transmission equipment at Network Communications is 20% per year and that the expected inflation rate is 10% per year. Nominal rate of return is

$$\begin{aligned}\text{Nominal rate} &= (1 + \text{Real rate})(1 + \text{Inflation rate}) - 1\\ &= (1 + 0.20)(1 + 0.10) - 1\\ &= (1.20 \times 1.10) - 1 = 1.32 - 1 = 0.32, \text{ or } 32\%\end{aligned}$$

The nominal rate of return is related to the real rate of return and the inflation rate:

Real rate of return	0.20
Inflation rate	0.10
Combination (0.20 × 0.10)	0.02
Nominal rate of return	0.32

Note the nominal rate, 0.32, is slightly higher than 0.30, the real rate (0.20) plus the inflation rate (0.10). That's because the nominal rate recognizes that inflation of 10% also decreases the purchasing power of the real rate of return of 20% earned during the year. The combination component represents the additional compensation investors seek for the decrease in the purchasing power of the real return earned during the year because of inflation.[4]

Net Present Value Method and Inflation

When incorporating inflation into the NPV method, always keep in focus *internal consistency*. There are two internally consistent approaches:

- *Nominal approach*—predicts cash inflows and outflows in nominal monetary units *and* uses a nominal rate as the required rate of return.

[4]The real rate of return can be expressed in terms of the nominal rate of return as follows:

$$\text{Real rate} = \frac{1 + \text{Nominal rate}}{1 + \text{Inflation rate}} - 1 = \frac{1 + 0.32}{1 + 0.10} - 1 = 0.20, \text{ or } 20\%$$

- *Real approach*—predicts cash inflows and outflows in real monetary units *and* uses a real rate as the required rate of return.

We will limit our discussion to the simpler nominal approach. Consider an investment that is expected to generate sales of 100 units and a net cash inflow of $1,000 ($10 per unit) each year for two years *absent inflation*. If inflation of 10% is expected each year, net cash inflows from the sale of each unit would be $11 ($10 × 1.10) in year 1 and $12.10 ($11 × 1.10, or $10 × $(1.10)^2$) in year 2, resulting in net cash inflows of $1,100 in year 1 and $1,210 in year 2. The net cash inflows of $1,100 and $1,210 are nominal cash inflows because they include the effect of inflation. *Nominal cash flows are the cash flows that are recorded in the accounting system.* The cash inflows of $1,000 each year are real cash flows. The accounting system does not record these cash flows. The nominal approach is easier to understand and use because it uses nominal cash flows from accounting systems and nominal rates of return from financial markets.

Assume that Network Communications can purchase equipment to make and sell a cellular data transmission product at a net initial investment of $750,000. It is expected to have a four-year useful life with a $0 terminal disposal value. An annual inflation rate of 10% is expected over this four-year period. Network Communications requires an after-tax nominal rate of return of 32% (see p. 739).

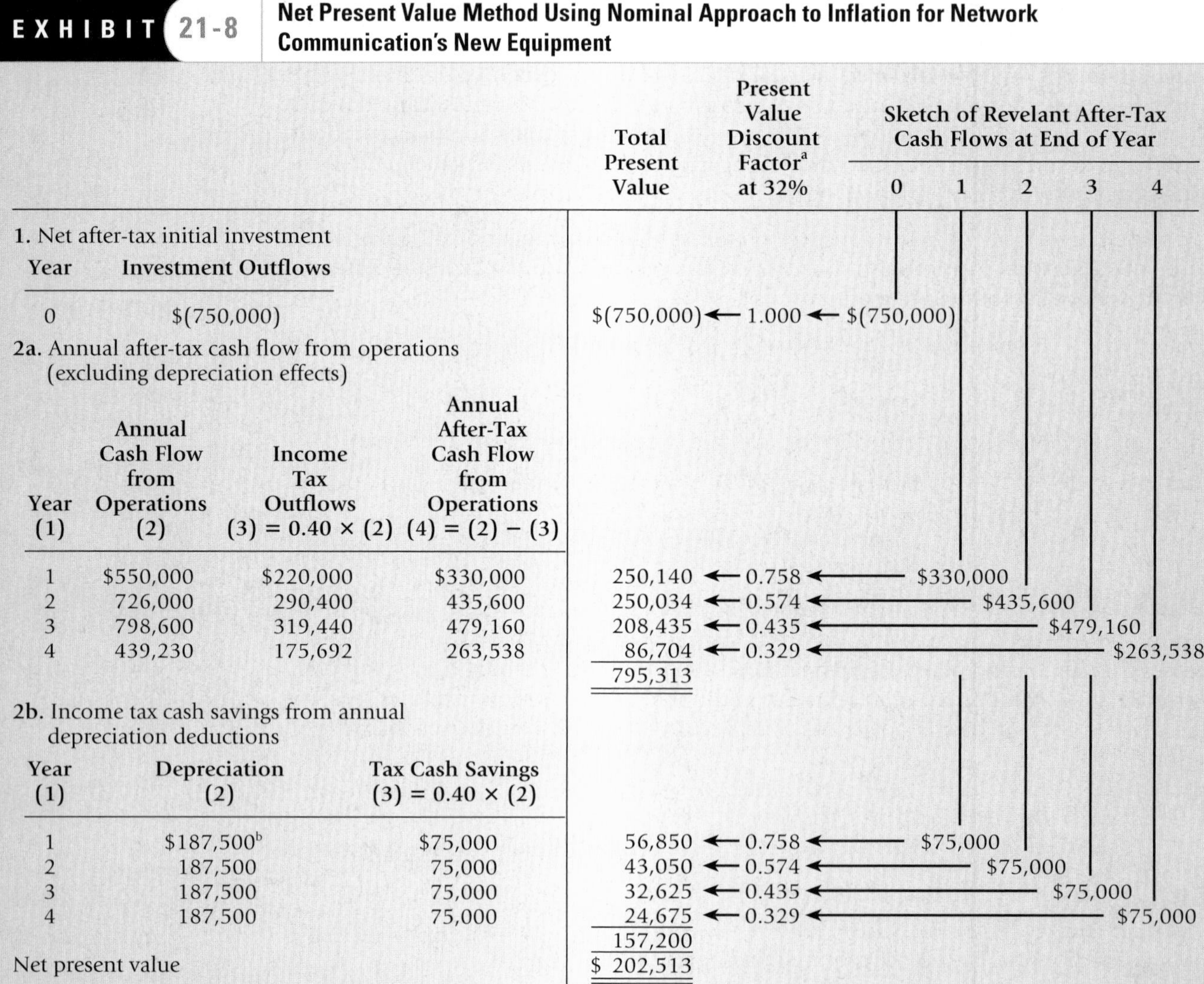

EXHIBIT 21-8 Net Present Value Method Using Nominal Approach to Inflation for Network Communication's New Equipment

	Total Present Value	Present Value Discount Factor[a] at 32%	Sketch of Revelant After-Tax Cash Flows at End of Year: 0	1	2	3	4
1. Net after-tax initial investment							
Year 0 — Investment Outflows $(750,000)	$(750,000)	1.000	$(750,000)				

2a. Annual after-tax cash flow from operations (excluding depreciation effects)

Year (1)	Annual Cash Flow from Operations (2)	Income Tax Outflows (3) = 0.40 × (2)	Annual After-Tax Cash Flow from Operations (4) = (2) − (3)	Total Present Value	Present Value Discount Factor at 32%	0	1	2	3	4
1	$550,000	$220,000	$330,000	250,140	0.758		$330,000			
2	726,000	290,400	435,600	250,034	0.574			$435,600		
3	798,600	319,440	479,160	208,435	0.435				$479,160	
4	439,230	175,692	263,538	86,704	0.329					$263,538
				795,313						

2b. Income tax cash savings from annual depreciation deductions

Year (1)	Depreciation (2)	Tax Cash Savings (3) = 0.40 × (2)	Total Present Value	Present Value Discount Factor at 32%	0	1	2	3	4
1	$187,500[b]	$75,000	56,850	0.758		$75,000			
2	187,500	75,000	43,050	0.574			$75,000		
3	187,500	75,000	32,625	0.435				$75,000	
4	187,500	75,000	24,675	0.329					$75,000
			157,200						
Net present value			$ 202,513						

[a]The nominal discount rate of 32% is made up of the real rate of return of 20% and the inflation rate of 10% [(1 + 0.20) (1 + 0.10)] − 1 = 0.32.
[b]$750,000 ÷ 4 = $187,500

The following table presents the predicted amounts of real (that's assuming no inflation) and nominal (that's after considering cumulative inflation) net cash inflows from the equipment over the next four years (excluding the $750,000 investment in the equipment and before any income tax payments):

Year (1)	Before-Tax Cash Inflows in Real Dollars (2)	Cumulative Inflation Rate Factor[a] (3)	Before-Tax Cash Inflows in Nominal Dollars (4) = (2) × (3)
1	$500,000	$(1.10)^1 = 1.1000$	$550,000
2	600,000	$(1.10)^2 = 1.2100$	726,000
3	600,000	$(1.10)^3 = 1.3310$	798,600
4	300,000	$(1.10)^4 = 1.4641$	439,230

[a]1.10 = 1.00 + 0.10 inflation rate.

We continue to make the simplifying assumption that cash flows occur at the end of each year. The income tax rate is 40%. For tax purposes, the cost of the equipment will be depreciated using the straight-line method.

Exhibit 21-8 shows the calculation of NPV with cash flows in nominal dollars and using a nominal discount rate. The calculations in Exhibit 21-8 include the net initial machine investment, annual after-tax cash flows from operations (excluding depreciation effects), and income tax cash savings from annual depreciation deductions. The project has a net present value of $202,513 and should be accepted.

Under the nominal approach, first express all amounts in terms of *future-year dollars* (using the cumulative inflation rate factors), and then discount the resulting amounts to their present value using the *nominal discount rate factors.*

TERMS TO LEARN

This chapter and the Glossary at the end of the book contain definitions of:

accounting rate of return (p. 726)
accrual accounting rate of return (AARR) (726)
capital budgeting (719)
cost of capital (720)
discounted cash flow (DCF) method (720)
discount rate (720)
hurdle rate (720)
inflation (739)
internal rate-of-return (IRR) method (722)
net present value (NPV) method (720)
nominal rate of return (739)
opportunity cost of capital (720)
payback (724)
real rate of return (739)
required rate of return (RRR) (720)
time value of money (720)

ASSIGNMENT MATERIAL

Questions

21-1 "Capital budgeting has the same focus as accrual accounting." Do you agree? Explain.

21-2 List and briefly describe each of the six stages in capital budgeting.

21-3 What is the essence of the discounted cash flow method?

21-4 "Only quantitative outcomes are relevant in capital budgeting analyses." Do you agree? Explain.

21-5 How can sensitivity analysis be incorporated in DCF analysis?

21-6 What is the payback method? What are its main strengths and weaknesses?

21-7 Describe the accrual accounting rate-of-return method. What are its main strengths and weaknesses?

21-8 "The trouble with discounted cash flow techniques is that they ignore depreciation costs." Do you agree? Explain.

21-9 "Let's be more practical. DCF is not the gospel. Managers should not become so enchanted with DCF that strategic considerations are overlooked." Do you agree? Explain.

21-10 "All overhead costs are relevant in NPV analysis." Do you agree? Explain.

21-11 Bill Watts, president of Western Publications, accepts a capital budgeting project advocated by Division X. This is the division in which the president spent his first 10 years with the company. On the same day, the president rejects a capital budgeting project proposal from Division Y. The manager of Division Y is incensed. She believes that the Division Y project has an internal rate of return at least 10 percentage points above the Division X project. She comments, "What is the point of all our detailed DCF analysis? If Watts is panting over a project, he can arrange to have the proponents of that project massage the numbers so that it looks like a winner." What advice would you give the manager of Division Y?

21-12 Distinguish different categories of cash flows that an equipment replacement decision by a tax-paying company should consider.

21-13 Describe three ways income taxes can affect the cash inflows or outflows in a motor vehicle replacement decision by a taxpaying company.

21-14 How can capital budgeting tools assist in evaluating a manager who is responsible for retaining customers of a cellular telephone company?

21-15 Distinguish the nominal rate of return from the real rate of return.

Exercises

21-16 Exercises in compound interest, no income taxes. To be sure that you understand how to use the tables in Appendix C at the end of this book, solve the following exercises. Ignore income tax considerations. The correct answers, rounded to the nearest dollar, appear on pages 749–750.

Required

1. You have just won $5,000. How much money will you have at the end of 10 years if you invest it at 6% compounded annually? At 14% ?
2. Ten years from now, the unpaid principal of the mortgage on your house will be $89,550. How much do you have to invest today at 6% interest compounded annually to accumulate the $89,550 in 10 years?
3. If the unpaid mortgage on your house in 10 years will be $89,550, how much money do you have to invest annually at 6% to have exactly this amount on hand at the end of the tenth year?
4. You plan to save $5,000 of your earnings at the end of each year for the next 10 years. How much money will you have at the end of the tenth year if you invest your savings compounded at 12% per year?
5. You have just turned 65 and an endowment insurance policy has paid you a lump sum of $200,000. If you invest the sum at 6%, how much money can you withdraw from your account in equal amounts each year so that at the end of 10 years (age 75) there will be nothing left?
6. You have estimated that for the first 10 years after you retire you will need an annual cash inflow of $50,000. How much money must you invest at 6% at your retirement age to obtain this annual cash inflow? At 20%?
7. The following table shows two schedules of prospective operating cash inflows, each of which requires the same net initial investment of $10,000 now:

	Annual Cash Inflows	
Year	**Plan A**	**Plan B**
1	$ 1,000	$ 5,000
2	2,000	4,000
3	3,000	3,000
4	4,000	2,000
5	5,000	1,000
Total	$15,000	$15,000

The required rate of return is 6% compounded annually. All cash inflows occur at the end of each year. In terms of net present value, which plan is more desirable? Show your computations.

21-17 Comparison of approaches to capital budgeting, no income taxes. The Building Distributors Group is thinking of buying, at a cost of $220,000, some new packaging equipment that is expected to save $50,000 in cash-operating costs per year. Its estimated useful life is 10 years, and it will have $0 terminal disposal value. The required rate of return is 16%. Ignore income tax issues in your answers.

Required Compute the following:

1. Net present value
2. Payback period
3. Internal rate of return
4. Accrual accounting rate of return based on net initial investment (Assume straight-line depreciation.)

21-18 Capital budgeting methods, no income taxes. City Hospital, a not-for-profit organization, estimates that it can save $28,000 a year in cash operating costs for the next 10 years if it buys a special-purpose eye-testing machine at a cost of $110,000. A $0 terminal disposal value is expected. City Hospital's required rate of return is 14%.

Required

1. Compute the following:
   a. Net present value
   b. Payback period
   c. Internal rate of return
   d. Accrual accounting rate of return based on net initial investment (Assume straight-line depreciation.)
2. What factors should City Hospital consider in deciding whether to purchase the special-purpose eye-testing machine?

21-19 Capital budgeting, income taxes. Assume the same facts as in Exercise 21-18 except that City Hospital is now a taxpaying entity. The income tax rate is 30% for all transactions that affect income taxes.

Required

1. Redo your computations in requirement 1 of Exercise 21-18.
2. How would your computations in requirement 1 be affected if the special-purpose machine has a $10,000 terminal disposal value at the end of 10 years? Assume depreciation deductions are based on the $110,000 purchase cost using a straight-line method. Answer briefly in words without new computations.

21-20 Capital budgeting with uneven cash flows, no income taxes. Southern Cola is considering the purchase of a special-purpose bottling machine for $23,000. It is expected to have a useful life of four years with a $0 terminal disposal value. The plant manager estimates the following savings in cash operating costs:

Year	Amount
1	$10,000
2	8,000
3	6,000
4	5,000
Total	$29,000

Southern Cola uses a required rate of return of 16% in its capital budgeting decisions. Ignore income taxes in your analysis.

Required

Compute the following:

1. Net present value
2. Payback period
3. Internal rate of return
4. Accrual accounting rate of return based on net initial investment (Assume straight-line depreciation. Use the average annual savings in cash operating costs when computing the numerator of the accrual accounting rate of return.)

21-21 Comparison of projects, no income taxes. (CMA, adapted) Fox Valley Healthcare, Inc., is a nonprofit organization. Jim Ruffalo, president of Fox Valley, has developed a plan to add a new building. He has selected a building contractor, Vukacek Construction Co. Vukacek is ready to start as soon as the contract is signed and will complete the work in two years.

The building contractor has offered Fox Valley a choice of three payment plans, as follows:

- *Plan I* Payment of $200,000 on the signing of the contract and $3,000,000 at the time of completion. The end of the second year is the completion date.
- *Plan II* Payment of $1,000,000 on the signing of the contract and $1,000,000 at the end of each of the two succeeding years.
- *Plan III* Payment of $100,000 on the signing of the contract and $1,000,000 at the end of each of the three succeeding years.

Ruffalo has asked the treasurer, Lisa Monroe, for her assessment of the three payment plans. Fox Valley has a required rate of return of 12%.

Required

1. Using the net present value method, calculate the comparative cost of each of the three payment plans being considered by Fox Valley Healthcare.
2. Which payment plan should the treasurer recommend? Explain.
3. Discuss the financial factors, other than the cost of the plan, and the nonfinancial factors that should be considered in selecting an appropriate payment plan.

21-22 Payback and NPV methods, no income taxes. (CMA, adapted) Cording Manufacturing is a small company currently analyzing capital expenditure proposals for the purchase of equipment. The capital budget is limited to $500,000, which Cording believes is the maximum capital it can raise.

Richard King, an outside financial adviser, is preparing an analysis of four projects that Walter Minden, Cording's president, is considering. King has projected the future cash flows for each potential purchase. The information concerning the four projects is as follows:

	Project A	Project B	Project C	Project D
Projected cash outflow				
Net initial investment	$200,000	$190,000	$250,000	$210,000
Projected cash inflows				
Year 1	$50,000	$40,000	$75,000	$75,000
Year 2	50,000	50,000	75,000	75,000
Year 3	50,000	70,000	60,000	60,000
Year 4	50,000	75,000	80,000	40,000
Year 5	50,000	75,000	100,000	20,000

Required

1. Because Cording Manufacturing's cash is limited, Walter Minden thinks the payback method for calculating investments would be the best method for choosing capital budgeting projects.
   a. Explain what the payback method measures and how it is used. Include in your explanation several benefits and limitations of the method.
   b. Calculate the payback period for each of the four projects. Ignore income tax considerations.
2. King would like to compare the projects using the net present value method. The required rate of return for Cording is 12%. All cash flows occur at the end of the year. Calculate the net present value for each project. Ignore income tax considerations.
3. Which projects, if any, would you recommend funding? Briefly state your reasons.

21-23 **DCF, accrual accounting rate of return, working capital, evaluation of performance, no income taxes.** Hammerlink Company has been offered a special-purpose metal-cutting machine for $110,000. The machine is expected to have a useful life of eight years, with a terminal disposal value of $30,000. Savings in cash operating costs are expected to be $25,000 per year. However, additional working capital is needed to keep the machine running efficiently and without stoppages. Working capital includes such items as filters, lubricants, bearings, abrasives, flexible exhaust pipes, and belts. These items must continually be replaced, so an investment of $8,000 must be maintained in them at all times, but this investment is fully recoverable (will be "cashed in") at the end of the useful life. Hammerlink's required rate of return is 14%. Ignore income taxes in your analysis.

Required

1. Compute net present value.
2. Compute internal rate of return.
3. Compute accrual accounting rate of return based on net initial investment. Assume straight-line depreciation.
4. You have the authority to make the purchase decision. Why might you be reluctant to base your decision on the DCF methods?

21-24 **New equipment purchase, income taxes.** National College Publishing, Inc., publishes accounting and finance textbooks. The company estimates it can save $100,000 in cash operating costs each year for the next four years if it buys PR2020, a modern printing machine, at a cost of $230,000. The printing machine will have a $30,000 terminal disposal value at the end of year 4. No change in working capital will be required. National has a 12% after-tax required rate of return. Its income tax rate is 40%.

Required

1. Assume that National uses straight-line depreciation on its tax return. Compute (a) net present value, (b) payback period, and (c) internal rate of return.
2. Compare the capital budgeting methods in requirement 1.

21-25 **New equipment purchase, income taxes.** Presentation Graphics prepares slides and other aids for individuals making presentations. It estimates it can save $35,000 a year in cash operating costs for the next five years if it buys a special-purpose color-slide workstation at a cost of $75,000. The workstation will have a $0 terminal disposal value at the end of year 5. No change in working capital will be required. Presentation Graphics has a 12% after-tax required rate of return. Its income tax rate is 40%.

Required

1. Assume that Presentation Graphics uses straight-line depreciation on its tax return. Compute (a) net present value, (b) payback period, and (c) internal rate of return.
2. Compare and contrast the capital budgeting methods in requirement 1.

Excel Application For students who wish to practice their spreadsheet skills, the following is a step-by-step approach to creating an Excel spreadsheet to work this problem.

Step-by-step:

1. Open a new spreadsheet. At top, create an "Original Data" section for the data provided by Presentation Graphics, with rows for "After-Tax Required Rate of Return, Income Tax Rate, Recurring Savings in Cash-Operating Costs," and "Initial Workstation Investment."

(Program your spreadsheet to perform all necessary calculations. Do not "hard-code" any amounts, such as the payback period, requiring addition, subtraction, multiplication, or division operations.)

2. Skip two rows, create a "1a. Net Present Value" section similar to Exhibit 21-7. Create one row for "Initial Workstation Investment." Next, under each of the following items, create five rows for year 1 through year 5: Annual After-Tax Cash Flow from Operations (Excluding Depreciation Effects) and "Income Tax Cash Savings from Annual Depreciation Deductions". Create columns labeled "Relevant After-Tax Cash Flows," "Present Value Discount Factors at 12%," and "Total Present Value."
3. Use your Original Data section to fill in the "Relevant Cash Flows" column. Next, enter calculations for the present value discount factors and total present value of these cash flows in the next two columns. Include a calculation for the "Net Present Value of the Workstation Investment" on a separate row in this section.
4. Skip two rows, create a "1b. Payback Period" section. Enter a calculation for the payback period in this section.
5. To calculate internal rate of return, go to the tools menu, select "Solver." Set the target cell equal to the cell where you calculated net present value of the workstation investment in step 3. Tell Solver to set this target cell to a value of zero. Under "By changing cells," choose the cell in your Original Data section that contains the After-Tax Required Rate of Return. Click "Solve." A new window will open. Under "Reports," choose "Answer," click on "Restore original values," and click "OK." You will now have a new worksheet titled "Answer Report I" that contains Solver's calculation of the internal rate of return.
6. *Check the validity of your spreadsheet:* Go to your Original Data section and change the after-tax required rate of return from 12% to 15%. If you programmed your spreadsheet correctly, net present value of the workstation investment should *decrease* to $15,508.

21-26 **Selling a plant, income taxes.** (CMA, adapted) Waterford Corporation, a clothing manufacturer, has a plant that will become idle on December 31, 2002. John Landry, corporate controller, has been asked to look at three options regarding the plant.

- *Option 1:* The plant, which has been fully depreciated for tax purposes, can be sold immediately for $9,000,000.
- *Option 2:* The plant can be leased to Auburn Mills, one of Waterford's suppliers, for four years. Under the lease terms, Auburn would pay Waterford $2,400,000 rent per year (payable at year-end) and would grant Waterford a $474,000 annual discount off the normal price of fabric purchased by Waterford (assume discount received at year-end for each of the four years). Auburn would bear all of the plant's ownership costs. Waterford expects to sell this plant for $2,000,000 at the end of the four-year lease.
- *Option 3:* The plant could be used for four years to make souvenir jackets for the Olympics. Fixed overhead costs (a cash outflow) before any equipment upgrades are estimated to be $200,000 annually for the four-year period. The jackets are expected to sell for $42 each. Variable costs per unit are expected to be $33. The following production and sales of jackets are expected: 2003, 200,000 units; 2004, 300,000 units; 2005, 400,000 units; 2006, 100,000 units. In order to manufacture the jackets, some of the plant equipment would need to be upgraded at an immediate cost of $1,500,000, which would be depreciated using straight-line depreciation over the four years it would be in use. Because of the equipment upgrades, Waterford could sell the plant for $3,000,000 at the end of four years. No change in working capital would be required.

Waterford treats all cash flows as if they occur at the end of the year, and it uses an after-tax required rate of return of 12%. Waterford is subject to a 40% income tax rate.

Required

1. Calculate net present value of each of the options and determine which option Waterford should select using the NPV criterion.
2. What nonfinancial factors should Waterford consider before making its choice?

Problems

21-27 **Equipment replacement, no income taxes.** Superfast Chips manufactures and delivers prototype chips to customers within 24 hours. The current production facility was set up when the company began operations in Dublin, Ireland, in 1997. It is outdated and constrains future growth. Next year, in 2004, Superfast expects to deliver 460 prototype chips at an average price of $80,000 per prototype. Superfast's marketing vice president forecasts growth of 50 prototype chips per year through 2010. That is, demand is 460 in 2004, 510 in 2005, 560 in 2006, and so on.

The current facility cannot produce more than 450 prototypes annually. To meet future demand, Superfast must either modernize the current facility or replace it. The old equipment is fully depreciated and can be sold for $3,000,000. If the current facilities are modernized, such costs are to be capitalized and depreciated over the useful life of the updated facility. The old equipment is retained as part of the modernize alternative. Following is some data on the two options available to Superfast:

	Modernize	Replace
Initial investment in 2004	$28,000,000	$49,000,000
Terminal disposal price in 2010	$5,000,000	$12,000,000
Useful life	7 years	7 years
Total annual cash operating costs per prototype	$62,000	$56,000

Superfast uses straight-line depreciation for income reporting, assuming zero terminal disposal value. For simplicity, we assume no change in prices or costs in future years. The investment will be made at the beginning of 2004, and all transactions thereafter occur on the last day of the year. Superfast's required rate of return is 12%.

There is no difference between the modernize and replace alternatives in terms of required working capital. Superfast Chips has a special waiver on income taxes until 2010.

Required

1. Sketch the cash inflows and outflows of the modernize and replace alternatives over the 2004 to 2010 period.
2. Compute payback period for the modernize and replace alternatives.
3. Compute net present value of the modernize and replace alternatives.
4. What factors should Superfast Chips consider in choosing between the alternatives?

21-28 **Equipment replacement, income taxes (continuation of 21-27).** Assume the same facts as in Problem 21-27, except that the plant is located in Austin, Texas. Superfast has no special waiver on income taxes. It pays a 30% tax rate on all income. Proceeds from sale of equipment above book value are taxed at the same 30% rate.

Required

1. Sketch the after-tax cash inflows and outflows of the modernize and replace alternatives over the 2004 to 2010 period.
2. Compute net present value of the modernize and replace alternatives.
3. Suppose Superfast is planning to build several more plants. It wants to have the most advantageous tax position possible. It has been approached by Spain, Malaysia, and Australia to construct a plant in their country. Use the data in Problem 21-27 and this problem to briefly describe income tax features that would be attractive and advantageous to Superfast. You should discuss the magnitude and timing of cost deductions in your description.

21-29 **DCF, sensitivity analysis, no income taxes.** (CMA, adapted) Bristol Engineering, Inc., manufactures electronic components. The company has developed a device that management believes could be modified and marketed as an electronic game.

The following information for the new product was developed from the best estimates of the marketing and production managers:

Annual sales volume	1,000,000 units
Selling price	$10 per unit
Cash variable costs	$4 per unit
Cash fixed costs	$2,000,000 per year
Investment required	$12,000,000
Project life	5 years

At the end of the five-year useful life, there will be a $0 terminal disposal value. Bristol Engineering's required rate of return on this project is 14%.

The electronic game industry is a new market for Bristol, and management is concerned about the reliability of the estimates. The controller has proposed applying sensitivity analysis to selected factors. Ignore income taxes in your computations.

Required

1. What is the net present value of this investment proposal?
2. What is the effect on the net present value of the following two changes in assumptions? (Treat each item independently of the other.)
   a. 10% reduction in the selling price
   b. 10% increase in the variable cost per unit
3. Discuss how management would use the data developed in requirements 1 and 2 in its consideration of the proposed capital investment.

21-30 **NPV and customer profitability, no income taxes.** Christen Granite sells granite countertops to the construction industry. Christen Granite has three customers: Homebuilders, Kitchen Constructors, and Subdivision Erectors. Following are Christen Granite's revenue and cost data by customer for the year ended December 31, 2003:

	Homebuilders	Kitchen Constructors	Subdivision Erectors
Revenues	$45,000	$325,000	$860,000
Cost of goods sold	22,000	180,000	550,000
Operating costs	10,000	75,000	235,000

Jay Christen, the owner, estimates that revenue and costs will increase as follows on an annual basis:

	Homebuilders	Kitchen Constructors	Subdivision Erectors
Revenues	5%	6%	8%
Cost of goods sold	4%	4%	4%
Operating costs	4%	4%	4%

Christen Granite's required rate of return is 10%. Assume that (a) all transactions occur at year-end, (b) all revenues are cash inflows, and (c) all costs are cash outflows. Ignore income tax considerations.

Required

1. Calculate operating income per customer for 2003 and for each year of the 2004 to 2008 period.
2. Christen estimates the value of each customer by calculating the customer's projected net present value over the next five years (2004 to 2008). Use the operating incomes calculated in requirement 1 to compute the value of each of its three customers.
3. Recently, Kitchen Constructors (KC) has been threatening to switch suppliers. KC demands a 20% price discount on the revenues for 2004 to 2008 that were estimated for KC in requirement 1 above, if it is to continue using Christen as a supplier. What is the five-year NPV of KC after incorporating the 20% discount? What other factors should Christen consider before making its final decision?

21-31 NPV of JIT, income taxes. (CMA, adapted) Rosen Manufacturing Corporation produces office furniture and sells it wholesale to furniture distributors. Rosen's management is reviewing a proposal to purchase a just-in-time inventory (JIT) system to better serve its customers. The JIT system will include a computer system and materials-handling equipment. The decision will be based on whether the new JIT system is cost effective to the organization for the next five years.

The computer system, including hardware and software, will initially cost $1,250,000. Materials-handling equipment will cost $450,000. Both groups of equipment will have a five-year useful life for tax reporting of depreciation (straight-line) calculated assuming a $0 terminal disposal value. At the end of the five years, the newly acquired materials-handling equipment is expected to be sold for $150,000. The computer system will have a $0 terminal disposal value at the end of five years.

Other factors to be considered over the next five years for this proposal include the following:

- Due to the service improvement resulting from this new JIT system, Rosen will realize a $800,000 increase in revenues during the first year. Rosen expects this initial $800,000 revenue increase to continue to grow by 10% per year thereafter.
- The contribution margin is 60% .
- Annual material-ordering costs will increase $50,000 due to a greater level of purchase orders.
- There will be a one-time decrease in working-capital investment of $150,000 at the end of the first year.
- There will be a 20% savings in warehouse rent due to less space being needed. The current annual rent is $300,000.

Rosen uses an after-tax required rate of return of 10% and is subject to an income tax rate of 40%. Assume that all cash flows occur at year-end for tax purposes except for any initial purchase amounts.

Required

1. Prepare an analysis of the after-tax effects for the purchase of the JIT system at Rosen using the net present value method for evaluating capital expenditures. Be sure to show all of your computations.
2. Determine whether Rosen should purchase the JIT system. Explain your answer.

21-32 Replacement of a machine, income taxes, sensitivity. (CMA, adapted) WRL Company operates a snack-food center at the Hartsfield Airport. On January 1, 2000, WRL purchased a special cookie-cutting machine, which has been used for three years. WRL is considering purchasing a newer, more-efficient machine. If purchased, the new machine would be acquired today, January 1, 2003. WRL expects to sell 300,000 cookies in each of the next four years. The selling price of each cookie is expected to average $0.50.

WRL has two options: (1) continue to operate the old machine or (2) sell the old machine and purchase the new machine. The seller of the new machine offered no trade-in. The following information has been assembled to help management decide which option is more desirable:

	Old Machine	New Machine
Initial purchase costs of machine	$80,000	$120,000
Terminal disposal value at the end of useful life assumed for depreciation purposes	$10,000	$20,000
Useful life from date of acquisition	7 years	4 years
Expected annual cash operating costs:		
Variable cost per cookie	$0.20	$0.14
Total fixed costs	$15,000	$14,000
Depreciation method used for tax purposes	Straight-line	Straight-line
Estimated disposal prices of machines:		
January 1, 2003	$40,000	$120,000
December 31, 2006	$7,000	$20,000

WRL is subject to a 40% income tax rate. Assume that any gain or loss on the sale of machines is treated as an ordinary tax item and will affect the taxes paid by WRL in the year in which it occurs. WRL has an after-tax required rate of return of 16%.

Required

1. Use the net present value method to determine whether WRL should retain the old machine or acquire the new machine.
2. How much more or less would the recurring after-tax cash operating savings have to be for WRL to exactly earn the 16% after-tax required rate of return? Assume all other data about the investment do not change.
3. Assume that the financial differences between the net present values of the two options are so slight that WRL is indifferent between the two proposals. Identify and discuss the nonfinancial and qualitative factors that WRL should consider.

21-33 **Capital budgeting, inflation, income taxes, appendix.** (J. Fellingham, adapted) Abbie Young is manager of the customer-service division of an electrical appliance store. Abbie is considering buying a repair machine that costs $10,000 on December 31, 2003. The machine will last five years. Abbie estimates that the incremental pretax cash savings from using the machine will be $3,000 annually. The $3,000 is measured at current prices and will be received at the end of each year. For tax purposes, she will depreciate the machine using the straight-line method, assuming $0 terminal disposal value. Abbie requires a 10% after-tax real rate of return (that is, the rate of return is 10% when all cash flows are denominated in December 31, 2003, dollars).

Required Treat each of the following cases independently.

1. There are no income taxes, but the annual inflation rate is 20%. What is the net present value of the machine? The cash savings each year will be increased by a factor equal to the cumulative inflation rate. Use the nominal discount rate in your computations.
2. The annual inflation rate is 20%, and the income tax rate is 40%. What is the net present value of the machine? Use the same nominal discount rate as in requirement 1 in your computations.

21-34 **Ethics, capital budgeting.** (CMA, adapted) Evans Company must expand its manufacturing capabilities to meet the growing demand for its products. The first alternative is to expand its current manufacturing facility, which is located next to a vacant lot in the heart of the city. The second alternative is to convert a warehouse, already owned by Evans, that is located 20 miles outside the city. Evans's controller, George Watson, directs Helen Dodge, assistant controller, to use net present value computations to evaluate both proposals. On completing her analysis, Dodge reports to Watson that the proposal to expand the current manufacturing facility has a slightly positive net present value. The proposal to convert the warehouse has a large negative net present value.

Watson is upset over Dodge's conclusions. He returns the proposal to her with the comment, "You must have made an error. The warehouse proposal should look better and have a positive net present value. Work on the projections and estimates."

Dodge suspects that Watson is anxious to have the warehouse proposal selected because this location would eliminate his long commute into the city. Feeling some pressure, she checks her calculations but finds no errors. Dodge reviews her projections and estimates. These, too, are quite reasonable. Even so, she replaces some of her original estimates with new estimates that are more favorable to the warehouse proposal, although these new estimates are less likely to occur. The revised proposal still has a negative net present value. Dodge is confused about what she should do.

Required

1. Referring to the "Standards of Ethical Conduct for Management Accountants" described in Chapter 1 (p. 18), explain:
   a. whether George Watson's conduct was unethical when he gave Helen Dodge specific instructions on reviewing the proposal.
   b. whether Helen Dodge's revised proposal for the warehouse conversion is unethical.
2. Identify the steps that Helen Dodge should take in attempting to resolve this situation.

Collaborative Learning Problem

21-35 **Relevant costs, outsourcing, capital budgeting, income taxes.** The Strubel Company currently makes as many units of Part No. 789 as it needs. David Lin, general manager of the Strubel Company, has received a bid from the Gabriella Company for supplying Part No. 789. Current plans call for Gabriella to supply 1,000 units of Part No. 789 per year at $50 a unit. Gabriella can begin supplying on January 1, 2004, and continue for five years, after which time Strubel will not need the part. Gabriella can accommodate any change in Strubel's demand for the part and will supply it for $50 a unit, regardless of quantity.

Jack Tyson, controller of the Strubel Company, reports the following costs for manufacturing 1,000 units of Part No. 789:

Direct materials	$22,000
Direct manufacturing labor	11,000
Variable manufacturing overhead	7,000
Depreciation on machine	10,000
Product and process engineering	4,000
Rent	2,000
Allocation of general plant overhead costs	5,000
Total costs	$61,000

The following additional information is available:

a. Part No. 789 is made on a machine used exclusively for the manufacture of Part No. 789. The machine was acquired on January 1, 2003, at a cost of $60,000. The machine has a useful life of six years and $0 terminal disposal value. Depreciation is calculated on the straight-line method.

b. The machine could be sold today for $15,000.

c. Product and process engineering costs are incurred to ensure that the manufacturing process for Part No. 789 works smoothly. Although these costs are fixed in the short run with respect to units of Part No. 789 produced, they can be saved in the long run if this part is no longer produced. If Part No. 789 is outsourced, product and process engineering costs of $4,000 will be incurred for 2004 but not thereafter.

d. Rent costs of $2,000 are allocated to products on the basis of the floor space used for manufacturing the product. If Part No. 789 is discontinued, the space currently used to manufacture it would become available. The company could then use the space for storage and save $1,000 currently paid for outside storage.

e. General plant overhead costs are allocated to each department on the basis of direct manufacturing labor dollars. These costs will not change in total, but no general plant overhead will be allocated to Part No. 789 if the part is outsourced.

Assume that Strubel requires a 12% required rate of return for this project.

Required

1. Should David Lin outsource Part No. 789? Prepare a quantitative analysis using the net present value method. Assume all cash flows other than disposal of machine occur at the end of each year.
2. Describe any sensitivity analysis that seems advisable, but you need not perform any sensitivity calculations.
3. What other factors should Lin consider in making a decision?
4. Lin is particularly concerned about his bonus for 2004. The bonus is based on Strubel's accounting income. What decision will Lin make if he wants to maximize his bonus in 2004?

Answers to Exercises in Compound Interest (Exercise 21-16)

The general approach to these exercises centers on a key question: Which of the four basic tables in Appendix C should be used? No computations should be made until this basic question has been answered with confidence.

1. *From Table 1.* The $5,000 is the present value P of your winnings. Their future value S in 10 years will be

$$S = P(1 + r)^n$$

The conversion factor, $(1 + r)^n$, is on line 10 of Table 1.

$$\text{Substituting at 6\%: } S = 5{,}000(1.791) = \$8{,}955$$
$$\text{Substituting at 14\%: } S = 5{,}000(3.707) = \$18{,}535$$

2. *From Table 2.* The $89,550 is an *amount of future worth.* You want the present value of that amount. $P = S \div (1 + r)^n$, The conversion factor, $1 \div (1 + r)^n$, is on line 10 of Table 2. Substituting,

$$P = \$89{,}550(0.558) = \$49{,}969$$

3. *From Table 3.* The $89,550 is *future worth.* You are seeking the uniform amount (annuity) to set aside annually. Note that $1 invested each year for 10 years at 6% has a future worth of $13.181 after 10 years, from line 10 of Table 3.

$$S_n = \text{Annual deposit (F)}$$
$$\$89{,}550 = \text{Annual deposit (13.181)}$$
$$\text{Annual deposit} = \frac{\$89{,}550}{13.181} = \$6{,}794$$

4. *From Table 3.* You are seeking the *amount of future worth* of an annuity of $5,000 per year. Note that $1 invested each year for 10 years at 12% has a future worth of $17.549 after 10 years.

$$S_n = \$5{,}000F, \text{ where } F \text{ is the conversion factor}$$
$$S_n = \$5{,}000(17.549) = \$87{,}745$$

5. *From Table 4.* When you reach age 65, you will get $200,000, a present value at that time. You must find the annuity that will exactly exhaust the invested principal in 10 years. To pay yourself $1 each year for 10 years when the interest rate is 6% requires you to have $7.360 today, from line 10 of Table 4.

$$P_n = \text{Annual withdrawal } (F)$$
$$\$200{,}000 = \text{Annual withdrawal } (7.360)$$
$$\text{Annual withdrawal} = \frac{\$200{,}000}{7.360} = \$27{,}174$$

6. *From Table 4.* You need to find the present value of an annuity for 10 years.

At 6%:

$$P_n = \text{Annual withdrawal (F)}$$
$$P_n = \$50{,}000\ (7.360)$$
$$P_n = \$368{,}000$$

At 20%:

$$P_n = \$50{,}000\ (4.192)$$
$$P_n = \$209{,}600, \text{ a much lower figure}$$

7. Plan B is preferable. The net present value of plan B exceeds that of plan A by $980 ($3,126 – $2,146):

		Plan A		**Plan B**	
Year	**PV Factor at 6%**	**Cash Inflows**	**PV of Cash Inflows**	**Cash Inflows**	**PV of Cash Inflows**
0	1.000	$(10,000)	$(10,000)	$(10,000)	$(10,000)
1	0.943	1,000	943	5,000	4,715
2	0.890	2,000	1,780	4,000	3,560
3	0.840	3,000	2,520	3,000	2,520
4	0.792	4,000	3,168	2,000	1,584
5	0.747	5,000	3,735	1,000	747
			$ 2,146		$ 3,126

Even though plans B and A have the same total cash inflows over the five years, plan B is preferred to plan A because it has greater cash inflows occurring earlier.

CHAPTER 21 INTERNET EXERCISE

Capital budgeting refers to the process of evaluating long-term investment projects. Its focus is on the present value of cash flows rather than traditional accrual-based accounting measures. CCH offers an excellent on-line tool kit to assist small business owners in making capital budgeting decisions. To learn more, go to www.prenhall.com/horngren, click on *Cost Accounting,* 11th ed., and access the Internet exercise for Chapter 21.

DEER VALLEY RESORT: Capital Budgeting

Nestled deep in the Wasatch Mountains near Park City, Utah, Deer Valley Ski Resort strives for excellence everywhere possible. Each winter since its opening in 1980, a growing number of skiers have chosen to experience the "Deer Valley Difference"—meticulously groomed slopes, friendly staff, and gourmet cuisine. With owners and managers eager to pamper skiers beyond expectations, a $13 million renovation of the base lodge and facilities was approved for 1995.

The project began in April 1995 and added nearly 50,000 square feet of guest service space. The number of ticket windows doubled to 16, child-care space was expanded, and lockers and basket-check service were added. The lodge's retail and ski rental spaces were remodeled and expanded, and new retail and ski rental spaces were built. The project was completed in December 1995, just in time for the opening of the 1995–1996 ski season.

How did the renovation project come into existence? Deer Valley management follows a structured approach to capital budgeting and planning. First, management maintains a rolling 10-year capital plan, which contains a master list of all projects planned for funding in the next decade. It is updated each spring, reflecting how well the resort performed during the preceding winter season.

In the identification stage, ideas for capital projects come from each major operating department: ski school, food and beverage, mountain operations, accounting, and more. Each idea submitted must come with a description of the project, its anticipated benefits, and detailed cost estimates, including bids. During the search stage, proposed ideas are reviewed by the ski area's "Futures Committee," which is composed of senior management and area owners. Proposals are ranked and prioritized for funding. The final decision on how much to spend and which projects to pursue each year rests with the ski resort's general manager and owners.

The base lodge renovation was assigned a high priority in 1995 because the owners saw the immediate benefit to enhancing Deer Valley's image and reputation through expanded restaurant and ski-lift services, as well as through reduced bottlenecks in guest services areas, such as ticket sales and rentals.

For the information-acquisition stage in the capital budgeting process, managers considered which areas to renovate and where to add square footage to the lodge. Although preliminary plans and drawings were used to review the project for funding, management worked with architects to finalize the plans. Quantitative measures, such as return on skier days (increased demand), speed of lift-ticket and ski-school sales, increased child-care revenues, and greater food and beverage sales, were determined. Net present value and payback periods comprised part of the analysis. Qualitative measures, such as increased customer satisfaction and enhanced resort image, were considered as well. Deer Valley regularly ranks at or near the top of ski magazines' consumer surveys in these areas. Because the base lodge is such an integral part of each guest's overall impression of their ski experience, the qualitative measures carried significant weight in the final decision to fund the project, which was made in the selection stage of the capital budgeting process.

The financing stage came next. Deer Valley routinely starts and completes its capital projects between April and December of each year, so standing lines of credit at local banks were used for funding. Resort owners expected to pay off the balance owed on the project in two years, based on increases in lift-tickets and restaurant revenues from additional skier days. With the renovation complete, a postinvestment audit as part of the implementation and control stage was performed to evaluate the project's contribution to the resort's profitability and image.

QUESTIONS:

1. What other types of capital budgeting projects would you expect Deer Valley to have in its rolling 10-year plan? If you were making the decision to allocate funds for projects, what factors would you consider in your analysis?
2. What influence might competition and events such as the 2002 Winter Olympics—held in Park City—have on Deer Valley's capital budgeting and planning?
3. What risks do you expect Deer Valley faced with the base lodge renovation project?
4. Based on the facts, What is your overall impression of the decision to pursue this project? Explain.

CHAPTER

22

Management Control Systems, Transfer Pricing, and Multinational Considerations

LEARNING OBJECTIVES

1. Describe a management control system and its three key properties
2. Describe the benefits and costs of decentralization
3. Explain transfer prices and four criteria used to evaluate them
4. Calculate transfer prices using three methods
5. Illustrate how market-based transfer prices promote goal congruence in perfectly competitive markets
6. Avoid making suboptimal decisions when transfer prices are based on full cost plus a markup
7. Understand the range over which two divisions negotiate the transfer price when there is unused capacity
8. Construct a general guideline for determining a minimum transfer price
9. Incorporate income tax considerations in multinational transfer pricing

www.prenhall.com/horngren

Why buy the components that go into the electronic products your company produces when your company can make those components at less cost? Making the components internally would achieve significant cost savings. Sounds like the thing to do, right? Maybe not always. Sometimes the transfer price—the price one division of a company charges for the product it supplies to another division—makes it difficult for managers to purchase parts from divisions inside the company. They then buy the components from outside suppliers, resulting in idle capacity in the division that manufactures these components. Many companies, such as Information Systems Corporation, regularly struggle with this issue, with varying degrees of success.

Which company has the better management control system: Ford or Toyota? Michelin or Pirelli? The answer lies in how well each control system achieves its stated goal of guiding and improving decisions for the benefit of the company as a whole in a cost-effective way, and how the system influences the behavior of the people who use it. This chapter develops the links between strategy, organization structure, management control systems, and accounting information. We'll examine the benefits and costs of centralized and decentralized organization structures, and we'll look at the pricing of products or services transferred between subunits of the same company. We emphasize how accounting information such as costs, budgets, and prices help in planning and coordinating actions of subunits. Some of the material in the chapter is "softer" than material in other chapters, that is, it presents relatively few numbers. Nevertheless, the concepts are relevant for a management accountant to understand.

1 Describe a management control system

...gathering information for planning and control decisions

and its three key properties

...align with strategy, fit with structure, and motivate employees

MANAGEMENT CONTROL SYSTEMS

A **management control system** is a means of gathering and using information to aid and coordinate the planning and control decisions throughout an organization and to guide the behavior of its managers and employees. General Electric's management control system gathers and reports information for management control at various levels:

1. *Total-organization level*—for example, stock price, net income, return on investment, cash flow from operations, total employment, pollution control, and contributions to the community.
2. *Customer/market level*—for example, customer satisfaction, time taken to respond to customer requests for products, and cost of competitors' products.
3. *Individual-facility level*—for example, material costs, labor costs, absenteeism rates, and accidents in various divisions or business functions (such as R&D, production, and distribution).
4. *Individual-activity level*—for example, time taken and costs incurred for receiving, storing, assembling, and dispatching goods in a warehouse; scrap rates, defects, and units reworked on a manufacturing line; number of sales transactions and revenue per salesperson; and number of shipments per employee at distribution centers.

As these examples indicate, management control systems collect both financial information (for example, net income, material costs, and storage costs) and nonfinancial information (for example, time taken to respond to customer requests, absenteeism rates, and accidents). Some of the information is obtained from within the company, such as net income and number of shipments per employee. Other information is obtained from outside the company, such as stock price and costs of competitors' products. Some companies present financial and nonfinancial information in a single report called the *balanced scorecard* (see Chapter 13 for details).

The four levels in General Electric's management control system indicate the different kinds of information needed by managers performing different tasks. For example, stock price information is needed by upper management at the total-company level to evaluate how much shareholder value the company has created. Stock price is less important for line managers managing individual activities in a warehouse, where the information they need is time taken for receiving and storing inventory and materials.

Management control systems refer to formal and informal control systems. The formal management control system of a company includes those explicit rules, procedures, performance measures, and incentive plans that guide the behavior of its managers and employees. The formal control system itself consists of several systems. The management accounting system is a formal accounting system that provides information regarding costs, revenues, and income. Other formal control systems are human resources systems that provide information on recruiting, training, absenteeism, and accidents, and quality systems that provide information on scrap, defects, rework, and late deliveries to customers.

The informal management control system includes such aspects as shared values, loyalties, and mutual commitments among members of the company, company culture, and the unwritten norms about acceptable behavior for managers and employees. Examples of company slogans that reinforce values and loyalties are "At Ford, Quality Is Job 1," and "At Home Depot, Low Prices Are Just the Beginning."

EVALUATING MANAGEMENT CONTROL SYSTEMS

To be effective, management control systems should be closely aligned to the company's strategies and goals. Examples of strategies are developing innovative products to increase market share in key product areas, or maximizing short-run income by reducing costs and forgoing risky long-run investments in R&D. Suppose management decides, wisely or unwisely, to maximize short-run income. The management control system must then reinforce this goal. The control system should provide managers with information—such as contribution margins on individual products—that will help them make short-run decisions. The control system should also tie managers' rewards to short-run income.

Management control systems should be designed to fit the company's structure and the decision-making responsibility of individual managers. Consider the R&D manager at GlaxoSmithKline, a pharmaceutical company. The management control system for this manager should focus on the R&D activities required for different drug projects, the number of scientists needed, the scheduled dates for completing different projects, and the preparation of reports comparing actual and budgeted performance.

Accountants must have the interpersonal and analytical skills necessary to evaluate and implement accounting systems, as well as the ability to interpret outputs of these systems. The behavioral issues in this chapter and throughout this book are very important to accountants' careers.

Now consider a product-line manager responsible for the manufacture, sale, and distribution of ketchup at Heinz, a food products company. The company's management control system should provide this manager with information about customer satisfaction, market share, manufacturing costs and product-line profitability—information that helps the manager plan and control the operations better. The manager of the Heinz ketchup product line requires very different information than the information required by the R&D manager at GlaxoSmithKline. But, in both cases, the information provided is designed to aid the manager's decision making.

Effective management control systems should also motivate managers and employees. **Motivation** is the desire to attain a selected goal (the goal-congruence aspect) combined with the resulting pursuit of that goal (the effort aspect).

McDonald's uses QSCV (quality, service, cleanliness, and value) as shared objectives. Top management designs the performance-evaluation system based on these objectives.

Goal congruence exists when individuals and groups work toward achieving the organization's goals—that is, managers working in their own best interest take actions that align with the overall goals of top management. We discussed goal-congruence issues in earlier chapters. For example, in capital budgeting, making decisions based on discounting long-run cash flows at the required rate of return best achieves company goals. But if the management control system evaluates managers on the basis of short-run accrual accounting income, managers will be tempted to make decisions to maximize accrual accounting income, which may not be in the long-run best interest of the organization as a whole.

Effort is exertion toward achieving a goal. Effort goes beyond physical exertion, such as a worker producing at a faster rate, to include both physical and mental actions.

Management control systems motivate managers and employees to exert effort through a variety of rewards tied to the achievement of those goals. These rewards can be monetary (such as cash, shares of company stock, use of a company car, or membership in a club) or nonmonetary (such as power or pride in working for a successful company).

2 Describe the benefits of decentralization

...responsiveness to customers, faster decision making, management development

and the costs of decentralization

...loss of control, duplication of activities

ORGANIZATION STRUCTURE AND DECENTRALIZATION

Management control systems must fit an organization's structure. An organization whose structure is decentralized has additional issues to consider for its management control system to be effective.

Decentralization is the freedom for managers at lower levels of the organization to make decisions. **Autonomy** refers to the degree of freedom to make decisions. The greater the freedom, the greater the autonomy. As we discuss the issues of decentralization and autonomy, we use *subunit* to refer to any part of an organization. A subunit may be a large division, such as the Chevrolet Division of General Motors, or a small group, such as a two-person advertising department of a local clothing chain. Decentralization empowers managers and employees of subunits to take decisive actions.

Total decentralization means minimum constraints and maximum freedom for managers at the lowest levels of an organization to make decisions. Total centralization means maximum constraints and minimum freedom for managers at the lowest levels of an organization to make decisions. Companies' structures fall somewhere in between these two extremes because there are both benefits and costs of decentralization.

Benefits of Decentralization

How much decentralization is optimal? Managers try to choose the degree of decentralization that maximizes benefits over costs. From a practical standpoint, top management can seldom quantify either the benefits or the costs of decentralization. Still, the cost-benefit approach helps them focus on the issues.

Supporters of decentralizing decision making and granting responsibilities to managers of subunits advocate the following benefits:

1. *Creates greater responsiveness to local needs.* Good decisions cannot be made without good information. Compared with top managers, subunit managers are better informed about their customers, competitors, suppliers, and employees, as well as about local factors, such as ways to decrease costs and improve quality, that affect performance. Eastman Kodak reports that two advantages of decentralization are an "increase in the company's knowledge of the marketplace and improved service to customers."
2. *Leads to gains from faster decision making.* Decentralization speeds decision making, creating a competitive advantage over centralized organizations. Centralization slows decision making as responsibility for decisions creeps upward through layer after layer of management. Interlake, a manufacturer of materials-handling equipment, cites the benefit of decentralization: "We have distributed decision-making powers more broadly to the cutting edge of product and market opportunity." Interlake's materials-handling equipment must often be customized to fit individual customers' needs. Delegating decision making to the salesforce allows Interlake to respond faster to changing customer requirements.
3. *Increases motivation of subunit managers.* Subunit managers are more motivated when they can exercise initiative. Johnson & Johnson, a highly decentralized company, maintains "Decentralization = Creativity = Productivity."
4. *Assists management development and learning.* Giving managers more responsibility helps develop an experienced pool of management talent to fill higher-level management positions. The company also learns which people are not management material. According to Tektronix, an electronics instruments company: "Decentralized units provide a training ground for general managers, and a visible field of combat where product champions may fight for their ideas."
5. *Sharpens the focus of subunit managers.* In a decentralized setting, the manager of a small subunit has a concentrated focus. A small subunit is more flexible and nimble than a larger subunit and can adapt quickly to changing market opportunities. Also, top management, relieved of the burden of day-to-day operating decisions, can spend more time and effort on strategic planning for the entire organization.

Costs of Decentralization

Advocates of more-centralized decision making point out the following costs of decentralizing decision making:

1. *Leads to* ***suboptimal decision making*** *(also called* ***incongruent*** *or* ***dysfunctional decision making****), which arises when a decision's benefit to one subunit is more than offset by the costs or loss of benefits to the organization as a whole.* This cost arises because top management has given up control over decision making.

Suboptimal decision making may occur when (1) there is a lack of harmony or congruence among the overall company goals, the subunit goals, and the individual goals of decision makers, or (2) there is no guidance to subunit managers concerning the effects of their decisions on other parts of the company. Suboptimal decision making is most likely to occur when the subunits in the company are highly interdependent, such as when the end product of one subunit is used or sold by another subunit. For example, a manufacturing manager evaluated on the basis of manufacturing costs may be unresponsive to requests from marketing to schedule a rush order for a customer if altering production schedules will increase manufacturing costs. From the company's viewpoint, however, supplying the product to the customer may be preferred both because the customer is willing to pay a premium price and because the company expects the customer to place many orders in the future.

2. *Focuses the manager's attention on the subunit rather than the company as a whole.* Individual subunit managers may regard themselves as competing with managers of other subunits in the same company as if they were external rivals. Consequently, managers may be unwilling to share information or to assist when another subunit faces an emergency. Also, subunit managers may use information they have about local conditions to further their own self-interest rather than the company's goals. For example, they may ask for more resources than they need from the company to reduce the effort they need to exert.

3. *Increases the costs of gathering information.* Managers may spend too much time obtaining information about different subunits of the company to coordinate their actions.

4. *Results in duplication of activities.* Several individual subunits of the company may undertake the same activity separately. For example, there may be a duplication of staff functions (accounting, human resources, and legal) if a company is highly decentralized. Centralizing these functions helps to consolidate, streamline, and use less resources for these activities.

Comparison of Benefits and Costs

To choose an organization structure that will implement a company's strategy, top managers must compare the benefits and costs of decentralization, often on a function-by-function basis. For example, the controller's function may be highly decentralized for many problem-solving and attention-directing purposes (such as preparing operating budgets and performance reports) but highly centralized for other purposes (such as processing accounts receivables and developing income tax strategies). Decentralizing budgeting and reporting enables the marketing manager of a subunit, for example, to tailor the report to specific information that the manager needs to make better decisions and increase income. Centralizing income tax strategies allows the organization to trade off income in a subunit with losses in other subunits to evaluate the impact on the organization as a whole.

Surveys of U.S. and European companies report that the decisions made most frequently at the decentralized level and least frequently at the corporate level are related to sources of supplies, product mix, and product advertising. In these areas, subunit managers must make faster decisions based on local information. Decisions related to the type and source of long-term financing are made least frequently at the decentralized level and most frequently at the corporate level. In these cases, corporate managers have better information about financing terms in different markets and can obtain the best rates. The benefits of decentralization are generally greater when companies face uncertainties in their environments, require detailed local knowledge for performing various jobs, and have few interdependencies among divisions.

Decentralization in Multinational Companies

Multinational companies—companies that operate in multiple countries—are often decentralized because centralized control of a company with subunits around the world is often physically and practically impossible. Also, language, customs, cultures, business practices, rules, laws, and regulations vary significantly across countries. Decentralization enables managers in different countries to make decisions that exploit their knowledge of local business and political conditions and to deal with uncertainties in their individual environments. Philips, a global electronics company headquartered in the Netherlands, delegates marketing and pricing decisions for its television business in the Indian and Singaporean markets to the managers in those countries. Multinational corporations often rotate managers between foreign locations and corporate headquarters. Job rotation combined with decentralization helps develop managers' abilities to operate in the global environment.

Of course, there are drawbacks to decentralizing multinational companies. One of the most important is the lack of control. Barings PLC, a British investment banking firm, went bankrupt and had to be sold when one of its traders in Singapore caused the firm to lose more than £1 billion on unauthorized trades that were not detected until after the trades were made. Similarly, a trader at Sumitomo Corporation racked up $2.6 billion in copper-trading losses because poor controls failed to detect the magnitude of the trader's activities. Multinational corporations that implement decentralized decision making usually also design their management control systems to measure and monitor division performance. Information and communications technology facilitates the flow of information for reporting and control.

Choices About Responsibility Centers

To measure the performance of subunits in centralized or decentralized companies, the management control system uses one or a mix of the four types of responsibility centers presented in Chapter 6:

- *Cost center*—the manager is accountable for costs only.
- *Revenue center*—the manager is accountable for revenues only.
- *Profit center*—the manager is accountable for revenues and costs.
- *Investment center*—the manager is accountable for investments, revenues, and costs.

Centralization or decentralization is not mentioned in the descriptions of these centers because each type of responsibility center can be found in either centralized or decentralized companies.

A common misconception is that *profit center*—and, in some cases, *investment center*—is a synonym for a decentralized subunit and *cost center* is a synonym for a centralized subunit. *Profit centers can be coupled with a highly centralized organization, and cost centers can be coupled with a highly decentralized organization.* For example, managers in a division organized as a profit center may have little freedom in making decisions. They may need to obtain approval from corporate headquarters for every expenditure over, say, $10,000 and may be forced to do what the central staff wants. In another company, divisions may be organized as cost centers, but their managers may have great latitude on capital expenditures and on where to purchase materials and services. In short, the labels "profit center" and "cost center" are independent of the degree of centralization or decentralization in a company.

TRANSFER PRICING

3 Explain transfer prices ...price one subunit charges another for product **and four criteria used to evaluate them** ...goal congruence, management effort, subunit performance evaluation, and subunit autonomy

In decentralized organizations, much of the decision-making power resides in its individual subunits. In these cases, the management control system often uses *transfer prices* to coordinate the actions of the subunits and to evaluate their performance.

A **transfer price** is the price one subunit (department or division) charges for a product or service supplied to another subunit of the same organization. If, for example, a car manufacturer has a separate division that manufactures engines, the transfer price is the price the engine division charges when it transfers engines to the car assembly division. The transfer price creates revenues for the selling subunit (the engine division in our example) and purchase costs for the buying subunit (the assembly division in our example), affecting each subunit's operating income. These operating incomes can be used to evaluate subunit performance and to motivate their managers. The product or service transferred between subunits of an organization is called an **intermediate product**. This product may either be further worked on by the receiving subunit or, if transferred from production to marketing, sold to an external customer.

In one sense, transfer pricing is a curious phenomenon. Activities within an organization are clearly nonmarket in nature; products and services are not bought and sold as they are in open-market transactions. Yet, establishing prices for transfers among subunits of a company has a distinctly market flavor. The rationale for transfer prices is that subunit managers (such as the manager of the engine division), when making decisions, need only focus on how their decisions will affect their subunit's performance without evaluating their impact on companywide performance. In this sense, transfer prices ease the subunit managers' information-processing and decision-making tasks. In a well-designed transfer-pricing system, optimizing subunit performance (the performance of the engine division) leads to optimizing the performance of the company as a whole.

To help organize transfer-pricing concepts, top management must address two questions. One is a policy question: Should divisions be permitted to source externally when the same goods are available internally? The other is an operational question: At what price will the transfer be made? To answer this question involves deciding (1) which transfer-pricing method will be used (market, cost, or negotiated) and (2) how disputes are to be resolved (negotiations, arbitration, or top management directives).

As in all management control systems, transfer prices should help achieve a company's strategies and goals and fit its organization structure. In particular, they should promote *goal congruence* and a sustained high level of *management effort*. Subunits selling a product or service should be motivated to hold down their costs; subunits buying the product or service should be motivated to acquire and use inputs efficiently. The transfer price should also help top management evaluate the performance of individual subunits and their managers. If top management favors a high degree of decentralization, transfer prices should also promote a high degree of subunit autonomy in decision making. That is, a subunit manager seeking to maximize the operating income of his or her subunit should have the freedom to transact with other subunits of the company (on the basis of transfer prices) or to transact with outside parties.

Transfer-Pricing Methods

4 Calculate transfer prices using three methods

...market-based, cost-based, negotiated

There are three methods for determining transfer prices:

1. *Market-based transfer prices.* Top management may choose to use the price of a similar product or service publicly listed in, say, a trade association Web site. Also, top management may select, for the internal price, the external price that a subunit charges to outside customers.

2. *Cost-based transfer prices.* Top management may choose a transfer price based on the costs of producing the product in question. Examples include variable production costs, variable and fixed production costs, and full costs of the product. Full costs of the product include all production costs plus costs from the other business functions (R&D, design, marketing, distribution, and customer service). The costs used in cost-based transfer prices can be actual costs or budgeted costs. Sometimes, the cost-based transfer price includes a markup or profit margin that represents a return on subunit investment.

3. *Negotiated transfer prices.* In some cases, the subunits of a company are free to negotiate the transfer price between themselves and then to decide whether to buy and sell internally or deal with outside parties. Subunits may use information about costs and market prices in these negotiations, but there is no requirement that the chosen transfer price bear any specific relationship to either cost or market-price data. Negotiated transfer prices are often employed when market prices are volatile and change occurs constantly. The negotiated transfer price is the outcome of a bargaining process between the selling and buying subunits.

To see how each of the three transfer-pricing methods works, and to see the differences among them, we examine transfer pricing at Horizon Petroleum Inc. against the four criteria: goal congruence, management effort, subunit performance evaluation, and subunit autonomy (if desired).

AN ILLUSTRATION OF TRANSFER PRICING

Horizon Petroleum has two divisions. Each operates as a profit center. The Transportation Division purchases crude oil in Matamoros, Mexico. It also operates a pipeline that transports crude oil from Matamoros to Houston, Texas. The Refining Division manages a refinery at Houston that processes crude oil into gasoline. Let's assume gasoline is the only salable product the refinery makes and that it takes two barrels of crude oil to yield one barrel of gasoline.

Variable costs in each division are variable with respect to a single cost driver in each division: barrels of crude oil transported by the Transportation Division, and barrels of gasoline produced by the Refining Division. The fixed costs per unit are based on the budgeted annual output of crude oil to be transported and the budgeted annual output of gasoline to be produced. Horizon Petroleum reports all costs and revenues of its non-U.S. operations in U.S. dollars using the prevailing exchange rate.

- The Transportation Division has obtained the rights to certain oil fields in the Matamoros area. It has a long-term contract to purchase crude oil produced from these fields at $12 per barrel. The division transports the oil to Houston and then "sells" it to the Refining Division. The pipeline from Matamoros to Houston has the capacity to carry 40,000 barrels of crude oil per day.
- The Refining Division has been operating at capacity (30,000 barrels of crude oil a day), using oil supplied by Horizon's Transportation Division (an average of 10,000 barrels per day) and oil bought from other producers and delivered to the Houston Refinery (an average of 20,000 barrels per day at $21 per barrel).
- The Refining Division sells the gasoline it produces at $58 per barrel.

Exhibit 22-1 summarizes Horizon Petroleum's variable and fixed costs per barrel of crude oil in the Transportation Division and variable and fixed costs per barrel of gasoline in the Refining Division, the external market prices of buying crude oil, and the external market prices of selling gasoline. What's missing in the exhibit is the actual transfer price from the Transportation Division to the Refining Division. This transfer price will vary depending on the transfer-pricing method used. Transfer prices from the Transportation Division to the Refining Division under each of the three methods are

- Method A: Market-based transfer price of $21 per barrel of crude oil based on the competitive market price in Houston.
- Method B: Cost-based transfer prices at, say, 110% of full costs, when full costs are the costs of the crude oil purchased plus the Transportation Division's own variable and fixed costs: $1.10 \times (\$12 + \$1 + \$3) = \$17.60$.
- Method C: Negotiated transfer price of $19.25 per barrel of crude oil, which is between the market-based and cost-based transfer prices.

Exhibit 22-2 presents division operating incomes per 100 barrels of crude oil purchased under each transfer-pricing method. Transfer prices create income for the selling division and corresponding costs for the buying division that cancel out when division results are consolidated. The exhibit assumes all three transfer-pricing methods yield transfer prices that are in a range that does not cause division managers to change the business relationships shown in Exhibit 22-1. That is, Horizon Petroleum's total operating income from purchasing, transporting, and refining the 100 barrels of crude oil and selling the 50 barrels of gasoline is the same, $600—*equal to* revenues of $2,900 minus costs of crude oil purchases of $1,200, *minus* transportation costs of $400, and *minus* refining costs of $700—*regardless of the internal transfer prices used.* Note further that in all

EXHIBIT 22-1

Operating Data for Horizon Petroleum

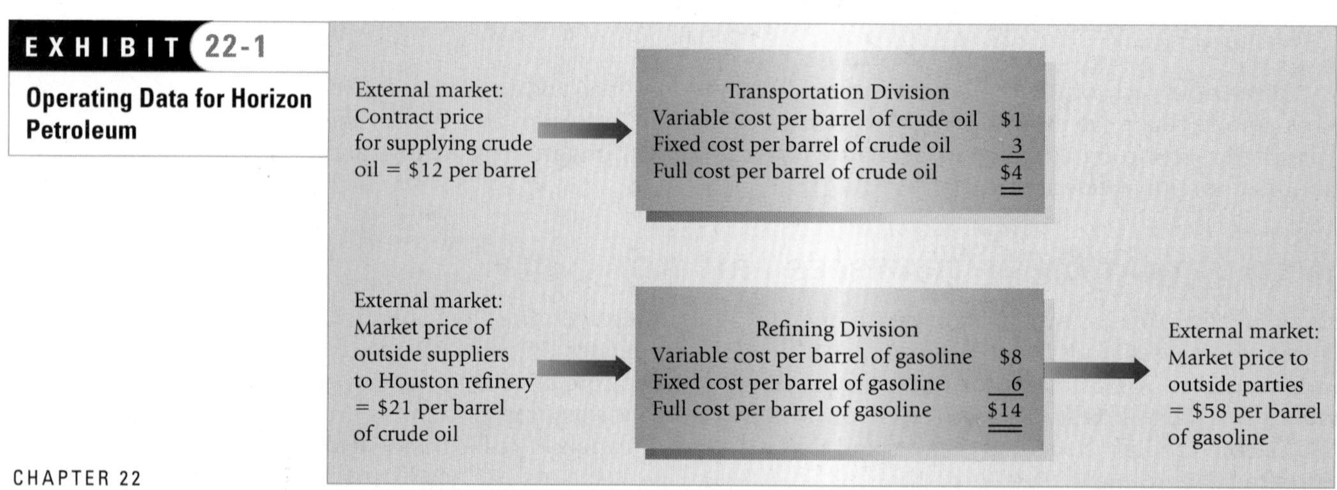

EXHIBIT 22-2 **Division Operating Income of Horizon Petroleum for 100 Barrels of Crude Oil Under Alternative Transfer-Pricing Methods**

	Method A: Internal Transfers at Market Prices	Method B: Internal Transfers at 110% of Full Costs	Method C: Internal Transfers at Negotiated Prices
Transportation Division			
Revenues, \$21, \$17.60, \$19.25 × 100 barrels of crude oil	\$2,100	\$1,760	\$1,925
Deduct:			
Crude oil purchase costs, \$12 × 100	1,200	1,200	1,200
Division variable costs, \$1 × 100 barrels of crude oil	100	100	100
Division fixed costs, \$3 × 100 barrels of crude oil	300	300	300
Division operating income	\$ 500	\$ 160	\$ 325
Refining Division			
Revenues, \$58 × 50 barrels of gasoline	\$2,900	\$2,900	\$2,900
Deduct:			
Transferred-in costs, \$21, \$17.60, \$19.25 × 100 barrels of crude oil	2,100	1,760	1,925
Division variable costs, \$8 × 50 barrels of gasoline	400	400	400
Division fixed costs, \$6 × 50 barrels of gasoline	300	300	300
Division operating income	\$ 100	\$ 440	\$ 275
Operating income of both divisions together	\$ 600	\$ 600	\$ 600

three methods, summing the two division operating incomes equals Horizon Petroleum's total operating income of \$600. By keeping total operating income the same, we focus attention on the effects of different transfer-pricing methods on the operating income of each division. Subsequent sections of this chapter relax this assumption.

Consider first methods A and B in the first two columns of Exhibit 22-2. The operating income of the Transportation Division is \$340 more (\$500 − \$160) if transfer prices are based on market prices (using method A) rather than on 110% of full costs (using method B). However, the operating income of the Refining Division is \$340 more (\$440 − \$100) if transfer prices are based on 110% of full costs (using method B) rather than market prices (using method A). If the Transportation Division's sole criterion were to maximize its own division operating income, it would favor transfer prices at market prices. In contrast, the Refining Division would prefer transfer prices at 110% of full costs to maximize its own division operating income. Little wonder that subunit managers take considerable interest in setting transfer prices, especially those managers whose compensation or promotion directly depends on subunit operating income. To reduce the excessive focus of subunit managers on their own subunits, many companies compensate subunit managers on the basis of both subunit and companywide operating incomes.

If market prices of crude oil in the Houston area fluctuated in response to local supply-and-demand conditions, then under market-based method A, the operating incomes of the Transportation and Refining divisions would fluctuate as well. The Transportation and Refining divisions may instead prefer to negotiate a more stable, long-run transfer price. Method C assumes a $19.25 transfer price, which is between the full cost and market-based transfer prices. In our example, the negotiated transfer price splits the $600 of operating income almost equally between the divisions ($325 for the Transportation Division and $275 for the Refining Division). Note, method B also has the effect of shielding both divisions from fluctuations in crude oil prices in Houston. As Exhibit 22-2 shows, the $17.60 transfer price depends only on the full costs of the Transportation Division. The market price of crude oil in Houston is irrelevant to this calculation.

This example illustrates how the choice of a transfer-pricing method divides the companywide operating income pie among individual divisions. Subsequent sections of this chapter illustrate that the choice of a transfer-pricing method and managers' sourcing decisions can determine the size of the operating income pie itself. We consider this effect as we expand our discussion of market-based, cost-based, and negotiated transfer prices.

5 Illustrate how market-based transfer prices promote goal congruence in perfectly competitive markets

...transacting internally is like transacting externally

MARKET-BASED TRANSFER PRICES

Perfectly Competitive Market Case

Transferring products or services at market prices generally leads to optimal decisions when three conditions are satisfied: (1) The market for the intermediate product is perfectly competitive, (2) interdependencies of subunits are minimal, and (3) there are no additional costs or benefits to the company as a whole from buying or selling in the external market instead of transacting internally. A **perfectly competitive market** exists when there is a homogeneous product with buying prices equal to selling prices and no individual buyers or sellers can affect those prices by their own actions. By using market-based transfer prices in perfectly competitive markets, a company can achieve (1) goal congruence, (2) management effort, (3) subunit performance evaluation, and (4) subunit autonomy.

In perfectly competitive markets, the minimum price the selling division is willing to accept from the buying division is the market price, because the selling division can always sell its output in the external market at that price. The maximum price the buying division is willing to pay to the selling division is the market price, because the buying division can always buy its input in the external market at that price.

Reconsider Horizon Petroleum. Assume there is a perfectly competitive market for crude oil in the Houston area. As a result, the Transportation Division can sell and the Refining Division can buy as much crude oil as each wants at $21 per barrel. Horizon would like its managers to buy or sell crude oil internally. Think about the decisions that Horizon's division managers would make if each had the option to sell or buy crude oil externally. If the transfer price between Horizon's Transportation and Refining divisions is set below $21, the manager of the Transportation Division will be motivated to sell all crude oil to outside buyers in the Houston area at $21 per barrel. If the transfer price is set above $21, the manager of the Refining Division will be motivated to purchase all crude oil requirements from outside suppliers. Only a $21 transfer price will motivate the Transportation Division *and* the Refining Division to buy and sell internally. That is, neither division profits by buying or selling in the external market.

Suppose division managers are evaluated on their individual division's operating income. The Transportation Division will sell, either internally or externally, as much crude oil as it can profitably transport, and the Refining Division will buy, either internally or externally, as much crude oil as it can profitably refine. At a $21 per barrel transfer price, the actions that maximize division operating income are also the actions that maximize operating income of Horizon Petroleum as a whole. Furthermore, division managers will be motivated to exert management effort to maximize their own division's operating income. Market prices also serve to evaluate the economic viability and profitability of each division individually. For example, if under market-based transfer prices, the Refining Division consistently shows small or negative profits, Horizon may decide to shut down the Refining Division and simply transport and sell the oil to other refineries in the Houston area.

Distress Prices

When supply outstrips demand, market prices may drop well below their historical averages. If the drop in prices is expected to be temporary, these low market prices are sometimes called "distress prices." Deciding whether a current market price is a distress price is often difficult. The market prices of several agricultural commodities, such as wheat and oats, have stayed for many years at what observers initially believed were temporary distress levels!

Which transfer price should be used for judging performance if distress prices prevail? Some companies use the distress prices themselves, but others use long-run average prices, or "normal" market prices. In the short run, the manager of the selling subunit should meet the distress price as long as it exceeds the incremental costs of supplying the product or service. If not, the selling division should stop selling the product or service to the buying division; the buying division should buy the product or service from an outside supplier. These actions would increase division and companywide operating income. If the long-run average market price is used, forcing the manager to buy internally at a price above the current market price will hurt the buying division's short-run performance and understate its profitability. Using the long-run average market price, however, provides a better measure of the long-run viability of the supplier division. If the price remains low in the long run, though, the company should use the distress price as the transfer price. If the distress price is lower than the variable and fixed costs that can be saved if manufacturing facilities are shut down, the manager of the selling subunit should dispose of its production facilities, and the buying subunit should purchase the product from an outside supplier.

Be aware of the conflict caused by distress prices. Because the selling division receives very low revenues from distress prices, that manager may decide to produce other products that may not be in the company's long-run best interest. Alternatively, if the transfer price is based on the long-run average market price, the buying division would prefer to buy externally. If top management requires buying internally (at the long-run average market price), autonomy will be violated.

COST-BASED TRANSFER PRICES

6 Avoid making suboptimal decisions when transfer prices are based on full cost plus a markup

...as a result of buying divisions regarding the fixed costs and the markup as variable costs

Cost-based transfer prices are helpful when market prices are unavailable, inappropriate, or too costly to obtain. For example, the product may be specialized or the internal product may be different from the products available externally in terms of quality and customer service.

Full-Cost Bases

In practice, many companies use transfer prices based on full costs. To approximate market prices, cost-based transfer prices are sometimes set at full cost plus a margin. These transfer prices, however, can lead to suboptimal decisions. Suppose Horizon Petroleum makes internal transfers at 110% of full cost. Recall, the Refining Division purchases, on average, 20,000 barrels of crude oil per day from a local Houston supplier, who delivers the crude oil to the refinery at a price of $21 per barrel. To reduce crude oil costs, the Refining Division has located an independent producer in Matamoros—Gulfmex Corporation—that is willing to sell 20,000 barrels of crude oil per day at $16 per barrel, delivered to Horizon's pipeline in Matamoros. Given Horizon's organization structure, the Transportation Division would purchase the 20,000 barrels of crude oil in Matamoros from Gulfmex, transport it to Houston, and then sell it to the Refining Division. The pipeline has unused capacity and can ship the 20,000 barrels at its variable cost of $1 per barrel without affecting the shipment of the 10,000 barrels of crude oil per day acquired under its existing long-term contract arrangement. Will Horizon Petroleum incur lower costs by purchasing crude oil from Gulfmex in Matamoros or by purchasing crude oil from the Houston supplier? Will the Refining Division show lower crude oil purchasing costs by using oil from Gulfmex or by using its current Houston supplier?

The following analysis shows Horizon Petroleum's operating income would be maximized by purchasing oil from Gulfmex. The analysis compares the incremental costs in both divisions under the two alternatives. The analysis assumes the fixed costs of the Transportation Division will be the same regardless of the alternative chosen. That is, the Transportation Division cannot save any of its fixed costs if it does not transport Gulfmex's 20,000 barrels of crude oil per day.

- *Alternative 1*: Buy 20,000 barrels from Houston supplier at $21 per barrel. Total costs to Horizon Petroleum are 20,000 barrels × $21 per barrel = $420,000.
- *Alternative 2*: Buy 20,000 barrels in Matamoros at $16 per barrel and transport it to Houston at a variable cost of $1 per barrel. Total costs to Horizon Petroleum are 20,000 barrels × ($16 + $1) per barrel = $340,000.

There is a reduction in total costs to Horizon Petroleum of $80,000 ($420,000 − $340,000) by acquiring oil from Gulfmex.

Suppose the Transportation Division's transfer price to the Refining Division is 110% of full cost. The Refining Division will see its reported division costs increase if the crude oil is purchased from Gulfmex:

$$\text{Transfer price} = 1.10 \times \left(\begin{array}{c}\text{Purchase price}\\ \text{from}\\ \text{Gulfmex}\end{array} + \begin{array}{c}\text{Variable cost per unit}\\ \text{of Transportation}\\ \text{Division}\end{array} + \begin{array}{c}\text{Fixed cost per unit}\\ \text{of Transportation}\\ \text{Division}\end{array}\right)$$

$$= 1.10 \times (\$16 + \$1 + \$3) = 1.10 \times \$20 = \$22$$

- *Alternative 1*: Buy 20,000 barrels from Houston supplier at $21 per barrel. Total costs to Refining Division are 20,000 barrels × $21 per barrel = $420,000.
- *Alternative 2*: Buy 20,000 barrels from the Transportation Division of Horizon Petroleum purchased from Gulfmex. Total costs to Refining Division are 20,000 barrels × $22 per barrel = $440,000.

As a profit center, the Refining Division can maximize its short-run division operating income by purchasing from the Houston supplier at $420,000.

The transfer-pricing method has led the Refining Division to regard the fixed cost (and the 10% markup) of the Transportation Division as a variable cost. That's because the Refining Division looks at each barrel that it obtains from the Transportation Division as a variable cost of $22 per barrel; if 10 barrels are transferred, it costs the Refining Division $220; if 100 barrels are transferred, it costs $2,200. From the viewpoint of Horizon Petroleum as a whole, its variable cost per barrel is $17 ($16 to purchase the oil from Gulfmex plus $1 to transport it to Houston). The remaining $5 ($22 − $17) per barrel is the Transportation Division's fixed cost and markup. Buying crude oil in Houston costs Horizon Petroleum an additional $21 per barrel. For the company, it is cheaper to buy from Gulfmex in Matamoros. But the Refining Division sees the problem differently. From its perspective, it prefers buying from the Houston supplier at a cost of $420,000 (20,000 barrels × $21 per barrel) because buying from Gulfmex costs the division $440,000 (20,000 barrels × $22 per barrel). In this example, the transfer price based on full cost plus a markup does not induce goal congruence.

What transfer price will promote goal congruence for both the Transportation and Refining divisions? The minimum transfer price is $17 per barrel. A transfer price below $17 does not provide the Transportation Division with an incentive to purchase crude oil from Gulfmex in Matamoros, whereas a transfer price above $17 generates contribution margin to cover its fixed costs. The maximum transfer price is $21 per barrel. A transfer price above $21 will cause the Refining Division to purchase crude oil from the external market rather than from the Transportation Division. A transfer price between the minimum and maximum transfer prices of $17 and $21 will promote goal congruence: Each division will increase its own reported division operating income by purchasing crude oil from Gulfmex in Matamoros while increasing Horizon Petroleum's operating income. For example, a transfer price based on the full costs of $20 without a markup will achieve goal congruence; the Transportation Division will show no operating income and will be evaluated as a cost center.

In the absence of a market-based transfer price, senior management at Horizon Petroleum cannot easily determine the profitability of the investment made in the Transportation Division and hence whether Horizon should keep or sell the pipeline. Furthermore, if the transfer price had been based on the actual costs of the Transportation Division, it would provide the division with no incentive to control costs. That's because all cost inefficiencies of the Transportation Division would get passed along as part of the actual full-cost transfer price. However, surveys indicate (see p. 767) that, despite their limitations, managers prefer to use full-cost-based transfer prices because they represent relevant costs for long-run decisions, they facilitate external pricing based on variable and fixed costs, and they are the least costly to administer.

Some recent research examines cost-based transfer prices in which margins over and above cost are not constant but increase as the actual costs decrease. The goal is to create incentives for division managers to decrease the costs of the products they are supplying.

Using full-cost-based transfer prices requires an allocation of each subunit's fixed costs to products. Full-cost transfer pricing raises many issues. How are indirect costs allocated to products? Have the correct activities, cost pools, and cost-allocation bases been identified? Should the chosen fixed-cost rates be actual or budgeted? The issues here are similar to the issues that arise in allocating fixed costs, introduced in Chapter 14. Calculations of full-cost-based transfer prices using activity-based cost drivers can provide more-refined allocation of costs to products. Using budgeted costs and budgeted rates lets both divisions know the transfer price in advance. It overcomes the problem of inefficiencies in actual costs getting passed along to the buying division. That's because the transfer prices are based on budgeted (efficient) costs, not what the actual costs turn out to be. Also, variations in the total quantity of units produced by the selling division do not affect the transfer price.

Variable Cost Bases

Transferring 20,000 barrels of crude oil from the Transportation Division to the Refining Division at the variable cost of $17 per barrel achieves goal congruence, as shown in the preceding section. The Refining Division would buy from the Transportation Division because the Transportation Division's variable cost (which is also the relevant incremental cost for Horizon Petroleum as a whole) is less than the $21 price charged by outside suppliers. At the $17 per barrel transfer price, the Transportation Division would record an operating loss. At the same time, the Refining Division would show large profits because it would be charged only for the variable costs of the Transportation Division. One approach to addressing this problem is to have the Refining Division make a lump-sum transfer payment to cover fixed costs and generate some operating income for the Transportation Division while the Transportation Division continues to make transfers at variable cost. The fixed payment is the price the Refining Division pays for using the capacity of the Transportation Division. The income earned by each division can then be used to evaluate the performance of each division and its manager.

Prorating the Difference Between Maximum and Minimum Transfer Prices

An alternative cost-based approach is for Horizon Petroleum to choose a transfer price that splits, on some fair basis, the $4 difference between the $21 per barrel maximum transfer price the Refining Division is willing to pay and the $17 per barrel minimum transfer price the Transportation Division is willing to charge. Suppose Horizon Petroleum allocates the $4 difference on the basis of the budgeted variable costs of the Transportation Division and the Refining Division for a given quantity of crude oil. Using the data in Exhibit 22-2 (p. 761), the variable costs are as follows:

Transportation Division's variable costs to transport 100 barrels of crude oil	$100
Refining Division's variable costs to refine 100 barrels of crude oil and produce 50 barrels of gasoline	400
	$500

Of the $4 difference in transfer prices ($21 − $17), the Transportation Division gets to keep ($100 ÷ $500) × $4.00 = $0.80, and the Refining Division gets to keep ($400 ÷ $500) × $4.00 = $3.20. That is, the transfer price between the Transportation Division and the Refining Division would be $17.80 per barrel of crude oil ($16 purchase cost + $1 variable cost + $0.80 that the Transportation Division gets to keep). This approach is a budgeted variable-cost-plus transfer price. The "plus" indicates the setting of a transfer price above variable cost.

To decide on the $0.80 and $3.20 allocation of the $4.00 contribution to total company operating income per barrel, the divisions must share information about their variable costs. In effect, each division does not operate (at least for this transaction) in a totally decentralized manner. Because most organizations are hybrids of centralization and decentralization anyway, this approach deserves serious consideration when transfers are significant. Note, each division has an incentive to overstate its variable costs to receive a more-favorable transfer price.

Because transfer pricing allocates profits across divisions, division managers often view each other as competitors; this attitude could limit their willingness to share information.

Dual Pricing

There is seldom a single cost-based transfer price that simultaneously meets the criteria of goal congruence, management effort, subunit performance evaluation, and subunit autonomy. As a result, some companies choose **dual pricing**, using two separate transfer-pricing methods to price each transfer from one subunit to another. An example of dual pricing arises when the selling division receives a full-cost-based price and the buying division pays the market price for the internally transferred products. Assume Horizon Petroleum purchases crude oil from Gulfmex in Matamoros at $16 per barrel. One way of recording the journal entry for the transfer between the Transportation Division and the Refining Division is

1. Debit the Refining Division (the buying division) with the market-based transfer price of $21 per barrel of crude oil.
2. Credit the Transportation Division (the selling division) with the 110%-of-full-cost transfer price of $22 per barrel of crude oil.
3. Debit a corporate cost account for the $1 ($22 − $21) per barrel difference between the two transfer prices.

The dual-pricing system promotes goal congruence because it makes the Refining Division no worse off if it purchases the crude oil from the Transportation Division rather than from the outside supplier at $21 per barrel. The dual-pricing system gives the Transportation Division a corporate subsidy. The effect of dual pricing is that the operating income for Horizon Petroleum as a whole is less than the sum of the operating incomes of the divisions.

Dual pricing is not widely used in practice even though it reduces goal incongruence associated with a pure cost-based transfer-pricing method. One concern with dual pricing is that it leads to problems in computing the taxable income of subunits located in different tax jurisdictions, such as in our example, where the Transportation Division is taxed in Mexico while the Refining Division is taxed in the United States. A second concern is that the manager of the supplying subunit does not have sufficient incentive to control costs with a dual-pricing system because the supplying division records revenues based on actual costs. A third concern is that dual pricing insulates managers from the frictions of the marketplace because costs, not market prices, affect the revenues of the supplying division.

7 Understand the range over which two divisions negotiate the transfer price when there is unused capacity

...variable cost and market price of the product transferred

NEGOTIATED TRANSFER PRICES

Negotiated transfer prices result from a bargaining process between selling and buying subunits. Consider again a transfer price between the Transportation and Refining divisions of Horizon Petroleum. The Transportation Division has unused capacity it can use to transport oil from Matamoros to Houston. The Transportation Division will only purchase oil from Gulfmex and sell oil to the Refining Division if the transfer price equals or exceeds $17 per barrel of crude oil—that's its variable cost. The Refining Division will only buy crude oil from the Transportation Division if the price does not exceed $21 per barrel—that's the price at which the Refining Division can buy crude oil in Houston.

From the perspective of Horizon Petroleum as a whole, operating income is maximized if the Refining Division purchases crude oil from the Transportation Division rather than from the Houston market (incremental cost per barrel of $17 versus $21). Both divisions would be interested in transacting with each other (thereby achieving goal congruence) if the transfer price is set between $17 and $21. For example, a transfer price of $19.25 per barrel will increase the Transportation Division's operating income by $19.25 − $17 = $2.25 per barrel. It will increase the Refining Division's operating income by $21 − $19.25 = $1.75 per barrel because the Refining Division can now buy the crude oil for $19.25 internally rather than for $21 in the outside market.

Where between $17 and $21 will the transfer price per barrel be set? Under a negotiated transfer price, the answer depends on several things: the bargaining strengths of the two divisions; the information the Transportation Division has about the demand for its services from outside refineries; and the information the Refining Division has about its other available sources of crude oil. Negotiations become particularly sensitive because Horizon Petroleum can now evaluate each division's performance on the basis of division operating income. The price negotiated by the two divisions will, in general, have no specific relationship to either costs or market price. But cost and price information are often useful starting points in the negotiation process. A negotiated transfer price strongly preserves division autonomy because the transfer price is the outcome of negotiations between division managers. It also has the advantage that each division manager is motivated to put forth effort to increase division operating income. Its disadvantage is the time and energy spent on the negotiations.

SURVEYS OF COMPANY PRACTICE

Domestic and Multinational Transfer-Pricing Practices

What transfer-pricing practices are used around the world? The following tables indicate how predominantly particular transfer-pricing methods are used in different countries.

A. Domestic Transfer-Pricing Methods

Methods	United States[a]	Australia[b]	Canada[c]	Japan[a]	India[d]	United Kingdom[e]	New Zealand[f]
Market-based	26%	13%	34%	34%	47%	26%	18%
Cost-based:							
Variable costs	3	—	6	2	6	10	10
Absorption or full costs	49	—	37	44	47	38	61
Other	1	—	3	—	—	1	—
Total	53%	65%	46%	46%	53%	49%	71%
Negotiated	17%	11%	18%	19%	—	24%	11%
Other	4%	11%	2%	1%	—	1%	—
	100%	100%	100%	100%	100%	100%	100%

B. Multinational Transfer-Pricing Methods

Methods	United States[a]	Australia[b]	Canada[c]	Japan[a]	India[d]	United Kingdom[g]	New Zealand[f]
Market-based	35%	—	37%	37%	—	31%	—
Cost-based:							
Variable costs	0	—	5	3	—	5	—
Absorption or full costs	42	—	26	38	—	28	—
Other	1	—	2	—	—	5	—
Total	43%	—	33%	41%	—	38%	—
Negotiated	14%	—	26%	22%	—	20%	—
Other	8%	—	4%	—	—	11%	—
	100%	—	100%	100%	—	100%	—

Note: Dashes indicate information was not disclosed in survey.

The surveys indicate that for domestic transfer pricing, managers in all countries use cost-based transfer prices more frequently than market-based transfer prices. For multinational transfer pricing, managers use market-based and cost-based methods equally as often. Many multinational companies have market-based transfer prices in some divisions and cost-based transfer prices in others.

What factors do managers consider important in decisions on domestic transfer pricing? Survey evidence indicates the following (in order of importance): (1) maximizing consolidated after-tax profits, (2) performance evaluation, (3) management motivation, (4) pricing and product mix, and (5) external market recognition.[a,h]

Factors cited as important in decisions on multinational transfer-pricing policy are (in order of importance) (1) income tax rate and other tax differences among countries, (2) total income of the company, (3) income or dividend repatriation restrictions, (4) availability of market price information, and (5) competitive position of subsidiaries in their respective markets.[a,c,i]

[a]Adapted from Tang, "Transfer Pricing."
[b]Joye and Blayney, "Cost and Management Accounting."
[c]Tang, "Canadian Transfer."
[d]Govindarajan and Ramamurthy, "Transfer Pricing."
[e]Drury, Braund, Osborne, and Tayles, *A Survey of Management Accounting.*
[f]Hoque and Alam, "Organization Size."
[g]Mostafa, Sharp, and Howard, "Transfer Pricing."
[h]Price Waterhouse, *Transfer Pricing Practices.*
[i]J. Elliott, "International Transfer Pricing." Full citations are in Appendix A at the end of the book.

The Surveys of Company Practice (p. 767) indicates how frequently the different transfer pricing methods are used around the world.

8 Contruct a general guideline for determining a minimum transfer price

...incremental cost plus opportunity cost of supplying division

A GENERAL GUIDELINE FOR TRANSFER-PRICING SITUATIONS

Exhibit 22-3 summarizes the properties of the different transfer-pricing methods using the criteria described in this chapter. As the exhibit indicates, there is no transfer-pricing method that meets all the criteria. Market conditions, the goal of the transfer-pricing system, and the criteria of goal congruence, management effort, subunit performance evaluation, and subunit autonomy (if desired), must all be considered simultaneously. The transfer price a company will eventually choose depends on the economic circumstances and the decision at hand. The following general guideline (formula) is a helpful first step in setting a minimum transfer price in many situations:

$$\text{Minimum transfer price} = \begin{array}{c}\text{Incremental cost}\\\text{per unit}\\\text{incurred up}\\\text{to the point of transfer}\end{array} + \begin{array}{c}\text{Opportunity cost}\\\text{per unit}\\\text{to the selling subunit}\end{array}$$

Incremental cost in this context means the additional cost of producing and transferring the products or services. *Opportunity cost* here is the maximum contribution margin forgone by the selling subunit if the products or services are transferred internally. For example, if the selling subunit is operating at capacity, the opportunity cost of transferring a unit internally rather than selling it externally is equal to the market price minus variable cost. That's because by transferring a unit internally, the subunit forgoes the contribution margin it could have obtained by selling the unit in the outside market. We distinguish incremental cost from opportunity cost because the financial accounting system typically records incremental cost but not opportunity cost. The guideline measures a *minimum* transfer price because the selling subunit will be motivated to sell the product to the buying subunit only if the transfer price covers the incremental cost the selling subunit incurs to produce the product and the opportunity cost it forgoes by selling the product internally rather than in the external market. We illustrate the general guideline in some specific situations using data from Horizon Petroleum.

In the transfer-pricing context, opportunity cost is the profit the selling division (SD) forgoes by selling internally rather than externally. Assume the SD has no idle capacity and can sell all it produces at $4 per unit. Incremental cost is $1 per unit. If the SD sells internally, the profit forgone (opportunity cost) is $3 per unit ($4 revenue per unit – $1 outlay cost per unit). In contrast, if the SD has unused capacity with no alternative use, no profit is forgone by selling internally (opportunity cost is $0).

1. *A perfectly competitive market for the intermediate product exists, and the selling division has no idle capacity.* If the market for crude oil in Houston is perfectly competitive, the Transportation Division can sell all the crude oil it transports to the external market at $21

EXHIBIT 22-3

Comparison of Different Transfer-Pricing Methods

Criteria	Market Price	Cost-Based	Negotiated
Achieves goal congruence	Yes, when markets are competitive	Often, but not always	Yes
Useful for evaluating subunit performance	Yes, when markets are competitive	Difficult unless transfer price exceeds full costs	Yes, but transfer prices are affected by bargaining strengths
Motivates management effort	Yes	Yes, when based on budgeted costs; less incentive to control costs if transfers are based on actual costs	Yes
Preserves subunit autonomy	Yes, when markets are competitive	No, because it is rule-based	Yes, because it is based on negotiations between subunits
Other factors	No market may exist or markets may be imperfect or in distress	Useful for determining full cost of products and services; easy to implement	Bargaining and negotiations take time and may need to be reviewed repeatedly as conditions change

per barrel, and it will have no idle capacity. The Transportation Division's incremental cost (as shown in Exhibit 22-1, p. 760) is $13 per barrel (purchase cost of $12 per barrel plus variable transportation cost of $1 per barrel) for oil purchased under the long-term contract or $17 per barrel (purchase cost of $16 plus variable transportation cost of $1) for oil purchased at current market prices from Gulfmex. The Transportation Division's opportunity cost per barrel of transferring the oil internally is the contribution margin per barrel forgone by not selling the crude oil in the external market: $8 for oil purchased under the long-term contract (market price, $21, minus variable cost, $13) and $4 for oil purchased from Gulfmex (market price, $21, minus variable cost, $17). In either case,

$$\begin{aligned}\text{Minimum transfer price per barrel} &= \text{Incremental cost per barrel} + \text{Opportunity cost per barrel}\\ &= \$13 + \$8 = \$21\\ &\quad\text{or}\\ &= \$17 + \$4 = \$21\end{aligned}$$

The minimum transfer price per barrel is the market price of $21. Market-based transfer prices are ideal in perfectly competitive markets when there is no idle capacity in the selling division.

2. *An intermediate market exists that is not perfectly competitive, and the selling division has idle capacity.* In markets that are not perfectly competitive, capacity utilization can only be increased by decreasing prices. Idle capacity exists because decreasing prices is often not worthwhile—it decreases operating income.

If the Transportation Division has idle capacity, its opportunity cost of transferring the oil internally is zero because the division does not forgo any external sales or contribution margin from internal transfers. In this case,

$$\text{Minimum transfer price per barrel} = \text{Incremental cost per barrel} = \begin{array}{c}\$13\text{ per barrel for oil purchased under the}\\ \text{long-term contract, or }\$17\text{ per barrel for}\\ \text{oil purchased from Gulfmex in Matamoros}\end{array}$$

Any transfer price above incremental cost but below $21—the price at which the Refining Division can buy crude oil in Houston—motivates the Transportation Division to transport crude oil to the Refining Division and the Refining Division to buy crude oil from the Transportation Division. In this situation, the company could either use a cost-based transfer price or allow the two divisions to negotiate a transfer price between themselves.

In general, when markets are not perfectly competitive, the potential to influence demand and operating income through prices complicates the measurement of opportunity costs. The transfer price depends on constantly changing levels of supply and demand. There is not just one transfer price. Rather, a transfer-pricing schedule presents the transfer prices for various quantities supplied and demanded, depending on the incremental costs and opportunity costs of the units transferred.

3. *No market exists for the intermediate product.* This situation would occur for the Horizon Petroleum case if the crude oil transported by the Transportation Division could be used only by the Houston refinery (due to, say, its high tar content) and would not be wanted by outside parties. Here, the opportunity cost of supplying crude oil internally is zero because the inability to sell crude oil externally means no contribution margin is forgone. For the Transportation Division of Horizon Petroleum, the minimum transfer price under the general guideline is the incremental cost per barrel (either $13 or $17). As in the previous case, any transfer price between the incremental cost and $21 will achieve goal congruence.

MULTINATIONAL TRANSFER-PRICING AND TAX CONSIDERATIONS

9 Incorporate income tax considerations in multinational transfer pricing

...set transfer prices to minimize tax payments to the extent permitted by tax laws

Transfer prices often have tax implications. Tax factors include not only income taxes, but also payroll taxes, customs duties, tariffs, sales taxes, value-added taxes, environment-related taxes, and other government levies. Our aim here is to highlight tax factors and, in particular, income taxes as an important consideration in determining transfer prices. (Fuller consideration of the tax aspects of transfer-pricing decisions is beyond the scope of this book.)

Consider the Horizon Petroleum data in Exhibit 22-2 (p. 761). Assume that the Transportation Division based in Mexico pays Mexican income taxes at 30% of operating income and that the Refining Division based in the United States pays income taxes at 20% of operating income. Horizon Petroleum would minimize its total income tax payments with the 110%-of-full-costs transfer-pricing method, as shown in the following table, because this method minimizes income reported in Mexico, where income is taxed at a higher rate than in the United States.

	Operating Income for 100 Barrels of Crude Oil			Income Tax on 100 Barrels of Crude Oil		
Transfer-Pricing Method	**Transportation Division (Mexico) (1)**	**Refining Division (U.S.) (2)**	**Total (3) = (1) + (2)**	**Transportation Division (Mexico) (4) = 0.30 × (1)**	**Refining Division (U.S.) (5) = 0.20 × (2)**	**Total (6) = (4) + (5)**
Market price	$500	$100	$600	$150.00	$20	$170.00
110% of full costs	160	440	600	48.00	88	136.00
Negotiated price	325	275	600	97.50	55	152.50

Income tax considerations raise additional issues. Tax issues may conflict with other objectives of transfer pricing. Suppose the market for oil in Houston is perfectly competitive. In this case, the market-based transfer price achieves goal congruence and provides incentives for management effort. It also helps Horizon to evaluate the economic profitability of the Transportation Division. But it is costly from the perspective of income taxes. To minimize income taxes, Horizon would favor using 110% of full costs for tax reporting. Tax laws in the United States and Mexico, however, constrain this option. In particular, the Mexican tax authorities, aware of Horizon's incentives to minimize income taxes by reducing the income reported in Mexico, would challenge any attempts to shift income to the Refining Division through an unreasonably low transfer price (see also Concepts in Action, p. 771).

Section 482 of the U.S. Internal Revenue Code governs taxation of multinational transfer pricing. Section 482 requires that transfer prices between a company and its foreign division or subsidiary, for both tangible and intangible property, equal the price that would be charged by an unrelated third party in a comparable transaction. Regulations related to Section 482 recognize that transfer prices can be market-based or cost-plus-based, where the plus represents margins on comparable transactions.[1]

If the market for crude oil in Houston is perfectly competitive, Horizon would be required to use the market price for transfers from the Transportation Division to the Refining Division. Horizon might successfully argue that the transfer price should be set below the market price because the Transportation Division incurs no marketing and distribution costs when selling crude oil to the Refining Division. Under the U.S. Internal Revenue Code, Horizon could obtain advanced approval of the transfer-pricing arrangements from the tax authorities, which is called an *advanced pricing agreement (APA)*. The APA is a binding agreement for a specified numbers of years. The goal of the APA program is to avoid costly transfer-pricing disputes between taxpayers and tax authorities.

To meet multiple transfer-pricing objectives, such as minimizing income taxes, achieving goal congruence, and motivating management effort, a company may choose to keep one set of accounting records for tax reporting and a second set for internal management reporting. The difficulty here is that tax authorities may interpret two sets of books as meaning the company manipulated its reported taxable income to avoid tax payments. To avoid the problems caused by maintaining two sets of books, companies that choose tax-minimizing transfer-pricing strategies may use other management control techniques.

Consider a U.S. company that makes high-end data storage machines that it sells through its own sales organization in different countries. To minimize taxes, suppose

[1]R. Feinschreiber (Ed.), *Transfer Pricing Handbook*, 3rd ed. (New York, John Wiley & Sons, 2001); L. Eden, *Taxing Multinationals: Transfer Pricing and Corporate Income Taxation in North America* (Toronto, University of Toronto Press, 1998); M. Levey, "Transfer Pricing—What Next?" *International Financial Law Review* (June 2001); J. Henshall, S. Wrappe, and K. Chung, "Transfer Pricing," *International Tax Review* (April 2001).

the U.S. company sets a very high transfer price. Setting the transfer price deliberately high lowers the operating income of the sales organization in each country, even though the country sales organization has no say or control in determining the transfer price. To neutralize this negative effect on income, the company evaluates sales managers only on revenues minus marketing costs incurred in their respective countries. That is, the transfer prices incurred to acquire the product by the sales organizations in the countries are added back to the operating income of the sales organizations for performance-evaluation purposes. The difficulty with this approach is that it creates incentives for the sales organization in each country to maximize revenues rather than profits per dollar of marketing costs. Corporate managers must then step in and enumerate product priorities based on the full product-profitability information available to them.

CONCEPTS IN ACTION

U.S. Internal Revenue Service, Japanese National Tax Agency, and Transfer-Pricing Games

Tax authorities and government officials all over the world pay close attention to taxes paid by foreign corporations operating within their boundaries. At the heart of the issue are the transfer prices that companies use to transfer products from one country to another.

For example, in 1993, the U.S. Internal Revenue Service (IRS) investigated and concluded that Nissan Motor Company had understated U.S. taxes by setting transfer prices on passenger cars and trucks imported from Japan at "unrealistically" high levels. Nissan argued that it had maintained low margins in the United States to increase long-run market share in a very competitive market. Eventually, Nissan agreed to pay the IRS $170 million, but Nissan suffered no loss. That's because the Japanese National Tax Agency (NTA), Japan's tax authority, refunded Nissan the full amount of the IRS payment.

Conversely, in May 1994, Japan's NTA alleged that Coca-Cola Corporation had underreported its taxable income in Japan by charging "excessive" transfer prices to its local subsidiary for materials and concentrate imported from the parent company and by levying "excessive" royalty payments on its Japanese subsidiary for use of its brand name and sales and manufacturing expertise. The NTA pointed out that the royalties paid by Coca-Cola's Japanese subsidiary were higher than those paid by other companies in the same industry. It also said that the Japanese subsidiary paid royalties even for products it had developed on its own. The NTA imposed taxes and penalties of $150 million. Coca-Cola filed a complaint with the IRS charging that the levying of the Japanese tax resulted in the same income being taxed twice, because Coca-Cola had already paid tax on this income in the United States. This complaint led to negotiations between Japanese and U.S. tax authorities to decide which country gets to tax Coke's Japanese income. In a 1998 compromise settlement, Japan's NTA reduced its tax levy against Coke from $150 million to $50 million. For its part, the IRS reduced Coca-Cola's U.S. income tax liability.

In 2000, Japan's NTA and the IRS had to settle another dispute regarding transfer prices. This time Coca-Cola's Japanese subsidiary had to record an additional $450 million in taxable income for 1993 through 1999, which meant that it owed approximately $170 million in back taxes and penalties. To avoid double taxation, the IRS refunded Coca-Cola the tax it had paid to the United States.

Disputes over what constitutes a "fair" transfer price arise because of the absence of an easily observable market price for the transferred product. Multinational transfer-pricing disputes are likely to remain significant, given the substantial and increasing amounts of multinational investments.

Source: Adapted from C. Pass, "Transfer Pricing in Multinational Companies," *Management Accounting* (September 1994); "Coca-Cola Gets 10 Billion Yen Reprieve in Back Taxes," *The Yomiuri Shimbun* (February 24, 1998); *Financial Times* (September 3, 1999); and *Daily Yomiuri* (February 24, 1998 and April 30, 2000).

Additional factors that arise in multinational transfer pricing include tariffs and customs duties levied on imports of products into a country. The issues here are similar to income tax considerations; companies will have incentives to lower transfer prices for products imported into a country to reduce the tariffs and customs duties charged on those products.

In addition to the motivations for choosing transfer prices already described, multinational transfer prices are sometimes influenced by restrictions that some countries place on dividend or income-related payments to parties outside their national borders. By increasing the prices of goods or services transferred into divisions in these countries, companies can seek to increase the cash paid out of these countries without violating dividend or income-related restrictions.

PROBLEM FOR SELF-STUDY

The Pillercat Corporation is a highly decentralized company. Each division manager has full authority for sourcing decisions and selling decisions. The Machining Division of Pillercat has been the major supplier of the 2,000 crankshafts that the Tractor Division needs each year.

The Tractor Division, however, has just announced that it plans to purchase all its crankshafts in the forthcoming year from two external suppliers at $200 per crankshaft. The Machining Division of Pillercat recently increased its price for the forthcoming year to $220 per unit (from $200 per unit in the current year).

Juan Gomez, manager of the Machining Division, feels that the 10% price increase is justified. It results from a higher depreciation charge on some new specialized equipment used to manufacture crankshafts and an increase in labor costs. Gomez wants the president of Pillercat Corporation to direct the Tractor Division to buy all its crankshafts from the Machining Division at the price of $220. The incremental cost per unit that Pillercat incurs to produce each crankshaft is the Machining Division's variable cost of $190. The fixed cost per crankshaft in the Machining Division is $20.

Required

1. Compute the advantage or disadvantage in terms of annual operating income to the Pillercat Corporation as a whole if the Tractor Division buys crankshafts internally from the Machining Division under each of the following cases.
   a. The Machining Division has no alternative use for the facilities used to manufacture crankshafts.
   b. The Machining Division can use the facilities for other production operations, which will result in annual cash operating savings of $29,000.
   c. The Machining Division has no alternative use for its facilities, and the external supplier drops the price to $185 per crankshaft.
2. As the president of Pillercat, how would you respond to Juan Gomez's request to order the Tractor Division to purchase all of its crankshafts from the Machining Division? Would your response differ according to the scenarios described in a, b, and c of requirement 1? Explain.

SOLUTION

1. Computations for the Tractor Division buying crankshafts internally for one year are

	Case		
	a	b	c
Total purchase costs if buying from an external supplier (2,000 shafts × $200, $200, $185 per shaft)	$400,000	$400,000	$370,000
Incremental costs if buying from the Machining Division (2,000 shafts × $190 per shaft)	380,000	380,000	380,000
Total opportunity costs of the Machining Division	—	29,000	—
Total relevant costs	$380,000	$409,000	$380,000
Annual operating income advantage (disadvantage) to Pillercat of buying from the Machining Division	$ 20,000	$ (9,000)	$(10,000)

The "general guideline" that was introduced in the chapter (p. 768) as a first step in setting a transfer price can be used to highlight the alternatives:

Case	Incremental Cost per Unit Incurred to Point of Transfer	+	Opportunity Cost per Unit to the Supplying Division	=	Transfer Price	External Market Price
a	$190	+	$0	=	$190	$200
b	$190	+	$14.50 ($29,000 ÷ 2,000)	=	$204.50	$200
c	$190	+	$0	=	$190	$185

Comparing transfer price to external market price, the Tractor Division will maximize annual operating income of Pillercat Corporation as a whole by purchasing from the Machining Division in case **a** and by purchasing from the external supplier in cases **b** and **c**.

2. Pillercat Corporation is a highly decentralized company. If no forced transfer were made, the Tractor Division would use an external supplier, a decision that would be in the best interests of the company as a whole in cases **b** and **c** of requirement 1 but not in case **a**.

   Suppose in case **a**, the Machining Division refuses to meet the price of $200. This decision means that the company will be $20,000 worse off in the short-run. Should top management interfere and force a transfer at $200? This interference would undercut the philosophy of decentralization. Many top managements would not interfere because they would view the $20,000 as an inevitable cost of a suboptimal decision that can occur under decentralization. But how high must this cost be before the temptation to interfere would be irresistible? $30,000? $40,000?

   Any top management interference with lower-level decision making weakens decentralization. Of course, such interference may occasionally be necessary to prevent costly blunders. But recurring interference and constraints simply transform a decentralized company into a centralized company.

DECISION POINTS — SUMMARY

The following question-and-answer format summarizes the chapter's learning objectives. Each decision presents a key question related to a learning objective. The guidelines are the answer to that question.

Decision	Guidelines
1. What is a management control system and how should it be designed?	A management control system is a means of gathering and using information to aid and coordinate the planning and control decisions throughout the organization, and to guide the behavior of managers and employees. Effective management control systems are (a) closely aligned to the organization's strategy, (b) fit the organization's structure, and (c) motivate managers and employees to give effort to achieve the organization's goals.
2. What are the benefits and costs of decentralization?	The benefits of decentralization include (a) greater responsiveness to local needs, (b) gains from faster decision making, (c) increased motivation of subunit managers, (d) greater management development and learning, and (e) sharpened focus of subunit managers. The costs of decentralization include (a) suboptimal decision making (loss of control), (b) duplication of activities, (c) decreased loyalty toward the organization, and (d) increased costs of information gathering.
3. What is a transfer price, and what is it intended to achieve?	A transfer price is the price one subunit charges for a product or service supplied to another subunit of the same organization. Transfer prices seek to achieve (a) goal congruence, (b) management effort, (c) subunit performance evaluation, and (d) subunit autonomy (if desired).
4. What methods can be used to calculate transfer prices?	Transfer prices can be (a) market-based, (b) cost-based, or (c) negotiated. Different transfer-pricing methods produce different revenues and costs for individual subunits, and hence, different operating incomes for them.

Continued

5. What transfer price should be used if the market for the product to be transferred is perfectly competitive?	In perfectly competitive markets, there is no idle capacity, and division managers can buy and sell as much as they want at the market price. Setting the transfer price at the market price motivates division managers to transact internally and to take exactly the same actions as they would if they were transacting in the external market.
6. What problems can arise when full cost plus a markup is used as a transfer price?	A transfer price based on full cost plus a markup may lead to suboptimal decisions because it leads the buying division to regard the fixed costs and the markup of the selling division as variable costs. The buying division may then purchase products from an outside vendor expecting savings in variable costs that, in fact, will not occur.
7. What is the range over which two divisions will negotiate a transfer price when there is unused capacity?	When there is unused capacity, the transfer-price range for negotiations generally lies between the minimum price at which the selling division is willing to sell (its variable cost per unit) and the maximum price the buying division is willing to pay (the price at which the product is available from outside suppliers).
8. What is the general guideline for determining a minimum transfer price?	The general guideline states that the minimum transfer price equals the incremental cost per unit incurred up to the point of transfer plus the opportunity cost per unit to the selling division resulting from transferring products or services internally.
9. What are the income tax considerations when determining transfer prices?	Transfer prices can reduce income tax payments by recognizing more income in low-tax-rate countries and less income in high-tax-rate countries. However, tax regulations of different countries restrict the transfer prices that companies can use.

TERMS TO LEARN

This chapter and the Glossary at the end of this book contain definitions of:

autonomy (p. 756)
decentralization (756)
dual pricing (756)
dysfunctional decision making (756)
effort (755)
goal congruence (755)
incongruent decision making (756)
intermediate product (758)
management control system (754)
motivation (755)
perfectly competitive market (762)
suboptimal decision making (756)
transfer price (758)

ASSIGNMENT MATERIAL

Questions

22-1 What is a management control system?

22-2 Describe three criteria you would use to evaluate whether a management control system is effective.

22-3 What is the relationship among motivation, goal congruence, and effort?

22-4 Name three benefits and two costs of decentralization.

22-5 "Organizations typically adopt a consistent decentralization or centralization philosophy across all their business functions." Do you agree? Explain.

22-6 "Transfer pricing is confined to profit centers." Do you agree? Explain.

22-7 What are the three methods for determining transfer prices?

22-8 What properties should transfer-pricing systems have?

22-9 "All transfer-pricing methods give the same division operating income." Do you agree? Explain.

22-10 Under what conditions is a market-based transfer price optimal?

22-11 What is one potential limitation of full-cost-based transfer prices?

22-12 Give two reasons why the dual-pricing system of transfer pricing is not widely used.

22-13 "Cost and price information play no role in negotiated transfer prices." Do you agree? Explain.

22-14 "Under the general guideline for transfer pricing, the minimum transfer price will vary depending on whether the supplying division has idle capacity or not." Do you agree? Explain.

22-15 Why should managers consider income tax issues when choosing a transfer-pricing method?

Exercises

22-16 Decentralization, responsibility centers. Quinn Corporation manufactures and sells lighting products. Quinn's sales and marketing divisions are organized along product lines—wall sconces, recessed lights, track lights, and so on. The Manufacturing Division produces lighting products for all the sales and marketing divisions.

During the planning process, each sales and marketing division specifies the quantity of each style of light to be manufactured. Senior management then assigns the task of manufacturing the lights to different plants in the Manufacturing Division. Because manufacturing capacity is limited, some of the production is also outsourced. Senior management determines the manufacturing schedule on the basis of detailed studies that have been done to measure the time and cost of manufacturing different types of lighting products. Manufacturing managers are evaluated based on achieving target output within budgeted costs.

Required

1. Are the manufacturing plants in the Manufacturing Division cost centers or profit centers? Explain.
2. Quinn Corporation is considering decentralizing its marketing and manufacturing decisions by letting manufacturing and marketing managers directly negotiate the prices for manufacturing various products.
   a. How should Quinn evaluate manufacturing plant managers under this proposal?
   b. Would you recommend that Quinn Corporation decentralize its marketing and manufacturing decisions? Explain.

22-17 Decentralization, goal congruence, responsibility centers. Hexton Chemicals consists of seven operating divisions that operate independently. The operating divisions are assisted by a number of support groups, such as R&D, human resources, and environmental management. The environmental management group consists of 20 environmental engineers. These engineers must seek business from the operating divisions—that is, the projects they work on must be mutually agreed to and paid for by one of the operating divisions. Under Hexton's rules, the environmental group is required to charge the operating divisions for environmental services at cost.

Required

1. Is the environmental management group centralized or decentralized?
2. What type of responsibility center is the environmental management group?
3. What benefits and problems do you see in structuring the environmental management group in this way? Does it lead to goal congruence and motivation? Explain.

22-18 Multinational transfer pricing, effect of alternative transfer-pricing methods, global income tax minimization. User Friendly Computer, Inc., with headquarters in San Francisco, manufactures and sells desktop computers. User Friendly has three divisions, each of which is located in a different country:

a. China Division—manufactures memory devices and keyboards
b. South Korea Division—assembles desktop computers using internally manufactured parts and memory devices and keyboards from the China Division
c. U.S. Division—packages and distributes desktop computers

Each division is run as a profit center. The costs for the work done in each division for a single desktop computer are as follows:

China Division:	Variable cost =	1,000 yuan
	Fixed cost =	1,800 yuan
South Korea Division:	Variable cost =	360,000 won
	Fixed cost =	480,000 won
U.S. Division:	Variable cost =	$100
	Fixed cost =	$200

- Chinese income tax rate on China Division's operating income: 40%
- South Korean income tax rate on South Korea Division's operating income: 20%
- U.S. income tax rate on U.S. Division's operating income: 30%

Each desktop computer is sold to retail outlets in the United States for $3,200. Assume that the current foreign exchange rates are

8 yuan = $1 U.S.
1,200 won = S1 U.S.

Both the China and the South Korea divisions sell part of their production under a private label. The China Division sells the comparable memory/keyboard package used in each User Friendly desktop computer to a Chinese manufacturer for 3,600 yuan. The South Korea Division sells the comparable desktop computer to a South Korean distributor for 1,560,000 won.

Required

1. Calculate the after-tax operating income per unit earned by each division under the following transfer-pricing methods: (a) market price, (b) 200% of full costs, and (c) 300% of variable costs. (Income taxes are *not* included in the computation of the cost-based transfer prices.)
2. Which transfer-pricing method(s) will maximize the net income per unit of User Friendly Computer?

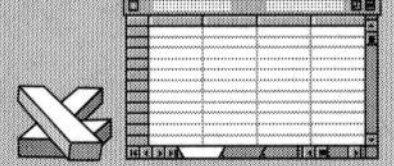

Excel Application For students who wish to practice their spreadsheet skills, the following is a step-by-step approach to creating an Excel spreadsheet to work this problem.

Step-by-Step

1. Open a new spreadsheet. At the top, create an "Original Data" section for the data provided by User Friendly Computer. Create rows for the exchange-rate data labeled "Yuan per U.S. Dollar" and "Won per U.S. Dollar." Skip two rows. Under the heading "China Division," create rows for "Price per Unit, Variable Cost per Unit, Fixed Cost per Unit," and "Income Tax Rate." Create two more sets of the same rows under the headings "South Korea Division" and "U.S. Division." Enter price and cost data in the division country's currency.

(Program your spreadsheet to perform all necessary calculations. Do not "hard-code" any amounts, such as net income per unit, requiring addition, subtraction, multiplication, or division operations.)

2. Skip two rows, create a "Problem 1" section in a similar format to Exhibit 22-2. Create columns for each of the three transfer-pricing methods. Under the heading "China Division," create rows for "Division Revenues per Unit, Division Variable Cost per Unit, Division Fixed Cost per Unit, Division Operating Income per Unit, Income Tax," and "Division Net Income per Unit." Under the headings "South Korea Division" and "U.S. Division," create rows for "Division Revenues per Unit, Transferred-In Cost per Unit, Division Variable Cost per Unit, Division Fixed Cost per Unit, Division Operating Income per Unit, Income Tax," and "Division Net Income per Unit." When entering calculations in this section, use the exchange rate data from your Original Data section to convert to U.S. dollars.
3. Skip two rows, create a "Problem 2" section. Create columns for each of the three transfer-pricing methods. Create rows for "China Division, South Korea Division, U.S. Division," and "User Friendly Computer." Enter the division net income under each of the transfer-pricing methods that you calculated in step 2 in this section. In the User Friendly Computer row, enter total net income under each of the transfer-pricing methods.
4. *Check the accuracy of your spreadsheet*: Go to your Original Data section and change the income tax rate for the South Korea Division from 20% to 35%. If you programmed your spreadsheet correctly, total net income for User Friendly Computer under the market price method should change to $1,278.

22-19 **Transfer-pricing methods, goal congruence.** British Columbia Lumber has a Raw Lumber Division and a Finished Lumber Division. The variable costs are

- Raw Lumber Division: $100 per 100 board-feet of raw lumber
- Finished Lumber Division: $125 per 100 board-feet of finished lumber

Assume that there is no board-feet loss in processing raw lumber into finished lumber. Raw lumber can be sold at $200 per 100 board-feet. Finished lumber can be sold at $275 per 100 board-feet.

Required

1. Should British Columbia Lumber process raw lumber into its finished form? Show your computations.
2. Assume that internal transfers are made at 110% of variable costs. Will each division maximize its division operating income contribution by adopting the action that is in the best interest of British Columbia Lumber? Explain.
3. Assume that internal transfers are made at market prices. Will each division maximize its division operating income contribution by adopting the action that is in the best interest of British Columbia Lumber? Explain.

22-20 **Effect of alternative transfer-pricing methods on division operating income.** (CMA, adapted) Ajax Corporation has two divisions. The Mining Division makes toldine, which is then transferred to the Metals Division. The toldine is further processed by the Metals Division and is sold to customers at a price of $150 per unit. The Mining Division is currently required by Ajax to transfer its total yearly output of 400,000 units of toldine to the Metals Division at 110% of full manufacturing cost. Unlimited quantities of toldine can be purchased and sold on the outside market at $90 per unit.

The following table gives the manufacturing costs per unit in the Mining and Metals divisions for 2004:

	Mining Division	Metals Division
Direct materials	$12	$ 6
Direct manufacturing labor costs	16	20
Manufacturing overhead costs	32[a]	25[b]
Total manufacturing costs per unit	$60	$51

[a]Manufacturing overhead costs in the Mining Division are 25% fixed and 75% variable.

[b]Manufacturing overhead costs in the Metals Division are 60% fixed and 40% variable.

Required

1. Calculate the operating incomes for the Mining and Metals divisions for the 400,000 units of toldine transferred under the following transfer-pricing methods: (a) market price and (b) 110% of full manufacturing costs.

2. Suppose Ajax rewards each division manager with a bonus, calculated as 1% of division operating income (if positive). What is the amount of bonus that will be paid to each division manager under the transfer-pricing methods in requirement 1? Which transfer-pricing method will each division manager prefer to use?
3. What arguments would Brian Jones, manager of the Mining Division, make to support the transfer-pricing method that he prefers?

22-21 Transfer pricing, general guideline, goal congruence. (CMA, adapted). Nogo Motors, Inc., operates as a decentralized multidivision company. The Igo Division of Nogo Motors purchases most of its airbags from the Airbag Division. The Airbag Division's incremental costs for manufacturing the airbags are $110 per unit. The Airbag Division is currently working at 80% of capacity. The current market price of the airbags is $140 per unit.

Required

1. Using the general guideline presented in the chapter, what is the minimum price at which the Airbag Division would sell airbags to the Igo Division?
2. Suppose that Nogo Motors requires that whenever divisions with idle capacity sell products internally, they must do so at incremental costs. Evaluate this transfer-pricing policy using the criteria of goal congruence, evaluating division performance, motivating management effort, and preserving division autonomy.
3. If the two divisions were to negotiate a transfer price, what is the range of possible transfer prices? Evaluate this negotiated transfer-pricing policy using the criteria of goal congruence, evaluating division performance, motivating management effort, and preserving division autonomy.
4. Do you prefer the transfer-pricing policy in requirement 2 or requirement 3? Explain your answer briefly.

22-22 General guideline, transfer-price range. The Shamrock Company manufactures and sells television sets. The Assembly Division assembles the television sets. It buys the screens for the television sets from the Screen Division. The Screen Division is operating at capacity. The incremental cost of manufacturing the screens is $70 per unit. The Screen Division can sell as many screens as it wants in the outside market at a price of $110 per screen. If it sells screens in the outside market, the Screen Division will incur variable marketing and distribution costs of $4 per unit. Similarly, if the Assembly Division purchases screens from outside suppliers, it will incur variable purchasing costs of $2 per screen.

Required

1. Using the general guideline presented in the chapter, what is the minimum transfer price at which the Screen Division will sell screens to the Assembly Division?
2. Suppose division managers act autonomously to maximize their own division's operating income, either by transacting internally or buying and selling in the market. If the two division managers were to negotiate a transfer price, what is the range of acceptable transfer prices?

22-23 Multinational transfer pricing, global tax minimization. The Mornay Company manufactures telecommunications equipment at its Wisconsin plant in the United States. The company has marketing divisions throughout the world. A Mornay marketing division in Vienna, Austria, imports 1,000 units of Product 4A36 from the United States. The following information is available:

U.S. income tax rate on the U.S. division's operating income	40%
Austrian income tax rate on the Austrian division's operating income	44%
Austrian import duty	10%
Variable manufacturing cost per unit of Product 4A36	$350
Full manufacturing cost per unit of Product 4A36	$500
Selling price (net of marketing and distribution costs) in Austria	$750

Suppose the U.S. and Austrian tax authorities only allow transfer prices that are between the full manufacturing cost per unit and a market price of $650, based on comparable imports into Austria. The Austrian import duty is charged on the price at which the product is transferred into Austria. Any import duty paid to the Austrian authorities is a deductible expense for calculating Austrian income taxes due.

Required

1. Calculate the after-tax operating income earned by the U.S. and Austrian divisions from transferring 1,000 units of Product 4A36 (a) at full manufacturing cost per unit and (b) at market price of comparable imports. (Income taxes are not included in the computation of the cost-based transfer prices.)
2. Which transfer price should the Mornay Company select to minimize the total of company import duties and income taxes? Remember that the transfer price must be between the full manufacturing cost per unit of $500 and the market price of $650 of comparable imports into Austria. Explain your reasoning.

22-24 Multinational transfer pricing, goal congruence (continuation of 22-23). Suppose that the U.S. division could sell as many units of Product 4A36 as it makes at $600 per unit in the U.S. market, net of all marketing and distribution costs.

Required

1. From the viewpoint of the Mornay Company as a whole, would after-tax operating income be maximized if it sold the 1,000 units of Product 4A36 in the United States or in Austria? Show your computations.

2. Suppose division managers act autonomously to maximize their division's after-tax operating income. Will the transfer price calculated in requirement 2 of Exercise 22-23 result in the U.S. division manager taking the actions determined to be optimal in requirement 1 of this exercise? Explain.
3. What is the minimum transfer price that the U.S. division manager would agree to? Does this transfer price result in the Mornay Company as a whole paying more import duty and taxes than the answer to requirement 2 of Exercise 22-23? If so, by how much?

22-25 Transfer-pricing dispute. The Allison-Chambers Corporation, manufacturer of tractors and other heavy farm equipment, is organized along decentralized lines, with each manufacturing division operating as a separate profit center. Each division manager has been delegated full authority on all decisions involving the sale of that division's output both to outsiders and to other divisions of Allison-Chambers. Division C has in the past always purchased its requirement of a particular tractor-engine component from Division A. However, when informed that Division A is increasing its selling price to $150, Division C's manager decides to purchase the engine component from outside suppliers.

Division C can purchase the component for $135 in the open market. Division A insists that, because of the recent installation of some highly specialized equipment and the resulting high depreciation charges, it will not be able to earn an adequate return on its investment unless it raises its price. Division A's manager appeals to top management of Allison-Chambers for support in the dispute with Division C and supplies the following operating data:

C's annual purchases of the tractor-engine component	1,000 units
A's variable costs per unit of the tractor-engine component	$120
A's fixed costs per unit of the tractor-engine component	$20

Required

1. Assume that there are no alternative uses for internal facilities. Determine whether the company as a whole will benefit if Division C purchases the component from outside suppliers for $135 per unit. What should the transfer price for the component be set at so that division managers acting in their own divisions' interests take actions that are in the best interest of the company as a whole?
2. Assume that internal facilities of Division A would not otherwise be idle. By not producing the 1,000 units for Division C, Division A's equipment and other facilities would be used for other production operations that would result in annual cash-operating savings of $18,000. Should Division C purchase from outside suppliers? Show your computations.
3. Assume that there are no alternative uses for Division A's internal facilities and that the price from outsiders drops $20. Should Division C purchase from outside suppliers? What should the transfer price for the component be set at so that division managers acting in their own divisions' interests take actions that are in the best interest of the company as a whole?

22-26 Transfer-pricing problem (continuation of 22-25). Refer to Exercise 22-25. Assume that Division A can sell the 1,000 units to other customers at $155 per unit, with variable marketing costs of $5 per unit.

Required Determine whether Allison-Chambers will benefit if Division C purchases the 1,000 components from outside suppliers at $135 per unit. Show your computations.

Problems

22-27 Pertinent transfer price. Europa, Inc., has two divisions, A and B, which manufacture expensive bicycles. Division A produces the bicycle frame, and Division B assembles the rest of the bicycle onto the frame. There is a market for both the subassembly and the final product. Each division has been designated as a profit center. The transfer price for the subassembly has been set at the long-run average market price. The following data are available for each division:

Selling price for final product	$300
Long-run average selling price for intermediate product	200
Incremental costs for completion in Division B	150
Incremental costs in Division A	120

The manager of Division B has made the following calculation:

Selling price for final product		$300
Transferred-in costs (market)	$200	
Incremental costs for completion	150	350
Contribution (loss) on product		$(50)

Required

1. Should transfers be made to Division B if there is no unused capacity in Division A? Is the market price the correct transfer price? Show your computations.
2. Assume that Division A's maximum capacity for this product is 1,000 units per month, and sales to the intermediate market are now 800 units. Should 200 units be transferred to Division B? At what transfer price? Assume that for a variety of reasons, Division A will maintain the $200 selling price indefinitely. That is, Division A is not considering lowering the price to outsiders even if idle capacity exists.

3. Suppose Division A quoted a transfer price of $150 for up to 200 units. What would be the contribution to the company as a whole if a transfer were made? As manager of Division B, would you be inclined to buy at $150? Explain.

22-28 Pricing in imperfect markets (continuation of 22-27). Refer to Problem 22-27.

Required

1. Suppose the manager of Division A has the option of (a) cutting the external price to $195, with the certainty that sales will rise to 1,000 units, or (b) maintaining the outside price of $200 for the 800 units and transferring the 200 units to Division B at a price that would produce the same operating income for Division A. What transfer price would produce the same operating income for Division A? Is that price consistent with that recommended by the general guideline in the chapter so that the desirable decision for the company as a whole would result?
2. Suppose that if the selling price for the intermediate product is dropped to $195, outside sales can be increased to 900 units. Division B wants to acquire as many as 200 units if the transfer price is acceptable. For simplicity, assume that there is no outside market for the final 100 units of Division A's capacity.
   a. Using the general guideline, what is (are) the minimum transfer price(s) that should lead to the correct economic decision? Ignore performance-evaluation considerations.
   b. Compare the total contributions under the alternatives to show why the transfer price(s) recommended lead(s) to the optimal economic decision.

22-29 Effect of alternative transfer-pricing methods on division operating income. Oceanic Products, a tuna fishing company, has two divisions:

a. Tuna Harvesting—operates a fleet of 20 trawling vessels.
b. Tuna Processing—processes the raw tuna into tuna fillets. Tuna fillets are sold to wholesale distributors at $5 per pound.

The Tuna Processing Division has a yield of 500 pounds of processed tuna fillets from 1,000 pounds of raw tuna provided by the Tuna Harvesting Division. Cost data for each division are as follows:

Tuna Harvesting Division		Tuna Processing Division	
Variable cost per pound of raw tuna	$0.20	Variable cost per pound of processed tuna	$0.80
Fixed cost per pound of raw tuna	$0.40	Fixed cost per pound of processed tuna	$0.60

Oceanic Products has chosen to process internally all raw tuna brought in by the Tuna Harvesting Division. Other tuna processors purchase raw tuna from boat operators at $1.00 per pound.

Required

1. Compute the overall operating income to Oceanic Products of harvesting 1,000 pounds of raw tuna and processing it into tuna fillets.
2. Compute the transfer prices that will be used for internal transfers from the Tuna Harvesting Division to the Tuna Processing Division under the following transfer-pricing methods:
   a. *150% of full costs.* Full costs are the costs of the division's own variable and fixed costs.
   b. *Market price.*
3. Oceanic rewards the division manager with a bonus, calculated as 10% of division operating income (if positive). What bonus will be paid to each division manager under the two transfer-pricing methods in requirement 2? Which transfer-pricing method will each division manager prefer to use?

22-30 Goal-congruence problems with cost-plus transfer-pricing methods, dual-pricing system (continuation of 22-29). Assume that Oceanic Products uses a transfer price of 150% of full cost. Pat Forgione decides to implement decentralization at Oceanic Products. A memorandum is sent to all division managers: "Starting immediately, each division of Oceanic Products is free to make its own decisions regarding the purchase of its direct materials and the sale of its finished product."

Required

1. Give two examples of goal-congruence problems that may arise if Oceanic were to continue to use the 150%-of-full-costs transfer-pricing method and a policy of decentralization is adopted.
2. Forgione is investigating whether a dual transfer-pricing policy will reduce goal-congruence problems at Oceanic Products. Transfers out of the Harvesting Division will be made at 150% of full costs. Transfers into the Processing Division will be made at market price. Using this dual transfer-pricing policy, compute the operating income of each division for a harvest of 1,000 pounds of raw tuna that is processed and marketed by Oceanic Products.
3. Compute the sum of the division operating incomes in requirement 2. Why might this sum not equal the overall corporate operating income from the harvesting of 1,000 pounds of raw tuna and its processing?
4. What problems may arise if Oceanic Products uses the dual transfer-pricing system described in requirement 2?

22-31 Multinational transfer pricing, global tax minimization. Industrial Diamonds, Inc., based in Los Angeles, has two divisions:

a. *Philippine Mining Division*—operates a mine in the Philippines containing a rich body of raw diamonds
b. *U.S. Processing Division*—processes the raw diamonds into polished diamonds used in industrial applications

The costs of the Philippine Mining Division are

- Variable cost, 4,000 pesos per pound of raw industrial diamonds
- Fixed cost, 8,000 pesos per pound of raw industrial diamonds

Industrial Diamonds has a corporate policy of further processing diamonds in Los Angeles. Several diamond-polishing companies in the Philippines buy raw diamonds from other local mining companies at 16,000 pesos per pound. Assume that the current foreign exchange rate is 40 pesos = $1 U.S. The costs of the U.S. Processing Division are

- Variable cost, $200 per pound of polished industrial diamonds
- Fixed cost, $600 per pound of polished industrial diamonds

Assume that it takes 2 pounds of raw industrial diamonds to yield 1 pound of polished industrial diamonds. Polished diamonds sell for $4,000 per pound.

Required

1. Compute the transfer price (in $U.S.) for 1 pound of raw industrial diamonds transferred from the Philippine Mining Division to the U.S. Processing Division under two methods: (a) 300% of full costs and (b) market price.
2. Assume a world of no income taxes. Also assume that 1,000 pounds of raw industrial diamonds are mined by the Philippine Division and then processed and sold by the U.S. Processing Division. Compute the operating income (in $U.S.) for each division of Industrial Diamonds under the two transfer-pricing methods in requirement 1.
3. Assume that the corporate income tax rate is 20% in the Philippines and 35% in the United States. Compute the after-tax operating income (in $U.S.) for each division under the transfer-pricing methods in requirement 1. (Income taxes are not included in the computation of the cost-based transfer price. Industrial Diamonds does not pay U.S. taxes on income already taxed in the Philippines.)
4. Which transfer-pricing method in requirement 1 will maximize the total after-tax operating income of Industrial Diamonds? Show your computations.
5. What factors, in addition to global tax minimization, might Industrial Diamonds consider in choosing a transfer-pricing method for transfers between its two divisions?

22-32 **Multinational transfer pricing and taxation.** (Richard Lambert, adapted) Anita Corporation, headquartered in the United States, manufactures state-of-the-art milling machines in the United States. It has two marketing subsidiaries, one in Brazil and one in Switzerland, that sell its products. Anita is building one new machine, at a cost of $500,000. There is no market for the equipment in the United States. The equipment can be sold in Brazil for $1,000,000, but the Brazilian subsidiary would incur transportation and modification costs of $200,000. Alternatively, the equipment can be sold in Switzerland for $950,000, but the Swiss subsidiary would incur transportation and modification costs of $250,000. The U.S. company can sell the equipment to either its Brazilian or its Swiss subsidiary, but not to both. The Anita Corporation and its subsidiary companies operate in a very decentralized manner. Managers in each company have considerable autonomy, with managers interested in maximizing their own company's income.

Required

1. From the viewpoint of Anita and its subsidiaries taken together, should the Anita Corporation manufacture the equipment? If it does, where should it sell the equipment to maximize total operating income? What would the operating income for Anita and its subsidiaries be from the sale? Ignore any income tax effects.
2. What range of transfer prices will result in achieving the actions determined to be optimal in requirement 1? Explain your answer.
3. The effective income tax rates are as follows: 40% in the United States, 60% in Brazil, and 15% in Switzerland. The tax authorities in the three countries are uncertain about the cost of the intermediate product and will allow any transfer price between $500,000 and $700,000. If Anita and its subsidiaries want to maximize after-tax operating income, (a) should the equipment be manufactured, and (b) where and at what price should it be transferred and sold? Show your computations.
4. Now suppose managers act autonomously to maximize their own subsidiary's after-tax operating income. The tax authorities will allow transfer prices only between $500,000 and $700,000. Which subsidiary will get the product and at what price? Is your answer the same as your answer in requirement 3? Explain why or why not.

22-33 **Transfer pricing, goal congruence**. The Sather Corporation manufactures and sells 10,000 boom boxes per year. The Assembly Division assembles the boom boxes. It buys the cassette deck for the boom box from the Cassette Deck Division. The Cassette Deck Division can manufacture at most 12,000 cassette decks. The demand for cassette decks is strong. Any cassette deck not sold to the Assembly Division can be sold in the outside market for $35 per unit. The Cassette Deck Division currently sells 10,000 cassette decks to the Assembly Division and 2,000 cassette decks in the outside market. The incremental cost of manufacturing the cassette deck is $25 per unit.

A crucial component for producing high-quality cassette decks is the (cassette) head mechanism. The Cassette Deck Division manufactures the head mechanism for its cassette decks. Many outside suppliers have offered to supply cassette decks to Sather. To ensure quality, Sather requires that any outside supplier wanting to supply cassette decks to Sather must purchase the head mechanism from the Cassette Deck

Division. The Cassette Deck Division will charge $18 per unit for the head mechanism. The incremental cost of manufacturing the head mechanism is $12 per unit out of the total incremental costs of $25 per unit to manufacture the cassette deck. The Cassette Deck Division has unused capacity for manufacturing the head mechanism. That is, even if the Cassette Deck Division manufactures the head mechanism for outside suppliers, it will still be able to manufacture 12,000 cassette decks for sale in the outside market at $35 per unit.

Johnson Corporation, an outside supplier, is currently negotiating to supply 10,000 cassette decks to the Assembly Division for a price in the range of $37 to $43. If Johnson gets the business, it will buy the head mechanism from the Cassette Deck Division for $18 per unit.

Required

Consider each question independently.

1. From the standpoint of Sather Corporation as a whole, should the Assembly Division accept Johnson Corporation's offer (a) at a price of $37 per cassette deck? (b) at a price of $43 per cassette deck? Show your computations.
2. What transfer price for cassette decks will result in the Cassette Deck Division and the Assembly Division taking actions that are optimal for Sather Corporation as a whole? Explain your answer.

22-34 Transfer pricing, utilization of capacity. (J. Patell, adapted) The California Instrument Company (CIC) consists of the Semiconductor Division and the Process-Control Division, each of which operates as an independent profit center. The Semiconductor Division employs craftsmen who produce two different electronic components, the new high-performance Super-chip and an older product called Okay-chip. These two products have the following cost characteristics:

	Super-chip	Okay-chip
Direct materials	$2	$1
Direct manufacturing labor 2 hours × $14; 0.5 hour × $14	28	7

Annual overhead in the Semiconductor Division totals $400,000, all fixed. Due to the high skill level necessary for the craftsmen, the Semiconductor Division's capacity is set at 50,000 hours per year.

One customer orders a maximum of 15,000 Super-chips per year, at a price of $60 per chip. If CIC cannot meet this entire demand, the customer curtails its own production. The rest of the Semiconductor Division's capacity is devoted to the Okay-chip, for which there is unlimited demand at $12 per chip.

The Process-Control Division produces only one product, a process-control unit, with the following cost structure:

- Direct materials (circuit board): $60
- Direct manufacturing labor (5 hours × $10): $50

Fixed overhead costs of the Process-Control Division are $80,000 per year. The current market price for the control unit is $132 per unit.

A joint research project has just revealed that a single Super-chip could be substituted for the circuit board currently used to make the process-control unit. Using Super-chip would require an extra one hour of labor per control unit for a new total of six hours per control unit.

Required

1. Calculate the contribution margin per hour of selling Super-chip and Okay-chip. If no transfers of Super-chip were made to the Process-Control Division, how many Super-chips and Okay-chips should the Semiconductor Division sell? Show your computations.
2. The Process-Control Division expects to sell 5,000 control units this year. From the viewpoint of California Instruments as a whole, should 5,000 Super-chips be transferred to the Process-Control Division to replace circuit boards? Show your computations.
3. If demand for the control unit is certain to be 5,000 units but its *price is uncertain,* what should the transfer price of Super-chip be to ensure that the division managers' actions maximize operating income for CIC as a whole? (All other data are unchanged.)
4. If demand for the control unit is certain to be 12,000 units, but its *price is uncertain,* what should the transfer price of Super-chip be to ensure that the division managers' actions maximize operating income for CIC as a whole? (All other data are unchanged.)

22-35 Ethics, transfer pricing. The Belmont Division of Durham Industries manufactures component R47, which it transfers to the Alston Division at 200% of variable costs. The variable cost of R47 is $14 per unit. Joe Lasker, the management accountant of the Belmont Division, calls Hal Tanner, his assistant, into his office. Lasker says, "I am not sure about the fixed- and variable-cost distinctions you are making. I think the variable cost is higher than $14 per unit."

Tanner knows that showing higher variable costs will increase the Belmont Division's profits and lead to higher bonuses for the division employees. However, Tanner is uncomfortable about making any changes because he has used the same method to classify costs as either variable or fixed over the last few years. Nevertheless, Tanner recognizes that fixed- and variable-cost distinctions are not always clear-cut.

Required

1. Calculate Belmont Division's contribution margin from transferring 10,000 units of R47 in 2001 (a) if variable cost is $14 per unit, and (b) if variable cost is $16 per unit.
2. Evaluate whether Lasker's suggestion to Tanner regarding variable costs is ethical. Would it be ethical for Tanner to revise the variable cost per unit? What steps should Tanner take to resolve this situation?

Collaborative Learning Problem

22-36 Goal congruence, income taxes, different market conditions. The San Ramon Corporation makes water pumps. The Engine Division makes the engines and supplies them to the Assembly Division, where the pumps are assembled. San Ramon is a successful and profitable corporation that attributes much of its success to its decentralized operating style. Each division manager is compensated on the basis of division operating income.

The Assembly Division currently acquires all its engines from the Engine Division. The Assembly Division manager could purchase similar engines in the market for $400 each.

The Engine Division is currently operating at 80% of its capacity of 4,000 units and has the following costs:

Direct materials ($125 per unit × 3,200 units)	$400,000
Direct manufacturing labor ($50 per unit × 3,200 units)	160,000
Variable manufacturing overhead costs ($25 per unit × 3,200 units)	80,000
Fixed manufacturing overhead costs	520,000

All the Engine Division's 3,200 units are currently transferred to the Assembly Division. No engines are sold in the outside market.

The Engine Division has just received an order for 2,000 units at $375 per engine that would utilize half the capacity of the plant. The order must either be taken in full or rejected. The order is for a slightly different engine than what the Engine Division currently makes, but it takes the same amount of manufacturing time. To produce the new engine would require direct materials per unit of $100, direct manufacturing labor per unit of $40, and variable manufacturing overhead costs per unit of $25.

Required

1. From the viewpoint of the San Ramon Corporation as a whole, should the Engine Division accept the order for the 2,000 units? Show your computations.
2. What range of transfer prices will result in achieving the actions determined to be optimal in requirement 1 if division managers act in a decentralized manner?
3. The manager of the Assembly Division has proposed a transfer price for the engines equal to the full costs of the engines, including an allocation of overhead costs. The Engine Division allocates overhead costs to engines on the basis of the total capacity of the plant used to manufacture the engines.
   a. Calculate the transfer price for the engines transferred to the Assembly Division under this arrangement.
   b. Do you think that the transfer price calculated in requirement 3a will result in achieving the actions determined to be optimal in requirement 1 if division managers act in a decentralized manner?
   c. Comment in general on one advantage and one disadvantage of using full costs of the producing division as the basis for setting transfer prices.
4. Now consider the effect of income taxes.
   a. Suppose the Assembly Division is located in a state that imposes a 10% tax on income earned within its boundaries, and the Engine Division is located in a state that imposes no tax on income earned within its boundaries. What transfer price would be chosen by the San Ramon Corporation to minimize state income tax payments for the corporation as a whole? Assume that only transfer prices that are greater than or equal to full manufacturing costs and less than or equal to the market price of "substantially similar" engines are acceptable to the tax authorities.
   b. Suppose that the San Ramon Corporation announces the transfer price computed in requirement 4a to price all transfers between the Engine and Assembly divisions. Each division manager then acts autonomously to maximize division operating income. Will division managers acting in a decentralized manner achieve the actions determined to be optimal in requirement 1? Explain.
5. Consider your responses to requirements 1 through 4 and assume the Engine Division will continue to have opportunities for outside business as described in requirement 1. What transfer-pricing policy would you recommend San Ramon use, and why? Would you continue to evaluate division performance on the basis of division operating incomes? Explain.

CHAPTER 22 INTERNET EXERCISE

Due to the rapid growth in e-commerce and cross-border intercompany transactions, transfer pricing is becoming increasingly important. In fact, it may be one of the most important tax issues facing multinational corporations today. To learn more, go to www.prenhall.com/horngren, click on *Cost Accounting,* 11th ed., and access the Internet exercise for Chapter 22.

INFORMATION SYSTEMS CORPORATION: Transfer Prices and Goal Congruence

Information Systems Corporation (ISC) makes computer systems and has high interdependence among its profit centers. Interdivisional transfers are made at full cost plus a profit margin.

The semiconductor division produces random access memories (RAMs) for ultimate consumption by several product divisions. For approximately 75% to 80% of the plant's total annual output, product divisions can purchase RAMs either from the semiconductor division or from outside suppliers in the United States and abroad. The remainder of the plant's annual output (20% to 25%) is comprised of unique, proprietary logic modules and chips used in selected products. These modules and chips can only be purchased from the semiconductor division.

Until five years ago, the semiconductor division supplied all the company's requirements for RAMs. But five years ago it was necessary, despite continued plant expansion, to purchase RAMs from outside suppliers to meet demand. Non-U.S. companies entered the U.S. market with high-quality products and aggressive pricing. In a short time, market prices for many products were at or below the semiconductor division's costs.

The manager of each product division is evaluated as a profit center. Product division managers have considerable autonomy in choosing where to buy the components they use in their products. Not surprisingly, these managers began purchasing components from outside vendors rather than pay more for the higher-cost RAMs produced internally by the semiconductor division.

The semiconductor division has idle capacity. Manufacturing costs are primarily fixed. As production decreased, these fixed costs were spread over fewer production units, resulting in higher costs and transfer prices for RAMs. In response, more product division managers sought outside suppliers, and so it went.

The semiconductor division began to focus on cutting its fixed costs to remain cost competitive. It began to increase productivity significantly, reduce indirect human resources, and control spending. The plan was to reduce its cost of RAMs from $25 to around $10 over a three-year period.

This plan would be difficult to achieve if the demand for RAMs produced by the semiconductor division declined or if the planned cuts in fixed costs were not made. In this case, the higher cost per RAM would be passed along to the product divisions when the RAMs are transferred at actual cost. In committing to buy RAMs from the semiconductor division, a product division manager did not have any guarantee that the cost and price would not increase later if planned volumes did not materialize or if the plant was unable to meet its cost objectives.

The semiconductor division manager, recognizing this dilemma, asked the financial staff to recommend a different system for interdivisional transfers. He wanted this new system, at a minimum, to convey to its internal customers the steps the division was taking on cost control and productivity and to indicate a commitment to lower prices.

The financial staff noted that many outside vendors did forward pricing—that is, they set prices not on the basis of current costs but rather on the basis of what they expected future costs to be. The prices that vendors offered were firm commitments, regardless of their own costs to produce RAMs. The prices and margins did, of course, vary with the type of RAM (lower for standard products and higher for specialized products).

QUESTIONS

1. Why are the plant's costs for semiconductors higher than competitors' market prices?
2. What alternatives could the controller recommend to the general manager for interdivisional transfers?
3. What would you recommend as an appropriate transfer-pricing method?

CHAPTER

23

Performance Measurement, Compensation, and Multinational Considerations

LEARNING OBJECTIVES

1. Measure performance from a financial and a nonfinancial perspective
2. Design an accounting-based performance measure
3. Analyze return on investment (ROI) using the DuPont method
4. Use the residual-income (RI) measure and understand its advantages
5. Describe the economic value added (EVA®) method
6. Contrast current-cost and historical-cost asset measurement methods
7. Indicate the difficulties when comparing the performance of divisions operating in different countries
8. Understand the role of salaries and incentives when rewarding managers
9. Describe the management accountant's role in helping organizations design better incentive systems

www.prenhall.com/horngren

At the end of this school term, you're going to receive a grade that represents a measure of your performance in this course. Your grade may consist of numerous elements—homework, quizzes, exams, and perhaps class participation. Some of these are objective and easily measured; others are subjective, relying on your professor's insights about your contribution. In many ways, corporations go through a similar "grading" process. Performance is measured regularly along financial and nonfinancial perspectives.

McDonald's, one of the world's largest restaurant operations, uses a variety of performance measures that align with its financial goals. Managers participate in setting the performance targets and then receive regular feedback on how they're doing. The company advertises that its employees "love to see you smile." Perhaps as important as customer smiles are the smiles from employees who have met or exceeded expectations.

We have discussed performance measurement in many earlier chapters, each time within a specific accounting context. Chapter 11 described a situation in which the correct decision based on a relevant-cost analysis (buying new equipment) might not be implemented because a performance measurement system induced the manager to make some other decision. This chapter discusses more generally the design, implementation, and uses of performance measures.

Measuring performance is an integral part of any management control system. Making strategic planning and control decisions requires information about how different subunits of the organization have performed. To be effective, performance measures (both financial and nonfinancial) and rewards must motivate managers and employees at all levels to strive to achieve company strategies and goals.

1 Measure performance from a financial perspective
...return on investment, residual income
and a nonfinancial perspective
...customer satisfaction ratings, number of defects

FINANCIAL AND NONFINANCIAL PERFORMANCE MEASURES

Many performance measures, such as operating income, rely on internal financial information. Increasingly, companies are supplementing internal financial measures with measures based on (a) external financial information (such as stock prices), (b) internal nonfinancial information (such as defect rates, manufacturing lead times, and number of new patents), and (c) external nonfinancial information (such as customer satisfaction ratings and market share). These measures are all often benchmarked against other subunits within the company and other companies.

Some organizations present financial and nonfinancial performance measures for their subunits in a single report called the *balanced scorecard* (Chapter 13, p. 449). Different organizations stress different elements in their scorecards, but most scorecards include (1) profitability measures; (2) customer-satisfaction measures; (3) internal measures of efficiency, quality, and time; and (4) innovation measures.[1] Companies (for example, ExxonMobil and Citibank) use balanced scorecard measures to evaluate the performance of subunits and subunit managers.

Some performance measures, such as the number of new patents developed, have a long time horizon. Other measures, such as direct materials efficiency variances and overhead spending variances, have a short time horizon. In this chapter, we focus on the most widely used performance measures for organization subunits covering an intermediate to long time horizon. These are internal financial measures based on accounting numbers routinely reported by organizations.

Designing such accounting-based performance measures requires six steps:

2 Design an accounting-based performance measure
...to align with top management's goals, measure subunit performance, and motivate managers

Step 1: Choose Performance Measures That Align with Top Management's Financial Goals. For example, is operating income, net income, return on assets, or revenues the best measure of a subunit's financial performance?

[1] See R. Kaplan and D. Norton, *The Balanced Scorecard* (Boston: Harvard Business School Press, 1996); and S. Hronec, *Vital Signs* (New York: American Management Association, 1993).

Step 2: Choose the Time Horizon of Each Performance Measure in Step 1. For example, should performance measures, such as return on assets, be calculated for one year or for a multiyear horizon?

Step 3: Choose a Definition of the Components in Each Performance Measure in Step 1. For example, should assets be defined as total assets or net assets (total assets minus total liabilities)?

Step 4: Choose a Measurement Alternative for Each Performance Measure in Step 1. For example, should assets be measured at historical cost or current cost?

Step 5: Choose a Target Level of Performance. For example, should all subunits have identical targets, such as the same required rate of return on assets?

Step 6: Choose the Timing of Feedback. For example, should manufacturing performance reports be sent to top management daily, weekly, or monthly?

These six steps need not be done sequentially. The issues considered in each step are interdependent, and top management will often proceed through these steps several times before deciding on one or more accounting-based performance measures. The answers to the questions raised at each step depend on top management's beliefs about how well each alternative measure fulfills the behavioral criteria of goal congruence, management effort, subunit performance evaluation, and subunit autonomy discussed in Chapter 22.

CHOOSING AMONG DIFFERENT PERFORMANCE MEASURES: STEP 1

Four measures are commonly used to evaluate the economic performance of company subunits. We illustrate these measures through Hospitality Inns.

Hospitality Inns owns and operates three hotels—one each in San Francisco, Chicago, and New Orleans. Exhibit 23-1 summarizes data for each hotel for the most recent year, 2003. At present, Hospitality Inns does not allocate the total long-term debt of the company to the three separate hotels. The exhibit indicates that the New Orleans hotel generates the highest operating income, $510,000, compared with Chicago's $300,000 and San Francisco's $240,000. But does this comparison mean the New Orleans hotel is the most "successful"? The main weakness of comparing operating

EXHIBIT 23-1 Annual Financial Data for Hospitality Inns for 2003 (in Thousands)

	San Francisco Hotel (1)	Chicago Hotel (2)	New Orleans Hotel (3)	Total (4) = (1) + (2) + (3)
Hotel revenues	$1,200,000	$1,400,000	$3,185,000	$5,785,000
Hotel variable costs	310,000	375,000	995,000	1,680,000
Hotel fixed costs	650,000	725,000	1,680,000	3,055,000
Hotel operating income	$ 240,000	$ 300,000	$ 510,000	1,050,000
Interest costs on long-term debt at 10%	—	—	—	450,000
Income before income taxes	—	—	—	600,000
Income taxes at 30%	—	—	—	180,000
Net income	—	—	—	$ 420,000
Net book values for 2003:				
Current assets	$ 400,000	$ 500,000	$ 660,000	$1,560,000
Long-term assets	600,000	1,500,000	2,340,000	4,440,000
Total assets	$1,000,000	$2,000,000	$3,000,000	$6,000,000
Current liabilities	$ 50,000	$ 150,000	$ 300,000	$ 500,000
Long-term debt	—	—	—	4,500,000
Stockholders' equity	—	—	—	1,000,000
Total liabilities and stockholders' equity				$6,000,000

incomes alone is ignoring differences in *the size of the investment* in each hotel. **Investment** refers to the resources or assets used to generate income. The question is not, How large is operating income? But, How large is operating income in relation to the investment made to earn it?

Three of the approaches to measuring performance include a measure of investment: return on investment, residual income, and economic value added. A fourth approach, return on sales, does not measure investment.

3 Analyze return on investment (ROI) using the DuPont method

...by calculating return on sales and investment turnover

Return on Investment

Return on investment (ROI) is an accounting measure of income divided by an accounting measure of investment.

$$\text{Return on investment (ROI)} = \frac{\text{Income}}{\text{Investment}}$$

Return on investment is the most popular approach to measure performance. ROI is popular for two reasons: it blends all the ingredients of profitability—revenues, costs, and investment—into a single percentage; and it can be compared with the rate of return on opportunities elsewhere, inside or outside the company. Like any single performance measure, however, ROI should be used cautiously and in conjunction with other measures.

ROI is also called the *accounting rate of return* or the *accrual accounting rate of return* (Chapter 21, p. 726). Managers usually use the term ROI when evaluating the performance of a division or subunit, and the term accrual accounting rate of return when an ROI measure is used to evaluate a project. Companies vary in the way they define what goes in income in the numerator and in investment in the denominator of the ROI calculation. Some companies use operating income for the numerator; others prefer to calculate ROI on an after-tax basis and use net income. Some companies use total assets in the denominator, others prefer to focus only on those assets financed by long-term debt and equity and use total assets minus current liabilities.

Hospitality Inns can increase ROI by increasing revenues or decreasing costs (each of which increases the numerator), or by decreasing investment (which decreases the denominator). ROI can provide more insight into performance when it is represented as its components:

$$\frac{\text{Income}}{\text{Investment}} = \frac{\text{Income}}{\text{Revenues}} \times \frac{\text{Revenues}}{\text{Investment}}$$

also written as,

$$\text{ROI} = \text{Return on sales} \times \text{Investment turnover}$$

ROI tells how much income each dollar of investment generates. The intuition behind the two ROI components: (1) Return on sales tells how much of each revenue dollar becomes income; the goal is to get higher income per revenue dollar. (2) Investment turnover tells how many revenue dollars are generated by each dollar of investment; the goal is to make each investment dollar "work harder" to generate more revenues.

This approach is known as the *DuPont method of profitability analysis*. The DuPont method recognizes the two basic ingredients in profit-making: increasing income per dollar of revenues and using assets to generate more revenues. An improvement in either ingredient without changing the other increases ROI.

Consider the ROIs of each of the three Hospitality hotels in Exhibit 23-1. For our calculations, we use the operating income of each hotel for the numerator and total assets of each hotel for the denominator.

Hotel	Operating Income	÷	Total Assets	=	ROI
San Francisco	$240,000	÷	$1,000,000	=	24%
Chicago	300,000	÷	2,000,000	=	15%
New Orleans	510,000	÷	3,000,000	=	17%

Using these ROI figures, the San Francisco hotel appears to make the best use of its total assets.

Assume that top management at Hospitality Inns adopts a 30% target ROI for the San Francisco hotel. How can this return be attained? We illustrate the DuPont method for the San Francisco hotel and show how this method can be used to describe three alternative ways in which the San Francisco hotel can increase its ROI from 24% to 30%.

Other alternatives, such as increasing the selling price per room, could increase both the revenues per dollar of total assets and the operating income per dollar of revenues.

	$\frac{\textbf{Operating Income}}{\textbf{Revenues}} \times \frac{\textbf{Revenue}}{\textbf{Total Assets}} = \frac{\textbf{Operating Income}}{\textbf{Total Assets}}$
Current ROI	$\frac{\$240,000}{\$1,200,000} \times \frac{\$1,200,000}{\$1,000,000} = 0.20 \times 1.20 = 0.24 \text{ or } 24\%$
Alternative	
A. Decrease assets (such as receivables), keeping revenues and operating income per dollar of revenue constant.	$\frac{\$240,000}{\$1,200,000} \times \frac{\$1,200,000}{\$800,000} = 0.20 \times 1.50 = 0.30 \text{ or } 30\%$
B. Increase revenues (via a higher occupancy rate), keeping assets and operating income per dollar of revenues constant.	$\frac{\$300,000}{\$1,500,000} \times \frac{\$1,500,000}{\$1,000,000} = 0.20 \times 1.50 = 0.30 \text{ or } 30\%$
C. Decrease costs (via, say, efficient maintenance) to increase operating income per dollar of revenues, keeping revenues and assets constant.	$\frac{\$300,000}{\$1,200,000} \times \frac{\$1,200,000}{\$1,000,000} = 0.25 \times 1.20 = 0.30 \text{ or } 30\%$

ROI makes clear the benefits that managers can obtain by reducing their investment in current or long-term assets. Some managers are conscious of the need to boost revenues or to control costs, but they pay less attention to reducing their investment base. Reducing the investment base means decreasing idle cash, managing credit judiciously, determining proper inventory levels, and spending carefully on long-term assets.

Residual Income

4 Use the residual income (RI) measure
...income minus a dollar amount for required return on investment
and recognize its advantages
...motivates managers to act in the best interest of the company

Residual income (RI) is an accounting measure of income minus a dollar amount for required return on an accounting measure of investment.

$$\text{Residual income (RI)} = \text{Income} - (\text{Required rate of return} \times \text{Investment})$$

Required rate of return multiplied by the investment is the *imputed cost of the investment.* **Imputed costs** are costs recognized in particular situations that are not usually recognized in financial accounting systems.

Suppose Hospitality Inns' investments are financed 50% by long-term debt and 50% by equity. Long-term debt carries an interest cost of 10% per year that is recorded in Hospitality Inn's books under accrual accounting procedures. Hospitality Inns' equity carries a cost of 14% per year. This 14% represents the opportunity cost to equity investors of investing in Hospitality Inns—the return forgone by not investing in other equity securities of similar risk. The cost of equity, like all opportunity costs, is not recorded in Hospitality Inns' financial accounting system. It is an imputed cost that is, nevertheless, a real economic cost of the amount of investment financed by equity. The weighted-average cost of capital for investments in Hospitality Inns is 50% × cost of debt + 50% × cost of equity = 0.50 × 10% + 0.50 × 14% = 5% + 7% = 12%. This is the required rate of return used when calculating RI for Hospitality Inns. A large component of this required rate of return is an imputed cost.

Question: What required rate of return should management use to compute residual income?
Answer: The cost of capital. Conceptually, it should be the cost of capital based on each division's risk level. For example, an oil exploration division would warrant a higher required rate of return than an oil refining division.

Assume each hotel faces similar risks. Hospitality Inns defines residual income for each hotel as a hotel's operating income minus the required rate of return of 12% of the total assets of the hotel:

Hotel	Operating Income	−	Required Rate of Return	×	Investment	=	Residual Income
San Francisco	$240,000	−	$120,000 (0.12	×	$1,000,000)	=	$120,000
Chicago	$300,000	−	$240,000 (0.12	×	$2,000,000)	=	$ 60,000
New Orleans	$510,000	−	$360,000 (0.12	×	$3,000,000)	=	$150,000

Companies using RI vary in the way they define income (for example, operating income or net income) and investment (for example, total assets or total assets minus current liabilities).

Given the 12% required annual rate of return, the New Orleans hotel has the best RI.

Some companies favor the RI measure because managers will concentrate on maximizing an absolute amount, such as dollars of RI, rather than a percentage, such as ROI. The objective of maximizing RI means that as long as a subunit earns a return in excess of the required return for investments, that subunit should expand.

Generally, RI is more likely than ROI to induce goal congruence. This preference for RI over ROI parallels the preference for net present value over internal rate of return in capital budgeting.

The objective of maximizing ROI may induce managers of highly profitable subunits to reject projects that, from the viewpoint of the company as a whole, should be accepted. Suppose Hospitality Inns is considering upgrading room features and furnishings at the San Francisco hotel. The upgrade will increase operating income of the San Francisco hotel by \$70,000 and increase its total assets by \$400,000. The ROI for the expansion is 17.5% (\$70,000 ÷ \$400,000), which is attractive to Hospitality Inns because it exceeds the required rate of return. By making this expansion, however, the San Francisco hotel's ROI will decrease:

$$\text{Pre-upgrade ROI} = \frac{\$240{,}000}{\$1{,}000{,}000} = 0.24, \text{ or } 24\%$$

$$\text{Post-upgrade ROI} = \frac{\$240{,}000 + \$70{,}000}{\$1{,}000{,}000 + \$400{,}000} = \frac{\$310{,}000}{\$1{,}400{,}000} = 0.221, \text{ or } 22.1\%$$

The annual bonus paid to the San Francisco manager may decrease if ROI affects the bonus calculation and the upgrading option is selected. Consequently, the manager may not look upon the expansion favorably. In contrast, if the annual bonus is a function of RI, the San Francisco manager will view the expansion favorably:

$$\text{Pre-upgrade RI} = \$240{,}000 - (0.12 \times \$1{,}000{,}000) = \$120{,}000$$

$$\text{Post-upgrade RI} = \$310{,}000 - (0.12 \times \$1{,}400{,}000) = \$142{,}000$$

Goal congruence (ensuring that subunit managers work toward achieving the company's goals) is more likely to be achieved by using RI rather than ROI as a measure of the subunit manager's performance.

5 Describe the economic value added (EVA®) method

...a variation of residual income using after-tax amounts

Economic Value Added[2]

Economic value added is a specific type of residual income calculation that has recently attracted considerable attention. **Economic value added (EVA®)** equals after-tax operating income *minus* the (after-tax) weighted-average cost of capital *multiplied* by total assets minus current liabilities.

$$\text{Economic value added (EVA}^{\circledR}) = \text{After-tax operating income} - \left[\text{Weighted-average cost of capital} \times \left(\text{Total assets} - \text{Current liabilities}\right)\right]$$

EVA® substitutes the following numbers in the RI calculations: (1) income equal to after-tax operating income, (2) a required rate of return equal to the (after-tax) weighted-average cost of capital, and (3) investment equal to total assets minus current liabilities.[3]

We use the Hospitality Inns data in Exhibit 23-1 to illustrate the basic EVA® calculations. The weighted-average cost of capital (WACC) equals *after-tax* average cost of all the long-term funds used by Hospitality Inns. The company has two sources of long-term funds: (a) long-term debt with a market value and book value of \$4.5 million issued at an interest rate of 10%, and (b) equity capital that also has a market value of \$4.5 million (but a book value of \$1 million).[4] Because interest costs are

[2]S. O'Byrne and D. Young, *EVA and Value-Based Management: A Practical Guide to Implementation* (New York: McGraw-Hill, 2000); J. Stein, J. Shiely, and I. Ross, *The EVA Challenge: Implementing Value Added Change in an Organization,* (New York: John Wiley and Sons, 2001).

[3]When implementing EVA®, companies make several adjustments to the operating income and asset numbers reported under generally accepted accounting principles (GAAP). For example, when calculating EVA®, costs such as R&D, restructuring costs, and leases that have long-run benefits are recorded as assets (which are then amortized), rather than as current operating costs. The goal of these adjustments is to obtain a better representation of the economic assets, particularly intangible assets, used to earn income. Naturally, the specific adjustments applicable to a company will depend on its individual circumstances.

[4]The market value of Hospitality Inns' equity exceeds book value because book values, based on historical costs, do not measure the current values of the company's assets and because various intangible assets, such as the company's brand name, are not shown at current value in the balance sheet under GAAP.

tax-deductible and the income tax rate is 30%, the after-tax cost of debt financing is $0.10 \times (1 - \text{Tax rate}) = 0.10 \times (1 - 0.30) = 0.10 \times 0.70 = 0.07$, or 7%. The cost of equity capital is the opportunity cost to investors of not investing their capital in another investment that is similar in risk to Hospitality Inns. Hospitality's cost of equity capital is 14%.[5] The WACC computation, which uses market values of debt and equity, is

Finance courses explain the calculation of WACC in greater detail.

$$\text{WACC} = \frac{(7\% \times \text{Market value of debt}) + (14\% \times \text{Market value of equity})}{\text{Market value of debt} + \text{Market value of equity}}$$
$$= \frac{(0.07 \times \$4{,}500{,}000) + (0.14 \times \$4{,}500{,}000)}{\$4{,}500{,}000 + \$4{,}500{,}000}$$
$$= \frac{\$945{,}000}{\$9{,}000{,}000} = 0.105, \text{ or } 10.5\%$$

The company applies the same WACC to all its hotels because each hotel faces similar risks.

Total assets minus current liabilities (see Exhibit 23-1) can also be computed as:

$$\text{Total assets} - \text{Current liabilities} = \text{Long-term assets} + \text{Current assets} - \text{Current liabilities}$$
$$= \text{Long-term assets} + \text{Working capital}$$

where working capital = current assets − current liabilities.

After-tax hotel operating income is

$$\text{Hotel operating income} \times (1 - \text{Tax rate}) = \text{Hotel operating income} \times (1 - 0.30) = \text{Hotel operating income} \times 0.70$$

EVA® calculations for Hospitality Inns are as follows:

Hotel	After-Tax Operating Income	−	[Weighted-Average Cost of Capital	× (Total Assets − Current Liabilities)]	=	Economic Value Added (EVA®)
San Francisco	$240,000 × 0.7	−	[0.105	× ($1,000,000 − $ 50,000)]	=	$168,000 − $ 99,750 = $68,250
Chicago	$300,000 × 0.7	−	[0.105	× ($2,000,000 − $150,000)]	=	$210,000 − $194,250 = $15,750
New Orleans	$510,000 × 0.7	−	[0.105	× ($3,000,000 − $300,000)]	=	$357,000 − $283,500 = $73,500

The New Orleans hotel has the highest EVA®. Economic value added, like residual income, charges managers for the cost of their investments in long-term assets and working capital. Value is created only if after-tax operating income exceeds the cost of investing the capital. To improve EVA®, managers must (a) earn more after-tax operating income with the same capital, (b) use less capital to earn the same after-tax operating income, or (c) invest capital in high-return projects.

Managers in companies such as Briggs and Stratton, Coca-Cola, CSX, Equifax, and FMC use the estimated impact on EVA® to guide their decisions. Division managers find EVA® helpful because it allows them to incorporate into decisions at the division level the cost of capital, which is generally only available at the companywide level. Comparing the actual EVA® achieved to the estimated EVA® is useful for evaluating performance and providing feedback to managers about performance. CSX, a railroad company, credits EVA® for decisions such as running trains with three locomotives instead of four and scheduling arrivals just in time for unloading rather than having trains arrive at their destination several hours in advance. The result? Higher income because of lower fuel costs and lower capital investments in locomotives.

Return on Sales

The income-to-revenues (or sales) ratio—often called *return on sales* (*ROS*)—is a frequently used financial performance measure. ROS is one component of ROI in the DuPont method of profitability analysis. To calculate ROS for each of Hospitality's hotels, we use operating income divided by revenues:

[5]For details on calculating cost of equity capital adjusted for risk, see J. Van Horne, *Financial Management and Policy*, 12th ed. (Upper Saddle River, NJ: Prentice Hall, 2002).

Hotel	Operating Income	÷	Revenues (Sales)	=	Return on Sales (ROS)
San Francisco	$240,000	÷	$1,200,000	=	0.200, or 20.0%
Chicago	$300,000	÷	$1,400,000	=	0.214, or 21.4%
New Orleans	$510,000	÷	$3,185,000	=	0.160, or 16.0%

The Chicago hotel has the highest ROS, but its performance is rated worse than the other hotels using measures such as ROI, RI, and EVA®.

Comparing Performance Measures

The following table summarizes the performance and ranks (in parentheses) of each hotel under the four performance measures:

Hotel	ROI	RI	EVA®	ROS
San Francisco	24% (1)	$120,000 (2)	$68,250 (2)	20.0% (2)
Chicago	15% (3)	$ 60,000 (3)	$15,750 (3)	21.4% (1)
New Orleans	17% (2)	$150,000 (1)	$73,500 (1)	16.0% (3)

The RI and EVA® rankings are the same. They differ from the ROI and ROS rankings. Consider the ROI and RI rankings for the San Francisco and New Orleans hotels. The New Orleans hotel has a smaller ROI. Although its operating income is only slightly

SURVEYS OF COMPANY PRACTICE

Examples of Key Financial Performance Measures in Different Companies Around the Globe[a]

Surveys indicate extensive use of net income as a performance measure and reliance on multiple measures.[b] The percentage of the largest U.S. firms that view specific financial performance measures as most important follow: income in comparison with budget, 49%; return on investment, 29%; economic value added, 14%; return on sales, 3%; other measures, 5%.[c] When comparing U.S. and Japanese companies, it appears that U.S. companies favor ROI (or EVA®) over ROS, whereas Japanese companies use ROS more than ROI.[d] Some researchers speculate that Japanese managers favor ROS because it is easier to calculate and because achieving a sufficient sales margin is likely to benefit ROI sooner or later. Deemphasizing ROI has other advantages. For example, managers are not induced to delay investment in facilities or equipment because of the negative effects it might have on ROI in the short run. The following table presents representative examples of financial measures used in different countries.

Company	Country Headquarters	Product/Business	Key Financial Performance Measures
Ford Motor	U.S.	Automotive	Income, ROS, and ROI
Quaker Oats	U.S.	Food products	Income, RI, EVA®
Guinness	U.K.	Consumer products	Income, ROS
Krones	Germany	Machinery/equipment	Revenues, income
Mayne Nickless	Australia	Security/transportation	ROI and ROS
Mitsui	Japan	Trading	Revenues, income
Pirelli	Italy	Tires/manufacturing	Income, cash flow
Swedish Match	Sweden	Consumer products	ROI

[a]Adapted from R. Schlank, "Evaluating the Performance"; Business International Corporation, "101 More Checklists"; and G. B. Stewart, "EVA®, Fact and Fantasy."

[b]S. Kalagnanam, "The Use of Nonfinancial"; K. Yasukata, "A survey of."

[c]R. Tang, "Transfer Pricing."

[d]K. Smith and C. Sullivan, "Survey of Cost Management"; P. Scarbrough, A. Nanni, and M. Sakurai, "Japanese Management Accounting." Full citations are in Appendix A at the end of the book.

more than twice the operating income of the San Francisco hotel—$510,000 versus $240,000—its total assets are three times as large—$3 million versus $1 million. The New Orleans hotel has a higher RI because it earns a higher income after covering the 12% required return on investment. The Chicago hotel has the highest ROS but the lowest ROI. That's because, although it earns very high income per dollar of revenues, it generates very low revenues per dollar of assets invested. Is any one method better than the others for measuring performance? No, because each evaluates a different aspect of performance. For example, in markets in which revenue growth is limited and investment levels are fixed, ROS is the most meaningful indicator of a subunit's performance.

To evaluate overall aggregate performance, ROI, RI, or EVA® measures are more appropriate than ROS because they consider both income earned and investments made. ROI indicates which investment yields the highest return. RI and EVA® measures overcome some of the goal-congruence problems of ROI. Some managers favor EVA® because it explicitly considers tax effects and pre-tax RI measures do not. Other managers favor pre-tax RI because it is easier to compute and because, in most cases, it leads to the same conclusions as EVA®. The Surveys of Company Practice (p. 792) indicate that, generally, companies use multiple financial measures to evaluate performance.

CHOOSING THE TIME HORIZON OF THE PERFORMANCE MEASURES: STEP 2

Step 2 of designing accounting-based performance measures is choosing the time horizon of the performance measures. The ROI, RI, EVA®, and ROS calculations represent the results for a single period, one year in our example. Managers could take actions that cause short-run increases in these measures but conflict with the long-run interest of the company. For example, managers may curtail R&D and plant maintenance in the last three months of a fiscal year to achieve a target level of annual operating income. For this reason, many companies evaluate subunits on the basis of ROI, RI, EVA®, and ROS over multiple years.

Another reason to evaluate subunits over a multiyear horizon is that the benefits of actions taken in the current period may not show up in short-run performance measures, such as the current year's ROI or RI. For example, the investment in a new hotel may adversely affect ROI and RI in the short run but benefit ROI and RI in the long-run.

A multiyear analysis highlights another advantage of the RI measure: The net present value of all the cash flows over the life of an investment equals the net present value of the RIs.[6] This characteristic means that if managers use the net present value method to make investment decisions (as prescribed in Chapter 21), then using multiyear RI to evaluate managers' performances achieves goal congruence.

Another way to motivate managers to take a long-run perspective is by compensating them on the basis of changes in the market price of the company's stock. This extends managers' time horizons because stock prices more rapidly incorporate the expected future effects of current decisions.

[6] We are grateful to S. Reichelstein for pointing out this equality. To see the equivalence, suppose the $400,000 investment in the San Francisco hotel increases operating income by $70,000 per year as follows: Increase in operating cash flows of $150,000 each year for five years minus depreciation of $80,000 ($400,000 ÷ 5) per year, assuming straight-line depreciation and $0 terminal disposal value. Depreciation reduces the investment amount by $80,000 each year. Assuming a required rate of return of 12%, net present values of cash flows and residual incomes are as follows:

Year	0	1	2	3	4	5	Net Present Value
(1) After-tax cash flow	–$400,000	$150,000	$150,000	$150,000	$150,000	$150,000	
(2) Present value of $1 discounted at 12%	1	0.89286	0.79719	0.71178	0.63552	0.56743	
(3) Present value: (1) × (2)	–$400,000	$133,929	$119,578	$106,767	$ 95,328	$ 85,114	$140,716
(4) Operating income		$ 70,000	$ 70,000	$ 70,000	$ 70,000	$ 70,000	
(5) Assets at start of year		$400,000	$320,000	$240,000	$160,000	$ 80,000	
(6) Capital charge: (5) × 12%		$ 48,000	$ 38,400	$ 28,800	$ 19,200	$ 9,600	
(7) Residual income: (4) – (6)		$ 22,000	$ 31,600	$ 41,200	$ 50,800	$ 60,400	
(8) Present value of RI: (7) × (2)		$ 19,643	$ 25,191	$ 29,325	$ 32,284	$ 34,273	$140,716

CHOOSING ALTERNATIVE DEFINITIONS FOR PERFORMANCE MEASURES: STEP 3

Distinguish step 3 from step 4. Step 3 requires managers to define the components of the performance measure chosen in step 1. For example, step 3 requires managers to define "investment" as, say, total assets or total assets minus current liabilities. After choosing the definition in step 3, managers choose the basis for measuring dollar values in the definition (for example, historical cost or current cost) in step 4.

To illustrate step 3 of designing accounting-based performance measures, we consider four alternative definitions of investment that companies use:

1. *Total assets available*—includes all assets, regardless of their intended purpose.
2. *Total assets employed*—total assets available minus the sum of idle assets plus assets purchased for future expansion. For example, if the New Orleans hotel in Exhibit 23-1 has unused land set aside for potential expansion, the total assets employed by the hotel would exclude the cost of that land.
3. *Total assets employed minus current liabilities*—total assets excluding those employed assets financed by short-term creditors. One negative feature of defining investment in this way is that it may encourage subunit managers to use an excessive amount of short-term debt because short-term debt reduces the amount of investment.
4. *Stockholders' equity*—calculated by assigning liabilities among subunits and deducting the amount assigned from the total assets of each subunit. One drawback of this method is that it combines operating decisions made by hotel managers with financing decisions made by top management.

Companies that use ROI or RI generally define investment as the total assets available. When top management directs a subunit manager to carry extra or idle assets, total assets employed can be more informative than total assets available. Companies that adopt EVA® define investment as total assets employed minus current liabilities. The most common rationale for using total assets employed minus current liabilities is that the subunit manager often influences decisions on current liabilities of the subunit.

CHOOSING MEASUREMENT ALTERNATIVES FOR PERFORMANCE MEASURES: STEP 4

6 **Contrast current-cost**
...cost today of purchasing an asset
and historical-cost asset measurement methods
...original cost of asset minus accumulated depreciation

To design accounting-based performance measures, we need to consider different ways to measure assets included in the investment calculations. Should assets be measured at historical cost or current cost? Should gross book value (that's original cost), or net book value (original cost minus accumulated depreciation) be used for depreciable assets?

Current Cost

Current cost is the cost of purchasing an asset today identical to the one currently held, or the cost of purchasing an asset that provides services like the one currently held if an identical one cannot be purchased. Of course, measuring assets at current costs will result in different ROIs compared with the ROIs calculated on the basis of historical costs.

We illustrate the current-cost ROI calculations using the data for Hospitality Inns (Exhibit 23-1) and then compare current-cost-based ROIs and historical-cost-based ROIs. Assume the following information about the long-term assets of each hotel:

	San Francisco	Chicago	New Orleans
Age of facility (at end of 2003)	8 years	4 years	2 years
Gross book value (original cost)	$1,400,000	$2,100,000	$2,730,000
Accumulated depreciation	$800,000	$600,000	$390,000
Net book value (at end of 2003)	$600,000	$1,500,000	$2,340,000
Depreciation for 2003	$100,000	$150,000	$195,000

Hospitality Inns assumes a 14-year estimated useful life, zero terminal disposal value for the physical facilities, and straight-line depreciation.

An index of construction costs indicating how the cost of construction has changed over the eight-year period that Hospitality Inns has been operating (1995 year-end = 100) is

When a specific cost index (such as the construction cost index) is not available, companies often use a general index (such as the consumer price index) to approximate current costs.

Year	1996	1997	1998	1999	2000	2001	2002	2003
Construction cost index	110	122	136	144	152	160	174	180

Earlier in this chapter, we computed an ROI of 24% for San Francisco, 15% for Chicago, and 17% for New Orleans (p. 788). One possible explanation of the high ROI for the San Francisco hotel is that this hotel's long-term assets are expressed in 1995 construction price levels—prices that prevailed eight years ago—and the long-term assets for the Chicago and New Orleans hotels are expressed in terms of higher, more-recent construction price levels, which depress ROIs for these two hotels.

Exhibit 23-2 illustrates a step-by-step approach for incorporating current-cost estimates of long-term assets and depreciation into the ROI calculation. We make these calculations to approximate what it would cost today to obtain assets that would produce the same expected operating income that the subunits currently earn. (Similar adjustments to represent the current costs of capital employed and depreciation can also be made in the RI and EVA® calculations.) The current-cost adjustment reduces by more than half the ROI of the San Francisco hotel.

	Historical Cost ROI	Current Cost ROI
San Francisco	24%	10.8%
Chicago	15%	11.1%
New Orleans	17%	14.8%

Adjusting assets to recognize current costs negates differences in the investment base caused solely by differences in construction price levels. Compared with historical-cost ROI, current-cost ROI is a better measure of the current economic returns from the investment. If Hospitality Inns were to invest in a new hotel today, investing in one like the New Orleans hotel offers the best ROI.

A drawback of using current costs is that it can be difficult to obtain current-cost estimates for some assets. That's because the estimate requires a company to consider, in addition to increases in price levels, technological advances such as in computers and in processes that could reduce the current cost of assets needed to earn today's operating income.

Long-Term Assets: Gross or Net Book Value?

Because the historical cost of assets is often used to calculate ROI, there has been much discussion about whether gross book value or net book value of assets should be used. Using the data in Exhibit 23-1 (p. 787), we calculate ROI with net book values and with gross book values of plant and equipment as follows:

	San Francisco	Chicago	New Orleans
ROI for 2003 using net book value of total assets given in Exhibit 23-1 and calculated earlier	$\frac{\$240,000}{\$1,000,000} = 24\%$	$\frac{\$300,000}{\$2,000,000} = 15\%$	$\frac{\$510,000}{\$3,000,000} = 17\%$
ROI for 2003 using gross book value of total assets obtained by adding accumulated depreciation from p. 794 to net book value of total assets in Exhibit 23-1	$\frac{\$240,000}{\$1,800,000} = 13.3\%$	$\frac{\$300,000}{\$2,600,000} = 11.5\%$	$\frac{\$510,000}{\$3,390,000} = 15.0\%$

Using gross book value, the 13.3% ROI of the older San Francisco hotel is lower than the 15.0% ROI of the newer New Orleans hotel. Those who favor using gross book value claim it enables more-accurate comparisons of ROI across subunits. For example, using gross book value calculations, the return on the original plant and equipment investment is higher for the newer New Orleans hotel than for the older San Francisco hotel. This difference probably reflects the decline in earning power of the San Francisco hotel. In contrast, using the net book value masks this decline in earning power because the constantly

EXHIBIT 23-2 **ROI for Hospitality Inns: Computed Using Current-Cost Estimates as of the End of 2003 for Depreciation and Long-Term Assets**

Step 1: Restate long-term assets from gross book value at historical cost to gross book value at current cost as of the end of 2003.

	Gross book value of long-term assets at historical cost	×	(Construction cost index at 2003	÷	Construction cost index in year of construction)	=	Gross book value of long-term assets at current cost at end of 2003
San Francisco	$1,400,000	×	(180	÷	100)	=	$2,520,000
Chicago	$2,100,000	×	(180	÷	144)	=	$2,625,000
New Orleans	$2,730,000	×	(180	÷	160)	=	$3,071,250

Step 2: Derive net book value of long-term assets at current cost as of the end of 2003. (Assume estimated useful life of each hotel is 14 years.)

	Gross book value of long-term assets at current cost at end of 2003	×	(Estimated useful life remaining	÷	Estimated total useful life)	=	Net book value of long-term assets at current cost at end of 2003
San Francisco	$2,520,000	×	(6	÷	14)	=	$1,080,000
Chicago	$2,625,000	×	(10	÷	14)	=	$1,875,000
New Orleans	$3,071,250	×	(12	÷	14)	=	$2,632,500

Step 3: Compute current cost of total assets in 2003. (Assume current assets of each hotel is expressed in 2003 dollars.)

	Current assets at end of 2003(from Exhibit 23-1)	+	Long-term assets from step 2 above	=	Current cost of total assets at end of 2003
San Francisco	$400,000	+	$1,080,000	=	$1,480,000
Chicago	$500,000	+	$1,875,000	=	$2,375,000
New Orleans	$660,000	+	$2,632,500	=	$3,292,500

Step 4: Compute current-cost depreciation expense in 2003 dollars.

	Gross book value of long-term assets at current cost at end of 2003 (from step 1)	×	(1 ÷ Estimated total useful life)	=	Current-cost depreciation expense in 2003 dollars
San Francisco	$2,520,000	×	(1 ÷ 14)	=	$180,000
Chicago	$2,625,000	×	(1 ÷ 14)	=	$187,500
New Orleans	$3,071,250	×	(1 ÷ 14)	=	$219,375

Step 5: Compute 2003 operating income using 2003 current-cost depreciation.

	Historical-cost operating income	−	(Current - cost depreciation expense in 2003 dollars (from step 4)	−	Historical-cost depreciation)	=	Operating income for 2003 using 2003 current - cost depreciation
San Francisco	$240,000	−	($180,000	−	$100,000)	=	$160,000
Chicago	$300,000	−	($187,500	−	$150,000)	=	$262,500
New Orleans	$510,000	−	($219,375	−	$195,000)	=	$485,625

Step 6: Compute ROI using current-cost estimates for long-term assets and depreciation.

	Operating income for 2003 using 2003 current-cost depreciation (from step 5)	÷	Current cost of total assets at end of 2003 (from step 3)	=	ROI using current-cost estimate
San Francisco	$160,000	÷	$1,480,000	=	10.8%
Chicago	$262,500	÷	$2,375,000	=	11.1%
New Orleans	$485,625	÷	$3,292,500	=	14.7%

decreasing investment base results in a higher ROI for the San Francisco hotel—24% in this example. This higher rate may mislead decision makers into thinking that the earning power of the San Francisco hotel has not decreased.

The proponents of using net book value as an investment base maintain it is less confusing because (1) it is consistent with the amount of total assets shown in the conventional balance sheet, and (2) it is consistent with income computations that include deductions for depreciation. Surveys of company practices report net book value to be the dominant measure of assets used by companies for internal performance evaluation.

When using net book value, the declining denominator increases ROI as an asset ages, all other things equal. Evaluating managers based on net assets rather than gross assets exacerbates incentives for retaining old property, plant, and equipment, rather than investing in new property, plant, and equipment.

CHOOSING TARGET LEVELS OF PERFORMANCE: STEP 5

We next consider setting targets for an accounting-based measure of performance against which to compare actual performance. Historical-cost-based accounting measures are usually inadequate for evaluating economic returns on new investments, and in some cases, they create disincentives for expansion. Despite these problems, historical-cost ROIs can be used to evaluate current performance by establishing *target* ROIs. For Hospitality Inns, we need to recognize that the hotels were built in different years, which means they were built at different levels of the construction cost index. Top management could adjust the target historical-cost-based ROIs accordingly, say by setting San Francisco's ROI at 26%, Chicago's at 18%, and New Orleans' at 19%.

The alternative of comparing actual results to target or budgeted performance is frequently overlooked. The budget should be carefully negotiated with full knowledge of historical-cost accounting pitfalls. *Companies should tailor a budget to a particular subunit, a particular accounting system, and a particular performance measure.* For example, many problems of asset valuation and income measurement can be resolved if top management gets subunit managers to focus on what is attainable in the forthcoming budget period—whether ROI, RI, or EVA® is used and whether the financial measures are based on historical cost or some other measure, such as current cost.

Because older assets valued at historical cost inflate ROI (particularly if investment is defined as net book value rather than gross book value), top management may set higher target ROIs for divisions with older assets.

A popular way to establish targets is to set continuous improvement targets. If a company is using EVA® as a performance measure, top management can evaluate operations on year-to-year changes in EVA®, rather than on absolute measures of EVA®. Evaluating performance on the basis of *improvements* in EVA® makes the initial method of calculating EVA® less important.

CHOOSING THE TIMING OF FEEDBACK: STEP 6

The final step in designing accounting-based performance measures is the timing of feedback. Timing of feedback depends largely on (a) how critical the information is for the success of the organization, (b) the specific level of management receiving the feedback, and (c) the sophistication of the organization's information technology. For example, hotel managers responsible for room sales want information on the number of rooms sold on a daily or weekly basis. That's because a large percentage of hotel costs are fixed costs, so achieving high room sales and taking quick action to reverse any declining sales trends are critical to the financial success of each hotel. Supplying managers with daily information about room sales is much easier if Hospitality Inns has a computerized room-reservation and check-in system. Top management, however, may look at information about daily room sales only on a monthly basis. In some instances, because of concern about the low sales-to-total-assets ratio of the Chicago hotel, they may want the information weekly.

Lower-level managers, who are responsible for day-to-day operations, usually require more-frequent feedback than top management.

PERFORMANCE MEASUREMENT IN MULTINATIONAL COMPANIES

7 Indicate the difficulties when comparing the performance of divisions operating in different countries

...adjustments needed for differences in inflation rates and changes in exchange rates

Comparing the performance of divisions of a multinational company—that is, a company, operating in different countries—creates additional difficulties.[7]

[7]See M. Z. Iqbal, *International Accounting—A Global Perspective* (Cincinnati: South-Western College Publishing, 2002).

- The economic, legal, political, social, and cultural environments differ significantly across countries.
- Governments in some countries may impose controls and limit selling prices of a company's products. For example, some countries in Asia, Latin America, and Eastern Europe impose tariffs and custom duties to restrict imports of certain goods.
- Availability of materials and skilled labor, as well as costs of materials, labor, and infrastructure (power, transportation, and communication), may also differ significantly across countries.
- Divisions operating in different countries keep score of their performance in different currencies. Issues of inflation and fluctuations in foreign-currency exchange rates affect performance measures.

Adjustments are necessary to compare performance measures across countries.

Calculating the Foreign Division's ROI in the Foreign Currency

Suppose Hospitality Inns invests in a hotel in Mexico City. The investment consists mainly of the costs of buildings and furnishings. Also assume:

- The exchange rate at the time of Hospitality's investment on December 31, 2001, is 10 pesos = $1.
- During 2002, the Mexican peso suffers a steady decline in its value. The exchange rate on December 31, 2002, is 15 pesos = $1.
- The average exchange rate during 2002 is [(10 + 15) ÷ 2] = 12.5 pesos = $1.
- The investment (total assets) in the Mexico City hotel is 30,000,000 pesos.
- The operating income of the Mexico City hotel in 2002 is 6,000,000 pesos.

What is the historical-cost-based ROI for the Mexico City hotel in 2002?

To answer, we first have to determine: Should we calculate the ROI in pesos or in dollars? If we calculate the ROI in dollars, what exchange rate should we use? We may also be interested in how the ROI of Hospitality Inns Mexico City (HIMC) compares with the ROI of Hospitality Inns New Orleans (HINO), which is also a relatively new hotel of approximately the same size? The answers provide information that will be helpful when making future investment decisions.

$$\text{HIMC's ROI (calculated using pesos)} = \frac{\text{Operating income}}{\text{Total assets}} = \frac{6{,}000{,}000 \text{ pesos}}{30{,}000{,}000 \text{ pesos}} = 0.20, \text{ or } 20\%$$

HIMC's ROI of 20% is higher than HINO's ROI of 17% (p. 788). Does this mean that HIMC outperformed HINO based on the ROI criterion? Not necessarily. Why not? Because HIMC operates in a very different economic environment than HINO.

The peso has declined in value relative to the dollar in 2002. Research shows that the peso's decline is correlated with correspondingly higher inflation in Mexico than in the United States.[8] As a result of the higher inflation in Mexico, HIMC will charge higher prices for its hotel rooms, which will increase HIMC's operating income and lead to a higher ROI. Inflation clouds the real economic returns on an asset and makes historical-cost-based ROI higher. Differences in inflation rates between the two countries make a direct comparison of HIMC's peso-denominated ROI with HINO's dollar-denominated ROI misleading.

Calculating the Foreign Division's ROI in U.S. Dollars

One way to make historical-cost-based ROIs more meaningfully comparable to each other is to restate HIMC's performance in dollars. But what exchange rate should we use to make the comparison meaningful? Assume operating income was earned evenly throughout 2002. We use the average exchange rate of 12.5 pesos = $1 to convert the operating income from pesos to dollars: 6,000,000 pesos ÷ 12.5 pesos per dollar = $480,000. The effect of dividing the operating income in pesos by the higher

[8]W. Beaver and M. Wolfson, "Foreign Currency Translation Gains and Losses: What Effect Do They Have and What Do They Mean?" *Financial Analysts Journal* (March–April 1984); F. D. S. Choi, "Resolving the Inflation/Currency Translation Dilemma," *Management International Review* (Vol. 34, Special Issue, 1994).

pesos-to-dollar exchange rate prevailing during 2002, rather than the 10 pesos = $1 exchange rate prevailing on December 31, 2001, is that any increase in operating income in pesos as a result of inflation during 2002 is eliminated when converting back to dollars.

At what rate should we convert HIMC's total assets of 30,000,000 pesos? At the 10 pesos = $1 exchange rate prevailing when the assets were acquired on December 31, 2001. That's because HIMC's assets are recorded in pesos at the December 31, 2001, cost, and they are not revalued as a result of inflation in Mexico in 2002. Because the cost of assets recorded on HIMC's books is unaffected by subsequent inflation, the exchange rate prevailing when the assets were acquired should be used to convert the assets into dollars. Using exchange rates after December 31, 2001, would be incorrect because these exchange rates incorporate the higher inflation in Mexico in 2002. Total assets are converted to 30,000,000 pesos ÷ 10 pesos per dollar = $3,000,000.

Then,

$$\text{HIMC's ROI (calculated using dollars)} = \frac{\text{Operating income}}{\text{Total assets}} = \frac{\$480{,}000}{\$3{,}000{,}000} = 0.16, \text{ or } 16\%$$

As we have discussed, these adjustments make the historical-cost-based ROIs of the Mexico City and New Orleans hotels comparable because they negate the effects of any differences in inflation rates between the two countries. HIMC's ROI of 16% is less than HINO's ROI of 17%.

Residual income calculated in pesos suffers from the same problems as ROI calculated using pesos. Calculating HIMC's RI in dollars adjusts for changes in exchange rates and makes for more-meaningful comparisons with Hospitality's other hotels:

$$\begin{aligned}\text{HIMC's RI} &= \$480{,}000 - (0.12 \times \$3{,}000{,}000)\\ &= \$480{,}000 - \$360{,}000 = \$120{,}000\end{aligned}$$

which is also less than HINO's RI of $150,000. In interpreting HIMC's and HINO's ROI and RI, keep in mind that they are historical-cost-based calculations. They do, however, pertain to relatively new hotels.

DISTINCTION BETWEEN MANAGERS AND ORGANIZATION UNITS[9]

The performance evaluation of a *manager* should be distinguished from the performance evaluation of that manager's *subunit,* such as a division of a company. Companies often put the most skillful division manager in charge of the division producing the poorest economic return in an attempt to improve it. The division may take years to show improvement. Furthermore, the manager's efforts may result merely in bringing the division up to a minimum acceptable ROI. The division may continue to be a poor performer in comparison with other divisions, but it would be a mistake to conclude from the poor performance of the division that the manager is performing poorly. The division's performance may be adversely affected by economic conditions over which the manager has no control.

As another example, consider again the Hospitality Inn Mexico City (HIMC) hotel. Suppose, despite the high inflation in Mexico, HIMC could not increase room prices because of price-control regulations imposed by the government. HIMC's performance in dollar terms would be very poor because of the decline in the value of the peso. But should top management conclude from HIMC's poor performance that the HIMC manager performed poorly? Probably not. Why not? Because most likely the poor performance of HIMC is largely the result of regulatory factors outside the manager's control.

In the following sections, we show the basic principles for evaluating the performance of an individual subunit manager, although these principles apply to managers at all organization levels. Later sections consider examples at the individual-worker level and the top-management level. We illustrate these principles using the RI performance measure.

[9]The presentations here draw (in part) from teaching notes prepared by S. Huddart, N. Melumad, and S. Reichelstein.

8 Understand the role of salaries and incentives when rewarding managers

...balancing risk and performance-based rewards

The Basic Trade-Off: Creating Incentives Versus Imposing Risk

How the performance of managers and employees is measured and evaluated affects their rewards. Compensation arrangements run the range from a flat salary with no direct performance-based incentive (or bonus), as in the case of many government employees, to rewards based only on performance, as in the case of real estate agents who get no salary and are compensated only via commissions paid on the properties they sell. Most managers' total compensation includes some combination of salary and a performance-based incentive. Therefore, in designing compensation arrangements, we need to consider *the trade-off between creating incentives and imposing risk.* We illustrate this trade-off in the context of our Hospitality Inns example.

Sally Fonda owns the Hospitality Inns chain of hotels. Roger Brett manages the Hospitality Inns San Francisco (HISF) hotel. Assume Fonda uses RI to measure performance. To improve RI, Fonda would like Brett to increase sales, control costs, provide prompt and courteous service, and reduce working capital. But even if Brett did all those things, high RI is not guaranteed. HISF's RI is affected by many factors outside Fonda's and Brett's control, such as a recession in the San Francisco economy or an earthquake that might negatively affect HISF. Or, there could be uncontrollable factors, such as road construction near competing hotels, that might have a positive effect on HISF's RI. Uncontrollable factors make HISF's profitability uncertain and, hence, risky.

People who decide to become entrepreneurs (owners) are generally more risk-tolerant than those who decide to work for others (managers). It is more efficient for owners to bear risk than managers, because managers demand a premium (extra compensation) for bearing risk. The objective of many compensation plans is to provide managers with incentives to work hard while minimizing the risk placed on them.

Fonda is an entrepreneur, so she expects to have to bear risk. But Brett does not like being subject to risk. One way of "insuring" Brett against risk is to pay Brett a flat salary, regardless of the actual amount of RI attained. All the risk would then be borne by Fonda. This arrangement creates a problem, however. That's because Brett's effort is difficult to monitor. The absence of performance-based compensation will provide Brett with no incentive to work harder or to undertake extra physical and mental effort beyond what is necessary to retain his job or to uphold his own personal values.

Moral hazard[10] describes situations in which an employee prefers to exert less effort (or report distorted information) compared with the effort (or accurate information) desired by the owner because the employee's effort (or validity of the reported information) cannot be accurately monitored and enforced. In some repetitive jobs, as in electronic assembly, a supervisor can monitor the workers' actions, and the moral hazard problem may not arise. However, a manager's job is to gather and interpret information and to exercise judgment on the basis of the information obtained. Monitoring a manager's effort is more difficult.

Paying no salary and rewarding Brett *only* on the basis of some performance measure—RI in our example—raises different concerns. In this case, Brett would be motivated to strive to increase RI because his rewards would increase with increases in RI. But compensating Brett on RI also subjects Brett to risk. That's because HISF's RI depends not only on Brett's effort, but also on factors such as local economic conditions over which Brett has no control.

Brett does not like being subject to risk. To compensate Brett for taking on risk, Fonda must pay him some extra compensation. That is, using performance-based bonuses will cost Fonda more money, *on average,* than paying Brett a flat salary. Why "on average"? Because Fonda's compensation payment to Brett will vary with RI outcomes. When averaged over these outcomes, the RI-based compensation will cost Fonda more than paying Brett a flat salary. The motivation for having some salary and some performance-based bonus in compensation arrangements is to balance the benefit of incentives against the extra cost of imposing risk on the manager.

9 Describe the management accountant's role in helping organizations design better incentive systems

...choosing performance measures sensitive to employee performance

Intensity of Incentives and Financial and Nonfinancial Measurements

What affects the intensity of incentives? That is, how large should the incentive component of a manager's compensation be relative to the salary component? To answer these questions, we need to understand how much the performance measure is affected by actions the manager takes to further the owner's objectives.

[10]The term *moral hazard* originated in insurance contracts to represent situations in which insurance coverage caused insured parties to take less care of their properties than they might otherwise. One response to moral hazard in insurance contracts is the system of deductibles (that is, the insured pays for damages below a specified amount).

Preferred performance measures are ones that are sensitive to or change significantly with the manager's performance. They do not change much with changes in factors that are beyond the manager's control. Sensitive performance measures motivate the manager as well as limit the manager's exposure to risk, reducing the cost of providing incentives. Less-sensitive performance measures are not affected by the manager's performance and fail to induce the manager to improve. The more that owners have sensitive performance measures available to them, the more they can rely on incentive compensation for their managers.

When possible, owners use performance-evaluation measures tightly linked to managers' efforts. Managers are evaluated based on things they can affect, even if not completely controllable. For example, salespersons often earn commissions based on the amount of sales revenues they generate. Salespersons can affect the amount of sales they generate by working harder, but they cannot completely control the level of sales because other factors (such as the economy and competitors' products) also affect sales.

Suppose Brett has no authority to determine investments, and suppose revenues are determined largely by external factors such as local economic conditions. Then Brett's actions would only influence costs. Using RI as a performance measure in these circumstances subjects Brett's bonus to excessive risk because two components of the performance measure—investments and revenues—are largely unrelated to his actions. The management accountant might suggest that, to create stronger incentives, Fonda should consider using a different performance measure for Brett. Perhaps Fonda should use HISF's costs, a measure that is directly affected by Brett's effort. In this case, RI may be a good measure of the economic viability of HISF, but it is not a good measure of Brett's performance.

The benefits of using performance measures that are directly affected by a manager's efforts encourage the use of nonfinancial measures. Consider two possible measures for evaluating the manager of the Housekeeping Department at one of Hospitality's hotels: (1) the costs of the Housekeeping Department and (2) the average time taken by the housekeeping staff to clean a room properly. Suppose housekeeping costs are affected by factors such as wage rates, which the housekeeping manager does not set. In this case, the average time taken to clean a room properly may be preferred as a performance measure because it is influenced more directly by the manager's performance.

The salary component of compensation dominates when performance measures that are sensitive to managers' actions are not available. This is the case, for example, for some corporate staff and government employees. A high salary component, however, does not mean incentives are completely absent. Promotions and salary increases do depend on some overall measure of performance, but the incentives are less direct. The incentive component of compensation is high when sensitive performance measures are available and when monitoring the employee's effort is difficult, such as for real estate agencies.

Surveys show that division managers' compensation arrangements include a mix of salary, bonus, and long-term compensation tied to earnings and stock price of the company. The goal of such compensation arrangements is to balance division and companywide incentives, as well as short-term and long-term incentives. One survey of companies reported the average annual incentive component of compensation as follows: (1) bonuses based on short-run performance equal to 40% of current salary, and (2) average annual cash and stock compensation based on long-run performance equal to 57% of current salary. These percentages vary widely over the sample; some companies use stronger performance incentives than others.[11]

Benchmarks and Relative Performance Evaluation

Owners often use benchmarks to evaluate performance. Benchmarks representing "best practice" may be available inside or outside the organization. For Hospitality Inns, benchmarks could be other similar hotels, either within or outside the Hospitality Inns chain. Suppose Brett has responsibility for revenues, costs, and investments. In evaluating Brett's performance, Fonda would want to use as a benchmark a hotel of a similar size influenced by the same uncontrollable factors — for example, location, demographic trends, and economic conditions — that affect HISF. If all these factors were the same, *differences* in performances of the two hotels would occur only because of differences in the two managers' performances. Benchmarking, also called *relative performance evaluation*, "filters out" the effects of the common uncontrollable factors.

[11]R. Bushman, R. Indjejikian, and A. Smith, "Aggregate Performance Measures in Business Unit Manager Compensation: The Role of Intrafirm Interdependencies," *Journal of Accounting Research* (Vol. 33 Supplement, 1995).

CONCEPTS IN ACTION

Should Companies Force Rank Employees?

In recent years a number of U.S. corporations have instituted employee evaluation programs that "force rank" employees—meaning, all employees are ranked based on their performance, with a certain number receiving the highest grade and a certain number receiving the lowest grade.

Companies do this to motivate employees and to combat excessive leniency in performance evaluations. Jack Welch, in his last letter to shareholders as CEO of General Electric, said: "A company that bets its future on its people must remove that lower 10%, and keep removing it every year...That is how real meritocracies are created and thrive."

Things don't always work out as planned, however. In January 2000, the Ford Motor Company instituted a forced-ranking system for all 18,000 of its managers. Supervisors were required to rate 10% of employees with the lowest grade, and receiving such a grade two years in a row could be grounds for dismissal. In July 2001, however, Ford's CEO, Jacques Nasser, announced that the program was being terminated. Nasser said that the program "was viewed as an inflexible system by some and as discriminatory by a few others." A few months earlier, the *Detroit News* reported that "at the least, the forced-ranking system has sparked resentment among many Ford workers. At the worst, it has fostered a working environment rife with paranoia and unhealthy competition. Many managers, regardless of the grade they received, say forced ranking undermines teamwork."

It is generally recognized that there is a subjective element in most employee evaluations. This subjectivity tends to magnify concerns about forced-ranking systems. Moreover, in 2000 and 2001, employees filed class-action suits against Ford Motor, Microsoft, and Conoco, alleging that these companies were using their employee evaluation programs to rationalize the firing of certain people they wanted to get rid of, irrespective of merit. In each case a different group of employees brought the charges: older workers at Ford, blacks and women at Microsoft, U.S. citizens at Conoco.

Forced-ranking systems are a particular problem when applied to small groups of employees. A former executive at Microsoft said it was very difficult to force-rank when a group had only five people in it. At the same time, evaluating employees who do very different kinds of work isn't easy. A bank executive said that his boss had to rank a vice president of research against vice presidents of marketing, credit risk management, market risk management, and private placement. He said his boss was "completely baffled."

Critics of forced-ranking acknowledge that leniency in performance evaluation is a widespread problem. The real goal they say is teaching people how to have difficult conversations with employees who are having problems, without having to benchmark everyone against each other.

Source: Detroit News (July 11 and April 29, 2001), *Chicago Sun-Times* (June 3, 2001), *Fortune* (May 28, 2001), *New York Times* (March 19, 2001), General Electric's 2000 Annual Report.

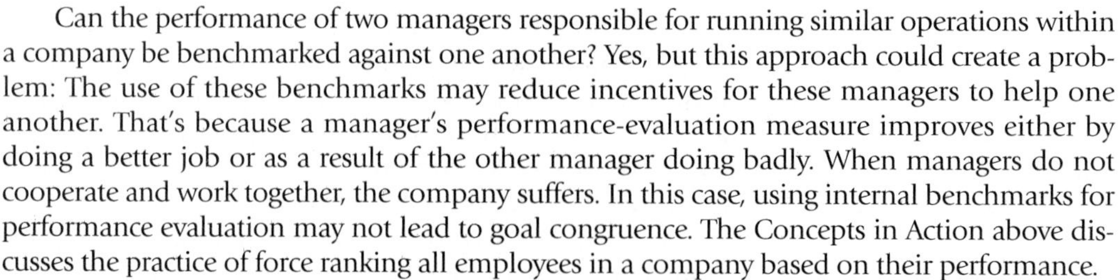

Can the performance of two managers responsible for running similar operations within a company be benchmarked against one another? Yes, but this approach could create a problem: The use of these benchmarks may reduce incentives for these managers to help one another. That's because a manager's performance-evaluation measure improves either by doing a better job or as a result of the other manager doing badly. When managers do not cooperate and work together, the company suffers. In this case, using internal benchmarks for performance evaluation may not lead to goal congruence. The Concepts in Action above discusses the practice of force ranking all employees in a company based on their performance.

PERFORMANCE MEASURES AT THE INDIVIDUAL ACTIVITY LEVEL

There are two issues when evaluating performance at the individual activity level: (a) designing performance measures for activities that require multiple tasks and (b) designing performance measures for activities done in teams.

Performing Multiple Tasks

Most employees perform more than one task as part of their jobs. Marketing representatives sell products, provide customer support, and gather market information. Manufacturing workers are responsible for both the quantity and quality of their output. Employers want employees to allocate their time and effort intelligently among various tasks or aspects of their jobs.

Consider mechanics at an auto repair shop. Their jobs have two distinct aspects: repair work—performing more repair work generates more revenues for the shop—and customer satisfaction—the higher the quality of the job, the more likely the customer will be pleased. If the employer wants an employee to focus on both aspects, then the employer must measure and compensate performance on both aspects.

Suppose the employer can easily measure the quantity, but not the quality, of auto repairs. If the employer rewards workers on a by-the-job rate, which pays workers only on the basis of the number of repairs actually performed, mechanics will likely increase the number of repairs they make and quality will likely suffer. Sears, Roebuck and Co. experienced this problem when it introduced by-the-job rates for its mechanics. Sears' managers responded by taking three steps to motivate workers to balance both quantity and quality. (1) They dropped the by-the-job rate system and paid mechanics an hourly salary, a step that deemphasized the quantity of repairs. Mechanics' promotions and pay increases were determined on the basis of management's assessment of each mechanic's overall performance regarding quantity and quality of repairs. (2) They began evaluating employees, in part, using data such as customer-satisfaction surveys, the number of dissatisfied customers, and the number of customer complaints. (3) They used staff from an independent outside agency to randomly monitor whether the repairs performed were of high quality.

If managers are evaluated on a single performance measure, they have incentives to subordinate all other measures to maximize that single measure. For example, managers might curtail advertising and maintenance to increase the current year's ROI. This is why performance evaluation should be based on a variety of factors, as in the balanced scorecard.

Note that nonfinancial measures, such as customer-satisfaction ratings, help motivate mechanics to emphasize both quantity and quality. The objective of performance measurement is to measure both aspects of the mechanics' jobs and to balance incentives so that both aspects are properly emphasized. Attaining this objective will align the incentives of the mechanics with Sears' goal of maximizing long-run profits and shareholder value.

Team-Based Compensation Arrangements

Many manufacturing, marketing, and design problems can be resolved when employees with multiple skills, knowledge, experiences, and judgments pool their talents. A team achieves better results than individual employees acting alone.[12] Companies reward individuals on a team on the basis of team performance. Such team-based incentives encourage individuals to help one another as they strive toward a common goal.

The specific forms of team-based compensation vary across companies. Colgate Palmolive rewards teams on the basis of each team's performance. Novartis, the Swiss pharmaceutical company, rewards teams on companywide performance—a certain amount of team-based bonuses are paid only if the company reaches certain goals. To encourage the development of team skills, Tennessee Eastman's skill-based plan rewards team members using a checklist of team skills, such as communication and willingness to help. Whether team-based compensation is desirable depends, to a great extent, on the culture and management style of a particular organization. For example, one criticism of team-based compensation, especially in the United States, is that incentives for individual employees to excel are diminished, harming overall performance. Another problem is to manage team members who are not productive contributors to the team's success but who, nevertheless, share in the team's rewards.

Team-based incentive compensation encourages employees to work together to achieve common goals. Individual-based incentive compensation rewards employees for their own performance, consistent with responsibility accounting. A mix of both types of incentives encourages employees to maximize their own performance while working together in the best interest of the company as a whole.

EXECUTIVE PERFORMANCE MEASURES AND COMPENSATION

The principles of performance evaluation described in the previous sections also apply to executive compensation plans. These plans are based on both financial and nonfinancial performance measures and consist of a mix of (1) base salary; (2) annual incentives, such

[12]J. Katzenbach and D. Smith, *The Wisdom of Teams* (Boston: Harvard Business School Press, 1993).

as cash bonus based on achieving a target annual RI; (3) long-run incentives, such as stock options (described later in this section) based on stock performance over, say, a five-year period; and (4) fringe benefits, such as life insurance, an office with a view, or a personal assistant. Designers of executive compensation plans emphasize three factors: achievement of organization goals, ease of administering the plans, and ensuring that affected executives perceive the plan as fair.

Well-designed plans use a compensation mix that balances risk (the effect of uncontrollable factors on the performance measure and hence compensation) with short-run and long-run incentives. For example, evaluating performance on the basis of annual EVA® sharpens an executive's short-run focus. And using EVA® and stock option plans over, say, five years motivates the executive to take a long-run view as well.

Stock options give executives the right to buy company stock at a specified price (called the exercise price) within a specified period. Suppose on April 26, 2001, Marriott International gave its CEO the option to buy 100,000 shares of Marriott stock at any time before June 30, 2005, at the April 26, 2001, market price of $43 per share. Let's say Marriott's stock price rises to $58 per share on March 24, 2005, and the CEO exercises his options on all 100,000 shares. The CEO would earn $15 ($58 – $43) per share on 100,000 shares, or $1.5 million. If Marriott's stock price stays below $43 during the entire period, the CEO will simply forgo his right to buy the shares. By linking CEO compensation to increases in the company's stock price, the stock option plan motivates the CEO to improve the company's long-run performance to increase the stock price.

In 1995, the Financial Accounting Standards Board (FASB) issued Statement Number 123 on accounting for stock options. For most stock options granted, the exercise price of the option equals or exceeds the market price of the stock on the day the options are granted. In these cases, Statement 123 encourages, but does not require, a company to record a compensation cost in its income statement. The company need not recognize cost even though the company has sacrificed something of value—the potentially large income from exercising the stock options that the executive will receive if the price of the stock increases. If the company records no cost in its income statement, it must disclose in a note to the financial statements the effect on net income and earnings per share had the company recognized cost equal to the estimated fair market value of the options on the grant date.[13]

Responding to some concerns about high executive compensation payments despite poor company performance, the Securities and Exchange Commission (SEC) issued rules requiring more-detailed disclosures of the compensation arrangements of top-level executives. In complying with these rules in 2001, Marriott International, for example, disclosed a compensation table showing the salaries, bonuses, stock options, other stock awards, and other compensation earned by its top five executives during the 1998, 1999, and 2000 fiscal years. Marriott also disclosed how well its stock performed relative to the overall market (S&P 500 Index) and stocks of other motels and hotels (the S&P Lodging Hotel Index). Investors use this information to evaluate the relationship between compensation and performance across companies generally, across companies of similar sizes, and across companies operating in similar industries.

The SEC rules also require companies to disclose the principles underlying their executive compensation plans and the performance criteria—such as profitability, revenue growth, and market share—used in determining compensation. In its annual report, Marriott International described these principles as "building a strong correlation between stockholder return and executive compensation, offering incentives that encourage attainment of short-run and long-run business goals, and providing a total level of pay that is commensurate with performance." Marriott uses cash flow, earnings per share, and guest satisfaction as performance criteria to determine annual cash incentives for its executives.

[13]If the exercise price is less than the market price of the stock on the date the options are granted, the company must recognize compensation cost equal to the difference between the two prices. This difference is less than the fair market value of the options. The company can choose to either recognize the full fair market value as a cost or disclose in a note to the financial statements the effect on net income and earnings per share.

INTRINSIC MOTIVATION AND ORGANIZATION CULTURE

Given the emphasis in this book on accounting, this chapter has emphasized the role of accounting measures in performance evaluation. Many other factors motivate managers and workers to perform well. Two of those other factors are intrinsic motivation and organization culture and values.

Sociologists and social psychologists argue that extrinsic motivators such as financial rewards and recognition for a job well done should be balanced by intrinsic motivators. *Intrinsic motivation* is the desire to achieve self-satisfaction from good performance regardless of external rewards such as bonuses or promotion. Intrinsic motivation comes from being given greater responsibility, doing interesting and creative work, having pride in doing that work, establishing commitment to the organization, and developing personal bonds with coworkers. High intrinsic motivation enhances performance because managers and workers have a sense of achievement, feel satisfied with their jobs, and see opportunities for personal growth.

Organization values and culture refer to the accepted norms and patterns of behavior expected of all managers and employees with respect to each other, shareholders, customers, and communities. Johnson and Johnson describes its values and culture in its credo statement:

> *We believe our first responsibility is to the doctors, nurses and patients, to mothers and fathers and all others who use our products and services.... Everything we do must be of high quality.*
>
> *We are responsible to our employees.... We must respect their dignity and recognize their merit. They must have a sense of security in their jobs.... We must be mindful of ways to help our employees fulfill their family responsibilities and provide opportunity for development and advancement....Our actions must be just and ethical.*
>
> *We are responsible to the communities in which we live.... We must support good works and charities and bear our fair share of taxes.... We must encourage better health and education.*
>
> *Our final responsibility is to our stockholders. Business must make a sound profit....We must experiment with new ideas ... develop innovative programs and pay for mistakes.*

Johnson and Johnson's credo is intended to inspire managers and employees to do their best. Values and culture generate organization commitment, pride, and belonging and are an important source of intrinsic motivation.

ENVIRONMENTAL AND ETHICAL RESPONSIBILITIES

As they strive to achieve the performance goals of their organizations, managers should be constantly aware of their environmental and ethical responsibilities. Environmental violations (such as water and air pollution) and unethical and illegal practices (such as bribery and corruption) carry heavy fines and are prison offenses under the laws of the United States and other countries. But environmental responsibilities and ethical conduct extend beyond legal requirements.

Socially responsible companies, such as BP, set aggressive environmental goals and measure and report their performance against them. German, Swiss, Dutch, and Scandinavian companies report on environmental performance as part of a larger set of social responsibility disclosures (for example, employee welfare and community development activities). Some companies, such as DuPont, make environmental performance a line item on every employee's salary appraisal report. Duke Power Company appraises employees on their part in reducing solid waste, cutting emissions and discharges, and implementing environmental plans. The result? Duke Power has met all its environmental goals.

Ethical behavior on the part of managers is paramount. In particular, the numbers that subunit managers report should not be tainted by "cooking the books." They should be uncontaminated by, for example, overstated assets, understated liabilities, fictitious revenues, and understated costs.

Codes of business conduct are circulated in some organizations to signal what is appropriate and what is inappropriate individual behavior. The following is from Caterpillar Tractor's "Code of Worldwide Business Conduct and Operating Principles":

The law is a floor. Ethical business conduct should normally exist at a level well above the minimum required by law. Caterpillar employees shall not accept costly entertainment or gifts (excepting mementos and novelties of nominal value) from dealers, suppliers and others with whom we do business. And we won't tolerate circumstances that produce, or reasonably appear to produce, conflict between personal interests of an employee and interests of the company.

Division managers often cite enormous top-management pressures "to make the budget" as excuses or rationalizations for not adhering to ethical accounting policies and procedures. A healthy amount of motivational pressure is not undesirable, as long as the "tone from the top" simultaneously communicates the absolute need for all managers to behave ethically at all times. Management should promptly and severely reprimand unethical conduct, irrespective of the benefits that might accrue to the company from such actions. Some companies such as Lockheed-Martin emphasize ethical behavior by routinely evaluating employees against a business code of ethics.

PROBLEM FOR SELF-STUDY

The Baseball Division of Home Run Sports manufactures and sells baseballs. Budgeted data for February 2003 are

Current assets	$ 400,000
Long-term assets	600,000
Total assets	$1,000,000
Production output	200,000 baseballs per month
Target ROI (Operating income ÷ Total assets)	30%
Fixed costs	$ 400,000 per month
Variable costs	$4 per baseball

Required

1. Compute the minimum selling price per baseball necessary to achieve the target ROI of 30%.
2. Using the selling price from requirement 1, separate the target ROI into its two components using the DuPont method.
3. Compute the RI of the Baseball Division for February 2003, using the selling price from requirement 1. Home Run Sports uses a 12% required rate of return on total division assets when computing division RI.
4. In addition to her salary, Pamela Stephenson, the division manager, receives 3% of the monthly RI of the Baseball Division as a bonus. Compute Stephenson's bonus. Why do you think Stephenson is rewarded using both salary and a performance-based bonus? Stephenson does not like bearing risk.

SOLUTION

1.

$$\begin{aligned}
\text{Target operating income} &= 30\% \text{ of } \$1{,}000{,}000 \text{ of total assets}\\
&= \$300{,}000\\
\text{Let } P &= \text{Selling price}\\
\text{Revenues} - \text{Variable costs} - \text{Fixed costs} &= \text{Operating income}\\
200{,}000P - (200{,}000 \times \$4) - \$400{,}000 &= \$300{,}000\\
200{,}000P &= \$300{,}000 + \$800{,}000 + \$400{,}000\\
&= \$1{,}500{,}000\\
P &= \$7.50 \text{ per baseball}
\end{aligned}$$

Proof:

Revenues, 200,000 baseballs × $7.50/baseball	$1,500,000
Variable costs, 200,000 baseballs × $4/baseball	800,000
Contribution margin	700,000
Fixed costs	400,000
Operating income	$ 300,000

2. The DuPont method describes ROI as the product of two components: return on sales (income ÷ revenues) and investment turnover (revenues ÷ investment).

$$\frac{\text{Income}}{\text{Revenues}} \times \frac{\text{Revenues}}{\text{Investment}} = \frac{\text{Income}}{\text{Investment}}$$

$$\frac{\$300{,}000}{\$1{,}500{,}000} \times \frac{\$1{,}500{,}000}{\$1{,}000{,}000} = \frac{\$300{,}000}{\$1{,}000{,}000}$$

$$0.2 \times 1.5 = 0.30, \text{ or } 30\%$$

3.
$$\begin{aligned} \text{RI} &= \text{Operating income} - \text{Required return on investment.} \\ &= \$300{,}000 - (0.12 \times \$1{,}000{,}000) \\ &= \$300{,}000 - \$120{,}000 \\ &= \$180{,}000 \end{aligned}$$

4.
$$\begin{aligned} \text{Stephenson's bonus} &= 3\% \text{ of RI} \\ &= 0.03 \times \$180{,}000 = \$5{,}400 \end{aligned}$$

The Baseball Division's RI is affected by many factors outside Stephenson's control, such as general economic conditions. These uncontrollable factors make the Baseball Division's profitability uncertain and risky. Because Stephenson does not like bearing risk, paying her a flat salary, regardless of RI would shield Stephenson from this risk. But there is a moral hazard problem with this compensation arrangement. Because Stephenson's effort is difficult to monitor, the absence of performance-based compensation will provide Stephenson with no incentive to undertake extra physical and mental effort beyond what is necessary to retain her job or uphold her personal values.

Paying no salary and rewarding Stephenson only on the basis of RI provides Stephenson with incentives to work hard but also subjects her to excessive risk because of uncontrollable factors that will affect RI and hence Stephenson's compensation. A compensation arrangement based only on RI would be more costly for Home Run Sports because it would have to compensate Stephenson for taking on uncontrollable risk.

A compensation arrangement that consists of both a salary and an RI-based performance bonus balances the benefits of incentives against the extra costs of imposing uncontrollable risk.

DECISION POINTS SUMMARY

The following question-and-answer format summarizes the chapter's learning objectives. Each decision presents a key question related to a learning objective. The guidelines are the answer to that question.

Decision	Guidelines
1. What financial and nonfinancial measures do companies use?	Financial measures such as return on investment and residual income measure aspects of both manager performance and organization-subunit performance. In many cases, financial measures are supplemented with nonfinancial measures of performance, such as customer satisfaction ratings, number of defects, and productivity.
2. What are the steps in designing an accounting-based performance measure?	The steps are (a) choose performance measures that align with top management's financial goals, (b) choose the time horizon of each performance measure, (c) choose a definition of the components in each performance measure, (d) choose a measurement alternative for each performance measure, (e) choose a target level of performance, and (f) choose the timing of feedback.
3. How does the DuPont method analyze return on investment?	The DuPont method describes return on investment (ROI) as the product of two components: income divided by revenues (return on sales) and revenues divided by investment (investment turnover). ROI can be increased in three ways: by increasing revenues, by decreasing costs, and by decreasing investment.
4. What is residual income and what are its advantages?	Residual income (RI) is income minus a dollar amount for required return on investment. RI is designed to overcome some of the limitations of ROI. For example, RI is more likely than ROI to promote goal congruence. ROI may induce managers of highly profitable divisions to reject projects that, from the perspective of the organization as a whole, should be accepted.

Continued

5. What is the economic value added method?	Economic value added (EVA®) is a variation of the RI calculation. It equals the after-tax operating income minus the product of after-tax weighted-average cost of capital and total assets minus current liabilities.
6. Should companies use current cost or historical cost of assets to measure performance?	Current cost of an asset is the cost now of purchasing an asset identical to the one currently held. Historical-cost asset-measurement methods generally consider net book value of the assets, which is original cost minus accumulated depreciation. Historical-cost measures are often inadequate for measuring economic returns. Current-cost measures do better. More generally, however, problems in any performance measure can be overcome by emphasizing budgets and targets that stress continuous improvement.
7. How can companies compare the performance of divisions operating in different countries?	Comparing the performance of divisions operating in different countries is difficult because of legal, political, social, economic, and currency differences. ROI calculations for subunits operating in different countries need to be adjusted for differences in inflation between the two countries and changes in exchange rates.
8. Why are managers compensated based on a mix of salary and incentives?	Companies create incentives by rewarding managers on the basis of performance. But managers may face risks because factors beyond their control may also affect their performance. Owners choose a mix of salary and incentive compensation to trade off the incentive benefit against the cost of imposing risk.
9. How can a company implement strong incentives?	Obtaining performance measures that are more sensitive to employee performance is necessary for implementing strong incentives. Many management accounting practices, such as the design of responsibility centers and the establishment of financial and nonfinancial measures, aid in better performance evaluation and, hence, allow for stronger incentives.

TERMS TO LEARN

This chapter and the Glossary at the end of this book contain definitions of:

current cost (p. 794)
economic value added (EVA®) (790)
imputed costs (789)
investment (788)
moral hazard (800)
residual income (RI) (789)
return on investment (ROI) (788)

ASSIGNMENT MATERIAL

Questions

23-1 Give two examples of financial performance measures and two examples of nonfinancial performance measures.

23-2 What are the six steps in designing accounting-based performance measures?

23-3 What factors affecting ROI does the DuPont method of profitability analysis highlight?

23-4 "RI is not identical to ROI, although both measures incorporate income and investment into their computations." Do you agree? Explain.

23-5 Describe EVA®.

23-6 Give three definitions of investment used in practice when computing ROI.

23-7 Distinguish between measuring assets based on current cost and historical cost.

23-8 What special problems arise when evaluating performance in multinational companies?

23-9 Why is it important to distinguish between the performance of a manager and the performance of the organization subunit for which the manager is responsible? Give an example.

23-10 Describe moral hazard.

23-11 "Managers should be rewarded only on the basis of their performance measures. They should be paid no salary." Do you agree? Explain.

23-12 Explain the management accountant's role in helping organizations design stronger incentive systems for their employees.

23-13 Explain the role of benchmarking in evaluating managers.

23-14 Explain the incentive problems that can arise when employees must perform multiple tasks as part of their jobs.

23-15 Describe two disclosures required by the SEC with respect to executive compensation.

Exercises

23-16 ROI, comparisons of three companies. (CMA, adapted) Return on investment (ROI) is often expressed as follows:

$$\frac{\text{Income}}{\text{Investment}} = \frac{\text{Revenues}}{\text{Investment}} \times \frac{\text{Income}}{\text{Revenues}}$$

Required

1. What advantages are there in the breakdown of the computation into two separate components?
2. Fill in the following blanks:

	Companies in Same Industry		
	A	**B**	**C**
Revenues	$1,000,000	$500,000	?
Income	$ 100,000	$ 50,000	?
Investment	$ 500,000	?	$5,000,000
Income as a percentage of revenues	?	?	0.5%
Investment turnover	?	?	2
ROI	?	1%	?

After filling in the blanks, comment on the relative performance of these companies as thoroughly as the data permit.

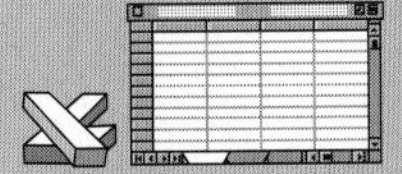

Excel Application For students who wish to practice their spreadsheet skills, the following is a step-by-step approach to creating an Excel spreadsheet to work this problem.

Step-by-Step

1. Open a new spreadsheet. At top, create a table in the same format as provided for this problem, with columns for companies A, B, and C and rows for "Revenues, Income, Investment, Income as a Percentage of Revenues, Investment Turnover," and "ROI." Enter the data provided in the table (leave cells blank when a "?" appears in the table).

(Program your spreadsheet to perform all necessary calculations. Do not "hard-code" any amounts, such as ROI for Company A, requiring addition, subtraction, multiplication, or division operations.)

2. Enter calculations for each of the missing items. For example, to calculate revenues for Company C, enter a calculation that multiplies Company C's investment by Company C's investment turnover.
3. *Verify the accuracy of your spreadsheet*: Change investment for Company A from $500,000 to $400,000. If you programmed your spreadsheet correctly, ROI for Company A should change to 25%.

23-17 Analysis of return on invested assets, comparison of two divisions. Quality Products, Inc., has two divisions: soft drinks and family restaurants. Results (in millions) for the past three years are as follows:

	Soft-Drink Division	Restaurant Division	Quality Products, Inc.
Operating Revenues			
2003	$2,800	$1,050	$3,850
2004	3,000	1,250	4,250
2005	3,600	1,530	5,130
Operating Income			
2003	120	105	225
2004	160	114	274
2005	240	100	340
Total Assets			
2003	1,200	800	2,000
2004	1,250	1,000	2,250
2005	1,400	1,300	2,700

Required Use the DuPont method of profitability analysis to explain changes in the operating-income-to-total-assets ratio over the 2003 to 2005 period for each division and Quality Products, Inc. Comment on the results.

23-18 ROI and RI. (D. Kleespie) The Gaul Company produces and distributes a wide variety of recreational products. One of its divisions, the Goscinny Division, manufactures and sells "menhirs," which are popular with cross-country skiers. The demand for these menhirs is relatively insensitive to price changes. The Goscinny Division is considered to be an investment center and in recent years has averaged a ROI of 20%. The following data are available for the Goscinny Division and its product:

Total annual fixed costs	$1,000,000
Variable costs per menhir	$300
Average number of menhirs sold each year	10,000
Average operating assets invested in the division	$1,600,000

Required

1. What is the minimum selling price per unit that the Goscinny Division could charge in order for Mary Obelix, the division manager, to get a favorable performance rating? Management considers an ROI below 20% to be unfavorable.
2. Assume that the Gaul Company judges the performance of its investment center managers on the basis of RI rather than ROI. The company's required rate of return is 15%. What is the minimum selling price that the Goscinny Division should charge for Obelix to receive a favorable performance rating?

23-19 Pricing and ROI. Hardy, Inc., assembles motorcycles and uses long-run average demand to set the budgeted production level and costs for pricing. You are given the following data:

- Variable costs: $1,320 per unit
- Fixed costs: $30 million per year
- Investment (total assets): $90 million

Required

1. What return on sales is needed to attain a ROI of 20% if Hardy assembles and sells 100,000 units?
2. What selling price is needed to attain a ROI of 20% if Hardy assembles and sells 100,000 units?
3. Using the selling price calculated in requirement 2, what ROI will be earned if Hardy assembles and sells 150,000 units? 50,000 units?
4. The company has a management bonus plan based on yearly division performance. Comment on the bonus plan.

23-20 Financial and nonfinancial performance measures, goal congruence. (CMA, adapted) Summit Equipment specializes in the manufacture of medical equipment, a field that has become increasingly competitive. Approximately two years ago, Ben Harrington, president of Summit, decided to revise the bonus plan (based, at the time, entirely on operating income) to encourage division managers to focus on areas that were important to customers and that added value without increasing cost. In addition to a profitability incentive, the revised plan includes incentives for reduced rework costs, reduced sales returns, and on-time deliveries. Bonuses are calculated and awarded semiannually on the following basis. A base bonus is calculated at 2% of operating income. This amount is then adjusted as follows:

a. (i) Reduced by excess of rework costs over and above 2% of operating income.
(ii) No adjustment if rework costs are less than or equal to 2% of operating income.
b. (i) Increased by $5,000 if more than 98% of deliveries are on time, and by $2,000 if 96% to 98% of deliveries are on time.
(ii) No adjustment if on-time deliveries are below 96%.
c. (i) Increased by $3,000 if sales returns are less than or equal to 1.5% of sales.
(ii) Decreased by 50% of excess of sales returns over 1.5% of sales.

Note: If the calculation of the bonus results in a negative amount for a particular period, the manager simply receives no bonus, and the negative amount is not carried forward to the next period.

Results for Summit's Charter Division and Mesa Division for 2003, the first year under the new bonus plan, follow. In 2002, under the old bonus plan, the Charter Division manager earned a bonus of $27,060 and the Mesa Division manager, a bonus of $22,440.

	CHARTER DIVISION		**MESA DIVISION**	
	January 1, 2003 to June 30, 2003	**July 1, 2003 to December 31, 2003**	**January 1, 2003 to June 30, 2003**	**July 1, 2003 to December 31, 2003**
Revenues	$4,200,000	$4,400,000	$2,850,000	$2,900,000
Operating income	$462,000	$440,000	$342,000	$406,000
On-time delivery	95.4%	97.3%	98.2%	94.6%
Rework costs	$11,500	$11,000	$6,000	$8,000
Sales returns	$84,000	$70,000	$44,750	$42,500

1. Why did Harrington need to introduce these new performance measures? That is, why does Harrington need to use these performance measures in addition to the operating income numbers for the period? **Required**
2. Calculate the bonus earned by each manager for each six-month period and for 2003.
3. What effect did the change in the bonus plan have on each manager's behavior? Did the new bonus plan achieve what Harrington desired? What changes, if any, would you make to the new bonus plan?

23-21 ROI, RI, EVA®. (D. Solomons, adapted) Consider the following data for the two geographical divisions of the Potomac Electric Company that operate as profit centers:

	Atlantic Division	Pacific Division
Total assets	$1,000,000	$5,000,000
Current liabilities	250,000	1,500,000
Operating income	200,000	750,000

Required

1. Calculate the ROI for each division using operating income as the measure of income and total assets as the measure of investment.
2. Potomac Electric has used RI as a measure of management performance, the variable it wants a manager to maximize. Using this criterion, what is the RI for each division using operating income and total assets, if the required rate of return on investment is 12%?
3. Potomac Electric has two sources of funds: long-term debt with a market value of $3,500,000 and an interest rate of 10%, and equity capital with a market value of $3,500,000 at a cost of equity of 14%. Potomac's income tax rate is 40%. Potomac applies the same weighted-average cost of capital to both divisions, because each division faces similar risks. Calculate the EVA® for each division. Which of the measures calculated in requirements 1, 2, and 3 would you recommend Potomac Electric use? Why? Explain briefly.

23-22 RI, EVA®. The Burlingame Transport Company operates two divisions: a Truck Rental Division that rents to individuals, and a Transportation Division that transports goods from one city to another. Results reported for the past year are as follows:

	Truck Rental Division	Transportation Division
Total assets	$650,000	$950,000
Current liabilities	120,000	200,000
Operating income	75,000	160,000

Required

1. Calculate the RI for each division using operating income and investment equal to total assets minus current liabilities. The required rate of return on investment is 12%.
2. The company has two sources of funds: long-term debt with a market value of $900,000 at an interest rate of 10% and equity capital with a market value of $600,000 at a cost of equity of 15%. Burlingame's income tax rate is 40%. Burlingame applies the same weighted-average cost of capital to both divisions, because each division faces similar risks. Calculate the EVA® for each division.
3. Using your answers to requirements 1 and 2, what would you conclude about the performance of each division? Explain briefly.

23-23 ROI, RI, measurement of assets. (CMA, adapted) Ashton Corporation recently announced a bonus plan to be awarded to the manager of the most profitable division. The three division managers are to choose whether ROI or RI will be used to measure profitability. In addition, they must decide whether investment will be measured using gross book value or net book value of assets. Ashton defines income as operating income and investment as total assets. The following information is available for the year just ended:

Division	Gross Book Value of Assets	Accumulated Depreciation	Operating Income
Bristol	$800,000	$430,000	$94,700
Darden	760,000	410,000	91,700
Gregory	500,000	280,000	61,400

Ashton uses a required rate of return of 10% on investment to calculate RI.

Required

Each division manager has selected a method of bonus calculation that ranks his or her division Number 1. Identify the method for calculating profitability that each manager selected, supporting your answer with appropriate calculations.

23-24 Multinational performance measurement, ROI, RI. The Sandvik Corporation manufactures electric motors in the United States and Sweden. The U.S. and Swedish operations are organized as decentralized divisions. The following information is available for 2003; ROI is calculated as operating income divided by total assets:

	U.S. Division	Swedish Division
Operating income	?	9,180,000 kronas
Total assets	$8,000,000	60,000,000 kronas
ROI	15%	?

The exchange rate at the time of Sandvik's investment in Sweden on December 31, 2002, was 8 kronas = $1. During 2003, the Swedish krona declined steadily in value so that the exchange rate on December 31, 2003, is 9 kronas = $1. The average exchange rate during 2003 is [(8 + 9) ÷ 2] = 8.5 kronas = $1.

Required

1. **a.** Calculate the U.S. division's operating income for 2003.
   b. Calculate the Swedish division's ROI for 2003 in kronas.
2. Senior management wants to know which division earned a better ROI in 2003. What would you tell them? Explain your answer.
3. Which division do you think had the better RI performance? Explain your answer. The required rate of return on investment (calculated in U.S. dollars) is 12%.

23-25 Multinational performance measurement, ROI, RI. Loren Press has two printing presses that operate as separate divisions, one located in Durham, North Carolina, and the other in Lyon, France. The following information is available for 2004. The required rate of return on investments is 15%.

	Durham Division	Lyon Division
Operating income	$765,000	3,600,000 francs
Total assets	$4,500,000	20,000,000 francs

Both investments were made on December 31, 2003. The exchange rate at the time of Loren's investment in France on December 31, 2003, was 4 francs = $1. During 2004, the French franc declined steadily in value, reaching an exchange rate on December 31, 2004, of 5 francs = $1. The average exchange rate during 2004 is [(4 + 5) ÷ 2] = 4.5 francs = $1.

Required

1. (a) Calculate Durham Division's ROI for 2004. (b) Calculate Lyon Division's ROI for 2004 in French francs. (c) Which division earned a better ROI in 2004? Explain.
2. Senior management wants to compare the performance of the two divisions using RI. Which division do you think had the better RI performance? Explain your answer.
3. On the basis of your answers to requirements 1 and 2, which division is performing better? If you had to promote one of the division managers to vice president, which manager would you choose? Explain.

23-26 Risk sharing, incentives, benchmarking, multiple tasks. The Dexter Division of AMCO sells car batteries. AMCO's corporate management gives Dexter management considerable operating and investment autonomy in running the division. AMCO is considering how it should compensate Jim Marks, the general manager of the Dexter Division. Proposal 1 calls for paying Marks a fixed salary. Proposal 2 calls for paying Marks no salary and compensating him only on the basis of the division's ROI, calculated based on operating income before any bonus payments. Proposal 3 calls for paying Marks some salary and some bonus based on ROI. Assume that Marks does not like bearing risk.

Required

1. Evaluate the three proposals, specifying the advantages and disadvantages of each.
2. Suppose that AMCO competes against Tiara Industries in the car battery business. Tiara is approximately the same size and operates in a business environment that is similar to Dexter's. The senior management of AMCO is considering evaluating Marks on the basis of Dexter's ROI minus Tiara's ROI. Marks complains that this approach is unfair because the performance of another company, over which he has no control, is included in his performance-evaluation measure. Is Marks's complaint valid? Why or why not?
3. Now suppose that Marks has no authority for making capital investment decisions. Corporate management makes these decisions. Is ROI a good performance measure to use to evaluate Marks? Is ROI a good measure to evaluate the economic viability of the Dexter Division? Explain.
4. Dexter's salespersons are responsible for selling and providing customer service and support. Sales are easy to measure. Although customer service is important to Dexter in the long run, it has not yet implemented customer-service measures. Marks wants to compensate his salesforce only on the basis of sales commissions paid for each unit of product sold. He cites two advantages to this plan: (a) It creates strong incentives for the salesforce to work hard, and (b) the company pays salespersons only when the company itself is earning revenues. Do you like his plan? Why or why not?

Problems

23-27 Relevant costs, performance evaluation, goal congruence. (N. Melumad, adapted) Pike Enterprises has three operating divisions. The managers of these divisions are evaluated on their division operating income, a figure that includes an allocation of corporate overhead proportional to the revenues of each division. The income statements (in thousands) for the first quarter of 2004 are as follows:

	Andorian Division	Orion Division	Tribble Division	Pike Enterprises
Revenues	$2,000	$1,200	$1,600	$4,800
Cost of goods sold	1,050	540	640	2,230
Gross margin	950	660	960	2,570
Division overhead	250	125	160	535
Corporate overhead	400	240	320	960
Division operating income	$ 300	$ 295	$ 480	$1,075

John Moore, the manager of the Andorian Division, is unhappy that his profitability is about the same as the Orion Division's and is much less than the Tribble Division's, even though his revenues are much higher than either of these divisions. Moore also knows that he is carrying one line of products with low profitability. He was going to replace this line of business as soon as more profitable product opportunities became available, but he has kept it because the line is marginally profitable and uses facilities that would otherwise be idle. Moore now realizes, however, that the sales from this product line are attracting a fair amount of corporate overhead because of the allocation procedure in use. This low-margin line of products had the following characteristics (in thousands) for the most recent quarter:

- Revenues: $800
- Cost of goods sold: $600
- Avoidable division overhead: $100

Required

1. Prepare the income statement for Pike Enterprises for the second quarter of 2004. Assume that revenues and operating results are identical to the first quarter except that Moore has discontinued the low-margin product line.
2. Is Pike Enterprises better off from discontinuing the low-margin product line?
3. Is Moore better off from discontinuing the low-margin product line?
4. Suggest changes for Pike's system of division reporting and evaluation that will motivate division managers to make decisions that are in the best interest of Pike Enterprises as a whole. Discuss any potential disadvantages of your proposal.

23-28 Historical-cost and current-cost ROI measures. Nobillo Corporation owns and manages convenience stores. The following information on three stores is collected for 2003:

	City Plaza	South Station	Central Park
Operating income	$ 90,000	$120,000	$ 60,000
Investment at historical cost	$300,000	$500,000	$240,000
Investment at current cost	$600,000	$700,000	$450,000
Age of store	10 years	5 years	8 years

Required

1. Compute the ROI for each store, with investment measured at (a) historical cost and (b) current cost.
2. How would you judge the performance of each store?

23-29 ROI performance measures based on historical cost and current cost. Mineral Waters Ltd. operates three divisions that process and bottle sparkling mineral water. The historical-cost accounting system reports the following information for 2004:

	Calistoga Division	Alpine Springs Division	Rocky Mountains Division
Revenues	$500,000	$ 700,000	$1,100,000
Operating costs (excluding plant depreciation)	300,000	380,000	600,000
Plant depreciation	70,000	100,000	120,000
Operating income	$130,000	$ 220,000	$ 380,000
Current assets	$200,000	$ 250,000	$ 300,000
Long-term assets—plant	140,000	900,000	1,320,000
Total assets	$340,000	$1,150,000	$1,620,000

Mineral Waters estimates the useful life of each plant to be 12 years, with a $0 terminal disposal value. The straight-line depreciation method is used. At the end of 2004, the Calistoga plant is 10 years old, the Alpine Springs plant is 3 years old, and the Rocky Mountains plant is 1 year old.

An index of construction costs for the 10-year period that Mineral Waters has been operating (1994 year-end = 100) is

1994	2001	2003	2004
100	136	160	170

Given the high turnover of current assets, management believes that the historical-cost and current-cost measures of current assets are approximately the same.

Required

1. Compute the ROI ratio (operating income to total assets) of each division using historical-cost measures. Comment on the results.
2. Use the approach in Exhibit 23-2 (p. 796) to compute the ROI of each division, incorporating current-cost estimates as of 2004 for depreciation and long-term assets. Comment on the results.
3. What advantages might arise from using current-cost asset measures as compared with historical-cost measures for evaluating the performance of the managers of the three divisions?

23-30 Evaluating managers, ROI, value-chain analysis of cost structure. User Friendly Computer is one of the largest personal computer companies in the world. The board of directors was recently informed that User Friendly's president is resigning. An executive search firm recommends that the board consider appointing Peter Diamond (current president of Computer Power) or Norma Provan (current president of Peach Computer). You collect the following financial information (in millions) on Computer Power and Peach Computer for 2002 and 2003:

	Computer Power		Peach Computer	
	2002	2003	2002	2003
Revenues	$400.0	$320.0	$200.0	$350.0
Costs				
R&D	36.0	16.8	18.0	43.5
Design	15.0	8.4	3.6	11.6
Production	102.0	112.0	82.8	98.6
Marketing	75.0	92.4	36.0	66.7
Distribution	27.0	22.4	18.0	23.2
Customer service	45.0	28.0	21.6	46.4
Total costs	300.0	280.0	180.0	290.0
Operating income	$100.0	$ 40.0	$ 20.0	$ 60.0
Total assets	$360.0	$340.0	$160.0	$240.0

In early 2004, a leading computer magazine gave Peach Computer's main product five stars, its highest rating. Computer Power's main product was given three stars, down from five stars a year ago, because of customer-service problems. The computer magazine also ran an article on new-product introductions. Peach Computer received high marks for new products in 2003. Computer Power's performance was called "mediocre."

Required

1. Use the DuPont method of profitability analysis to compute the ROI of Computer Power and Peach Computer in 2002 and 2003. Comment on the results.
2. Compute the percentage of costs in each of the six business-function cost categories for Computer Power and Peach Computer in 2002 and 2003. Comment on the results.
3. Rank Diamond and Provan as potential candidates for president of User Friendly Computer. Explain your ranking.

23-31 ROI, RI, ROS, management incentives. (CMA, adapted) The Jump-Start Division (JSD) of Mason Industries manufactures go-carts and other recreational vehicles. JSD is considering building a new plant in 2004. The investment will cost $2.5 million. The expected revenues and costs for the new plant in 2004 are

Revenues	$2,400,000
Variable costs	800,000
Fixed costs	1,120,000
Operating income	$ 480,000

JSD's ROI in 2003 is 24%, and its return on sales (ROS) is 19%. ROI is defined as operating income divided by total assets. The bonus of Maureen Grieco, the division manager of JSD, is based on division ROI.

Required

1. Explain why Grieco would be reluctant to build the new plant. Show your computations.
2. Suppose Mason Industries uses RI to determine Grieco's bonus. Suppose further that the required rate of return on investment is 15%. Will Grieco be more willing to build the new plant? Explain.
3. Suppose Mason Industries uses ROS to determine Grieco's bonus. Will Grieco be more willing to build the new plant? What are the advantages and disadvantages of using ROS to determine Grieco's bonus?

23-32 Division manager's compensation, risk sharing, incentives (continuation of 23-31). The management of Mason Industries is considering the following alternative compensation arrangements for Maureen Grieco, the division manager of JSD:

- Make Grieco's compensation a fixed salary without any bonus. Mason's management believes that one advantage of this arrangement is that Grieco will be less inclined to reject future investments just because of their impact on ROI or RI.

- Make all of Grieco's compensation depend on the division's RI. The benefit of this arrangement is that it creates incentives for Grieco to aggressively seek and accept all proposals that increase JSD's RI.
- Evaluate Grieco's performance using benchmarking by comparing JSD's RI against the RI achieved by managers of other companies that also manufacture and sell go-carts and recreational vehicles and have comparable levels of investment. Mason's management believes that the advantage of benchmarking is that it focuses attention on Grieco's performance relative to peers, rather than on the division's absolute performance.

Required

1. Assume Grieco is risk averse and does not like bearing risk. Using concepts of performance evaluation described in this chapter, evaluate the three proposals that Mason's management is considering. Indicate the positive and negative features of each proposal.
2. What compensation arrangement would you recommend? Explain briefly.

23-33 ROI, RI, investment decisions. The Media Group has three major divisions:

a. Newspapers—owns leading newspapers on four continents
b. Television—owns major television networks on three continents
c. Film studios—owns one of the five largest film studios in the world

Summary financial data (in millions) for 2002 and 2003 are as follows:

	Operating Income		Revenues		Total Assets	
	2002	2003	2002	2003	2002	2003
Newspapers	$900	$1,100	$4,500	$4,600	$4,400	$4,900
Television	130	160	6,000	6,400	2,700	3,000
Film studios	220	200	1,600	1,650	2,500	2,600

Division managers have an annual bonus plan based on division ROI. ROI is defined as operating income divided by total assets. Senior executives from divisions reporting increases in ROI from the prior year are automatically eligible for a bonus. Senior executives of divisions reporting a decline in the division ROI have to provide persuasive explanations for the decline to be eligible for a limited bonus.

Ken Kearney, manager of the Newspapers Division, is considering a proposal to invest $200 million in fast-speed printing presses with color-print options. The estimated increment to 2004 operating income would be $30 million. The Media Group has a 12% required rate of return for investments in all three divisions.

Required

1. Use the DuPont method of profitability analysis to explain differences among the three divisions in their ROIs for 2003. Use total assets in 2003 as the investment base.
2. Why might Kearney be less than enthusiastic about the fast-speed printing press investment proposal?
3. Rupert Prince, chairman of the Media Group, receives a proposal to base senior executive compensation at each division on division RI. Compute the RI of each division in 2003.
4. Would adoption of a RI measure reduce Kearney's reluctance to adopt the fast-speed printing press investment proposal?

23-34 Division managers' compensation (continuation of 23-33). Rupert Prince seeks your advice on revising the existing bonus plan for division managers of the Media Group. Assume division managers do not like bearing risk. He is considering three ideas:

- Make each division manager's compensation depend on division ROI.
- Make each division manager's compensation depend on companywide ROI.
- Use benchmarking, and compensate division managers on the basis of their division's ROI minus the average ROI of the other two divisions.

Required

Evaluate the three ideas Prince has put forth using performance-evaluation concepts described in this chapter. Indicate the positive and negative features of each proposal.

23-35 Ethics, manager's performance evaluation. (A. Spero, adapted) Hamilton Semiconductors manufactures specialized chips that sell for $20 each. Hamilton's manufacturing costs consist of variable costs of $2 per chip and fixed costs of $9,000,000. Hamilton also incurs $400,000 in fixed marketing costs each year.

Hamilton calculates operating income using absorption costing—that is, Hamilton calculates manufacturing costs per unit by dividing total manufacturing costs by actual production. Hamilton costs all units in inventory at this rate and expenses the costs in the income statement at the time when the units in inventory are sold. Next year, 2004, appears to be a difficult year for Hamilton. It expects to sell only 500,000 units. The demand for these chips fluctuates considerably, so Hamilton usually holds minimal inventory.

Required

1. Calculate Hamilton's operating income in 2004 if Hamilton manufactures (a) 500,000 units and (b) 600,000 units.
2. Would it be unethical for Randy Jones, the general manager of Hamilton Semiconductors, to produce more units than can be sold in order to show better operating results? Jones's compensation has a bonus component based on operating income. Explain your answer.
3. Would it be unethical for Jones to ask distributors to buy more product than they need? Hamilton follows the industry practice of booking sales when products are shipped to distributors. Explain your answer.

Collaborative Learning Problem

23-36 ROI, RI, division manager's compensation, nonfinancial measures. Key information for the Peoria Division (PD) of Barrington industries for 2003 follows.

Revenues	$15,000,000
Operating income	1,800,000
Total assets	10,000,000

PD's managers are evaluated and rewarded on the basis of ROI defined as operating income divided by total assets. Barrington Industries expects its divisions to increase ROI each year.

Next year, 2004, appears to be a difficult year for PD. PD had planned a new investment to improve quality but, in view of poor economic conditions, has postponed the investment. ROI for 2004 was certain to decrease had PD made the investment.

Management is now considering ways to meet its target ROI of 20% for next year. It anticipates revenues to be steady at $15,000,000 in 2004.

Required

1. Calculate PD's return on sales (ROS) and ROI for 2003.
2. **a.** By how much would PD need to cut costs in 2004 to achieve its target ROI of 20% in 2004, assuming no change in total assets between 2003 and 2004?
   b. By how much would PD need to decrease total assets in 2004 to achieve its target ROI of 20% in 2004, assuming no change in operating income between 2003 and 2004?
3. Calculate PD's RI in 2003 assuming a required rate of return on investment of 15%.
4. PD wants to increase RI by 50% in 2004. Assuming it could cut costs by $45,000 in 2004, by how much would PD need to decrease total assets in 2004?
5. Barrington Industries is concerned that the focus on cost cutting and asset sales will have an adverse long-run effect on PD's customers. Yet Barrington wants PD to meet its financial goals. What other measurements, if any, do you recommend that Barrington use? Explain briefly.

CHAPTER 23 INTERNET EXERCISE

Investors today have unparalleled access to financial information on the Web. To use the Web to evaluate a company's financial performance, go to www.prenhall.com/horngren, click on *Cost Accounting, 11th ed.*, and access the Internet exercise for Chapter 23.

CHAPTER 23 VIDEO CASE

McDONALD'S CORPORATION: Performance Measurement and Compensation Issues

Not long ago, McDonald's top management wanted to revise the compensation package for managers in all 1,800 of its U.S.-based company-owned restaurants. The revision was intended to make sure the company continued to offer a competitive compensation package to managers. Top management also was interested in improving the linkage between its corporate vision and management incentives. The question facing management was this: How best to structure the new plan?

McDonald's was founded in 1955 by Ray Kroc, a milkshake machine salesman of great personal ambition. On a chance visit to a restaurant in Southern California, he noted the long line of customers waiting to buy a milkshake. If customers would come and wait at one restaurant for shakes, he reasoned, certainly they would come if there were other locations. The restaurant was owned by the McDonald brothers. Ray Kroc approached the brothers about expanding to multiple locations—the rest is history.

Ray Kroc built McDonald's around a new food-production system that applied precise procedures that not only helped streamline operations for efficient service, but also created a pleasant family atmosphere for dining. Standards were established for food portions, and equipment was designed to prepare meals quickly. The words "quality, service, cleanliness, and value," or QSCV, stood behind every meal, every customer interaction, every day. Ray Kroc wanted each customer's restaurant experience to be the best.

The vision of being the best is still alive today at McDonald's. Managers are trained in all aspects of operations at the company's central training center in Oak Brook, Illinois. Called Hamburger University, the facility provides intensive courses of study to help managers understand how to deliver QSCV. The managers are quite loyal to McDonald's, but the job market is competitive. McDonald's knows that its compensation scheme and incentives must meet the expectations of its managers or they risk losing them. So, what should be rewarded and how?

For the managers at company-owned restaurants in some markets, McDonald's has chosen incentives tied to performance in four areas: operational excellence, customer satisfaction, people, and profitability. These areas are all linked to the corporate vision of being the best quick-service restaurant experience, and they are reported to the restaurants on a monthly report called a "scorecard."

Restaurant managers are evaluated on the elements of the four areas that are within their control. For example, McDonald's believes that taking care of its people is key to success, so managers are given incentives to reduce turnover and increase employee commitment. For profitability, sales are important, but they can't always be controlled by restaurant managers. For example, a restaurant located near roadway construction may see a decline in sales due to limited access. Weather also affects business. Instead, restaurant managers may be compensated more heavily for achieving adjusted "bottom line" targets or cost-control targets, or operational excellence as measured by mystery shoppers or restaurant performance grading.

The key is linking incentive payouts to actual results. If goals are not achieved, no payouts occur. The amount of each reward is appropriate for the effort required to achieve the desired result, so managers will feel the effort was worth it. If the rewards are presented frequently and in a timely manner, there is strong reinforcement of the actions that resulted in the performance initially, which increases the likelihood the actions will be repeated. That's a challenge McDonald's would like all its managers to take!

QUESTIONS

1. Of the 28,000-plus restaurants that McDonald's operates around the globe, 1,800 of them are company-owned. Does it make sense to devise a single compensation plan for use in all 1,800 locations? Why or why not?
2. Return on investment has been used in the past as part of a restaurant manager's performance evaluation. For company-owned restaurants, is this a viable measure of performance for restaurant managers? Why or why not?
3. Put yourself in the position of a restaurant manager at McDonald's. Because the restaurants operate with the same vision, should McDonald's use benchmarking and relative performance evaluation to compensate restaurant managers? What are the benefits? Costs?

Surveys of Company Practice

This appendix provides the full citations to the individual publications cited in the many Surveys of Company Practice boxes included in the text.

American Electronics Association, *Operating Ratios Survey 1993–94,* (Santa Clara, CA: American Electronics Association, 1993) — cited in Chapter 18.

APQC/CAM-I, *Activity Based Management Consortium Study* (American Productivity and Quality Center/CAM-I, 1995) — cited in Chapter 5.

Armitage, H., and R. Nicholson, "Activity-Based Costing: A Survey of Canadian Practice," Supplement to *CMA Magazine* (1993) — cited in Chapter 5.

Asada, T., J. Bailes, and M. Amano, "An Empirical Study of Japanese and American Budget Planning and Control Systems," (Working Paper, Tsukuba University and Oregon State University, 1989) — cited in Chapter 6.

Ask, U., and C. Ax, "A Survey of Cost Accounting Practice in a Manufacturing Setting — the Swedish Case," *Journal of Theory and Practice of Management* (1997) — cited in Chapters 7 and 9.

Atkinson, A., *Intrafirm Cost and Resource Allocations: Theory and Practice,* (Hamilton, Canada: Society of Management Accountants of Canada and Canadian Academic Accounting Association Research Monograph, 1987) — cited in Chapter 14.

Ax, C., and T. Bjornenak, "The Building and Diffusion of Management Accounting Innovations — The Case of Balanced Scorecard in Scandinavia," (European Accounting Association Congress, 2000) — cited in Chapter 13.

Berry, L. E., and J. Scheumann. "The Controller's Good Intentions," *Financial Executive,* (January/February 1998) — cited in Chapter 1.

Blayney, P., and I. Yokoyama, "Comparative Analysis of Japanese and Australian Cost Accounting and Management Practices," (Working Paper. The University of Sydney, Australia, 1991) — cited in chapters 2, 4, 6, 9, 12, 21, and 22.

Block, S., "Capital Budgeting Techniques Used by Small Business in the 1990's," *The Engineering Economist* (Summer 1998) — cited in Chapter 21.

Bruner, R., K. Eades, R. Harris, and R. Higgins, "Best Practices in Estimating the Cost of Capital: Survey and Synthesis," *Financial Practice and Education* (1998)—cited in Chapter 21.

Business International Corporation, *101, More Checklists for Global Financial Management* (New York, 1992) — cited in Chapter 23.

Chenhall, R. H., and K. Langfield-Smith, "Adoption and Benefits of Management Accounting Practices: An Australian Study," *Management Accounting Research* (March 1998) — cited in Chapter 6.

Clarke, B., and M. Lokman, "Activity-Based Costing in Australian Companies," 2000 — cited in Chapter 5.

Clarke, P., "Management Accounting Practices and Techniques in Irish Manufacturing Firms," (Working Paper, University College, Dublin, Ireland, 1995) — cited in Chapters 7 and 22.

Clarke, P., "A Survey of Activity-Based Costing in Large Manufacturing Firms in Ireland," (Working Paper, University College, Dublin, Ireland, 1996) — cited in Chapters 4 and 5.

Clarke, P., and C. Brislane, "An Investigation into JIT Systems in Ireland," (Working Paper, University College, Dublin, Ireland, 2000) — cited in Chapters 4 and 7.

Clarke, P., and T. Mullins, "Activity-Based Costing in the Nonmanufacturing Sector in Ireland," (Working Paper, University College, Dublin, Ireland, 2001) — cited in Chapter 5.

Clarke, P., and T. O'Dea, "Management Accounting Systems: Some Field Evidence from Sixteen Multinational Companies in Ireland," (Working Paper, University College, Dublin, Ireland, 1993) — cited in Chapter 21.

Cohen, J., and L. Paquette, "Management Accounting Practices: Perceptions of Controllers," *Journal of Cost Management* (Fall 1991) — cited in Chapter 4.

Cornick, M., W. Cooper, and S. Wilson, "How Do Companies Analyze Overhead," *Management Accounting* (June 1988) — cited in Chapters 7 and 12.

Cotton, W., "Activity Based Costing in New Zealand," (Working paper, SUNY Genesco, 1993) — cited in Chapter 5.

Dean, G., M. Joye, and P. Blayney, *Strategic Management Accounting Survey,* (Sydney, Australia: The University of Sydney, 1991) — cited in Chapter 14.

deWith, E., and E. Ijskes, "Current Budgeting Practices in Dutch Companies," (Working Paper, Vrije Universiteit, 1992, Amsterdam, Netherlands) — cited in Chapter 6.

Drury, C., S. Braund, P. Osborne, and M. Tayles, *A Survey of Management Accounting Practices in UK Manufacturing Companies,* (London, U.K., Chartered Association of Certified Accountants, 1993) — cited in chapters 4, 7, 8, 12, and 22.

Elliott, J., "International Transfer Pricing, A Survey of U.K. and Non-U.K. Groups," *Management Accounting,* CIMA, November 1998 — cited in Chapter 22.

Foster, G. and S. M. Young, "Frontiers of Management Accounting Research," *Journal of Management Accounting Research* (1997) — cited in Chapter 16.

Fremgen, J., and S. Liao, *The Allocation of Corporate Indirect Costs* (New York: National Association of Accountants, 1981) — cited in Chapter 14.

Frigo, M., "2001 CMG Survey on Performance Measurement Trends and Challenges in Performance Measurement," *Cost Management Update,* (Institute of Management Accountants, 2001) — cited in Chapter 13.

Gosselin, M., "Performance Measurement Competence in Manufacturing Firms: Empirical Evidence," (Working Paper, Université Laval, Quebec City, Canada, 2001)—cited in Chapter 7.

Govindarajan, V., and B. Ramamurthy, "Transfer Pricing Policies in Indian Companies: A Survey," *Chartered Accountant* (November 1983) — cited in Chapter 22.

Grant, Thornton, *Survey of American Manufacturers,* (New York: Grant Thornton, 1992) — cited in Chapter 12.

Groot, T., "Activity Based Costing in U.S. and Dutch food companies," *Advances in Management Accounting,* 1999 — cited in Chapter 5.

Hoque, Z., and M. Alam, "Organization Size, Business Objectives, Managerial Antonomy, Industry Conditions, and Management's Choice of Transfer Pricing Methods: A Contextual Analysis of New Zealand Companies," (Working Paper, Victoria University of Wellington, Wellington, New Zealand) — cited in Chapter 22.

Innes, J., and F. Mitchell, "A Survey of Activity-Based Costing in the U.K.'s Largest Companies," *Management Accounting Research* (June 1995) — cited in Chapters 5 and 16.

Inoue, S., "A Comparative Study of Recent Development of Cost Management Problems in U.S.A., U.K., Canada, and Japan," Kagawa University *Economic Review* (June 1988) — cited in Chapters 6, 7, and 9.

Jog, V., and A. Srivastava, "Corporate Financial Decision Making in Canada, *Canadian Journal of Administrative Sciences* (June 1994) — cited in Chapter 21.

Joye, M., and P. Blayney, "Cost and Management Accounting Practices in Australian Manufacturing Companies: Survey Results." (Accounting Research Centre, The University of Sydney, 1991) — cited in Chapters 10, 17, and 22.

Kalagnanam, S., "The Use of Nonfinancial Measures (NFM) by Managers," (Working Paper, University of Saskatchewan, Saskatoon, Canada, 2001) — cited in Chapter 23.

Kim, I., and J. Song, "U.S., Korea, and Japan: Accounting Practices in Three Countries," *Management Accounting* (August 1990) — cited in Chapter 21.

Koester, R. J., and D. J. Barnett, "Petroleum Refinery Joint Cost Allocation" (Working paper, California State University, Dominguez Hills, 1996) — cited in Chapter 15.

Lazere, C., "All Together Now," *CFO* (February 1998) — cited in Chapter 6.

Malmi, T., "Balanced Scorecard in Finnish Companies: Some Empirical Evidence," (European Accounting Association Congress, 2000) — cited in Chapter 13.

Management Accounting Research Group, "Investigation into the Actual State of Target Costing, Corporate Accounting," (Working Paper, Kobe University, Japan, May 1992) — cited in Chapter 12.

Mills, R., and C. Sweeting, "Pricing Decisions in Practice: How Are They Made in U.K. Manufacturing and Service Companies?" (London, U.K.: Chartered Institute of Management Accountants, Occasional Paper, 1988) — cited in Chapter 12.

Mostafa, A., J. Sharp, and K. Howard, "Transfer Pricing — A Survey Using Discriminant Analysis," *Omega,* 12, no. 5 (1984) — cited in Chapter 22.

Mowen, M., *Accounting for Costs as Fixed and Variable* (National Association of Accountants: Montvale, NJ, 1986) — cited in Chapter 2.

NAA Tokyo Affiliate, "Management Accounting in the Advanced Manufacturing Surrounding: Comparative Study on Survey in Japan and U.S.A.," (Tokyo, Japan, 1988) — cited in Chapter 10.

Price Waterhouse, *Transfer Pricing Practices of American Industry* (New York: Price Waterhouse, 1984) — cited in Chapter 22.

Ramadan, S., "The Rationale for Cost Allocation: A Study of U.K. Divisionalised Companies," *Accounting and Business Research* (Winter 1989) — cited in Chapter 14.

Research Incorporated, "Synchronizing the Supply Chain Through Collaborative Design," (Alpharetta, Georgia, 1998) — cited in Chapter 20.

Rodrigues, L., and G. Sonsa, "The Use of the Balanced Scorecard in Portugal," (Universidade do Minho, Portugal, 2000)—cited in Chapter 13.

Sangster, A., "Capital Investment Appraisal Techniques: A Survey of Current Usage," *Journal of Business Finance & Accounting* (April 1993) — cited in Chapter 21.

Scarbrough, P., A. Nanni, and M. Sakurai, "Japanese Management Accounting Practices and the Effects of Assembly and Process Automation," *Management Accounting Research* (March 1991) — cited in Chapters 7 and 23.

Schlank, R., "Evaluating the Performance of International Operations," (New York: Business International Corporation, 1989) — cited in Chapter 23.

Siegel, G. and J. Sorensen, "The Practice Analysis of Management Accounting," *Management Accounting* (March 1999) — cited in Chapter 1.

Smith, K., and C. Sullivan, "Survey of Cost Management Systems in Manufacturing," (Working Paper, Purdue University, West Lafayette, Indiana, 1990) — cited in Chapters 21 and 23.

Stewart, G.B., "Eva®, Fact and Fantasy," *Journal of Applied Corporate Finance* (Summer, 1994) — cited in Chapter 23.

Tang, R., "Canadian Transfer Pricing in the 1990s," *Management Accounting* (February 1992) — cited in Chapter 22.

Tang, R., *Transfer Pricing Systems Management: Practical Issues and Cases* (Montvale, NJ: Institute of Management Accountants, 2001) — cited in Chapters 22 and 23.

Towers, Perrin, "CompScan Report: Inside the Balanced Scorecard," January 1996 — cited in Chapter 13.

Yasukata, K., "A Survey of Performance Measurement and Evaluation Systems in Japan: Strategic Management Accounting Perspective (Working Paper, Kobe University, Japan, 2001) — cited in Chapter 23.

Recommended Readings

The literature on cost accounting and related areas is vast and varied. The following books illustrate recent publications that capture current developments:

Ansari, S., J. Bell, and CAM-I Target Cost Core Group, *Target Costing: The Next Frontier in Strategic Cost Management.* Chicago: Irwin Professional Publishing, 1996.

Brimson, J., *Activity Accounting: An Activity-Based Costing Approach.* New York: John Wiley & Sons, 1997.

Connell, R., *Measuring Customer and Service Profitability in the Finance Sector.* London, U.K.: Chapman & Hall, 1996.

Cooper, R., and R. Kaplan, *The Design of Cost Management Systems.* Upper Saddle River, NJ: Prentice Hall, 1999.

Ditz, D., J. Ranganathan, and R. Banks, *Green Ledgers: Case Studies in Corporate Environmental Accounting.* World Resources Institute, 1995.

Hronec, S., *Vital Signs.* New York: American Management Association, 1993.

Johnson, T., *Relevance Regained.* New York: Free Press, 1992.

Miller, J., *Implementing Activity-Based Management in Daily Operation.* New York: John Wiley & Sons, 1996.

Player, S., and D. Keys, *Activity-Based Management.* New York: MasterMedia Limited, 1995.

Schweitzer, M., E. Trossmann, and G. Lawson, *Break-even Analyses: Basic Model, Variants, Extensions.* Chichester, U.K.: Wiley, 1992.

Shank, J., and V. Govindarajan, *Strategic Management Accounting.* New York: The Free Press, 1993.

Simons, R., Performance Measurement and Control Systems for Implementing Strategy, Upper Saddle River, N.J.: Prentice Hall, 2000.

Books of readings related to cost or management accounting include:

Aly, I., ed., *Readings in Management Accounting.* Dubuque, Iowa: Kendall/Hunt, 1995.

Brinker, B., ed., *Emerging Practices in Cost Management.* Boston, MA: Warren, Gorham, and Lamont, 1995.

Ratnatunga, J., J. Miller, N. Mudalige, and A. Sohalled, eds., *Issues in Strategic Management Accounting.* Sydney, Australia: Harcourt Brace Jovanovich, 1993.

Young, M., ed., *Readings in Management Accounting.* Upper Saddle River, N.J.: Prentice Hall, 2001.

The Harvard Business School series in accounting and control offers important contributions to the cost accounting literature, including:

Anthony, R., *The Management Control Function.* Boston: Harvard Business School Press, 1988.

Berliner, C., and J. Brimson, eds., *Cost Management for Todays Advanced Manufacturing: The CAMI Conceptual Design.* Boston: Harvard Business School Press, 1988.

Bruns, W., ed., *Performance Measurement, Evaluation, and Incentives.* Boston: Harvard Business School Press, 1992.

Bruns, W., and R. Kaplan, eds., *Accounting and Management: Field Study Perspectives.* Boston: Harvard Business School Press, 1987.

Cooper, R., *When Lean Enterprises Collide.* Boston: Harvard Business School Press, 1995.

Johnson, H., and R. Kaplan, *Relevance Lost: The Rise and Fall of Management Accounting.* Boston: Harvard Business School Press, 1987.

Kaplan, R., ed., *Measures for Manufacturing Excellence.* Boston: Harvard Business School Press, 1990.

Kaplan, R., and R. Cooper, *Cost and Effect.* Boston: Harvard Business School Press, 1998.

Kaplan, R., and D. P. Norton, *The Balanced Scorecard.* Boston: Harvard Business School Press, 1996.

Kaplan, R., and D. P. Norton, *The Strategy-Focused Organization,* Harvard Business School Press, 2001.

Merchant, K.A., *Rewarding Results: Motivating Profit Center Managers.* Boston: Harvard Business School Press, 1989.

Simons R., *Levers of Control.* Boston: Harvard Business School Press, 1995.

Productivity Press publishes many books with a global focus on cost and management accounting, including:

Cooper, R., and R. Slagmulder, *Target Costing and Value Engineering.* Portland: Productivity Press, 1997.

Monden, Y., *Cost Management in the New Manufacturing Age: Innovations in the Japanese Automotive Industry.* Cambridge, MA: Productivity Press, 1993.

Sakurai, M., *Integrated Cost Management.* Portland, OR: Productivity Press, 1996.

The Institute of Management Accountants publishes monographs and books covering cost accounting topics, such as:

Atkinson, A., J. Hamburg, and C. Ittner, *Linking Quality to Profits,* Montvale, NJ: Institute of Management Accountants and Milwaukee, WI: ASQC Quality Press, 1994.

Cooper, R., R. Kaplan, L. Maisel, E. Morrissey, and R. Oehm, *Implementing Activity-Based Cost Management: Moving from Analysis to Action.* Montvale, NJ: Institute of Management Accountants, 1993.

Dhavale, D., *Management Accounting Issues in Cellular Manufacturing and Focused-Factory Systems.* Montvale, NJ: Institute of Management Accountants, 1996.

Epstein, M., *Measuring Corporate Environmental Performance.* Montvale, NJ: IMA Foundation of Applied Research, 1995.

Klammer, T., *Managing Strategic and Capital Investment Decisions.* Burr Ridge, IL: Irwin and IMA, 1994.

Martinson, O., *Cost Accounting in the Service Industry.* Montvale, NJ: Institute of Management Accountants, 1994.

Noreen, E., D. Smith, and J.T. Mackey, *The Theory of Constraints and Its Implications for Management Accounting.* Great Barrington, MA: North River Press, 1995.

The Financial Executives Research Foundation publishes monographs and books concerning topics of interest to financial executives, such as:

Howell, R., J. Shank, S. Soucy, and J. Fisher, *Cost Management for Tomorrow: Seeking the Competitive Edge.* Morristown, NJ: Financial Executives Research Foundation, 1992.

Keating, P., and S. Jablonsky, *Changing Roles of Financial Management.* Morristown, NJ: Financial Executives Research Foundation, 1990.

The Chartered Institute of Management Accountants, London, U.K., publishes monographs and books, including:

Drury, C., ed., *Management Accounting Handbook.* London, U.K.: Butterworth Heinemann and Chartered Institute of Management Accountants, 1997.

Ezzamel, M., C. Green, S. Lilley, and H. Willmott, *Changing Managers and Managing Change.* London, UK: Chartered Institute of Management Accountants, 1995.

Friedman, A., and S. Lylne, *Activity-Based Techniques: The Real Life Consequences.* London, UK: Chartered Institute of Management Accountants, 1995.

Murphy, C., J. Currie, M. Fahy, and W. Golden, *Deciding the Future: Management Accountants as Decision Support Personnel.* London, UK: Chartered Institute of Management Accountants, 1995.

Ward, K., *Strategic Management Accounting.* Oxford, U.K.: Butterworth Heinemann and Chartered Institute of Management Accountants, 1992.

Jai Press publishes *Advances in Management Accounting* on an annual basis. It is edited by M. Epstein and K. Poston and includes a broad cross-section of research articles and case studies.

Case books on cost and management accounting include:

Rotch, W., B. Allen, and E. Brownlee, *Cases in Management Accounting and Control Systems.* Upper Saddle River, NJ: Prentice Hall, 1995.

Shank, J., *Cases in Cost Management: A Strategic Emphasis.* Cincinnati, Ohio: South Western Publishing, 1996.

The following are detailed annotated bibliographies of the cost and management accounting research literatures:

Clancy, D., *Annotated Management Accounting Readings.* Management Accounting Section of the American Accounting Association, 1986.

Deakin, E., M. Maher, and J. Cappel, *Contemporary Literature in Cost Accounting.* Homewood, IL: Richard D. Irwin, 1988.

Klemstine, C., and M. Maher, *Management Accounting Research: 1926–1983.* New York: Garland Publishing, 1984.

The *Journal of Cost Management for the Manufacturing Industry* contains numerous articles on modern management accounting. It is published by Warren, Gorham, and Lamont, 210 South Street, Boston, MA 02111.

Two journals bearing on management accounting are published by sections of the American Accounting Association, 5717 Bessie Drive, Sarasota, FL 34233: *Journal of Management Accounting Research* and *Behavioral Research in Accounting.*

Professional associations that specialize in serving members with cost and management accounting interests include:

- *Institute of Management Accountants,* 10 Paragon Drive, P.O. Box 433, Montvale, NJ 07645. Publishes the *Strategic Finance* journal.
- *Financial Executives Institute,* 10 Madison Avenue, P.O. Box 1938, Morristown, NJ 07960. Publishes *Financial Executive.*
- *Society of Cost Estimating and Analysis,* 101 South Whiting Street, Suite 313, Alexandria, VA 22304. Publishes the *Journal of Cost Analysis* and monographs related to cost estimation and price analysis in government and industry.
- *The Institute of Internal Auditors,* 249 Maitland Avenue, Altamonte Springs, FL 32701. Publishes *The Internal Auditor* journal. Also publishes monographs on topics related to internal control.
- *Society of Management Accountants of Canada,* 154 Main Street East, MPO Box 176, Hamilton, Ontario, L8N 3C3. Publishes the *CMA Magazine.*
- *The Chartered Institute of Management Accountants,* 63 Portland Place, London, WIN 4AB. Publishes the *Management Accounting* journal. Also publishes monographs covering cost and managerial accounting topics.

In many countries, individuals with cost and management accounting interests belong to professional bodies that serve members with financial reporting and taxation, as well as cost and management accounting, interests.

Notes on Compound Interest and Interest Tables

APPENDIX C

Interest is the cost of using money. It is the rental charge for funds, just as renting a building and equipment entails a rental charge. When the funds are used for a period of time, it is necessary to recognize interest as a cost of using the borrowed ("rented") funds. This requirement applies even if the funds represent ownership capital and if interest does not entail an outlay of cash. Why must interest be considered? Because the selection of one alternative automatically commits a given amount of funds that could otherwise be invested in some other alternative.

Interest is generally important, even when short-term projects are under consideration. Interest looms correspondingly larger when long-run plans are studied. The rate of interest has significant enough impact to influence decisions regarding borrowing and investing funds. For example, $100,000 invested now and compounded annually for 10 years at 8% will accumulate to $215,900; at 20%, the $100,000 will accumulate to $619,200.

INTEREST TABLES

Many computer programs and pocket calculators are available that handle computations involving the time value of money. You may also turn to the following four basic tables to compute interest.

Table 1—Future Amount of $1

Table 1 shows how much $1 invested now will accumulate in a given number of periods at a given compounded interest rate per period. Consider investing $1,000 now for three years at 8% compound interest. A tabular presentation of how this $1,000 would accumulate to $1,259.70 follows:

Year	Interest per Year	Cumulative Interest Called Compound Interest	Total at End of Year
0	$ —	$ —	$1,000.00
1	80.00 (0.08 × $1,000)	80.00	1,080.00
2	86.40 (0.08 × $1,080)	166.40	1,166.40
3	93.30 (0.08 × $1,166.40)	259.70	1,259.70

This tabular presentation is a series of computations that could appear as follows, where S is the future amount and the subscripts 1, 2, and 3 indicate the number of time periods.

$$S_1 = \$1,000(1.08)^1 = \$1.080$$
$$S_2 = \$1,080(1.08) = \$1,000(1.08)^2 = \$1,166.40$$
$$S_3 = \$1,166.40 \times (1.08) = \$1,000(1.08)^3 = \$1,259.70$$

The formula for the "amount of 1," often called the "future value of $1" or "future amount of $1," can be written

$$S = P(1 + r)^n$$
$$S = \$1,000(1 + .08)^3 = \$1,259.70$$

S is the future value amount; P is the present value, $1,000 in this case; r is the rate of interest; and n is the number of time periods.

Fortunately, tables make key computations readily available. A facility in selecting the *proper* table will minimize computations. Check the accuracy of the preceding answer using Table 1, p. 828.

Table 2—Present Value of $1

In the previous example, if $1,000 compounded at 8% per year will accumulate to $1,259.70 in 3 years, then $1,000 must be the present value of $1,259.70 due at the end of 3 years. The formula for the present value can be derived by reversing the process of *accumulation* (finding the future amount) that we just finished.

If
$$S = P(1 + r)n$$

then
$$P = \frac{S}{(1 + r)^n}$$

$$P = \frac{\$1,259.70}{(1.08)^3} = \$1,000$$

Use Table 2, p. 829, to check this calculation.

When accumulating, we advance or roll forward in time. The difference between our original amount and our accumulated amount is called *compound interest*. When discounting, we retreat or roll back in time. The difference between the future amount and the present value is called *compound discount*. Note the following formulas (where P = $1,000):

$$\text{Compound interest} = P[(1 + \text{r})^n - 1] = \$259.70$$

$$\text{Compound discount} = S\left[1 - \frac{1}{(1 + r)^n}\right] = \$259.70$$

Table 3—Amount of Annuity of $1

An (ordinary) *annuity* is a series of equal payments (receipts) to be paid (or received) at the end of successive periods of equal length. Assume that $1,000 is invested at the end of each of 3 years at 8%:

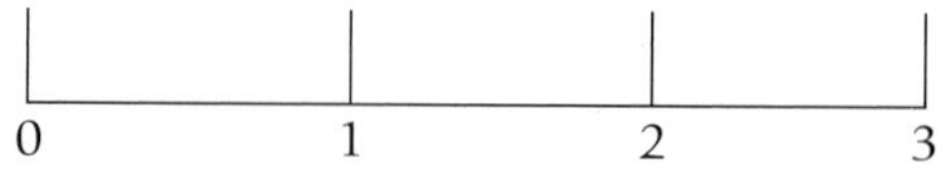

End of Year			Amount
1st payment	$1,000.00 →	$1,080.00 →	$1,166.40, which is $1,000(1.08)^2
2nd payment		$1,000.00 →	1,080.00, which is $1,000(1.08)^1
3rd payment			1,000.00
Accumulation (future amount)			$3,246.40

The preceding arithmetic may be expressed algebraically as the amount of an ordinary annuity of $1,000 for 3 years = $\$1,000(1 + r)^2 + \$1,000(1 + r)^1 + \$1,000$.

We can develop the general formula for S_n, the amount of an ordinary annuity of $1, by using the example above as a basis:

1. $S_n = 1 + (1 + \text{r})^1 + (1 + \text{r})^2$
2. Substitute: $S_n = 1 + (1.08)^1 + (1.08)^2$
3. Multiply (2) by (1 + r): $(1.08)S_n = (1.08)^1 + (1.08)^2 + (1.08)^3$
4. Subtract (2) from (3): Note that all terms on the right-hand side are removed except $(1.08)^3$ in equation (3) and 1 in equation (2). $1.08S_n - S_n = (1.08)^3 - 1$
5. Factor (4): $S_n(1.08 - 1) = (1.08)^3 - 1$

6. Divide (5) by (1.08 – 1): $$S_n = \frac{(1.08)^3 - 1}{1.08 - 1} = \frac{(1.08)^3 - 1}{.08}$$

7. The general formula for the amount of an ordinary annuity of \$1 becomes: $$S_n = \frac{(1 + r)^n - 1}{r} \text{ or } \frac{\text{Compound interest}}{\text{Rate}}$$

This formula is the basis for Table 3, p. 830. Look at Table 3 or use the formula itself to check the calculations.

Table 4—Present Value of an Ordinary Annuity of \$1

Using the same example as for Table 3, we can show how the formula of P_n, *the present value of an ordinary annuity,* is developed.

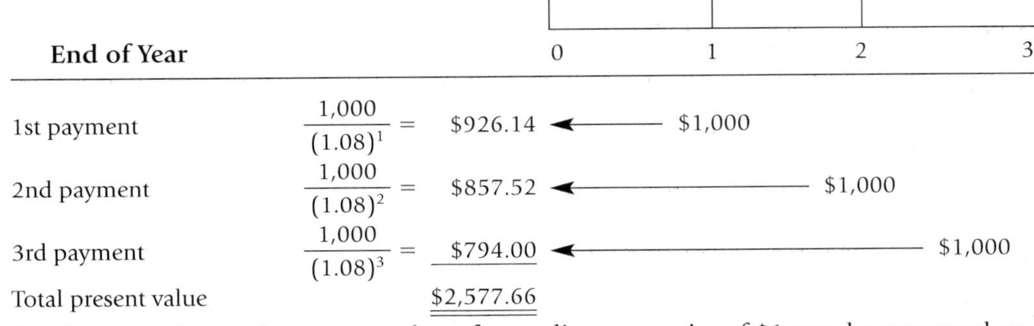

For the general case, the present value of an ordinary annuity of \$1 may be expressed as:

1. $$P_n = \frac{1}{1 + r} + \frac{1}{(1 + r)^2} + \frac{1}{(1 + r)^3}$$

2. Substitute $$P_n = \frac{1}{1.08} + \frac{1}{(1.08)^2} + \frac{1}{(1.08)^3}$$

3. Multiply by $\frac{1}{1.08}$: $$P_n \frac{1}{1.08} = \frac{1}{(1.08)^2} + \frac{1}{(1.08)^3} + \frac{1}{(1.08)^4}$$

4. Subtract (3) from (2): $$P_n - P_n \frac{1}{1.08} = \frac{1}{1.08} - \frac{1}{(1.08)^4}$$

5. Factor: $$P_n\left(1 - \frac{1}{(1.08)}\right) = \frac{1}{1.08}\left[1 - \frac{1}{(1.08)^3}\right]$$

6. or $$P_n\left(\frac{.08}{1.08}\right) = \frac{1}{1.08}\left[1 - \frac{1}{(1.08)^3}\right]$$

7. Multiply by $\frac{1.08}{.08}$: $$P_n = \frac{1}{.08}\left[1 - \frac{1}{(1.08)^3}\right]$$

The general formula for the present value of an annuity of \$1.00 is:

$$P_n = \frac{1}{r}\left[1 - \frac{1}{(1 + r)^n}\right] = \frac{\text{Compound discount}}{\text{Rate}}$$

Solving, $$P_n = \frac{.2062}{.08} = 2.577$$

The formula is the basis for Table 4, p. 831. Check the answer in the table. The present value tables, Tables 2 and 4, are used most frequently in capital budgeting.

The tables for annuities are not essential. With Tables 1 and 2, compound interest and compound discount can readily be computed. It is simply a matter of dividing either of these by the rate to get values equivalent to those shown in Tables 3 and 4.

TABLE 1
Compound Amount of $1.00 (The Future Value of $1.00)
$S = P(1 + r)^n$. In this table $P = \$1.00$

Periods	2%	4%	6%	8%	10%	12%	14%	16%	18%	20%	22%	24%	26%	28%	30%	32%	40%	Periods
1	1.020	1.040	1.060	1.080	1.100	1.120	1.140	1.160	1.180	1.200	1.220	1.240	1.260	1.280	1.300	1.320	1.400	1
2	1.040	1.082	1.124	1.166	1.210	1.254	1.300	1.346	1.392	1.440	1.488	1.538	1.588	1.638	1.690	1.742	1.960	2
3	1.061	1.125	1.191	1.260	1.331	1.405	1.482	1.561	1.643	1.728	1.816	1.907	2.000	2.097	2.197	2.300	2.744	3
4	1.082	1.170	1.262	1.360	1.464	1.574	1.689	1.811	1.939	2.074	2.215	2.364	2.520	2.684	2.856	3.036	3.842	4
5	1.104	1.217	1.338	1.469	1.611	1.762	1.925	2.100	2.288	2.488	2.703	2.932	3.176	3.436	3.713	4.007	5.378	5
6	1.126	1.265	1.419	1.587	1.772	1.974	2.195	2.436	2.700	2.986	3.297	3.635	4.002	4.398	4.827	5.290	7.530	6
7	1.149	1.316	1.504	1.714	1.949	2.211	2.502	2.826	3.185	3.583	4.023	4.508	5.042	5.629	6.275	6.983	10.541	7
8	1.172	1.369	1.594	1.851	2.144	2.476	2.853	3.278	3.759	4.300	4.908	5.590	6.353	7.206	8.157	9.217	14.758	8
9	1.195	1.423	1.689	1.999	2.358	2.773	3.252	3.803	4.435	5.160	5.987	6.931	8.005	9.223	10.604	12.166	20.661	9
10	1.219	1.480	1.791	2.159	2.594	3.106	3.707	4.411	5.234	6.192	7.305	8.594	10.086	11.806	13.786	16.060	28.925	10
11	1.243	1.539	1.898	2.332	2.853	3.479	4.226	5.117	6.176	7.430	8.912	10.657	12.708	15.112	17.922	21.199	40.496	11
12	1.268	1.601	2.012	2.518	3.138	3.896	4.818	5.936	7.288	8.916	10.872	13.215	16.012	19.343	23.298	27.983	56.694	12
13	1.294	1.665	2.133	2.720	3.452	4.363	5.492	6.886	8.599	10.699	13.264	16.386	20.175	24.759	30.288	36.937	79.371	13
14	1.319	1.732	2.261	2.937	3.797	4.887	6.261	7.988	10.147	12.839	16.182	20.319	25.421	31.691	39.374	48.757	111.120	14
15	1.346	1.801	2.397	3.172	4.177	5.474	7.138	9.266	11.974	15.407	19.742	25.196	32.030	40.565	51.186	64.359	155.568	15
16	1.373	1.873	2.540	3.426	4.595	6.130	8.137	10.748	14.129	18.488	24.086	31.243	40.358	51.923	66.542	84.954	217.795	16
17	1.400	1.948	2.693	3.700	5.054	6.866	9.276	12.468	16.672	22.186	29.384	38.741	50.851	66.461	86.504	112.139	304.913	17
18	1.428	2.026	2.854	3.996	5.560	7.690	10.575	14.463	19.673	26.623	35.849	48.039	64.072	85.071	112.455	148.024	426.879	18
19	1.457	2.107	3.026	4.316	6.116	8.613	12.056	16.777	23.214	31.948	43.736	59.568	80.731	108.890	146.192	195.391	597.630	19
20	1.486	2.191	3.207	4.661	6.727	9.646	13.743	19.461	27.393	38.338	53.358	73.864	101.721	139.380	190.050	257.916	836.683	20
21	1.516	2.279	3.400	5.034	7.400	10.804	15.668	22.574	32.324	46.005	65.096	91.592	128.169	178.406	247.065	340.449	1171.356	21
22	1.546	2.370	3.604	5.437	8.140	12.100	17.861	26.186	38.142	55.206	79.418	113.574	161.492	228.360	321.184	449.393	1639.898	22
23	1.577	2.465	3.820	5.871	8.954	13.552	20.362	30.376	45.008	66.247	96.889	140.831	203.480	292.300	417.539	593.199	2295.857	23
24	1.608	2.563	4.049	6.341	9.850	15.179	23.212	35.236	53.109	79.497	118.205	174.631	256.385	374.144	542.801	783.023	3214.200	24
25	1.641	2.666	4.292	6.848	10.835	17.000	26.462	40.874	62.669	95.396	144.210	216.542	323.045	478.905	705.641	1033.590	4499.880	25
26	1.673	2.772	4.549	7.396	11.918	19.040	30.167	47.414	73.949	114.475	175.936	268.512	407.037	612.998	917.333	1364.339	6299.831	26
27	1.707	2.883	4.822	7.988	13.110	21.325	34.390	55.000	87.260	137.371	214.642	332.955	512.867	784.638	1192.533	1800.927	8819.764	27
28	1.741	2.999	5.112	8.627	14.421	23.884	39.204	63.800	102.967	164.845	261.864	412.864	646.212	1004.336	1550.293	2377.224	12347.670	28
29	1.776	3.119	5.418	9.317	15.863	26.750	44.693	74.009	121.501	197.814	319.474	511.952	814.228	1285.550	2015.381	3137.935	17286.737	29
30	1.811	3.243	5.743	10.063	17.449	29.960	50.950	85.850	143.371	237.376	389.758	634.820	1025.927	1645.505	2619.996	4142.075	24201.432	30
35	2.000	3.946	7.686	14.785	28.102	52.800	98.100	180.314	327.997	590.668	1053.402	1861.054	3258.135	5653.911	9727.860	16599.217	130161.112	35
40	2.208	4.801	10.286	21.725	45.259	93.051	188.884	378.721	750.378	1469.772	2847.038	5455.913	10347.175	19426.689	36118.865	66520.767	700037.697	40

TABLE 2 *(Place a clip on this page for easy reference.)*

Present Value of $1.00

$$P = \frac{S}{(1 + r)^n}.$$ In this table $S = \$1.00$.

Periods	2%	4%	6%	8%	10%	12%	14%	16%	18%	20%	22%	24%	26%	28%	30%	32%	40%	Periods
1	0.980	0.962	0.943	0.926	0.909	0.893	0.877	0.862	0.847	0.833	0.820	0.806	0.794	0.781	0.769	0.758	0.714	1
2	0.961	0.925	0.890	0.857	0.826	0.797	0.769	0.743	0.718	0.694	0.672	0.650	0.630	0.610	0.592	0.574	0.510	2
3	0.942	0.889	0.840	0.794	0.751	0.712	0.675	0.641	0.609	0.579	0.551	0.524	0.500	0.477	0.455	0.435	0.364	3
4	0.924	0.855	0.792	0.735	0.683	0.636	0.592	0.552	0.516	0.482	0.451	0.423	0.397	0.373	0.350	0.329	0.260	4
5	0.906	0.822	0.747	0.681	0.621	0.567	0.519	0.476	0.437	0.402	0.370	0.341	0.315	0.291	0.269	0.250	0.186	5
6	0.888	0.790	0.705	0.630	0.564	0.507	0.456	0.410	0.370	0.335	0.303	0.275	0.250	0.227	0.207	0.189	0.133	6
7	0.871	0.760	0.665	0.583	0.513	0.452	0.400	0.354	0.314	0.279	0.249	0.222	0.198	0.178	0.159	0.143	0.095	7
8	0.853	0.731	0.627	0.540	0.467	0.404	0.351	0.305	0.266	0.233	0.204	0.179	0.157	0.139	0.123	0.108	0.068	8
9	0.837	0.703	0.592	0.500	0.424	0.361	0.308	0.263	0.225	0.194	0.167	0.144	0.125	0.108	0.094	0.082	0.048	9
10	0.820	0.676	0.558	0.463	0.386	0.322	0.270	0.227	0.191	0.162	0.137	0.116	0.099	0.085	0.073	0.062	0.035	10
11	0.804	0.650	0.527	0.429	0.350	0.287	0.237	0.195	0.162	0.135	0.112	0.094	0.079	0.066	0.056	0.047	0.025	11
12	0.788	0.625	0.497	0.397	0.319	0.257	0.208	0.168	0.137	0.112	0.092	0.076	0.062	0.052	0.043	0.036	0.018	12
13	0.773	0.601	0.469	0.368	0.290	0.229	0.182	0.145	0.116	0.093	0.075	0.061	0.050	0.040	0.033	0.027	0.013	13
14	0.758	0.577	0.442	0.340	0.263	0.205	0.160	0.125	0.099	0.078	0.062	0.049	0.039	0.032	0.025	0.021	0.009	14
15	0.743	0.555	0.417	0.315	0.239	0.183	0.140	0.108	0.084	0.065	0.051	0.040	0.031	0.025	0.020	0.016	0.006	15
18	0.728	0.534	0.394	0.292	0.218	0.163	0.123	0.093	0.071	0.054	0.042	0.032	0.025	0.019	0.015	0.012	0.005	16
17	0.714	0.513	0.371	0.270	0.198	0.146	0.108	0.080	0.060	0.045	0.034	0.026	0.020	0.015	0.012	0.009	0.003	17
18	0.700	0.494	0.350	0.250	0.180	0.130	0.095	0.069	0.051	0.038	0.028	0.021	0.016	0.012	0.009	0.007	0.002	18
19	0.686	0.475	0.331	0.232	0.164	0.116	0.083	0.060	0.043	0.031	0.023	0.017	0.012	0.009	0.007	0.005	0.002	19
20	0.673	0.456	0.312	0.215	0.149	0.104	0.073	0.051	0.037	0.026	0.019	0.014	0.010	0.007	0.005	0.004	0.001	20
21	0.660	0.439	0.294	0.199	0.135	0.093	0.064	0.044	0.031	0.022	0.015	0.011	0.008	0.006	0.004	0.003	0.001	21
22	0.647	0.422	0.278	0.184	0.123	0.083	0.056	0.038	0.026	0.018	0.013	0.009	0.006	0.004	0.003	0.002	0.001	22
23	0.634	0.406	0.262	0.170	0.112	0.074	0.049	0.033	0.022	0.015	0.010	0.007	0.005	0.003	0.002	0.002	0.000	23
24	0.622	0.390	0.247	0.158	0.102	0.066	0.043	0.028	0.019	0.013	0.008	0.006	0.004	0.003	0.002	0.001	0.000	24
25	0.610	0.375	0.233	0.146	0.092	0.059	0.038	0.024	0.016	0.010	0.007	0.005	0.003	0.002	0.001	0.001	0.000	25
26	0.598	0.361	0.220	0.135	0.084	0.053	0.033	0.021	0.014	0.009	0.006	0.004	0.002	0.002	0.001	0.001	0.000	26
27	0.586	0.347	0.207	0.125	0.076	0.047	0.029	0.018	0.011	0.007	0.005	0.003	0.002	0.001	0.001	0.001	0.000	27
28	0.574	0.333	0.196	0.116	0.069	0.042	0.026	0.016	0.010	0.006	0.004	0.002	0.002	0.001	0.001	0.000	0.000	28
29	0.563	0.321	0.185	0.107	0.063	0.037	0.022	0.014	0.008	0.005	0.003	0.002	0.001	0.001	0.000	0.000	0.000	29
30	0.552	0.308	0.174	0.099	0.057	0.033	0.020	0.012	0.007	0.004	0.003	0.002	0.001	0.001	0.000	0.000	0.000	30
35	0.500	0.253	0.130	0.068	0.036	0.019	0.010	0.006	0.003	0.002	0.001	0.001	0.000	0.000	0.000	0.000	0.000	35
40	0.453	0.208	0.097	0.046	0.022	0.011	0.005	0.003	0.001	0.001	0.000	0.000	0.000	0.000	0.000	0.000	0.000	40

TABLE 3

Compound Amount of Annuity of $1.00 in Arrears* (Future Value of Annuity)

$$S_n = \frac{(1 + r)^n - 1}{r}$$

Periods	2%	4%	6%	8%	10%	12%	14%	16%	18%	20%	22%	24%	26%	28%	30%	32%	40%	Periods
1	1.000	1.000	1.000	1.000	1.000	1.000	1.000	1.000	1.000	1.000	1.000	1.000	1.000	1.000	1.000	1.000	1.000	1
2	2.020	2.040	2.060	2.080	2.100	2.120	2.140	2.160	2.180	2.200	2.220	2.240	2.260	2.280	2.300	2.320	2.400	2
3	3.060	3.122	3.184	3.246	3.310	3.374	3.440	3.506	3.572	3.640	3.708	3.778	3.848	3.918	3.990	4.062	4.360	3
4	4.122	4.246	4.375	4.506	4.641	4.779	4.921	5.066	5.215	5.368	5.524	5.684	5.848	6.016	6.187	6.362	7.104	4
5	5.204	5.416	5.637	5.867	6.105	6.353	6.610	6.877	7.154	7.442	7.740	8.048	8.368	8.700	9.043	9.398	10.946	5
6	6.308	6.633	6.975	7.336	7.716	8.115	8.536	8.977	9.442	9.930	10.442	10.980	11.544	12.136	12.756	13.406	16.324	6
7	7.434	7.898	8.394	8.923	9.487	10.089	10.730	11.414	12.142	12.916	13.740	14.615	15.546	16.534	17.583	18.696	23.853	7
8	8.583	9.214	9.897	10.637	11.436	12.300	13.233	14.240	15.327	16.499	17.762	19.123	20.588	22.163	23.858	25.678	34.395	8
9	9.755	10.583	11.491	12.488	13.579	14.776	16.085	17.519	19.086	20.799	22.670	24.712	26.940	29.369	32.015	34.895	49.153	9
10	10.950	12.006	13.181	14.487	15.937	17.549	19.337	21.321	23.521	25.959	28.657	31.643	34.945	38.593	42.619	47.062	69.814	10
11	12.169	13.486	14.972	16.645	18.531	20.655	23.045	25.733	28.755	32.150	35.962	40.238	45.031	50.398	56.405	63.122	98.739	11
12	13.412	15.026	16.870	18.977	21.384	24.133	27.271	30.850	34.931	39.581	44.874	50.895	57.739	65.510	74.327	84.320	139.235	12
13	14.680	16.627	18.882	21.495	24.523	28.029	32.089	36.786	42.219	48.497	55.746	64.110	73.751	84.853	97.625	112.303	195.929	13
14	15.974	18.292	21.015	24.215	27.975	32.393	37.581	43.672	50.818	59.196	69.010	80.496	93.926	109.612	127.913	149.240	275.300	14
15	17.293	20.024	23.276	27.152	31.772	37.280	43.842	51.660	60.965	72.035	85.192	100.815	119.347	141.303	167.286	197.997	386.420	15
16	18.639	21.825	25.673	30.324	35.950	42.753	50.980	60.925	72.939	87.442	104.935	126.011	151.377	181.868	218.472	262.356	541.988	16
17	20.012	23.698	28.213	33.750	40.545	48.884	59.118	71.673	87.068	105.931	129.020	157.253	191.735	233.791	285.014	347.309	759.784	17
18	21.412	25.645	30.906	37.450	45.599	55.750	68.394	84.141	103.740	128.117	158.405	195.994	242.585	300.252	371.518	459.449	1064.697	18
19	22.841	27.671	33.760	41.446	51.159	63.440	78.969	98.603	123.414	154.740	194.254	244.033	306.658	385.323	483.973	607.472	1491.576	19
20	24.297	29.778	36.786	45.762	57.275	72.052	91.025	115.380	146.628	186.688	237.989	303.601	387.389	494.213	630.165	802.863	2089.206	20
21	25.783	31.969	39.993	50.423	64.002	81.699	104.768	134.841	174.021	225.026	291.347	377.465	489.110	633.593	820.215	1060.779	2925.889	21
22	27.299	34.248	43.392	55.457	71.403	92.503	120.436	157.415	206.345	271.031	356.443	469.056	617.278	811.999	1067.280	1401.229	4097.245	22
23	28.845	36.618	46.996	60.893	79.543	104.603	138.297	183.601	244.487	326.237	435.861	582.630	778.771	1040.358	1388.464	1850.622	5737.142	23
24	30.422	39.083	50.816	66.765	88.497	118.155	158.659	213.978	289.494	392.484	532.750	723.461	982.251	1332.659	1806.003	2443.821	8032.999	24
25	32.030	41.646	54.865	73.106	98.347	133.334	181.871	249.214	342.603	471.981	650.955	898.092	1238.636	1706.803	2348.803	3226.844	11247.199	25
26	33.671	44.312	59.156	79.954	109.182	150.334	208.333	290.088	405.272	567.377	795.165	1114.634	1561.682	2185.708	3054.444	4260.434	15747.079	26
27	35.344	47.084	63.706	87.351	121.100	169.374	238.499	337.502	479.221	681.853	971.102	1383.146	1968.719	2798.706	3971.778	5624.772	22046.910	27
28	37.051	49.968	68.528	95.339	134.210	190.699	272.889	392.503	566.481	819.223	1185.744	1716.101	2481.586	3583.344	5164.311	7425.699	30866.674	28
29	38.792	52.966	73.640	103.966	148.631	214.583	312.094	456.303	669.447	984.068	1447.608	2128.965	3127.798	4587.680	6714.604	9802.923	43214.343	29
30	40.568	56.085	79.058	113.263	164.494	241.333	356.787	530.312	790.948	1181.882	1767.081	2640.916	3942.026	5873.231	8729.985	12940.859	60501.081	30
35	49.994	73.652	111.435	172.317	271.024	431.663	693.573	1120.713	1816.652	2948.341	4783.645	7750.225	12527.442	20188.966	32422.868	51869.427	325400.279	35
40	60.402	95.026	154.762	259.057	442.593	767.091	1342.025	2360.757	4163.213	7343.858	12936.535	22728.803	39792.982	69377.460	120392.883	207874.272	1750091.741	40

*Payments (or receipts) at the end of each period.

TABLE 4 *(Place a clip on this page for easy reference.)*
Present Value of Annuity $1.00 in Arrears*

$$P_n = \frac{1}{r}\left[1 - \frac{1}{(1+r)^n}\right]$$

Periods	2%	4%	6%	8%	10%	12%	14%	16%	18%	20%	22%	24%	26%	28%	30%	32%	40%	Periods
1	0.980	0.962	0.943	0.926	0.909	0.893	0.877	0.862	0.847	0.833	0.820	0.806	0.794	0.781	0.769	0.758	0.714	1
2	1.942	1.886	1.833	1.783	1.736	1.690	1.647	1.605	1.566	1.528	1.492	1.457	1.424	1.392	1.361	1.331	1.224	2
3	2.884	2.775	2.673	2.577	2.487	2.402	2.322	2.246	2.174	2.106	2.042	1.981	1.923	1.868	1.816	1.766	1.589	3
4	3.808	3.630	3.465	3.312	3.170	3.037	2.914	2.798	2.690	2.589	2.494	2.404	2.320	2.241	2.166	2.096	1.849	4
5	4.713	4.452	4.212	3.993	3.791	3.605	3.433	3.274	3.127	2.991	2.864	2.745	2.635	2.532	2.436	2.345	2.035	5
6	5.601	5.242	4.917	4.623	4.355	4.111	3.889	3.685	3.498	3.326	3.167	3.020	2.885	2.759	2.643	2.534	2.168	6
7	6.472	6.002	5.582	5.206	4.868	4.564	4.288	4.039	3.812	3.605	3.416	3.242	3.083	2.937	2.802	2.677	2.263	7
8	7.325	6.733	6.210	5.747	5.335	4.968	4.639	4.344	4.078	3.837	3.619	3.421	3.241	3.076	2.925	2.786	2.331	8
9	8.162	7.435	6.802	6.247	5.759	5.328	4.946	4.607	4.303	4.031	3.786	3.566	3.366	3.184	3.019	2.868	2.379	9
10	8.983	8.111	7.360	6.710	6.145	5.650	5.216	4.833	4.494	4.192	3.923	3.682	3.465	3.269	3.092	2.930	2.414	10
11	9.787	8.760	7.887	7.139	6.495	5.938	5.453	5.029	4.656	4.327	4.035	3.776	3.543	3.335	3.147	2.978	2.438	11
12	10.575	9.385	8.384	7.536	6.814	6.194	5.660	5.197	4.793	4.439	4.127	3.851	3.606	3.387	3.190	3.013	2.456	12
13	11.348	9.986	8.853	7.904	7.103	6.424	5.842	5.342	4.910	4.533	4.203	3.912	3.656	3.427	3.223	3.040	2.469	13
14	12.106	10.563	9.295	8.244	7.367	6.628	6.002	5.468	5.008	4.611	4.265	3.962	3.695	3.459	3.249	3.061	2.478	14
15	12.849	11.118	9.712	8.559	7.606	6.811	6.142	5.575	5.092	4.675	4.315	4.001	3.726	3.483	3.268	3.076	2.484	15
16	13.578	11.652	10.106	8.851	7.824	6.974	6.265	5.668	5.162	4.730	4.357	4.033	3.751	3.503	3.283	3.088	2.489	16
17	14.292	12.166	10.477	9.122	8.022	7.120	6.373	5.749	5.222	4.775	4.391	4.059	3.771	3.518	3.295	3.097	2.492	17
18	14.992	12.659	10.828	9.372	8.201	7.250	6.467	5.818	5.273	4.812	4.419	4.080	3.786	3.529	3.304	3.104	2.494	18
19	15.678	13.134	11.158	9.604	8.365	7.366	6.550	5.877	5.316	4.843	4.442	4.097	3.799	3.539	3.311	3.109	2.496	19
20	16.351	13.590	11.470	9.818	8.514	7.469	6.623	5.929	5.353	4.870	4.460	4.110	3.808	3.546	3.316	3.113	2.497	20
21	17.011	14.029	11.764	10.017	8.649	7.562	6.687	5.973	5.384	4.891	4.476	4.121	3.816	3.551	3.320	3.116	2.498	21
22	17.658	14.451	12.042	10.201	8.772	7.645	6.743	6.011	5.410	4.909	4.488	4.130	3.822	3.556	3.323	3.118	2.498	22
23	18.292	14.857	12.303	10.371	8.883	7.718	6.792	6.044	5.432	4.925	4.499	4.137	3.827	3.559	3.325	3.120	2.499	23
24	18.914	15.247	12.550	10.529	8.985	7.784	6.835	6.073	5.451	4.937	4.507	4.143	3.831	3.562	3.327	3.121	2.499	24
25	19.523	15.622	12.783	10.675	9.077	7.843	6.873	6.097	5.467	4.948	4.514	4.147	3.834	3.564	3.329	3.122	2.499	25
26	20.121	15.983	13.003	10.810	9.161	7.896	6.906	6.118	5.480	4.956	4.520	4.151	3.837	3.566	3.330	3.123	2.500	26
27	20.707	16.330	13.211	10.935	9.237	7.943	6.935	6.136	5.492	4.964	4.524	4.154	3.839	3.567	3.331	3.123	2.500	27
28	21.281	16.663	13.406	11.051	9.307	7.984	6.961	6.152	5.502	4.970	4.528	4.157	3.840	3.568	3.331	3.124	2.500	28
29	21.844	16.984	13.591	11.158	9.370	8.022	6.983	6.166	5.510	4.975	4.531	4.159	3.841	3.569	3.332	3.124	2.500	29
30	22.396	17.292	13.765	11.258	9.427	8.055	7.003	6.177	5.517	4.979	4.534	4.160	3.842	3.569	3.332	3.124	2.500	30
35	24.999	18.665	14.498	11.655	9.644	8.176	7.070	6.215	5.539	4.992	4.541	4.164	3.845	3.571	3.333	3.125	2.500	35
40	27.355	19.793	15.046	11.925	9.779	8.244	7.105	6.233	5.548	4.997	4.544	4.166	3.846	3.571	3.333	3.125	2.500	40

*Payments (or receipts) at the end of each period.

Cost Accounting in Professional Examinations

This appendix describes the role of cost accounting in professional examinations. We use professional examinations in the United States, Canada, Australia, Japan, and the United Kingdom to illustrate the role.[1] A conscientious reader who has solved a representative sample of the problems at the end of the chapters will be well prepared for the professional examination questions dealing with cost accounting. This appendix aims to provide perspective, instill confidence, and encourage readers to take the examinations.

AMERICAN PROFESSIONAL EXAMINATIONS

CPA and CMA Designations

Many American readers may eventually take the Certified Public Accountant (CPA) examination, the Certified Management Accountant (CMA) examination, or the CFM (Certified in Financial Management) examination. Certification is important to professional accountants for many reasons, such as:

1. Recognition of achievement and technical competence by fellow accountants and by users of accounting services
2. Increased self-confidence in one's professional abilities
3. Membership in professional organizations offering programs of career-long education
4. Enhancement of career opportunities
5. Personal satisfaction

The CPA certificate is issued by individual states; it is necessary for obtaining a state's license to practice as a Certified Public Accountant. A prominent feature of public accounting is the use of independent (external) auditors to give assurance about the reliability of the financial statements supplied by managers. These auditors are called Certified Public Accountants in the United States and Chartered Accountants in many other English-speaking nations. The major U.S. professional association in the private sector that regulates the quality of external auditing is the American Institute of Certified Public Accountants (AICPA).

The CMA and CFM designations are offered by the Institute of Management Accountants (IMA). The IMA is the largest association of management accountants in the world.[2] The major objective of the CMA and CFM certifications is to enhance the development of the management accounting profession. In particular, focus is placed on the modern role of the management accountant as an active contributor to and a participant in management. The CMA and CFM designations are gaining increased stature in the business community as a credential parallel to the CPA designation.

The CMA and CFM examinations are given in a computer-based format and consists of 4 parts. They consist of carefully constructed multiple-choice questions that test all levels of cognitive skills. The CMA exam consists of

- Part 1: Economics, finance, and management
- Part 2: Financial accounting, reporting, and analysis
- Part 3: Management reporting, analysis, and behavioral issues
- Part 4: Decision analysis, information systems, and management controls.

A person who has successfully completed the U.S. CPA examination is exempt from Part 2. Parts 1, 3, and 4 of the CFM exam are the same as those for the CMA examination. Part 2 deals with corporate financial management. Questions regarding ethical issues can appear on any part of the CMA and CFM examinations.

---

[1]We appreciate help from Tom Craven (United States), Bill Langdon (Canada), John Goodwin (Australia), Michi Sakurai (Japan), and Louise Drysdale and Andrea Jeffries (U.K.).

[2]The IMA has a wide range of activities driven by many committees. For example, the Management Accounting Practices Committee issues statements on both financial accounting and management accounting. The IMA also has an extensive continuing-education program.

Cost/management accounting questions are prominent in the CMA examination. The CPA examination also includes such questions, although they are less extensive than questions regarding financial accounting, auditing, and business law. On the average, cost/managerial accounting represents 35% to 40% of the CMA examination and 5% of the CPA examination. This book includes many questions and problems used in past CMA and CPA examinations. In addition, a supplement to this book, *Student Guide and Review Manual* [John K. Harris (Upper Saddle River, NJ: Prentice Hall, 2003)], contains over one hundred CMA and CPA questions and explanatory answers. Careful study of appropriate topics in this book will give candidates sufficient background for succeeding in the cost accounting portions of the professional examinations.

The IMA publishes *Strategic Finance* monthly. Each issue includes advertisements for courses that help students prepare for the CMA examination.[3]

CANADIAN PROFESSIONAL EXAMINATIONS

Three professional accounting designations are available in Canada:

Designation	Sponsoring Organization
Certified Management Accountant (CMA)	Society of Management Accountants (SMA)
Certified General Accountant (CGA)	Certified General Accountants' Association (CGA)
Chartered Accountant (CA)	Canadian Institute of Chartered Accountants (CICA)

The SMA represents over 27,000 certified management accountants employed throughout Canadian business, industry, and government.

The CMA Entrance Examination is a two-day examination covering eleven topics: Management accounting, corporate finance, operations management, information technology, strategic management, international business, human resources, marketing, financial accounting, taxation, and internal control. These topics are tested in roughly equal proportion, although management accounting, information technology, and financial accounting may be tested to a somewhat greater extent.

Multiple-choice questions comprise 50% and case studies the other 50% of the exam. Topics covered on recent examinations in the management accounting area include relevant costing, transfer pricing, capital budgeting, performance measures, activity-based costing, cost allocation, and productivity.

The Society of Management Accountants publishes *CMA Management* monthly. This magazine includes details of courses that assist students in preparing for the CMA exam.

AUSTRALIAN PROFESSIONAL EXAMINATIONS

CPA Australia is the largest body representing accountants in Australia. Their professional designation is termed a CPA (Certified Practising Accountant). The basic entry requirement for Associate membership of the Society is having an approved Bachelors degree. Associates of the Society can advance to CPA status by passing the CPA program and having the required amount of relevant work experience. There are two compulsory core segments in the program. Core I covers the practical application of the more common accounting standards and ethics, while more technical standards (such as foreign currency translation) are covered in the Core II segment. Candidates are then required to take three segments from nine elective subjects. These subjects include external reporting, insolvency and reconstruction, strategic management accounting, management of information systems, auditing, treasury, taxation, and personal financial planning and superannuation.

The strategic management accounting segment topics include:

1. Management accounting in the contemporary business environment
2. Accounting for strategic management

[3]Other U.S. professional associations also require detailed knowledge of cost accounting. For example, the Certified Cost Estimator/Analyst (CCEA) program is administered by the Society of Cost Estimating and Analysis, 101 South Whiting Street, Suite 313, Alexandria, VA 22304. The society's primary purpose is to improve the effectiveness of cost estimation, especially contract cost estimation and price analysis.

3. Long-term project planning and management
4. Costing for decision making
5. Performance measurement and reward systems.

The Australian CPA, published each month (except January), includes advertisements for courses that help students prepare for the CPA examination.

The Institute of Chartered Accountants in Australia (ICAA) offers the Chartered Accountant Certification that has membership requirements that include passing four core modules (Taxation, Accounting I, Accounting II, and Ethics) and one elective module (one of which is Advanced Management Accounting). Management-accounting-related topics are in both the Accounting II and Advanced Management Accounting modules. These include:

- purpose and perspective (including strategic and operational management, organizations, goals, ethics, operational environments, and cost concepts);
- strategic management accounting (including strategic applications, project evaluation and capital budgeting);
- operational management accounting (including decision analysis, financial planning and management, product and service costing, control and performance evaluation).

JAPANESE PROFESSIONAL EXAMINATIONS

There are two major management accounting organizations—Japanese Industrial Management and Accounting Association and Enterprise Management Association. The JIMAA is the oldest, largest, and most authoritative accounting organization of its kind in Japan. It directs a School of Cost Control and a School of Corporate Tax Accounting. There are two courses in the School of Cost Control—Preparatory Course and Cost Control Course. These courses are taught by university professors and executives from member corporations. The Enterprise Management Association is the Japanese chapter of the U.S.-based Institute of Management Accountants.

The Japanese Institute of Certified Public Accountants (JICPA) is the organization of the CPA profession in Japan. The CPA exam, conducted by the Certified Public Accountants Board, consists of three stages. The second stage covers cost accounting.

UNITED KINGDOM PROFESSIONAL EXAMINATIONS

The Chartered Institute of Management Accountants (CIMA) is the largest professional management accounting body in the United Kingdom. CIMA provides a wide range of services to members in commerce, education, government, and the accounting profession.

The syllabus for the CIMA examination consists of three levels:

1. *Foundation:* includes papers on financial accounting, management accounting, business economics, business law, and business mathemathics.
2. *Intermediate:* includes papers on finance, taxation, financial accounting, and management accounting.
3. *Final:* includes papers on different applications of management accounting to business strategy, financial strategy, and information strategy.

Management Accounting, published monthly by CIMA, includes details of courses assisting students in preparing for their examinations.

Management accounting topics are also covered by several other professional bodies. The syllabus for the examinations of the Chartered Association of Certified Accountants (ACCA) has three stages: I (Foundation), II (Certificate), and III (Professional). Skills examined in III include information for control and decision making, management and strategy, and financial strategy. Other accounting bodies include the Institute of Chartered Accountants in England and Wales (ICAEW) and the Institute for Chartered Accountants of Scotland (ICAS). Both institutes have requirements that cover proficiency in "general management" topics as well as professional accounting topics.

Abnormal spoilage. Spoilage that would not arise under efficient operating conditions; it is not inherent in a particular production process. (628)

Absorption costing. Method of inventory costing in which all variable manufacturing costs and all fixed manufacturing costs are included as inventoriable costs. (287)

Account analysis method. Approach to cost estimation that classifies cost accounts in the subsidiary ledger as variable, fixed, or mixed with respect to the identified level of activity. Typically, qualitative rather than quantitative analysis is used when making these cost-classification decisions. (329)

Accounting rate of return. See *accrual accounting rate-of-return (AARR)*.

Accrual accounting rate of return (AARR). Divides an accrual accounting measure of average annual income of a project by an accrual accounting measure of its investment. Also called *accounting rate of return* or *return on investment (ROI)*. (726)

Activity. An event, task, or unit of work with a specified purpose. (141)

Activity-based budgeting (ABB). Budgeting approach that focuses on the budgeted cost of activities necessary to produce and sell products and services. (190)

Activity-based costing (ABC). Approach to costing that focuses on individual activities as the fundamental cost objects. It uses the costs of these activities as the basis for assigning costs to other cost objects such as products or services. (141)

Activity-based management (ABM). Management decisions that use activity-based costing information to satisfy customers and improve profitability. (148)

Actual cost. Cost incurred (a historical cost), as distinguished from a budgeted or forecasted cost. (30)

Actual costing. A costing method that traces direct costs to a cost object by using the actual direct-cost rates times the actual quantity of the direct-cost inputs and allocates indirect costs based on the actual indirect-cost rates times the actual quantity of the cost-allocation bases. (99)

Adjusted allocation-rate approach. Restates all overhead entries in the general ledger and subsidiary ledgers using actual cost rates rather than budgeted cost rates. (115)

Allowable cost. Cost that parties to a contract agree to include in the costs to be reimbursed. (536)

Appraisal costs. Costs incurred to detect which of the individual units of products do not conform to specifications. (655)

Artificial cost. See *complete reciprocated cost*.

Attention directing. Helping managers focus on opportunities and problems role of management accounting. (8)

Autonomy. The degree of freedom to make decisions. (756)

Average cost. See *unit cost*.

Average waiting time. The average amount of time that an order will wait in line before it is set up and processed. (666)

Backflush costing. Costing system that omits recording some or all of the journal entries relating to the cycle from purchase of direct material to the sale of finished goods. (700)

Balanced Scorecard. A framework for implementing strategy by translating an organization's mission and strategy into a set of performance measures. (447)

Batch-level costs. The costs of activities related to a group of units of products or services rather than to each individual unit of product or service. (143)

Benchmarking. The continuous process of comparing the levels of performance in producing products and services and executing activities against the best levels of performance. (234)

Book value. The original cost minus accumulated depreciation of an asset. (386)

Bottleneck. An operation where the work to be performed approaches or exceeds the capacity available to do it. (665)

Breakeven point. Quantity of output sold at which total revenues equal total costs, that is where the operating income is zero. (64)

Budget. Quantitative expression of a proposed plan of action by management for a specified period and is an aid to coordinating what needs to be done to implement that plan. (6)

Budgetary slack. The practice of underestimating budgeted revenues, or overestimating budgeted costs, to make budgeted targets more easily achievable. (193)

Budgeted indirect-cost rate. Budgeted annual indirect cost in a cost pool divided by the budgeted annual quantity of the cost-allocation base. (106)

Bundled product. A package of two or more products (or services) that is sold for a single price, but individual components of the bundle also may be sold as separate items at their own "stand-alone" prices. (537)

Business function costs. The sum of all costs (variable and fixed) in a particular business function in the value chain. (373)

Byproducts. Products from a joint production process that have low sales values compared with the sales value of the main product or joint products. (556)

Capital budgeting. The making of long-run planning decisions for investments in projects. (719)

Carrying costs. Costs that arise while holding inventory of goods for sale. (686)

Cash budget. Schedule of expected cash receipts and disbursements. (197)

Cause-and-effect diagram. Diagram that identifies the potential causes of defects. Four categories of potential causes of failure are human factors, methods and design factors, machine-related factors, and materials and components factors. Also called a *fishbone diagram.* (659)

Certified in Financial Management (CFM). Certifies that the holder has met the admission criteria and demonstrated the competency of technical knowledge in financial management required by the *Institute of Management Accountants.* (17)

Certified Management Accountant (CMA). Certifies that the holder has met the admission criteria and demonstrated the competency of technical knowledge in management accounting required by the *Institute of Management Accountants.* (17)

Chief financial officer (CFO). Executive responsible for overseeing the financial operations of an organization. Also called *finance director.* (15)

Choice criterion. Objective that can be quantified in a decision model. (80)

Coefficient of determination (r^2). Measures the percentage of variation in a dependent variable explained by one or more independent variables. (348)

Collusive pricing. Companies in an industry conspire in their pricing and production decisions to achieve a price above the competitive price and so restrain trade. (429)

Common cost. Cost of operating a facility, activity, or like cost object that is shared by two or more users. (533)

Complete reciprocated cost. The support department's own costs plus any interdepartmental cost allocations. Also called the *artificial cost* of the support department. (530)

Composite unit. Hypothetical unit with weights based on the mix of individual units. (498)

Conference method. Approach to cost estimation that develops cost estimates on the basis of analysis and opinions about costs and their drivers gathered from various departments of a company (purchasing, process engineering, manufacturing, employee relations, and so on). (329)

Conformance quality. Refers to the performance of a product or service relative to its design and product specifications. (655)

Constant. The component of total cost that, within the relevant range, does not vary with changes in the level of the activity. Also called *intercept.* (325)

Constant gross-margin percentage NRV method. Method that allocates joint costs to joint products in such a way that the overall gross-margin percentage is identical for the individual products. (563)

Constraint. A mathematical inequality or equality that must be satisfied by the variables in a mathematical model. (392)

Continuous Budget. See *rolling budget.*

Continuous improvement budgeted cost. Budgeted cost that is progressively reduced over succeeding periods. (230)

Contribution income statement. Income statement that groups costs into variable costs and fixed costs to highlight the contribution margin. (64)

Contribution margin. Total revenues minus total variable costs. (63)

Contribution margin per unit. Difference between the selling price and the variable cost per unit. (63)

Contribution margin percentage. Contribution margin per unit divided by selling price. Also called *contribution margin ratio.* (64)

Contribution margin ratio. See *contribution margin percentage.*

Control. Taking actions that implement the planning decisions, and deciding how to evaluate performance and what feedback to provide that will help future decision making. (6)

Control chart. Graph of a series of successive observations of a particular step, procedure, or operation taken at regular intervals of time. Each observation is plotted relative to specified ranges that represent the limits within which the observations are expected to fall. (657)

Controllability. Degree of influence that a specific manager has over costs, revenues, and related items for which he or she is responsible. (192)

Controllable cost. Any cost that is primarily subject to the influence of a given responsibility center manager for a given period. (192)

Controller. The financial executive primarily responsible for management accounting and financial accounting. Also called *chief accounting officer.* (16)

Conversion costs. All manufacturing costs other than direct material costs. (43)

Cost. Resource sacrificed or forgone to achieve a specific objective. (30)

Cost accounting. Measures and reports financial and nonfinancial information relating to the cost of acquiring or consuming resources in an organization. It provides information for both management accounting and financial accounting. (3)

Cost Accounting Standards Board (CASB). Government agency that has the exclusive authority to make, put into effect, amend, and rescind cost accounting standards and interpretations thereof designed to achieve uniformity and consistency in regard to measurement, assignment, and allocation of costs to contracts within the United States. (535)

Cost accumulation. Collection of cost data in some organized way by means of an accounting system. (30)

Cost allocation. The assignment of indirect costs to a particular cost object. (31)

Cost-allocation base. A factor that links in a systematic way an indirect cost or group of indirect costs to a cost object. (97)

Cost-application base. Cost-allocation base when the cost object is a job, product or customer. (97)

Cost assignment. General term that encompasses both (1) tracing accumulated costs that have a direct relationship to a cost object, and (2) allocating accumulated costs that have an indirect relationship to a cost object. (30)

Cost-benefit approach. Approach to decision-making and resource allocation based on a comparison of the expected benefits from attaining company goals and the expected costs. (13)

Cost center. Responsibility center where the manager is accountable for costs only. (191)

Cost driver. A variable, such as the level of activity or volume, that causally affects costs over a given time span. (34)

Cost estimation. The attempt to measure a past relationship based on data from past costs and the related level of an activity. (326)

Cost function. Mathematical description of how a cost changes with changes in the level of an activity relating to the cost. (324)

Cost hierarchy. Categorization of costs into different cost pools on the basis of different types of cost drivers, or cost-allocation bases, or different degrees of difficulty in determining cause-and-effect (or benefits received) relationships. (143)

Cost incurrence. Describes when a resource is consumed (or benefit forgone) to meet a specific objective. (417)

Cost leadership. Organization's ability to achieve lower costs relative to competitors through productivity and efficiency improvements, elimination of waste, and tight cost control. (447)

Cost management. The approaches and activities of managers in short-run and long-run planning and control decisions that increase value for customers and lower costs of products and services. (3)

Cost object. Anything for which a measurement of costs is desired. (30)

Cost of capital. See *required rate of return (RRR)*.

Cost of goods manufactured. Cost of goods brought to completion, whether they were started before or during the current accounting period. (40)

Cost pool. A grouping of individual cost items. (97)

Cost predictions. Forecasts about future costs. (327)

Cost smoothing. A costing approach that uses broad averages for assigning (spreading) the cost of resources uniformly to cost objects (such as products or services) when the individual products or services, in fact, use those resources in a nonuniform way. Also called *peanut-butter costing*. (136)

Cost tracing. Describes the assignment of direct costs to the particular cost object. (31)

Costs of quality (COQ). Costs incurred to prevent, or costs arising as a result of, producing a low-quality product. (655)

Cost-volume-profit (CVP) analysis. Examines the behavior of total revenues, total costs, and operating income as changes occur in the output level, the selling price, the variable cost per unit, and/or the fixed costs of a product. (62)

Cumulative average-time learning model. Learning curve model in which the cumulative average time per unit declines by a constant percentage each time the cumulative quantity of units produced doubles. (340)

Current cost. Asset measure based on the cost of purchasing an asset today identical to the one currently held, or the cost of purchasing an asset that provides services like the one currently held if an identical one cannot be purchased. (794)

Customer cost hierarchy. Hierarchy that categorizes costs related to customers into different cost pools on the basis of different types of cost drivers, or cost-allocation bases, or different degrees of difficulty in determining cause-and-effect or benefits received relationships. (491)

Customer life-cycle costs. Focuses on the total costs incurred by a customer to acquire and use a product or service until it is replaced. (427)

Customer-profitability analysis. The reporting and analysis of revenues earned from customers and the costs incurred to earn those revenues. (490)

Customer-response time. Duration from the time a customer places an order for a product or service to the time the product or service is delivered to the customer. (664)

Customer service. Providing after-sale support to customers. (10)

Decentralization. The freedom for managers at lower levels of the organization to make decisions. (756)

Decision model. Formal method for making a choice, often involving both quantitative and qualitative analyses. (370)

Decision table. Summary of the alternative actions, events, outcomes, and probabilities of events in a decision. (81)

Degree of operating leverage. Contribution margin divided by operating income at any given level of sales. (72)

Denominator level. The denominator of the budgeted fixed overhead rate computation. (257)

Denominator-level variance. See *production-volume variance*.

Dependent variable. The cost to be predicted. (330)

Design of products, services, or processes. The detailed planning and engineering of products, services, or processes. (10)

Designed-in costs. See *locked-in costs*.

Differential cost. Difference in total cost between two alternatives. (377)

Differential revenue. Difference in total revenue between two alternatives. (377)

Direct allocation method. Cost allocation method that allocates each support department's costs directly to the operating departments. Also called *direct method*. (527)

Direct costing. See *variable costing*.

Direct costs of a cost object. Costs related to the particular cost object and can be traced to that object in an economically feasible (cost-effective) way. (31)

Direct manufacturing labor costs. Include the compensation of all manufacturing labor that can be traced to the cost object (work in process and then finished goods) in an economically feasible way. (39)

Direct material costs. Acquisition costs of all materials that eventually become part of the cost object (work in process and then finished goods), and that can be traced to the cost object in an economically feasible way. (39)

Direct materials inventory. Direct materials in stock and awaiting use in the manufacturing process. (38)

Direct materials mix variance. The difference between (1) the budgeted cost for the actual mix of the actual total quantity of direct materials used and (2) the budgeted costs of the budgeted mix of the actual total quantity of direct materials used. (506)

Direct materials yield variance. The difference between (1) the budgeted cost of direct materials based on the actual total quantity of direct materials used and (2) the flexible-budget cost of direct materials based on the budgeted total quantity of direct materials allowed for the actual output produced. (506)

Direct method. See *direct allocation method.*

Discount rate. See *required rate of return (RRR).*

Discounted cash flow (DCF) methods. Capital budgeting methods that measure all expected future cash inflows and outflows of a project as if they occurred at a single point in time. (720)

Discretionary costs. Arise from periodic (usually annual) decisions regarding the maximum amount to be incurred and have no measurable cause-and-effect relationship between output and resources used. (462)

Distribution. Delivering products or services to customers. (10)

Downsizing. An integrated approach of configuring processes, products, and people to match costs to the activities that need to be performed to operate effectively and efficiently in the present and future. Also called *rightsizing.* (464)

Downward demand spiral. Pricing context where prices are raised to spread capacity costs over a smaller number of output units. Continuing reduction in the demand for products that occurs when the prices of competitors' products are not met and as demand drops further higher and higher unit costs result in more and more reluctance to meet competitors' prices. (303)

Dual pricing. Approach to transfer pricing using two separate transfer-pricing methods to price each transfer from one subunit to another. (765)

Dual-rate cost-allocation method. Allocation method that classifies costs in each cost pool into two pools (a variable-cost pool and a fixed-cost pool) with each pool using a different cost-allocation base. (522)

Dumping. Under U.S. laws, occurs when a non-U.S. company sells a product in the United States at a price below the market value in the country where it is produced, and this lower price materially injures or threatens to materially injure an industry in the United States. (429)

Dysfunctional decision making. See *suboptimal decision making.*

Economic order quantity (EOQ). Decision model that calculates the optimal quantity of inventory to order under a set of assumptions. (687)

Economic value added (EVA®). After-tax operating income minus the (after-tax) weighted average cost of capital multiplied by total assets minus current liabilities. (790)

Effectiveness. The degree to which a predetermined objective or target is met. (228)

Efficiency variance. The difference between the actual quantity of input used and the budgeted quantity of input that should have been used to produce the actual output, multiplied by the budgeted price. Also called *usage variance.* (224)

Efficiency. The relative amount of inputs used to achieve a given output level. (228)

Effort. Exertion toward achieving a goal. (755)

Engineered costs. Costs that result from a cause-and-effect relationship between the cost driver, output, and the (direct or indirect) resources used to produce that output. (461)

Equivalent units. Derived amount of output units that (a) takes the quantity of each input (factor of production) in units completed or in incomplete units of work in process, and (b) converts the quantity of input into the amount of completed output units that could be made with that quantity of input. (590)

Event. A possible relevant occurrence in a decision model. (80)

Expected monetary value. See *expected value.*

Expected value. Weighted average of the outcomes of a decision with the probability of each outcome serving as the weight. Also called *expected monetary value.* (81)

Experience curve. Function that measures the decline in cost per unit in various value-chain functions such as manufacturing, marketing, distribution, and so on, as units produced increase. (340)

External failure costs. Costs incurred on a defective product after it is shipped to customers. (655)

Facility-sustaining costs. The costs of activities that cannot be traced to individual products or services but support the organization as a whole. (148)

Factory overhead costs. See *indirect manufacturing costs.*

Favorable variance. Variance that has the effect of increasing operating income relative to the budgeted amount. Denoted F. (217)

Feedback. Involves managers examining past performance and systematically exploring alternative ways to make better informed decisions in the future. (6)

Finance director. See *chief financial officer (CFO).*

Financial accounting. Measures and records business transactions and provides financial statements that are based on generally accepted accounting principles. It focuses on reporting to external parties. (3)

Financial budget. Part of the master budget that focuses on the impact of operations and planned capital outlays on cash. It is made up of the capital expenditures budget, cash budget, budgeted balance sheet, and budgeted statement of cash flows. (180)

Financial planning models. Mathematical representations of the relationships among operating activities, financial activities, and other factors that affect the master budget. (187)

Finished goods inventory. Goods fully completed but not yet sold. (39)

First-in, first-out (FIFO) process-costing method. Method of process costing that assigns the cost of the previous accounting period's equivalent units in beginning work-in-process inventory to the first units completed and transferred out of the process, and assigns the cost of the equivalent units worked on during the current period first to complete beginning inventory, next to start and complete new units, and finally to units in ending work-in-process inventory. (596)

Fixed cost. Cost that remains unchanged in total for a given time period, despite wide changes in the related level of total activity or volume. (32)

Fixed overhead flexible-budget variance. The difference between actual fixed overhead costs and the fixed overhead costs in the flexible budget. (258)

Fixed overhead spending variance. Same as the fixed overhead flexible-budget variance. The difference between actual fixed overhead costs and the fixed overhead costs in the flexible budget. (258)

Flexible budget. Budget developed using budgeted revenues and budgeted costs based on the actual output level in the budget period. (216)

Flexible-budget variance. The difference between an actual result and the corresponding flexible-budget amount based on the actual output level in the budget period. (220)

Full costs of the product. The sum of all variable and fixed costs in all business functions in the value chain (R&D, design, production, marketing, distribution, and customer service). (373)

Goal congruence. Exists when individuals and groups work toward achieving the organization's goals. Managers working in their own best interest take actions that align with the overall goals of top management. (755)

Gross margin percentage. Gross margin divided by revenues. (78)

Growth component. Change in operating income attributable solely to the change in the quantity of output sold between one period and the next. (455)

High-low method. Method used to estimate a cost function that uses only the highest and lowest observed values of the cost driver within the relevant range and their respective costs. (332)

Homogeneous cost pool. Cost pool in which all the costs have the same or a similar cause-and-effect or benefits-received relationship with the cost-allocation base. (488)

Hurdle rate. See *required rate of return (RRR)*.

Hybrid costing system. Costing system that blends characteristics from both job-costing systems and process-costing systems. (609)

Idle time. Wages paid for unproductive time caused by lack of orders, machine breakdowns, material shortages, poor scheduling, and the like. (44)

Imputed costs. Costs recognized in particular situations that are not usually recognized in financial accounting systems. (789)

Incongruent decision making. See *suboptimal decision making*.

Incremental cost. Additional total cost incurred for an activity. (377)

Incremental cost-allocation method. Method that ranks the individual users of a cost object in the order of users most responsible for the common costs and then uses this ranking to allocate costs among those users. (534)

Incremental revenue. Additional total revenue from an activity. (377)

Incremental revenue-allocation method. Method that ranks individual products in a bundle according to criteria determined by management (for example, sales), and then uses this ranking to allocate bundled revenues to the individual products. (539)

Incremental unit-time learning model. Learning curve model in which the incremental unit time needed to produce the last unit declines by a constant percentage each time the cumulative quantity of units produced doubles. (340)

Independent variable. Level of activity or cost driver used to predict the dependent variable (costs) in a cost estimation or prediction model. (330)

Indirect costs of a cost object. Costs related to the particular cost object but cannot be traced to that object in an economically feasible (cost-effective) way. (31)

Indirect-cost rate. Total overhead costs in a cost pool divided by the total quantity of the cost-allocation base for that cost pool. (100)

Indirect manufacturing costs. All manufacturing costs that are related to the cost object (work in process and then finished goods) but that cannot be traced to that cost object in an economically feasible way. Also called *manufacturing overhead costs* and *factory overhead costs*. (39)

Industrial engineering method. Approach to cost estimation that analyzes the relationship between inputs and outputs in physical terms. Also called *work measurement method*. (329)

Inflation. The decline in the general purchasing power of the monetary unit. (739)

Input-price variance. See *price variance*.

Insourcing. Process of producing goods or providing services within the organization rather than purchasing those same goods or services from outside vendors. (375)

Inspection point. Stage of the production cycle at which products are examined to determine whether they are acceptable or unacceptable units. (629)

Institute of Management Accountants (IMA). A profession accounting organization. It is the largest association of management accountants in the United States. (17)

Intercept. See *constant*.

Intermediate product. Product transferred from one subunit to another subunit of an organization. This product may either be further worked on by the receiving subunit or sold to an external customer. (758)

Internal failure costs. Costs incurred on a defective product before it is shipped to customers. (655)

Internal rate-of-return (IRR) method. Capital budgeting DCF method that calculates the discount rate at which the present value of expected cash inflows from a project equals the present value of its expected cash outflows. (722)

Inventoriable costs. All costs of a product that are regarded as assets when they are incurred and then become cost of goods sold when the product is sold. (39)

Inventory management. The planning, coordinating, and controlling activities related to the flow of inventory into, through, and out of an organization. (686)

Investment. Resources or assets used to generate income. (788)

Investment center. Responsibility center where the manager is accountable for investments, revenues, and costs. (191)

Job. A unit or multiple units of a distinct product or service. (98)

Job-cost record. Source document that records and accumulates all the costs assigned to a specific job, starting when work begins. Also called *job-cost sheet.* (101)

Job-cost sheet. See *job-cost record.*

Job-costing system. Costing system in which the cost object is a unit or multiple units of a distinct product or service called a job. (98)

Joint costs. Costs of a production process that yields multiple products simultaneously. (556)

Joint products. Two or more products that have high sales values compared with the sales values of other products yielded by a joint production process. (556)

Just-in-time (JIP) production. Demand-pull manufacturing system in which each component in a production line is produced as soon as and only when needed by the next step in the production line. Also called *lean production.* (697)

Just-in-time (JIT) purchasing. The purchase of goods or materials so that they are delivered just as needed for production. (692)

Kaizen budgeting. Budgetary approach that explicitly incorporates continuous improvement during the budget period into the budget numbers. (189)

Labor-time record. Source document that contains information about the labor time used on a specific job and in a specific department. (102)

Lean production. See *just-in-time (FIT) production.*

Learning curve. Function that measures how labor-hours per unit decline as units of production increase because workers are learning and becoming better at their jobs. (339)

Life-cycle budgeting. Budget that estimates the revenues and individual value-chain costs attributable to each product from its initial R&D to its final customer servicing and support. (425)

Life-cycle costing. System that tracks and accumulates individual value-chain costs attributable to each product from its initial R&D to its final customer servicing and support. (425)

Line management. Mangers who are directly responsible for attaining the goals of the organization. (15)

Linear cost function. Cost function in which the graph of total costs versus the level of a single activity related to that cost is a straight line within the relevant range. (324)

Linear programming (LP). Optimization technique used to maximize an objective function (for example, contribution margin of a mix of products), when there are multiple constraints. (393)

Locked-in costs. Costs that have not yet been incurred but, based on decisions that have already been made, will be incurred in the future. Also called *designed-in costs.* (417)

Main product. Product from a joint production process that has a high sales value compared with the sales values of all other products of the joint production process. (556)

Make-or-buy decisions. Decisions about whether a producer of goods or services will insource (produce goods or services within the firm) or outsource (purchase them from outside vendors). (375)

Management accounting. Measures and reports financial and nonfinancial information that helps managers make decisions to fulfill the goals of an organization. It focuses on internal reporting. (2)

Management by exception. Practice of concentrating on areas not operating as expected and giving less attention to areas operating as expected. (216)

Management control system. Means of gathering and using information to aid and coordinate the planning and control decisions throughout an organization and to guide the behavior of its managers and employees. (754)

Manufacturing cells. Grouping of all the different types of equipment used to make a given product. (697)

Manufacturing cycle time. See *manufacturing lead time.* (664)

Manufacturing lead time. Duration between the time an order is received by manufacturing to the time it becomes a finished good. Also called *manufacturing cycle time.* (664)

Manufacturing overhead allocated. Indirect manufacturing costs allocated to a job, product, or service based on the budgeted rate multiplied by the actual quantity used of the cost-allocation base. Also called *manufacturing overhead applied.* (112)

Manufacturing overhead applied. See *manufacturing overhead allocated.*

Manufacturing overhead costs. See *indirect manufacturing costs.*

Manufacturing-sector companies. Companies that purchase materials and components and convert them into various finished goods. (38)

Margin of safety. Amount of budgeted revenues over and above breakeven revenues. (70)

Marketing. Promoting and selling products or services to customers or prospective customers. (10)

Market-share variance. The difference in budgeted contribution margin for actual market size in units caused solely by actual market share being different from budgeted market share. (500)

Market-size variance. The difference in budgeted contribution margin at the budgeted market share caused solely by actual market size in units being different from budgeted market size in units (501)

Master budget. Expression of management's operating and financial plans for a specified period (usually a year) and comprises a set of budgeted financial statements. Also called *pro forma statements.* (176)

Master-budget capacity utilization. The expected level of capacity utilization for the current budget period (typically one year). (301)

Materials requirements planning (MRP). Push-through system that manufactures finished goods for inventory on the basis of demand forecasts. (696)

Materials-requisition record. Source document that contains information about the cost of direct materials used on a specific job and in a specific department. (101)

Merchandising-sector companies. Companies that purchase and then sell tangible products without changing their basic form. (38)

Mixed cost. A cost that has both fixed and variable elements. Also called a *semivariable cost.* (325)

Moral hazard. Describes situations in which an employee prefers to exert less effort (or report distorted information) compared with the effort (or accurate information) desired by the owner because the employee's effort (or validity of the reported information) cannot be accurately monitored and enforced. (800)

Motivation. The desire to attain a selected goal (the goal-congruence aspect) combined with the resulting pursuit of that goal (the effort aspect). (755)

Multicollinearity. Exists when two or more independent variables in a multiple regression model are highly correlated with each other. (353)

Multiple regression. Regression model that estimates the relationship between the dependent variable and two or more independent variables. (334)

Net income. Operating income plus nonoperating revenues (such as interest revenue) minus nonoperating costs (such as interest cost) minus income taxes. (63)

Net present value (NPV) method. Capital budgeting DCF method that calculates the expected monetary gain or loss from a project by discounting all expected future cash inflows and outflows to the present point in time, using the required rate of return. (720)

Net realizable value (NRV) method. Method that allocates joint costs to joint products on the basis of the final sales value minus the separable costs of the total production of the joint products during the accounting period. (562)

Nominal rate of return. Made up of three elements: (a) a risk-free element when there is no expected inflation, (b) a business-risk element, and (c) and an inflation element. (739)

Nonlinear cost function. Cost function in which the graph of total costs based on the level of a single activity is not a straight line within the relevant range. (338)

Nonvalue-added cost. A cost that, if eliminated, would not reduce the actual or perceived value or utility (usefulness) customers obtain from using the product or service. (417)

Normal capacity utilization. The level of capacity utilization that satisfies average customer demand over a period (say, 2–3 years) that includes seasonal, cyclical, and trend factors. (300)

Normal costing. A costing method that traces direct costs to a cost object by using the actual direct cost rates times the actual quantity of the direct cost inputs and allocates indirect costs based on the budgeted indirect cost rates times the actual quantity of the cost allocation bases. (106)

Normal spoilage. Spoilage inherent in a particular production process that arises even under efficient operating conditions. (628)

Objective function. Expresses the objective to be maximized (for example, operating income) or minimized (for example, operating costs) in a decision model (for example, a linear programming model). (392)

On-time performance. Situations in which the product or service is actually delivered by the time it was scheduled to be delivered. (664)

One-time-only special order. Orders that have no long-run implications. (373)

Operating budget. Budgeted income statement and its supporting budget schedules. (180)

Operating department. Department that directly adds value to a product or service. Also called a *production department* in manufacturing companies. (526)

Operating income. Total revenues from operation minus cost of goods sold and operating costs (excluding interest expense and income taxes). (40)

Operating leverage. Effects that fixed costs have on changes in operating income as changes occur in units sold and hence in contribution margin. (72)

Operation. A standardized method or technique that is performed repetitively, often on different materials resulting in different finished goods. (612)

Operation-costing system. Hybrid-costing system applied to batches of similar, but not identical products. Each batch of products is often a variation of a single design and it proceeds through a sequence of operations but each batch does not necessarily move through the same operations as other batches. Within each operation, all product units use identical amounts of the operation's resources. (612)

Opportunity cost. The contribution to income that is forgone or rejected by not using a limited resource in its next-best alternative use. (379)

Opportunity cost of capital. See *required rate of return (RRR)*.

Ordering costs. Costs of preparing, issuing, and paying purchase orders, plus receiving and inspecting the items included in the orders. (686)

Organization structure. Arrangement of lines of responsibility within the organization. (191)

Outcomes. Predicted economic results of the various possible combinations of actions and events in a decision model. (81)

Output unit-level costs. The costs of activities performed on each individual unit of product or service. (143)

Output-level overhead variance. See *production-volume variance*.

Outsourcing. Process of purchasing goods and services from outside vendors rather than producing the same goods or providing the same services within the organization. (375)

Overabsorbed indirect costs. See *overallocated indirect costs*.

Overallocated indirect costs. Allocated amount of indirect costs in an accounting period is greater than the actual (incurred) amount in that period. Also called *overapplied indirect costs* and *overabsorbed indirect costs.* (114)

Overapplied indirect costs. See *overallocated indirect costs.*

Overtime premium. Wage rate paid to workers (for both direct labor and indirect labor) in *excess* of their straight-time wage rates. (44)

Pareto diagram. Chart that indicates how frequently each type of defect occurs, ordered from the most frequent to the least frequent. (658)

Partial productivity. Measures the quantity of output produced divided by the quantity of an individual input used. (468)

Payback. Capital budgeting method that measures the time it will take to recoup, in the form of expected future cash flows, the net initial investment in a project. (724)

Peak-load pricing. Practice of charging a higher price for the same product or service when demand for it approaches the physical limit of the capacity to produce that product or service. (427)

Peanut-butter costing. See *cost smoothing.*

Perfectly competitive market. Exists when there is a homogeneous product with buying prices equal to selling prices and no individual buyers or sellers can affect those prices by their own actions. (762)

Period costs. All costs in the income statement other than cost of goods sold. (39)

Physical measure method. Method that allocates joint costs to joint products on the basis of the relative weight, volume, or other physical measure at the splitoff point of the total production of these products during the accounting period. (560)

Planning. Selecting organization goals, predicting results under various alternative ways of achieving those goals, deciding how to attain the desired goals, and communicating the goals and how to attain them to the entire organization. (6)

Practical capacity. The level of capacity that reduces theoretical capacity by unavoidable operating interruptions such as scheduled maintenance time, shutdowns for holidays, and so on. (300)

Predatory pricing. Company deliberately prices below its costs in an effort to drive out competitors and restrict supply and then raises prices rather than enlarge demand. (428)

Prevention costs. Costs incurred to preclude the production of products that do not conform to specifications. (655)

Previous department costs. See *transferred-in costs.*

Price discounting. Reduction of selling prices below list selling prices to encourage increases in customer purchases. (491)

Price discrimination. Practice of charging different customers different prices for the same product or service. (427)

Price-recovery component. Change in operating income attributable solely to changes in prices of inputs and outputs between one period and the next. (456)

Price variance. The difference between the actual price and the budgeted price multiplied by the actual quantity of input. Also called *input-price variance* or *rate variance* (224)

Prime costs. All direct manufacturing costs. (43)

Pro forma statements. *Budgeted financial statements.*

Probability. Likelihood or chance that an event will occur. (80)

Probability distribution. Describes the likelihood (or probability) that each of the mutually exclusive and collectively exhaustive set of events will occur. (80)

Problem solving. Comparative analysis for decision making role of a management accountant. (8)

Process-costing system. Costing system in which the cost object is masses of identical or similar units of a product or service. (98)

Product. Any output that has a positive sales value (or an output that enables an organization to avoid incurring costs). (556)

Product cost. Sum of the costs assigned to a product for a specific purpose. (45)

Product-cost cross-subsidization. Costing outcome where one undercosted (overcosted) product results in at least one other product being overcosted (undercosted) in the organization. (136)

Product differentiation. An organization's ability to offer products or services perceived by its customers to be superior and unique relative to the products and services of its competitors. (447)

Product life cycle. Spans the time from initial R&D on a product to when customer servicing and support is no longer offered for that product. (425)

Product-mix decisions. Decisions about which products to sell and in what quantities. (382)

Product overcosting. A product consumes a low level of resources but is reported to have a high cost per unit. (136)

Product-sustaining costs. The costs of activities undertaken to support individual products regardless of the number of units or batches in which the units are produced. (144)

Product undercosting. A product consumes a high level of resources but is reported to have a low cost per unit. (136)

Production. Acquiring, coordinating, and assembling resources to produce a product or deliver a service. (10)

Production department. See *operating department.*

Production-denominator level. The denominator of the budgeted manufacturing fixed overhead rate computation. (257)

Production-volume variance. The difference between budgeted fixed overhead and fixed overhead allocated on the basis of actual output produced. Also called *denominator-level variance* and *output-level overhead variance.* (259)

Productivity. Measures the relationship between actual inputs used (both quantities and costs) and actual outputs produced; the lower the inputs for a given quantity of outputs or the higher the outputs for a given quantity of inputs, the higher the productivity. (468)

Productivity component. Change in costs attributable to a change in the quantity of inputs used in the current period relative to the quantity of inputs that would have been used in the prior period to produce the quantity of current period output. (456)

Profit center. Responsibility center where the manager is accountable for revenues and costs. (191)

Proration. The spreading of underallocated or overallocated overhead among ending work in process, finished goods, and cost of goods sold. (116)

Purchase-order lead time. The time between placing an order and its delivery. (687)

Purchasing costs. Cost of goods acquired from suppliers including incoming freight or transportation costs. (686)

PV graph. Shows how changes in the quantity of units sold affects operating income. (67)

Qualitative factors. Outcomes that are difficult to measure accurately in numerical terms. (372)

Quality costs. See *costs of quality (COQ)*.

Quality of design. Refers to how closely the characteristics of a product or service meets the needs and wants of customers. (655)

Quantitative factors. Outcomes that are measured in numerical terms. (372)

Rate variance. See *price variance*.

Real rate of return. The rate of return demanded to cover investment risk (with no inflation). It has a risk-free element and a business-risk element. (739)

Reciprocal allocation method. Cost allocation method that explicitly includes the mutual services provided among all support departments. (529)

Reengineering. The fundamental rethinking and redesign of business processes to achieve improvements in critical measures of performance, such as cost, quality, service, speed, and customer satisfaction. (448)

Refined costing system. Costing system that reduces the use of broad averages for assigning the cost of resources to cost objects (jobs, products, services) and provides better measurement of the costs of overhead resources used by different cost objects—no matter how differently the different cost objects use overhead resources. (140)

Regression analysis. Statistical method that measures the average amount of change in the dependent variable associated with a unit change in one or more independent variables. (333)

Relevant costs. Expected future costs that differ among alternative courses of action being considered. (370)

Relevant range. Band of normal activity level or volume in which there is a specific relationship between the level of activity or volume and the cost in question (35)

Relevant revenues. Expected future revenues that differ among alternative courses of action being considered. (370)

Reorder point. The quantity level of the inventory on hand that triggers a new order. (688)

Required rate of return (RRR). The minimum acceptable annual rate of return on an investment. Also called the *discount rate, hurdle rate, cost of capital*, or opportunity cost of capital. (720)

Research and development. Generating and experimenting with ideas related to new products, services, or processes. (9)

Residual income (RI). Accounting measure of income minus a dollar amount of required return on an accounting measure of investment. (789)

Residual term. The vertical difference or distance between the actual cost and the estimated cost for each observation in a regression model. (334)

Responsibility accounting. System that measures the plans (by budgets) and actions (by actual results) of each responsibility center. (191)

Responsibility center. Part, segment, or subunit of an organization whose manager is accountable for a specified set of activities. (191)

Return on investment (ROI). An accounting measure of income divided divided by an accounting measure of investment. See also *accrual accounting rate of return*. (788)

Revenues. Inflows of assets (usually cash or accounts receivable) received for products or services provided to customers. (40)

Revenue allocation. The allocation of revenues that are related to a particular revenue object but cannot be traced to it in an economically feasible (cost-effective) way. (537)

Revenue center. Responsibility center where the manager is accountable for revenues only. (191)

Revenue driver. A variable, such as volume, that causally affects revenues. (62)

Revenue object. Anything for which a separate measurement of revenue is desired. (537)

Rework. Units of production that do not meet the standards required by customers for finished units that are subsequently repaired and sold as acceptable finished units. (626)

Rightsizing. See *downsizing*.

Rolling budget. Budget or plan that is always available for a specified future period by adding a period (month, quarter or year) in the future as the period just ended is dropped. Also called *continuous budget*. (180)

Safety stock. Inventory held at all times regardless of the quantity of inventory ordered using the EOQ model. (689)

Sales mix. Quantities of various products or services that constitute total unit sales. (74)

Sales-mix variance. The difference between (1) the budgeted contribution margin for the actual sales mix, and (2) the budgeted contribution margin for the budgeted sales mix. (498)

Sales-quantity variance. The difference between (1) the budgeted contribution margin based on actual units sold of all products at the budgeted-mix and (2) the contribution margin in the static budget (which is based on the budgeted units of all products to be sold at the budgeted mix). (499)

Sales value at splitoff method. Method that allocates joint costs to joint products on the basis of the relative total sales value at the splitoff point of the total production of these products during the accounting period. (560)

Sales-volume variance. The difference between a flexible-budget amount and the corresponding static-budget amount. (220)

Scorekeeping. Role of a management accountant focusing on accumulating data and reporting results to all levels of management describing how the organization is doing. (8)

Scrap. Material leftover when making a product. (626)

Self-liquidating cycle. The movement from cash to inventories to receivables and back to cash. (198)

Selling-price variance. The difference between the actual selling price and the budgeted selling price multiplied by the actual units sold. (221)

Semivariable cost. See *mixed cost.*

Sensitivity analysis. A what-if technique that managers use to examine how a result will change if the original predicted data are not achieved or if an underlying assumption changes. (70)

Separable costs. All costs (manufacturing, marketing, distribution, and so on) incurred beyond the splitoff point that are assignable to each of the specific products identified at the splitoff point. (556)

Sequential allocation method. See *step-down allocation method.*

Sequential tracking. Approach in a product-costing method in which recording of the journal entries occurs in the same order as actual purchases and progress in production. (700)

Service department. See *support department.*

Service-sector companies. Companies that provide services or intangible products to their customers. (38)

Service-sustaining costs. The costs of activities undertaken to support individual services. (144)

Simple regression. Regression model that estimates the relationship between the dependent variable and one independent variable. (334)

Single-rate cost-allocation method. Allocation method that allocates costs in each cost pool to cost objects using the same rate per unit of the single allocation base. (522)

Slope coefficient. Coefficient term in a cost estimation model that indicates the amount by which total cost changes when a one-unit change occurs in the level of activity within the relevant range. (325)

Source document. An original record that supports journal entries in an accounting system. (101)

Specification analysis. Testing of the assumptions of regression analysis. (349)

Splitoff point. The juncture in a joint-production process when two or more products become separately identifiable. (556)

Spoilage. Units of production that do not meet the standards required by customers for good units and that are discarded or sold for reduced prices. (626)

Staff management. Staff who provide advice and assistance to line management. (15)

Stand-alone cost-allocation method. Method that uses information pertaining to each user of a cost object as a separate entity to determine the cost-allocation weights. (533)

Stand-alone revenue-allocation method. Method that uses product-specific information on the products in the bundle as weights for allocating the bundled revenues to the individual products. (538)

Standard. A carefully predetermined price, cost, or quantity. It is usually expressed on a per unit basis. (222)

Standard cost. A carefully determined cost of a unit of output. (222)

Standard costing. Costing method that traces direct costs to output produced by multiplying the standard prices or rates by the standard quantities of inputs allowed for actual outputs produced and allocates indirect costs on the basis of the standard indirect rates times the standard quantities of the allocation bases allowed for the actual outputs produced. (253)

Standard error of the estimated coefficient. Regression statistic that indicates how much the estimated value of the coefficient is likely to be affected by random factors. (348)

Standard input. A carefully predetermined quantity of input required for one unit of output. (222)

Standard price. A carefully determined price that a company expects to pay for a unit of input. (222)

Static budget. Budget based on the level of output planned at the start of the budget period. (216)

Static-budget variance. Difference between an actual result and the corresponding budgeted amount in the static budget. (217)

Step cost function. A cost function in which the cost remains the same over various ranges of the level of activity, but the cost increases by discrete amounts (that is, increases in steps) as the level of activity changes from one range to the next. (338)

Step-down allocation method. Cost allocation method that allows for partial recognition of the services provided by support departments to other support departments. Also called *sequential allocation method.* (528)

Stockout costs. Costs that result when a company runs out of a particular item for which there is customer demand. The company must act to meet that demand or suffer the costs of not meeting it. (686)

Strategic cost management describes cost management that specifically focuses on strategic issues. (4)

Strategy. Specifies how an organization matches its own capabilities with the opportunities in the marketplace to accomplish its objectives. (4)

Suboptimal decision making. Decisions in which the benefit to one subunit is more than offset by the costs or loss of benefits to the organization as a whole. Also called *incongruent decision making* or *dysfunctional decision making.* (756)

Sunk costs. Past costs that are unavoidable because they cannot be changed no matter what action is taken. (371)

Super-variable costing. See *throughput costing.*

Supply chain. Describes the flow of goods, services, and information from the initial sources of materials and services to the delivery of products to consumers, regardless of whether those activities occur in the same organization or in other organizations. (10)

Support department. Department that provides the services that assist other internal departments (operating departments and other support departments) in the company. Also called a *service department.* (526)

Target cost per unit. Estimated long-run cost per unit of a product or service that enables the company to achieve its target operating income per unit when selling at the target price. Target cost per unit is derived by subtracting the target operating income per unit from the target price. (416)

Target operating income per unit. Operating income that a company aims to earn per unit of a product or service sold. (416)

Target price. Estimated price for a product or service that potential customers will pay. (415)

Target rate of return on investment. The target annual operating income that an organization aims to achieve divided by invested capital. (422)

Theoretical capacity. The level of capacity based on producing at full efficiency all the time. (300)

Theory of constraints (TOC). Describes methods to maximize operating income when faced with some bottleneck and some nonbottleneck operations. (668)

Throughput contribution. Revenues minus the direct materials cost of the goods sold. (668)

Throughput costing. Method of inventory costing in which only variable direct material costs are included as inventoriable costs. Also called *super-variable costing.* (295)

Time driver. Any factor in which a change in the factor causes a change in the speed of an activity. (665)

Time value of money. Takes into account that a dollar (or any other monetary unit) received today is worth more than a dollar received at any future time. (720)

Total factor productivity (TFP). The ratio of the quantity of output produced to the costs of all inputs used, based on current period prices. (470)

Total-overhead variance. The sum of the flexible-budget variance and the production-volume variance. (p. 263)

Transfer price. Price one subunit (department or division) charges for a product or service supplied to another subunit of the same organization. (758)

Transferred-in costs. Costs incurred in previous departments that are carried forward as the product's costs when it moves to a subsequent process in the production cycle. Also called *previous department costs.* (604)

Trigger point. Refers to a stage in the cycle from purchase of direct materials to sale of finished goods at which journal entries are made in the accounting system. (700)

Uncertainty. The possibility that an actual amount will deviate from an expected amount. (71)

Underabsorbed indirect costs. See *underallocated indirect costs.*

Underallocated indirect costs. Allocated amount of indirect costs in an accounting period is less than the actual (incurred) amount in that period. Also called *underapplied indirect costs* or *underabsorbed indirect costs.* (114)

Underapplied indirect costs. See *underallocated indirect costs.*

Unfavorable variance. Variance that has the effect of decreasing operating income relative to the budgeted amount. Denoted U. (217)

Unit cost. Cost computed by dividing some amount of total costs by the related number of units. Also called *average cost.* (37)

Unused capacity. The amount of productive capacity available over and above the productive capacity employed to meet consumer demand in the current period. (461)

Usage variance. See *efficiency variance.*

Value-added cost. A cost that, if eliminated, would reduce the actual or perceived value or utility (usefulness) customers obtain from using the product or service. (417)

Value chain. The sequence of business functions in which usefulness is added to the products of services of a company. (9)

Value engineering. Systematic evaluation of all aspects of the value-chain business functions, with the objective of reducing costs while satisfying customer needs. (417)

Variable cost. Cost that changes in total in proportion to changes in the related level of total activity or volume. (32)

Variable costing. Method of inventory costing in which all variable manufacturing costs are included as inventoriable costs. Also called *direct costing.* (287)

Variable overhead efficiency variance. The difference between the actual quantity of variable overhead cost-allocation base used and the budgeted quantity of variable overhead cost-allocation base that should have been used to produce the actual output, multiplied by the budgeted variable overhead cost per unit of cost-allocation base (255)

Variable overhead flexible-budget variance. The difference between actual variable overhead costs and flexible-budget variable overhead costs. (254)

Variable overhead spending variance. The difference between the actual variable overhead cost per unit and the budgeted variable overhead cost per unit of the cost-allocation base, multiplied by the actual quantity of the variable overhead cost-allocation base used for actual output. (255)

Variance. The difference between an amount based on an actual result and the corresponding budgeted amount. (216)

Weighted-average process-costing method. Method of process costing that assigns the equivalent-unit cost of the work done to date (regardless of when it was done) to equivalent units completed and transferred out of the process and to equivalent units in ending work-in-process inventory. (593)

Work-in-process inventory. Goods partially worked on but not yet fully completed. Also called *work in progress.* (38)

Work in progress. See *work-in-process inventory.*

Work-measurement method. See *industrial-engineering method.*

Alam, M., 767
Alston, F., 535
Amano, M., 179
Ansari, S., 416
Areeda, P., 429
Armitage, H., 153
Asada, T., 179
Ask, U., 223, 298
Atkinson, A., 403, 488, 649, 671
Atkinson, A. A., 194, 533
Ax, C., 223, 298

Bagley, C., 429, 430
Bailes, J., 179
Bailey, C., 342
Bamber, L., 647
Banker, R., 454
Barnett, D. J., 566
Beaver, W., 798
Bell, J., 416
Blayney, P., 34, 100, 298, 328, 424, 488, 533, 587, 727, 767
Block, S., 727
Borjesson, S., 191
Braund, S., 223, 424, 767
Bruner, R., 727
Bruns, W., 159
Bushman, R., 801

Capettini, R., 576, 580
Chambers, K., 662
Champy, J., 448
Cheatham, C., 568, 577
Chenhal, R. H., 179
Choi, F. D. S., 798
Chung, K., 770
Clarke, P., 100, 153, 223, 727
Cohen, J., 100
Cooper, R., 141, 189, 420, 491
Cooper, W., 223, 424
Cornick, M., 223, 424
Cotton, W., 153
Cox, J., 668
Crespi, J., 558
Crum, W., 548, 577

Datar, S., 454
Davenport, T. H., 698
Dean, G., 488
Demski, J., 534
Drury, C., 223, 265, 424, 767

Eades, K., 727
Eden, L., 770
Eisenmann, T., 35
Elliott, J., 767
Eppen, G., 82, 392

Feinschreiber, R., 770
Fellingham, J., 748
Foster, G., 659
Fremgen, J., 488
Friedland, J., 378

Goering, L., 378
Goldratt, E., 668
Goldsman, L., 535
Goldstein, J. L., 428
Good, T., 100
Gould, F., 82
Govindarajan, V., 767
Grant, T., 424
Green, D., 356
Green, M., 568, 577
Greene, W. H., 349
Grinnell, D. J., 735
Groot, T., 153

Hall, G., 448
Hammer, M., 448
Harrington, J., 428, 429
Harris, J., 558
Harris, J. K., 497
Harris, R., 727
Hartman, A., 14
Heath, C., 178
Henshall, J., 770
Higgins, R., 727
Hoque, Z., 767
Hout, T., 663
Howard, K., 767
Huddart, S., 554, 799
Hunt, H. G., 735

Indjejikian, R., 801
Innes, J., 153
Inoue, S., 179, 223, 298
Iqbal, Z., 129, 797

Jaekicke, R., 92
Jog, V., 727
Joye, M., 328, 488, 587, 767

Kador, J., 14
Kalagnanam, S., 792
Kaplan, R., 454, 475
Kaplan, R. S., 141, 194, 447, 491, 533, 786
Kaplow, L., 484
Katzenbach, J., 803
Kennedy, D., 554
Keys, D., 182
Kim, I., 727
Klammer, T., 304
Koester, R. J., 566

Laimon, S., 626
Lambert, R., 86, 780
Langefeld-Smith, K., 179
Larnick, R., 178
Lavery, R., 35
Lazare, C., 179
Lee, H., 695
Levey, M., 770
Liao, S., 488
Lokman, M., 153

Mackey, J., 668
Marple, R., 316
Martin, D., 640
Mayne, F., 648
Melamud, N., 402, 403, 799, 812
Mills, R., 424
Mitchell, F., 153
Moore, J., 82, 392
Moriarty, S., 534
Mostafa, A., 767
Mowen, M., 34

Nanni, A., 223, 792
Neshlin, S., 338
Nicholson, R., 153
Noreen, E., 668
Norton, D. P., 447, 786

O'Byrne, S., 790
O'Dea, T., 727
Osborne, P., 223, 424, 767

Padmanabhan, V., 695
Paquette, L., 100
Pass, C., 770
Patell, J., 781
Paton, W. A., 396
Player, S., 182

Porter, M., 446
Pothen, S., 35
Powell, T., 188

Rajan, M., 88, 130
Ramadan, S., 488
Ramamurthy, B., 767
Reichelstein, S., 403, 793, 799
Robichek, A., 92
Rosenthal, J., 448
Ross, I., 790
Ruhli, E., 448

Sakurai, M., 223, 792
Sangster, A., 727
Scarbrough, P., 223, 792
Schaefer, H., 401
Schemo, D. J., 378
Schlank, R., 792
Schmidt, C., 82, 392
Schmidt, S., 448
Sedgwick, D., 378
Sharp, J., 767
Shavell, S., 484
Shiely, J., 790
Siegel, G., 11
Sifonis, J., 14
Sjoblom, L., 659
Slagmulder, R., 420
Smith, A., 801
Smith, D., 668, 803
Smith, K., 727, 792
Solomons, D., 811
Song, J., 727
Sorenson, J., 11
Spero, A., 400, 815
Sridhar, S., 130, 436
Srivastava, A., 727
Stalk, G., 663
Stein, J., 790
Stewart, G. B., 792
Stout, D., 568
Sullivan, C., 727, 792
Sweeting, C., 424
Swenson, D., 493

Tang, R., 767, 792
Tayles, M., 223, 424, 767
Towers, P., 454
Treichler, C., 448
Trujillo, T. J., 428
Turban, E., 493
Turner, D., 429

Van Horne, J., 791
Vernon, J., 428, 429
Villers, R., 207
Viscusi, W., 428, 429

Wade, J., 448
Weatherford, L., 82, 392
Whang, S., 695
Williamson, R., 80
Wilson, S., 223, 424
Winchell, W., 329
Wolfson, M., 798
Worthington, M., 535
Wrappe, S., 770
Wright, H., 551
Wu, G., 178
Wygal, D., 568

Yasukata, K., 792
Yokoyama, I., 34, 100, 298, 424, 533, 727
Young, D., 790

Zeller, T. L., 154

COMPANY INDEX

Adjustor's Replace-a-Car, 428–429
Agency Rent-a-Car, 428–429
Airbus Industries, 482–483
Alaska Airlines, 235
Amazon.com, 5, 14, 73, 154
American Airlines, 5, 73, 235, 381
American Electronics Association, 627
American Express, 136
America West Airlines, 235
Analog Devices, Inc., 226, 297, 343, 662
Anderson Construction, 123–124
AOL Time Warner, 31
Apple Computer, 427
AT&T, 436, 449, 464, 663
Avis Corporation, 427–428

Baker & Taylor, 698
Banca di America e di Italia, 449
Band-X, 430
Barings PLC, 758
Barnes and Noble, 5, 21, 73, 734
BASF, 428
BCTel, 152
Bechtel Corporation, 98, 413
Behlen Manufacturing, 471
Beijing Engineering, 377
BMW, 382
Boeing Company, 136, 320, 324, 326, 328, 664, 665
Braintree Hospital, 152
Briggs and Stratton, 791
British Petroleum, 191, 805
British Telecom, 654
Brooke Group, 428

Cadbury Schweppes, 212
Campbell Soup Company, 19
Canseco Company, 55
Caterpillar Tractor, 11, 338, 805–806
Chevrolet, 177
Chrysler, 22
Cigna Insurance, 449
CISCO Systems, 430
Citibank, 98
Citizen Watch, 189
Clorox, 252
Coca-Cola Company, 10, 375, 447, 692, 771, 791
Colgate Palmolive, 803
Collins Industries, 320
Colorscope, Inc., 104
Compaq Computer, 22, 427, 556, 661
Continental Airlines, 12, 235
Cooperative Bank, 152, 155, 329, 338
Corio, 35
Crysel, 654
CSX, 791

DaimlerChrysler, 96, 177–178, 426, 662
Deckers Outdoor Corporation, 283
Deer Valley Resort, 718, 751
Dell Computer Corporation, 4, 14, 96, 133–134, 136, 173, 320, 375, 430, 556, 654, 661, 662
Del Monte, 504
Delta Airlines, 235, 464
Duke Power Company, 805
DuPont Corporation, 640, 654, 735, 805

Eastman Kodak, 194, 375, 756
Eaton, 471
Electrolux, 180
EMC Corporation, 4, 665
Emerson Electric, 447
Equifax, 791
Excite, 54
Exodus Communications, 665
Exxon, 654
Exxon Mobil, 136

Federal Express, 78, 283, 493, 661, 664, 734
Fidelity Investments, 2
FMC, 791
Ford Motor Company, 22–23, 32–33, 37, 377, 426, 427, 449, 608–609, 654, 718, 792, 802
Four Points Hotels, 441
Frito-Lay, Inc., 620–621
FRx Software Corporation, 188
Fujitsu, 654, 699

General Chemicals, 98
General Electric, 4, 21, 22, 54, 178, 194, 626, 654, 661, 663, 734, 754, 802
General Foods Corporation, 413
General Motors, 53, 136, 426, 464, 734, 756
Glaxo Smith Kline, 755
Grand Canyon Railway, 410, 443–444
GTE Corporation, 2
Guinsess, 792

Harley-Davidson, 180
Harvard University, 22, 522
Heinz, 482, 755
Hewlett-Packard Company, 21, 163–164, 177, 447, 449, 519, 654, 692
Hitachi, 98, 665
Hoffman Beverage Company, 367
Home Depot, 447, 735
Hyundai, 377

IBM, 21, 22, 194, 375, 447, 464, 556
Information Systems Corporation, 754, 782
Ingram, 698
Insight, Inc., 425–426
Intel Corporation, 98, 134
Interface, Inc., 622, 651
Interlake, 756
Isuzu, 177

J. Walter Thompson, 104, 377
Jamcracker, 35
John Deere and Company, 338
Johnson & Johnson, 8, 53–54, 194, 756, 805

Kodak, 194, 375, 756
Kraft Foods, 5
Kroger, 686
Krones, 792

La Quinta Corporation, 472
Lever Brothers, 462
Levi Strauss, 608
Libbey-Owens-Ford Company, 651–652
Lightning Source, 698
Lockheed-Martin, 806
Loral Aerospace, 2

Mark's Work Warehouse Ltd., 214, 479
Marriott International, 191–192, 804
MasterCard, 518
Mayne Nickless, 792
Maytag, 216
McDonald's Corporation, 5, 216, 248–249, 446, 479–480, 663, 755, 786, 816–817
Memory Manufacturing Company, 584
Merck & Company, 5, 14, 22, 734
Meridian Finance, 243
Microsoft, 22, 35, 802
MIT, 522
Mitsubishi, 22
Mitsui, 792
Mobil, 452
Mobile Communications, 178
Motorola, 471
Mount Sinai Hospital, 22

Nantucket Nectars, 482, 519, 586, 623
National Football League, 327
NBC, 734
New York Stock Exchange, 327
Nike, 2, 5, 10, 16
Nissan Motor Company, 177, 343, 426, 771
Nortel Networks, 8
Northwest Airlines, 235
Novartis, 14, 338, 803

Oracle, 699
Owens Corning, 177

Pabst Brewing Company, 367
Pace, 178
Panasonic, 377
Pepsi, 31, 122
Pepsi Bottling Group, 10
PetsMart, 60
Pfizer, 4, 14
PHH, 493
Philips, 758
Pirelli, 792
Pizza Hut, 193, 734
Polysar, 261
PriceWaterhouseCoopers, 96
Procter & Gamble, 5, 30, 191, 695–696

Quaker Oats, 792

Raytheon Corporation, 98
Regal Marine, 2, 26–27, 686, 716
Replica Books, 698
R.H. Macy, 104
Richfield Oil Company, 512–513
Ritz-Carlton Hotel Company, 176, 214, 654, 683

Saatchi and Saatchi, 98, 104
Safeway, 54, 686
Samsung, 654
Scott Paper, 464
Sears, Roebuck and Co., 5, 22, 803
Sears Appliance Services, 44
Sheraton Hotels, 441
Siemens Nixdorf, 449
Sony Corporation, 9–10, 62, 377
Southwest Airlines, 4, 12, 173, 234–235
Sprint, 35
Stanford University, 522, 553–554
Store 24, 62, 93–94, 370, 407–408
Subaru, 177
Sumitomo Corporation, 12, 758

Super Shuttle, 326
Suzuki Company, 201 – 202
Swedish Match, 792

Tektronix, 756
Tennessee Eastman, 803
Teva Sport Sandals, 252, 283 – 284
Texas Instruments, 447
Three Dog Bakery, 30, 60
Toronto Blue Jays, 127
Toyota, 4, 10, 22, 53, 377, 426, 628, 654, 661, 662, 686, 703
Toys R Us, 5, 154
TRW, 471

Union Pacific, 152
United Airlines, 78 – 79, 234 – 235, 734
United Libbey-Nippon, 651 – 652
United Van Lines, 663
University of Chicago Press, 125 – 126
U.S. Airways, 235

Visa, 518
Volkswagen, 377, 378

Wal-Mart, 5, 96, 154, 663, 686, 692
Walt Disney, 104
Webvan, 461
Westin Hotels, 441, 734
Wheeled Coach Industries, 286, 320 – 321
Whirlpool, 471

Xerox Corporation, 22

Yahoo!, 14, 430
Yokogowa Hewlett-Packard, 343

SUBJECT INDEX

Entries appearing in footnotes are indicated by an italicized n following the page number.

Ability to bear, as criterion in cost-allocation decisions, 484
Abnormal rework, 638
Abnormal spoilage
  definition of, 628
  job costing and, 637
Absorption costing
  about, 286 – 289
  breakeven points in, 309 – 310
  comparative income effects *vs.* variable costing, 293
  definition of, 287
  denominator choice for budgeted fixed manufacturing cost per case, 304
  denominator-level capacity for, 300 – 301
  operating income and, 294
  performance measures and, 293 – 295
  revising performance evaluation, 295
  variable costing compared to, 290 – 292
Account analysis method of cost estimation, 329 – 330
Accounting rate of return, 726, 788. *See also* Return on investment (ROI)
Accrual accounting rate of return (AARR), 726, 788. *See also* Return on investment (ROI)
Activity, definition of, 141
Activity-based budgeting, 189 – 191
Activity-based costing (ABC)
  about, 141 – 144
  cost-allocation bases in, 142 – 143
  cost drivers and, 337, 338
  department-costing systems and, 151
  e-retailing and, 154
  flexible budgeting and, 232 – 234
  global practices, 153
  implementing, 151 – 152
  improving cost management and profitability, 148 – 151
  indirect-cost pool system compared with, 148, 149
  in manufacturing sector, 144 – 148
  in merchandising sector, 152, 155
  product costs with, 146, 147
  revenue drivers and, 338
  in service sector, 152, 155
  variance analysis and, 268 – 271
Activity-based management (ABM), 148 – 151
Activity cost pools, 485
Activity-cost rates, for indirect-cost pools, 145
Actual cost(s), 30
Actual costing
  comparison of inventory-costing systems, 296
  definition of, 99
Actual cost rates, 524 – 525
Actual market share, 500
Actual market size in units, 501
Actual sales mix, 498
Actual units sold of all products, 499
Actual usage allocation bases, 525 – 526
Adjusted allocation-rate approach, 115 – 116, 305, 306*n*
Adjustment issues, cost functions, 343 – 344
Adjustor's Replace-a-Car v. Agency Rent-a-Car, 428 – 429
Administration, and budgeting, 179 – 180
Advanced pricing agreement, 770
Advertising decisions, 69
After-tax cash flows, 729 – 733
Allocability, 535*n*
Allowable costs, 536
American Society for Quality Control, 654
Antitrust laws, and pricing, 428 – 429
Application Service Providers, 35
Appraisal costs, 655
Artificial costs, 530
Assets
  current assets, 4 – 5
  intangible assets, 5, 734 – 736
  long term, gross or net book value, 795, 797
  long-term productive assets, 5
  total assets, 794
Attention directing, 8
Australia
  budgeting practices, 179
  capital budgeting, 727
  corporate cost allocation, 488
  cost classifications, 328
  financial performance measures, 792
  manufacturing overhead cost allocation, 100
  process costing, 587
  support department cost allocation, 533
  transfer pricing, 767
  value engineering, 424
  variable costing, 298
Autocorrelation, 350
Autonomy, 756
Average costs, 36 – 37. *See also* Unit costs
Average waiting time, 666

B2B (business-to-business exchanges), 430
Backflush costing
  about, 700 – 707
  general ledger overview, 705
  journal entries in, 704
  special considerations, 706 – 707
Balanced scorecard
  about, 447 – 448
  aligning to strategy, 451
  example of, 450
  excellence in, 452 – 453
  frequently cited measures of, 452
  implementing, 451 – 452
  performance measurement broadening, 454
  perspectives of, 449, 451
  pitfalls of implementation, 453
Balance sheet
  budgeted balance sheet, 199
  examples of, 196
Bargaining power, 447
Batch-level costs, 143, 232 – 233
Beckloff, Mark, 30, 60
Benchmarking
  continuous improvement and, 12 – 13
  definition of, 234
  relative performance evaluation and, 801 – 802
  variances and, 234 – 235
Benefits received, as criterion in cost-allocation decisions, 484
Black boxes, 462
Books on demand, 698
Book value, 386 – 388
Bottlenecks
  definition of, 665
  on Internet, 665
  theory of constraints and, 669
  as time driver, 665 – 667
Breakeven points
  about, 64 – 69
  in absorption costing, 309 – 310
  contribution margin method, 65 – 66
  equation method, 65
  graph method, 66 – 67
  in variable costing, 309 – 310
Breakthrough strategies, 14
Broad averaging, 136 – 137
Brooke Group v. Brown & Williamson Tobacco, 429
Budget(s)
  about, 176 – 177
  administration of, 179 – 180
  advantages of, 177 – 180
  cash budget, 195 – 199
  continuous budget, 180
  definitions of, 6, 176
  feedback and, 192
  financial budget, 180
  flexible budget, 216 – 217, 218 – 219, 232 – 234
  learning curves and, 342 – 343
  manufacturing overhead budget, 185
  master budget, 176, 181
  nonmanufacturing costs budget, 186
  operating budget development, 180 – 187
  preparing, 197 – 199
  production budget, 183 – 184
  revenue budget, 183
  rolling budget, 180
  static budget, 216 – 217
  time coverage of, 180
Budgetary slack, 193 – 194
Budgeted balance sheet, 199
Budgeted cost rates, 524 – 525
Budgeted fixed manufacturing overhead cost rate, 301, 306
Budgeted income statement, 187, 198, 373
Budgeted indirect-cost rate, 106
Budgeted indirect costs, 114 – 118
Budgeted input prices, obtaining, 222
Budgeted input quantities, obtaining, 222
Budgeted market share, 500
Budgeted market size in units, 501
Budgeted sales mix, 498
Budgeted units of all products to be sold, 499
Budgeted usage allocation bases, 525 – 526
Budgeted variable manufacturing overhead cost rates, 253 – 254
Budgeting. *See also* Capital budgeting
  activity-based budgeting, 189 – 191
  behavioral considerations, 13
  global practices, 179
  human aspects of, 193 – 194
  kaizen budgeting, 189
  life-cycle budgeting, 425 – 427
  responsibility accounting and, 191 – 192
Bullwhip effect, 695
Bundled products, 537
Business conduct, codes of, 805 – 806
Business function costs, 373
Business-to-business (B2B) exchanges, 430
Byproducts
  accounting for, 568 – 571
  costing of, 570
  definition of, 556
  distinguishing from joint products, 568
  recognition of
    at time of sale, 570 – 571
    at time production is completed, 569–570

Calabrese, Jerry, 249
Canada
  activity-based costing, 153
  capital budgeting, 727
  corporate cost allocation, 488
  quality practices, 654
  transfer pricing, 767
  variable costing, 298
Capabilities, building, 4
Capacity
  practical capacity, 300
  theoretical capacity, 300
  unused capacity, 461, 463, 464
Capacity constraints
  opportunity costs, outsourcing and, 377 – 382
  product-mix decisions under, 382 – 383
Capacity costs, and denominator-level issues, 306 – 307
Capacity level(s)
  alternative denominator-level capacity for absorption costing, 300 – 301
  choosing, 301 – 306
  effect on product costing and capacity management, 302 – 303
Capacity-level allocation bases, 525 – 526
Capacity management, 302 – 303, 460 – 463
Capital, relevant opportunity cost of, 691
Capital budgeting
  accrual accounting rate of return (AARR) method of, 726
  global practices, 727
  inflation and, 739 – 741
  intangible assets and, 734 – 736
  management decisions, 727 – 728
  for pollution prevention, 735
  stages of, 719 – 720
  strategic considerations, 734
  taxation and, 728 – 733
Carrying costs, 380 – 382, 686, 689
Cash budgets, 195 – 199
Cash flows
  in discounted cash flow analysis, 728 – 733
  of net initial investment, 730 – 731
  nonuniform cash flows, 725 – 726

Cash flows (*cont.*)
  from operations, 731 – 732
  relevant after-tax flows, 729 – 733
  sensitivity analysis and, 200
  uniform cash flows, 724 – 725
Cause and effect
  as criterion in choosing cost drivers, 327 – 328
  as criterion in cost-allocation decisions, 484
Cause-and-effect diagrams, 659
Celebrity endorsements, 496
Certified in Financial Management (CFM), 17
Certified Management Accountant (CMA), 17
Cha, Andrew, 104
Chicken processing industry, 570
Chief accounting officer, 16
Chief Executive Officer (CEO), 16
Chief financial officer (CFO), 15
Chief Operating Officer (COO), 16
Choice criterion, 80
Clean Air Act, 426, 654
Codes of business conduct, 805 – 806
Coefficient of determination, 348
Collusive pricing, 429
Common costs, 533 – 534
Communication, 178
Compensation arrangements
  designing, 800 – 801
  disclosure of, 804
  executive performance measures and, 803 – 804
  team-based compensation, 803
Competence, as ethical standard, 18
Competitors
  pricing decisions and, 410
  strategy and, 446
Complete reciprocated costs, 530
Composite unit, 498 – 499
Computer-based financial planning models, 187 – 189
Computer-integrated manufacturing (CIM), 5
Computers. *See* Information technology; Software
Conference method of cost estimation, 329
Confidentiality, as ethical standard, 18
Conformance quality, 655
Constant, definition of, 325
Constant gross-margin percentage NRV method of joint-cost allocation, 558, 563 – 564
Constant variance of residuals, 349 – 350
Constraints, 392, 393. *See also* Theory of constraints
Continuous budget, 180
Continuous improvement, 12 – 13, 230, 420
Continuous improvement budgeted cost, 230
Contracts
  disputes over reimbursable costs, 536
  with U.S. government, 535 – 537
Contribution income percentage, 64
Contribution income ratio, 64
Contribution income statements, 64
Contribution margin
  definition of, 63
  quality and, 660
  vs. gross margin, 77 – 78
Contribution margin method, breakeven point, 65 – 66
Contribution margin percentage, 64
Contribution margin per unit, 63
Contribution margin ratio, 64
Control
  definition of, 6
  in JIT production, 699 – 700
  management accountants and, 6 – 8
  obtaining information for, 47
Control accounts, 107
Control charts, 657 – 658
Control decisions, 6 – 8, 265
Controllability, 192 – 193
Controllable costs, 192
Controller, 16
Conversion costs
  definition of, 43, 455
  growth and, 457
  productivity and, 459
Coordination, 178
Corporate administration costs, 486
Corporate costs
  allocating to divisions and products, 486 – 489
  categories of, 486
  global allocation practices, 488
  implementing allocations, 489 – 490
  reasons to allocate to divisions, 488
Corporate-sustaining costs, 492
Cost(s)
  actual cost, 30
  allocation of (*See* Cost allocation)
  alternative classifications of, 47
  alternative computation methods, 13, 15
  appraisal costs, 655
  artificial costs, 530
  associated with goods for sale, 686 – 687
  batch-level costs, 143
  business function costs, 373
  carrying costs, 380 – 382, 686, 689
  classification of, 326 – 327
  common costs, 533 – 534
  controllable costs, 192
  conversion costs, 43
  corporate costs, 486
  cost drivers relationships, 344
  current costs, 794 – 795
  customer life-cycle costs, 427
  of decentralization, 756 – 757
  direct costs
    of cost object, 31 – 32, 97
    examples in combinations, 32
    factors affecting classifications, 32
    of quality, 656
  direct manufacturing labor costs, 39
  direct material costs, 39
  discretionary costs, 462
  division costs, 486
  efficiency and, 11 – 12
  environmental costs, 640
  examples in combinations, 37
  external failure costs, 655
  facility-sustaining costs, 144
  fixed costs
    cost-behavior patterns, 32–36
    distinguishing from variable costs, 34
    examples in combinations, 37
  fixed overhead costs, 252 – 253
  full costs of product, 373
  imputed costs, 789
  incremental costs, 377, 768
  indirect costs of cost object, 31 – 32
  indirect manufacturing costs, 39
  information-gathering technology and, 32
  infrastructure costs, 462*n*
  internal failure costs, 655
  inventoriable costs, 39
  joint costs (*See* Joint costs)
  materiality of, 32
  measuring, 43 – 46
  mixed costs, 325
  nonvalue-added cost, 417
  opportunity costs, 379 – 382, 768
  ordering costs, 686, 689
  output unit-level costs, 143
  overallocated (underallocated) indirect costs, 114
  overhead costs (*See* Overhead cost(s))
  past costs, irrelevance of, 386 – 388
  period costs, 39 – 40
  prevention costs, 655
  previous department costs, 604
  pricing decisions and, 410 – 411
  prime costs, 43
  product costs (*See* Product cost(s))
  product-sustaining costs, 144
  purchasing costs, 686
  relationships among types, 36
  relevant costs (*See* Relevant cost(s))
  semivariable costs, 325
  separable costs, 556, 557
  service-sustaining costs, 144
  standard costs, 222
  of time, 667 – 668
  transferred-in costs (*See* Transferred-in costs)
  underabsorbed (overabsorbed) indirect costs, 115
  underapplied (overapplied) indirect costs, 115
  value-added cost, 417
  variable costs, 32 – 36
  variable overhead costs, 252
Cost accounting, 3
Cost Accounting Standards Board (CASB), 535
Cost accumulation, 30
Cost allocation
  byproducts accounting, 568 – 571
  common costs, 533 – 534
  contracts and, 535 – 537
  cost driver compared to, 255
  costing systems and, 485 – 490
  decision criteria, 484 – 485
  definition of, 31
  dual rate method of, 522 – 524
  incremental method of, 534
  irrelevance of joint costs for decision making, 566 – 568
  joint cost allocation approaches, 558 – 566
  joint-cost basics, 556 – 558
  of multiple support departments, 526 – 533
  purposes of, 482 – 484
  single rate method of, 522 – 524
  stand alone method of, 533 – 534
  of support department to operating divisions, 522 – 526
Cost-allocation bases
  in activity-based costing, 142 – 143
  definition of, 97
  example of, 485
  for manufacturing overhead, 100
Cost analysis
  accounting-period dimension, 718
  customer cost analysis, 491 – 492
  project dimension, 718
Cost-application base, 97. *See also* Cost-allocation bases
Cost assignment
  to cost object, 31
  definition of, 30, 97
  federal standards for, 484*n*
Cost base alternatives, 422 – 423
Cost-based transfer prices, 759, 763 – 766
Cost-behavior patterns, 32 – 36
Cost-benefit approach, 13, 485
Cost center, 191
Cost classifications, global practices, 328
Cost drivers
  about, 34 – 35
  activity-based costing and, 337, 338
  cause-and-effect criterion in choosing, 327 – 328
  choosing for cost functions with regression output, 351
  cost allocation compared to, 255
  economic plausibility, 336
  evaluating for cost functions, 335 – 337
  goodness of fit, 336
  multiple, 76 – 77
  relationship with cost, 344
  significance of independent variable, 336
Cost effect of growth, 456
Cost effect of price recovery, 457 – 458
Cost estimation
  about, 326 – 327
  methods of, 328 – 330
  specification analysis of assumptions, 349 – 351
Cost functions
  adjustment issues, 343 – 344
  basic assumptions, 324 – 326
  comparison of alternatives, 352
  data collection issues, 343 – 344
  definition of, 324
  estimation with quantitative analysis, 330 – 335
  evaluating cost drivers of, 335 – 337
  nonlinearity and, 337 – 339
  regression analysis of, 333 – 335
  regression output to choose cost drivers, 351
  step cost functions, 338 – 339
Cost hierarchy
  about, 143 – 144
  customer cost hierarchy, 491
  flexible budget focus on, 234
  multiple regression analysis and, 351 – 352
Cost incurrence, 417 – 418
Costing
  absorption costing (*See* Absorption costing)
  activity-based costing (ABC) (*See* Activity-based costing (ABC))
  actual costing
    comparison of inventory-costing systems, 296
    definition of, 99
  backflush costing, 700 – 707
  direct costing, 289
  job costing (*See* Job costing)
  life-cycle budgeting and, 426 – 427
  life-cycle costing, 425
  pricing for long run and, 413 – 415
  pricing for short run and, 411 – 413
  standard costing (*See* Standard costing)
  throughput costing, 295 – 296
  variable costing (*See* Variable costing)
Costing systems
  about, 96 – 98
  comparing indirect-cost pool and activity-based costing, 148, 149
  cost allocation and, 485 – 490
  JIT's effect on, 700
  job-costing systems, 98 – 99
  in manufacturing environment, 137 – 140
  process-costing systems, 98 – 99
  refining, 140 – 141
Cost leadership, 447
Cost management
  accounting systems and, 3
  framework for, 46 – 47
  improving with activity-based costing, 148 – 151

Cost objects
calculating cost of, 46
choosing, 326
cost assignment to, 31
definition of, 30, 96
departments, 97 – 98
direct costs of, 31 – 32
examples of, 30
indirect costs of, 31 – 32, 97
products, 97 – 98
responsibility centers, 97
Cost of capital, 720
Cost of goods manufactured, 40
Cost of goods sold budgets, 186
Cost planning, and cost-volume-profit (CVP) analysis, 71 – 74
Cost-plus pricing, 421 – 424
Cost pools
activity cost pools, 485
definition of, 97
homogenous cost pool, 140, 488
indirect-cost pools, 140, 142, 145
overhead cost pools, 118
Cost predictions, 327
Cost reduction decisions, 150
Cost smoothing, 136
Costs of quality (COQ), 655 – 657, 663
Cost structures, 71 – 73
Cost terminology, 30
Cost tracing, 31
Cost-volume-profit (CVP) analysis
about, 62 – 64
breakeven point and, 64 – 69
contribution margin *vs.* gross margin, 77 – 78
cost planning and, 71 – 74
for decision making, 69 – 70
effects of sales mix on income, 74 – 75
graph example, 66
multiple cost drivers and, 76 – 77
in nonprofit organizations, 75 – 76
sensitivity analysis and, 70 – 71
in service organizations, 75 – 76
spreadsheet analysis of relationships, 70
uncertainty and, 71
Cross-sectional data, 331
Cumulative average-time learning model, 340, 341
Current assets, 4 – 5
Current costs, 794 – 795
Customer batch-level costs, 491
Customer cost analysis, 491 – 492
Customer cost hierarchy, 491
Customer costs, 490 – 492
Customer focus, 9
Customer-level costs, 492, 494
Customer life-cycle costs, 427
Customer output unit-level costs, 491
Customer perspective, balanced scorecard, 449, 450, 452, 454
Customer profitability, 383 – 386, 493
Customer-profitability analysis, 490, 493
Customer-profitability profiles, 494 – 496
Customer-response time, 664
Customer revenue analysis, 491
Customer revenues, 490 – 492
Customers
bargaining power of, 447
celebrity endorsements, 496
growth potential of, 495
learning from, 496
long-run customer profitability, 495
pricing decisions and, 410
retention of, 495
value assessment of, 495 – 496
Customer satisfaction, nonfinancial measures of, 661 – 662
Customer service, in value chain, 10
Customer-sustaining costs, 491
Customized products, 608
CVP analysis. *See* Cost-volume-profit (CVP) analysis

Data collection, cost functions, 343 – 344
Decentralization
benefits of, 756
costs of, 756 – 757
definition of, 756
management control systems and, 755 – 756
in multinational companies, 757 – 758
transfer pricing and, 758 – 759
Decision making. *See also* Pricing decisions
analyzing relevant information, 47
capital budgeting decisions, 727 – 728
cost allocation decision criteria, 484 – 485
cost reduction decisions, 150
with cost-volume-profit (CVP) analysis, 69 – 70
customer profitability, 383 – 386
design decisions, 150
equipment replacement, 386 – 388
five-step decision process, 371
good decisions and good outcomes, 82
information and, 370
insourcing *vs.* outsourcing, 375 – 377
inventory management decisions, 692
irrelevance of joint costs, 566 – 568
irrelevance of past costs, 386 – 388
key themes, 9
make-or-buy decisions, 375 – 377
management accountants and, 3 – 5
opportunity costs, outsourcing, and capacity constraints, 377 – 382
performance evaluation and, 388 – 389
planning and managing activities, 150 – 151
pricing and product-mix decisions, 45, 149
pricing decisions and downward demand spiral, 303
process improvement decisions, 150
product-mix decisions under capacity constraints, 382 – 383
relevance concept, 370 – 372
suboptimal decision making, 756 – 757
unit costs and, 37 – 38
variance analysis and control decisions, 265
Decision models
definition of, 370
performance evaluation and, 82
reference works, 392*n*
role of, 80 – 81
Decision tables, 81
Degree of operating leverage, 72
Delivery time, 664
Demand inelasticity, 427
Deming Prize, 654
Denominator level, 257, 306 – 307
Denominator-level capacity, for absorption costing, 300 – 301
Denominator-level variance, 259. *See also* Production-volume variance
Department-costing systems, 151
Departments, as cost objects, 97 – 98
Dependent variables, 330
Design
decision making and, 150
of operations, 32
processes of, 137 – 138
quality of, 655
in value chain, 10
Designed-in costs, 417 – 418
Design quality, costs of, 661
Devaney, Pat, 283
Differential costs, 377
Differential revenues, 377
Direct allocation method, 527 – 528
Direct costing, 289
Direct costs
of cost object, 31 – 32, 97
examples in combinations, 37
factors affecting classifications, 32
of quality, 656
Direct-cost tracing, 140, 141
Direct engineered costs, 461
Direct manufacturing labor budget, 185
Direct manufacturing labor costs, 39
Direct materials
growth and, 457
productivity and, 459
Direct materials costs, 39
Direct materials inventory, 38
Direct materials mix variances, 505 – 506
Direct materials prices, 505
Direct materials purchases budgets, 184
Direct materials usage budgets, 184
Direct materials yield variances, 505 – 506, 507
Direct method, 527 – 528
Discounted cash flow (DCF) methods
about, 720 – 724
relevant cash flows in, 728 – 733
Discount rate, 720
Discretionary costs
about, 462
engineered costs distinct from, 462
identifying unused capacity for, 463
Distress prices, 762 – 763
Distribution, in value chain, 10
Distribution-channel costs, 491
Distribution processes, 137 – 138
Disturbance term, 349
Division costs, 486
Divisions
allocating corporate costs to, 486 – 490
allocating costs of support department to, 522 – 526
Double-bilking, 536
Doucette, Paul, 93, 407
Downsizing, 464
Downward demand spiral, 303
Dual pricing, 765 – 766
Dual-rate cost-allocation method, 522 – 524
Dumping, 429
Dupont method of profitability analysis, 788
Durbin-Watson statistic, 349, 351
Dye, Dan, 30, 60
Dysfunctional decision making, 756 – 757. *See also* Suboptimal decision making

E-business strategies, and management accountants, 14
E-commerce, 665
Economic order quantity (EOQ) decision model
about, 687 – 688
JIT purchasing and, 692 – 693
Economic plausibility, 336
Economic value added (EVA®), 790 – 791
Effectiveness, 228
Efficiency, 228
Efficiency variances
comparing with yield improvements, 226
computation of, 225 – 226
definition of, 224
for direct-cost inputs, 221 – 226
direct materials price and, 505
flexible budget and, 233 – 234
variable overhead efficiency variance, 255, 256 – 257
Effort, 755
Electronic Data Interchange (EDI), 103 – 104
Electronics industry, and reject rates, 627
Employees
forced ranking of, 802
intrinsic motivation and organization culture, 805
morale during downsizing, 464
motivating, 178
Ending inventories budget, 185 – 186
End-of-period adjustments
adjusted allocation-rate approach, 115 – 116
budgeted indirect costs and, 114 – 118
choice among approaches, 117 – 118
proration approach, 116 – 117
write-off to cost of goods sold approach, 117
Engineered costs
about, 461 – 462
discretionary costs distinct from, 462
identifying unused capacity for, 463
Enterprise resource planning (ERP) systems, 698 – 699
Environmental issues
costs, 640
laws, 426 – 427
responsibilities, 654 – 655, 735, 805 – 806
Environmental Protection Agency (EPA), 640
Equation method, breakeven point, 65
Equipment-replacement decisions, 386 – 388
Equity, as criterion in cost-allocation decisions, 484
Equivalent products, 446 – 447
Equivalent-unit costs
in first-in, first-out (FIFO) process-costing method, 597
spoilage and, 630
in weighted-average process-costing method, 594
Equivalent units
definition of, 590
in first-in, first-out (FIFO) process-costing method, 596 – 597
physical units and, 588 – 590
spoilage and, 630
in weighted-average process-costing method, 593
E-retailing, activity-based costing and, 154
Error term, 349
Ethical issues
about, 16 – 17
guidelines, 17
responsibilities, 805 – 806
typical challenges, 17
Event, definition of, 80
Executive compensation arrangements, 803 – 804
Expected future costs, 370 – 371
Expected future revenues, 370 – 371
Expected monetary value, 81
Expected value, 81
Experience curves, 340
External failure costs, 655
Exxon Valdez oil spill, 654

Facility-sustaining costs, 144
Factory overhead costs, 39
Failure costs, 655

Fairness
as criterion in cost-allocation decisions, 484
of pricing, 535 – 537
Favorable variance, 217
Feedback
about, 6
budgets and, 192
choosing timing of, 797
Finance director, 15
Financial accounting, 3
Financial Accounting Standards Board (FASB), on stock options, 804
Financial budgets, 180
Financial performance measures
about, 230, 786 – 787
aligning with financial goals, 787 – 793
intensity of incentives and, 800 – 801
overhead variances as, 267
Financial perspective, balanced scorecard, 450, 452, 454
Financial perspective, of balanced scorecard, 449
Financial planning models, 187 – 189
Financial statements
alternative capacity level concepts and, 304 – 306
external reporting under GAAP, 46
inventoriable costs and period costs, 38 – 40
Financing stage of capital budgeting, 719
Finished-goods inventory, 39
First, Tom, 482, 519, 623
First-in, first-out (FIFO) process-costing method
about, 596
transferred-in costs and, 606 – 607
weighted-average process-costing method compared to, 599 – 600
Fishbone diagrams, 659
Fixed cost(s)
cost-behavior patterns, 32 – 36
distinguishing from variable costs, 34
examples in combinations, 37
Fixed cost structures, 71 – 73
Fixed direct manufacturing costs, 296
Fixed indirect manufacturing costs, 296
Fixed manufacturing overhead, 262
Fixed manufacturing overhead costs, 264, 288
Fixed overhead cost-allocation rates, 257 – 258
Fixed overhead costs, 252 – 253
Fixed overhead flexible-budget variances, 258
Fixed overhead spending variances, 258
Fixed setup overhead costs, 270 – 271
Flexible budget
about, 216 – 217
activity-based costing and, 232 – 234
cost hierarchy focus, 234
developing, 218 – 219
Flexible-budget analysis, 254 – 255
Flexible-budget variances
about, 221, 258
definition of, 220
fixed setup overhead costs, 270 – 271
sales-volume variances and, 219 – 220, 497
variable setup overhead costs, 268 – 270
Forced ranking of employees, 802
4-variance analysis, 262 – 263
FRx Forecaster, 188
Full costs of product, 373, 423
Full-cost transfer pricing, 763 – 765

General ledger. *See also* Journal entries
backflush costing overview, 705
for manufacturing job costing, 107 – 114
subsidiary ledgers with control in title, 107
Generally accepted accounting principles (GAAP)
economic value added (EVA®) calculation, 790*n*
financial statements for external reporting, 46
managers and, 3
Germany, financial performance measures, 792
Global practices
activity-based costing, 153
budgeting, 179
capital budgeting, 727
corporate cost allocation, 488
cost classification, 328
cost methods used in pricing decisions, 424
financial performance measures, 792
manufacturing overhead cost allocation, 100
pricing, 424
quality, 654
standard costs, 223
support department cost allocation, 533
transfer pricing, 767
variable costing, 298
Goal congruence
about, 755
manager evaluation and, 692, 727 – 728
promotion of, 759
Goodness of fit, 336, 347 – 348
Goods for sale, costs associated with, 686 – 687
Gordon, Bob, 407
Government agencies, contracting with, 45 – 46
Graphic approach, linear programming, 394
Graph method, breakeven point, 66 – 67
Gross book value, 795, 797
Gross margin
vs. contribution margin, 77 – 78, 288
vs. variable nonmanufacturing costs, 288
Gross margin percentage, 78
Gross revenues, distinct from net revenues, 491*n*
Growth component, of operating income, 455, 456 – 457, 459 – 460
Growth *vs.* profitability, 461

Hashman, Ken, 173
Hazardous waste management, 640
Heteroscedasticity, 350
High-low method, quantitative analysis, 332 – 333
Holland
activity-based costing, 153
budgeting practices, 179
Homogenous cost pool, 140, 488
Homoscedasticity, 350
Human resource management costs, 486, 489
Hurdle rate, 720
Hybrid costing, 608 – 609

Identification stage of capital budgeting, 719
Idle time, 44, 669 – 670
Implementation and control stage of capital budgeting, 719
Improvement. *See* Continuous improvement; Quality improvement; Yield improvement
Imputed costs, 789
Incentives, 800 – 801
Income
effect of sales mix on, 74 – 75
operating income
absorption costing and, 294
definition of, 40
inventory costing and, 289 – 293
sales and production effect, 292 – 293
strategic analysis of, 454 – 460
residual income, 789 – 790
Income statements
alternative capacity-level concepts, 305
budgeted income statement, 187, 198
with contribution margin emphasis, 77, 78
examples of, 41, 494, 564
with gross margin emphasis, 77, 78
variable costing compared to absorption costing, 288 – 289, 290 – 292
Income taxes, target net income and, 67 – 69. *See also* Taxation
Incongruent decision making, 756 – 757
Incremental cost-allocation method, 534
Incremental costs, 377, 768
Incremental revenue, 377
Incremental revenue-allocation method, 539 – 540
Incremental unit-time learning model, 340 – 341, 342
Independence of residuals, 350 – 351
Independent variables, 330, 348 – 349
India, transfer pricing, 767
Indirect cost(s)
budgeted indirect costs, 114 – 118
cost allocation and, 482
of cost object, 31 – 32, 97
examples in combinations, 37
factors affecting classifications, 32
job costing and, 114 – 118
overallocated (underallocated) indirect costs, 114
underabsorbed (overabsorbed) indirect costs, 115
underapplied (overapplied) indirect costs, 115
Indirect-cost pools, 140, 142, 145
Indirect-cost pool system, 149
Indirect-cost rates
calculating, 100
time period to compute, 105 – 106
Indirect costs of quality, 656 – 657
Indirect engineered costs, 461
Indirect manufacturing costs, 39
Industrial engineering method, cost estimation, 329, 338
Inflation, and capital budgeting, 739 – 741
Information, and decision process, 370
Information-acquisition stage of capital budgeting, 719
Information technology. *See also* Software
in job costing, 103 – 105
software
Application Service Providers, 35
financial planning models, 187 – 189
standard costs and, 232
Infrastructure costs, 462*n*
Innovation, 12
Input, standard, 222
Input-price variances, 224
Inputs, relationship with outputs, 462
Input suppliers, bargaining power of, 447
Insourcing *vs.* outsourcing, 375 – 377
Inspection points
allocating costs of normal spoilage, 634, 636
definition of, 629
spoilage at intermediate stages of completion in process costing, 642 – 644
Institute of Management Accountants (IMA)
about, 17
Standards of Ethical Conduct for Management Accountants, 17, 18 – 19
Intangible assets
about, 5
capital budgeting and, 734 – 736
Integrated variance analysis, 272
Integrity, as ethical standard, 18
Intercept, definition of, 325
Intermediate market, 769
Intermediate products, 758
Internal business process perspective, balanced scorecard, 449, 450, 452, 454
Internal failure costs, 655
Internal performance, nonfinancial measures of, 662 – 663
Internal rate-of-return (IRR) method
about, 722 – 723
net present value (NPV) method compared to, 723 – 724
Internal Revenue Code
adjusted allocation-rate approach, 306*n*
inventoriable costs, 298*n*
practical capacity, 306
proration approach, 306*n*
taxation of multinational transfer pricing, 770
International Organization for Standards, 654
International practices. *See* Global practices
Internet. *See also* World Wide Web
advantages of, 5
Application Service Providers, 35
bottlenecks on, 665
customer profitability and, 493
e-retailing with activity-based costing, 154
growth *vs.* profitability choices of dot-com companies, 461
opportunity costs and, 381
pricing and, 430
Intrinsic motivation, and organization culture, 805
Inventoriable costs
about, 39
flow of, 40 – 43
relationship with period costs, 42 – 43
Inventory(ies)
buildup of undesirable, 293 – 294
carrying costs of, 380 – 382
direct materials inventory, 38
finished-goods inventory, 39
impact on variances, 227
merchandising-sector companies and, 39
reorder point, 688 – 689, 690
safety stock, 689 – 690
service-sector companies and, 39
types of, 38
work-in-process inventory, 38
Inventory costing
comparison of methods, 296 – 298
operating income differences, 289 – 293
performance measures and absorption costing, 293 – 295
throughput costing, 295 – 296
variable costing and absorption costing, 286 – 289
Inventory management
definition of, 686
estimating inventory-related costs and their effects, 691 – 692
JIT production and, 697 – 700
JIT purchasing and, 692 – 695
materials requirement planning and, 696 – 697
in retail organizations, 686 – 690
supply-chain analysis and, 695 – 696
Investment, 788. *See also* Return on investment (ROI)
Investment activity, management control of, 733
Investment center, 191
Ireland
activity-based costing, 153
capital budgeting, 727

cost methods used in pricing decisions, 424
manufacturing overhead cost allocation, 100
pricing practices, 424
standard costs, 223
ISO 4000, 654 - 655
ISO 9000, 654
Italy, financial performance measures, 792

Japan
budgeting practices, 179
capital budgeting, 727
cost classifications, 328
financial performance measures, 792
manufacturing overhead cost allocation, 100
National Tax Agency and transfer pricing, 771
pricing practices, 424
quality practices, 654
standard costs, 223
support department cost allocation, 533
transfer pricing, 767
value engineering, 424
variable costing, 298
Job costing
budgeted indirect costs and end-of-period adjustments, 114 - 118
example of gains from, 104
general approach to, 99 - 101
general ledger in manufacturing sector, 107 - 114
in manufacturing-sector companies, 99 - 105
multiple overhead cost pools, 118
nonmanufacturing costs and, 114
normal job-costing, 106 - 107
overview for manufacturing company, 102
service sector example, 118 - 119
spoilage and, 636 - 638
technology's role in, 103 - 105
time period to compute indirect-cost rates, 105 - 106
Job-costing systems, 98 - 99
Job-cost record, 101, 103
Job-cost sheet. *See* Job-cost record
Joint costs
about, 556 - 558
allocation approaches, 558 - 564
choosing allocation method, 564 - 565
definition of, 556
irrelevance for decision making, 566 - 568
not allocating, 565 - 566
reasons to allocate, 558
Joint products
costing of, 570
definition of, 556
distinguishing from byproducts, 568
Jones, John, 173
Journal entries
in backflush costing, 704
in operation-costing systems, 613 - 614
for overhead costs, 264 - 267
in process costing, 591 - 592
for spoilage, 634
using standard costs, 230 - 232
for variances, 264 - 267
Just-in-time (JIT) production
about, 4 - 5
inventory management and, 697 - 700
JIT purchasing and, 698
Just-in-time (JIT) purchasing
definition of, 692
inventory management and, 692 - 695
JIT production and, 698

Kaizen budgeting, 189, 420
Kennedy, Donald, 553
Kroc, Ray, 480, 816

Labor costs
direct manufacturing labor costs, 39
measuring, 43 - 44
Labor-time record, 102, 103
Law. *See* Antitrust laws, and pricing
Lead time, manufacturing, 664, 697
Lean production, 697. *See also* Just-in-time (JIT) production
Learning and growth perspective, balanced scorecard, 450, 451, 452, 454
Learning curves, nonlinear cost functions and, 339 - 343
Ledgers, subsidiary, 107 - 114
Life cycle, product, 425
Life-cycle budgeting, 425 - 427
Life-cycle costing, 425
Linear cost functions, 324, 325
Linearity within relevant range, 349
Linear programming
about, 391 - 392
graphic approach, 394
problem solving steps, 392
trial-and-error approach, 393 - 394
Line management, 15
Locked-in costs, 417 - 418
Long-run alternative pricing, 414 - 415
Long-run costing and pricing, 413 - 415
Long-run customer profitability, 495
Long term assets, gross or net book value, 795, 797
Long-term productive assets, 5
Lopez, Maria, 93 - 94

Main products, 556
Make-or-buy decisions, 375 - 377, 379
Malcolm Baldridge Quality Award, 654, 683
Management accountants
control decisions, 6 - 8
daily activities, 11
e-business strategies and, 14
organization structure and, 15 - 16
planning decisions, 6 - 8
role in implementing strategy, 6 - 9
scorekeeping and attention-directing roles, 8 - 9
strategic decisions and, 3 - 5
Management accounting
about, 2 - 3
key guidelines, 13, 15
value enhancement of, 9 - 13
Management by exception, 216
Management control systems
about, 754 - 755
evaluating, 755
in organization structure, 755 - 756
Managers
capital budgeting decisions, 727 - 728
cost allocation and, 483
creating incentives *vs.* imposing risk, 800
generally accepted accounting principles (GAAP) and, 3
intrinsic motivation and organization culture, 805
inventory management decisions, 692
investment activity control, 733
motivating, 178, 483
performance distinct from organization units, 799 - 802
project control, 733 - 734
value chain and, 10
variances used by, 228 - 230
Manufacturing cells, 697
Manufacturing costs, 39, 423
Manufacturing cycle time, 664
Manufacturing lead time, 664, 697
Manufacturing overhead, cost-allocation bases for, 100
Manufacturing overhead allocated, 112
Manufacturing overhead applied, 112
Manufacturing overhead budget, 185
Manufacturing overhead cost analysis, 263 - 264
Manufacturing overhead costs, 39
Manufacturing-sector companies
about, 38
common cost classifications, 39
contribution margin *vs.* gross margin, 77 - 78
general ledger and subsidiary ledgers, 107 - 114
implementing activity-based costing, 144 - 148
income statement example, 41
inventoriable costs flow, 40 - 43
inventory costing, 286 - 299
job costing in, 98, 99 - 105
normal job-costing system in, 107 - 114
process costing in, 98
schedule of cost of goods manufactured example, 41
Margin of safety, 70
Market, potential entrants into, 446
Market-based transfer prices, 759, 762 - 763
Marketing, in value chain, 10
Market-share variances, 500 - 501
Market-size variances, 501 - 502
Marvin, Ken, 651 - 652
Mass customization, 608
Master budget, 176, 181. *See also* Static budget
Master-budget capacity utilization, 301, 303 - 304
Materials requirement planning (MRP), 696 - 697
Materials-requisition record, 101 - 102, 103
Maximum transfer prices, 765
Merchandising-sector companies
about, 38
activity-based costing and, 152, 155
contribution margin *vs.* gross margin, 77
inventory and, 39
job costing in, 98
process costing in, 98
Mexico, quality practices, 654
Minimum transfer prices, 765
Mixed costs, 325
Money, time value of, 720
Moral hazard, 800
Motivation, 178, 755, 805
Multicollinearity, 353 - 354
Multinational companies
decentralization in, 757 - 758
performance measures in, 797 - 799
transfer pricing tax considerations, 769 - 772
Multiple cost drivers, 76 - 77
Multiple overhead cost pools, 118
Multiple regression analysis, 334, 351 - 352, 353
Multiple task performance, 803

Nasser, Jacques, 802
Negotiated transfer prices, 759, 766
Net book value, 795, 797
Net income, 63
Net initial investment cash flows, 730 - 731
Net present value (NPV) method
about, 720 - 722
inflation and, 739 - 741
internal rate-of-return (IRR) method compared to, 723 - 724
Net realizable value (NRV) method of joint-cost allocation, 558, 561 - 563
Net revenues, distinct from gross revenues, 491*n*
New fundamentals, 14
New-product development time, 12
New Zealand
activity-based costing, 153
transfer pricing, 767
Nominal rate of return, 739
Nonfinancial performance measures
about, 230, 786 - 787
intensity of incentives and, 800 - 801
overhead costs and, 267
Nonlinear cost functions, and learning curves, 339 - 343
Nonlinearity, and cost functions, 337 - 339
Nonmanufacturing costs, and job costing, 114
Nonmanufacturing costs budget, 186
Nonprofit companies, 75 - 76
Nonuniform cash flows, 725 - 726
Nonvalue-added costs, 417
Normal capacity utilization, 300 - 301, 303 - 304
Normal costing, comparison of inventory-costing systems, 296. *See also* Normal job-costing
Normality of residuals, 351
Normal job-costing
about, 106 - 107
in manufacturing sector, 107 - 114
variations from, 118 - 119
Normal rework, 637 - 638
Normal spoilage
allocating costs of, 634, 636
attributable to specific job, 636
common to all jobs, 636 - 637
definition of, 628

Objective function, 392, 393
Objectivity, as ethical standard, 18
One-time-only special orders, 373 - 374
1-variance analysis, 263
On-time performance, 664
Operating budgets, developing, 180 - 187
Operating departments, 526
Operating divisions. *See* Divisions
Operating income
absorption costing and, 294
definition of, 40
inventory costing and, 289 - 293
sales and production effect, 292 - 293
strategic analysis of, 454 - 460
Operating leverage, 72
Operation, definition of, 612
Operational excellence, 14
Operational measures of time, 664
Operation-costing systems
about, 612
definition of, 612
illustration of, 612 - 613
journal entries in, 613 - 614
Operations, design of, 32
Opportunity cost(s), 379 - 382, 768
Opportunity-cost approach, make-or-buy decisions, 379
Opportunity cost of capital, 720
Ordering costs, 686, 689
Organizational learning, 228 - 229
Organizational structure
comparison of benefits and costs of decentralization, 757
decentralization and, 755 - 758

Organizational structure (*cont.*)
management accountants and, 15 - 16
responsibility and, 191
sample reporting relationships, 16
Organization culture, and intrinsic motivation, 805
Outcomes, 81, 82
Output(s)
relating batch costs to, 232 - 233
relationship with inputs, 462
Output-level overhead variance, 259. *See also* Production-volume variance
Output levels, choosing by relevance, 372 - 375
Output unit-level costs, 143
Outsourcing
capacity constraints and, 377 - 382
definition of, 375
example of, 378
strategic and qualitative factors, 377
vs. insourcing, 375 - 377
Overabsorbed indirect costs, 115
Overallocated indirect costs, 114
Overapplied indirect costs, 115
Overcharging, 536
Overcosting, 136
Overhead cost(s)
budgeted fixed overhead cost-allocation rates, 257 - 258
budgeted variable overhead cost-allocation rates, 253 - 254
cost allocation and, 486
journal entries for, 264 - 267
manufacturing overhead cost analysis, 263 - 264
planning of variable and fixed overhead costs, 252 - 253
Overhead cost pools, 118
Overhead cost variances
financial and nonfinancial performance, 267
fixed overhead cost variances, 258
integrated analysis of, 260 - 263
in nonmanufacturing settings, 267 - 268
variable overhead cost variances, 254 - 257
Overtime premium, 44

Pareto diagrams, 658 - 659
Partial productivity
definition of, 468
evaluating changes in, 469
measures of, 468 - 471
using measures, 471
Past costs, irrelevance of, 386 - 388
Payback, 724 - 726
Peak-load pricing, 427 - 428
Peanut-butter costing, 136
Perfectly competitive market, 762, 768 - 769
Performance
choosing target levels of, 797
evaluation of
benchmarks and, 801 - 802
capacity utilization and, 303 - 304
decision making and, 388 - 389
decision model and, 82
joint-cost allocation and, 567 - 568
managers distinct from organization units, 799 - 802
obtaining information for, 47
relative performance evaluation, 801 - 802
revision under absorption costing, 295
framework for judging, 178
measures of
absorption costing and, 293 - 295
aligning with financial goals, 787 - 793
alternative definitions for, 794
balanced scorecard and, 454
executive compensation, 803 - 804
financial and nonfinancial, 230, 267, 786 - 787, 800 - 801
at individual activity level, 802 - 803
in JIT production, 699 - 700
measurement alternatives for, 794 - 797
in multinational companies, 797 - 799
nonfinancial measures of internal performance, 662 - 663
time horizon of, 793
variances used for, 228
Period costs
about, 39 - 40
relationship with inventoriable costs, 42 - 43
Personalized pricing, 430
Physical-measure method of joint-cost allocation, 558, 560 - 561
Physical units
of output
equivalent units and, 588 - 590
in first-in, first-out (FIFO) process-costing method, 596
spoilage and, 630
in weighted-average process-costing method, 593
in stand-alone revenue-allocation method, 538
Planning
decision making and, 150 - 151
definition of, 6
financial planning models, 187 - 189
management accountants and, 6 - 8
obtaining information for, 47
of variable and fixed overhead costs, 252 - 253
Plans, implementation of, 177 - 178
Pollution prevention, 735
Postinvestment audit, 733 - 734
Poultry processing industry, 570
Practical capacity, 300
Predatory pricing, 428
Prediction errors, cost of, 691 - 692
Premio Nacional de Calidad, 654
Prevention costs, 655
Previous department costs, 604. *See also* Transferred-in costs
Price(s)
distress prices, 762 - 763
learning curves and, 342 - 343
standard, 222
target price, 415
Price discounting, 491
Price discrimination, 427
Price-recovery component, of operating income, 456, 457 - 458, 459 - 460
Price variances
computing, 224 - 225
definition of, 224
for direct-cost inputs, 221 - 226
flexible budget and, 233 - 234
Pricing. *See also* Transfer pricing
antitrust laws and, 428 - 429
collusive pricing, 429
dual pricing, 765 - 766
fairness of, 535 - 537
global practices, 424
Internet strategies, 430
long-run alternative pricing, 414 - 415
peak-load pricing, 427 - 428
predatory pricing, 428
short-run costing and, 411 - 413
Pricing decisions
achieving target cost per unit, 419 - 421
antitrust law effects on, 428 - 429
considerations other than costs, 427 - 428
cost-plus pricing, 421 - 424
downward demand spiral and, 303
global practices, 424
life-cycle product budgeting and costing, 425 - 427
long-run costing and pricing, 413 - 415
major influences on, 410 - 411
short-run costing and pricing, 411 - 413
target costing and target pricing, 415 - 418
time horizon of, 411
Prime costs, 43
Print-on-demand technology, 698
Probability, 80
Probability distribution, 80
Problem solving, 8
Process costing
in Australia, 587
comparison of weighted-average and FIFO methods, 599 - 600
first-in, first-out (FIFO) method, 596 - 600
illustrating, 586 - 588
journal entries in, 591 - 592
in manufacturing sector, 98
in merchandising sector, 98
in service sector, 98
with some beginning and some ending work-in-process inventory, 592 - 593
spoilage and, 628 - 636
spoilage at intermediate stages of completion in, 642 - 644
standard-costing method of, 600 - 603
transferred-in costs, 603 - 608
weighted-average method, 593 - 595, 599 - 600
with zero beginning inventory
and some ending work-in-process inventory, 588 - 592
and zero ending work-in-process inventory, 588
Process-costing systems, 98 - 99
Product(s)
allocating corporate costs to, 486 - 489
calculating cost of, 46
celebrity endorsements of, 496
as cost objects, 97 - 98
customized products, 608
definition of, 556
Product cost(s)
with activity-based costing, 146, 147
alternative for different purposes, 46
calculating, 413 - 414, 590 - 591
definition of, 45 - 46
with single overhead cost pool, 139
Product-cost cross-subsidization, 136 - 137
Product costing, and capacity level, 302 - 303
Product differentiation, 447
Production. *See also* Just-in-time (JIT) production
effect on operating income, 292 - 293
in value chain, 10
Production budget, 183 - 184
Production-denominator level, 257
Production departments, 526
Production processes, 137 - 138
Production-volume variance, 258 - 260, 297
Productive assets, 5
Productivity
conversion costs and, 459
definition of, 468
direct materials and, 459
measurement of, 468 - 471
operating income component, 456, 458 - 459, 459 - 460
partial productivity, 468 - 471
R & D costs and, 459
total factor productivity (TFP), 470 - 471
Product life cycle, 425
Product-mix decisions
under capacity constraints, 382 - 383
pricing and, 45
Product overcosting, 136
Product-sustaining costs, 144
Product undercosting, 136
Professional accounting organizations, 17
Professional ethical issues. *See* Ethical issues
Profitability. *See also* Customer profitability
Dupont method of profitability analysis, 788
improving with activity-based costing, 148 - 151
strategic analysis of, 459
vs. growth, 461
Profit centers, 191
Profit plan, 177
Profit-volume graph, 67, 68, 71
Pro forma statements, 177
Projects, management control of, 733 - 734
Proration approach, 116 - 117, 305, 306*n*
Prospective prices, 423 - 424
Purchase-order lead time, 687
Purchasing costs, 686
PV graph, 67, 68, 71

Qualitative relevant information, 372
Quality
advantages of nonfinancial measures of, 663
analysis techniques, 657 - 659
as competitive tool, 654 - 655
costs of design quality, 661
costs of quality (COQ), 655 - 657, 663
evaluating quality performance, 663
examples of, 662
global practices, 654
nonfinancial measures of, 661 - 663
total quality management (TQM), 12
Quality costs, 687
Quality improvement, 448, 659 - 661
Quality of design, 655
Quality performance, evaluating, 663
Quantitative analysis
cost estimation methods, 330
cost function estimation with, 330 - 335
high-low method, 332 - 333
Quantitative relevant information, 372
QUEST (Quality Underlies Every Single Task), 662

RAID (redundant arrays of inexpensive disks), 665
Rate variances, 224
Rational experimentation, 14
Real rate of return, 739
Receipt time, 664
Reciprocal allocation method, 529 - 532
Reengineering, 448 - 449
Refined costing systems, 140 - 141
Regression analysis, 333 - 335, 338, 347 - 354
Regression line, estimating, 347
Reimbursable costs, disputes over, 536
Reject rates, 627
Relative performance evaluation, 801 - 802
Relevance, 370 - 372, 372 - 375
Relevant after-tax flows, 729 - 733
Relevant benefits, of JIT purchasing, 693
Relevant cash flow analysis, 728 - 733

Relevant cost(s)
about, 370 – 371
considerations in obtaining estimates of, 691
cost of prediction error, 691 – 692
determining, 372
financial benefits of JIT and, 699
of JIT purchasing, 693
for pricing special order, 411 – 412
of quality and timely deliveries, 693 – 695
Relevant-cost analysis
adding customer, 385 – 386
discontinuing customer, 384 – 385
discontinuing or adding branches or segments, 386
potential problems, 374 – 375
Relevant incremental costs, 691
Relevant information, 372
Relevant opportunity cost of capital, 691
Relevant range
about, 35 – 36
in cost classification, 326
linearity within, 327, 349
Relevant revenue(s)
about, 370 – 371
costs of time and, 667 – 668
determining, 372
Relevant-revenue analysis
adding customer, 385 – 386
discontinuing customer, 384 – 385
discontinuing or adding branches or segments, 386
Reorder point, 688 – 689, 690
Representative high, 333
Representative low, 333
Required rate of return (RRR), 720
Research and development (R&D)
costs
capitalizing, 484*n*
as discretionary costs, 462
growth and, 457
in value chain, 9 – 10
Residual income, 789 – 790
Residuals
constant variance of, 349 – 350
independence of, 350 – 351
normality of, 351
Residual term, 334, 349
Resources, building, 4
Responsibility, and controllability, 192 – 193
Responsibility accounting
budgeting and, 191 – 192
definition of, 191
emphasis on information and behavior, 193
Responsibility centers
choices about, 758
as cost objects, 97
definition of, 191
Retail inventory management, 686 – 690
Return on investment (ROI)
about, 788 – 789
foreign divisions calculations
in foreign currency, 798
in U.S. dollars, 798 – 799
target rate of, 421 – 422
Return on sales, 791 – 793
Revenue(s)
customer revenue analysis, 491
definition of, 40, 537
differential revenues, 377
Revenue allocation
bundled products and, 537
definition of, 537
Revenue-allocation methods, 537 – 540
Revenue budgets, 183
Revenue centers, 191
Revenue drivers
activity-based costing and, 338
definition of, 62
Revenue effect
of growth, 456
of price recovery, 457
Revenue object, 537
Rework
about, 637 – 638
definition of, 626
Rightsizing, 464
Risk-return tradeoff, 73
Rolling budgets, 180

Safety, margin of, 70
Safety stock, 689 – 690
Salary. *See* Compensation arrangements
Sales, effect on operating income, 292 – 293
Sales mix, effects on income, 74 – 75
Sales-mix variances, 498 – 499
Sales-quantity variances, 499 – 500
Sales value at splitoff method of joint-cost allocation, 558, 560
Sales-volume variances
about, 220 – 221
definition of, 220
flexible-budget variances and, 219 – 220, 497 – 498
Schedule of cost of goods manufactured, 41
Scorekeeping, 8
Scotland, capital budgeting, 727
Scott, Tom, 482, 519, 623
Scrap
accounting for, 638
attributable to specific job, 639
common to all jobs, 639
definition of, 626
recognizing
at time of production, 639 – 641
at time of sale, 638 – 639
Search engines, and personalized pricing, 430
Search stage of capital budgeting, 719
Securities and Exchange Commission (SEC), 804
Selection stage of capital budgeting, 719
Self-liquidating cycle, 198
Selling price
decisions, 69 – 70
stand-alone revenue-allocation method, 538
Selling-price variances, 221
Sell-or-process-further decisions, 567
Semivariable costs, 325
Sensitivity analysis
about, 724
cash flows and, 200
effects on short-term budgeting, 199
linear programming and, 394 – 395
uncertainty and, 70 – 71
Separable costs, 556, 557
Sequential allocation method, 528 – 529
Sequential tracking, 700
Serial correlation, 350
Service departments, 526. *See also* Support departments
Services, calculating cost of, 46
Service-sector companies
about, 38
activity-based costing and, 152, 155
cost-volume-profit (CVP) analysis in, 75 – 76
inventory and, 39
job costing in, 98, 118 – 119
overhead cost variances, 267 – 268
process costing in, 98
Service-sustaining costs, 144
Setup time, 697
Shapley value, 534*n*, 540*n*
Short-run costing and pricing, 411 – 413
Significance of independent variable, 336
Simple regression analysis, 334, 351
Simplex method, linear programming, 393*n*
Single indirect-cost pool system, 138 – 140
Single-rate cost-allocation method, 522 – 524
Slope coefficient, 325
Social responsibilities, 805 – 806
Software. *See also* Information technology
Application Service Providers, 35
financial planning models, 187 – 189
Source documents, 101, 103
South Korea
capital budgeting, 727
quality practices, 654
Special orders
one-time-only special orders, 373 – 374
relevant costs for pricing, 411 – 412
strategic and other factors in pricing, 412 – 413
Specification analysis, 349 – 351
Splitoff point, 556
Spoilage
counting, 629 – 630
definition of, 626
job costing and, 636 – 638
journal entries for, 634
procedure for process costing with, 630 – 631
process costing and, 628
standard costing and, 631, 634, 635
types of, 626, 628
weighted-average process-costing method and, 631, 633
Staff management, 15
Stand-alone cost-allocation method, 533 – 534
Stand-alone product revenues, 538
Stand-alone revenue-allocation method, 538 – 539
Standard(s)
definition of, 222
learning curves and, 342 – 343
Standard cost(s)
definition of, 222
global use of, 223
information technology and, 232
journal entries using, 230 – 232
wide applicability of, 232
Standard costing
comparison of inventory-costing systems, 296
definition of, 253
process costing
about, 600
accounting for variances, 601 – 603
computations, 600 – 601
spoilage and, 631, 634, 635
variance analysis and, 261
Standard error of the estimated coefficient, 348
Standard inputs, 222
Standard price, 222
Standards of Ethical Conduct for Management Accountants, 18 – 19
Stata, Ray, 297
Static budget, 216 – 217. *See also* Master budget
Static-budget variances, 217 – 218, 497
Statistical process control, 657 – 658
Statistical quality control, 657 – 658
Step cost functions, 338 – 339
Step-down allocation method, 528 – 529
Step-fixed cost function, 339
Step-variable cost function, 339
Stockholders' equity, 794
Stock options, 804
Stockout costs, 686
Strategic analysis, 454 – 460
Strategic cost management, 4
Strategy
about, 446 – 447
balanced scorecard and, 447 – 453
in capital budgeting and, 734
developing, 4
evaluating success of, 453 – 454
plan implementation, 177 – 178
Suboptimal decision making, 756 – 757
Subsidiary ledgers, in manufacturing job costing, 107 – 114
Substitutable inputs, 504
Success, key factors, 10 – 12
Sung Park, 608
Sunk costs, 371
Superfund Amendment and Reauthorization Act, 426
Super-variable costing, 295 – 296
Supplier evaluation, 693 – 695
Supplier-managed inventory, 696
Supply chain, 10, 695
Supply-chain analysis
challenges in obtaining benefits from, 696
inventory management and, 695 – 696
Support costs, allocating, 488
Support departments
cost allocation to operating divisions, 522 – 526
definition of, 526
global allocation cost practices, 533
multiple department cost allocation, 526 – 533
overview of allocation methods, 532 – 533
Supreme Court, and pricing decisions, 428 – 429
Sweden
financial performance measures, 792
standard costs, 223
variable costing, 298

T-accounts, for manufacturing cost flow, 41
Target costing
implementing, 416 – 417
for target pricing, 415 – 418
Target cost per unit
achieving, 419 – 421
definition of, 416
Targeting, 177. *See also* Budgeting
Target net income, and income taxes, 67 – 69
Target operating income, 67
Target operating income per unit, 416
Target prices
cost-plus pricing and, 423 – 424
definition of, 415
implementing, 416 – 417
target costing for, 415 – 418
Target rate of return on investment, 421 – 422
Taxation
adjusted allocation-rate approach, 306*n*
capital budgeting and, 728 – 733
inventoriable costs, 298*n*
multinational transfer pricing considerations, 769 – 772
practical capacity, 306
proration approach, 306*n*
target net income and, 67 – 69

Taxation (*cont.*)
transfer-pricing games with foreign corporations, 771
Team-based compensation arrangements, 803
Technical support, and quality, 662
Technology. *See also* Information technology
for cost information gathering, 32
job costing role of, 103 - 105
print-on-demand, 698
Terminal disposal of investment, 732 - 733
Terminology
benefits of defining accounting terms, 45
costs, 30
cost-volume-profit (CVP) analysis, 62 - 63
rework, 626
scrap, 626
spoilage, 626
Thatcher, Mark, 283
Theoretical capacity, 300
Theory of constraints, 668 - 671
3-variance analysis, 263
Throughput contribution analysis, 668 - 671
Throughput costing, 295 - 296
Time
as competitive tool, 663 - 664
components of, 12
costs of, 664 - 668
manufacturing lead time, 664, 697
on-time performance, 664
relevant revenues and costs of, 667 - 668
Time drivers, 664 - 668
Time horizon
costs and, 326
effect of, 73 - 74
of performance measures, 793
of pricing decisions, 411
Time-series data, 331
Time value of money, 720
Total-alternatives approach, make-or-buy decisions, 379
Total assets available, 794
Total assets employed, 794
Total assets employed minus current liabilities, 794
Total costs
to account for
in first-in, first-out (FIFO) process-costing method, 597
spoilage and, 630
in weighted-average process-costing method, 594
spoilage and assignment, 631
unit costs and, 36 - 38
Total costs line, 66
Total factor productivity
about, 470
calculating and comparing, 470 - 471
using measures, 471
Total-overhead variance, 263
Total quality management (TQM), 12
Total revenues line, 66 - 67
Trade regulation, 429
Transfer price, definition of, 758
Transfer pricing
about, 758 - 759
cost-based transfer prices, 763 - 766
general guidelines for, 768 - 769
global practices, 767
illustration of, 759 - 762
market-based transfer prices, 762 - 763
methods of, 759
multinational tax considerations, 769 - 772
negotiated transfer prices, 766
prorating between minimum and maximum prices, 765
taxation games with foreign corporations, 771
Transferred-in costs
definition of, 604
first-in, first-out (FIFO) process-costing method and, 606 - 607
points to remember, 607 - 608
in process costing, 603 - 604
weighted-average process-costing method and, 604 - 606
Treasury costs, 486
Trial-and-error approach, linear programming, 393 - 394
Trigger points
as completion of good finished units of product, 706
at completion of good finished units of product, 701 - 703
definition of, 700
as purchase of direct materials, 703 - 706
at purchase of direct materials, 701 - 703
as sale of finished goods, 703 - 706
at sale of finished goods, 701 - 703
2-sigma rule, 658
2-variance analysis, 263

Uncertainty
coping with, 80 - 81
cost-volume-profit (CVP) analysis and, 71
definition of, 462
as time driver, 665 - 667
Underabsorbed indirect costs, 115
Underallocated indirect costs, 114
Underapplied indirect costs, 115
Undercosting, 136
Unfavorable variances, 217
Uniform cash flows, 724 - 725
Unit costs
about, 36 - 37
decision making and, 37 - 38
stand-alone revenue-allocation method, 538
total costs and, 36 - 38
United Kingdom
activity-based costing, 153
budgeting practices, 179
capital budgeting, 727
corporate cost allocation, 488
cost methods used in pricing decisions, 424
financial performance measures, 792
manufacturing overhead cost allocation, 100
pricing practices, 424
quality practices, 654
standard costs, 223
support department cost allocation, 533
transfer pricing, 767
value engineering, 424
variable costing, 298
variance analysis, 265
United States
activity-based costing, 153
budgeting practices, 179
capital budgeting, 727
corporate cost allocation, 488
cost classifications, 328
cost methods used in pricing decisions, 424
Department of Defense, 398 - 399, 522, 535, 554, 639
financial performance measures, 792
government contracts with, 535 - 537
manufacturing overhead cost allocation, 100
pricing practices, 424
quality practices, 654, 659
standard costs, 223
transfer pricing, 767
variable costing, 298
Units completed
assigning costs
in first-in, first-out (FIFO) process-costing method, 597 - 598
in weighted-average process-costing method, 594
Units in ending work in process
assigning costs
in first-in, first-out (FIFO) process-costing method, 597 - 598
in weighted-average process-costing method, 594
Unused capacity
definition of, 461
identifying for engineered and discretionary overhead costs, 463
managing, 464
Usage variances, 224
Utilization
master-budget capacity, 301, 303 - 304
normal capacity, 300 - 301, 303 - 304

Value-added costs, 417
Value chain
about, 9
managers and, 10
product costs and, 483
Value engineering, 417
Variable cost(s)
cost-behavior patterns, 32 - 36
distinguishing from fixed costs, 34
examples in combinations, 37
of product, 423
variable cost structures, 71 - 73
Variable costing
about, 286 - 289
absorption costing compared to, 290 - 292
breakeven points in, 309 - 310
comparative income effects *vs.*absorption costing, 293
definition of, 287
example of, 297
global practices, 298
Variable-cost transfer pricing, 763 - 765
Variable direct manufacturing costs, 296
Variable indirect manufacturing costs, 296
Variable manufacturing cost, 423
Variable manufacturing overhead, 262
Variable manufacturing overhead costs, 263 - 264
Variable overhead cost-allocation rates, 253 - 254
Variable overhead costs, 252
Variable overhead cost variances, 254 - 257
Variable overhead efficiency variance, 255, 256 - 257
Variable overhead flexible-budget analysis, 254 - 255
Variable overhead spending variance, 255 - 257
Variable setup overhead costs, 268 - 270
Variance(s). *See also* Efficiency variances; Overhead cost variances
about, 216
between actual and standard costs, 703
benchmarking and, 234 - 235
favorable variance, 217
feedback and, 192
flexible-budget variances, 218 - 219, 221
inventories' impact on, 227
journal entries for, 264 - 267
management uses of, 228 - 230
market-share variances, 500 - 501
market-size variances, 501 - 502
mix and yield variances for substitutable inputs, 504 - 507
multiple causes of, 228 - 229
organizational learning and, 228 - 229
for performance evaluation, 228
price variances, 221 - 226, 233 - 234
in process-costing systems, 601 - 603
production-volume variance, 258 - 260
sales-mix variances, 498 - 499
sales-quantity variances, 499 - 500
sales variances, 496 - 498
sales-volume variances, 218 - 219, 220 - 221
static budget variances, 217 - 218
summary of, 226 - 227
unfavorable variance, 217
when to investigate, 229 - 230
Variance analysis
activity-based costing and, 268 - 271
control decisions and, 265
fixed manufacturing overhead, 262
4-, 3-, 2-, and 1-variance analysis, 262 - 263
standard costing and, 261
variable manufacturing overhead, 262
Vendor-managed inventory, 696

Waiting time, 666
Waste management, 640
Weighted-average contribution margin per unit, 75
Weighted-average process-costing method
about, 593 - 595
first-in, first-out (FIFO) process-costing method compared to, 599 - 600
spoilage and, 631, 633
transferred-in costs and, 604 - 606
Welch, Jack, 178, 626, 802
Whiplash effect, 695
Work-in-process inventory, 38, 588 - 592, 592 - 593, 604*n*
Work-measurement method, cost estimation, 329. *See also* Industrial engineering method, cost estimation
World Trade Organization, 429
World Wide Web. *See also* Internet
advantages of, 5
budgeting with, 188
customer profitability and, 493
e-retailing with activity-based costing, 154
growth *vs.* profitability choices of dot-com companies, 461
remote mirroring techniques, 665
rerouting traffic, 665
virtual business models, 73
Write-off to cost of goods sold approach, 117, 305

Yield improvement, 226